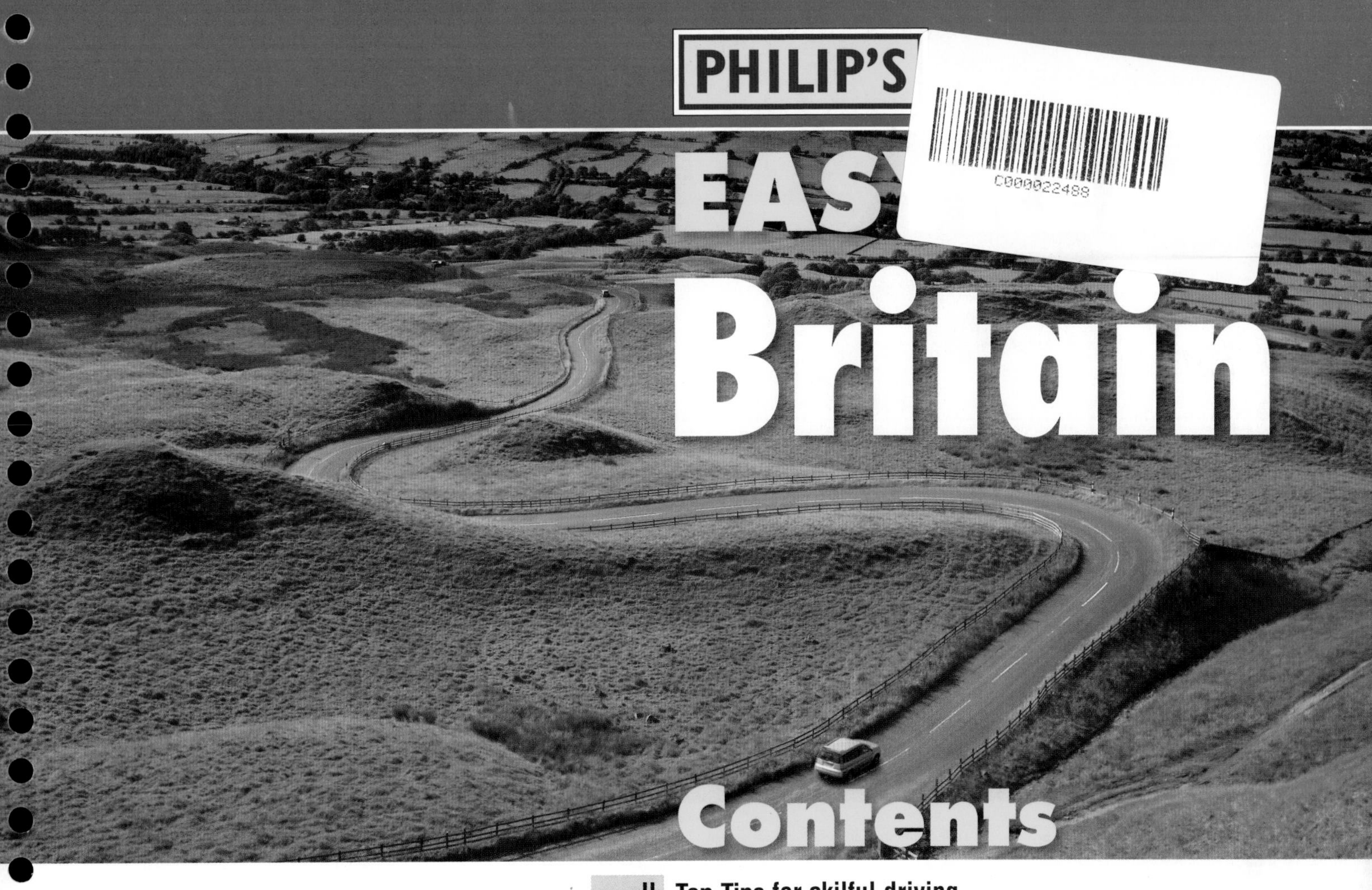

Contents

II Top Tips for skilful driving
IV Mobile speed camera sites
X Route planning maps with list of restricted motorway junctions
XVI Key to map symbols
1 Key to road map pages
2 Road maps at 2⅓ miles to 1 inch
289 Town plans and urban approach maps

- 289 Aberdeen, Bath
- 290 Birmingham approaches
- 292 Birmingham
- 293 Blackpool, Brighton
- 294 Bristol
- 295 Bristol approaches
- 296 Cambridge, Canterbury
- 297 Cardiff
- 298 Cardiff approaches
- 299 Carlisle, Chester
- 300 Coventry, Derby
- 301 Durham, Exeter
- 302 Edinburgh
- 303 Edinburgh approaches
- 304 Glasgow
- 305 Glasgow approaches
- 306 Gloucester, Leicester
- 307 Leeds
- 308 Leeds approaches
- 309 Liverpool
- 310 Liverpool approaches
- 311 London
- 312 London approaches
- 316 Manchester
- 317 Manchester approaches
- 318 Newcastle
- 319 Newcastle approaches
- 320 Norwich, Nottingham
- 321 Nottingham approaches
- 322 Oxford, Plymouth
- 323 Salisbury, Stratford-upon-Avon
- 324 Sheffield
- 325 Sheffield approaches
- 326 Swansea, Winchester
- 327 Worcester, York

328 M25 and routes into London
329 Index to road maps of Great Britain
376 Distance table

Top Tips for skilful driving

Are you concerned about speed cameras and worried about points on your licence?

Do tailgaters loom in your rear-view mirror and set out to intimidate you, driving inches from your bumper?

Have you had a near miss that was too close for comfort, but dismissed it as the other driver's fault?

Do other drivers cut you up frequently and leave you fuming at the wheel?

Does the ever-rising price of fuel make your heart sink every time you fill the tank?

Well, you're not alone. Britain's 32 million licence-holders are probably finding the joys of motoring a bit few and far between these days. It wasn't so long ago that we used to talk about going for a drive as a leisure activity we actually enjoyed doing, but that golden age of motoring now feels well and truly tarnished. Who really gets in the car these days just for fun?

Drivers seem to be under fire from all directions: if it's not aggressive road users or road rage, it's parking charges or road pricing, and if it's not the unpredictable behaviour of some cyclists, it's traffic attendants stalking your every move.

We have teamed up with the Institute of Advanced Motorists (IAM, www.iam.org.uk), the UK's leading advanced driving organization, to give you some practical advice that will save you money and keep you and your passengers less stressed and safer on the road. Who knows, we might even be able to inject a bit of enjoyment back into your driving.

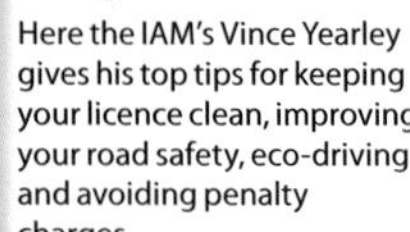

Here the IAM's Vince Yearley gives his top tips for keeping your licence clean, improving your road safety, eco-driving and avoiding penalty charges.

Keep the points off your licence

There are two sorts of speeder – the deliberate speeder and the accidental speeder. The vast majority of drivers are accidental speeders, misjudging the road and the conditions. Keeping the following points in mind should help you avoid becoming one of them.

Make a point of knowing the speed limit, wherever you are, and stick at, or below, it. You don't want to see a yellow speed camera at the last moment and panic because you don't know the speed you should be doing. Too many drivers get taken by surprise like this – as the skid marks by speed cameras testify.

Nowadays, most cameras have a sign before them, telling you the speed limit. But this isn't universally true: there are still plenty of the box-brownie-type signs that tell you absolutely nothing other than there may or may not be a speed camera coming up.

As a rule of thumb, in any urban area with street lighting the speed limit is 30mph. If in doubt, don't go any faster than this.

There are also some 20mph zones – such as those outside some schools and in designated 'home zones' and 'play streets' – and we are set to see more of them in future, but at least these are always clearly marked. However, arcane regulations prevent local authorities from putting up 30mph repeater signs, so it is up to you to remember what the limit is.

There will be roads – particularly wider, two-lane carriageways – where you just 'feel' that you can go faster. It's a temptation you should avoid, until you are certain that the 30mph rule does not apply on that stretch.

Strictly speaking, you could be prosecuted for driving at 31mph in a 30mph zone. In reality, this is extremely rare as a 10% of error is normally allowed, but don't rely on it.

A favourite point where speeding motorists are caught is where the speed limit drops from 40mph to 30mph – and inattentive drivers who don't respond, or do so too late, are faced with a flash, a fine and three points on their licence.

> ⚠ Remember, the speed limit is the *maximum* speed

Bear in mind that the same sign can mean different things. On a dual carriageway or a motorway the national speed limit sign (the round white sign with a black diagonal flash through it) means a maximum speed of 70mph, but on a single carriageway, the same sign indicates a limit of only 60mph.

Remember that the speed limit is the *maximum* speed and in difficult conditions, such as fog and ice, your speed should be modified to suit the road conditions.

Whatever the form of speed camera – Gatso, mobile safety camera units, SPECS or Truvelo – remember, it can't catch you if you are driving at the correct speed. The best speed camera is the one that doesn't go off.

Top tips to boost your driving

Read the road ahead and always drive at the correct speed for the conditions – the farther ahead you look, the more time you give yourself to recognise and respond to potential road hazards.

Anticipate – drivers often pride themselves on their quick reactions to events. But the really good driver anticipates the problem that's coming and slows down well in advance to avoid the need for any last-minute evasion. Successful anticipation relies not just on what is ahead of you, but also regular mirror checks (rear and door), and over-the shoulder checks before you move out so you can see what is happening or may develop behind you. It's that 360-degree awareness of possible hazards, before they develop, that will help keep you safe.

> ⚠ ...there should be no 'suddenly' about it...

If you've not been keeping on eye on him, you may not see that motorcyclist preparing to overtake you at speed precisely when you try to move out for a slow-moving cyclist. Good anticipation would have spotted both hazards emerging and helped you avoid a dangerous situation.

Crash-scene investigators hear people explain what happened by starting a sentence with the word 'Suddenly'. If you have spotted a hazard early enough, there should be no 'suddenly' about it.

If you anticipate the traffic flow, you can avoid having to make 'late' lane changes on the motorway, which are the single most dangerous manoeuvre.

Create space – the more space there is around your vehicle, the more time you have to respond if something goes wrong, and the more likely you will be to find an escape route.

In town, it's a good idea to make sure that when you are pulling up behind a vehicle at lights or a junction, you leave a reasonable amount of space ahead of you. If you can see the tyres vehicle of the in front, and the tarmac between them, you probably have sufficient headway to avoid problems. If that vehicle rolls back for some reason, you have a bit of a buffer. Likewise, if you are hit from behind, you are hopefully far enough back to avoid being pushed into him and becoming the 'meat in the sandwich'.

Your brake lights are the only indicators on your vehicle that work retrospectively – you are already braking when the lights go on. So always aim to brake gently and in good time to give following vehicles an extra second or two to react to you slowing or stopping.

There is an old sticker on many lorries that says, 'If you can't see my mirrors, I can't see you.' The ability to see and be seen is even more crucial in these days of congestion. Lorries and coaches that are obviously from Europe and so have left-hand drive should be given a particularly wide berth as the driver's view of the road behind and to the right is restricted.

The two-second rule – applying this phrase could save your life. Spot a marker ahead, such as a bridge or a lamp-post, and when the vehicle ahead of you goes past it say quietly to yourself, 'Only a fool breaks the two-second rule.' If you reach the marker before you have finished the sentence, then you are too close and you should pull back gently to create enough space for your-

Speed limits (mph)	Built-up area	Single carriageway	Dual carriageway	Motorway
Cars and motorcycles	30	60	70	70
Cars towing caravans and trailers	30	50	60	60
Buses and Coaches	30	50	60	60
Goods vehicles under 7.5 tonnes	30	50	60	70 (60 if articulated or towing)
Goods vehicles over 7.5 tonnes	30	40	50	60

self and other vehicles. Double the gap to four seconds if the road is wet, icy or greasy.

This two-second rule also stops aggressive 'cutting up'. If a driver needs to get in front of you in a hurry, perhaps because they have had to give up on overtaking the vehicle in front of you, they can take advantage of your 'buffer space' without you having to brake suddenly and feeling aggrieved.

If you are being tailgated, the first thing to do is to try to clear a way – perhaps by changing lanes if you can do so safely – and allow the tailgater to overtake. Even though it's galling, it's better to give way to an aggressive driver than to risk a crash.

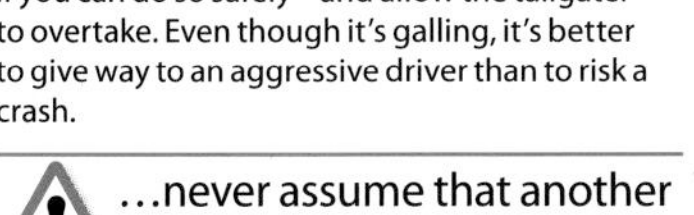

If you literally have nowhere to go, and that tail-gater is still too close for comfort, then leaving a two-second gap between you and the car in front means that you have time to react and stop in safety and, again, buy a crucial extra second that might prevent a rear-end shunt.

Assume the worst: never assume that another motorist has seen you or will react or behave as you expect, and never rely on anyone else's reactions to keep you safe. It can be difficult to interpret other drivers' body language.

In town, for example, if you are at a pinch-point between parked vehicles, and there is not enough room for you and an oncoming vehicle to pass, don't assume that the car coming towards you is going to give way.

He may flash his headlamps, but does that mean 'Come on, go faster,' 'Get out the way, I'm coming through,' or even a polite 'You go first'?

Make your intentions obvious to help everybody through a pinch-point. By pulling in behind the obstruction, you give the other driver a clear, unambiguous message that you are a civilized person, actively giving way and asking them to go first.

▲ Leave a two-second gap between yourself and the vehicle in front

In this way, everyone gets through more easily and quickly, and it's much neater than both of you slowing to a snail's pace, squeezing through and risking both your door mirrors and high blood pressure.

A useful advanced driving concept is that of the escape route – at any given moment, make sure you have a space to go to, to get you out of a tight squeeze. This could be a gap between parked cars or, on a motorway, a clear space in an adjacent lane.

Concentrate – at 70mph your car covers more than 100ft (30 m) per second. Looking away at a crucial moment can be fatal.

Whilst using handheld mobile phones is now a specific offence while driving, there are a host of other distractions inside and outside the vehicle. Even fiddling with the radio, lighting a cigarette or paying too much attention to your Sat Nav can be dangerous. We still have on file the multi-vehicle crash caused by a driver on a motorway reaching for a packet of mints.

Learn from your mistakes: near-misses happen to everyone. Afterwards, think calmly about the circumstances and how you could have avoided getting into that situation; never mind what the 'other guy' did – was there anything you could have done differently?

Camera enforcement

The UK is said to be one of the most closely watched societies in the world. In just 15 years we have seen the introduction of, and a huge growth in, speed and red-light cameras and CCTV and the list is growing with cameras being used to monitor, detect and send fines for ever more traffic offences.

Whatever your views about the 'surveillance society' and the use of cameras to issue parking tickets, technology can and does play an important role in enforcing important road-user safety and traffic-management regulations.

Motorway speed limits

Motorway speed limits have previously not been rigorously enforced by an increasingly stretched traffic police and – while our motorways are our safest roads – the potential for disaster if drivers ignore speed limits is always present, especially where lower limits are set at road works, or on controlled motorways at peak hours. Each year, motorists who ignore the lower limits and speed through motorway road works cause injury, damage and misery to themselves, other road users and those carrying out the road works.

However, the Highways Agency is increasingly using digital average-speed cameras to monitor the speed of all vehicles. The yellow painted cameras, known as 'specs', are typically mounted much higher from the ground than normal speed cameras and record the speed of all vehicles between cameras, and are intended to deter drivers from slowing on the approach to the camera and speeding away. They are an effective way of slowing traffic through road works or variable speed limits and will become an integral part of motorway driving.

Urban driving

We are also on the threshold of an increase in the use of cameras to enforce traffic-management regulations, with local authorities throughout the UK able to use them to enforce a growing number of measures intended to safeguard pedestrians and cyclists, improve bus reliability, and improve the lot of drivers with physical disabilities.

▲ The probability that a pedestrian will be killed if struck by a vehicle travelling between 20mph and 40mph

Pedestrian crossings whether traffic light controlled, or the increasingly rare 'zebra' crossing, work extremely well but only if the view of drivers and pedestrians using the crossing is not blocked by parked vehicles. For this reason, waiting is prohibited on the approach to and exit from crossings. Local authorities can use approved cameras to enforce the no-waiting rule as well as police and 'civil enforcement officers'.

Cycle lanes are increasingly being used by local government in an attempt to make cycling a safer proposition and encourage more of to consider cycling on shorter journeys. Cycle lanes are clearly marked on the road and have a white longitudinal separation line. Busy cycle lanes will be marked with a solid white line which – like all solid white lines – must not be crossed by any motor vehicle. It is illegal to drive into, wait, or park in these lanes, unless the vehicle has broken down and is temporarily awaiting recovery or immediate repair, a regulation which can and will be enforced by approved cameras.

Bus lanes are a feature of the urban and suburban street scene throughout the UK and are intended to improve the reliability of buses by providing a lane almost exclusively for them. Hours of operation and the lanes themselves are clearly marked. Whilst enforcement has not been consistent in the past, local authorities up and down the country have been given enforcement powers and will use them readily.

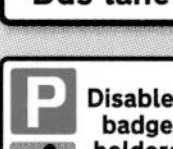

Disabled parking bays are self-explanatory and are provided on the street and in car parks to allow car users with a physical disability to get between their car and home, shop, cinema, etc with minimal hassle. They are always clearly marked and yet able-bodied motorists selfishly and illegally persist in parking in them, especially if other bays are occupied. Disabled parking bays are increasingly being monitored both on the street and in car parks and able-bodied motorists who do park, can expect a hefty penalty, or perhaps find their car removed.

Charges and fines

Parking – not only has London got the first congestion charge, which will in future vary, depending on the size of your vehicle, but from 2008 drivers who breach parking regulations can no longer rely on the absence of parking attendants: infringements can now be detected by CCTV and a penalty notice sent to the vehicle's registered keeper in the same way as speeding tickets, etc. This system is set to roll out over other towns and cities, too.

Nowadays, it's easy to get caught out: not every yellow line has to display a time plate showing the restriction. In the Controlled Parking Zones (CPZs) that are springing up all over the place, the general parking, waiting, returning and loading restrictions are displayed at points of entry to the CPZ, usually at major junctions. Inside the CPZ, time plates need only be displayed where the restrictions differ from those shown on the CPZ entry plate. It's up to you to make sure that you know what the restrictions are: single yellow lines can indicate either hours when no waiting is allowed, or where 24-hour restrictions apply at certain seasons.

If you are successful in finding a meter or parking space, you are still only a minute or two away from a penalty notice, so it's important to pay immediately. Similarly, 'overstaying' doesn't feel like illegal parking – but that just makes the pain all the more intense. A fine of between £30 and £140 is a bitter pill to swallow for anybody.

Know your rights

If you get a parking ticket (or PCN) you must decide quickly if you are going to pay, or contest it.

You can't do both. If you are going to pay, then do so quickly (usually within two weeks) or you will lose the 50% discount for prompt payment.

If you are going to query or contest the ticket (again, two weeks is usually the limit), you will need to follow the procedure described on the PCN. You write to the address shown and make what the law calls 'representations'. These are considered by, or on behalf of the local authority, who have a very wide discretion to cancel PCNs. If your representations are rejected (and many of them are) you can then appeal to the independent adjudication service (there are three, one for London, one for the rest of England and Wales, and one for Scotland). The Notice of Rejection sent by the local authority must tell you how to proceed. However, the independent adjudication service can only hear appeals based on specified grounds involving fact or law. The adjudicators cannot intervene on compassionate grounds, or if the driver thinks they have had a raw deal or just encountered an over-zealous parking attendant.

Three sources of information are

The London Parking and Traffic Appeals Service [LPATAS]

The National Appeals Service (formerly the NPAS)

www.appealnow.com – a web site run by Barry Segal (described as the 'UK's leading parking ticket authority')

Eco-driving

With fuel prices continuing to rise, there has never been a better time to learn about 'eco-driving'. Regardless of the size of vehicle you drive – which of course is key in terms of fuel efficiency overall – there are things you can do as a driver to squeeze that tank of petrol harder, so you go a bit farther for that bit less.

Ask yourself, 'Do I really need to drive? – it's the shortest journeys – less than two miles – which cause the most pollution and are most inefficient in terms of fuel consumption. A straining cold engine will produce 60% more pollution than a warm one. Yet it's these shorter journeys that are ideal for walking or cycling.

Plan your route – a bit of forethought can save much wear and tear - for the car, and the driver. Try to take the most direct route and go off peak if possible. Sitting in congestion means you are often doing zero miles per gallon. If you get stuck in stationary traffic, be ready to switch off the engine after a few minutes.

Have your vehicle serviced regularly – this helps maintain efficient running and good economy. Inefficient, under-serviced engines can reduce fuel economy by 10% or more. Catalytic converters are environmentally friendly – but only if they are properly maintained.

Check your tyres weekly – correct tyre pressures will keep wear down and fuel economy up. Under-inflated tyres need replacing more often (itself an environmental problem) as well as being dangerous. Anybody who has cycled on under-inflated tyres will appreciate how much extra effort is involved! Make a point of checking them at least once a week.

Keep to the speed limits – try to 'feather' the throttle as you reach your cruising speed. Doing 70mph could use up to 17.2% more fuel than 60mph, according to the AA. A smoother driving style, changing gear to avoid straining the engine, can also bring significant fuel savings.

Use 'accelerator' sense – do you go straight from the accelerator to the brake? You would save fuel if you planned ahead. There is no point in rushing to join a queue.

Reverse in when you park – when you start off again, the engine will be cold and at its most fuel inefficient. If you can drive smoothly away without having to reverse when the engine is cold, not only will you save fuel you will also have better visibility.

Be a tank miser – why fill the tank up to the very brim? Carrying around the extra weight of the fuel means you burn more fuel. By filling up less frequently, you are not only saving money, you are also dong your bit to reduce CO2 emissions.

For advice on any aspect of advanced driving, please contact the IAM on 020 8996 9600 or visit iam.org.uk.

Mobile speed camera sites

The vast majority of speed cameras used on Britain's roads are operated by safety camera partnerships. This table lists the sites where each safety camera partnership may enforce speed limits through the use of mobile cameras or detectors. These are usually set up on the roadside or a bridge spanning the road and operated by a police or civilian enforcement officer. The speed limit at each site (if available) is shown in red type, followed by the approximate location in black type.

Abbreviations	
adj	adjacent
btwn	between
j/w	junction with
nr	near
NSL	National Speed Limit
o/s	outside
rdbts	roundabouts
twds	towards

England

Avon and Somerset

Bath and North East Somerset, Bristol, North Somerset, Somerset, South Gloucestershire

A4
30 Bath, Newbridge Rd
30 Bristol, Anchor Rd
30 Bristol, Totterdown Bridge
50 Keynsham Bypass Jct A4175 Durley Hill
50 Portway
30 Portway, nr A4176 Bridge Valley Rd

A4/B4054
30 Bristol, Avonmouth Rd

A30
50 Cricket St Thomas
30 East Chinnock
40 Roundham
40 Yeovil, Hospital Rdbt
30 Yeovil, Sherborne Rd

A37
30 Bristol, Wells Rd (nr Jct Airport Rd)
30 Bristol, Wells Rd (nr St Johns La)
60 Chilthorne Domer
50 Emborough
60 Fosse Way, north of Podimore Rdbt
30 Gurney Slade
60 Lydford to Bristol
40 Lydford to Yeovil
30 Shepton Mallet

A38
30 Bathpool
40 Bedminster Down, Bridgwater Rd
40 Bristol, Bedminster Down Rd nr Bishopsworth Rd
30 Bristol, Bedminster Down Rd/West St
30 Bristol, Cheltenham Rd/Gloucester Rd, nr Cranbrook Rd
30 Bristol, Gloucester Rd nr B4052 Ashley Down Rd
30 Bristol, Stokes Croft nr Bond St
40 Churchill – Langford
40 Cross
30 East Reach/Toneway
50 Heatherton Grange
40,30 North Petherton
40 Patchway, Gloucester Rd nr Highwood Rd
50 Pawlett
50 Redhill
30 Rooks Bridge
30 Taunton – Bridgwater
30 Taunton, Wellington Rd
30 West Huntspill
30 Winscombe, Sidcot Lane nr Jct A371

A39
30 Ashcott
30 Bilbrook
30 Bridgwater, Bath Rd
30 Bridgwater, North Broadway
30 Chewton Mendip
50 Green Ore
40 Horsey, Bath Rd
30 Quantock Rd
30 Walton
40 Wells, Coxley

A46
60 Bath to Wickwar Rd
40 Dunkirk

A303
50 Buckland St Mary
50 Downhead nr Ilchester

A303/A358
60 Southfields Rdbt

A303/A3088
70 Cartgate Rdbt

A357
30 Templecombe

A358
60 Ashill
30 Donyatt
30 Henlade, nr M5 Jct 25
40 Hornsbury Mill
40 Pen Elm
30 Staplegrove Rd
30 Taunton Deane, Priorswood Rd
30 Taunton, Greenway Rd

A359
30 Mudford

A361
30 Doulting
40 Durston
60 Frome Bypass
30 Othery
30 Pilton
30 West Pennard

A362
40 Terry Hill

A367
30 Bath, Bear Flat
30 Bath, Green Park Rd
30 Radstock, Wells Rd

A369
40 Abbots Leigh
60 Easton-in-Gordano, Martcombe Rd nr M5 Jct 19

A370
30 Backwell
40 Bristol End, Long Ashton Bypass
30 Cleeve Village
30 Congresbury, Station Rd, Bristol Rd
30 Flax Bourton nr B3130
50 West Wick, Somerset Ave, west of M5 Jct 21
30 Weston-super-Mare, Beach Rd
50 Weston-super-Mare, Herluin Wy
30 Weston-super-Mare, Somerset Ave
30 Weston-super-Mare, Winterstoke Rd

A371
30 Draycott
40 Priestleigh

A372
30 Aller
50 Red Post

A378
30 Curry Rivel
40 Wrantage

A403
40 Avonmouth Docks

A420
30 Bristol, Lawrence Hill
30 Old Market, nr Temple Way/Bond St
30 St George, Clouds Hill Rd/Bell Hill Rd
30 Warmley, High St London Rd nr A4175 Bath Rd
60 Wick, Tog Hill

A432
30 Bristol, Fishponds Rd nr B4469 Royate Hill
30 Bristol, Fishponds Rd nr B4048 Lodge Causeway
30 Bristol, Fishponds Rd with B4469 Muller Rd
30 Bristol, Stapleton Rd nr Jct A4320 Easton Wy
40 Hambrook, Badminton Rd nr A4174 Avon Ring Rd
40 Kendleshire
30 Yate, Station Rd/B4059 Stover Rd

A3039
30 Devonshire Rd

A3088
30 Yeovil, Lysander Rd

A3259
30 Monkton Heathfield

A4018
30 Bristol, Black Boy Hill/ Whiteladies Rd
30 Bristol, Cribbs Causeway Jct 17 M5
30 Bristol, Westbury Rd nr B4054 North View
30 Bristol, Whiteladies Rd into Queens Rd
30 Westbury on Trym, Falcondale Rd

A4044
30 Bristol, Temple Wy/ Redcliffe Wy

A4081
50 Catbrain

A4162
30 Bristol, Sylvan Wy/Dingle Rd/Canford Lane

A4174
50 Avon Ring Rd nr Jct 1 M32
30 Bristol, Hartcliffe Wy
40 Bristol, Hengrove Wy/ Airport Rd nr Creswicke Rd
50 Bromley Heath
50 Filton, Filton Rd/Avon Ring Rd nr Coldharbour Lane
40 Filton, Station Rd, nr Great Stoke Wy

A4320
30 Bristol, at A4 Bath Rd nr Sandy Park Rd

B3124
30 Clevedon, Walton Rd

B3130
30 Nailsea, Stockway (north)/ Chapel Ave
30,40 Wraxall

B3133
30 Clevedon, Central Wy

B3139
30 Chilcompton
30 Mark Causeway

B3140
30 Berrow, Coast Rd

B3141
30 East Huntspill

B3151
30 Compton Dundon
30 Ilchester
30 Street, Somerton Rd

B3153
30 Keinton Mandeville (east Somerton)

B3170
30 Shoreditch Rd

B3440
30 Weston-super-Mare, Locking Rd/Regent St/Alexandra Parade

B4051
30 Bristol, Park Row/Perry Rd

B4054
30 Sea Mills, Shirehampton Rd

B4056
30 Bristol, Northumbria Drive/Linden Rd/ Westbury Park
30 Bristol, Southmead Rd nr Pen Park Rd
30 Bristol, Southmead Rd nr Wellington Hill

B4057
30 Bristol, Crow Lane nr A4018 Passage Rd
30 Gypsy Patch Lane nr Hatchet Rd
40 Winterbourne Rd nr B4427 Gloucester Rd

B4058
30 Bristol, Frenchay Park Rd
30 Winterbourne, Winterbourne Hill/High St

B4059
30 Yate, Goose Green Wy

B4060
30 Yate, Station Rd/Bowling Hill/Rounceval St

B4061
30 Thornbury, Bristol Rd
30 Thornbury, Gloucester Rd

B4465
30 Mangotsfield, Broad St
30 Staple Hill, Staple Hill Rd/High St nr Forest Rd

Unclassified
30 Bristol, Bishopsworth, Whitchurch/Hareclive Rd
30 Bristol, Bishport Ave
30 Bristol, Hengrove, Hawkfield Rd nr A4174 Hengrove Wy
30 Bristol, Kingsway
30 Bristol, Long Cross, Lawrence Weston
30 Bristol, Stoke Hill/Stoke Rd nr Saville Rd, Clifton
30 Bristol, Sturminster Rd
30 Knowle Bristol, Broadwalk
30 Taunton, Cheddon Rd
30 Taunton, Chestnut Drive
30 Taunton, Lisieux Wy
30 Taunton, Trull Rd
50 Watergore, Harp Rd
30 Yeovil, Combe St

Bedfordshire and Luton

A1
50 Sandy

A5
60 Battlesden
40 Hockcliffe
60 Kensworth

A6
60 Pulloxhill
60 Silsoe

A421
50 Brogborough/ Apsley Guise
60 Wootton

A428
30 Bedford, Bromham Rd
30 Bedford, Goldington Rd

A505
60 Leighton Buzzard Bypass

A507
60 Clifton, nr New Rd
30 Ridgemont, High St

A603
30 Bedford, Cardington Rd
40 Willington

A1081
60 Luton, Airport Wy

A5120
40 Harlington
40 Houghton Regis, Bedford Rd

B531
30 Kempston, Bedford Rd

B1040
30 Biggleswade

Unclassified
30 Apsley Guise, Bedford Rd – West Hill
30 Arlesey, Hitchin Rd
30 Bedford, Park Ave
30 Bedford, Roff Ave
30 Bedford, Wentworth Drive
30 Bromham, Stagsden Rd
30 Bromham, Village Rd
30 Caddington, Dunstable Rd
30 Clapham, High Street
30 Cranfield, High St
30 Dunstable, Luton Rd
30 Eaton Bray, The Rye
30 Flitwick, High Street
30 Harlington, Barton Rd
30 Heath & Reach, Woburn Rd
30 Kempston, High Street
30 Leighton Buzzard, Billington Rd
30 Leighton Buzzard, Heath Rd
30 Luton, Crawley Green Rd
40 Luton, Dunstable Rd
30 Luton, Leagrave High St
30 Luton, New Bedford Rd
30 Luton, Park Viaduct
30 Luton, Waller Ave
30 Luton, Whitehorse Vale
30 Slip End, Markyate Rd
30 Toddington, Station Rd
30 Upper Caldecote, Hitchin Rd
30 Wrestlingworth, High St
30 Wrestlingworth, Potton Rd

Berkshire

see Thames Valley

Buckinghamshire

see Thames Valley

Cambridgeshire

A10
Littleport

A14
Little Stukeley

A15
New Fletton, London Rd

A141
Clews Corner
Warboys
Wimblington/ Doddington Bypass

A142
Soham Bypass
Witchford Bypass

A505
Whittlesford

A605
Elton, Bullock Rd
Kings Dyke

A1073
Eye Green, Peterborough Rd

A1123
Bluntisham, Needingworth Bypass
St Ives, Houghton Hill
Wiburton Village

A1134
Cambridge

A1303
Cambridge

A1307
Bartlow crossroads
Hills Rd
Linton Bypass

Cheshire

A50
30 Grappenhall, Knutsford Rd
30 Knutsford, Manchester/ Toft Rd
30 Warrington, Long Lane

A51
40 Nantwich, Alpraham

A54
60,70 Ashton, Kelsall Rd

A56
40 Lymm, Camsley Lane

A57
40 Paddington, New Manchester Rd

A523
30 Poynton, London Rd

A532
30 Crewe, West St

A533
40 Middlewich, Booth Lane

A537
50 Macclesfield, Buxton Rd nr Wildboarclough

A5019
30 Crewe, Mill St

A5032
30 Whitby, Chester Rd

A5034
60 Mere, Mereside Rd

A5104
30 Chester, Hough Green

B5071
30 Crewe, Gresty Rd

B5078
30 Alsager, Sandbach Rd North

B5082
30 Northwich, Middlewich Rd

B5132
30 Ellesmere Port, Overpool Rd

B5153
30 Mill Lane/Hollow Lane (speed indicator sign)

B5463
30 Little Sutton, Station Rd

B5470
30 Macclesfield, Rainow Rd

Unclasssified
30 Burtonwood, Lumber Lane
30 Ellesmere Port, Overpool Rd
30 Fearnhead, Harpers Rd
30 Hough Green, Prescot Rd
30 Howley, Battersby Lane
40 Runcorn, Astmoor Rd
30 Runcorn, Boston Ave
30 Runcorn, Clifton Rd
30 Runcorn, Halton Rd
30 Runcorn, Heath Rd
30 Runcorn, Northwich Rd
30 Runcorn, Warrington Rd
30 Vale Royal, Woodford Lane (St John's Drive)
30 Whitecross, Lovely Lane
30 Widnes, Birchfield Rd
30 Widnes, Hough Green Rd
30 Wilmslow, Hough Lane
40 Winsford, Bradford Rd

Cleveland

Darlington, Hartlepool, Middlesbrough, Redcar and Cleveland

A171
50 Redcar, Charltons

A172
40 Middlesbrough, Morton Rd from crossroads to St Lukes
30 Middlesbrough, Morton Rd from Longlands to St Lukes
40 Middlesbrough, Stokesley – from Guisborough Rd Jct to Captain Cooks Crescent

A177
50,60 Stockton, Durham Rd

A178
30 Seaton Carew, The Front

A179
30,40,50 Hartlepool, Easington Rd/Powlett Rd

A689
50 to 40 Hartlepool, from Sappers Corner

B1380
40 Middlesbrough, Ladgate Lane
30 Redcar, Eston

Unclassified
30 Hartlepool, Catcote Rd
40,30 Hartlepool, Coronation Drive
30 Hartlepool, Elwick Rd
30 Hartlepool, King Oswy Drive
30 Hartlepool, Owton Manor Lane & Wynyard Rd
30 Hartlepool, Oxford Rd
30 Hartlepool, Raby Rd
30 Hartlepool, Seaton Lane
30 Hartlepool, Station Lane
30 Hartlepool, Throston Grange Lane
30 Hartlepool, Winterbottom Ave
30 Middlesbrough, Acklam Rd
40 Middlesbrough, Acklam Rd from Blue Bell to the Crematorium
30 Middlesbrough, Mandale Rd
30 Middlesbrough, Ormesby, Normanby Rd
30 Middlesbrough, Ormesby Rd
30 Middlesbrough, Trimdon Ave
30 Redcar, Bankfields Rd
30 Redcar, Carlin How
30 Redcar, Church Lane
30 Redcar, Dormanstow, Broadway
30 Redcar, Flatts Lane
30 Redcar, Greenstones Rd
30,40 Redcar, Kirkleatham Lane
30 Redcar, Marske High St
30 Redcar, Normanby Rd
30 Redcar, Ormesby Bank
30 Redcar, Redcar Lane
30 Redcar, Redcar Rd
30 Redcar, Stanghow Rd
30 Redcar, West Dyke Rd
30 Stockton, Thornaby, Acklam Rd
40 Stockton, Bishopton Ave
30 Stockton, Bishopton Rd West
30 Stockton, Thornaby, Cunningham Drive
30 Stockton, Darlington Lane
30 Stockton, Harrogate Lane
30 Stockton, Junction Rd
30 Stockton, Thames Rd
30 Stockton, Thornaby Rd
30 Stockton, Whitehouse Rd
30 Stockton, Eaglescliffe, Yarm Rd

Cumbria

Mobile cameras may be located on any road.

Derbyshire

A6
30 Allestree
Alvaston
Alvaston to Raynesway
Ashford in the Water
30 Bakewell
Bakewell to Buxton
30 Belper
Belper to Ambergate
Buxton to Dove Holes
Cromford
Darley Dale
30 Derby, London Rd
Dove Holes
Dove Holes to Chapel
Duffield
Furness Vale to Newtown
Matlock
Matlock Bath
Milford to Belper
Northwood
Rowsley to Bakewell
50 Taddington to Buxton

A52
Brailsford
30 Derby, Ashbourne Rd
40 Mackworth
Shirley Hollow

A57
Snake Rd

A511
Swadlincote, Ashby Rd East

A514
Hartshorne
30 Swadlincote
40 Swadlincote to Hartshorne
30 Ticknall

A515
Alsop-en-le-Dale
Sudbury

A516
Derby, Uttoxeter New Rd
Derby, Uttoxeter Rd

A537
30 Cat & Fiddle Rd

A601
30 Derby, Abbey St

A608
30 Heanor, Heanor Rd
30 Smalley

A609
30 Ilkeston, Nottingham Rd
30 Kilburn to Horsley Woodhouse
Stanley Common

A610
40 Codnor
40 Sawmills

A615
30 Tansley
Tansley to Wessington

A616
30 Clowne
30 Creswell
30 North Wingfield

A617
40 Bramley Vale
40 Glapwell to Pleasley

A619
Eastmoor

A623
Peak to Barmoor Clough
Peak Forest
30 Stoney Middleton

A624
50 Chunal to Little Hayfield
Glossop
Hayfield to Chinley

A628
Tintwistle to Boundary

A632
30 Bolsover
Hady to Calow
30 Matlock

A5004
Buxon, Long Hill

A5250
30 Derby, Burton Rd
30 Littleover, Burton Rd

A6005
30 Draycott to Breaston
Long Eaton, Derby Rd
Spondon, Derby Rd

A6007
30 Codnor to Heanor

A6175
30 Holmewood
30 North Wingfield

B600
Somercotes

B5010
Sandiacre, Derby Rd

B5353
30 Newhall, Park Rd

B6019
South Normanton

B6051
30 Chesterfield, Newbold Rd
30 Newbold, Newbold Rd

B6052
30 Whittington

B6057
Chesterfield, Sheffield Rd

B6062
30 Chinley

B6179
Denby
30 Little Eaton
40 Lower Kilburn
50 Lower Kilburn to Little Eaton
30 Ripley to Marehay

B6540
30 Long Eaton, Tamworth Rd

Unclassified
Bolsover, Shuttlewood Rd
30 Chesterfield, Boythorpe Rd
30 Chesterfield, Old Rd
30 Derby, Blagreaves Lane
30 Derby, Kedleston Rd
30 Derby, Stenson Rd
Mickleover, Station Rd
Newhall, Union Rd
30 Shardlow, London Rd
40 Stenson Fields, Stenson Rd
30 Whitwell Common – Barlborough to Whitwell

Devon and Cornwall

A30
60 Chiverton Cross
70 Highgate (Eastbound)
70 Highgate Hill
40 Exeter, Sowton
60 Temple

A38
70 Bittaford Straight, Wrangaton
70 Deep Lane
70 Lee Mill, Lee Mill on-slip
70 Lower Clicker Tor
70 Overbridge, Smithaleigh
70 Smithaleigh, Smithaleigh Overbridge
70 Wrangaton, Bittaford Straight

A39
60 Barras Moor
30 Camelford, Valley Truckle
40 Perranarworthal, nr Truro

A361
50 Barnstaple, Ashford
30 Barnstaple, Eastern Ave
40 Braunton, Knowle
30 Braunton, Knowle (Westerland)
30 Wrafton

A374
40 Plymouth, Plymouth Rd
30 Torpoint, Anthony Rd

A376
30 Ebford
30 Exmouth, Exeter Rd

A377
30 Copplestone
30 Crediton, Western Rd
30 Exeter, Alphington Rd

A379
30 Brixton Village
30 Paignton, Dartmouth Rd
30 Starcross
30 Starcross, The Strand
30 Teignmouth, Teignmouth Rd
30 Torquay, Babbacombe Rd
30 Yealmpton

A380
40 Kingskerswell, Newton Rd

A381
30 Newton Abbott, East St

A385
30 Paignton, Collaton St Mary, Totnes Rd
30 Totnes, Ashburton Rd

A386
60 Chubb Tor
30 Plymouth, Outland Rd
60 Plymouth, Roborough Down
40 Plymouth, Tavistock Rd

A388
30,40 Callington, Kelly Bray

A390
60 Penstraze
60 Sticker Bypass

A394
40 Kenneggy Downs

A396
30 Rewe
30 Stoke Canon, Exeter Rd

A3015
30 Exeter, Topsham Rd

A3047
30 St Ives, Carbis Bay
30 Camborne, Pool, Trevenson Rd
30 Camborne, Tuckingmill

A3058
30 St Austell, Trewoon

A3064
30 Plymouth, St Budeaux Bypass

A3075
60 Newquay, Rosecliston

B3165
30 Raymonds Hill, Crewkerne Rd

B3174
30 Ottery St Mary, Barrack Rd

B3183
30 Exeter, Heavitree Rd
30 Exeter, New North Rd

B3212
30 Exeter, Dunsford Rd
30 Exeter, Pinhoe Rd

B3213
30 Wrangaton Village, nr South Brent

B3233
30 Barnstaple, Bickington Rd

B3250
30 Plymouth, North Hill

B3284
30 Chudleigh, Station Hill
60 Liskey
30 Perranporth, Liskey

B3396
30 Plymouth, Milehouse Rd

Unclassified
30 Avonwick Village
30 Buddle Lane, Exwick Rd
30 Elburton, Haye Rd
30 Exeter, Exwick Lane
30 Fraddon Village, nr Indian Queens
60 Goss Moor, Castle an Dinas
30 Honicknowle, Shakespeare Rd
30 Ivybridge, Exeter Rd
40 Monkton Village
30 Paignton, Colley End Rd
30 Paignton, Preston Down Rd
30 Plymouth, Beacon Park Rd
30 Plymouth, Church Hill
30 Plymouth, Devonport Rd
30 Plymouth, Eggbuckland Rd
30 Plymouth, Glen Rd
30 Plymouth, Honicknowle Lane
30 Plymouth, Lipson Rd
30 Plymouth, Mannamead Rd
30 Plymouth, Molesworth Rd
30 Plymouth, North Prospect Rd
40 Plymouth, Novorrossiysk Rd
30 Plymouth, Pomphlett Rd
30 Plymouth, St Levan Rd
30 Plymouth, Southway Drive
30 Plymouth, Tamerton Foliot Rd
30 Plymouth, Union St
30 Plymouth, Weston Park Rd
30 Plymouth, Wolseley Rd (Both Directions)
30 Plympton, Glen Rd
30 St Judes, Grenville Rd
30 Saltash, Callington Rd

Dorset

A30
Babylon Hill
Shaftesbury, Long Cross

A31
St Leonards, Ringwood Rd
Winterbourne Zelston

A35
Bakers Arms Rdbt
Bridport, Cross Dykes nr Whiteway Cross
Christchurch Bypass
Dorchester, Friary Press
Kingston Russell
Lyndhurst Rd
Morden Mill & Slepe
Poole, Upton Rd
Sea Rd South
Vinney Cross

A37
Grimstone, Dorchester Rd
Holywell Cross
Long Ash Lane
Staggs Folly

A338
Cooper Dean, Wessex Wy
Spur Rd

A348
Bear Cross, Ringwood Rd

A349
Poole, Gravel Hill

A350
Holes Bay Rd to Sterte Rd
Poole Rd
Poole, Upton Country Park
Stourplane, Shashton Rd

A351
Wareham, Sandford Rd

A352
Charminster, North Street
Longburton
Wool, Dorchester Rd

A354
Dorchester Rd Manor Rdbt
Redlands, Dorchester Rd
Ridgeway Hill, Dorchester Rd
Upwey, Dorchester Rd
Weymouth, Buxton Rd
Whitechurch, Winterbourne

A3040
Poole, Alder Rd

A3049
Bournemouth, Alma Rd

A3066
Bridport, Sea Rd North

B3065
Poole, Pinecliff Rd
Poole, The Ave

B3068
Hamworthy, Blandford Rd

B3072
Verwood, Manor Rd

B3073
West Parley, Christchurch Rd
Wimborne, Oakley Hill
Wimborne, Poole Rd

B3074
Poole, Higher Blandford Rd
Poole, Lower Blandford Rd

B3075
Gore Heath, Morden Rd
Stoborough, Corfe Rd
Stoborough, South Causeway

B3081
Ebblake, Ringwood Rd

B3082
Bradbury Rings, Blandford Rd

B3091
Shaftesbury, Salisbury Street

B3092
East Stour, Scotchey Hill
Gillingham, Colesbrook

B3150
Dorchester, Bridport Rd

B3157
Dorchester, Swrye
Lanehouse Rocks Rd
Limekiln Hill
Portesham
Weymouth, Chickerell Rd

B3165
Marshwood School

B3369
Poole, Sandbanks Rd
Poole, Shore Rd

B3390
Crossways, Warmwell Rd

Unclassified
Blandford, Salisbury Rd
Bournemouth, Branksome Wood Rd
Bournemouth, Charminster Ave
Bournemouth, Crabery Ave
Bournemouth, Littledown Ave
Bournemouth, Southbourne Overcliff Drive
Bournemouth, West Way
Bovington, King George V Rd
Broadmayne, Knighton Lane
Canford Heath, Arrowsmith Rd
Christchurch, Ringwood Rd
Christchurch, Walkford, Chewton Farm Rd
Christchurch, Walkford Rd
Constitution Hill Rd
Corfe Mullen, Old Wareham Rd
Gillingham, Bay Rd
Hamworthy, Lulworth Ave
Hamworthy, Rockley Rd
Horton Heath, Horton Rd
Poole, Lilliput Rd
Poole, Old Wareham Rd
Poole, Pound Lane
Portland, Weston Rd
Staplehill, Wimbourne Rd
Upton, Blandford Rd North
Upton, Poole Rd
Wareham/Bere Regis, nr Sugar Hill
Weymouth, Chickerell Rd
Weymouth, Field Barn Drive
Wimborne, Burts Hill
Wimborne, Stone Lane

Essex

A12
Braintree, Overbridge nr Kelvedon Interchange

A13
30 Castle Point, High St (Hadleigh twds London)
Southend, North Shoebury
Southend, Southchurch Boulevard

A104
Epping New Rd

A121
30 Epping, High Rd
Epping, Honey Lane

A126
30 Grays, London Rd

A128
30 Ingrave/Herongate, Brentwood Rd

A129
30 Billericay, Southend Rd
Rayleigh, London Rd
30 Wickford, London Rd
Wickford, Southend Rd

A131
Bournebridge Hill

A133
Colchester, St Andrews Ave
Frating Hill
Little Bentley, Colchester Rd
Tendring
Weeley

A414
Danbury, Main Rd
Epping Rd
Ongar Rd

A1016
30 Chelmsford, Waterhouse Lane

A1023
30 Brentwood, Shenfield Rd

A1025
40 Harlow, Third Ave

A1090
30 Purfleet, London Rd

A1124
30 Colchester, Lexden Rd
Halstead, Hedingham Road

A1158
30 Westcliff on Sea, Southbourne Grove

A1232
30 Colchester, Ipswich Rd

A1235
40 Basildon, Cranes Farm Road

B170
30 Chigwell, Chigwell Rise

B173
Chigwell

B184
Great Dunmow

B186
30 South Ockendon, South Rd

B1002
30 Ingatestone, High St

B1006
Benfleet

B1007
30 Billericay, Stock Rd
40 Chelmsford, Stock Rd

B1008
30 Chelmsford, Broomfield Rd

B1009
Chelmsford

B1010&B1012
Maldon, Lower Burnham Road

B1013
30 Rayleigh, Hockley Rd

B1014
Canvey Island

B1016
30 Southend, Shoebury Common Road

B1019
30 Hatfield Peveral, Maldon Rd

B1022
Maldon

B1027
30 Clacton-on-Sea, St Johns Rd

B1033
30 Kirby Cross, Frinton Rd

B1335
40 South Ockendon, Stifford Rd

B1352
Harwich, Main Rd

B1383
30 Newport, London Rd

B1389
30 Witham, Hatfield Rd

B1393
Epping

B1442
30 Clacton-on-Sea, Thorpe Rd

B1464
Basildon
30 Bowers Gifford, London Rd

Unclassified
40 Alresford, St Osyth Rd
30 Aveley, Purfleet Rd
30 Basildon, Clay Hill Rd
Basildon, Pound Lane
30 Basildon, Vange Hill Drive
30 Basildon, Whitmore Wy
30 Braintree, Coldnailhurst Ave
Brentwood, Coxtie Green Road
30 Canvey Island, Link Rd
Chadwell St Mary, Brentwood Rd
30 Chelmsford, Chignall Rd
Chelmsford, Galleywood Rd
30 Chelmsford, New Bowers Way
30 Clacton-on-Sea, St Johns Rd
30 Colchester, Abbots Rd
30 Colchester, Avon Wy
30 Corringham, Springhouse Rd
Danbury, Maldon Rd
30 Eastwood, Green Lane j/w Kendal Wy
30 Eastwood, Western Approaches j/w Rockall
30 Grays, Blackshots Lane
30 Grays, Lodge Lane
Grays, London Rd (nr Bransons Wy)
40 Harlow, Howard Wy
30 Laindon, Wash Rd
30 Leigh on Sea, Belton Way East
30 Leigh on Sea, Belton Wy West
30 Leigh on Sea, Grand Parade/Cliff Parade
30 Leigh on Sea, Mountdale Gardens
30 Leigh on Sea, Western Rd
Loughton, Valley Hill
30 Pitsea, Rectory Rd
30 Prittlewell, Kenilworth Gardens
30 Prittlewell, Prittlewell Chase
Rayleigh, Downhall Rd
30 Rayleigh, Trinity Rd, nr Church Rd
30 Rochford, Ashingdon Rd
30 Shoeburyness, Ness Rd
Southend, Bournemouth Park Rd
30 Southend, Hamstel Rd
30 Southend, Lifstan Wy
30 Stanford le Hope, London Rd
30 Thorpe Bay, Barnstaple Rd
30 Thorpe Bay, Thorpe Hall Ave
30 Waltham Abbey, Paternoster Hill
Weeley Heath, Clacton Rd
30 Westcliff on Sea, Chalkwell Ave
30 Westcliff on Sea, Kings Rd
30 Wickford, Clayhill Rd
30 Wickford, London Rd
30 Witham, Powers Hall End

Gloucestershire

A38
40 Twigworth

A40
60 Andoversford
60 The Barringtons
50 Churcham
60 Farmington
40 Gloucester Rd
60 Hampnett
60 Hazleton
60 Northleach
60 Whittington Area

A46
30 Ashchurch
40 North of Nailsworth

A48
60 Stroat

A417
70 Burford Jct
30 Corse, Gloucester Rd
70 Dartley Bottom
40 nr Hartpury
40 Lechlade
30 Maisemore

A419
40 Oldends Lane to Stonehouse Ct

A429
60 nr Bourton-on-the-Water
40 Fossebridge

A430
40 Hempsted Bypass

A435
60 Colesbourne

A436
60 Jct with B4068 Westfield

A4013
30 Gloucester, Princess Elizabeth Wy
30 Gloucester, Princess Elizabeth Wy (Arle)

A4019
50 Uckington

A4136
40 Brierley
40 Coleford, Lower Lane
40 Harrow Hill
40 Little London

A4151
40 Steam Mills

A4173
30 nr St Peters School

B4008
30 Hardwicke, Bristol Rd south of Tesco rdbt
30 Olympus Park, Bristol Rd
30 Stonehouse, Gloucester Rd

B4060
30 Katherine Lady Berkeley's School

B4215
50 South of Newent Bypass
50 South east of Rudford

B4221
40 Kilcot Village
30 Picklenash School

B4226
60 Speech House

B4228
30 Coleford, Old Station Wy
40 Perrygrove

B4231
30 Bream, Coleford Rd

B4633
30 Cheltenham, Gloucester Rd

Unclassified
30 Gloucester, Abbeymead Ave
30 Gloucester, Barrow Hill
30 Gloucester, Chesterton Lane
30 Gloucester, Parkend, Fancy Rd
30 Gloucester, St Georges Rd
30 Gloucester, Swindon Lane
30 Gloucester, Wymans Lane
30 Lydney, Highfield Rd
40 Minchinhampton Common
30 Siddington
40 Tewkesbury, Gloucester Rd

Greater Manchester

A6
Manchester, Stockport Rd
Salford, Manchester Rd

A34
Manchester, Birchfield Road

A49
Marus Bridge, Warrington Rd

A56
Bury, Bury New Rd
Bury, Walmersley Rd
Bury, Whalley Rd

A57
Manchester, Hyde Rd
Salford, Liverpool Rd
Tameside, Manchester Rd

A58
Bury, Bury & Bolton Rd
Bury, Rochdale Rd

A62
Manchester, Oldham Rd
Oldham, Oldham Rd
Oldham, Oldham Wy

A575
Salford, Walkden Rd

A580
Salford, East Lancashire Rd

A627
Oldham, Ashton Rd
Oldham, Chadderton Wy

A662
Manchester, Ashton New Rd

A663
Oldham, Broadway

A664
Manchester, Rochdale Rd

A665
Bury, New Rd
Bury, Radcliffe New Rd

A666
Bolton, Blackburn Rd
Bolton, St Peter's Wy
Salford, Manchester Rd

A667
Bury, Ringley Rd West

A5103
Manchester, Princess Parkway/Road

A6010
Manchester, Alan Turing Wy

A6044
Prestwich, Hilton Lane
Prestwich, Sheepfoot Lane

A6053
Radcliffe, Dumers Lane

A6104
Blackley, Victoria Ave

B6196
Ainsworth, Church Street
Ainsworth, Cockey Moor Rd

B6213
Tottington, Turton Rd

B6214
Greenmount, Brandlesholme Rd
Holcombe, Helmshore Rd
Holcombe Brook, Longsight Rd

B6226
Horwich, Chorley Old Rd

Unclassified
Ashton on Mersey, Ashton Lane
Bolton, Chorley Old Rd
Bolton, Hardy Mill Rd
Bolton, Hulton Lane
Bolton, Lever Park Ave
Bolton, Plodder Lane
Bolton, Stitch Mi Lane
Bredbury, Ashton Rd
Bury, Croft Lane
Bury, Higher Lane
Bury, Stand Lane
Bury, Walshaw Rd
Manchester, Blackley New Rd
Manchester, Kingsway
Manchester, Mancunian Wy
Oldham, Abbey Hills Rd
Oldham, Manchester Rd
Rochdale, Bagslate Moor Rd
Rochdale, Broad Lane
Rochdale, Bury Old Rd
Rochdale, Caldershaw Rd
Rochdale, Edenfield Rd
Rochdale, Halifax Rd
Rochdale, Heywood Old Rd
Rochdale, Hollin Lane
Rochdale, Manchester Rd
Rochdale, Queens Park Rd
Rochdale, Shawclough Rd
Rochdale, Smithybridge Rd
Rochdale, Todmorden Rd
Rochdale, Wildhouse Lane
Salford, Belvedere Rd
Salford, Langley Rd
Stockport, Birdhall Lane
Stockport, Bridge Lane
Stockport, Buxton Rd
Stockport, Chester Rd
Stockport, Councillor Lane
Stockport, Dialstone Lane
Stockport, Harrytown
Stockport, Jacksons Lane
Stockport, Kingsway
Stockport, Longhurst Lane
Stockport, Marple Rd
Stockport, Sandy Lane
Stockport, Schools Hill
Stockport, Strines Rd
Stockport, Styal Rd
Stockport, Wellington Rd North
Tameside, Mossley Rd
Tameside, Mottram Old Rd
Tameside, Mottram Rd
Tameside, Stamford Rd
Tameside, Stamford Street
Trafford, Church Rd
Trafford, Edge Lane
Trafford, Glebelands Rd
Trafford, Hope Rd
Trafford, Mosley Rd
Trafford, Norris Rd
Trafford, Park Rd
Trafford, Seymour Grove
Trafford, Warburton Lane
Trafford, Westinghouse Rd
Wigan, Almond Brook Rd
Wigan, Bickershaw Lane
Wigan, Bolton Rd
Wigan, Chaddock Lane
Wigan, Chorley Rd
Wigan, Crow Orchard Rd
Wigan, Lily Lane
Wigan, Newton Rd
Wigan, Pemberton Rd
Wigan, Scot Lane
Wigan, Victoria Street
Wigan, Wigan Rd

Hampshire and Isle of Wight

A27
30/40 Fareham
30 Fareham, Portchester Rd

A30
30/40 Blackwater
30/40 Hook

A33
50 Basingstoke
50 Southampton, Millbrook Rd

A325
30/40/60 East Hampshire (south)
30/40/60/70 Rushmoor (north)

A334/B2177
30/40/60 Wickham

A335
30/40 Eastleigh

A337
30/40 New Forest

A338
40/60 New Forest

A339
60 Lasham

A340
30/60 Basingstoke

A2047
30 Portsmouth, Fratton Rd

A3020
40 Newport, Blackwater Rd
40 Newport, Horsebridge Hill

A3021
30 East Cowes, York Ave

A3024
30/40 Southampton, Bursledon Rd
30 Southampton, Northam Rd/Bitterne Rd West

A3054
30 Binstead, Binstead Hill
30/40 Newport, Fairlee Rd
30 Wootton / Lushington Hill, High St

A3055
30 Brading, High Street/New Rd

B2149
30 Hampshire, New Rd
40 Hampshire, Petersfield Rd

B3037/A335
30/40 Eastleigh

B3055
30/40 New Forest

B3272
30/40 Yateley

B3330
30 Ryde, St Johns Hill

B3395
30 Sandown, Culver Parade

Unclassified
30 East Cowes, Victoria Grove/Adelaide Grove
40 Gosport, Grange Rd
30 Isle of Wight, Carisbrooke Rd
30 Newport, Staplers Rd/Long Lane
30 Portsmouth, Clarence Esplanade
30 Portsmouth, Northern Rd
40 Southampton, The Ave

Herefordshire

see West Mercia

Hertfordshire

A409
30 Bushey, Heathbourne Rd

A411
30 Bushey, London Rd
30 Elstree, Barnet Lane
30 Watford, Hempstead Rd

A414
40 Hemel Hempstead, St Albans Rd
40 Hertford, Hertingfordbury Rd

A505
30 Hitchin, Cambridge Rd

A600
30 Hitchin, Bedford Rd

A602
40 Hitchin, Stevenage Rd
40 Stevenage, Broadhall Wy

A1000
40 Potters Bar, Barnet Rd

A1057
30/40 St Albans, Hatfield Rd

A1170
30 Turnford, High Rd Wormley

A4125
40 South Oxhey, Sandy Lane

A4147
30 Hemel Hempstead, Leverstock Green Rd

A4251
30 Bourne End, London Rd

A5183
30 Elstree, Elstree Hill South
30 Frogmore, Park Street

A6141
40 Letchworth, Letchworth Gate

B156
30 Cheshunt, Goffs Lane

B176
30 Cheshunt, High Street

B197
30 Baldock, London Rd
30 Stevenage, North Rd

B462
30 Bushey, Aldenham Rd

B487
30 Hatching Green, Redbourn Lane

B488
40 Tring, Icknield Wy

B556
30 Potters Bar, Mutton Lane

B1004
30 Bishops Stortford, Windhill

B1197
30 Hertford, London Rd

B1502
30 Hertford, Stanstead Rd

B4505
30 Bovingdon, Chesham Rd

B4630
30 Chiswell Green, Watford Rd

B5378
30 Borehamwood, Allum Lane

B6426
30 Hatfield, Cavendish Wy

Unclassified
30 Cheshunt, Hammondstreet Rd
30 Hemel Hempstead, Bennetts End Rd
30 Hemel Hempstead, High Street Green
30 Hemel Hempstead, Long Chaulden
40 Hemel Hempstead, Queensway
30 Hoddesdon, Essex Rd
30 Letchworth, Pixmore Wy
30 Royston, Old North Rd
30 St Albans, Sandpit Lane
30 South Oxhey, Hayling Rd
30 Stevenage, Clovelly Wy
30 Stevenage, Grace Wy
40 Stevenage, Gresley Wy
40 Stevenage, Monkswood Wy
30 Watford, Radlett Rd
30 Watford, Tolpits Lane
30 Welwyn Garden City, Heronswood Rd
30 Welwyn Garden City, Howlands

Humberside

East Riding of Yorkshire, Hull, North East Lincolnshire, North Lincolnshire

M180
NSL West of River Trent

A18
NSL Barton St Central
NSL Barton St North
NSL Barton St South

A63
40 Hull, Castle St
40 Hull, Daltry St Flyover
50 Melton

A161
30 Belton

A163
30 Holme on Spalding Moor

A164
30 Leconfield

A165
30 Beeford
40 Coniston
30 Hull, Freetown Wy
40 Hull, Holderness Rd
30 Skirlaugh

A180
NSL Great Coates Jct

A614
40 Holme on Spalding Moor
30 Middleton on the Wolds
NSL Shiptonthorpe

A1033
40 Hull, Thomas Clarkson Wy
30 Thorngumbald, Main St
30 Withernsea

A1077
30 Barton

A1079
50 Barmby Moor
30 Bishop Burton
30 Hull, Beverley Rd (Desmond Ave to Riverdale Rd)
40 Hull, Beverley Rd (Sutton Rd to Mizzen Rd)

A1084
30 Brigg, Bigby High Rd

A1174
30 Dunswell
30 Woodmansey

B1206
30 Barrow, Wold Rd

B1230
40 Gilberdyke
40 Newport

B1398
40 Greetwell

Unclassified
30 Ashby, Grange Lane South
30 Ashby, Messingham Rd
30 Belton, Westgate Rd
30 Beverley, Hull Bridge Rd
30 Bilton, Main Rd
30 Bridlington, Kingsgate
30 Bridlington, Quay Rd/St John's St
30 Broughton, High St
30 Cleethorpes, Clee Rd
30 East Halton, College Rd
30 Goole, Airmyn Rd
30 Grimsby, Cromwell Rd
30 Grimsby, Great Coates Rd
30 Grimsby, Laceby Rd
30 Grimsby, Louth Rd
30 Grimsby, Waltham Rd
30 Grimsby, Weelsby Rd
30 Hessle, Beverley Rd
30 Hornsea, Rolston Rd
30 Howden, Thorpe Rd
30 Hull, Anlaby Rd
40 Hull, Boothferry Rd
30 Hull, Bricknell Ave
30 Hull, Greenwood Ave
30 Hull, Hall Rd
30 Hull, John Newton Wy/Bude Rd
30 Hull, Leads Rd
30 Hull, Marfleet Ave
30 Hull, Marfleet Lane
30 Hull, Priory Rd
30 Hull, Saltshouse Rd
40 Hull, Spring Bank West
30 Hull, Wawne Rd
30 Humberston, Tetney Rd
30 Immingham, Pelham Rd
NSL Laceby Bypass
30 Preston, Station Rd
30 Scunthorpe, Ashby Rd
30 Scunthorpe, Cambridge Ave
30 Scunthorpe, Cottage Beck Rd
40 Scunthorpe, Doncaster Rd
30 Scunthorpe, Luneburg Wy
40 Scunthorpe, Queensway
30 Scunthorpe, Rowland Rd
30 South Killingholme, Top Rd
30 Yaddlethorpe, Moorwell Rd

Kent and Medway

A2
70 Dunkirk/Upper Harbledown
60 Guston
70 Lydden
40 Rochester, London Rd

A20
70,40 Dover, Dover Rd/Archcliffe
40,50 Tonbridge & Malling, London Rd

A21
60 Key's Green
70 Sevenoaks Bypass
60 Tonbridge, Castle Hill

A25
30 Sevenoaks, Seal Rd

A26
40 Hadlow, Maidstone Rd

A28
40 Bethersden, Ashford Rd

A224
30 Sevenoaks, Tubs Hill

A225
30 Otford, Sevenoaks Rd

A226
50 Chalk, Rochester Rd/Gravesend Rd
40 Higham, Rochester Rd/Gravesend Rd
50 Shorne, Rochester Rd/Gravesend Rd

A227
30 Culverstone Green
40 Istead Rise

A228
40 Chattenden, Ratcliffe Highway
40 Sundridge, Sundridge Hill
30 Tonbridge, Seven Mile Lane

A229
- 40 Cranbrook, Angley Rd
- 50 Maidstone, Bluebell Hill
- 40,30 Maidstone, Linton Rd/Loose Rd
- 30 Rochester, City Wy

A249
- 50 Newington, Chestnut St
- 70 South Street

A253
- 30 Cliffsend, Canterbury Rd West

A256
- 70 Betteshanger
- 70 Tilmanstone

A258
- 50 Ringwould, Dover Rd

A259
- 60 Brookland, Guldeford Lane
- 30 New Romney, High St
- 40 St Marys Bay

A262
- 30 Biddenden, High St

A268
- 30 Sandhurst, Queen St

A289
- 50 Chatham, Medway Tunnel
- 70 Wainscott, Wainscott Bypass

A290
- 30 Blean

A291
- 30 Herne, Canterbury Rd

A2033
- 30 Folkestone, Dover Rd

A2990
- 60 Swalecliffe, Old Thanet Wy

B258
- 30 Wilmington, Barn End Lane

B2000
- 40 Strood

B2015
- 40 Nettlestead Green, Maidstone Rd

B2017
- 30 Five Oak Green, Badsell Rd

B2019
- 30 Seal Hollow Rd

B2097
- 30 Rochester, Maidstone Rd

Unclassified
- 30 Cobham, Sole St
- 30 Gillingham, Beechings Wy
- 30 Herne Bay, Mickleburgh Hill
- 30 Longfield, Ash Rd/ Hartley Rd
- 30 Margate, Shottendane Rd
- 30 Rainham, Maidstone Rd
- 30 Rochester, Esplanade
- 30 Sevenoaks, Ash Rd/ Hartley Rd
- 30,40 Sheerness, Marine Parade
- 30 Sittingbourne, Mill Wy
- 30 Teynham, Lower Rd

Lancashire

A6
- 40 Broughton, Garstang Rd (north of M55)
- 30 Chorley, Bolton Rd
- 30 Fulwood, Garstang Rd (south of M55)
- 30 Fulwood, Garstang Rd, north of Blackpool Rd
- 30 Lancaster, Greaves Rd
- 50 Lancaster, Scotforth Rd nr Burrow Lane Bailrigg
- 30 Preston, North Rd
- 30 Preston, Ringway

A56
- 30 Colne, Albert Rd
- 30 Colne, Burnley Rd
- 30 Nelson, Leeds Rd

A59
- 60 Gisburn, Gisburn Rd
- 50 Hutton, Liverpool Rd
- 30 Preston, New Hall Lane

A65
- 40 Lancaster, Cowan Bridge

A570
- 40 Scarisbrick, Southport Rd, Brook House Farm

A581
- 40 Ulnes Walton, Southport Rd

A583&A5073
- 30 Blackpool, Whitegate Drive/Waterloo Rd

A583&B5266
- 30 Blackpool, Church St/Newton Drive

A584
- 30 Blackpool, Promenade
- 30 Lytham, West/ Central Beach
- 30 Warton, Lytham Rd

A584&A587
- 30 Blackpool, Promenade/ Fleetwood Rd

A587
- 30 Blackpool, East/North Park Drive
- 30 Cleveleys, Rossall Rd/Crescent East

A588
- 60 Pilling, Head Dyke Lane
- 60 Wyre, Lancaster Rd, Cockerham at Gulf Lane

A666
- 30 Darwen, Blackburn Rd
- 30 Darwen, Bolton Rd nr Cross St
- 30 Darwen, Duckworth St

A671
- 30 Read, Whalley Rd

A674
- 30 Cherry Tree, Preston Old Rd

A675
- 50 Belmont, Belmont Rd (south of village)
- 50 Darwen, Belmont Rd, north of Belmont Village
- 60 Withnell, Bolton Rd (Dole Lane to Calf Hey Bridge)

A680
- 40 Edenfield, Rochdale Rd

A682
- 60 Barrowford, Gisburn Rd nr Moorcock Inn
- 30 Brierfield, Colne Rd
- 40 Crawshawbooth, Burnley Rd
- 60 Gisburn, Gisburn Rd
- 60 Gisburn, Long Preston Rd

A683
- 30 Lancaster, Morecambe Rd

A5073
- 30 Blackpool, Waterloo Rd

A5085
- 30 Lane Ends, Blackpool Rd

A5209
- 30 Newburgh, Course Lane/Ash Brow

A6062
- Blackburn, Livesey Branch Rd nr Green Lane

A6068
- 50 Barrowford, Barrowford Rd

A6114
- 30 Burnley, Casterton Ave

A6177
- Blackburn, Haslingden Rd/Elton Rd/Belthorn to Grey Mare Inn
- 50 Haslingden, Grane Rd West of Holcombe Rd

B5192
- 30 Kirkham, Preston St

B5242
- Scarisbrick, Bescar Brow Lane – Hall Road Bescar

B5251
- 30 Chorley, Pall Mall

B5254
- 30 Lostock Hall, Leyland Rd/Watkin Lane
- 30 South Ribble, Leyland Rd

B5256
- 30 Leyland, Turpin Green Lane

B6231
- 30 Oswaldtwistle, Union Rd

B6243
- Longridge, Preston Rd

Unclassified
- 60 Belmont, Egerton Rd
- 30 Blackburn, East Park Rd
- 30 Blackburn, Revidge Rd nr Pleckgate
- 30 Blackburn, Whalley Old Rd
- 30 Blackpool, Dickson Rd, Queens St to Pleasant St
- 30 Briercliffe, Burnley Rd
- 30 Darwen, Lower Eccleshill Rd
- 60 Galgate, Bay Horse Rd
- 30 Nelson, Netherfield Rd
- 30 Preston, Lytham Rd
- 30 Preston, St Georges Rd
- 30 St Anne's, Church Rd to Albany Rd, nr High School

Leicestershire and Rutland

A1
- NSL Empingham, Great North Rd
- NSL Stretton, Great North Rd

A5
- NSL Hinckley, Watling St (B578 to M69)
- Hinckley, Watling St (M69 to A47)
- NSL Sharnford, Watling St (Highcross to B4114)

A6
- 40 Birstall, Loughborough Rd
- 40 Leicester, Abbey Lane
- 30 Leicester, London Rd (Knighton Drive)
- 30 Loughborough, Derby Rd
- 40 Oadby, Glen Rd/ Harborough Rd

A47
- NSL Barrowden, Peterborough Rd
- NSL Bisbrooke, Uppingham Rd/Glaston, Main Rd
- 30 Earl Shilton, Hinckley Rd
- 40 Houghton on the Hill
- 30 Leicester, Hinckley Rd
- 30 Leicester, Humberstone Rd
- 30 Leicester, Uppingham Rd (Spencefield Lane)
- 50 Morcott, Glaston Rd

A50
- 40 Leicester/Glenfield, Groby Rd/Leicester Rd
- 30 Leicester, Woodgate/ Frog Island

A426
- 50 Dunton Bassett, Lutterworth Rd
- 40 Glen Parva, Leicester Rd
- NSL Lutterworth, Leicester Rd
- NSL Whetstone, Lutterworth Rd

A444
- 50 Norton Juxta Twycross
- 30 Twycross Village, Main Rd

A447
- NSL Cadeby, Hinckley Rd
- 40 Ravenstone, Wash Lane/Melbourne Rd

A512
- 30 Loughborough, Ashby Rd
- 40 Shepshed, Ashby Rd Central

A563
- 30 Leicester, Asquith Wy
- 30 Leicester, Attlee Wy
- 30 Leicester, Colchester Rd/Hungarton Boulevard
- 30 Leicester, Glenhills Wy
- 40 Leicester, Krefield Wy
- 30 Leicester, New Parks Wy

A594
- 30 Leicester, St Georges Wy

A606
- NSL Barnsdale, Stamford Rd
- NSL Leicester, Broughton/ Old Dalby
- NSL Tinwell, Stamford Rd

A607
- 30 Leicester, Melton Rd
- 50 Thurmaston, Newark Rd
- NSL Waltham, Melton Rd

A4304
- 30 Market Harborough, Lubbenham Hill

A5199
- 30 Leicester, Welford Rd
- 30 Wigston, Bull Head St
- 30 Wigston, Leicester Rd

A5460
- 40 Leicester, Narborough Rd

A6004
- 30 Loughborough, Alan Moss Rd

A6030
- 30 Leicester, Wakerley Rd/Broad Ave

A6121
- 30 Ketton, Stamford Rd

B568
- 30 Leicester, Victoria Park Rd

B581
- 30 Broughton Astley, Broughton Wy/Station Rd

B582
- 30 Blaby, Little Glen Rd

B590
- 30 Hinckley, Rugby Rd

B591
- NSL Charley, Loughborough Rd

B4114
- 40 Enderby, Leicester Rd/Narborough, King Edward Ave
- 30 Sharnford

B4666
- 30 Hinckley, Coventry Rd

B5003
- 40 Norris Hill, Ashby Rd

B5006
- 30 Ashby, Tamworth Rd

B5350
- 30 Loughborough, Forest Rd
- 30 Loughborough, Nanpantan Rd

B6416
- 30 Leicester, East Park Rd

Unclassified
- 30 Barrow upon Soar, Sileby Rd
- 30 Blaby, Lutterworth Rd
- 30 Glenfield, Station Rd
- 30 Ibstock, Leicester Rd
- 30 Leicester, Beaumont Leys Lane
- 30 Leicester, Fosse Rd South
- 30 Shepshed, Leicester Rd

Lincolnshire

A15
- 60 Ashby Lodge
- 60 Aswarby

A15-B1191
- 60 Dunsby Hollow

A16
- 60 Boston, Boston Tytton Lane
- 40 Burwell
- 50/60 Deeping Bypass
- 60 North Thoresby
- 60 Stickney Fenside

A17
- 60 Fleet Hargate
- 60 Hoffleet Stow
- 60 Moulton Common

A52
- 60 Bridge End
- 60 Horbling & Swaton
- 60 Ropsley

A153
- 40 Billinghay
- 50 Tattershall

A158
- 40/50 Scremby to Candlesby

A631
- 60 Dale Bridge
- 50/60 Hemswell

B1188
- 30 Branston
- 60 Canwick, Highfield House
- 60 Potterhanworth

B1191
- 60 Martin Dales

London

M11
- Chadwell

M25
- Egham
- Elmbridge, Byfleet
- Hillingdon
- Hillingdon, Colnbrook
- Runneymeade
- Spelthorne
- Wraysbury

A3
- Kingston Bypass
- Wandsworth, Kingston Rd

A4
- Hounslow, Brentford, Great West Rd
- Hounslow, Great West Rd

A5
- Barnet, Hendon Broadway
- Brent, Edgware Rd

A10
- Enfield, Great Cambridge Rd
- Hackney, Stamford Hill

A13
- Barking & Dagenham, Alfreds Wy
- Barking & Dagenham, Ripple Rd
- Dagenham, Ripple Rd
- Newham, Alfreds Wy

A20
- Bexley, Sidcup Rd
- Bromley, Sidcup Bypass
- Greenwick, Sidcup Rd

A21
- Lewisham, Bromley Rd

A22
- Croydon, Godstone Rd

A40
- City of Westminster, Westway
- Ealing, Perivale
- Ealing, Western Ave
- Hammersmith & Fulham, Westway
- Hillingdon, Ruislip, Western Ave

A110
- Enfield, Enfield Rd

A124
- Newham, Barking Rd

A205
- Richmond upon Thames
- Richmond upon Thames, Upper Richmond Rd West

A213
- Bromley, Croydon Rd

A214
- Wandsworth, Trinity Rd

A215
- Croydon, Beulah Hill

A217
- Croydon, Garratt Lane

A219
- Hammersmith & Fulham, Scrubs Lane

A222
- Bromley, Bromley Rd

A232
- Sutton, Cheam Rd

A298
- West Barnes, Bushey Rd

A312
- Hillingdon

A315
- Hounslow, High St

A406
- Barking & Dagenham, Barking Relief Rd
- Barnet, North Circular Rd
- Redbridge, Southend Rd

A501
- Camden, Euston Rd

A503
- Haringey, Seven Sisters Rd

A3220
- Wandsworth, Latchmere Rd

A4006
- Brent, Kenton Rd

B178
- Barking & Dagenham, Ballards Rd

B272
- Sutton, Foresters Rd

B278
- Sutton, Green Lane

B279
- Sutton, Tudor Drive

Unclassified
- Barnet, Oakleigh Rd South
- Bexley, Abbey Rd
- Bexley, Bellegrove Rd
- Bexley, Erith Rd
- Bexley, Farady Ave
- Bexley, King Harolds Wy
- Bexley, Lower Rd
- Bexley, Penhill Rd
- Bexley, Pickford Lane
- Bexley, Well Hall Rd
- Bexley, Woolwich Rd
- Brent, Crest Rd
- Brent, Hillside
- Brent, Kingsbury Rd
- Brent, Kingsbury, Fryent Wy
- Brent, Sudbury, Watford Rd
- Brent, Wembley, Watford Rd
- Brent, Woodcock Hill
- Bromley, Beckenham Rd
- Bromley, Burnt Ash Lane
- Bromley, Crystal Palace Park Rd
- Bromley, Elmers End Rd
- Bromley, Main Rd
- Bromley, Sevenoaks Wy
- Bromley, Wickham Wy
- City of Westminster, Great Western Rd
- City of Westminster, Millbank
- City of Westminster, Vauxhall Bridge Rd
- Croydon, Addiscombe, Long Lane
- Croydon, Brigstock Rd
- Croydon, Coulsdon, Coulsdon Rd
- Croydon, Coulsdon, Portnalls Rd
- Croydon, Thornton Rd
- Ealing, Greenford, Greenford Rd
- Ealing, Horn Lane
- Ealing, Lady Margaret Rd
- Ealing, Ruislip Rd
- Ealing, Southall, Greenford Rd
- Ealing, Uxbridge Rd
- Eastcote, Field End Rd
- Enfield, Fore St
- Forest Hill, Stanstead Rd
- Greenwich, Beresford St
- Greenwich, Court Rd
- Greenwich, Creek Rd
- Greenwich, Glenesk Rd
- Greenwich, Rochester Wy
- Greenwich, Woolwich Church St
- Hackney, Clapton Common
- Hackney, Seven Sisters Rd
- Hackney, Upper Clapton Rd
- Hammersmith & Fulham, Fulham Palace Rd
- Hammersmith & Fulham, Uxbridge Rd
- Hammersmith & Fulham, Westway
- Haringey, Belmont Rd
- Haringey, Bounds Green Rd
- Haringey, Seven Sisters Rd
- Haringey, White Hart Lane
- Harrow, Alexandra Ave
- Harrow, Harrow View
- Harrow, Harrow Weald, Uxbridge Rd
- Harrow, Honeypot Lane
- Harrow, Porlock Ave
- Harrow, Watford Rd
- Havering, Chase Cross Rd
- Havering, Eastern Ave
- Havering, Hall Lane
- Havering, Hornchurch, Parkstone Ave
- Havering, Ockenden Rd
- Havering, Romford, Brentwood Rd
- Havering, Wingletye Lane
- Hillingdon, Cowley, Cowley Rd
- Hillingdon, Cowley, High Rd
- Hillingdon, Harefield, Church Hill
- Hillingdon, Hayes, Kingshill Ave
- Hillingdon, Hayes, Uxbridge Rd
- Hillingdon, Northwood Hills, Joel St
- Hillingdon, Park Rd
- Hillingdon, Stockley Rd
- Hillingdon, Uxbridge, Cowley Rd
- Hounslow, Bedfont, Hatton Rd
- Hounslow, Great West Rd
- Hounslow, Hanworth, Castle Wy
- Hounslow, Harlington Rd West
- Islington, Holloway Rd
- Islington, Seven Sisters Rd
- Islington, Upper St
- Kensington & Chelsea, Barlby Rd
- Kensington & Chelsea, Chelsea Embankment
- Kensington & Chelsea, Chesterton Rd
- Kensington & Chelsea, Holland Park Ave
- Kensington & Chelsea, Holland Villas Rd
- Kensington & Chelsea, Kensington Park Rd
- Kensington & Chelsea, Kensington Rd
- Kensington & Chelsea, Ladbroke Grove
- Kensington & Chelsea, Latimer Rd
- Kensington & Chelsea, Royal Hospital Rd
- Kensington & Chelsea, St Helens Gardens
- Kensington & Chelsea, Sloane St
- Kingston upon Thames, Kingston Rd
- Kingston upon Thames, Manor Drive North
- Kingston upon Thames, Richmond Rd
- Lambeth, Atkins Rd
- Lambeth, Brixton Hill
- Lambeth, Clapham Rd
- Lambeth, Herne Hill Rd
- Lambeth, Kennington Park Rd
- Lambeth, Kings Ave
- Lambeth, Streatham High Rd
- Lewisham, Brockley Rd
- Lewisham, Brownhill Rd
- Lewisham, Burnt Ash Hill
- Lewisham, Lee High Rd
- Lewisham, Lewisham Wy
- Lewisham, Westwood Hill
- Merton, Central Rd
- Merton, Colliers Wood, High St
- Merton, Hillcross
- Merton, London Rd
- Merton, Martin Wy
- Merton, Ridgway Place
- Merton, West Barnes Lane
- Newham, Barking Rd
- Newham, Romford Rd
- Newham, Royal Albert Dock, Spine Rd
- Newham, Royal Docks Rd
- North Dagenham, Rainham Rd
- Redbridge, Hainault, Manford Wy
- Redbridge, Woodford
- Redbridge, Woodford Rd
- Richmond upon Thames, Kew Rd
- Richmond upon Thames, Sixth Cross Rd
- Richmond upon Thames, Uxbridge Rd
- Southwark, Albany Rd
- Southwark, Alleyn Park
- Southwark, Brenchley Gardens
- Southwark, Camberwell New Rd
- Southwark, Denmark Hill
- Southwark, Kennington Park Rd
- Southwark, Linden Grove
- Southwark, Old Kent Rd
- Southwark, Peckham Rye
- Southwark, Salter Rd
- Southwark, Sunray
- Streatham, Streatham High Rd
- Sutton, Beddington Lane
- Sutton, Cheam Common Rd
- Sutton, Maiden Rd
- Sutton, Middleton Rd
- Tower Hamlets, Bow Rd
- Tower Hamlets, Cambridge Heath Rd
- Tower Hamlets, Homerton High Rd
- Tower Hamlets, Manchester Rd
- Tower Hamlets, Mile End Rd
- Tower Hamlets, Upper Clapton Rd
- Tower Hamlets, Westferry Rd
- Waltham Forest, Chingford Rd
- Waltham Forest, Hoe St
- Waltham Forest, Larksall Rd
- Wandsworth, Battersea Park Rd
- Wandsworth, Garratt Lane
- Wandsworth, Upper Richmond Rd
- Woolwich, Woolwich Church St

Merseyside

Unclassified
- 30 Knowsley, Bowring Rd/Roby Rd
- 40 Knowsley, East Prescot Rd
- 30 Liverpool, Great Homer Street
- 30 Liverpool, Green Lane
- 30 Liverpool, Hornby Rd
- 30 Liverpool, Longmore Lane
- 30 Liverpool, Lower House Lane/Dwerry House Lane
- 30 Liverpool, Muirhead Ave East
- 30 Liverpool, Netherfield Rd North
- 30 Liverpool, Parliament St/Upper Parliament St
- 40 Liverpool, Speke Rd/ Speke Boulevard
- 30 Liverpool, Townsend Ave
- 30 Liverpool, Utting Avevnue East
- 30 St Helens, Common Rd
- 60 St Helens, East Lancashire Rd
- 30 St Helens, Prescot Rd
- 30 Sefton, Park Lane
- 30 Sefton, Southport Rd
- 30 Wirral, Laird St
- 40 Wirral, Leasowe Rd
- 30 Wirral, New Chester Rd

Norfolk

A10
- Downham Market to Setchey

A47
- Burlingham to Great Yarmouth
- Swaffham to Dereham
- Tuddenham to Easton

A134
- Mundford to Whittington

A140
- Norwich (Ring Rd) to Aylsham
- Scole to Long Stratton

A140/A149
- Aylsham to Cromer

A143
- Scole to Harleston

A148
- Sculthorpe to Bale

A149
- Catfield to Cats Common
- Great Yarmouth to Catfield
- Knights Hill to Hunstanton

A1069
- Drayton to Foxley

Unclassified
- Kings Lynn, Wisbech to Saddlebow

Northamptonshire

A5
- Crick
- Kilsby
- Lilbourne
- Long Buckby to Watford (S)
- Towcester (N)
- Watford (N)

A6
- Burton Latimer (S)

A43
- Collyweston
- Collyweston to Easton on the Hill
- Duddington
- Easton on the Hill
- Little Cransley
- Weldon

A45
- Braunston
- Flore
- M1 Junc 16 to Weedon
- Stanwick to Raunds

A361
- Kilsby
- Welton

A422
- Brackley Bypass

A427
- Corby
- Upper Benefield

A428
- Brafield (W)
- East Haddon
- Northampton
- Little Houghton

A508
- Grafton Regis to Yardley Gobion
- Northampton, Broad Street
- Northampton, Harborough Street
- Stoke Bruerne to Grafton Regis (N)

A605
- Barnwell
- Elmington
- Oundle Bypass
- Thorpe Waterville
- Thrapston

A4246
- Daventry (E)

A4500
- Ecton Brook

A4525
- Helmdon (W)

A5028
- Rushden

A5086
- Corby

A5095
- Northampton, Kingsthorpe Grove
- St Andrews Rd

A5193
- Wellingborough

A6003
- Kettering to Great Oakley

A6014
- Corby

A6086
- Corby

A6116
- Brigstock
- Corby

B526
- Horton

B569
- Irchester
- Knuston Vale

B570
- Irchester

B574
- Gt Harrowden

B576
- Desborough, Harborough Rd
- Desborough, Rothwell Rd

B4100
- Aynho

B4525
- Helmdon
- Thorpe Mandeville

B5385
- Watford (W)

Unclassified
- Boughton
- Cranford St John
- Daventry, Royal Oak South
- Islip
- Northampton, Rowtree Rd
- Northampton, Wooldale Rd
- Overstone
- Wellingborough
- Yarwell

Northumbria

Gateshead, Newcastle-upon-Tyne, North Tyneside, Northumberland, South Tyneside, Sunderland

A1
- 60 Berwick Bypass, Dunns Jct (N)

A68
- 60 Colt Crag

A69
- 60 Haltwhistle Bypass
- 70 Hexham, Two Mile Cottage

A167
- 30 Newcastle, Stamfordham Rd

A182
- 30 Sunderland, Houghton Rd

A183
- 30 Broadway, Chester Rd

A186
- 40 Denton Burn, West Rd
- 30 Newcastle, City Rd at Beamish House
- 40 Newcastle, West Rd at Turret Rd
- 30 Newcastle, Westgate Rd at Elwick Row

A189
- 70 Cramlington, High Pitt
- 70 Cramlington, Spine Rd
- 30 South Gosforth, Haddricks Mill Rd

A191
- 30 Benton, Whitley Rd
- 30 Newcastle, Springfield Rd

A193
- 30 Seaton Sluice, Beresford Rd
- 30 Wallsend, Church Bank

A194
- 40 Simonside, Newcastle Rd

A196
- 30 Blackclose Bank

A690
- 30 Sunderland, Durham Rd
- 50 Sunderland, Stoneygate, Houghton, Durham Rd

A692
- 30 Gateshead, Church Street

A694
- 30 Rowlands Gill, Station Rd
- 40 Winlaton Mill (Spa Well Rd)

A695
- 60 Crawcrook Bypass
- 40 Prudhoe Jct B6395

A696
30 Belsay Village
60 Blaxter Cottages
60 Kirkwhelpington (S)
60 Otterburn Monkridge
30 Ponteland, West Rd

A697
60 Morpeth, Heighley Gate
60 Wooperton

A1018
30 Sunderland, Ryhope Rd, Irene

A1058
30 Newcastle, Jesmond Rd at Akenside Terrace

A1068
30 Amble Ind Est

A1147
30 Stakeford, Gordon Terrace

A1171
30 Cramlington, Dudley Lane

A1290
30 Sunderland, Southwick, Keir Hardie Wy

A1300
30 Nook, Prince Edward Rd

A6085
40 Newcastle, Lemington Rd

A6127
30 Barley Mow, Durham Rd

B1286
30 Sunderland, Burdon Rd
30 Sunderland, Tunstall Bank

B1288
40 Gateshead, Leam Lane/ A195

B1296
30 Sheriffs Highway, QE Hospital
30 Sheriffs Highway, Split Crow Rd

B1297
30 South Tyneside, Blacket Street

B1298
30 Boldon Colliery, New Rd

B1301
30 South Tyneside, Dean Rd (John Clay St)
30 South Tyneside, Laygate, Eglesfield Rd

B1316
30 North Shields, Lynn Rd

B1318
30 Seaton Burn, Bridge St

B1404
30 Sunderland, Seaham Rd

B1426
30 Felling, Sunderland Rd

B1505
30 West Moor, Great Lime Rd

B6315
30 High Spen, Hookergate Lane

B6317
30 Ryton, Main Rd
30 Whickham Highway

B6318
60 Whitchester, Military Rd
60 Whittington Fell, Military Rd

B6324
40 Newcastle, Stamfordham Rd SE of Walbottle Rd

B6918
30 Newcastle, Woolsington Village

Unclassified
30 Ashington, Barrington Rd
30 Ashington, Station Rd
30 Benton, Coach Lane
30 Blaydon, Shibdon Bank
30 Chopwell, Mill Rd
30 Crawcrook, Greenside Rd
30 Felling, Watermill Lane
30 Gateshead, Askew Rd West
30 Gateshead, Split Crow Rd
30 Hebburn, Campbell Park Rd
70 Nafferton
60 Newcastle, Dinnington Rd North Brunton Lane
40 Newcastle, West Denton Wy east of Hawksley
30 North Shields, Norham Rd
30 South Tyneside, Harton Lane
40 South Tyneside, Hedworth Lane, Abingdon Wy
30 Sunderland, Allendale Rd
30 Sunderland, Burdon Lane
40 Sunderland, Farringdon, North Moor Lane
40 Sunderland, North Hylton Rd, Castletown Wy
30 Sunderland, Parkway at Barrington Drive
30 Sunderland, St Aidens Terrace at the Vicarage
30 Sunderland, St Lukes Rd
30 Sunderland, Silksworth Rd, Rutland Ave
30 Sunderland, Springwell Rd
30 Sunderland, Warwick Terrace
30 Wallsend, Battle Hill Drive
30 Whickham, Fellside Rd
30 Whiteleas, Nevinson

Nottinghamshire

A60
Carlton in Lindrick/ Costhorpe
Mansfield, Nottingham Rd
Market Warsop/Cuckney
Nottingham, Bellar Gate to Woodthorpe Drive
Nottingham, London Rd
Ravenshead, Nottingham Rd/Mansfield Rd

A609
Nottingham, Ilkeston Rd/Wollaton Rd/Russell Drive

A610
Nottingham, Bobbers Mill

A611
Annelsey, Derby Rd
Nottingham, Hucknall Rd

A612
Southwell, Nottingham Rd

A614
Arnold, Burnt Stump

A617
Mansfield, Chesterfield Rd South

A620
Retford, Welham Rd

A631
Beckingham Bypass
Beckingham, Flood Plains Rd
Beckingham, nr Wood Lane
Gringley to Beckingham, nr Mutton Lane

A6005
Nottingham, Castle Boulevard/Abbey Bridge/ Beeston Rd

A6008
Nottingham, Canal St

A6130
Nottingham, Gregory Boulevard
Nottingham, Radford & Lenton Boulevards

A6200/A52
Nottingham, Derby Rd

B679
West Bridgford, Wilford Lane

B682
Nottingham, Sherwood Rise/Nottingham Rd/Vernon Rd

B6004
Arnold, Oxclose Lane
Strelley Rd/Broxtowe Lane/Stockhill Lane

B6010
Giltbrook, Nottingham Rd

B6011
Hucknall, Annesley Rd/Nottingham Rd/ Portland Rd

B6020
Rainworth, Kirklington Rd

B6033
Mansfield, Bath Lane/ Ravensdale Rd

B6040
Worksop, Retford Rd

B6166
Newark on Trent, Lincoln Rd/Northgate

B6326
Newark on Trent, London Rd

Unclassified
Newark, Balderton, Hawton Lane
Nottingham, Beechdale Rd/Wigman Rd
Nottingham, Bestwood Park Drive
Nottingham, Radford Boulevard/Lenton Boulevard
Nottingham, Ridge Wy/Top Valley Drive

Oxfordshire

see Thames Valley

Shropshire

see West Mercia

Somerset

see Avon and Somerset

South Yorkshire

A18
40 Doncaster, Carr House Rd/Leger Wy
NSL Doncaster, Slay Pits to Tudworth, Epworth Rd

A57
40,60 Rotherham, Anston, Sheffield Rd/Worksop Rd
60 Rotherham, Aston/ Todwick, Worksop Rd
60 Rotherham, Worksop Rd
NSL Sheffield, Mosborough ParkWy

A60
NSL Tickhill, Doncaster Rd
30,60 Tickhill, Worksop Rd

A61
30 Cutting Edge, Park Rd
30,40 Sheffield, Chesterfield Rd/Chesterfield Rd South
30,40 Sheffield, Halifax Rd
30 Sheffield, Penistone Rd

A614
NSL Thorne, Selby Rd

A618
40 Wales Bar, Mansfield Rd

A628
30,40 Barnsley, Cundy Cross to Shafton Two Gates
40,60 Barnsley, Dodworth
40 Penistone, Barnsley Rd

A629
NSL Barnsley, Wortley
30 Burncross, Hallwood Rd/Burncross Rd
40 Rotherham, New Wortley Rd
30,40 Rotherham, Wortley Rd/Upper Wortley Rd

A630
30,40,60 Dalton/Thrybergh, Doncaster Rd
30,40,60 Doncaster, Balby Flyover to Hill Top
40 Doncaster, Wheatley Hall Rd
40,50 Rotherham, Centenary Wy

A631
40 Brinsworth, Bawtry Rd
30,40 Hellaby/Maltby, Bawtry Rd/Rotherham Rd
50 Rotherham, West Bawtry Rd
40 Wickersley/Brecks, Bawtry Rd

A633
30 Athersley South, Rotherham Rd
40 Monk Bretton, Rotherham Rd
30 Wath upon Dearne, Sandygate
30,40 Wombwell, Barnsley Rd

A635
30,40,60 Barnsley, Doncaster Rd/Saltersbrook Rd

A638
40 Doncaster, Bawtry Rd
40,50 Doncaster, Great North Rd/York Rd

A6022
30 Rotherham, Swinton

A6101
40 Sheffield, Rivelin Valley Rd

A6102
30,40 Hillsborough/ Deepcar, Manchester Rd/ Langsett Rd

A6109
40 Rotherham, Meadow Bank Rd

A6123
40 Rotherham, Herringthorpe Valley Rd

A6135
40 Sheffield, Ecclesfield Rd/Chapeltown Rd

B6059
30,40 Rotherham, Kiveton/ Wales

B6089
40 Thorn Hill/Greasbrough, Greasbrough Rd/ Greasbrough St

B6096
30 Barnsley, Wombwell to Snape Hill

B6097
30,60 Wath upon Dearne, Doncaster Rd

B6100
30 Barnsley, Ardsley Rd/Hunningley Lane

B6411
30 Thurnscoe, Houghton Rd

B6463
NSL Tickhill, Stripe Rd

Unclassified
30 Armthorpe, Hatfield Lane/Mill St
30 Armthorpe, Nutwell Lane
30 Barnsley, Pogmoor Rd
30 Bolton upon Dearne, Dearne Rd
30 Doncaster, Melton Rd/Sprotbrough Rd
30 Doncaster, Urban Rd
30,60 Edlington/ Warmsworth, Broomhouse Lane/Springwell Lane
40,60 Finningley, Hurst Lane
30 Grimethorpe, Brierley Rd
30,60 Rotherham, Fenton Rd
30 Rotherham, Kilnhurst Rd
30,40 Rotherham, Rawmarsh, Haugh Rd
30 Stainforth, Station Rd
40 Wath upon Dearne, Barnsley Rd
30 Wheatley, Thorne Rd

Staffordshire

A5
A5127 to A38 – Wall Island to Weeford Island
btwn A34 Churchbridge & The Turf Pub Island (B4154)
from A38 to Hints Lane
from A461 to A5127 (Muckley Corner Island to Wall Island Lichfield/ Tamworth)
Hanney Hay/Barracks Lane Island to Muckley Corner Island
M6 Jct 12 to A460/A4601 Island
South Cannock
Weston under Lizard

A34
Cannock North, North of Holly Lane Jct to A34/B5012 rdbt
Cannock South to County Boundary
Cannock South, A34 from south of Jct of A5 Walstall Rd to north of Jct with Jones Lane
Newcastle North, from Wolstanton Rd/Dimsdale Parade west Island to Milehouse Lane/B5367
Newcastle Rd btwn Hanford Island to London Rd Bowling Club
Newcastle South, Barracks Rd to Stoke City Boundary
Newcastle under Lyme to Talke
Stafford South, from A449 Jct to Acton Hill Lane Jct
Stone Rd from Jct of Longton Rd/A5035 to Handford Island/A500
Stone Rd Redhill (A513/ A34) island to Lloyds Island, Eccleshall Rd
Talke, Jct A500 to Jct A5011
Tittensor
Yarlet

A50
Kidsgrove, btwn City Boundary & Oldcott Drive

A51
Lichfield, from A5127 Birmingham Rd to Heath Rd
btwn Armitage Lane, Rugeley & A515
Meaford to Stableford
Pasturefields, A51 from south of Jct with Amerton Lane to south of Hoomill Lane
Rugeley North, from A51 Jct with Bower Lane to island of A460 Sandy Lane & B5013 Elmore Lane
Rugeley South, from south of island of A460/Sandy Lane & B5013 Elmore Lane to Brereton Island
Tamworth, A51 Tamworth Rd/Dosthill Rd from south of Jct with Peelers Wy to Jct with A51 Ascot Drive
Weston, btwn New Rd & 500m past Sandy Lane

A52
Stoke on Trent, Werrington Rd

A53
Baldwins Gate
Blackshaw Moor
Endon
Loggerheads
Longsden

A444
Stanton Rd

A449
Coven, Station Drive
Gailey, btwn Rodbaston Drive & Station Drive
Penkridge, Lynehill Lane to 0.5mile north of Goodstation Lane
Stafford, Lichfield Rd to Gravel Lane
Stourton btwn Ashwood, Lower Lane & Dunsley Lane

A454
Trescott, Bridgenorth Rd btwn Brantley Lane & Shop Lane

A460
Eastern Way Cannock btwn Hemlock Way & A5 Watling St
Hednesford

A511
Burton North, btwn Anslow Lane to island of A5121
Burton South, island of A5121 to Brizlincote Lane

A513
Armitage, btwn Hawkesyard Lane & Rectory Lane
Elford
Walton-on-the-Hill to Milford

A518
Stafford, btwn M6 & Bridge St
Stafford, Riverway to Blackheath Lane

A519
Newcastle, Clayton Rd – from south of A519 Clayton Rd/Friars Wood

A520
Sandon Rd btwn Grange Rd & A50
Weston Rd – from north of the A50 to City boundary (Park Hall)

A4601
Cannock, btwn A34 Walsall Rd Jct to Longford Island A5
Wedges Mill, Longford Island twd Jct 11

A5005
Stoke on Trent, Lightwood Rd btwn A520 & A50

A5035
Trentham, Longton Rd btwn Trentham Rdbt A34 & A50 Jct at Longton

A5121
Burton, from Island Jct with B5108 Branston to Borough Rd
Burton, from Jct with Byrkley St, Horninglow to Jct with Hillfield Lane

A5127
Lichfield, from Jct with Upper St John St twds Streethay

A5189
Burton, btwn Wellington Rd Jct along St Peters Bridge to Stapenhill Rd rdbt

A5190
Burntwood, Cannock Rd from Attwood Rd to Stockhay Lane Jct
btwn Burntwood & Pipehill

A519
Newcastle, Clayton Rd – from south of A519 Clayton Rd/Friars Wood & Brook Lane to rdbt on A519
Woodseaves between Moss Lane & Lodge Lane

B531
Betley & Wrinehill

B5044
Silverdale, btwn Sneyd Terrace & the Jct of the B5368 (Church Lane/ Cemetery Rd)

B5051
btwn Sneyd Hill Rd & Brown Edge

B5080
Tamworth, Pennine Wy btwn B5000 & Pennymoor Rd

B5404
Tamworth, from Sutton Rd to Jct of A4091 (Coleshill Rd/Fazeley Rd)
Tamworth, Watling St btwn Jct with A51 & A5

B5500
Bignall End/Bignall Hill between Boon Hill Road & Deans Lane

Unclassified
Burntwood, Church Rd btwn Rugeley Rd & Farewell Lane
Burton, Rosliston Rd btwn A5189 St Peters Bridge & County Boundary by Railway Bridge
Cannock, Pye Green Rd
Cedar Rd btwn Crackley Bank & B5500 Audley Rd
Leek New Rd – btwn B5049 Hanley Rd & B5051 Jct with A53 at Endon
Oxford Rd/Chell Heath Rd btwn A527 & B5051
Pye Green Rd Cannock btwn A34 Stafford Road & the Jct of Pye Green Road/Brindley Rd
Stoke on Trent, Dividy Rd – btwn B5039 & A52
Stoke on Trent, Oxford Rd / ChellHeath Rd – btwn A527 & B5051

Suffolk

A137
30 Brantham

A143
30 Bury St Edmunds
30 Chedburgh
40 Stanton Bypass
40 Stradishall, Highpoint Prison

A144
40 Ilketshall St Lawrence

A1065
40 Eriswell

A1101
Flempton

A1156
40/NSL Foxhall
30 Ipswich, Norwich Rd

A1214
40 Ipswich, London Rd

A1302
30 Bury St Edmunds

A1304
NSL Newmarket, Golf Club

B1078
30 Barking
30 Needham Market

B1106
30 Fornham

B1113
40 Bramford

B1115
40 Chilton

B1384
30 Carlton Colville

B1438
30 Melton Hill

B1506
40 Kentford

Unclassified
30 Felixstowe, Grange Farm
30 Felixstowe, Trinity Ave
30 Ipswich, Ellenbrook Rd
30 Ipswich, Foxhall Rd
30 Ipswich, Landseer Rd
30 Ipswich, Nacton Rd
30 Kesgrave, Ropes Drive

Surrey

A23
30 Horley, Brighton Rd
40 Salfords, Brighton Rd

A31
60 Hogs Back, Guildford (from A3 to Searle)

A308
50 Staines, Staines Bypass

B380
Mayford

Unclassified
30 Staines, Kingston Rd

Thames Valley

Bracknell Forest, Buckinghamshire, Milton Keynes, Oxfordshire, Reading, Slough, West Berkshire, Windsor & Maidenhead, Wokingham

A5
70 Bletchley
70 Wolverton

A34
40,70 Chieveley
70 Kennington
70 Radley

A40
60 Cassington
70 Forest Hills

A44
50 Kiddington with Asterleigh

A338
50 Hungerford

A361
60 Little Faringdon

A413
60 Hardwick
60 Swanbourne
60 Weedon
60 Wendover Bypass

A417
30 East Challow

A421
70 Tingewick Bypass
60 Wavendon

A422
50 Radclive cum Chackmore

A509
60 Emberton Bypass

A4074
60 Dorchester
50 Nuneham Courteney

A4130
60 Nuffield
40 Remenham Hill

A4155
30 Shiplake

A4260
60 Rousham, Banbury Rd
60 Steeple Aston

B430
40 Weston on the Green

B471
40 Whitchurch Hill

B4009
50 Ewelme

B4011
60 Piddington

B4494
60 Leckhampstead

Unclassified
30 Abingdon, Drayton Rd
30 Abingdon, Oxford Rd
30 Aylesbury, Buckingham Rd
30 Aylesbury, Gatehouse Rd
30 Aylesbury, Oakfield Rd
30 Aylesbury, Tring Rd
30 Aylesbury, Walton St
30 Aylesbury, Wendover Rd
30 Barkham, Barkham Rd
60 Beenham, Bath Rd
30 Blackbird Leys, Watlington Rd
30 Bletchley, Buckingham Rd
30 Blewbury, Bessels Wy
30 Blewbury, London Rd
40 Bracknell, Bagshot Rd
30 Bracknell, Binfield Rd
50 Bracknell, Nine Mile Ride
30 Bracknell, Opladen Wy
40 Bray, Oakley Green Rd
30 Brightwell Cum Sotwell, Sires Hill
30,40 Buckingham, Stratford Rd
30 Burford, Witney Street
40 Calcot, Bath Rd
30 Caversham, Woodcote Rd
30 Chalfont St Peter, Denham Lane
30 Chalfont St Peter, Gravel Hill
30 Chesham, Botley Rd
30 Chipping Norton, Burford Rd
30,40 Chipping Norton, London Rd
30 Crowthorne, New Wokingham Rd
30 Culham, High Street
40 Curbridge, Bampton Rd
40 Denham, North Orbital Rd
30 Denham, Oxford Rd
30 Drayton, High Street
40 Earley, London Rd
30 Earley, Wilderness Rd
30 Ewelme, Green Lane
40 Farmoor, Oxford Rd
40 Freeland, Witney Rd
30 Great Missenden, Rignall Rd
60 Hardmead, Newport Rd
30 Hazelmere, Sawpit Hill
60 Henley on Thames, Fairmile
30 Henley on Thames, Greys Rd
30 High Wycombe, High Wycombe Rd
30 High Wycombe, Holmers Farm Wy
30,40 High Wycombe, Marlow Hill
30 High Wycombe, New Rd
30 High Wycombe, Totteridge Lane
30 High Wycombe, West Wycombe Rd
60 Hungerford, Bath Rd
30 Kidlington, Oxford Rd
60 Kintbury, Bath Rd
30 Long Crendon, Bicester Rd
30 Maidenhead, Bath Rd
40 Maidenhead, Braywick Rd
30 Maidenhead, Cookham Rd
30 Milton Keynes, Avebury Boulevard
30 Milton Keynes, Midsummer Boulevard
30 Milton Keynes, Silbury Boulevard
70 Milton Keynes, Woughton on the Green, Standing Wy
30 Monks Risborough, Aylesbury Rd
40 Newbury, London Rd
30 Newbury, Monks Lane
30 Oakley, Bicester Rd
30 Oxford, Church Cowley Rd
30 Oxford, Headington Rd
30 Oxford, London Rd
30 Oxford, Windmill Rd
30 Pangbourne, Shooters Hill
30 Prestwood, High Street
30 Reading, Berkeley
30 Reading, Castle Hill
30 Reading, Henley Rd
30 Reading, Kentwood Hill
30 Reading, Kings Rd
30 Reading, The Meadway
30 Reading, Overdown Rd
30 Reading, Park Lane
30 Reading, Vastern Rd
30 Reading, Wokingham Rd
50 Shipton on Cherwell, Banbury Rd
30 Slough, Buckingham Ave
30 Slough, Cippenham Lane
30 Slough, Farnham Rd
40 Slough, London Rd
30 Slough, Parlaunt Rd
30 Slough, Sussex Place
40 Slough, Uxbridge Rd
30 Sonning Common, Peppard Rd
30 Speen, Bath Rd
30 Stanford in the Vale, Faringdon Rd
30 Sunningdale, London Rd
40 Sunninghill, Brockenhurst Rd
30 Tadmarton, Main Street
30,40 Thatcham, Bath Rd
30 Thatcham, Bowling Green Rd
30 Tiddington, Oxford Rd
30 Wallingford, Wantage Rd
30 Wantage, Charlton Rd
70 Winkfield, Bagshot Rd
30 Witney, Corn St
30 Wokingham, London Rd
30 Woodcote, Goring Rd
30 Woodcote, Reading Rd
30 Woodley, Loddon Bridge Rd
30 Woolhampton, Bath Rd
30 Wootten, Besselsleigh Rd
60 Wroxton, Stratford Rd

Warwickshire

A5
NSL Churchover, Watling Street
50 Grendon to Hinckley

A44
NSL Little Compton, London Rd

A45
NSL Dunchurch
50 Rugby, nr Ryton

A46
NSL Stoneleigh, Kenilworth Bypass
NSL Stratford Northern Bypass, nr Snitterfield

A47
30 Nuneaton, Hinckley Rd
40 Nuneaton, Longshoot

A422
30 Pillerton Priors, Banbury Rd
30 Stratford, Alcester Rd

A423
NSL Farnborough
NSL Fenny Compton
30 Marton, Coventry Rd
NSL Rugby, nr Marton
NSL south of Southam, Southam Rd

A425
30 Radford Semele, Radford Rd
30 Ufton

A426
30 Dunchurch, Rugby Rd
30 Rugby, Dunchurch Rd
NSL Stockton, Rugby Rd

A428
30 Rugby, Binley Woods
NSL Rugby, Church Lawford
40 Rugby, Long Lawford

A429
NSL Stretton on Fosse
30 Warwick, Coventry Rd
NSL Wellesbourne

A435
40 Mappleborough Green

A439
50 Stratford to A46

A446
NSL Allen End

A448
40 Studley, Bromsgrove Rd

A452
NSL Greys Mallory
NSL Heathcote

A3400
30 Alderminster, Shipston Rd
40 Henley in Arden, Stratford Rd
NSL Little Wolford, London Rd
30 Long Compton, Main Street
30 Newbold on Stour, Stratford Rd
50 Pathlow, Birmingham Rd

A4091
NSL Middleton

A4189
NSL Lower Norton, Henley Rd

B439
NSL Cranhill, Evesham Rd

B4035
30 Upper Brailes, Main Rd

B4065
30 Ansty, Main Rd

B4087
30 Wellesbourne, Newbold Rd

B4089
30 Alcester, Arden Rd
30 Great Alne

B4090
NSL Alcester Heath

B4098
40 Corley, Tamworth Rd
40 Fillongley, Coventry Rd
30 Kingsbury

B4100
NSL Bishop's Tachbrook
NSL Gaydon
B4101
40 Tamworth in Arden, Broad Lane
B4102
30 Nuneaton, Arbury Rd
B4103
30 Kenilworth, Castle Rd
30 Kenilworth, Clinton Lane
B4109
40 Bulkington, Coventry Rd
B4111
30 Nuneaton, Mancetter Rd
B4112
40 Ansley Rd, Nuneaton Radial Route
B4113
30 Nuneaton, Hilltop
B4114
30 Ansley Common, Coleshill Rd
NSL Burton Hastings, Lutterworth Rd
NSL Church End
30 Tuttle Hill
B4117
30 Coleshill, Lower High Street
B4429
40 Rugby, Ashlawn Rd
B4455
NSL Rugby, Fosse Wy south of Princethorpe
B5414
30 Rugby, Clifton Rd
Unclassified
30 Ash Green, Royal Oak Lane
30 Ash Green, Vicarage Lane
30 Exhall, School Lane
NSL Monks Kirby, Coalpit Lane
30 Nuneaton, Donnithorne
40 Rugby, Ashlawn Rd
40 Salford Priors, Station Rd
40 Sambourne, Middletown Lane
30 Woodloes Park, Primrose Hill

West Mercia
Herefordshire, Shropshire, Telford and Wrekin, Worcestershire

A5
NSL Aston
NSL Gobowen, Moreton Bridge
60 Montford Bridge
NSL West Felton
A40
50 Pencraig
A41
40,NSL Albrighton Bypass
NSL Chetwynd nr Newport
40 Tern Hill
NSL Whitchurch Bypass
A44
40 Wickhamford
30 Worcester, Bromyard Rd
A46
50 Beckford
NSL Evesham Bypass
A49
NSL Ashton
30 Dorrington
40 Hereford, Harewood End
A417
40 Ledbury, Parkway
A438
60 Staunton-on-Wye
A442
40 Crudgington
A448
30 Bromsgrove, Kidderminster Rd
A456
30 Blakedown
30 Newnham Bridge
A458
40 Morville
30 Much Wenlock
A465
NSL Allensmore
A491
50 Bromsgrove, Stourbridge Rd
NSL Hagley, Sandy Lane
A528
30 Shrewsbury, Ellesmere Rd
A4103
NSL Hereford, Lumber Lane/Lugg Bridge
40 Newtown Cross
50 Stiffords Bridge/Storridge
A4104
30 Welland, Drake St / Marlbank Rd
A4110
30 Hereford, Three Elms Rd
A5064
30 Shrewsbury, London Rd
B4084
40 Cropthorne
B4096
30 Bromsgrove, Old Birmingham Rd
B4208
30 Welland
B4211
30 Malvern, Barnards Green Rd
B4368
40 Hungerford
B4373
40 Telford, Castlefields Wy
40 Telford, Wrockwardine Wood Wy
B4638
30 Worcester, Woodgreen Drive
B5060
40 Telford, Castle Farm Wy
B5062
60 Newport, Edgmond Rd
30 Shrewsbury, Sundorne Rd
Unclassified
30 Astwood Bank, Evesham Rd
30 Hereford, Yazor Rd
30 Kidderminster, Habberley Lane
30 Newport, Wellington Rd
40 Redditch, Alders Dr
30 Redditch, Bromsgrove Rd
40 Redditch, Coldfield Drive
30 Redditch, Studley Rd
30 Shrewsbury, Longden Rd (Rural)
30 Shrewsbury, Monkmoor Rd
30 Telford, Britannia Wy
30 Newport, Wellington Rd

West Midlands
Birmingham, Coventry, Dudley, Sandwell, Solihull, Walsall, Wolverhampton

A41
30 Silhill, Warwick Rd
A452
50 Collector Rd – Castle Bromwich
50 Smith's Wood, Collector Rd
A4034
40 Birchfield Lane
A4036
40 Netherton Woodside & St Andrew's, Pedmore Rd
A4040
30 Hodge Hill, Bromford Lane
A4123
40 Castle & Priory, Birmingham New Rd
A4600
40 Wyken, Ansty Rd
B425
30 Elmdon, Lode Lane
B4114
30 Hodge Hill, Washwood Heath Rd
B4121
40 Bartley Green, Barnes Hill
40 Weoley, Shenley Lane
B4135
30 Cranford Street / Heath Street
Unclassified
30 Oxley, The Droveway
40 St Alphege, Widney Manor Rd

West Yorkshire

M606
50 Mill Carr Hill Bridge
A58
40 Leeds, Easterly Rd
A61
40 Alwoodley, Harrogate Rd
40 Leeds, Scott Hall Rd
40 Rothwell, Wakefield Rd
A62
30 Birstall, Gelderd Rd
30 Huddersfield, Manchester Rd
30 Slaithwaite, Manchester Rd
A64
40 Leeds, York Rd
A65
30 Guiseley, Otley Rd
40 Ilkley, Ilkley Rd
A616
40 Huddersfield, Woodhead Rd
A629
30 Cullingworth, Halifax Rd
30 Halifax, Ovenden Rd
30 Halifax, Skircoat Rd
30 Keighley, Halifax Rd
A635
30 Holmfirth, Holmfirth Rd
A640
30 Huddersfield, Westbourne Rd
A642
30 Horbury, Northfield Lane
A644
30 Brighouse, Denholme Rd
30 Dewsbury, Huddersfield Rd
A645
30 Featherstone, Pontefract Rd
30 Featherstone, Wakefield Rd
A646
30 Cornholme, Burnley Rd
30 Luddenden Foot, Burnley Rd
30 Todmorden, Halifax Rd
A647
30 Bradford, Great Horton Rd
40 Pudsey, Bradford Rd
A650
30 Frizinghall, Bradford Rd
A651
30 Birkenshaw, Bradford Rd
A653
40 Shaw Cross, Leeds Rd
A657
30 Thackley, Leeds Rd
A6025
50 Elland, Elland Rd
A6036
30 Northowram, Bradford Rd
A6037/A650
40 Shipley, Airedale Rd
A6038
40 Baildon, Otley Rd
40 Esholt, Otley Rd
A6120
30 Cross Gates, Station Rd
A6177
30 Bradford, Ingleby Rd
40 Bradford, Rooley Lane
A6186
30 Durkar, Asdale Rd
B6124
30 Wakefield, Batley Rd
B6144
30 Bradford, Haworth Rd Daisy Hill
30 Bradford, Toller Lane
B6145
30 Bradford, Thornton Rd
30 Greenside, Thornton Rd
B6265
30 Stockbridge, Bradford Rd
B6273
30 Kinsley, Wakefield Rd
B6380
30 Bradford, Beacon Rd
Unclassified
30 Bradford, Cutler Heights Lane/Dick Lane
30 Bradford, Gain Lane
30 Bradford, Moore Ave
30 Burley, Willow Rd/ Cardigan Rd
30 Calderdale, Crag Lane
30 Dalton, Long Lane
30 Horsforth, Low Lane
30 Lawnswood, Otley Old Rd
30 Sandford, Broad Lane

Wiltshire and Swindon

M4
70 east & west of Jct 15
70 east & west of Jct 16
70 east & west of Jct 17
A30
40 nr Fovant
A346
50 Chiseldon
60 Chiseldon Firs
A354
30 Coombe Bissett
A361
40 Highworth, Swindon Rd
A419
Blunsdon (twds Cirencester)
70 nr Covingham
70 Widhill Blunsdon
A420
50 South Marston twds Oxford
A3102
30 Wootten Bassett
A4259
50 nr Coate
40 Swindon, Queens Drive
A4311
30 Swindon, Cricklade Rd
A4312
30 Swindon, Oxford Rd
A4361
30 Swindon, Croft Rd
30 Wroughton, Swindon Rd
B4006
30 Stratton St Margaret, Swindon Rd
40 Swindon, btwn Barnfield Rdbt & Meads Rdbt
40 Swindon, Marlborough Rd
30 Swindon, Pinehurst, Whitworth Rd
B4042
30 Malmesbury, Swindon Rd
B4141
30 Swindon, Kingsdown Rd
B4143
30 Swindon, Bridge End Rd
30 Swindon, Gipsy Lane
B4289
40 Swindon, Great Western Wy nr Bruce St Bridges
30 Swindon, Kingshill Rd
B4553
40 Swindon, Tewkesbury Wy
B4587
30 Swindon, Akers Wy
Unclassified
30 Sevenhampton nr Swindon
30 Swindon, Beech Ave
30 Swindon, Ermin St–Hyde Rd
30 Swindon, Liden Drive
30 Swindon, Merlin Wy
30 Swindon, Moredon Rd
30 Swindon, Nythe, The Drive
40 Swindon, Pinehurst Rd
40 Swindon, Thamesdown Dr
30 Swindon, Wanborough House
30 Trowbridge, Wiltshire Drive

Worcestershire
see West Mercia

Wales

Mid and South Wales
Blaenau Gwent, Bridgend, Caerphilly, Cardiff, Carmarthenshire, Merthyr Tydfil, Monmouthshire, Neath Port Talbot, Newport, Pembrokeshire, Rhondda Cynon Taff, Swansea, Torfaen, Vale of Glamorgan

M4
70 Cherry Orchard Rd, M4 bridge site
70 2km east of Jct35
70 east of Jct36, nr Sarn
50 Jct 36, Sarn-Jct 37, Pyle
50 Jct 38, Margam-Jct 40, Taibach
70 Llanmartin Overbridge
50 Toll Plaza
A40
30 Abergavenny, Brecon Rd, Neville Hall
70 Bancyfelin Bypass
60 Buckland Hall, Brecon to Abergavenny
70 Johnstown, Carmarthen to St Clears
60 Llanhamlach, Brecon to Abergavenny
60 Llansantffried Jct
30 Monmouth, Llangattock Lodge
40 Rhosmaen
60 Scethrog, Brecon to Abergavenny
40 Trecastle
60 Whitemill
A44
60 Forest Bends
60 Gwystre
30 Llanbadarn Fawr
60 Llanfihangel, Nant Melan
60 Rhydgaled, Sweet Lamb
A48
30 Baglan, Dinas Baglan
30 Berryhill
40 Bonvilston
30 Castleton
40 Corntown
70 Cowbridge, Cowbridge Bypass
70 Foelgastell
40 Langstone, Chepstow Rd
70 Llanddarog
30 Morriston, Clasemont Rd
30 Nantycaws
30 Parkwall, Parkwall Hill
70 north of Pont Abraham
30 Pontarddulais, Bolgoed Rd
30 Pontardualais, Carmarthen Rd
30 Pontarddulais, Fforest Rd
30 Port Talbot, Margam Rd
30 Sycamore Cross
30 Wenvoe, St Nicolas
A410
50 Porthcawl, The Porthway
A422
30 Cowbridge, Aberthin Rd
A438
30 Bronllys
40 Clyro
40 Three Cocks
A449
70 north of Coldra
70 Llandenny
70 Llantrissent nr Usk
A458
60 Cefn Bridge
60 Llanfair Caereinion (Neuadd Bridge)
40 Trewern
A465
60 btwn Aberbaden & Llanfoist
60 Abergavenny, llanfoist
30 Abergavenny, Triley Mill
70 Glynneath Bank
50 Pandy
70 Resolven north
70 Rheola
A466
30 Llandogo
30 Monmouth, High Beech Rdbt to Old Hospital
30 Monmouth, Redbrook Rd
30 Monmouth, Whitecross Street
30 St Arvans to Livox Ends
30 Tintern
A467
30 Aberbeeg, Aberbeeg Rd
60 Abertillery, Aberbeeg Rd
40 Blaina, Abertillery Rd
70 Danycraig, Risca
A468
30 Machen Village
30 Rhiwderin, Caerphilly Rd
A469
70 Llanbradach, Lower Rhymney Valley Relief Rd
30 Tir-Y-Berth, New Rd
A470
60 Aberduhonw, south of Builth
70 Aberfan
60 Abernant, south of Builth
60 Beacons Reservoir
40 Ash Grove nr Heol-y-Forlan Jct
30 Erwood
60 Erwood South
40 Llandinam Village
60 Llandinam to Caersws Jct
60 Llanidloes to Llandinam
60 Llwyn y Celyn, Brecon to Merthyr
30 Llyswen
60 Newbridge to Rhayader, Argoed Mill
30 Newbridge on Wye
70 Rhydyfelin
70 nr Taffs Well
60 Ysgiog, south of Builth
A472
60 Hafodrynys, Hafod yr ynys Rd
60 Monkswood, Little Mill
30 Usk Bridge to Old Saw Mill
A473
30 Bridgend, Bryntirion Hill
50 Bridgend, Coychurch Bypass
30 Bridgend, Inner Bypass
30 Bryncae, New Rd
30 Pencoed, Penybont Rd
30 Upper Boat, Main Rd
A474
40 Alltwen, Graig Rd
50 Briton Ferry, Briton Ferry Rd
30,40 Garnant, Glanffrwd Est Jct
30 Heol-y-Gors
30 Neath, Penywern Rd
30 Pontamman to Glanaman
30 Rhyd y Fro, Commercial St
A475
40 Lampeter, Pentrebach, County Rd
30 Llanwnen
A476
40 Carmel, Stag & Pheasant
40 Carmel to NSL at Temple Bar
40 Gorslas, The Gate
30 Llannon, Erw Non Jct to Clos Rebecca Jct
30 Swiss Valley, Thomas Arms
30 Upper Tumble, Llannon Rd & Bethania Rd
A477
30 Llanddowror
40 Bangeston To Nash Fingerpost
A478
30 Clunderwen
30 Llandissilio, Nr school
30 Pentlepoir
A482 & A475
30 Lampeter
A482
30 Aberaeron, Lampeter Rd
30 Cwmann, North
30 Cwmann, South
30 Llanwrda
A483
60 Abbey Cwm Hir Jct
30 Ammanford, Penybanc Rd
60 north of Crossgates
70 south of Cwmgwili, Pontarddulais Rd
30 Ffairfach to Llandeilo Bridge
50 Garthmyl, Refail Garage
60 Garthmyl, Welshpool
30 Llandeilo, Rhosmaen St
60 Llandrindod, Midway Bends
40 Swansea, Fabian Wy
A484
30 Bronwydd Village
30 Cenarth
40 Cwmffrwd
30 Cynwyl Elfed
40 Idole
30 Llanelli, Sandy Rd
60 Llanelli, Trostre Rdbt to Berwick Rdbt
30 Newcastle Emlyn
40 Pentrecagel
40 Rhos
40 Saron
A485
40 Alltwalis
30 Cwmann, from the A482 Jct N
40 Llanllwwni
30 Llanybydder
40 Peniel
A486
30 Llandysul, Well Street
30 New Quay
A487 & A4120
30 Aberystwyth, Southgate
A487
30 Aberaeron, Greenland Terrace
30 Bow Street
30 Eglwyswrw
40 Furnace
40 Llanarth, Alma Street
30 Llanfarian
40 Llanrhystud
30 Newgale
30 Newport
40 Penparc
40 Rhydyfelin
40 Rhydypennau
30 Talybont
30 Waunfawr, Penglais Hill
A489
60 Caersws Jct to Penstrowed
60 Kerry, County Rd, Glanmule Garage
40 Newtown, west of Hafren coll
60 Penstrowed to Newtown
A4042
60 Llanover
30 Mamhilad
A4043
40 Abersychan, Cwmavon Rd
A4046
30 Ebbw Vale (nr Tesco's)
30 Ebbw Vale, College Rd
30 Waunllwyd, Station Rd
A4047
30 Brynmawr, Beaufort Hill & High St
A4048
30 Cwmfelinfach Village
30 Hollybush
30 Pontllanfraith, Blackwood Rd
A4050
30 Barry, Jenner Rd
A4054
30 Cilfynydd, Cilfynydd Rd
30 Edwardsville, Nantddu
30 Merthyr Vale, Cardiff Rd
30 Mountain Ash, New Rd
30 Pontypridd, Pentrebach Rd
30 Upper Boat, Cardiff Rd
A4055
30 Barry, Gladstone Rd
A4058
30 Pontypridd, Broadway
A4061
30 Ogmore Vale, Cemetery Rd
30 Nant-Y-Moel, Aber Rd
A4063
30 Coytrahen to Llangynwyd
30 Llangynwydd, Bridgend Rd
30 Penyfai, Bridgend Rd
50 Sarn Bypass
A4066
40 Broadway
40 Pendine, Llanmiloe
A4067
60 Abercraf Bypass
60 Crai
40 Mumbles Rd
A4068
30 Cwmtwrch, Bethel Rd
30 Cwmtwrch, Heol Gleien
A4069
30 Brynamman, Brynamman Rd
30 Llandovery, Broad St
30 Llangadog, Station Rd
A4075
30 Pembroke
A4076
30 Hubberston, St Lawrence Hill
30 Johnston, Milford Rd
30 Johnston, Vine Rd
40 Steynton, Steynton Rd
A4078
30 Carew
A4093
30 Blackmill
30 Glynogwr
30 Hendreforgan, Gilfach Rd
A4102
30 Gellideg, Swansea Rd
A4106
40 Porthcawl, Bridgend Rd
30 Porthcawl, Newton Nottage Rd
A4107
30 Abergwynfi, High St
A4109
40 Aberdulais, Main Rd
30 Crynant, Main Rd
40 Glynneath
30 Seven Sisters, Dulais Rd
A4118
60 Fairwood Common
A4119
70 Cardiff, Llantrisant Rd
30 Groesfaen
50 Llantrisant, Mwyndy Cross
A4139
30 Pembroke, Orange Wy
30 Pembroke Dock, Bush Street
30 Tenby, Marsh Rd
A4216
30 Cockett, Cockett Rd
A4221
60 Brooklands Terrace
A4222
30 Brynsadler, Cowbridge Rd
30 Cowbridge, Cardiff Rd
30 Maendy, Maendy Rd
A4226
40 Rhoose, Waycock Rd
A4232
70 Cardiff, Ely Link
A4233
30 Ferndale, The Parade
B4181
30 Bridgend, Coyhurch Rd
30 Bridgend, Coity Rd
B4223
30 Gelli, Gelli Rd
30 Ton Pentre, Maindy Rd
30 Ton Pentre, Pentwyn Rd
B4235
60 Gwernesney nr Usk
B4236
30 Llanfrechfa, Caerleon Rd
B4237
30 Maesglas, Cardiff Rd
30 Somerton, Chepstow Rd
B4239
30 Newport, Lighthouse Rd
B4245
30 Langstone, Magor Rd
60 Leechpool, Cartref to Uplands
30 Penpedairheol, Pengam Rd
30 Rogiet, Caldicot Rd
B4246
40 Abersychan, Varteg
30 Garndiffaith, New Rd
B4248
30 Blaenavon, Garn Rd
B4251
30 Abergavenny, Hereford Rd
30 Caerphilly, Kendon Hill
B4257
30 Llechryd
B4265
50 Llantwit Major, Llantwit Major Bypass
30 St Brides Major, Ewenny Rd
30 St Brides Major, St Brides Rd
B4275
30 Abercynon, Abercynon Rd
B4278
30 Dinas, Dinas Rd
30 Tonyrefail, Penrhiwfer Rd
B4281
30 Cefn Cribwr, Cefn Rd
30 Kenfig Hill, High St
B4282
30 Bryn, Maesteg Rd
30 Maesteg, Bridgend Rd & Castle St
B4283
30 North Cornelly, Heol Fach
B4290
30 Jersey Marine, New Rd
30 Skewen, Burrows Rd
30 Skewen, Pen-yr-Heol & Crymlyn Rd
B4293
30 Trellech Village
30 Trellech, Monmouth Road
B4295
30 Crofty, New Rd
40 btwn Gowerton & Penclawdd
60 btwn Penclawdd & Llanrhidian
30 Cockett, Cwmbach Rd
B4296
30 Waungren, Pentre Rd
30 Killay, Goetre Fawr Rd
B4297
30 Bynea, Lougher Bridge Rdbt to Station Rd Jct
30 Capel Hendre
30 Fforest
30 Llanedi
30 Llangennech, Cleviston Park Jct to Park Lane Jct
30 Llangennech, Pontarddulais Rd
30 Llwynhendy, from Capel Soar to the Police Station
B4301
30 Bronwydd Village
B4302
30 Talley
B4303
30 Llanelli, Dafen Rdbt to Felinfoel Rdbt
B4304
40 Llanelli, Copperworks Rdbt to Morfa Rdbt
30 Llanelli, Lower Trostre Rd Rdbt to Trostre Rd Rdbt
30 Llanelli, New Dock Rd
B4306
30 Bancffosfelen, Heol Y Banc
30 Crwbin
30 Llangendeirn
30 Pontyberem, Llanon Rd
B4308
40 Penmynydd
B4309
30 Cynheidre
30 Five Roads
B4310
30 Drefach, Heol Caegwyn
B4312
40 Llangain
B4314
30 Moorfield Road, Nr school
30 Pendine
B4317
30 Carway
30 Ponthenri, Myrtle Hill
30 Pontyberem, Heol Capel Ifan
30 Pontyberem, Station Rd
B4320
30 Hundleton
B4322
40 Pembroke Dock, Pembroke Rd
B4325
30 Llanstadwell, Honeyborough Rd
30 Neyland, High Street
30 Neyland, The Promenade
B4328
30 Whitland, Trevaughan
B4333
30 Cynwyl Elfed
40 Hermon
30 Newcastle Emlyn, Aber-arad
B4336
30 Llandysul, Pont-tyweli
30 Llanfihangel Ar Arth
B4337
30 Llanybydder
40 Talsarn
B4347
30 Newcastle Village
B4350
60 Glasbury, Llwyn au bach
B4436
40 Bishopton, Northway
40 Kittle, Pennard Rd
B4459
40 Pencader
B4471
30 Llanhilleth, Oak Leaf Terrace, Commercial Rd
B4478
30 Beaufort, Letchworth Rd
B4486
30 Ebbw Vale, Steelworks Rd
B4524
30 Corntown, Corntown Rd
B4548
30 Cardigan, Cardigan North Rd
B4556
30 Blaenau, Penygroes Rd
30 Caerbryn
30 Penygroes, Norton Rd
B4560
30 Beaufort, Ebbw Vale, Llangynidr Rd
B4591
30 Highcross, Risca Rd
30 Pontymister, Risca Rd
30 Risca, opp Power Station, Risca Rd
B4596
30 Newport, Caerleon Rd
B4598
60 Abergavenny, Horse & Jockey
60 Llancayo
B4599
30 Ystradgynlais
B4603
30 Clydach, Pontardawe Rd
30 Ynystawe, Clydach Rd
B4622
30 Bridgend, Broadlands Link Rd
B4623
30 Caerphilly, Mountain Rd

Unclassified
30 Aberbargoed, Bedwellty & Coedymoeth Rd Jct
30 Abercwmboi, Park View Terrace
30 Abergwili, Ambulance Station to the Bypass Rdbt
30 Abersychan, Foundry Rd
30 Abertillery, Gwern Berthi
30 Abertillery, Roseheyworth Rd
30 Aberystwyth Town, Park
30 Ammanford, Dyffryn Rd
30 Ammanford, New Rd & Pantyffynnon Rd
30 Ammanford, layby outside Saron Church, Saron Rd
30 Barry, Barry Rd
30 Barry, Buttrills Rd
30 Barry, Holton Rd
30 Barry, Winston Rd
30 Beddau, Bryniteg Hill
30 Beddau, Gwaunmiskin Rd
30 Bedwellty, Heol y Bedw – Hirion
30 Betws, Betws Rd
30 Betws, Maesquarre Rd
30 Blaenavon, Upper Coedcae Rd
30 Blaina, Bourneville Rd
30 Blaina, Farm Rd
30 Blaina, Surgery Rd
30 Brackla, Brackla Wy
30 Bridgend, Heol Y Nant
30 Bridgend, Llangewydd Rd
30 Bridgend, Pen-Y-Cae Lane
30 Bridgend Ind Est, Kingsway
30 Bridgend Ind Est, North Rd
30 Bridgend Ind Est, South Rd
30 Briton Ferry, Old Rd
30 Brynna, Brynna Rd
30 Caerphilly, Lansbury Park Ring Rd
30 Caerphilly, Lon y Llyn Rd
30 Caerphilly, Pontllanfraith, Bryn Lane
30 Caerphilly, Waterloo Rd
30 Caldicot, Chepstow Rd
30 Cardiff, Ninian Park Rd
30 Cardiff, Pentwyn, Bryn Celyn
30 Cardiff, Cyncoed Rd
30 Cardiff, Excalibur Drive
30 Cardiff, Ferry Rd
30 Cardiff, Heath, Maescoed Rd
30 Cardiff, Heol Isaf
30 Cardiff, Lansdowne Rd
30 Cardiff, Leckwith Rd
30 Cardiff, Newport Rd
30 Cardiff, Oakdale Terrace
30 Cardiff, Pencisely Rd
30 Cardiff, Penylan, Colchester
30 Cardiff, Rhiwbina Hill
30 Cardiff, Roath, Lake Rd East/West
30 Cardiff, St Fagans Rd
30 Cardiff, Wentloog
30 Cardiff, Willowbrook Drive
30 Cardiff, Ystrad Mynach,Pengam Rd
30 Carmarthen, Lime Grove & Fountain Head Tce
30 Cefn Glas, Merlin Crescent
30 Cefneithin
30 Chepstow, Mathern Rd
30 Church Village, Station Rd
30 Clydach, Vadre Rd
30 Coity, Heol Spencer
60 Coldharbour, Usk to Raglan Rd
30 Crumlin, Hafodyrynys Hill
30 Cwm Govilon, Bryn Awelon Rd
30 Cwmavon, Cwmavon Rd
30 Cwmbran, Greenforge Wy
30 Cwmbran, Henllys Wy
30 Cwmbran, Hollybush Wy
30 Cwmbran, Llanfrechfa Wy
30 Cwmbran, Maendy Wy
30 Cwmbran, Pontnewydd, Chapel Street
30 Cwmbran, Thornhill Rd
30 Cwmbran, Ty Canol Wy
30 Cwmbran, Ty Gwyn Wy & Greenmeadow Wy
30 Cwmbran, Upper Cwmbran Rd
30 Cwmgwili
30 Cwmgwili, Thornhill Rd
30 Deri, New Rd
30 Derwen Fawr, Rhy-Y-Defaid Drive
30 Dinas Powys, Pen-y-turnpike Rd
30 Dowlais, High St
30 Drefach, Heol Blaenhirwaun
30 Ebbw Vale, Newchurch Rd
30 Felinfoel, Llethri Rd
30 Forest Fach, Carmarthen Rd
30 Fochrie, Olgivie Terrace
30 Foelgastell
30 Forden
30 Gelligaer, Church Rd
30 Gilwern, Cae Meldon (aka Ty Mawr Lane)
30 Glyncorrwg, Heol y Glyn
30 Gorseinon, Frampton Rd
30 Gorslas, Penygroes Rd
30 Grovesend
30 Haverfordwest, New Rd/Uzmaston Rd
30 Hendredenny, Hendredenny Drive
30 Hopkinstown, Hopkinstown Rd
30 Johnstown, St Clears Rd
30 Llanbradach, Coed y Brain Rd to Glyn Bedw
30 Llanelli, Denham
30 Llanelli, Heol Goffa
30 Llanfihangel Ar Arth (South)
30 Llangan
30 Llangyfelach, Swansea Rd
30 Llanharan, Brynna Rd
60 Llanhenock, Caerleon to Usk Rd – Apple tree farm
30 Llantwit Major, Llanmaes Rd
30 Maesteg, Heol-Ty-Gwyn
30 Magor (West)
30 Malpas, Rowan Wy
30 Merthyr Vale, Nixonvale
30 Merthyr Tydfil, Brecon Rd
30 Merthyr Tydfil, Goatmill Rd
30 Merthyr Tydfil, Gumos Rd
30 Merthyr Tydfil, Heolgerrig Rd
30 Merthyr Tydfil, Plymouth St
30 Merthyr Tydfil, Rocky Rd
30 Merthyr Tydfil, The Walk
30 Milford Haven, Priory Rd
40 Milford Haven, Thornton Rd
30 Monmouth, Devauden Village
30 Monmouth, Dixton Rd
30 Monmouth, Llangybi
30 Morriston, Caemawr Rd
30 Mountain Ash, Llanwonno Rd
30 Mountain Ash, Miskin Rd
30 Nantgarw, Oxford St
70 Nantycaws Hill
30 New Tredegar, White Roase Wy
30 Newbridge, Park Rd
30 Newport, Allt-Yr-Yn
30 Newport, Corporation Rd
30 North Connelly, Fairfield Rd
30 Pant, Pant Rd
30 Pembroke Rd
30 Pencoed, Felindre Rd
30 Pendine
30 Penpedairheol, Hengoed Rd
40 Pentrecagel
30 Penydarren, High Street
30 Pontardawe, Ynys-Meudwy Rd
40 Ponthir, Caerleon Rd
30 Pontllanfraith, Bryn Rd
30 Pontlottyn, Southend Terrace
30 Pontnewynydd, Plas Y Coed Rd
30 Pontyclun, Cowbridge Rd
30 Pontypool, Little Mill
30 Porthcawl, Fulmar Rd
30 Portskewett, Caldicot Rd
30 Rassau, Reservoir Rd
30 Rhydfelin, Gwalia Grove
30 Rhymney, Llys Joseph Parry (nr Farmers Arms)
30 Rhymney, Wellington Wy
30 Risca, Cromwell Rd
30 Risca, Holly Rd
30 Rogerstone, Pontymason Lane
30 St Athan, Cowbridge Rd
30 Sandfields, Village Rd
30 Saron
70 Seven Sisters, Golwg-y-Bryn
30 Sully, Hayes Rd
30 Sully, South Rd
30 Swansea, Mynydd Newydd Rd, Caemawr Rd, Parry Rd, Vicarage Rd
30 Swansea, Pentregethin Rd
30 Tiers Cross
30 Tonteg, Church Rd
30 Tonyrefail, Gilfach Rd
30 Trebanos, Swansea Rd
30 Treboeth, Llangyfelach Rd
30 Tredegar, Merthyr Rd
30 Tredegar, Vale Terrace
30 Trehafod, Gyfeillion Rd
30 Trelewis, Gelligaer Rd
30 Tylorstown, Penrhys Rd
30 Usk, Maryport St
30 Usk, Porthycarne St
30 Whitland
30 Whitland, Market St
30 Whitland (East), Spring Gardens
30 Willowtow, Gwaun Helyg Rd
30 Ynysawdre, Heol-Yr-Ysgol
30 Ynysybwl, New Rd

North Wales
Ceredigion, Conwy, Denbighshire, Flintshire, Gwynedd, Isle of Anglesey, Powys, Wrexham

A5
30 Holyhead
30/40 Llandygai to Bangor
A5/A5025
50 Holyhead to Llanfachraeth
A470
30,60 Conwy Valley
40,60 Dolgellau
40,60 (30 at rdbts) Llandudno to the A55
30,40,60 Tal-y-waenydd to Congl-y-wal (Blaenau)
A483/A5
60 Ruabon to Chirk
A487
30,40,50,60 Caernarfon to Dolbenmaen
30,40,60 Penmorfa to Gellilydan
A494
40,60 Bala to Glanrafon
30 Llyn Tegid, Bala
40,60 Ruthin to Llanferres
A496
30,40,60 Harlech to Llanbedr
A499
30,40,60 Pwllheli
A525
40,60 Denbigh to Ruthin
30,40,60 Llanfair Dyffryn Clwyd to Llandegla
30,60 Wrexham to Minera
30,40,60 Wrexham to Redbrook Maelor
A534
30 Wrexham, Holt Rd
A539
30,60 Llangollen, Mill St
30,40,60 Trevor to Erbistock
A541
30 Wrexham, Mold Rd
30,40,60,70 Mold to Caergwrle
30,40,60,70 Wrexham to Cefn-y-bedd
A541/525
30,40,60 St Asaph to Bodfari
A545
30,40 Menai Bridge to Beaumaris
A547
30,40,50 Colwyn Bay
30,40,60 Prestatyn to Rhuddlan
30 Rhyl, Vale Rd/Rhuddlan Rd
A548
30,40 Abergele to Kinmel Bay
30 Abergele, Dundonald
30,40,50,60,70 Gronant to Flint (Oakenholt)
30,40 Rhyl to Prestatyn
A549
30,60 Mynydd Isa to Buckley
A550/B5125
30 Hawarden
A4086
30,40,60 Cwm-y-glo to Llanrug
A4212
30/60 Bala
60 Graig Las/Tryweryn to Trawsfynydd
A4244
60 Ty Mawr to Cym-y-glo
A5025
30,40,50,60 Amlwch, Menai Bridge
A5104
30 Coed-Talon to Leeswood
A5112
30,40 Llandygai to Bangor
A5119
30,50,60 Mold to Flint
A5152
30,60 Bala
30 Wrexham, Chester Rd
30,40 Wrexham, Rhostyllen
B4545
30,40 Kingsland to Valley (Treaddur Bay)
B5108
30,60 Benllech
B5109
30 Llangefni
B5113
30 Colwyn Bay, Kings Rd/Kings Drive
B5115
30 Llandrillo, Llandudno Rd
30,40 Llandudno Promenade to Rhos Point
B5118
30 Rhyl Promenade
B5120
30 Prestatyn, Pendyffryn Rd
B5129
30,60 Kelsterton to Saltney Ferry
B5420
30 Menai Bridge
B5425
30,60 Wrexham, Llay New Rd
B5443
30 Wrexham, Rossett
Unclassified
30,40,60 Wrexham, Johnstown
30,60 Kinmel Bay, St Asaph
30,40,60 Menai Bridge to Gwalchmai

Scotland

Central Scotland
M9
70 at M876 (W)
70 Polmont (W)
70 Stirling, Craigforth
M80
70 Denny (N)
M876
70 Larbert, Torwood (N)
A9
70 Dunblane
A82
30 Crianlarich
A706
30 Bo'ness, Linlithgow Rd
A907
40 Cambus
A908
30 Sauchie
30 Tillicoultry, Devonside
A993
30 Bo'ness, Dean Rd

Dumfries and Galloway
A74(M)
70 Cogries
70 Greenhillstairs
70 J17 Torwood
70 J19 Ecclefechan
70 J21 Kirkpatick Fleming
A7
60 Old Irvine
A75
60 Barncrosh
30 Crocketford
60 Mouswaldbanks
60 Newton Stewart
A76
60 Auldgirth
60 Closeburn
60 Gateside
30 Dumfries, Glasgow Rd
A77
60 Balyett
60 Cairnryan
60 Whiteleys
A701
30 Moffat
60 Mollinburn/St Anns
A709
60 Burnside
A711
30 Kirkcudbright
A716
60 Stoneykirk
A718
60 Craichmore
B721
30 Eastriggs

Fife
A91
60 Cupar to Dairsie
60 Deer Centre to Stratheden Jct
60 Guardbridge to St Andrews
A92
50 Cadham to New Inn
70 Cardenden Overbridge to Chapel
70 Cowdenbeath to Lochgelly
60 Freuchie to Annsmuir
60 Melville Lodges to Lindifferon
60 Rathillet (south) to Easter Kinnear
A823
30 Dunfermline, Queensferry Rd
40 Dunfermline, St Margaret Drive
A907
30 Dunfermline, Halbeath Rd
A911
60 Glenrothes to Milton
A914
60 Dairsie to St Michaels
60 Edenwood to Cupar
60 Kettlebridge to Kingskettle
60 Pitlessie to Clushford Toll
A915
60 Checkbar Jct to Percival Jcts
A921
30 Kirkcaldy, Esplanade
30 Kirkcaldy, High St/Path
A955
30 Methil, Methilhaven Rd
30 Buckhaven, Methilhaven Rd
40 Dysart to Coaltown of Wemyss
A977
30 Kincardine, Fere Gait
A985
60 Culross (west) to C38 Valleyfield
30 Rosyth, Admiralty Rd
60 Waukmill to Brankholm
B920
30 Crosshill to Ballingry
B942
60 East of Colinsburgh
B980
30 Rosyth, Castlandhill Rd
B981
30 Cowdenbeath, Broad St
40 Kirkcaldy, Dunnikier Wy
B9157
60 Bankhead of Pitheadle to Kirkcaldy
60 Orrock to East Balbairdie
60 White Lodge Jct to Croftgary
Unclassified
30 Dunfermline, Masterton Rd
30 Dunfermline, Townhill Rd/Kingseat Rd
30 Glenrothes, Formonthills Rd
30 Glenrothes, Woodside Wy
30 Kirkcaldy, Hendry Rd

Lothian and Borders
East Lothian, Edinburgh, Midlothian, Scottish Borders, West Lothian

A7
30 Galashiels, Magdela Terrace
30 Hawick, Wilton Hill
30 Stow
A8
40 Edinburgh, at Ratho station
A68
30 Jedburgh
NSL Soutra Hill
A70
30 Edinburgh, Balerno
A71
30 Breich
30 Polbeth
A72
60 Horsbrugh
30 Peebles, Innerleithen Rd
A89
30 Armadale, West Main Street
A90
40 Edinburgh, Burnshot Lane
A697
30 Coldstream
30 Greenlaw
NSL Orange Lane
A698
60 Ashybank
60 Crailing, Eckford Rd End
A701
30 Broughton
60 Fingland
60 Tweedhopefoot
A702
60 Dolphinton
A703
60 Leadburn Moor
30 Peebles, Edinburgh Rd
A705
30 East Whitburn, Bridge End
30 Whitburn, West Main St
A706
30 Whitburn, Carnie Place
30 Longridge Village
A720
50 Edinburgh, City Bypass
A899
50 btwn Lizzie Bryce Rdbt & Almond Interchange
50 South of Deer Park Rdbt
A6091
NSL Melrose bypass
A6105
30 Gordon
B3764
30 Langlees
B7105
30 Livingston, Howden South Rd
Unclassified
40 Edinburgh, Comiston Rd
30 Edinburgh, Lower Granton Rd
30 Edinburgh, Muirhouse Parkway
40 Edinburgh, West Approach Rd

North East Scotland
Aberdeen, Aberdeenshire, Moray

A90
40 Aberdeen, Midstocket Rd to Whitestripes Rdbt
60 btwn bend at South of Leys & Bogbrae
60 btwn Bogbrae & north of Bridgend
70 btwn Candy & Upper Criggie
70 btwn Laurencekirk & north of Fourdon
70 btwn Mill of Barnes & Laurencekirk
70 Dundee to Aberdeen Rd at Jct with B9120 Laurencekirk
70 north of Newtonhill Jct to South of Schoolhill Rd
60 Peterhead, btwn north of Bridgend & Blackhills
70 south of Schoolhill Rd, Portlethen to South Damhead (northbound)
A92
NSL btwn Johnshaven & Inverbervie
NSL btwn rdside of Kinneff & Mill of Uras
A93
30 Aboyne
40 at Banchory eastbound from Caravan Site
30 at Banchory westbound from Church
NSL btwn Cambus O'May & Dinnet
NSL btwn Dinnet to Aboyne
NSL btwn Kincardine O'Neil & Haugh of Sluie
A95
30 Cornhill
NSL btwn 30mph at Keith & Davoch of Grange
A96
NSL btwn Forgie & A98 Jct at Fochabers
NSL btwn north of Pitmachie & Jct with A920 at Kirton of Culsalmond
NSL Keith to Huntly Rd betwn Auchairn and Coachford
30 Btwn Haudagain and Chapel of Stoneywood
NSL Huntly btwn A920 Dufftown and B9022 Portsey jcns
NSL Mosstodloch to Lhanbryde (East)
70 Inverurie btwn Thainstone Agricultural Centre and Port Elphinstone
60 Inverurie btwn Inveramsey and Conglass
A98
30 Banff
NSL btwn Carnoch Farm Rd, Buckie & 30mph at Cullen
NSL btwn Fochabers 30mph & Mill of Tynet
NSL Buckle, btwn Mill of Tynet & Barhill Rd Jct
A941
NSL btwn 30mph at Lossiemouth & 40mph at Elgin
NSL btwn Clackmarras Rd & South Netherglen
NSL btwn Glassgreen & Clackmarras Rd
NSL from South Netherglen & Rothes
A944
30/40/60 Westhill Rd btwn Gairloch & Westhill Rdbt
A947
NSL btwn Mains of Tulloch Jct & Fyvie
NSL btwn Newmachar & Whiterashes
A948
NSL btwn Ellon to Auchnagatt
A952
NSL btwn New Leeds & Jct with A90 at Cortes
A956
40 Aberdeen, Wellington Rd
30 Aberdeen, King St
30 Aberdeen, Ellon Rd
30 Aberdeen, North Esplanade West
B9040
NSL btwn Silver Sands Caravan Park to Jct with B9012
B9077
30 Aberdeen, Great Southern Rd
B9089
NSL from Kinloss & crossroads at Roseisle Maltings
Unclassified
30 Aberdeen, Beach Boulevard to Links Rd
30 Aberdeen, Beach Boulevard to Wales St
30 Aberdeen, Ellon, Craigs Rd
30 Aberdeen, Springhill Rd
30 Aberdeen, St Machar Drive
40 Aberdeen, Wellington Rd
40 Aberdeen, West Tullos Rd

Northern Scotland
Highland, Orkney, Shetland, Western Isles

A9
60 Altnasleanach by Inverness
60 Sutherland, Golspie, Caulmaillie Farm
60 Cuaich by Dalwhinnie
70 Daviot, by Inverness
60 Fearn, by Tain
70 North Kessock Jct (both directions)
60 nr Dalwhinnie South of the Mound, by Golspie
A82
60 Altsigh Youth Hostel, by Inverness
60 Drumnadrochit, Temple Pier
60 Invergarry Power Station
60 Kingshouse Hotel, Glencoe
60 White Corries, Rannoch Moor, Lochaber
A87
60 West of Bunloyne Jct
A95
60 by Grantown on Spey, Congash Farm
60 Drumuillie by Boat of Garten
60 North of Cromdale
A96
60 East Auldearn Jct, by Nairn
60 Gollanfield, by Nairn
60 Nairn, West Auldern Jct
60 West of Allanfearn Jct, by Inverness
A99
60 Hempriggs, south of Wick
A834
60 Dingwall, nr Foddarty Bridge
30 Dingwall, Strathpeffer Rd
A835
60 Inverlael straight nr Ullapool
A939
60 Ferness to Grantown on Spey
B9006
60 Sunnyside, Culloden, Inverness

Strathclyde
Argyll & Bute, East Ayrshire, East Dunbartonshire, East Renfrewshire, Glasgow, Inverclyde, North Ayrshire, North Lanarkshire, Renfrewshire, South Ayrshire, South Lanarkshire, West Dunbartonshire

M74
70 Abington, Jct 13 (northbound)
A70
60 East Tarelgin
A73
30 Airdrie, Carlisle Rd
A76
30 New Cumnock, nr Lime Rd
A78
30 Fairlie, Main Rd
A82
60 Bridge of Orchy
40 Milton, Dunbarton Rd
A85
60 west of Tyndrum
A89
30 Airdrie, Forrest St
A706
60 South of Forth
A730
30 Rutherglen, Blairbeth Rd
A730
30 Rutherglen, Mill St
A737
30 Dairy, New St/Kilwinning Rd
A749
40 East Kilbride Rd btwn Cathkin Rd & Cairnmuir Rd
A761
30 Paisley, Glasgow Rd nr Newtyle Rd
A807
30 Bardowie, Balmore Rd
A810
30 Bearsden, Duntocher Rd / Drymen Rd
A814
30 Clydebank, Glasgow Rd
A814
30 Dunbarton, Cardross Rd
A815
60 Near Ardkinglass
B768
30 Rutherglen, Burnhill St
B803
30 Airdrie to Glenmavis, Coatbridge Rd
B814
30 Duntocher Rd
B7078
30 Blackwood
B8048
30 Kirkintilloch, Waterside Rd
Unclassified
30 Barrhead, Aurs Rd
30 Bishopbriggs, Woodhill Rd
30 Coatbridge, Townhead Rd
30 Drymen Rd/Duntocher Rd
30 East Kilbride, Maxwellton Rd at Kirkoswald (South)
30 Johnstone, Beith Rd
30 Neilston, Kingston Rd
30 Newton Mearns, Mearns Rd
30 Rutherglen, Glasgow Rd
30 Troon, Craigend Rd

Tayside
Angus, Dundee, Perth & Kinross

M90
70 Jct 6
A9
70 Perth to Inverness
70 Stirling to Perth
A90
50 Dundee, Kingsway
70 Perth to Dundee
A91
60 Milnathort to Devon Bridge
A92
60 Arbroath to Montrose
30 Dundee, Greendykes Rd
40 Dundee, East Dock St
A93
60 Guildtown to Blairgowrie
60 Old Scone to Blairgowrie
60 Old Scone to Guildtown
A94
60 Scone to Coupar Angus
A822
60 Crieff to Braco
A923
60 Blairgowrie to Muirhead
60 Blairgowrie to Tullybaccart
A933
60 Arbroath to Brechin
60 Colliston to Redford
A935
60 Brechin to Montrose
A972
40 Dundee, Kingsway East
A977
60 Kinross to Crook of Devon
B961
30 Dundee, Drumgeith Rd
B996
60 Kinross to Kelty
Unclassified
30 Dundee, Broughty Ferry Rd
30 Dundee, Charleston Drive
30 Dundee, Laird St
30 Dundee, Old Glamis Rd
30 Dundee, Perth Rd
30 Dundee, Strathmartine Rd

Abbreviations

adj	adjacent
btwn	between
j/w	junction with
nr	near
NSL	National Speed Limit
o/s	outside
rdbts	roundabouts
twds	towards

Holyhead
Anglesey
Llangefni
Bangor
Llandudno
Colwyn Bay
Conwy
Rhyl
Flint
Denbigh
Mold
Ellesmere Port
Runcorn
Northwich
Macclesfield
Chester
Sandbach
Congleton
Crewe
Nantwich
Newcastle-Under-Lyme
STOKE-ON-TRENT
Wrexham
Whitchurch
Stone
Eccleshall
Caernarfon
Bethesda
Llanrwst
Betws-y-Coed
Ruthin
Penygroes
Blaenau Ffestiniog
Llangollen
Nefyn
Porthmadog
Pwllheli
Abersoch
Bala
Oswestry
Llanbedr
L. Vyrnwy
Barmouth
Dolgellau
Newport
Llwyngwril
Mallwyd
Welshpool
Shrewsbury
Telford
Tywyn
Machynlleth
WOLVERHAMPTON
Church Stretton
Bridgnorth
West Bromwich
Dudley
Talybont
Caersws
Newtown
Aberystwyth
Llangurig
Kidderminster
Knighton
Ludlow
Rhayader
Stourport-on-Severn
Aberaeron
Tregaron
Llandrindod Wells
Leominster
Kington
Builth Wells
Worcester
Lampeter
Cardigan
Hay-on-Wye
Great Malvern
Newcastle Emlyn
Goodwick
Fishguard
Llandovery
Hereford
Ledbury
Brecon
Tewkesbury
St. David's
Llandissilio
Carmarthen
Llandeilo
Llangadog
Ross-on-Wye
Gloucester
Haverfordwest
Abergavenny
Milford Haven
Merthyr Tydfil
Ebbw Vale
Monmouth
Stroud
Pembroke
Tenby
Llanelli
Pontypool
Lydney
Swansea
Neath
Rhondda
Cwmbran
Chepstow
Tetbury
Port Talbot
Pontypridd
Caerphilly
Newport
Port Eynon
Yate
Bridgend
CARDIFF
Porthcawl
Penarth
BRISTOL
Barry
Bath
Bristol Channel
Weston-super-Mare
Melksham
Radstock
Trowbridge
Ilfracombe
Lynton
Minehead
Wells
Frome
Glastonbury
Barnstaple
Bridgwater
Bideford
Great Torrington
Taunton
Wincanton
Mere
Shaftesbury
Wellington
Henstridge
Tiverton
Ilminster
Yeovil
Chard
Blandford Forum
Bude
Hatherleigh
Holsworthy
Crediton
Okehampton
Honiton
Beaminster
Cerne Abbas
Wimborne Minster
Exeter
Lyme Regis
Bridport
Dorchester
Poole
Launceston
Exmouth
Weymouth
Tavistock
Newton Abbot
Teignmouth
Easton
Newquay
Bodmin
Torquay
Liskeard
Paignton
Totnes
Brixham
PLYMOUTH
Fowey
St. Austell
Dartmouth
Redruth
St. Ives
Truro
Camborne
Salcombe
Penzance
Falmouth
Helston
Lizard
Greystones
Wicklow
ROSSLARE
ROSCOFF SANTANDER
GUERNSEY JERSEY ST. MALO
ENGLISH

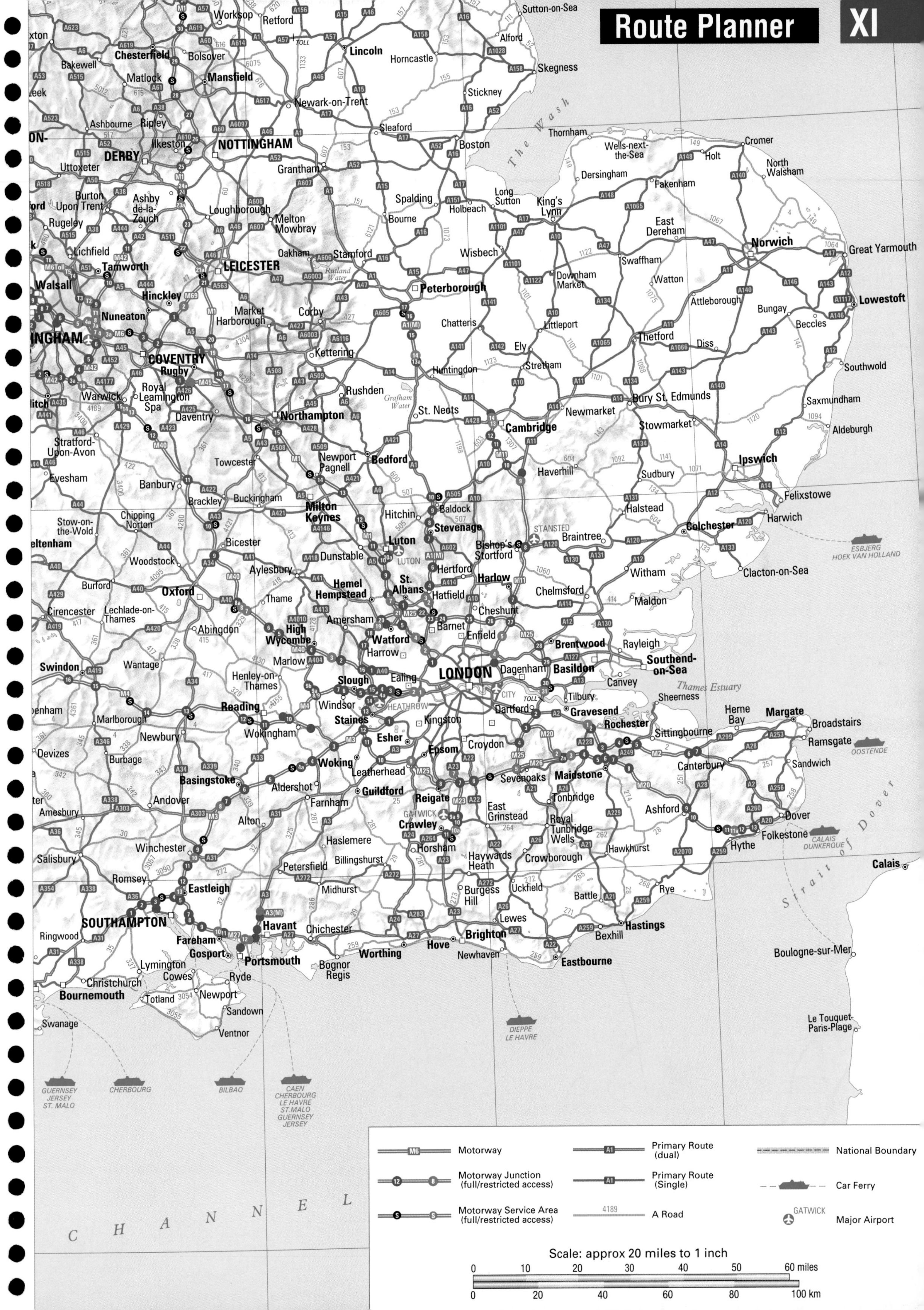
Worksop
Retford
Sutton-on-Sea
Lincoln
Alford
Horncastle
Skegness
Chesterfield
Bolsover
Bakewell
Matlock
Mansfield
Stickney
Newark-on-Trent
The Wash
Ashbourne
Ripley
Sleaford
Thornham
Cromer
Ilkeston
NOTTINGHAM
Boston
Wells-next-the-Sea
Holt
DERBY
Uttoxeter
Grantham
Dersingham
North Walsham
Fakenham
Burton Upon Trent
Ashby de-la-Zouch
Loughborough
Spalding
Long Sutton
King's Lynn
Melton Mowbray
Bourne
Holbeach
East Dereham
Rugeley
Lichfield
Oakham
Stamford
Rutland Water
Wisbech
Norwich
Great Yarmouth
Tamworth
LEICESTER
Swaffham
Downham Market
Watton
Walsall
Hinckley
Peterborough
Attleborough
Lowestoft
Nuneaton
Market Harborough
Corby
Chatteris
Bungay
Beccles
Littleport
COVENTRY
Kettering
Ely
Thetford
Diss
Rugby
Huntingdon
Stretham
Southwold
Royal Leamington Spa
Warwick
Rushden
Grafham Water
St. Neots
Bury St. Edmunds
Saxmundham
Daventry
Northampton
Cambridge
Newmarket
Stowmarket
Aldeburgh
Stratford-Upon-Avon
Towcester
Newport Pagnell
Bedford
Haverhill
Ipswich
Evesham
Banbury
Sudbury
Felixstowe
Brackley
Buckingham
Milton Keynes
Hitchin
Baldock
Stevenage
Halstead
Harwich
Stow-on-the-Wold
Chipping Norton
STANSTED
Braintree
Colchester
Bicester
Luton
Bishop's Stortford
ESBJERG
HOEK VAN HOLLAND
Woodstock
Dunstable
LUTON
Hertford
Aylesbury
St. Albans
Harlow
Witham
Clacton-on-Sea
Burford
Oxford
Hemel Hempstead
Hatfield
Chelmsford
Cirencester
Lechlade-on-Thames
Thame
Maldon
Abingdon
Amersham
Cheshunt
High Wycombe
Watford
Barnet
Enfield
Harrow
Brentwood
Rayleigh
Swindon
Wantage
Marlow
LONDON
Dagenham
Basildon
Southend-on-Sea
Henley-on-Thames
Slough
Ealing
Canvey
Thames Estuary
CITY
Windsor
Tilbury
Sheerness
Reading
HEATHROW
Dartford
Marlborough
Staines
Kingston
Gravesend
Herne Bay
Margate
Broadstairs
Wokingham
Rochester
Sittingbourne
Newbury
Esher
Epsom
Croydon
Ramsgate
OOSTENDE
Devizes
Burbage
Woking
Canterbury
Sandwich
Basingstoke
Leatherhead
Sevenoaks
Maidstone
Aldershot
Guildford
Reigate
Tonbridge
Andover
Farnham
Amesbury
GATWICK
East Grinstead
Ashford
Dover
Alton
Crawley
Royal Tunbridge Wells
Winchester
Haslemere
Horsham
Hythe
Folkestone
CALAIS
DUNKERQUE
Strait of Dover
Hawkhurst
Salisbury
Billingshurst
Haywards Heath
Crowborough
Calais
Petersfield
Romsey
Eastleigh
Midhurst
Burgess Hill
Uckfield
Rye
Battle
SOUTHAMPTON
Havant
Lewes
Hastings
Ringwood
Fareham
Chichester
Brighton
Bexhill
Gosport
Worthing
Hove
Newhaven
Eastbourne
Boulogne-sur-Mer
Portsmouth
Lymington
Cowes
Ryde
Bognor Regis
Christchurch
Bournemouth
Totland
Newport
Sandown
Swanage
Ventnor
DIEPPE
LE HAVRE
Le Touquet-Paris-Plage
GUERNSEY
JERSEY
ST. MALO
CHERBOURG
BILBAO
CAEN
CHERBOURG
LE HAVRE
ST.MALO
GUERNSEY
JERSEY
C H A N N E L
Motorway
Primary Route (dual)
National Boundary
Motorway Junction (full/restricted access)
Primary Route (Single)
Car Ferry
Motorway Service Area (full/restricted access)
A Road
GATWICK
Major Airport
Scale: approx 20 miles to 1 inch
0 10 20 30 40 50 60 miles
0 20 40 60 80 100 km

Helensburgh
Dunfermline
Cowdenbeath
Burntisland
Port Askaig
Feolin Ferry
Islay
Bridgend
Portnahaven
Port Ellen
Tarbert
Colintraive
Dunoon
Gourock
Greenock
Port Glasgow
Rothesay
Clydebank
Kilsyth
Falkirk
Cumbernauld
Airdrie
EDINBURGH
Haddington
Livingston
Bonnyrigg
Penicuik
Leadburn
Lauder
Paisley
GLASGOW
Hamilton
East Kilbride
Largs
Lochranza
Tayinloan
Arran
Stewarton
Ardrossan
Irvine
Brodick
Kilmarnock
Lanark
Carnwath
Peebles
Galashiels
Biggar
Troon
Prestwick
Ayr
Blackwaterfoot
Kilchenzie
Campbeltown
Mauchline
Cumnock
Selkirk
Hawick
Sanquhar
Firth of Clyde
Turnberry
Maybole
Dalmellington
Moffat
Ballintoy
Ballycastle
Coleraine
NORTH CHANNEL
L. Doon
Thornhill
Carsphairn
Ballymoney
Glenariff
Ballantrae
Barrhill
New Galloway
Lockerbie
Dumfries
Glenarm
Swatragh
Kirkcolm
Cairnryan
Newton Stewart
Castle Douglas
Crocketford
Longtown
Ballymena
Broughshane
Stranraer
Dalbeattie
Gretna
Carlisle
Brampton
Larne
FLEETWOOD
Glenluce
Wigtown
Kirkcudbright
Caulkerbush
Portpatrick
Magherafelt
Ballyclare
Antrim
Carrickfergus
High Hesket
Dundrennan
Solway Firth
Moneymore
Newtownabbey
Bangor
Drummore
Whithorn
Maryport
Bothel
Lough Neagh
BELFAST
Newtownards
LIVERPOOL DOUGLAS
Cockermouth
Workington
Penrith
Lisburn
Keswick
Whitehaven
Portadown
Lurgan
Saintfield
Strangford Lough
Egremont
Shap
Ballynahinch
Portaferry
Isle of Man
Ambleside
Armagh
Banbridge
Bride
Ramsey
Ballaugh
Coniston
Windermere
Downpatrick
Kendal
Ardglass
Laxey
Peel
Bootle
Kilcoo
Newcastle
Whicham
Newry
Warrenpoint
Annalong
Douglas
Ulverston
Cullaville
Kilkeel
Port Erin
Castletown
Barrow-in-Furness
Dundalk
Morecambe
Heysham
Lancaster
LIVERPOOL
BELFAST
Ardee
DUBLIN
LARNE
Fleetwood
Drogheda
Blackpool
Navan
Lytham St. Anne's
Preston
IRISH SEA
Balbriggan
Southport
Chorley
BELFAST DOUGLAS DUBLIN
Ormskirk
Wigan
DOUGLAS LIVERPOOL
Malahide
Kirkby
LIVERPOOL
St. Helens
Amlwch
Wallasey
Bootle
DUBLIN
Dun Laoghaire
Holyhead
Anglesey
Llandudno
Colwyn Bay
Prestatyn
Birkenhead
Widnes
Warrington
Runcorn
Bray
Llangefni
Bangor
Conwy
Rhyl
Ellesmere Port
Northwich
Flint
Greystones
Denbigh
Mold
Chester
Hollywood
Bethesda
Caernarfon
Llanrwst
Betws-y-Coed
Ruthin
Penygroes
Wicklow
Blaenau Ffestiniog
Wrexham
Nantwich
Nefyn
Porthmadog
Llangollen
Whitchurch
Pwllheli
Bala
Arklow
Abersoch
Oswestry
Llanbedr
L. Vyrnwy
Barmouth
Dolgellau
Gorey
Llwyngwril
Mallwyd
Welshpool
Shrewsbury
Camolin
Cardigan Bay
Tywyn
Machynlleth

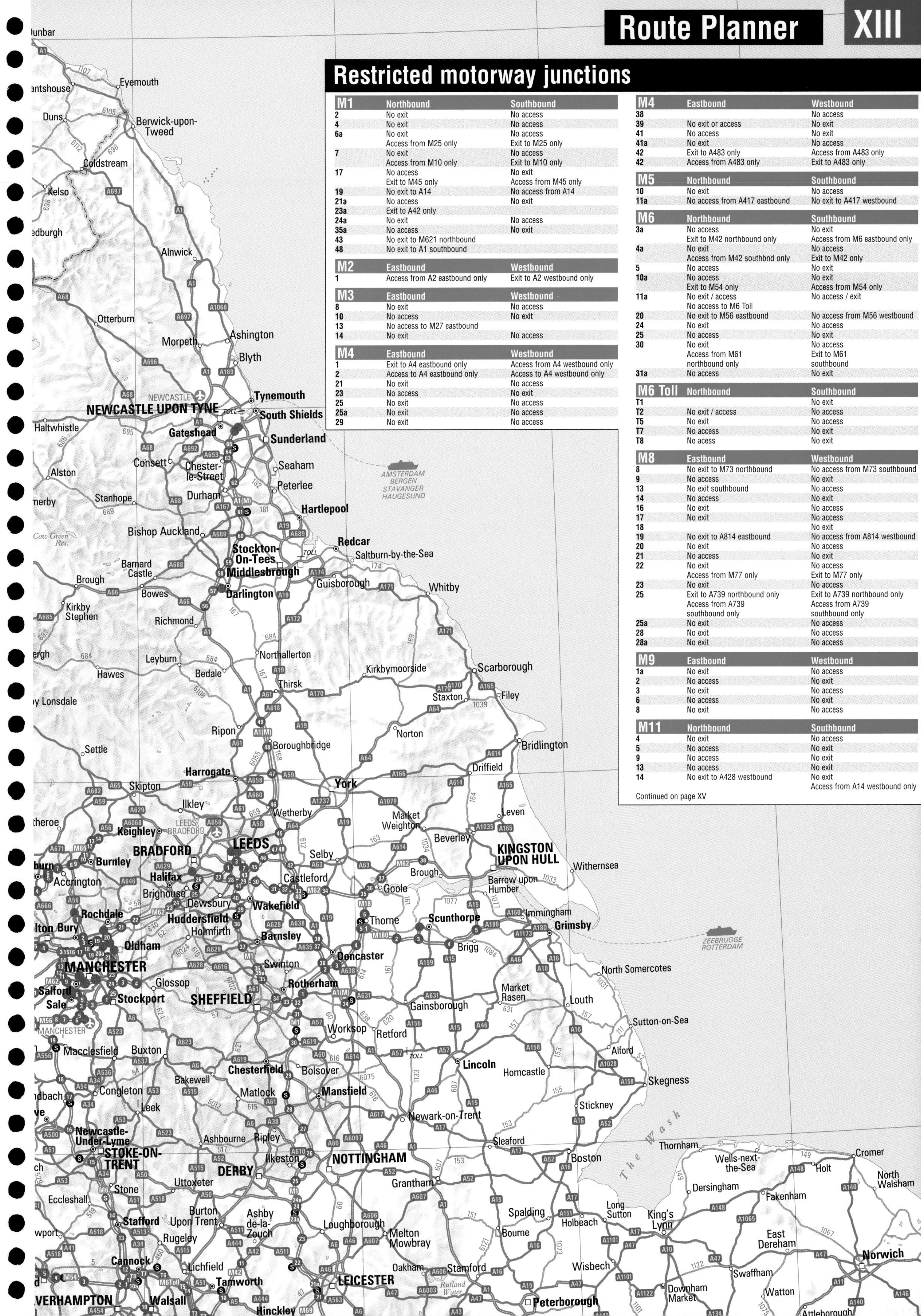

Restricted motorway junctions

M1	Northbound	Southbound
2	No exit	No access
4	No exit	No access
6a	No exit Access from M25 only	No access Exit to M25 only
7	No exit Access from M10 only	No access Exit to M10 only
17	No access Exit to M45 only	No exit Access from M45 only
19	No exit to A14	No access from A14
21a	No access	No exit
23a	Exit to A42 only	
24a	No exit	No access
35a	No access	No exit
43	No exit to M621 northbound	
48	No exit to A1 southbound	

M2	Eastbound	Westbound
1	Access from A2 eastbound only	Exit to A2 westbound only

M3	Eastbound	Westbound
8	No exit	No access
10	No access	No exit
13	No access to M27 eastbound	
14	No exit	No access

M4	Eastbound	Westbound
1	Exit to A4 eastbound only	Access from A4 westbound only
2	Access to A4 eastbound only	Access to A4 westbound only
21	No exit	No access
23	No access	No exit
25	No exit	No access
25a	No exit	No access
29	No exit	No access

M4	Eastbound	Westbound
38		No access
39	No exit or access	No exit
41	No access	No exit
41a	No exit	No access
42	Exit to A483 only	Access from A483 only
42	Access from A483 only	Exit to A483 only

M5	Northbound	Southbound
10	No exit	No access
11a	No access from A417 eastbound	No exit to A417 westbound

M6	Northbound	Southbound
3a	No access Exit to M42 northbound only	No exit Access from M6 eastbound only
4a	No exit Access from M42 southbnd only	No access Exit to M42 only
5	No access	No exit
10a	No access Exit to M54 only	No exit Access from M54 only
11a	No exit / access No access to M6 Toll	No access / exit
20	No exit to M56 eastbound	No access from M56 westbound
24	No exit	No access
25	No access	No exit
30	No exit Access from M61 northbound only	No access Exit to M61 southbound
31a	No access	No exit

M6 Toll	Northbound	Southbound
T1		No exit
T2	No exit / access	No access
T5	No exit	No access
T7	No access	No exit
T8	No acess	No exit

M8	Eastbound	Westbound
8	No exit to M73 northbound	No access from M73 southbound
9	No access	No exit
13	No exit southbound	No access
14	No access	No exit
16	No exit	No access
17	No exit	No access
18		No exit
19	No exit to A814 eastbound	No access from A814 westbound
20	No exit	No access
21	No access	No exit
22	No exit Access from M77 only	No access Exit to M77 only
23	No exit	No access
25	Exit to A739 northbound only Access from A739 southbound only	Exit to A739 northbound only Access from A739 southbound only
25a	No exit	No access
28	No exit	No access
28a	No exit	No access

M9	Eastbound	Westbound
1a	No exit	No access
2	No access	No exit
3	No exit	No access
6	No access	No exit
8	No exit	No access

M11	Northbound	Southbound
4	No exit	No access
5	No access	No exit
9	No access	No exit
13	No access	No exit
14	No exit to A428 westbound	No exit Access from A14 westbound only

Continued on page XV

Stromness
Pentland Firth
John o' Groats
Scrabster
Thurso
Durness
Melvich
Tongue
Eriboll
Dalhalvaig
Mybster
Wick
Laxford Bridge
Kylestrome
Kinloch
Altnaharra
Latheron
Kinbrace
Lochinver
Inchnadamph
Loch Shin
Helmsdale
Ledmore
Lairg
Brora
Rosehall
Inveran
Ullapool
Dornoch
Kincardine
Tain
Moray Firth
Aultbea
Ardessie
Fionn L.
Braemore
Gairloch
L. Maree
Invergordon
Cromarty
Lossiemouth
Elgin
Achnasheen
Garve
Dingwall
Nairn
Forres
Shieldaig
Muir of Ord
Rothes
Inverness
Ferness
L. Monar
Lochcarron
Dufftown
Mullardoch
Drumnadrochit
Grantown-on-Spey
Kyle of Lochalsh
Tomatin
Broadford
Shiel Bridge
Loch Ness
Invermoriston
Aviemore
Strathdon
Armadale
L. Quoich
Fort Augustus
L. Garry
L. Lochy
Newtonmore
Mallaig
Braemar
L. Arkaig
Spean Bridge
Dalwhinnie
Lochailort
Fort William
L. Treig
Spittal of Glenshee
Loch Shiel
L. Ericht
Acharacle
Onich
Strontian
Blair Atholl
Glencoe
L. Rannoch
L. Tummel
Pitlochry
Kirriemuir
Tobermory
Aberfeldy
Lochaline
Bridge of Orchy
Blairgowrie
Salen
L. Tay
Lawers
Coupar Angus
Mull
Connel
Amulree
Oban
Killin
Tyndrum
Fionnphort
Dalmally
Crianlarich
St. Fillans
Perth
Firth of Lorn
Loch Awe
L. Earn
Crieff
Newburgh
Strathyre
Kilmelford
L. Katrine
Auchtermuchty
Greenloaning
Inveraray
Furnace
Strachur
Tarbet
Dunblane
Glenrothes
Aberfoyle
Loch Lomond
Kilmartin
Stirling
Alloa
Kirkcaldy
Garelochhead
Cowdenbeath
Ardlussa
Lochgilphead
Dunfermline
Burntisland
Helensburgh
Kilsyth
Falkirk
Gourock
Greenock
Edinburgh
Dunoon
Cumbernauld
Colintraive
Clydebank
Port Glasgow
Port Askaig
Feolin Ferry
Tarbert
Airdrie
Livingston
Islay
Rothesay
Glasgow
Bonnyrigg
Jura
Bridgend
Largs
Paisley
Penicuik
East Kilbride
Hamilton
Leadburn
Portnahaven
Lochranza
Port Ellen
Tayinloan
Carnwath
Stewarton
Ardrossan
Arran
Lanark
Peebles
Irvine
Kilmarnock
Brodick
Biggar
Troon
Prestwick
Blackwaterfoot
Mauchline
Firth of Clyde
Ayr
Kilchenzie
Cumnock
Campbeltown
Larne
Sanquhar
Moffat
Turnberry
Maybole
Dalmellington
Ballintoy
Port Nis
Barabhas
Stornoway
Port Nan Giuran
Lewis
Outer Hebrides
North Minch
Tairbeart (Tarbert)
Roghadal
Little Minch
Kilmaluag
Loch nam Madadh (Lochmaddy)
North Uist
Clachan na Luib
Uig
Carbost
Dunvegan
Skye
Portree
Tobha Mor
South Uist
Sligachan
Loch Baghasdail (Lochboisdale)
Inner Hebrides
Bagh a Chaisteil (Castlebay)

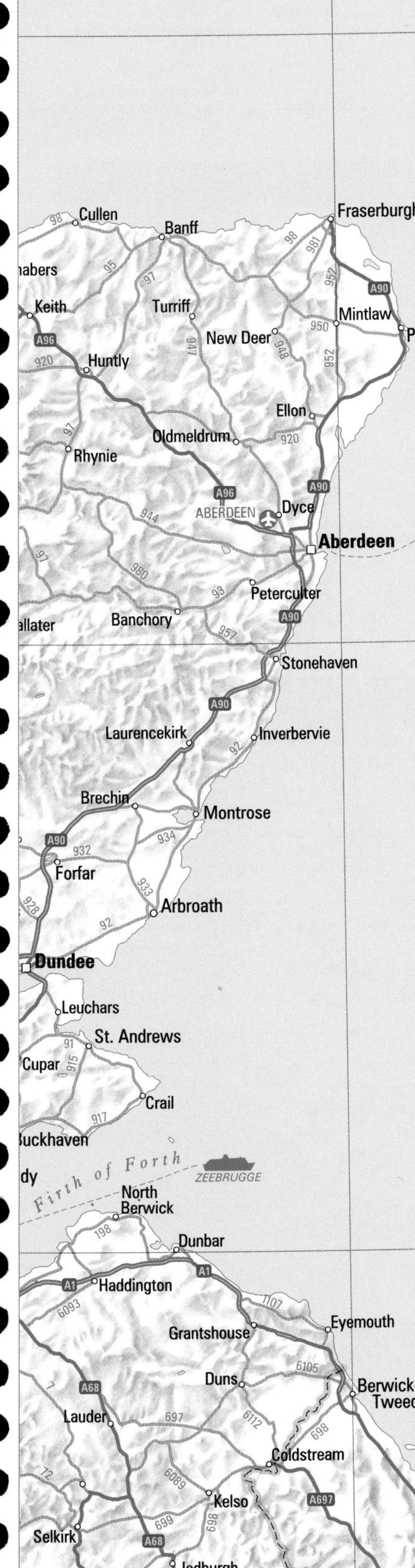

Restricted motorway junctions

Continuation from page XIII

M20	Eastbound	Westbound
2	No access	No exit
3	No exit Access from M26 eastbound only	No access Exit to M26 westbound only
11a	No access	No exit

M23	Northbound	Southbound
7	No exit to A23 southbound	No access from A23 northbound
10a	No exit	No access

M25	Clockwise	Anticlockwise
5	No exit to M26 eastbound	No access from M26 westbound
19	No access	No exit
21	No exit to M1 southbound Access from M1 southbound only	No exit to M1 southbound Access from M1 southbound only
31	No exit	No access

M27	Eastbound	Westbound
10	No exit	No access
12	No access	No exit

M40	Eastbound	Westbound
3	No exit	No access
7	No exit	No access
8	No exit	No access
13	No exit	No access
14	No access	No exit
16	No access	No exit

M42	Northbound	Southbound
1	No exit	No access
7	No access Exit to M6 northbound only	No exit Access from M6 northbound only
7a	No access Exit to M6 only	No exit Access from M6 northbound only
8	No exit Access from M6 southbound only	Exit to M6 northbound Access from M6 southbound only

M45	Eastbound	Westbound
M1 junc 17	Access to M1 southbound only	No access from M1 southbound
With A45 (Dunchurch)	No access	No exit

M48	Eastbound	Westbound
M4 junc 21	No exit to M4 westbound	No access from M4 eastbound
M4 junc 23	No access from M4 westbound	No exit to M4 eastbound

M49	Southbound
18a	No exit to M5 northbound

M53	Northbound	Southbound
11	Exit to M56 eastbound only Access from M56 westbound only	Exit to M56 eastbound only Access from M56 westbound only

M56	Eastbound	Westbound
2	No exit	No access
3	No access	No exit
4	No exit	No access
7		No access
8	No exit or access	No exit
9	No access from M6 northbound	No access to M6 southbound
15	No exit to M53	No access from M53 northbound

M57	Northbound	Southbound
3	No exit	No access
5	No exit	No access

M58	Eastbound	Westbound
1	No exit	No access

M60	Clockwise	Anticlockwise
2	No exit	No access
3	No exit to A34 northbound	No exit to A34 northbound
4	No access to M56	No exit to M56
5	No exit to A5103 southbound	No exit to A5103 northbound
14	No exit to A580	No access from A580
16	No exit	No access
20	No access	No exit
22		No access
25	No access	
26		No exit or access
27	No exit	No access

M61	Northbound	Southbound
2	No access from A580 eastbound	No exit to A580 westbound
3	No access from A580 eastbound No access from A666 southbound	No exit to A580 westbound
M6 junc 30	No exit to M6 southbound	No access from M6 northbound

M62	Eastbound	Westbound
23	No access	No exit

M65	Eastbound	Westbound
9	No access	No exit
11	No exit	No access

M66	Northbound	Southbound
1	No access	No exit

M67	Eastbound	Westbound
1a	No access	No exit
2	No exit	No access

M69	Northbound	Southbound
2	No exit	No access

M73	Northbound	Southbound
2	No access from M8 or A89 eastbound No exit to A89	No exit to M8 or A89 westbound No access from A89
3	Exit to A80 northbound only	Access from A80 southbound only

M74	Northbound	Southbound
2	No access	No exit
3	No exit	No access
7	No exit	No access
9	No exit or access	No access
10		No exit
11	No exit	No access
12	No access	No exit

M77	Northbound	Southbound
4	No exit	No access
6	No exit	No access
7	No exit or access	
8	No access	No access
M8 junc 22	Exit to M8 eastbound only	Access from M8 westbound only

M80	Northbound	Southbound
3	No access	No exit
5	No access from M876	No exit to M876

M90	Northbound	Southbound
2a	No access	No exit
7	No exit	No access
8	No access	No exit
10	No access from A912	No exit to A912

M180	Northbound	Southbound
1	No access	No exit

M621	Eastbound	Westbound
2a	No exit	No access
4	No exit or access	
5	No exit	No access
6	No access	No exit

M876	Northbound	Southbound
2	No access	No exit

A1(M)	Northbound	Southbound
2	No access	No exit
3		No access
5	No exit	No access
40	No access	No exit
44	No exit, access from M1 only	Exit to M1 only
57	No access	No exit
65	No access	No exit

A3(M)	Northbound	Southbound
1		No access
4	No access	No exit

A38(M)	Northbound	Southbound
With Victoria Road (Park Circus) Birmingham	No exit	No access

A48(M)	Northbound	Southbound
M4 Junc 29	Exit to M4 eastbound only	Access from M4 westbound only
29a	Access from A48 eastbound only	Exit to A48 westbound only

A57(M)	Eastbound	Westbound
With A5103	No access	No exit
With A34	No access	No exit

A58(M)	Southbound
With Park Lane and Westgate, Leeds	No access

A64(M)	Eastbound	Westbound
With A58 Clay Pit Lane, Leeds	No access	No exit
With Regent Street, Leeds	No access	No access

A74(M)	Northbound	Southbound
18	No access	No exit
22	No access	No exit

A167(M)	Northbound	Southbound
With Camden St, Newcastle	No exit	No exit or access

A194(M)	Northbound	Southbound
A1(M) junc 65 Gateshead Western Bypass	Access from A1(M) northbound only	Exit to A1(M) southbound only

Road map symbols

M6
Motorway, toll motorway
Motorway junction – full, restricted access
Motorway service area – full, restricted access
Motorway under construction

A453
Primary route – dual, single carriageway
Service area, roundabout, multi-level junction
Numbered junction – full, restricted access
Primary route under construction
Narrow primary route
Derby
Primary destination

A34
A road – dual, single carriageway
A road under construction, narrow A road

B2135
B road – dual, single carriageway
B road under construction, narrow B road

Minor road – over 4 metres, under 4 metres wide
Minor road with restricted access

Distance in miles
Scenic route
Speed camera – single, multiple
TOLL
Toll, steep gradient – arrow points downhill
Tunnel

National trail – England and Wales
Long distance footpath – Scotland

Railway with station
Level crossing, tunnel
Preserved railway with station

National boundary
County / unitary authority boundary

Car ferry, catamaran
Passenger ferry, catamaran
Hovercraft, freight ferry
CALAIS 1:15
Ferry destination, journey time – hrs : mins
Ferry
Car ferry – river crossing
Principal airport, other airport

National park
Area of Outstanding Natural Beauty – England and Wales **National Scenic Area** – Scotland
forest park / regional park / national forest
Woodland
Beach
Linear antiquity
Roman road
1066
Hillfort, battlefield – with date
795
Viewpoint, nature reserve, spot height – in metres
Golf course, youth hostel, sporting venue
Camp site, caravan site, camping and caravan site
P&R
Shopping village, park and ride
29
Adjoining page number – road maps

Road map scale 1: 150 000 or 2·37 miles to 1 inch

0 1 2 3 4 5 6 miles

0 1 2 3 4 5 6 7 8 9 10 km

Approach map symbols

M6
Motorway
Toll motorway
Motorway junction – full, restricted access
Service area
Under construction
A6
Primary route – dual, single carriageway
Service area
Multi-level junction
roundabout
Under construction
A195
A road – dual, single carriageway
B1288
B road – dual, single carriageway
Minor road – dual, single carriageway
Ring road
Distance in miles
COSELEY
Railway with station
LOXDALE
Tramway with station
Underground or metro station
Congestion charge area
Uncharged road in congestion charge area

Town plan symbols

Motorway
Primary route – dual, single carriageway
A road – dual, single carriageway
B road – dual, single carriageway
Minor through road
one-way street
Pedestrian roads
Shopping streets
Railway with station
City Hall
Tramway with station
Bus or railway station building
Shopping precinct or retail park
Park
Building of public interest
Theatre, cinema
Parking, shopmobility
Bank
Underground station
West St
Metro station
Hospital, Police station
Post office

Tourist information

Abbey, cathedral or priory
Ancient monument
Aquarium
Art gallery
Bird collection or aviary
Castle
Church
Country park
England and Wales
Scotland
Farm park
Garden
Historic ship
House
House and garden
Motor racing circuit
Museum
Picnic area
Preserved railway
Race course
Roman antiquity
Safari park
Theme park
Tourist information centre
open all year
open seasonally
Zoo
Other place of interest

Relief

Feet	metres
3000	914
2600	792
2200	671
1800	549
1400	427
1000	305
0	0

Speed Cameras

Fixed camera locations are shown using the (40) symbol.

In congested areas the (40) symbol is used to show that there are two or more cameras on the road indicated.

Due to the restrictions of scale the camera locations are only approximate and cannot indicate the operating direction of the camera. Mobile camera sites, and cameras located on roads not included on the mapping are not shown. Where two or more cameras are shown on the same road, drivers are warned that this may indicate that a SPEC system is in operation. These cameras use the time taken to drive between the two camera positions to calculate the speed of the vehicle.

Key to road map pages

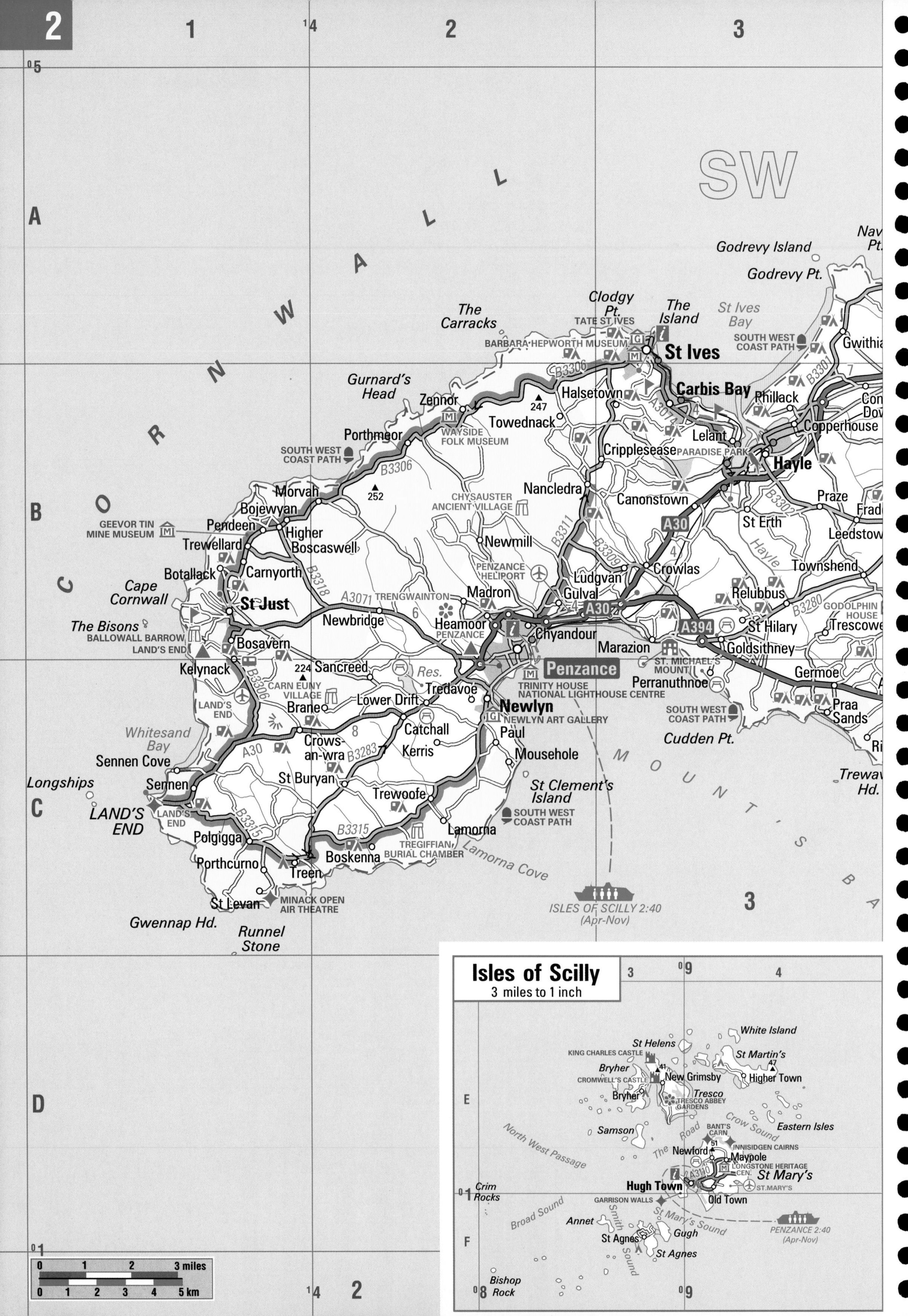
1
2
3
A
B
C
D
SW
C O R N W A L L
Godrevy Island
Godrevy Pt.
Nav Pt.
Clodgy Pt.
The Island
St Ives Bay
TATE ST IVES
The Carracks
BARBARA HEPWORTH MUSEUM
St Ives
SOUTH WEST COAST PATH
Gwithia
B3306
Carbis Bay
Halsetown
Phillack
B3301
Gurnard's Head
Zennor
247
Towednack
Lelant
Copperhouse
Porthmeor
WAYSIDE FOLK MUSEUM
A3074
SOUTH WEST COAST PATH
Cripplesease
PARADISE PARK
Hayle
B3306
Nancledra
Morvah
252
CHYSAUSTER ANCIENT VILLAGE
Canonstown
Praze
Bojewyan
B3302
GEEVOR TIN MINE MUSEUM
Pendeen
Higher Boscaswell
A30
St Erth
Trewellard
Newmill
B3311
Leedstow
B3309
Hayle
Botallack
Carnyorth
PENZANCE HELIPORT
Ludgvan
Crowlas
Townshend
B3318
Cape Cornwall
A3071
TRENGWAINTON
Madron
Gulval
Relubbus
St Just
Newbridge
A30
B3280
GODOLPHIN HOUSE
The Bisons
Heamoor
PENZANCE
Chyandour
A394
St Hilary
Trescowe
BALLOWALL BARROW
LAND'S END
Bosavern
Marazion
Goldsithney
Kelynack
224
Sancreed
Res.
Penzance
ST. MICHAEL'S MOUNT
Germoe
B3306
CARN EUNY VILLAGE
Tredavoe
TRINITY HOUSE NATIONAL LIGHTHOUSE CENTRE
Perranuthnoe
LAND'S END
Brane
Lower Drift
Newlyn
Praa Sands
NEWLYN ART GALLERY
SOUTH WEST COAST PATH
Whitesand Bay
Catchall
Paul
Crows-an-wra
B3283
Kerris
Cudden Pt.
A30
Sennen Cove
Mousehole
Trewav Hd.
Longships
Sennen
St Buryan
St Clement's Island
M O U N T ' S B A
LAND'S END
Trewoofe
LAND'S END
B3315
SOUTH WEST COAST PATH
Polgigga
B3315
Lamorna
TREGIFFIAN BURIAL CHAMBER
Lamorna Cove
Boskenna
Porthcurno
Treen
St Levan
MINACK OPEN AIR THEATRE
ISLES OF SCILLY 2:40 (Apr-Nov)
Gwennap Hd.
Runnel Stone
Isles of Scilly
3 miles to 1 inch
E
F
White Island
St Helens
KING CHARLES CASTLE
St Martin's
Bryher
New Grimsby
Higher Town
CROMWELL'S CASTLE
Bryher
Tresco
TRESCO ABBEY GARDENS
Eastern Isles
Crow Sound
Samson
BANT'S CARN
The Road
North West Passage
Newford
INNISIDGEN CAIRNS
Maypole
LONGSTONE HERITAGE CEN.
St Mary's
A3110
Hugh Town
ST.MARY'S
Crim Rocks
GARRISON WALLS
Old Town
Broad Sound
Annet
Smith Sound
St Mary's Sound
Gugh
PENZANCE 2:40 (Apr-Nov)
St Agnes
St Agnes
Bishop Rock
0 1 2 3 miles
0 1 2 3 4 5 km

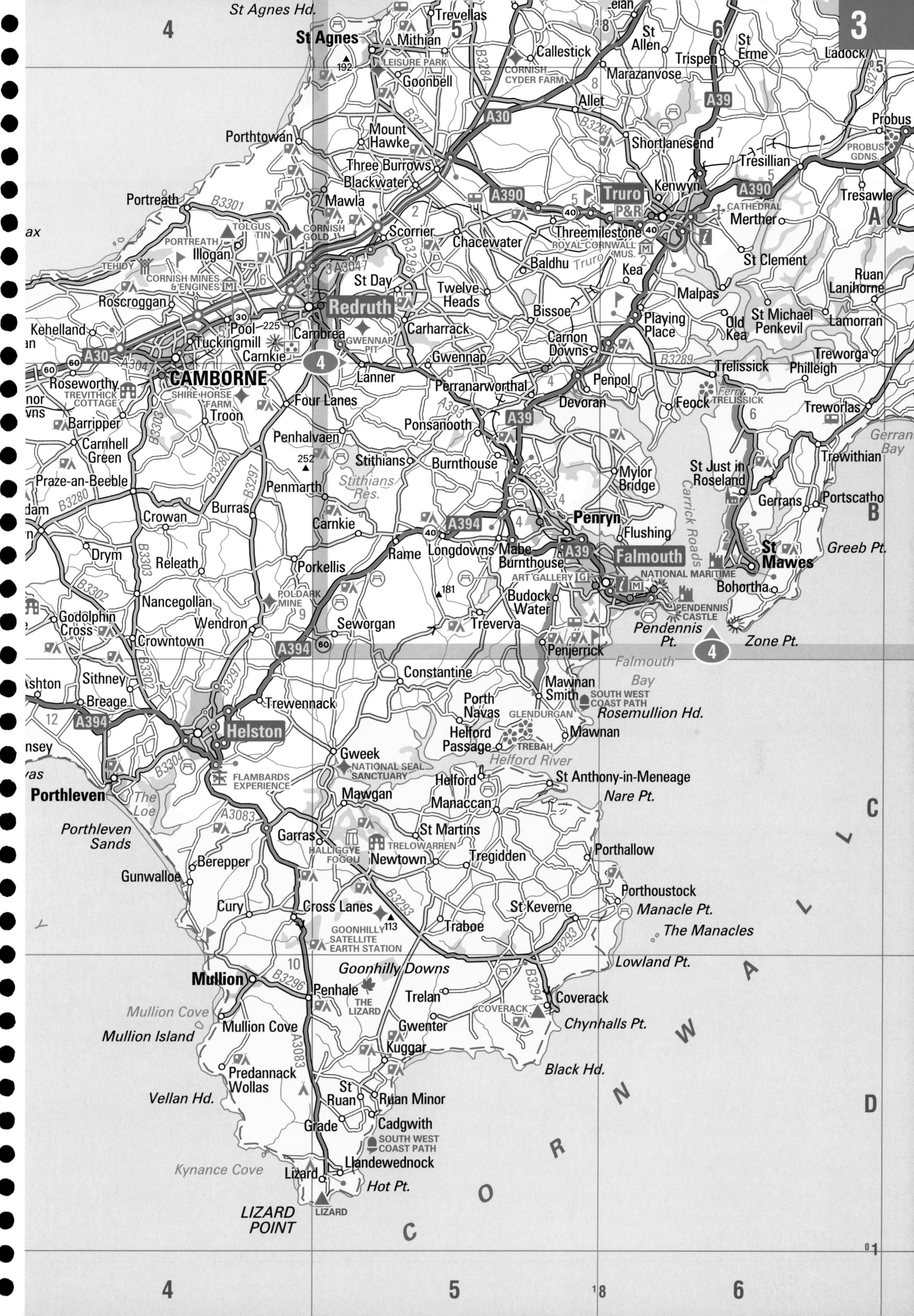
St Agnes Hd.
St Agnes
Trevellas
Mithian
LEISURE PARK
Callestick
CORNISH CYDER FARM
St Allen
Trispen
St Erme
Ladock
Marazanvose
Goonbell
Allet
A30
A39
Probus
PROBUS GDNS.
Porthtowan
Mount Hawke
Shortlanesend
Three Burrows
Blackwater
Tresillian
Truro
Kenwyn
A390
Tresawle
Portreath
Mawla
P&R
CATHEDRAL
Merther
TOLGUS TIN
CORNISH GOLD
Scorrier
Threemilestone
PORTREATH
Illogan
Chacewater
ROYAL CORNWALL MUS.
St Clement
TEHIDY
Baldhu
Kea
CORNISH MINES & ENGINES
St Day
Twelve Heads
Malpas
Ruan Lanihorne
Roscroggan
Redruth
Bissoe
Playing Place
Old Kea
St Michael Penkevil
Lamorran
Kehelland
Pool
Carnbrea
Carharrack
Carnon Downs
Tuckingmill
GWENNAP PIT
Treworga
A30
Carnkie
Gwennap
Trelissick
Philleigh
Roseworthy
CAMBORNE
Lanner
Penpol
TREVITHICK COTTAGE
SHIRE HORSE FARM
Perranarworthal
Feock
TRELISSICK
Devoran
Treworlas
Four Lanes
Troon
Barripper
Ponsanooth
Penhalvaen
Gerrans Bay
Carnhell Green
252
Stithians
Burnthouse
Trewithian
Praze-an-Beeble
Mylor Bridge
St Just in Roseland
Penmarth
Stithians Res.
Carrick Roads
Gerrans
Portscatho
Crowan
Burras
Penryn
Carnkie
A394
Flushing
St Mawes
Greeb Pt.
Drym
Longdowns
Mabe Burnthouse
Rame
Falmouth
Releath
Porkellis
ART GALLERY
NATIONAL MARITIME
181
Bohortha
Nancegollan
POLDARK MINE
Budock Water
Godolphin Cross
Wendron
PENDENNIS CASTLE
Sewrogan
Treverva
Pendennis Pt.
Zone Pt.
Crowntown
A394
Penjerrick
Falmouth Bay
Constantine
Sithney
Mawnan Smith
SOUTH WEST COAST PATH
Breage
Porth Navas
Trewennack
GLENDURGAN
Rosemullion Hd.
Helston
Helford Passage
Mawnan
TREBAH
Gweek
Helford River
NATIONAL SEAL SANCTUARY
FLAMBARDS EXPERIENCE
Helford
St Anthony-in-Meneage
Porthleven
The Loe
Mawgan
Manaccan
Nare Pt.
Porthleven Sands
St Martins
Garras
Porthallow
HALLIGGYE FOGOU
TRELOWARREN
Newtown
Tregidden
Berepper
Gunwalloe
Porthoustock
Cury
Cross Lanes
St Keverne
Manacle Pt.
GOONHILLY SATELLITE EARTH STATION
Traboe
The Manacles
Lowland Pt.
Goonhilly Downs
Mullion
Penhale
Trelan
Coverack
THE LIZARD
COVERACK
Mullion Cove
Gwenter
Chynhalls Pt.
Mullion Island
Kuggar
Black Hd.
Predannack Wollas
St Ruan
Ruan Minor
Vellan Hd.
Cadgwith
Grade
SOUTH WEST COAST PATH
Kynance Cove
Lizard
Llandewednock
Hot Pt.
LIZARD
LIZARD POINT
CORNWALL
A
B
C
D
4
5
6

4
SW
Park Hd.
Penrose
St Ervan
Rumford
St Issey
Tredinnick
RARE BREEDS CENTRE
St Jidgey
CREALY GREAT ADVENTURE PARK
St Eval
Trenance
Berryl's Pt.
Trevarrian
St Mawgan
CORNISH BIRDS OF PREY CENTRE
Talskiddy
WATERGATE BAY
Tregurrian
NEWQUAY
St Columb Major
CASTLE AN DINAS
Towan Hd.
Newquay Bay
Porth
St Columb Minor
Fistral Bay
Pentire
Trebudannon
SPRINGFIELDS FUN & PONY CENTRE
ANIMAL WORLD
Kelsey Hd.
SEA LIFE CENTRE
Newquay
Quintrell Downs
Colan
Mountjoy
Ruthvoes
West Pentire
Crantock
Lane
Trevarren
Indian Queens
Penhale Pt.
HOLYWELL BAY FUN PARK
Kestle Mill
St Columb Road
DAIRYLAND FARM WORLD
Holywell
Carines
Fraddon
Penhale
St Dennis
TRERICE
Ligger or Perran Bay
Cubert
St Newlyn East
Gummow's Shop
St Enoder
Retew
Penhale Sands
Mount
Rejerrah
LAPPA VALLEY STEAM RAILWAY
Treviscoe
SOUTH WEST COAST PATH
PERRAN ROUND
Summercourt
Rose
Brighton
Trethosa
Perranporth
PERRANPORTH
WORLD IN MINIATURE
Newlyn Downs
Mitchell
Goonhavern
Carland Cross
Bolingey
Trelassick
St Stephen
Perranzabuloe
Zelah
St Agnes Hd.
Trevellas
New Mills
Coombe
St Agnes
Mithian
St Allen
St Erme
Ladock
Grampound Road
LEISURE PARK
Callestick
Trispen
CORNISH CYDER FARM
Marazanvose
Goonbell
Allet
Probus
Grampound
TREWITHEN
Porthtowan
Mount Hawke
Shortlanesend
PROBUS GDNS.
Creed
Three Burrows
Tresillian
Blackwater
Truro
Kenwyn
Tresawle
Portreath
Mawla
P&R
CATHEDRAL
Merther
Tregony
TOLGUS TIN
CORNISH GOLD
Scorrier
Chacewater
Threemilestone
PORTREATH
ROYAL CORNWALL MUS.
Illogan
Baldhu
Kea
St Clement
Ruan Lanihorne
CORNISH MINES & ENGINES
St Day
Twelve Heads
Malpas
Redruth
Bissoe
Playing Place
Old Kea
St Michael Penkevil
Lamorran
Pool
Tuckingmill
Cambrea
Carharrack
Carnon Downs
Portholland
Carnkie
GWENNAP PIT
Gwennap
Treworga
CAMBORNE
Lanner
Trelissick
Philleigh
Perranarworthal
Penpol
Veryan
Portloe
SHIRE HORSE FARM
Four Lanes
Devoran
Feock
TRELISSICK
Treworlas
SOUTH WEST COAST PATH
Troon
Ponsanooth
Carne
Penhalvaen
Gerrans Bay
Stithians
Burnthouse
Mylor Bridge
St Just in Roseland
Trewithian
Nare Hd.
Stithians Res.
Penmarth
Carrick Roads
Gerrans
Portscatho
Crows
Burras
Carnkie
Penryn
Flushing
Longdowns
Mabe Burnthouse
Rame
Falmouth
St Mawes
Greeb Pt.
Releath
Porkellis
ART GALLERY
NATIONAL MARITIME
Bohortha
Nancegollan
POLDARK MINE
Budock Water
PENDENNIS CASTLE
Wendron
Seworgan
Treverva
Pendennis Pt.
Zone Pt.
Crowntown
Penjerrick
Falmouth Bay
Constantine
Mawnan Smith
Porth Navas
SOUTH WEST COAST PATH
GLENDURGAN
Rosemullion Hd.
0 1 2 3 miles
0 1 2 3 4 5 km
A39
A30
A390
A392
A3059
A3075
A3058
A3076
A394
A393
A3047
A3078
B3276
B3274
B3275
B3279
B3285
B3284
B3277
B3298
B3301
B3289
B3292
B3297
B3280
B3303
B3302
A
B
C
D
1
2
3
4

4
5
6
7
PENCARROW HOUSE
Helland
268
Maidenwell
Burlawn
Egloshayle
A389
9
10
Millpool
BODMIN
Commonmoor
Washaway
Bodmin Forest
Warleggan
GOLITHA FALLS
ST.BREOCK DOWNS MONOLITH
A30
Cardinham
KING DONIERT'S STONE
St Cleer
Bodmin
St Neot
Mount
Ruthernbridge
Nanstallon
MUSEUM
Rosenannon
CARNGLAZE SLATE CAVERNS
Ley
Withiel
St Lawrence
DOBWALLS ADVENTURE PARK
BODMIN AND WENFORD RAILWAY
Fowey
St Wenn
Dobwalls
B3268
A38
A
Tregonetha
LANHYDROCK HOUSE
East Taphouse
Doublebois
West Taphouse
A390
Lanivet
St Pinnock
227
Trebyan
Belowda
Victoria
A30
RESTORMEL CASTLE
Braddock
Sweethouse
Lockengate
Redmoor
B3269
Herodsfoot
St Keyne
Tregoss
GOSS MOOR
Bilberry
Lostwithiel
6
Trewidland
Roche
Trezaise
Lanlivery
Couch's Mill
208
Bugle
B3274
Duloe
LANREATH FOLK FARM MUS.
B3254
Milltown
A391
Hensbarrow
Luxulyan
Bocaddon
Whitemoor
312
Lerryn
Downs
Stenalees
A390
Sandplace
Nanpean
Penwithick
Penpillick
Lanreath
B3359
Muchlarnick
Carthew
Fowey
GOLANT
Trethurgy
St Blazey
Golant
St Veep
Pelynt
Foxhole
WHEAL MARTYN CHINA CLAY HER. CENTRE
EDEN PROJECT
Penpoll
B
B3279
Carclaze
Tywardreath
High Street
St Austell
Boscoppa
B3269
Lanteglos Highway
Trenewan
Looe
Par
A3082
West Looe
Trewoon
Holmbush
Polkerris
Bodinnick
Porthallow
St Mewan
SHIPWRECK & HERITAGE CENTRE
Menabilly
Fowey
Ferry
Charlestown
Lansallos
Talland Bay
Sticker
Polgooth
ST.AUSTELL BREWERY
ST.CATHERINE'S CASTLE
Polruan
Polperro
SMUGGLERS MUSEUM
Porthpean
ST. AUSTELL BAY
SOUTH WEST COAST PATH
Pencarrow Hd.
Hewas Water
TORTOISE GARDEN
Gribbin Hd.
B3273
Trenarren
Black Hd.
SX
Pentewan
THE LOST GARDENS OF HELIGAN
St Ewe
Mevagissey Bay
Kestle
Polmassick
WORLD OF MODEL RAILWAYS
Mevagissey
C
Portmellon
Chapel Pt.
Trevarrick
Gorran Churchtown
St Michael Caerhays
Gorran Haven
Boswinger
BOSWINGER
Penare
114
Veryan Bay
Dodman Pt.
D
4
5
6
7

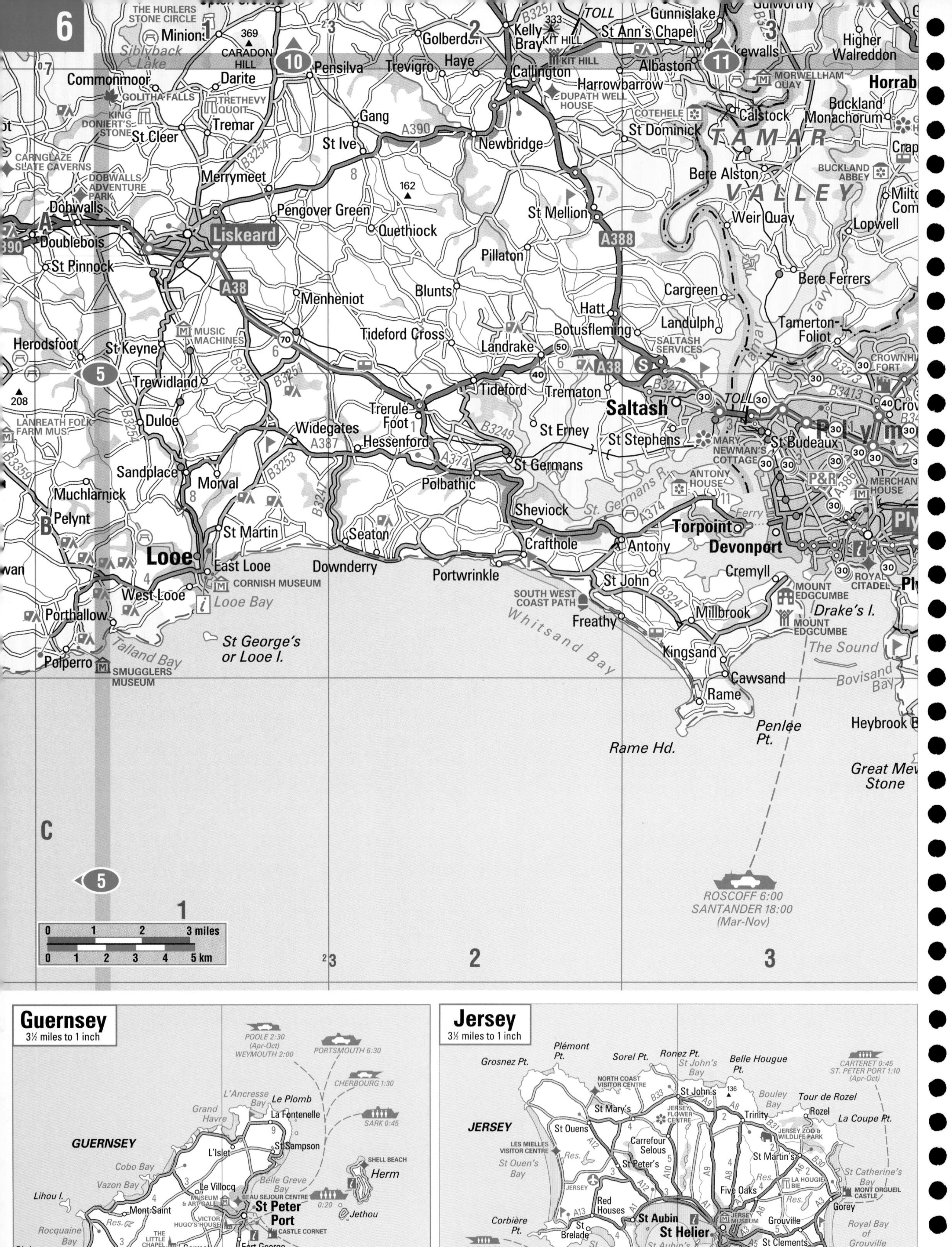

Guernsey

3½ miles to 1 inch

POOLE 2:30 (Apr-Oct)
WEYMOUTH 2:00
PORTSMOUTH 6:30
CHERBOURG 1:30
L'Ancresse Bay
Le Plomb
Grand Havre
La Fontenelle
SARK 0:45
GUERNSEY
St Sampson
SHELL BEACH
Herm
L'Islet
Cobo Bay
Vazon Bay
Belle Greve Bay
Le Villocq
Lihou I.
BEAU SEJOUR CENTRE
MUSEUM & ART GALL.
St Peter Port
0:20
Mont Saint
Jethou
VICTOR HUGO'S HOUSE
Res.
CASTLE CORNET
Rocquaine Bay
THE LITTLE CHAPEL
Carmel
Fort George
Pleinmont Pt.
GUERNSEY
Mouilpied
ST. HELIER 2:00
Le Planel
La Planque
St Martin's Pt.
ST. HELIER 0:50
ST. MALO 2:40
Pointe de la Moye
Icart Pt.
Moulin Huet Bay
DIELETTE 1:00
CARTERET 1:00 (Apr-Oct)
ALDERNEY 1:00

Jersey

3½ miles to 1 inch

Plémont Pt.
Grosnez Pt.
Sorel Pt.
Ronez Pt.
St John's Bay
Belle Hougue Pt.
CARTERET 0:45
ST. PETER PORT 1:10 (Apr-Oct)
NORTH COAST VISITOR CENTRE
St John's
136
Bouley Bay
Tour de Rozel
St Mary's
JERSEY FLOWER CENTRE
Trinity
Rozel
La Coupe Pt.
JERSEY
St Ouens
JERSEY ZOO & WILDLIFE PARK
LES MIELLES VISITOR CENTRE
Carrefour Selous
St Martin's
St Ouen's Bay
Res.
St Peter's
St Catherine's Bay
Five Oaks
LA HOUGUE BIE
MONT ORGUEIL CASTLE
JERSEY
Res.
Gorey
Red Houses
Corbière Pt.
St Aubin
JERSEY MUSEUM
Grouville
Royal Bay of Grouville
St Brelade
St Helier
SARK 0:50 (Apr-Oct)
St Aubin's Bay
St Clements
St Brelades Bay
ELIZABETH CASTLE
FORT REGENT LEISURE CENTRE
ST. PETER PORT 0:50
WEYMOUTH 3:15
POOLE 3:45 (Apr-Oct)
Noirmont Pt.
Le Nez Pt.
St Clements Bay
La Rocque Pt.
GRANVILLE 1:00
ST. PETER PORT 1:00 (Apr-Oct)
CARTERET 1:00
ST. PETER PORT 2:00
PORTSMOUTH 10:00
ST. MALO 1:10

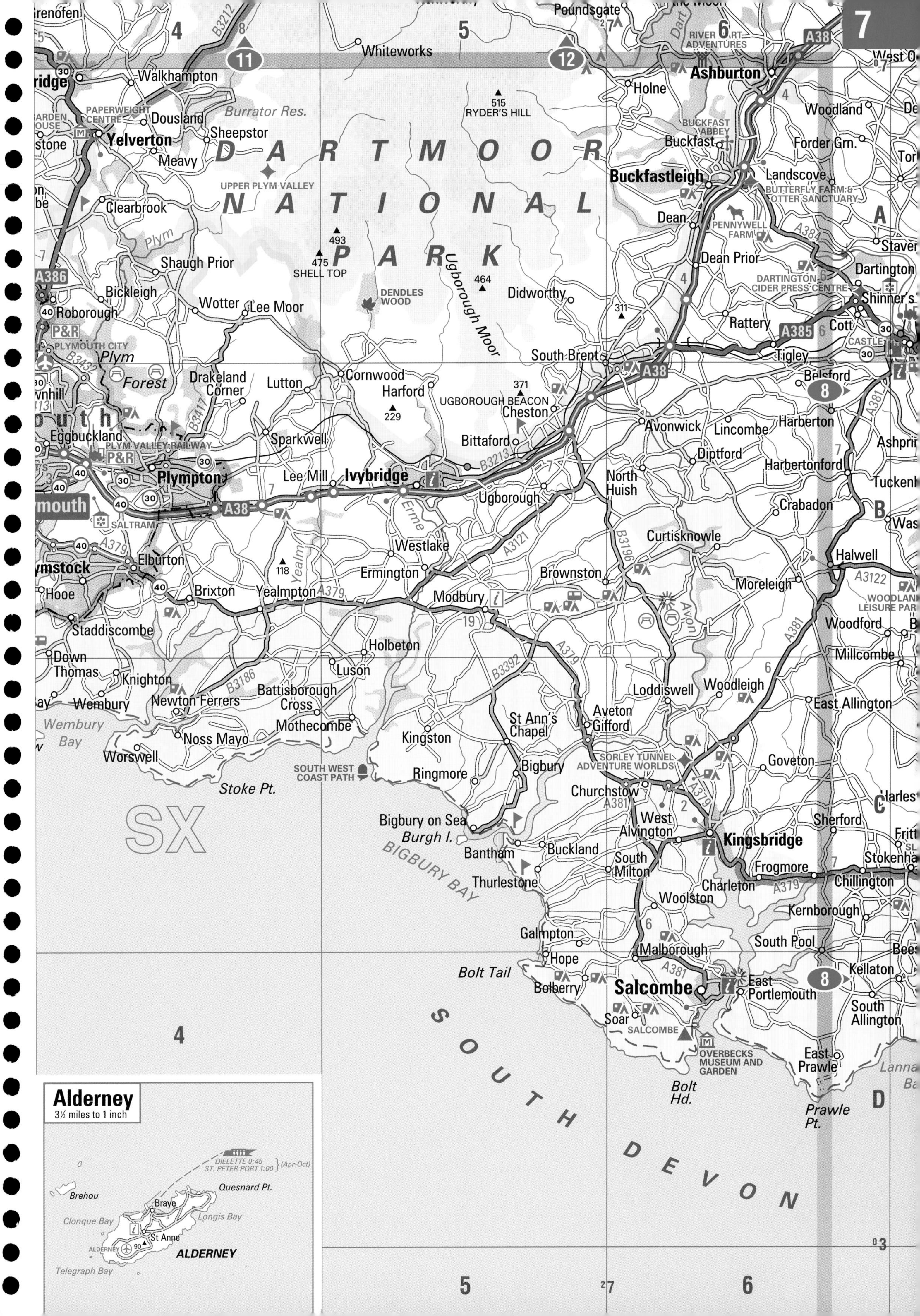
DARTMOOR NATIONAL PARK
Poundsgate
Whiteworks
RIVER ART ADVENTURES
Ashburton
Walkhampton
Holne
RYDER'S HILL
Woodland
PAPERWEIGHT CENTRE
Dousland
Burrator Res.
BUCKFAST ABBEY
Buckfast
Forder Grn.
Yelverton
Sheepstor
Meavy
Landscove
Buckfastleigh
UPPER PLYM VALLEY
BUTTERFLY FARM & OTTER SANCTUARY
Clearbrook
Dean
PENNYWELL FARM
Plym
Dean Prior
Shaugh Prior
SHELL TOP
Ugborough Moor
Dartington
DARTINGTON CIDER PRESS CENTRE
Bickleigh
DENDLES WOOD
Didworthy
Shinner's
Roborough
Wotter
Lee Moor
Rattery
Cott
PLYMOUTH CITY
Tigley
South Brent
Plym Forest
Drakeland Corner
Lutton
Cornwood
Harford
Belsford
UGBOROUGH BEACON
Cheston
Eggbuckland
PLYM VALLEY RAILWAY
Sparkwell
Bittaford
Avonwick
Lincombe
Harberton
Diptford
Plympton
Lee Mill
Ivybridge
Harbertonford
North Huish
Ugborough
SALTRAM
Erme
Crabadon
Westlake
Curtisknowle
Elburton
Halwell
Yealm
Ermington
Brownston
Hooe
Brixton
Yealmpton
Modbury
Moreleigh
Avon
WOODLANDS LEISURE PARK
Woodford
Staddiscombe
Holbeton
Millcombe
Down Thomas
Luson
Knighton
Battisborough Cross
Loddiswell
Woodleigh
East Allington
Wembury
Newton Ferrers
Aveton Gifford
Wembury Bay
Mothecombe
St Ann's Chapel
Noss Mayo
Kingston
SORLEY TUNNEL ADVENTURE WORLDS
Worswell
SOUTH WEST COAST PATH
Goveton
Ringmore
Bigbury
Stoke Pt.
Churchstow
SX
West Alvington
Sherford
Bigbury on Sea
Burgh I.
Kingsbridge
BIGBURY BAY
Bantham
Buckland
South Milton
Frogmore
Stokenham
Thurlestone
Charleton
Chillington
Woolston
Kernborough
Galmpton
South Pool
Hope
Malborough
Bolt Tail
Kellaton
Bolberry
Salcombe
East Portlemouth
South Allington
Soar
SALCOMBE
OVERBECKS MUSEUM AND GARDEN
East Prawle
Bolt Hd.
Prawle Pt.
SOUTH DEVON
Alderney
3½ miles to 1 inch
DIELETTE 0:45
ST. PETER PORT 1:00 (Apr-Oct)
Quesnard Pt.
Brehou
Braye
Longis Bay
Clonque Bay
St Anne
ALDERNEY
Telegraph Bay

NEWTON ABBOT
SHALDON WILDLIFE TRUST
Combeinteignhead
Netherton
SOUTH WEST COAST PATH
Stokeinteignhead
Wolborough
BRADLEY
PLANT WORLD
East Ogwell
PRICKLY BALL HEDGEHOG HOSPITAL
BABBACOMBE BAY
Woodland
Denbury
Abbotskerswell
Coffinswell
Kingskerswell
Maidencombe
Forder Grn.
Barton
Torbryan
Ipplepen
North Whilborough
Watcombe
Landscove
Broadhempston
MODEL VILLAGE
BUTTERFLY FARM & OTTER SANCTUARY
Shiphay
Babbacombe
Compton
COMPTON CASTLE
Torquay
Staverton
Torre
TORRE ABBEY
Cockington
KENT'S CAVERN PREHISTORIC CAVES
Wellswood
Hope's Nose
Dartington
Littlehempston
COCKINGTON
DARTINGTON CIDER PRESS CENTRE
DARTINGTON HALL GARDENS
Marldon
LIVING COASTS
OLDWAY MANSION
BERRY POMEROY CASTLE
Shinner's Bridge
Hollicombe
SOUTH DEVON RAILWAY
Blagdon
Tor bay
Rattery
Cott
Totnes
Berry Pomeroy
KIRKHAM
Paignton
CASTLE
Tigley
PAIGNTON & DARTMOUTH STEAM RAILWAY
Collaton St Mary
TORBAY
Belsford
MOTOR MUSEUM
ZOO & ENVIRONMENTAL PARK
TOR BAY
Harberton
Dart
Goodrington
Ashprington
Stoke Gabriel
Brixham
AQUARIUM
Berry Head
Harbertonford
Galmpton
Churston Ferrers
BERRY HEAD
Tuckenhay
Cornworthy
St Mary's Bay
Crabadon
Washbourne
Dittisham
RIVER DART
Sharkham Pt.
Halwell
Allaleigh
Capton
Hillhead
SX
SY
Moreleigh
WOODLAND LEISURE PARK
Ferry
Dartmouth
NEWCOMEN ENGINE HOUSE
Woodford
Blackawton
Kingswear
Scabbacombe Hd.
P&R
Ferry
Millcombe
BAYARDS COVE FORT
Warfleet
COLETON FISHACRE
Bowden
DARTMOUTH CASTLE
Mew Stone
East Allington
Stoke Fleming
Blackpool
Strete
Goveton
SOUTH WEST COAST PATH
Harleston
Slapton
Sherford
Slapton Sands
START BAY
Kingsbridge
Frittiscombe
SLAPTON LEY
Stokenham
Frogmore
Chillington
Torcross
Kernborough
Beeson
South Pool
Beesands
Kellaton
East Portlemouth
Hallsands
South Allington
START POINT
East Prawle
Lannacombe Bay
Prawle Pt.
SOUTH DEVON
A38
A383
A379
A3022
A380
A381
A384
A385
A3122
B3205
0 1 2 3 miles
0 1 2 3 4 5 km

4
5
6
A
B
C
D
SR
SS
SW
SX
10
CORNWALL
Fire Beacon Pt.
BOSCASTLE HARBOUR
Trevalga
CASTLE
Tintagel Hd.
OLD POST OFFICE TINTAGEL
Bossiney
Tintagel
308
Treknow
Trewarmett
B3263
B3266
Start Pt.
Trebarwith
BRITISH CYCLING MUS.
Treligga
SOUTH WEST COAST PATH
Delabole
Valley Truckle
Port Isaac Bay
B3314
B3267
Helstone
Port Isaac
Port Quin
Port Gaverne
St Teath
Pentire Pt.
Port Quin Bay
New Polzeath
LONG CROSS
Trelights
Pendoggett
Treveighan
Gulland Rock
Padstow Bay
Polzeath
St Endellion
Trelill
A39
Michaelstow
Trebetherick
Gunver Hd.
St Minver
St Tudy
Row
TREVOSE HEAD
Crugmeer
Pityme
Trewethern
St Kew
PRIDEAUX PLACE
Trevone
Chapel Amble
Rock
B3314
St Kew Highway
TREYARNON BAY
Constantine Bay
NATIONAL LOBSTER HATCHERY
Padstow
St Merryn
Camel
Treyarnon
Shop
Bodieve
Trevanson
SOUTH WEST COAST PATH
Little Petherick
Wadebridge
St Mabyn
Porthcothan
Whitecross
Camel
B3276
St Issey
St Breock
Egloshayle
A389
PENCARROW HOUSE
Helland
Park Hd.
Penrose
St Ervan
Rumford
Tredinnick
Burlawn
RARE BREEDS CENTRE
St Jidgey
Washaway
Bodmin Forest
CREALY GREAT ADVENTURE PARK
ST BREOCK DOWNS MONOLITH
208
St Eval
Trenance
A30
Bodmin

10
1
2
3
4
A
B
C
D
24
9
5
6
Coombe
Kilkhampton
Alfardisworthy
Stibb
Soldon Cross
A39
BUDE
BAY
Poughill
Flexbury
Hersham
DUNSDON
Holsworthy Beacon
Bude Haven
1643
Stratton
Grimscott
Bude
Chilsworthy
A3072
Launcells
Pancrasweek
Tamar
Upton
B3254
Derril
Marhamchurch
Bridgerule
Derriton
Pyworthy
162
Chasty
Widemouth Bay
Widemouth Sand
Budd's Titson
Coppathorne
Leworthy
Millook
Dizzard Pt.
Poundstock
SOUTH WEST COAST PATH
Tregole
Treskinnick Cross
Whitstone
St Gennys
Trewint
Week St Mary
North Tamerton
PENHALLAM
Cambeak
Crackington Haven
Rosecare
Jacobstow
Tetcott
Lana
Wainhouse Corner
Luffincott
Trespareett Posts
B3263
South Wheatley
West Curry
Fire Beacon Pt.
260
Beeny
Maxworthy
BOSCASTLE HARBOUR
Tresparrett
Marshgate
Bennacott
Northcott
Canworthy Water
Boyton
Brazacott
Boscastle
Lesnewth
Otterham
256
Warbstow
Trevalga
Trelash
Langdon
Tremaine
Ottery
Bridgetown
Bossiney
North Petherwin
B3266
B3262
Tintagel
Hallworthy
Treneglos
Werrington
308
Davidstow
Yeolmbridge
Trewarmett
Tresmeer
Tremail
Egloskerry
Langore
Trewassa
Tregeare
THE ARTHURIAN CENTRE
Cold Northcott
St Stephens
Trebarwith
HIDDEN VALLEY DISCOVERY PARK
BRITISH CYCLING MUS.
B3314
Davidstow Moor
A395
Piper's Pool
Launceston
TRETHORNE LEISURE FARM
Tregadillett
Delabole
St Clether
Laneast
CASTLE
A30
Camelford
Crowdy Res.
Trewen
Daw's House
Valley Truckle
Polyphant
Helstone
B3267
Inny
South Petherwin
400 ROUGH TOR
High Moor
Altarnun
Lewannick
St Teath
Treveighan
420 BROWN WILLY
Trewint
B3257
Lezant
369
Michaelstow
Codda
Congdon's Shop
331 GARROW TOR
Trebullett
St Breward
Trebartha
Treburley
MUSEUM OF SMUGGLING
Row
St Tudy
Bolventor
North Hill
Coad's Green
BODMIN
Bradford
Bray Shop
Wenfordbridge
396 KILMAR TOR
Dozmary Pool
Bathpool
Blisland
COLLIFORD LAKE
Henwood
Linkinhorne
St Mabyn
MOOR
Temple
Rilla Mill
South Hill
342
Colliford Lake
Upton Cross
Camel
THE HURLERS STONE CIRCLE
Helland
268
Minions
369 CARADON HILL
Golberdon
Siblyback Lake
Millpool
Maidenwell
Pensilva
Trevigro
Commonmoor
Darite
Warleggan
GOLITHA FALLS
TRETHEVY QUOIT
St Neot
KING DONIERT'S STONE
Tremar
Gang
A390
Bodmin
0 1 2 3 miles
0 1 2 3 4 5 km

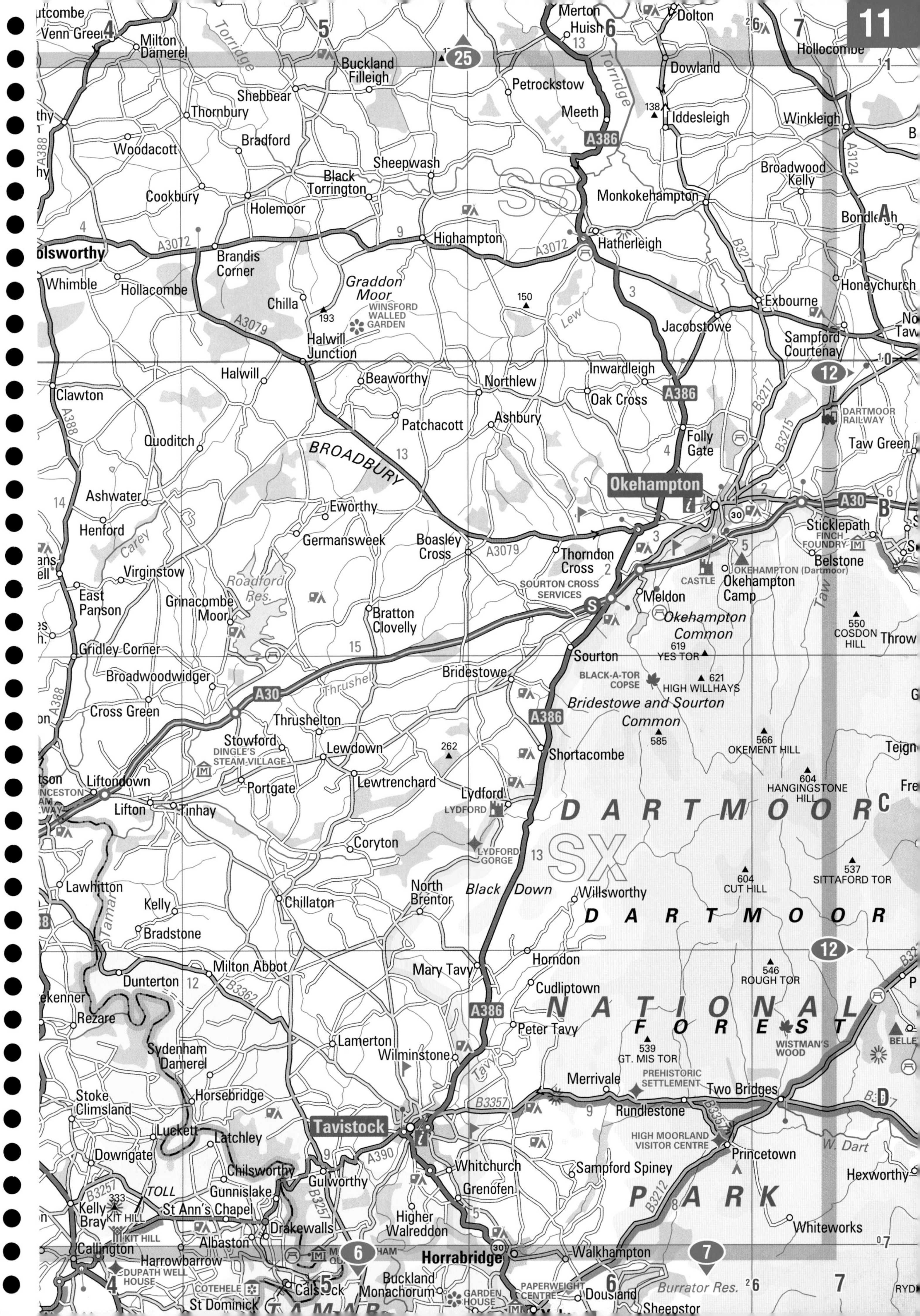
11
Merton
Huish
Dolton
Hollocombe
Buckland Filleigh
Milton Damerel
Venn Green
Torridge
Shebbear
Thornbury
Petrockstow
Dowland
Meeth
Iddesleigh
Winkleigh
Woodacott
Bradford
A386
Sheepwash
Broadwood Kelly
Black Torrington
Cookbury
Holemoor
Monkokehampton
SS
Bondleigh
Highampton
A3072
Hatherleigh
Brandis Corner
Whimble
Hollacombe
Graddon Moor
Honeychurch
Exbourne
Chilla
WINSFORD WALLED GARDEN
Lew
Jacobstowe
A3079
Halwill Junction
Sampford Courtenay
Halwill
Inwardleigh
Beaworthy
Northlew
Oak Cross
Clawton
Ashbury
DARTMOOR RAILWAY
Patchacott
Folly Gate
Taw Green
Quoditch
BROADBURY
Okehampton
Ashwater
Eworthy
A30
Sticklepath
Henford
FINCH FOUNDRY
Germansweek
Boasley Cross
Thorndon Cross
Belstone
Carey
Virginstow
Roadford Res.
SOURTON CROSS SERVICES
CASTLE
OKEHAMPTON (Dartmoor)
Okehampton Camp
East Panson
Grinacombe Moor
Meldon
Bratton Clovelly
Okehampton Common
550 COSDON HILL
Gridley Corner
Sourton
619 YES TOR
Broadwoodwidger
Bridestowe
BLACK-A-TOR COPSE
621 HIGH WILLHAYS
Thrushel
Cross Green
Bridestowe and Sourton Common
Thrushelton
585
566 OKEMENT HILL
Stowford
DINGLE'S STEAM VILLAGE
Lewdown
262
Shortacombe
Liftondown
Portgate
Lewtrenchard
604 HANGINGSTONE HILL
Lifton
Tinhay
Lydford
LYDFORD CASTLE
DARTMOOR
Coryton
LYDFORD GORGE
SX
Lawhitton
North Brentor
Black Down
Willsworthy
604 CUT HILL
537 SITTAFORD TOR
Kelly
Chillaton
DARTMOOR
Bradstone
Tamar
Horndon
546 ROUGH TOR
Milton Abbot
Mary Tavy
Dunterton
Cudliptown
B3362
NATIONAL
Rezare
Peter Tavy
FOREST
Sydenham Damerel
Lamerton
539 GT. MIS TOR
WISTMAN'S WOOD
Wilminstone
Merrivale
PREHISTORIC SETTLEMENT
Two Bridges
Stoke Climsland
Horsebridge
B3357
Rundlestone
Tavistock
Luckett
Latchley
HIGH MOORLAND VISITOR CENTRE
Princetown
W. Dart
Downgate
A390
Whitchurch
Sampford Spiney
Hexworthy
Chilsworthy
Gulworthy
Grenofen
B3257
TOLL
Gunnislake
333 KIT HILL
Kelly Bray
St Ann's Chapel
Higher Walreddon
PARK
B3212
Whiteworks
Drakewalls
Albaston
Callington
Harrowbarrow
Horrabridge
Walkhampton
DUPATH WELL HOUSE
COTEHELE
Calstock
Buckland Monachorum
GARDEN HOUSE
PAPERWEIGHT CENTRE
Dousland
Burrator Res.
St Dominick
Sheepstor

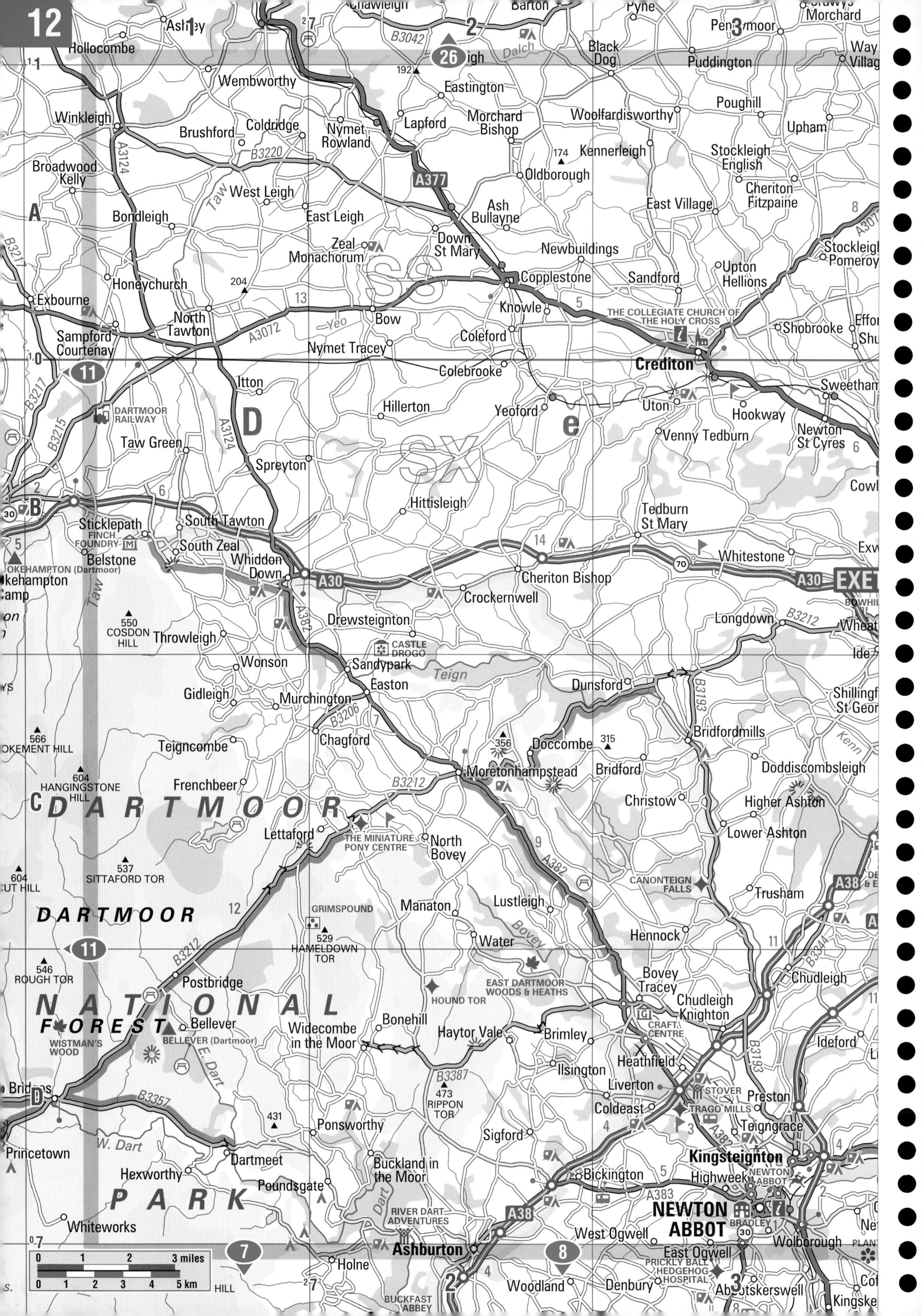

Ashley
Hollocombe
Wembworthy
Eastington
Black Dog
Puddington
Poughill
Winkleigh
Brushford
Coldridge
Nymet Rowland
Lapford
Morchard Bishop
Woolfardisworthy
Upham
Kennerleigh
Stockleigh English
Broadwood Kelly
Oldborough
West Leigh
Cheriton Fitzpaine
Bondleigh
East Leigh
Ash Bullayne
East Village
Zeal Monachorum
Down St Mary
Newbuildings
Stockleigh Pomeroy
Honeychurch
Copplestone
Sandford
Upton Hellions
Exbourne
Knowle
North Tawton
Bow
THE COLLEGIATE CHURCH OF THE HOLY CROSS
Sampford Courtenay
Coleford
Shobrooke
Nymet Tracey
Crediton
Colebrooke
Itton
Sweetham
DARTMOOR RAILWAY
Hillerton
Yeoford
Uton
Hookway
Venny Tedburn
Newton St Cyres
Taw Green
Spreyton
Hittisleigh
Tedburn St Mary
Sticklepath
South Tawton
FINCH FOUNDRY
South Zeal
Belstone
Whiddon Down
Cheriton Bishop
Whitestone
OKEHAMPTON (Dartmoor)
Crockernwell
Drewsteignton
Longdown
550 COSDON HILL
Throwleigh
CASTLE DROGO
Wonson
Sandypark
Teign
Dunsford
Gidleigh
Murchington
Easton
Chagford
Bridfordmills
566 OKEMENT HILL
Teigncombe
Doccombe
Bridford
Doddiscombsleigh
604 HANGINGSTONE HILL
Moretonhampstead
Frenchbeer
Christow
Higher Ashton
DARTMOOR
Lettaford
THE MINIATURE PONY CENTRE
North Bovey
Lower Ashton
537 SITTAFORD TOR
CANONTEIGN FALLS
Trusham
Manaton
Lustleigh
GRIMSPOUND
Water
Hennock
529 HAMELDOWN TOR
546 ROUGH TOR
Postbridge
Bovey Tracey
Chudleigh
EAST DARTMOOR WOODS & HEATHS
HOUND TOR
NATIONAL
Chudleigh Knighton
FOREST
Bellever
Bonehill
BELLEVER (Dartmoor)
Widecombe in the Moor
Haytor Vale
Brimley
CRAFT CENTRE
WISTMAN'S WOOD
Ideford
Heathfield
Ilsington
B3387
473 RIPPON TOR
Liverton
STOVER
Preston
Coldeast
TRAGO MILLS
431
Ponsworthy
Teigngrace
Sigford
Princetown
W. Dart
Dartmeet
Kingsteignton
Hexworthy
Buckland in the Moor
Bickington
Highweek
NEWTON ABBOT
Poundsgate
PARK
RIVER DART ADVENTURES
NEWTON ABBOT
BRADLEY
Whiteworks
West Ogwell
Wolborough
Ashburton
East Ogwell
PRICKLY BALL HEDGEHOG HOSPITAL
Holne
Woodland
Denbury
Abbotskerswell
BUCKFAST ABBEY
Kingskerswell
0 1 2 3 miles
0 1 2 3 4 5 km

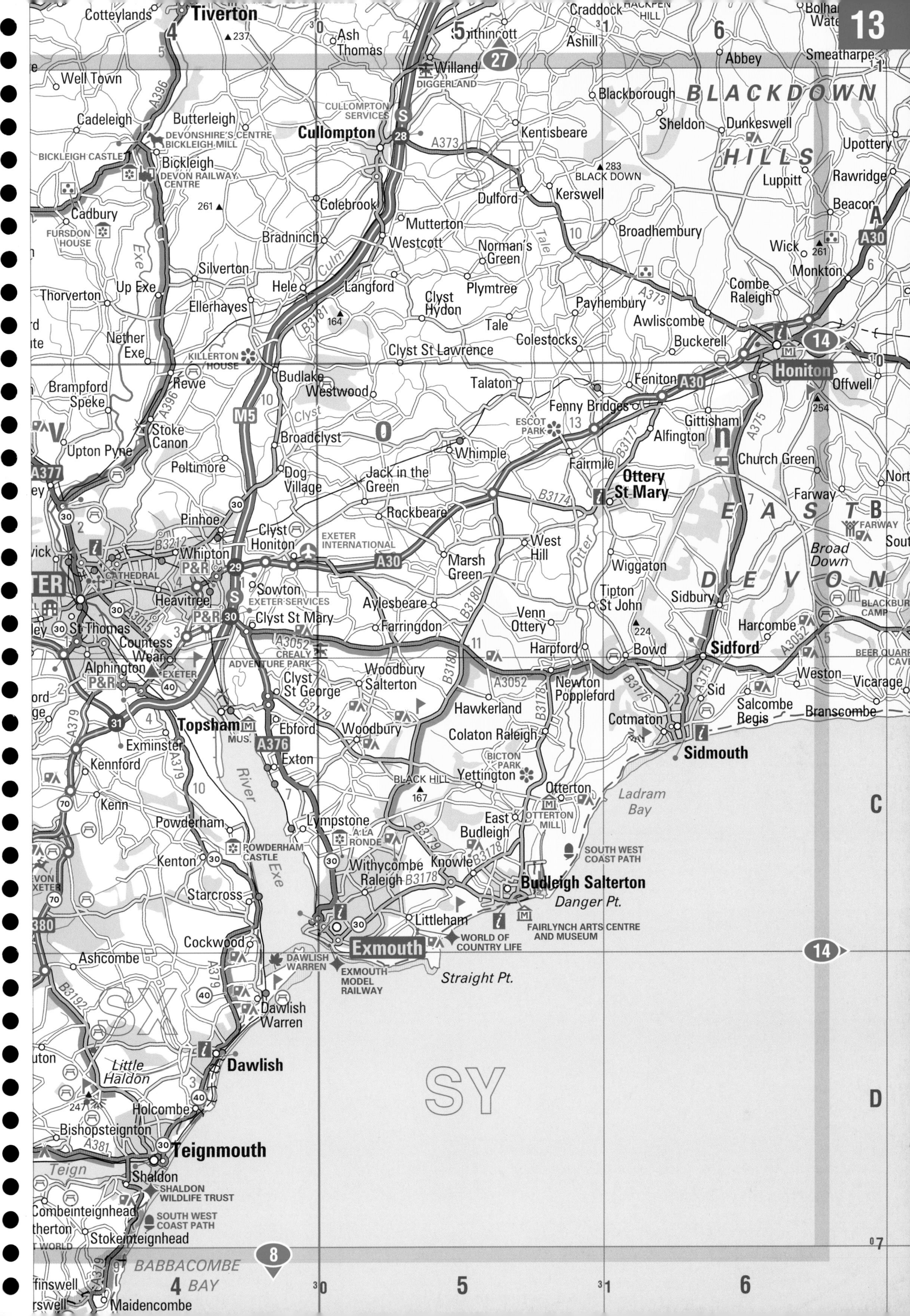
Tiverton
Cotteylands
Ash Thomas
Smithincott
Craddock
Ashill
Abbey
Smeatharpe
Willand
DIGGERLAND
Well Town
Blackborough
BLACKDOWN HILLS
Sheldon
Dunkeswell
Upottery
Cadeleigh
Butterleigh
CULLOMPTON SERVICES
Cullompton
Kentisbeare
DEVONSHIRE'S CENTRE BICKLEIGH MILL
BICKLEIGH CASTLE
Bickleigh
DEVON RAILWAY CENTRE
BLACK DOWN
Luppitt
Rawridge
Kerswell
Dulford
Colebrook
Cadbury
FURSDON HOUSE
Mutterton
Broadhembury
Beacon
Bradninch
Westcott
Norman's Green
Wick
Monkton
Silverton
Thorverton
Up Exe
Hele
Langford
Plymtree
Clyst Hydon
Combe Raleigh
Ellerhayes
Payhembury
Awliscombe
Nether Exe
Tale
Colestocks
Buckerell
Clyst St Lawrence
KILLERTON HOUSE
Budlake
Westwood
Talaton
Feniton
Honiton
Offwell
Brampford Speke
Rewe
Fenny Bridges
ESCOT PARK
Gittisham
Alfington
Stoke Canon
Broadclyst
Whimple
Upton Pyne
Fairmile
Ottery St Mary
Church Green
Poltimore
Dog Village
Jack in the Green
Farway
Rockbeare
EAST DEVON
Pinhoe
Clyst Honiton
EXETER INTERNATIONAL
FARWAY
West Hill
Broad Down
Whipton
Marsh Green
Wiggaton
CATHEDRAL
Sowton
EXETER SERVICES
Tipton St John
Sidbury
Heavitree
Aylesbeare
BLACKBURY CAMP
St Thomas
Clyst St Mary
Venn Ottery
Farringdon
Harcombe
Countess Wear
CREALY ADVENTURE PARK
Harpford
Bowd
Sidford
BEER QUARRY CAVES
Alphington
EXETER
Woodbury Salterton
Newton Poppleford
Weston
Vicarage
Clyst St George
Sid
Salcombe Regis
Branscombe
Hawkerland
Cotmaton
Topsham
MUS.
Ebford
Woodbury
Colaton Raleigh
Sidmouth
Exminster
Kennford
Exton
BICTON PARK
BLACK HILL
Yettington
Otterton
OTTERTON MILL
Ladram Bay
Kenn
Powderham
Lympstone
A LA RONDE
East Budleigh
POWDERHAM CASTLE
SOUTH WEST COAST PATH
Kenton
Withycombe Raleigh
Knowle
Budleigh Salterton
Starcross
Danger Pt.
Littleham
FAIRLYNCH ARTS CENTRE AND MUSEUM
WORLD OF COUNTRY LIFE
Cockwood
Exmouth
Ashcombe
DAWLISH WARREN
EXMOUTH MODEL RAILWAY
Straight Pt.
Dawlish Warren
SX
Dawlish
Little Haldon
SY
Holcombe
Bishopsteignton
Teignmouth
Teign
Shaldon
SHALDON WILDLIFE TRUST
Combeinteignhead
SOUTH WEST COAST PATH
Stokeinteignhead
BABBACOMBE BAY
Maidencombe
River Exe
Culm
Clyst
Otter
M5
A30
A373
A396
A3052
A376
A379
A381
B3181
B3180
B3174
B3177
B3176
B3178
B3179
B3192
B3212
A3015
A375
A377
27
28
29
30
31
14
8
4
5
6
C
D

Bolham Water
Combe St Nicholas
St George
Marsh
Whitestaunton
Cricket Malherbie
Chillington
Smeatharpe
A303
28
Wadeford
Cudworth
Abbey
Chaffcombe
Crewkerne
BLACKDOWN
Newcott
Howley
A30
Cricket St Thomas
Yarcombe
Wambrook
Chard
WILDLIFE PARK
Hewish
B3165
Dunkeswell
Misterton
Upottery
B3162
Whatley
Wayford
Forton
Winsham
Clapton
Luppitt
Rawridge
A30
Tatworth
Seaborough
HILLS
Beacon
South Chard
Drimpton
A
Stockland
FORDE ABBEY AND GARDENS
Furley
Millhayes
Chardstock
B3167
Wick
Monkton
Membury
Tytherleigh
Thorncombe
Burstock
Combe Raleigh
Heathstock
Alston
Holditch
Cotleigh
Churchill
A358
Birdsmoor Gate
Yarty
Ham
B3165
B3164
Dalwood
Smallridge
Axe
Hawkchurch
Wilmington
Marshalsea
Bettiscombe
Honiton
Weycroft
13
Offwell
Marshwood
Pilsdon
A35
Axminster
A375
Shute
Kilmington
SHUTE BARTON
B3261
Church Green
A358
Broad Oak
Northleigh
Wootton Fitzpaine
Whitchurch Canonicorum
Farway
Whitford
Ryall
EAST DEVON
FARWAY
Musbury
Char
Morcombelake
Colyton
Southleigh
B3165
Broad Down
Charmouth
Symondsbury
Uplyme
Chideock
A35
Colyford
Combpyne
CHARMOUTH HERITAGE COAST CENTRE
BLACKBURY CAMP
Lyme Regis
Eype
B3172
Rousdon
Seatown
Axmouth
AQUARIUM
A3052
DINOSAURLAND
Harcombe
SOUTH WEST COAST PATH
SEATON ELECTRIC TRAMWAY COMPANY
B3174
AXMOUTH TO LYME REGIS UNDERCLIFFS
A3052
Sidford
BEER QUARRY CAVES
BEER
Weston
Vicarage
PECORAMA
Seaton
Charlton Bay
SOUTH WEST COAST PATH
Beer
MARINE HOUSE
LYME BAY
Salcombe Regis
Branscombe
Seaton Bay
Beer Hd.
C
D
13
0 1 2 3 miles
0 1 2 3 4 5 km
1
2
3
4

Hardington Mandeville
Haselbury Plucknett
North Perrott
Hardington Marsh
182
Pendomer
Closworth
Ryme Intrinseca
Beer Hackett
29
Holwell
Crouch Hill
Holnest
Leigh
Glanvilles Wootton
Pulham
Hazelbury Bryan
Halstock
Melbury Osmond
Chetnole
Hermitage
Middlemarsh
South Perrott
Mosterton
Chedington
Corscombe
West Chelborough
Melbury Sampford
Melbury Bubb
Hilfield
Lyon's Gate
Duntish
Westfields
Mappowder
238
Evershot
Holywell
Batcombe
265
Minterne Magna
MINTERNE GARDENS
Buckland Newton
Higher Ansty
Melcombe Bingham
261
Alton Pancras
Plush
CRAFT AND DESIGN CENTRE
Broadwindsor
Beaminster
Rampisham
Frome St Quintin
Up Cerne
Up Sydling
CERNE ABBAS GIANT
Cerne Abbas
16
Dorset
Stoke Abbott
Wraxall
Cattistock
Sydling St Nicholas
Piddletrenthide
Netherbury
Mapperton
MAPPERTON
Hooke
Toller Porcorum
Chilfrome
Maiden Newton
Nether Cerne
White Lackington
Melplash
North Poorton
Toller Fratrum
HOG CLIFF
Godmanstone
Piddlehinton
Salwayash
West Milton
Powerstock
Wynford Eagle
Forston
Dottery
Nettlecombe
DORSET
135
Eggardon Down
252
Frampton
Charlton Down
Puddletown
Athelhampton
Bradpole
Loders
West Compton
Grimstone
Bridport
Uploders
Askerswell
Muckleford
Stratton
Charminster
Compton Valence
Bradford Peverell
Dorchester
HARDY'S COTTAGE GARDEN
Tincleton
Walditch
Bothenhampton
170
Kingston Russell
Winterbourne Abbas
THE TUTANKHAMUN EXHIBITION
Stinsford
Kingston Maurward
Shipton Gorge
Chilcombe
Long Bredy
Litton Cheney
NINE STONES
MILITARY MUSEUM
THE DINOSAUR MUSEUM
West Stafford
West Bay
LITTON CHENEY
POOR LOT BARROWS
Winterbourne Steepleton
Martinstown
MAIDEN CASTLE
Burton Bradstock
Littlebredy
Whitcombe
130
Swyre
Puncknowle
Black Down
HARDY MONUMENT
Winterborne Monkton
Winterborne Herringston
West Knighton
VALLEY OF STONES
KINGSTON RUSSELL STONE CIRCLE
West Bexington
Broadmayne
Portesham
SOUTH WEST COAST PATH
Abbotsbury
TITHE BARN CHILDREN'S FARM
SUB TROPICAL GARDENS
ST. CATHERINES CHAPEL
96
Rodden
SWANNERY
Upwey
WHITE HORSE
Bincombe
Poxwell
Broadwey
Littlemoor
Preston
Upton
SOUTH WEST COAST PATH
Langton Herring
Nottington
Overcombe
JORDAN HILL ROMAN TEMPLE
Osmington
TOLL
Radipole
Osmington Mills
CHESIL BEACH
Chickerell
WATER GARDENS
WEYMOUTH SEA LIFE PARK
Melcombe Regis
Ringstead Bay
Westham
Weymouth
16
Charlestown
WEYMOUTH BAY
NOTHE FORT
BREWER'S QUAY AND TIMEWALK
Rodwell
Wyke Regis
Portland Harbour
GUERNSEY 2:00
JERSEY 3:15
ST. MALO 5:00
SY
PORTLAND CASTLE
PORTLAND
Fortuneswell
West Bay
130
Grove
Easton
Weston
PORTLAND
MUSEUM
Southwell
Bill of Portland
A37
A30
A356
A3066
B3163
A35
A352
B3143
B3146
B3142
A354
B3157
B3159
B3156
A353
B3162
A
B
C
D
4
5
6
7

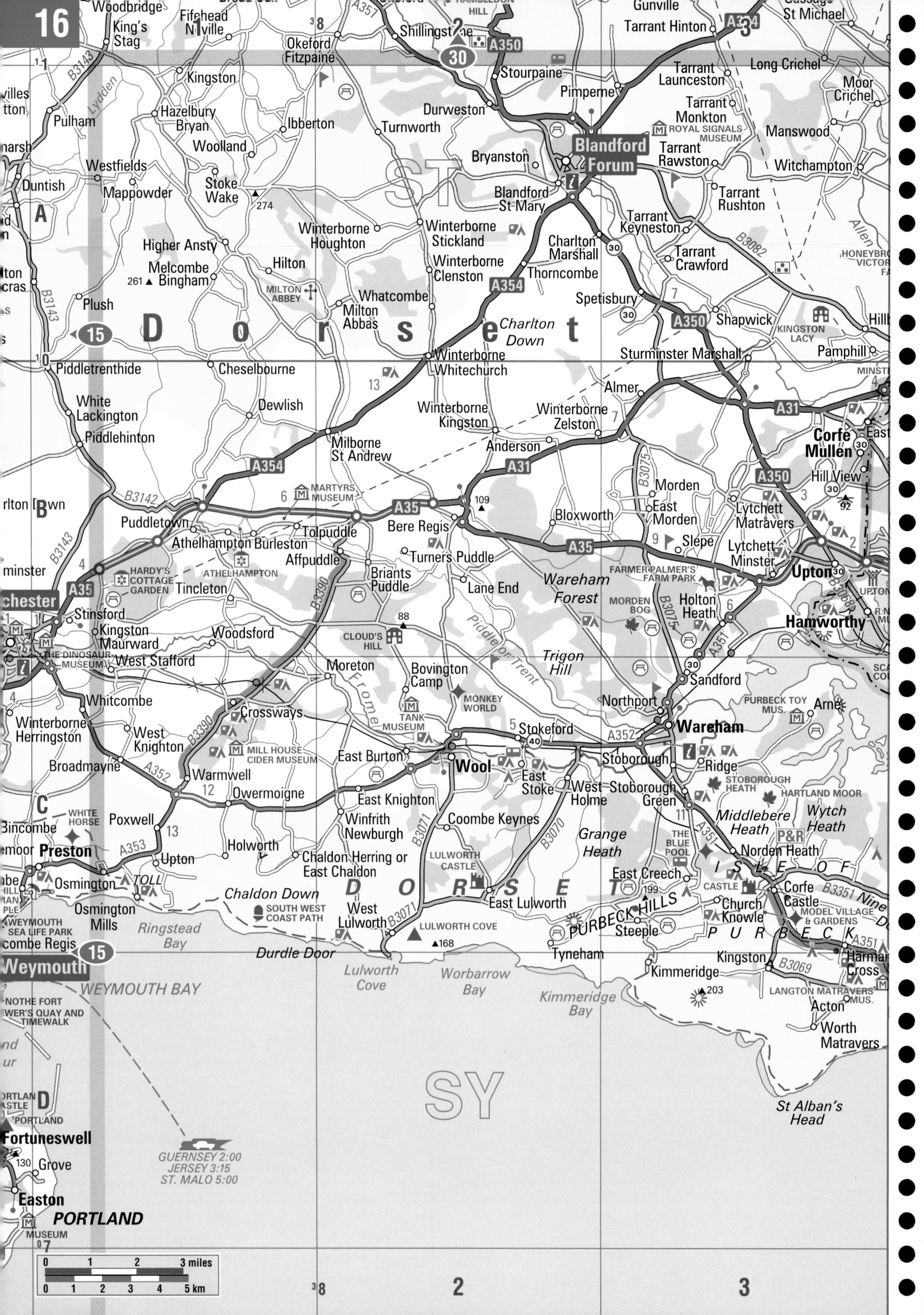
16
Woodbridge
King's Stag
Fifehead Neville
Okeford Fitzpaine
Shillingstone
Gunville
Tarrant Hinton
St Michael
A350
30
A354
Long Crichel
Moor Crichel
B3143
Kingston
Stourpaine
Tarrant Launceston
Pimperne
Tarrant Monkton
ROYAL SIGNALS MUSEUM
Hazelbury Bryan
Pulham
Ibberton
Turnworth
Durweston
Woolland
Blandford Forum
Manswood
Tarrant Rawston
Witchampton
Westfields
Mappowder
Duntish
Stoke Wake
274
Bryanston
Blandford St Mary
Tarrant Rushton
A
Higher Ansty
Winterborne Houghton
Winterborne Stickland
Charlton Marshall
Tarrant Keyneston
B3082
Allen
Melcombe Bingham
261
Hilton
Winterborne Clenston
Thorncombe
Tarrant Crawford
HONEYBROOK VICTORIAN FARM
MILTON ABBEY
Whatcombe
Milton Abbas
A354
Spetisbury
Plush
Shapwick
KINGSTON LACY
15
Dorset
Charlton Down
A350
Sturminster Marshall
Pamphill
Piddletrenthide
Cheselbourne
Winterborne Whitechurch
13
Almer
White Lackington
Dewlish
Winterborne Kingston
Winterborne Zelston
A31
Piddlehinton
Milborne St Andrew
Anderson
Corfe Mullen
A354
A31
B3075
Hill View
MARTYRS MUSEUM
Morden
A350
B3142
A35
109
East Morden
Lytchett Matravers
B
Puddletown
Tolpuddle
Bere Regis
Bloxworth
92
Athelhampton
Burleston
Turners Puddle
Slepe
Lytchett Minster
B3143
Affpuddle
A35
Upton
HARDY'S COTTAGE GARDEN
ATHELHAMPTON
Briants Puddle
FARMER PALMER'S FARM PARK
A35
Tincleton
Lane End
Wareham Forest
Dorchester
Stinsford
B3390
MORDEN BOG
Holton Heath
B3068
Hamworthy
Kingston Maurward
88
Piddle or Trent
Woodsford
CLOUD'S HILL
THE DINOSAUR MUSEUM
West Stafford
Trigon Hill
A351
Moreton
Bovington Camp
Sandford
Frome
Whitcombe
MONKEY WORLD
Northport
PURBECK TOY MUS.
Arne
Crossways
TANK MUSEUM
Winterborne Herringston
West Knighton
B3390
Stokeford
Wareham
A352
MILL HOUSE CIDER MUSEUM
East Burton
40
Stoborough
Ridge
Broadmayne
Wool
A352
Warmwell
East Stoke
West Holme
Stoborough Green
STOBOROUGH HEATH
HARTLAND MOOR
12
Owermoigne
East Knighton
C
WHITE HORSE
Poxwell
Winfrith Newburgh
Coombe Keynes
Middlebere Heath
Wytch Heath
Bincombe
13
B3071
Grange Heath
P&R
Preston
A353
Holworth
B3070
THE BLUE POOL
Norden Heath
Upton
Chaldon Herring or East Chaldon
LULWORTH CASTLE
Osmington
TOLL
East Creech
ISLE OF PURBECK
Corfe Castle
CASTLE
B3351
Chaldon Down
DORSET
199
Church Knowle
Osmington Mills
SOUTH WEST COAST PATH
West Lulworth
East Lulworth
PURBECK HILLS
MODEL VILLAGE & GARDENS
WEYMOUTH SEA LIFE PARK
Ringstead Bay
B3071
LULWORTH COVE
Steeple
Preston
A351
Weymouth
15
Durdle Door
168
Tyneham
Kingston
B3069
Harman's Cross
Lulworth Cove
Worbarrow Bay
Kimmeridge
WEYMOUTH BAY
Kimmeridge Bay
203
LANGTON MATRAVERS MUS.
NOTHE FORT
BREWER'S QUAY AND TIMEWALK
Acton
Worth Matravers
SY
PORTLAND CASTLE
D
PORTLAND
St Alban's Head
Fortuneswell
GUERNSEY 2:00
JERSEY 3:15
ST. MALO 5:00
130
Grove
Easton
PORTLAND
MUSEUM
0 1 2 3 miles
0 1 2 3 4 5 km
8
2
3

Verwood
Ringwood Forest
Ringwood
Ferndown
Wimborne Minster
Bournemouth
Poole
CHRISTCHURCH
Boscombe
Southbourne
Mudeford
Highcliffe
Barton on Sea
New Milton
Milford on Sea
LYMINGTON
Brockenhurst
Burley
Sway
Christchurch Bay
Hengistbury Head
POOLE BAY
SZ
Sandbanks
Poole Harbour
Brownsea I.
Studland
Studland Bay
The Foreland
Swanage
Swanage Bay
Peveril Pt.
Durlston Head
Tilly Whim Caves
Langton Matravers
Newton Heath
Totland Bay
Alum Bay
The Needles
GUERNSEY 2:30
JERSEY 3:45
(Apr-Oct)
ST. MALO 5:25
CHERBOURG 2:15
(May-Sept)
CHERBOURG 4:15

SOUTHAMPTON
Woodlands
Ashurst
Lyndhurst
NEW FOREST MUSEUM
Emery Down
Clayhill
Bank
Denny Lodge
Newtown
Pooksgreen
LONGDOWN FARM
WILDLIFE CONSERVATION PARK
Marchwood
Dibden
Hythe
Dibden Purlieu
Buttsash
Hardley
Holbury
Fawley
Ashlett
Blackfield
Langley
Calshot
CALSHOT CASTLE
Itchen
Woolston
Old Netley
Netley
NETLEY ABBEY
ROYAL VICTORIA
Bursledon
Hound
Lowford
Hamble-le-Rice
ST ANDREWS
Warsash
Newtown
Locks Heath
Park Gate
HOLLY HILL WOODLAND PARK
Lower Swanwick
Swanwick
Burridge
Curbridge
MANOR FARM
WHITELEY VILLAGE
Titchfield
ABBEY
TITCHFIELD HAVEN
Stubbington
Hill Head
Lee-on-the-Solent
Northam
Sholing
Hamble
SOUTHAMPTON WATER
REPTILIARY
Lymington
New Park
Balmerlawn
Brockenhurst
Setley
Hatchet Gate
Beaulieu
PALACE HO.
NATIONAL MOTOR MUS.
ABBEY
Beaulieu Heath
Hill Top
East Boldre
Bucklers Hard
MARITIME MUSEUM
EXBURY
Exbury
LEPE
Lepe
Stone Pt.
Battramsley
Boldre
Bull Hill
Pilley
SPINNERS
Norleywood
East End
Portmore
Walhampton
Wootton
Sway
Marley Mount
Mount Pleasant
Golden Hill
Hordle
Buckland
LYMINGTON
Pennington
Waterford
Woodside
Everton
Ashley
Milton
Downton
Lymore
Lower Pennington
KEYHAVEN & PENNINGTON MARSHES
Keyhaven
Milford on Sea
HURST CASTLE
FORT VICTORIA
MARINE AQUARIUM
Sconce Pt.
Needs Ore Pt.
THE SOLENT
Cowes
MARITIME MUSEUM
East Cowes
OSBORNE HOUSE
Osborne
Gurnard Bay
Gurnard
Rew Street
Northwood
Thorness Bay
Whippingham
Fishbourne
Wootton Bridge
Newtown Bay
NEWTOWN HARBOUR
Porchfield
Parkhurst Forest
Parkhurst
Hamstead
OLD TOWN HALL
Newtown
Cranmore
Shalfleet
Hunny Hill
BUTTERFLY WORLD
Staplers
Wootton Common
Norton
Yarmouth
Thorley Street
Ningwood
Gunville
Carisbrooke
NEWPORT
ROMAN VILLA
Shide
Downend
Colwell Bay
Totland
Norton Green
Wellow
Newbridge
CALBOURNE WATER MILL
Clatterford
CARISBROOKE CASTLE
Isle of Wight
Totland Bay
TOTLAND BAY
Pound Green
Freshwater
CHESSELL POTTERY BARNS
Calbourne
Bowcombe
ARRETON MANOR
Arreton
Alum Bay
Freshwater Bay
Afton
Blackwater
Merstone
Shalcombe
The Needles
NEEDLES PLEASURE PARK
THE NEEDLES OLD BATTERY
Freshwater Bay
Hulverstone
Brook
Brighstone Forest
Mottistone
Gatcombe
Chillerton
Rookley
Horringford
AMAZON WORLD
Branstone
Moortown
Shorwell
The Undercliff
Brighstone
Limerstone
Kingston
MODEL VILLAGE
Godshill
Sandford
Thorncross
DINOSAUR FARM MUS.
Yafford
Little Atherfield
Brighstone Bay
Chale Green
Roud
Pyle
Atherfield Pt.
Stenbury Down
Bierley
Chale
Whitwell
Chale Bay
Blackgang
ST. CATHERINE'S ORATORY
Niton
Blackgang Chine
BLACKGANG CHINE FANTASY PARK
St Lawrence
The Undercliff
St Catherine's Point
0 1 2 3 miles
0 1 2 3 4 5 km

Wickham
Hundred Acres
North Boarhunt
Denmead
Cowplain
FOREST OF BERE
Rowlands Castle
Stoughton
Walderton
BOW HILL
Waterlooville
Leigh Park
Funtley
Boarhunt
Southwick
SOUTHWICK BREWHOUSE
Purbrook
Ports Down
Wallington
Fareham
Portchester
PORTCHESTER CASTLE
Wymering
Drayton
Cosham
Hilsea
Bedhampton
HAVANT
Warblington
Stockheath
Westbourne
Funtington
Woodmancote
Woodend
West Stoke
Mid Lavant
East Ashling
West Ashling
Summersdale
Hermitage
Hambrook
Nutbourne
Emsworth
Southbourne
Broadbridge
Fishbourne
Chidham
Bosham
BOSHAM WALK
FISHBOURNE PALACE
Apuldram
Langstone
FARLINGTON MARSHES
Northney
North Hayling
Thorney
West Thorney
CHICHESTER HARBOUR
Donnington
Hunston
West Itchenor
Shipton Green
Birdham
Peel Common
Fleetlands
Bridgemary
Portsmouth
FORT BROCKHURST
Brockhurst
Hardway
Portsmouth Harbour
EXPLOSION
HMS VICTORY, MARY ROSE
GUNWHARF QUAYS
DICKENS BIRTHPLACE
North End
Langstone Harbour
Stoke
Fleet
HAYLING ISLAND
Chichester Harbour
LITTLE WOODHAM 17TH CENTURY VILLAGE
GOSPORT
Portsea
PORTSMOUTH
CATHEDRAL
Fratton
Milton
West Town
SUBMARINE WORLD
Alverstoke
Stokes Bay
BLUE REEF AQUARIUM
ROYAL MARINES MUSEUM
FORT
Eastney
Southsea
CASTLE AND MUSEUM
South Hayling
Eastoke
EAST HAYLING LIGHT RLY
West Wittering
Acre Street
Somerley
Highleigh
EARNLEY BUTTERFLIES AND GARDENS
Earnley
East Wittering
Bracklesham
Gilkicker Pt.
SPITHEAD
Norton
Selsey
RYDE
Binstead
Nettlestone Pt.
FLAMINGO PARK
TOLL
BRICKFIELD HORSE COUNTRY
Elmfield
Seaview
Nettlestone
Havenstreet
ISLE OF WIGHT STEAM RAILWAY
WALTZING WATERS
St Helens
Bembridge
Foreland
Lane End
WINDMILL
Steyne Cross
Brading
BEMBRIDGE
Hillway
ROMAN VILLA
MORTON MANOR
Alverstone
DINOSAUR ISLE
Whitecliff Bay
Culver Cliff
Yaverland
ISLE OF WIGHT ZOO
Newchurch
ISLE OF WIGHT (SANDOWN)
Winford
Sandown
Lake
Apse Heath
Sandown Bay
Shanklin
SHANKLIN CHINE
Whiteley Bank
Wroxall
Luccombe Village
Luccombe Chine
Dunnose
Bonchurch
Ventnor
BOTANIC GARDEN & VISITOR CENTRE
CAEN 6:00
CHERBOURG 3:00 (March-Nov)
LE HAVRE 7:30
ST. MALO 8:45
BILBAO 35:00
GUERNSEY 6:30
JERSEY 10:00
SZ

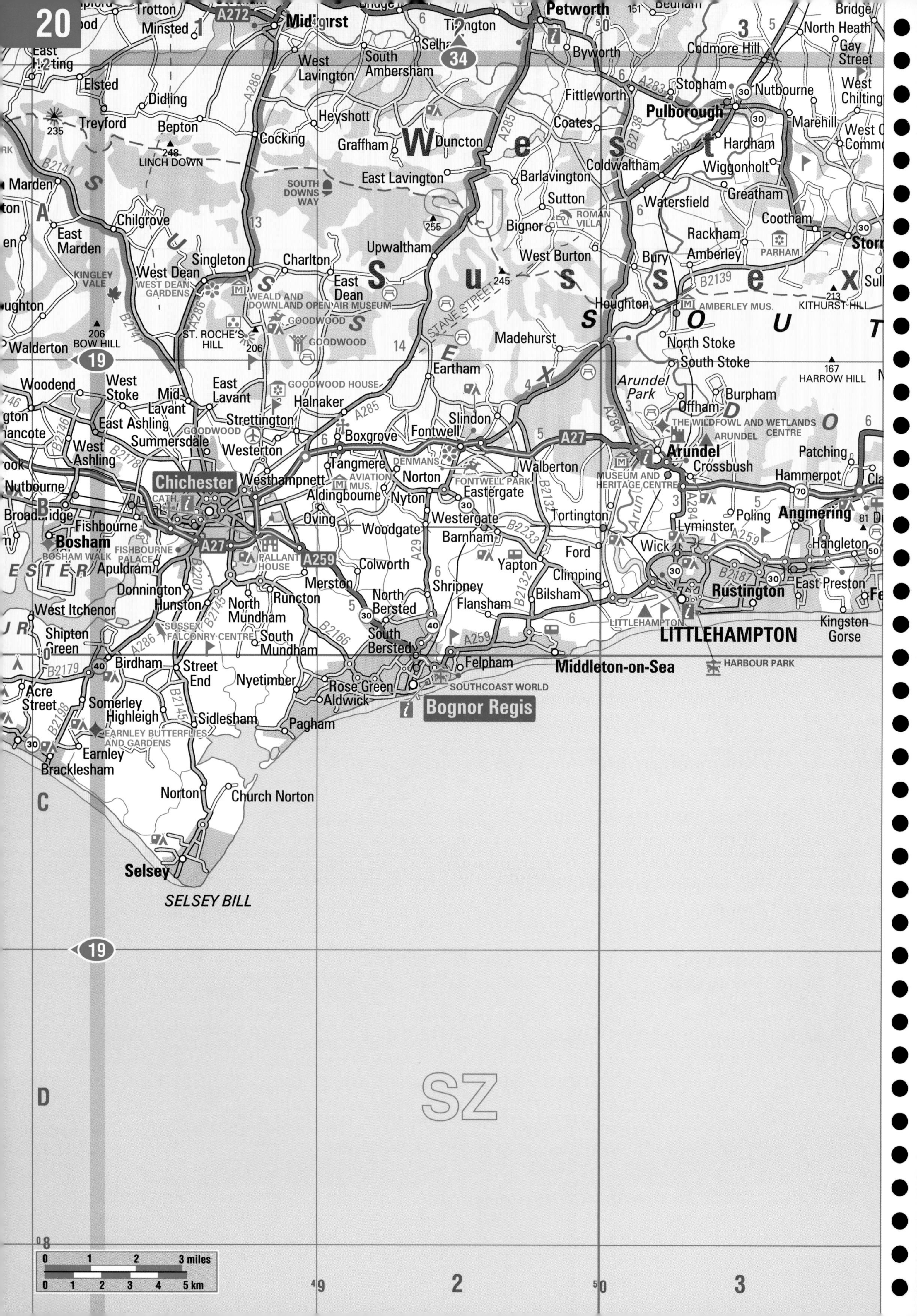
Trotton
Minsted
Midhurst
Tillington
Petworth
Byworth
Codmore Hill
North Heath
Gay Street
West Lavington
South Ambersham
Selham
34
Elsted
Didling
Treyford
Bepton
Cocking
Heyshott
Graffham
Duncton
Fittleworth
Coates
Stopham
Pulborough
Nutbourne
West Chiltington
Marehill
Hardham
Coldwaltham
Wiggonholt
LINCH DOWN
SOUTH DOWNS WAY
East Lavington
Barlavington
Sutton
Watersfield
Greatham
Cootham
Marden
Chilgrove
East Marden
ROMAN VILLA
Bignor
Rackham
Amberley
PARHAM
Upwaltham
Singleton
Charlton
West Burton
Bury
KINGLEY VALE
West Dean
WEST DEAN GARDENS
East Dean
WEALD AND DOWNLAND OPEN AIR MUSEUM
GOODWOOD
Houghton
AMBERLEY MUS.
KITHURST HILL
ST. ROCHE'S HILL
BOW HILL
Walderton
19
Madehurst
North Stoke
South Stoke
HARROW HILL
Eartham
Woodend
West Stoke
Mid Lavant
East Lavant
GOODWOOD HOUSE
Halnaker
Arundel Park
Burpham
Offham
East Ashling
Strettington
Slindon
THE WILDFOWL AND WETLANDS CENTRE
ARUNDEL
West Ashling
Summersdale
Westerton
Boxgrove
Fontwell
Arundel
Crossbush
Patching
Tangmere
DENMANS
Walberton
Nutbourne
Chichester
Westhampnett
AVIATION MUS.
Norton
FONTWELL PARK
MUSEUM AND HERITAGE CENTRE
Hammerpot
CATH.
Aldingbourne
Nyton
Eastergate
Tortington
Poling
Angmering
Broadbridge
Oving
Westergate
Lyminster
Fishbourne
Bosham
Woodgate
Barnham
Wick
Hangleton
BOSHAM WALK
FISHBOURNE PALACE
PALLANT HOUSE
Colworth
Yapton
Ford
Apuldram
Merston
Climping
Rustington
East Preston
Donnington
Shripney
Bilsham
Hunston
North Mundham
Runcton
North Bersted
Flansham
West Itchenor
SUSSEX FALCONRY CENTRE
South Mundham
South Bersted
LITTLEHAMPTON
Kingston Gorse
Shipton Green
Birdham
Street End
Felpham
Middleton-on-Sea
HARBOUR PARK
Nyetimber
Rose Green
SOUTHCOAST WORLD
Acre Street
Somerley
Aldwick
Highleigh
Sidlesham
Bognor Regis
Pagham
EARNLEY BUTTERFLIES AND GARDENS
Earnley
Bracklesham
Norton
Church Norton
Selsey
SELSEY BILL
19
SZ
WEST SUSSEX
SOUTH DOWNS
0 1 2 3 miles
0 1 2 3 4 5 km

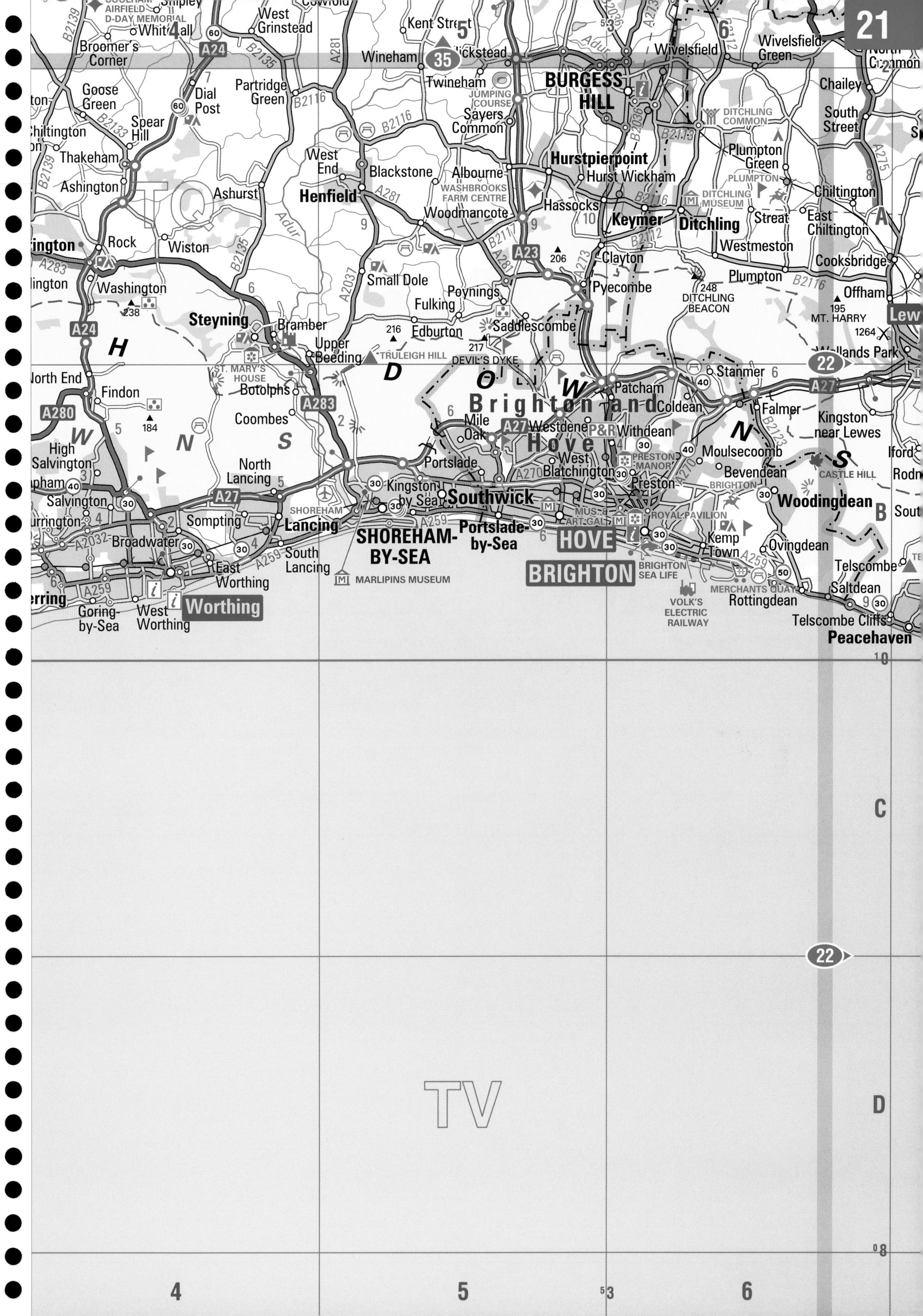
West Grinstead
Kent Street
Broomer's Corner
Wineham
Twineham
BURGESS HILL
Wivelsfield
Wivelsfield Green
Goose Green
Dial Post
Partridge Green
Spear Hill
Sayers Common
Chailey
South Street
Thakeham
Ashington
West End
Blackstone
Albourne
Hurstpierpoint
Hurst Wickham
Plumpton Green
Ashurst
Henfield
Hassocks
Keymer
Ditchling
Streat
East Chiltington
Woodmancote
Rock
Wiston
Clayton
Westmeston
Cooksbridge
Washington
Small Dole
Pyecombe
Plumpton
Offham
Fulking
Poynings
Steyning
Bramber
Edburton
Saddlescombe
Upper Beeding
TRULEIGH HILL
DEVIL'S DYKE
North End
Findon
ST. MARY'S HOUSE
Botolphs
Stanmer
Patcham
Brighton and Hove
Coldean
Falmer
Coombes
Mile Oak
Westdene
Withdean
Kingston near Lewes
High Salvington
North Lancing
Portslade
West Blatchington
Moulsecoomb
Iford
Salvington
Kingston by Sea
Southwick
Preston
Bevendean
Woodingdean
Sompting
Lancing
SHOREHAM-BY-SEA
Portslade-by-Sea
HOVE
ROYAL PAVILION
Kemp Town
Ovingdean
Broadwater
South Lancing
East Worthing
BRIGHTON
BRIGHTON SEA LIFE
Telscombe
Saltdean
Goring-by-Sea
West Worthing
Worthing
MARLIPINS MUSEUM
VOLK'S ELECTRIC RAILWAY
MERCHANTS QUAY
Rottingdean
Telscombe Cliffs
Peacehaven
TV

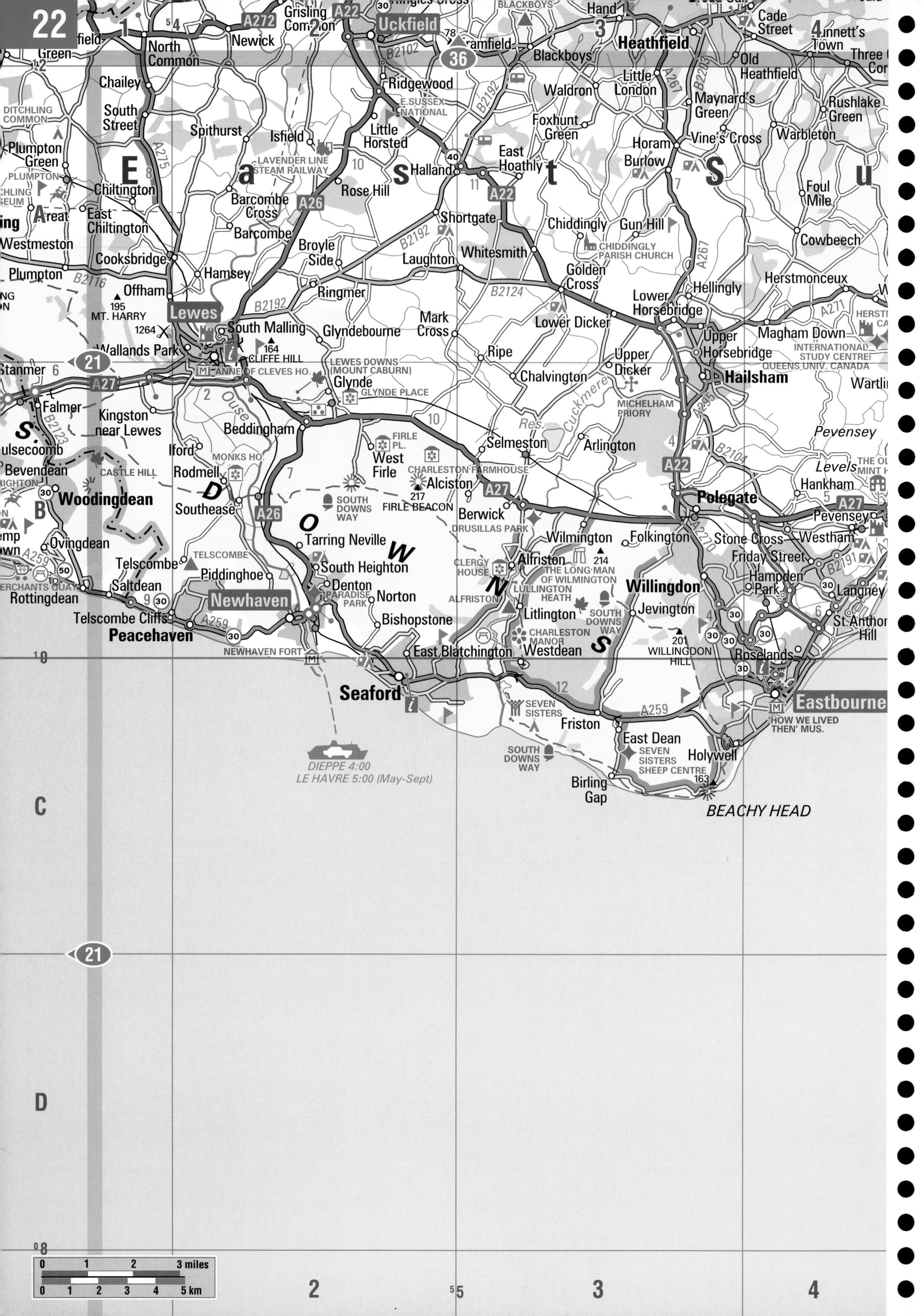
A272
Grisling Common
A22
Uckfield
Blackboys
Hand
Heathfield
Cade Street
Newick
North Common
Framfield
36
B2102
Old Heathfield
Chailey
Ridgewood
Waldron
Little London
Maynard's Green
Rushlake Green
DITCHLING COMMON
South Street
E. SUSSEX NATIONAL
Foxhunt Green
Spithurst
Isfield
Little Horsted
Horam
Vine's Cross
Warbleton
Plumpton Green
LAVENDER LINE STEAM RAILWAY
East Hoathly
Burlow
PLUMPTON
Chiltington
Halland
Foul Mile
Barcombe Cross
Rose Hill
A26
A22
East Chiltington
Barcombe
Shortgate
Chiddingly
Gun Hill
Cowbeech
Westmeston
Broyle Side
Laughton
Whitesmith
CHIDDINGLY PARISH CHURCH
Cooksbridge
Hamsey
Golden Cross
Plumpton
B2116
Ringmer
Hellingly
Herstmonceux
Offham
195
MT. HARRY
B2192
B2124
Lower Horsebridge
Lewes
Mark Cross
Lower Dicker
A271
1264
South Malling
Glyndebourne
Upper Horsebridge
Magham Down
Wallands Park
164
Ripe
Upper Dicker
INTERNATIONAL STUDY CENTRE
QUEENS UNIV. CANADA
CLIFFE HILL
Stanmer
21
A27
ANNE OF CLEVES HO.
LEWES DOWNS (MOUNT CABURN)
Glynde
Chalvington
Hailsham
GLYNDE PLACE
Cuckmere
MICHELHAM PRIORY
Falmer
Kingston near Lewes
Ouse
Beddingham
Res.
Pevensey
Selmeston
Arlington
Coldean
FIRLE PL.
Iford
MONKS HO.
West Firle
A22
Levels
Bevendean
CASTLE HILL
Rodmell
CHARLESTON FARMHOUSE
B2104
Hankham
Alciston
A27
Woodingdean
217
FIRLE BEACON
Polegate
SOUTH DOWNS WAY
Berwick
A27
Southease
A26
DRUSILLAS PARK
Pevensey
Ovingdean
Tarring Neville
Wilmington
Folkington
Stone Cross
Westham
A259
Telscombe
TELSCOMBE
CLERGY HOUSE
Alfriston
214
Friday Street
South Heighton
THE LONG MAN OF WILMINGTON
Piddinghoe
Saltdean
Denton
Willingdon
Hampden Park
Langney
Rottingdean
PARADISE PARK
Norton
LULLINGTON HEATH
Newhaven
ALFRISTON
Jevington
Telscombe Cliffs
Litlington
Bishopstone
SOUTH DOWNS WAY
St. Anthony's Hill
Peacehaven
A259
CHARLESTON MANOR
201
NEWHAVEN FORT
East Blatchington
Westdean
WILLINGDON HILL
Roselands
Seaford
SEVEN SISTERS
A259
Eastbourne
Friston
HOW WE LIVED THEN' MUS.
East Dean
SOUTH DOWNS WAY
SEVEN SISTERS SHEEP CENTRE
Holywell
DIEPPE 4:00
LE HAVRE 5:00 (May-Sept)
Birling Gap
163
BEACHY HEAD
C
D
21
0 1 2 3 miles
0 1 2 3 4 5 km
2
3
4

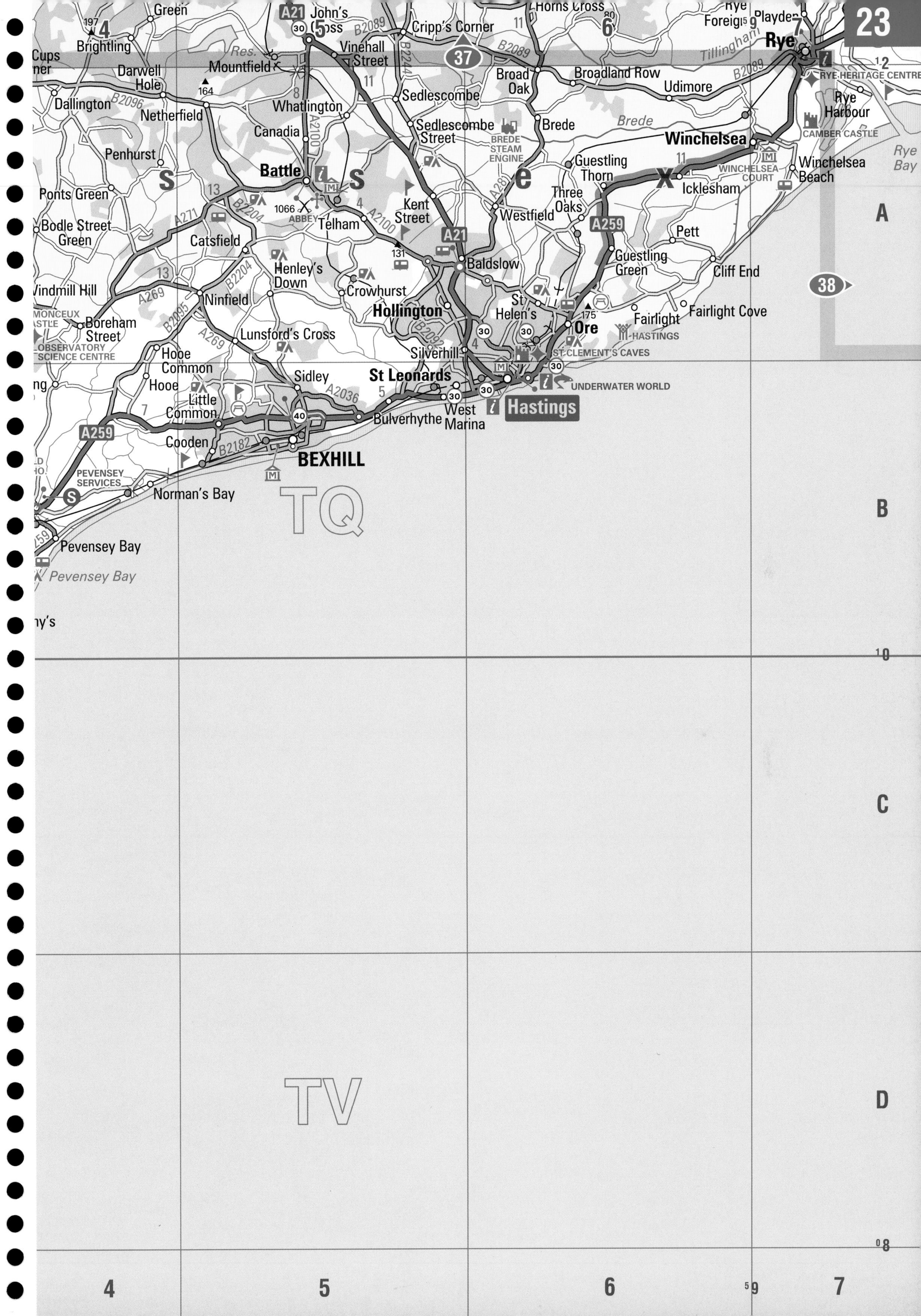
Brightling
Mountfield
Darwell Hole
Dallington
Netherfield
Whatlington
Canadia
Penhurst
Battle
Ponts Green
Bodle Street Green
Catsfield
Telham
Kent Street
Henley's Down
Crowhurst
Hollington
Ninfield
Boreham Street
Lunsford's Cross
Hooe Common
Hooe
Little Common
Sidley
St Leonards
Silverhill
Bulverhythe
West Marina
Hastings
Cooden
BEXHILL
Norman's Bay
Pevensey Bay
Cripp's Corner
Vinehall Street
Sedlescombe
Sedlescombe Street
Broad Oak
Brede
BREDE STEAM ENGINE
Broadland Row
Udimore
Rye
Playden
RYE HERITAGE CENTRE
Rye Harbour
CAMBER CASTLE
Winchelsea
WINCHELSEA COURT
Winchelsea Beach
Rye Bay
Guestling Thorn
Three Oaks
Westfield
Icklesham
Pett
Guestling Green
Cliff End
Baldslow
St Helen's
Ore
Fairlight
Fairlight Cove
HASTINGS
ST CLEMENT'S CAVES
UNDERWATER WORLD
OBSERVATORY SCIENCE CENTRE
PEVENSEY SERVICES
ABBEY
TQ
TV
A
B
C
D
4
5
6
7
37
38

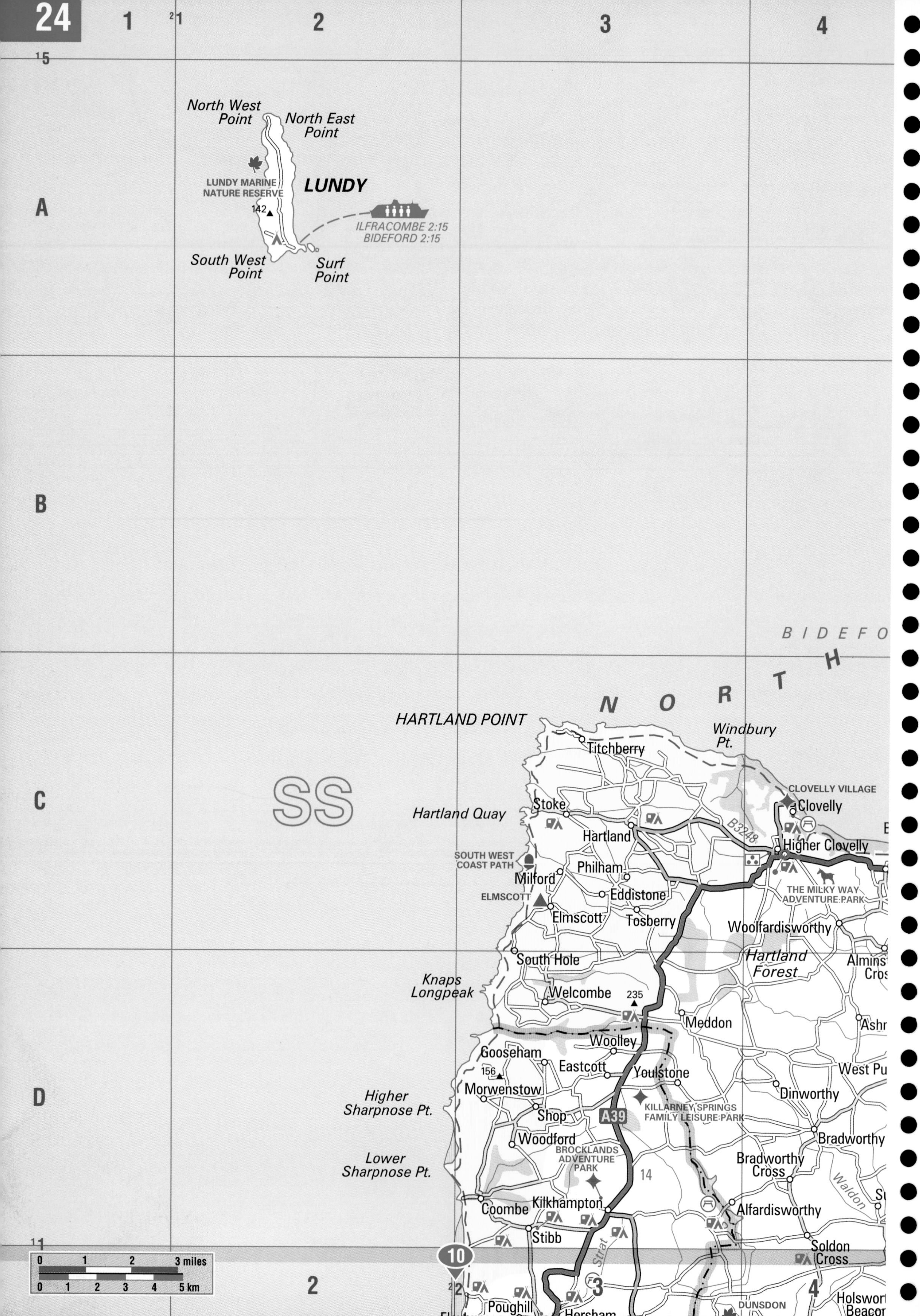

North West Point
North East Point
LUNDY MARINE NATURE RESERVE
LUNDY
142
ILFRACOMBE 2:15
BIDEFORD 2:15
South West Point
Surf Point
SS
B I D E F O
N O R T H
HARTLAND POINT
Windbury Pt.
Titchberry
CLOVELLY VILLAGE
Clovelly
Stoke
Hartland Quay
Hartland
B3248
Higher Clovelly
SOUTH WEST COAST PATH
Philham
Milford
Eddistone
THE MILKY WAY ADVENTURE PARK
ELMSCOTT
Elmscott
Tosberry
Woolfardisworthy
South Hole
Hartland Forest
Knaps Longpeak
Welcombe
235
Meddon
Woolley
Gooseham
Eastcott
Youlstone
156
Morwenstow
Dinworthy
Higher Sharpnose Pt.
Shop
KILLARNEY SPRINGS FAMILY LEISURE PARK
A39
Woodford
Bradworthy
BROCKLANDS ADVENTURE PARK
Lower Sharpnose Pt.
Bradworthy Cross
14
Waldon
Coombe
Kilkhampton
Alfardisworthy
Stibb
Strat
Soldon Cross
10
Poughill
DUNSDON
0 1 2 3 miles
0 1 2 3 4 5 km

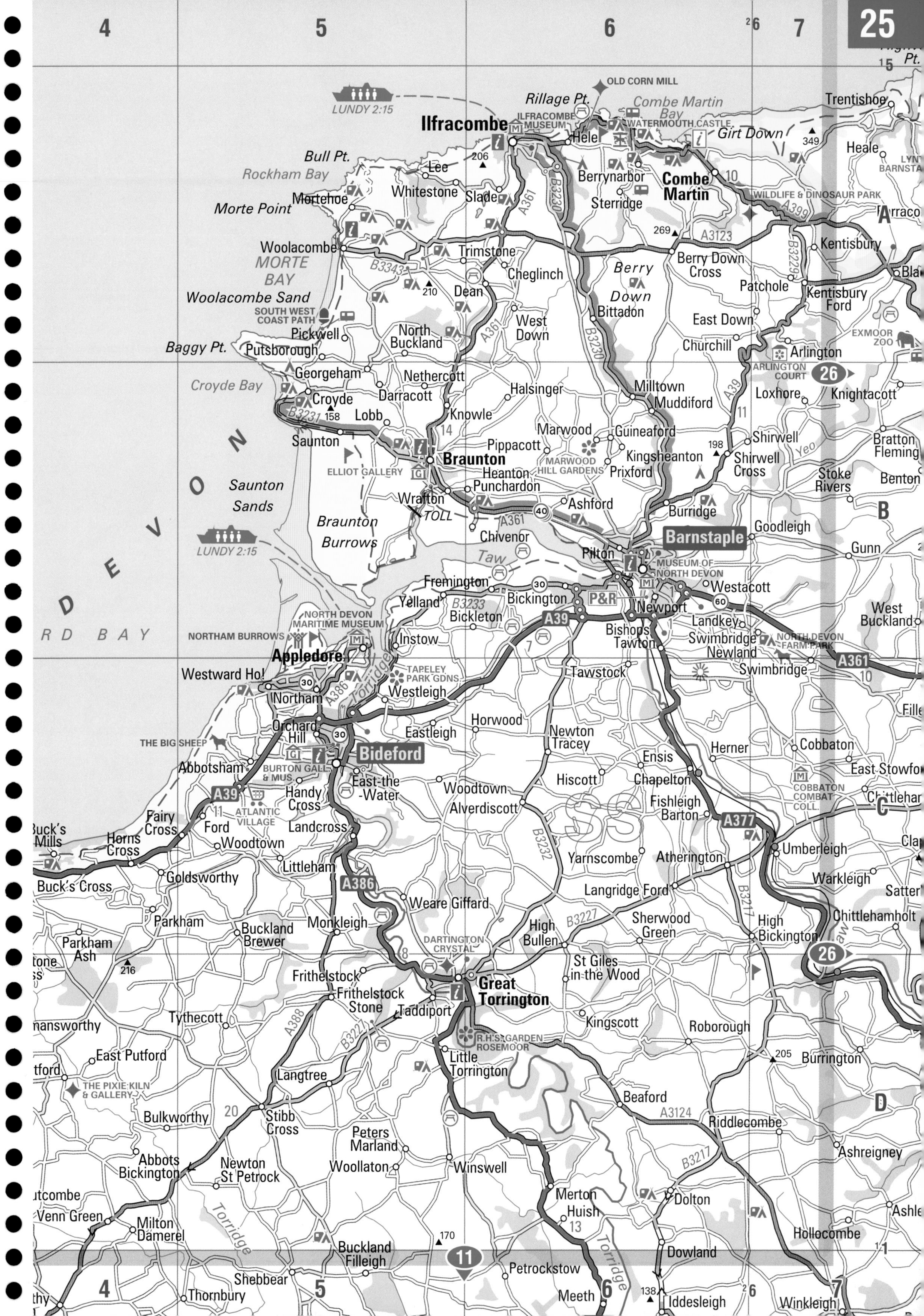

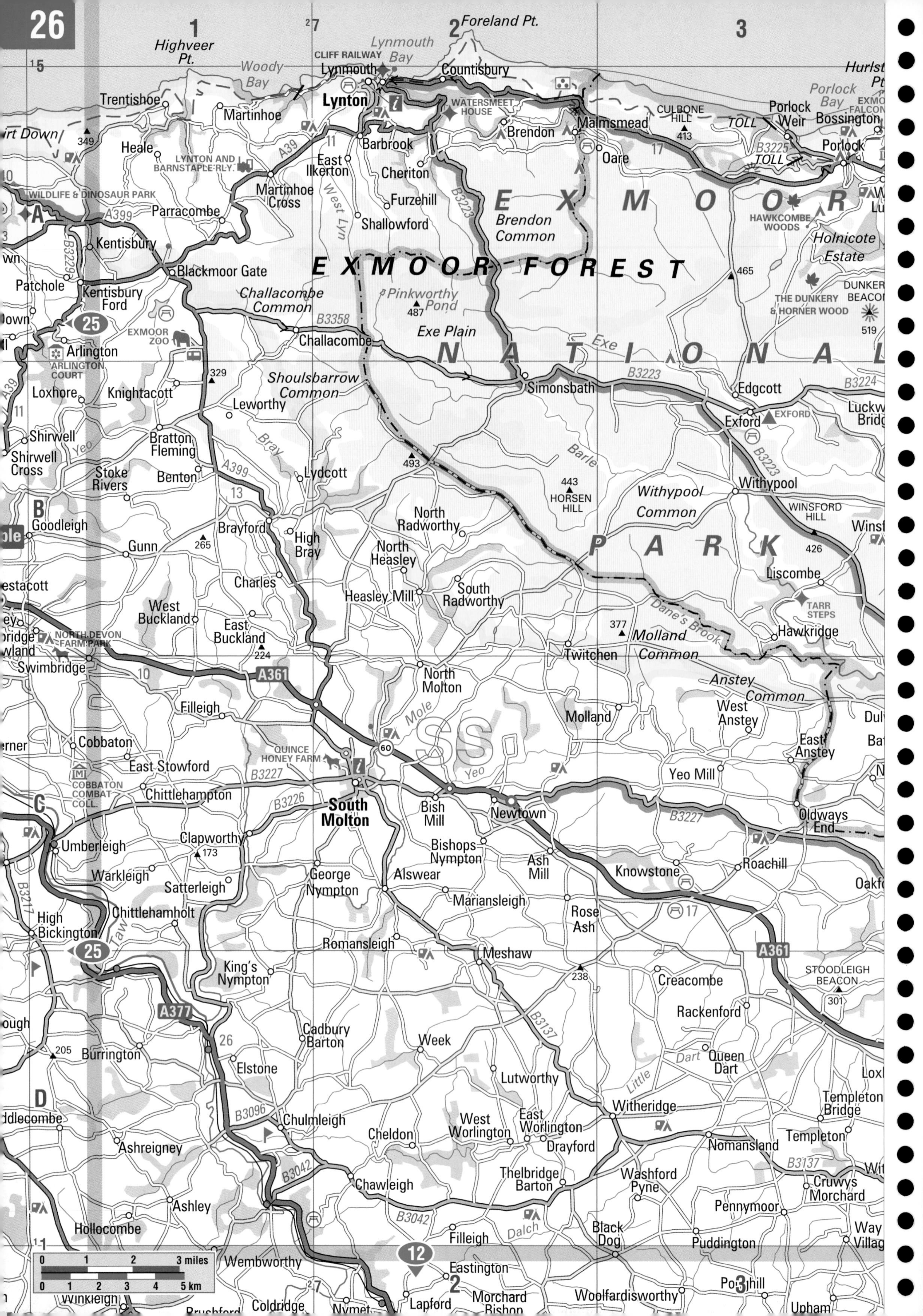
1
2
3
Foreland Pt.
Highveer Pt.
Lynmouth Bay
Woody Bay
CLIFF RAILWAY
Lynmouth
Countisbury
Lynton
Trentishoe
Martinhoe
WATERSMEET HOUSE
Brendon
Malmsmead
CULBONE HILL
413
TOLL
Porlock Bay
Porlock Weir
Bossington
Hurlstone Pt.
Porlock
B3225
Oare
17
Barbrook
East Ilkerton
Cheriton
Furzehill
Shallowford
West Lyn
B3223
Heale
349
LYNTON AND BARNSTAPLE RLY.
A39
11
Martinhoe Cross
WILDLIFE & DINOSAUR PARK
A399
Parracombe
Kentisbury
B3229
Blackmoor Gate
Patchole
Kentisbury Ford
25
Challacombe Common
B3358
Challacombe
EXMOOR ZOO
Arlington
ARLINGTON COURT
329
Loxhore
Knightacott
Shoulsbarrow Common
Leworthy
Shirwell
Shirwell Cross
Yeo
Bratton Fleming
Stoke Rivers
Benton
A399
Bray
Lydcott
493
13
B
Goodleigh
Gunn
265
Brayford
High Bray
North Radworthy
North Heasley
Charles
Heasley Mill
South Radworthy
West Buckland
East Buckland
224
NORTH DEVON FARM PARK
Swimbridge
10
A361
North Molton
Filleigh
Cobbaton
East Stowford
QUINCE HONEY FARM
Mole
60
SS
Yeo
COBBATON COMBAT COLL.
B3227
Chittlehampton
B3226
South Molton
Bish Mill
Newtown
C
Umberleigh
Clapworthy
173
Bishops Nympton
Ash Mill
Warkleigh
Satterleigh
George Nympton
Alswear
Mariansleigh
B3217
Chittlehamholt
High Bickington
Taw
Romansleigh
Meshaw
King's Nympton
A377
Cadbury Barton
205
Burrington
26
Week
Elstone
Lutworthy
B3137
D
Chulmleigh
B3096
Cheldon
West Worlington
East Worlington
Drayford
Ashreigney
B3042
Chawleigh
Thelbridge Barton
Ashley
Hollocombe
B3042
Filleigh
Dalch
Black Dog
12
Wembworthy
Eastington
Lapford
Morchard Bishop
Coldridge
Nymet
Winkleigh
Woolfardisworthy
Poughill
Upham
0 1 2 3 miles
0 1 2 3 4 5 km
EXMOOR
Brendon Common
EXMOOR FOREST
Pinkworthy Pond
487
Exe Plain
NATIONAL
Exe
Simonsbath
B3223
HAWKCOMBE WOODS
Holnicote Estate
465
DUNKERY BEACON
THE DUNKERY & HORNER WOOD
519
Edgcott
B3224
Exford
EXFORD
Barle
B3223
443
HORSEN HILL
Withypool
Withypool Common
WINSFORD HILL
426
PARK
Liscombe
TARR STEPS
Dane's Brook
377
Molland Common
Hawkridge
Twitchen
Anstey Common
West Anstey
Molland
East Anstey
Yeo Mill
B3227
Oldways End
Roachill
Knowstone
17
Rose Ash
A361
238
Creacombe
STOODLEIGH BEACON
301
Rackenford
Dart
Queen Dart
Little Dart
Witheridge
Templeton Bridge
Templeton
Nomansland
Washford Pyne
B3137
Cruwys Morchard
Pennymoor
Puddington
Way Village

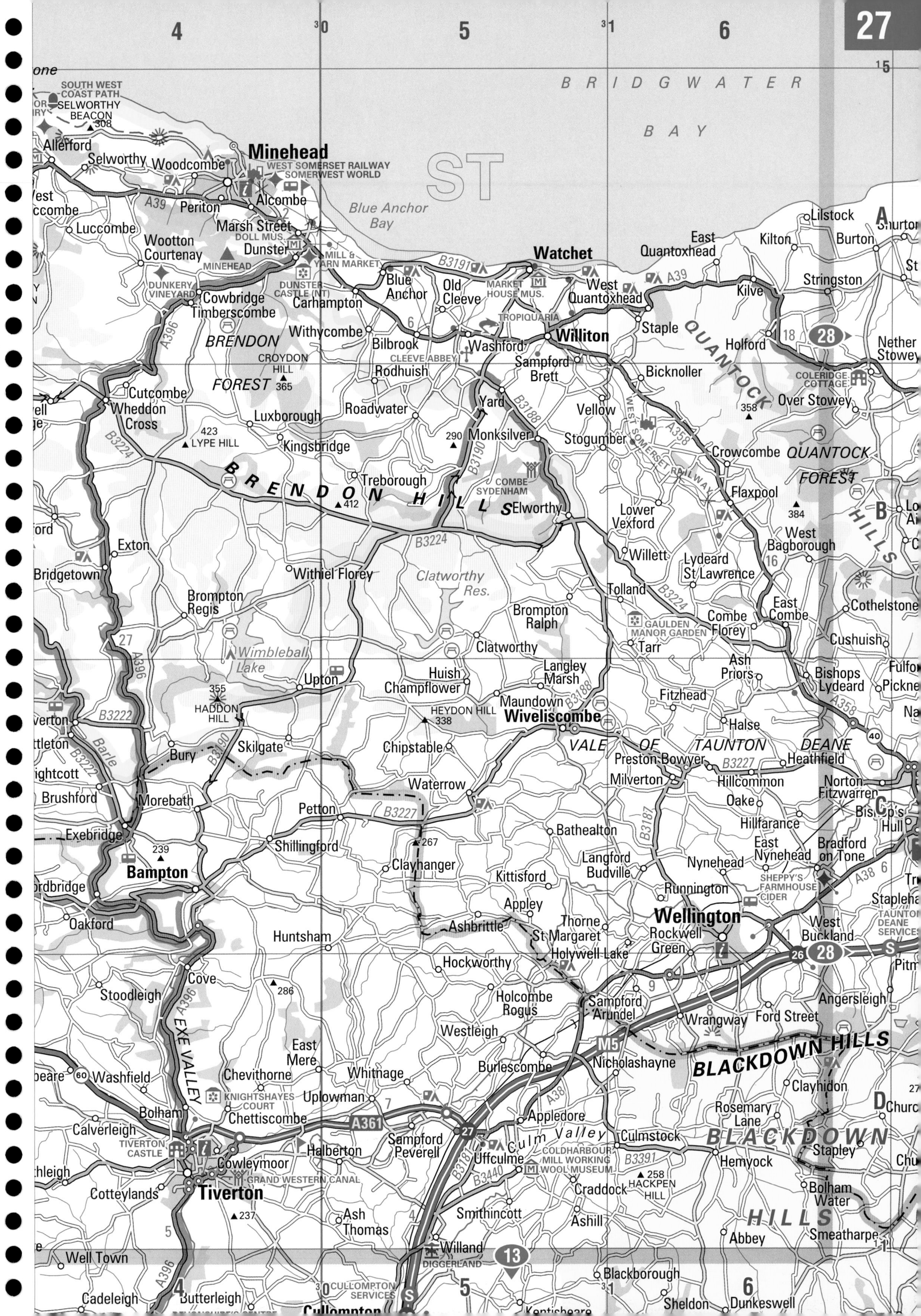

4
5
6
BRIDGWATER
BAY
ST
SOUTH WEST COAST PATH
SELWORTHY BEACON
308
Allerford
Selworthy
Woodcombe
Minehead
WEST SOMERSET RAILWAY
SOMERWEST WORLD
A39
Periton
Alcombe
Blue Anchor Bay
Luccombe
Marsh Street
DOLL MUS.
Wootton Courtenay
Dunster
MINEHEAD
MILL & YARN MARKET
B3191
Watchet
East Quantoxhead
Lilstock
Kilton
Burton
DUNKERY VINEYARD
DUNSTER CASTLE (NT)
Cowbridge
Carhampton
Blue Anchor
Old Cleeve
MARKET HOUSE MUS.
West Quantoxhead
Stringston
Kilve
Timberscombe
A396
BRENDON
Withycombe
Bilbrook
TROPIQUARIA
Washford
Williton
Staple
QUANTOCK
Holford
28
Nether Stowey
CROYDON HILL
CLEEVE ABBEY
Sampford Brett
Bicknoller
COLERIDGE COTTAGE
FOREST
365
Rodhuish
Cutcombe
Wheddon Cross
Luxborough
Roadwater
Yard
B3188
Vellow
358
Over Stowey
423
LYPE HILL
Kingsbridge
290
Monksilver
Stogumber
WEST SOMERSET RAILWAY
A358
Crowcombe
QUANTOCK FOREST
B3224
Treborough
B3190
COMBE SYDENHAM
BRENDON HILLS
412
Elworthy
Flaxpool
384
Lower Vexford
West Bagborough
Exton
Withiel Florey
Clatworthy Res.
Willett
Lydeard St Lawrence
16
Bridgetown
Brompton Regis
Tolland
Brompton Ralph
GAULDEN MANOR GARDEN
Combe Florey
East Combe
Cothelstone
27
Wimbleball Lake
Clatworthy
Tarr
Cushuish
Ash Priors
Bishops Lydeard
Upton
Huish Champflower
Langley Marsh
355
HADDON HILL
HEYDON HILL
338
Maundown
Wiveliscombe
Fitzhead
Halse
B3222
Barle
Bury
Skilgate
Chipstable
VALE OF TAUNTON DEANE
Preston Bowyer
B3227
Heathfield
40
Brushford
Morebath
Waterrow
Milverton
Hillcommon
Norton Fitzwarren
Oake
Petton
Exebridge
Shillingford
267
Bathealton
B3187
Hillfarance
239
Bampton
Clayhanger
Langford Budville
East Nynehead
Nynehead
Bradford on Tone
Kittisford
Runnington
SHEPPY'S FARMHOUSE CIDER
A38
Oakford
Appley
Ashbrittle
Thorne St Margaret
Wellington
Rockwell Green
West Buckland
Huntsham
Holywell Lake
26
Cove
Stoodleigh
286
Hockworthy
Sampford Arundel
Wrangway
Ford Street
Angersleigh
Holcombe Rogus
Westleigh
EXE VALLEY
East Mere
M5
BLACKDOWN HILLS
Nicholashayne
Burlescombe
Washfield
60
Chevithorne
Whitnage
Clayhidon
KNIGHTSHAYES COURT
Uplowman
Bolham
Chettiscombe
A361
Appledore
Rosemary Lane
Calverleigh
TIVERTON CASTLE
Halberton
Sampford Peverell
Culm Valley
Culmstock
BLACKDOWN
Stapley
Cowleymoor
Uffculme
COLDHARBOUR MILL WORKING WOOL MUSEUM
B3391
258
HACKPEN HILL
Hemyock
GRAND WESTERN CANAL
B3181
B3440
Cotteylands
Tiverton
Craddock
Bolham Water
237
Ash Thomas
Smithincott
Ashill
HILLS
Abbey
Smeatharpe
Well Town
Willand
DIGGERLAND
13
Blackborough
Cadeleigh
Butterleigh
CULLOMPTON SERVICES
Sheldon
Dunkeswell

1
2
3
4
A
B
C
D
Berrow
East Brent
Brent Knoll
Rooks Bridge
Badgworth
Stone Allerton
Chapel Allerton
Burnham-on-Sea
Edithmead
Cocklake
West Stoughton
Mark Causeway
Mark
Blackford
STERT FLATS
Highbridge
BRIDGWATER BAY
Watchfield
Westham
Stolford
Steart
Bason Bridge
Heath House
Huntspill
SECRET WORLD
East Huntspill
Lilstock
Kilton
Burton
Shurton
Stockland Bristol
Stretcholt
HUNTSPILL RIVER
Burtle
Brue
Stogursey
Stringston
Otterhampton
Combwich
Pawlett
Westhay
Kilve
Puriton
Woolavington
Holford
Nether Stowey
Fiddington
Dunball
Cossington
Chilton Polden
Edington
Rodway
Cannington
CANNINGTON COLLEGE
COLERIDGE COTTAGE
Bawdrip
POLDEN HILLS
Catcott
SHAPWICK HEATH
Over Stowey
Chilton Trinity
THE PEAT MOORS VISITOR CENTRE
Charlynch
BLAKE MUS.
Stawell
Shapwick
Wembdon
BRIDGWATER AND TAUNTON CANAL AND DOCKS
Spaxton
QUANTOCK FOREST
Four Forks
Durleigh
Chedzoy
Moorlinch
Sutton Mallet
Greinton
Ashcott
Pedwell
Bridgwater
VINEYARD
Flaxpool
BARFORD PARK
Enmore
Westonzoyland
Lower Aisholt
BRIDGWATER SERVICES
Goathurst
West Bagborough
Courtway
North Petherton
Huntworth
King's Sedge Moor
TEMPLE OF HARMONY
SOMERSET LEVELS
FYNE COURT
Northmoor Green or Moorland
Middlezoy
Henley
East Combe
Cothelstone
Broomfield
Othery
Pathe
High Ham
STEMBRIDGE
Cushuish
North Newton
Thurloxton
BRIDGWATER & TAUNTON CANAL MAUNSEL LOCKS
Burrowbridge
Ash Priors
Bishops Lydeard
Fulford
Kingston St Mary
HESTERCOMBE GARDENS
Lyng
Stathe
Aller
Low Ham
Pickney
Hedging
Athelney
Parrett
Halse
Nailsbourne
West Monkton
Durston
West Lyng
DEANE
Heathfield
Cheddon Fitzpaine
Monkton Heathfield
Creech Heathfield
Tone
Stoke St Gregory
Langport
Huish Episcopi
Staplegrove
Bathpool
North End
Meare Green
WILLOWS & WETLANDS VISITOR CENTRE
West Sedge Moor
Curry Rivel
LANGPORT & R. PARRETT VISITOR CENTRE
Norton Fitzwarren
Creech St Michael
Knapp
Bishop's Hull
Ruishton
North Curry
Drayton
Muchelney
ABBEY
Hillfarance
SOMERSET CRICKET MUS.
Thornfalcon
Taunton
East Nynehead
Bradford on Tone
Henlade
Fivehead
Isle
SHEPPY'S FARMHOUSE CIDER
Trull
Stoke St Mary
Wrantage
TAUNTON
Curry Mallet
Isle Brewers
Staplehay
Orchard Portman
Hatch Beauchamp
Isle Abbotts
Hambridge
TAUNTON DEANE SERVICES
West Buckland
Thurlbear
West Hatch
Beercrocombe
Westport
East Lambrook
West Lambrook
Pitminster
Corfe
Hatch Green
Staple Fitzpaine
E. LAMBROOK MANOR
Angersleigh
Blagdon Hill
BARRINGTON COURT
Ford Street
Bickenhall
Puckington
Barrington
South Petherton
Ilton
BLACKDOWN HILLS
Curland
BARRINGTON HILL
Ashill
Stocklinch
Shepton Beauchamp
STAPLE HILL
Windmill Hill
Ashwell
Clayhidon
Broadway
DILLINGTON HOUSE
Seavington St Michael
Churchstanton
Horton
Ilminster
Seavington St Mary
Lopen
Fyfett
Donyatt
Buckland St Mary
Stapley
Crock Street
Kingstone
Dinnington
Hemyock
Churchinford
Dowlish Wake
Bishopswood
Hinton St George
Bolham Water
Combe St Nicholas
Cricket Malherbie
Chillington
Marsh
Whitestaunton
HORNSBURY MILL
Smeatharpe
Cudworth
Wadeford
Chaffcombe
Crewkerne
Newcott
Howley
Cricket St Thomas
WILDLIFE PARK
Yarcombe
Wambrook
Chard
Hewish
Dunkeswell
Misterton
0 1 2 3 miles
0 1 2 3 4 5 km

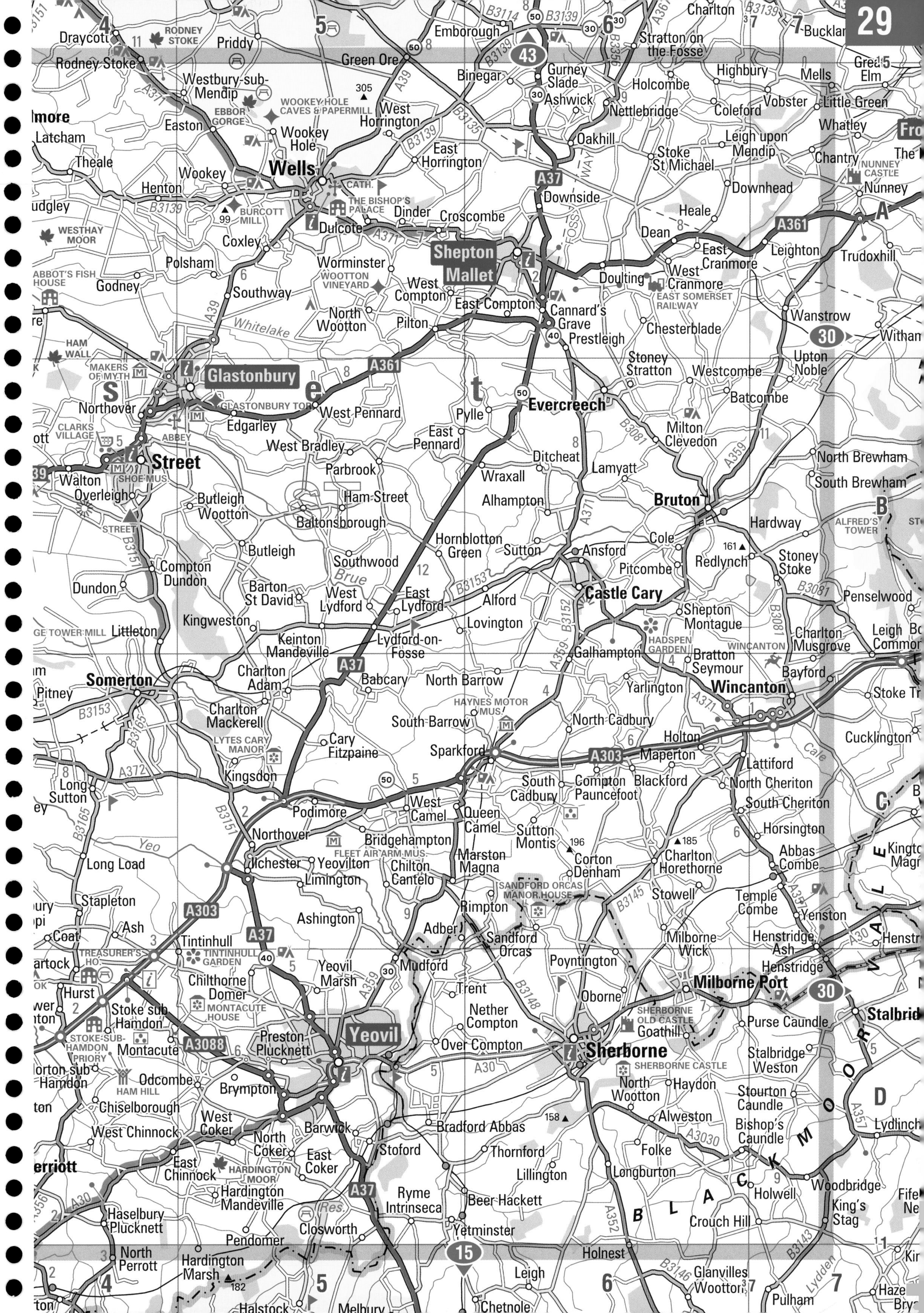
Wells
Shepton Mallet
Glastonbury
Street
Somerton
Yeovil
Sherborne
Wincanton
Castle Cary
Bruton
Evercreech
Milborne Port
Draycott
Rodney Stoke
Priddy
Green Ore
Emborough
Binegar
Gurney Slade
Ashwick
Oakhill
Stratton on the Fosse
Holcombe
Nettlebridge
Highbury
Coleford
Vobster
Mells
Great Elm
Little Green
Whatley
Westbury-sub-Mendip
Wookey Hole
Caves & Papermill
Ebbor Gorge
Easton
Wookey Hole
West Horrington
East Horrington
Wookey
Henton
Theale
Latcham
Leigh upon Mendip
Stoke St Michael
Chantry
Nunney Castle
Nunney
Downhead
Downside
Croscombe
Dinder
Dulcote
Coxley
Burcott Mill
Westhay Moor
Polsham
Godney
Abbot's Fish House
Southway
Worminster
Wootton Vineyard
West Compton
East Compton
North Wootton
Pilton
Cannard's Grave
Prestleigh
Doulting
East Cranmore
West Cranmore
East Somerset Railway
Leighton
Trudoxhill
Heale
Dean
Chesterblade
Wanstrow
Witham
Upton Noble
Stoney Stratton
Westcombe
Batcombe
Ham Wall
Makers of Myth
Northover
Glastonbury Tor
West Pennard
Edgarley
Clarks Village
Abbey
West Bradley
East Pennard
Pylle
Walton
Overleigh
Shoe Mus.
Parbrook
Ditcheat
Wraxall
Lamyatt
Milton Clevedon
North Brewham
South Brewham
Butleigh Wootton
Ham Street
Baltonsborough
Alhampton
Hardway
Alfred's Tower
Butleigh
Hornblotton Green
Sutton
Cole
Ansford
Redlynch
Stoney Stoke
Compton Dundon
Dundon
Southwood
Pitcombe
Penselwood
Barton St David
West Lydford
East Lydford
Alford
Shepton Montague
Kingweston
Lovington
Hadspen Garden
Charlton Musgrove
Leigh Common
Littleton
Keinton Mandeville
Lydford-on-Fosse
Galhampton
Bratton Seymour
Bayford
Pitney
Charlton Adam
Babcary
North Barrow
Yarlington
Stoke Trister
Charlton Mackerell
Haynes Motor Mus.
South Barrow
North Cadbury
Cucklington
Lytes Cary Manor
Cary Fitzpaine
Sparkford
Holton
Maperton
Lattiford
Kingsdon
South Cadbury
Compton Pauncefoot
Blackford
North Cheriton
South Cheriton
Long Sutton
Podimore
West Camel
Queen Camel
Horsington
Northover
Bridgehampton
Sutton Montis
Abbas Combe
Long Load
Ilchester
Yeovilton
Fleet Air Arm Mus.
Chilton Cantelo
Marston Magna
Corton Denham
Charlton Horethorne
Limington
Stapleton
Sandford Orcas Manor House
Rimpton
Stowell
Temple Combe
Yenston
Ash
Ashington
Adber
Sandford Orcas
Milborne Wick
Henstridge Ash
Henstridge
Coat
Tintinhull
Tintinhull Garden
Treasurer's Ho.
Yeovil Marsh
Mudford
Poyntington
Hurst
Chilthorne Domer
Trent
Oborne
Sherborne Old Castle
Stoke sub Hamdon
Montacute House
Nether Compton
Goathill
Purse Caundle
Stalbridge
Stoke-sub-Hamdon Priory
Montacute
Preston Plucknett
Over Compton
Sherborne Castle
Stalbridge Weston
Norton sub Hamdon
Odcombe
Ham Hill
Brympton
North Wootton
Haydon
Stourton Caundle
Chiselborough
West Coker
Alweston
Bishop's Caundle
Lydlinch
West Chinnock
Barwick
Bradford Abbas
North Coker
Stoford
Thornford
Folke
East Chinnock
Hardington Moor
East Coker
Lillington
Longburton
Woodbridge
Hardington Mandeville
Ryme Intrinseca
Beer Hackett
Holwell
King's Stag
Haselbury Plucknett
Closworth
Yetminster
Crouch Hill
Pendomer
North Perrott
Hardington Marsh
Holnest
Leigh
Glanvilles Wootton
Pulham
Halstock
Melbury
Chetnole
Blackmoor Vale
A37
A39
A361
A371
A359
A303
A372
A3088
A30
A352
A3030
A357
B3139
B3135
B3151
B3153
B3152
B3081
B3165
B3148
B3145
B3143
B3146
B3114
B3356
43
30
15

Buckland Dinham
Lullington
Beckington
Rudge
BRATTON CAMP & WHITE HORSE
Littleton Down
Westbury
Oldford
Great Elm
Mells
Vobster
Little Green
Clink
Berkley
Dilton Marsh
Upton Scudamore
Summer Down
West Lavington Down
Frome
Whatley
Leigh upon Mendip
Chantry
The Butts
NUNNEY CASTLE
Nunney
Downhead
Chapmanslade
Corsley
WARMINSTER SERVICES
Corsley Heath
Warminster
Wilts
SAL
WARMINSTER DEWEY MUSEUM
Tytherington
West Woodlands
LONGLEAT
Bugley
Boreham
Chitterne
Leighton
Trudoxhill
Bishopstrow
Norton Bavant
Heytesbury
Crockerton
Shear Cross
Sutton Veny
Knook
Upton Lovell
Horningsham
Wanstrow
Witham Friary
Gare Hill
Longbridge Deverill
Tytherington
Corton
Codford St Peter
Upton Noble
Bruton Forest
Batcombe
Maiden Bradley
Brixton Deverill
Monkton Deverill
Boyton
Sherrington
Stockton
Kilmington
North Brewham
Norton Ferris
Kingston Deverill
CRANBORNE
Great Ridge
Pertwood
South Brewham
Hardway
ALFRED'S TOWER
STOURHEAD
Stourton
WHITE SHEET HILL
Keysley Down
Chicklade
Berwick St Leonard
Fonthill Bishop
Stoney Stoke
Penselwood
Zeals
Queen Oak
Mere
West Knoyle
Hindon
Chilmark
Teffont Magna
BUSH FARM BISON CENTRE
The Green
Fonthill Gifford
Ridge
Teffont Evias
Charlton Musgrove
Leigh Common
Bourton
Barrow Street
CHASE
East Knoyle
Chicksgrove
Bayford
Wincanton
Huntingford
Tisbury
Stoke Trister
Milton on Stour
Sedgehill
Newtown
Hatch
Sutton Mandeville
Cucklington
Swallowcliffe
Gillingham
Elm Hill
OLD WARDOUR CASTLE
Lattiford
Wyke
Ham Common
Semley
Ansty
PRESCOMBE DOWN
North Cheriton
Motcombe
Donhead St Andrew
West End
Buckhorn Weston
Horsington
Knap Corner
Donhead St Mary
WHITE SHEET HILL
Milkwell
Abbas Combe
Kington Magna
West Stour
Ivy Cross
Berwick St John
Alvediston
Shaftesbury
East Stour
Ludwell
Temple Combe
Charlton
Cann
Cann Common
Yenston
Fifehead Magdalen
Stour Provost
Stour Row
Guy's Marsh
WILTSHIRE
Win Green
Henstridge Ash
Henstridge Marsh
Todber
Melbury Abbas
Melbury Down
Henstridge
Pillwell
Marnhull
Tollard Royal
Margaret Marsh
Compton Abbas
Ashmore
Stalbridge
Purse Caundle
Bedchester
Woodcutts
East Orchard
West Orchard
Fontmell Magna
LARMER TREE VICTORIAN PLEASURE GARDEN
Sixpenny Handley
Stalbridge Weston
Hinton St Mary
Sutton Waldron
Dean
Manston
Sturminster Newton
Farnham
Lydlinch
Hammoon
Iwerne Courtney or Shroton
Iwerne Minster
Stubhampton
CHETTLE HOUSE
Bishop's Caundle
Fiddleford
Chettle
Cashmoor
Newton
FIDDLEFORD MANOR
Child Okeford
HAMBLEDON HILL
Tarrant Gunville
Gussage St Michael
Broad Oak
Holwell
Woodbridge
Fifehead Neville
King's Stag
Shillingstone
Tarrant Hinton
Okeford Fitzpaine
DOWNS
Long Crichel
Stourpaine
Tarrant Launceston
Pimperne
Moor Crichel
Tarrant Monkton
Durweston
Pulham
Bryan
Ibberton
Turnworth
ROYAL SIGNALS
BLACKMORE VALE
CRANBORNE CHASE AND WEST WILTSHIRE DOWNS
0 1 2 3 miles
0 1 2 3 4 5 km

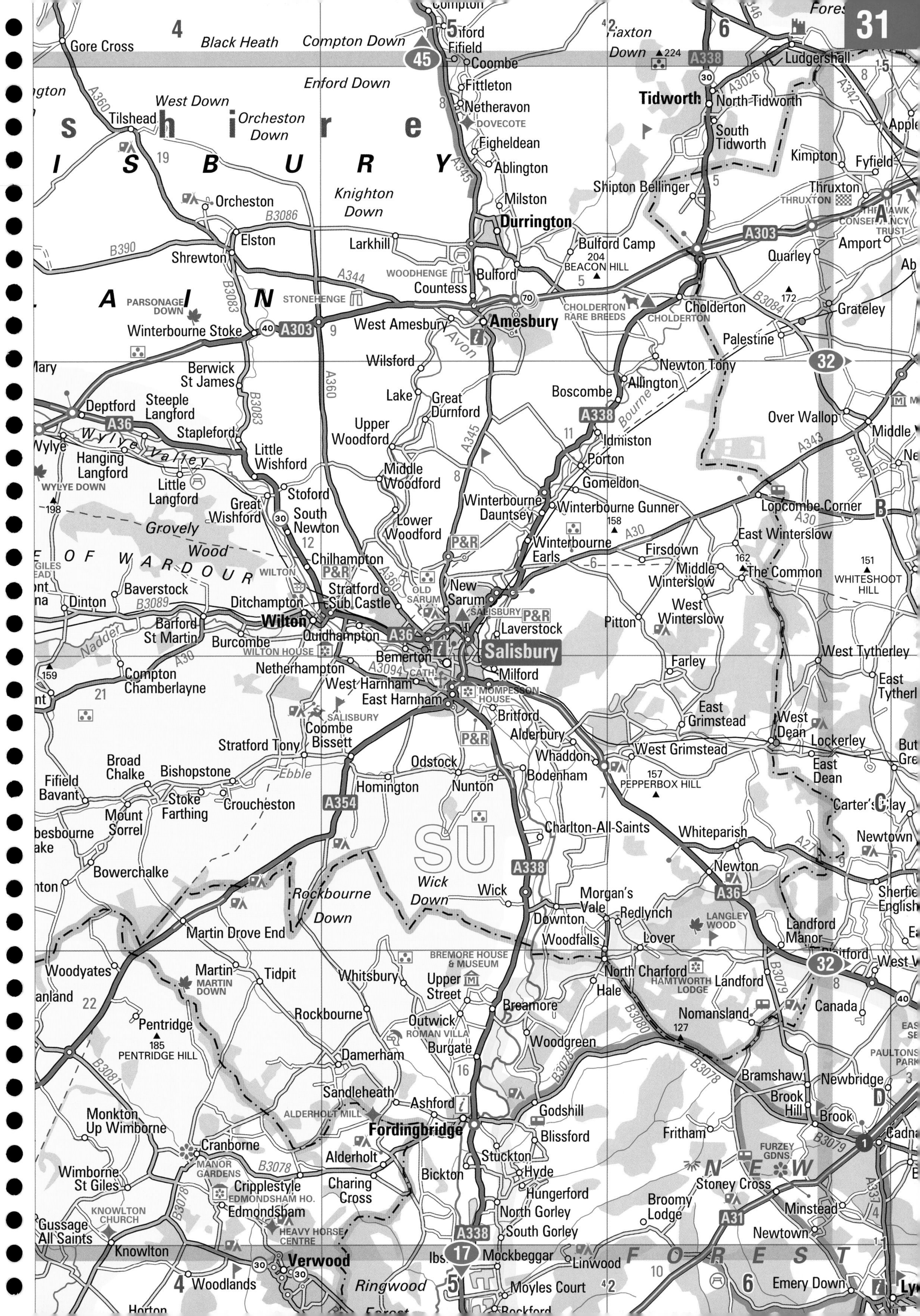

Gore Cross
Black Heath
Compton Down
Enford Down
West Down
Tilshead
Orcheston Down
Orcheston
Elston
Shrewton
Larkhill
Knighton Down
Durrington
Bulford Camp
Bulford
Countess
Amesbury
Stonehenge
Woodhenge
Winterbourne Stoke
West Amesbury
Wilsford
Lake
Great Durnford
Upper Woodford
Middle Woodford
Lower Woodford
Berwick St James
Deptford
Steeple Langford
Stapleford
Wylye
Hanging Langford
Little Langford
Little Wishford
Great Wishford
Stoford
South Newton
Grovely Wood
Wylye Down
Chilhampton
Baverstock
Dinton
Barford St Martin
Ditchampton
Wilton
Burcombe
Quidhampton
Stratford sub Castle
Old Sarum
New Sarum
Laverstock
Salisbury
Bemerton
Netherhampton
West Harnham
East Harnham
Milford
Compton Chamberlayne
Coombe Bissett
Stratford Tony
Britford
Alderbury
Whaddon
Bodenham
Odstock
Nunton
Homington
Broad Chalke
Bishopstone
Fifield Bavant
Stoke Farthing
Croucheston
Mount Sorrel
Bowerchalke
Rockbourne Down
Wick Down
Wick
Martin Drove End
Woodyates
Martin
Martin Down
Tidpit
Whitsbury
Upper Street
Rockbourne
Outwick
Burgate
Damerham
Pentridge
Pentridge Hill
Sandleheath
Ashford
Alderholt Mill
Fordingbridge
Monkton Up Wimborne
Cranborne
Manor Gardens
Alderholt
Wimborne St Giles
Cripplestyle
Edmondsham
Charing Cross
Bickton
Gussage All Saints
Knowlton Church
Heavy Horse Centre
Knowlton
Verwood
Woodlands
Ringwood
Ibsley
Mockbeggar
Linwood
Moyles Court
Rockford
South Gorley
North Gorley
Hungerford
Hyde
Stuckton
Blissford
Godshill
Woodgreen
Breamore
Hale
North Charford
Woodfalls
Downton
Redlynch
Morgan's Vale
Lover
Charlton-All-Saints
Whiteparish
Newton
Langley Wood
Landford Manor
Landford
Hamtworth Lodge
Nomansland
Bramshaw
Brook
Fritham
Stoney Cross
Broomy Lodge
Minstead
Newtown
Emery Down
Furzey Gdns.
New Forest
Canada
Newbridge
West Grimstead
East Grimstead
Pepperbox Hill
Farley
West Dean
East Dean
Lockerley
Carter's Clay
Newtown
West Tytherley
The Common
Middle Winterslow
West Winterslow
Pitton
Firsdown
East Winterslow
Lopcombe Corner
Whiteshoot Hill
Winterbourne Gunner
Winterbourne Dauntsey
Winterbourne Earls
Gomeldon
Porton
Idmiston
Boscombe
Allington
Newton Tony
Over Wallop
Middle Wallop
Palestine
Grateley
Cholderton
Cholderton Rare Breeds
Beacon Hill
Quarley
Amport
Thruxton
Kimpton
Fyfield
Shipton Bellinger
South Tidworth
North Tidworth
Tidworth
Ludgershall
Milston
Ablington
Figheldean
Netheravon
Fittleton
Coombe
Fifield
Enford
Compton
Wilton House
Mompesson House
Bremore House & Museum
Roman Villa
Edmondsham Ho.
Salisbury Plain
Vale of Wardour
A303
A36
A338
A345
A360
A354
A30
A31
A343
A3026
B3083
B3086
B390
B3089
A3094
B3081
B3078
B3080
B3079
B3084
SU

Forest
1
2
3
4
Doles Wood
Stoke
Wildhern
St Mary Bourne
46
A34
Cole Henley
Quidhampton
Overton
Deane
Ashe
Ludgershall
Hatherden
Little London
A3026
North Tidworth
South Tidworth
Clanville
Enham Alamein
Smannell
Appleshaw
Penton Mewsey
Picket Piece
B3048
B3400
Whitchurch
Laverstoke
Steventon
Kimpton
Fyfield
A342
Weyhill
Charlton
FINKLEY DOWN FARM PARK
Hurstbourne Priors
Tufton
A3093
B3400
Thruxton
THRUXTON
THE HAWK CONSERVANCY TRUST
WEYHILL SERVICES
Andover
Andover Down
A
A303
Amport
Monxton
Middleton
Longparish
Quarley
Abbotts Ann
Anna Valley
Upper Clatford
Harewood Forest
Forton
TIDBURY RING
MICHELDEVER SERVICES
183
172
B3084
Grateley
Goodworth Clatford
B3420
A3057
Wherwell
B3048
Newton Stacey
Bullington
Barton Stacey
A303
West Stratton
Palestine
A343
31
Fullerton
Chilbolton
SUTTON SCOTNEY SERVICES
B3420
A30
Wonston
Sutton Scotney
Micheldever
Stoke Charity
MUSEUM OF ARMY FLYING
Over Wallop
Middle Wallop
143
Nether Wallop
Longstock
Leckford
A272
A34
Michel Wood
South Wonston
B3084
H
a
m
p
s
h
A30
B
Lopcombe Corner
Stockbridge
158
Crawley
Worthy Down
A33
M3
WINCHESTER SERVICES
East Winterslow
A3057
B3049
Kings Worthy
Martyr Worthy
Itchen Abbas
B3047
162
The Common
151
WHITESHOOT HILL
Broughton
Little Somborne
ALL SAINTS CHURCH
Up Somborne
Littleton
B3420
Headbourne Worthy
Houghton
FLOWERDOWN BARROWS
Easton
Avington
Horsebridge
King's Somborne
Ashley
Sparsholt
Weeke
Winnall
West Tytherley
FARLEY MOUNT
Winchester
CATH.
P&R
INTECH SCIENCE TECHNOLOGY
East Tytherley
174
FARLEY MOUNT
Stanmore
Brook
MOTTISFONT ABBEY
West Dean
B3084
A3090
Chilcomb
176
A272
Lockerley
Butt's Green
Mottisfont
Standon
Oliver's Battery
ST. CATHERINE'S HILL
Longwood Warren
East Dean
Michelmersh
Braishfield
A3057
Compton
Morestead
C
Carter's Clay
Kent's Oak
Timsbury
Pucknall
HILLIER GARDENS AND ARBORETUM
Hursley
Twyford
Shawford
Newtown
Awbridge
Owslebury
Upper Ratley
Abbotswood
A3090
Ampfield
M3
Otterbourne
Baybridge
Sherfield English
Cupernham
A27
Colden Common
Romsey
ABBEY
Whitenap
B3043
Chandler's Ford
B3335
B3354
MARWELL ZOOLOGICAL PARK
Landford Manor
A36
East Wellow
A27
Fisher's Pond
Plaitford
West Wellow
BROADLANDS
North Baddesley
EASTLEIGH
Lower Upham
B3079
31
Landford
Chilworth
Bishopstoke
B3037
Toothill
A3090
Canada
LAKESIDE
A335
Itchen
Fair Oak
Wintershill
Horton Heath
Ridge
A3057
Lee
EASTLEIGH SERVICES
Wigley
Upton
ROWNHAMS SERVICES
Rownhams
SOUTHAMPTON
B3354
Owen
PAULTONS PARK
M27
Nursling
Bassett
A35
A27
M27
ITCHEN VALLEY
Durley
Bramshaw
Newbridge
Calmore
Coxford
Swaythling
D
Brook Hill
Brook
A36
Testwood
M271
Southampton
B3035
Long Common
Copythorne
Wimpson
Portswood
West End
B3079
Cadnam
Winsor
A336
Totton
Shirley
A33
A334
Curdridge
Millbrook
Bitterne
B3036
Hedge End
Botley
NEW
FURZEY GDNS.
Bartley
Netley Marsh
ELING TIDE MILL
Eling
CITY ART GALL.
Northam
Thornhill
Shedfield
A337
Woodlands
A3024
Sholing
A31
Minstead
SOUTHAMPTON
Hamble
MANOR FARM
Curbridge
Burridge
A3025
A3051
WHITELEY VILLAGE
Newtown
FOREST
Ashurst
LONGDOWN FARM
MARITIME MUS.
Itchen
Woolston
Pooksgreen
A35
WILDLIFE CONSERVATION PARK
Marchwood
18
Old Netley
Lowford
Swanwick
NETLEY ABBEY
Bursledon
Lower Swanwick
0 1 2 3 miles
0 1 2 3 4 5 km
hurst
NEW FOREST MUSEUM
A326
Netley
Hound
HOLLY HILL WOODLAND PARK
Park Gate

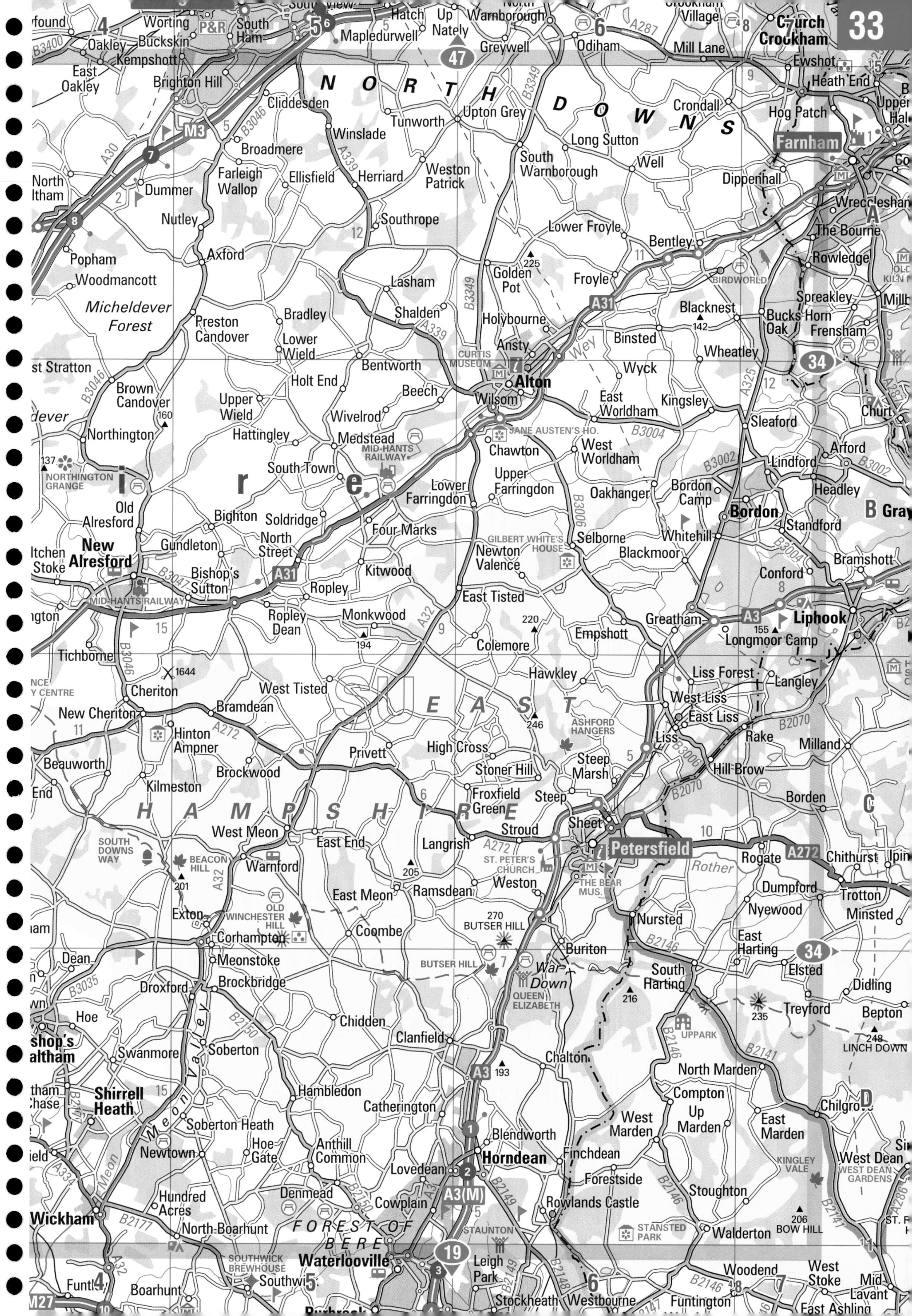

NORTH DOWNS
Farnham
Alton
Bordon
Liphook
Petersfield
New Alresford
HAMPSHIRE
SOUTH EAST
Horndean
Waterlooville
Wickham
Shirrell Heath
Church Crookham
Odiham
Micheldever Forest
FOREST OF BERE
Liss
Greatham
Selborne
Chawton
East Meon
West Meon
Hambledon
Clanfield
Buriton
South Harting
Rogate
Headley
Binsted
Bentley
Crondall
Long Sutton
Upton Grey
Herriard
Cliddesden
Preston Candover
Medstead
Four Marks
Ropley
Bishop's Sutton
Cheriton
Bramdean
Privett
Steep
Rowlands Castle
Westbourne
Denmead
Cowplain
Lovedean

Sandhurst
CAMBERLEY
Yateley
Frogmore
York Town
YATELEY COMMON
Blackwater
Hawley
Frimley
Fox Lane
Farnborough Green
Cove
West Heath
FLEET SERVICES
M3
Fleet
ST MICHAEL'S ABBEY
FARNBOROUGH
Pondtail
Mytchett
BASINGSTOKE CANAL CENTRE
Pirbright
Frimley Green
Deepcut
Brookwood
Chobham Ridges
LIGHTWATER
West End
Donkey Town
Bisley
Chobham
Castle Green
Knaphill
Horsell
WOKING
Woodham
Cheapside
Byfleet
West Byfleet
Wisley
RHS GARDEN WISLEY
PAINSHILL PARK
M25
Pyrford
Old Woking
Ripley
Ockham
St John's
Mayford
Send Marsh
Send
Burntcommon
B380
Fox Corner
Sutton Green
Worplesdon
Pitch Place
Slyfield
Burpham
West Clandon
CLANDON PARK
West Horsley
East Horsley
East Clandon
HATCHLANDS PARK
Merrow
Newland's Corner
Ash Vale
Willey Green
Stoughton
Wood Street
Normandy
Wyke
Church Crookham
ALDERSHOT
Long Valley
THE GALLERIES
Ash
Flexford
DAPDUNE WHARF
CATH.
Guildford
Heath End
Badshot Lea
Upper Hale
Tongham
Hogs Back
Wanborough
Onslow Village
Littleton
Compton
LOSELEY HO.
Shalford
Chilworth
Albury
Shere
Gomshall
Hog Patch
Farnham
Dippenhall
Runfold
Seale
Puttenham
The Sands
Wrecclesham
WAVERLEY ABBEY
Shackleford
Hurtmore
Farncombe
Blackheath
Brook
Sutton
Wonersh
Bramley
Farley Green
Norney
Peper Harow
Eashing
Godalming
GODALMING MUS.
Shamley Green
Hurt Wood
The Bourne
Rowledge
BIRDWORLD
OLD KILN MUS.
Tilford
Elstead
Milford
Thorncombe Street
Grafham
Rowly
Ewhurst
Spreakley
Millbridge
Bucks Horn Oak
Frensham
FRENSHAM COMMON
Rushmoor
THURSLEY
Wheelerstreet
Tuesley
WINKWORTH ARBORETUM
Hydestile
Hascombe
Cranleigh
Wheatley
Thursley
Witley
Bowlhead Green
Wormley
Hambledon
Churt
Sleaford
Brook
Sandhills
OAKHURST COTTAGE
Loxhill
Beacon Hill
HINDHEAD
Arford
Lindford
Headley
Hindhead
GIBBET HILL
Combe Common
Dunsfold
Chiddingfold
Alfold Crossways
Ellen's Green
Grayshott
Standford
Grayswood
RAMSTER GDN.
Alfold
Bramshott
Shottermill
Haslemere
Ramsnest Common
Alfold Bars
Tisman's Common
Conford
Hammer
Liphook
Camelsdale
Fisherstreet
Loxwood
Plaistow
Ifold
Longmoor Camp
Linchmere
Kingsley Green
HOLLYCOMBE STEAM COLLECTION
BLACK DOWN
Langley
Northchapel
Mackerel's Common
Roundstreet Common
Liss
Fernhurst
EBERNOE COMMON
Rake
Milland
Lurgashall
Balls Cross
Kirdford
Wisborough Green
Newpound Common
Hill Brow
Henley
Lickfold
Strood Green
Borden
Parbrook
Arun
Adversane
Rogate
Chithurst
Iping
Woolbeding
Easebourne
Lodsworth
Upperton
Halfway Bridge
PETWORTH HO.
Petworth
Bedham
Broadford Bridge
Dumpford
Trotton
Stedham
Midhurst
Tillington
North Heath
Nyewood
Minsted
Selham
Byworth
Codmore Hill
Gay Street
East Harting
West Lavington
South Ambersham
Stopham
Nutbourne
West Chiltington
Fittleworth
Pulborough
Heyshott
Coates
Marehill
Treyford
Bepton
S U R R E Y
D O W N S
N. H I L L S
0 1 2 3 miles
0 1 2 3 4 5 km

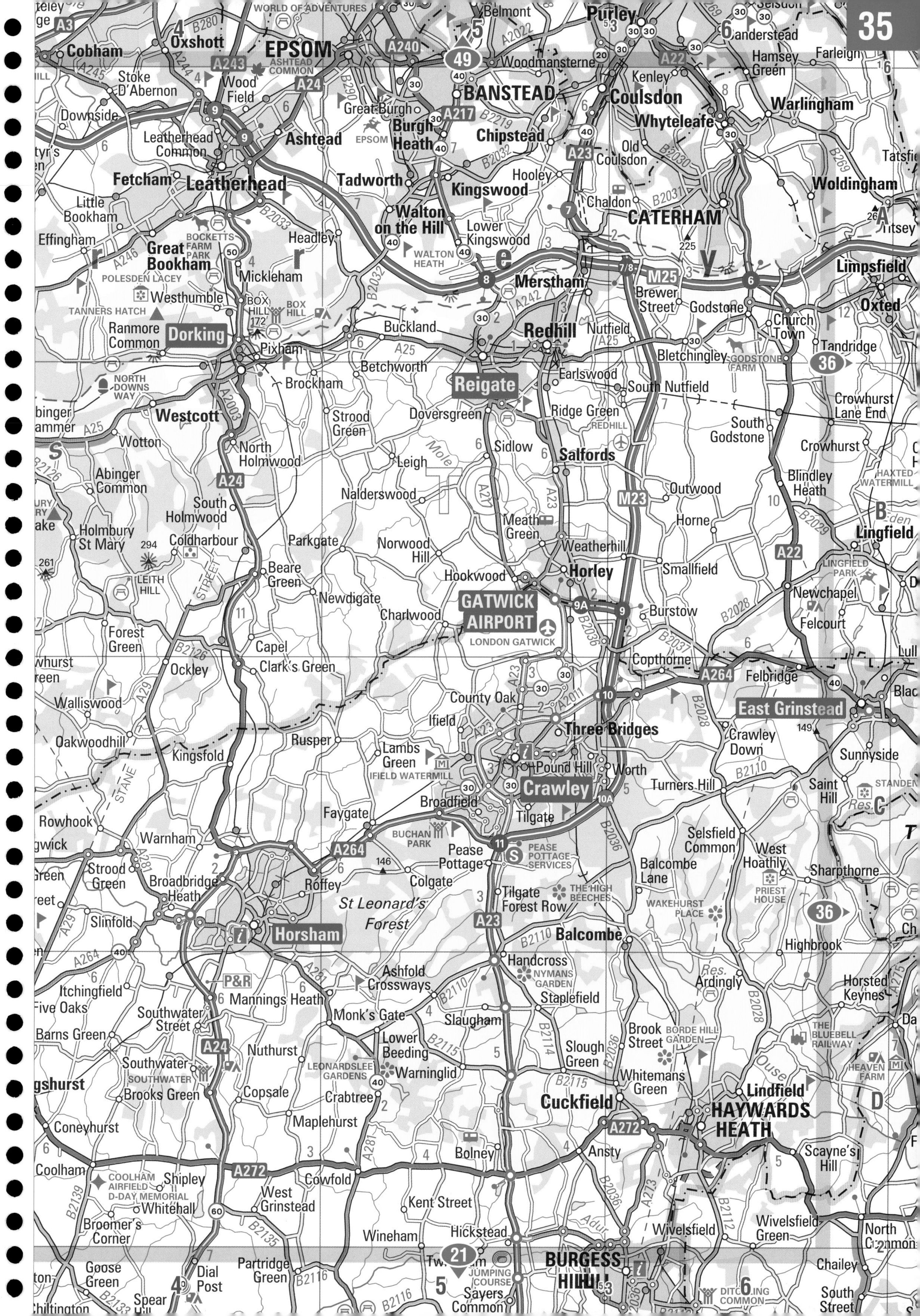

Cobham
Oxshott
EPSOM
Purley
Sanderstead
Belmont
Woodmansterne
BANSTEAD
Coulsdon
Kenley
Hamsey Green
Farleigh
Warlingham
Whyteleafe
Stoke D'Abernon
Wood Field
Downside
Great Burgh
Burgh Heath
Chipstead
Old Coulsdon
Ashtead
Leatherhead Common
Fetcham
Leatherhead
Tadworth
Kingswood
Hooley
Woldingham
Little Bookham
Walton on the Hill
Lower Kingswood
Chaldon
CATERHAM
Effingham
Great Bookham
Headley
Mickleham
Merstham
Limpsfield
Oxted
Westhumble
Brewer Street
Godstone
Church Town
Ranmore Common
Dorking
Pixham
Buckland
Redhill
Nutfield
Bletchingley
Tandridge
Brockham
Betchworth
Reigate
Earlswood
South Nutfield
Westcott
Doversgreen
Ridge Green
Crowhurst Lane End
Strood Green
South Godstone
Wotton
North Holmwood
Leigh
Sidlow
Salfords
Crowhurst
Abinger Common
Nalderswood
Outwood
Blindley Heath
South Holmwood
Meath Green
Horne
Lingfield
Holmbury St Mary
Coldharbour
Parkgate
Norwood Hill
Weatherhill
Beare Green
Hookwood
Horley
Smallfield
Newdigate
GATWICK AIRPORT
Newchapel
Charlwood
Burstow
Felcourt
Forest Green
Capel
Copthorne
Ockley
Clark's Green
Felbridge
Walliswood
County Oak
East Grinstead
Ifield
Three Bridges
Crawley Down
Oakwoodhill
Rusper
Kingsfold
Lambs Green
Pound Hill
Worth
Sunnyside
Crawley
Turners Hill
Saint Hill
Rowhook
Faygate
Broadfield
Tilgate
Warnham
Selsfield Common
West Hoathly
Pease Pottage
Strood Green
Balcombe Lane
Sharpthorne
Broadbridge Heath
Roffey
Colgate
St Leonard's Forest
Tilgate Forest Row
Slinfold
Horsham
Balcombe
Highbrook
Handcross
Ashfold Crossways
Ardingly
Itchingfield
Staplefield
Horsted Keynes
Five Oaks
Mannings Heath
Monk's Gate
Slaugham
Southwater Street
Barns Green
Lower Beeding
Brook Street
Nuthurst
Slough Green
Southwater
Warninglid
Whitemans Green
Lindfield
Brooks Green
Copsale
Crabtree
Cuckfield
HAYWARDS HEATH
Maplehurst
Coneyhurst
Bolney
Ansty
Scayne's Hill
Coolham
Shipley
Cowfold
West Grinstead
Kent Street
Whitehall
Broomer's Corner
Wineham
Hickstead
Wivelsfield
Wivelsfield Green
North Chailey
Goose Green
Dial Post
Partridge Green
Twineham
BURGESS HILL
Chailey
Spear Hill
Sayers Common
South Street

Leaves Green
Downe
DARWIN MUSEUM
Pratt's Bottom
Badger's Mount
Halstead
M25
Shoreham
Fairseat
Hamsey Green
Farleigh
BIGGIN HILL
50
Biggin Hill
Cudham
Knockholt Pound
Knockholt
Otford
Wrotham
Warlingham
Kemsing
Heaverham
M20
M26
Wrotham Heath
South Street
Chevening
NORTH DOWNS WAY
Tatsfield
Dunton Green
Seal
Borough Green
Platt
Woldingham
Chipstead
Riverhead
Ightham
Crouch
CLACKET LANE SERVICES
Titsey
Brasted
Sundridge
Sevenoaks
Stone Street
Claygate Cross
Westerham
QUEBEC HO.
KNOLE
Ivy Hatch
Plaxtol
Merewo
Limpsfield
Brasted Chart
The Chart
IGHTHAM MOTE
OLD SOAR MANOR
Dunk's Green
Oxted
Limpsfield Chart
SQUERRYES COURT
EMMETTS
Cross Keys
Whitley Row
Underriver
Shipbourne
West Peckham
Church Town
Tandridge
CHARTWELL
Ide Hill
Crockham Hill
Toy's Hill
Sevenoaks Weald
Oakhurst
Coldharbour
BROADVIEW GARDEN
Pittswood
Hadlow
GODSTONE FARM
35
Pootings
Four Elms
Res.
Hildenborough
Higham Wood
East Peckham
Crowhurst Lane End
Marlpit Hill
Hilden Park
Golden Green
South Godstone
Crowhurst
Crouch House Green
How Green
Chiddingstone Causeway
TONBRIDGE CASTLE
Medway
Blindley Heath
HAXTED WATERMILL
Edenbridge
Bough Beech
CHIDDINGSTONE CASTLE
Leigh
Brook Street
TONBRIDGE
Five Oak Green
Hever
Chiddingstone
PENSHURST PLACE
HAYSDEN
Tudeley
ALL SAINTS CHURCH
Lingfield
Marsh Green
HEVER CASTLE AND GARDENS
Bidborough
LINGFIELD PARK
Dormansland
Markbeech
Penshurst
Southborough
High Brooms
Newchapel
Chiddingstone Hoath
GREATHED MANOR
Speldhurst
Matfield
Felcourt
Cowden
MUS. & ART GALL.
Pembury
Lullenden
Hammerwood
Blackham
Fordcombe
Rusthall
ROYAL TUNBRIDGE WELLS
Felbridge
Blackwell
Ashurst
Langton Green
East Grinstead
HAMMERWOOD PARK
Hawkenbury
Lamberhurst Quarter
Crawley Down
Sunnyside
Ashurstwood
SPA VALLEY RAILWAY
Groombridge
Bells Yew Green
Saint Hill
STANDEN
Forest Row
Hartfield
Withyham
Eridge Green
Frant
West Hoathly
Coleman's Hatch
Upper Hartfield
Lye Green
Wood's Green
Sharpthorne
Friar's Gate
Boarshead
Durgates
PRIEST HOUSE
Wych Cross
Mark Cross
Highbrook
Chelwood Gate
ASHDOWN FOREST LLAMA PARK
Crowborough
Bestbeech Hill
ASHDOWN FOREST
Poundfield
Town Row
Riseden
Horsted Keynes
Chelwood Common
Jarvis Brook
Rotherfield
Tidebrook
Nutley
Duddleswell
Danehill
Coggins Mill
Cackle Street
Fairwarp
High Hurstwood
Mayfield
HEAVEN FARM
Butcher's Cross
Lindfield
Sheffield Green
Splayne's Green
Hadlow Down
Five Ashes
Rother
HAYWARDS HEATH
SHEFFIELD PARK
Maresfield
Pound Green
Burwash Common
Fletching
THE BLUEBELL RAILWAY
Scayne's Hill
Buxted
Ringles Cross
Cross in Hand
Broad Oak
Burwash Weald
Grisling Common
BLACKBOYS
Cade Street
Uckfield
Newick
Wivelsfield Green
North Common
Framfield
Blackboys
Heathfield
Punnett's Town
Old Heathfield
Ridgewood
22
Waldron
Little London
E. SUSSEX NATIONAL
Maynard's Green
Rushlake Green
Foxhunt Green
DITCHLING COMMON
KENT
EAST SUSSEX
HIGH WEALD

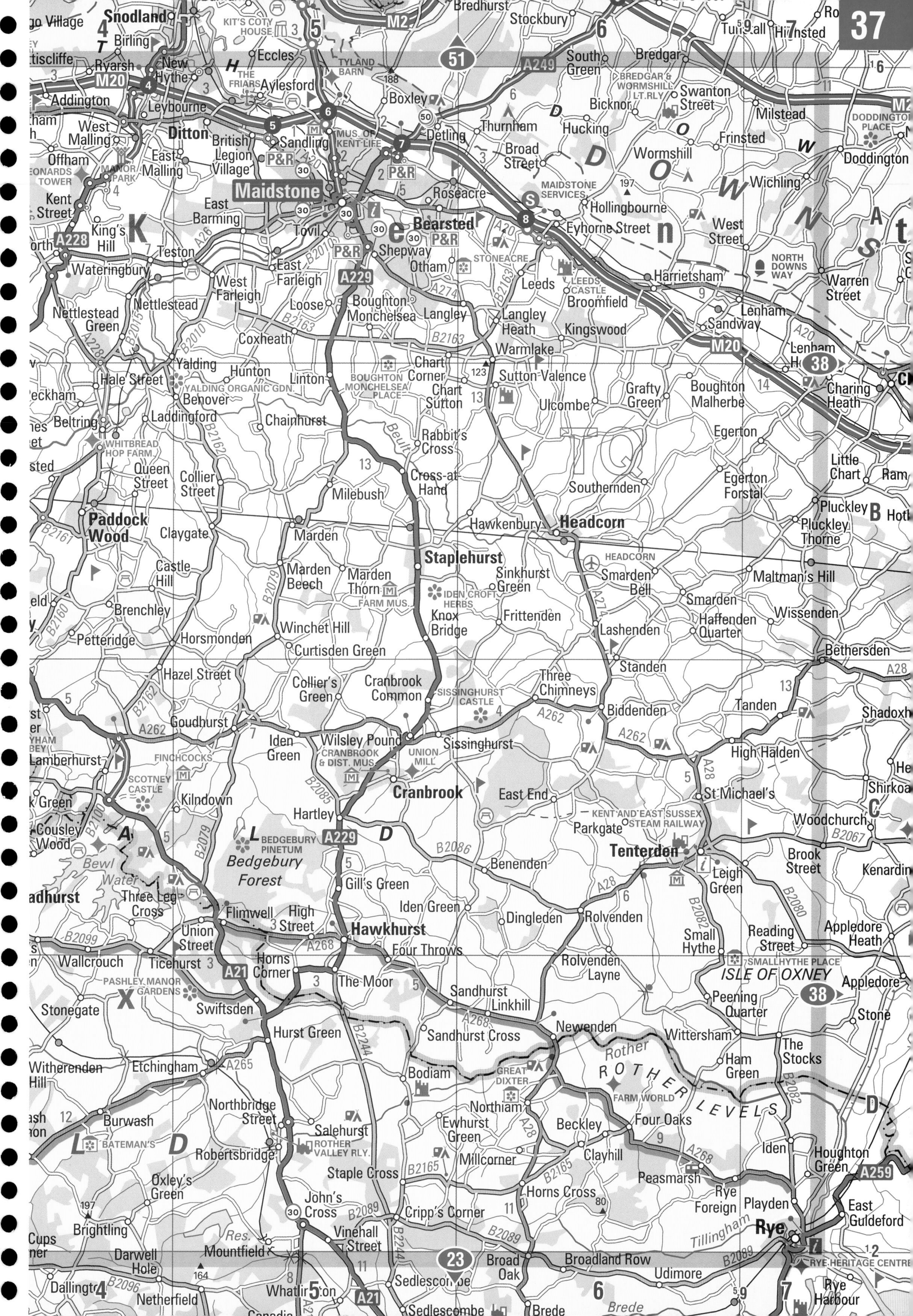

Snodland
Birling
Ryarsh
New Hythe
Eccles
Aylesford
Addington
Leybourne
West Malling
Ditton
British Legion Village
Sandling
East Malling
Offham
Maidstone
Boxley
Detling
Thurnham
Bredhurst
Stockbury
South Green
Bredgar
Bicknor
Hucking
Swanton Street
Milstead
Frinsted
Wormshill
Doddington
Wichling
Broad Street
Roseacre
Hollingbourne
Eyhorne Street
Bearsted
Shepway
Otham
East Barming
Barming
Tovil
King's Hill
Teston
Wateringbury
West Farleigh
East Farleigh
Nettlestead
Nettlestead Green
Loose
Boughton Monchelsea
Langley
Langley Heath
Leeds
Broomfield
Harrietsham
Lenham
Sandway
Warren Street
West Street
Kingswood
Coxheath
Yalding
Hunton
Linton
Chart Corner
Warmlake
Sutton Valence
Chart Sutton
Ulcombe
Grafty Green
Boughton Malherbe
Lenham Heath
Charing Heath
Hale Street
Benover
Laddingford
Beltring
Chainhurst
Rabbit's Cross
Egerton
Queen Street
Collier Street
Milebush
Cross-at-Hand
Southernden
Egerton Forstal
Little Chart
Paddock Wood
Claygate
Marden
Staplehurst
Hawkenbury
Headcorn
Pluckley
Pluckley Thorne
Castle Hill
Marden Beech
Marden Thorn
Sinkhurst Green
Smarden Bell
Maltman's Hill
Brenchley
Knox Bridge
Frittenden
Smarden
Haffenden Quarter
Wissenden
Petteridge
Horsmonden
Winchet Hill
Curtisden Green
Lashenden
Bethersden
Hazel Street
Collier's Green
Cranbrook Common
Three Chimneys
Standen
Biddenden
Tanden
Goudhurst
Iden Green
Wilsley Pound
Sissinghurst
High Halden
Lamberhurst
Kilndown
Cranbrook
East End
St Michael's
Hartley
Parkgate
Woodchurch
Tenterden
Benenden
Brook Street
Leigh Green
Bedgebury Forest
Gill's Green
Iden Green
Dingleden
Rolvenden
Three Leg Cross
Flimwell
High Street
Hawkhurst
Small Hythe
Reading Street
Appledore Heath
Union Street
Wallcrouch
Ticehurst
Horns Corner
Four Throws
The Moor
Rolvenden Layne
ISLE OF OXNEY
Appledore
Stonegate
Swiftsden
Sandhurst
Linkhill
Peening Quarter
Newenden
Wittersham
Stone
Hurst Green
Sandhurst Cross
The Stocks
Ham Green
Etchingham
Bodiam
ROTHER LEVELS
Northbridge Street
Northiam
Beckley
Four Oaks
Burwash
Salehurst
Ewhurst Green
Robertsbridge
Millcorner
Clayhill
Iden
Houghton Green
Staple Cross
Peasmarsh
Oxley's Green
Horns Cross
Rye Foreign
Playden
East Guldeford
John's Cross
Cripp's Corner
Brightling
Vinehall Street
Rye
Darwell Hole
Mountfield
Broad Oak
Broadland Row
Udimore
Dallington
Netherfield
Whatlington
Sedlescombe
Brede
Rye Harbour

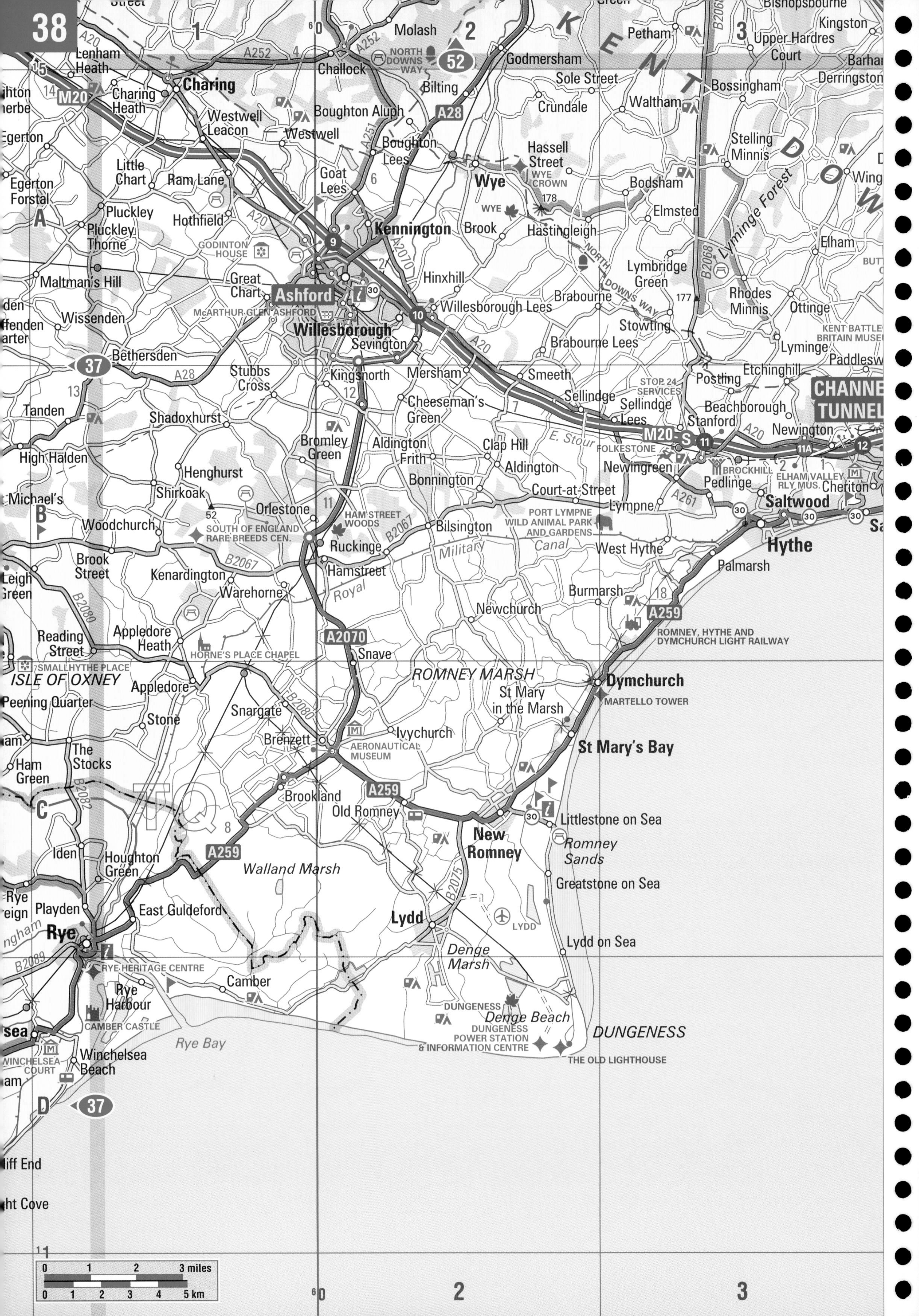
Molash
NORTH DOWNS WAY
Godmersham
KENT DOWNS
Petham
Bishopsbourne
Kingston
Upper Hardres Court
Barham
Derringston
Lenham Heath
Charing
Charing Heath
Challock
Bilting
Sole Street
Crundale
Waltham
Bossingham
Westwell Leacon
Westwell
Boughton Aluph
Boughton Lees
Egerton
Egerton Forstal
Little Chart
Ram Lane
Goat Lees
Hassell Street
WYE CROWN
Wye
Bodsham
Stelling Minnis
Wing
Lyminge Forest
Pluckley
Pluckley Thorne
Hothfield
GODINTON HOUSE
Kennington
Brook
WYE
Hastingleigh
Elmsted
Elham
Maltman's Hill
Great Chart
Ashford
McARTHUR GLEN ASHFORD
Hinxhill
Willesborough Lees
Lymbridge Green
Brabourne
Rhodes Minnis
Ottinge
Wissenden
Willesborough
Sevington
Stowting
Brabourne Lees
KENT BATTLE OF BRITAIN MUSEUM
Lyminge
Paddlesworth
Bethersden
Stubbs Cross
Kingsnorth
Mersham
Smeeth
STOP 24 SERVICES
Postling
Etchinghill
CHANNEL TUNNEL
Tanden
Shadoxhurst
Cheeseman's Green
Sellindge
Sellindge Lees
Beachborough
Stanford
Newington
High Halden
Bromley Green
Aldington Frith
Clap Hill
E. Stour
FOLKESTONE
Henghurst
Aldington
Newingreen
BROCKHILL
Pedlinge
ELHAM VALLEY RLY MUS.
Cheriton
Shirkoak
Bonnington
Court-at-Street
St Michael's
Orlestone
PORT LYMPNE WILD ANIMAL PARK AND GARDENS
Lympne
Saltwood
Woodchurch
SOUTH OF ENGLAND RARE BREEDS CEN.
HAM STREET WOODS
Bilsington
Hythe
Ruckinge
Royal Military Canal
West Hythe
Brook Street
Kenardington
Hamstreet
Palmarsh
Leigh Green
Warehorne
Burmarsh
Newchurch
Reading Street
Appledore Heath
HORNE'S PLACE CHAPEL
Snave
ROMNEY, HYTHE AND DYMCHURCH LIGHT RAILWAY
SMALLHYTHE PLACE
ISLE OF OXNEY
Appledore
ROMNEY MARSH
Dymchurch
MARTELLO TOWER
Peening Quarter
Stone
Snargate
St Mary in the Marsh
Brenzett
Ivychurch
AERONAUTICAL MUSEUM
St Mary's Bay
The Stocks
Ham Green
TQ
Brookland
Old Romney
Littlestone on Sea
New Romney
Romney Sands
Iden
Houghton Green
Walland Marsh
Greatstone on Sea
Rye Foreign
Playden
East Guldeford
Lydd
LYDD
Rye
Denge Marsh
Lydd on Sea
RYE HERITAGE CENTRE
Camber
Rye Harbour
DUNGENESS
Denge Beach
CAMBER CASTLE
DUNGENESS POWER STATION & INFORMATION CENTRE
DUNGENESS
THE OLD LIGHTHOUSE
Rye Bay
Winchelsea
WINCHELSEA COURT
Winchelsea Beach
Cliff End
Fairlight Cove
0 1 2 3 miles
0 1 2 3 4 5 km

Nonington
Snowdown
Tilmanstone
Elvington
Northbourne
Great Mongeham
DEAL CASTLE
THE DOWNS
Walmer
WALMER CASTLE AND GARDENS
Womenswold
Barfrestone
EAST KENT RLY.
Woolage Green
Eythorne
East Studdal
Sutton
Ripple
Kingsdown
Coxhill
Shepherdswell
West Langdon
Ringwould
Coldred
East Langdon
Martin
Martin Mill
Denton
LYDDEN
Wootton
Whitfield
Guston
St Margaret's at Cliffe
Selsted
Lydden
LYDDEN TEMPLE EWELL
ST. JOHN'S COMMANDERY
Ewell Minnis
Temple Ewell
West Cliffe
THE BAY MUSEUM
St Margaret's Bay
Swingfield Street
CRABBLE CORN MILL
THE PINES GARDEN
Swingfield Minnis
Buckland
SOUTH FORELAND
Alkham
ROMAN PAINTED HOUSE
WHITE CLIFFS (N.T.)
Densole
Drellingore
Maxton
CASTLE & HELLFIRE CORNER
CALAIS 1:10
DUNKERQUE 1:50
Hawkinge
West Hougham
Farthingloe
DOVER
Aycliff
DE BRADELEI WHARF
Capel le Ferne
SAMPHIRE HO.
BOULOGNE 0:50
EASTCLIFFS AND WARREN
East Wear Bay
Folkestone
ROTUNDA
CLIFF LIFT
Sandgate
A2
A20
A256
A258
A260
B2011
TR
CHANNEL TUNNEL
ENGLISH CHANNEL
A
B
C
D
4
5
6

Pontardawe
Clydach
Ynystawe
Morriston
Llansamlet
Swansea
(Abertawe)
Port Tennant
Foxhole
SWANSEA MUSEUM
NATIONAL WATERFRONT MUSEUM
PLANTASIA
Skewen
Llandarcy
Neath
(Castell-Nedd)
NEATH MUSEUM
Neath Abbey
Cadoxton-Juxta-Neath
Tonna
Aberdulais
Cilfrew
Bryn-coch
Birchgrove
Rhydding
Heol-las
Glais
Alltwen
Trebanos
Rhyd-y-fro
Cilybebyll
Gellinudd
Rhôs
Crynant
Mynydd March-Hywel
CEFNCOED COLLIERY MUS.
VALE OF NEATH
CWM NEDD
Resolven
RESOLVEN MTN.
Melincourt
Clyne
Blaengwrach
Cwmgwrach
Rhigos
Cwm-hwnt
Blaenrhondda
Tynewydd
Treherbert
Neath
Port Talbot
(Castell-Nedd
Port Talbot)
Glyncorrwg
Blaen-gwynfi
Aber-gwynfi
Cwm-parc
Cymer
Croeserw
Duffryn
Caerau
Spelter
SOUTH WALES MINERS MUSEUM
AFAN ARGOED
FOEL Y DYFFRYN
Dyffryn
Nantyffyllon
Blaengarw
Pontycymer
Nant-y-moel
WERFA
Wyndham
Price Town
MAESTEG
Cwmfelin
Garth
Llangynwyd
Pont Rhyd-y-cyff
Ogmore Vale
Baglan
Briton Ferry
Cimla
THE GNOLL
Pontrhydyfen
Pwll-y-glaw
Brynbryddan
MYNYDD DINAS
Cwmafan
Bryn
Aberavon
Port Talbot
Goybre
Taibach
Margam
Groes
MYNYDD MARGAM
MOEL TON-MAWR
MARGAM
MARGAM ABBEY AND STONES MUSEUM
SWANSEA BAY
BAE ABERTAWE
Bridgend
(Pen-y-bont ar Ogwr)
Bettws
Llangeinor
Coytrahen
Tondu
Aberkenfig
Brynmenyn
Bryncethin
Sarn
SARN PARK SERVICES
McARTHUR GLEN BRIDGEND
Kenfig Hill
Cefn Cross
Cefn Cribbwr
Pyle
(Y Pîl)
North Cornelly
Kenfig
Mawdlam
KENFIG POOL AND DUNES
Kenfig Burrows
South Cornelly
Pen-y-fai
Pendre
Coity
COITY CASTLE
Bridgend
(Pen-y-bont ar Ogwr)
Laleston
Oldcastle
Coychurch
Treoes
Corntown
ROYAL PORTHCAWL
Nottage
Hutchwns
Newton
Tythegston
Merthyr Mawr
OGMORE CASTLE
Clevis
Porthcawl
MERTHYR MAWR WARREN
Ogmore
Ewenny
Ogmore-by-Sea
St Brides Major
Colwinston
Southerndown
Penuchadre
GLENMORGAN HERITAGE COAST CENTRE
Wick
Broughton
Monknash
Marcross
St Donat's
Nash Pt.
Trwyn yr As
Tusker Rock
SS
M4
A465
A48
A4107
A4063
A4061
0 1 2 3 miles
0 1 2 3 4 5 km

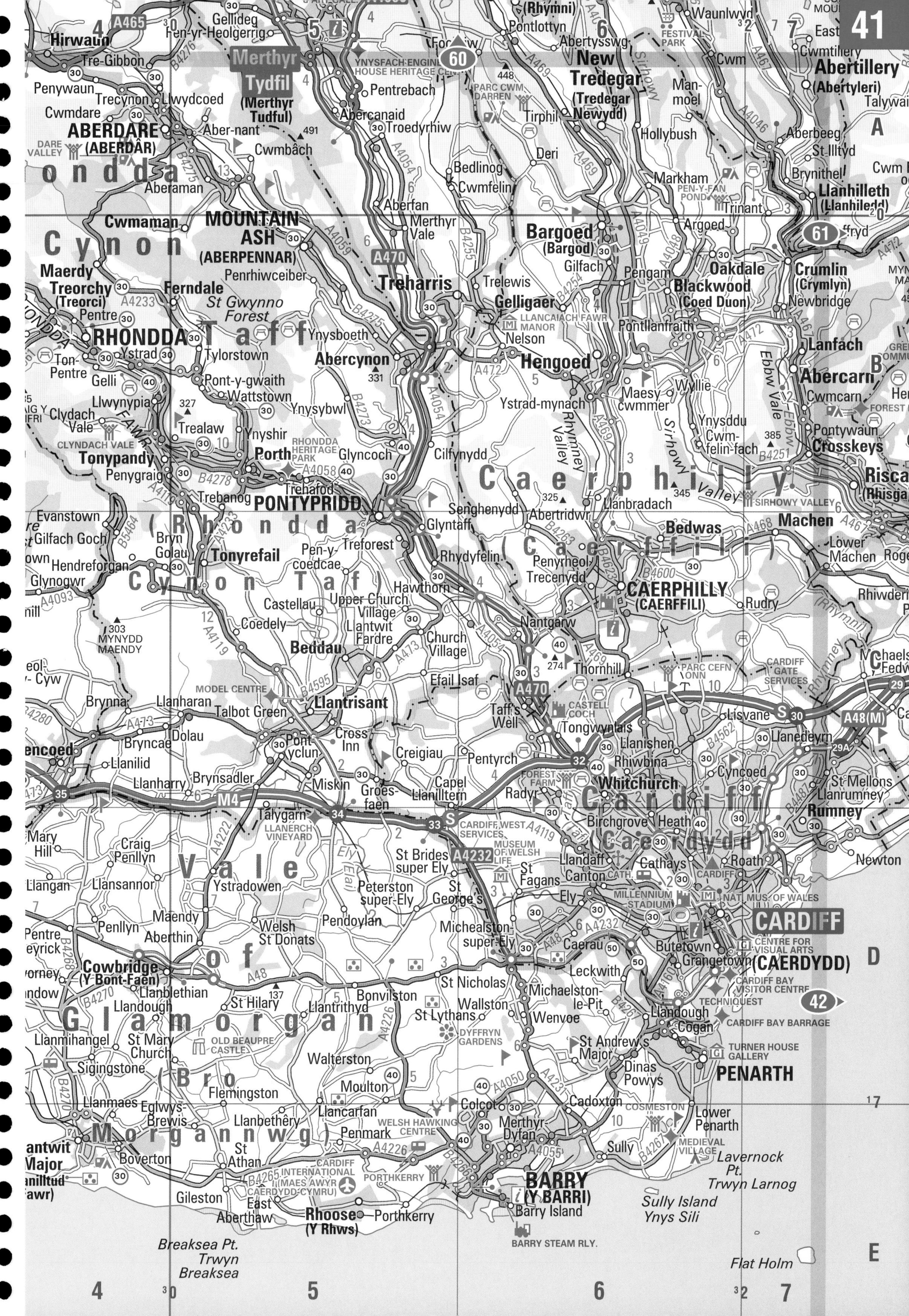
Hirwaun
Tre-Gibbon
Penywaun
Trecynon
Llwydcoed
Cwmdare
ABERDARE
(ABERDÂR)
DARE VALLEY
Aber-nant
Cwmbâch
Aberaman
Gellideg
Pen-yr-Heolgerrig
Merthyr Tydfil
(Merthyr Tudful)
YNYSFACH ENGINE HOUSE HERITAGE CENTRE
Pentrebach
Abercanaid
Troedyrhiw
Aberfan
Merthyr Vale
Rhondda
Cwmaman
MOUNTAIN ASH
(ABERPENNAR)
Penrhiwceiber
Cynon
Maerdy
Treorchy
(Treorci)
Ferndale
St Gwynno Forest
Pentre
RHONDDA
Ystrad
Ton-Pentre
Gelli
Tylorstown
Ynysboeth
Abercynon
Treharris
Pont-y-gwaith
Wattstown
Llwynypia
Clydach Vale
CLYNDACH VALE
Trealaw
Ynyshir
Ynysybwl
Tonypandy
Penygraig
Porth
RHONDDA HERITAGE PARK
Glyncoch
Trebanog
Trehafod
PONTYPRIDD
Evanstown
Gilfach Goch
Bryn Golau
Tonyrefail
Hendreforgan
Glynogwr
(Rhondda Cynon Taf)
Pen-y-coedcae
Treforest
Glyntaff
Rhydyfelin
Hawthorn
Castellau
Upper Church Village
Llantwit Fardre
Coedely
Beddau
Church Village
MYNYDD MAENDY
Efail Isaf
MODEL CENTRE
Llantrisant
Brynna
Llanharan
Talbot Green
Dolau
Bryncae
Pont-yclun
Cross Inn
Creigiau
Pentyrch
Llanilid
Llanharry
Brynsadler
Miskin
Groes-faen
Capel Llanilltern
Radyr
Talygarn
LLANERCH VINEYARD
CARDIFF WEST SERVICES
M4
Mary Hill
Craig Penllyn
Llangan
Llansannor
Vale of Glamorgan
(Bro Morgannwg)
Ystradowen
Peterston super-Ely
St Brides super Ely
St George's
MUSEUM OF WELSH LIFE
St Fagans
Pendoylan
Welsh St Donats
Penllyn
Maendy
Aberthin
Pentre Meyrick
Cowbridge
(Y Bont-Faen)
Llanblethian
Llandough
St Hilary
Llantrithyd
Bonvilston
Michealston-super-Ely
St Nicholas
Wallston
St Lythans
DYFFRYN GARDENS
Llanmihangel
St Mary Church
OLD BEAUPRE CASTLE
Sigingstone
Walterston
Flemingston
Moulton
Llanmaes
Eglwys-Brewis
Llanbethery
Llancarfan
WELSH HAWKING CENTRE
Penmark
Llantwit Major
(Llanilltud Fawr)
Boverton
St Athan
CARDIFF INTERNATIONAL (MAES AWYR CAERDYDD-CYMRU)
PORTHKERRY
Gileston
East Aberthaw
Rhoose
(Y Rhws)
Porthkerry
Breaksea Pt.
Trwyn Breaksea
(Rhymni)
Pontlottyn
Abertysswg
Fochriw
PARC CWM DARREN
New Tredegar
(Tredegar Newydd)
Tirphil
Deri
Bedlinog
Cwmfelin
Bargoed
(Bargod)
Gilfach
Trelewis
Gelligaer
LLANCAIACH FAWR MANOR
Nelson
Hengoed
Ystrad-mynach
Rhymney Valley
Cilfynydd
Caerphilly
(Caerffili)
Senghenydd
Abertridwr
Llanbradach
Penyrheol
Trecenydd
CAERPHILLY
(CAERFFILI)
Nantgarw
Thornhill
Taff's Well
CASTELL COCH
Tongwynlais
Waunlwyd
FESTIVAL PARK
Cwm
Man-moel
Hollybush
Markham
PEN-Y-FAN POND
Trinant
Argoed
Pengam
Blackwood
(Coed Duon)
Oakdale
Pontllanfraith
Maesycwmmer
Wyllie
Ynysddu
Cwm-felin-fach
Sirhowy Valley
SIRHOWY VALLEY
Bedwas
Machen
Lower Machen
Rudry
Abertillery
(Abertyleri)
Cwmtillery
Aberbeeg
St Illtyd
Brynithel
Llanhilleth
(Llanhiledd)
Crumlin
(Crymlyn)
Newbridge
Lanfach
Abercarn
Cwmcarn
FOREST DRIVE
Pontywaun
Crosskeys
Risca
(Rhisga)
Ebbw Vale
PARC CEFN ONN
CARDIFF GATE SERVICES
Lisvane
Llanedeyrn
Llanishen
Rhiwbina
Cyncoed
St Mellons
Llanrumney
Rumney
FOREST FARM
Whitchurch
Cardiff
(Caerdydd)
Birchgrove
Heath
Llandaff
Cathays
Roath
Canton
CARDIFF CASTLE
Ely
MILLENNIUM STADIUM
NAT. MUS. OF WALES
CARDIFF
CENTRE FOR VISUAL ARTS
(CAERDYDD)
Caerau
Butetown
Grangetown
Leckwith
CARDIFF BAY VISITOR CENTRE
TECHNIQUEST
Michaelston-le-Pit
Wenvoe
Llandough
Cogan
CARDIFF BAY BARRAGE
St Andrew's Major
TURNER HOUSE GALLERY
Dinas Powys
PENARTH
Cadoxton
COSMESTON
Lower Penarth
MEDIEVAL VILLAGE
Merthyr-Dyfan
Colcot
Sully
Lavernock Pt.
Trwyn Larnog
BARRY
(Y BARRI)
Barry Island
BARRY STEAM RLY.
Sully Island
Ynys Sili
Flat Holm
Newton
A465
A470
A4232
A48(M)
A48
A4119
A4054
A4059
A469
A467
A4226
A4050
A4055
60
61
42
4
5
6
7
A
B
D
E

Crosskeys
Risca
(Rhisga)
Machen
Lower Machen
Rogerstone
Rudry
Rhiwderin
Pentre-poeth
Bassaleg
Bettws
Malpas
Caerleon
(Caerllion)
LEGIONARY MUS.
Cat's Ash
Seymour
Llanvaches
Llanbeder
Penhow
PENHOW WOODLANDS
Caerwent
Crick
RUNSTON CHAPEL
Highmoor Hill
Christchurch
FOURTEEN LOCKS
Maindee
Newport
(Casnewydd)
CATH
MUS. & GALLERY
Liswerry
WELSH NATIONAL VELODROME
Langstone
Llanmartin
St Bride's Netherwent
MAGOR SERVICES
Llanwern
Wilcrick
Bishton
Llandevenny
Magor
Llanfihangel-Rogiet
Rogiet
Undy
Caldicot
TOLL
Duffryn
TREDEGAR HOUSE
Michaelston-y-Fedw
CARDIFF GATE SERVICES
Newport
(Casnewydd)
Caldicot Level
Pye Corner
Redwick
Summerleaze
Nash
Whitson
Goldcliff
Usk (Wysg)
Lisvane
Castleton
Coedkernew
Llanedeyrn
Marshfield
Cyncoed
Blacktown
St Brides Wentlooge
St Mellons
Llanrumney
Peterstone Wentlooge
Rumney
Roath
Newton
NAT. MUS. OF WALES
CARDIFF
CENTRE FOR VISUAL ARTS
(CAERDYDD)
CARDIFF BAY VISITOR CENTRE
CARDIFF BAY BARRAGE
TURNER HOUSE GALLERY
PENARTH
Lavernock Pt.
Flat Holm
Steep Holm
ABER HAFREN
MOUTH OF THE SEVERN
ST
Avonmouth
Battery Pt.
Portishead
West Hill
Redcliff Bay
Sheepway
Weston-in-Gordano
Clapton-in-Gordano
Walton-in-Gordano
GORDANO VALLEY
NOAH'S ARK ZOO FARM
Clevedon
CLEVEDON COURT
Stone-edge Batch
Tickenham
Nailsea
North Somerset
West End
East End
Farleigh
Kenn
Chelvey
Brockley
West Town
Kingston Seymour
North End
Claverham
Yatton
Cleeve
BRISTOL INTERNATIONAL
Sand Pt.
Wick St Lawrence
Sand Bay
Bourton
Hewish
Congresbury
Puxton
Wrington
Kewstoke
Worle
Milton
TOLL
Brinsea
Lower Langford
Weston-super-Mare
West Wick
Weston Bay
HELICOPTER MUS.
Locking
Hutton
Banwell
Churchill
Sandford
Burrington
Blagdon
Star
Brean Down
Uphill
BLEADON HILL
Christon
Bleadon
Winscombe
Sidcot
Shipham
Charterhouse
Brean
Loxton
Compton Bishop
KING JOHN'S HUNTING LODGE
Cross
BERROW
ANIMAL FARM ADVENTURE PARK
FLATS
Lympsham
Eastertown
Lower Weare
Axbridge
Cheddar Res.
CHEDDAR SHOWCAVES AND GORGE
Cheddar
Biddisham
Weare
SEDGEMOOR SERVICES
Gore Sands
East Brent
Rooks Bridge
Badgworth
Berrow
Brent Knoll
Stone Allerton
Chapel Allerton
Clewer
Draycott
Rodney Stoke
Burnham-on-Sea
Edithmead
Cocklake
West Stoughton
Mark Causeway
Mark
Blackford
Wedmore
0 1 2 3 miles
0 1 2 3 4 5 km

South Gloucestershire
BRISTOL
Bristol
Bath and N.E. Somerset
Bath
FILTON
MANGOTSFIELD
KEYNSHAM
Kingswood
Thornbury
Yate
Chipping Sodbury
Patchway
Hanham
Long Ashton
Paulton
Radstock
Midsomer Norton
Peasedown St John
COTSWOLDS
M4
M5
M32
M48
M49
A4
A36
A37
A38
A46
A4174

Alderley
Leighterton
Doughton
A433
63
Shipton Moyne
Brokenborough
Hankerton
Upper Minety
Minety
Hillesley
WESTONBIRT ARBORETUM
Westonbirt
Oldbury on the Hill
Filands
A350
Perry Green
Charlton
B4040
Easton Grey
Garsdon
Hawkesbury Upton
Hawkesbury
Didmarton
Sopworth
Sherston
Malmesbury
Queen Street
HORTON COURT
Foxley
Lea
Cleverton
The Common
FOSS WAY
Norton
Corston
Little Somerford
B4042
Luckington
Little Badminton
Brinkworth
Callow Hill
A46
Rodbourne
Old Sodbury
Badminton
Alderton
Hullavington
Startley
Dauntsey
Great Somerford
Grittenham
B4040
Lower Stanton St Quintin
Lower Seagry
Tockenham Wick
A3102
Acton Turville
Littleton Drew
Grittleton
Leigh Delamere
Stanton St Quintin
Upper Seagry
B4069
43
Tormarton
Burton
M4
17
Bradenstoke
Lyneham
Church End
B4122
Sutton Benger
Christian Malford
18
LEIGH DELAMERE SERVICES
Kington St Michael
A350
Foxham
Preston
Goatacre
West Kington
Nettleton
Castle Combe
B4039
Yatton Keynell
Kington Langley
West End
Spirthill
CASTLE COMBE
Langley Burrell
50
West Littleton
North Wraxall
Ford
A420
Hardenhuish
CHIPPENHAM MUS.
East Tytherton
Hilmarton
SHELDEN MANOR
West Tytherton
B4528
Chippenham
Marshfield
Slaughterford
Biddestone
128
A420
141
Bremhill
Cold Ashton
Thickwood
A4
Studley
Colerne
A4
Corsham
CORSHAM COURT
Easton
LACKHAM COUNTRYSIDE CENTRE
Derry Hill
Calne
Cherhill
St Catherine
BOWOOD HOUSE
189
Alcombe
Notton
A342
Mile Elm
A46
Hawthorn
Quemerford
Northend
LACOCK ABBEY
Calstone Wellington
Gastard
172
Sandy Lane
Batheaston
Box
B3109
Lacock
FOX TALBOT MUS.
Blackland
TOLL
A4
Neston
B3353
Bowden Hill
Stockley
Bath
Bathford
A365
Whitley
A350
Chittoe
260
MORGAN'S HILL
POSTAL MUS.
Shaw
Beanacre
Heddington
Bathampton
Monkton Farleigh
Atworth
Norrington Common
Sandridge
Bromham
1643
ABBEY
AMERICAN MUS.
South Wraxall
Broughton Common
A3102
St Edith's
242
ROUNDWAY HILL
BATH
Claverton
Broughton Gifford
Melksham
ROMAN BATHS
PRIOR PARK
Combe Down
GREAT CHALFIELD MANOR
Bradford Leigh
Bowerhill
A365
Rowde
Roundway
A36
A363
CANAL
Monkton Combe
B3110
Bradford-on-Avon
Holt
B3107
Avon
Sells Green
B3101
Devizes
B3108
THE COURTS
Seend Cleeve
Winsley
Kennet & Avon Canal
Turleigh
Staverton
Semington
Seend
BROADLEAS GARDENS
190
Limpley
Freshford
TITHE BARN
Poulshot
43
IFORD MANOR
BARTON FARM
Hilperton
A361
A360
A342
Twinhoe
Westwood
Trowle Common
Great Hinton
Stert
WESTWOOD MANOR
Potterne
Hinton Charterhouse
Farleigh Hungerford
Ashton Common
Bulkington
Keevil
Worton
Wedham
NORWOOD FARM
Trowbridge
Potterne Wick
Urchfont
A366
Steeple Ashton
BARROW
Norton St Philip
Wingfield
Marston
A363
Tellisford
B3098
Southwick
A361
West Ashton
Eastcott
A366
RODE BIRD GARDENS
B3109
North Bradley
Yarnbrook
Great Cheverell
Littleton Pannell
Easterton
Faulkland
Woolverton
Coulston
Heywood
Rode
Hawkeridge
Erlestoke
Market Lavington
BROKERSWOOD
Laverton
Little Cheverell
West Lavington
B3098
Hardington
Edington
Bratton
A362
Lullington
Beckington
BRATTON CAMP & WHITE HORSE
230
W i l t
Dinham
Rudge
Littleton Down
Gore Cross
Oldford
A36
Westbury Leigh
Westbury
A360
30
Dilton Marsh
Summer Down
West Lavington Down
Upton Scudamore
A350
Tilshead
0 1 2 3 miles
0 1 2 3 4 5 km

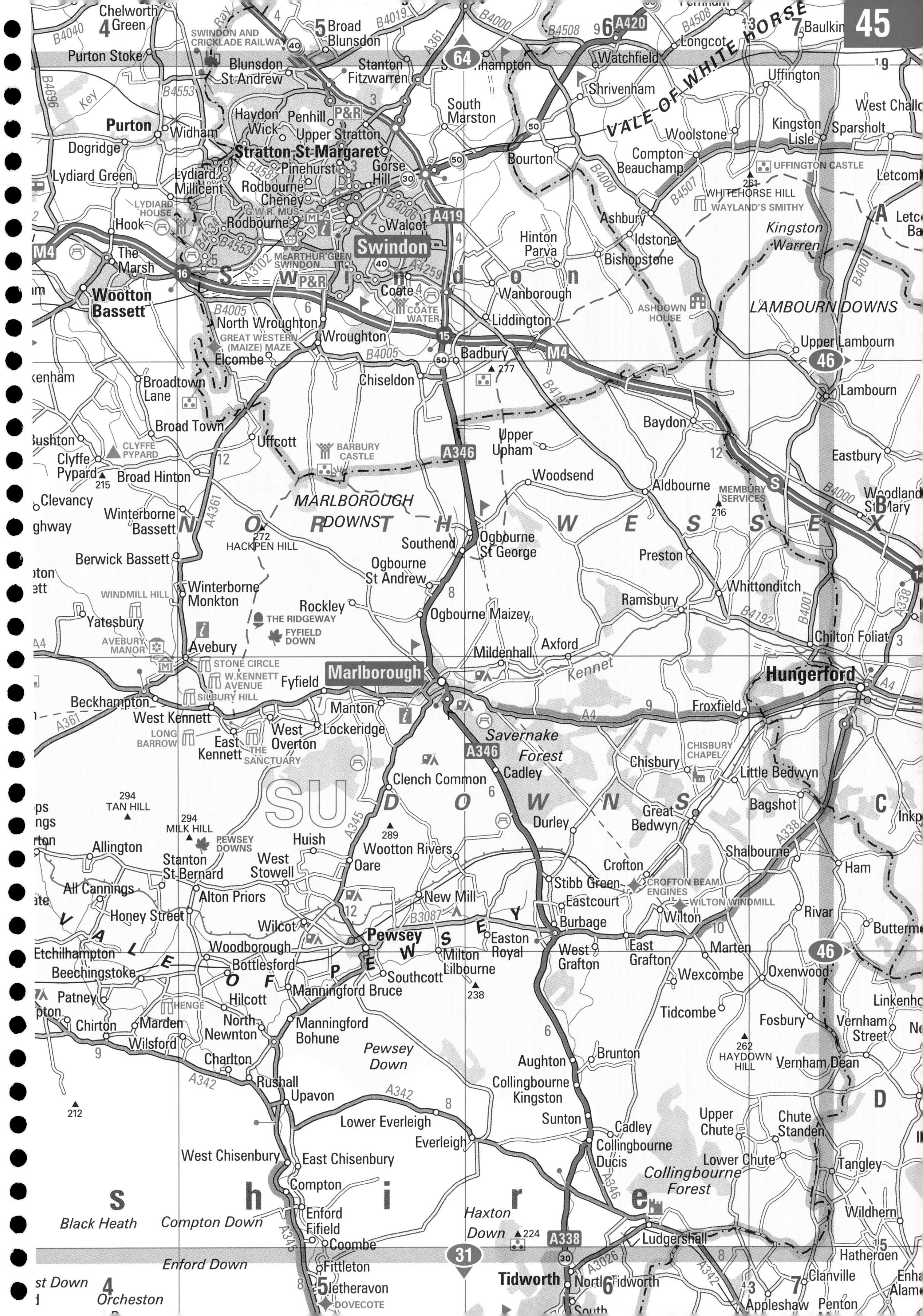
Chelworth Green
Broad Blunsdon
SWINDON AND CRICKLADE RAILWAY
Purton Stoke
Blunsdon St Andrew
Stanton Fitzwarren
South Marston
Watchfield
Longcot
VALE OF WHITE HORSE
Baulking
Uffington
Shrivenham
West Challow
Kingston Lisle
Sparsholt
Woolstone
Compton Beauchamp
UFFINGTON CASTLE
WHITEHORSE HILL
WAYLAND'S SMITHY
Letcombe
Purton
Widham
Haydon Wick
Penhill
Upper Stratton
Stratton St Margaret
Dogridge
Lydiard Green
Lydiard Millicent
Pinehurst
Gorse Hill
Rodbourne Cheney
LYDIARD HOUSE
G.W.R. MUS.
Rodbourne
Walcot
Hook
Bourton
Hinton Parva
Ashbury
Idstone
Bishopstone
Kingston Warren
The Marsh
Swindon
McARTHUR GLEN SWINDON
Wootton Bassett
Coate
COATE WATER
Wanborough
Liddington
ASHDOWN HOUSE
LAMBOURN DOWNS
North Wroughton
Wroughton
GREAT WESTERN (MAIZE) MAZE
Elcombe
Badbury
Upper Lambourn
Lambourn
Broadtown Lane
Chiseldon
Broad Town
Uffcott
Upper Upham
Baydon
Bushton
CLYFFE PYPARD
Clyffe Pypard
BARBURY CASTLE
Eastbury
Broad Hinton
Woodsend
Aldbourne
MEMBURY SERVICES
Woodlands St Mary
Clevancy
MARLBOROUGH DOWNS
Winterborne Bassett
HACKPEN HILL
Southend
Ogbourne St George
Preston
Berwick Bassett
Ogbourne St Andrew
WINDMILL HILL
Winterborne Monkton
Whittonditch
Ramsbury
Rockley
Ogbourne Maizey
Yatesbury
THE RIDGEWAY
FYFIELD DOWN
AVEBURY MANOR
Avebury
Chilton Foliat
Mildenhall
Axford
STONE CIRCLE
W.KENNETT AVENUE
Fyfield
Marlborough
Kennet
Hungerford
SILBURY HILL
Beckhampton
West Kennett
Manton
Froxfield
LONG BARROW
West Overton
Lockeridge
Savernake Forest
East Kennett
THE SANCTUARY
Cadley
Chisbury
CHISBURY CHAPEL
Little Bedwyn
Clench Common
TAN HILL
MILK HILL
Durley
Great Bedwyn
Bagshot
PEWSEY DOWNS
Huish
Wootton Rivers
Shalbourne
Allington
Stanton St Bernard
West Stowell
Oare
Crofton
Ham
All Cannings
Alton Priors
Stibb Green
CROFTON BEAM ENGINES
New Mill
Eastcourt
WILTON WINDMILL
Honey Street
Wilton
Rivar
VALE OF PEWSEY
Wilcot
Burbage
Pewsey
Easton Royal
Buttermere
Etchilhampton
Woodborough
West Grafton
East Grafton
Marten
Milton Lilbourne
Beechingstoke
Bottlesford
Southcott
Wexcombe
Oxenwood
Manningford Bruce
Patney
Hilcott
HENGE
Linkenholt
Chirton
Marden
North Newnton
Manningford Bohune
Tidcombe
Fosbury
Vernham Street
Wilsford
Charlton
Pewsey Down
Brunton
Aughton
HAYDOWN HILL
Vernham Dean
Rushall
Upavon
Collingbourne Kingston
Lower Everleigh
Sunton
Upper Chute
Chute Standen
Everleigh
Cadley
West Chisenbury
East Chisenbury
Collingbourne Ducis
Lower Chute
Tangley
Collingbourne Forest
Compton
Wiltshire
Enford
Fifield
Black Heath
Compton Down
Haxton Down
Wildhern
Coombe
Ludgershall
Hatherden
Enford Down
Fittleton
Tidworth
North Tidworth
Clanville
Netheravon
Orcheston
DOVECOTE
Appleshaw
Penton
SU

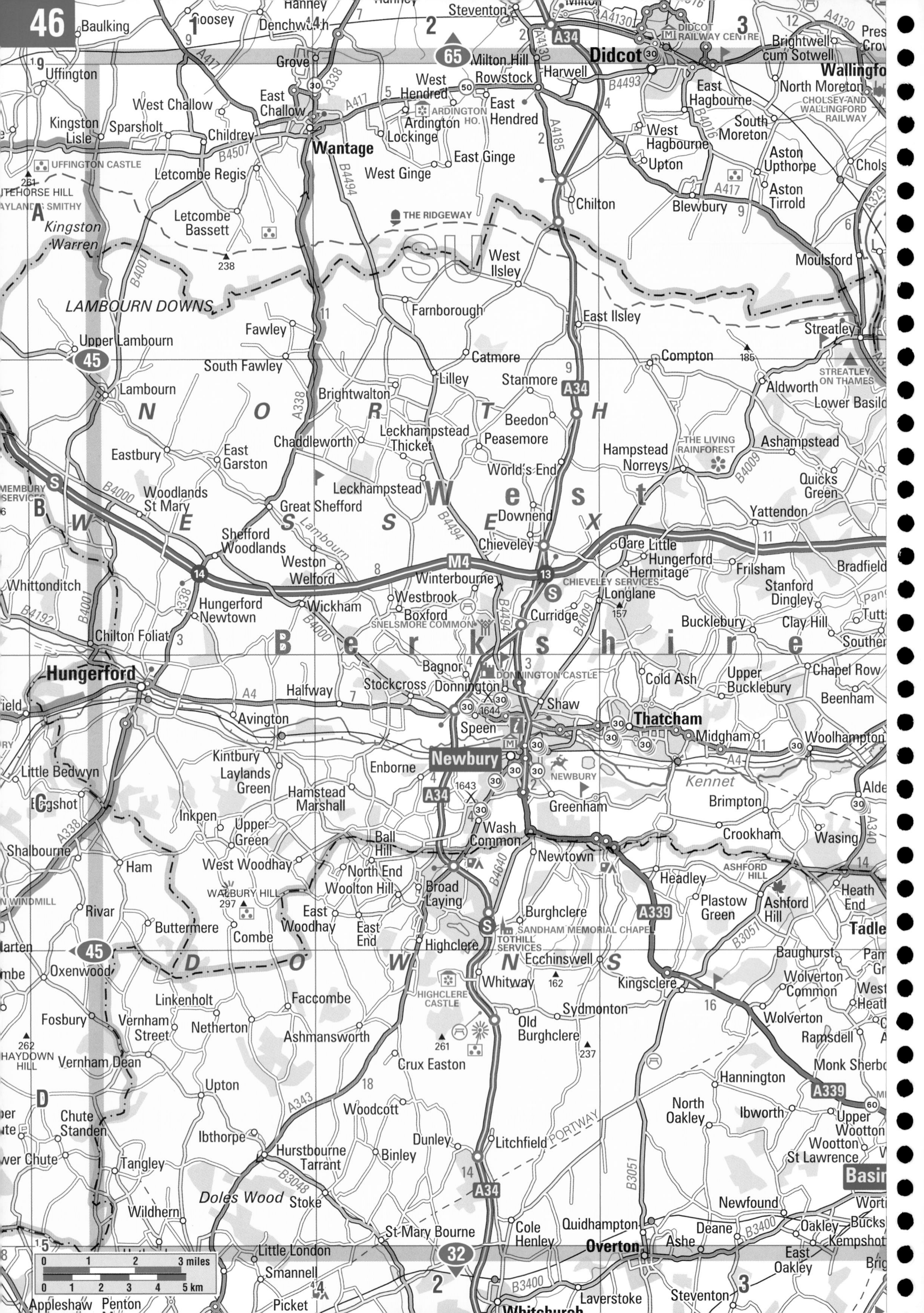

Baulking
Goosey
Denchworth
Hanney
Steventon
Milton
Didcot
DIDCOT RAILWAY CENTRE
Brightwell-cum-Sotwell
Wallingford
65
Milton Hill
Rowstock
Harwell
Grove
West Hendred
ARDINGTON HO.
Ardington
Lockinge
East Hendred
East Challow
West Challow
Uffington
Kingston Lisle
Sparsholt
Childrey
Wantage
East Ginge
West Ginge
UFFINGTON CASTLE
WHITEHORSE HILL
WAYLAND'S SMITHY
Letcombe Regis
Letcombe Bassett
THE RIDGEWAY
Chilton
Blewbury
East Hagbourne
West Hagbourne
Upton
South Moreton
North Moreton
CHOLSEY AND WALLINGFORD RAILWAY
Aston Upthorpe
Aston Tirrold
Cholsey
Moulsford
Kingston Warren
West Ilsley
East Ilsley
LAMBOURN DOWNS
Farnborough
Fawley
Upper Lambourn
South Fawley
Catmore
Compton
Streatley
STREATLEY ON THAMES
Aldworth
Lower Basildon
45
Lambourn
Lilley
Stanmore
Brightwalton
Beedon
Leckhampstead Thicket
Peasemore
Chaddleworth
Eastbury
East Garston
World's End
Hampstead Norreys
THE LIVING RAINFOREST
Ashampstead
Quicks Green
MEMBURY SERVICES
Woodlands St Mary
Great Shefford
Leckhampstead
Downend
Yattendon
Shefford Woodlands
Chieveley
Oare
Little Hungerford
Hermitage
Frilsham
Bradfield
Weston
Welford
Winterbourne
CHIEVELEY SERVICES
Stanford Dingley
Longlane
Whittonditch
Hungerford Newtown
Wickham
Westbrook
Boxford
SNELSMORE COMMON
Curridge
Bucklebury
Clay Hill
Tutts Clump
Southend
Chilton Foliat
Berkshire
West Berkshire
NORTH WESSEX DOWNS
Bagnor
DONNINGTON CASTLE
Cold Ash
Upper Bucklebury
Chapel Row
Hungerford
Halfway
Stockcross
Donnington
Shaw
Thatcham
Beenham
Avington
Speen
Midgham
Woolhampton
Kintbury
Laylands Green
Newbury
Enborne
NEWBURY
Kennet
Little Bedwyn
Froxfield
Oxford
Hamstead Marshall
Greenham
Brimpton
Aldermaston
Inkpen
Upper Green
Wash Common
Crookham
Wasing
Shalbourne
Ham
West Woodhay
Ball Hill
Newtown
ASHFORD HILL
Heath End
North End
Woolton Hill
Broad Laying
Headley
Plastow Green
Ashford Hill
WALBURY HILL
Rivar
East Woodhay
Burghclere
SANDHAM MEMORIAL CHAPEL
Tadley
Buttermere
Combe
East End
Highclere
TOTHILL SERVICES
Ecchinswell
Baughurst
Oxenwood
Whitway
Kingsclere
Wolverton Common
HIGHCLERE CASTLE
Linkenholt
Faccombe
Sydmonton
Wolverton
Fosbury
Vernham Street
Netherton
Old Burghclere
Ramsdell
Ashmansworth
HAYDOWN HILL
Vernham Dean
Crux Easton
Monk Sherborne
Upton
Hannington
North Oakley
Ibworth
Woodcott
Chute Standen
Upper Wootton
Wootton St Lawrence
Ibthorpe
Dunley
Litchfield
PORTWAY
Lower Chute
Hurstbourne Tarrant
Binley
Tangley
Basingstoke
Doles Wood
Stoke
Newfound
Wildhern
St Mary Bourne
Cole Henley
Quidhampton
Deane
Oakley
Worting
Kempshott
Little London
32
Overton
Ashe
East Oakley
Smannell
Laverstoke
Steventon
Appleshaw
Penton
Picket
Whitchurch
0 1 2 3 miles
0 1 2 3 4 5 km

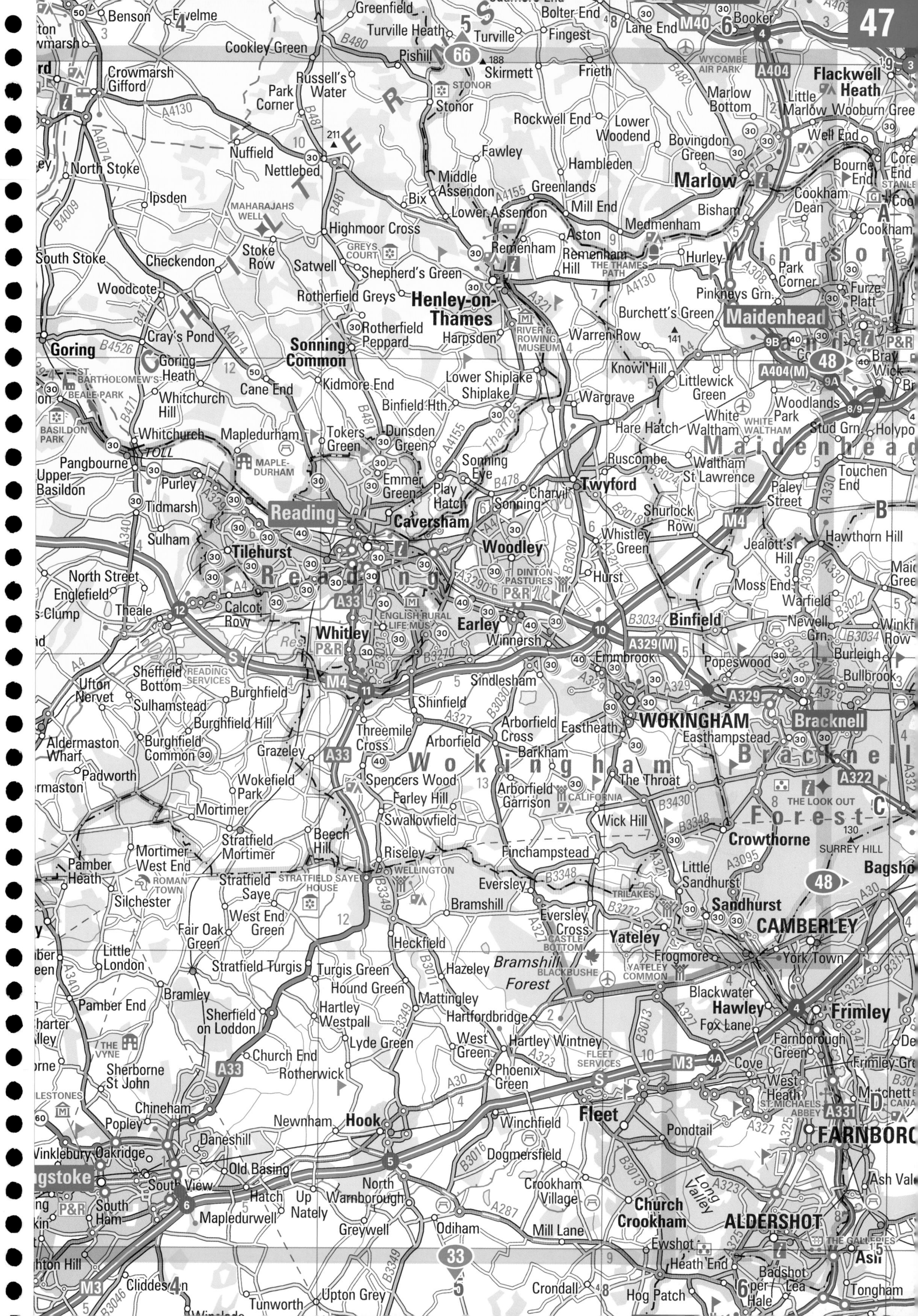

Benson
Ewelme
Greenfield
Turville Heath
Turville
Bolter End
Fingest
Lane End
Booker
Cookley Green
Pishill
66
Skirmett
Frieth
WYCOMBE AIR PARK
A404
Flackwell Heath
Crowmarsh Gifford
Russell's Water
Park Corner
STONOR
Stonor
Marlow Bottom
Little Marlow
Wooburn Green
Rockwell End
Lower Woodend
Bovingdon Green
Well End
Nuffield
Nettlebed
Fawley
Hambleden
North Stoke
Middle Assendon
Greenlands
Marlow
Bourne End
Ipsden
MAHARAJAHS WELL
Bix
Lower Assendon
Mill End
Bisham
Cookham Dean
Cookham
Highmoor Cross
Medmenham
Aston
South Stoke
Checkendon
Stoke Row
GREYS COURT
Remenham
Remenham Hill
Hurley
THE THAMES PATH
Park Corner
Satwell
Shepherd's Green
Woodcote
Rotherfield Greys
Henley-on-Thames
Pinkneys Grn.
Furze Platt
Burchett's Green
Maidenhead
Rotherfield Peppard
Goring
Cray's Pond
Sonning Common
Harpsden
RIVER & ROWING MUSEUM
Warren Row
Goring Heath
ST. BARTHOLOMEW'S
BEALE PARK
Cane End
Kidmore End
Lower Shiplake
Shiplake
Knowl Hill
Littlewick Green
Bray Wick
Whitchurch Hill
Binfield Hth.
Wargrave
White Waltham
Woodlands Park
BASILDON PARK
Whitchurch
Mapledurham
MAPLEDURHAM
Tokers Green
Dunsden Green
Hare Hatch
WHITE WALTHAM
Stud Grn.
Holyport
Pangbourne
Upper Basildon
Purley
Emmer Green
Sonning Eye
Ruscombe
Waltham St Lawrence
Touchen End
Tidmarsh
Reading
Play Hatch
Charvil
Sonning
Twyford
Paley Street
Caversham
Shurlock Row
Sulham
Tilehurst
Woodley
Whistley Green
Jealott's Hill
Hawthorn Hill
North Street
Englefield
DINTON PASTURES
Hurst
Moss End
Warfield
Theale
Calcot Row
Reading
ENGLISH RURAL LIFE MUS.
Earley
Winnersh
Binfield
Newell Grn.
Winkfield Row
Whitley
Emmbrook
Popeswood
Burleigh
Sheffield Bottom
READING SERVICES
Burghfield
Sindlesham
Bullbrook
Ufton Nervet
Sulhamstead
Shinfield
WOKINGHAM
Bracknell
Burghfield Hill
Threemile Cross
Arborfield
Arborfield Cross
Eastheath
Easthampstead
Aldermaston Wharf
Burghfield Common
Grazeley
Barkham
Padworth
Wokefield Park
Spencers Wood
Wokingham
The Throat
Bracknell
Farley Hill
Arborfield Garrison
CALIFORNIA
THE LOOK OUT
Mortimer
Swallowfield
Wick Hill
Forest
Stratfield Mortimer
Beech Hill
Crowthorne
Mortimer West End
Riseley
Finchampstead
SURREY HILL
Pamber Heath
ROMAN TOWN
Stratfield Saye
STRATFIELD SAYE HOUSE
WELLINGTON
Eversley
Little Sandhurst
Bagshot
Silchester
West End Green
Bramshill
TRILAKES
Sandhurst
Fair Oak Green
Eversley Cross
CASTLE BOTTOM
Yateley
CAMBERLEY
Little London
Heckfield
Stratfield Turgis
Turgis Green
Hazeley
Bramshill Forest
BLACKBUSHE
YATELEY COMMON
Frogmore
York Town
Hound Green
Bramley
Pamber End
Sherfield on Loddon
Hartley Westpall
Mattingley
Blackwater
Hawley
Frimley
Hartfordbridge
Fox Lane
THE VYNE
Lyde Green
West Green
Hartley Wintney
FLEET SERVICES
Farnborough Green
Church End
Cove
Sherborne St John
Rotherwick
Phoenix Green
West Heath
Chineham
Fleet
ST. MICHAELS ABBEY
Popley
Newnham
Hook
Winchfield
Pondtail
FARNBOROUGH
Daneshill
Oakridge
Old Basing
Dogmersfield
South View
North Warnborough
Crookham Village
Ash Vale
South Ham
Hatch
Up Nately
Church Crookham
ALDERSHOT
Mapledurwell
Long Valley
Greywell
Odiham
Mill Lane
Ewshot
THE GALLERIES
Heath End
Badshot Lea
Ash
Cliddesden
Upton Grey
Crondall
Hog Patch
Upper Hale
Tongham
Tunworth
33
48

Loudwater
Beaconsfield
Forty Green
Bekonscot Model Village
Jordans
Chalfont Common
Chalfont St Peter
67
Northwood
Harefield
Bayhurst Wood
Ruislip Woods
Hatch End
Pinner
Harrow
Flackwell Heath
Little Marlow
Wooburn Green
Gerrards Cross
Denham Green
Ruislip Common
Eastcote
Rayners Lane
Well End
Wooburn
Odds Farm Park
Hedgerley
Denham
Tatling End
Ruislip
Bourne End
Cores End
Hedsor
Burnham Beeches
M40
Fulmer
Ickenham
Stanley Spencer Gallery
Cookham Dean
Cookham
Farnham Common
Stoke Poges
Northolt
Cliveden
Cookham Rise
Black Park
Iver Heath
M25
Uxbridge
Windsor
Farnham Royal
Wexham Street
Stoke Green
Hillingdon
London Motorcycle Mus.
Park Corner
Burnham
Furze Platt
Yeading
Greenford
Taplow
Langley Park
Cowley
George Green
Maidenhead
Slough
Iver
Yiewsley
Hayes
Southall
P&R
Bray Wick
Bray
Dorney
Eton Wick
Upton
Langley
Richings Park
West Drayton
Thorney
Heston Services
47
Woodlands Park
White Waltham
Dorney Court
Eton
M4
Harmondsworth
Sipson
Harlington
Cranford
Heston
Stud Grn.
Holyport
Boveney
Windsor Castle
Datchet
Colnbrook
Longford
London Heathrow
Fifield
Touchen End
Oakley Green
Poyle
Heathrow Airport
Hounslow
Paley Street
Household Cavalry Mus.
Horton
Windsor Legoland
Old Windsor
Wraysbury
Stanwell Moor
West Bedfont
East Bedfont
Twickenham Mus. of Rugby
Hawthorn Hill
Jealott's Hill
Forest
Stanwell
Cranbourne
Maiden's Green
Hythe End
Runnymede
Moss End
Warfield
Winkfield
Great Park
Englefield Green
Egham
Feltham
Newell Grn.
Winkfield Row
Woodside
The Savill Garden
Staines
Ashford
Hanworth
Kempton Park
Burleigh
Valley Gdns
Hampton
Bullbrook
Ascot
Virginia Water
Thorpe
Laleham
Littleton
Sunbury-on-Thames
Bracknell
Sunninghill
Wentworth
Thorpe Park
M3
West Molesey
East Molesey
South Ascot
Sunningdale
Shepperton
Broomhall
Chertsey
Walton-on-Thames
Sandown Park
The Look Out
Lyne
Addlestone
Weybridge
Hersham
Chobham Common
Claremont Landscape Garden
Crowthorne
Surrey Hill
Windlesham
Ottershaw
Bagshot
New Haw
Brooklands Mus.
Whiteley Village
Burrowhill
Lightwater
Fairoaks
Woodham
Byfleet
Chobham
West End
Camberley
West Byfleet
Cobham
Donkey Town
Castle Green
Chobham Ridges
York Town
34
Cheapside
Painshill Park
Stoke D'Abernon
Bisley
Knaphill
Horsell
Wisley
RHS Garden Wisley
Downside
Frimley
Woking
Pyrford
Farnborough Green
Deepcut
Brookwood
St John's
Old Woking
Ripley
Martyr's Green
Cove
Frimley Green
Mayford
Ockham
Fetcham
West Heath
Mytchett
Basingstoke Canal Centre
Send Marsh
Send
Little Bookham
St Michael's Abbey
Pirbright
Fox Corner
Burntcommon
Effingham
Farnborough
Worplesdon
Sutton Green
East Horsley
West Horsley
Polesden Lacey
Ash Vale
Willey Green
Pitch Place
Slyfield
Burpham
Clandon Park
West Clandon
Hatchlands Park
Tanners Hatch
Aldershot
Normandy
Stoughton
Merrow
East Clandon
Ranmore Common
The Galleries
Wyke
Wood Street
Dapdune Wharf
Newland's Corner
North Downs Way
Guildford
Wanborough
Hogs Back
Onslow Village
Albury
Gomshall
Abinger Hammer
0 1 2 3 miles
0 1 2 3 4 5 km

Edgware
Finchley
Hornsey
Wood Green
Tottenham
Woodford
Wealdstone
Hendon
Walthamstow
Wanstead
Harrow on the Hill
Highgate
Hampstead
Stoke Newington
Leytonstone
Leyton
Ilford
Wembley
Willesden
Camden
Islington
Hackney
Stratford
East Ham
Acton
Paddington
Holborn
City
Shoreditch
Poplar
West Ham
Beckton
EALING
Kensington
Westminster
Southwark
Bermondsey
Blackwall Tunnel
Woolwich Ferry
Woolwich
Chiswick
Hammersmith
Chelsea
LAMBETH
Greenwich
Deptford
Charlton
Fulham
Battersea
Camberwell
Lewisham
Richmond
Wandsworth
Brixton
Dulwich
Catford
Eltham
Twickenham
Wimbledon
Streatham
Sydenham
Chislehurst
BROMLEY
Kingston upon Thames
Mitcham
Beckenham
Surbiton
New Malden
Morden
Croydon
Carshalton
Sutton
Cheam
Wallington
EPSOM
Purley
BANSTEAD
Coulsdon
Warlingham
Biggin Hill
Leatherhead
Tadworth
Kingswood
CATERHAM
Woldingham
Westerham
Limpsfield
Oxted
Redhill
Reigate
Merstham
Godstone
M25
M23
A22
A23
A24
A3
A2
A20
A21
A40
A406
A13
A12
A10
A1

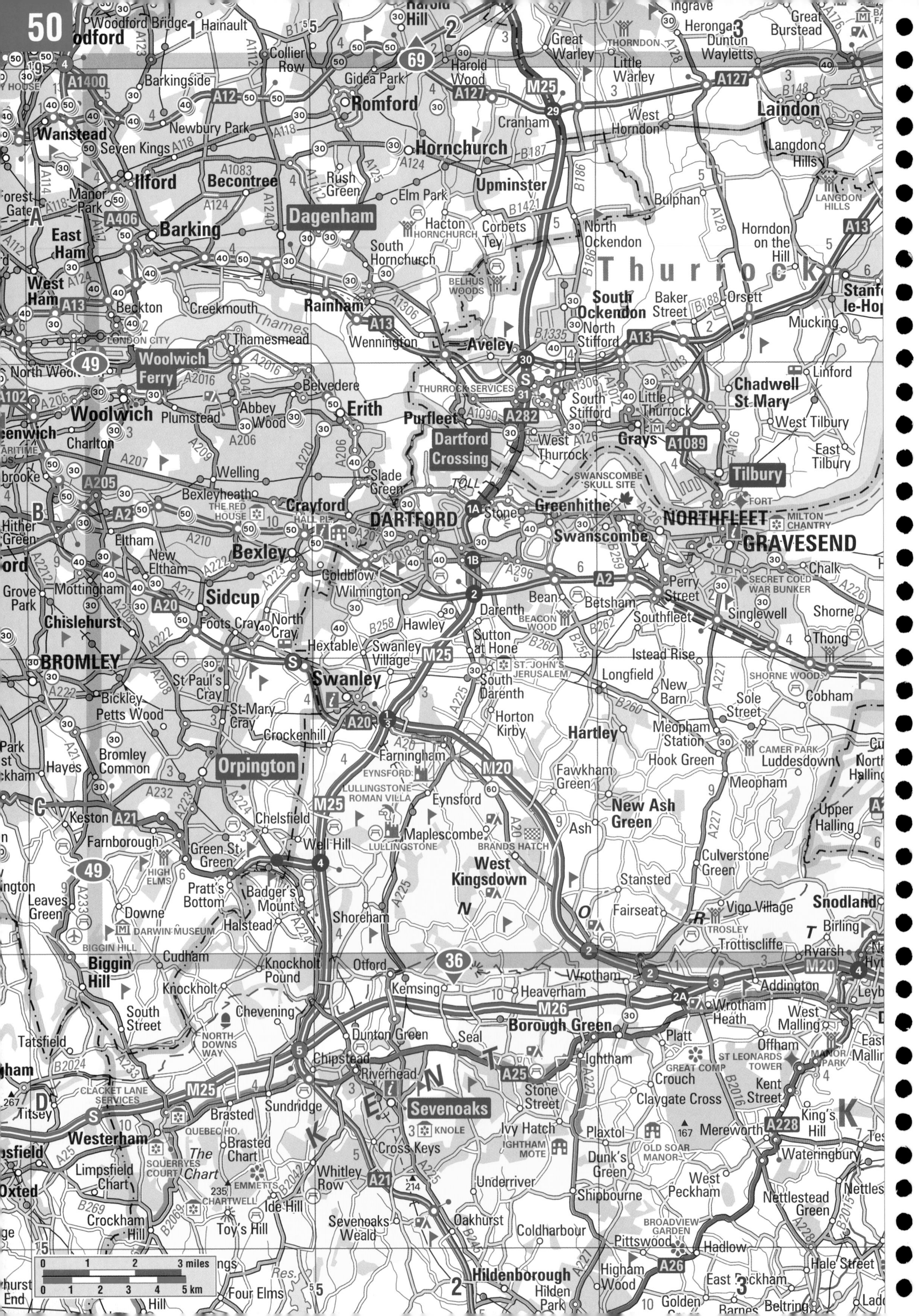

Woodford Bridge
Hainault
Harold Hill
Ingrave
Herongate
Great Burstead
Collier Row
Gidea Park
Harold Wood
Great Warley
Little Warley
Dunton Wayletts
Barkingside
Romford
Cranham
West Horndon
Laindon
Newbury Park
Wanstead
Seven Kings
Hornchurch
Langdon Hills
Ilford
Becontree
Rush Green
Upminster
Bulphan
Manor Park
Forest Gate
Elm Park
Barking
Dagenham
Hacton
Corbets Tey
North Ockendon
East Ham
South Hornchurch
Horndon on the Hill
West Ham
Thurrock
Beckton
Creekmouth
Rainham
Belhus Woods
South Ockendon
Baker Street
Orsett
Stanford-le-Hope
Thames
Wennington
Aveley
North Stifford
Mucking
London City
Thamesmead
Woolwich Ferry
Belvedere
Thurrock Services
South Stifford
Little Thurrock
Chadwell St Mary
Linford
North Woolwich
Woolwich
Plumstead
Abbey Wood
Erith
Purfleet
Grays
West Tilbury
Greenwich
Charlton
Dartford Crossing
West Thurrock
East Tilbury
Tilbury
Welling
Slade Green
Swanscombe Skull Site
Bexleyheath
Crayford
Stone
Greenhithe
Northfleet
Milton Chantry
The Red House
Hall Place
Dartford
Swanscombe
Gravesend
Hither Green
Eltham
New Eltham
Bexley
Coldblow
Chalk
Wilmington
Perry Street
Secret Cold War Bunker
Grove Park
Mottingham
Sidcup
Darenth
Bean
Betsham
Singlewell
Shorne
Chislehurst
Foots Cray
North Cray
Hawley
Beacon Wood
Southfleet
Thong
Hextable
Swanley Village
Sutton at Hone
Istead Rise
Bromley
St Paul's Cray
Swanley
St John's Jerusalem
South Darenth
Longfield
New Barn
Shorne Wood
Cobham
Bickley
Petts Wood
St Mary Cray
Horton Kirby
Hartley
Sole Street
Crockenhill
Meopham Station
Farningham
Camer Park
Luddesdown
Bromley Common
Hayes
Orpington
Eynsford
Fawkham Green
Hook Green
Lullingstone Roman Villa
Meopham
Keston
Chelsfield
Maplescombe
New Ash Green
Upper Halling
Farnborough
Well Hill
Lullingstone
Brands Hatch
Ash
Green St Green
West Kingsdown
High Elms
Culverstone Green
Stansted
Pratt's Bottom
Badger's Mount
Leaves Green
Downe
Shoreham
Fairseat
Vigo Village
Snodland
Darwin Museum
Halstead
Trosley
Birling
Biggin Hill
Trottiscliffe
Ryarsh
Cudham
Knockholt Pound
Otford
Wrotham
Knockholt
Kemsing
Heaverham
Addington
South Street
Chevening
Wrotham Heath
West Malling
Borough Green
Tatsfield
North Downs Way
Dunton Green
Seal
Platt
Offham
Chipstead
Ightham
St Leonards Tower
Manor Park
East Malling
Riverhead
Great Comp
Crouch
Clacket Lane Services
Stone Street
Kent Street
Sundridge
Brasted
Claygate Cross
Titsey
Sevenoaks
Westerham
Quebec Ho.
Knole
Ivy Hatch
Plaxtol
Mereworth
King's Hill
Ightham Mote
Limpsfield
Brasted Chart
Cross Keys
Dunk's Green
Old Soar Manor
Wateringbury
The Chart
Squerryes Court
Limpsfield Chart
Emmetts
Whitley Row
Underriver
West Peckham
Nettlestead
Oxted
Chartwell
Ide Hill
Shipbourne
Nettlestead Green
Crockham Hill
Toy's Hill
Sevenoaks Weald
Oakhurst
Coldharbour
Broadview Gardens
Hadlow
Pittswood
Higham Wood
Hale Street
Hildenborough
Hilden Park
East Peckham
Four Elms
Golden Green
Beltring
Barnes
KENT

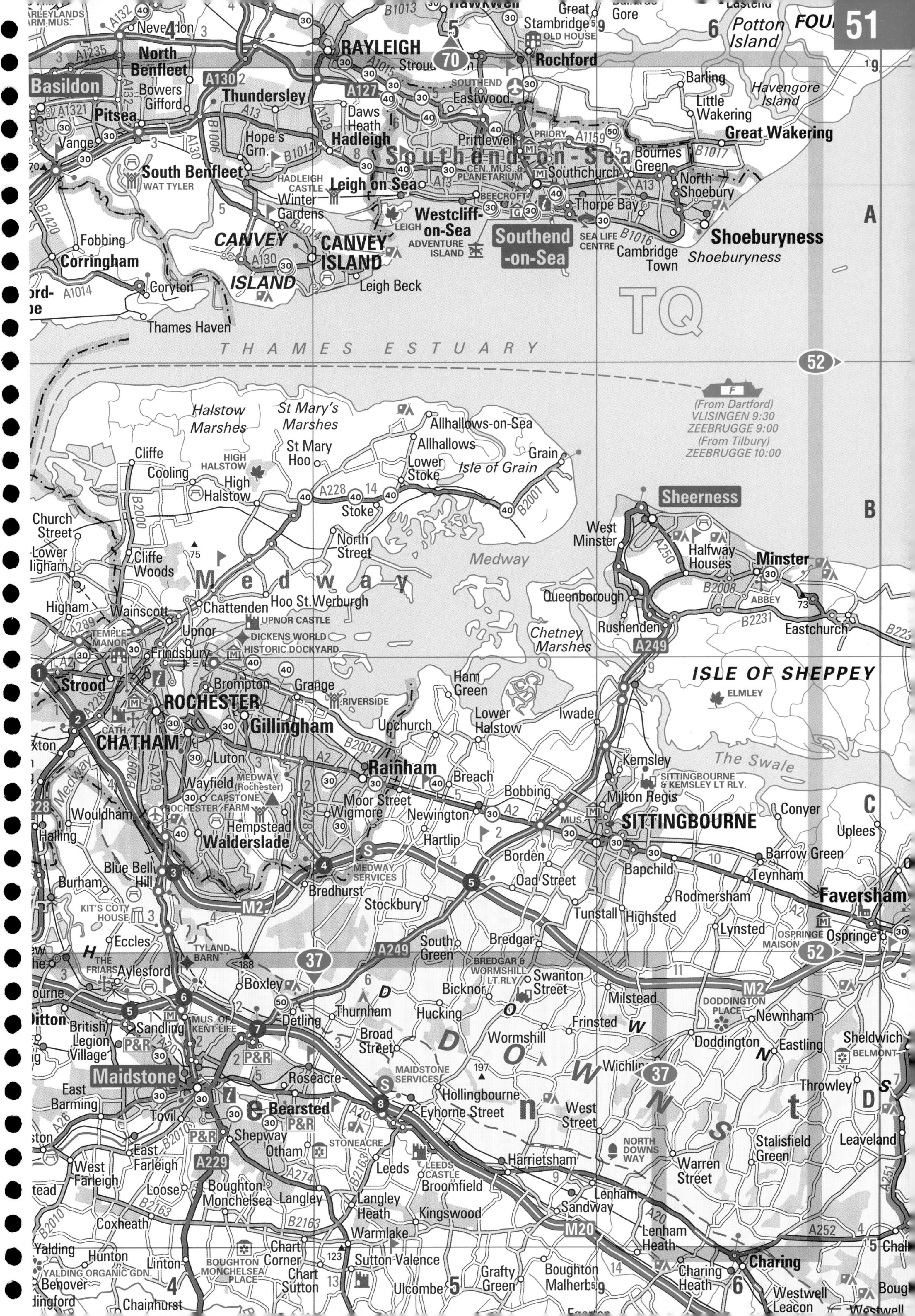

Rayleigh
Hawkwell
Great Stambridge
Ballards Gore
Potton Island
Foulness
Nevendon
North Benfleet
Basildon
Bowers Gifford
Pitsea
Vange
Thundersley
Daws Heath
Hadleigh
Hope's Grn.
South Benfleet
Wat Tyler
Stroud Green
Rochford
Southend Airport
Eastwood
Prittlewell
Priory
Southend-on-Sea
Cen. Mus. & Planetarium
Southchurch
Bournes Green
Barling
Little Wakering
Havengore Island
Great Wakering
North Shoebury
Shoeburyness
Hadleigh Castle
Leigh on Sea
Winter Gardens
Westcliff-on-Sea
Beecroft
Thorpe Bay
Sea Life Centre
Adventure Island
Cambridge Town
Leigh
Canvey Island
Leigh Beck
Fobbing
Corringham
Coryton
Thames Haven
TQ
Thames Estuary
(From Dartford)
Vlisingen 9:30
Zeebrugge 9:00
(From Tilbury)
Zeebrugge 10:00
Halstow Marshes
St Mary's Marshes
Allhallows-on-Sea
Allhallows
St Mary Hoo
Cliffe
Cooling
High Halstow
Lower Stoke
Isle of Grain
Grain
Stoke
Church Street
Lower Higham
Cliffe Woods
North Street
Medway
Sheerness
West Minster
Halfway Houses
Minster
Queenborough
Abbey
Rushenden
Eastchurch
Higham
Wainscott
Chattenden
Hoo St. Werburgh
Upnor Castle
Upnor
Temple Manor
Dickens World
Historic Dockyard
Frindsbury
Chetney Marshes
Strood
Brompton
Grange
Riverside
Rochester
Gillingham
Ham Green
Isle of Sheppey
Elmley
Chatham
Cath.
Lower Halstow
Iwade
Upchurch
Luton
Rainham
The Swale
Kemsley
Sittingbourne & Kemsley Lt Rly.
Breach
Bobbing
Milton Regis
Wayfield
Medway (Rochester)
Capstone Farm
Moor Street
Wigmore
Newington
Mus.
Sittingbourne
Conyer
Uplees
Wouldham
Rochester Farm
Hempstead
Halling
Walderslade
Hartlip
Borden
Barrow Green
Blue Bell Hill
Medway Services
Oad Street
Bapchild
Teynham
Burham
Bredhurst
Rodmersham
Faversham
Kit's Coty House
Stockbury
Tunstall
Highsted
Lynsted
Ospringe Maison
Ospringe
Eccles
South Green
Bredgar
Tyland Barn
The Friars
Aylesford
Bredgar & Wormshill Lt.Rly.
Swanton Street
Boxley
Bicknor
Milstead
Doddington Place
Thurnham
Detling
Hucking
Frinsted
Newnham
Ditton
British Legion Village
Sandling
Mus. of Kent Life
Broad Street
Wormshill
Doddington
Eastling
Sheldwich
Belmont
Maidstone
East Barming
Roseacre
Maidstone Services
Wichling
Throwley
Bearsted
Hollingbourne
Eyhorne Street
West Street
Tovil
Shepway
Otham
Stoneacre
North Downs Way
Stalisfield Green
Leaveland
East Farleigh
West Farleigh
Leeds
Leeds Castle
Broomfield
Harrietsham
Warren Street
Loose
Boughton Monchelsea
Langley
Langley Heath
Kingswood
Sandway
Lenham
Coxheath
Warmlake
Lenham Heath
Yalding
Hunton
Linton
Chart Corner
Sutton Valence
Charing
Chart Sutton
Boughton Monchelsea Place
Yalding Organic Gdn.
Benover
Grafty Green
Boughton Malherbe
Charing Heath
Ulcombe
Westwell Leacon
Chainhurst
Westwell
Medway
Downs

FOULNESS ISLAND
Potton Island
Barling
Havengore Island
Little Wakering
Great Wakering
MAPLIN SANDS
Bournes Green
North Shoebury
Thorpe Bay
SEA LIFE CENTRE
Cambridge Town
Shoeburyness
Shoeburyness
TQ
(From Dartford)
VLISINGEN 9:30
ZEEBRUGGE 9:00
(From Tilbury)
ZEEBRUGGE 10:00
Sheerness
West Minster
Halfway Houses
Minster
ABBEY
Warden Pt.
Warden
Rushenden
Eastchurch
Leysdown-on-Sea
ISLE OF SHEPPEY
ELMLEY
Shell Ness
Isle of Harty
THE SWALE
The Swale
HERNE BAY
WHITSTABLE
Tankerton
Swalecliffe
MUSEUM & GALLERY
Greenhill
Herne
Kemsley
SITTINGBOURNE & KEMSLEY LT RLY.
Milton Regis
SITTINGBOURNE
Conyer
Seasalter
Chestfield
South Street
Uplees
Barrow Green
Bapchild
Teynham
Oare
Graveney
Yorkletts
Calcott
CHART GUNPOWDER MILLS
Rodmersham
Faversham
Goodnestone
Dargate
Honey Hill
Broadoak
Tunstall
Highsted
FLEUR DE LIS HERITAGE CENTRE
Hernhill
Tyler Hill
Lynsted
OSPRINGE MAISON DIEU
Ospringe
Preston
FARMING WORLD
MOUNT EPHRAIM
BLEAN WOODS
Blean
Sturry
Hales Place
Boughton Street
Rough Common
Milstead
Dunkirk
Canterbury
DODDINGTON PLACE
North Street
South Street
Harbledown
Frinsted
Newnham
ST. AUGUSTINE'S ABBEY
Doddington
Eastling
Sheldwich
BELMONT
Oversland
Chartham Hatch
CANTERBURY TALES
Thanington
ROMAN MUS
CANTERBURY
Wichling
Throwley
Selling
KENT
Old Wives Lees
Chartham
D
Badlesmere
Shottenden
Shalmsford Street
Nackington
Bridge
NORTH DOWNS WAY
Stalisfield Green
Leaveland
Chilham
Street End
Lower Hardres
Warren Street
Garlinge Green
Bishopsbourne
DOWNS
Lenham
Molash
Kingston
Petham
Upper Hardres Court
Lenham Heath
NORTH DOWNS WAY
Godmersham
Challock
Sole Street
Bossingham
Derringstone
Crundale
Waltham
Westwell
Leacon
Oughton Aluph
Westwell
0 1 2 3 miles
0 1 2 3 4 5 km

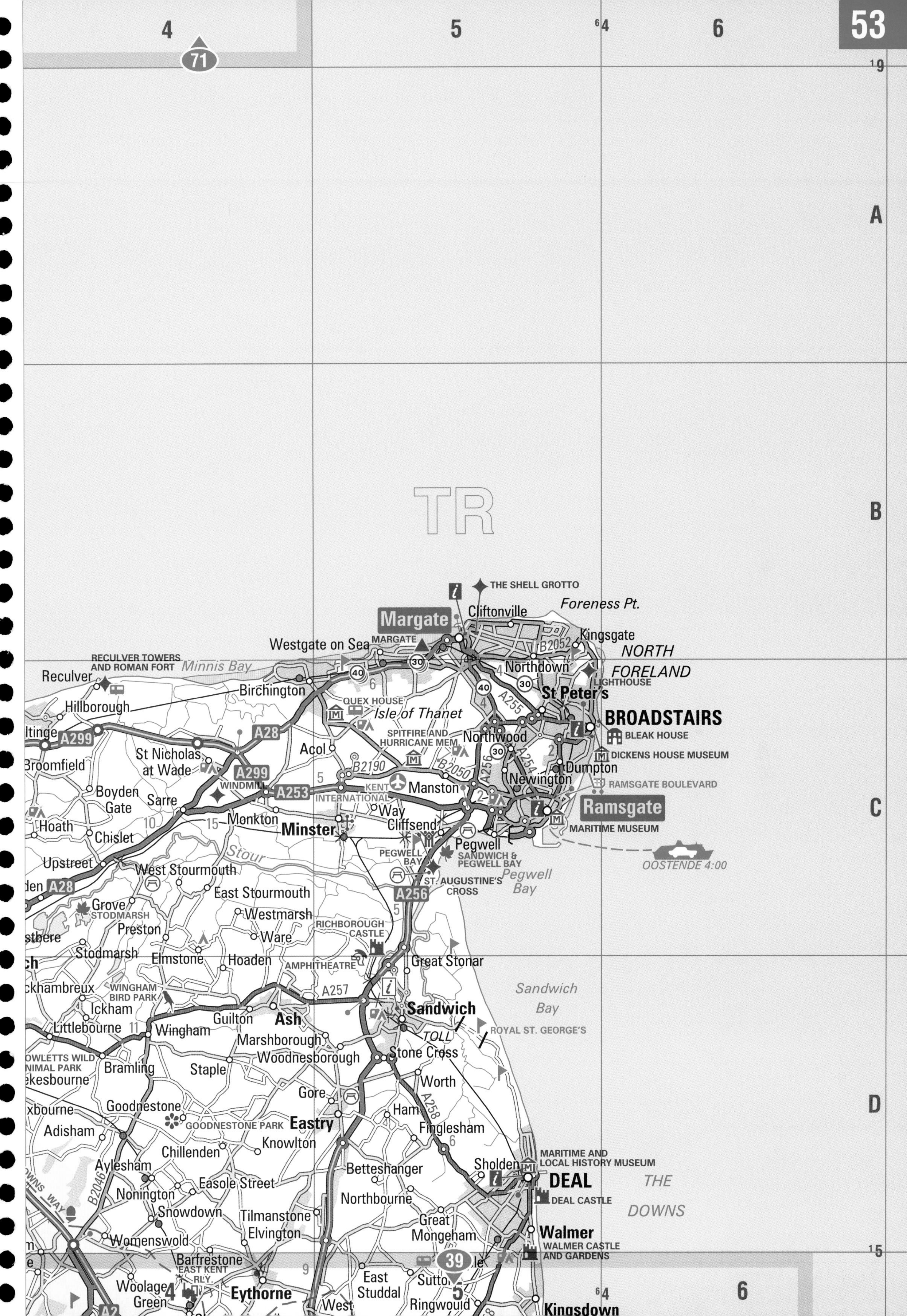
4
5
6
71
19
A
B
C
D
TR
THE SHELL GROTTO
Margate
Cliftonville
Foreness Pt.
Kingsgate
NORTH FORELAND
LIGHTHOUSE
Westgate on Sea
MARGATE
B2052
Northdown
St Peter's
BROADSTAIRS
BLEAK HOUSE
DICKENS HOUSE MUSEUM
RAMSGATE BOULEVARD
Ramsgate
MARITIME MUSEUM
OOSTENDE 4:00
RECULVER TOWERS AND ROMAN FORT
Minnis Bay
Reculver
Birchington
QUEX HOUSE
Isle of Thanet
A255
Hillborough
A299
A28
St Nicholas at Wade
Acol
SPITFIRE AND HURRICANE MEM.
Northwood
Dumpton
Newington
B2190
B2050
A256
A254
Broomfield
WINDMILL
A253
KENT INTERNATIONAL
Manston
Boyden Gate
Sarre
Hoath
Chislet
Monkton
Minster
Way
Cliffsend
Pegwell
SANDWICH & PEGWELL BAY
PEGWELL BAY
ST. AUGUSTINE'S CROSS
Pegwell Bay
Stour
Upstreet
West Stourmouth
East Stourmouth
Grove
STODMARSH
Westmarsh
Preston
RICHBOROUGH CASTLE
Ware
Stodmarsh
Elmstone
Hoaden
AMPHITHEATRE
Great Stonar
WINGHAM BIRD PARK
Ickham
A257
Sandwich
Sandwich Bay
Littlebourne
Wingham
Guilton
Ash
ROYAL ST. GEORGE'S
Marshborough
TOLL
Stone Cross
Woodnesborough
Bramling
Staple
Worth
Gore
Goodnestone
GOODNESTONE PARK
Eastry
Ham
A258
Finglesham
Adisham
Knowlton
Chillenden
Aylesham
B2046
Betteshanger
Sholden
MARITIME AND LOCAL HISTORY MUSEUM
DEAL
THE DOWNS
DEAL CASTLE
Nonington
Easole Street
Northbourne
Snowdown
Tilmanstone
Elvington
Great Mongeham
Walmer
WALMER CASTLE AND GARDENS
Womenswold
Barfrestone
EAST KENT RLY.
39
15
Woolage Green
Eythorne
East Studdal
Sutton
Ringwould
West
Kingsdown

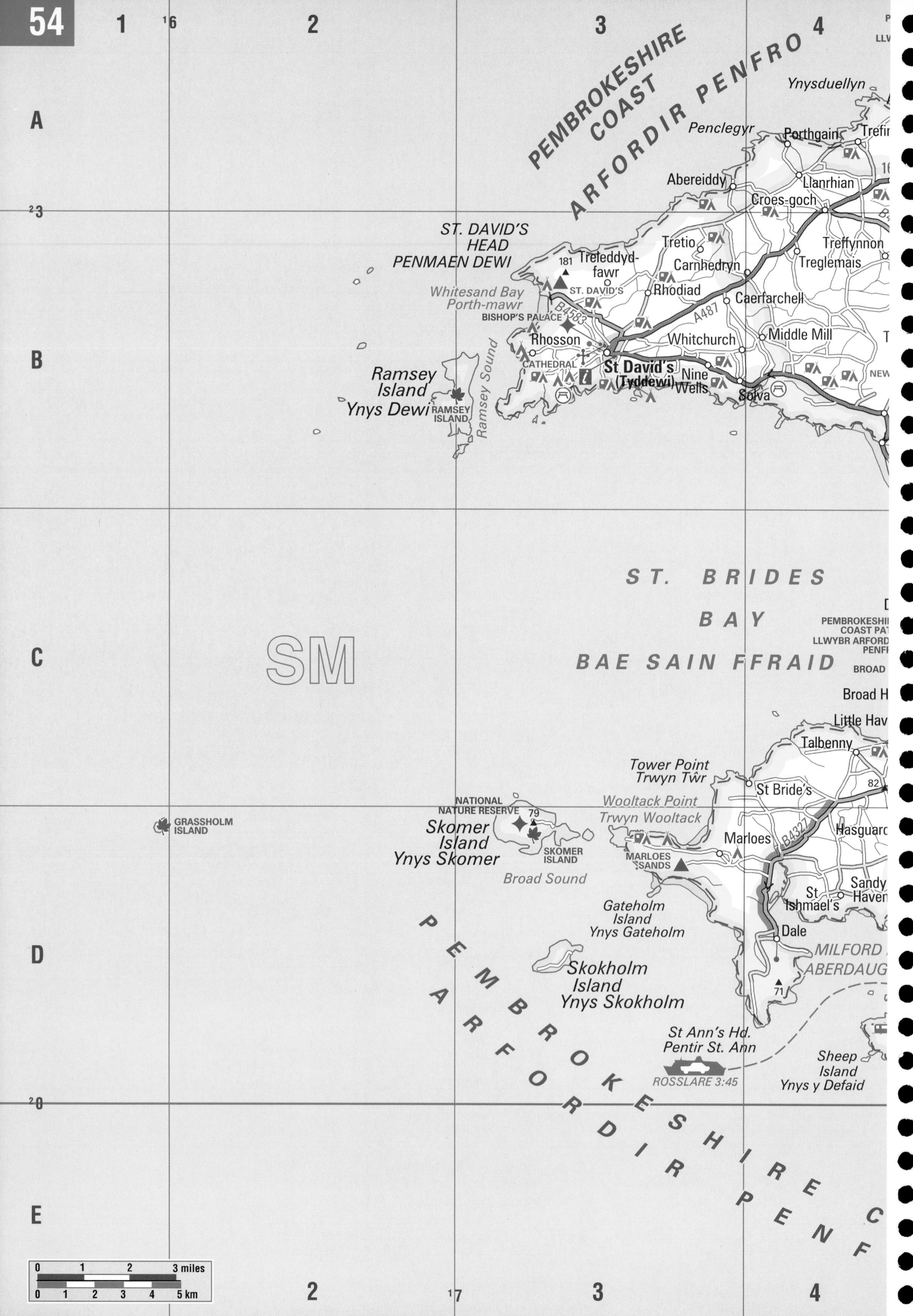
1
2
3
4
A
B
C
D
E
PEMBROKESHIRE COAST
ARFORDIR PENFRO
Ynysduellyn
Penclegyr
Porthgain
Abereiddy
Llanrhian
Croes-goch
Treffynnon
Treglemais
Tretio
Carnhedryn
Treleddyd-fawr
Rhodiad
Caerfarchell
ST. DAVID'S HEAD
PENMAEN DEWI
Whitesand Bay
Porth-mawr
ST. DAVID'S
BISHOP'S PALACE
Rhosson
CATHEDRAL
St David's
(Tyddewi)
Whitchurch
Middle Mill
Nine Wells
Solva
A487
B4583
Ramsey Island
Ynys Dewi
RAMSEY ISLAND
Ramsey Sound
ST. BRIDES BAY
BAE SAIN FFRAID
SM
Broad H
Little Hav
Talbenny
Tower Point
Trwyn Tŵr
St Bride's
Wooltack Point
Trwyn Wooltack
NATIONAL NATURE RESERVE
Skomer Island
Ynys Skomer
SKOMER ISLAND
GRASSHOLM ISLAND
Marloes
MARLOES SANDS
B4327
Hasguard
Broad Sound
Gateholm Island
Ynys Gateholm
St Ishmael's
Sandy Haven
Dale
Skokholm Island
Ynys Skokholm
St Ann's Hd.
Pentir St. Ann
ROSSLARE 3:45
Sheep Island
Ynys y Defaid
PEMBROKESHIRE C
PARFORDIR PENF
0 1 2 3 miles
0 1 2 3 4 5 km

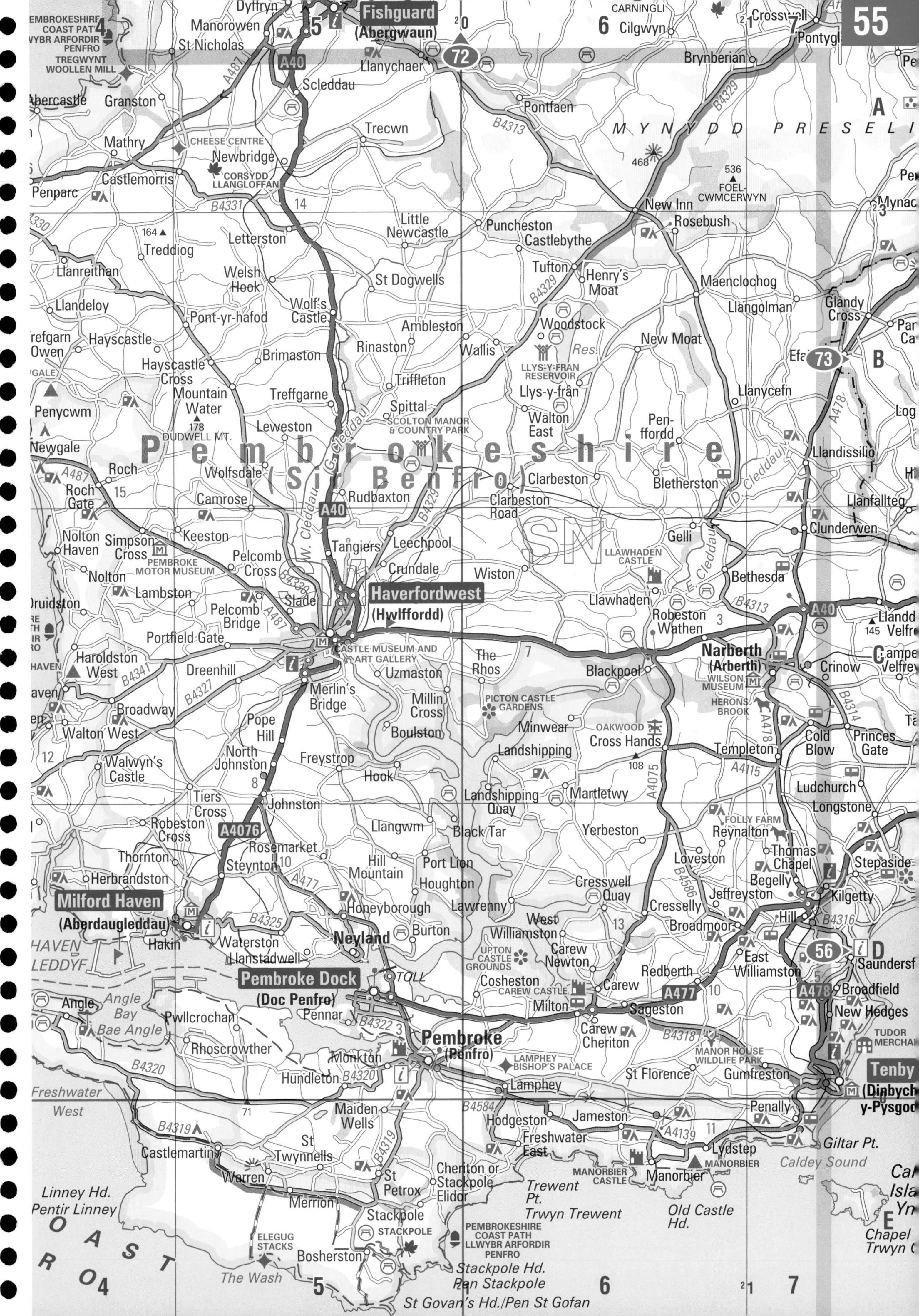

Fishguard
(Abergwaun)
Haverfordwest
(Hwlffordd)
Milford Haven
(Aberdaugleddau)
Pembroke Dock
(Doc Penfro)
Pembroke
(Penfro)
Narberth
(Arberth)
Neyland
Pembrokeshire
(Sir Benfro)
MYNYDD PRESELI
PEMBROKESHIRE COAST PATH
LLWYBR ARFORDIR PENFRO
TREGWYNT WOOLLEN MILL
CHEESE CENTRE
CORSYDD LLANGLOFFAN
SCOLTON MANOR & COUNTRY PARK
LLYS-Y-FRAN RESERVOIR
PEMBROKE MOTOR MUSEUM
CASTLE MUSEUM AND ART GALLERY
LLAWHADEN CASTLE
PICTON CASTLE GARDENS
OAKWOOD
WILSON MUSEUM
HERONS BROOK
FOLLY FARM
UPTON CASTLE GROUNDS
CAREW CASTLE
LAMPHEY BISHOP'S PALACE
MANOR HOUSE WILDLIFE PARK
MANORBIER CASTLE
TUDOR MERCHANT
ELEGUG STACKS
STACKPOLE
FOEL-CWMCERWYN
DUDWELL MT.
Dyffryn
Manorowen
St Nicholas
Llanychaer
Scleddau
Abercastle
Granston
Mathry
Newbridge
Castlemorris
Penparc
Trecwn
Pontfaen
Carningli
Cilgwyn
Crosswell
Pontyglasier
Brynberian
New Inn
Rosebush
Treddiog
Letterston
Little Newcastle
Puncheston
Castlebythe
Llanreithan
Welsh Hook
St Dogwells
Tufton
Henry's Moat
Maenclochog
Llandeloy
Wolf's Castle
Pont-yr-hafod
Ambleston
Woodstock
Llangolman
Glandy Cross
Trefgarn Owen
Hayscastle
Brimaston
Rinaston
Wallis
New Moat
Hayscastle Cross
Triffleton
Llys-y-frân
Llanycefn
Mountain Water
Treffgarne
Spittal
Walton East
Penycwm
Leweston
Pen-ffordd
Newgale
Roch
Wolfsdale
Clarbeston
Bletherston
Llandissilio
Roch Gate
Camrose
Rudbaxton
Clarbeston Road
Llanfallteg
Nolton Haven
Simpson Cross
Keeston
Tangiers
Leechpool
Gelli
Clunderwen
Nolton
Pelcomb Cross
Crundale
Wiston
Bethesda
Lambston
Slade
Llawhaden
Druidston
Pelcomb Bridge
Robeston Wathen
Portfield Gate
Haroldston West
Dreenhill
The Rhos
Uzmaston
Blackpool
Crinow
Merlin's Bridge
Millin Cross
Broadway
Pope Hill
Boulston
Minwear
Cross Hands
Walton West
Cold Blow
Princes Gate
Templeton
Walwyn's Castle
North Johnston
Freystrop
Landshipping
Hook
Ludchurch
Landshipping Quay
Martletwy
Tiers Cross
Johnston
Longstone
Robeston Cross
Llangwm
Black Tar
Yerbeston
Reynalton
Thornton
Rosemarket
Thomas Chapel
Stepaside
Steynton
Hill Mountain
Port Lion
Loveston
Herbrandston
Houghton
Cresswell Quay
Begelly
Jeffreyston
Kilgetty
Honeyborough
Lawrenny
Cresselly
Hakin
Waterston
Burton
West Williamston
Broadmoor
Hill
Llanstadwell
Carew Newton
East Williamston
Saundersfoot
Redberth
Cosheston
Carew
Broadfield
Angle
Angle Bay
Bae Angle
Milton
Sageston
New Hedges
Pwllcrochan
Pennar
Carew Cheriton
Rhoscrowther
Monkton
St Florence
Gumfreston
Tenby
(Dinbych-y-Pysgod)
Hundleton
Lamphey
Freshwater West
Maiden Wells
Hodgeston
Jameston
Penally
St Twynnells
Freshwater East
Lydstep
Giltar Pt.
Castlemartin
Caldey Sound
Warren
St Petrox
Cheriton or Stackpole Elidor
Trewent Pt.
Trwyn Trewent
Manorbier
Caldey Island
Linney Hd.
Pentir Linney
Merrion
Old Castle Hd.
Stackpole
Chapel Pt.
Bosherston
Stackpole Hd.
Pen Stackpole
The Wash
St Govan's Hd./Pen St Gofan
A40
A487
A477
A478
A4076
A4075
A4115
A4139
B4329
B4313
B4331
B4330
B4341
B4327
B4325
B4322
B4320
B4319
B4584
B4318
B4316
B4586
B4314
72
73
56
TOLL
SN
SM
468
536
164
178
108
145
71
A
B
C
D
E

Llandissilio
Henllan Amgoed
Llanfallteg
Clunderwen
Meidrim
73
Merthyr
Tre-vaughan
LOVESPOON GALLERY
Carmarthen
(Caerfyrddin)
Llangynin
Cwmfelin Boeth
Sarnau
B4298
Llanllwch
Johnstown
GROVELANDS
B4299
Bancyfelin
CORS GOCH, LLANLLWCH
Bethesda
A478
B4313
A40
Pwll-trap
Llanddewi Velfrey
145
Whitland
Trevaughan
Backe
St Clears
(Sanclêr)
Afon Cywyn
Llangynog
153
Llangain
Afon Tâf
Crinow
Lampeter Velfrey
Llwyn-y-brain
Llanddowror
B4328
A4066
Morfa Bach
Afon Tywi
B4314
Tavernspite
A477
Halfpenny Furze
Llanybri
Cold Blow
Princes Gate
Red Roses
178
Llandawke
DYLAN THOMAS BOATHOUSE
B4312
Llandyfaelog
Templeton
A4115
Ludchurch
Llanteg
B4314
Llansteffan
Laugharne
CASTLE
Ferryside
55
FOLLY FARM
Llansadurnen
Brook
Broadway
Marros
MUSEUM OF SPEED
Broadlay
Thomas Chapel
Begelly
Stepaside
COLBY WOODLAND GARDEN
152
Pendine
East Marsh
Llansaint
Kilgetty
Amroth
Pendine Sands
Traeth Pentywyn
Hill
B4316
East Williamston
Saundersfoot
PEMBROKESHIRE COAST
ARFORDIR PENFRO
A478
Broadfield
SN
Pembrey Forest
New Hedges
TUDOR MERCHANT'S HOUSE
CARMARTHEN
Tenby
(Dinbych-y-Pysgod)
Gumfreston
PEMBREY
Penally
BAY
Giltar Pt.
Caldey Sound
BAE CAERFYRDDIN
Caldey Island
Ynys Bŷr
Chapel Pt.
Trwyn Capel
SS
Burry Holms
Rhossili Bay
Bae Rhossili
Worms Head
Penrhyn-Gŵyr
A
B
C
D
1
2
3
0 1 2 3 miles
0 1 2 3 4 5 km

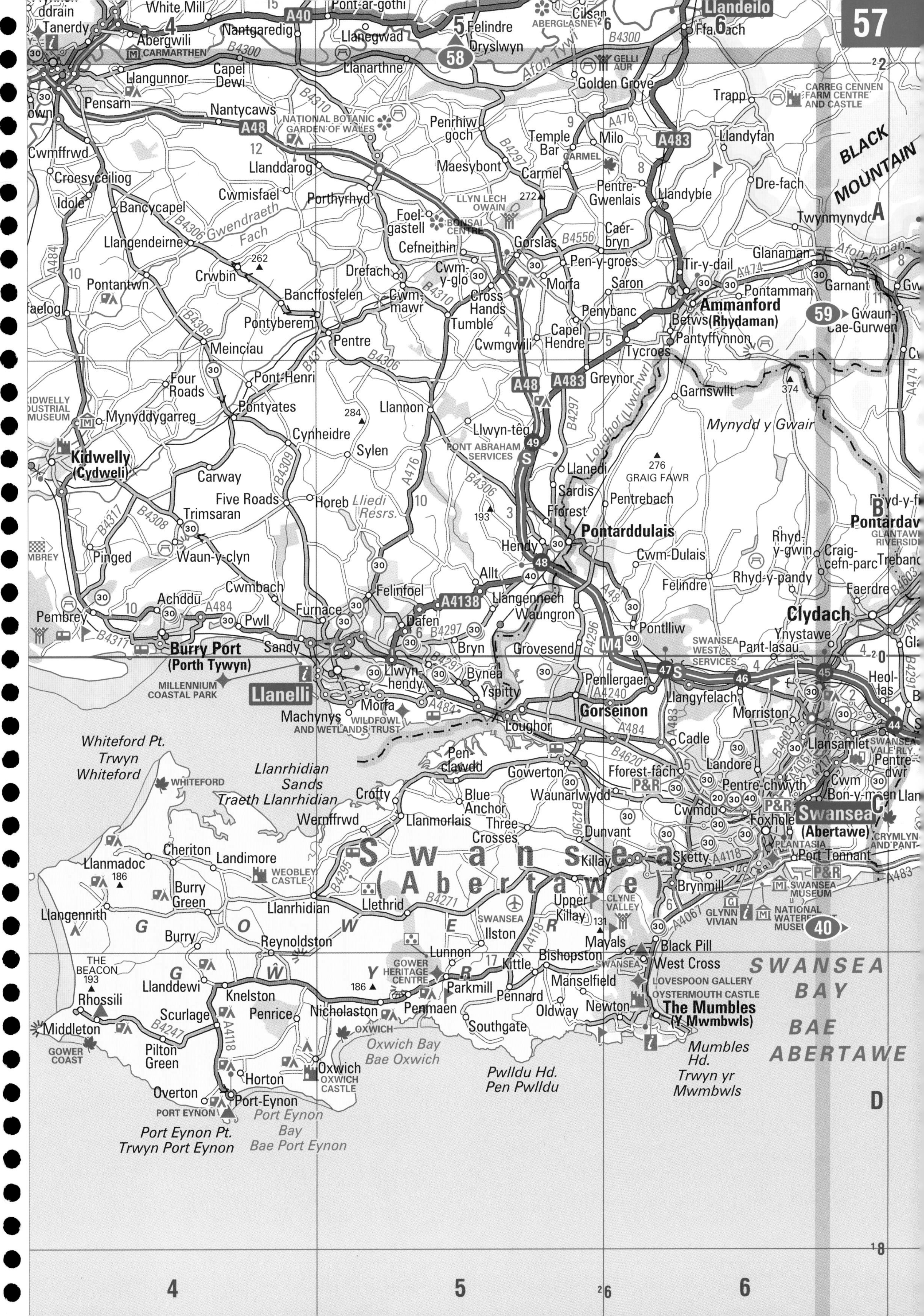

White Mill
Pont-ar-gothi
Llandeilo
Tanerdy
Abergwili
Nantgaredig
Felindre
Cilsan
ABERGLASNEY
Ffairfach
Dryslwyn
CARMARTHEN
Llanegwad
58
Llangunnor
Capel Dewi
Llanarthne
Afon Tywi
GELLI AUR
Golden Grove
CARREG CENNEN FARM CENTRE AND CASTLE
Trapp
Pensarn
Nantycaws
A48
NATIONAL BOTANIC GARDEN OF WALES
Penrhiw-goch
Temple Bar
Milo
A483
Llandyfan
BLACK MOUNTAIN
Cwmffrwd
Llanddarog
CARMEL
Maesybont
Carmel
Croesyceiliog
Pentre-Gwenlais
Llandybie
Dre-fach
Cwmisfael
Porthyrhyd
LLYN LLECH OWAIN
Idole
Bancycapel
Foel-gastell
BONSAI CENTRE
Caer-bryn
Twynmynydd
Gwendraeth Fach
Gorslas
Llangendeirne
Cefneithin
Pen-y-groes
Glanaman
Afon Aman
Tir-y-dail
Pontantwn
Crwbin
Drefach
Cwm-y-glo
Morfa
Saron
Pontamman
Garnant
Ammanford (Rhydaman)
Bancffosfelen
Cwm-mawr
Cross Hands
Penybanc
59
Gwaun-Cae-Gurwen
Betws
Pontyberem
Tumble
Capel Hendre
Pantyffynnon
Meinciau
Pentre
Cwmgwili
Tycroes
Four Roads
Pont-Henri
Greynor
KIDWELLY INDUSTRIAL MUSEUM
Pontyates
Llannon
Garnswllt
Mynyddygarreg
Cynheidre
Llwyn-têg
Mynydd y Gwair
Sylen
PONT ABRAHAM SERVICES
Kidwelly (Cydweli)
Loughor (Llwchwr)
Llanedi
GRAIG FAWR
Carway
Sardis
Five Roads
Horeb
Lliedi Resrs.
Pentrebach
Trimsaran
Fforest
Pontarddulais
Pontardawe
Rhyd-y-gwin
Craig-cefn-parc
GLANTAWE RIVERSIDE
Trebanos
Pinged
Waun-y-clyn
Hendy
Cwm-Dulais
Allt
Rhyd-y-pandy
Felindre
Cwmbach
Felinfoel
Llangennech
Waungron
Faerdre
Achddu
Pembrey
Pwll
Furnace
Dafen
A4138
Pontlliw
Clydach
Ynystawe
Burry Port (Porth Tywyn)
Sandy
Bryn
Grovesend
SWANSEA WEST SERVICES
Pant-lasau
Llwyn-hendy
Bynea
Ysbitty
Penllergaer
Heol-las
MILLENNIUM COASTAL PARK
Llanelli
Morfa
Gorseinon
Llangyfelach
Morriston
Machynys
WILDFOWL AND WETLANDS TRUST
Loughor
Cadle
Llansamlet
SWANSEA VALE RLY.
Whiteford Pt. Trwyn Whiteford
Pen-clawdd
Fforest-fach
Landore
Pentre-dwr
WHITEFORD
Llanrhidian Sands Traeth Llanrhidian
Gowerton
Pentre-chwyth
Cwm
Crofty
Blue Anchor
Waunarlwydd
Cwmdu
Bon-y-maen
Swansea (Abertawe)
Wernffrwd
Llanmorlais
Three Crosses
Dunvant
Foxhole
CRYMLYN AND PANT-Y-SAIS
Cheriton
Landimore
Swansea (Abertawe)
Killay
Sketty
PLANTASIA
Port Tennant
Llanmadoc
WEOBLEY CASTLE
Burry Green
Brynmill
SWANSEA MUSEUM
Llangennith
Llanrhidian
Llethrid
Upper Killay
CLYNE VALLEY
GLYNN VIVIAN
NATIONAL WATERFRONT MUSEUM
40
Gower
Burry
Reynoldston
SWANSEA
Ilston
Mayals
Black Pill
THE BEACON
Lunnon
Kittle
Bishopston
West Cross
SWANSEA BAY
Rhossili
Llanddewi
Knelston
GOWER HERITAGE CENTRE
Parkmill
Manselfield
LOVESPOON GALLERY
OYSTERMOUTH CASTLE
BAE ABERTAWE
Scurlage
Penrice
Nicholaston
Penmaen
Pennard
Oldway
Newton
The Mumbles (Y Mwmbwls)
Middleton
OXWICH
Southgate
Oxwich Bay Bae Oxwich
Mumbles Hd. Trwyn yr Mwmbwls
GOWER COAST
Pilton Green
Oxwich
OXWICH CASTLE
Horton
Pwlldu Hd. Pen Pwlldu
Overton
Port-Eynon
PORT EYNON
Port Eynon Bay Bae Port Eynon
Port Eynon Pt. Trwyn Port Eynon
A
B
C
D
4
5
6

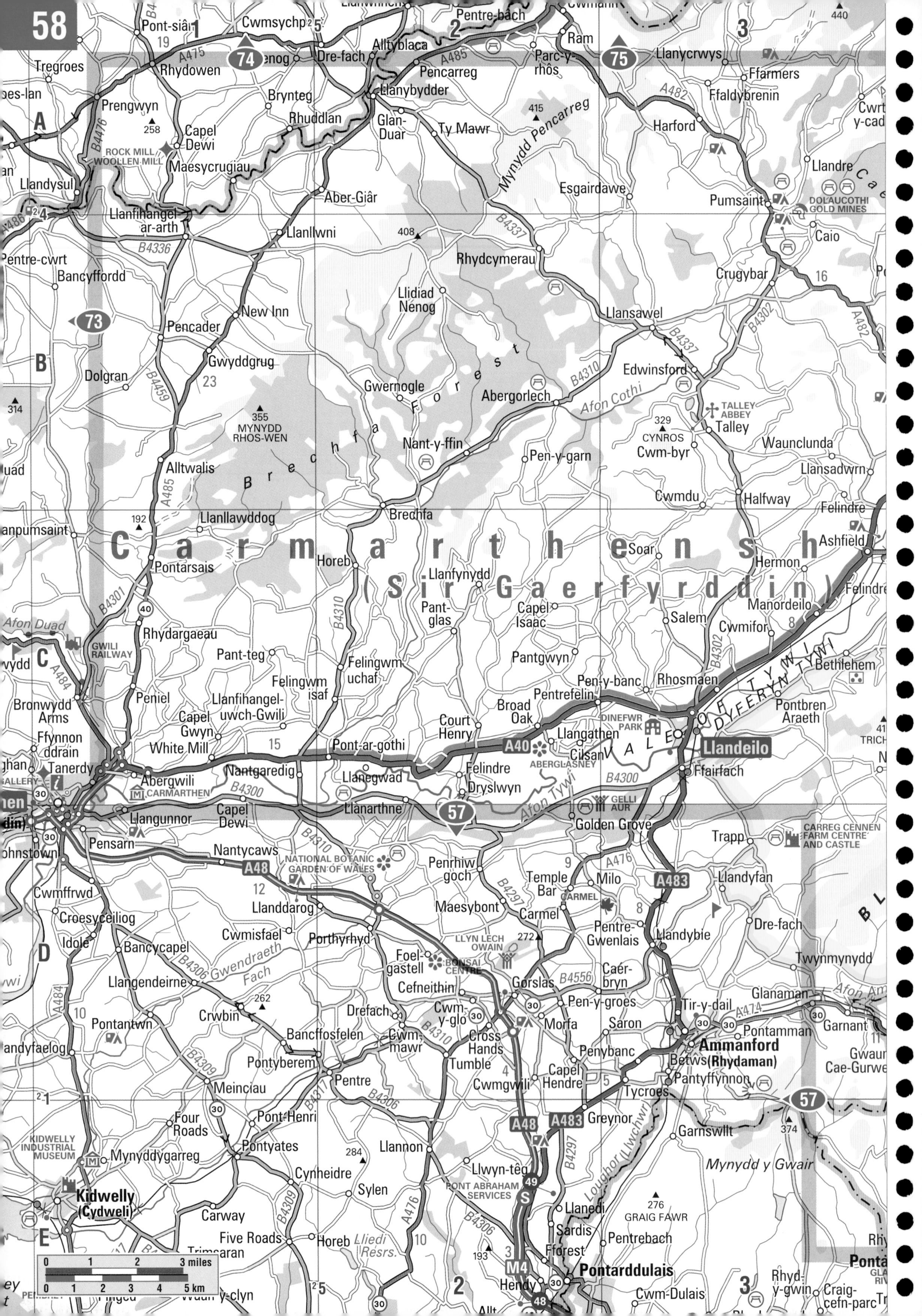

Pont-siân
Cwmsychpant
Pentre-bach
Ram
Tregroes
Rhydowen
Dre-fach
Alltyblaca
Pencarreg
Parc-y-rhôs
Llanycrwys
Ffarmers
Ffaldybrenin
Prengwyn
Brynteg
Llanybydder
Rhuddlan
Glan-Duar
Ty Mawr
Mynydd Pencarreg
Harford
Capel Dewi
ROCK MILL WOOLLEN MILL
Maesycrugiau
Llandysul
Aber-Giâr
Esgairdawe
Llandre
Pumsaint
DOLAUCOTHI GOLD MINES
Caio
Llanfihangel-ar-arth
Llanllwni
Rhydcymerau
Crugybar
Pentre-cwrt
Bancyffordd
Llidiad Nenog
Llansawel
New Inn
Pencader
Gwyddgrug
Edwinsford
Gwernogle
Abergorlech
Afon Cothi
Dolgran
MYNYDD RHOS-WEN
TALLEY ABBEY
CYNROS
Talley
Cwm-byr
Wauncluna
Llansadwrn
Nant-y-ffin
Pen-y-garn
Alltwalis
Brechfa Forest
Cwmdu
Halfway
Felindre
Brechfa
Llanllawddog
Llanpumsaint
Carmarthenshire (Sir Gaerfyrddin)
Soar
Ashfield
Horeb
Hermon
Pontarsais
Llanfynydd
Felindre
Manordeilo
Pant-glas
Capel Isaac
Salem
Cwmifor
Afon Duad
Rhydargaeau
GWILI RAILWAY
Pant-teg
Pantgwyn
Bethlehem
Felingwm uchaf
Felingwm isaf
Pen-y-banc
Rhosmaen
Vale of Tywi
Dyffryn Tywi
Bronwydd Arms
Peniel
Llanfihangel-uwch-Gwili
Pentrefelin
Broad Oak
Court Henry
Pontbren Araeth
Capel Gwyn
DINEFWR PARK
Ffynnon ddrain
White Mill
Pont-ar-gothi
Llangathen
Cilsan
Llandeilo
Tanerdy
Nantgaredig
Felindre
ABERGLASNEY
Ffairfach
Abergwili
Llanegwad
Dryslwyn
CARMARTHEN
Llangunnor
Capel Dewi
Llanarthne
Afon Tywi
GELLI AUR
Golden Grove
Trapp
CARREG CENNEN FARM CENTRE AND CASTLE
Pensarn
Nantycaws
NATIONAL BOTANIC GARDEN OF WALES
Penrhiw-goch
Temple Bar
Milo
Llandyfan
Cwmffrwd
Llanddarog
Maesybont
CARMEL
Carmel
Pentre-Gwenlais
Llandybie
Dre-fach
Croesyceiliog
Idole
Bancycapel
Cwmisfael
Porthyrhyd
LLYN LLECH OWAIN
Foel-gastell
BONSAI CENTRE
Gwendraeth Fach
Twynmynydd
Llangendeirne
Cefneithin
Gorslas
Caer-bryn
Glanaman
Crwbin
Drefach
Cwm-y-glo
Pen-y-groes
Tir-y-dail
Pontantwn
Morfa
Saron
Garnant
Pontamman
Ammanford
Bancffosfelen
Cwm-mawr
Cross Hands
Penybanc
Betws
(Rhydaman)
Gwaun-Cae-Gurwen
Pontyberem
Tumble
Pantyffynnon
Pentre
Meinciau
Cwmgwili
Capel Hendre
Tycroes
Four Roads
Pont-Henri
Greynor
Garnswllt
KIDWELLY INDUSTRIAL MUSEUM
Pontyates
Mynyddygarreg
Llannon
Mynydd y Gwair
Cynheidre
Llwyn-têg
Kidwelly
(Cydweli)
Sylen
PONT ABRAHAM SERVICES
Llanedi
GRAIG FAWR
Carway
Loughor (Llwchwr)
Sardis
Five Roads
Horeb
Lliedi Resrs.
Pentrebach
Trimsaran
Fforest
Pontarddulais
Hendy
Rhyd-y-gwin
Craig-cefn-parc
Cwm-Dulais
A475
A485
A482
B4476
B4336
B4337
B4459
B4310
B4302
B4301
A484
A40
B4300
A48
A476
B4297
A483
B4306
B4556
A474
B4309
B4317
M4
0 1 2 3 miles
0 1 2 3 4 5 km

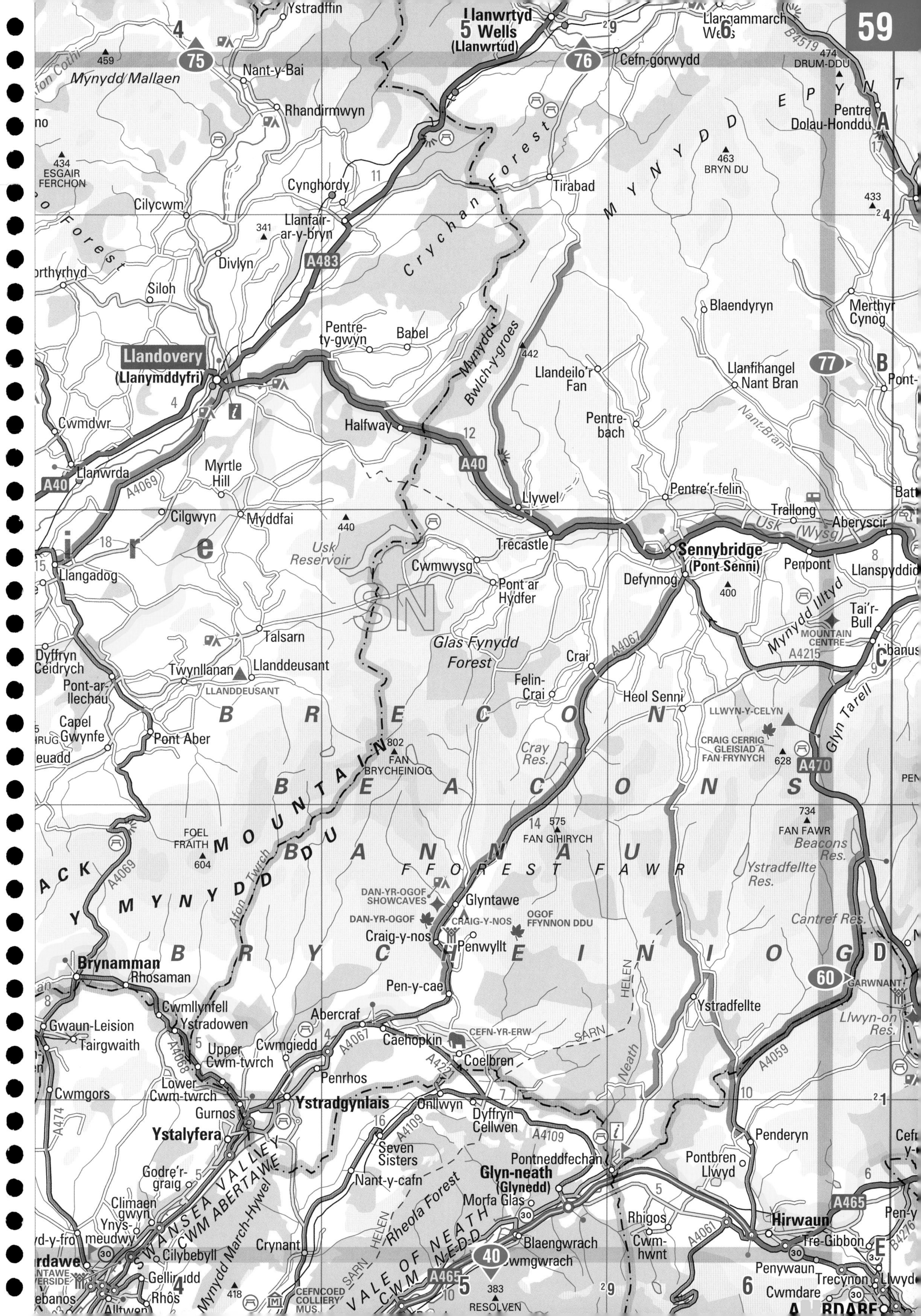
Ystradffin
Llanwrtyd Wells (Llanwrtud)
Llangammarch Wells
75
76
Mynydd Mallaen
Nant-y-Bai
Cefn-gorwydd
474 DRUM-DDU
Rhandirmwyn
MYNYDD EPYNT
Pentre Dolau-Honddu
434 ESGAIR FERCHON
Cynghordy
Tirabad
463 BRYN DU
Cilycwm
Llanfair-ar-y-bryn
Crychan Forest
Divlyn
A483
Siloh
Blaendyryn
Merthyr Cynog
Pentre-ty-gwyn
Babel
Mynydd Bwlch-y-groes
442
Llandovery (Llanymddyfri)
Llandeilo'r Fan
Llanfihangel Nant Bran
77
Cwmdwr
Halfway
Pentre-bach
Nant-Bran
Llanwrda
A40
Myrtle Hill
A4069
Llywel
Pentre'r-felin
Cilgwyn
Myddfai
440
Trallong
Aberyscir
Usk Reservoir
Trecastle
Sennybridge (Pont Senni)
Penpont
Llanspyddid
Llangadog
Cwmwysg
Defynnog
Pont ar Hydfer
400
SN
Mynydd Illtyd
Tai'r-Bull
MOUNTAIN CENTRE
Talsarn
Glas Fynydd Forest
A4067
A4215
Dyffryn Ceidrych
Twynllanan
Llanddeusant
Crai
LLANDDEUSANT
Pont-ar-llechau
Felin-Crai
Heol Senni
Capel Gwynfe
LLWYN-Y-CELYN
Glyn Tarell
Pont Aber
BRECON BEACONS
802 FAN BRYCHEINIOG
Cray Res.
CRAIG CERRIG GLEISIAD A FAN FRYNYCH
628
A470
BLACK MOUNTAIN
734 FAN FAWR
575 FAN GIHIRYCH
FOEL FRAITH 604
Beacons Res.
FFOREST FAWR
Ystradfellte Res.
MYNYDD DU
Afon Twrch
DAN-YR-OGOF SHOWCAVES
Glyntawe
DAN-YR-OGOF
CRAIG-Y-NOS
OGOF FFYNNON DDU
Cantref Res.
Craig-y-nos
Penwyllt
FFOREST FAWR GEOPARK
Brynamman
Rhosaman
60
GARWNANT
Pen-y-cae
Cwmllynfell
Ystradfellte
Gwaun-Leision
Ystradowen
Abercraf
Llwyn-on Res.
Tairgwaith
Cwmgiedd
Caehopkin
CEFN-YR-ERW
SARN HELEN
Upper Cwm-twrch
Coelbren
Neath
A4059
A4068
Penrhos
A4221
Cwmgors
Lower Cwm-twrch
Ystradgynlais
Onllwyn
Gurnos
Dyffryn Cellwen
Ystalyfera
A4109
Penderyn
Seven Sisters
Pontneddfechan
Pontbren Llwyd
Godre'r-graig
Nant-y-cafn
Glyn-neath (Glynedd)
SWANSEA VALLEY CWM ABERTAWE
Rheola Forest
Morfa Glas
A465
Climaen gwyn
Rhigos
Hirwaun
Ynys-meudwy
Mynydd March-Hywel
VALE OF NEATH CWM NEDD
Cwm-hwnt
A4061
Tre-Gibbon
Cilybebyll
Crynant
Blaengwrach
Penywaun
Gellinudd
40
Cwmgwrach
Trecynon
Rhôs
418
CEFNCOED COLLIERY MUS.
383 RESOLVEN
Cwmdare

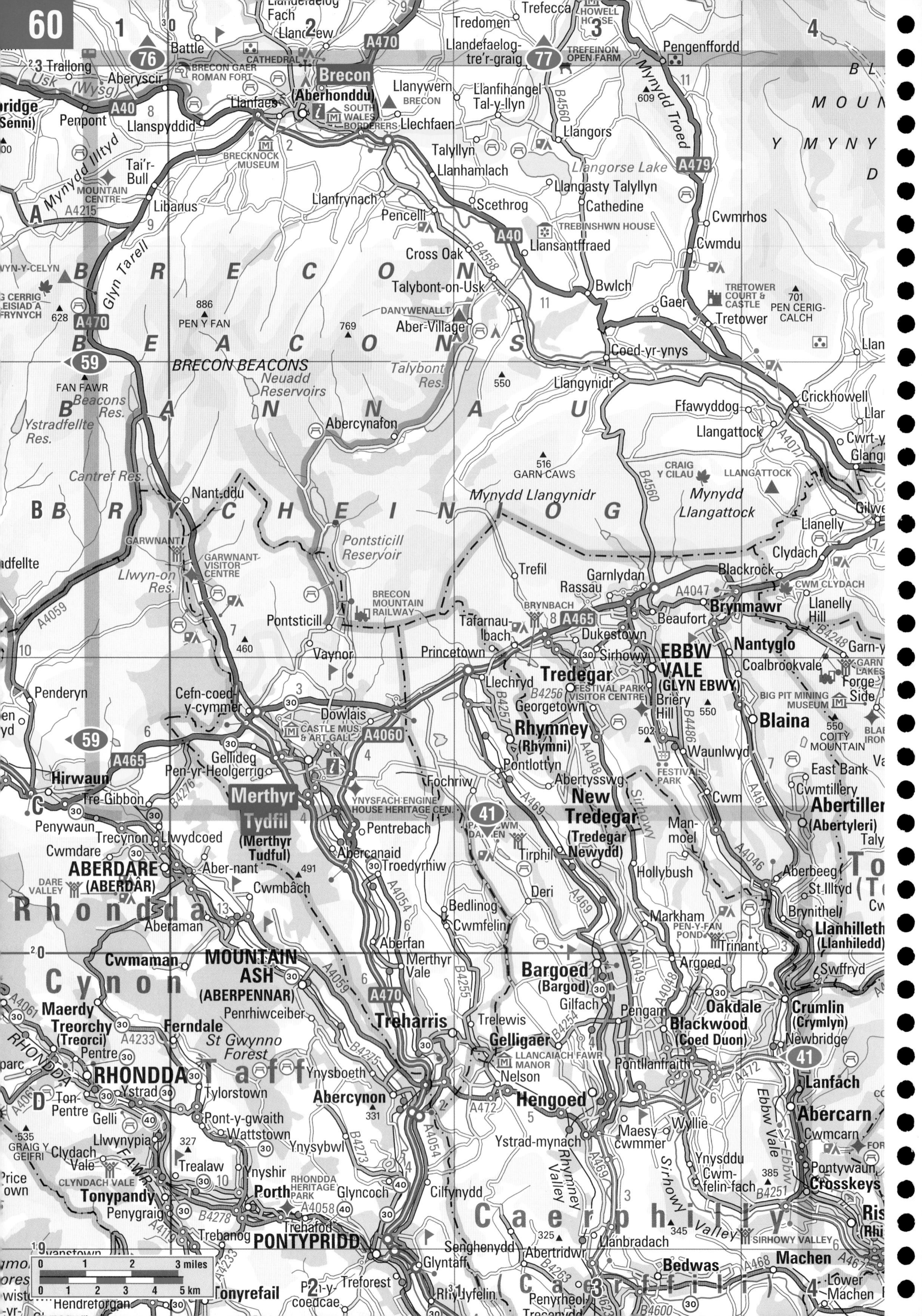

Brecon
(Aberhonddu)
BRECON BEACONS
Brecon Beacons
Fforest Fawr
Merthyr Tydfil
(Merthyr Tudful)
ABERDARE
(ABERDÂR)
MOUNTAIN ASH
(ABERPENNAR)
RHONDDA
PONTYPRIDD
EBBW VALE
(GLYN EBWY)
Tredegar
Rhymney
(Rhymni)
New Tredegar
(Tredegar Newydd)
Bargoed
(Bargod)
Blackwood
(Coed Duon)
Abertillery
(Abertyleri)
Crickhowell
Brynmawr
Nantyglo
Blaina
Hirwaun
Treharris
Abercynon
Gelligaer
Hengoed
Oakdale
Crumlin
(Crymlyn)
Abercarn
Crosskeys
Machen
Bedwas
Porth
Tonypandy
Treorchy
(Treorci)
Ferndale
Maerdy
Llangorse Lake
Talybont-on-Usk
Pontsticill Reservoir
Mynydd Llangynidr
Mynydd Llangattock
Rhondda
Cynon
Taff
Caerphilly
(Caerffili)
Brycheiniog
0 1 2 3 miles
0 1 2 3 4 5 km

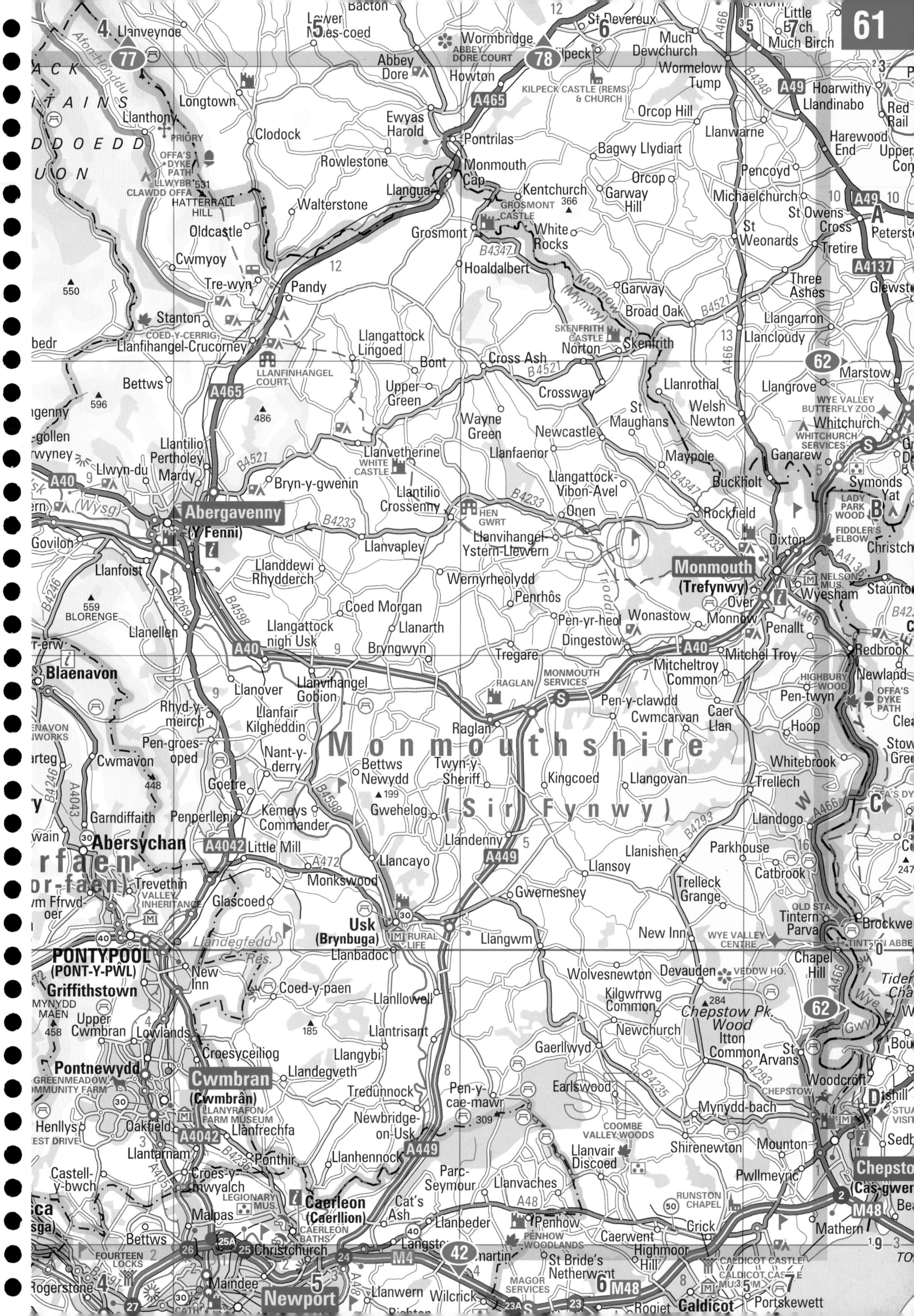

Llanveynoe
Lower Maes-coed
Bacton
Wormbridge
ABBEY DORE COURT
St Devereux
Kilpeck
Much Dewchurch
Little Birch
Much Birch
Abbey Dore
Howton
KILPECK CASTLE (REMS) & CHURCH
Wormelow Tump
Hoarwithy
Llandinabo
Longtown
Llanthony
PRIORY
Clodock
Ewyas Harold
Pontrilas
Orcop Hill
Llanwarne
Red Rail
Harewood End
Bagwy Llydiart
Rowlestone
OFFA'S DYKE PATH
LLWYBR CLAWDD OFFA
HATTERRALL HILL
531
Monmouth Cap
Llangua
Kentchurch
Orcop
Garway Hill
Pencoyd
Michaelchurch
Walterstone
GROSMONT CASTLE
366
St Owens Cross
Oldcastle
Grosmont
White Rocks
St Weonards
Tretire
Cwmyoy
Hoaldalbert
Tre-wyn
Pandy
550
Garway
Three Ashes
Broad Oak
Monnow (Mynwy)
Stanton
COED-Y-CERRIG
Llanfihangel-Crucorney
SKENFRITH CASTLE
Norton
Skenfrith
Llangarron
Llancloudy
Llangattock Lingoed
Bont
Cross Ash
LLANFINHANGEL COURT
Bettws
596
Upper Green
Crossway
Llanrothal
Marstow
Llangrove
486
St Maughans
Welsh Newton
WYE VALLEY BUTTERFLY ZOO
Wayne Green
Newcastle
Whitchurch
WHITCHURCH SERVICES
Llantilio Pertholey
Mardy
Llwyn-du
Llanvetherine
WHITE CASTLE
Llanfaenor
Maypole
Ganarew
Bryn-y-gwenin
Llangattock-Vibon-Avel
Buckholt
Symonds Yat
Llantilio Crossenny
HEN GWRT
Onen
Rockfield
LADY PARK WOOD
FIDDLER'S ELBOW
Abergavenny (Y Fenni)
Govilon
Llanvapley
Llanvihangel-Ystern-Llewern
Dixton
Monmouth (Trefynwy)
Llanfoist
Llanddewi Rhydderch
Wernyrheolydd
NELSON MUS.
Wyesham
Penrhôs
559 BLORENGE
Coed Morgan
Llanarth
Pen-yr-heol
Wonastow
Over Monnow
Penallt
Llanellen
Llangattock nigh Usk
Dingestow
Mitchel Troy
Redbrook
Blaenavon
Bryngwyn
Tregare
Mitcheltroy Common
Newland
Llanover
Llanvihangel Gobion
RAGLAN
MONMOUTH SERVICES
HIGHBURY WOOD
OFFA'S DYKE PATH
Rhyd-y-meirch
Llanfair Kilgheddin
Pen-y-clawdd
Pen-twyn
Cwmcarvan
Caer Llan
Raglan
Hoop
Pen-groes-oped
Nant-y-derry
Monmouthshire (Sir Fynwy)
Cwmavon
Bettws Newydd
Twyn-y-Sheriff
Kingcoed
Llangovan
Whitebrook
Trellech
Goetre
199
448
Garndiffaith
Penperlleni
Kemeys Commander
Gwehelog
Llandogo
Abersychan
Little Mill
Llandenny
Llanishen
Parkhouse
Llancayo
Torfaen (Tor-faen)
Trevethin
VALLEY INHERITANCE
Monkswood
Llansoy
Catbrook
Trelleck Grange
Glascoed
Gwernesney
Usk (Brynbuga)
RURAL LIFE
OLD STA.
Tintern Parva
Brockweir
New Inn
WYE VALLEY CENTRE
Llandegfedd Res.
Llangwm
PONTYPOOL (PONT-Y-PŴL)
Llanbadoc
Chapel Hill
Griffithstown
New Inn
Wolvesnewton
Devauden
VEDDW HO.
MYNYDD MAEN
458
Coed-y-paen
Kilgwrrwg Common
284
Chepstow Pk. Wood
Upper Cwmbran
Lowlands
Llanllowell
Itton Common
Newchurch
185
Llantrisant
Croesyceiliog
Gaerllwyd
St Arvans
Pontnewydd
Llangybi
GREENMEADOW COMMUNITY FARM
Llandegveth
Cwmbran (Cwmbrân)
Tredunnock
Pen-y-cae-mawr
Earlswood
CHEPSTOW
Woodcroft
Henllys
Oakfield
LLANYRAFON FARM MUSEUM
Newbridge-on-Usk
309
COOMBE VALLEY WOODS
Mynydd-bach
Llanfrechfa
Llantarnam
Ponthir
Llanhennock
Llanvair Discoed
Shirenewton
Mounton
Chepstow (Cas-gwent)
Castell-y-bwch
Croes-y-mwyalch
Parc-Seymour
Llanvaches
Pwllmeyric
LEGIONARY MUS.
Caerleon (Caerllion)
Cat's Ash
RUNSTON CHAPEL
Malpas
CAERLEON BATHS
Llanbeder
Penhow
PENHOW WOODLANDS
Crick
Mathern
Bettws
Christchurch
Langstone
Caerwent
Highmoor Hill
FOURTEEN LOCKS
Llanmartin
St Bride's Netherwent
CALDICOT CASTLE
CALDICOT CASTLE MUSEUM
Rogerstone
Maindee
Newport
Llanwern
Wilcrick
MAGOR SERVICES
Rogiet
Caldicot
Portskewett
A465
A40
A449
A4042
A466
A49
A4137
A48
M4
M48
B4521
B4233
B4347
B4598
B4269
B4246
B4293
B4235
77
78
62

Dewchurch
Ballingham
Falcon
Crossway
Lyne Down
Dymock
Ryton
Redmarley D'Abitot
Playley Green
Care
78
Fawley Chapel
Penalt
How Caple
Hoarwithy
Llandinabo
Red Rail
King's Caple
Foy
Hole-in-the-Wall
Fishpool
Kempley
ST MARY'S CHURCH
79
M50
Poolhill
Brand Green
Staunton
Corse
Leadon
Harewood End
Upper Grove Common
Sellack
Brampton Abbotts
Phocle Green
Crow Hill
Upton Bishop
Upleadon
Pencoyd
ROSS SPUR SERVICES
Gorsley
Newent
Michaelchurch
St Owens Cross
Bridstow
Rudhall
Linton
Kilcot
Malswick
Hartpury
St Weonards
Peterstow
Ross-on-Wye
Bromsash
Aston Ingham
BIRDS OF PREY
Tretire
CANDLEMAKERS
Aston Crews
Kent's Green
Highleadon
Three Ashes
A4137
Tudorville
Weston under Penyard
Clifford's Mesne
Glewstone
Hom Green
Coughton
Pontshill
Lea
Tibberton
Taynton
Rudford
Lassington
Llangarron
Pencraig
Llancloudy
Walford
Glasshouse Hill
Highnam Green
61
Goodrich
Hope Mansell
Marstow
Kerne Bridge
Mitcheldean
Longhope
Huntley
Bulley
Highnam
Llangrove
WYE VALLEY BUTTERFLY ZOO
JUBILEE MAZE
Birdwood
Churcham
Whitchurch
WHITCHURCH SERVICES
Welsh Bicknor
WELSH BICKNOR
Ruardean
Drybrook
Oakle Street
Ganarew
Greater Doward
Ruardean Woodside
Blaisdon
Minsterworth
Lower Lydbrook
Upper Lydbrook
Nailbridge
Northwood Green
Elmore Back
Elmore
Symonds Yat
English Bicknor
Flaxley
Westbury-on-Severn
Farleys End
LADY PARK WOOD
Brierley
FIDDLER'S ELBOW
Dixton
Christchurch
Edge End
Cinderford
Elton
Quedgeley
Bilson Green
Littledean
Monmouth
NELSON MUS.
Berry Hill
Five Acres
FOREST
200
LITTLEDEAN HALL
WESTBURY COURT
Boxbush
Longney
Hardwicke
Over
Wyesham
Staunton
Mile End
COLLIERY MUSEUM
OF
Ruspidge
Newnham
Rodley
Penallt
Coleford
Broadwell
DEAN
Upper Soudley
DEAN HERITAGE CENTRE
WORKING FARM
Arlingham
Upper Framilode
Mitchel Troy
Redbrook
G.W.R. MUSEUM
Coalway
Fretherne
Saul
Moreton Valence
HIGHBURY WOOD
Newland
IRON MINES
OFFA'S DYKE PATH
CAVES
Milkwall
Ellwood
Parkend
Awre
Whitminster
Pen-twyn
Hoop
Clearwell
Yorkley
Frampton on Severn
Stowe Green
Trow Green
Whitecroft
Pillowell
Viney Hill
Blakeney
Whitebrook
Trellech
OFFA'S DYKE
The Eaves
Bream
DEAN FOREST RAILWAY & MUSEUM
WWT SLIMBRIDGE WETLAND CENTRE
Eastington
Llandogo
St Briavels
ST. BRIAVELS
Purton
SLIMBRIDGE
Cambridge
Leonard Stanley
Parkhouse
Coldharbour
Lydney
Newerne
Sharpness
Slimbridge
Moorend
Frocester
Catbrook
247
Hewelsfield
Halmore
Newtown
Gossington
Coaley
OLD STA.
Tintern Parva
Brockweir
Aylburton
Wanswell
Breadstone
Lower Cam
TINTERN ABBEY
Netherend
Alvington
The Quarry
Nympsfield
Chapel Hill
Woolaston
Brookend
Berkeley
Cam
ULEY TUMULUS
BERKELEY CASTLE
JENNER MUSEUM
Stinchcombe
Dursley
Ham
Uley
Wibdon
Stroat
Woodmancote
Bevington
St Arvans
Boughspring
249
Woodcroft
Tidenham
Shepperdine
Hill
Woodford
Stone
Nibley Green
North Nibley
MICHAELWOOD SERVICES
CHEPSTOW
Tutshill
STUART CRYSTAL VISITOR CENTRE
OLDBURY POWER STA. & VISITOR CENTRE
Mounton
Sedbury
Rockhampton
Falfield
Tortworth
Wotton-under-Edge
Chepstow
(Cas-gwent)
Oldbury-on-Severn
Charfield
Pwllmeyric
Whitfield
Kingswood
ABBEY GATEHOUSE
Beachley
Morton
SEVERN ROAD BRIDGE PONT HAFREN
Littleton-on-Severn
Mathern
Milbury Heath
Cromhall
Churchend
Alderley
SEVERN VIEW SERVICES
Thornbury
43
Cromhall Common
Hillesley
Elberton
Alveston
Ingst
Tytherington
Wickwar
Portskewett
OLDOWN
A49
A449
A40
A4136
A48
A466
A38
A4135
M5
M48
A417
B4234
B4224
B4228
B4226
B4231
B4221
B4215
B4222
B4058
B4060
B4059
B4061
B4461
B4066
B4293
B4235
0 1 2 3 miles
0 1 2 3 4 5 km

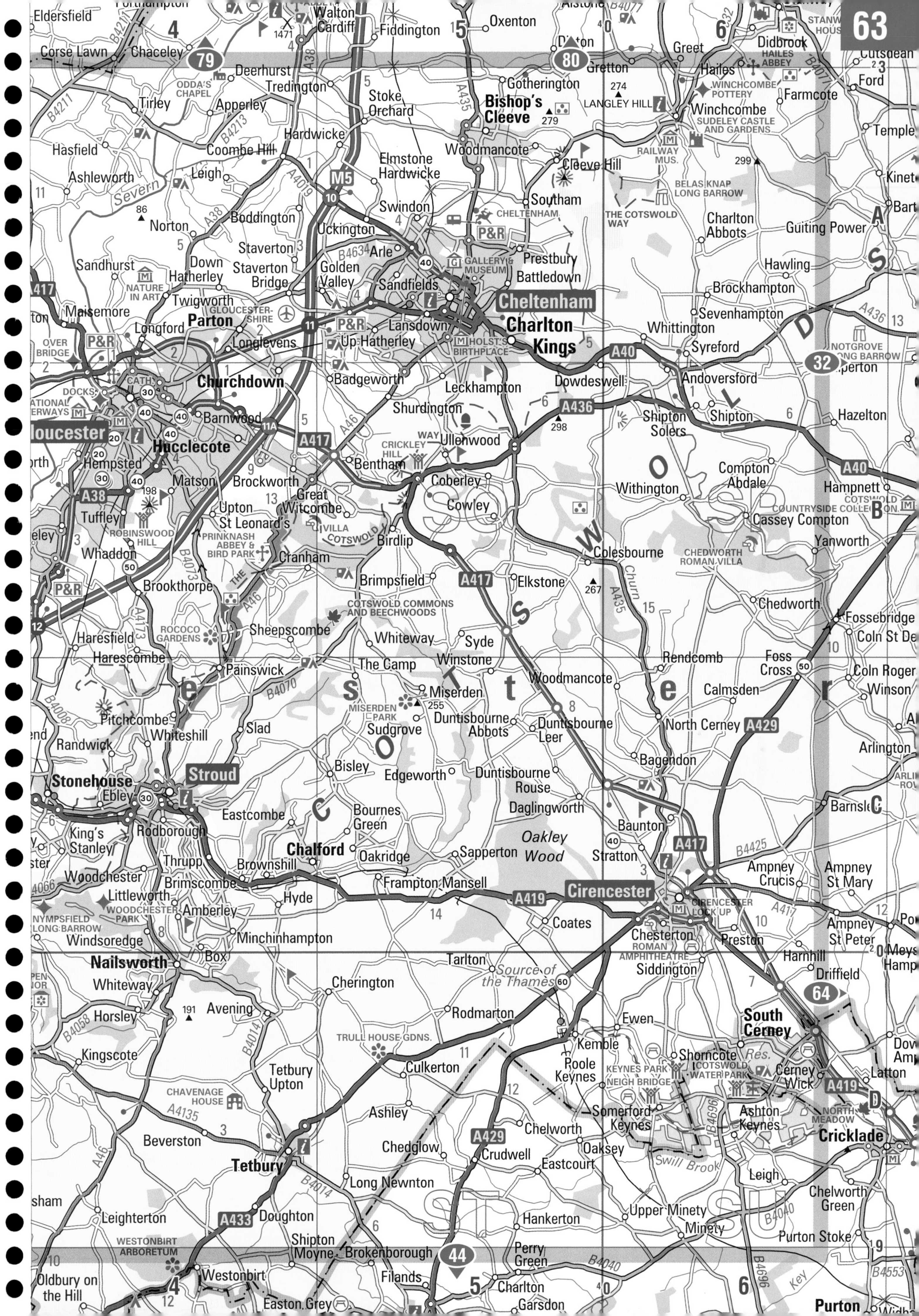
Eldersfield
Walton Cardiff
Fiddington
Oxenton
Alstone
Dixton
Greet
Didbrook
HAILES ABBEY
STANWAY HOUSE
Cutsdean
Corse Lawn
Chaceley
79
80
Deerhurst
ODDA'S CHAPEL
Tredington
Stoke Orchard
Gotherington
Gretton
Hailes
Ford
Tirley
Apperley
Bishop's Cleeve
LANGLEY HILL
WINCHCOMBE POTTERY
Farmcote
Winchcombe
SUDELEY CASTLE AND GARDENS
Temple
Hasfield
Hardwicke
Coombe Hill
Woodmancote
Elmstone Hardwicke
RAILWAY MUS.
Cleeve Hill
Ashleworth
Leigh
Severn
M5
BELAS KNAP LONG BARROW
Kineton
Southam
Swindon
Norton
Boddington
Uckington
CHELTENHAM
THE COTSWOLD WAY
Charlton Abbots
Guiting Power
Barton
Staverton
Arle
P&R
GALLERY & MUSEUM
Prestbury
Sandhurst
Down Hatherley
Staverton Bridge
Golden Valley
Sandfields
Battledown
Hawling
NATURE IN ART
Twigworth
GLOUCESTER-SHIRE
Cheltenham
Brockhampton
Maisemore
Parton
Longford
Lansdown
Charlton Kings
Sevenhampton
Whittington
A436
OVER BRIDGE
Longlevens
Up Hatherley
HOLST'S BIRTHPLACE
Syreford
NOTGROVE LONG BARROW
A40
32
Churchdown
CATH.
Badgeworth
Leckhampton
Dowdeswell
Andoversford
DOCKS
Shurdington
A436
Shipton Solers
Shipton
Hazelton
Barnwood
Gloucester
Hucclecote
A417
CRICKLEY HILL
WAY
Ullenwood
Hempsted
Bentham
Compton Abdale
A40
Matson
Brockworth
Coberley
Withington
Hampnett
Great Witcombe
Cowley
COTSWOLD COUNTRYSIDE COLLECTION
A38
Tuffley
Upton St Leonard's
Cassey Compton
ROBINSWOOD HILL
VILLA
COTSWOLD
Birdlip
Yanworth
PRINKNASH ABBEY & BIRD PARK
Whaddon
Cranham
Colesbourne
CHEDWORTH ROMAN VILLA
THE
Brimpsfield
A417
Elkstone
Brookthorpe
COTSWOLD COMMONS AND BEECHWOODS
Churn
Chedworth
Fossebridge
ROCOCO GARDENS
Haresfield
Sheepscombe
Whiteway
Syde
Coln St Dennis
Harescombe
Painswick
The Camp
Winstone
Rendcomb
Foss Cross
Coln Rogers
Winson
Woodmancote
Miserden
MISERDEN PARK
Calmsden
Pitchcombe
Whiteshill
Slad
Sudgrove
Duntisbourne Abbots
Duntisbourne Leer
North Cerney
A429
Randwick
Arlington
Bisley
Bagendon
Stroud
Stonehouse
Edgeworth
Duntisbourne Rouse
Ebley
Eastcombe
Bournes Green
Daglingworth
Barnsley
King's Stanley
Rodborough
Chalford
Oakley Wood
Baunton
Stratton
Thrupp
Oakridge
Sapperton
A417
Woodchester
Brimscombe
Brownshill
Frampton Mansell
Ampney Crucis
Ampney St Mary
Littleworth
Hyde
A419
Cirencester
CIRENCESTER LOCK UP
NYMPSFIELD LONG BARROW
WOODCHESTER PARK
Amberley
Coates
Ampney St Peter
Windsoredge
Minchinhampton
Chesterton
ROMAN AMPHITHEATRE
Preston
Nailsworth
Box
Tarlton
Source of the Thames
Siddington
Harnhill
Driffield
Meysey Hampton
Whiteway
Cherington
64
Horsley
Avening
Rodmarton
Ewen
South Cerney
TRULL HOUSE GDNS.
Kemble
Kingscote
Poole Keynes
KEYNES PARK
NEIGH BRIDGE
Shorncote
COTSWOLD WATER PARK
Res.
Cerney Wick
Latton
Tetbury Upton
Culkerton
CHAVENAGE HOUSE
A419
Ashley
Somerford Keynes
Ashton Keynes
NORTH MEADOW
Cricklade
A4135
Beverston
A429
Chelworth
Oaksey
Chedglow
Crudwell
Eastcourt
Swill Brook
Tetbury
Leigh
Long Newnton
Chelworth Green
B4014
Leighterton
A433
Doughton
Hankerton
Upper Minety
Minety
Purton Stoke
Shipton Moyne
Brokenborough
Perry Green
44
WESTONBIRT ARBORETUM
Oldbury on the Hill
Westonbirt
Filands
Charlton
B4040
Key
Easton Grey
Garsdon
Purton

Stow-on-the-Wold
Chipping Norton
Burford
Carterton
Fairford
Lechlade-on-Thames
Faringdon
Highworth
Cricklade
South Cerney
COTSWOLDS
VALE OF WHITE HORSE
Sezincote
Longborough
Donnington
Condicote
Temple Guiting
Kineton
Barton
Guiting Power
Naunton
Hawling
Brockhampton
Upper Swell
Lower Swell
Upper Slaughter
Lower Slaughter
THE OLD MILL
Wyck Rissington
Bourton-on-the-Water
MINIATURE WORLD
BIRDLAND PARK
Notgrove
NOTGROVE LONG BARROW
Salperton
Cold Aston
Hazelton
Turkdean
Clapton-on-the-Hill
Little Rissington
Great Rissington
Upper Rissington
Farmington
Hampnett
COTSWOLD COUNTRYSIDE COLLECTION
Northleach
Cassey Compton
Compton Abdale
Yanworth
Eastington
LODGE PARK
Sherborne
Windrush
Great Barrington
Little Barrington
Taynton
Fulbrook
Chedworth
Fossebridge
Coln St Dennis
Foss Cross
Coln Rogers
Winson
Aldsworth
Ablington
Arlington
ARLINGTON MILL
Bibury
ARLINGTON ROW (N.T.)
Coln St Aldwyn's
Barnsley
Hatherop
Quenington
Eastleach Turville
Eastleach Martin
Fyfield
Southrop
Ampney Crucis
Ampney St Mary
Ampney St Peter
Poulton
Milton End
Horcott
Meysey Hampton
Harnhill
Driffield
Preston
Marston Meysey
Whelford
Dunfield
Kempsford
Down Ampney
Latton
Cerney Wick
Ashton Keynes
NORTH MEADOW
THE THAMES PATH
Castle Eaton
Hannington Wick
Hannington
Inglesham
Upper Inglesham
Leigh
Chelworth Green
Purton Stoke
SWINDON AND CRICKLADE RAILWAY
Broad Blunsdon
Blunsdon St Andrew
Stanton Fitzwarren
Haydon Wick
Penhill
Purton
South Marston
Severnhampton
Watchfield
Shrivenham
Longcot
Fernham
Uffington
Baulking
Kingston
Sparsholt
Great Coxwell
Little Coxwell
Shellingford
GREAT BARN
BADBURY HILL
Coleshill
Buscot
BUSCOT PARK
Kelmscot
KELMSCOTT MANOR
Eaton Hastings
Radcot
Grafton
Littleworth
Hatford
Carswell Marsh
CHIMNEY MEADOWS
Clanfield
Bampton
Weald
Aston
Langford
Little Faringdon
Kencot
Broadwell
Broughton Poggs
Filkins
Alvescot
Black Bourton
BRIZE NORTON
Brize Norton
Lew
Curbridge
Ducklington
Shilton
COTSWOLD WILD LIFE PARK
Bradwell Grove
Holwell
Westwell
Signet
Asthall
Asthall Leigh
Swinbrook
Minster Lovell
MINSTER LOVELL HALL AND DOVECOTE
Charterville Allotments
Fordwells
Leafield
Shipton-under-Wychwood
Milton under Wychwood
Ascott-under-Wychwood
Chilson
Fifield
Idbury
Westcote
Icomb
Bruern Abbey
Lyneham
Chadlington
Spelsbury
Sarsden
Churchill
Kingham
Bledington
Daylesford
Oddington
Maugersbury
Broadwell
Adlestrop
Evenlode
Chastleton
CHASTLETON HOUSE
Little Compton
Compton
Rollright
ROLLRIGHT STONES
Salford
Over Norton
Cornwell
Lidstone
WELLINGTON AVIATION ART MUSEUM
SEZINCOTE
STANWAY HOUSE
HAILES ABBEY
WINCHCOMBE POTTERY
SUDELEY CASTLE AND GARDENS
Farmcote
Ford
COTSWOLD FARM PARK
STOW-ON-THE-WOLD
A40
A429
A424
A44
A436
A361
A417
A419
A420
A4095
A3400
B4077
B4068
B4450
B4425
B4437
B4047
B4020
B4477
B4449
B4019
B4000
B4508
B4040
AKEMAN STREET
Windrush
Leach
Coln
Thames
Ray
80
81
63
45
1
2
3
4
A
B
C
D
0 1 2 3 miles
0 1 2 3 4 5 km

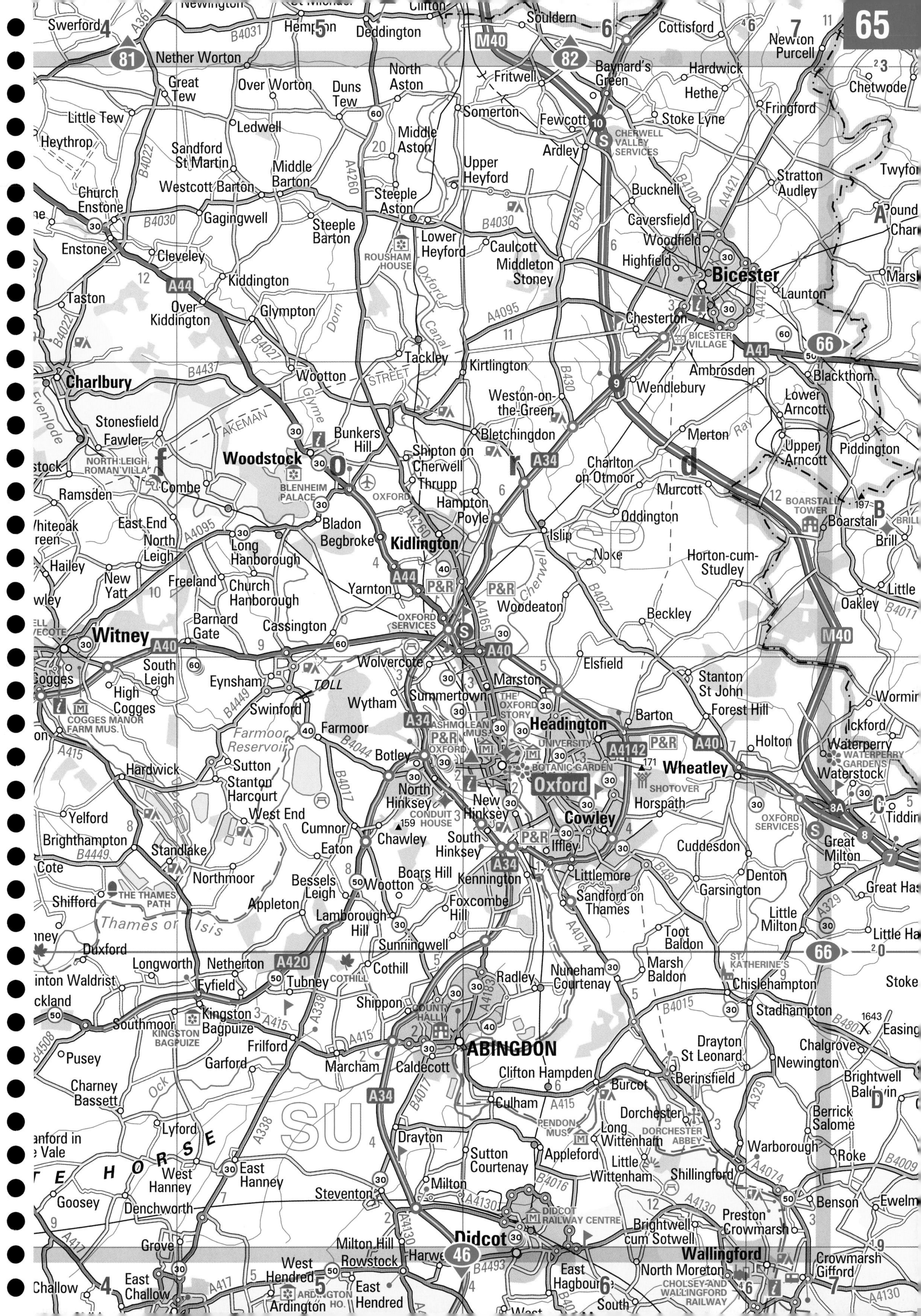

Swerford
Hempton
Deddington
Souldern
Cottisford
Newton Purcell
81
Nether Worton
M40
82
Baynard's Green
Hardwick
Hethe
Chetwode
Great Tew
Over Worton
Duns Tew
North Aston
Fritwell
Little Tew
Ledwell
Middle Aston
Somerton
Fewcott
Stoke Lyne
Fringford
Heythrop
Sandford St Martin
Upper Heyford
Ardley
CHERWELL VALLEY SERVICES
Church Enstone
Westcott Barton
Middle Barton
Steeple Aston
Bucknell
Stratton Audley
Twyford
Gagingwell
Steeple Barton
Caversfield
Pound
Enstone
Cleveley
ROUSHAM HOUSE
Lower Heyford
Caulcott
Woodfield
Highfield
Bicester
Middleton Stoney
Marsh
Launton
Taston
Kiddington
Over Kiddington
Glympton
Dorn
Oxford Canal
Chesterton
BICESTER VILLAGE
Tackley
Kirtlington
Ambrosden
Blackthorn
Charlbury
Wootton
STREET
Weston-on-the-Green
Wendlebury
Lower Arncott
Evenlode
Stonesfield
Fawler
AKEMAN
Glyme
Bunkers Hill
Bletchingdon
Merton
Ray
Upper Arncott
Piddington
NORTH LEIGH ROMAN VILLA
Woodstock
Shipton on Cherwell
Thrupp
Charlton on Otmoor
Combe
BLENHEIM PALACE
OXFORD
Murcott
Ramsden
Hampton Poyle
BOARSTALL TOWER
Boarstall
Brill
Whiteoak Green
East End
North Leigh
Bladon
Begbroke
Kidlington
Islip
Oddington
Long Hanborough
Noke
Horton-cum-Studley
Hailey
New Yatt
Freeland
Church Hanborough
Yarnton
P&R
Cherwell
Woodeaton
Little Oakley
Crawley
Witney
Barnard Gate
Cassington
OXFORD SERVICES
Beckley
South Leigh
Eynsham
Wolvercote
Elsfield
Cogges
High Cogges
COGGES MANOR FARM MUS.
TOLL
Swinford
Wytham
Summertown
Marston
Stanton St John
Forest Hill
Worminghall
Farmoor Reservoir
Farmoor
ASHMOLEAN MUS.
THE OXFORD STORY
Headington
Barton
Ickford
Botley
UNIVERSITY
Holton
Waterperry
WATERPERRY GARDENS
Hardwick
Sutton
Stanton Harcourt
BOTANIC GARDEN
Oxford
Wheatley
SHOTOVER
Waterstock
North Hinksey
New Hinksey
Horspath
Yelford
West End
CONDUIT HOUSE
Cowley
OXFORD SERVICES
Tiddington
Brighthampton
Cumnor
Chawley
South Hinksey
Iffley
Cuddesdon
Great Milton
Cote
Standlake
Eaton
Northmoor
Bessels Leigh
Wootton
Boars Hill
Kennington
Littlemore
Garsington
Denton
Great Haseley
Shifford
THE THAMES PATH
Appleton
Foxcombe Hill
Sandford on Thames
Little Milton
Thames or Isis
Lamborough Hill
Toot Baldon
Little Haseley
Duxford
Sunningwell
Marsh Baldon
Longworth
Netherton
Cothill
COTHILL
Radley
Nuneham Courtenay
ST. KATHERINE'S
Chislehampton
Stoke
Hinton Waldrist
Fyfield
Tubney
Shippon
Stadhampton
Buckland
Kingston Bagpuize
COUNTY HALL
Southmoor
KINGSTON BAGPUIZE
Easington
Pusey
Frilford
Marcham
ABINGDON
Drayton St Leonard
Chalgrove
Newington
Garford
Caldecott
Clifton Hampden
Berinsfield
Burcot
Brightwell Baldwin
Charney Bassett
Ock
Culham
PENDON MUS.
Dorchester
DORCHESTER ABBEY
Long Wittenham
Berrick Salome
Stanford in the Vale
Lyford
Drayton
Sutton Courtenay
Appleford
Warborough
Roke
WHITE HORSE
West Hanney
East Hanney
Milton
Little Wittenham
Shillingford
Goosey
Denchworth
Steventon
DIDCOT RAILWAY CENTRE
Preston Crowmarsh
Benson
Ewelme
Brightwell cum Sotwell
Grove
Milton Hill
Rowstock
Harwell
Didcot
46
Wallingford
Crowmarsh Gifford
West Hendred
East Hendred
East Hagbourne
North Moreton
CHOLSEY AND WALLINGFORD RAILWAY
Challow
East Challow
ARDINGTON HO.
Ardington
South
West
SU
SP
A34
A40
A44
A41
A420
A415
A4142
A4095
A4260
A4165
A4074
A4183
A4130
A4421
A338
A361
A417
A329
A4011
B4027
B4030
B4031
B4022
B4437
B4449
B4044
B4017
B4100
B4430
B4480
B4015
B4016
B4493
B4009
B4508
66

Buckingham
Winslow
Aylesbury
Thame
Haddenham
Princes Risborough
Chinnor
Wendover
High Wycombe
Bicester
Weston Turville
Aston Clinton
Prestwood
Flackwell Heath
Padbury
Adstock
Great Horwood
Little Horwood
Newton Longville
Singleborough
Preston Bissett
Barton Hartshorn
Chetwode
Fringford
Hillesden
Addington
Mursley
Drayton Parslow
Stoke Hammond
Swanbourne
North End
Soulbury
Steeple Claydon
Twyford
Stratton Audley
Middle Claydon
Poundon
Charndon
East Claydon
Granborough
Hoggeston
Stewkley
South End
Calvert
Botolph Claydon
Dunton
Burcott
Marsh Gibbon
Launton
Edgcott
North Marston
Creslow
Cublington
Wing
Grendon Underwood
Oving
Whitchurch
Aston Abbotts
Quainton
Pitchcott
Blackthorn
Kingswood
Hardwick
Wingrave
Lower Arncott
Upper Arncott
Ludgershall
Piddington
Westcott
Waddesdon
Weedon
Rowsham
Hulcott
Wotton Underwood
Long Marston
Bierton
Puttenham
Boarstall
Brill
Dorton
Ashendon
Upper Winchendon
Upper Pollicott
Lower Winchendon
Stone
Southcourt
Buckland
Little London
Oakley
Chilton
Cuddington
Dinton
Westlington
Stoke Mandeville
Easington
Chearsley
Bishopstone
Halton
Townsend
Ford
Long Crendon
Worminghall
Kimble Wick
North Lee
Terrick
Nash Lee
Aston Sandford
Butler's Cross
Ickford
Holton
Shabbington
Waterperry
Waterstock
Kingsey
Owlswick
Little Kimble
Meadle
Ellesborough
Great Kimble
Towersey
Ilmer
Longwick
Askett
Dunsmore
Tiddington
Moreton
Monks Risborough
Great Milton
Little Hampden
Emmington
Pitch Green
Henton
Bledlow
Denton
Great Haseley
Tetsworth
Sydenham
Saunderton
Great Hampden
Little Milton
Little Haseley
Oakley
Loosley Row
Postcombe
Crowell
Kingston Blount
Aston Rowant
Chislehampton
Stoke Talmage
Adwell
South Weston
Lacey Green
Speen
Little Kingshill
Great Kingshill
Stadhampton
Easington
Lewknor
Radnage
Bledlow Ridge
Walters Ash
Upper North Dean
Cryers Hill
Chalgrove
Newington
The City
Bradenham
Naphill
Widmer End
Hughenden Valley
Brightwell Baldwin
Pyrton
Stokenchurch
Shirburn
Cuxham
West Wycombe
Downley
Beacon's Bottom
Berrick Salome
Watlington
Christmas Common
Tylers Green
Warborough
Roke
Ibstone
Britwell Salome
Northend
Cadmore End
Bolter End
Benson
Ewelme
Greenfield
Lane End
Booker
Preston Crowmarsh
Turville Heath
Turville
Fingest
Cookley Green
Pishill
Skirmett
Frieth
Russell's Water
Park Corner
Stonor
Rockwell End
Lower
Marlow Bottom
Little Marlow
Wooburn
WINSLOW HALL
CLAYDON HOUSE
QUAINTON WINDMILL
BUCKINGHAMSHIRE RAILWAY CENTRE
WADDESDON MANOR
AKEMAN STREET
BOARSTALL TOWER
BRILL WINDMILL
NETHER WINCHENDON HOUSE
WATERPERRY GARDENS
RYCOTE CHAPEL
OXFORD SERVICES
MANOR HOUSE
CHINNOR & PRINCES RISBOROUGH RAILWAY
ST KATHERINE'S
ASTON ROWANT
THE RIDGEWAY
WEST WYCOMBE CAVES
WEST WYCOMBE PARK
HUGHENDEN MANOR
WYCOMBE AIR PARK
ASCOTT
Thame
Ray
Ouse
A41
A413
A418
A4010
A4146
A4157
A4129
A4128
A4421
A329
A40
A404
A4074
M40
B4033
B4032
B4011
B4012
B4445
B4443
B4009
B480
B482
B481
Chase
3 miles
5 km

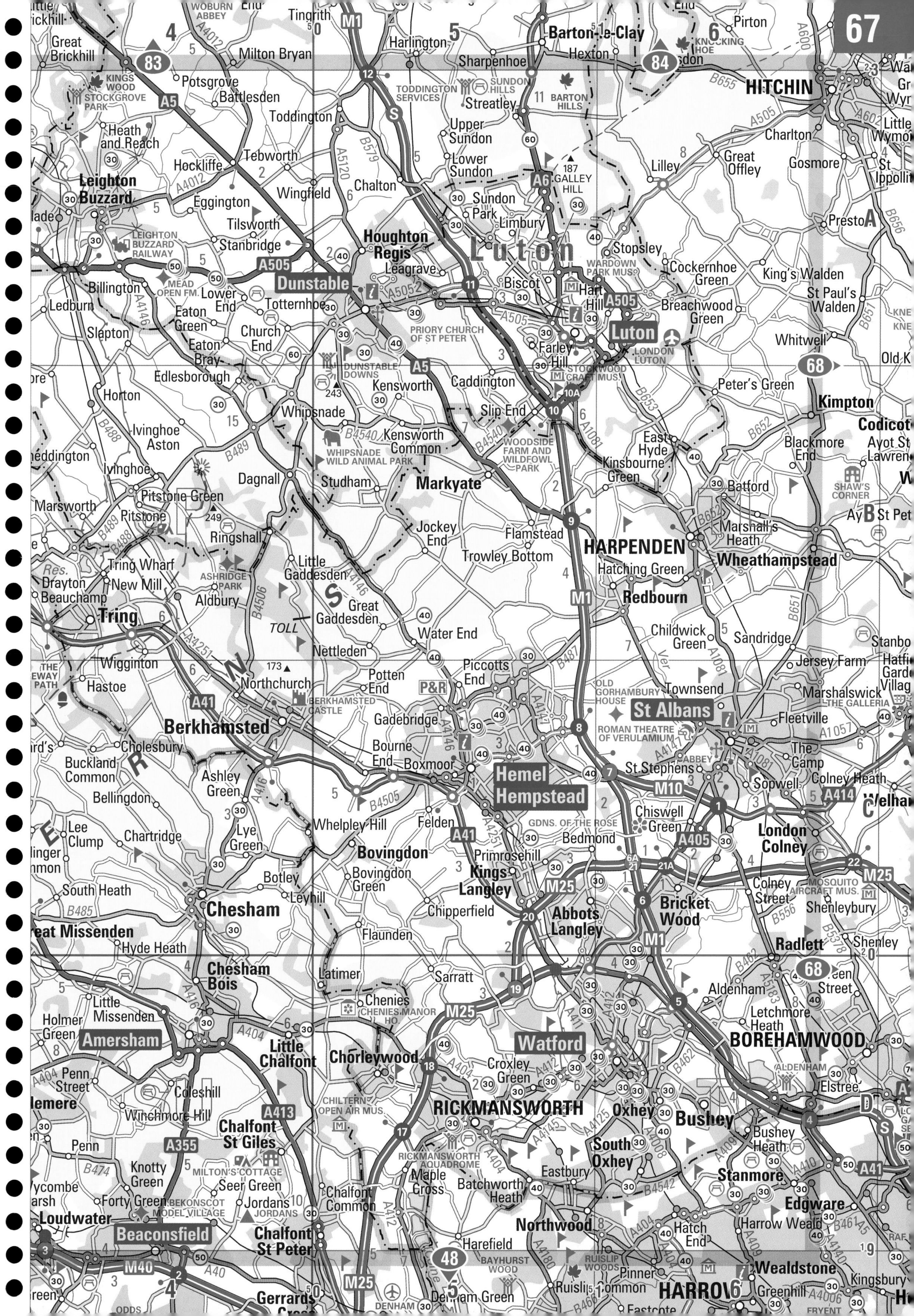
Great Brickhill
Milton Bryan
Tingrith
Harlington
Sharpenhoe
Barton-le-Clay
Hexton
Pirton
HITCHIN
Potsgrove
Battlesden
KINGS WOOD
STOCKGROVE PARK
TODDINGTON SERVICES
SUNDON HILLS
BARTON HILLS
Streatley
Toddington
Heath and Reach
Upper Sundon
Lower Sundon
Charlton
Little Wymondley
Tebworth
Hockliffe
Lilley
Great Offley
Gosmore
St Ippollitts
Leighton Buzzard
Eggington
Wingfield
Chalton
Sundon Park
Limbury
187 GALLEY HILL
Tilsworth
Stanbridge
LEIGHTON BUZZARD RAILWAY
Houghton Regis
Luton
Stopsley
Preston
Leagrave
WARDOWN PARK MUS.
Cockernhoe Green
King's Walden
Billington
MEAD OPEN FM.
Lower End
Dunstable
Biscot
Hart Hill
St Paul's Walden
Ledburn
Eaton Green
Totternhoe
Breachwood Green
Church End
PRIORY CHURCH OF ST PETER
Slapton
Eaton Bray
Farley Hill
LONDON LUTON
Whitwell
DUNSTABLE DOWNS
STOCKWOOD CRAFT MUS.
Old Knebworth
Edlesborough
Kensworth
Caddington
Peter's Green
Horton
243
Kimpton
Whipsnade
Slip End
Codicote
Ivinghoe Aston
Kensworth Common
East Hyde
Blackmore End
Ayot St Lawrence
Cheddington
WHIPSNADE WILD ANIMAL PARK
WOODSIDE FARM AND WILDFOWL PARK
Kinsbourne Green
Ivinghoe
Dagnall
Studham
Markyate
Batford
SHAW'S CORNER
Pitstone Green
Marsworth
Pitstone
249
Jockey End
Flamstead
HARPENDEN
Marshall's Heath
Ayot St Peter
Ringshall
Trowley Bottom
Wheathampstead
Tring Wharf
Little Gaddesden
Hatching Green
Drayton Beauchamp
New Mill
ASHRIDGE PARK
Redbourn
Aldbury
Great Gaddesden
Tring
TOLL
Water End
Childwick Green
Sandridge
Stanborough
Nettleden
Jersey Farm
Hatfield Garden Village
Wigginton
173
Piccotts End
THE RIDGEWAY PATH
Potten End
Hastoe
Northchurch
OLD GORHAMBURY HOUSE
Townsend
Marshalswick
THE GALLERIA
BERKHAMSTED CASTLE
Berkhamsted
Gadebridge
St Albans
Fleetville
Cholesbury
ROMAN THEATRE OF VERULAMIUM
Buckland Common
Bourne End
Boxmoor
ABBEY
The Camp
St Stephens
Ashley Green
Hemel Hempstead
Sopwell
Colney Heath
Bellingdon
Welham Green
Lee Clump
Whelpley Hill
Felden
GDNS. OF THE ROSE
Chiswell Green
Chartridge
Lye Green
London Colney
Bovingdon
Bedmond
Primrosehill
Kings Langley
Botley
Bovingdon Green
Colney Street
MOSQUITO AIRCRAFT MUS.
South Heath
Leyhill
Chesham
Chipperfield
Bricket Wood
Shenleybury
Great Missenden
Abbots Langley
Hyde Heath
Flaunden
Radlett
Shenley
Chesham Bois
Latimer
Sarratt
Green Street
Little Missenden
Chenies
CHENIES MANOR HO.
Aldenham
Letchmore Heath
Holmer Green
Amersham
Watford
BOREHAMWOOD
Little Chalfont
Chorleywood
Croxley Green
ALDENHAM
Penn Street
Elstree
Coleshill
Winchmore Hill
CHILTERN OPEN AIR MUS.
RICKMANSWORTH
Oxhey
Bushey
Chalfont St Giles
Penn
Bushey Heath
South Oxhey
RICKMANSWORTH AQUADROME
Knotty Green
MILTON'S COTTAGE
Seer Green
Maple Cross
Batchworth Heath
Eastbury
Stanmore
Forty Green
BEKONSCOTT MODEL VILLAGE
Jordans
JORDANS
Chalfont Common
Edgware
Loudwater
Northwood
Harrow Weald
Beaconsfield
Chalfont St Peter
Harefield
Hatch End
BAYHURST WOOD
RUISLIP WOODS
Wealdstone
Pinner
Ruislip Common
Kingsbury
HARROW
Greenhill
Denham Green
Gerrards Cross
DENHAM
Eastcote
M1
M25
M10
M40
A5
A6
A41
A505
A413
A355
A405
A414
A4146
A4251
A4012
A5120
A1081
B489
B4540
B4505
B579
B651
B652
B653
B655
B656
B656
B462
B4542
83
84
68
48

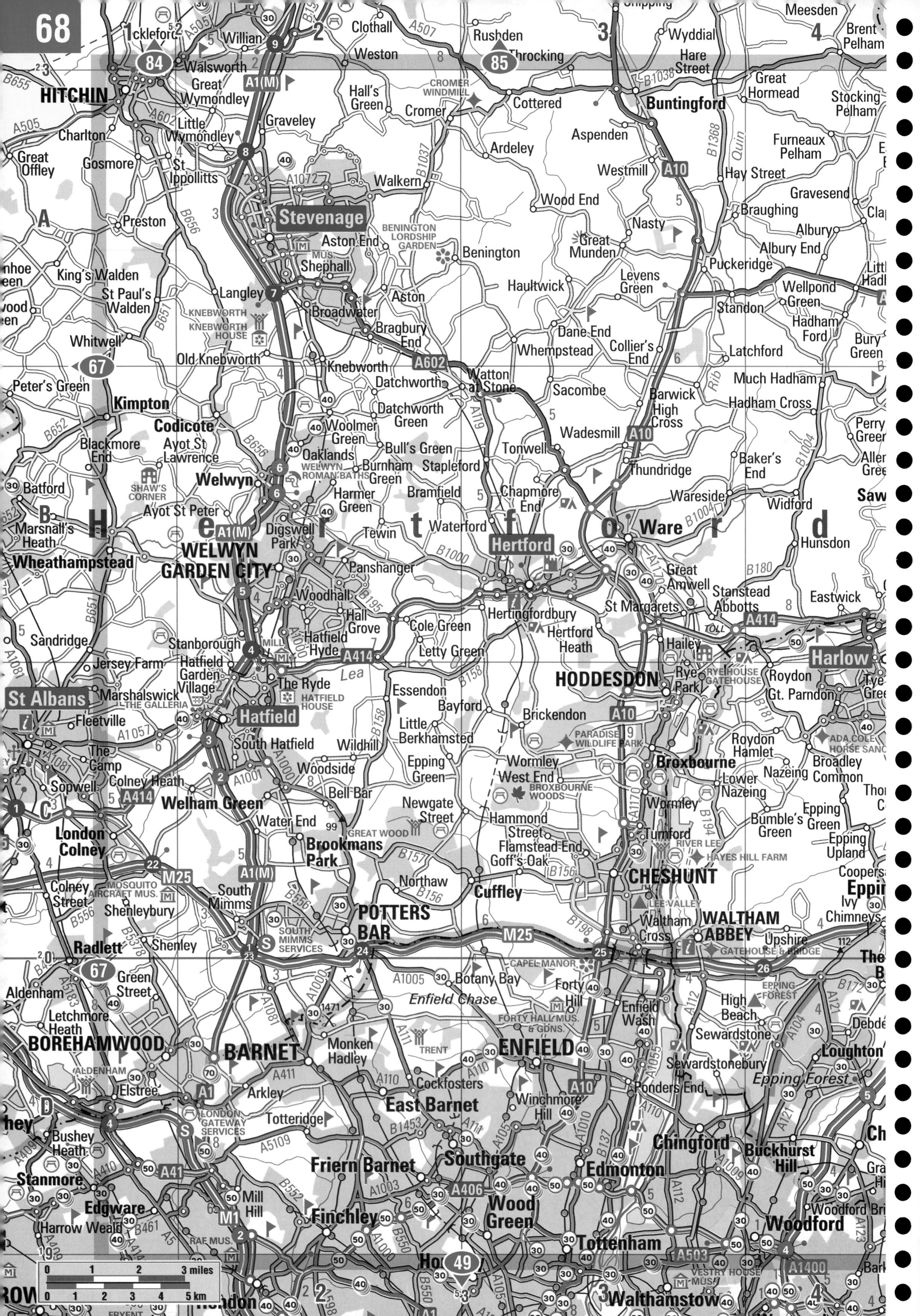
0 1 2 3 miles
0 1 2 3 4 5 km

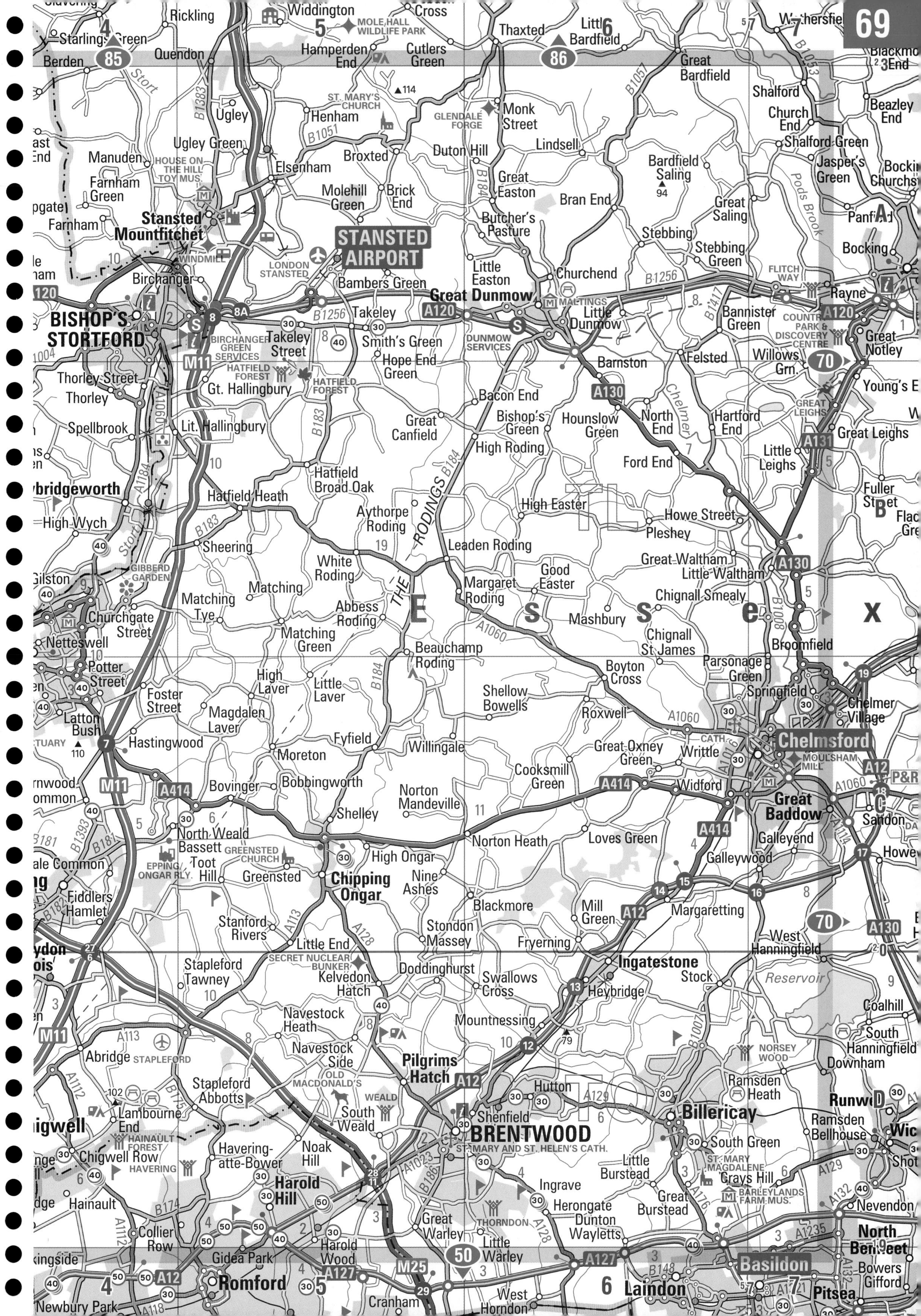
85
86
70
50
STANSTED AIRPORT
BISHOP'S STORTFORD
Stansted Mountfitchet
Great Dunmow
Chelmsford
BRENTWOOD
Billericay
Chipping Ongar
Ingatestone
Harold Hill
Romford
Basildon
Laindon
Sawbridgeworth
Thaxted
Takeley
Felsted
Writtle
Great Baddow
Pilgrims Hatch
Shenfield
Hutton
Galleywood
Margaretting
Stock
Broomfield
Springfield
Great Leighs
Great Notley
Rayne
Bocking
Great Bardfield
Finchingfield
Widdington
Rickling
Quendon
Berden
Manuden
Ugley
Elsenham
Henham
Broxted
Hatfield Broad Oak
Hatfield Heath
Sheering
Matching
Matching Tye
Matching Green
White Roding
Aythorpe Roding
Leaden Roding
High Roding
Margaret Roding
Abbess Roding
Beauchamp Roding
High Laver
Little Laver
Magdalen Laver
Moreton
Fyfield
Willingale
Shelley
Bobbingworth
High Ongar
Norton Mandeville
Norton Heath
Blackmore
Stondon Massey
Doddinghurst
Kelvedon Hatch
Navestock Heath
Navestock Side
Stapleford Tawney
Stapleford Abbotts
Abridge
Lambourne End
Chigwell Row
Havering-atte-Bower
Noak Hill
Great Warley
Little Warley
West Horndon
Herongate
Ingrave
Dunton Wayletts
Little Burstead
Great Burstead
Ramsden Heath
Ramsden Bellhouse
South Green
Crays Hill
Mountnessing
Fryerning
Mill Green
Loves Green
Cooksmill Green
Great Oxney Green
Roxwell
Shellow Bowells
Boyton Cross
Chignall St James
Chignall Smealy
Mashbury
Good Easter
High Easter
Pleshey
Great Waltham
Little Waltham
Barnston
Little Dunmow
Bacon End
Great Canfield
Bishop's Green
Hounslow Green
North End
Ford End
Howe Street
Hartford End
Little Leighs
Lindsell
Great Easton
Duton Hill
Monk Street
Little Easton
Churchend
Stebbing
Stebbing Green
Great Saling
Bardfield Saling
Bran End
Shalford
Shalford Green
Church End
Bannister Green
Willows Grn.
Young's End
Fuller Street
Gt. Hallingbury
Lit. Hallingbury
Thorley
Thorley Street
Spellbrook
High Wych
Gilston
Netteswell
Churchgate Street
Potter Street
Foster Street
Latton Bush
Hastingwood
Bovinger
North Weald Bassett
Toot Hill
Greensted
Stanford Rivers
Little End
Epping
Fiddlers Hamlet
Theydon Bois
Chigwell
Hainault
Collier Row
Gidea Park
Harold Wood
Cranham
Newbury Park
West Hanningfield
South Hanningfield
Downham
Runwell
Wickford
Nevendon
North Benfleet
Pitsea
Bowers Gifford
Sandon
Galleyend
Coalhill
Heybridge
Swallows Cross
ESSEX
TL
TQ
M11
A120
A130
A12
A414
A1060
A131
A127
M25
B1256
B184
B183
THE RODINGS
Stort
Chelmer
Pods Brook
Reservoir

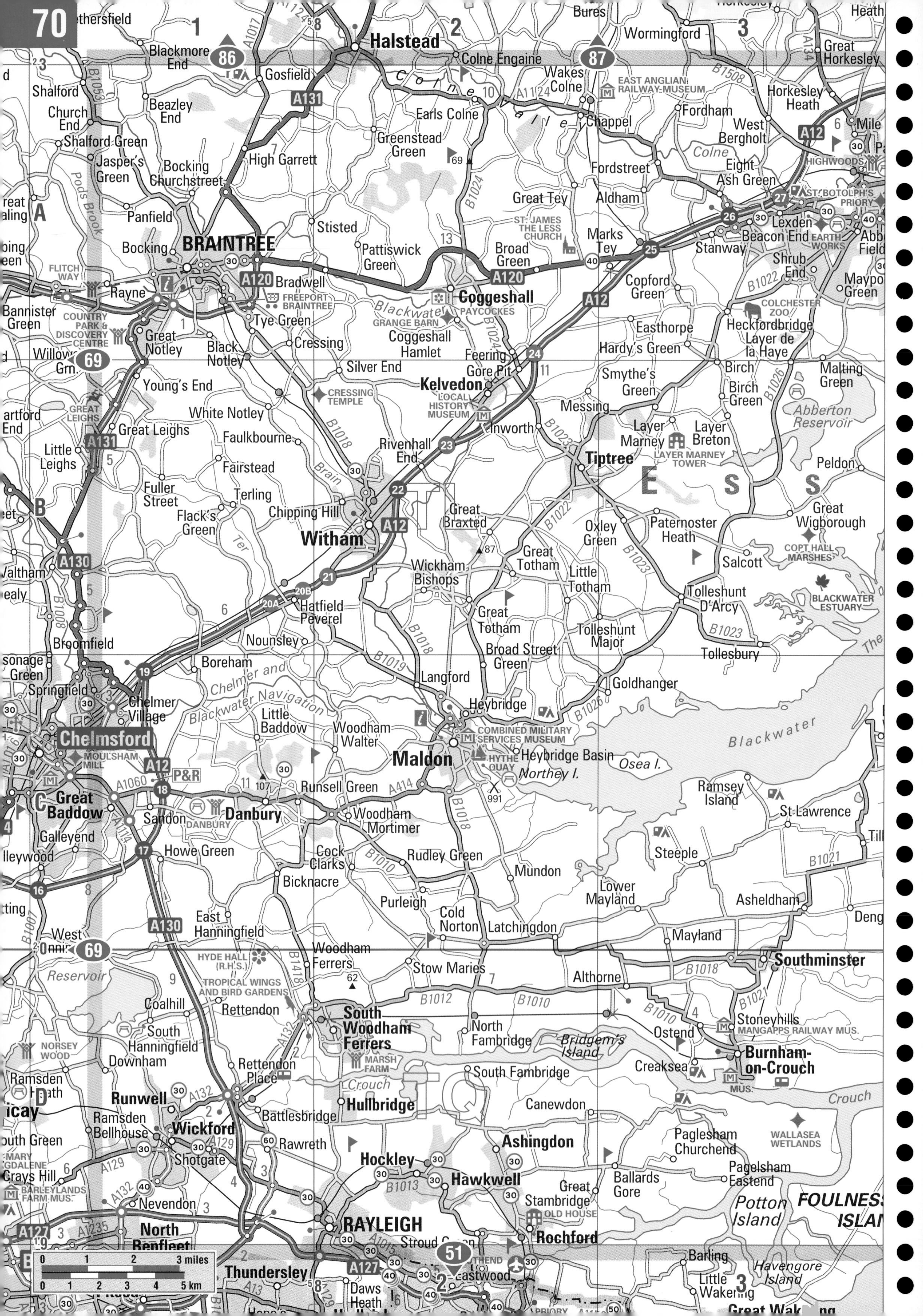
Halstead
Colne Engaine
Bures
Wormingford
Great Horkesley
Heath
Blackmore End
Gosfield
Wakes Colne
EAST ANGLIAN RAILWAY MUSEUM
Shalford
Church End
Beazley End
Earls Colne
Chappel
Fordham
Horkesley Heath
Shalford Green
Jasper's Green
Bocking Churchstreet
High Garrett
Greenstead Green
West Bergholt
Colne Valley
Colne
Fordstreet
Eight Ash Green
HIGHWOODS
Panfield
Great Tey
Aldham
ST. BOTOLPH'S PRIORY
Stisted
ST. JAMES THE LESS CHURCH
Marks Tey
Lexden
Bocking
BRAINTREE
Pattiswick Green
Broad Green
Stanway
Beacon End
EARTH WORKS
Shrub End
FLITCH WAY
Rayne
Bradwell
Coggeshall
Copford Green
Maypole Green
FREEPORT BRAINTREE
PAYCOCKES
Blackwater
GRANGE BARN
COLCHESTER ZOO
Bannister Green
COUNTRY PARK & DISCOVERY CENTRE
Great Notley
Tye Green
Cressing
Coggeshall Hamlet
Easthorpe
Heckfordbridge
Layer de la Haye
Willows Grn.
Black Notley
Silver End
Feering
Gore Pit
Hardy's Green
Birch
Malting Green
Young's End
CRESSING TEMPLE
Kelvedon
Smythe's Green
Birch Green
LOCAL HISTORY MUSEUM
Messing
Abberton Reservoir
Great Leighs
White Notley
Inworth
Layer Marney
Layer Breton
LAYER MARNEY TOWER
Little Leighs
Faulkbourne
Rivenhall End
Tiptree
Peldon
Fairstead
Brain
Fuller Street
Terling
ESSEX
Flack's Green
Chipping Hill
Great Braxted
Oxley Green
Paternoster Heath
Great Wigborough
Witham
Ter
Great Totham
COPT HALL MARSHES
Wickham Bishops
Little Totham
Salcott
Waltham
Hatfield Peverel
Tolleshunt D'Arcy
BLACKWATER ESTUARY
Broomfield
Great Totham
Tolleshunt Major
Nounsley
Tollesbury
Broad Street Green
Boreham
Langford
Goldhanger
Springfield
Chelmer and Blackwater Navigation
Chelmer Village
Heybridge
Little Baddow
Woodham Walter
COMBINED MILITARY SERVICES MUSEUM
Chelmsford
MOULSHAM MILL
Maldon
Heybridge Basin
Osea I.
HYTHE QUAY
Northey I.
Blackwater
Runsell Green
Ramsey Island
Great Baddow
Sandon
Danbury
Woodham Mortimer
St Lawrence
Galleyend
Howe Green
Cock Clarks
Rudley Green
Steeple
Mundon
Bicknacre
Lower Mayland
Purleigh
Asheldham
East Hanningfield
Cold Norton
Latchingdon
Mayland
West Hanningfield
Woodham Ferrers
HYDE HALL (R.H.S.)
Stow Maries
Southminster
Reservoir
Althorne
TROPICAL WINGS AND BIRD GARDENS
Coalhill
Rettendon
South Woodham Ferrers
North Fambridge
Bridgemarsh Island
Ostend
Stoneyhills
MANGAPPS RAILWAY MUS.
South Hanningfield
NORSEY WOOD
Downham
MARSH FARM
Burnham-on-Crouch
Rettendon Place
South Fambridge
Creeksea
Crouch
Ramsden Heath
Runwell
Hullbridge
Canewdon
Battlesbridge
Ramsden Bellhouse
Wickford
Ashingdon
Paglesham Churchend
WALLASEA WETLANDS
Shotgate
Rawreth
Crays Hill
Hockley
Paglesham Eastend
BARLEYLANDS FARM MUS.
Hawkwell
Great Stambridge
Ballards Gore
Nevendon
Potton Island
FOULNESS ISLAND
OLD HOUSE
North Benfleet
RAYLEIGH
Rochford
Stroud Green
Barling
Thundersley
Eastwood
Havengore Island
Little Wakering
Daws Heath
0 1 2 3 miles
0 1 2 3 4 5 km

Dedham
Langham
Lawford
Mistley
Manningtree
Bradfield
Wrabness
Parkeston
Ramsey
Upper Dovercourt
Dovercourt
HARWICH REDOUBT
Bradfield Heath
Ardleigh
Little Bromley
Horsleycross Street
Horsley Cross
Wix
Little Oakley
Great Oakley
Great Bromley
Fox Street
Crockleford Heath
Colchester
Elmstead Market
Stone's Green
Tendring Green
Little Bentley
Beaumont
Horsey Island
The Naze
Hare Green
Balls Green
Wivenhoe Cross
Old Heath
BOURNE MILL
BETH CHATTO GDNS.
Tendring
Thorpe Green
Thorpe-le-Soken
Kirby-le-Soken
HAMFORD WATER
MARITIME MUSEUM
Wivenhoe
Frating Green
Great Bentley
Weeley
Weeley Heath
Blackheath
Rowhedge
Alresford
Aingers Green
Walton-on-the-Naze
Kirby Cross
Frinton-on-Sea
Fingringhoe
Thorrington
Row Heath
Little Clacton
CLACTON VILLAGE
Abberton
Langenhoe
Great Holland
HOLLAND HAVEN
River Colne
St Osyth Heath
Brightlingsea
Mersea Island
East Mersea
ST OSYTH'S PRIORY
St Osyth
Great Clacton
Holland-on-Sea
Clacton-on-Sea
CUDMORE GROVE
Point Clear
Blue Row
COLNE ESTUARY
Jaywick
West Mersea
MERSEA ISLAND MUSEUM
Colne Pt.
Virley Channel
Sales Pt.
ST. PETERS ON THE WALL
Bradwell Waterside
Bradwell on Sea
TM
DENGIE
Ray Sand
Montsale
Deal Hall
Foulness Sand
Foulness Pt.
TR
Courtsend
Churchend
MAPLIN SANDS
A12
A120
A133
B1029
B1035
B1033
B1414
B1027
B1028
B1025
B1032
B1336
B1352
A137
A1232
87
88
52
53
A
B
C
D
4
5
6

SM
Cemaes Head
Pen Cemaes
PEMBROKESHIRE COAST
ARFORDIR PENFRO
ROSSLARE 3:30
ROSSLARE 1:50
(Apr-Sept)
Strumble Head
Pen Caer
Dinas Head
Newport
Bay
Bae
Trefdraeth
Fishguard
Bay
Bae
Abergwaun
Tresinwen
Llanwnda
Brynhenllan
PWLL
DERI
213
Goodwick
(Wdig)
191
Trefasser
Penbwchdy
Lower
Town
Dyffryn
Manorowen
St Nicholas
Fishguard
(Abergwaun)
PEMBROKESHIRE
COAST PATH
LLWYBR ARFORDIR
PENFRO
TREGWYNT
WOOLLEN MILL
Abercastle
Granston
Scleddau
Llanychaer
A40
A487
55
Dinas
Cross
TREFDRAETH
Parrog
Berry
Hill
Newport
(Trefdraeth)
347
CARNINGLI
Cilgwyn
TY CANOL
Nevern
B4582
Felindre
Farchog
PENGELLI
FOREST
CASTELL
HENLLYS
FORT
Moylgrove
Monington
Glanrhyd
197
Pont-gareg
Cippyn
POPPIT SANDS
St Dogmaels
Crosswell
Pontyglasier
Brynberian
Afon Nevern
DYFED SHIRE
LEISURE
Pontfaen
B4313
Trecwn
MYNYDD PRESELI
468
536
FOEL-
CWMCERWYN
B4329
Trefin
Mathry
CHEESE CENTRE
Newbridge
CORSYDD
LLANGLOFFAN
Penparc
Castlemorris
16
B4330
B4331
14
164
Treddiog
Letterston
Little
Newcastle
Puncheston
Castlebythe
New Inn
Rosebush
55
Llanreithan
Welsh
Hook
St Dogwells
Tufton
Henry's
Moat
Maenclochog
Llangolman
Glandy
Cross
Llandeloy
Wolf's
Castle
Pont-yr-hafod
Ambleston
Woodstock
Res.
New Moat
Efailwen
Trefgarn
Owen
Hayscastle
NEWGALE
Hayscastle
Cross
Brimaston
Rinaston
Wallis
LLYS-Y-FRAN
RESERVOIR
Llys-y-frân
Triffleton
Mountain
Water
178
DUDWELL MT.
Treffgarne
Spittal
SCOLTON MANOR
& COUNTRY PARK
Walton
East
Llanycefn
Penycwm
Newgale
Leweston
Pen-
ffordd
A478
Pembrokeshire
(Sir Benfro)
Llandissilio
A487
Roch
Wolfsdale
Clarbeston
Bletherston
Roch
Gate
15
Camrose
Rudbaxton
Clarbeston
Road
W. Cleddau
G. Cleddau
E. Cleddau
B4329
Llanfallteg
Tangiers
Leechpool
Gelli
Clunderwen
Pelcomb
Cross
PEMBROKE
MOTOR MUSEUM
Nolton
Crundale
Wiston
LAWHADEN
CASTLE
0 1 2 3 miles
0 1 2 3 4 5 km

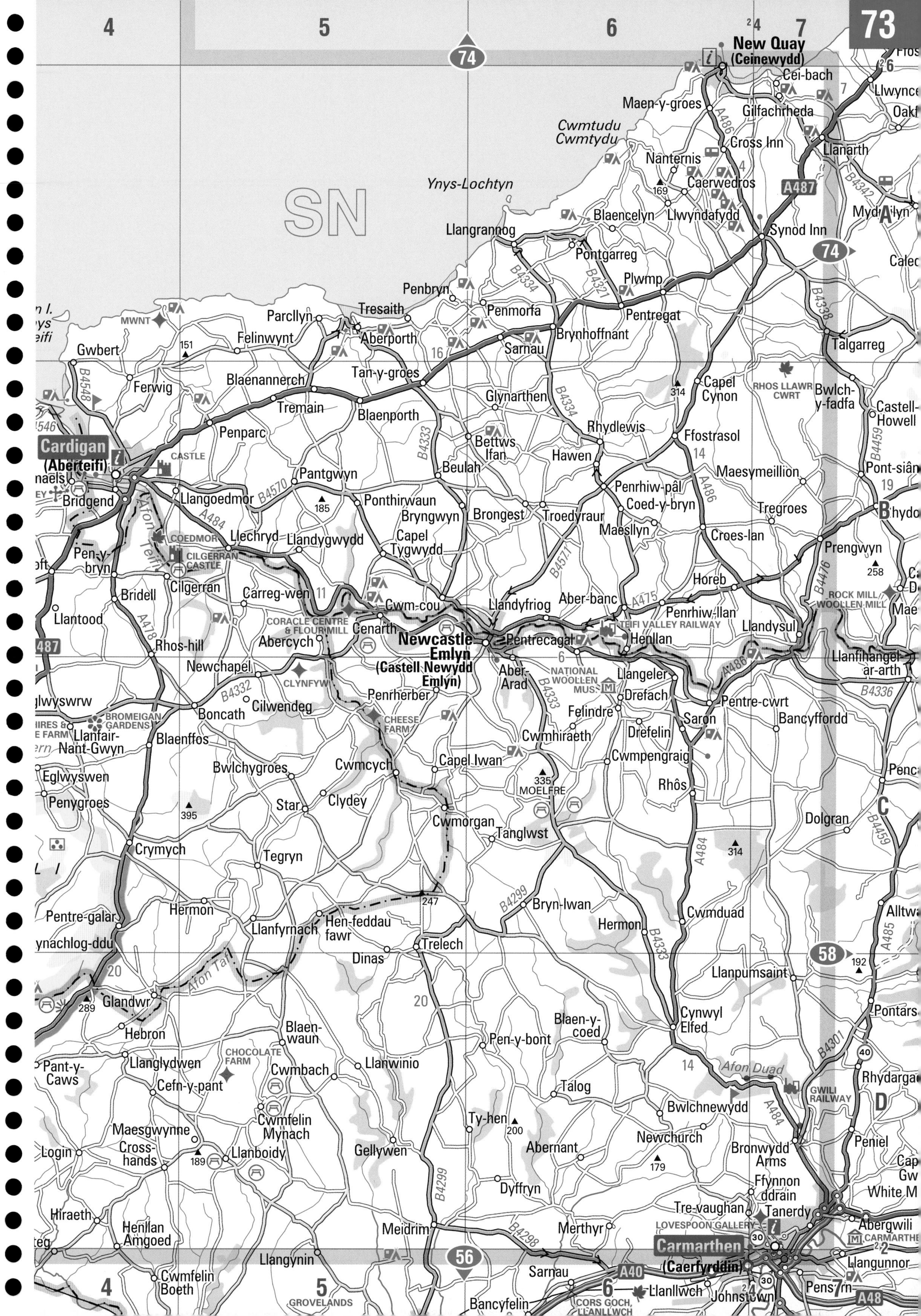
SN
New Quay (Ceinewydd)
Cei-bach
Maen-y-groes
Gilfachrheda
Cwmtudu Cwmtydu
Cross Inn
Llanarth
Nanternis
Caerwedros
Ynys-Lochtyn
Blaencelyn
Llwyndafydd
Synod Inn
Llangrannog
Pontgarreg
Plwmp
Penbryn
Penmorfa
Pentregat
Tresaith
Parcllyn
Aberporth
Brynhoffnant
Sarnau
Gwbert
Felinwynt
Tan-y-groes
Talgarreg
Ferwig
Blaenannerch
Glynarthen
Capel Cynon
Tremain
Blaenporth
Cardigan (Aberteifi)
Penparc
Rhydlewis
Ffostrasol
Bettws Ifan
Hawen
Beulah
Pantgwyn
Maesymeillion
Penrhiw-pâl
Coed-y-bryn
Bridgend
Llangoedmor
Ponthirwaun
Bryngwyn
Brongest
Troedyraur
Tregroes
Maesllyn
Croes-lan
Llechryd
Llandygwydd
Capel Tygwydd
Prengwyn
Pen-y-bryn
Cilgerran
Carreg-wen
Cwm-cou
Llandyfriog
Aber-banc
Horeb
Bridell
Llantood
Penrhiw-llan
Llandysul
Abercych
Cenarth
Newcastle Emlyn (Castell Newydd Emlyn)
Pentrecagal
Henllan
Rhos-hill
Newchapel
Aber-Arad
Llangeler
Llanfihangel-ar-arth
Boncath
Cilwendeg
Penrherber
Drefach
Felindre
Pentre-cwrt
Saron
Bancyffordd
Llanfair-Nant-Gwyn
Blaenffos
Drefelin
Cwmhiraeth
Cwmpengraig
Eglwyswen
Bwlchygroes
Cwmcych
Capel Iwan
Rhôs
Penygroes
Star
Clydey
Cwmorgan
Tanglwst
Dolgran
Crymych
Tegryn
Bryn-Iwan
Hermon
Cwmduad
Pentre-galar
Llanfyrnach
Hen-feddau fawr
Trelech
Dinas
Llanpumsaint
Glandwr
Hebron
Blaen-waun
Pen-y-bont
Blaen-y-coed
Cynwyl Elfed
Pant-y-Caws
Llanglydwen
Cwmbach
Llanwinio
Cefn-y-pant
Talog
Rhydargaeau
Cwmfelin Mynach
Bwlchnewydd
Ty-hen
Maesgwynne
Cross-hands
Llanboidy
Gellywen
Abernant
Newchurch
Bronwydd Arms
Peniel
Login
Dyffryn
Ffynnon ddrain
Hiraeth
Henllan Amgoed
Meidrim
Merthyr
Tre-vaughan
Tanerdy
Abergwili
Carmarthen (Caerfyrddin)
Llangynin
Sarnau
Llangunnor
Cwmfelin Boeth
Llanllwch
Johnstown
Bancyfelin

74
1
2
3
A
B
C
D
Llansantff
Aberarth
Aberaeron
Monacht
New Quay
(Ceinewydd)
Cei-bach
Ffos-y-ffin
LLANERCHAE
Llwyncelyn
Oakford
Ciliau Aeron
Maen-y-groes
Gilfachrheda
Cwmtudu
Cwmtydu
Cross Inn
Llanarth
Nanternis
Caerwedros
Dihewyd
Ynys-Lochtyn
169
A487
Mydroilyn
B4342
Blaencelyn
Llwyndafydd
Synod Inn
Llangrannog
Pontgarreg
Caledrhydiau
B4334
B4321
Plwmp
Penbryn
Penmorfa
Pentregat
B4338
Tresaith
Parcllyn
Aberporth
Brynhoffnant
Talgarreg
Gorsgoch
Felinwynt
151
Sarnau
16
B4338
324
Tan-y-groes
Capel Cynon
RHOS LLAWR CWRT
Bwlch-y-fadfa
Blaenannerch
A487
Glynarthen
314
Castell-Howell
Aber
Cwrt-new
Tremain
Blaenporth
B4334
Penparc
B4333
Bettws Ifan
Rhydlewis
Ffostrasol
B4459
CASTLE
Hawen
14
Beulah
Maesymeillion
Pont-siân
Cwmsychpa
Pantgwyn
Llangoedmor
B4570
185
Ponthirwaun
Penrhiw-pâl
A486
19
Llanwenog
Coed-y-bryn
A484
Bryngwyn
Brongest
Troedyraur
Tregroes
Rhydo
58
Maesllyn
Croes-lan
COEDMOR
Llechryd
Llandygwydd
Capel Tygwydd
Prengwyn
Brynteg
CILGERRAN CASTLE
B4571
258
Capel Dewi
Rhuc
Cilgerran
Carreg-wen
11
Horeb
B4476
Cwm-cou
Llandyfriog
Aber-banc
A475
ROCK MILL WOOLLEN MILL
Maesycrugiau
CORACLE CENTRE & FLOUR MILL
Cenarth
Penrhiw-llan
TEIFI VALLEY RAILWAY
Llandysul
Abercych
Newcastle Emlyn
(Castell Newydd Emlyn)
Pentrecagal
Henllan
Rhos-hill
6
Llanfihangel-ar-arth
0 1 2 3 miles
0 1 2 3 4 5 km
Aber-Arad
NATIONAL WOOLLEN MUS.
Llangeler
A486
Llanll
B4333
Penrherber
Drefach
B4336
Boncath
Felindre
Pentre-cwrt
Saron
Bancyfford
CHEESE
73

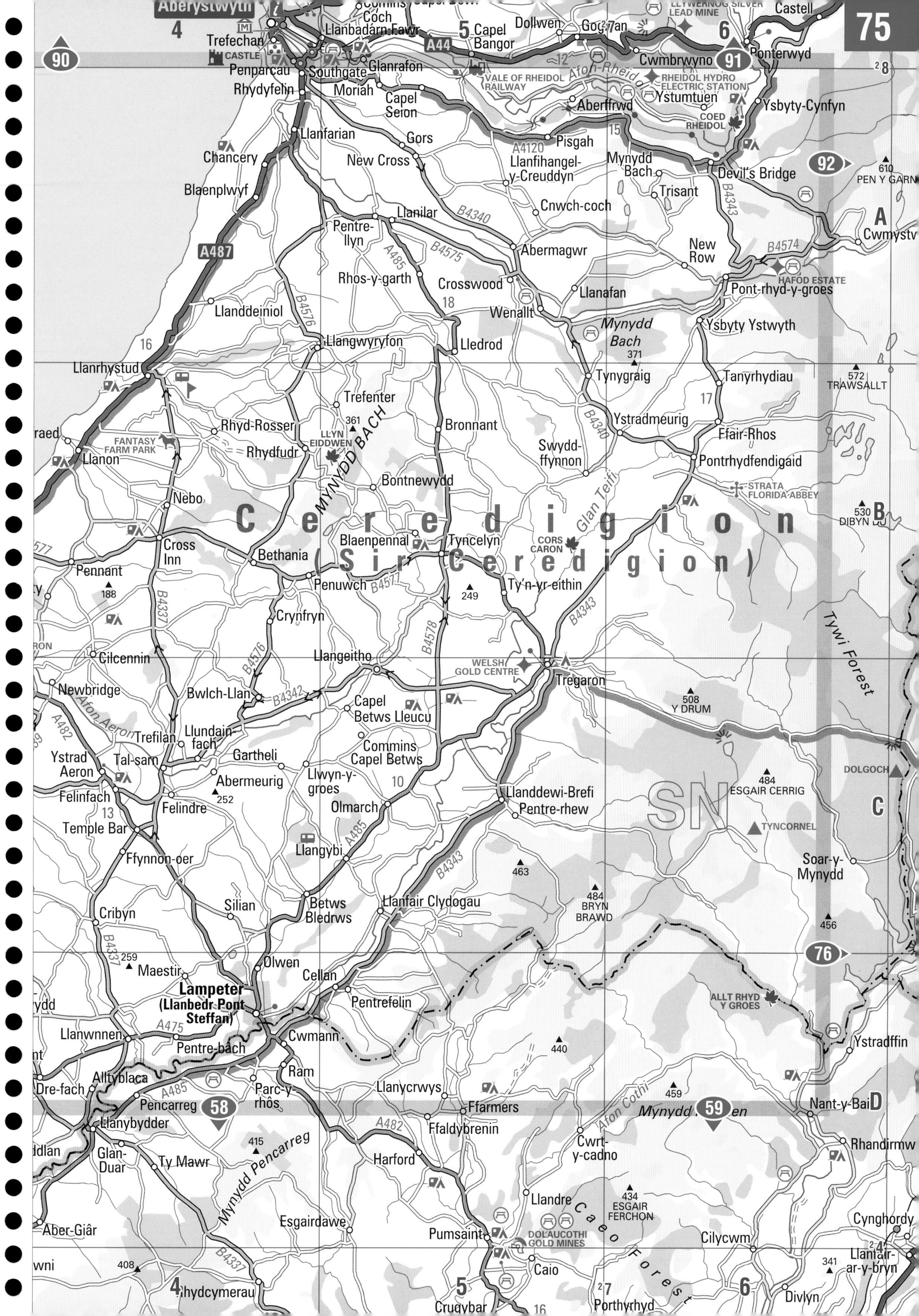
Aberystwyth
4
Trefechan
CASTLE
Penparcau
Southgate
Rhydyfelin
Llanbadarn Fawr
Coch
Glanrafon
Moriah
Capel Seion
5
Capel Bangor
A44
Dollwen
Goginan
LLYWERNOG SILVER LEAD MINE
6
Castell
Cwmbrwyno
Ponterwyd
VALE OF RHEIDOL RAILWAY
Afon Rheidol
RHEIDOL HYDRO ELECTRIC STATION
Ystumtuen
Ysbyty-Cynfyn
Aberffrwd
COED RHEIDOL
Llanfarian
Gors
Pisgah
A4120
Llanfihangel-y-Creuddyn
Mynydd Bach
Trisant
Devil's Bridge
PEN Y GARN
610
Chancery
New Cross
Blaenplwyf
Cnwch-coch
B4343
A
Cwmystwyth
Llanilar
B4340
Pentre-llyn
A485
B4575
Abermagwr
New Row
B4574
HAFOD ESTATE
Pont-rhyd-y-groes
A487
Rhos-y-garth
Crosswood
Llanafan
18
Wenallt
Llanddeiniol
B4576
16
Llangwyryfon
Lledrod
Mynydd Bach
371
Ysbyty Ystwyth
Llanrhystud
Tynygraig
Tanyrhydiau
572
TRAWSALLT
Trefenter
361
17
Rhyd-Rosser
LLYN EIDDWEN
MYNYDD BACH
Bronnant
Ystradmeurig
B4340
Efair-Rhos
FANTASY FARM PARK
Rhydfudr
Llanon
Swydd-ffynnon
Pontrhydfendigaid
STRATA FLORIDA ABBEY
Bontnewydd
Nebo
Glan Teifi
530
DIBYN DU
B
Ceredigion
(Sir Ceredigion)
Cross Inn
Blaenpennal
Tyncelyn
CORS CARON
Bethania
Pennant
188
Penuwch
B4577
249
Ty'n-yr-eithin
B4337
Crynfryn
B4343
B4578
Tywi Forest
Cilcennin
B4576
Llangeitho
WELSH GOLD CENTRE
Tregaron
Newbridge
Bwlch-Llan
B4342
Capel Betws Lleucu
508
Y DRUM
Afon Aeron
A482
Trefilan
Llundain-fach
Commins Capel Betws
Ystrad Aeron
Tal-sarn
Gartheli
Abermeurig
252
Llwyn-y-groes
10
484
ESGAIR CERRIG
DOLGOCH
Felinfach
Felindre
Olmarch
Llanddewi-Brefi
Pentre-rhew
SN
C
13
Temple Bar
TYNCORNEL
Llangybi
A485
Ffynnon-oer
B4343
463
Soar-y-Mynydd
Betws Bledrws
Llanfair Clydogau
484
BRYN BRAWD
Cribyn
Silian
456
B4337
259
Maestir
Olwen
76
Cellan
Lampeter
(Llanbedr Pont Steffan)
Pentrefelin
ALLT RHYD Y GROES
A475
Llanwnnen
Cwmann
Pentre-bach
440
Ystradffin
Ram
Alltyblaca
Parc-y-rhôs
Llanycrwys
459
Dre-fach
A485
Pencarreg
58
Ffarmers
Afon Cothi
Mynydd
59
Nant-y-Bai
D
Llanybydder
A482
Ffaldybrenin
Cwrt-y-cadno
Rhandirmwyn
Glan-Duar
415
Ty Mawr
Mynydd Pencarreg
Harford
434
ESGAIR FERCHON
Llandre
Caeo Forest
Aber-Giâr
Esgairdawe
Pumsaint
DOLAUCOTHI GOLD MINES
Cilycwm
Cynghordy
408
B4337
Caio
341
Llanfair-ar-y-bryn
4
Rhydcymerau
5
Crugybar
16
Porthyrhyd
6
Divlyn
90
91
92

Tanyrhydiau
572 TRAWSALLT
CLAERWEN
Rhayader
(Rhaeadr Gwy)
WELSH ROYAL CRYSTAL
Gaufron
Llansantffraed Cwmdeuddwr
Elan Village
Penygarreg Res.
Garreg-ddu-Res.
Claerwen Reservoir
THE GIGRIN FARM RED KITE FEEDING CENTRE
Nantmel
STRATA FLORIDA ABBEY
530 DIBYN DU
Nant-glas
Llanwrthwl
Caban-coch Res.
Argoed Mill
Llanyre
Afon Claerwen
537 DRUM-DDU
Newbridge on Wye
Tywi Forest
645 DRYGARN FAWR
532 BRYN CRWN
Disserth
DOLGOCH
484 ESGAIR CERRIG
TYNCORNEL
Llanafan-fawr
CORS Y LLYN
500
NANT IRFON
Pentre-llwyn-llwyd
Cwmbach
Builth Road
Troed-rhiwdalar
Soar-y-Mynydd
Llyn Brianne Res.
Abergwesyn
Beulah
Cilmery
456
Llanfechan
Mynydd Trawsnant
Cwm Irfon
487
Garth
Tyn-y-graig
441
CAMBRIAN WOOLLEN MILL
Llanwrtyd
Maesmynis
Ystradffin
Llanwrtyd Wells (Llanwrtud)
Llangammarch Wells
Cefn-gorwydd
474 DRUM-DDU
Nant-y-Bai
Rhandirmwyn
MYNYDD EPYNT
Pentre Dolau-Honddu
463 BRYN DU
Crychan Forest
Tirabad
Cynghordy
Upper Chapel
433
341
Llanfair-ar-y-bryn
Divlyn
Siloh
Blaendyryn
Merthyr Cynog
Lower Chapel
423
Honddu
Pentre-ty-gwyn
Babel
Mynydd Bwlch-y-groes
442
Llandeilo'r Fan
Llanfihangel Nant Bran
Pont-faen
Pwllgloyw
Llandovery (Llanymddyfri)
Halfway
Pentre-bach
Sarnau
Nant Bran
Myrtle Hill
Pentre'r-felin
Battle
Llywel
Trallong
Aberyscir
BRECON GAER ROMAN FORT
CATHEDRAL
Usk (Wysg)
Trecastle
Sennybridge (Pont Senni)
Penpont
Llanspyddid
Cwmwysg
A470
A44
A483
A40
B4518
B4358
B4519
B4520
A4081
0 1 2 3 miles
0 1 2 3 4 5 km

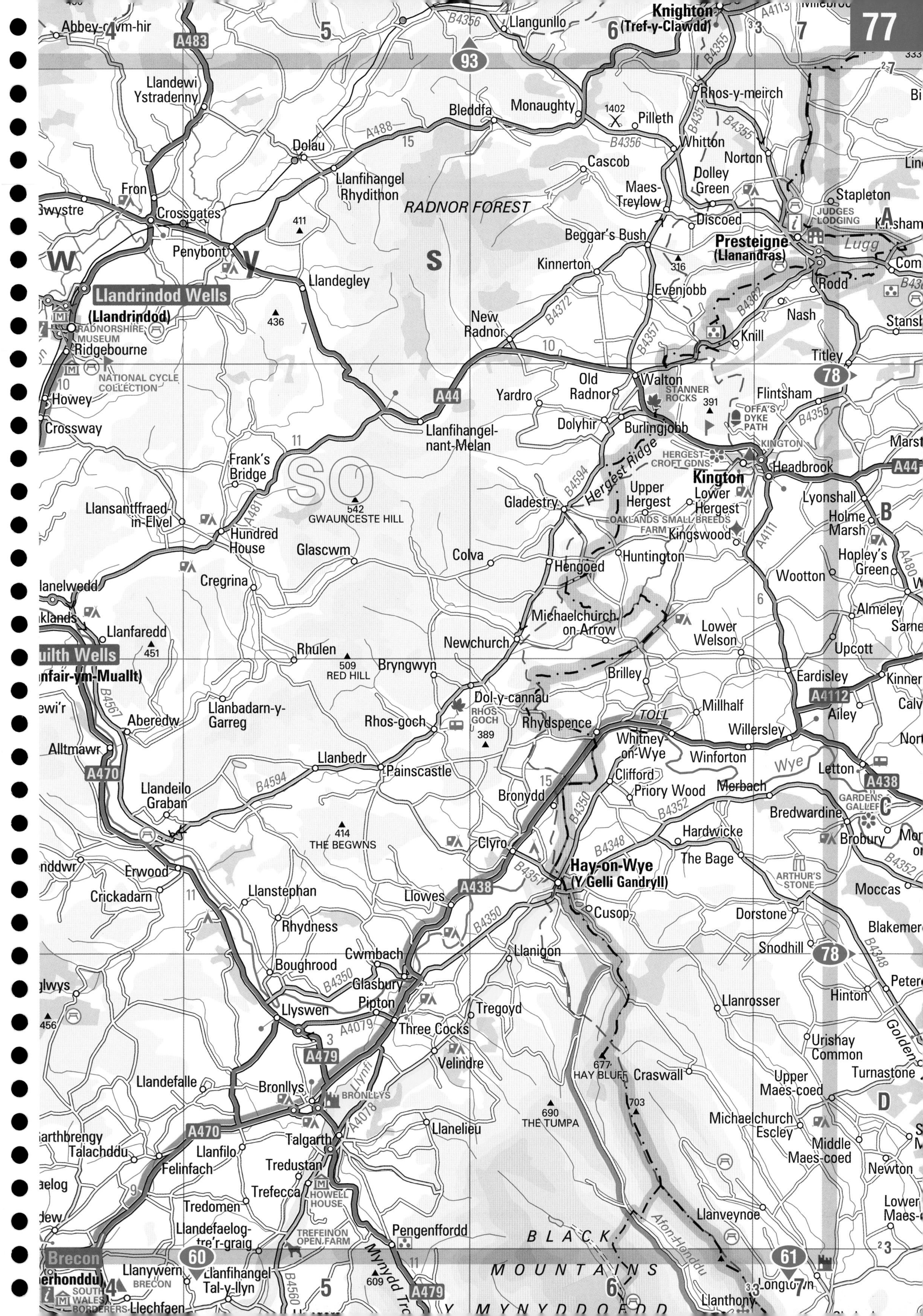
Knighton
(Tref-y-Clawdd)
Abbey-cwm-hir
Llangunllo
Llandewi Ystradenny
Bleddfa
Monaughty
Pilleth
Rhos-y-meirch
Whitton
Norton
Dolau
Llanfihangel Rhydithon
RADNOR FOREST
Cascob
Dolley Green
Maes-Treylow
Discoed
Stapleton
JUDGES LODGING
Presteigne
(Llanandras)
Lugg
Fron
Crossgates
Gwystre
Penybont
Beggar's Bush
Kinnerton
Evenjobb
Rodd
Llandegley
Llandrindod Wells
(Llandrindod)
RADNORSHIRE MUSEUM
Ridgebourne
NATIONAL CYCLE COLLECTION
Howey
Crossway
New Radnor
Nash
Knill
Titley
Walton
Old Radnor
Yardro
STANNER ROCKS
Flintsham
OFFA'S DYKE PATH
Dolyhir
Burlingjobb
Llanfihangel-nant-Melan
HERGEST CROFT GDNS.
KINGTON
Kington
Headbrook
Frank's Bridge
SO
GWAUNCESTE HILL
Gladestry
Hergest Ridge
Upper Hergest
Lower Hergest
OAKLANDS SMALL BREEDS FARM
Kingswood
Lyonshall
Holme Marsh
Llansantffraed-in-Elvel
Hundred House
Glascwm
Colva
Hengoed
Huntington
Hopley's Green
Wootton
Cregrina
Michaelchurch-on-Arrow
Lower Welson
Almeley
Llanfaredd
Builth Wells
(Llanfair-ym-Muallt)
Rhulen
RED HILL
Bryngwyn
Newchurch
Upcott
Eardisley
Brilley
Dol-y-cannau
RHOS GOCH
Llanbadarn-y-Garreg
Aberedw
Rhos-goch
Rhydspence
TOLL
Millhalf
Willersley
Ailey
Alltmawr
Whitney-on-Wye
Winforton
Llanbedr
Painscastle
Wye
Letton
Clifford
Priory Wood
Merbach
Llandeilo Graban
Bronydd
Bredwardine
Hardwicke
THE BEGWNS
Clyro
Hay-on-Wye
(Y Gelli Gandryll)
The Bage
Brobury
Erwood
ARTHUR'S STONE
Moccas
Crickadarn
Llanstephan
Llowes
Cusop
Dorstone
Rhydness
Snodhill
Cwmbach
Llanigon
Boughrood
Glasbury
Hinton
Llyswen
Pipton
Tregoyd
Llanrosser
Three Cocks
Urishay Common
Velindre
HAY BLUFF
Craswall
Turnastone
Upper Maes-coed
Llandefalle
Bronllys
BRONLLYS
Llynfi
THE TUMPA
Michaelchurch Escley
Talgarth
Llanelieu
Llanfilo
Felinfach
Talachddu
Middle Maes-coed
Tredustan
Newton
Trefecca
HOWELL HOUSE
Tredomen
Llanveynoe
Llandefaelog-tre'r-graig
TREFEINON OPEN FARM
Pengenffordd
Afon Honddu
BLACK MOUNTAINS
Brecon
(Aberhonddu)
Llanywern
BRECON
SOUTH WALES BORDERERS
Llanfihangel Tal-y-llyn
Llechfaen
Mynydd Troed
Longtown
Llanthony
Y MYNYDD DDU
A483
A488
A44
A481
A470
A438
A479
A4079
A4078
A4111
A4112
A480
B4356
B4355
B4357
B4372
B4362
B4594
B4567
B4350
B4351
B4352
B4348
B4560
1402
93
78
60
61

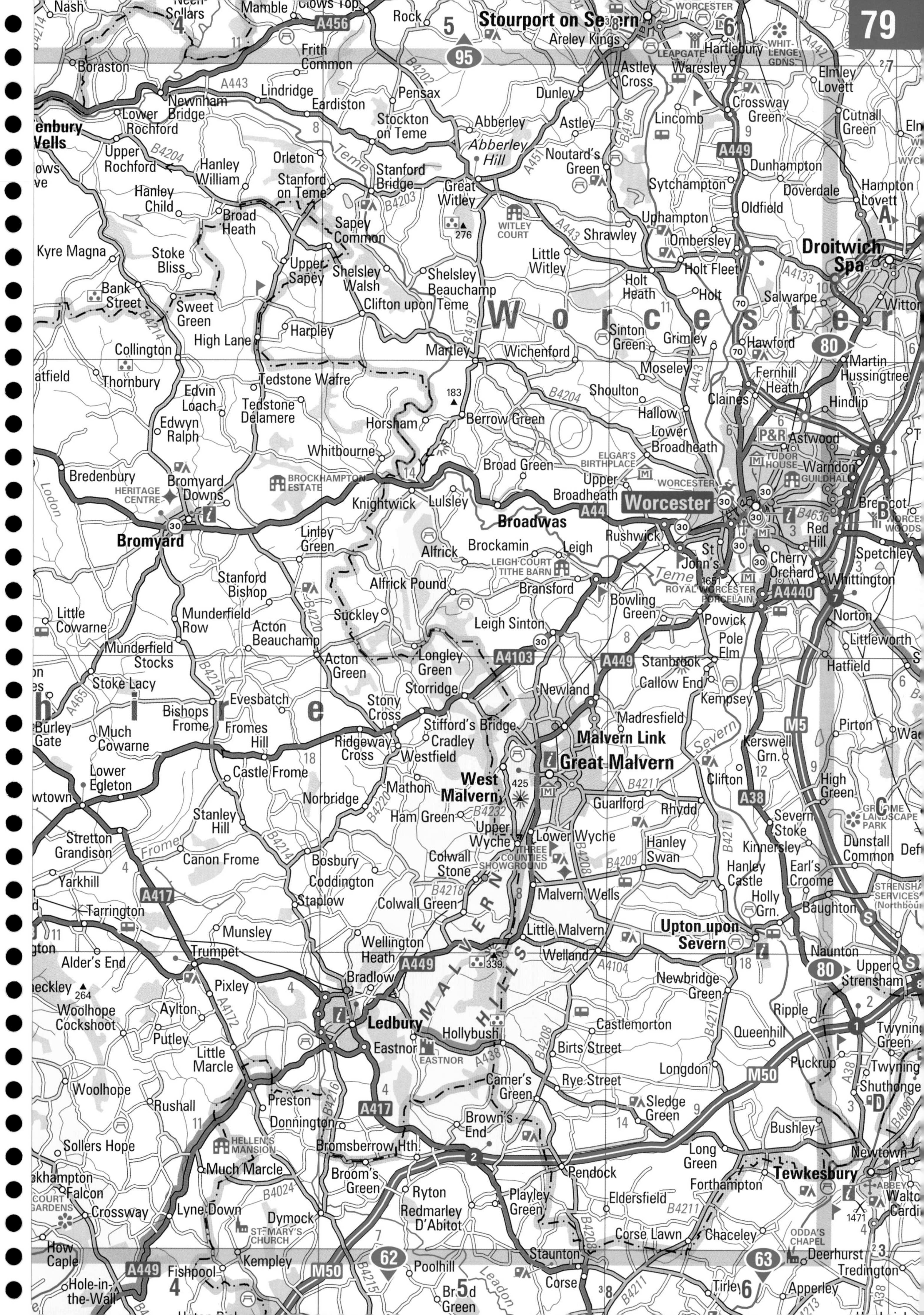
Stourport on Severn
Worcester
Droitwich Spa
Great Malvern
Malvern Link
West Malvern
Bromyard
Ledbury
Upton upon Severn
Tewkesbury
Broadwas
Worcestershire
Malvern Hills
Tenbury Wells
Mamble
Rock
Areley Kings
Hartlebury
Frith Common
Boraston
Lindridge
Pensax
Dunley
Astley Cross
Waresley
Elmley Lovett
Newnham Bridge
Eardiston
Stockton on Teme
Abberley
Astley
Lincomb
Crossway Green
Cutnall Green
Lower Rochford
Upper Rochford
Hanley William
Orleton
Abberley Hill
Noutard's Green
Dunhampton
Hanley Child
Stanford on Teme
Stanford Bridge
Great Witley
Sytchampton
Hampton Lovett
Doverdale
Oldfield
Broad Heath
Sapey Common
Witley Court
Uphampton
Shrawley
Ombersley
Kyre Magna
Stoke Bliss
Upper Sapey
Shelsley Walsh
Shelsley Beauchamp
Little Witley
Holt Fleet
Holt Heath
Holt
Salwarpe
Bank Street
Sweet Green
Clifton upon Teme
Sinton Green
Grimley
Hawford
Harpley
High Lane
Collington
Martley
Wichenford
Moseley
Martin Hussingtree
Thornbury
Tedstone Wafre
Fernhill Heath
Shoulton
Claines
Edvin Loach
Tedstone Delamere
Hallow
Hindlip
Edwyn Ralph
Horsham
Berrow Green
Lower Broadheath
Astwood
Whitbourne
Elgar's Birthplace
Tudor House
Warndon
Guildhall
Bredenbury
Heritage Centre
Bromyard Downs
Brockhampton Estate
Broad Green
Upper Broadheath
Knightwick
Lulsley
Rushwick
Red Hill
Brockamin
Leigh
St John's
Cherry Orchard
Linley Green
Alfrick
Leigh Court Tithe Barn
Spetchley
Stanford Bishop
Alfrick Pound
Bransford
Royal Worcester Porcelain
Whittington
Little Cowarne
Munderfield Row
Suckley
Bowling Green
Powick
Norton
Acton Beauchamp
Leigh Sinton
Pole Elm
Littleworth
Munderfield Stocks
Acton Green
Longley Green
Stanbrook
Callow End
Hatfield
Stoke Lacy
Evesbatch
Storridge
Newland
Kempsey
Bishops Frome
Stony Cross
Madresfield
Burley Gate
Much Cowarne
Fromes Hill
Stifford's Bridge
Cradley
Ridgeway Cross
Westfield
Kerswell Grn.
Pirton
Lower Egleton
Castle Frome
Clifton
Mathon
Guarlford
Rhydd
High Green
Norbridge
Ham Green
Severn Stoke
Croome Landscape Park
Stretton Grandison
Stanley Hill
Upper Wyche
Lower Wyche
Hanley Swan
Kinnersley
Dunstall Common
Canon Frome
Bosbury
Colwall Stone
Three Counties Showground
Hanley Castle
Earl's Croome
Yarkhill
Coddington
Malvern Wells
Holly Grn.
Baughton
Tarrington
Staplow
Colwall Green
Strensham Services
Munsley
Little Malvern
Wellington Heath
Naunton
Alder's End
Trumpet
Welland
Upper Strensham
Pixley
Bradlow
Newbridge Green
Woolhope Cockshoot
Aylton
Ripple
Putley
Hollybush
Castlemorton
Twyning Green
Queenhill
Little Marcle
Eastnor
Birts Street
Puckrup
Woolhope
Camer's Green
Rye Street
Longdon
Twyning
Shuthonger
Rushall
Preston
Sledge Green
Donnington
Brown's End
Bushley
Sollers Hope
Hellen's Mansion
Bromsberrow Hth.
Long Green
Newtown
Much Marcle
Broom's Green
Pendock
Falcon
Ryton
Forthampton
Abbey
Crossway
Lyne Down
Playley Green
Eldersfield
Dymock
Redmarley D'Abitot
St Mary's Church
Corse Lawn
Chaceley
Odda's Chapel
How Caple
Kempley
Staunton
Deerhurst
Tredington
Fishpool
Poolhill
Corse
Tirley
Apperley
Hole-in-the-Wall
Bro'd Green
A456
A443
A449
A451
A44
A4103
A4440
A38
A417
A4172
A438
A4104
A4133
A465
M5
M50
B4214
B4202
B4204
B4203
B4197
B4196
B4220
B4232
B4211
B4208
B4209
B4218
B4216
B4024
B4215
B4636
B4080
B4213
95
80
62
63
276
183
425
339
264
1651
1471
Teme
Severn
Frome
Leadon
Lodon

Bromsgrove
96
Sidemoor
Rowney Green
Branson's Cross
Wood End
Umberslade Farm
Tanworth-in-Arden
Kemp Green
Elmley Lovett
Charford
Finstall
Tardebigge
Beoley
Holt End
Aston Fields
Crossway Green
Cutnall Green
Elmbridge
Avoncroft Historic Buildings
Redditch
Needle Mus.
Gorcott Hill
Webbs of Wychbold
Stoke Prior
Upton Warren
Ullenhall
Dunhampton
Woodgate
Webheath
Ipsley
Oldberrow
Doverdale
Hampton Lovett
Wychbold
Bentley
Headless Cross
Mappleborough Green
Oldfield
Fosters Green Meadows
Crabbs Cross
Morton Bagot
Droitwich Spa
Hanbury Hall
Hanbury
Hunt End
Studley
Woolmere Green
Ham Green
Salwarpe
Witton
Hadzor
Astwood Bank
Shelfield
Worcester
Sambourne
Coughton Court
Little Alne
Hawford
79
Shernal Green
Bradley Green
Feckenham
Coughton
Great Alne
Martin Hussingtree
Fernhill Heath
Oddingley
Stock Wood
Holberrow Green
New End
King's Coughton
Hindlip
Himbleton
Stock Green
Cookhill
Alcester
Walcote
Sale Green
Astwood
Tibberton
Huddington
Dormston
Overley Green
Haselor
Tudor House
Warndon
Guildhall
Inkberrow
Arrow
Billesley
Crowle
Grafton Flyford
Kington
Abbots Morton
Exhall
Ragley Hall
Bredicot
Broughton Hackett
Weethley Gate
Temple Grafton
Worcester Woods
Red Hill
North Piddle
Flyford Flavell
Wixford
Ardens Grafton
Cherry Orchard
Spetchley
Churchill
Upton Snodsbury
Rous Lench
Dunnington
Abberton
Iron Cross
Broom
Whittington
White Ladies Aston
Naunton Beauchamp
Ab Lench
Church Lench
Norton
Egdon
Bishampton
Salford Priors
Bidford-on-Avon
Littleworth
Peopleton
Atch Lench
Abbots Salford
Barton
Marlcliff
Annard Woollen Mill
Hatfield
Stoulton
Pinvin
Throckmorton
Harvington Cross
Dorsington
Drake's Broughton
Harvington
Cleeve Prior
Norton
North Littleton
Pirton
Wadborough
Lenchwick
Pebworth
Evesham Country Park
Kerswell Grn.
Wyre Piddle
Lower Moor
Middle Littleton
Fladbury
Pershore
Charlton
Offenham
Broad Marston
High Green
Abbey
Wick
South Littleton
Besford
Cropthorne
Severn Stoke
Groome Landscape Park
Evesham
Aldington
Domestic Fowl Trust
Honeybourne
Kinnersley
Dunstall Common
Defford
Little Comberton
Bengeworth
Bretforton
Hanley Castle
Earl's Croome
Birlingham
Hampton
Fairfield
Badsey
Fleece Inn
Holly Grn.
Great Comberton
Bricklehampton
Strensham Services (Northbound Only)
Baughton
Eckington
Netherton
Wickhamford
Lower Strensham
Bredon Hill
Elmley Castle
Vale of Evesham
Weston-Sub-Edge
Naunton
Strensham Services (Southbound Only)
Kersoe
Hinton on the Green
Childswickham
Willersey
Saintbury
Upper Strensham
Bredon's Norton
Ashton under Hill
Sedgeberrow
Ripple
Bredon Barn
Kemerton
Overbury
Conderton Pottery
Aston Somerville
Broadway
Queenhill
Twyning Green
Conderton
Puckrup
Twyning
Bredon
Silk Centre
Dumbleton
Wormington
Buckland
Shuthonger
Kinsham
Beckford
Alderton Hill
Laverton
Broadway Tower
Northway
Great Washbourne
Snowshill Manor
Stanton
Snowshill Lavender
Bushley
Newtown
Aston Cross
Teddington
Alderton
Snowshill
Cotswolds
Tewkesbury
Ashchurch
Toddington
Gloucestershire Warwickshire Steam Railway
Abbey
Alstone
Stanway
Walton Cardiff
Stanway House
Fiddington
Oxenton
Dixton
Greet
Didbrook
Hailes Abbey
Odda's Chapel
Gretton
Hailes
Cutsdean
Deerhurst
63
Gotherington
Winchcombe Pottery
Ford
64
Stoke Orchard
Bishop's Cleeve
Langley Hill
Winchcombe
Sudeley Castle and Gardens
Farmcote
Condicote
Temple Guiting
0 1 2 3 miles
0 1 2 3 4 5 km

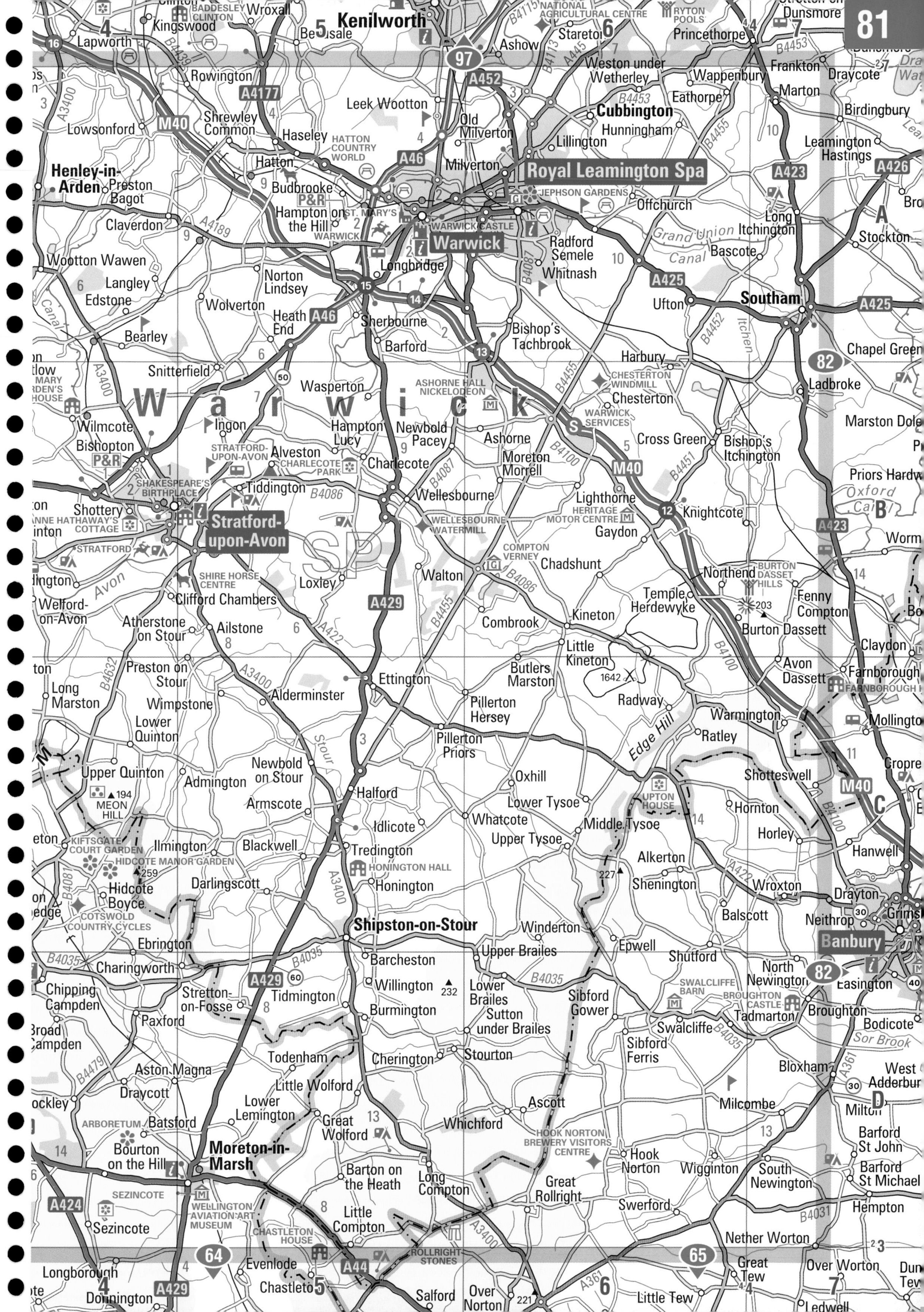
Kenilworth
Royal Leamington Spa
Warwick
Stratford-upon-Avon
Southam
Banbury
Shipston-on-Stour
Moreton-in-Marsh
Cubbington
Henley-in-Arden
Warwick
Kingswood
Lapworth
Rowington
Lowsonford
Shrewley Common
Haseley
Hatton
Leek Wootton
Old Milverton
Milverton
Lillington
Hunningham
Weston under Wetherley
Wappenbury
Eathorpe
Frankton
Draycote
Marton
Birdingbury
Leamington Hastings
Offchurch
Long Itchington
Stockton
Bascote
Ufton
Radford Semele
Whitnash
Budbrooke
Hampton on the Hill
Preston Bagot
Claverdon
Wootton Wawen
Langley
Edstone
Wolverton
Norton Lindsey
Heath End
Longbridge
Sherbourne
Barford
Bishop's Tachbrook
Harbury
Chapel Green
Ladbroke
Bearley
Snitterfield
Wasperton
Wilmcote
Bishopton
Ingon
Hampton Lucy
Newbold Pacey
Ashorne
Chesterton
Moreton Morrell
Charlecote
Alveston
Tiddington
Wellesbourne
Lighthorne
Gaydon
Cross Green
Bishop's Itchington
Marston Doles
Priors Hardwick
Knightcote
Shottery
Walton
Chadshunt
Northend
Loxley
Temple Herdewyke
Fenny Compton
Clifford Chambers
Welford-on-Avon
Atherstone on Stour
Ailstone
Combrook
Kineton
Burton Dassett
Little Kineton
Claydon
Preston on Stour
Ettington
Butlers Marston
Avon Dassett
Farnborough
Long Marston
Wimpstone
Alderminster
Pillerton Hersey
Radway
Warmington
Mollington
Lower Quinton
Pillerton Priors
Ratley
Upper Quinton
Newbold on Stour
Admington
Oxhill
Shotteswell
Cropredy
Armscote
Halford
Lower Tysoe
Hornton
Whatcote
Middle Tysoe
Idlicote
Upper Tysoe
Horley
Ilmington
Blackwell
Tredington
Hanwell
Alkerton
Hidcote Boyce
Darlingscott
Honington
Shenington
Wroxton
Drayton
Balscott
Neithrop
Shipston-on-Stour
Winderton
Ebrington
Epwell
Charingworth
Barcheston
Upper Brailes
Shutford
North Newington
Easington
Chipping Campden
Stretton-on-Fosse
Tidmington
Willington
Lower Brailes
Sibford Gower
Broughton
Paxford
Burmington
Sutton under Brailes
Swalcliffe
Tadmarton
Bodicote
Broad Campden
Sibford Ferris
Todenham
Cherington
Stourton
Aston Magna
Bloxham
West Adderbury
Little Wolford
Draycott
Lower Lemington
Ascott
Milcombe
Milton
Batsford
Great Wolford
Whichford
Barford St John
Bourton on the Hill
Hook Norton
Wigginton
South Newington
Barford St Michael
Barton on the Heath
Long Compton
Great Rollright
Swerford
Hempton
Sezincote
Little Compton
Nether Worton
Evenlode
Great Tew
Over Worton
Longborough
Donnington
Chastleton
Salford
Over Norton
Little Tew
Ledwell
Warwick
SP
M40
A46
A429
A3400
A425
A423
A452
A4177
A422
A44
A424
A361
Grand Union Canal
Avon
Stour
Edge Hill
NATIONAL AGRICULTURAL CENTRE
RYTON POOLS
HATTON COUNTRY WORLD
JEPHSON GARDENS
WARWICK CASTLE
ST. MARY'S
ASHORNE HALL NICKELODEON
CHESTERTON WINDMILL
WARWICK SERVICES
CHARLECOTE PARK
SHAKESPEARE'S BIRTHPLACE
ANNE HATHAWAY'S COTTAGE
MARY ARDEN'S HOUSE
HERITAGE MOTOR CENTRE
WELLESBOURNE WATERMILL
COMPTON VERNEY
SHIRE HORSE CENTRE
BURTON DASSETT HILLS
FARNBOROUGH HALL
UPTON HOUSE
MEON HILL
KIFTSGATE COURT GARDEN
HIDCOTE MANOR GARDEN
COTSWOLD COUNTRY CYCLES
HONINGTON HALL
SWALCLIFFE BARN
BROUGHTON CASTLE
HOOK NORTON BREWERY VISITORS CENTRE
ARBORETUM
SEZINCOTE
WELLINGTON AVIATION ART MUSEUM
CHASTLETON HOUSE
ROLLRIGHT STONES

97
82
64
65

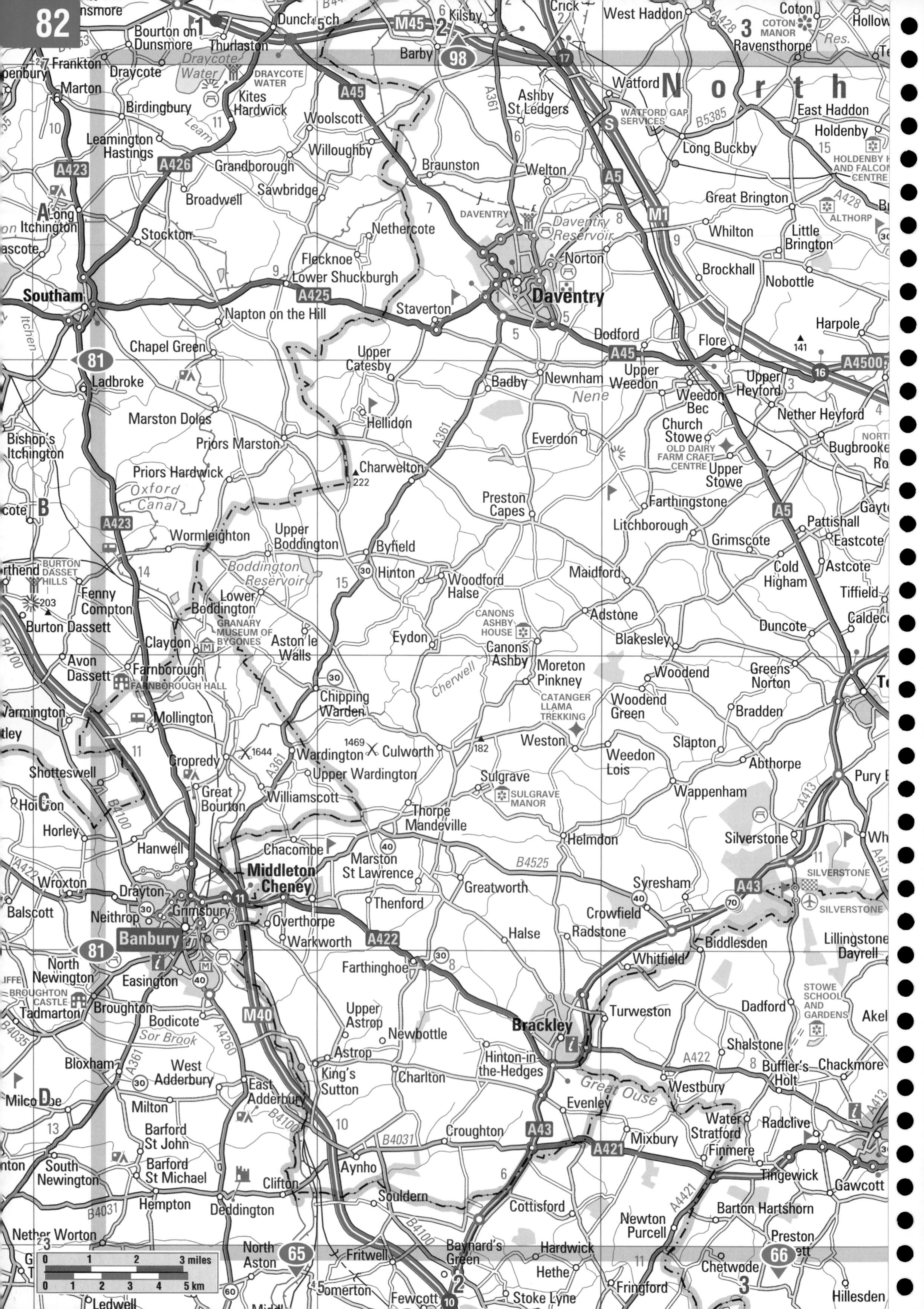
Bourton on Dunsmore
Thurlaston
Dunchurch
M45
Kilsby
Crick
West Haddon
Coton
COTON MANOR
Ravensthorpe
Res.
Hollow
Frankton
Draycote
Draycote Water
DRAYCOTE WATER
Barby
98
Marton
Birdingbury
Kites Hardwick
Leam
A45
Ashby St Ledgers
Watford
North
East Haddon
WATFORD GAP SERVICES
B5385
Holdenby
HOLDENBY H AND FALCON CENTRE
Leamington Hastings
Woolscott
Willoughby
Long Buckby
A423
A426
Grandborough
Braunston
Welton
A5
Sawbridge
Broadwell
Great Brington
A428
DAVENTRY
Daventry Reservoir
M1
ALTHORP
Long Itchington
Stockton
Nethercote
Whilton
Little Brington
Flecknoe
Norton
Brockhall
Lower Shuckburgh
Nobottle
Southam
A425
Daventry
Napton on the Hill
Staverton
Harpole
Dodford
Flore
Itchen
Chapel Green
Upper Catesby
A45
Upper Weedon
Upper Heyford
A4500
81
Ladbroke
Badby
Newnham
Weedon Bec
Nene
Nether Heyford
Marston Doles
Hellidon
A361
Church Stowe
Bishop's Itchington
Priors Marston
Everdon
OLD DAIRY FARM CRAFT CENTRE
Upper Stowe
Bugbrooke
Priors Hardwick
Charwelton
222
Oxford Canal
Preston Capes
Farthingstone
Litchborough
Pattishall
A423
Wormleighton
Upper Boddington
Byfield
Grimscote
Eastcote
BURTON DASSETT HILLS
Boddington Reservoir
Hinton
Woodford Halse
Maidford
Cold Higham
Astcote
Fenny Compton
203
Lower Boddington
CANONS ASHBY HOUSE
Adstone
Tiffield
Burton Dassett
GRANARY MUSEUM OF BYGONES
Duncote
Claydon
Aston le Walls
Eydon
Canons Ashby
Blakesley
Avon Dassett
Farnborough
FARNBOROUGH HALL
Moreton Pinkney
Woodend
Greens Norton
Cherwell
Chipping Warden
CATANGER LLAMA TREKKING
Woodend Green
Bradden
Warmington
Mollington
Weston
Slapton
1469
Culworth
182
Cropredy
1644
Wardington
Weedon Lois
Abthorpe
Shotteswell
Upper Wardington
Sulgrave
SULGRAVE MANOR
Pury End
Hornton
Great Bourton
Williamscott
Wappenham
B4100
Thorpe Mandeville
Horley
Silverstone
Hanwell
Chacombe
Helmdon
Marston St Lawrence
B4525
Middleton Cheney
Wroxton
A422
Syresham
SILVERSTONE
Drayton
Greatworth
A43
Balscott
Neithrop
Grimsbury
Thenford
Crowfield
Overthorpe
Banbury
Halse
Radstone
Biddlesden
Lillingstone Dayrell
Warkworth
A422
81
North Newington
Farthinghoe
Whitfield
BROUGHTON CASTLE
Easington
Turweston
STOWE SCHOOL AND GARDENS
Tadmarton
Broughton
Dadford
Bodicote
Upper Astrop
M40
Brackley
Akeley
Sor Brook
Newbottle
A4260
Shalstone
Astrop
Hinton-in-the-Hedges
A422
Buffler's Holt
Chackmore
Bloxham
West Adderbury
King's Sutton
Charlton
Great Ouse
Westbury
East Adderbury
Milcombe
Evenley
Milton
B4100
Water Stratford
Radclive
Croughton
Barford St John
A43
Mixbury
B4031
A421
Finmere
South Newington
Barford St Michael
Aynho
Tingewick
Gawcott
Clifton
Souldern
Cottisford
Hempton
Deddington
Newton Purcell
Barton Hartshorn
B4031
A4421
Preston Bissett
Nether Worton
B4100
North Aston
65
Fritwell
Baynard's Green
Hardwick
Chetwode
66
Hethe
Fringford
Somerton
Fewcott
Stoke Lyne
Hillesden
Ledwell
0 1 2 3 miles
0 1 2 3 4 5 km

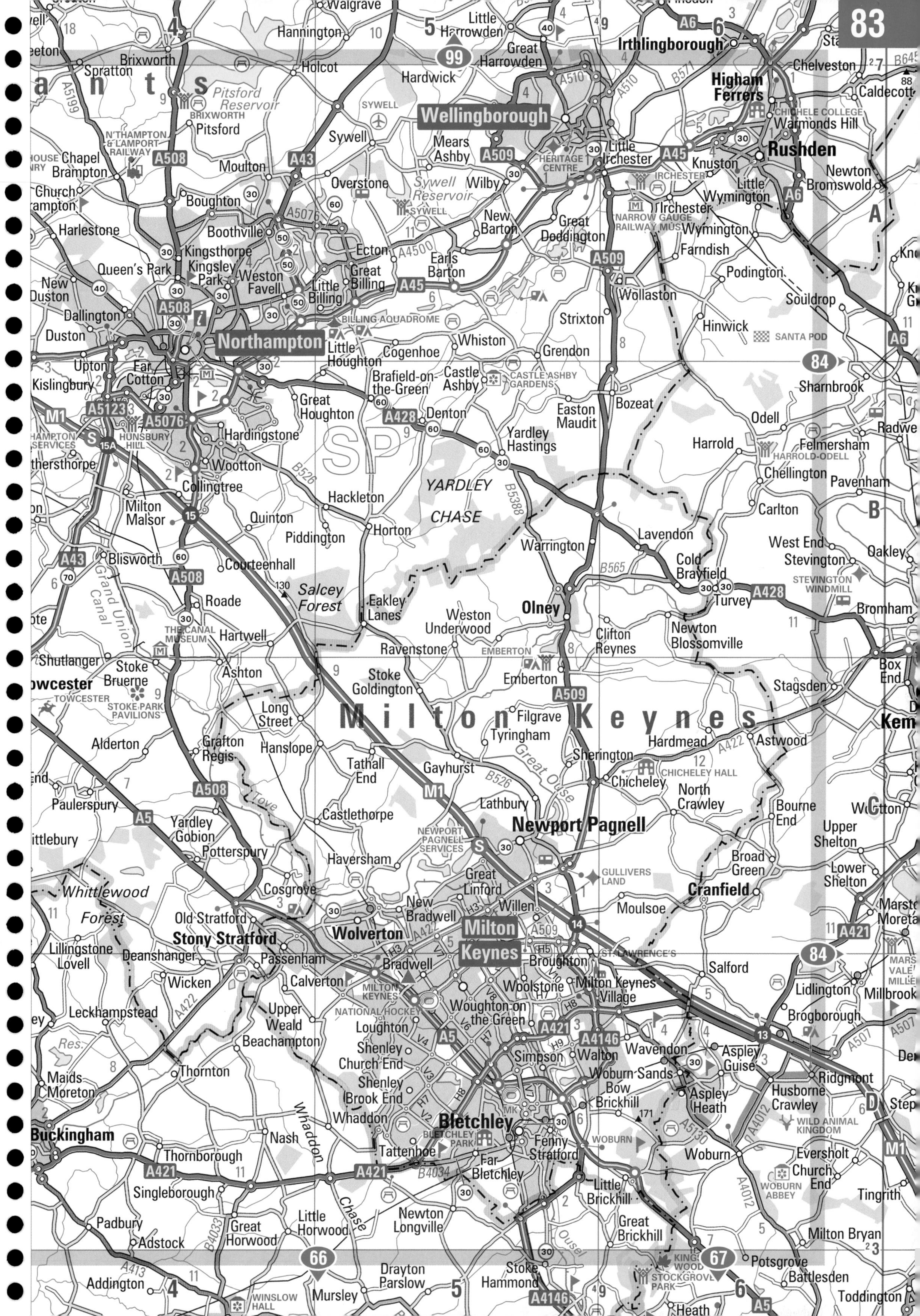
Walgrave
Hannington
Little Harrowden
Great Harrowden
Irthlingborough
Brixworth
Spratton
Holcot
Hardwick
Chelveston
Caldecott
Higham Ferrers
Chichele College
Warmonds Hill
Pitsford Reservoir
Brixworth
Pitsford
Sywell
Wellingborough
N'Thampton & Lamport Railway
Chapel Brampton
Church Brampton
Moulton
Mears Ashby
Heritage Centre
Little Irchester
Knuston
Rushden
Newton Bromswold
Overstone
Sywell Reservoir
Wilby
Irchester
Little Wymington
Boughton
New Barton
Great Doddington
Irchester Narrow Gauge Railway Mus
Wymington
Harlestone
Boothville
Kingsthorpe
Ecton
Earls Barton
Farndish
Queen's Park
Kingsley Park
Weston Favell
Great Billing
Little Billing
Podington
New Duston
Wollaston
Souldrop
Dallington
Billing Aquadrome
Strixton
Hinwick
Duston
Northampton
Little Houghton
Cogenhoe
Whiston
Grendon
Santa Pod
Upton
Far Cotton
Brafield-on-the-Green
Castle Ashby
Castle Ashby Gardens
Sharnbrook
Kislingbury
Great Houghton
Denton
Easton Maudit
Bozeat
Odell
Radwell
Hunsbury Hill
Hardingstone
Yardley Hastings
Harrold
Felmersham
Harrold-Odell
Rothersthorpe
Wootton
Chellington
Pavenham
Collingtree
Yardley Chase
Milton Malsor
Quinton
Hackleton
Horton
Carlton
Piddington
Lavendon
Warrington
West End
Stevington
Oakley
Blisworth
Courteenhall
Cold Brayfield
Stevington Windmill
Grand Union Canal
Salcey Forest
Eakley Lanes
Turvey
Bromham
Roade
Weston Underwood
Olney
Clifton Reynes
Newton Blossomville
The Canal Museum
Hartwell
Ravenstone
Emberton
Shutlanger
Stoke Bruerne
Ashton
Stoke Goldington
Box End
Towcester
Stoke Park Pavilions
Long Street
Stagsden
Milton Keynes
Filgrave
Tyringham
Alderton
Grafton Regis
Hanslope
Hardmead
Astwood
Tathall End
Gayhurst
Sherington
Great Ouse
Chicheley
Chicheley Hall
Paulerspury
North Crawley
Yardley Gobion
Castlethorpe
Lathbury
Bourne End
Wootton
Newport Pagnell Services
Newport Pagnell
Upper Shelton
Potterspury
Haversham
Broad Green
Whittlewood Forest
Great Linford
Gullivers Land
Lower Shelton
Cosgrove
Cranfield
Old Stratford
New Bradwell
Willen
Moulsoe
Stony Stratford
Wolverton
Milton Keynes
Lillingstone Lovell
Deanshanger
Passenham
Bradwell
Broughton
St Lawrence's
Salford
Wicken
Calverton
Woolstone
Milton Keynes Village
Lidlington
Millbrook
Milton Keynes National Hockey
Leckhampstead
Upper Weald
Loughton
Woughton on the Green
Brogborough
Beachampton
Shenley Church End
Simpson
Walton
Wavendon
Aspley Guise
Thornton
Maids Moreton
Woburn Sands
Ridgmont
Shenley Brook End
Bow Brickhill
Aspley Heath
Husborne Crawley
Whaddon
Bletchley
Wild Animal Kingdom
Buckingham
Nash
Bletchley Park
Fenny Stratford
Woburn
Eversholt
Thornborough
Tattenhoe
Far Bletchley
Church End
Singleborough
Little Brickhill
Woburn Abbey
Tingrith
Padbury
Little Horwood
Newton Longville
Great Brickhill
Adstock
Great Horwood
Milton Bryan
Potsgrove
Kings Wood
Addington
Drayton Parslow
Stoke Hammond
Stockgrove Park
Battlesden
Winslow Hall
Mursley
Heath
Toddington
Ouzel
Whaddon Chase
Res.

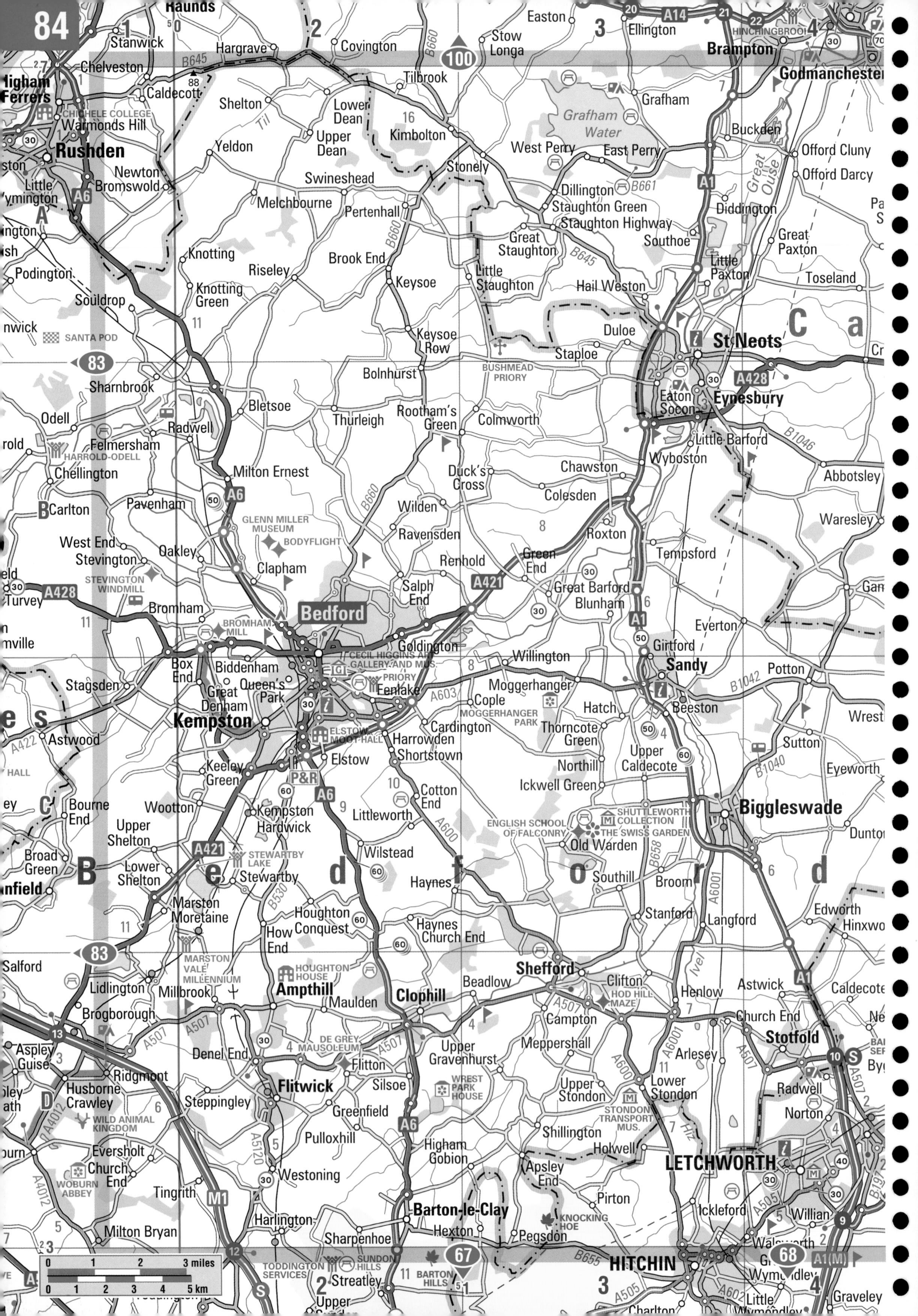
Raunds
Stanwick
Hargrave
Covington
Easton
Stow Longa
Ellington
A14
Brampton
HINCHINGBROOKE
Godmanchester
100
Chelveston
B645
Higham Ferrers
Caldecott
Tilbrook
Shelton
Lower Dean
Upper Dean
Kimbolton
Grafham
Grafham Water
CHICHELE COLLEGE
Wymington Hill
Rushden
Yeldon
West Perry
East Perry
Buckden
Offord Cluny
Offord Darcy
Newton Bromswold
Stonely
Swineshead
Dillington
B661
Great Ouse
Little Irchester
Wymington
A6
Melchbourne
Pertenhall
Staughton Green
Staughton Highway
Diddington
Podington
Knotting
Riseley
Brook End
B660
Great Staughton
B645
Southoe
Great Paxton
Little Paxton
Knotting Green
Keysoe
Little Staughton
Hail Weston
Toseland
Souldrop
St Neots
Duloe
Keysoe Row
Staploe
SANTA POD
83
Bolnhurst
BUSHMEAD PRIORY
A428
Eynesbury
Eaton Socon
Sharnbrook
Odell
Bletsoe
Thurleigh
Rootham's Green
Colmworth
Little Barford
B1046
Felmersham
Radwell
HARROLD-ODELL
Wyboston
Chellington
Milton Ernest
Duck's Cross
Chawston
Abbotsley
Colesden
Carlton
Pavenham
B660
Wilden
Waresley
GLENN MILLER MUSEUM
BODYFLIGHT
Ravensden
Roxton
West End
Stevington
Oakley
Renhold
Green End
Tempsford
Clapham
STEVINGTON WINDMILL
Salph End
A421
Great Barford
Blunham
Turvey
Bromham
Bedford
BROMHAM MILL
Everton
Goldington
CECIL HIGGINS ART GALLERY AND MUS.
Willington
Girtford
Sandy
Potton
Box End
Biddenham
PRIORY
Moggerhanger
B1042
Stagsden
Great Denham
Queen's Park
Fenlake
A603
Cople
MOGGERHANGER PARK
Hatch
Beeston
Wrestlingworth
Kempston
Cardington
Thorncote Green
ELSTOW MOOT HALL
Harrowden
Shortstown
Upper Caldecote
Sutton
Astwood
A422
Keeley Green
Elstow
Northill
B1040
Eyeworth
Ickwell Green
P&R
Cotton End
Bourne End
Wootton
Kempston Hardwick
Littleworth
SHUTTLEWORTH COLLECTION
Biggleswade
Upper Shelton
ENGLISH SCHOOL OF FALCONRY
THE SWISS GARDEN
Old Warden
Dunton
Broad Green
A421
STEWARTBY LAKE
Wilstead
A600
B658
Lower Shelton
Stewartby
Southill
Broom
Cranfield
Haynes
A6001
Marston Moretaine
B530
Houghton Conquest
Stanford
Langford
Edworth
Hinxworth
How End
Haynes Church End
MARSTON VALE MILLENNIUM
Salford
Shefford
Ivel
Beadlow
HOUGHTON HOUSE
Clifton
Astwick
Caldecote
Lidlington
Millbrook
Ampthill
HOD HILL MAZE
Henlow
A1
Clophill
Maulden
A507
Campton
Church End
Brogborough
Stotfold
Aspley Guise
Denel End
DE GREY MAUSOLEUM
Flitton
Upper Gravenhurst
Meppershall
Arlesey
Ridgmont
Flitwick
Silsoe
WREST PARK HOUSE
Upper Stondon
Lower Stondon
Radwell
Husborne Crawley
Steppingley
Greenfield
STONDON TRANSPORT MUS.
Norton
WILD ANIMAL KINGDOM
Pulloxhill
Shillington
Hiz
Eversholt
A5120
Higham Gobion
Holwell
LETCHWORTH
Church End
WOBURN ABBEY
Westoning
Apsley End
Tingrith
M1
Pirton
Ickleford
A505
William
Harlington
Barton-le-Clay
KNOCKING HOE
Milton Bryan
Hexton
Pegsdon
Sharpenhoe
Walsworth
TODDINGTON SERVICES
SUNDON HILLS
67
BARTON HILLS
B655
HITCHIN
68
A1(M)
Streatley
Great Wymondley
Little Wymondley
Graveley
Upper Sundon
Charlton
A602
0 1 2 3 miles
0 1 2 3 4 5 km
B
e
d
f
o
r
d
C
a

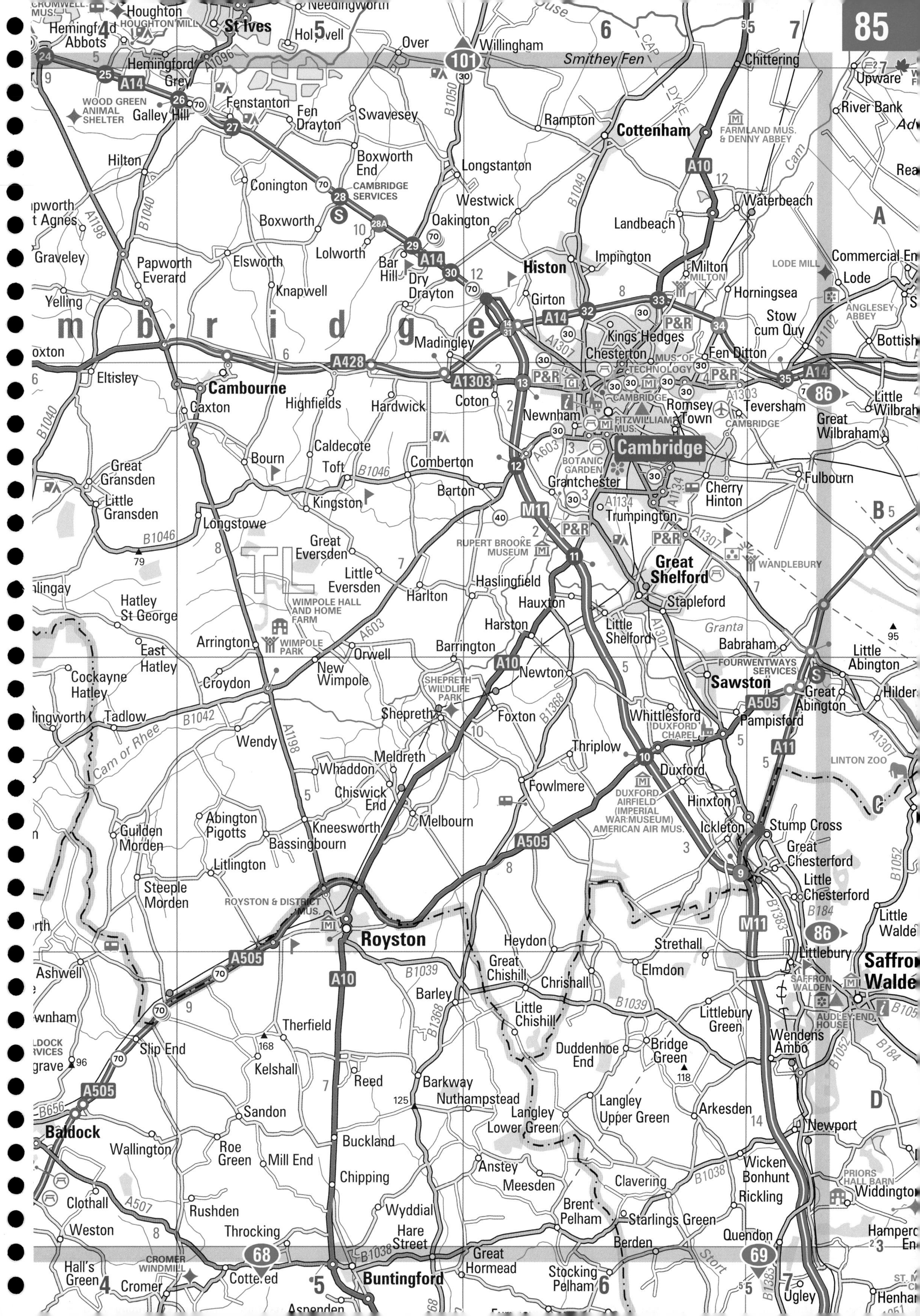

St Ives
Houghton
Hemingford Abbots
Hemingford Grey
Holywell
Needingworth
Over
Willingham
Smithey Fen
Chittering
Upware
River Bank
Fenstanton
Fen Drayton
Swavesey
Galley Hill
WOOD GREEN ANIMAL SHELTER
Rampton
Cottenham
FARMLAND MUS. & DENNY ABBEY
Hilton
Boxworth End
Longstanton
Conington
CAMBRIDGE SERVICES
Westwick
Waterbeach
Papworth St Agnes
Boxworth
Oakington
Landbeach
Graveley
Papworth Everard
Elsworth
Lolworth
Bar Hill
Dry Drayton
Histon
Impington
Milton
LODE MILL
Commercial End
Lode
Yelling
Knapwell
Girton
Horningsea
ANGLESEY ABBEY
Stow cum Quy
Bottisham
Cambridge
Madingley
Kings Hedges
Chesterton
Fen Ditton
Toxton
Eltisley
Cambourne
Caxton
Highfields
Hardwick
Coton
Newnham
FITZWILLIAM MUS.
Romsey Town
Teversham
Little Wilbraham
Great Wilbraham
Cambridge
Caldecote
Toft
Comberton
BOTANIC GARDEN
Grantchester
Cherry Hinton
Fulbourn
Great Gransden
Little Gransden
Bourn
Kingston
Barton
Trumpington
Longstowe
Great Eversden
RUPERT BROOKE MUSEUM
Great Shelford
WANDLEBURY
Little Eversden
Harlton
Haslingfield
Hauxton
Stapleford
Gamlingay
Hatley St George
WIMPOLE HALL AND HOME FARM
Harston
Little Shelford
Babraham
Granta
East Hatley
Arrington
WIMPOLE PARK
Orwell
Barrington
Little Abington
FOURWENTWAYS SERVICES
Cockayne Hatley
Croydon
New Wimpole
SHEPRETH WILDLIFE PARK
Newton
Sawston
Great Abington
Hildersham
Tadlow
Wrestlingworth
Shepreth
Foxton
Whittlesford
DUXFORD CHAPEL
Pampisford
Wendy
Cam or Rhee
Thriplow
LINTON ZOO
Meldreth
Whaddon
Duxford
Fowlmere
Chiswick End
DUXFORD AIRFIELD (IMPERIAL WAR MUSEUM) AMERICAN AIR MUS.
Hinxton
Guilden Morden
Abington Pigotts
Melbourn
Kneesworth
Bassingbourn
Ickleton
Stump Cross
Great Chesterford
Litlington
Little Chesterford
Steeple Morden
ROYSTON & DISTRICT MUS.
Royston
Heydon
Strethall
Little Walden
Ashwell
Great Chishill
Elmdon
Littlebury
Saffron Walden
SAFFRON WALDEN
Chrishall
Barley
Little Chishill
Littlebury Green
AUDLEY END HOUSE
Therfield
Duddenhoe End
Bridge Green
Wendens Ambo
Slip End
Kelshall
Reed
Barkway
Nuthampstead
Langley
Langley Upper Green
Langley Lower Green
Arkesden
Newport
Sandon
Baldock
Wallington
Roe Green
Mill End
Buckland
Chipping
Anstey
Meesden
Clavering
Wicken Bonhunt
Rickling
PRIORS HALL BARN
Widdington
Clothall
Rushden
Wyddial
Brent Pelham
Starlings Green
Weston
Throcking
Hare Street
Berden
Quendon
CROMER WINDMILL
Great Hormead
Hall's Green
Cromer
Cottered
Buntingford
Stocking Pelham
Ugley
Henham
Aspenden
Stort
A14
A10
A428
A1303
M11
A11
A505
A603
A1198
A1307
A1134
A1301
A1096
A507
B1040
B1046
B1042
B1049
B1050
B1039
B1038
B1368
B1383
B1052
B1102
B184
B656
TL

Newmarket
Haverhill
Saffron Walden
Burwell
Wicken
Upware
Fordham
Chippenham
Tuddenham
Herringswell
Cavenham
Red Lodge
Kennett
Kentford
Snailwell
Landwade
Exning
Reach
Swaffham Prior
Swaffham Bulbeck
Commercial End
Lode
Bottisham
Horningsea
Stow cum Quy
Waterbeach
Teversham
Little Wilbraham
Great Wilbraham
Fulbourn
Six Mile Bottom
Dullingham
Stetchworth
Woodditton
Saxon Street
Cheveley
Ashley
Moulton
Gazeley
Dalham
Higham
Barrow
Denham
Risby
Little Saxham
Dunstall Green
Hargrave
Ousden
Lidgate
Depden Green
Upend
Kirtling
Kirtling Green
Ditton Green
Westley Waterless
Burrough Green
Brinkley
Weston Colville
Weston Green
Carlton
Great Bradley
Little Bradley
Little Thurlow
Great Thurlow
Cowlinge
Thorns
Wickhambrook
Clopton Green
Wickham Street
Denston
Stradishall
Balsham
West Wratting
West Wickham
Streetly End
Horseheath
Withersfield
Great Wratting
Little Wratting
Kedington
Barnardiston
Hundon
Poslingford
Chilton Street
Clare
Boyton End
Stoke by Clare
Wixoe
Baythorn End
Sturmer
Babraham
Little Abington
Great Abington
Hildersham
Pampisford
Linton
Bartlow
Hadstock
Shudy Camps
Castle Camps
Ashdon
Helions Bumpstead
Steeple Bumpstead
Birdbrook
Ridgewell
Ashen
Ovington
Tilbury Juxta Clare
Little Yeldham
Great Yeldham
Stump Cross
Great Chesterford
Little Chesterford
Little Walden
Church End
Sewards End
Radwinter
Hempstead
Wimbish
Tye Green
Wimbish Green
Great Sampford
Little Sampford
Stambourne
Stambourne Green
Toppesfield
Cornish Hall End
Gainsford End
Highstreet Green
Sible Hedingham
Castle Hedingham
Howe Street
Finchingfield
Morris Green
Wethersfield
Blackmore End
Great Bardfield
Little Bardfield
Thaxted
Debden
Debden Cross
Howlett End
Newport
Wendens Ambo
Wicken Bonhunt
Rickling
Widdington
Quendon
Hamperden End
Cutlers Green
Monk Street
Shalford
Church End
Gosfield
Beazley End
Newmarket Heath
Adventures Fen
New River
River Bank
WICKEN CORN MILL
WICKEN FEN
CHIPPENHAM FEN
DOWN FIELD WINDMILL
PACKHORSE BRIDGE
NATIONAL HORSERACING MUSEUM
NATIONAL STUD
LODE MILL
ANGLESEY ABBEY
FARMLAND MUS. & DENNY ABBEY
WANDLEBURY
FOURWENTWAYS SERVICES
LINTON ZOO
CLARE CASTLE
CLARE ANCIENT HOUSE
SUE RYDER FOUNDATION MUSEUM
COLNE VALLEY RAILWAY
HEDINGHAM CASTLE
AUDLEY END HOUSE
PRIORS HALL BARN
MOLE HALL WILDLIFE PARK
GLENDALE FORGE
E s s e x
A11
A14
A142
A1123
A1303
A1304
A1307
A143
A1017
A505
M11
B1102
B1103
B1085
B1506
B1063
B1061
B1052
B1054
B1053
B1057
B1051
B184
B1383
102
85
69
70
0 1 2 3 miles
0 1 2 3 4 5 km

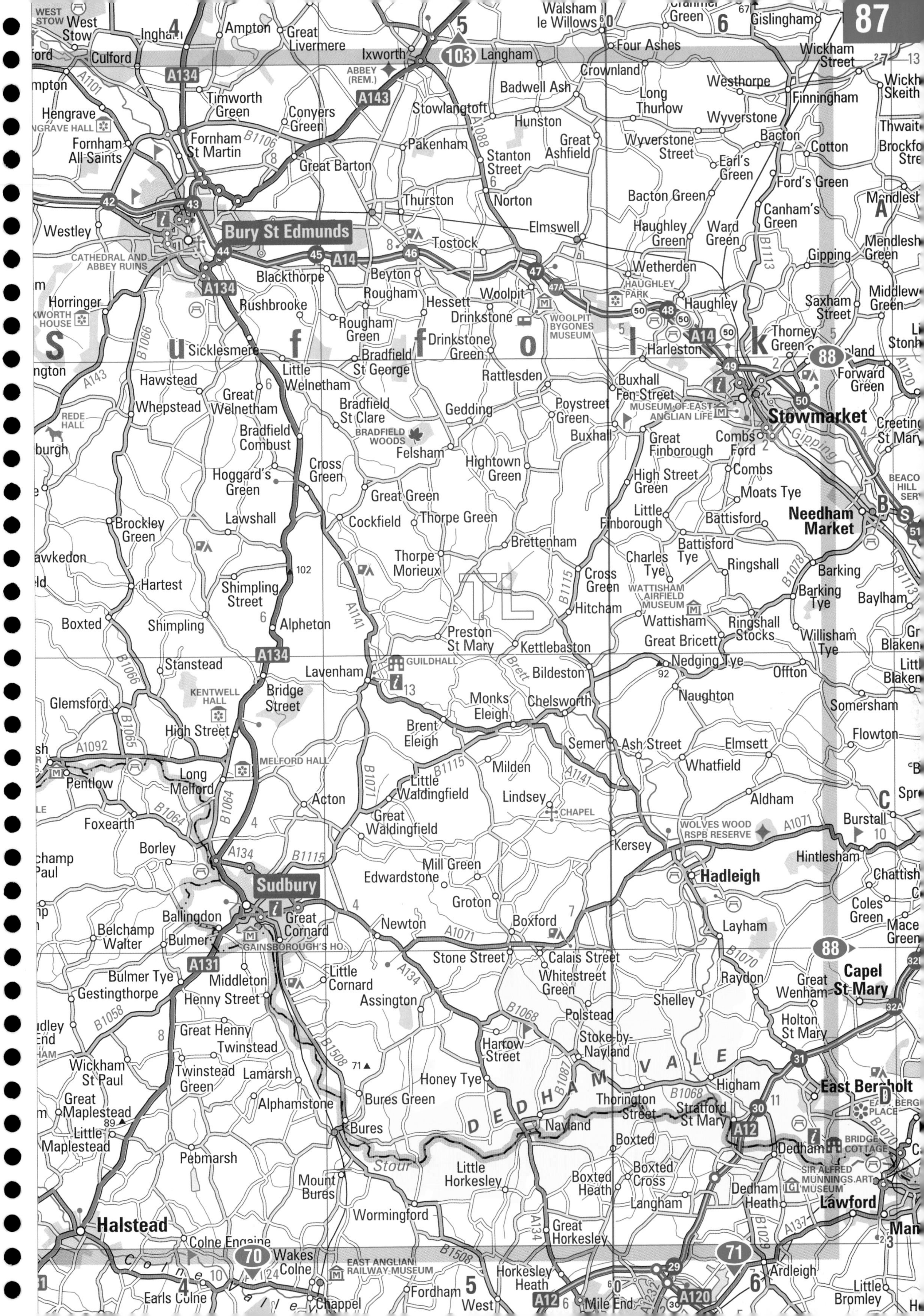

Thornham Magna
Braiseworth
Redlingfield
Athelington
Foals Green
Laxfield
Ubbeston Green
Wickham Street
Stoke Ash
Occold
Thorndon
Brundish Street
Crown Corner
Finningham
Wickham Skeith
Rishangles
Southolt
Stanway Green
Brundish
Owl's Green
Bedingfield
Worlingworth
Badingham
Bacton
Thwaite
Tannington
Cotton
Brockford Street
Bedfield
Maypole Green
Dennington
Bruisyard
Wetheringsett
Ford's Green
Kenton
Blacksmith's Green
Mendlesham
Monk Soham
Saxtead
Brabling Green
Cransford
Canham's Green
SAXTEAD GREEN POST MILL
Saxtead Green
Mendlesham Green
Wetherup Street
Debenham
Gipping
Framlingham
Ashfield
Earl Soham
Middlewood Green
Mickfield
Winston
Lampardbrook
Great Glemham
Cole's Green
Saxham Street
Winston Green
Brandeston
Thorney Green
Little Stonham
Peats Corner
Parham
Stonham Aspal
Cretingham
Kettleburgh
Forward Green
Framsden
Hacheston
Pettaugh
Easton
Earl Stonham
Monewden
EASTON FARM PARK
Marlesford
Stowmarket
HELMINGHAM HALL GARDENS
Creeting St Mary
Creeting Bottoms
Helmingham
Letheringham
Combs Ford
AKENFIELD
Crowfield
Charsfield
Lower Hacheston
Combs
BEACON HILL SERVICES
Gosbeck
Otley
Clopton Corner
Wickham Market
Moats Tye
Campsey Ash
Needham Market
Ashbocking
Dallinghoo
Coddenham
Debach
Pettistree
Hemingstone
Rendlesham
Ringshall
Barking
Swilland
Bredfield
Clopton
Ufford
Barking Tye
Baylham
Witnesham
Burgh
Eyke
Ringshall Stocks
Barham
Henley
Grundisburgh
Hasketon
Willisham Tye
Great Blakenham
Claydon
Melton
Bromeswell
Offton
Little Blakenham
Culpho
Boot Street
Great Bealings
Akenham
Tuddenham St Martin
Woodbridge
Rendlesham Forest
Somersham
SUTTON HOO ARCHAEOLOGICAL SITE
Playford
Maidensgrave
Capel
Whitton
Westerfield
Flowton
Elmsett
Rushmere St Andrew
Little Bealings
Martlesham
Sutton
Bramford
Westbourne
CHRISTCHURCH MANSION
Waldringfield Heath
Sproughton
IPSWICH MUS.
Ipswich
Kesgrave
Martlesham Heath
Waldringfield
Shottisham
Aldham
Burstall
Rose Hill
MARTLESHAM HEATH CONTROL TOWER
Hintlesham
Chantry
Stoke
Brightwell
Warren Heath
Newbourne
Chattisham
Maidenhall
Copdock
Gainsborough
Bucklesham
Hemley
Coles Green
Mace Green
Belstead
Wherstead
ORWELL
Nacton
Kirton
Capel St Mary
Great Wenham
Freston
Falkenham
Woolverstone
Levington
Thorpe Common
Pin Mill
Trimley St Martin
Holton St Mary
Chelmondiston
Trimley Lower Street
Felixstowe
Bentley
Tattingstone
Alton Water Reservoir
Holbrook
The Heath
Trimley St Mary
East Bergholt
Lower Holbrook
Stutton
Erwarton
Shotley
Walton
Old Felixstowe
TRIMLEY MARSHES NATURE RESERVE
EAST BERGHOLT PLACE
Upper Street
Harkstead
Shotley Gate
Brantham
STOUR VALLEY
Holbrook Bay
Shop Corner
FELIXSTOWE
Dedham
BRIDGE COTTAGE
Cattawade
Stour
HARWICH
CHARLES MANNING'S AMUSEMENT PARK
SIR ALFRED MUNNINGS ART MUSEUM
MISTLEY TOWERS
Dedham Heath
Lawford
Mistley
Parkeston
HARWICH REDOUBT
Bradfield
Wrabness
Manningtree
Ramsey
Upper Dovercourt
Dovercourt
OOSTENDE (From Ipswich)
Bradfield Heath
Horsleycross Street
Little Oakley
Bromley
Wix
Horsley
S u f f o l k
Gipping
Deben
Orwell
Alde
A140
A14
A12
A1120
A1214
A1156
A1071
A137
A120
A154
A1152
B1077
B1078
B1079
B1113
B1116
B1118
B1119
B1120
B1117
B1438
B1084
B1083
B1080
B1456
B1070
B1352
B1035
0 1 2 3 miles
0 1 2 3 4 5 km

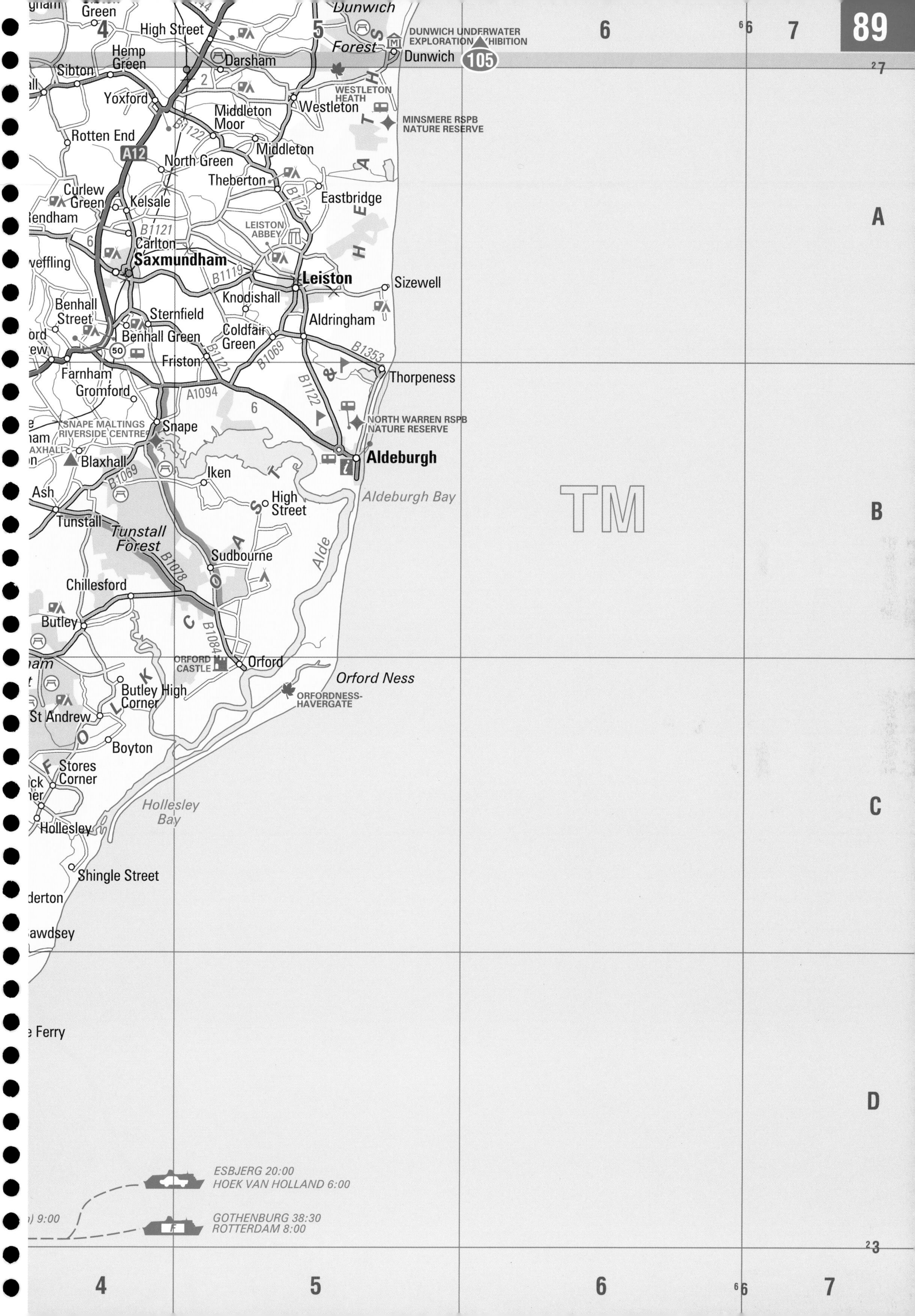
Dunwich
Forest
DUNWICH UNDERWATER EXPLORATION EXHIBITION
Dunwich
105
Green
High Street
Hemp Green
Darsham
Sibton
Yoxford
Middleton Moor
Westleton
WESTLETON HEATH
MINSMERE RSPB NATURE RESERVE
Rotten End
B1122
A12
Middleton
North Green
Theberton
Eastbridge
Curlew Green
Kelsale
LEISTON ABBEY
B1121
Carlton
Saxmundham
B1119
Leiston
Sizewell
Knodishall
Benhall Street
Sternfield
Aldringham
Coldfair Green
Benhall Green
B1069
B1353
Friston
Farnham
Thorpeness
Gromford
A1094
B1122
Snape
SNAPE MALTINGS RIVERSIDE CENTRE
NORTH WARREN RSPB NATURE RESERVE
Blaxhall
Aldeburgh
Iken
Aldeburgh Bay
High Street
Ash
Tunstall
Tunstall Forest
Sudbourne
Alde
Chillesford
B1078
Butley
B1084
ORFORD CASTLE
Orford
Orford Ness
ORFORDNESS-HAVERGATE
Butley High Corner
St Andrew
Boyton
Stores Corner
Hollesley Bay
Hollesley
Shingle Street
Ferry
ESBJERG 20:00
HOEK VAN HOLLAND 6:00
GOTHENBURG 38:30
ROTTERDAM 8:00
TM
A
B
C
D

1
2
3
4
107
SH
A
B
C
D
Tal-y-bont
Plas-canol
Llanaber
Caerdeon
Cutiau
A496
Afon Mawdd
Barmouth
(Abermaw)
RNLI LIFEBOAT MUSEUM
BARMOUTH BAY
The Bar
Arthog
Ynysgyffl
FAIRBOURNE & BARMOUTH
STEAM RAILWAY
BAE BERMO
Fairbourne
Friog
SNOWDO
NATION
PARK
Llwyngwril
A493
Llangelynin
Rhoslefain
Llanegryn
Llanfendigaid
Peniarth
309
Tonfanau
Bryncrug
Pandy
Rhyd-yr-onen
TALYLLYN RAILWAY
Tywyn
Caethle
C A R D I G A N
279
Aberdovey
A493
Aberdovey Bar
Bae Aberdyfi
DYFI
B A Y
Ynyslas
B4353
Llancynfelyn
BORTH
B A E
Borth
Upper Borth
Tal-y-bon
Dôl-y-Bont
C E R E D I G I O N
Llandre
Pen-y-garn
SN
B4572
ARTS CENTRE
Bow
Street
NATIONAL
LIBRARY
Clarach
148
Plas Goger
CLIFF RAILWAY
A4159
Aberystwyth
Comins
Coch
Capel De
P&R
Llanbadarn Fawr
Trefechan
A44
CASTLE
Penparcau
Southgate
Glanrafon
Rhydyfelin
Moriah
Capel
Seion
A4120
74
75
0 1 2 3 miles
0 1 2 3 4 5 km

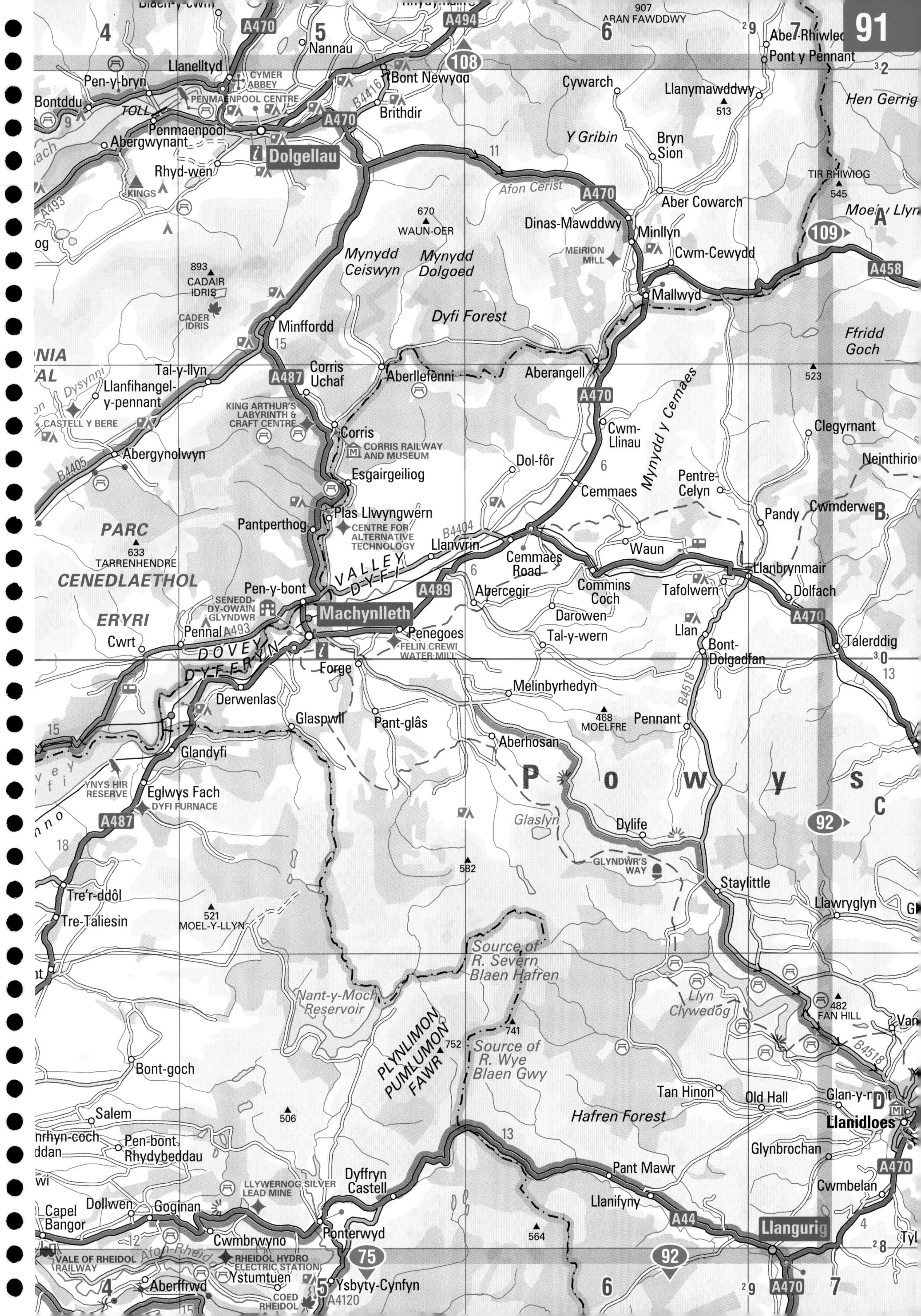

4
5
6
7
A470
A494
Nannau
907
ARAN FAWDDWY
Abe Rhiwlech
Pont y Pennant
108
Llanelltyd
CYMER ABBEY
Pen-y-bryn
Bontddu
TOLL
PENMAENPOOL CENTRE
Penmaenpool
Bont Newydd
B4416
Brithdir
Cywarch
Llanymawddwy
513
Hen Gerrig
Abergwynant
Dolgellau
11
Y Gribin
Bryn Sion
Rhyd-wen
KINGS
A493
Afon Cerist
A470
TIR RHIWIOG
545
Aber Cowarch
670
WAUN-OER
Dinas-Mawddwy
Minllyn
Moel y Llyn
109
MEIRION MILL
Cwm-Cewydd
893
CADAIR IDRIS
Mynydd Ceiswyn
Mynydd Dolgoed
A458
Mallwyd
CADER IDRIS
Dyfi Forest
Minffordd
15
Ffridd Goch
Tal-y-llyn
Corris Uchaf
Aberllefenni
Aberangell
523
Llanfihangel-y-pennant
A487
Dysynni
A470
Mynydd y Cemaes
KING ARTHUR'S LABYRINTH & CRAFT CENTRE
CASTELL Y BERE
Corris
Cwm-Llinau
Clegyrnant
CORRIS RAILWAY AND MUSEUM
Abergynolwyn
B4405
Dol-fôr
Neinthirion
Esgairgeiliog
6
Pentre-Celyn
Cemmaes
Plas Llwyngwern
Pandy
Cwmderwen
PARC
Pantperthog
CENTRE FOR ALTERNATIVE TECHNOLOGY
B4404
Llanwrin
Waun
633
TARRENHENDRE
VALLEY
DYFI
Cemmaes Road
Llanbrynmair
CENEDLAETHOL
6
Commins Coch
Tafolwern
Dolfach
Pen-y-bont
A489
Abercegir
SENEDD-DY-OWAIN GLYNDWR
Machynlleth
Darowen
A470
ERYRI
Llan
Cwrt
Pennal
A493
Penegoes
Tal-y-wern
Talerddig
DOVEY
DYFFRYN
FELIN CREWI WATER MILL
Bont-Dolgadfan
Forge
13
Derwenlas
Melinbyrhedyn
B4518
Glaspwll
Pant-glâs
468
MOELFRE
Pennant
15
Aberhosan
Glandyfi
Powys
YNYS HIR RESERVE
Eglwys Fach
DYFI FURNACE
A487
Glaslyn
Dylife
92
18
582
GLYNDWR'S WAY
Tre'r-ddôl
Staylittle
521
MOEL-Y-LLYN
Llawryglyn
Tre-Taliesin
Source of R. Severn
Blaen Hafren
Nant-y-Moch Reservoir
Llyn Clywedog
482
FAN HILL
741
PLYNLIMON
PUMLUMON FAWR
752
Source of R. Wye
Blaen Gwy
B4518
Bont-goch
Tan Hinon
Old Hall
Glan-y-nant
Salem
506
Hafren Forest
Llanidloes
13
Pen-bont Rhydybeddau
Glynbrochan
Dyffryn Castell
Pant Mawr
A470
LLYWERNOG SILVER LEAD MINE
Cwmbelan
Capel Bangor
Dollwen
Goginan
Llanifyny
A44
Ponterwyd
Cwmbrwyno
564
Llangurig
VALE OF RHEIDOL RAILWAY
Afon Rheidol
RHEIDOL HYDRO ELECTRIC STATION
75
92
Ystumtuen
Aberffrwd
COED RHEIDOL
Ysbyty-Cynfyn
A4120
6
A470
7

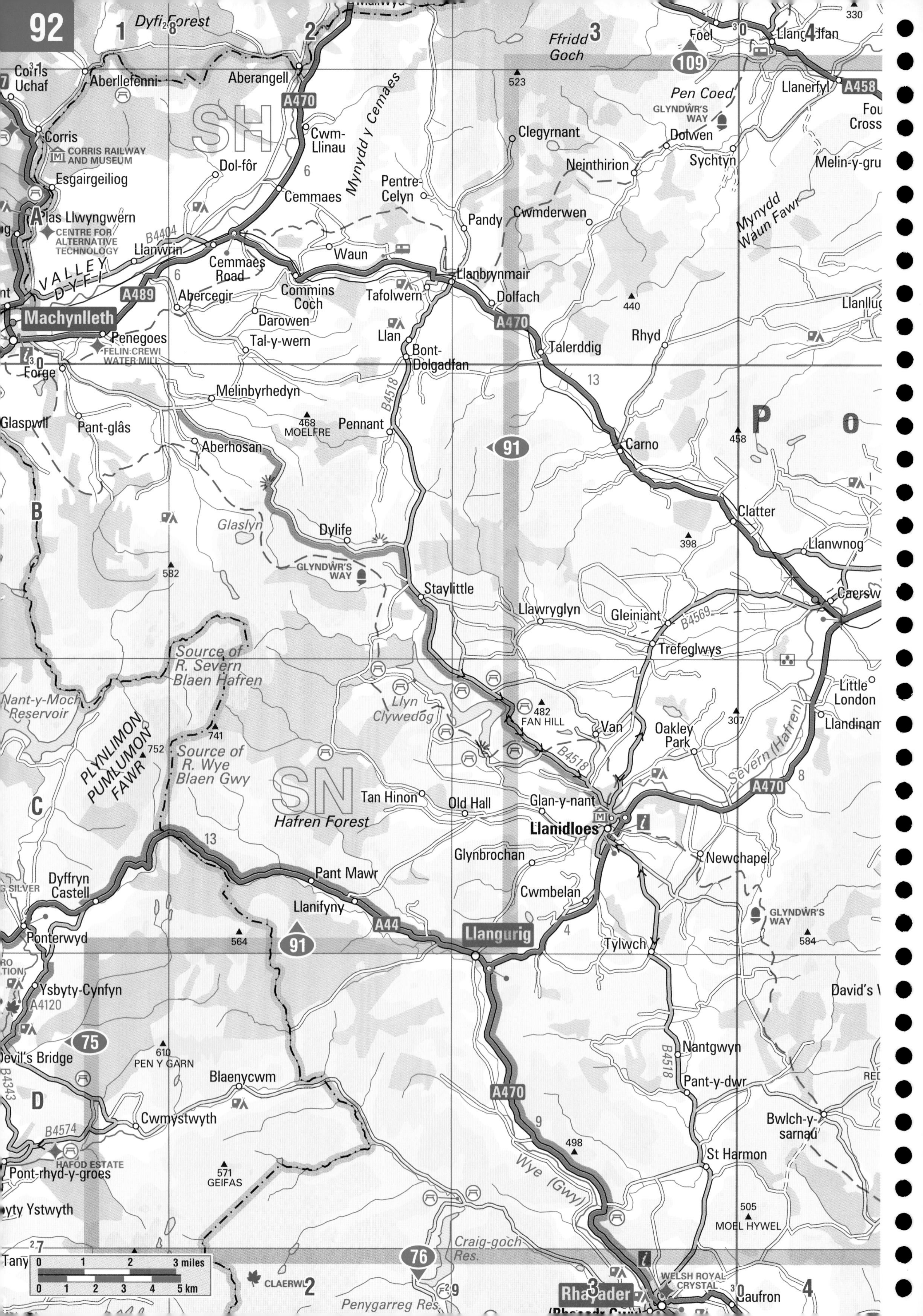
Dyfi Forest
Corris Uchaf
Aberllefenni
Aberangell
A470
Corris
CORRIS RAILWAY AND MUSEUM
Esgairgeiliog
Dol-fôr
Cwm-Llinau
Mynydd y Cemaes
Cemmaes
Pentre-Celyn
Plas Llwyngwern
CENTRE FOR ALTERNATIVE TECHNOLOGY
B4404
Llanwrin
Cemmaes Road
Waun
Commins Coch
Tafolwern
Llanbrynmair
Dolfach
DYFI VALLEY
A489
Abercegir
Darowen
Machynlleth
Penegoes
FELIN CREWI WATER MILL
Tal-y-wern
Llan
Bont-Dolgadfan
Forge
Melinbyrhedyn
Glaspwll
Pant-glâs
468 MOELFRE
Pennant
B4518
Aberhosan
Glaslyn
Dylife
GLYNDŴR'S WAY
582
Staylittle
Source of R. Severn Blaen Hafren
Nant-y-Moch Reservoir
PLYNLIMON PUMLUMON FAWR
752
741
Source of R. Wye Blaen Gwy
SN
Hafren Forest
Llyn Clywedog
Tan Hinon
Old Hall
Glan-y-nant
Llanidloes
Glynbrochan
Cwmbelan
Pant Mawr
Llanifyny
A44
Llangurig
Dyffryn Castell
Ponterwyd
564
91
Ysbyty-Cynfyn
A4120
75
Devil's Bridge
610 PEN Y GARN
Blaenycwm
B4343
Cwmystwyth
B4574
HAFOD ESTATE
Pont-rhyd-y-groes
571 GEIFAS
Ysbyty Ystwyth
Tany
CLAERWEN
76
Craig-goch Res.
Penygarreg Res.
A470
Wye (Gwy)
498
Rhayader
WELSH ROYAL CRYSTAL
Cwmdauddwr
Ffridd Goch
523
109
Foel
Llangadfan
Llanerfyl
A458
Pen Coed
Dolwen
Sychtyn
Clegyrnant
Neinthirion
Melin-y-grug
Mynydd Waun Fawr
Pandy
Cwmderwen
440
A470
Talerddig
Rhyd
Llanllugan
P O
458
Carno
91
Clatter
398
Llanwnog
Caersws
Llawryglyn
Gleiniant
B4569
Trefeglwys
Little London
Llandinam
482 FAN HILL
Van
Oakley Park
307
Severn (Hafren)
A470
Newchapel
GLYNDŴR'S WAY
584
Tylwch
David's Well
B4518
Nantgwyn
Pant-y-dwr
Bwlch-y-sarnau
St Harmon
505 MOEL HYWEL
0 1 2 3 miles
0 1 2 3 4 5 km

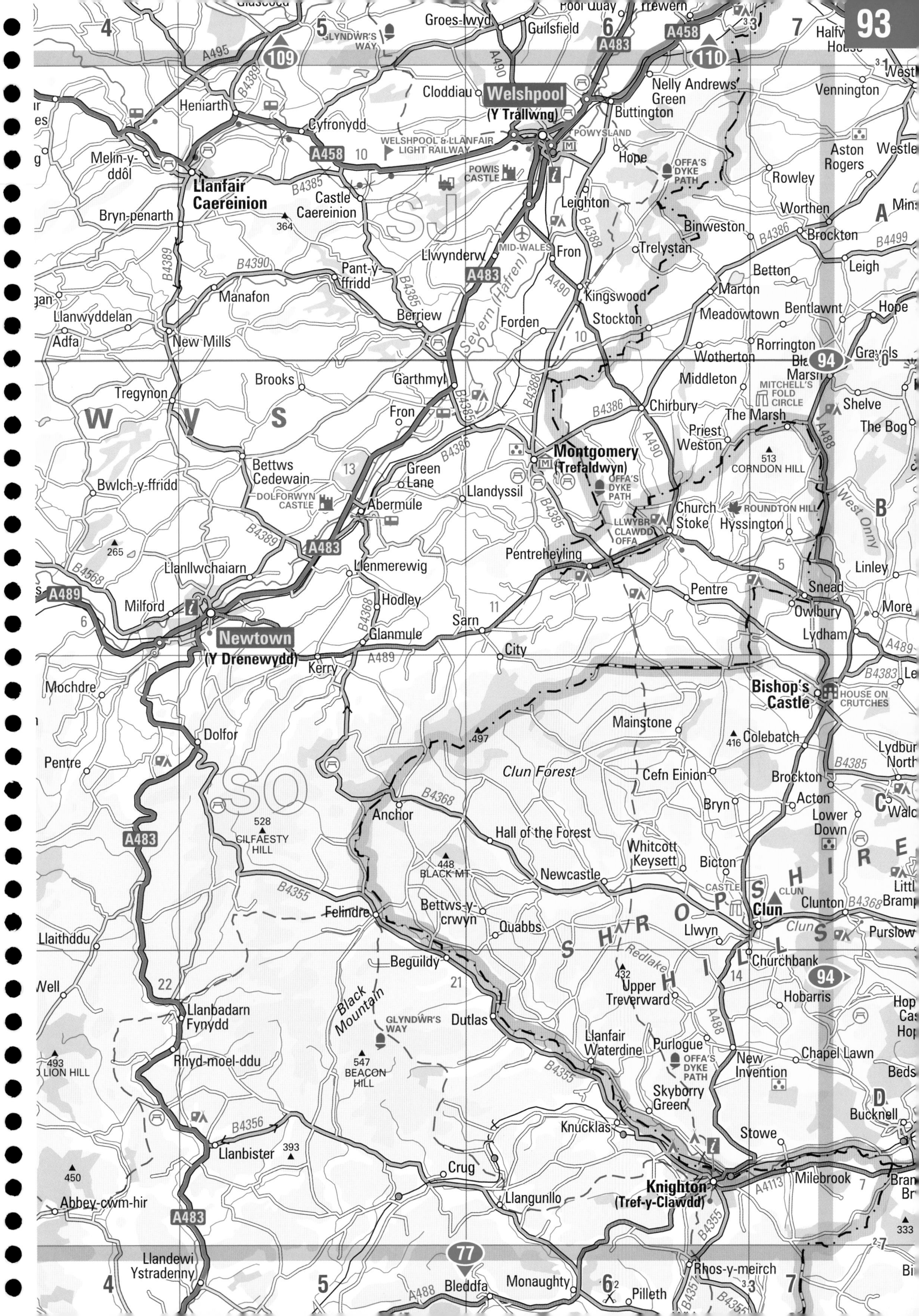
Welshpool
(Y Trallwng)
Llanfair
Caereinion
Newtown
(Y Drenewydd)
Montgomery
(Trefaldwyn)
Bishop's
Castle
Knighton
(Tref-y-Clawdd)
Clun
Guilsfield
Groes-lwyd
Heniarth
Cyfronydd
Castle
Caereinion
Bryn-penarth
Melin-y-
ddôl
Manafon
Llanwyddelan
Adfa
New Mills
Tregynon
Brooks
Garthmyl
Berriew
Forden
Pant-y-
ffridd
Llwynderw
Fron
Kingswood
Stockton
Leighton
Trelystan
Binweston
Buttington
Nelly Andrews
Green
Hope
Rowley
Worthen
Brockton
Vennington
Aston
Rogers
Marton
Betton
Leigh
Meadowtown
Bentlawnt
Rorrington
Wotherton
Middleton
Chirbury
Priest
Weston
The Marsh
Shelve
The Bog
Church
Stoke
Hyssington
Pentreheyling
Llandyssil
Green
Lane
Abermule
Bettws
Cedewain
Bwlch-y-ffridd
Llanllwchaiarn
Milford
Llanmerewig
Hodley
Glanmule
Sarn
City
Kerry
Pentre
Snead
Owlbury
Lydham
More
Linley
Mochdre
Dolfor
Mainstone
Colebatch
Cefn Einion
Brockton
Acton
Lower
Down
Bryn
Anchor
Hall of the Forest
Clun Forest
Whitcott
Keysett
Bicton
Newcastle
Clunton
Purslow
Felindre
Bettws-y-
crwyn
Quabbs
Llwyn
Churchbank
Beguildy
Hobarris
Llaithddu
Llanbadarn
Fynydd
Upper
Treverward
Dutlas
Llanfair
Waterdine
Purlogue
New
Invention
Chapel Lawn
Rhyd-moel-ddu
Skyborry
Green
Knucklas
Stowe
Bucknell
Llanbister
Crug
Llangunllo
Milebrook
Abbey-cwm-hir
Llandewi
Ystradenny
Bleddfa
Monaughty
Pilleth
Rhos-y-meirch
Black Mountain
Redlake
Severn (Hafren)
West Onny
GLYNDŴR'S WAY
OFFA'S DYKE PATH
WELSHPOOL & LLANFAIR LIGHT RAILWAY
POWIS CASTLE
POWYSLAND
MID-WALES
MITCHELL'S FOLD CIRCLE
CORNDON HILL
ROUNDTON HILL
DOLFORWYN CASTLE
LLWYBR CLAWDD OFFA
HOUSE ON CRUTCHES
CILFAESTY HILL
BLACK MT.
BEACON HILL
CLUN
SJ
SO
POWYS
SHROPSHIRE
SHROPSHIRE HILLS
A458
A483
A490
A495
A489
A488
A4113
B4385
B4389
B4390
B4386
B4388
B4368
B4355
B4356
B4568
B4499
B4383
109
110
94
77
4
5
6
7
A
B
C
D

Shrewsbury
Bayston Hill
Church Stretton
Bishop's Castle
Craven Arms
Clun
Ludlow
SHROPSHIRE
Shropshire Hills
THE LONG MYND
WENLOCK EDGE
Ape Dale
Corve Dale
STIPERSTONES
BRIDGES LONG MYND
ALL STRETTON
WILDERHOPE MANOR
ACTON BURNELL
LANGLEY CHAPEL AND GATEHOUSE
ATTINGHAM PARK
WROXETER ROMAN CITY
MITCHELL'S FOLD CIRCLE
CORNDON HILL
HOUSE ON CRUTCHES
STOKESAY CASTLE
THE WERNLAS COLLECTION
WORKING FARM
BURFORD HOUSE & MEADOW GALLERY
0 1 2 3 miles
0 1 2 3 4 5 km

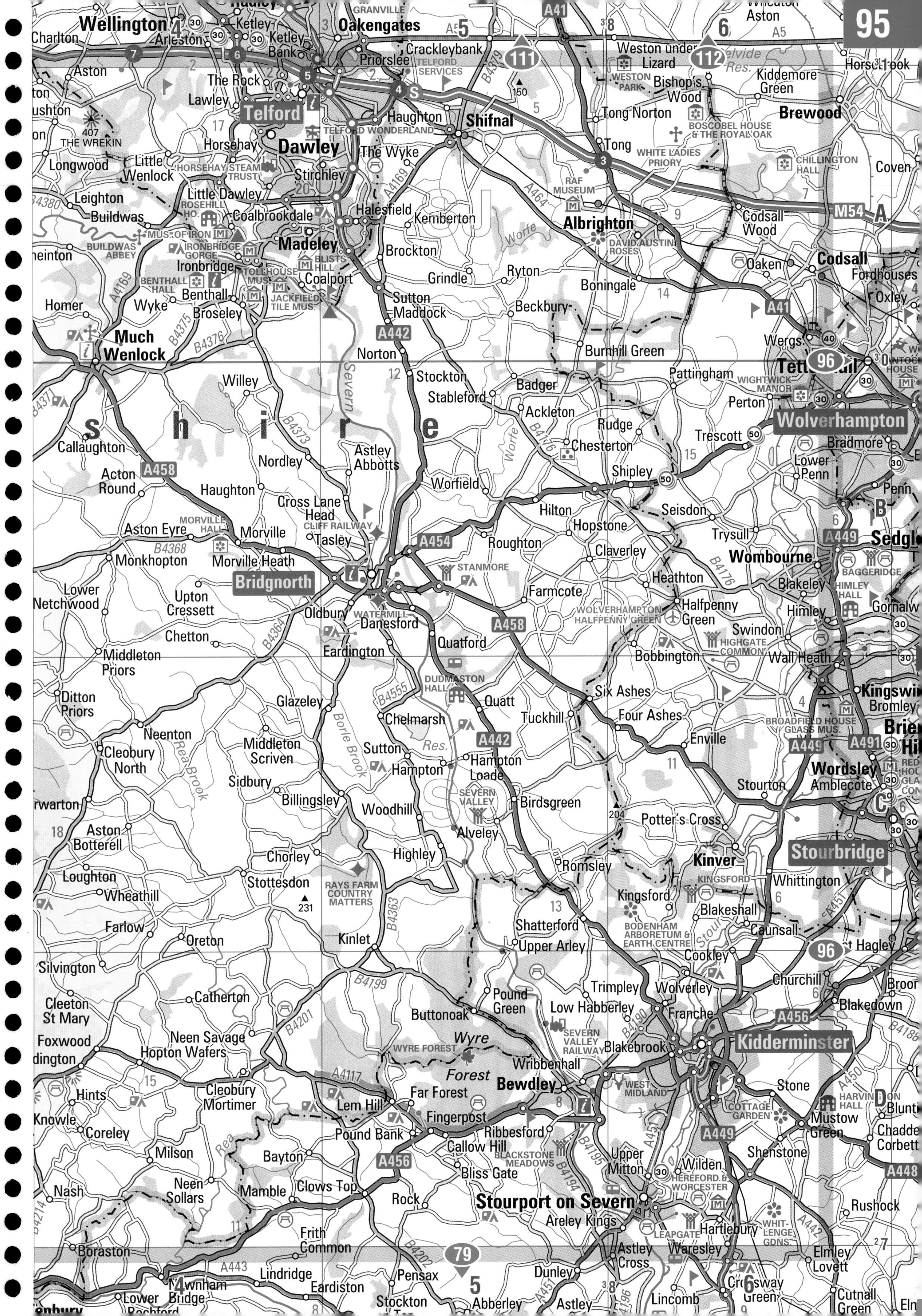

Wellington
Charlton
Arleston
Ketley
Ketley Bank
Oakengates
GRANVILLE
Crackleybank
Priorslee
TELFORD SERVICES
A41
111
Weston under Lizard
WESTON PARK
112
Belvide Res.
Aston
Horsebrook
A5
Kiddemore Green
Bishop's Wood
The Rock
Lawley
Telford
Haughton
Shifnal
Tong Norton
Brewood
THE WREKIN
407
TELFORD WONDERLAND
BOSCOBEL HOUSE & THE ROYAL OAK
Tong
Horsehay
Dawley
The Wyke
WHITE LADIES PRIORY
CHILLINGTON HALL
Coven
Longwood
Little Wenlock
HORSEHAY STEAM TRUST
Stirchley
A4169
RAF MUSEUM
A464
Leighton
Little Dawley
ROSEHILL HO.
Halesfield
Kemberton
Albrighton
Codsall Wood
M54
Buildwas
Coalbrookdale
MUS. OF IRON
Madeley
DAVID AUSTIN ROSES
Worfe
BUILDWAS ABBEY
IRONBRIDGE GORGE
BLISTS HILL
Brockton
Oaken
Codsall
Fordhouses
Ironbridge
TOLLHOUSE MUS.
Coalport
Grindle
Ryton
Boningale
BENTHALL HALL
Benthall
JACKFIELD TILE MUS.
Sutton Maddock
Oxley
Homer
Wyke
Broseley
Beckbury
A41
B4375
B4376
A442
Much Wenlock
Norton
Burnhill Green
Wergs
Tettenhall
96
Severn
Stockton
Badger
Pattingham
WIGHTWICK MANOR
Willey
Stableford
Ackleton
Perton
A4371
Rudge
Wolverhampton
s h i r e
B4373
Chesterton
Trescott
Bradmore
Callaughton
Astley Abbotts
B4176
Lower Penn
Acton Round
A458
Nordley
Worfield
Shipley
Penn
Haughton
Cross Lane Head
Hilton
Seisdon
CLIFF RAILWAY
MORVILLE HALL
Hopstone
Trysull
Aston Eyre
Morville
Tasley
A454
Roughton
A449
Sedgley
B4368
Claverley
Wombourne
Monkhopton
Morville Heath
STANMORE
BAGGERIDGE
Bridgnorth
Heathton
Blakeley
HIMLEY HALL
Gornalw
Lower Netchwood
Upton Cressett
Farmcote
Oldbury
WATERMILL
Danesford
WOLVERHAMPTON HALFPENNY GREEN
Halfpenny Green
Himley
Swindon
Chetton
B4364
A458
Quatford
HIGHGATE COMMON
Wall Heath
Middleton Priors
Eardington
Bobbington
DUDMASTON HALL
Kingswinford
Ditton Priors
Six Ashes
Bromley
B4555
Glazeley
Quatt
Tuckhill
Four Ashes
Chelmarsh
BROADFIELD HOUSE GLASS MUS.
Brierley Hill
Neenton
Borle Brook
A442
Enville
A491
Cleobury North
Rea Brook
Middleton Scriven
Sutton
Res.
Hampton Loade
Hampton
Wordsley
Amblecote
Sidbury
SEVERN VALLEY
Stourton
Burwarton
Billingsley
Woodhill
Birdsgreen
204
Potter's Cross
Aston Botterell
Alveley
Stourbridge
Chorley
Highley
Kinver
Loughton
Romsley
KINGSFORD
Whittington
Stottesdon
RAYS FARM COUNTRY MATTERS
231
Kingsford
Wheathill
Blakeshall
BODENHAM ARBORETUM & EARTH CENTRE
B4363
Shatterford
Farlow
Caunsall
A451
Oreton
Kinlet
Upper Arley
Hagley
Stour
96
Silvington
Cookley
B4199
Trimpley
Churchill
Wolverley
Broom
Pound Green
Cleeton St Mary
Catherton
Low Habberley
Blakedown
Buttonoak
Franche
A456
Foxwood
Neen Savage
Wyre
SEVERN VALLEY RAILWAY
B4190
B4201
Kidderminster
Hopton Wafers
WYRE FOREST
Blakebrook
B4188
Wribbenhall
Forest
A4117
Bewdley
WEST MIDLAND
Stone
A450
Hints
Cleobury Mortimer
Far Forest
HARVINGTON HALL
Blunti
Lem Hill
COTTAGE GARDEN
Knowle
Fingerpost
Mustow Green
Coreley
Pound Bank
Ribbesford
A449
Chaddesley Corbett
Milson
Callow Hill
Shenstone
Rea
Bayton
A456
BLACKSTONE MEADOWS
B4195
B4194
A451
Upper Mitton
Wilden
A448
Bliss Gate
HEREFORD & WORCESTER
Nash
Neen Sollars
Mamble
Clows Top
Rock
Stourport on Severn
Rushock
A4214
Areley Kings
LEAPGATE
Hartlebury
WHITLENGE GDNS.
A442
Frith Common
Boraston
B4202
79
Astley Cross
Waresley
Elmley Lovett
A443
Lindridge
Newnham Bridge
Pensax
Dunley
Crossway Green
Eardiston
Lower Rochford
Stockton on Teme
Abberley
Astley
A451
Lincomb
Cutnall Green
A
B
C
D
4
5
6

96
Stretton
Gailey
Oldfallow
Littleworth
Wimblebury
Gentleshaw
Farewell
Chorley
Elmhurst
Horsebrook
Hatherton
Heath Hayes
Cannock
Burntwood
Lichfield
Kiddemore Green
Norton East
Norton Canes
SAMUEL JOHNSON BIRTHPLACE MUS.
Leamonsley
Brewood
Bridgtown
Chasetown
CHASE WATER
Hammerwich
Standeford
Churchbridge
NORTON CANES SERVICES
TOLL
CHILLINGTON HALL
Coven
Shareshill
Great Wyrley
Cheslyn Hay
Muckley Corner
WALL (LETOCETUM)
Wall
BROWNHILLS COMMON
Featherstone
HILTON PARK SERVICES
Little Wyrley
Brownhills
M54
Springhill
Clayhanger
Shenstone
M6 Toll
Weeford
Codsall
MOSELEY OLD HALL
Essington
Pelsall
Walsall Wood
Stonnall
Oaken
Fordhouses
Bushbury
Shelfield
Little Hay
Oxley
New Invention
Bloxwich
Leighswood
RYKNILD STREET
Wood Hayes
Harden
Watford Gap
Short Heath
Rushall
Aldridge
Little Aston
Tettenhall
WOLVERHAMPTON
Wednesfield
BANTOCK HOUSE
Heath Town
Hill
WIGHTWICK MANOR
Willenhall
ARBORETUM
Hardwick
Roughley
Perton
Streetly
Four Oaks
Mere Grn.
Wolverhampton
Walsall
Moseley
GALL. & MUS.
Palfrey
SUTTON COLDFIELD
Bradmore
Bilston
Darlaston
Lower Penn
Blakenhall
Ettingshall
Great Barr
SUTTON PARK
Penn
Moxley
Kingstanding
Wylde Green
Bradley
Wednesbury
Coseley
Hill Top
New Oscott
Sedgley
Walmley
Wombourne
Toll End
Grove Vale
BAGGERIDGE
Tipton
SANDWELL VALLEY
Hamstead
Upper Witton
Blakeley
HIMLEY HALL
Upper Gornal
WRENS NEST
Gt. Bridge
Churchfield
Erdington
Himley
Gornalwood
DUDLEY ZOO & CASTLE
Dudley Port
West Bromwich
Perry Barr
Swindon
Tividale
Gravelly Hill
HIGHGATE COMMON
Wall Heath
Dudley
Handsworth
Aston
Oldbury
Sandwell
Winson Grn.
ASTON HALL
CASTLE BROMWICH HALL
Kingswinford
Netherton
Bromley
Rowley Regis
SMETHWICK
NAT. SEA LIFE BIRMINGHAM
Ward End
BROADFIELD HOUSE GLASS MUS.
Brierley Hill
Old Hill
BIRMINGHAM
Bearwood
Wordsley
RED HOUSE GLASS CONE
Blackheath
BLAKESLEY HALL
Stourton
Amblecote
Quarry Bank
Cradley Heath
Chad Valley
Yardley
Quinton
BOTANICAL GDNS.
Wollescote
West Midlands
Lye
WOODGATE VALLEY
Harborne
Edgbaston
Balsall Hth.
RAILWAY MUS.
Acock's Green
Stourbridge
HALESOWEN
Sparkhill
Hasbury
Bartley Green
Selly Oak
Moseley
Whittington
Woodgate
Pedmore
SELLY MANOR MUS.
King's Heath
Springfield
Olton
SAREHOLE MILL
Illey
Hall Green
Caunsall
FRANKLEY SERVICES
Bartley Res.
Bournville
CADBURY WORLD
West Hagley
Hagley
CLENT HILLS
Frankley
Clent
Romsley
Northfield
Cotteridge
Shirley
Solihull
Churchill
Broom
Holy Cross
King's Norton
Blakedown
Longbridge
Hollywood
Kidderminster
Bell End
WASELEY HILLS
Rubery
Drakes Cross
Whitlock's End
Belbroughton
Monkspath
Drayton
Wildmoor
LICKEY HILLS
Cofton Hackett
Hopwood
Stone
HARVINGTON HALL
Fairfield
Lickey
Wythall
MANOR FARM CRAFT CENTRE
COTTAGE GARDEN
Bluntington
Mustow Green
Marlbrook
Barnt Green
HOPWOOD PARK SERVICES
Chaddesley Corbett
Bournheath
Catshill
Earlswood
CHADDESLEY WOODS
Shenstone
Dodford
Lickey End
Blackwell
Alvechurch
M42
Portway
Rowney Green
Rushock
Sidemoor
Bromsgrove
Branson's Cross
Wood End
UMBERSLADE FARM
WHITLENGE GDNS.
Tutnall
Tanworth-in-Arden
Charford
Finstall
Bordesley
Beoley
Aston Fields
Holt End
NEEDLE MUS.
AVONCROFT HISTORIC BUILDINGS
Redditch
Gorcott Hill
Elmbridge
miles
km

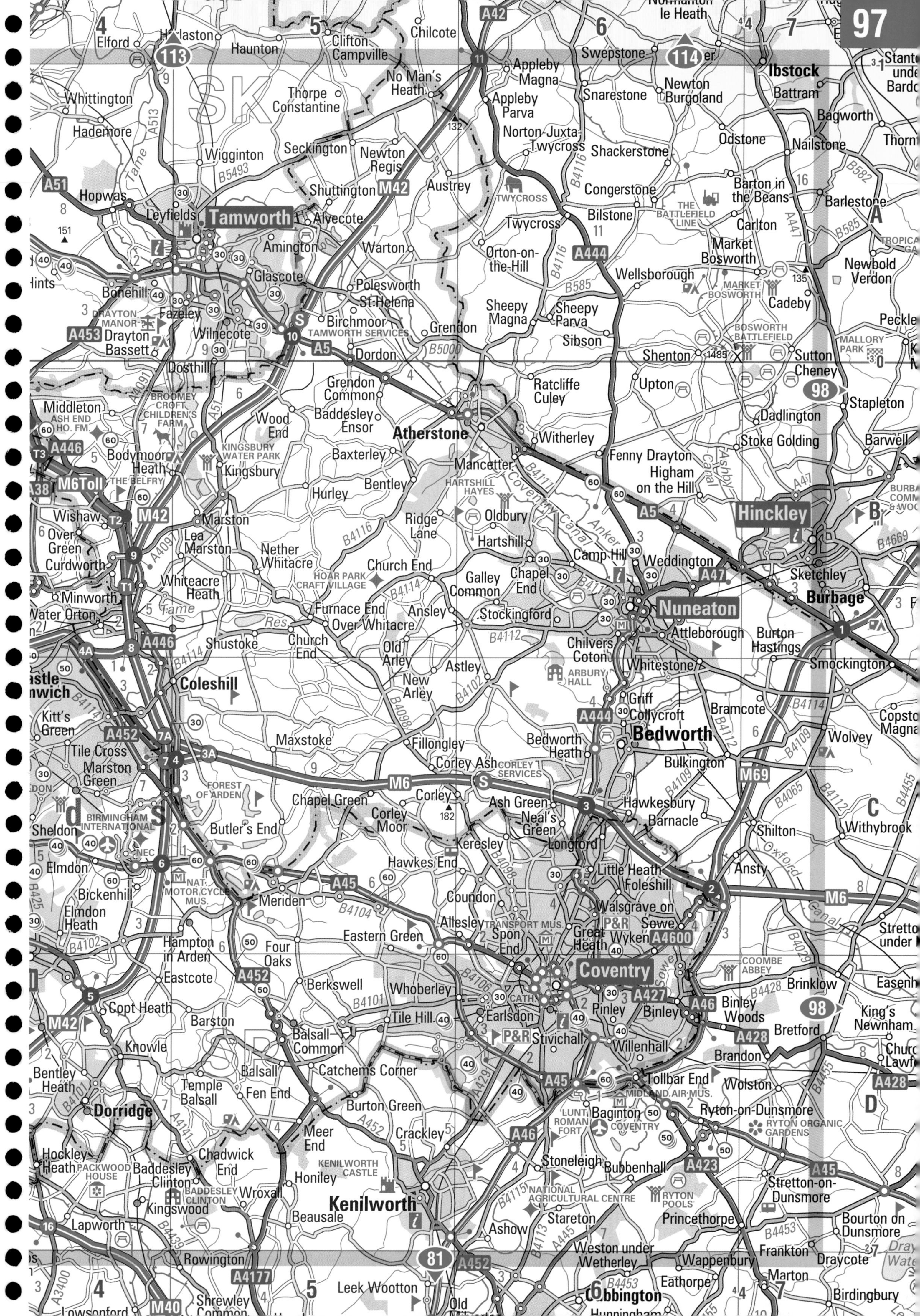
Tamworth
Atherstone
Nuneaton
Hinckley
Burbage
Bedworth
Coleshill
Coventry
Kenilworth
Ibstock
Dorridge
Elford
Haunton
Clifton Campville
Chilcote
No Man's Heath
Appleby Magna
Appleby Parva
Swepstone
Snarestone
Newton Burgoland
Norton-Juxta-Twycross
Shackerstone
Odstone
Nailstone
Bagworth
Battram
Whittington
Hademore
Thorpe Constantine
Seckington
Newton Regis
Wigginton
Shuttington
Austrey
Hopwas
Leyfields
Alvecote
Amington
Warton
Twycross
Bilstone
Congerstone
Barton in the Beans
Carlton
Barlestone
Market Bosworth
Wellsborough
Newbold Verdon
Cadeby
Orton-on-the-Hill
Glascote
Polesworth
St Helena
Birchmoor
Bonehill
Fazeley
Drayton Manor
Drayton Bassett
Wilnecote
Dosthill
Grendon
Dordon
Sheepy Magna
Sheepy Parva
Sibson
Shenton
Sutton Cheney
Upton
Ratcliffe Culey
Grendon Common
Baddesley Ensor
Wood End
Middleton
Bodymoor Heath
Kingsbury
Kingsbury Water Park
Witherley
Fenny Drayton
Stapleton
Dadlington
Stoke Golding
Higham on the Hill
Barwell
Baxterley
Mancetter
Hurley
Bentley
Hartshill Hayes
Oldbury
Hartshill
Ridge Lane
Wishaw
Over Green
Curdworth
Marston
Lea Marston
Nether Whitacre
Whiteacre Heath
Church End
Hoar Park Craft Village
Galley Common
Chapel End
Camp Hill
Weddington
Sketchley
Minworth
Water Orton
Furnace End
Over Whitacre
Ansley
Stockingford
Attleborough
Burton Hastings
Shustoke
Old Arley
New Arley
Astley
Chilvers Coton
Arbury Hall
Whitestone
Smockington
Kitt's Green
Tile Cross
Marston Green
Maxstoke
Fillongley
Bedworth Heath
Griff
Collycroft
Bramcote
Wolvey
Bulkington
Corley Ash
Corley Services
Forest of Arden
Chapel Green
Corley
Corley Moor
Ash Green
Neal's Green
Hawkesbury
Barnacle
Shilton
Withybrook
Sheldon
Birmingham International
NEC
Butler's End
Keresley
Longford
Elmdon
Hawkes End
Little Heath
Foleshill
Ansty
Bickenhill
Nat. Motorcycle Mus.
Meriden
Coundon
Walsgrave on Sowe
Elmdon Heath
Allesley
Transport Mus.
Spon End
Great Heath
Wyken
Hampton in Arden
Four Oaks
Eastern Green
Coombe Abbey
Brinklow
Eastcote
Berkswell
Whoberley
Pinley
Binley
Binley Woods
King's Newnham
Copt Heath
Barston
Tile Hill
Earlsdon
Stivichall
Willenhall
Bretford
Balsall Common
Knowle
Catchems Corner
Brandon
Bentley Heath
Balsall
Temple Balsall
Fen End
Tollbar End
Wolston
Midland Air Mus.
Burton Green
Lunt Roman Fort
Baginton
Coventry
Ryton-on-Dunsmore
Ryton Organic Gardens
Meer End
Crackley
Hockley Heath
Packwood House
Baddesley Clinton
Chadwick End
Kenilworth Castle
Honiley
Wroxall
Stoneleigh
Bubbenhall
Stretton-on-Dunsmore
Kingswood
National Agricultural Centre
Ryton Pools
Lapworth
Beausale
Stareton
Ashow
Princethorpe
Bourton on Dunsmore
Rowington
Weston under Wetherley
Wappenbury
Frankton
Draycote
Leek Wootton
Eathorpe
Marton
Birdingbury
Shrewley Common
Lowsonford
Hunningham
Cubbington
Old Milverton
Tamworth Services
Bosworth Battlefield
Mallory Park
The Battlefield Line
Broomey Croft Children's Farm
Ash End Ho. Fm.
The Belfry
M42
M6
M6Toll
M69
M40
A5
A42
A444
A47
A446
A452
A45
A46
A4600
A427
A428
A423
A4177
A51
A453
A38
B5000
B4116
B585
B5493
B4114
B4112
B4102
B4098
B4104
B4101
B4106
B4428
B4029
B4455
B4065
B4109
B4669
B582
B4453
A447
A513
A4091
A429
A4141
B4439
A3400
B4115
B4113
A445
113
114
98
81

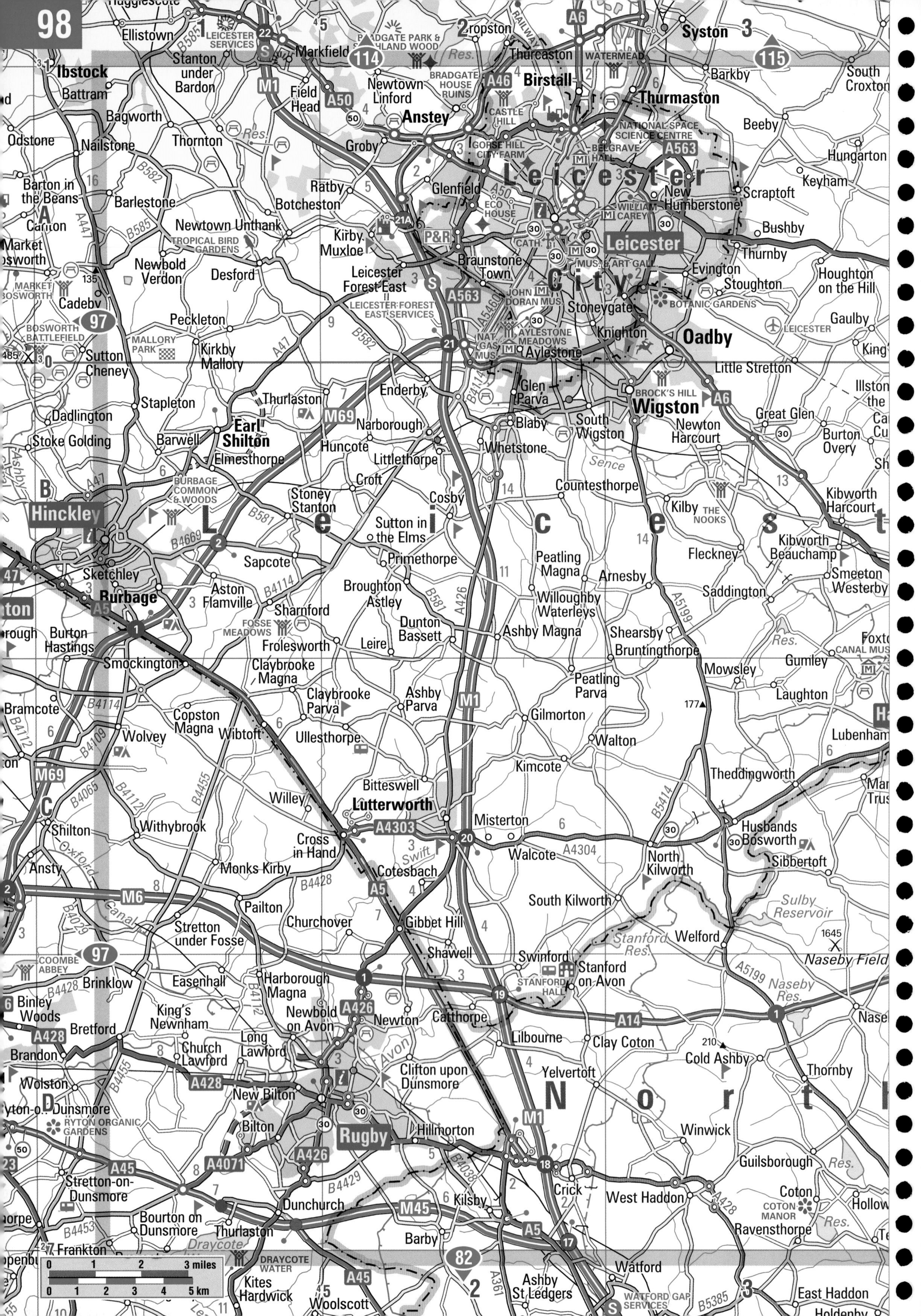
Ellistown
Stanton under Bardon
Markfield
Ropston
Thurcaston
Syston
Ibstock
Battram
Bagworth
Odstone
Nailstone
Thornton
Field Head
Newtown Linford
Anstey
Birstall
Thurmaston
Barkby
South Croxton
Beeby
Groby
Hungarton
Leicester
Barton in the Beans
Barlestone
Ratby
Botcheston
Glenfield
Keyham
Scraptoft
New Humberstone
Carlton
Market Bosworth
Newtown Unthank
Kirby Muxloe
Bushby
Thurnby
Leicester City
Newbold Verdon
Desford
Leicester Forest East
Braunstone Town
Evington
Stoughton
Houghton on the Hill
Cadeby
Peckleton
Stoneygate
Knighton
Oadby
Gaulby
Sutton Cheney
Kirkby Mallory
Aylestone
Little Stretton
Stapleton
Thurlaston
Enderby
Glen Parva
Wigston
Dadlington
Earl Shilton
Narborough
Blaby
South Wigston
Newton Harcourt
Great Glen
Stoke Golding
Barwell
Elmesthorpe
Huncote
Littlethorpe
Whetstone
Burton Overy
Croft
Countesthorpe
Hinckley
Stoney Stanton
Cosby
Kilby
Kibworth Harcourt
Sutton in the Elms
Kibworth Beauchamp
Sketchley
Sapcote
Primethorpe
Peatling Magna
Arnesby
Fleckney
Smeeton Westerby
Burbage
Aston Flamville
Broughton Astley
Willoughby Waterleys
Saddington
Sharnford
Dunton Bassett
Ashby Magna
Shearsby
Burton Hastings
Frolesworth
Leire
Bruntingthorpe
Smockington
Claybrooke Magna
Peatling Parva
Mowsley
Gumley
Laughton
Bramcote
Claybrooke Parva
Ashby Parva
Gilmorton
Copston Magna
Wolvey
Wibtoft
Ullesthorpe
Walton
Lubenham
Kimcote
Theddingworth
Bitteswell
Willey
Lutterworth
Misterton
Shilton
Withybrook
Cross in Hand
Walcote
Husbands Bosworth
North Kilworth
Sibbertoft
Ansty
Monks Kirby
Cotesbach
South Kilworth
Pailton
Churchover
Gibbet Hill
Welford
Stretton under Fosse
Shawell
Swinford
Stanford on Avon
Brinklow
Easenhall
Harborough Magna
Binley Woods
King's Newnham
Newbold on Avon
Newton
Catthorpe
Bretford
Church Lawford
Long Lawford
Lilbourne
Clay Coton
Cold Ashby
Brandon
Clifton upon Dunsmore
Yelvertoft
Thornby
Wolston
New Bilton
Ryton-on-Dunsmore
Bilton
Rugby
Hillmorton
Winwick
Guilsborough
Stretton-on-Dunsmore
Crick
West Haddon
Coton
Dunchurch
Kilsby
Ravensthorpe
Bourton on Dunsmore
Thurlaston
Barby
Frankton
Watford
Ashby St Ledgers
Kites Hardwick
Woolscott
East Haddon
Holdenby
Leicester
Northampton
M1
M6
M45
M69
A5
A6
A14
A45
A46
A50
A426
A428
A563
A4303
A4304
A5199
A4071
0 1 2 3 miles
0 1 2 3 4 5 km

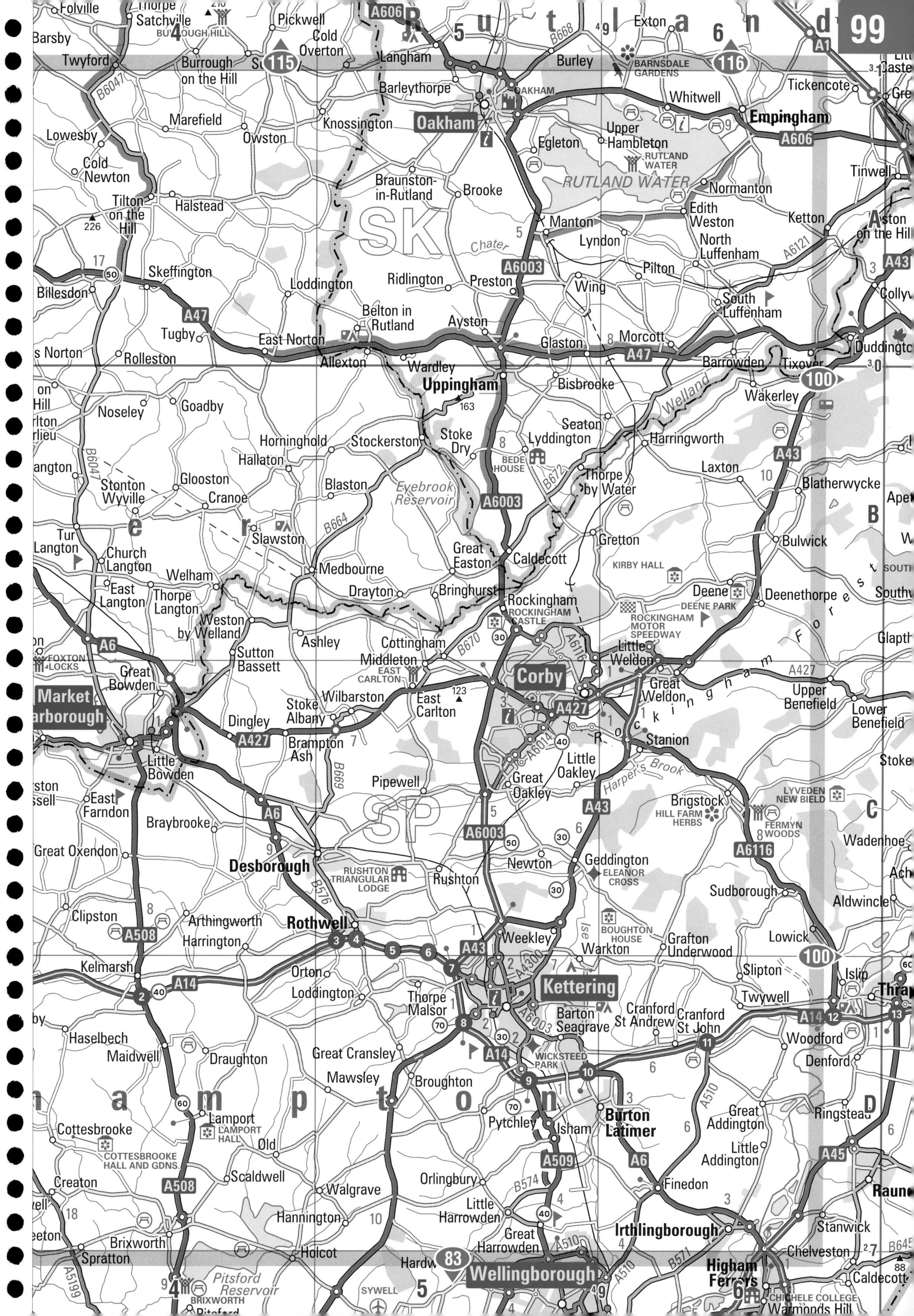
Oakham
Uppingham
Corby
Kettering
Market Harborough
Wellingborough
Desborough
Rothwell
Burton Latimer
Irthlingborough
Higham Ferrers
Empingham
RUTLAND WATER
Eyebrook Reservoir
Pitsford Reservoir
ROCKINGHAM CASTLE
KIRBY HALL
DEENE PARK
BOUGHTON HOUSE
LYVEDEN NEW BIELD
RUSHTON TRIANGULAR LODGE
WICKSTEED PARK
LAMPORT HALL
COTTESBROOKE HALL AND GDNS.
BARNSDALE GARDENS
BEDE HOUSE
ELEANOR CROSS
FOXTON LOCKS
A47
A6003
A427
A43
A6
A14
A508
A509
A6116
A606
A45
SK
SP
100
115
116
83

Stamford
Empingham
Market Deeping
Deeping St James
Crowland
Peterborough
Oundle
Thrapston
Raunds
Huntingdon
Yaxley
Sawtry
Brampton
Godmanchester
Wansford
Stibbington
Elton
Fotheringhay
King's Cliffe
Nassington
Duddington
Collyweston
Easton on the Hill
Ketton
Tinwell
Uffington
Tallington
Barnack
Ufford
Helpston
Glinton
Peakirk
Northborough
Maxey
Etton
Bainton
Southorpe
Wittering
Thornhaugh
Upton
Marholm
Werrington
Walton
Dogsthorpe
Gunthorpe
Newark
Eye
Newborough
Castor
Ailsworth
Sutton
Water Newton
Alwalton
Orton Waterville
Orton Longueville
Stanground
Fengate
Old Fletton
Farcet
Chesterton
Haddon
Morborne
Folksworth
Norman Cross
Stilton
Caldecote
Denton
Holme
Conington
Glatton
Lutton
Polebrook
Ashton
Barnwell St Andrew
Barnwell All Saints
Hemington
Luddington in the Brook
Thurning
Great Gidding
Little Gidding
Steeple Gidding
Winwick
Clopton
Titchmarsh
Thorpe Waterville
Wigsthorpe
Aldwincle
Achurch
Wadenhoe
Pilton
Stoke Doyle
Lower Benefield
Upper Benefield
Glapthorn
Cotterstock
Tansor
Eaglethorpe
Warmington
Southwick
Woodnewton
Apethorpe
Blatherwycke
Bulwick
Deenethorpe
Wakerley
Islip
Lowick
Slipton
Twywell
Woodford
Denford
Ringstead
Great Addington
Little Addington
Stanwick
Hargrave
Chelveston
Keyston
Bythorn
Molesworth
Brington
Old Weston
Catworth
Covington
Tilbrook
Lower Dean
Shelton
Spaldwick
Easton
Stow Longa
Ellington
Leighton Bromswold
Barham
Woolley
Buckworth
Alconbury
Alconbury Weston
Upton
Hamerton
Coppingford
Wood Walton
Great Raveley
Church End
Ramsey Heights
Wennington
Abbots Ripton
Little Stukeley
Great Stukeley
Grafham
Farcet Fen
Whittlesey Mere
Bedford Level (North)
Eye Green
Rockingham Forest
BURGHLEY
BARNACK HILLS AND HOLES
SACREWELL FARM & COUNTRY CENTRE
CASTOR HANGLANDS
BEDFORD PURLIEUS
COLLYWESTON GREAT WOOD
LONGTHORPE TOWER
FERRY MEADOWS
NENE VALLEY RAILWAY
RAILWORLD
CROWN LAKES
PETERBOROUGH SERVICES
ELTON HALL
CASTLE SITE
SOUTHWICK HALL
LYVEDEN NEW BIELD
FERMYN WOODS
BARNWELL
HOLME FEN
WOODWALTON FEN
UPWOOD MEADOWS
MONKS WOOD
HAMERTON ZOO PARK
HINCHINGBROOKE
TOLETHORPE HALL RUTLAND OPEN AIR THEATRE
FLAG FEN BRONZE AGE EXCAVATION
SIBSON
A1
A1(M)
A14
A15
A16
A43
A45
A47
A605
A606
A1139
A6116
A141
A427
B660
B1043
B1090
B1091
B662
B663
B645
B671
B1443
0 1 2 3 miles
0 1 2 3 4 5 km

116
117
99
84

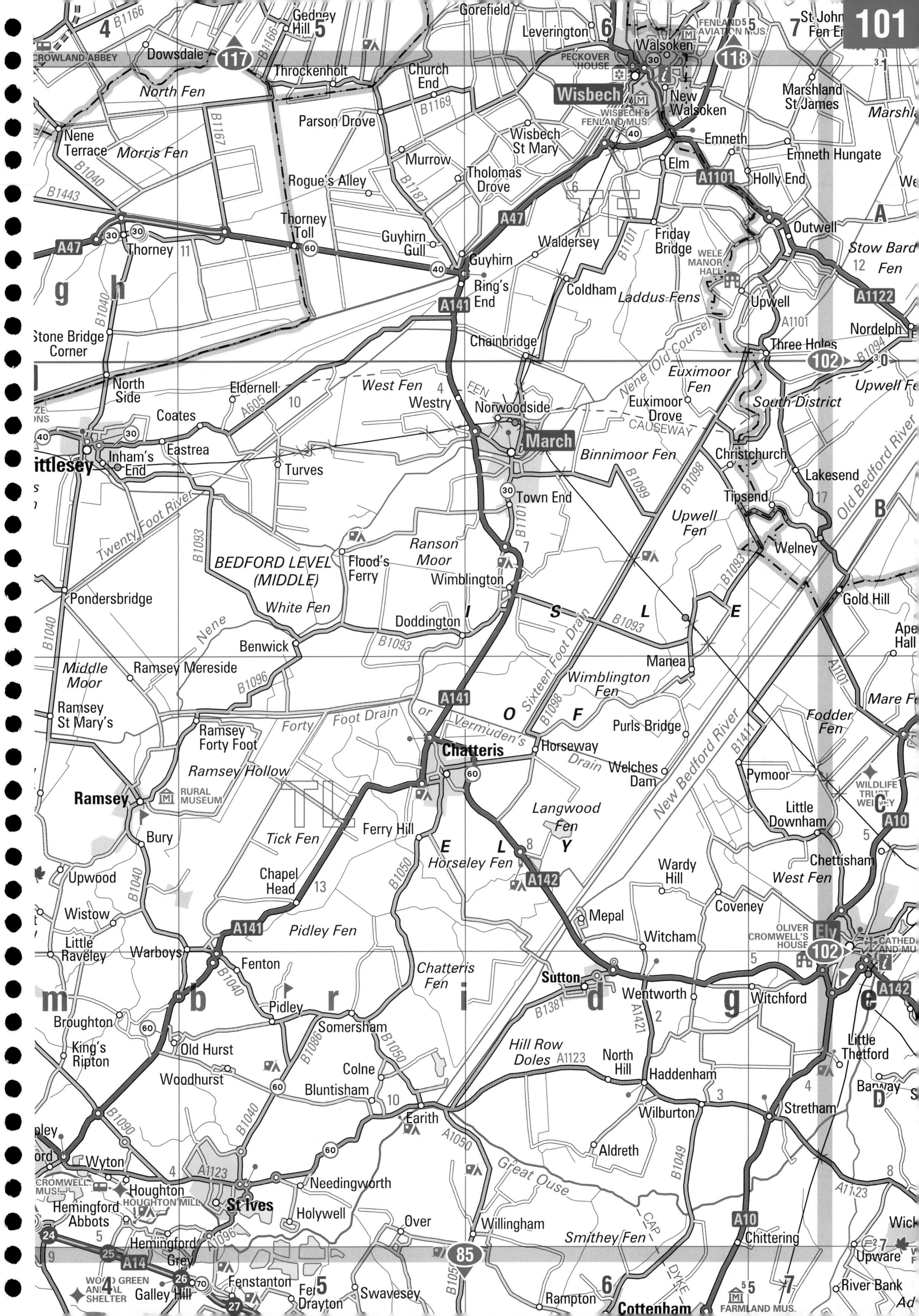

Gedney Hill
Gorefield
Leverington
St John's Fen End
FENLAND AVIATION MUS.
CROWLAND ABBEY
Dowsdale
117
118
Throckenholt
Church End
PECKOVER HOUSE
Walsoken
Wisbech
New Walsoken
Marshland St James
North Fen
Parson Drove
WISBECH & FENLAND MUS.
Wisbech St Mary
Emneth
Nene Terrace
Morris Fen
Murrow
Elm
Emneth Hungate
Rogue's Alley
Tholomas Drove
A1101
Holly End
Thorney Toll
A47
Outwell
Thorney
Guyhirn Gull
Waldersey
Friday Bridge
WELE MANOR HALL
Stow Bardolph Fen
Guyhirn
Ring's End
Coldham
Laddus Fens
Upwell
A1122
A141
Stone Bridge Corner
Chainbridge
Nordelph
Three Holes
102
North Side
Eldernell
West Fen
Westry
Euximoor Fen
Nene (Old Course)
Upwell Fen
Coates
Norwoodside
Euximoor Drove
South District
CAUSEWAY
Whittlesey
Inham's End
Eastrea
March
Binnimoor Fen
Christchurch
Turves
Old Bedford River
Lakesend
Town End
Tipsend
Twenty Foot River
Upwell Fen
Ranson Moor
Welney
BEDFORD LEVEL (MIDDLE)
Flood's Ferry
Wimblington
Pondersbridge
White Fen
Gold Hill
ISLE
Doddington
Nene
Benwick
Apes Hall
Middle Moor
Ramsey Mereside
Manea
Wimblington Fen
Sixteen Foot Drain
Ramsey St Mary's
Mare Fen
Forty Foot Drain or Vermuden's Drain
Purls Bridge
Fodder Fen
Ramsey Forty Foot
OF
Chatteris
Horseway
New Bedford River
Ramsey Hollow
Welches Dam
Pymoor
Ramsey
RURAL MUSEUM
WILDLIFE TRUST WELNEY
Langwood Fen
Little Downham
Bury
Tick Fen
Ferry Hill
ELY
Horseley Fen
A142
Chettisham
Upwood
Chapel Head
Wardy Hill
West Fen
Wistow
Pidley Fen
Coveney
Mepal
Little Raveley
Warboys
Witcham
OLIVER CROMWELL'S HOUSE
Ely
CATHEDRAL AND MUS.
Fenton
Chatteris Fen
Sutton
Cambridge
Pidley
Wentworth
Witchford
Broughton
Somersham
King's Ripton
Old Hurst
Hill Row Doles
North Hill
Little Thetford
Colne
Haddenham
Woodhurst
Bluntisham
Barway
Earith
Wilburton
Stretham
Wyton
Aldreth
Great Ouse
Needingworth
Houghton
CROMWELL MUS.
HOUGHTON MILL
St Ives
Holywell
Hemingford Abbots
Over
Willingham
Chittering
Hemingford Grey
Smithey Fen
Upware
CAR DYKE
WOOD GREEN ANIMAL SHELTER
Fenstanton
Fen Drayton
Swavesey
Rampton
Cottenham
FARMLAND MUS.
River Bank
Galley Hill
85
A10
A14
A1123
A605
B1040
B1093
B1098
B1099
B1101
B1050
B1086
B1090
B1096
B1166
B1167
B1169
B1187
B1443
B1381
B1411
A1421
B1049
B1094
A1050
A1096
TF
TL

St John's Fen End
Wiggenhall St Mary Magdalen
Watlington
Tottenhill
Wormegay
118
119
A47
Marham
Shouldham
Runcton Holme
Marshland St James
Marshland Fen
South Runcton
Shouldham Thorpe
Beachamwell Warren
A1122
Emneth Hungate
Stowbridge
Stow Bardolph
A134
Holly End
West Head
Fincham
Barton Bendish
Wimbotsham
Beachamwell
Outwell
Downham Market
Stradsett
Shingham
Stow Bardolph Fen
Broomhill
Crimplesham
Cockley Cley
Barroway Drove
Bexwell
Eastmoor
Upwell
A1122
Denver
Boughton
GOODERSTONE WATER GARDENS
Gooderstone
Wereham
Oxborough
A1101
Nordelph
A10
OXBURGH HALL
Three Holes
B1094
West Dereham
101
Fordham
Wretton
Stoke Ferry
Whittington
Foulden
Upwell Fen
South District
Old Bedford River
Hilgay
Wissey
A134
Northwold
Ten Mile Bank
B1160
B1112
Christchurch
Brookville
Lakesend
Tipsend
Hilgay Fen
Southery
Cranwich
Methwold Hythe
Methwold
B1160
Welney
Methwold Fens
Southery Fens
Queen's Ground
THETFORD
B1093
Gold Hill
Brandon Creek
B1112
Apes Hall
60
Feltwell
A1101
Brandon Bank
Feltwell Fens
Hockwold cum Wilton
Weeting
Mare Fen
Burnt Fen
Fodder Fen
Hockwold Fens
WEETING HEATH
B1411
Littleport
Little Ouse
Brandon
Pymoor
WILDLIFE TRUST WELNEY
BEDFORD LEVEL (SOUTH)
A1101
30
Little Downham
A10
BRANDON PARK
Shippea Hill Sta.
Great Ouse
Chettisham
Lakenheath
West Fen
Prickwillow
A1065
B1382
B1106
Coveney
101
Wangford Warren
B1112
Queen Adelaide
OLIVER CROMWELL'S HOUSE
Ely
CATHEDRAL AND MUS.
Kenny Hill
Lakenheath Warren
Middle Fen
Mildenhall Fen
Witchford
Great Fen
Stuntney
Eriswell
B1104
Lark
A11
A142
Holywell Row
Broad Hill
Beck Row
A10
Little Thetford
A1101
Thistley Green
WINDMILL
Isleham Fen
West Row
Barway
PRIORY CHURCH
Soham Cotes
Stretham
Isleham
Mildenhall
B1112
Soham
Worlington
A1101
Barton Mills
Icklingham
Soham Mere
B1102
CAVENHAM HEATH
Freckenham
DOWN FIELD WINDMILL
Tuddenham
A11
Fordham
Kennett
Wicken
A1123
A142
Chittering
WICKEN CORN MILL
Red Lodge
Herringswell
Lackford
New River
86
Chippenham
B1085
WICKEN
Cavenham
Fle
0 1 2 3 miles
0 1 2 3 4 5 km
CHIPPENHAM FEN
FARMLAND MUS.
Adventures
Kennett

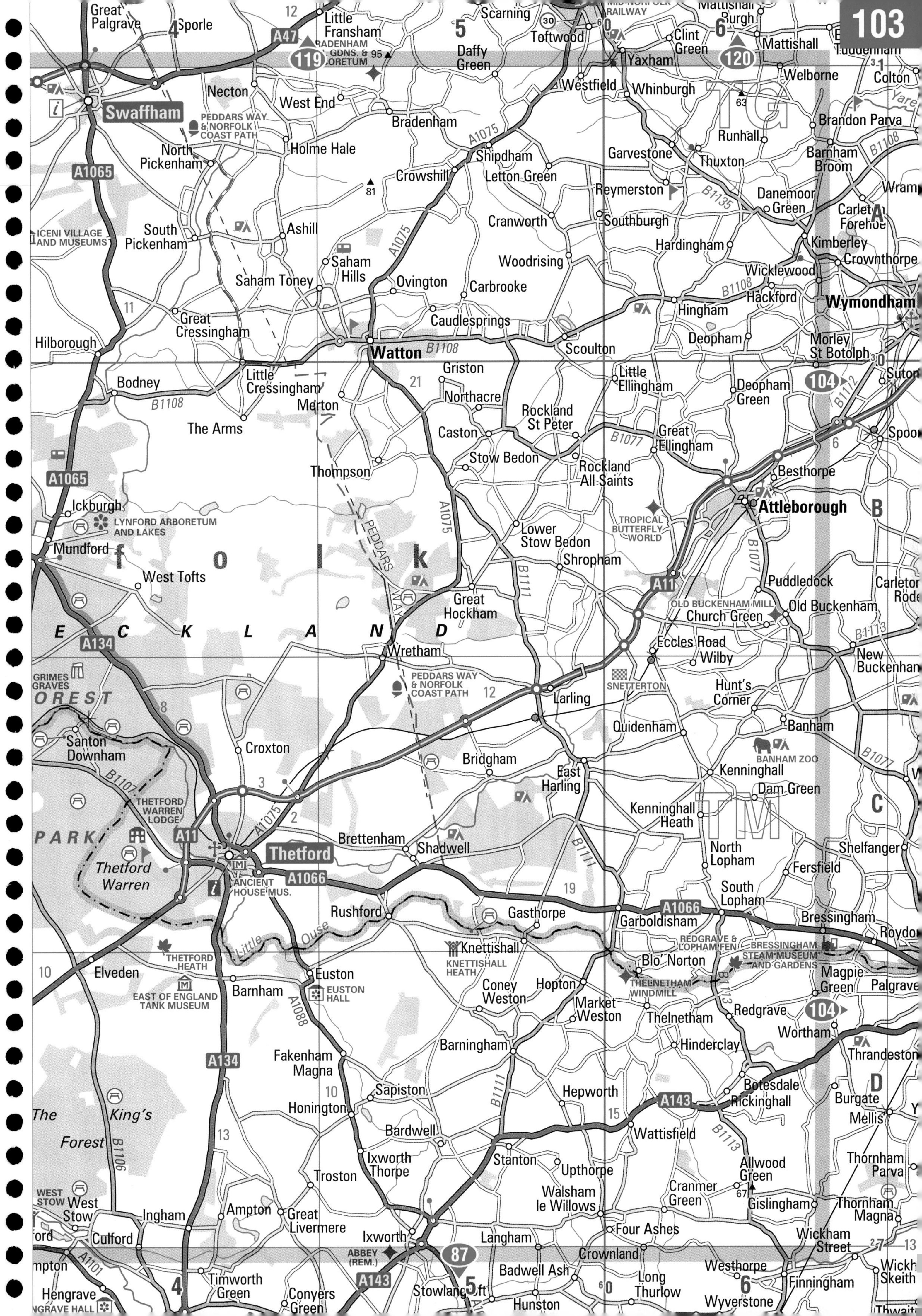

Great Palgrave
Sporle
Little Fransham
A47
BRADENHAM GDNS. & ARBORETUM
119
Scarning
Toftwood
Daffy Green
Yaxham
Clint Green
Mattishall Burgh
Mattishall
120
Welborne
Colton
Swaffham
Necton
West End
Bradenham
Westfield
Whinburgh
PEDDARS WAY & NORFOLK COAST PATH
Brandon Parva
Runhall
Holme Hale
North Pickenham
A1065
A1075
Shipdham
Garvestone
Thuxton
Barnham Broom
B1108
Crowshill
Letton Green
Reymerston
B1135
Danemoor Green
Carleton Forehoe
Cranworth
Southburgh
ICENI VILLAGE AND MUSEUMS
South Pickenham
Ashill
Hardingham
Kimberley
Crownthorpe
Woodrising
Saham Hills
Saham Toney
Ovington
Carbrooke
Wicklewood
Hackford
Hingham
Wymondham
Great Cressingham
Caudlesprings
Deopham
Hilborough
Watton
B1108
Scoulton
Morley St Botolph
Griston
Little Ellingham
Deopham Green
104
Bodney
Little Cressingham
Northacre
Merton
Rockland St Peter
Great Ellingham
The Arms
Caston
B1077
Stow Bedon
Rockland All Saints
Thompson
Besthorpe
A1065
Ickburgh
LYNFORD ARBORETUM AND LAKES
TROPICAL BUTTERFLY WORLD
Attleborough
Lower Stow Bedon
A1075
Mundford
Shropham
West Tofts
PEDDARS WAY
B1111
B1077
Puddledock
A11
Great Hockham
OLD BUCKENHAM MILL
Church Green
Old Buckenham
E C K L A N D
A134
Eccles Road
Wilby
B1113
New Buckenham
Wretham
GRIMES GRAVES
PEDDARS WAY & NORFOLK COAST PATH
SNETTERTON
Larling
Hunt's Corner
Quidenham
Banham
Santon Downham
Croxton
BANHAM ZOO
Bridgham
B1077
B1107
East Harling
Kenninghall
Dam Green
THETFORD WARREN LODGE
A1075
Kenninghall Heath
PARK
A11
Brettenham
Shadwell
B1111
North Lopham
Shelfanger
Thetford
Thetford Warren
A1066
ANCIENT HOUSE MUS.
Fersfield
South Lopham
Rushford
Gasthorpe
Garboldisham
A1066
Bressingham
Roydon
Little Ouse
Knettishall
KNETTISHALL HEATH
REDGRAVE & LOPHAM FEN
BRESSINGHAM STEAM MUSEUM AND GARDENS
THETFORD HEATH
Elveden
Euston
Blo' Norton
THELNETHAM WINDMILL
Magpie Green
Palgrave
EAST OF ENGLAND TANK MUSEUM
Barnham
EUSTON HALL
A1088
Coney Weston
Hopton
B1113
Market Weston
Thelnetham
Redgrave
104
Wortham
Barningham
Hinderclay
Thrandeston
A134
Fakenham Magna
Sapiston
B1111
Hepworth
Botesdale
Rickinghall
Burgate
Mellis
The King's Forest
Honington
A143
Wattisfield
B1106
Bardwell
B1113
Ixworth Thorpe
Stanton
Upthorpe
Allwood Green
Thornham Parva
Troston
Walsham le Willows
Cranmer Green
WEST STOW
West Stow
Ingham
Ampton
Great Livermere
Gislingham
Thornham Magna
Culford
Four Ashes
Ixworth
Langham
Wickham Street
ABBEY (REM.)
87
Crownland
A101
A143
Badwell Ash
Westhorpe
Timworth Green
Conyers Green
Stowlangtoft
Long Thurlow
Finningham
Hengrave
HENGRAVE HALL
Hunston
Wyverstone
TG
TM
A
B
C
D
4
5
6

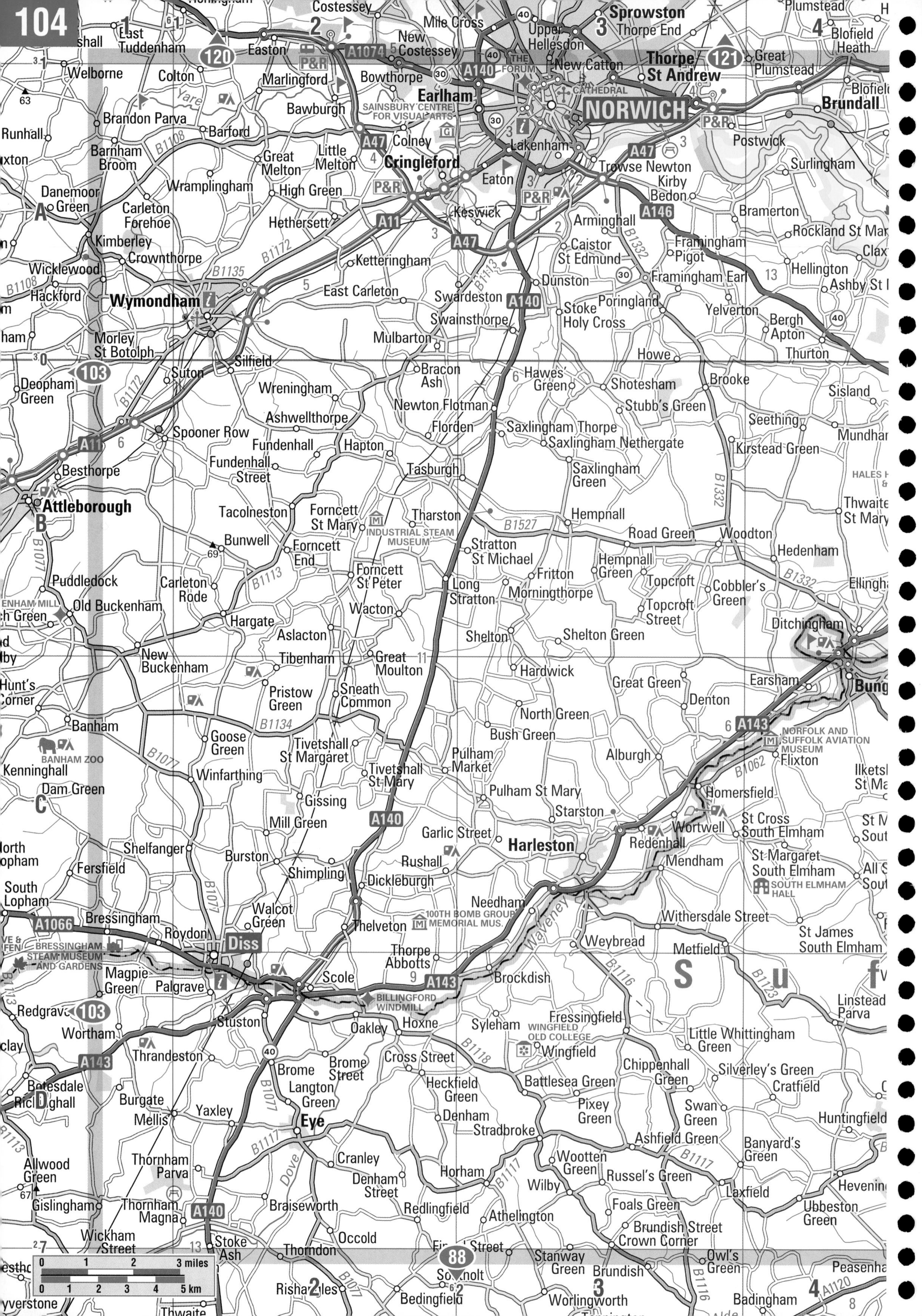
East Tuddenham
Costessey
Mile Cross
Sprowston
Thorpe End
Plumstead
Blofield Heath
Easton
New Costessey
Upper Hellesdon
New Catton
Thorpe St Andrew
Great Plumstead
Welborne
Colton
Marlingford
Bowthorpe
Earlham
THE FORUM
CATHEDRAL
NORWICH
Brundall
Blofield
Brandon Parva
Barford
Bawburgh
SAINSBURY CENTRE FOR VISUAL ARTS
Runhall
Barnham Broom
Great Melton
Little Melton
Colney
Cringleford
Lakenham
Postwick
Trowse Newton
Surlingham
Kirby Bedon
Danemoor Green
Carleton Forehoe
Wramplingham
High Green
Eaton
Keswick
Bramerton
Hethersett
Arminghall
Rockland St Mary
Kimberley
Crownthorpe
Caistor St Edmund
Framingham Pigot
Wicklewood
Ketteringham
Hellington
Hackford
East Carleton
Dunston
Framingham Earl
Ashby St Mary
Wymondham
Swardeston
Stoke Holy Cross
Poringland
Yelverton
Bergh Apton
Morley St Botolph
Swainsthorpe
Mulbarton
Thurton
Howe
Silfield
Suton
Bracon Ash
Hawes' Green
Shotesham
Brooke
Deopham Green
Wreningham
Newton Flotman
Stubb's Green
Sisland
Ashwellthorpe
Seething
Spooner Row
Florden
Saxlingham Thorpe
Saxlingham Nethergate
Mundham
Fundenhall
Hapton
Kirstead Green
Besthorpe
Fundenhall Street
Tasburgh
Saxlingham Green
HALES HALL
Attleborough
Tacolneston
Forncett St Mary
INDUSTRIAL STEAM MUSEUM
Tharston
Hempnall
Thwaite St Mary
Bunwell
Forncett End
Stratton St Michael
Road Green
Woodton
Hedenham
Puddledock
Carleton Rode
Forncett St Peter
Long Stratton
Fritton
Hempnall Green
Topcroft
Cobbler's Green
Old Buckenham
Morningthorpe
Topcroft Street
Hargate
Wacton
Aslacton
Shelton
Shelton Green
Ditchingham
New Buckenham
Tibenham
Great Moulton
Hardwick
Pristow Green
Sneath Common
Great Green
Earsham
Denton
Bungay
Banham
North Green
Bush Green
BANHAM ZOO
Goose Green
Tivetshall St Margaret
Pulham Market
Alburgh
NORFOLK AND SUFFOLK AVIATION MUSEUM
Flixton
Kenninghall
Winfarthing
Tivetshall St Mary
Dam Green
Gissing
Pulham St Mary
Homersfield
Starston
Mill Green
Garlic Street
Harleston
St Cross South Elmham
Wortwell
Redenhall
Shelfanger
Burston
Rushall
Mendham
St Margaret South Elmham
Fersfield
Shimpling
Dickleburgh
SOUTH ELMHAM HALL
South Lopham
Needham
Bressingham
Walcot Green
100TH BOMB GROUP MEMORIAL MUS.
Withersdale Street
Roydon
Thelveton
Waveney
St James South Elmham
BRESSINGHAM STEAM MUSEUM AND GARDENS
Diss
Thorpe Abbotts
Weybread
Metfield
Magpie Green
Palgrave
Scole
Brockdish
Suffolk
Linstead Parva
BILLINGFORD WINDMILL
Redgrave
Stuston
Oakley
Hoxne
Syleham
Fressingfield
Wortham
WINGFIELD OLD COLLEGE
Little Whittingham Green
Thrandeston
Cross Street
Wingfield
Chippenhall Green
Silverley's Green
Brome
Brome Street
Botesdale
Rickinghall
Burgate
Langton Green
Heckfield Green
Battlesea Green
Cratfield
Pixey Green
Swan Green
Yaxley
Mellis
Eye
Denham
Stradbroke
Huntingfield
Ashfield Green
Banyard's Green
Thornham Parva
Cranley
Allwood Green
Wootten Green
Horham
Denham Street
Wilby
Russel's Green
Laxfield
Heveningham
Gislingham
Thornham Magna
Braiseworth
Redlingfield
Athelington
Foals Green
Ubbeston Green
Brundish Street
Crown Corner
Wickham Street
Occold
Stoke Ash
Thorndon
Finningham Street
Stanway Green
Brundish
Owl's Green
Peasenhall
Rishangles
Southolt
Bedingfield
Worlingworth
Badingham
Thwaite
Wyverstone
0 1 2 3 miles
0 1 2 3 4 5 km

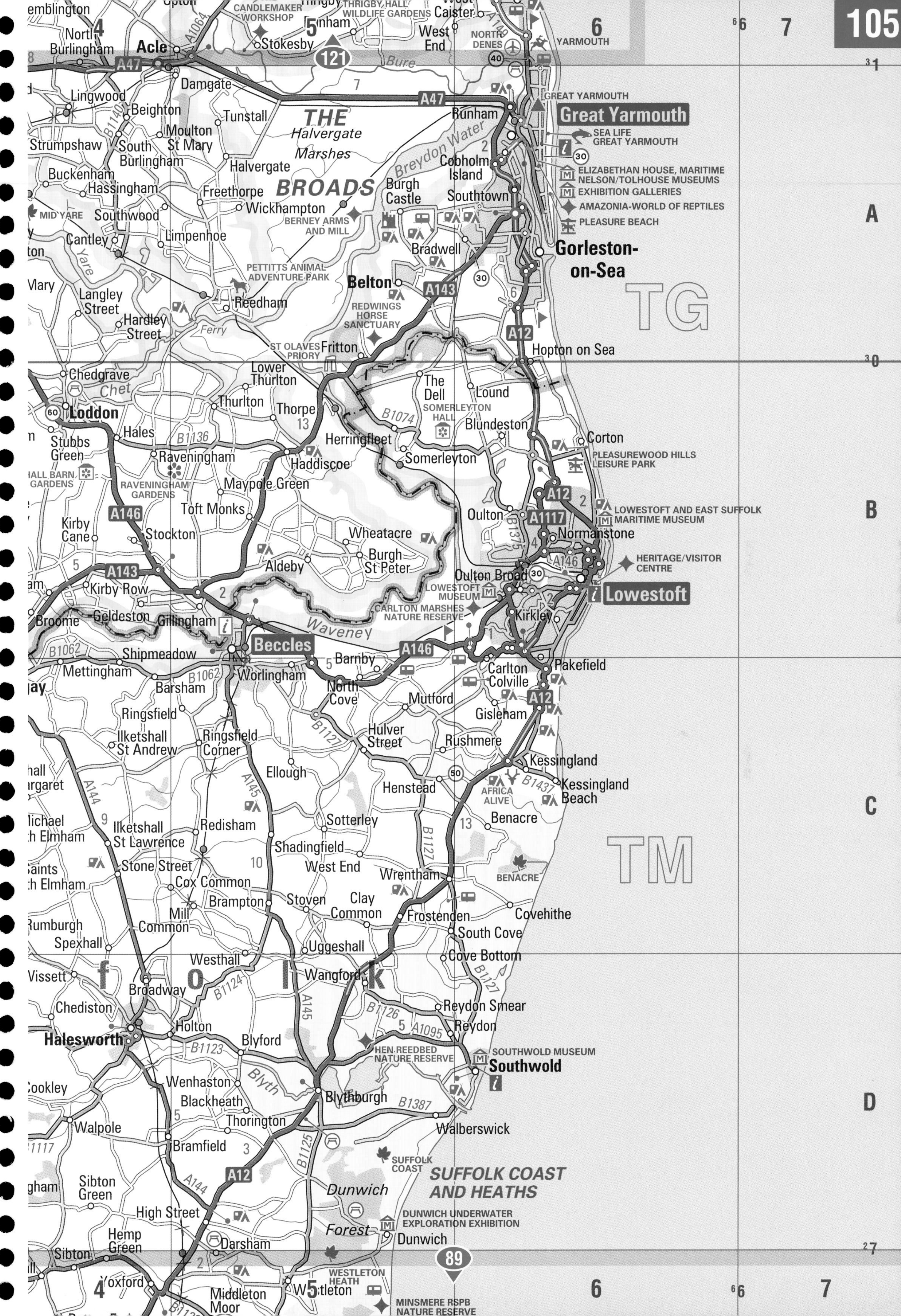

Acle
Great Yarmouth
THE Halvergate Marshes
BROADS
Breydon Water
GREAT YARMOUTH
SEA LIFE GREAT YARMOUTH
ELIZABETHAN HOUSE, MARITIME
NELSON/TOLHOUSE MUSEUMS
EXHIBITION GALLERIES
AMAZONIA-WORLD OF REPTILES
PLEASURE BEACH
Gorleston-on-Sea
TG
Belton
Reedham
Hopton on Sea
Loddon
Lowestoft
LOWESTOFT AND EAST SUFFOLK MARITIME MUSEUM
HERITAGE/VISITOR CENTRE
PLEASUREWOOD HILLS LEISURE PARK
Beccles
Waveney
Kessingland
TM
Halesworth
Southwold
SOUTHWOLD MUSEUM
SUFFOLK COAST AND HEATHS
Dunwich
DUNWICH UNDERWATER EXPLORATION EXHIBITION
MINSMERE RSPB NATURE RESERVE

122
CAERNARFON BAY
BAE CAERNARFON
SH
LLEYN
LLŶN
Carreg Ddu
Porth Dinllaen
Morfa Nefyn
Nefyn
LLEYN HISTORICAL MARITIME MUSEUM
Porth Ysgadan
Edern
Glanrhyd
Rhos-y-llan
Tudweiliog
CORS GEIRCH
Boduan
BODVEL HALL ADVENTURE PARK
PENRHYN LLYN
Dinas
Garnfadryn
Porth Golmon
Bryn-mawr
Llaniestyn
Pen-y-graig
Llangwnnadl
Penrhyn Mawr
Sarn Meyllteyrn
Pen-y-groeslon
Ty-hen
Methlem
Rhydlios
Bryncroes
Botwnnog
Nanhoron
Rhoshirwaun
304
MYNYDD RHIW
PLAS-YN-RHIW
Llandegwning
Capel Carmel
Rhiw
Llawr Dref
191
Uwchmynydd
Aberdaron
Llanfaelrhys
Bodermid
Pen-y-cil
Bardsey Sound
Swnt Enlli
167
YNYS ENLLI
Bardsey Island
Ynys Enlli
Porth Neigwl or Hell's Mouth
Llanengan
Sarn Bach
Bwlchtocyn
Marchroes
Cilan Uchaf
Trwyn Cilan
Llangian
Abersoch
Mynytho
Llanbedrog
Trwyn Llanbedrog
St Tudwal's Road
Angorfa St Tudwal
St Tudwal's Island East
Ynys St Tudwal Dwyrain
St Tudwal's Island West
Ynys St Tudwal Gorllewin
Rhedyn
Penrhos
Rhyd-y-clafdy
Tan-y-graig
Fron
Llannor
Efailnewydd
Denio
Pwllheli
South Beach
Rhos-fawr
Llwyndyrys
Pistyll
Llithfaen
564
YR EIFL
Trefor
Bryn-yr-eryr
Gyrn-goch
Clynnog
B4417
B4415
B4413
B4354
A497
A499
0 1 2 3 miles
0 1 2 3 4 5 km

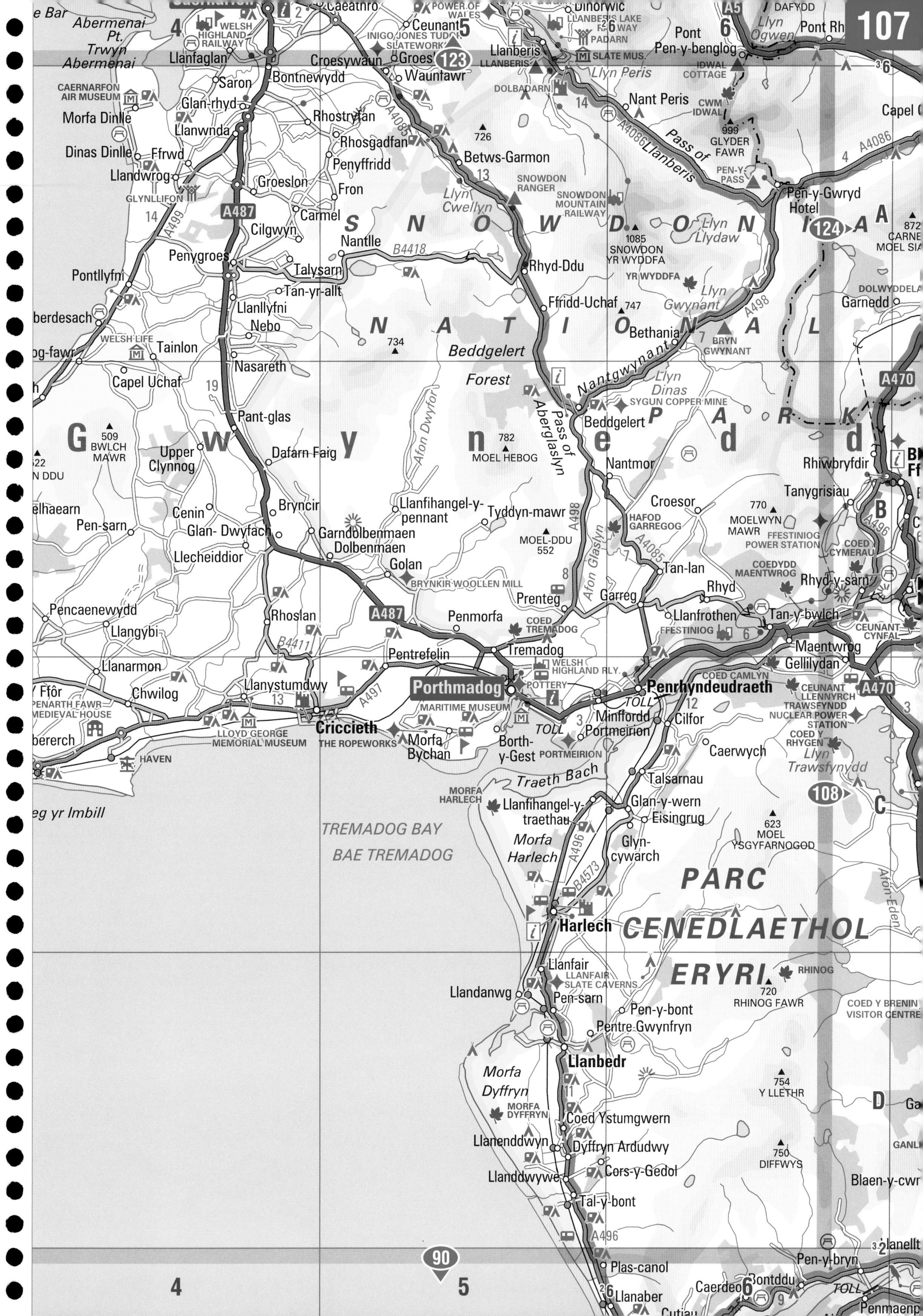

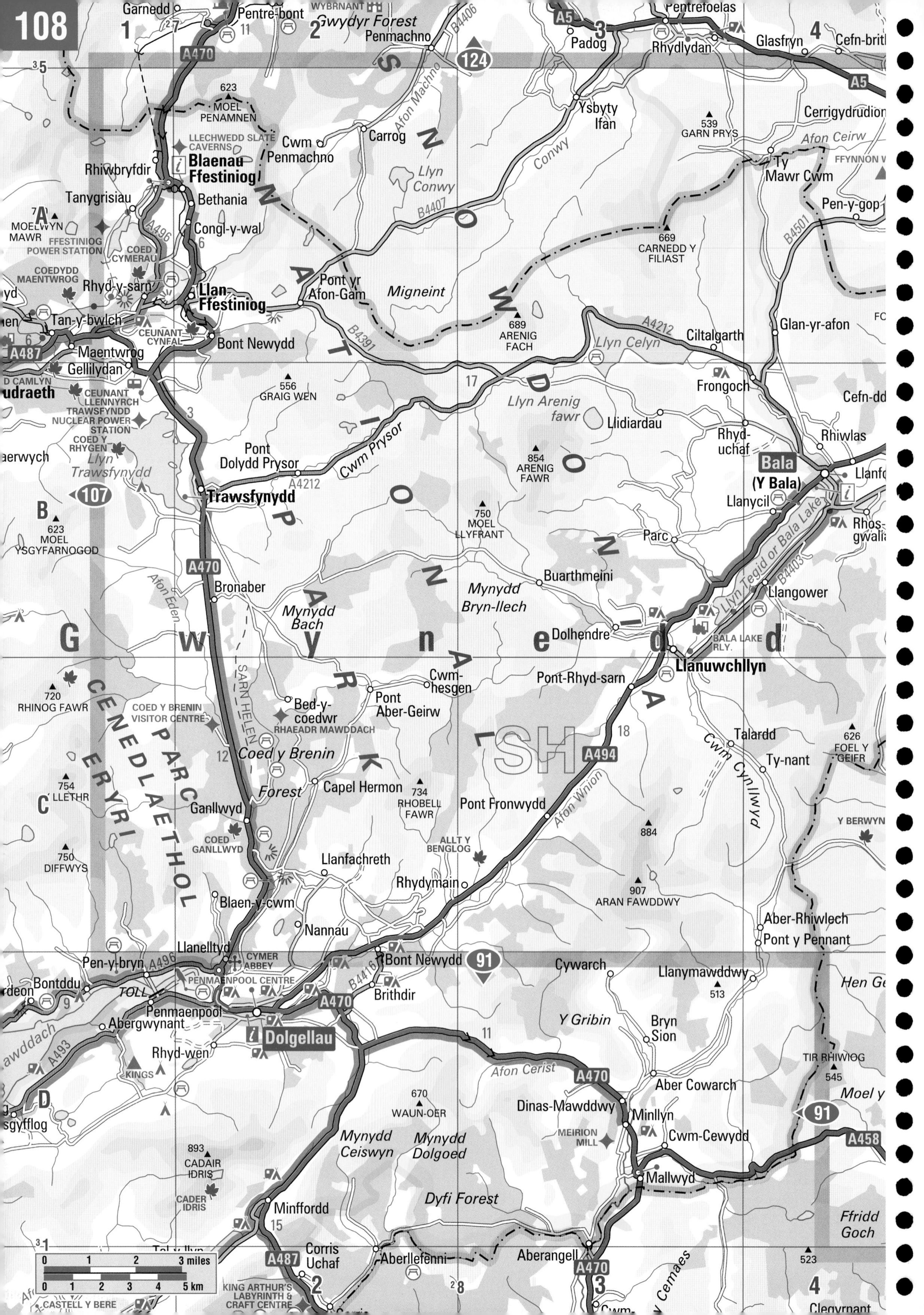
Garnedd
Pentre-bont
Gwydyr Forest
Penmachno
Pentrefoelas
Padog
Rhydlydan
Glasfryn
Cefn-brith
A470
A5
124
623 MOEL PENAMNEN
LLECHWEDD SLATE CAVERNS
Blaenau Ffestiniog
Cwm Penmachno
Carrog
Afon Machno
Ysbyty Ifan
539 GARN PRYS
Cerrigydrudion
Afon Ceirw
Ty Mawr Cwm
Rhiwbryfdir
Tanygrisiau
Bethania
Congl-y-wal
Llyn Conwy
Conwy
B4407
Pen-y-gop
MOELWYN MAWR
FFESTINIOG POWER STATION
COED CYMERAU
COEDYDD MAENTWROG
Rhyd-y-sarn
Llan-Ffestiniog
Pont yr Afon-Gam
Migneint
669 CARNEDD Y FILIAST
B4501
Tan-y-bwlch
CEUNANT CYNFAL
Bont Newydd
Maentwrog
A487
Gellilydan
B4391
689 ARENIG FACH
A4212
Llyn Celyn
Ciltalgarth
Glan-yr-afon
CEUNANT LLENNYRCH
TRAWSFYNYDD NUCLEAR POWER STATION
COED Y RHYGEN
Llyn Trawsfynydd
556 GRAIG WEN
Frongoch
Cefn-ddwysarn
Llyn Arenig fawr
Llidiardau
Rhyd-uchaf
Rhiwlas
Pont Dolydd Prysor
Cwm Prysor
854 ARENIG FAWR
Bala (Y Bala)
Llanycil
Trawsfynydd
107
623 MOEL YSGYFARNOGOD
750 MOEL LLYFRANT
Parc
Rhos-gwaliau
Llyn Tegid or Bala Lake
B4403
Afon Eden
Bronaber
Buarthmeini
Llangower
Mynydd Bach
Mynydd Bryn-llech
Dolhendre
BALA LAKE RLY.
Llanuwchllyn
G w y n e d d
720 RHINOG FAWR
COED Y BRENIN VISITOR CENTRE
SARN HELEN
Bed-y-coedwr
RHAEADR MAWDDACH
Pont Aber-Geirw
Cwm-hesgen
Pont-Rhyd-sarn
Coed y Brenin Forest
SH
A494
Talardd
626 FOEL Y GEIFR
Ty-nant
Cwm Cynllwyd
754 LLETHR
Capel Hermon
734 RHOBELL FAWR
Pont Fronwydd
Afon Wnion
884
Y BERWYN
Ganllwyd
COED GANLLWYD
ALLT Y BENGLOG
750 DIFFWYS
Llanfachreth
Rhydymain
907 ARAN FAWDDWY
Blaen-y-cwm
Nannau
Aber-Rhiwlech
Pont y Pennant
PARC CENEDLAETHOL ERYRI
SNOWDONIA NATIONAL PARK
Llanelltyd
CYMER ABBEY
Bont Newydd
91
Cywarch
Llanymawddwy
513
Pen-y-bryn
Bontddu
A496
TOLL
PENMAENPOOL CENTRE
B4416
Brithdir
Hen Gerrig
Penmaenpool
Abergwynant
A470
Dolgellau
Y Gribin
Bryn Sion
Mawddach
A493
Rhyd-wen
KINGS
Afon Cerist
TIR RHIWIOG 545
Aber Cowarch
670 WAUN-OER
Dinas-Mawddwy
Minllyn
Moel y Cerrig Duon
Tywyn
D
Llwyngwril
Mynydd Ceiswyn
Mynydd Dolgoed
MEIRION MILL
Cwm-Cewydd
A458
893 CADAIR IDRIS
Mallwyd
CADER IDRIS
Dyfi Forest
Minffordd
Ffridd Goch
Corris Uchaf
Aberllefenni
Aberangell
A487
Cemaes
523
KING ARTHUR'S LABYRINTH & CRAFT CENTRE
CASTELL Y BERE
Cwm
Cleyrnant
0 1 2 3 miles
0 1 2 3 4 5 km

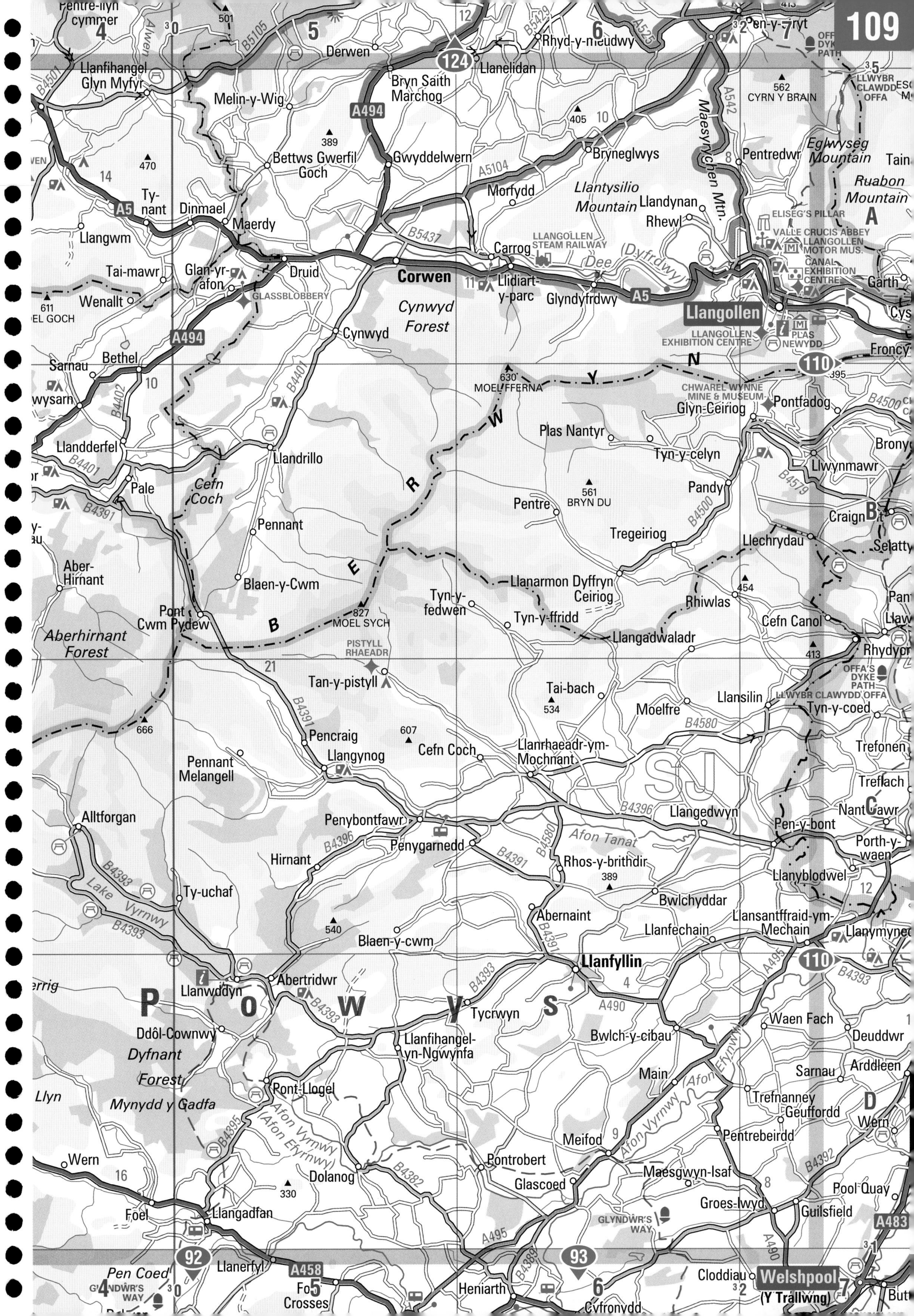
Llanfihangel Glyn Myfyr
Melin-y-Wig
Derwen
Bryn Saith Marchog
Llanelidan
Rhyd-y-meudwy
Pen-y-stryt
Cyrn y Brain
Bettws Gwerfil Goch
Gwyddelwern
Bryneglwys
Pentredwr
Eglwyseg Mountain
Ruabon Mountain
Llantysilio Mountain
Llandynan
Rhewl
Maesyrychen Mtn.
Ty-nant
Dinmael
Maerdy
Llangwm
Morfydd
Eliseg's Pillar
Valle Crucis Abbey
Llangollen Motor Mus.
Llangollen Steam Railway
Carrog
Dee (Dyfrdwy)
Canal Exhibition Centre
Garth
Tai-mawr
Glan-yr-afon
Druid
Corwen
Llidiart-y-parc
Glyndyfrdwy
Wenallt
Glassblobbery
Cynwyd Forest
Llangollen
Llangollen Exhibition Centre
Plas Newydd
Cynwyd
Bethel
Sarnau
Moel Fferna
Berwyn
Chwarel Wynne Mine & Museum
Pontfadog
Glyn Ceiriog
Plas Nantyr
Tyn-y-celyn
Llandderfel
Llandrillo
Llwynmawr
Pale
Cefn Coch
Pandy
Bryn Du
Pentre
Craignant
Pennant
Tregeiriog
Llechrydau
Selattyn
Aber-Hirnant
Blaen-y-Cwm
Llanarmon Dyffryn Ceiriog
Rhiwlas
Tyn-y-fedwen
Moel Sych
Tyn-y-ffridd
Cefn Canol
Pont Cwm Pydew
Aberhirnant Forest
Llangadwaladr
Rhydycroesau
Pistyll Rhaeadr
Tan-y-pistyll
Tai-bach
Llansilin
Offa's Dyke Path
Llwybr Clawdd Offa
Moelfre
Tyn-y-coed
Pencraig
Cefn Coch
Llanrhaeadr-ym-Mochnant
Trefonen
Pennant Melangell
Llangynog
Treflach
Alltforgan
Penybontfawr
Llangedwyn
Nantmawr
Pen-y-bont
Afon Tanat
Penygarnedd
Porth-y-waen
Hirnant
Rhos-y-brithdir
Llanyblodwel
Ty-uchaf
Lake Vyrnwy
Bwlchyddar
Abernaint
Llansantffraid-ym-Mechain
Llanfechain
Llanymynech
Blaen-y-cwm
Llanfyllin
Abertridwr
Llanwddyn
Powys
Tycrwyn
Waen Fach
Ddôl-Cownwy
Llanfihangel-yn-Ngwynfa
Bwlch-y-cibau
Deuddwr
Dyfnant Forest
Sarnau
Arddleen
Main
Pont-Llogel
Mynydd y Gadfa
Llyn
Trefnanney
Geufordd
Afon Vyrnwy (Afon Efyrnwy)
Pentrebeirdd
Wern
Meifod
Wern
Pontrobert
Maesgwyn-Isaf
Dolanog
Glascoed
Pool Quay
Groes-lwyd
Guilsfield
Foel
Llangadfan
Glyndŵr's Way
Llanerfyl
Pen Coed
Heniarth
Cloddiau
Welshpool (Y Trallwng)
Cyfronydd
Fron Crosses

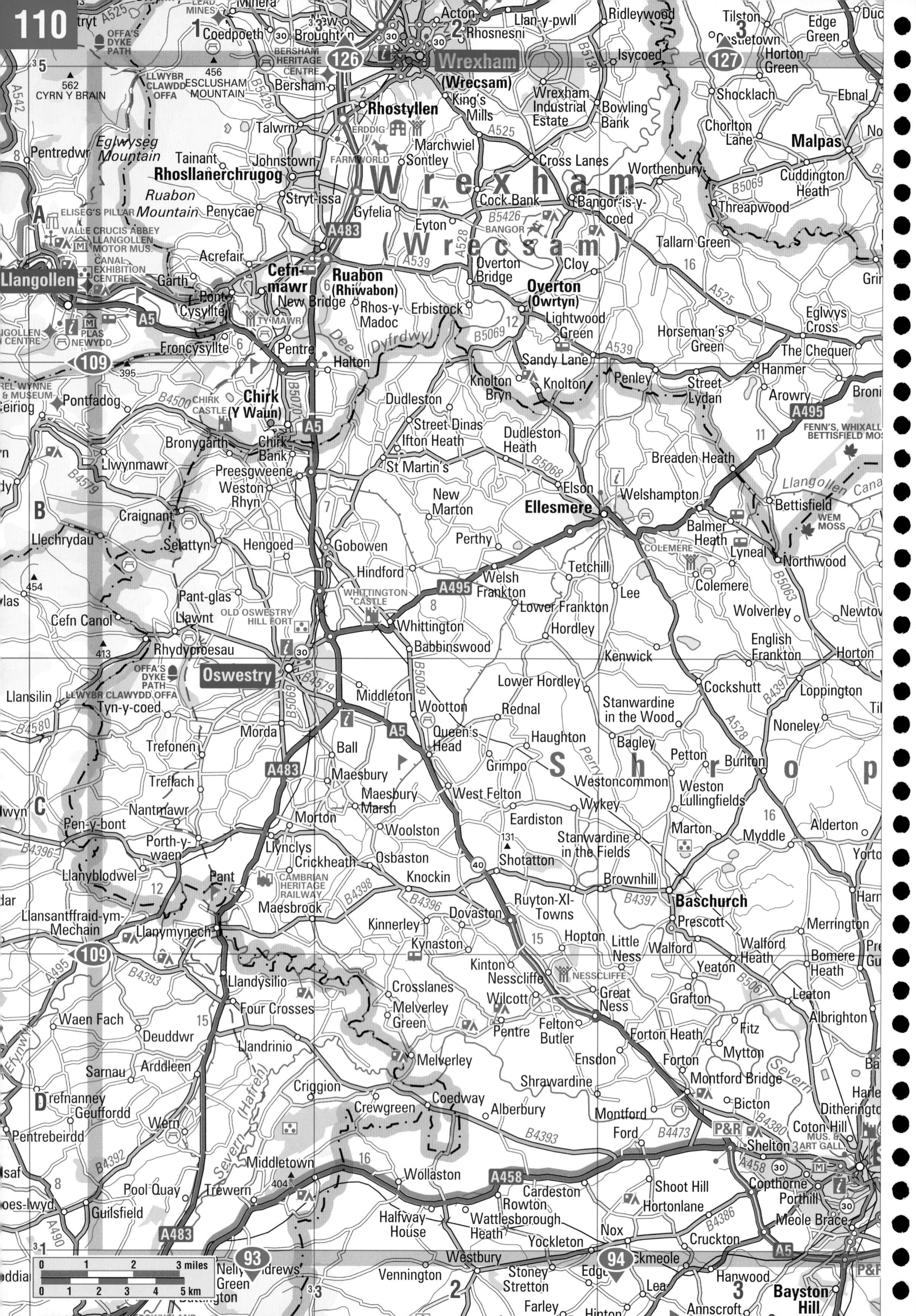
Wrexham
(Wrecsam)
Rhostyllen
Coedpoeth
Broughton
Acton
Rhosnesni
Llan-y-pwll
Ridleywood
Tilston
Castletown
Edge Green
Horton Green
Isycoed
Bersham
Minera
OFFA'S DYKE PATH
BERSHAM HERITAGE CENTRE
CYRN Y BRAIN
ESCLUSHAM MOUNTAIN
LLWYBR CLAWDD OFFA
King's Mills
Wrexham Industrial Estate
Bowling Bank
Shocklach
Ebnal
Chorlton Lane
Malpas
Talwrn
ERDDIG
FARMWORLD
Marchwiel
Sontley
Cross Lanes
Worthenbury
Cuddington Heath
Threapwood
Pentredwr
Eglwyseg Mountain
Tainant
Johnstown
Rhosllanerchrugog
Ruabon Mountain
Stryt-issa
Penycae
Gyfelia
Cock Bank
Bangor-is-y-coed
Eyton
BANGOR
ELISEG'S PILLAR
VALLE CRUCIS ABBEY
LLANGOLLEN MOTOR MUS.
CANAL EXHIBITION CENTRE
Tallarn Green
Acrefair
Cefn-mawr
Ruabon
(Rhiwabon)
Overton Bridge
Cloy
Overton
(Owrtyn)
Llangollen
Garth
Pont Cysyllte
New Bridge
Rhos-y-Madoc
Erbistock
Lightwood Green
Horseman's Green
Eglwys Cross
TY MAWR
PLAS NEWYDD
Froncysyllte
Pentre
Halton
Dee (Dyfrdwy)
Sandy Lane
The Chequer
Hanmer
Knolton Bryn
Knolton
Penley
Street Lydan
Arowry
Pontfadog
CHIRK CASTLE
Chirk
(Y Waun)
Dudleston
Street Dinas
Ifton Heath
Dudleston Heath
FENN'S, WHIXALL & BETTISFIELD MOSS
Bronygarth
Chirk Bank
Llwynmawr
Preesgweene
Weston Rhyn
St Martin's
Breaden Heath
Elson
Welshampton
Llangollen Canal
Bettisfield
Craignant
New Marton
Ellesmere
Balmer Heath
WEM MOSS
Llechrydau
Selattyn
Hengoed
Gobowen
Perthy
COLEMERE
Lyneal
Northwood
Hindford
Tetchill
Welsh Frankton
Colemere
Pant-glas
WHITTINGTON CASTLE
Lee
Lower Frankton
Wolverley
Newtown
Cefn Canol
Llawnt
OLD OSWESTRY HILL FORT
Whittington
Hordley
English Frankton
Rhydycroesau
Babbinswood
Kenwick
Horton
Oswestry
Middleton
Lower Hordley
Cockshutt
Loppington
Llansilin
Tyn-y-coed
Wootton
Rednal
Stanwardine in the Wood
Noneley
Morda
Queen's Head
Haughton
Bagley
Trefonen
Ball
Grimpo
Petton
Burlton
Shropshire
Maesbury
Westoncommon
Weston Lullingfields
Treflach
West Felton
Maesbury Marsh
Wykey
Nantmawr
Morton
Eardiston
Marton
Myddle
Alderton
Pen-y-bont
Woolston
Stanwardine in the Fields
Porth-y-waen
Llynclys
Crickheath
Osbaston
Shotatton
Llanyblodwel
Pant
CAMBRIAN HERITAGE RAILWAY
Knockin
Brownhill
Ruyton-XI-Towns
Baschurch
Llansantffraid-ym-Mechain
Maesbrook
Dovaston
Kinnerley
Prescott
Merrington
Llanymynech
Kynaston
Hopton
Little Ness
Walford
Walford Heath
Bomere Heath
Kinton
Nesscliffe
NESSCLIFFE
Yeaton
Llandysilio
Crosslanes
Wilcott
Great Ness
Grafton
Leaton
Four Crosses
Melverley Green
Waen Fach
Pentre
Felton Butler
Forton Heath
Albrighton
Deuddwr
Llandrinio
Fitz
Sarnau
Arddleen
Melverley
Ensdon
Forton
Mytton
Criggion
Shrawardine
Montford Bridge
Severn
Drefnanney
Geufordd
Crewgreen
Coedway
Alberbury
Bicton
Wern
Severn (Hafren)
Montford
Pentrebeirdd
Ford
Coton Hill
Shelton
Middletown
Wollaston
Pool Quay
Trewern
Cardeston
Shoot Hill
Copthorne
Porthill
Guilsfield
Rowton
Hortonlane
Halfway House
Wattlesborough Heath
Yockleton
Nox
Cruckton
Meole Brace
Westbury
Hanwood
Vennington
Stoney Stretton
Edge
Lea
Bayston Hill
Annscroft
Farley
0 1 2 3 miles
0 1 2 3 4 5 km

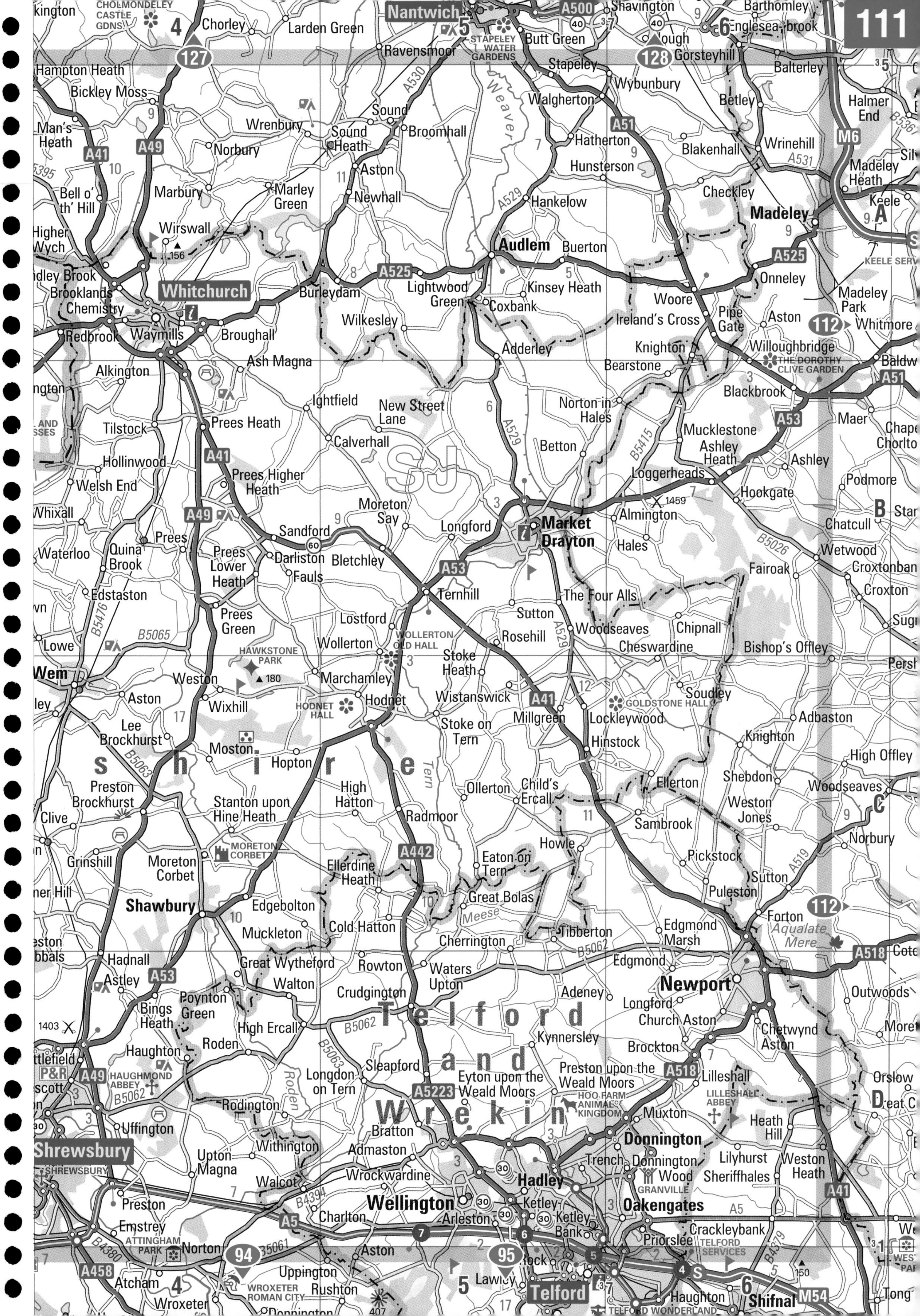
Nantwich
Whitchurch
Audlem
Market Drayton
Madeley
Wem
Shawbury
Newport
Shrewsbury
Wellington
Hadley
Donnington
Oakengates
Telford
Shifnal
Telford and Wrekin
Shropshire
SJ
Weaver
Tern
Roden
Meese
Aqualate Mere
Chorley
Larden Green
Ravensmoor
Wrenbury
Sound
Sound Heath
Broomhall
Aston
Newhall
Marbury
Marley Green
Norbury
Wirswall
Hankelow
Buerton
Hatherton
Hunsterson
Walgherton
Wybunbury
Stapeley
Butt Green
Shavington
Barthomley
Englesea-brook
Gorsteyhill
Balterley
Betley
Wrinehill
Blakenhall
Checkley
Keele
Halmer End
Madeley Heath
Onneley
Woore
Pipe Gate
Ireland's Cross
Knighton
Bearstone
Adderley
Kinsey Heath
Coxbank
Lightwood Green
Burleydam
Wilkesley
Broughall
Ash Magna
Alkington
Redbrook
Waymills
Brooklands
Chemistry
Tilstock
Prees Heath
Ightfield
New Street Lane
Calverhall
Norton in Hales
Betton
Mucklestone
Ashley Heath
Ashley
Loggerheads
Almington
Hales
Blackbrook
Willoughbridge
Aston
Whitmore
Madeley Park
Maer
Hookgate
Podmore
Chatcull
Wetwood
Fairoak
Croxton
Hollinwood
Welsh End
Whixall
Prees Higher Heath
Prees
Quina Brook
Waterloo
Prees Lower Heath
Darliston
Fauls
Sandford
Bletchley
Moreton Say
Longford
Ternhill
Edstaston
Prees Green
Lostford
Wollerton
Sutton
Rosehill
Woodseaves
The Four Alls
Chipnall
Cheswardine
Bishop's Offley
Lowe
Hawkstone Park
Weston
Aston
Wixhill
Marchamley
Hodnet
Hodnet Hall
Stoke Heath
Wistanswick
Stoke on Tern
Millgreen
Goldstone Hall
Lockleywood
Hinstock
Soudley
Adbaston
Knighton
High Offley
Lee Brockhurst
Moston
Hopton
Preston Brockhurst
Stanton upon Hine Heath
High Hatton
Radmoor
Ollerton
Child's Ercall
Ellerton
Shebdon
Woodseaves
Weston Jones
Sambrook
Norbury
Clive
Grinshill
Moreton Corbet
Ellerdine Heath
Eaton on Tern
Howle
Pickstock
Sutton
Puleston
Edgebolton
Great Bolas
Muckleton
Cold Hatton
Cherrington
Tibberton
Edgmond Marsh
Forton
Hadnall
Great Wytheford
Rowton
Waters Upton
Edgmond
Astley
Walton
Crudgington
Adeney
Longford
Church Aston
Outwoods
Bings Heath
Poynton Green
High Ercall
Kynnersley
Chetwynd Aston
Haughton
Roden
Brockton
Lilleshall
Haughmond Abbey
Longdon on Tern
Sleapford
Eyton upon the Weald Moors
Preston upon the Weald Moors
Hoo Farm Animal Kingdom
Lilleshall Abbey
Rodington
Muxton
Heath Hill
Uffington
Bratton
Withington
Admaston
Upton Magna
Trench
Donnington Wood
Lilyhurst
Sheriffhales
Weston Heath
Walcot
Wrockwardine
Granville
Preston
Charlton
Ketley
Arleston
Ketley Bank
Priorslee
Crackleybank
Emstrey
Attingham Park
Norton
Aston
Atcham
Uppington
Rushton
Wroxeter
Wroxeter Roman City
Lawley
Haughton
Telford Services
Telford Wonderland
Tong
Stapeley Water Gardens
The Dorothy Clive Garden
Wollerton Old Hall
Moreton Corbet
Cholmondeley Castle Gdns
Hampton Heath
Bickley Moss
Man's Heath
Bell o' th' Hill
Higher Wych
Keele Serv
A500
A530
A51
A529
A525
A49
A41
A53
A442
A5223
A518
A5
A458
A519
A531
B5415
B5026
B5065
B5476
B5063
B5062
B4394
B4380
B5061
B4379
M6
M54
127
128
112
94
95

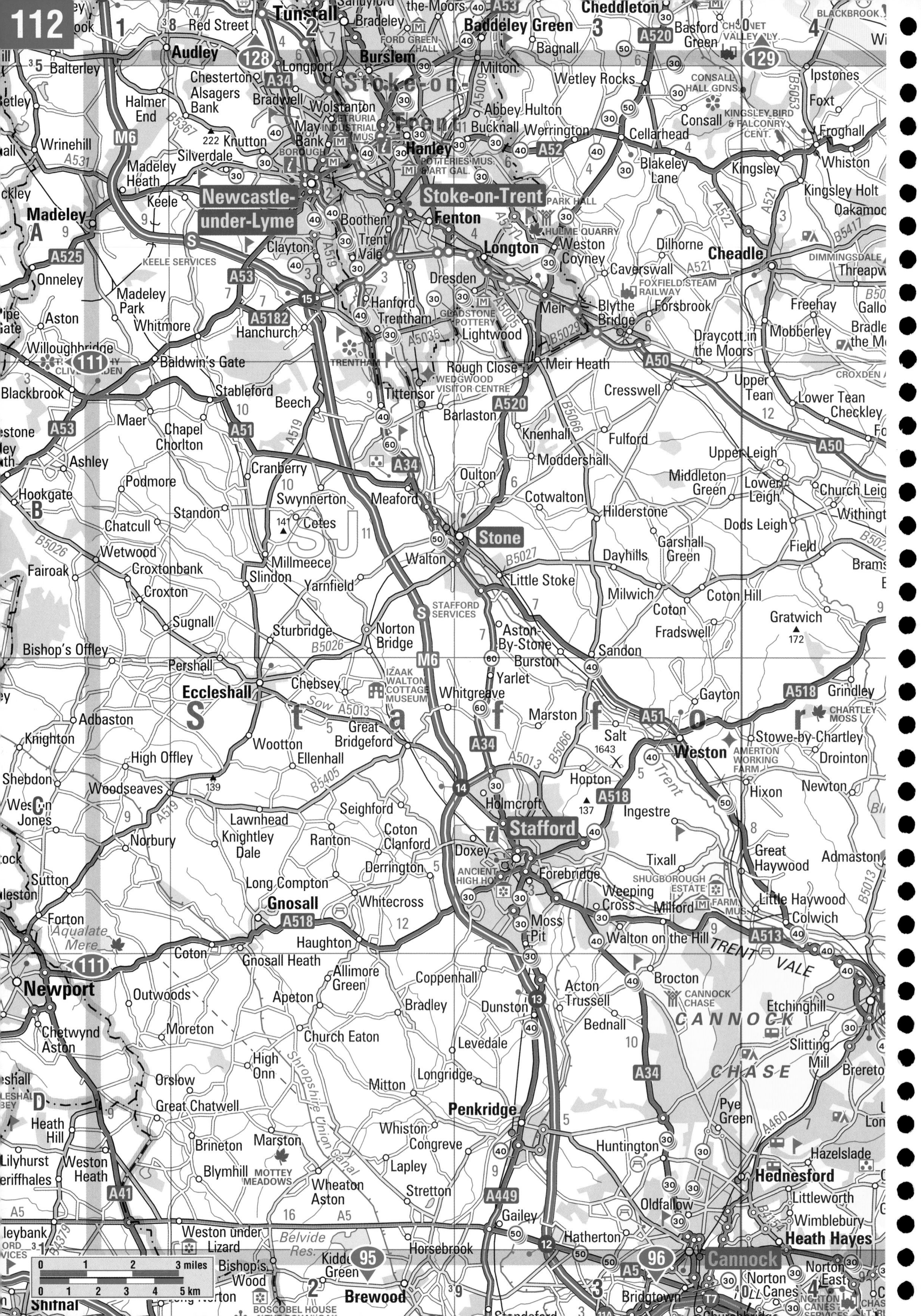
Tunstall
Cheddleton
Red Street
Bradeley
Baddeley Green
Audley
Burslem
Basford Green
Bagnall
Balterley
Longport
Milton
Wetley Rocks
Ipstones
Chesterton
Alsagers Bank
Stoke-on-Trent
Abbey Hulton
Foxt
Halmer End
Bradwell
Wolstanton
Bucknall
Werrington
Consall
Froghall
Wrinehill
Knutton
Hanley
Cellarhead
Whiston
Silverdale
Madeley Heath
Blakeley Lane
Kingsley
Keele
Newcastle-under-Lyme
Kingsley Holt
Madeley
Boothen
Fenton
Oakamoor
Clayton
Trent Vale
Longton
Weston Coyney
Dilhorne
Cheadle
Caverswall
Threapwood
Onneley
Dresden
Madeley Park
Hanford
Trentham
Meir
Blythe Bridge
Forsbrook
Freehay
Aston
Whitmore
Lightwood
Hanchurch
Draycott in the Moors
Mobberley
Willoughbridge
Baldwin's Gate
Rough Close
Meir Heath
Blackbrook
Stableford
Tittensor
Cresswell
Upper Tean
Lower Tean
Beech
Barlaston
Checkley
Maer
Chapel Chorlton
Knenhall
Fulford
Ashley
Upper Leigh
Cranberry
Moddershall
Podmore
Oulton
Middleton Green
Lower Leigh
Church Leigh
Hookgate
Swynnerton
Meaford
Cotwalton
Hilderstone
Standon
Withington
Chatcull
Cotes
Stone
Dods Leigh
Garshall Green
Wetwood
Millmeece
Walton
Dayhills
Field
Fairoak
Croxtonbank
Slindon
Yarnfield
Little Stoke
Croxton
Milwich
Coton
Coton Hill
Sugnall
Norton Bridge
Aston-By-Stone
Fradswell
Gratwich
Sturbridge
Bishop's Offley
Sandon
Pershall
Burston
Eccleshall
Chebsey
Yarlet
Grindley
Whitgreave
Gayton
Marston
Adbaston
Great Bridgeford
Salt
Stowe-by-Chartley
Knighton
Wootton
Weston
Drointon
Ellenhall
High Offley
Hopton
Shebdon
Woodseaves
Hixon
Newton
Holmcroft
Ingestre
Seighford
Lawnhead
Knightley Dale
Coton Clanford
Stafford
Norbury
Ranton
Doxey
Great Haywood
Tixall
Admaston
Derrington
Forebridge
Sutton
Long Compton
Weeping Cross
Milford
Little Haywood
Gnosall
Whitecross
Colwich
Forton
Moss Pit
Walton on the Hill
Aqualate Mere
Haughton
Coton
Gnosall Heath
Newport
Allimore Green
Coppenhall
Acton Trussell
Brocton
Outwoods
Apeton
Bradley
Dunston
Etchinghill
Bednall
Chetwynd Aston
Moreton
Church Eaton
Levedale
Slitting Mill
Cannock Chase
High Onn
Orslow
Longridge
Mitton
Great Chatwell
Penkridge
Pye Green
Heath Hill
Whiston
Brineton
Marston
Congreve
Huntington
Hazelslade
Lilyhurst
Weston Heath
Blymhill
Lapley
Hednesford
Wheaton Aston
Stretton
Oldfallow
Littleworth
Wimblebury
Gailey
Weston under Lizard
Hatherton
Heath Hayes
Horsebrook
Bishops Wood
Cannock
Norton East
Brewood
Bridgtown
Norton Canes
Shifnal
Boscobel House
Belvide Res.
Shropshire Union Canal
Trent Vale
Keele Services
Stafford Services
Izaak Walton Cottage Museum
Wedgwood Visitor Centre
Trentham
Park Hall
Hulme Quarry
Foxfield Steam Railway
Consall Hall Gdns.
Kingsley Bird & Falconry Cent.
Shugborough Estate
Amerton Working Farm
Chartley Moss
Mottey Meadows
Cannock Chase
0 1 2 3 miles
0 1 2 3 4 5 km

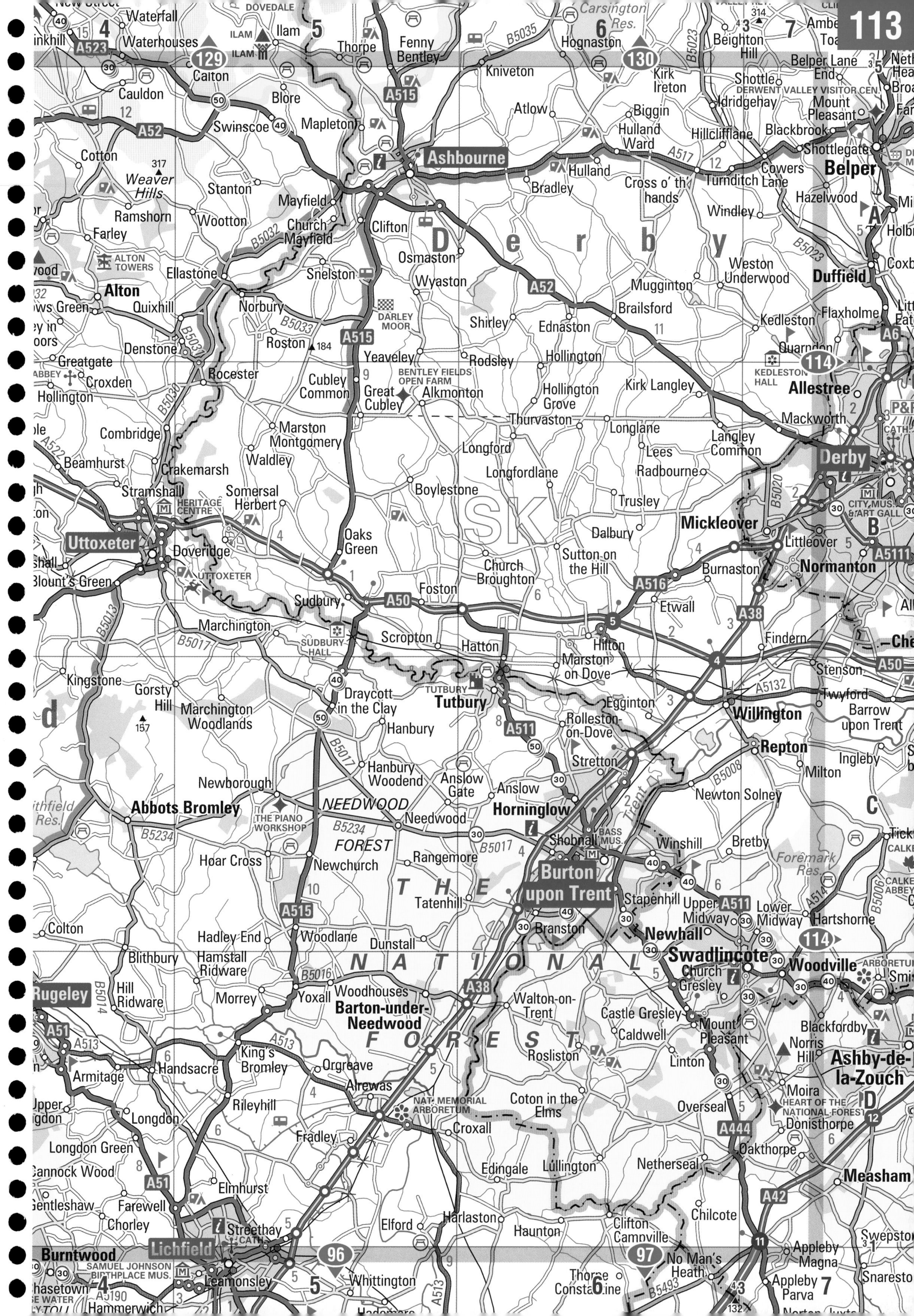

Ashbourne
Uttoxeter
Derby
Belper
Duffield
Allestree
Mickleover
Normanton
Burton upon Trent
Swadlincote
Woodville
Lichfield
Rugeley
Burntwood
Measham
Ashby-de-la-Zouch
Tutbury
Alton
Abbots Bromley
Barton-under-Needwood
Willington
Repton
Newhall
Horninglow
Littleover
NEEDWOOD FOREST
THE NATIONAL FOREST
Derby
SK
Waterfall
Waterhouses
Ilam
Thorpe
Fenny Bentley
Hognaston
Kniveton
Calton
Cauldon
Blore
Swinscoe
Mapleton
Atlow
Biggin
Hulland Ward
Hulland
Bradley
Mayfield
Stanton
Cotton
Weaver Hills
Ramshorn
Wootton
Farley
Ellastone
Church Mayfield
Clifton
Osmaston
Snelston
Wyaston
Norbury
Roston
Denstone
Rocester
Croxden
Hollington
Yeaveley
Rodsley
Shirley
Ednaston
Brailsford
Mugginton
Kirk Langley
Longford
Longlane
Thurvaston
Marston Montgomery
Waldley
Somersal Herbert
Doveridge
Sudbury
Foston
Hatton
Scropton
Hilton
Etwall
Marchington
Kingstone
Gorsty Hill
Marchington Woodlands
Draycott in the Clay
Hanbury
Hanbury Woodend
Anslow
Anslow Gate
Rolleston-on-Dove
Stretton
Newborough
Needwood
Hoar Cross
Newchurch
Rangemore
Tatenhill
Branston
Stapenhill
Winshill
Bretby
Dunstall
Yoxall
Woodhouses
Walton-on-Trent
Rosliston
Coton in the Elms
Croxall
Edingale
Lullington
Netherseal
Overseal
Linton
Caldwell
Castle Gresley
Church Gresley
Alrewas
Fradley
Orgreave
King's Bromley
Handsacre
Armitage
Longdon
Rileyhill
Elmhurst
Farewell
Chorley
Streethay
Elford
Harlaston
Haunton
Clifton Campville
No Man's Heath
Whittington
Appleby Magna
Appleby Parva
Snarestone
Oakthorpe
Donisthorpe
Moira
Blackfordby
Hartshorne
Ingleby
Milton
Newton Solney
Findern
Stenson
Twyford
Barrow upon Trent
Burnaston
Egginton
Marston on Dove
Dalbury
Sutton on the Hill
Church Broughton
Trusley
Radbourne
Lees
Langley Common
Mackworth
Kedleston
Quarndon
Weston Underwood
Windley
Hazelwood
Cowers Lane
Turnditch
Shottlegate
Blackbrook
Hillcliffane
Idridgehay
Shottle
Kirk Ireton
Beighton Hill
Mount Pleasant
Flaxholme
Cross o' th' hands
Hollington Grove
Alkmonton
Great Cubley
Cubley Common
Boylestone
Oaks Green
Longfordlane
Crakemarsh
Stramshall
Beamhurst
Combridge
Greatgate
Quixhill
Blithbury
Hamstall Ridware
Hill Ridware
Morrey
Hadley End
Woodlane
Colton
Longdon Green
Cannock Wood
Gentleshaw
Leamonsley
Hammerwich
Thorpe Constantine
Mount Pleasant
Norris Hill
Lower Midway
Upper Midway
ALTON TOWERS
DARLEY MOOR
BENTLEY FIELDS OPEN FARM
KEDLESTON HALL
SUDBURY HALL
TUTBURY
THE PIANO WORKSHOP
BASS MUS.
NAT. MEMORIAL ARBORETUM
HEART OF THE NATIONAL FOREST
SAMUEL JOHNSON BIRTHPLACE MUS.
CITY MUS. & ART GALL.
DERWENT VALLEY VISITOR CEN.
Carsington Res.
Foremark Res.
A52
A515
A50
A38
A511
A516
A5132
A444
A51
A513
A42
A5111
A6
B5017
B5234
B5033
B5032
B5030
B5013
B5016
B5014
B5035
B5023
B5008
B5020
B5493
129
130
114
96
97

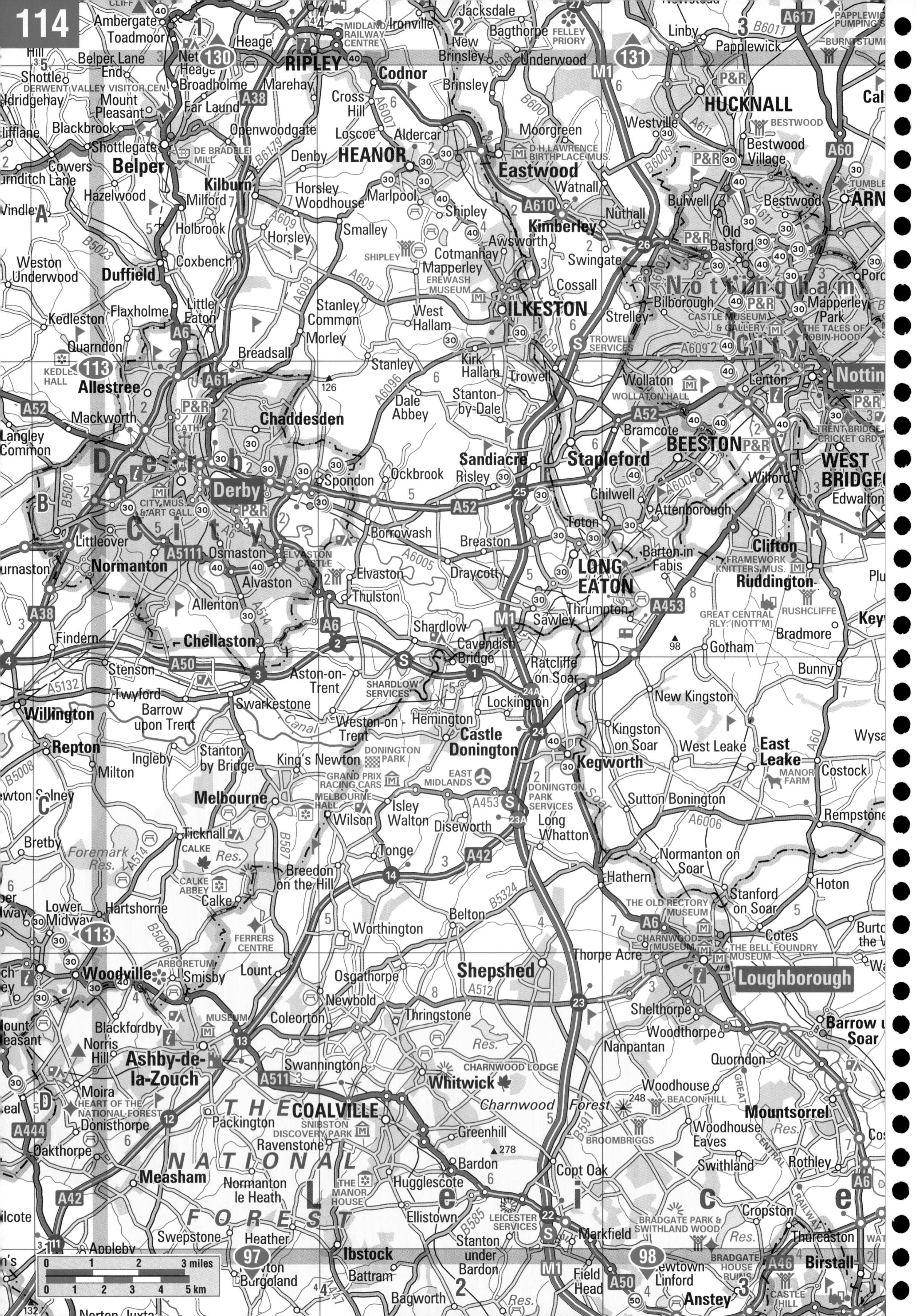
Ambergate
Toadmoor
Heage
RIPLEY
MIDLAND RAILWAY CENTRE
Ironville
Jacksdale
Bagthorpe
FELLEY PRIORY
New Brinsley
Underwood
Linby
Papplewick
PAPPLEWICK PUMPING STN
Shottle
Belper Lane End
Nether Heage
Broadholme
Marehay
Codnor
Brinsley
Cross Hill
DERWENT VALLEY VISITOR CEN.
Idridgehay
Mount Pleasant
Far Laund
Openwoodgate
Loscoe
Aldercar
Moorgreen
HUCKNALL
Westville
BESTWOOD
Bestwood Village
Blackbrook
Shottlegate
DE BRADELEI MILL
Denby
HEANOR
D.H.LAWRENCE BIRTHPLACE MUS.
Eastwood
Cowers Lane
Belper
Kilburn
Horsley Woodhouse
Marlpool
Watnall
Bulwell
Bestwood
ARN
Hazelwood
Milford
Shipley
Nuthall
Kimberley
Holbrook
Horsley
Smalley
Awsworth
Old Basford
Weston Underwood
Duffield
Coxbench
SHIPLEY
Cotmanhay
Mapperley
EREWASH MUSEUM
Swingate
Cossall
Nottingham
Bilborough
Mapperley Park
Kedleston
Flaxholme
Little Eaton
Stanley Common
West Hallam
ILKESTON
Strelley
CASTLE MUSEUM & GALLERY
THE TALES OF ROBIN HOOD
Quarndon
Morley
TROWELL SERVICES
City
KEDLESTON HALL
Allestree
Breadsall
Stanley
Kirk Hallam
Trowell
Wollaton
Lenton
Nottin
WOLLATON HALL
Mackworth
Chaddesden
Dale Abbey
Stanton-by-Dale
Bramcote
TRENT BRIDGE CRICKET GRD.
Langley Common
CATH.
BEESTON
WEST BRIDGF
Derby
Sandiacre
Stapleford
Spondon
Ockbrook
Risley
Chilwell
Wilford
Edwalton
CITY MUS. & ART GALL.
Attenborough
City
Borrowash
Toton
Clifton
Littleover
Osmaston
ELVASTON CASTLE
Breaston
Barton in Fabis
Normanton
Elvaston
Draycott
LONG EATON
FRAMEWORK KNITTERS MUS.
Ruddington
Alvaston
Thulston
Thrumpton
Allenton
Sawley
GREAT CENTRAL RLY. (NOTT'M)
RUSHCLIFFE
Findern
Chellaston
Shardlow
Cavendish Bridge
Bradmore
Gotham
Stenson
Aston-on-Trent
Ratcliffe on Soar
Bunny
SHARDLOW SERVICES
Twyford
Willington
Barrow upon Trent
Swarkestone
Weston-on-Trent
Hemington
Lockington
New Kingston
Kingston on Soar
Repton
Ingleby
Stanton by Bridge
King's Newton
Castle Donington
DONINGTON PARK
West Leake
East Leake
Costock
Milton
GRAND PRIX RACING CARS
EAST MIDLANDS
Kegworth
MANOR FARM
Newton Solney
Melbourne
MELBOURNE HALL
DONINGTON PARK SERVICES
Sutton Bonington
Wilson
Isley Walton
Diseworth
Long Whatton
Rempstone
Bretby
Ticknall
Foremark Res.
CALKE
Tonge
Normanton on Soar
Breedon on the Hill
Hathern
Hoton
CALKE ABBEY
Calke
THE OLD RECTORY MUSEUM
Stanford on Soar
Lower Midway
Hartshorne
Belton
Worthington
CHARNWOOD MUSEUM
Cotes
THE BELL FOUNDRY MUSEUM
FERRERS CENTRE
Thorpe Acre
Loughborough
Woodville
ARBORETUM
Smisby
Lount
Osgathorpe
Shepshed
Newbold
Shelthorpe
Coleorton
Thringstone
Blackfordby
MUSEUM
Woodthorpe
Barrow upon Soar
Norris Hill
Ashby-de-la-Zouch
Nanpantan
Quorndon
Moira
Swannington
CHARNWOOD LODGE
Whitwick
Woodhouse
HEART OF THE NATIONAL FOREST
THE NATIONAL FOREST
COALVILLE
Charnwood Forest
BEACON HILL
Mountsorrel
Donisthorpe
Packington
SNIBSTON DISCOVERY PARK
Greenhill
BROOMBRIGGS
Woodhouse Eaves
Oakthorpe
Ravenstone
Bardon
Copt Oak
Swithland
Rothley
Measham
Normanton le Heath
THE MANOR HOUSE
Hugglescote
Leicester
Cropston
Ellistown
LEICESTER SERVICES
BRADGATE PARK & SWITHLAND WOOD
Swepstone
Heather
Markfield
Thurcaston
Appleby
Stanton under Bardon
Ibstock
Newton Burgoland
Battram
Field Head
Newtown Linford
BRADGATE HOUSE RUINS
Birstall
Bagworth
Anstey
CASTLE HILL
0 1 2 3 miles
0 1 2 3 4 5 km

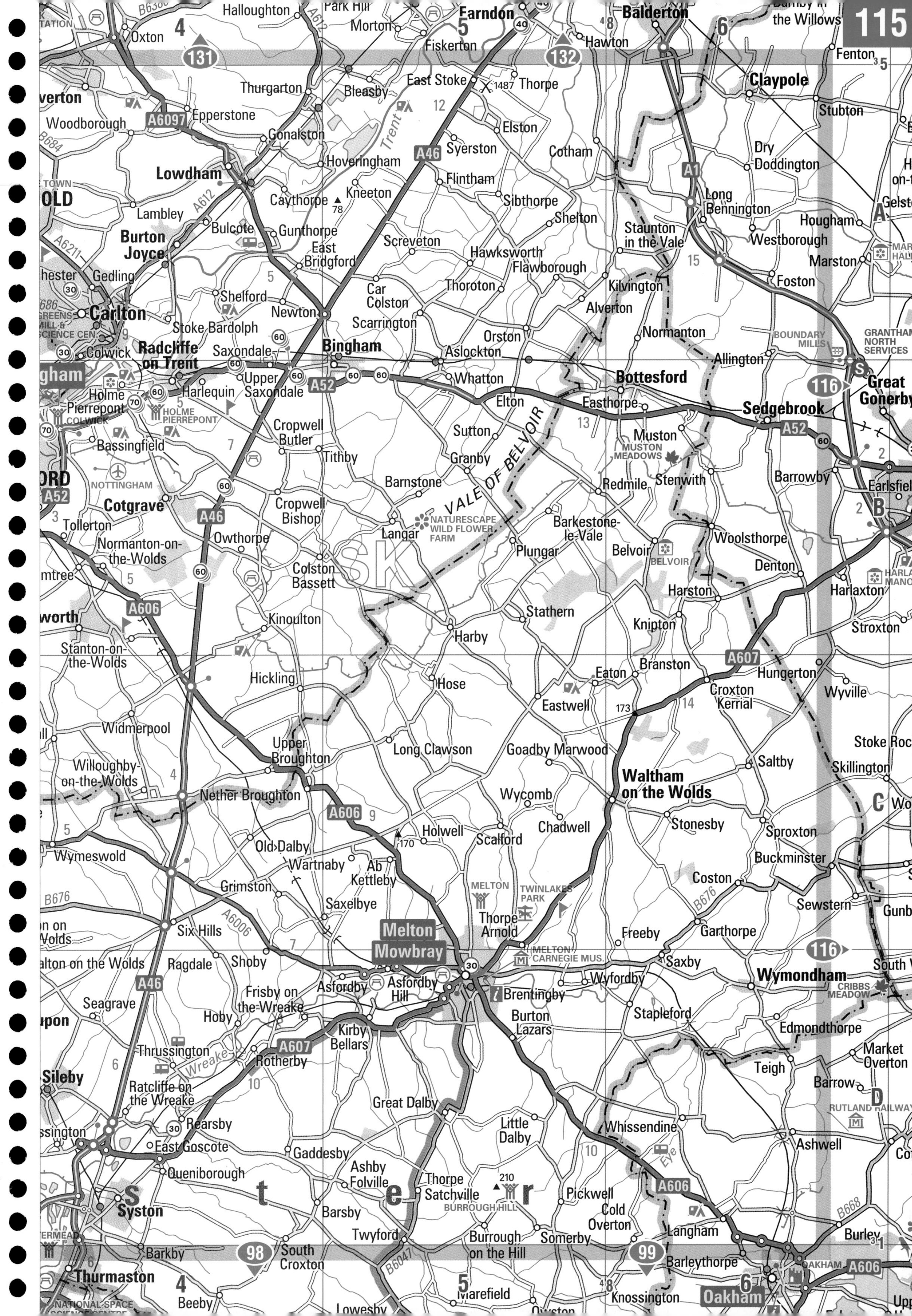

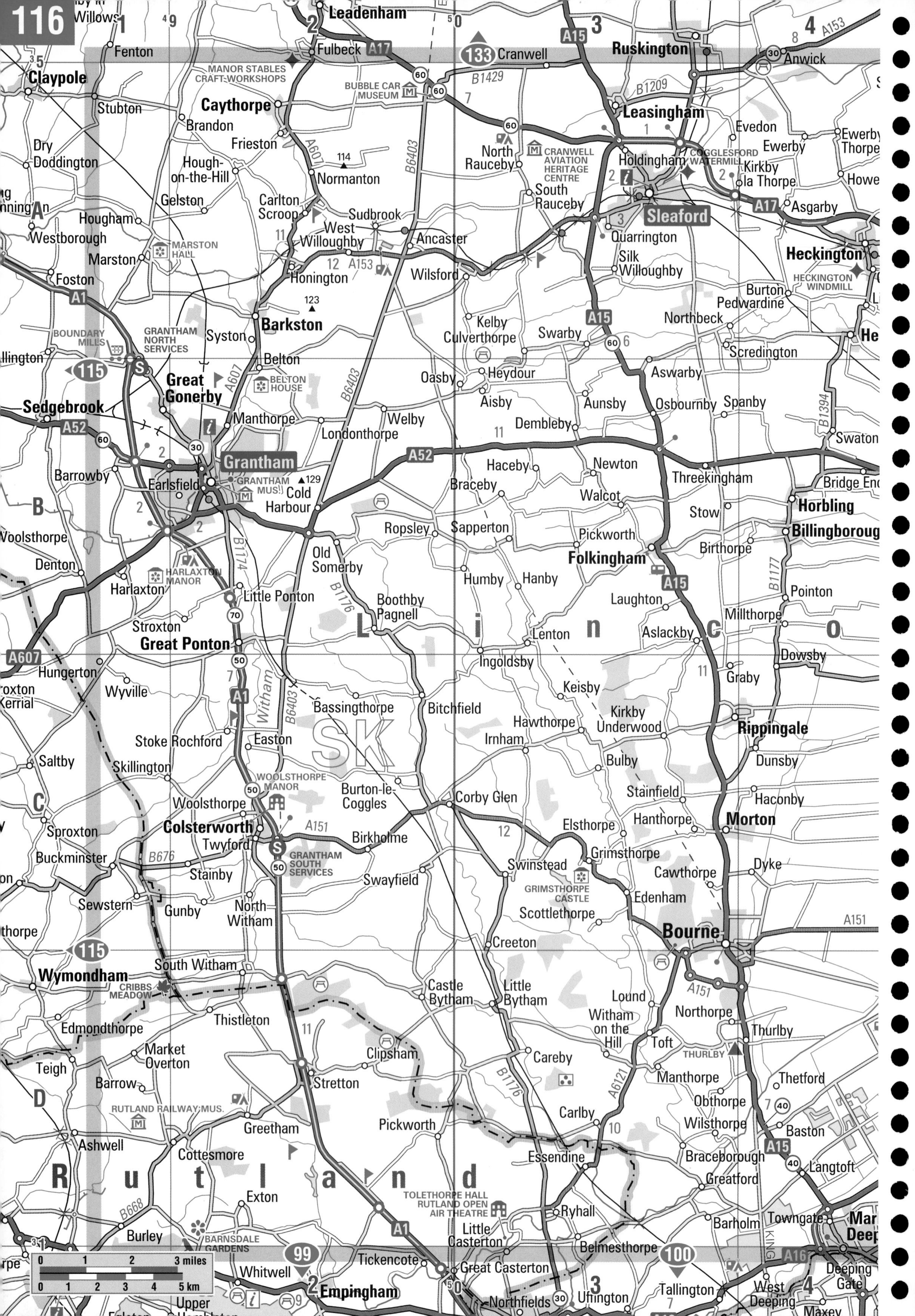
Leadenham
Fulbeck
Fenton
Claypole
MANOR STABLES CRAFT WORKSHOPS
133 Cranwell
Ruskington
Anwick
BUBBLE CAR MUSEUM
B1429
B1209
Stubton
Caythorpe
Brandon
Leasingham
Evedon
Ewerby
Ewerby Thorpe
Frieston
Dry Doddington
Hough-on-the-Hill
Normanton
North Rauceby
CRANWELL AVIATION HERITAGE CENTRE
Holdingham
COGGLESFORD WATERMILL
Kirkby la Thorpe
Howell
South Rauceby
Sleaford
Asgarby
Gelston
Carlton Scroop
Sudbrook
Hougham
Westborough
West Willoughby
Ancaster
Quarrington
MARSTON HALL
Marston
A153
Wilsford
Silk Willoughby
Heckington
Foston
Honington
HECKINGTON WINDMILL
Burton Pedwardine
A1
Barkston
Northbeck
BOUNDARY MILLS
GRANTHAM NORTH SERVICES
Syston
Kelby
Culverthorpe
Swarby
Scredington
Belton
115
Great Gonerby
BELTON HOUSE
Oasby
Heydour
Aswarby
Aisby
Aunsby
Osbournby
Spanby
Sedgebrook
A607
B6403
B1394
Manthorpe
Welby
Londonthorpe
Dembleby
Swaton
A52
Grantham
Barrowby
Earlsfield
GRANTHAM MUS.
Cold Harbour
Haceby
Newton
Braceby
Threekingham
Bridge End
Horbling
Billingborough
Walcot
Stow
Woolsthorpe
Ropsley
Sapperton
Pickworth
Folkingham
Birthorpe
Denton
Old Somerby
HARLAXTON MANOR
Harlaxton
Humby
Hanby
B1174
B1177
Pointon
Little Ponton
Boothby Pagnell
Laughton
Millthorpe
Stroxton
Great Ponton
Lenton
Aslackby
Ingoldsby
Dowsby
Hungerton
Graby
Keisby
Croxton Kerrial
Wyville
Bassingthorpe
Bitchfield
Hawthorpe
Kirkby Underwood
Rippingale
Witham
Irnham
Saltby
Stoke Rochford
Easton
Bulby
Dunsby
Skillington
WOOLSTHORPE MANOR
Burton-le-Coggles
Stainfield
Corby Glen
Haconby
Woolsthorpe
Colsterworth
Hanthorpe
Elsthorpe
Morton
Sproxton
A151
Birkholme
Twyford
Grimsthorpe
Buckminster
B676
GRANTHAM SOUTH SERVICES
Swinstead
Stainby
Dyke
Swayfield
Cawthorpe
GRIMSTHORPE CASTLE
Sewstern
Gunby
North Witham
Edenham
Scottlethorpe
Bourne
Creeton
South Witham
Wymondham
CRIBBS MEADOW
Castle Bytham
Little Bytham
Lound
Witham on the Hill
Northorpe
Thistleton
Edmondthorpe
Thurlby
Toft
Clipsham
Market Overton
Careby
Teigh
THURLBY
Barrow
Stretton
Manthorpe
Thetford
B1176
A6121
Obthorpe
RUTLAND RAILWAY MUS.
Carlby
Baston
Wilsthorpe
Greetham
Pickworth
Ashwell
Cottesmore
Essendine
Braceborough
Langtoft
R u t l a n d
Greatford
Exton
TOLETHORPE HALL RUTLAND OPEN AIR THEATRE
Ryhall
B668
Barholm
Towngate
Market Deeping
Burley
BARNSDALE GARDENS
Little Casterton
Belmesthorpe
99
100
A16
Tickencote
Great Casterton
Whitwell
Deeping Gate
West Deeping
Empingham
Uffington
Tallington
Northfields
Maxey
0 1 2 3 miles
0 1 2 3 4 5 km
SK
L i n c o

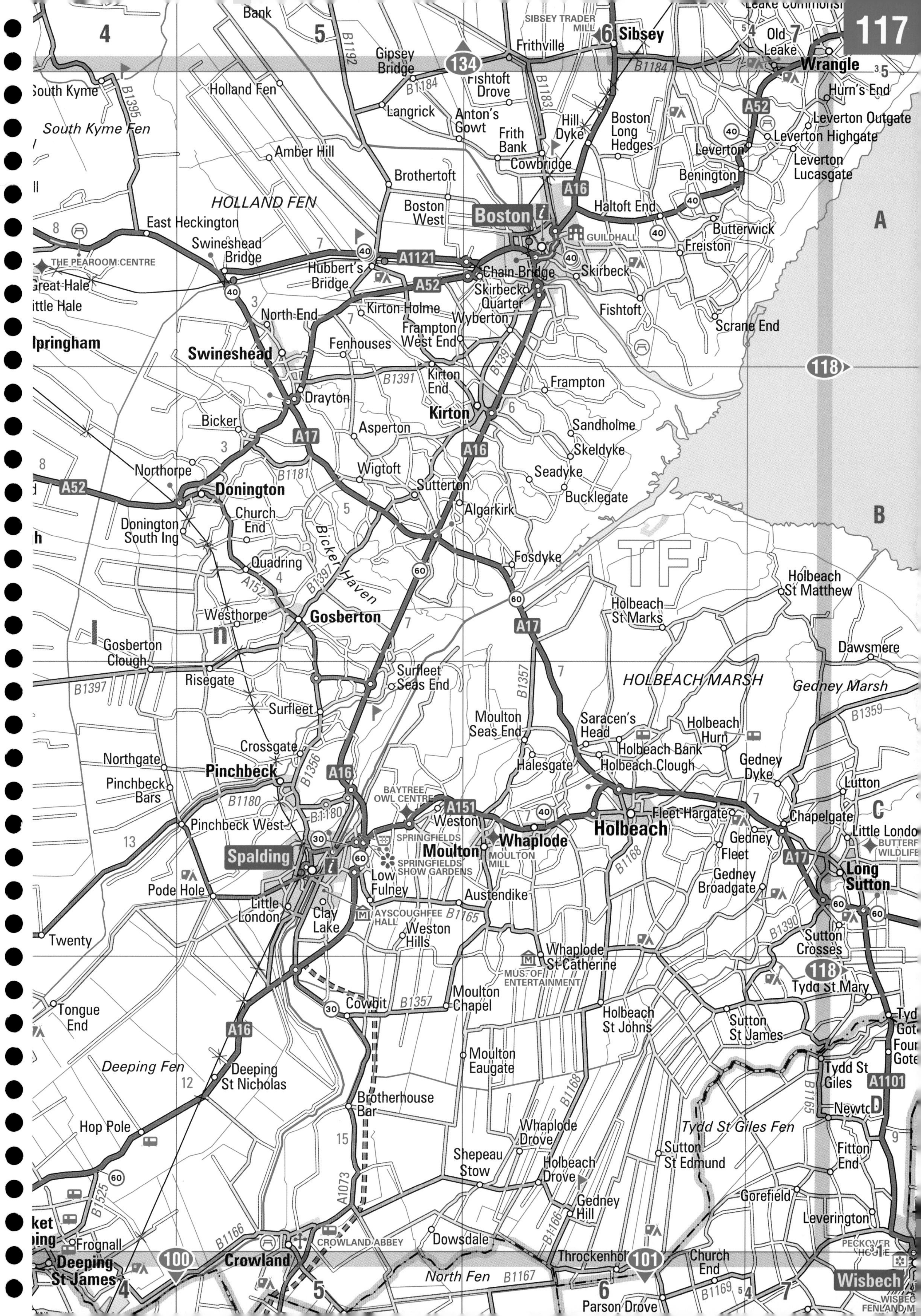

Boston
Spalding
Holbeach
Long Sutton
Wisbech
Crowland
Deeping St James
Sibsey
Wrangle
Kirton
Swineshead
Donington
Gosberton
Pinchbeck
Moulton
Whaplode
HOLLAND FEN
HOLBEACH MARSH
Gedney Marsh
South Kyme Fen
Deeping Fen
Tydd St Giles Fen
Bicker Haven
TF
A16
A17
A52
A151
A1121
A1101
A1073
B1397
B1357
B1168
B1165
B1166
134
118
100
101
THE PEAROOM CENTRE
GUILDHALL
BAYTREE OWL CENTRE
SPRINGFIELDS
SPRINGFIELDS SHOW GARDENS
MOULTON MILL
AYSCOUGHFEE HALL
MUS. OF ENTERTAINMENT
CROWLAND ABBEY
SIBSEY TRADER MILL
BUTTERFLY WILDLIFE
PECKOVER HOUSE

Wrangle
Lowgate
Friskney Flats
Hurn's End
Leverton Outgate
Leverton Highgate
Leverton Lucasgate
BOSTON DEEPS
LYNN DEEPS
THE WASH
NORFOLK
BIRD OBSERVATORY RESERVE
Old Hunstanton
Hunstanton
SEA LIFE SANCTUARY
Heacham
Lynn Channel
SNETTISHAM NATURE RESERVE
Shepherd's Port
Holbeach St Matthew
Dawsmere
Gedney Marsh
Gedney Drove End
THE WASH
DERSINGHAM BOG
SANDRINGHAM
Wolferton
Gedney Dyke
Lutton
Guy's Head
Chapelgate
Little London
BUTTERFLY & WILDLIFE PARK
Long Sutton
Terrington Marsh
Ongar Hill
Castle Rising
CASTLE RISING
North Wootton
South Wootton
Roydon
ROYDON COMMON
King's Lynn
MARITIME EXHIBITION
Gaywood
Sutton Bridge
Orange Row
Clenchwarton
Sutton Crosses
Walpole Cross Keys
Terrington St Clement
West Lynn
GUILDHALL
Fairstead
Tydd St Mary
Hardwick
Leziate
Sutton St James
Tydd Gote
Walpole St Andrew
Hay Green
Tilney High End
Tilney All Saints
Fair Green
Tower End
Four Gotes
Walpole Marsh
Walpole St Peter
West Winch
Middleton
Tydd St Giles
Saddle Bow
North Runcton
East Winch
Newton
Ingleborough
St John's Highway
Terrington St John
Wiggenhall St Germans
Blackborough End
St Giles Fen
West Walton
Tilney St Lawrence
Setchey
Fitton End
Walpole Highway
Wiggenhall St Mary the Virgin
Tottenhill Row
West Walton Highway
Marshland
Gorefield
St John's Fen End
Wiggenhall St Mary Magdalen
Watlington
Wormegay
Leverington
FENLAND AVIATION MUS.
Walsoken
Tottenhill
PECKOVER HOUSE
Runcton Holme
Shouldham
New Walsoken
Marshland St James
Marshland Fen
FENLAND MUS.
South
0 1 2 3 miles
0 1 2 3 4 5 km

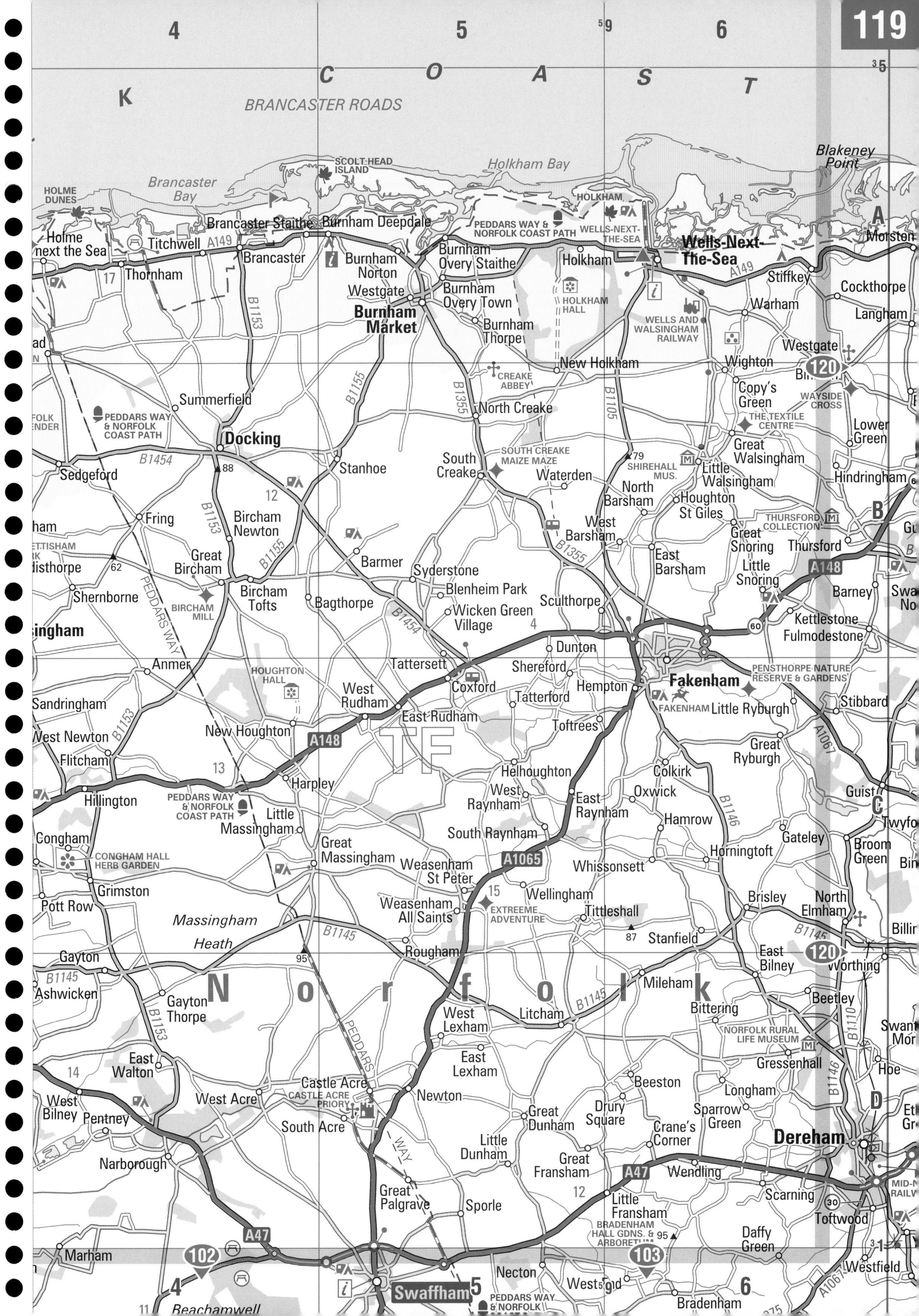
4
5
6
C O A S T
K
BRANCASTER ROADS
SCOLT HEAD ISLAND
Holkham Bay
Blakeney Point
Brancaster Bay
HOLME DUNES
Holme next the Sea
Titchwell
Brancaster Staithe
Burnham Deepdale
Brancaster
Thornham
Burnham Norton
Westgate
Burnham Market
Burnham Overy Staithe
Burnham Overy Town
Burnham Thorpe
PEDDARS WAY & NORFOLK COAST PATH
HOLKHAM
WELLS-NEXT-THE-SEA
Holkham
HOLKHAM HALL
Wells-Next-The-Sea
Stiffkey
Morston
Cockthorpe
Warham
Langham
WELLS AND WALSINGHAM RAILWAY
Westgate
Wighton
New Holkham
CREAKE ABBEY
Copy's Green
WAYSIDE CROSS
THE TEXTILE CENTRE
Lower Green
Summerfield
Docking
North Creake
SOUTH CREAKE MAIZE MAZE
South Creake
Waterden
SHIREHALL MUS.
Little Walsingham
Great Walsingham
Hindringham
Sedgeford
Stanhoe
North Barsham
Houghton St Giles
Fring
Bircham Newton
West Barsham
Great Snoring
THURSFORD COLLECTION
Thursford
Great Bircham
Barmer
East Barsham
Little Snoring
Shernborne
Bircham Tofts
Syderstone
Blenheim Park
Sculthorpe
Barney
BIRCHAM MILL
Bagthorpe
Wicken Green Village
Kettlestone
Fulmodestone
PEDDARS WAY
Dunton
Anmer
HOUGHTON HALL
Tattersett
Shereford
Coxford
Hempton
Fakenham
PENSTHORPE NATURE RESERVE & GARDENS
FAKENHAM
Little Ryburgh
Stibbard
Sandringham
West Rudham
East Rudham
Tatterford
Toftrees
West Newton
New Houghton
TF
Great Ryburgh
Flitcham
Helhoughton
Colkirk
Harpley
Hillington
West Raynham
East Raynham
Oxwick
Guist
PEDDARS WAY & NORFOLK COAST PATH
Little Massingham
Hamrow
Congham
South Raynham
Gateley
CONGHAM HALL HERB GARDEN
Great Massingham
Weasenham St Peter
Whissonsett
Horningtoft
Broom Green
Grimston
Wellingham
Brisley
North Elmham
Pott Row
Weasenham All Saints
EXTREME ADVENTURE
Tittleshall
Massingham Heath
Stanfield
Rougham
Gayton
East Bilney
Worthing
Ashwicken
Gayton Thorpe
N o r f o l k
Mileham
Beetley
West Lexham
Litcham
Bittering
NORFOLK RURAL LIFE MUSEUM
East Lexham
Gressenhall
Hoe
East Walton
Castle Acre
CASTLE ACRE PRIORY
Beeston
West Bilney
West Acre
Newton
Longham
Pentney
Great Dunham
Drury Square
Sparrow Green
South Acre
Crane's Corner
Dereham
Little Dunham
Narborough
Great Fransham
Wendling
Scarning
Great Palgrave
Little Fransham
Sporle
BRADENHAM HALL GDNS. & ARBORETUM
Toftwood
Daffy Green
Marham
Necton
Westfield
Swaffham
West End
Bradenham
Beachamwell
A149
A148
A1065
A47
A1067
B1153
B1155
B1355
B1105
B1454
B1145
B1146
B1110
102
103
120

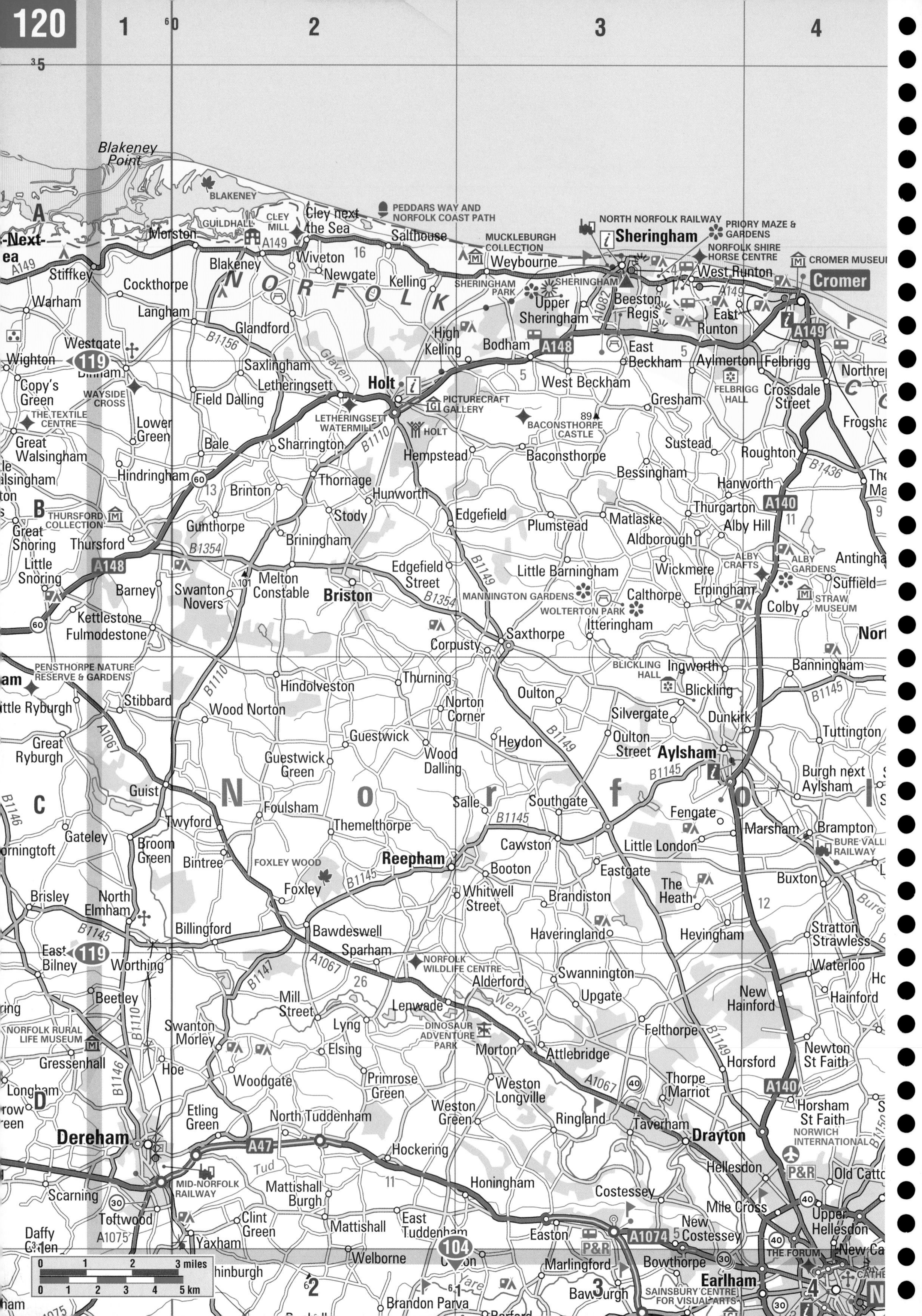

120
Blakeney Point
BLAKENEY
GUILDHALL
CLEY MILL
Cley next the Sea
PEDDARS WAY AND NORFOLK COAST PATH
Salthouse
MUCKLEBURGH COLLECTION
NORTH NORFOLK RAILWAY
Sheringham
PRIORY MAZE & GARDENS
NORFOLK SHIRE HORSE CENTRE
CROMER MUSEUM
Cromer
Morston
Stiffkey
Blakeney
Wiveton
Newgate
Kelling
Weybourne
SHERINGHAM PARK
SHERINGHAM
Upper Sheringham
Beeston Regis
West Runton
East Runton
Cockthorpe
Warham
Langham
Glandford
NORFOLK
High Kelling
Bodham
East Beckham
Aylmerton
Felbrigg
Westgate
Wighton
Binham
Copy's Green
WAYSIDE CROSS
THE TEXTILE CENTRE
Saxlingham
Glaven
Letheringsett
Holt
PICTURECRAFT GALLERY
LETHERINGSETT WATERMILL
HOLT
West Beckham
Gresham
FELBRIGG HALL
Crossdale Street
Northrepps
Frogshall
Field Dalling
Lower Green
Great Walsingham
Bale
Sharrington
Hindringham
Brinton
Thornage
Hunworth
Hempstead
BACONSTHORPE CASTLE
Baconsthorpe
Sustead
Roughton
Bessingham
Hanworth
THURSFORD COLLECTION
Great Snoring
Thursford
Gunthorpe
Stody
Briningham
Edgefield
Plumstead
Matlaske
Thurgarton
Alby Hill
Aldborough
Little Snoring
Barney
Swanton Novers
Melton Constable
Briston
Edgefield Street
Little Barningham
Wickmere
ALBY CRAFTS
ALBY GARDENS
Antingham
Suffield
Kettlestone
Fulmodestone
MANNINGTON GARDENS
WOLTERTON PARK
Calthorpe
Erpingham
Colby
STRAW MUSEUM
Corpusty
Saxthorpe
Itteringham
PENSTHORPE NATURE RESERVE & GARDENS
Hindolveston
Thurning
BLICKLING HALL
Ingworth
Blickling
Banningham
Little Ryburgh
Stibbard
Wood Norton
Norton Corner
Oulton
Silvergate
Dunkirk
Great Ryburgh
Guestwick
Heydon
Oulton Street
Aylsham
Tuttington
Guestwick Green
Wood Dalling
Burgh next Aylsham
Guist
NORFOLK
Salle
Southgate
Fengate
Gateley
Twyford
Foulsham
Themelthorpe
Cawston
Marsham
Brampton
BURE VALLEY RAILWAY
Broom Green
Bintree
FOXLEY WOOD
Reepham
Booton
Little London
Eastgate
Buxton
Brisley
North Elmham
Foxley
Whitwell Street
Brandiston
The Heath
Bawdeswell
Billingford
Haveringland
Hevingham
Stratton Strawless
East Bilney
Worthing
Sparham
NORFOLK WILDLIFE CENTRE
Alderford
Swannington
Waterloo
Beetley
Mill Street
Lenwade
Upgate
New Hainford
Hainford
Wensum
NORFOLK RURAL LIFE MUSEUM
Swanton Morley
Lyng
DINOSAUR ADVENTURE PARK
Felthorpe
Gressenhall
Hoe
Elsing
Morton
Attlebridge
Horsford
Newton St Faith
Woodgate
Primrose Green
Weston Longville
Thorpe Marriot
Longham
Etling Green
Weston Green
Ringland
Taverham
Horsham St Faith
NORWICH INTERNATIONAL
Dereham
North Tuddenham
Drayton
Hockering
Hellesdon
MID-NORFOLK RAILWAY
Tud
Mattishall Burgh
Honingham
Old Catton
Scarning
Costessey
Toftwood
Clint Green
Mattishall
East Tuddenham
Easton
Mile Cross
New Costessey
Upper Hellesdon
Daffy Green
Yaxham
Welborne
Marlingford
Bowthorpe
THE FORUM
New Catton
Earlham
SAINSBURY CENTRE FOR VISUAL ARTS
Bawburgh
Brandon Parva
Yare
0 1 2 3 miles
0 1 2 3 4 5 km

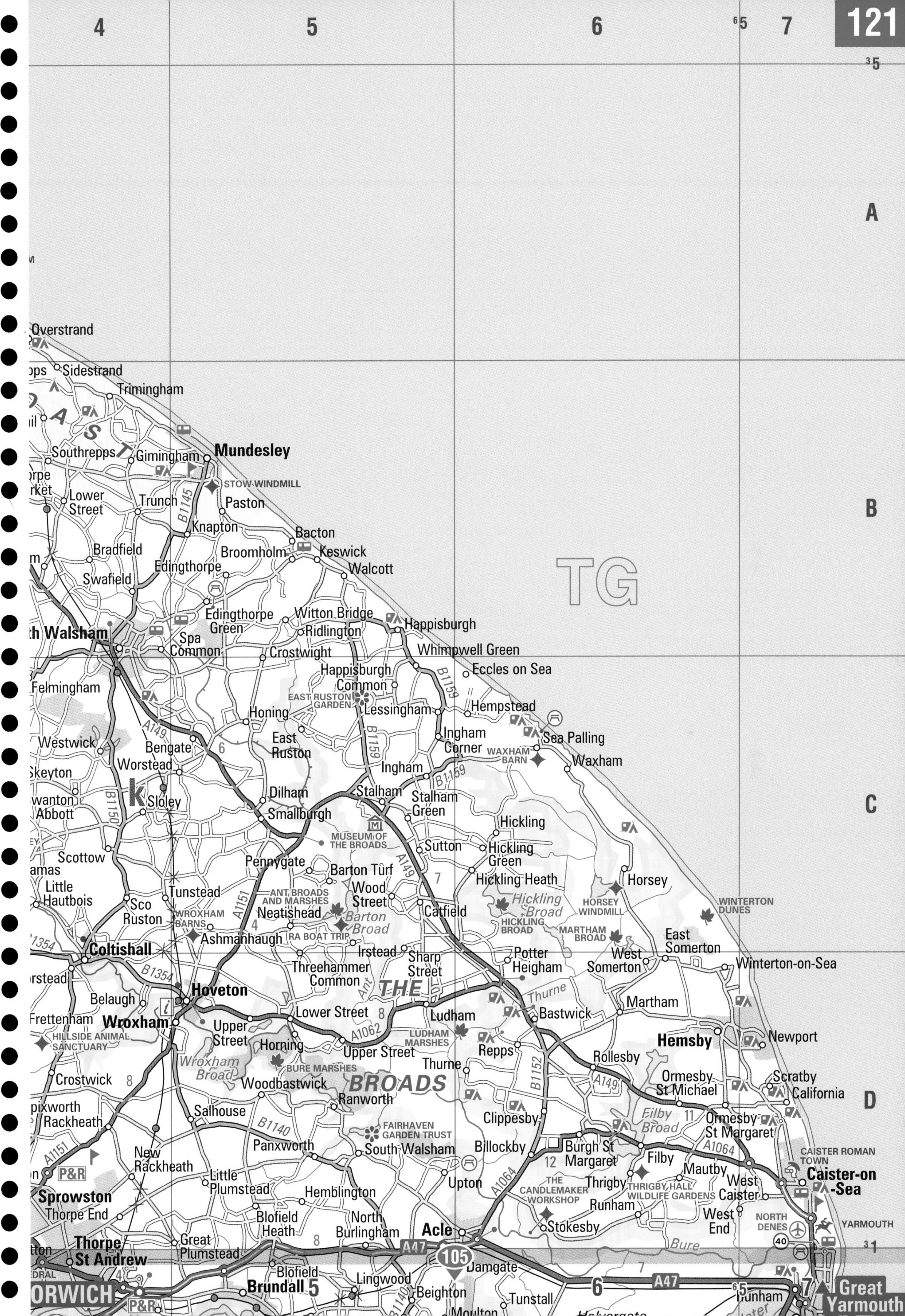
4
5
6
7
A
B
C
D
TG
Overstrand
Sidestrand
Trimingham
Southrepps
Gimingham
Mundesley
STOW WINDMILL
Lower Street
Trunch
Paston
Knapton
Bacton
Bradfield
Broomholm
Keswick
Walcott
Swafield
Edingthorpe
Edingthorpe Green
Witton Bridge
Happisburgh
Ridlington
Spa Common
Crostwight
Whimpwell Green
Eccles on Sea
Happisburgh Common
Felmingham
EAST RUSTON GARDEN
Lessingham
Hempstead
Honing
Westwick
Bengate
East Ruston
Ingham Corner
Sea Palling
WAXHAM BARN
Waxham
Worstead
Ingham
Skeyton
Sloley
Dilham
Stalham
Stalham Green
Smallburgh
Hickling
MUSEUM OF THE BROADS
Sutton
Hickling Green
Scottow
Pennygate
Barton Turf
Little Hautbois
Tunstead
Wood Street
Hickling Heath
Horsey
ANT BROADS AND MARSHES
Sco Ruston
Neatishead
Catfield
Hickling Broad
HORSEY WINDMILL
WINTERTON DUNES
WROXHAM BARNS
Barton Broad
HICKLING BROAD
MARTHAM BROAD
Ashmanhaugh
RA BOAT TRIP
East Somerton
Coltishall
Irstead
Sharp Street
Potter Heigham
West Somerton
Winterton-on-Sea
Threehammer Common
Belaugh
Hoveton
THE
Thurne
Bastwick
Martham
Frettenham
Wroxham
Lower Street
Ludham
Upper Street
HILLSIDE ANIMAL SANCTUARY
Horning
LUDHAM MARSHES
Repps
Hemsby
Newport
Upper Street
Rollesby
Wroxham Broad
Thurne
Crostwick
BURE MARSHES
Ormesby St Michael
Scratby
California
Woodbastwick
BROADS
Ranworth
Salhouse
Clippesby
Filby Broad
Ormesby St Margaret
Rackheath
FAIRHAVEN GARDEN TRUST
Panxworth
South Walsham
Billockby
Burgh St Margaret
Filby
New Rackheath
CAISTER ROMAN TOWN
Caister-on-Sea
Mautby
Little Plumstead
Upton
Thrigby
THRIGBY HALL WILDLIFE GARDENS
West Caister
Sprowston
THE CANDLEMAKER WORKSHOP
Hemblington
Runham
Thorpe End
Blofield Heath
North Burlingham
West End
NORTH DENES
YARMOUTH
Acle
Stokesby
Thorpe St Andrew
Great Plumstead
Bure
Damgate
Blofield
Lingwood
Brundall
Beighton
NORWICH
Tunstall
Runham
Great Yarmouth
Moulton
A47
A149
A1151
A1062
A1064
B1145
B1159
B1150
B1354
B1152
B1140
A1064
P&R

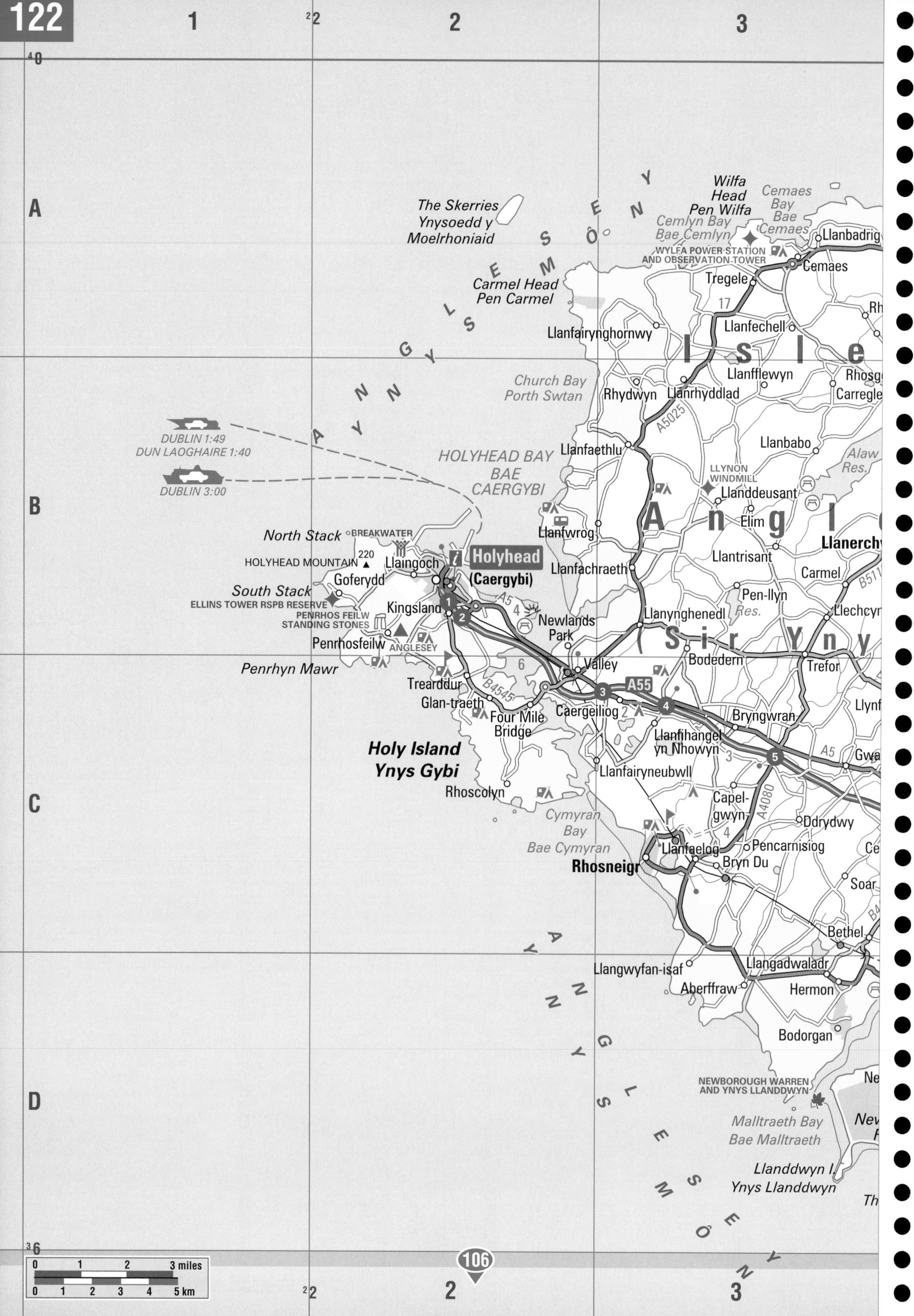
1
2
3
A
B
C
D
The Skerries
Ynysoedd y
Moelrhoniaid
Wilfa
Head
Pen Wilfa
Cemaes
Bay
Bae
Cemaes
Cemlyn Bay
Bae Cemlyn
WYLFA POWER STATION
AND OBSERVATION TOWER
Llanbadrig
Cemaes
Tregele
Carmel Head
Pen Carmel
Llanfechell
Llanfairynghornwy
Isle
Church Bay
Porth Swtan
Rhydwyn
Llanrhyddlad
Llanfflewyn
Rhosgo
Carregle
A5025
Llanbabo
Llanfaethlu
Alaw
Res.
HOLYHEAD BAY
BAE
CAERGYBI
LLYNON
WINDMILL
Llanddeusant
DUBLIN 1:49
DUN LAOGHAIRE 1:40
DUBLIN 3:00
Anglesey
Elim
Llanfwrog
North Stack
BREAKWATER
HOLYHEAD MOUNTAIN
220
Llaingoch
Holyhead
(Caergybi)
Llantrisant
Llanerch
Llanfachraeth
Carmel
Goferydd
South Stack
ELLINS TOWER RSPB RESERVE
Pen-llyn
Kingsland
PENRHOS FEILW
STANDING STONES
A5
Newlands
Park
Llanynghenedl
Res.
Llechcyn
Penrhosfeilw
ANGLESEY
Sir Ynys
Bodedern
Trefor
Penrhyn Mawr
Valley
Trearddur
A55
B4545
Glan-traeth
Four Mile
Bridge
Caergeiliog
Bryngwran
Llanfihangel
yn Nhowyn
Llynf
A5
Holy Island
Ynys Gybi
Llanfairyneubwll
A4080
Rhoscolyn
Capel-
gwyn
Ddrydwy
Cymyran
Bay
Bae Cymyran
Llanfaelog
Pencarnisiog
Rhosneigr
Bryn Du
Soar
Bethel
Llangwyfan-isaf
Llangadwaladr
Aberffraw
Hermon
Bodorgan
NEWBOROUGH WARREN
AND YNYS LLANDDWYN
Malltraeth Bay
Bae Malltraeth
Llanddwyn I.
Ynys Llanddwyn
ANGLESEY
YNYS MÔN
0
1
2
3 miles
0
1
2
3
4
5 km

4
5
6
A
B
D
SH
ANGLESEY MÔN
Isle of Anglesey (Ynys Môn)
Bull Bay
Porth Llechog
Porthllechog
Burwen
Amlwch Port
Amlwch
Point Lynas
Trwyn Eilian
Llaneilian
Pengorffwysfa
Rhosbeirio
Bodewryd
Penysarn
Nebo
Dulas
Dulas Bay
Bae Dulas
A5025
B5111
Rhosybol
Tyn-y-pwll
City Dulas
Brynrefail
Moelfre
Gwredog
Ty-mawr
Llanallgo
Llandyfrydog
Mynydd Bodafon
Hebron
Marianglas
Llannerch-y-medd
Bachau
Maenaddwyn
Tynygongl
Brynteg
Benllech
B5108
Capel Coch
CORS ERDDREINIOG
Red Wharf Bay
Traeth-coch
Red Wharf Bay
Llanfihangel Ysgeifiog
Llanfarwy
CORS GOCH
Llanbedrgoch
Puffin Island
Ynys Seiriol
Mariandyrys
Glan-yr-afon
Caim
Penmon
Tregaian
B5110
Llangwyllog
Tan-y-graig
Llanddona
Llangoed
Llanddyfnan
Pentraeth
B5109
Glan Gors
THE STONE SCIENCE
Rhosmeirch
CORS BODEILIO
Llanfaes
Res.
Bodffordd
ORIEL YNYS MON
Talwrn
Pen-y-garnedd
B5109
Llechcynfarwy
Heneglwys
Rhoscefnhir
Llansadwrn
GAOL AND COURTHOUSE
Beaumaris
Penmaenmawr
Llangefni
Ceint
A5114
Lavan Sands
Traeth Lafan
Llanfairfechan
Nant-y-pandy
Penmynydd
B5420
Llandegfan
A545
Trefor
Gwalchmai
Llangristiolus
JAMES PRINGLE WEAVERS
PILI PALAS
Menai Bridge
(Porthaethwy)
TEGFRYN
Garth
Hirael
PENRHYN
A55
Abergwyngregyn
Bodorgan
Llangaffo
HENBLAS COUNTRY PARK
A5
Capel Mawr
Pentre Berw
Gaerwen
Llanfairpwll -gwyngyll
Coed Mawr
Bangor
Llandegai
BANGOR
Crymlyn
COEDYDD ABER
Aber Falls
Rhaeadr Aber
Trefdraeth
Afon Cefni
B4419
Llanddaniel Fab
Glan Adda
Minffordd
Tal-y-bont
PLAS NEWYDD
COCHWILLAN OLD HALL
Llanllechid
A4080
Capel-y-graig
Glasinfryn
BANGOR SERVICES
Rachub
SNOWDONIA NATIONAL PARK
Malltraeth
PLAS COCH GARDEN ZOO
Tregarth
B4409
942 FOEL FRAS
MENAI STRAIT AFON MENAI
GREENWOOD CENTRE
Pentir
Bethesda
Brynsiencyn
Seion
A4244
Sling
Gerlan
PARC
B4421
Y Felinheli
Braichmelyn
Dwyran
B4419
SEA ZOO
Saron
Llanddeiniolen
Rhiwlas
CENEDLAETHOL
Newborough
A487
B4366
Pen-lon
BIRD WORLD
FOEL FARM PARK
MODEL VILLAGE
Bethel
Penisarwaun
Ty'n-y-maes
ERYRI
1064 CARNEDD LLYWELYN
Newborough Forest
Waterloo Port
BRYN BRAS CASTLE
Deiniolen
Llanrug
SEIONT II MARITIME MUSEUM
CASTLE & REGIMENTAL MUS.
Pont-rug
Clwt-y-bont
Marchlyn Mawr Res.
1044 CARNEDD DAFYDD
SEGONTIUM FORT
Brynrefail
Caernarfon
Cwm-y-glo
Llyn Padarn
Dinorwic
A5
Llyn Ogwen
Pont Rhyd-goch
Caeathro
POWER OF WALES
LLANBERIS LAKE RAILWAY
PADARN
Abermenai Pt.
Trwyn Abermenai
Abermenai Bar
WELSH HIGHLAND RAILWAY
Ceunant
INIGO JONES TUDOR SLATEWORKS
Llanberis
SLATE MUS.
Pont Pen-y-benglog
Llanfaglan
Croesywaun
Groeslon
LLANBERIS
IDWAL COTTAGE
Llyn Peris
Saron
Bontnewydd
Waunfawr
107
CAERNARFON AIR MUSEUM
Glan-rhyd
DOLBADARN
Nant Peris
CWM IDWAL
Capel Curig
Morfa Dinlle
Rhostryfan
A4085
999
124
15A
15
14
13
12
11
10
9
8
8A
7
7A
6
S
16
20

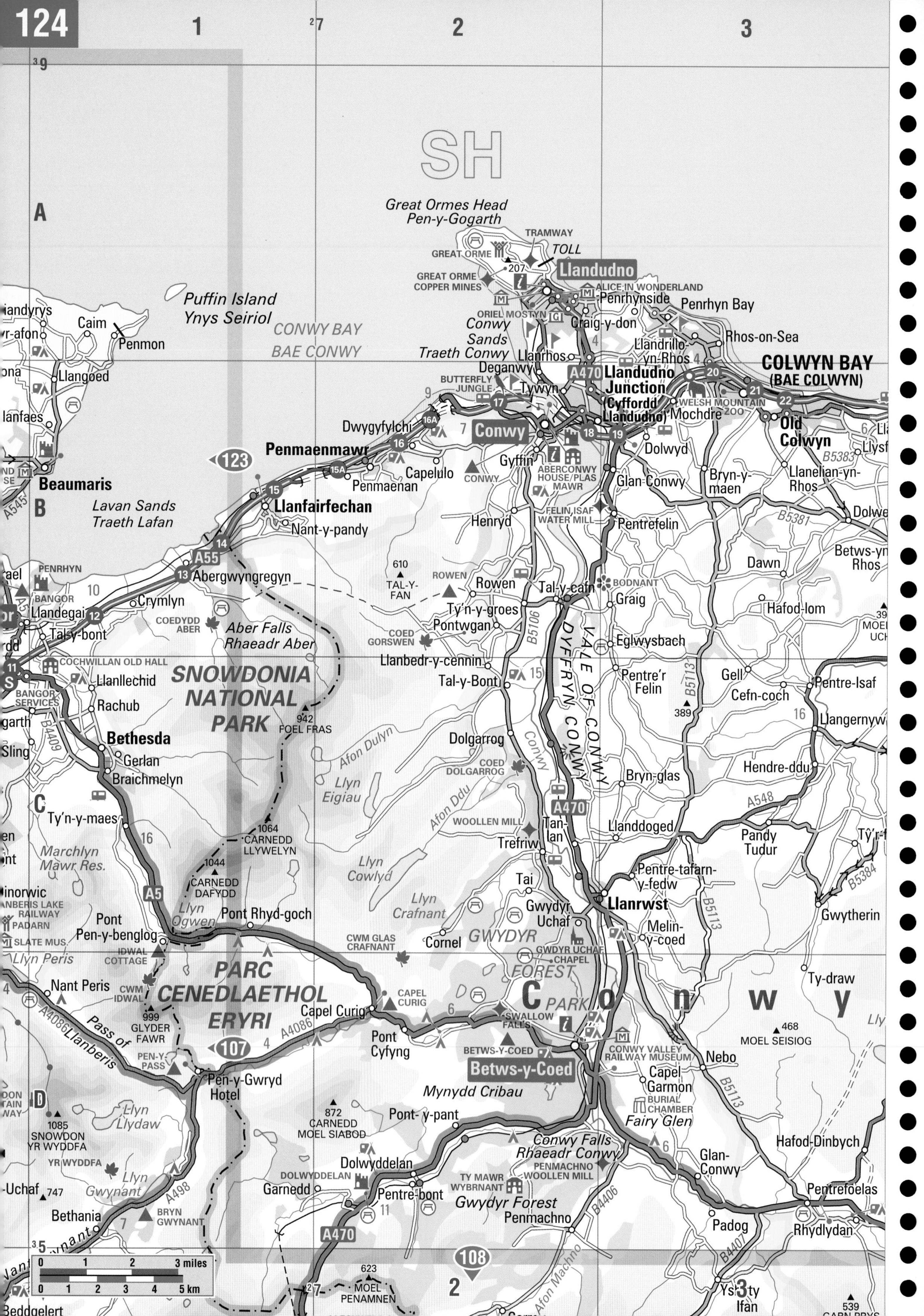
1
2
3
A
B
C
D
SH
Great Ormes Head
Pen-y-Gogarth
TRAMWAY
GREAT ORME
TOLL
207
Llandudno
GREAT ORME COPPER MINES
ALICE IN WONDERLAND
Penrhynside
Penrhyn Bay
ORIEL MOSTYN
Craig-y-don
Rhos-on-Sea
Conwy Sands
Traeth Conwy
Llanrhos
Llandrillo-yn-Rhos
COLWYN BAY
(BAE COLWYN)
Deganwy
A470
Llandudno Junction
(Cyffordd Llandudno)
BUTTERFLY JUNGLE
Tywyn
WELSH MOUNTAIN ZOO
Mochdre
Old Colwyn
Dwygyfylchi
Conwy
Dolwyd
Penmaenmawr
Gyffin
Capelulo
Penmaenan
CONWY
ABERCONWY HOUSE/PLAS MAWR
Glan-Conwy
Bryn-y-maen
Llanelian-yn-Rhos
B5383
Puffin Island
Ynys Seiriol
CONWY BAY
BAE CONWY
Caim
Penmon
Llangoed
Beaumaris
Lavan Sands
Traeth Lafan
Llanfairfechan
Nant-y-pandy
Henryd
FELIN ISAF WATER MILL
Pentrefelin
B5381
Dawn
Betws-yn-Rhos
A55
PENRHYN
Abergwyngregyn
610
TAL-Y-FAN
ROWEN
Rowen
Tal-y-cafn
BODNANT
Graig
Hafod-lom
BANGOR
Llandegai
Crymlyn
Tal-y-bont
COEDYDD ABER
Aber Falls
Rhaeadr Aber
Ty'n-y-groes
Pontwgan
COED GORSWEN
B5106
DYFFRYN CONWY
VALE OF CONWY
Eglwysbach
COCHWILLAN OLD HALL
Llanllechid
SNOWDONIA NATIONAL PARK
Llanbedr-y-cennin
Tal-y-Bont
Pentre'r Felin
B5113
Gell
Cefn-coch
Pentre-Isaf
BANGOR SERVICES
Rachub
942
FOEL FRAS
389
Llangernyw
B4409
Bethesda
Afon Dulyn
Dolgarrog
Gerlan
Braichmelyn
Llyn Eigiau
COED DOLGARROG
Conwy
Bryn-glas
Hendre-ddu
A548
Ty'n-y-maes
Afon Ddu
WOOLLEN MILL
Tan-lan
Llanddoged
Pandy Tudur
Marchlyn Mawr Res.
1064
CARNEDD LLYWELYN
Trefriw
Llyn Cowlyd
1044
CARNEDD DAFYDD
Pentre-tafarn-y-fedw
B5384
A5
Tai
Llanrwst
Llyn Crafnant
Gwydyr Uchaf
Gwytherin
LLANBERIS LAKE RAILWAY
PADARN
SLATE MUS.
Pont Pen-y-benglog
Llyn Ogwen
Pont Rhyd-goch
CWM GLAS CRAFNANT
Cornel
GWYDYR
Melin-y-coed
Llyn Peris
IDWAL COTTAGE
GWYDYR UCHAF CHAPEL
PARC CENEDLAETHOL ERYRI
FOREST PARK
Nant Peris
CWM IDWAL
CAPEL CURIG
Capel Curig
Conwy
Ty-draw
999
GLYDER FAWR
A4086
Pass of Llanberis
SWALLOW FALLS
Pont Cyfyng
468
MOEL SEISIOG
PEN-Y-PASS
BETWS-Y-COED
Betws-y-Coed
CONWY VALLEY RAILWAY MUSEUM
Nebo
Pen-y-Gwryd Hotel
Mynydd Cribau
Capel Garmon
B5113
BURIAL CHAMBER
Llyn Llydaw
872
CARNEDD MOEL SIABOD
Pont-y-pant
Fairy Glen
1085
SNOWDON
YR WYDDFA
Conwy Falls
Rhaeadr Conwy
Hafod-Dinbych
PENMACHNO WOOLLEN MILL
Glan-Conwy
YR WYDDFA
Llyn Gwynant
Dolwyddelan
747
DOLWYDDELAN
TY MAWR WYBRNANT
Garnedd
Pentre-bont
Gwydyr Forest
Pentrefoelas
A498
B4406
Bethania
BRYN GWYNANT
Penmachno
Padog
Rhydlydan
A470
B4407
0 1 2 3 miles
0 1 2 3 4 5 km
623
MOEL PENAMNEN
Afon Machno
Ysbyty Ifan
539
Beddgelert
123
107
108

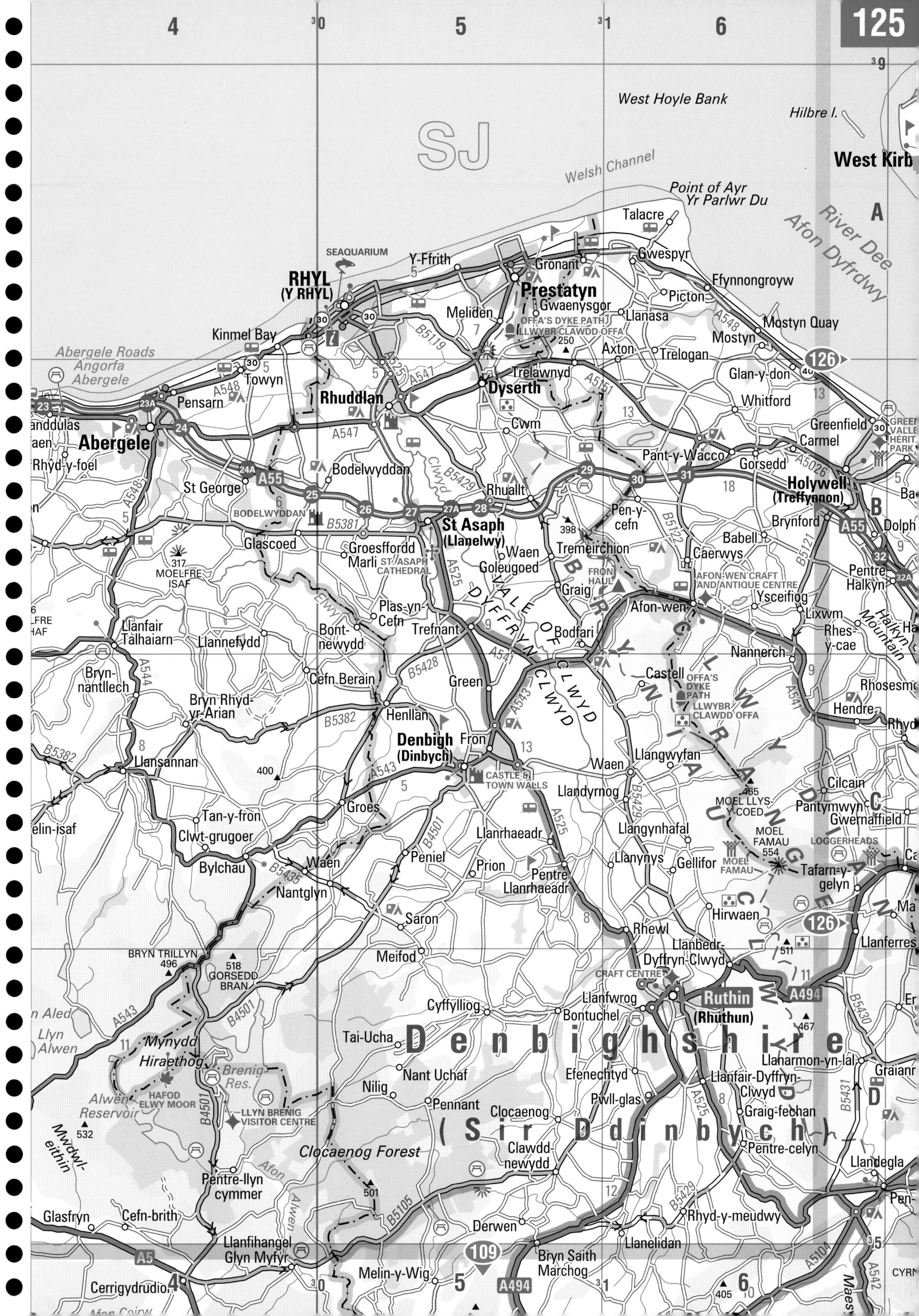

SJ
West Hoyle Bank
Hilbre I.
West Kirb
Welsh Channel
Point of Ayr
Yr Parlwr Du
River Dee
Afon Dyfrdwy
Talacre
Gwespyr
Gronant
Prestatyn
Gwaenysgor
Picton
Ffynnongroyw
Llanasa
Mostyn Quay
Mostyn
SEAQUARIUM
Y-Ffrith
RHYL
(Y RHYL)
Meliden
OFFA'S DYKE PATH
LLWYBR CLAWDD OFFA
Axton
Trelogan
Kinmel Bay
Abergele Roads
Angorfa
Abergele
Towyn
Pensarn
Rhuddlan
Trelawnyd
Dyserth
Glan-y-don
Whitford
Greenfield
Carmel
GREENFIELD VALLEY HERITAGE PARK
Abergele
Llanddulas
Rhŷd-y-foel
Cwm
Pant-y-Wacco
Gorsedd
Bodelwyddan
St George
BODELWYDDAN
Rhuallt
Holywell
(Treffynnon)
Brynford
Babell
Caerwys
St Asaph
(Llanelwy)
Pen-y-cefn
Tremeirchion
Glascoed
Groesffordd Marli
ST ASAPH CATHEDRAL
Waen
Goleugoed
MOELFRE ISAF
FRON HAUL
Graig
AFON-WEN CRAFT AND ANTIQUE CENTRE
Afon-wen
Ysceifiog
Pentre Halkyn
Halkyn Mountain
Lixwm
Rhes-y-cae
Plas-yn-Cefn
Trefnant
Bont-newydd
Bodfari
Llanfair Talhaiarn
Llannefydd
VALE OF CLWYD
DYFFRYN CLWYD
Nannerch
Bryn-nantllech
Cefn Berain
Green
Castell
OFFA'S DYKE PATH
LLWYBR CLAWDD OFFA
Rhosesmor
Hendre
Bryn Rhyd-yr-Arian
Henllan
Denbigh
(Dinbych)
Fron
CLWYDIAN RANGE
BRYNIAU CLWYD
Llansannan
CASTLE & TOWN WALLS
Waen
Llangwyfan
Llandyrnog
MOEL LLYS-Y-COED
Cilcain
Pantymwyn
Gwernaffield
Tan-y-fron
Groes
Llangynhafal
MOEL FAMAU
LOGGERHEADS
Clwt-grugoer
Llanrhaeadr
Peniel
Llanynys
Gellifor
Tafarn-y-gelyn
Bylchau
Waen
Prion
Pentre Llanrhaeadr
Nantglyn
Hirwaen
Saron
Rhewl
Llanferres
Llanbedr-Dyffryn-Clwyd
BRYN TRILLYN
GORSEDD BRAN
Meifod
CRAFT CENTRE
Ruthin
(Rhuthun)
Llanfwrog
Bontuchel
Cyffylliog
Llyn Alwen
Mynydd Hiraethog
Tai-Ucha
Denbighshire
(Sir Ddinbych)
Llanarmon-yn-Ial
Gwaenysgor
Brenig Res.
Nant Uchaf
Efenechtyd
Llanfair-Dyffryn-Clwyd
Alwen Reservoir
HAFOD ELWY MOOR
LLYN BRENIG VISITOR CENTRE
Nilig
Pennant
Pwll-glas
Clocaenog
Graig-fechan
Mwdwl-eithin
Clocaenog Forest
Clawdd-newydd
Pentre-celyn
Llandegla
Pentre-llyn cymmer
Afon Alwen
Glasfryn
Cefn-brith
Derwen
Rhyd-y-meudwy
Llanfihangel Glyn Myfyr
Llanelidan
Bryn Saith Marchog
Cerrigydrudion
Melin-y-Wig
Maes

HOYLAKE
West Hoyle Bank
Hilbre I.
West Kirby
Welsh Channel
Point of Ayr
Yr Parlwr Du
River Dee
Afon Dyfrdwy
Talacre
Gwespyr
Ffynnongroyw
Picton
Llanasa
Mostyn Quay
Mostyn
Axton
Trelogan
Glan-y-don
Whitford
Greenfield
Carmel
Pant-y-Wacco
Gorsedd
Holywell
(Treffynnon)
Brynford
Babell
Caerwys
Ysceifiog
Afon-wen
Lixwm
Nannerch
Castell
Rhes-y-cae
Halkyn Mountain
Halkyn
Pentre Halkyn
Rhosesmor
Hendre
Rhydymwyn
Flintshire
(Sir y Fflint)
Cilcain
Pantymwyn
Gwernaffield
Mold
(Yr Wyddgrug)
Cadole
Tafarn-y-gelyn
Gwernymynydd
Maeshafn
Llanferres
Eryrys
Treuddyn
Llanarmon-yn-Ial
Graianrhyd
Rhydtalog
Four Crosses
Llandegla
Pen-y-stryt
Gwynfryn
Minera
Coedpoeth
Bersham
Llangwyfan
Llangynhafal
Llanynys
Gellifor
Hirwaen
Rhewl
Llanbedr-Dyffryn-Clwyd
Ruthin
(Rhuthun)
Llanfwrog
Llanfair-Dyffryn-Clwyd
Graig-fechan
Pentre-celyn
Rhyd-y-meudwy
Llanelidan
Meols
Moreton
Greasby
Grange
Woodchurch
Frankby
Upton
Caldy
Thurstaston
Irby
Pensby
Heswall
Thingwall
Barnston
Brimstage
Gayton
Thornton Hough
Raby
Parkgate
Neston
Little Neston
Ness
Hinderton
Willaston
Burton
Puddington
Dawpool Bank
Holywell Bank
Gayton Sands
Bagillt
Dolphin
Flint (Y Fflint)
Mount Pleasant
Oakenholt
Flint Mountain
Northop
Northop Hall
Connah's Quay
Shotton
Soughton
New Brighton
Buckley
(Bwcle)
Mynydd-isa
Llong
Spon Green
Drury
Ewloe
Ewloe Grn.
Queensferry
Sandycroft
Mancot
Hawarden
(Penarlâg)
Broughton
Bretton
Saltney
Penyffordd
Nercwys
Pontblyddyn
Leeswood
Coed-Talon
Caergwrle
Hope
(Yr Hôb)
Llanfynydd
Cefn-y-bedd
Ffrith
Brymbo
Bwlchgwyn
Moss
Gwersyllt
Rhosrobin
Llay
Garden Village
New Broughton
Wrexham
(Wrecsam)
Rhostyllen
Gresford
Marford
Rossett
Trevalyn
Burton Green
Borras Head
Acton
Llan-y-pwll
Rhosnesni
Wrexham Industrial Estate
Dodleston
Higher Kinnerton
Lower Kinnerton
Balderton
Pulford
Lavister
Wallasey
Poulton
Seacombe
Bidston
Claughton
Birkenhead
Tranmere
Rock Ferry
Prenton
BEBINGTON
Storeton
Port Sunlight
New Ferry
Bromborough
Eastham
Eastham Ferry
Hooton
Childer Thornton
Little Sutton
Overpool
Great Sutton
Ledsham
Two Mills
Capenhurst
Backford Cross
Shotwick
Saughall
Garden City
Sealand
Mollington
Blacon
Chester
LIVERPOOL
Edge Hill
Toxteth
Dingle
Mossley Hill
Aigburth
Grassendale
Wavertree
Everton
Garston
Mostyn
Ben-y-cefn
Waen
Tremeirchion
Moel Famau
Llwybr Clawdd Offa
Offa's Dyke Path
Cyrn y Brain
Esclus Mountain
Talwrn
Clwydian Range
Dee
Alyn
0 1 2 3 miles
0 1 2 3 4 5 km

Warrington
Widnes
Runcorn
Halton
Speke
Liverpool Airport
Liverpool John Lennon
Ellesmere Port
Ince Banks
Mersey
Frodsham
Helsby
Northwich
Weaverham
Hartford
Davenham
Moulton
Wharton
WINSFORD
Kelsall
Tarporley
Delamere Forest Park
Cheshire
Farndon
Holt
Nantwich
Wistaston
Crewe
Willaston
Lymm
Huyton
Roby
Knotty Ash
Whiston
Rainhill
Sutton Manor
Clock Face
Bold Heath
Great Sankey
Penketh
Latchford
Thelwall
Grappenhall
Stockton Heath
Appleton Thorn
Stretton
Lower Stretton
Higher Walton
Moore
Daresbury
Keckwick
Hatton
Norton
Halton
Preston Brook
Preston on the Hill
Dutton
Sutton Weaver
Aston
Weston
Hale
Hale Bank
Halewood
Hunt's Cross
Woolton
Gateacre
Childwall
Netherley
Tarbock Green
Cronton
Hough Green
Ditton
Farnworth
Appleton
Barrow's Green
Doe Green
Newtown
Overton
Fivecrosses
Newton
Alvanley
Hapsford
Elton
Stanlow
Ince
Whitby
Whitbyheath
Thornton-le-Moors
Stoak
Picton
Wervin
Backford
Mickle Trafford
Bridge Trafford
Dunham-on-the-Hill
Manley
Mouldsworth
Ashton
Little Barrow
Great Barrow
Guilden Sutton
Stamford Bridge
Tarvin
Oscroft
Kelsall Hill
Willington Corner
Utkinton
Cotebrook
Duddon
Clotton
Burton
Kingsley
Crowton
Commonside
Birch Hill
Norley
Hatchmere
Sandiway
Cuddington
Oakmere
Delamere
Acton Bridge
Dones Green
Comberbach
Little Leigh
Barnton
Anderton
Marston
Wincham
Great Budworth
Higher Whitley
Lower Whitley
Gib Hill
Bate Heath
Arley
Whitegate
Foxwist Green
Wharton Green
Salterswall
Little Budworth
Over
Church Hill
School Green
Rushton
Eaton
Rhuddall Heath
Four Lane Ends
Tilstone Fearnall
Wettenhall
Church Minshull
Alpraham
Calveley
Cholmondeston
Wardle
Aston juxta Mondrum
Barbridge
Haughton Moss
Radmore Green
Burland
Burford
Acton
Faddiley
Larden Green
Chorley
Ravensmoor
Bunbury
Bunbury Heath
Spurstow
Peckforton
Beeston
Beeston Castle
Tiverton
Brassey Green
Birch Heath
Huxley
Hargrave
Milner's Heath
Waverton
Brown Heath
Christleton
Littleton
Hoole
Newton
Handbridge
Rowton
Eccleston
Saighton
Hatton Heath
Bruera
Gatesheath
Newton
Tattenhall
Milton Green
Aldford
Handley
Aldersey Green
Churton
Chowley
Coddington
Clutton
Broxton
Barnhill
Harthill
Burwardsley
Higher Burwardsley
Bulkeley
Gallantry Bank
Fuller's Moor
Bickerton
Duckington
Cholmondeley Castle Gdns
Barton
Crewe
Stretton
Tilston
Castletown
Edge Green
Horton Green
Ridleywood
Isycoed
Stretton
Hampton Heath
Bickley Moss
Ebnal
Stocklach
Bowling Bank
Chorlton
No Man's Heath
Wrenbury
Sound
Broomhall
Walgherton
Stapeley
Butt Green
Wistaston Green
Woolstanwood
Worleston
Barrows Green
Bradfield Green
Warmingham
Moston
Bostock Green
Rudheath
Broken Cross
Broomedge
Swettenham
Sworton Heath
Martinscroft
Woolston
Birchwood
Fearnhead
Houghton Green
Dallam
Pex Hill
Cheshire Oaks
Chester
Shropshire Union Canal
Weaver
Dee
M62
M6
M56
A49
A51
A54
A556
A533
A534
A41
A55
A500
A530
A5300
A557
A561
A562
A57
127
128
136
137
110
111

Hollins Green
Partington
Manchester Ship Canal
Warburton
Mossbrow
Heatley
Broadheath
Dunham Town
Timperley
SALE
Brooklands
Northenden
Wythenshawe
GATLEY
Cheadle
Cheadle Heath
Cheadle Hulme
Woodhouse Park
Altrincham
Hale
Halebarns
Bowdon
Bowgreen
Oughtrington
DUNHAM MASSEY
Little Bollington
Broomedge
Lymm
Thelwall
Latchford
Grappenhall
Stockton Heath
WALTON HALL
Appleton Thorn
Stretton
Lower Stretton
Woolston
Martinscroft
Orford
LYMM SERVICES
Sworton Heath
High Legh
ROSTHERNE MERE
Rostherne
Ashley
Thorns Green
MANCHESTER
Manchester Airport
Styal
QUARRY BANK MILL
Heald Green
Handforth
Woodford
Bucklow Hill
Hoo Green
Mere
New Mills
Morley Green
TATTON HOUSE
TATTON PARK
ARLEY HALL
Arley
Higher Whitley
Lower Whitley
Bate Heath
Holehouses
Over Tabley
Mobberley
Knolls Green
Davenport Green
WILMSLOW
Dean Row
Knutsford
Over Knutsford
Alderley Edge
Hough
Mottram St Andrew
Prestbury
Dones Green
Comberbach
Gib Hill
Great Budworth
CHESHIRE COUNTY SHOW
Pickmere
TABLEY
KNUTSFORD SERVICES
Ollerton
Marthall
Nether Alderley
NETHER ALDERLEY MILL
Little Leigh
ANDERTON BOAT LIFT
MARBURY
Barnton
Anderton
Marston
Higher Wincham
Wincham
Plumley
Smithy Green
Over Peover
Chelford
Monks Heath
Broken Cross
Henbury
Northwich
Weaverham
Broken Cross
Lostock Gralam
Lostock Green
Rudheath
SALT MUS
Lower Peover
Swan Green
PEOVER HALL
Peover Heath
CAPESTHORNE HALL
Lower Pexhill
FARMER FOR A DAY
Cuddington
Hartford
Lach Dennis
JODRELL BANK VISITOR CENTRE
Blackden Heath
Withington Green
Siddington
Warren
Gawsworth
Davenham
Moulton
Whitegate
Bostock Green
Puddinglake
Goostrey
Twemlow Green
Lower Withington
Gleadsmoss
Marton
Foxwist Green
Wharton Green
Byley
Cranage
Holmes Chapel
Swettenham
Sproston Green
Saltersw all
Wharton
WINSFORD
LITTLE BUDWORTH
Middlewich
Sandlow Green
Newsbank
Rodeheath
North Rode
Little Budworth
Over
Church Hill
Cheshire
Brereton Green
BRERETON HEATH
Brereton Heath
Hulme Walfield
Eaton
School Green
Occlestone Green
Bradwall Green
Lower Heath
Buglawton
Congleton
Wettenhall
Moston Green
Elworth
SANDBACH CROSSES
Arclid
West Heath
Hightown
Church Minshull
Warmingham
Sandbach
SANDBACH SERVICES
Brookhouse Green
Brownlow
Astbury
Mossley
Brownlow Heath
Alpraham
Cholmondeston
Bradfield Green
Coppenhall Moss
Fourlanes End
Calveley
Wheelock
Hassall Green
LITTLE MORETON HALL
Marsh Green
Wheelock Heath
Gillow Heath
Wardle
Aston juxta Mondrum
Barrows Green
Maw Green
Thurlwood
Rode Heath
Scholar Green
Mow Cop
MOW COP CASTLE
Barbridge
Winterley
Hassall
Mount Pleasant
Worleston
Church Lawton
Woolstanwood
Haslington
Radmore Green
Crewe
Wistaston Green
Alsager
Kidsgrove
Newchapel
Brindley
Burford
Burland
Wistaston
Wells Green
Radway Green
Talke
Goldenhill
Gresty Green
ST MARY'S
Faddiley
Acton
Willaston
Weston
FREEPORT TALKE OUTLET MALL
Chell Heath
Nantwich
Shavington
Barthomley
Red Street
Tunstall
Sandyford
Bradeley
Englesea-brook
Butt Green
Hough
STAPELEY WATER GARDENS
Ravensmoor
Gorsteyhill
Audley
Burslem
FORD GREEN HALL
Stapeley
Balterley
Chesterton
Walgherton
Halmer End
Alsagers Bank
Bradwell
Wolstanton
ETRURIA INDUSTRIAL
Broomhall
Sound
0 1 2 3 miles
0 1 2 3 4 5 km

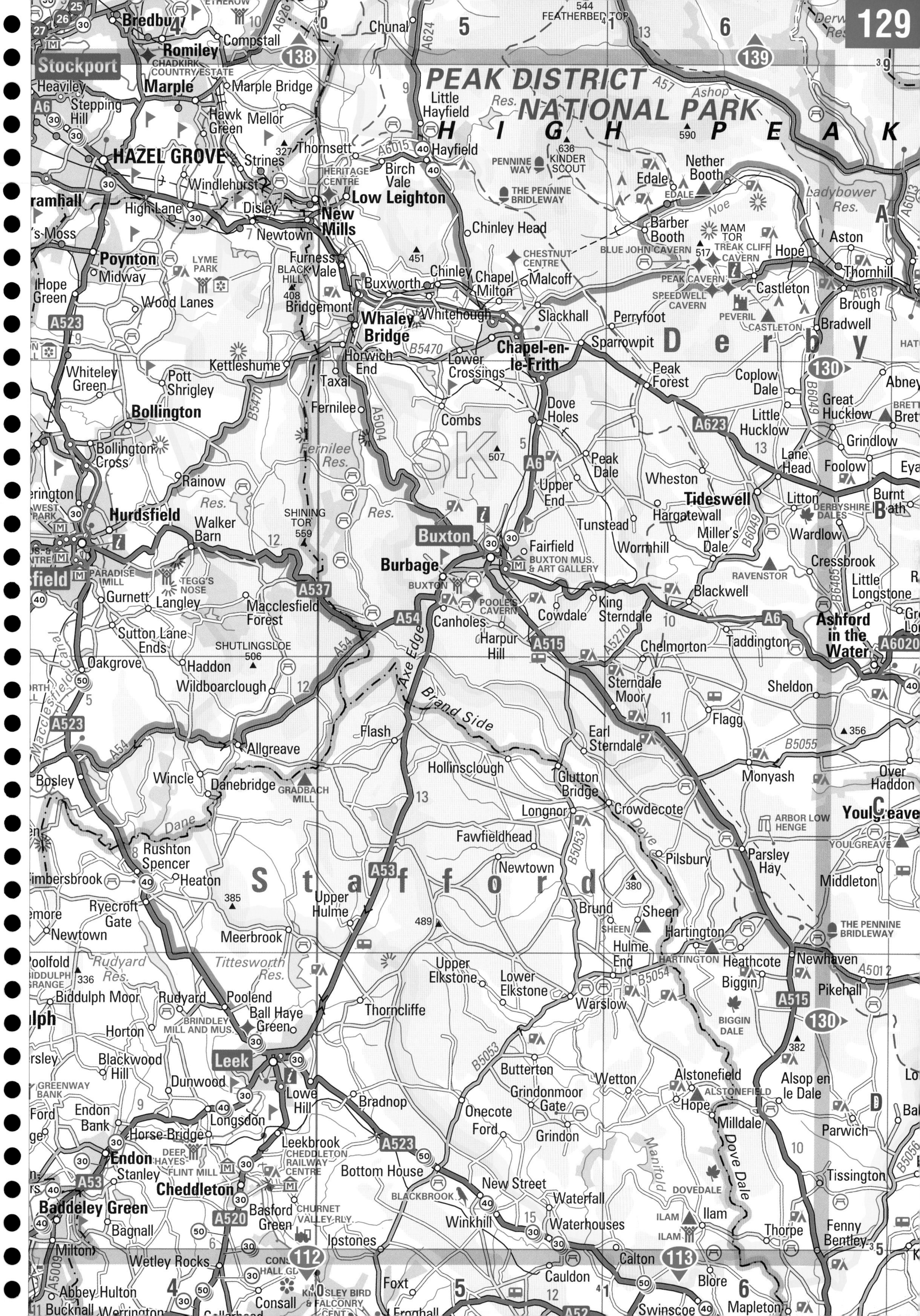
PEAK DISTRICT NATIONAL PARK
HIGH PEAK
Derby
Stafford
SK
Stockport
Marple
HAZEL GROVE
Romiley
Bredbury
Compstall
Marple Bridge
Mellor
Hawk Green
Strines
Thornsett
Hayfield
Little Hayfield
Birch Vale
Low Leighton
New Mills
Newtown
Disley
High Lane
Windlehurst
Poynton
Lyme Park
Furness Vale
Buxworth
Chinley
Chapel Milton
Malcoff
Chinley Head
Whaley Bridge
Bridgemont
Whitehough
Chapel-en-le-Frith
Slackhall
Perryfoot
Sparrowpit
Edale
Nether Booth
Barber Booth
Mam Tor
Blue John Cavern
Treak Cliff Cavern
Peak Cavern
Speedwell Cavern
Castleton
Peveril
Hope
Aston
Thornhill
Brough
Bradwell
Ladybower Res.
Kinder Scout
Pennine Way
The Pennine Bridleway
Chestnut Centre
Peak Forest
Coplow Dale
Great Hucklow
Little Hucklow
Grindlow
Foolow
Lane Head
Tideswell
Litton
Wheston
Burnt Heath
Bollington
Pott Shrigley
Kettleshulme
Whiteley Green
Taxal
Horwich End
Lower Crossings
Combs
Fernilee
Fernilee Res.
Dove Holes
Peak Dale
Upper End
Tunstead
Hargatewall
Miller's Dale
Wormhill
Wardlow
Cressbrook
Little Longstone
Ravenstor
Blackwell
Rainow
Hurdsfield
Walker Barn
Shining Tor
Buxton
Burbage
Fairfield
Buxton Mus. & Art Gallery
Poole's Cavern
Harpur Hill
Canholes
Cowdale
King Sterndale
Chelmorton
Taddington
Ashford in the Water
Sheldon
Flagg
Sterndale Moor
Earl Sterndale
Macclesfield Forest
Langley
Gurnett
Tegg's Nose
Sutton Lane Ends
Shutlingsloe
Oakgrove
Haddon
Wildboarclough
Allgreave
Flash
Axe Edge
Brand Side
Hollinsclough
Glutton Bridge
Crowdecote
Longnor
Monyash
Over Haddon
Youlgreave
Arbor Low Henge
Bosley
Wincle
Danebridge
Gradbach Mill
Rushton Spencer
Heaton
Fawfieldhead
Newtown
Pilsbury
Parsley Hay
Middleton
Ryecroft Gate
Upper Hulme
Meerbrook
Brund
Sheen
Hartington
Heathcote
Newhaven
Hulme End
Biggin
Pikehall
Tittesworth Res.
Rudyard Res.
Rudyard
Poolend
Ball Haye Green
Horton
Biddulph Moor
Thorncliffe
Upper Elkstone
Lower Elkstone
Warslow
Biggin Dale
Leek
Blackwood Hill
Dunwood
Lowe Hill
Bradnop
Butterton
Wetton
Alstonefield
Alsop en le Dale
Grindonmoor Gate
Onecote
Ford
Grindon
Hope
Milldale
Parwich
Endon
Endon Bank
Horse Bridge
Longsdon
Leekbrook
Cheddleton
Deep Hayes
Stanley
Baddeley Green
Bagnall
Basford Green
Bottom House
New Street
Waterfall
Waterhouses
Winkhill
Ipstones
Dovedale
Dove Dale
Manifold
Ilam
Thorpe
Tissington
Fenny Bentley
Wetley Rocks
Calton
Cauldon
Blore
Foxt
Consall
Mapleton
Swinscoe
Abbey Hulton
Bucknall
Milton
A6
A523
A537
A54
A53
A515
A520
A623
A6020
A5004
A5270
B5470
B5053
B5054
B5055
B6049
130
138
139
112
113

PEAK DISTRICT NATIONAL PARK
Derwent Res.
Moors
Low Bradfield
Worrall
P&R
Wadsley
Wadsley Bridge
Wincobank
Stacey Bank
139
Ughill
Dungworth
Loxley
B6077
Owlerton
Pitsmoor
Attercliffe
Ashop
A57
590
B6076
Stopes
Stannington
Walkley
KELHAM ISLAND MUSEUM
Hollow Meadows
A6101
Crookes
P&R
A57
Nether Booth
Edale
EDALE
HIGH NEB 458
Ladybower Res.
A6013
BOTANICAL GARDENS
Ranmoor
Sheffield
Highfield
Fulwood
HEELEY CITY FARM
Arbourthorne
Noe
Barber Booth
MAM TOR
TREAK CLIFF CAVERN
BLUE JOHN CAVERN
517
Aston
Hope
Reservoirs
Ecclesall
BISHOPS HOUSE
Norton
Gleadless
Ringinglow
Millhouses
Bamford
Thornhill
Whirlow
P&R
Woodseats
PEAK CAVERN
Castleton
SPEEDWELL CAVERN
A6187
Brough
PEVERIL CASTLE
Abbeydale
A6102
RIDGEWAY COTTAGE INDUSTRY CENTRE
Perryfoot
Hathersage
HATHERSAGE
Bradwell
A625
Dore
Beauchief
Jordanthorpe
Sparrowpit
New Totley
Bradway
Coal Aston
B6056
129
Upper Padley
LONGSHAW
Peak Forest
Coplow Dale
Abney
B6001
B6521
Dronfield Woodhouse
Dronfield
Great Hucklow
BRETTON
Bretton
429
Owler Bar
B6057
Apperknowle
A623
Little Hucklow
Grindlow
Grindleford
Nether Padley
B6054
Holmesfield
Unstone
202
Peak Dale
Lane Head
Foolow
Eyam
EYAM
EYAM HALL
A625
Froggatt
A621
B6051
Unstone Green
A61
REVOLUTION HOUSE
Wheston
Tideswell
Litton
Burnt Heath
DERBYSHIRE DALES
Stoney Middleton
Common Side
Moorhall
Barlow
Hargatewall
Tunstead
Miller's Dale
Wardlow
Calver
Curbar
Wilday Green
Old Whittington
Wormhill
Cressbrook
B6001
B6050
Newbold
RAVENSTOR
Baslow
Overgreen
Cutthorpe
Blackwell
Little Longstone
Rowland
Old Brampton
King Sterndale
B6465
Great Longstone
Hassop
Chesterfield
A6
Ashford in the Water
A619
CHATSWORTH
Eastmoor
Brampton
A5270
Chelmorton
Taddington
A6020
Pilsley
Wadshelf
A619
ST MARY & ALL SAINTS
Wye
East Moor
Sterndale Moor
Sheldon
Edensor
HOB HURSTS HOUSE
Holymoorside
Walton
Birdholme
Bakewell
B6012
367
Slatepit Dale
Swathwick
Flagg
356
HADDON HALL
PEAK VILLAGE
Beeley
B5057
Earl Sterndale
B5055
Wingerworth
Rowsley
Over Haddon
Monyash
Old Tupton
CAUDWELL'S MILL
Uppertown
Crowdecote
A515
ARBOR LOW HENGE
Youlgreave
Alport
Stanton in Peak
Northwood
Brockhurst
Alton
Dove
YOULGREAVE
Bradford
NINE LADIES STONE CIRCLE
Derwent
Kelstedge
Clay Cross
Pilsbury
Parsley Hay
Churchtown
Two Dales
B6036
Ashover
Fallgate
380
Middleton
B5056
Darley Bridge
PEAK RAIL
Upper Hackney
A632
Birchover
A61
Milltown
Brund
Sheen
129
SHEEN
Hartington
THE PENNINE BRIDLEWAY
Elton
B5057
Wensley
Tansley Knoll
B6014
Hulme End
Winster
Matlock
Woolley
HARTINGTON
Heathcote
Newhaven
Tansley
Res.
B5054
Biggin
Brightgate
THE HEIGHTS OF ABRAHAM
Brackenfield
Pikehall
A5012
Starkholmes
A615
Warslow
Bonsall
GULLIVER'S KINGDOM
Matlock Bath
Lea
Wessington
Shirland
BIGGIN DALE
Grangemill
ARKWRIGHT'S CROMFORD MILL
382
Aldwark
Ible
Cromford
MASSON MILLS
Wheatcroft
Holloway
THE NATIONAL TRAMWAY MUS.
Middleton
NATIONAL STONE CEN.
LEAWOOD PUMPHOUSE
B5035
South Wingfield
Wetton
Alstonefield
ALSTONEFIELD
Alsop en le Dale
Longcliffe
MIDDLETON TOP ENGINE HOUSE
Bolehill
Hope
Ballidon
Wirksworth
Wirksworth Moor
Whatstandwell
Oakerthorpe
Milldale
WINGFIELD MANOR
A515
Parwich
Crich
Manifold
Dove Dale
Brassington
Miller's Green
Fritchley
Swanwick
B5056
Bradbourne
Carsington
Alderwasley
A6
Bullbridge
Pentrich
Tissington
ECCLESBOURNE VALLEY RLY.
SHINING CLIFF
DOVEDALE
Carsington Res.
314
Ambergate
Ilam
ILAM
Thorpe
Fenny Bentley
B5035
Hognaston
B5023
Beighton Hill
Toadmoor
Heage
Nether Heage
Belper Lane End
Kniveton
113
Kirk Ireton
Shottle
114
DERWENT VALLEY VISITOR
Broadholme
Marehay
Idridgehay
Mount Pleasant
Far Laund
Swinscoe
Mapleton
Atlow
Biggin
Hulland
Blackbrook
0 1 2 3 miles
0 1 2 3 4 5 km

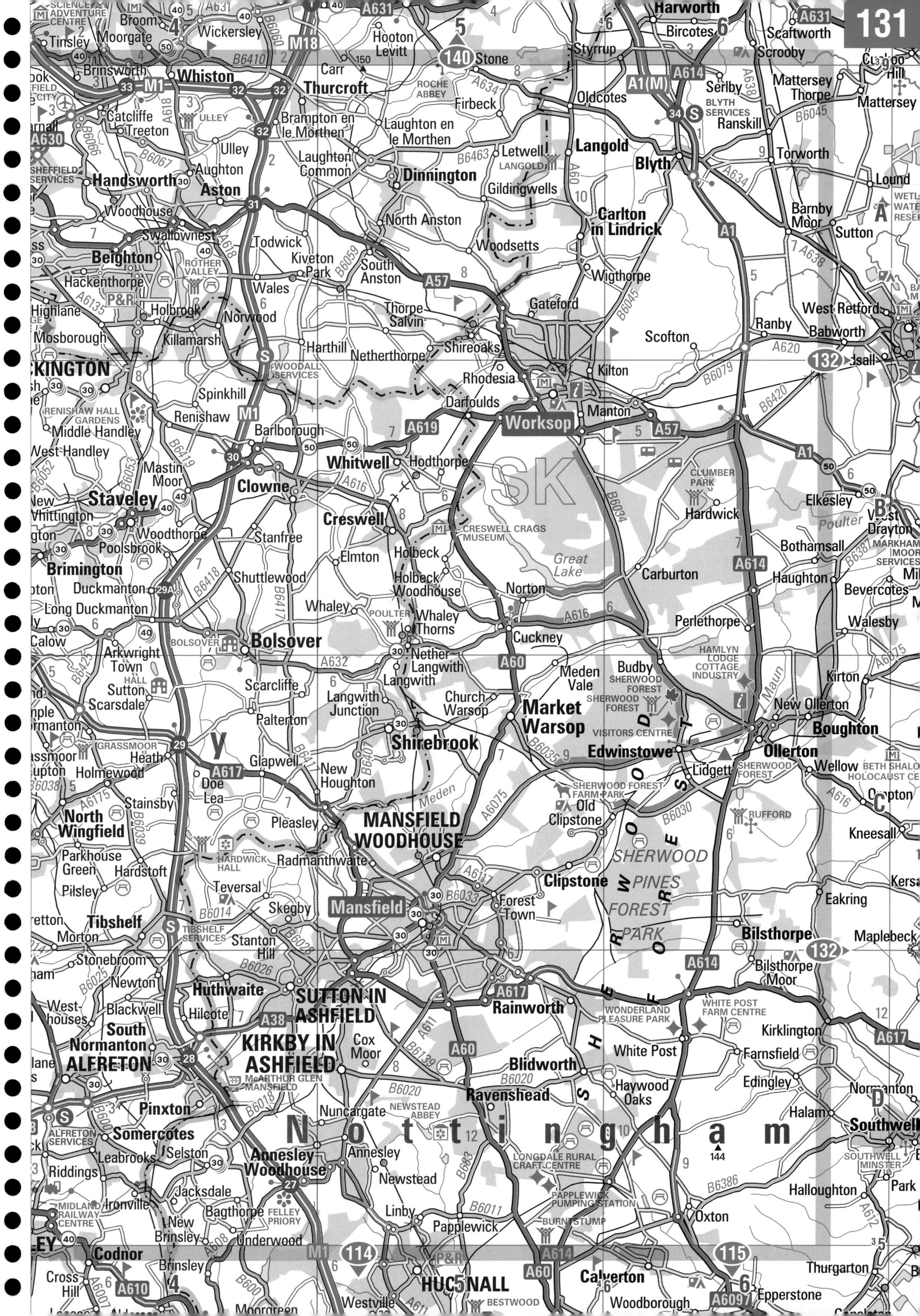

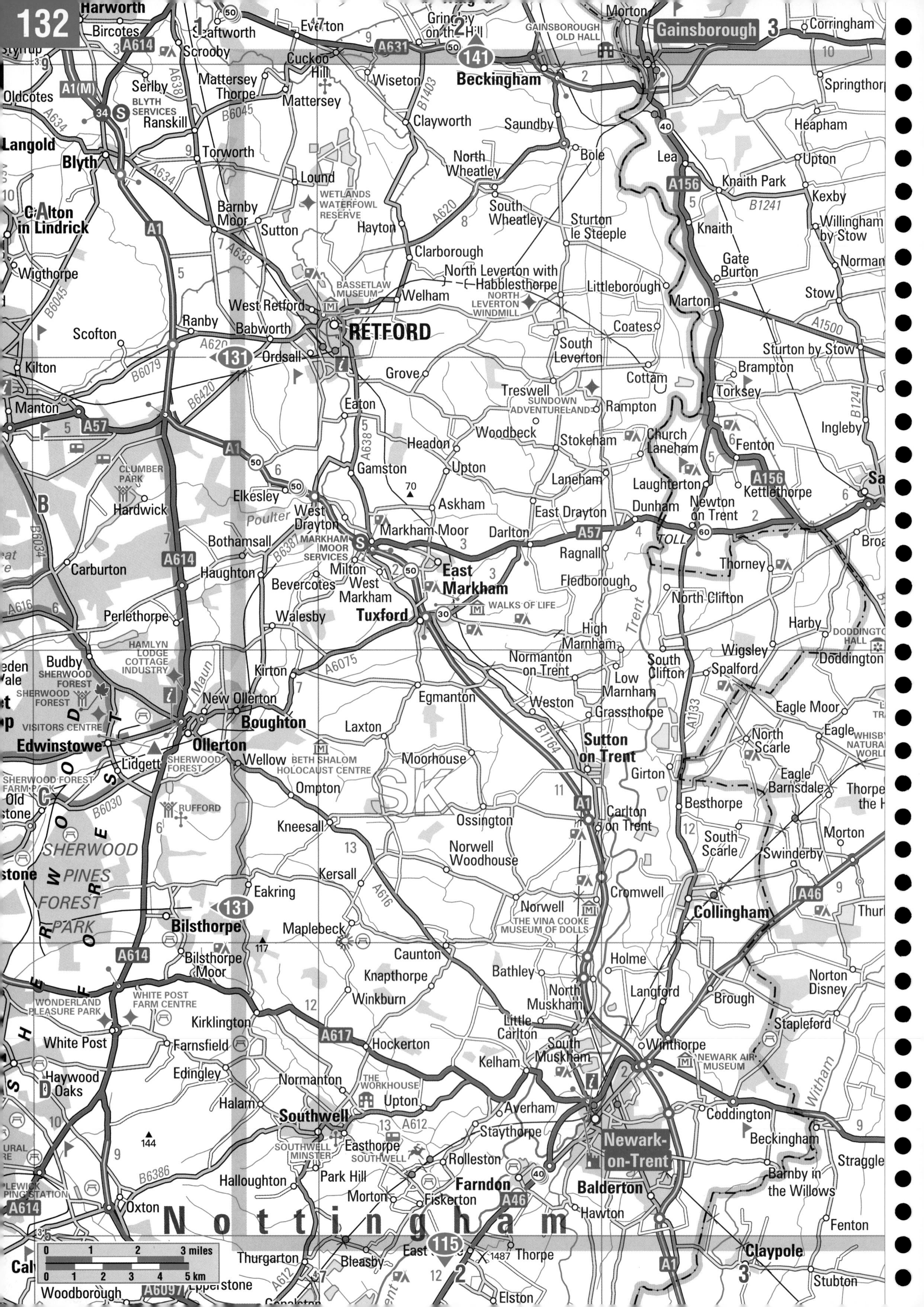
Harworth
Bircotes
Scaftworth
Everton
Gringley on the Hill
Morton
Gainsborough
Corringham
GAINSBOROUGH OLD HALL
Scrooby
Cuckoo Hill
Beckingham
Oldcotes
Serlby
Mattersey Thorpe
Mattersey
Wiseton
Springthorpe
BLYTH SERVICES
Ranskill
Clayworth
Saundby
Heapham
Langold
Blyth
Torworth
North Wheatley
Bole
Lea
Upton
Lound
Knaith Park
WETLANDS WATERFOWL RESERVE
South Wheatley
Kexby
Carlton in Lindrick
Barnby Moor
Sutton
Hayton
Sturton le Steeple
Knaith
Willingham by Stow
Clarborough
Gate Burton
Norman
Wigthorpe
North Leverton with Habblesthorpe
BASSETLAW MUSEUM
Welham
Littleborough
NORTH LEVERTON WINDMILL
Marton
Stow
West Retford
RETFORD
Ranby
Scofton
Babworth
Coates
South Leverton
Sturton by Stow
Kilton
Ordsall
Grove
Brampton
Cottam
Treswell
Torksey
Manton
SUNDOWN ADVENTURELAND
Rampton
Eaton
Woodbeck
Church Laneham
Ingleby
Headon
Stokeham
Fenton
CLUMBER PARK
Upton
Gamston
Laneham
Laughterton
Kettlethorpe
Hardwick
Elkesley
Askham
Dunham
Newton on Trent
West Drayton
East Drayton
Poulter
Markham Moor
Darlton
Bothamsall
MARKHAM MOOR SERVICES
Ragnall
TOLL
Thorney
Carburton
Haughton
Milton
East Markham
Bevercotes
West Markham
Fledborough
North Clifton
WALKS OF LIFE
Perlethorpe
Walesby
Tuxford
Harby
High Marnham
DODDINGTON HALL
HAMLYN LODGE COTTAGE INDUSTRY
Budby
Normanton on Trent
Wigsley
Doddington
SHERWOOD FOREST
Kirton
South Clifton
Spalford
Low Marnham
SHERWOOD FOREST VISITORS CENTRE
New Ollerton
Egmanton
Weston
Eagle Moor
Grassthorpe
Boughton
Laxton
Eagle
Sutton on Trent
North Scarle
Edwinstowe
Ollerton
Lidgett
Wellow
BETH SHALOM HOLOCAUST CENTRE
Moorhouse
Girton
SHERWOOD FOREST FARM PARK
Eagle Barnsdale
Thorpe on the Hill
Ompton
Besthorpe
RUFFORD
Kneesall
Ossington
Carlton on Trent
South Scarle
Morton
Norwell Woodhouse
Swinderby
SHERWOOD PINES FOREST PARK
Kersall
Cromwell
Eakring
Norwell
Collingham
THE VINA COOKE MUSEUM OF DOLLS
Bilsthorpe
Maplebeck
Caunton
Holme
Bilsthorpe Moor
Bathley
Norton Disney
Knapthorpe
North Muskham
Langford
WONDERLAND PLEASURE PARK
WHITE POST FARM CENTRE
Winkburn
Brough
Kirklington
Little Carlton
Stapleford
White Post
Farnsfield
Hockerton
South Muskham
Winthorpe
NEWARK AIR MUSEUM
Kelham
Haywood Oaks
Edingley
Normanton
THE WORKHOUSE
Halam
Upton
Averham
Coddington
Southwell
Staythorpe
Newark-on-Trent
Beckingham
SOUTHWELL MINSTER
Easthorpe
SOUTHWELL
Rolleston
Straggle
Park Hill
Barnby in the Willows
Halloughton
Farndon
Balderton
Morton
Fiskerton
Oxton
Hawton
Nottingham
Fenton
Thurgarton
East
Thorpe
Claypole
Bleasby
Woodborough
Epperstone
Stubton
Elston
0 1 2 3 miles
0 1 2 3 4 5 km
SK
Trent
Witham
Maun
A614
A1(M)
A634
A638
B6045
B1403
A631
A620
A156
B1241
A1500
B1241
A57
B6079
B6420
A1
B6034
B6387
A616
A6075
B1164
A1133
A46
A617
A612
B6386
B6030
A6097
A614
131
141
115
50
40
60
30

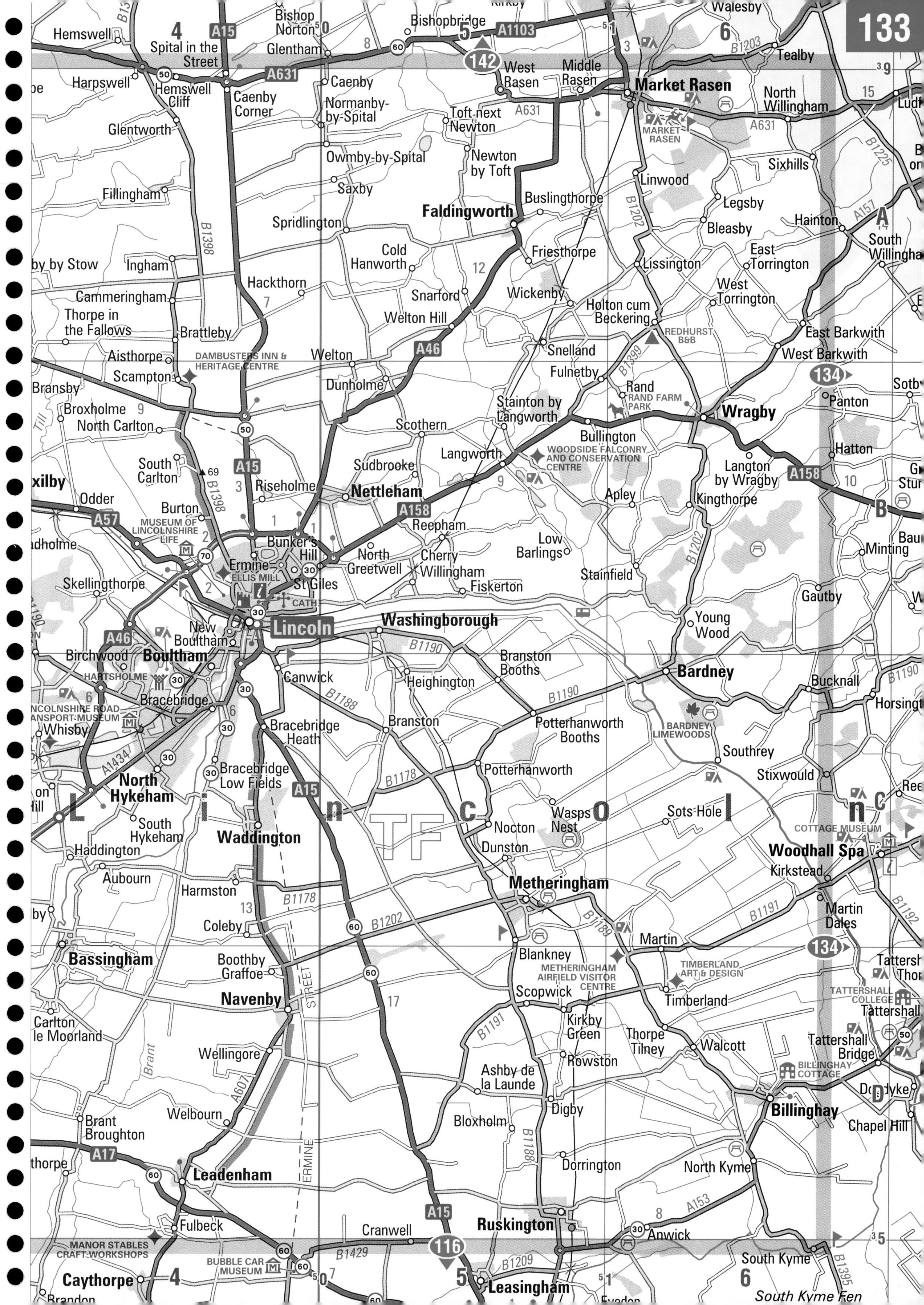
Hemswell
Spital in the Street
Bishop Norton
Glentham
Bishopbridge
Walesby
Tealby
West Rasen
Middle Rasen
Market Rasen
North Willingham
Harpswell
Hemswell Cliff
Caenby
Caenby Corner
Normanby-by-Spital
Toft next Newton
Glentworth
Owmby-by-Spital
Newton by Toft
Sixhills
Linwood
Fillingham
Saxby
Buslingthorpe
Legsby
Faldingworth
Spridlington
Bleasby
Hainton
South Willingham
Ingham
Cold Hanworth
Friesthorpe
Lissington
East Torrington
Hackthorn
West Torrington
Cammeringham
Snarford
Wickenby
Holton cum Beckering
Thorpe in the Fallows
Brattleby
Welton Hill
East Barkwith
West Barkwith
Aisthorpe
Welton
Snelland
Scampton
Dambusters Inn & Heritage Centre
Dunholme
Fulnetby
Rand
Rand Farm Park
Panton
Bransby
Broxholme
Stainton by Langworth
Wragby
North Carlton
Scothern
Bullington
Hatton
South Carlton
Langworth
Woodside Falconry and Conservation Centre
Sudbrooke
Langton by Wragby
Riseholme
Nettleham
Apley
Kingthorpe
Odder
Burton
Museum of Lincolnshire Life
Reepham
Low Barlings
Bunker's Hill
North Greetwell
Cherry Willingham
Minting
Ermine
Ellis Mill
Stainfield
Skellingthorpe
St Giles
Fiskerton
Gautby
Cath
New Boultham
Lincoln
Washingborough
Young Wood
Birchwood
Boultham
Branston Booths
Bardney
Hartsholme
Canwick
Heighington
Bucknall
Bracebridge
Lincolnshire Road Transport Museum
Potterhanworth Booths
Whisby
Bracebridge Heath
Branston
Bardney Limewoods
Southrey
Bracebridge Low Fields
Potterhanworth
Stixwould
North Hykeham
Wasps Nest
Sots Hole
Nocton
South Hykeham
Waddington
Dunston
Cottage Museum
Woodhall Spa
Haddington
Kirkstead
Aubourn
Harmston
Metheringham
Martin Dales
Coleby
Martin
Bassingham
Blankney
Boothby Graffoe
Metheringham Airfield Visitor Centre
Timberland Art & Design
Tattershall College
Tattershall
Navenby
Scopwick
Timberland
Carlton le Moorland
Kirkby Green
Thorpe Tilney
Walcott
Tattershall Bridge
Wellingore
Rowston
Billinghay Cottage
Ashby de la Launde
Dogdyke
Billinghay
Welbourn
Digby
Chapel Hill
Brant Broughton
Bloxholm
Dorrington
North Kyme
Leadenham
Ermine Street
Fulbeck
Ruskington
Anwick
Cranwell
Manor Stables Craft Workshops
Bubble Car Museum
South Kyme
Caythorpe
Leasingham
South Kyme Fen
Lincolnshire
TF
A15
A631
A1103
A46
A57
A158
A15
A1434
A607
A17
A153
B1398
B1202
B1399
B1190
B1188
B1178
B1202
B1189
B1191
B1429
B1209
B1395
B1225
A157
B1203
142
134
116

Market Rasen
Tealby
North Willingham
Ludford
Great Tows
Kelstern
North Elkington
Fotherby
Little Grimsby
Alvingham
North Cockerington
South Cockerington
South Elkington
Louth
Keddington
Grimoldby
Stewton
Welton le Wold
Burgh on Bain
Sixhills
Linwood
Legsby
Bleasby
Hainton
Gayton le Wold
Grimblethorpe
Biscathorpe
Hallington
Raithby
Little Carlton
Legbourne
Lissington
East Torrington
West Torrington
South Willingham
Donington on Bain
Withcall
Tathwell
Little Cawthorpe
North Reston
Holton cum Beckering
Benniworth
Haugham
Muckton
East Barkwith
West Barkwith
Stenigot
Cawkwell
Cadwell Park
Market Stainton
Maidenwell
Burwell
Rand
Wragby
Panton
Sotby
Ranby
Goulceby
Scamblesby
Farforth
Woody's Top
Ruckland
Belleau
White Pit
Bullington
Hatton
Oxcombe
Ketsby
Langton by Wragby
Great Sturton
Belchford
South Ormsby
Calceby
Apley
Kingthorpe
Baumber
Hemingby
Tetford
Driby
Minting
Fulletby
Salmonby
Brinkhill
Somersby
Stainfield
Gautby
Wispington
West Ashby
Bag Enderby
Harrington
Young Wood
Edlington
Ashby Puerorum
High Toynton
Greetham
Aswardby
Bardney
Bucknall
Thimbleby
Langton
Horncastle
Scrafield
Hagworthingham
Snipe Dales
Horsington
Thornton
Mareham on the Hill
Hameringham
Lusby
Mavis Enderby
Raithby
Bardney Limewoods
Southrey
Old Woodhall
Martin
Scrivelsby
Asgarby
Stixwould
Reeds Beck
Dalderby
Hareby
Old Bolingbroke
Hundleby
Roughton
Wood Enderby
Oslinc Ostrich Farm
Miningsby
Bolingbroke
West Keal
East Keal
Sots Hole
Cottage Museum
Roughton Moor
Moorby
Woodhall Spa
Haltham
Kirkstead
Kirkby on Bain
Toft Hill
East Kirkby
Toynton Fen Side
Mareham le Fen
Revesby
Lincolnshire Aviation Heritage Centre
Keal Cotes
Martin Dales
Martin
Revesby Bridge
Stickford
Timberland Art & Design
Tattershall Thorpe
New Bolingbroke
Timberland
Tattershall College
Tattershall
Coningsby
Fen Side
Battle of Britain Memorial Flight
Tumby Woodside
Midville
Thorpe Tilney
Walcott
Tattershall Bridge
Collegiate Church of the Holy Trinity
Medlam
Stickney
Billinghay Cottage
Hawthorn Hill
New York
Dogdyke
Sandy Bank
Scrub Hill
Carrington
Billinghay
Chapel Hill
Hundle Houses
Bunker's Hill
West Fen
Northlands
Haven Bank
Wildmore Fen
North Kyme
Sibsey Trader Mill
Sibsey
Frithville
Anwick
Gipsey Bridge
Fishtoft Drove
Holland Fen
Langrick
Anton's Gowt
Boston Long
South Kyme Fen
Lincolnshire Wolds
Lincolnshire
A631
A157
A153
A16
A158
A155
B1225
B1202
B1399
B1190
B1191
B1192
B1183
B1195
B1189
B1184
B1395
0 1 2 3 miles
0 1 2 3 4 5 km

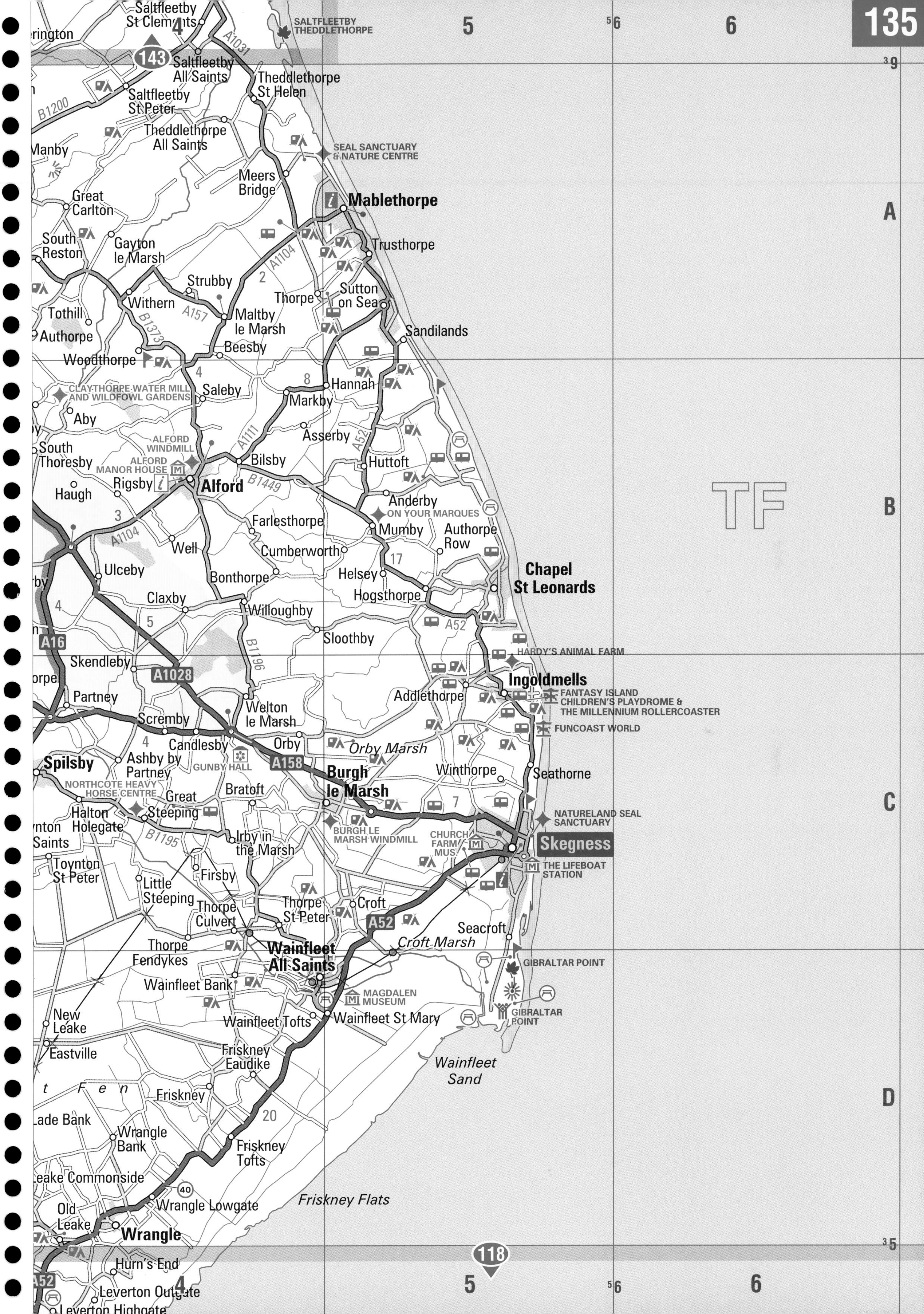
Saltfleetby St Clements
SALTFLEETBY THEDDLETHORPE
143
Saltfleetby All Saints
Theddlethorpe St Helen
Saltfleetby St Peter
B1200
A1031
Theddlethorpe All Saints
Manby
SEAL SANCTUARY & NATURE CENTRE
Meers Bridge
Mablethorpe
Great Carlton
South Reston
Gayton le Marsh
Trusthorpe
A1104
Strubby
Withern
A157
Maltby le Marsh
Thorpe
Sutton on Sea
Tothill
Authorpe
B1373
Sandilands
Beesby
Woodthorpe
CLAYTHORPE WATER MILL AND WILDFOWL GARDENS
Saleby
Hannah
Markby
Aby
ALFORD WINDMILL
A1111
Asserby
A52
South Thoresby
ALFORD MANOR HOUSE
Bilsby
Huttoft
Rigsby
Alford
B1449
Haugh
Anderby
ON YOUR MARQUES
TF
Farlesthorpe
Mumby
Authorpe Row
A1104
Well
Cumberworth
Ulceby
Bonthorpe
Helsey
Hogsthorpe
Chapel St Leonards
Claxby
Willoughby
A52
A16
Sloothby
B1196
HARDY'S ANIMAL FARM
Skendleby
A1028
Ingoldmells
FANTASY ISLAND CHILDREN'S PLAYDROME & THE MILLENNIUM ROLLERCOASTER
Partney
Addlethorpe
Welton le Marsh
Scremby
FUNCOAST WORLD
Candlesby
Orby
Orby Marsh
Spilsby
Ashby by Partney
GUNBY HALL
A158
Burgh le Marsh
Winthorpe
Seathorne
NORTHCOTE HEAVY HORSE CENTRE
Great Steeping
Bratoft
Halton Holegate
NATURELAND SEAL SANCTUARY
Toynton All Saints
B1195
Irby in the Marsh
BURGH LE MARSH WINDMILL
CHURCH FARM MUS.
Skegness
Toynton St Peter
Firsby
THE LIFEBOAT STATION
Little Steeping
Thorpe Culvert
Thorpe St Peter
Croft
A52
Seacroft
Thorpe Fendykes
Wainfleet All Saints
Croft Marsh
GIBRALTAR POINT
Wainfleet Bank
MAGDALEN MUSEUM
GIBRALTAR POINT
New Leake
Wainfleet Tofts
Wainfleet St Mary
Eastville
Friskney Eaudike
Wainfleet Sand
Friskney
Lade Bank
Wrangle Bank
Friskney Tofts
Leake Commonside
Wrangle Lowgate
Friskney Flats
Old Leake
Wrangle
118
Hurn's End
A52
Leverton Outgate
Leverton Highgate
A
B
C
D
4
5
6

1
2
3
4
A
B
C
D
Squires Gate
BLACKPOOL INTERNATIONAL
Westby
Moss Side
Wrea Green
Dowbridge
Lea Town
Ingol
Fulwood
Cadley
144
145
Higher Ballam
Newton
Scales
Clifton
Preston
TOY AND TEDDY BEAR MUSEUM
ROYAL LYTHAM & ST ANNES
LYTHAM HALL
Ansdell
St Annes
Lytham St Anne's
Lytham
Fairhaven
Salters Bank
Warton
Freckleton
A584
Bottom of Hutton
Higher Penwortham
Walton-le-Dale
Middleforth Green
Hutton
Longton
Ribble
A582
Lostock Hall
New Longton
Farington
Banks Sands
RIBBLE MARSHES
Great Bank
Hesketh Bank
Walmer Bridge
Midge Hall
BRITISH COMMERCIAL VEHICLE MUS.
Becconsall
Much Hoole
LEYLAND
Hundred End
Broadfield
Banks
Tarleton
B5248
Horse Bank
Bretherton
WORDEN
Crossens
Marshside
A565
B5247
B5249
Ulnes Walton
Shaw Green
Sollom
Croston
M6
ECO VISITOR CENTRE
Southport
Churchtown
Mere Brow
A581
Yarrow
NEW MODEL VILLAGE
Holmeswood
Eccleston
B5246
RUFFORD OLD HALL
CAMELOT
Blowick
MARTIN MERE WILDFOWL AND WETLAND CENTRE
Rufford
Mawdesley
Heskin Green
Birkdale
Brown Edge
Tarlscough
B5243
Snape Green
Bescar
Douglas
Canal
Bispham Green
Hillside
ROYAL BIRKDALE
Scarisbrick
New Lane
A59
Wrightington Bar
Ainsdale-on-Sea
Ainsdale
Shirdley Hill
ECCLES FARM CRAFT CENTRE
Hill Dale
Mossy Lea
Woodvale
Pinfold
Liverpool
Burscough
Burscough Bridge
Dangerous Corner
Parbold
A570
B5242
A5209
Formby Hills
Halsall
Newburgh
Leeds and
AINSDALE SAND DUNES
Barton
Haskayne
ORMSKIRK
B5240
Appley Bridge
Shevington
Freshfield
A577
Dalton
BEACON PARK
Roby Mill
Formby
Westhead
Stanley
Downholland Cross
Formby Pt.
Little Altcar
Aughton Park
Blaguegate
Skelmersdale
Great Altcar
B5195
Digmoor
Up Holland
Orrell
CABIN HILL
Stanley Gate
Aughton
Royal Oak
A506
M58
Hightown
Ince Blundell
Lydiate
B5197
Bickerstaffe
Rainford Junction
Higher End
Alt
A59
B5193
Barrow Nook
B5206
Maghull
Crawford
Lunt
Longshaw
Little Crosby
M58
Melling Mount
Rainford
A571
B5422
Sefton
Thornton
Netherton
Billinge
B5205
Melling
Crank
Garswood
Great Crosby
Kirkby
Moss Bank
Chadwick Green
BELFAST 8:00
Crosby Channel
A565
AINTREE
Aintree
B5203
LITHERLAND
Southdene
A506
DOUGLAS 4:00 (Winter Only)
DUBLIN 7:45
Waterloo
Seaforth
Orrell
A59
A580
Denton's Green
Fazakerley
Knowsley
Blackbrook
Broad Oak
Bootle
St Helens
Gillar's Green
M57
Eccleston
DUBLIN 4:00 (Mar-Dec)
DOUGLAS 2:30
New Brighton
Walton
Norris Green
KNOWSLEY SAFARI PARK
Peasley Cross
NEW PALACE
CROXTETH
Kirkdale
Merseyside
A58
Sutton
WALKER GALL.
Anfield
West Derby
Thatto Heath
Liscard
Egremont
Longview
Eccleston Park
A570
Sutton Leach
Wallasey
Everton
A57
Prescot
Rainhill
Leasowe
Seacombe
LIVERPOOL
Knotty Ash
Whiston
Sutton Manor
Clock Face
MARITIME MUS.
TOLL
Moreton
Poulton
Huyton
Roby
A57
M62
Bidston
Edge Hill
A5058
Rainhill Stoops
Bold Heath
126
127
B5178
A5080
PEX HILL
Wavertree
Childwall
TATE
Toxteth
Netherley
Farnworth
Barrow's Green
Greasby
Birkenhead
ALBERT DOCK
Mossley
A562
Tarbock Green
Cronton
0 1 2 3 miles
0 1 2 3 4 5 km

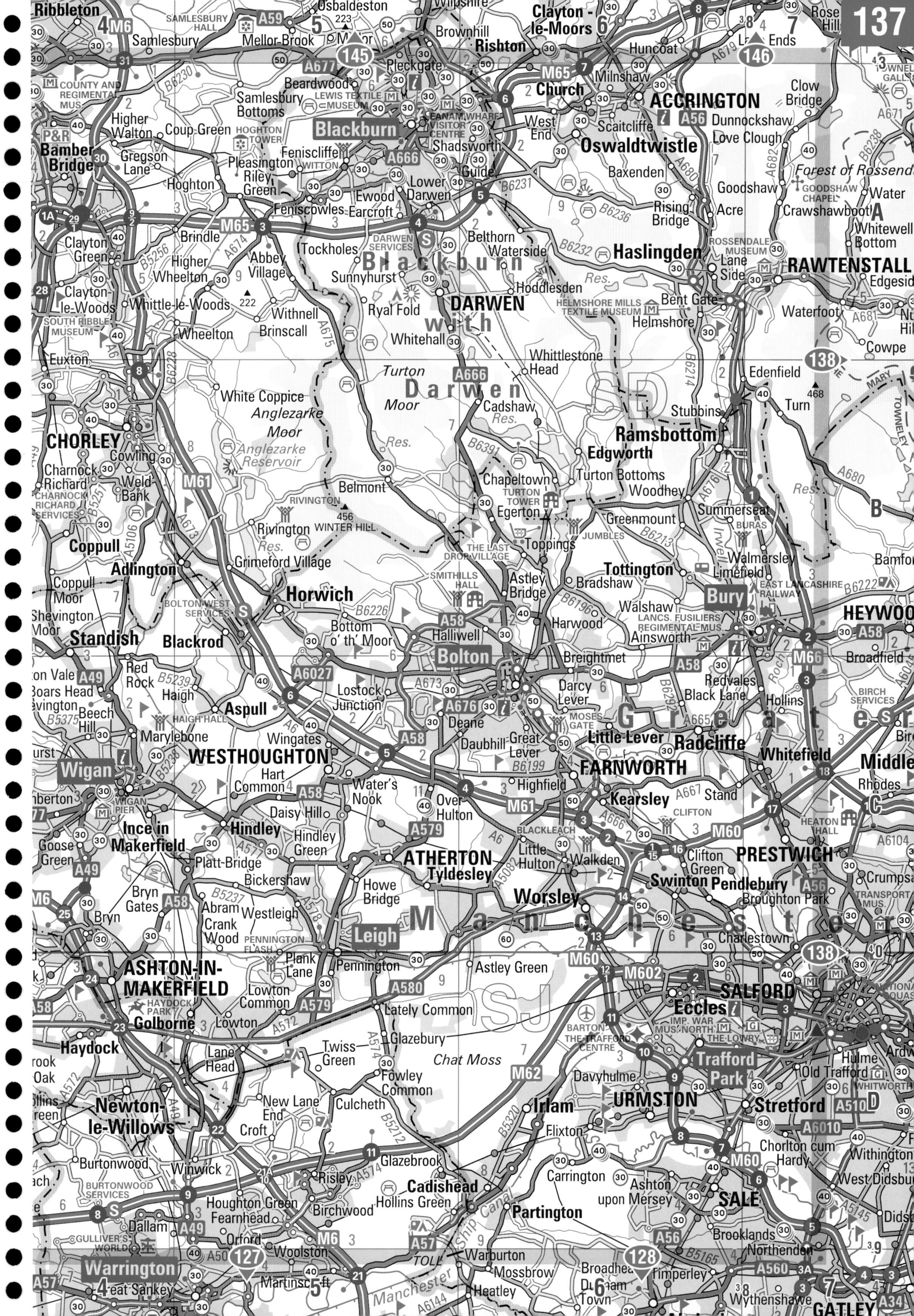
137
Ribbleton
Samlesbury
Osbaldeston
Mellor Brook
Clayton-le-Moors
Brownhill
Rishton
Huncoat
Ends
Pleckgate
Beardwood
Samlesbury Bottoms
Blackburn
Church
Milnshaw
ACCRINGTON
Clow Bridge
COUNTY AND REGIMENTAL MUS.
LEWIS TEXTILE MUSEUM
Higher Walton
Coup Green
Bamber Bridge
Gregson Lane
Pleasington
Feniscliffe
Shadsworth
West End
Scaitcliffe
Oswaldtwistle
Dunnockshaw
Love Clough
Riley Green
Hoghton
Guide
Baxenden
Forest of Rossendale
Goodshaw
GOODSHAW CHAPEL
Water
Feniscowles
Ewood
Lower Darwen
Eccleston
Rising Bridge
Acre
Crawshawbooth
Clayton Green
Brindle
Tockholes
DARWEN SERVICES
Belthorn
Waterside
Haslingden
ROSSENDALE MUSEUM
Whitewell Bottom
Higher Wheelton
Abbey Village
Sunnyhurst
Blackburn
Hoddlesden
Lane Side
RAWTENSTALL
Edgeside
Clayton-le-Woods
Whittle-le-Woods
Withnell
Ryal Fold
DARWEN
HELMSHORE MILLS TEXTILE MUSEUM
Bent Gate
Helmshore
Waterfoot
SOUTH RIBBLE MUSEUM
Wheelton
Brinscall
with
Whitehall
Euxton
Turton Moor
Whittlestone Head
Cowpe
Edenfield
Darwen
White Coppice
Anglezarke Moor
Cadshaw
Stubbins
Turn
CHORLEY
Anglezarke Reservoir
Ramsbottom
Cowling
Edgworth
Charnock Richard
Weld Bank
CHARNOCK RICHARD SERVICES
Belmont
Chapeltown
Turton Bottoms
Woodhey
RIVINGTON
WINTER HILL
TURTON TOWER
Egerton
Summerseat
Greenmount
BURAS
Rivington
Coppull
THE LAST DROP VILLAGE
Toppings
JUMBLES
Walmersley
Grimeford Village
SMITHILLS HALL
Adlington
Tottington
Limefield
Bamford
Coppull Moor
Astley Bridge
Bradshaw
EAST LANCASHIRE RAILWAY
Horwich
BOLTON WEST SERVICES
Bury
Walshaw
HEYWOOD
Shevington Moor
Bottom o' th' Moor
Halliwell
Harwood
LANCS. FUSILIERS REGIMENTAL MUS.
Ainsworth
Standish
Blackrod
Bolton
Breightmet
Broadfield
Red Rock
Lostock Junction
Darcy Lever
Redvales
Haigh
Aspull
Black Lane
Hollins
BIRCH SERVICES
Beech Hill
HAIGH HALL
Deane
MOSES GATE
Greater
Wingates
Marylebone
Daubhill
Great Lever
Little Lever
Radcliffe
Whitefield
WESTHOUGHTON
Middleton
Wigan
Hart Common
FARNWORTH
Water's Nook
Highfield
Rhodes
Kearsley
Stand
WIGAN PIER
Daisy Hill
Over Hulton
CLIFTON
HEATON HALL
Ince in Makerfield
Hindley
Hindley Green
BLACKLEACH
Little Hulton
Clifton Green
PRESTWICH
Goose Green
Platt Bridge
ATHERTON
Tyldesley
Walkden
Swinton
Pendlebury
Crumpsall
Bickershaw
Howe Bridge
Broughton Park
TRANSPORT MUS.
Bryn Gates
Abram
Westleigh
Worsley
Bryn
Crank Wood
Manchester
PENNINGTON FLASH
Leigh
Charlestown
Plank Lane
Pennington
Astley Green
ASHTON-IN-MAKERFIELD
SALFORD
Lowton Common
Lately Common
Eccles
HAYDOCK PARK
Golborne
Lowton
BARTON
THE TRAFFORD CENTRE
IMP. WAR MUS. NORTH
THE LOWRY
Haydock
Twiss Green
Glazebury
Chat Moss
Trafford Park
Hulme
Old Trafford
Lane Head
Fowley Common
Davyhulme
Newton-le-Willows
New Lane End
Culcheth
Irlam
URMSTON
Stretford
Croft
Flixton
Chorlton cum Hardy
Withington
Burtonwood
Winwick
Glazebrook
Carrington
BURTONWOOD SERVICES
Risley
Cadishead
Ashton upon Mersey
West Didsbury
Houghton Green
Hollins Green
Partington
SALE
Fearnhead
Birchwood
Dallam
Brooklands
Orford
GULLIVER'S WORLD
Woolston
Warburton
Northenden
Warrington
Broadheath
Timperley
Martinscroft
Mossbrow
Manchester Ship Canal
Great Sankey
Heatley
Dunham Town
Wythenshawe
GATLEY
Res.
SD
SJ
M6
M61
M62
M65
M66
M60
M602
M56
A58
A49
A579
A580
A6027
A676
A666
A677
A56
A6010
A560
A57
A50
A5103
145
146
138
127
128

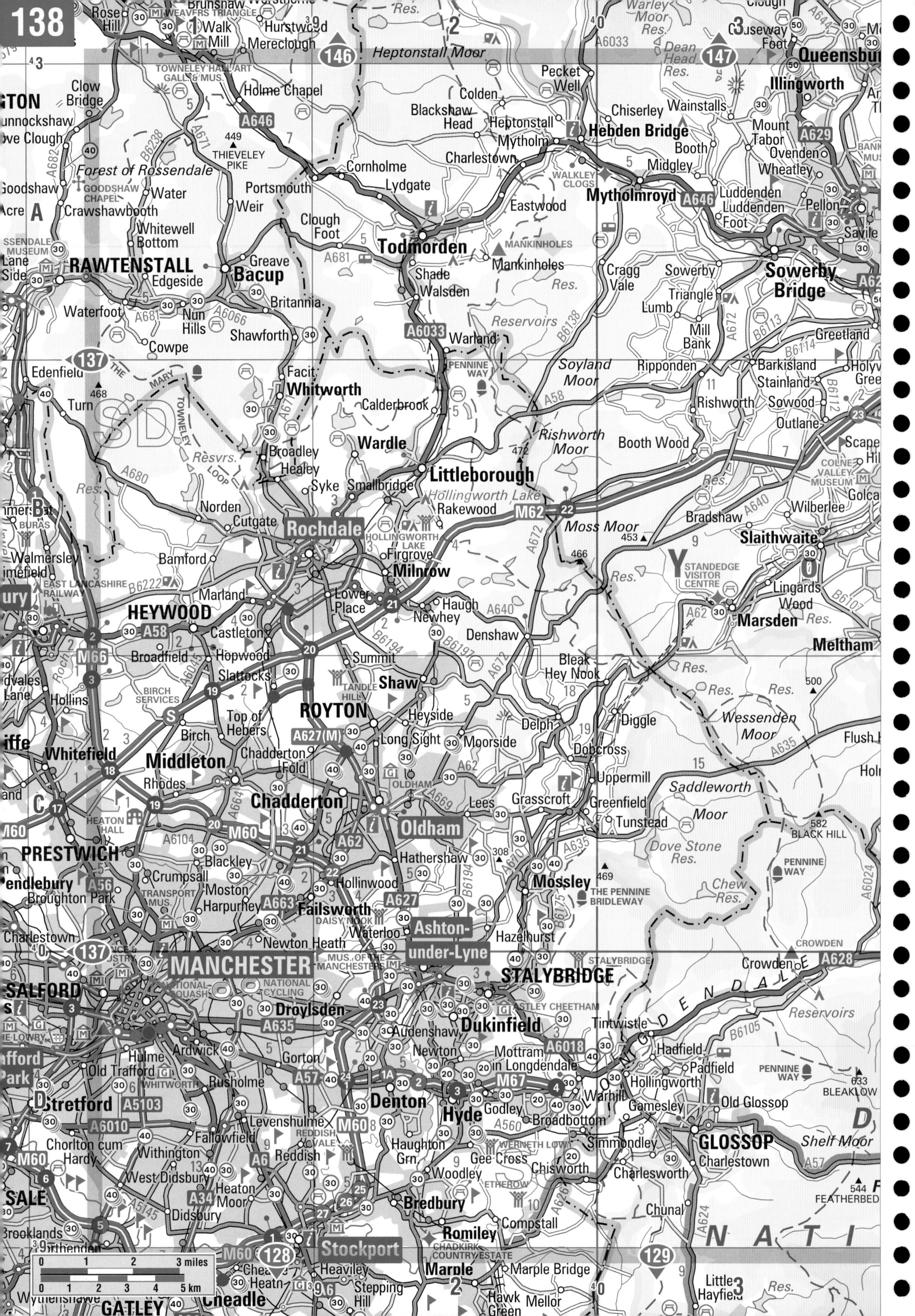

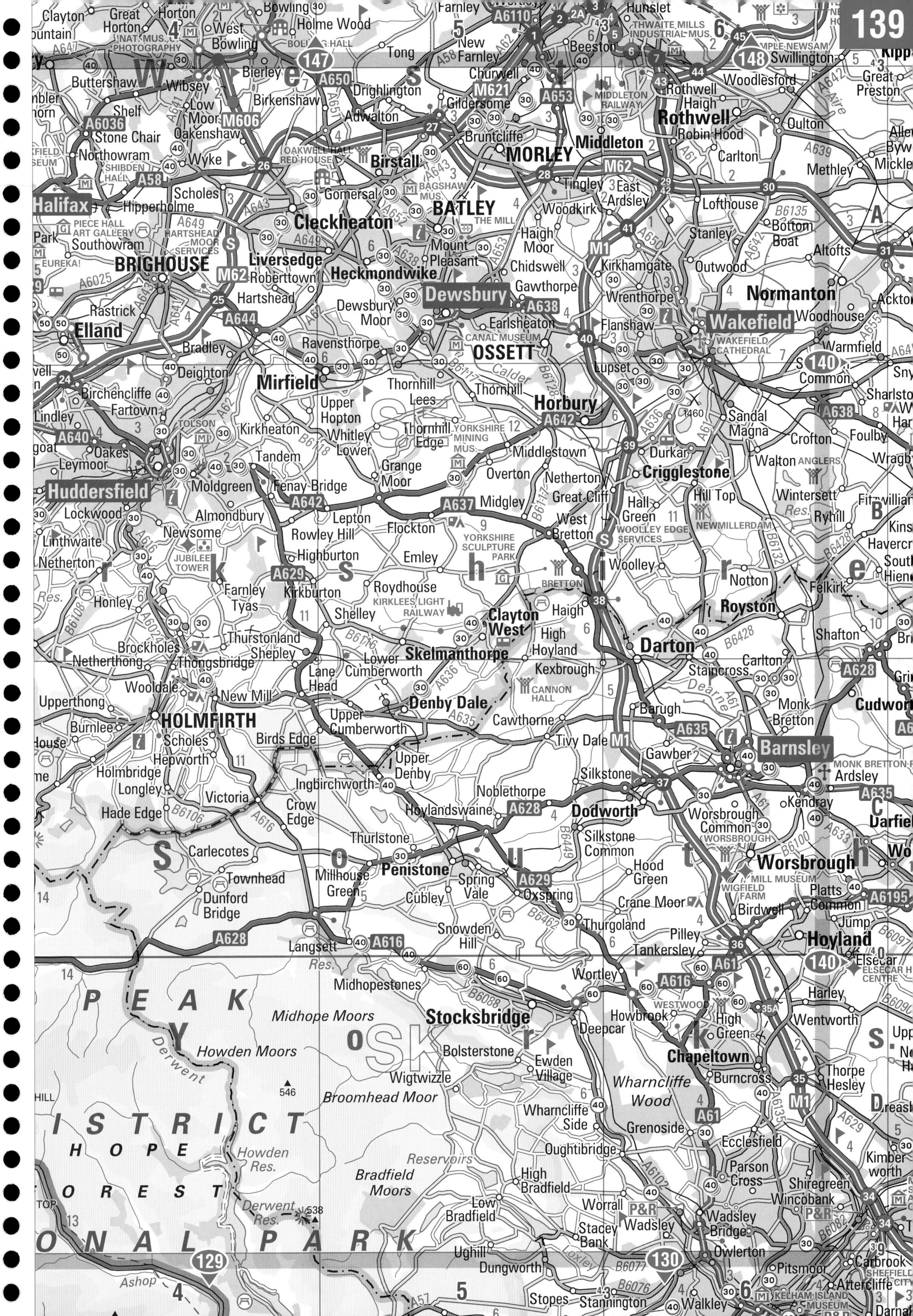

Clayton
Great Horton
Bowling
Holme Wood
Farnley
Hunslet
THWAITE MILLS INDUSTRIAL MUS.
West Bowling
NAT. MUS. PHOTOGRAPHY
BOLLING HALL
Tong
New Farnley
Beeston
TEMPLE NEWSAM
Swillington
Great Preston
Buttershaw
Wibsey
Bierley
Drighlington
Churwell
Woodlesford
Rothwell
Haigh
Shelf
Low Moor
Birkenshaw
Adwalton
Gildersome
MIDDLETON RAILWAY
Rothwell
Oulton
Stone Chair
Oakenshaw
Bruntcliffe
Middleton
Robin Hood
Northowram
Wyke
OAKWELL HALL RED HOUSE
Birstall
MORLEY
Carlton
SHIBDEN HALL
Methley
Scholes
Gomersal
BAGSHAW MUS.
Tingley
East Ardsley
Halifax
Hipperholme
BATLEY
THE MILL
Woodkirk
Lofthouse
Bottom Boat
PIECE HALL ART GALLERY
HARTSHEAD MOOR SERVICES
Cleckheaton
Haigh Moor
Stanley
Park
Southowram
Mount Pleasant
Altofts
EUREKA!
BRIGHOUSE
Liversedge
Heckmondwike
Chidswell
Kirkhamgate
Outwood
Robertown
Gawthorpe
Normanton
Rastrick
Hartshead
Dewsbury Moor
Dewsbury
Wrenthorpe
Ackton
Elland
Earlsheaton
Flanshaw
Wakefield
Woodhouse
Bradley
Ravensthorpe
CANAL MUSEUM
WAKEFIELD CATHEDRAL
OSSETT
Warmfield
Deighton
Mirfield
Thornhill
Calder
Lupset
Common
Birchencliffe
Upper Hopton
Thornhill Lees
Thornhill
Horbury
Sandal Magna
Sharlston
Lindley
Fartown
TOLSON MUS.
Kirkheaton
Whitley Lower
Thornhill Edge
YORKSHIRE MINING MUS.
Middlestown
Durkar
Crofton
Foulby
Oakes
Leymoor
Tandem
Grange Moor
Overton
Netherton
Crigglestone
Walton
ANGLERS
Huddersfield
Moldgreen
Fenay Bridge
Lepton
Midgley
Great Cliff
Hill Top
Wintersett
Lockwood
Almondbury
Flockton
Hall Green
West Bretton
NEWMILLERDAM
Res.
Ryhill
Newsome
Rowley Hill
YORKSHIRE SCULPTURE PARK
Bretton
WOOLLEY EDGE SERVICES
Linthwaite
JUBILEE TOWER
Highburton
Emley
Woolley
Notton
Netherton
Farnley Tyas
Kirkburton
Roydhouse
BRETTON
Felkirk
Royston
Honley
KIRKLEES LIGHT RAILWAY
Haigh
Shelley
Clayton West
High Hoyland
Darton
Shafton
Brockholes
Thurstonland
Shepley
Lower Cumberworth
Skelmanthorpe
Netherthong
Thongsbridge
Lane Head
Kexbrough
Staincross
Carlton
Wooldale
New Mill
Denby Dale
CANNON HALL
Dearne
Upperthong
Barugh
Monk Bretton
Cudworth
Burnlee
HOLMFIRTH
Upper Cumberworth
Cawthorne
Scholes
Birds Edge
Tivy Dale
Gawber
Barnsley
Hepworth
Upper Denby
Silkstone
MONK BRETTON
Ardsley
Holmbridge
Longley
Ingbirchworth
Noblethorpe
Kendray
Victoria
Crow Edge
Hoylandswaine
Dodworth
Worsbrough Common
Darfield
Hade Edge
Thurlstone
Silkstone Common
WORSBROUGH
Carlecotes
Penistone
Millhouse Green
Spring Vale
Hood Green
Worsbrough
MILL MUSEUM
Townhead
Dunford Bridge
Cubley
Oxspring
Crane Moor
WIGFIELD FARM
Platts Common
Birdwell
Thurgoland
Jump
Snowden Hill
Pilley
Langsett
Res.
Tankersley
Hoyland
Elsecar
ELSECAR HERITAGE CENTRE
Midhopestones
Wortley
Harley
PEAK
Midhope Moors
Stocksbridge
WESTWOOD
Howbrook
High Green
Wentworth
Deepcar
Howden Moors
Derwent
Bolsterstone
Chapeltown
Ewden Village
Wharncliffe Wood
Burncross
Thorpe Hesley
Wigtwizzle
546
Broomhead Moor
DISTRICT
Wharncliffe Side
Grenoside
HOPE
Howden Res.
Oughtibridge
Ecclesfield
Kimberworth
Reservoirs
Bradfield Moors
High Bradfield
Parson Cross
Shiregreen
FOREST
Derwent Res.
538
Low Bradfield
Worrall
Wadsley
Wincobank
NATIONAL PARK
Stacey Bank
Wadsley Bridge
Ughill
Owlerton
Carbrook
Dungworth
Loxley
Pitsmoor
Attercliffe
Ashop
Stopes
Stannington
Walkley
KELHAM ISLAND MUSEUM
Darnall
M1
M62
M621
M606
A61
A628
A629
A616
A635
A642
A638
A644
A637
147
148
140
129
130

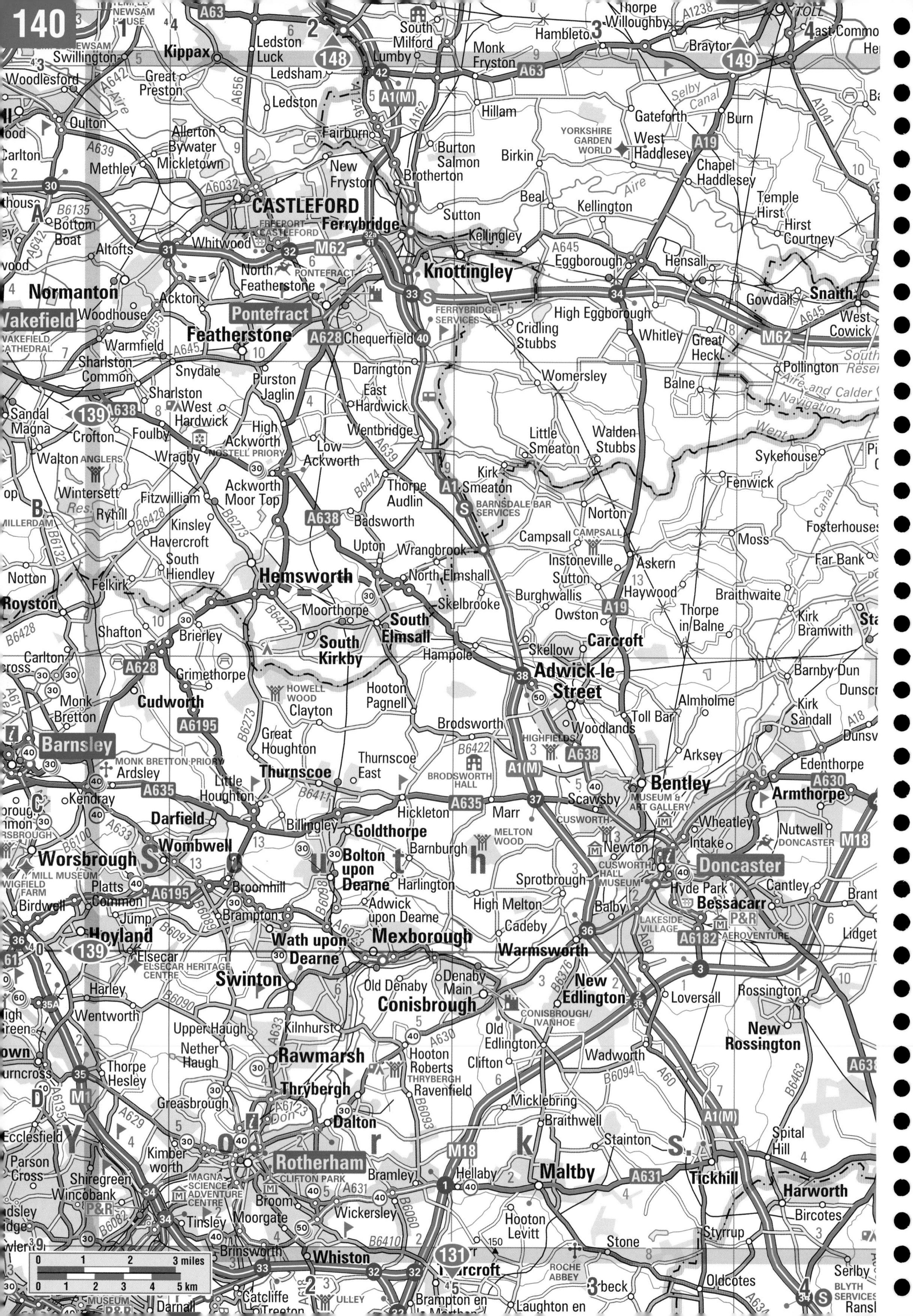
Swillington
Kippax
Ledston Luck
South Milford
Lumby
Monk Fryston
Hambleton
Thorpe Willoughby
Brayton
148
149
A63
Woodlesford
Great Preston
Ledsham
Ledston
A1(M)
A162
A1246
Hillam
Selby Canal
Gateforth
Burn
A1041
Oulton
Allerton Bywater
Fairburn
Burton Salmon
Birkin
YORKSHIRE GARDEN WORLD
West Haddlesey
A19
Chapel Haddlesey
Methley
Mickletown
New Fryston
Brotherton
A639
A6032
CASTLEFORD
Aire
Beal
Kellington
Temple Hirst
Hirst Courtney
B6135
Bottom Boat
FREEPORT CASTLEFORD
Ferrybridge
Sutton
Kellingley
Altofts
Whitwood
M62
A645
Eggborough
Hensall
North Featherstone
PONTEFRACT
Knottingley
Normanton
Ackton
FERRYBRIDGE SERVICES
High Eggborough
Gowdall
Snaith
Wakefield
Woodhouse
Pontefract
Cridling Stubbs
Whitley
Great Heck
West Cowick
WAKEFIELD CATHEDRAL
Featherstone
A628
Chequerfield
Warmfield
A655
Sharlston Common
Snydale
Purston Jaglin
Darrington
Womersley
Balne
Pollington
Aire and Calder Navigation
Sandal Magna
139
A638
Sharlston
West Hardwick
East Hardwick
Crofton
Foulby
High Ackworth
Wentbridge
Little Smeaton
Walden Stubbs
Went
Walton
ANGLERS
NOSTELL PRIORY
Wragby
Low Ackworth
A639
Sykehouse
Wintersett
Fitzwilliam
Ackworth Moor Top
Thorpe Audlin
B6474
Kirk Smeaton
A1
Fenwick
Ryhill
Res.
B6428
Kinsley
B6273
A638
Badsworth
BARNSDALE BAR SERVICES
Norton
Canal
Fosterhouses
Havercroft
South Hiendley
Upton
Wrangbrook
Campsall
CAMPSALL
Moss
Instoneville
Askern
Far Bank
Notton
Felkirk
Hemsworth
North Elmshall
Sutton
B6132
Royston
Moorthorpe
Skelbrooke
Burghwallis
Haywood
Braithwaite
Shafton
Brierley
B6422
South Elmsall
Owston
Thorpe in Balne
Kirk Bramwith
B6428
South Kirkby
Hampole
Skellow
Carcroft
Carlton
A628
Grimethorpe
Adwick le Street
Barnby Dun
HOWELL WOOD
Hooton Pagnell
Almholme
Monk Bretton
Cudworth
Clayton
Woodlands
Toll Bar
Kirk Sandall
A6195
B6273
Brodsworth
Barnsley
Great Houghton
HIGHFIELDS
A638
Arksey
A18
MONK BRETTON PRIORY
Ardsley
Thurnscoe
Thurnscoe East
B6422
BRODSWORTH HALL
A1(M)
Bentley
Edenthorpe
Little Houghton
Scawsby
A630
Armthorpe
Kendray
A635
B6411
A635
MUSEUM & ART GALLERY
Darfield
Billingley
Hickleton
Marr
CUSWORTH
Wheatley
Nutwell
A633
Goldthorpe
MELTON WOOD
Intake
DONCASTER
M18
Wombwell
Barnburgh
Newton
Worsbrough
Bolton upon Dearne
CUSWORTH HALL MUSEUM
Doncaster
S
o
u
t
h
MILL MUSEUM
Platts Common
A6195
Broomhill
Harlington
Sprotbrough
Hyde Park
Cantley
WIGFIELD FARM
Birdwell
Brampton
B6098
Adwick upon Dearne
High Melton
Bessacarr
LAKESIDE VILLAGE
P&R
Jump
Cadeby
A60
A6182
AEROVENTURE
Hoyland
B6097
Wath upon Dearne
A6023
Mexborough
Warmsworth
Lidget
Elsecar
ELSECAR HERITAGE CENTRE
Swinton
Denaby Main
B6376
New Edlington
Rossington
Harley
B6090
Old Denaby
Conisbrough
Loversall
Wentworth
Upper Haugh
Kilnhurst
CONISBROUGH/ IVANHOE
New Rossington
A633
Nether Haugh
A630
Old Edlington
Wadworth
Rawmarsh
Hooton Roberts
Clifton
B6463
Thorpe Hesley
THRYBERGH
Thrybergh
Ravenfield
B6094
A60
M1
Greasbrough
A6123
Don
B6093
Micklebring
Braithwell
A1(M)
A629
Dalton
Spital Hill
Ecclesfield
Y
o
r
k
s.
Kimberworth
Stainton
Parson Cross
Rotherham
M18
Maltby
A631
Tickhill
Harworth
Shiregreen
CLIFTON PARK
Bramley
Hellaby
MAGNA SCIENCE ADVENTURE CENTRE
Wincobank
A631
Broom
Hooton Levitt
Bircotes
P&R
Tinsley
B6082
Moorgate
Wickersley
B6060
Styrrup
Brinsworth
B6410
Stone
Whiston
131
Harcroft
ROCHE ABBEY
Serlby
Oldcotes
BLYTH SERVICES
A618
MUSEUM
Catcliffe
Treeton
ULLEY
Brampton en le Morthen
Laughton en
Letwell
A634
Darnall
0 1 2 3 miles
0 1 2 3 4 5 km

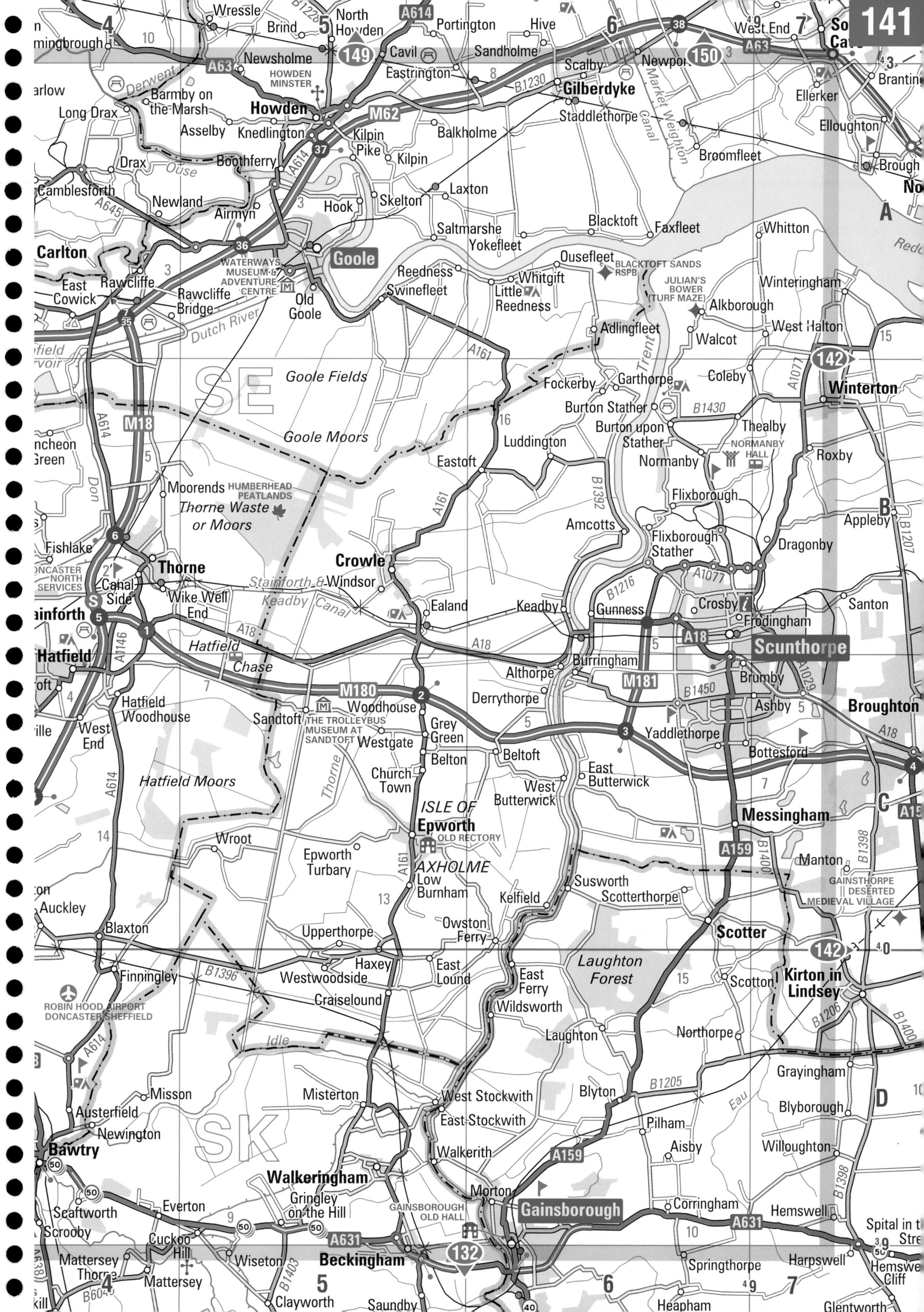
Wressle
Brind
North Howden
A614
Portington
Hive
West End
Newsholme
Cavil
Sandholme
Scalby
Newport
Howden Minster
Eastrington
Gilberdyke
Ellerker
Brantingham
Barmby on the Marsh
Long Drax
Howden
Asselby
Knedlington
Kilpin Pike
Kilpin
Balkholme
Staddlethorpe
Market Weighton Canal
Elloughton
Broomfleet
Brough
Drax
Boothferry
Ouse
Camblesforth
Newland
Airmyn
Hook
Skelton
Laxton
Saltmarshe
Yokefleet
Blacktoft
Faxfleet
Whitton
Carlton
Goole
Waterways Museum & Adventure Centre
Reedness
Ousefleet
Blacktoft Sands RSPB
Whitgift
Julian's Bower (Turf Maze)
Winteringham
East Cowick
Rawcliffe
Rawcliffe Bridge
Old Goole
Swinefleet
Little Reedness
Alkborough
Adlingfleet
West Halton
Walcot
Dutch River
Trent
SE
Goole Fields
Fockerby
Garthorpe
Coleby
Winterton
Burton Stather
Burton upon Stather
Thealby
Goole Moors
Luddington
Normanby
Normanby Hall
Roxby
Eastoft
Moorends
Humberhead Peatlands
Thorne Waste or Moors
Flixborough
Amcotts
Appleby
Flixborough Stather
Dragonby
Fishlake
Crowle
Thorne
Doncaster North Services
Canal Side
Stainforth & Keadby Canal
Windsor
Wike Well End
Stainforth
Ealand
Keadby
Gunness
Crosby
Frodingham
Santon
Hatfield
Hatfield Chase
Althorpe
Burringham
Scunthorpe
Brumby
Hatfield Woodhouse
Woodhouse
Derrythorpe
Ashby
Broughton
Sandtoft
The Trolleybus Museum at Sandtoft
Grey Green
Westgate
Yaddlethorpe
West End
Belton
Beltoft
Bottesford
Hatfield Moors
Church Town
East Butterwick
West Butterwick
Isle of Axholme
Epworth
Old Rectory
Messingham
Wroot
Epworth Turbary
Low Burnham
Manton
Gainsthorpe Deserted Medieval Village
Susworth
Scotterthorpe
Kelfield
Auckley
Owston Ferry
Scotter
Blaxton
Upperthorpe
Haxey
East Lound
Laughton Forest
Kirton in Lindsey
Finningley
Westwoodside
East Ferry
Scotton
Craiselound
Wildsworth
Robin Hood Airport Doncaster Sheffield
Laughton
Northorpe
Idle
Grayingham
Misson
Misterton
West Stockwith
Blyton
Austerfield
East Stockwith
Pilham
Blyborough
Newington
SK
Aisby
Willoughton
Bawtry
Walkerith
Walkeringham
Morton
Gringley on the Hill
Corringham
Scaftworth
Everton
Gainsborough
Hemswell
Gainsborough Old Hall
Spital in the Street
Scrooby
Cuckoo Hill
Mattersey Thorpe
Wiseton
Beckingham
Springthorpe
Harpswell
Hemswell Cliff
Mattersey
Clayworth
Saundby
Heapham
Glentworth
M62
M18
M180
M181
A63
A18
A161
A614
A645
A1146
A1077
A159
A631
B1230
B1392
B1216
B1430
B1450
B1396
B1205
B1398
B1400
B1403
B1206
B1207
149
150
142
132

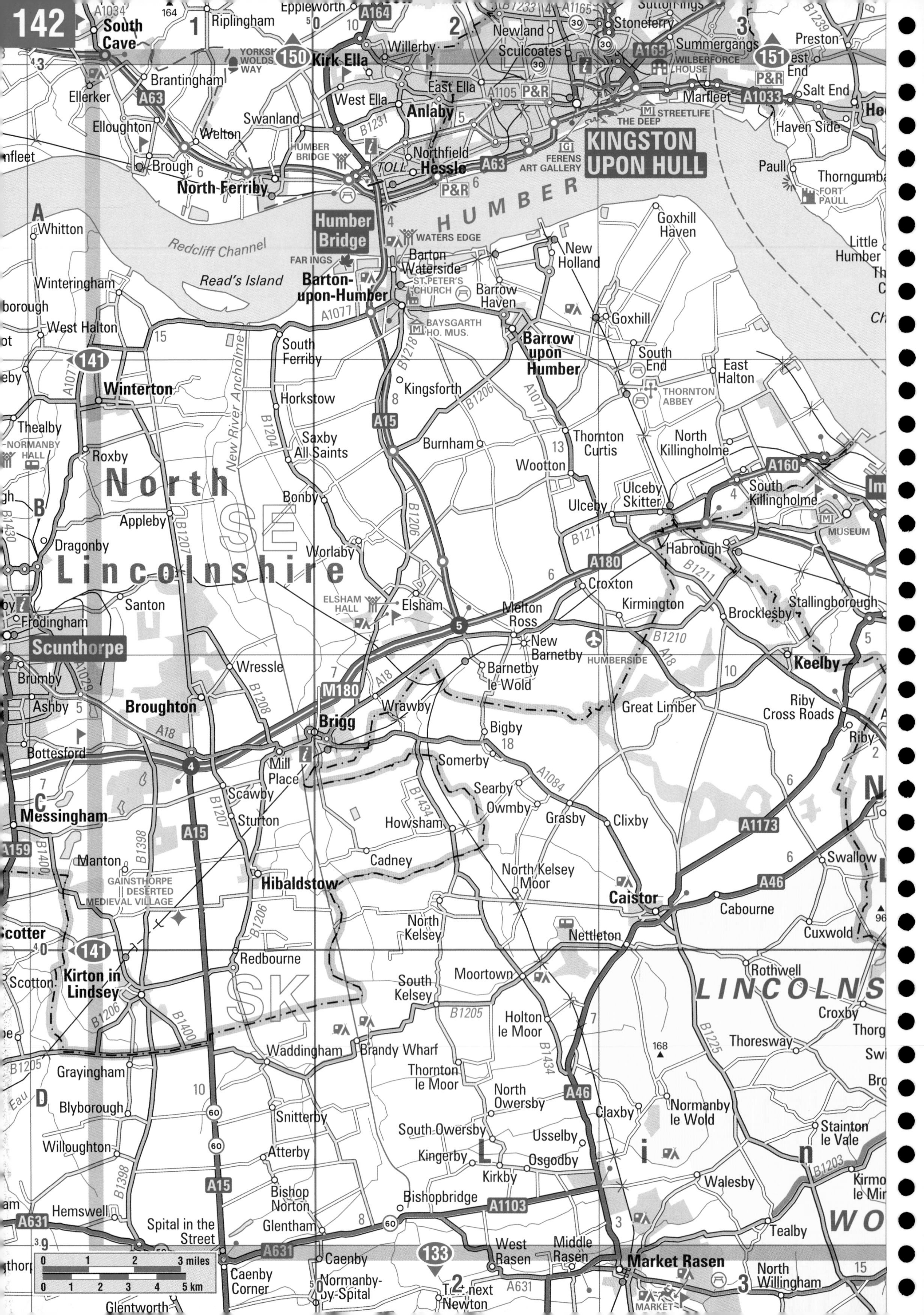
South Cave
Riplingham
Eppleworth
Kirk Ella
Willerby
Newland
Stoneferry
Sculcoates
Summergangs
Preston
Brantingham
Ellerker
West Ella
Anlaby
East Ella
Marfleet
Salt End
Swanland
Elloughton
Welton
Haven Side
Brough
Northfield
Hessle
North Ferriby
KINGSTON UPON HULL
Paull
Thorngumbald
FERENS ART GALLERY
THE DEEP
STREETLIFE
WILBERFORCE HOUSE
HUMBER BRIDGE
FORT PAULL
HUMBER
Whitton
Humber Bridge
WATERS EDGE
Goxhill Haven
Little Humber
Redcliff Channel
New Holland
FAR INGS
Barton Waterside
Read's Island
Winteringham
Barton-upon-Humber
ST PETER'S CHURCH
Barrow Haven
West Halton
BAYSGARTH HO. MUS.
Goxhill
South Ferriby
Barrow upon Humber
South End
East Halton
Winterton
Kingsforth
Horkstow
THORNTON ABBEY
Thealby
NORMANBY HALL
Saxby All Saints
Burnham
Thornton Curtis
North Killingholme
Roxby
New River Ancholme
Wootton
North
Ulceby Skitter
South Killingholme
Bonby
Ulceby
Appleby
MUSEUM
Dragonby
Worlaby
Habrough
Lincolnshire
Croxton
Santon
ELSHAM HALL
Elsham
Kirmington
Stallingborough
Frodingham
Melton Ross
Brocklesby
Scunthorpe
New Barnetby
HUMBERSIDE
Keelby
Wressle
Barnetby le Wold
Brumby
Ashby
Broughton
Wrawby
Great Limber
Riby Cross Roads
Brigg
Bigby
Riby
Bottesford
Somerby
Mill Place
Searby
Scawby
Owmby
Grasby
Clixby
Messingham
Sturton
Howsham
Manton
Cadney
Swallow
GAINSTHORPE DESERTED MEDIEVAL VILLAGE
Hibaldstow
North Kelsey Moor
Caistor
Cabourne
North Kelsey
Nettleton
Scotter
Cuxwold
Redbourne
Kirton in Lindsey
Rothwell
Scotton
Moortown
South Kelsey
LINCOLNSHIRE
Holton le Moor
Croxby
Waddingham
Brandy Wharf
Thoresway
Grayingham
Thornton le Moor
North Owersby
Blyborough
Snitterby
Claxby
Normanby le Wold
South Owersby
Usselby
Stainton le Vale
Willoughton
Atterby
Kingerby
Osgodby
Kirkby
Walesby
Hemswell
Bishop Norton
Bishopbridge
Spital in the Street
Glentham
Tealby
West Rasen
Middle Rasen
Market Rasen
Caenby
Caenby Corner
Normanby-by-Spital
Toft next Newton
North Willingham
Glentworth
MARKET
0 1 2 3 miles
0 1 2 3 4 5 km

Elstronwick
Burton Pidsea
Roos
North End
Tunstall
Waxholme
Owthorne
Withernsea
Rimswell
Burstwick
Halsham
East End
Camerton
Ryehill
Keyingham
Ottringham
Hollym
Winestead
Patrington
Holmpton
Out Newton
Welwick
Weeton
Sunk Island
Skeffling
Easington
Cherry Cob Sands
ROTTERDAM 12:30
ZEEBRUGGE 12:45
ROTTERDAM
ZEEBRUGGE
Kilnsea
TA
SPURN
SPURN HEAD
HOEK VAN HOLLAND 13:00
OOSTENDE 15:00
Grimsby
Pyewipe
Healing
West Marsh
Great Coates
CLEETHORPES
Old Clee
NATIONAL FISHING HERITAGE CENTRE
CLEETHORPES COAST LIGHT RAILWAY
PLEASURE ISLAND THEME PARK
MOUTH OF THE HUMBER
BREVIK 33:00
CUXHAVEN 22:00
ESBJERG 22:00
GOTHENBURG 26:00
KRISTIANSAND 30:00
ROTTERDAM 11:45
ZEEBRUGGE 14:00
Laceby
Nunsthorpe
Bradley
Scartho
Humberston
North East Lincolnshire
Irby upon Humber
Barnoldby le Beck
Waltham
New Waltham
WALTHAM WINDMILL
Holton le Clay
Beelsby
Brigsley
Ashby cum Fenby
Tetney Lock
North Cotes
Hatcliffe
Tetney
Waithe
East Ravendale
Grainsby
Marshchapel
Donna Nook
TF
Eskham
Wragholme
Grainthorpe
North Thoresby
Wold Newton
Fulstow
North Somercotes
DONNA NOOK
LINCOLNSHIRE WOLDS RLY.
Skidbrooke North End
Ludborough
Covenham St Bartholomew
Conisholme
South Somercotes
Saltfleet
North Ormsby
Binbrook
Covenham St Mary
Utterby
Yarburgh
Skidbrooke
Fotherby
ALVINGHAM MILL
Alvingham
Saltfleetby St Clements
Little Grimsby
North Cockerington
North Elkington
Great Tows
Kelstern
RUSHMOOR
Saltfleetby All Saints
Theddlethorpe St Helen
South Cockerington
South Elkington
Ludford
Welton le Wold
Louth
Keddington
Grimoldby
Saltfleetby St Peter
Theddlethorpe
A180
A46
A1098
B1219
A16
A18
B1203
A1031
B1201
A631
B1200
B1242
B1362
A1033
B1445
151
134
135
A
B
C
D
4
5
6

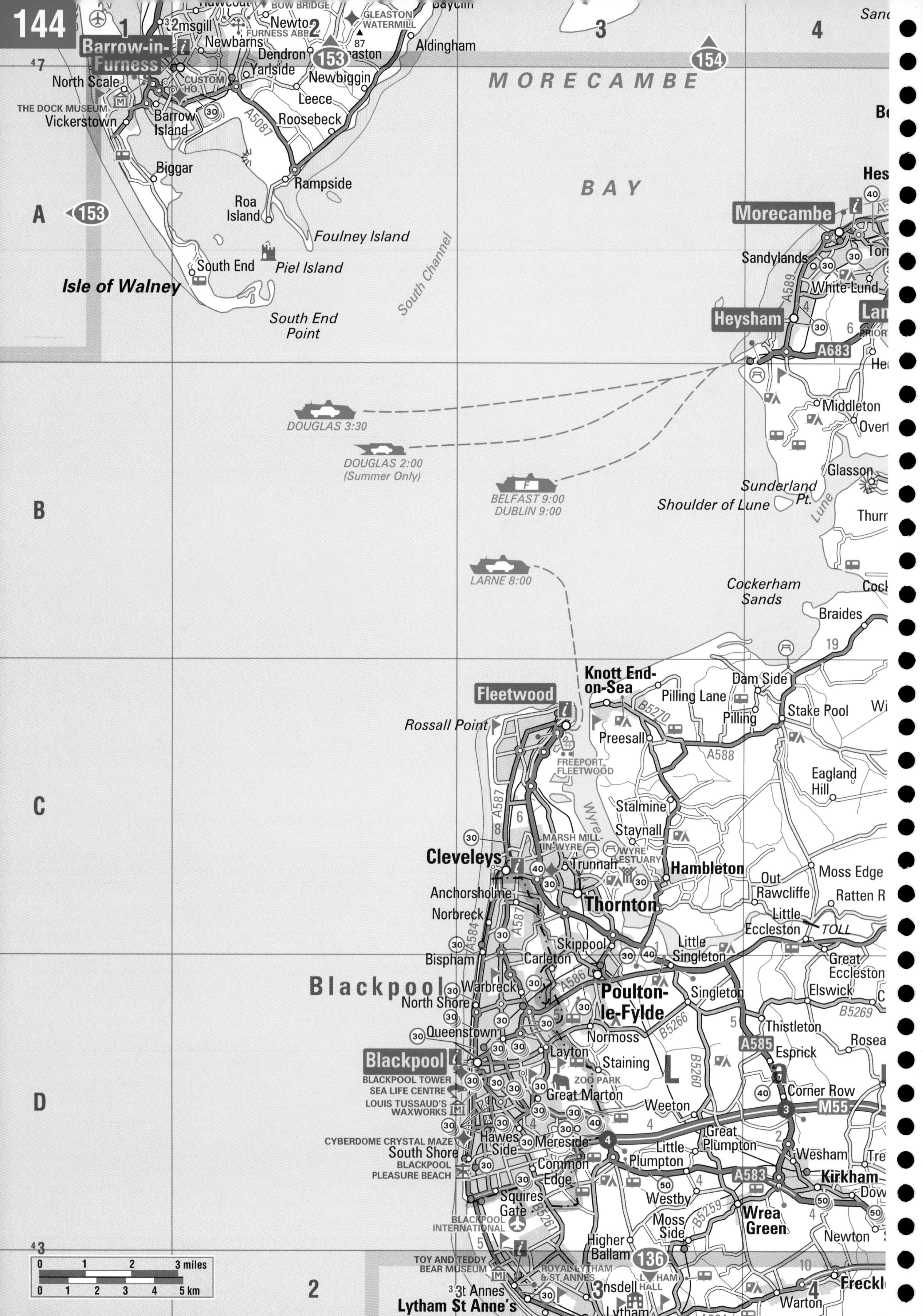

1
2
3
4
A
B
C
D
153
154
136
Barrow-in-Furness
Newbarns
FURNESS ABBEY
BOW BRIDGE
GLEASTON WATERMILL
Dendron
Aldingham
Yarlside
Newbiggin
North Scale
CUSTOM HO
THE DOCK MUSEUM
Vickerstown
Barrow Island
Leece
Roosebeck
A5087
Biggar
Rampside
Roa Island
Foulney Island
Piel Island
South End
Isle of Walney
South End Point
MORECAMBE
BAY
South Channel
Morecambe
Sandylands
White Lund
A589
Heysham
A683
Middleton
Glasson
Sunderland Pt.
Shoulder of Lune
Lune
Cockerham Sands
Braides
DOUGLAS 3:30
DOUGLAS 2:00 (Summer Only)
BELFAST 9:00
DUBLIN 9:00
LARNE 8:00
Fleetwood
Rossall Point
Knott End-on-Sea
B5270
Pilling Lane
Dam Side
Pilling
Stake Pool
Preesall
A588
FREEPORT FLEETWOOD
Eagland Hill
Wyre
Stalmine
Staynall
A587
MARSH MILL-IN-WYRE
WYRE ESTUARY
Cleveleys
Trunnah
Hambleton
Out Rawcliffe
Moss Edge
Anchorsholme
Thornton
Little Eccleston
TOLL
Norbreck
A584
Skippool
Little Singleton
Great Eccleston
Bispham
Carleton
A586
Blackpool
Warbreck
Poulton-le-Fylde
Singleton
Elswick
North Shore
B5269
Queenstown
Normoss
B5266
Thistleton
Layton
A585
Esprick
Roseacre
BLACKPOOL TOWER
SEA LIFE CENTRE
LOUIS TUSSAUD'S WAXWORKS
ZOO PARK
Staining
B5260
Great Marton
Corner Row
Weeton
M55
CYBERDOME CRYSTAL MAZE
Hawes Side
Mereside
Great Plumpton
Little Plumpton
Wesham
South Shore
BLACKPOOL PLEASURE BEACH
Common Edge
A583
Kirkham
Squires Gate
Westby
B5259
Wrea Green
B5261
BLACKPOOL INTERNATIONAL
Moss Side
Newton
Higher Ballam
TOY AND TEDDY BEAR MUSEUM
ROYAL LYTHAM & ST ANNES
HALL
St Annes
Lytham St Anne's
Lytham
Warton
0 1 2 3 miles
0 1 2 3 4 5 km

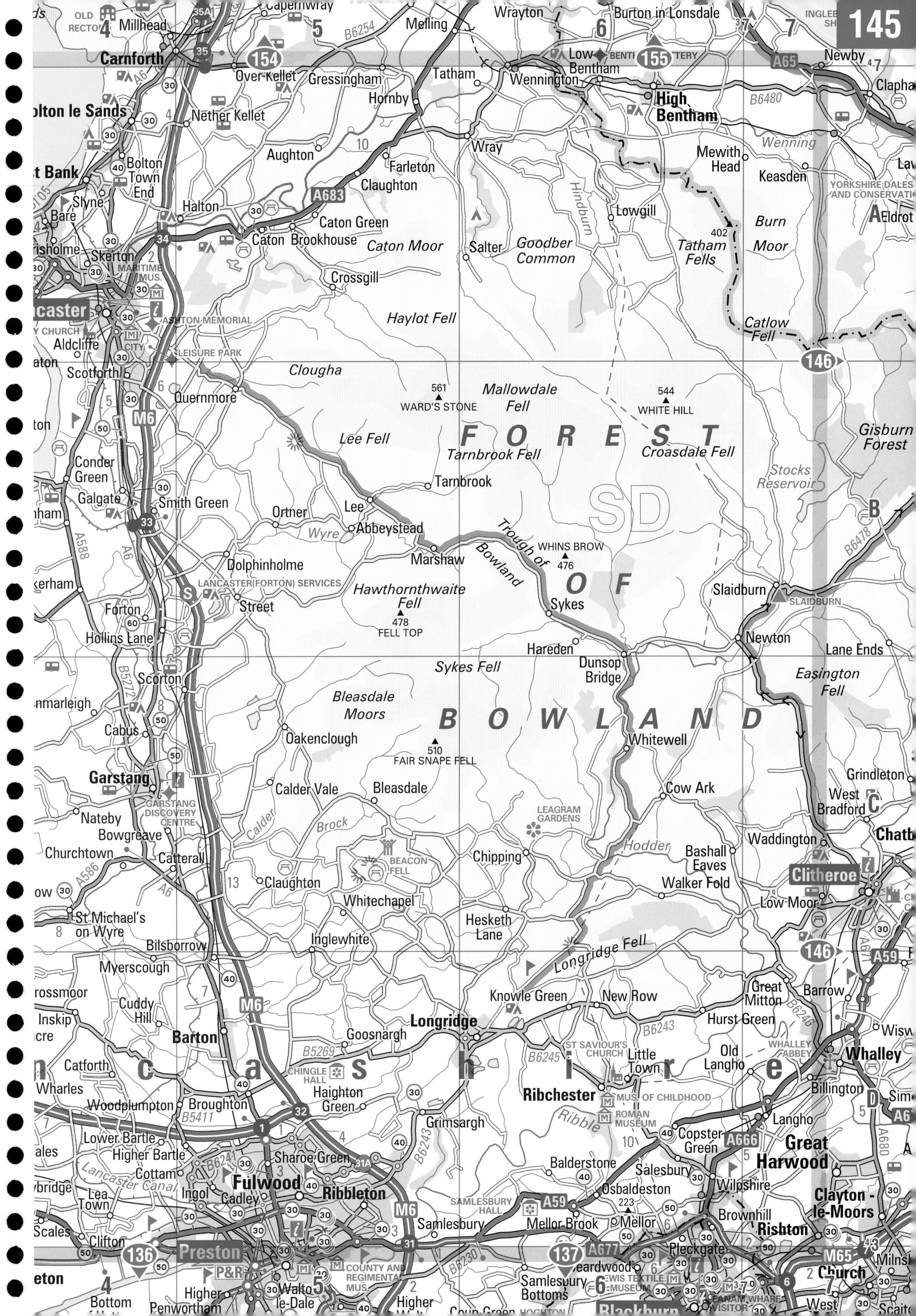
Carnforth
Millhead
Capernwray
Over Kellet
Gressingham
Melling
Wrayton
Burton in Lonsdale
Newby
Clapham
Low Bentham
High Bentham
Wennington
Tatham
Hornby
Nether Kellet
Bolton le Sands
Wray
Aughton
Farleton
Claughton
Mewith Head
Keasden
Wenning
Bolton Town End
Slyne
Bare
Halton
Caton Green
Caton
Brookhouse
Caton Moor
Salter
Goodber Common
Lowgill
Hindburn
Tatham Fells
Burn Moor
Skerton
Maritime Mus.
Lancaster
Ashton Memorial
Crossgill
Haylot Fell
Catlow Fell
Aldcliffe
Leisure Park
Scotforth
Clougha
Quernmore
Ward's Stone
Mallowdale Fell
White Hill
Lee Fell
Tarnbrook Fell
Croasdale Fell
Gisburn Forest
Stocks Reservoir
FOREST OF BOWLAND
Conder Green
Galgate
Smith Green
Tarnbrook
Lee
Ortner
Abbeystead
Wyre
Marshaw
Trough of Bowland
Whins Brow
Dolphinholme
Lancaster (Forton) Services
Hawthornthwaite Fell
Fell Top
Street
Forton
Hollins Lane
Sykes
Slaidburn
Newton
Lane Ends
Hareden
Dunsop Bridge
Sykes Fell
Easington Fell
Scorton
Bleasdale Moors
Cabus
Oakenclough
Fair Snape Fell
Whitewell
Garstang
Garstang Discovery Centre
Calder Vale
Bleasdale
Cow Ark
Grindleton
West Bradford
Nateby
Bowgreave
Leagram Gardens
Brock
Calder
Hodder
Bashall Eaves
Waddington
Churchtown
Catterall
Chipping
Beacon Fell
Claughton
Walker Fold
Clitheroe
Low Moor
Whitechapel
St Michael's on Wyre
Hesketh Lane
Bilsborrow
Inglewhite
Longridge Fell
Myerscough
Knowle Green
New Row
Great Mitton
Barrow
Cuddy Hill
Inskip
Longridge
Hurst Green
Barton
Goosnargh
St Saviour's Church
Little Town
Old Langho
Whalley Abbey
Whalley
Catforth
Chingle Hall
Lancashire
Wharles
Woodplumpton
Broughton
Haighton Green
Ribchester
Mus. of Childhood
Roman Museum
Billington
Ribble
Lower Bartle
Higher Bartle
Grimsargh
Copster Green
Langho
Great Harwood
Cottam
Sharoe Green
Lancaster Canal
Balderstone
Salesbury
Wilpshire
Lea Town
Ingol
Fulwood
Cadley
Ribbleton
Osbaldeston
Samlesbury Hall
Clayton-le-Moors
Brownhill
Samlesbury
Mellor Brook
Mellor
Rishton
Clifton
Preston
Pleckgate
County and Regimental Mus.
Samlesbury Bottoms
Lewis Textile Museum
Walton-le-Dale
Higher Penwortham
Church
Blackburn
A65
A683
A6
A588
B5272
A586
A59
A666
A677
A680
B6480
B6254
B6478
B6243
B6245
B5269
B5411
B6241
B6230
B6246
M6
M65
SD

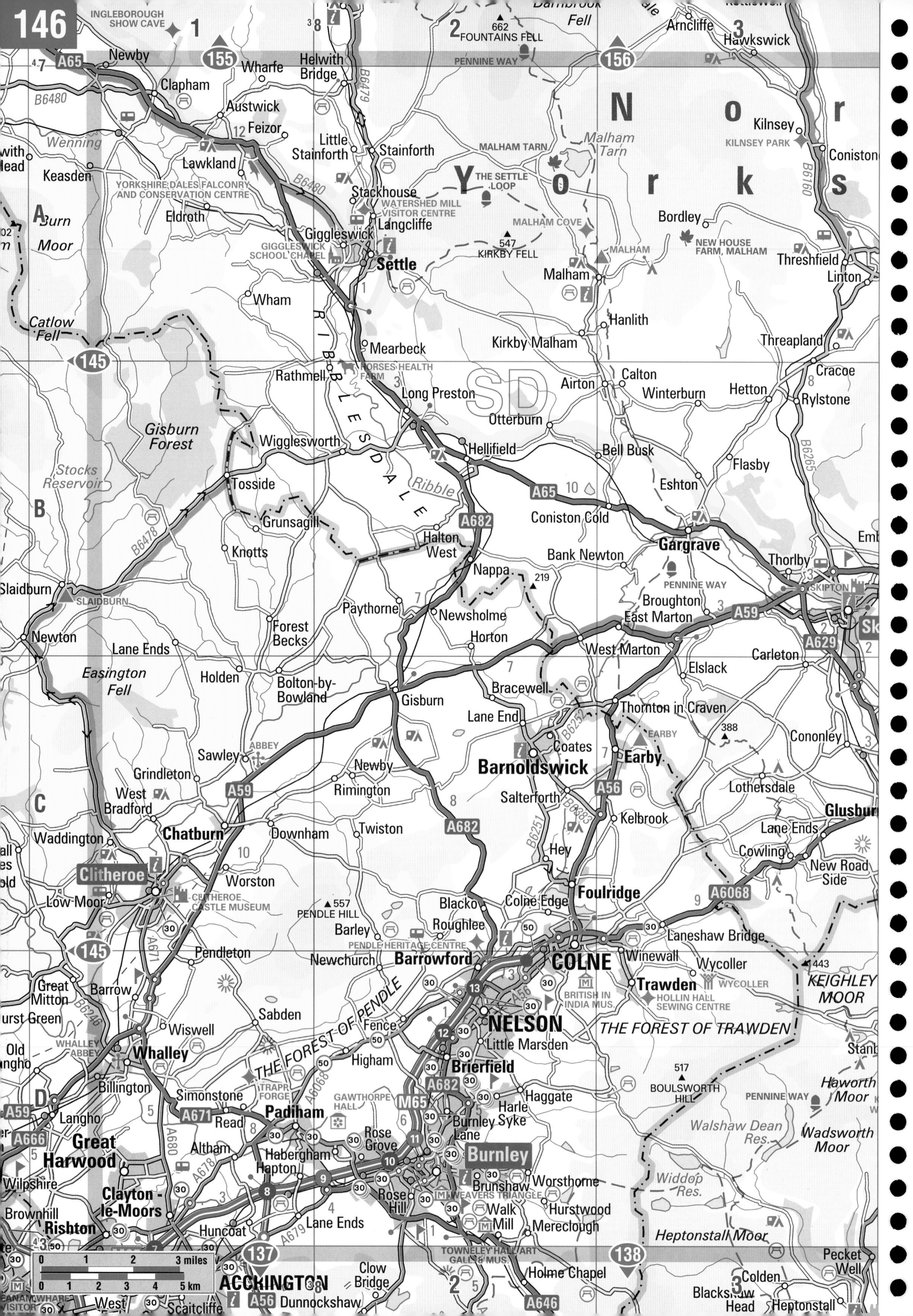

North Yorks
SD
Settle
Clapham
Austwick
Giggleswick
Langcliffe
Stainforth
Malham
Kirkby Malham
Long Preston
Hellifield
Gargrave
Skipton
Gisburn
Barnoldswick
Earby
Colne
Nelson
Brierfield
Burnley
Padiham
Whalley
Clitheroe
Chatburn
Great Harwood
Clayton-le-Moors
Rishton
Accrington
Trawden
Foulridge
Barrowford
Slaidburn
Newton
Gisburn Forest
Stocks Reservoir
Easington Fell
Pendle Hill
THE FOREST OF PENDLE
THE FOREST OF TRAWDEN
KEIGHLEY MOOR
Haworth Moor
Wadsworth Moor
Heptonstall Moor
PENNINE WAY
RIBBLESDALE

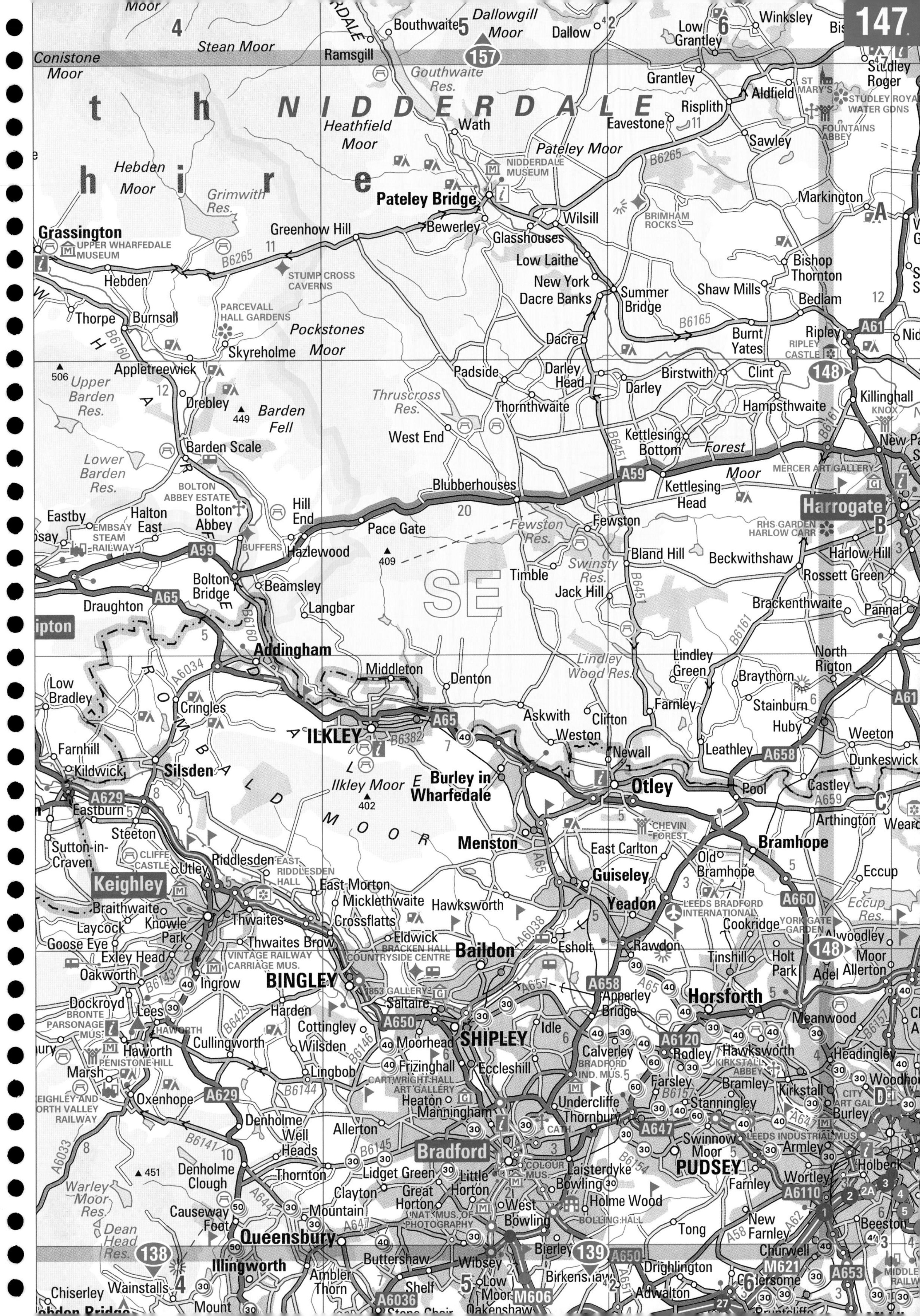
Moor
Stean Moor
Bouthwaite
Dallowgill Moor
Dallow
Low Grantley
Winksley
Conistone Moor
Ramsgill
157
Gouthwaite Res.
Grantley
Studley Roger
Aldfield
ST MARY'S
STUDLEY ROYAL WATER GDNS
t h NIDDERDALE
Risplith
Eavestone
FOUNTAINS ABBEY
Heathfield Moor
Wath
Sawley
Pateley Moor
B6265
NIDDERDALE MUSEUM
Hebden Moor
h i r e
Grimwith Res.
Pateley Bridge
Markington
Grassington
UPPER WHARFEDALE MUSEUM
Greenhow Hill
Beverley
Wilsill
Glasshouses
BRIMHAM ROCKS
B6265
Low Laithe
Bishop Thornton
Hebden
STUMP CROSS CAVERNS
New York
Dacre Banks
Summer Bridge
Shaw Mills
Bedlam
Thorpe
Burnsall
PARCEVALL HALL GARDENS
Pockstones Moor
B6165
Burnt Yates
Ripley
RIPLEY CASTLE
A61
B6160
Skyreholme
Dacre
Appletreewick
Padside
Darley Head
Birstwith
Clint
148
506
Upper Barden Res.
Drebley
Thruscross Res.
Darley
Hampsthwaite
Killinghall
449
Barden Fell
Thornthwaite
West End
Kettlesing Bottom
Forest
Barden Scale
B6451
Lower Barden Res.
Moor
MERCER ART GALLERY
BOLTON ABBEY ESTATE
Blubberhouses
A59
Kettlesing Head
Eastby
Halton East
Bolton Abbey
Hill End
Pace Gate
Fewston
Harrogate
EMBSAY STEAM RAILWAY
Fewston Res.
RHS GARDEN HARLOW CARR
BUFFERS
A59
Hazlewood
409
Swinsty Res.
Bland Hill
Beckwithshaw
Harlow Hill
Bolton Bridge
Beamsley
Timble
Jack Hill
Rossett Green
Draughton
A65
SE
B6451
Brackenthwaite
Pannal
Langbar
B6160
B6161
Addingham
Lindley Wood Res.
Lindley Green
North Rigton
A6034
Middleton
Denton
Braythorn
Low Bradley
Cringles
Askwith
Clifton
Farnley
Stainburn
A61
ILKLEY
A65
B6382
Weston
Huby
Weeton
Farnhill
Kildwick
Silsden
Newall
Leathley
A658
Dunkeswick
ROMBALDS MOOR
Ilkley Moor
Burley in Wharfedale
Otley
Pool
Castley
A629
402
A659
Eastburn
Steeton
CHEVIN FOREST
Arthington
Weardley
Sutton-in-Craven
CLIFFE CASTLE
Menston
Bramhope
Riddlesden
EAST RIDDLESDEN HALL
East Carlton
Old Bramhope
Utley
Keighley
A65
Guiseley
Eccup
East Morton
Micklethwaite
Hawksworth
Yeadon
LEEDS BRADFORD INTERNATIONAL
A660
Braithwaite
Laycock
Knowle Park
Thwaites
Crossflatts
Eccup Res.
Cookridge
YORK GATE GARDEN
Alwoodley
Goose Eye
Thwaites Brow
Eldwick
BRACKEN HALL COUNTRYSIDE CENTRE
Baildon
A6038
Esholt
Rawdon
148
Exley Head
VINTAGE RAILWAY CARRIAGE MUS.
Tinshill
Holt Park
Moor Allerton
Oakworth
Adel
BINGLEY
A657
A658
Ingrow
1853 GALLERY
Apperley Bridge
Horsforth
B6143
Saltaire
Dockroyd
Lees
BRONTE PARSONAGE MUS.
HAWORTH
Harden
A650
Cottingley
Idle
Meanwood
Cullingworth
Wilsden
Moorhead
SHIPLEY
A6120
Haworth
Calverley
Rodley
Hawksworth
PENISTONE HILL
BRADFORD IND. MUS.
KIRKSTALL ABBEY
Headingley
Marsh
Lingbob
Frizinghall
Eccleshill
Farsley
Bramley
Kirkstall
KEIGHLEY AND WORTH VALLEY RAILWAY
Oxenhope
A629
B6144
CARTWRIGHT HALL ART GALLERY
B6157
Heaton
Undercliffe
Stanningley
CITY ART GAL
Manningham
Thornbury
A647
Burley
Denholme
Allerton
CATH.
A647
Swinnow Moor
LEEDS INDUSTRIAL MUS.
B6141
Well Heads
Bradford
Armley
A6033
B6145
COLOUR MUS.
Laisterdyke
PUDSEY
Holbeck
451
Denholme Clough
Thornton
Lidget Green
Little Horton
Bowling
B6154
Farnley
Wortley
Warley Moor Res.
Clayton
Great Horton
West Bowling
Holme Wood
A6110
A644
NAT. MUS. OF PHOTOGRAPHY
BOLLING HALL
New Farnley
Beeston
Causeway Foot
Mountain
A647
Tong
A58
A62
Dean Head Res.
Queensbury
Bierley
Churwell
138
Illingworth
Buttershaw
Wibsey
139
A650
Drighlington
M621
Ambler Thorn
Birkenshaw
A651
Gildersome
A653
Chiserley
Wainstalls
Shelf
Low Moor
M606
Adwalton
A6036
Mount
Oakenshaw

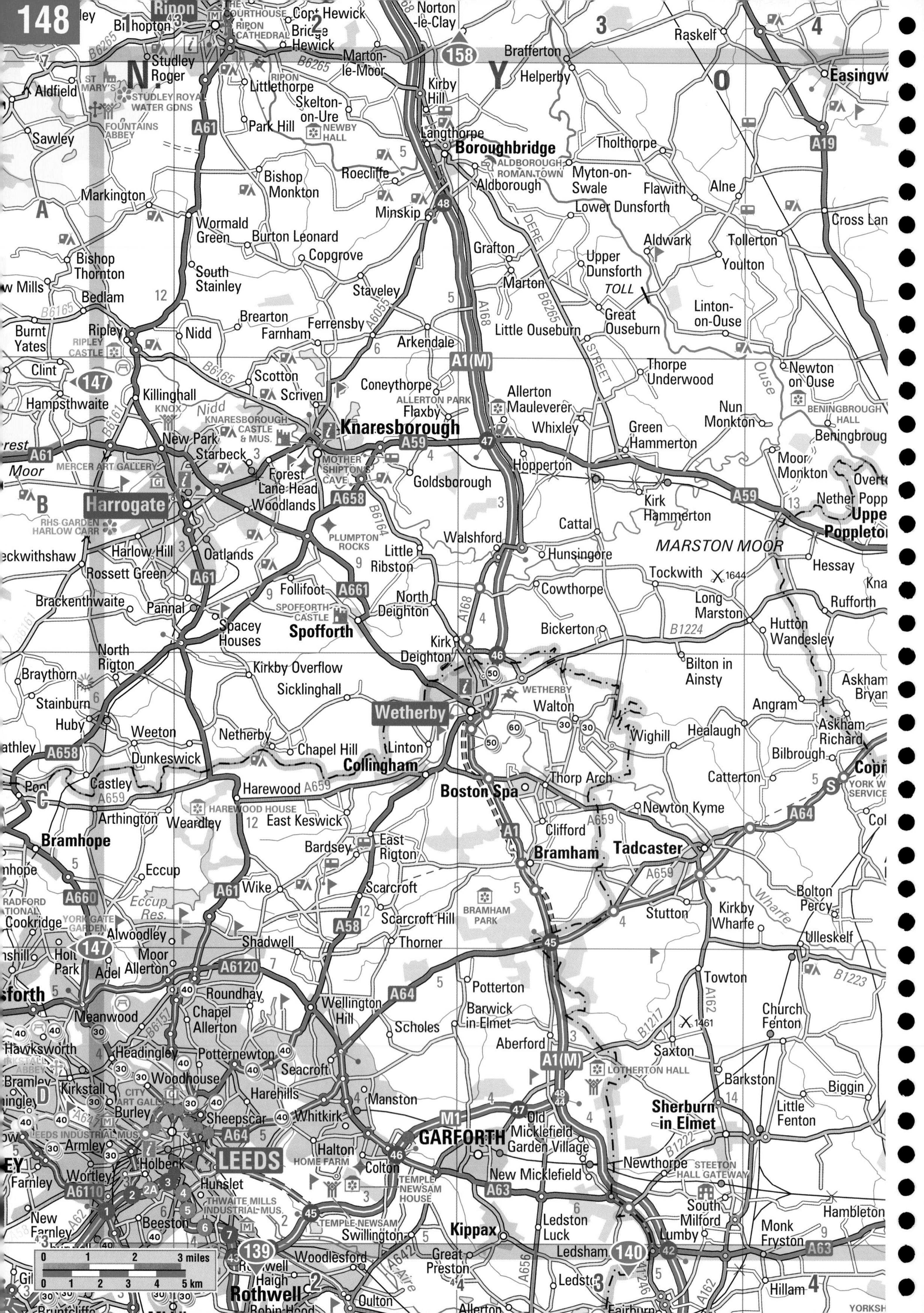
Ripon
Bishopton
Copt Hewick
Bridge Hewick
Norton -le-Clay
158
Brafferton
Raskelf
Easingwold
Studley Roger
Marton- le-Moor
Kirby Hill
Helperby
Aldfield
St Mary's
Studley Royal Water Gdns
Littlethorpe
Skelton- on-Ure
Newby Hall
Fountains Abbey
Sawley
Park Hill
Langthorpe
Boroughbridge
Tholthorpe
Aldborough Roman Town
Myton-on- Swale
Flawith
Alne
Bishop Monkton
Roecliffe
Aldborough
Markington
Minskip
Lower Dunsforth
Cross Lane
Wormald Green
Burton Leonard
Copgrove
Grafton
Aldwark
Tollerton
Youlton
Bishop Thornton
South Stainley
Upper Dunsforth
Toll
Marton
Staveley
Dere Street
Bedlam
Brearton
Great Ouseburn
Linton- on-Ouse
Burnt Yates
Ripley
Ripley Castle
Nidd
Farnham
Ferrensby
Arkendale
Little Ouseburn
Clint
147
Scotton
Coneythorpe
Thorpe Underwood
Newton on Ouse
Hampsthwaite
Killinghall
Knox
Nidd
Scriven
Allerton Park
Allerton Mauleverer
Flaxby
Nun Monkton
Beningbrough Hall
Beningbrough
Knaresborough Castle & Mus.
Knaresborough
Whixley
Green Hammerton
New Park
Starbeck
Mother Shipton's Cave
Goldsborough
Hopperton
Moor Monkton
Mercer Art Gallery
Forest Lane Head
Kirk Hammerton
Nether Poppleton
Upper Poppleton
Harrogate
Woodlands
RHS Garden Harlow Carr
Cattal
Walshford
Plumpton Rocks
Marston Moor
Harlow Hill
Little Ribston
Hunsingore
Hessay
Beckwithshaw
Rossett Green
Oatlands
Tockwith
1644
Follifoot
Cowthorpe
Brackenthwaite
Pannal
North Deighton
Long Marston
Rufforth
Spofforth Castle
Spacey Houses
Spofforth
Bickerton
Hutton Wandesley
Kirk Deighton
North Rigton
Bilton in Ainsty
Kirkby Overflow
Braythorn
Sicklinghall
Wetherby
Askham Bryan
Stainburn
Walton
Angram
Huby
Weeton
Netherby
Wighill
Healaugh
Askham Richard
Dunkeswick
Chapel Hill
Linton
Bilbrough
Collingham
Castley
Harewood
Thorp Arch
Catterton
Copmanthorpe
York West Service
Boston Spa
Newton Kyme
Harewood House
Arthington
Weardley
East Keswick
Clifford
Bramhope
Bardsey
East Rigton
Bramham
Tadcaster
Eccup
Wike
Scarcroft
Stutton
Bolton Percy
Cookridge
Eccup Res.
Scarcroft Hill
Bramham Park
Kirkby Wharfe
Yorkgate Garden
Alwoodley
Shadwell
Thorner
Ulleskelf
Moor Allerton
Adel
Holt Park
Towton
Roundhay
Potterton
Wellington Hill
Chapel Allerton
Barwick in-Elmet
Church Fenton
Meanwood
Scholes
1461
Headingley
Potternewton
Aberford
Saxton
Hawksworth
Kirkstall Abbey
Woodhouse
Seacroft
Lotherton Hall
Barkston
Kirkstall
Harehills
Biggin
City Art Gallery
Manston
Little Fenton
Bramley
Burley
Sheepscar
Whitkirk
Old Micklefield
Sherburn in Elmet
Leeds Industrial Mus.
Garforth
Armley
Micklefield Garden Village
Leeds
Halton
Home Farm
Colton
Newthorpe
Steeton Hall Gateway
Farnley
Wortley
Holbeck
Hunslet
Temple Newsam House
New Micklefield
Thwaite Mills Industrial Mus.
South Milford
Hambleton
New Farnley
Beeston
Temple Newsam
Ledston Luck
Lumby
Monk Fryston
Swillington
Kippax
139
Woodlesford
Great Preston
Ledsham
140
Rothwell
Haigh
Ledston
Hillam
Oulton
Allerton
Fairburn
Robin Hood
Wharfe
Ouse
Aire
A61
A1(M)
A59
A658
A661
A168
A19
A64
A659
A660
A6120
A58
A63
A6110
M1
A162
B6265
B6165
B6161
B1224
B1223
B1217
B1222
0 1 2 3 miles
0 1 2 3 4 5 km
Yorkshire

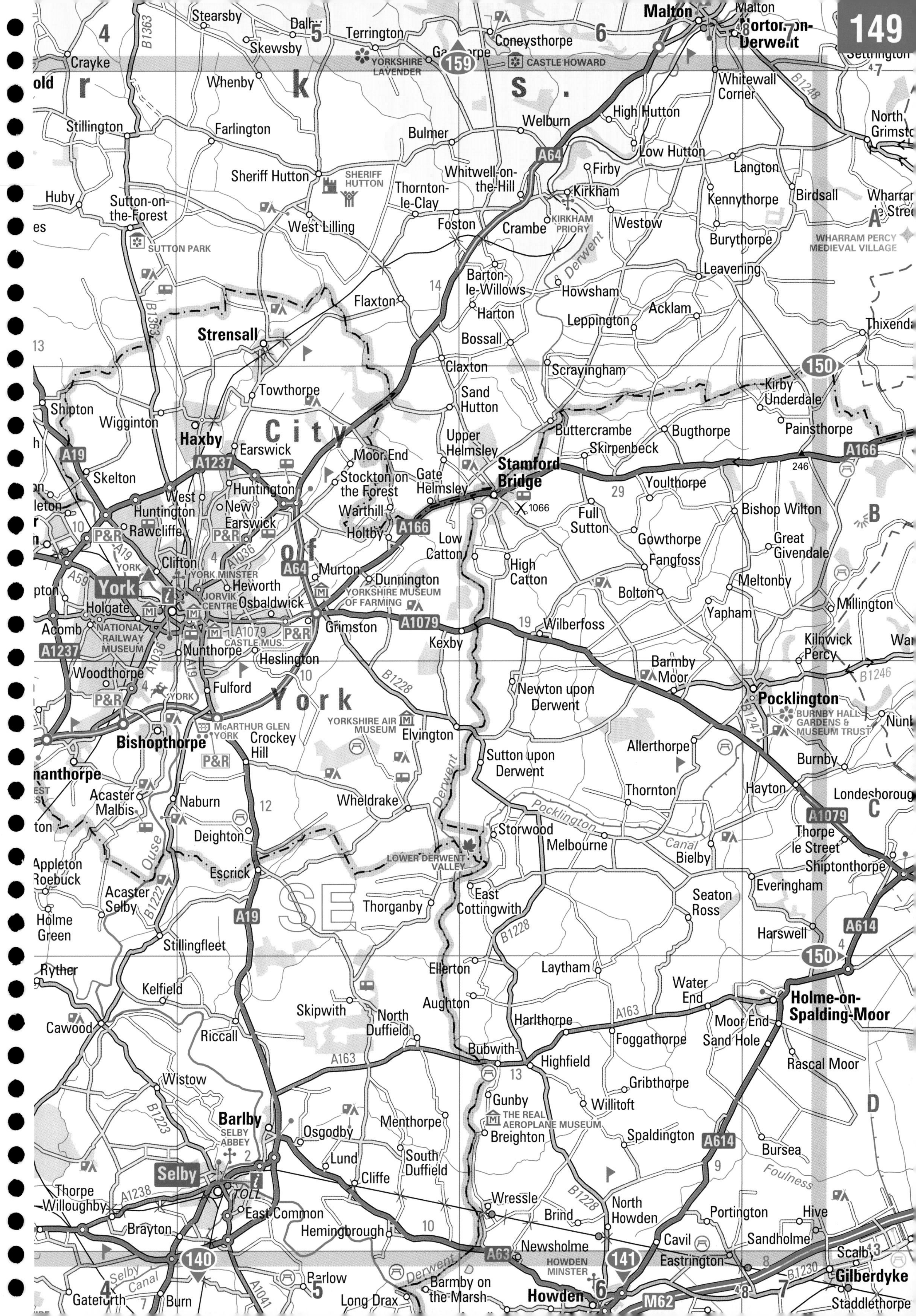

Stearsby
Dalby
Terrington
Coneysthorpe
Malton
Norton-on-Derwent
Crayke
Skewsby
YORKSHIRE LAVENDER
159
CASTLE HOWARD
Whenby
Whitewall Corner
B1248
B1363
Stillington
Farlington
Bulmer
Welburn
High Hutton
North Grimston
A64
Low Hutton
Langton
Sheriff Hutton
SHERIFF HUTTON
Whitwell-on-the-Hill
Firby
Thornton-le-Clay
Kirkham
Kennythorpe
Birdsall
Huby
Sutton-on-the-Forest
West Lilling
Foston
Crambe
KIRKHAM PRIORY
Westow
Burythorpe
SUTTON PARK
WHARRAM PERCY MEDIEVAL VILLAGE
Derwent
Leavening
Barton-le-Willows
Howsham
Flaxton
Harton
Acklam
Leppington
Thixendale
Strensall
Bossall
Claxton
Scrayingham
150
Towthorpe
Sand Hutton
Kirby Underdale
Shipton
Wigginton
Buttercrambe
Bugthorpe
Painsthorpe
Haxby
City
Upper Helmsley
Skirpenbeck
Earswick
Moor End
A166
A19
A1237
Stamford Bridge
Skelton
Stockton on the Forest
Gate Helmsley
Youlthorpe
Huntington
West Huntington
New Earswick
Warthill
29
Full Sutton
Bishop Wilton
1066
Rawcliffe
P&R
Holtby
Gowthorpe
Low Catton
of
Great Givendale
Clifton
A1036
A64
High Catton
Fangfoss
YORK
Murton
Dunnington
A59
York
YORK MINSTER
Heworth
Meltonby
YORKSHIRE MUSEUM OF FARMING
Bolton
JORVIK CENTRE
Osbaldwick
Holgate
Millington
Yapham
NATIONAL RAILWAY MUSEUM
Acomb
A1079
Grimston
Wilberfoss
Kexby
Kilnwick Percy
CASTLE MUS.
A1237
Nunthorpe
Heslington
Woodthorpe
Barmby Moor
B1228
B1246
Fulford
York
Newton upon Derwent
Pocklington
BURNBY HALL GARDENS & MUSEUM TRUST
McARTHUR GLEN YORK
YORKSHIRE AIR MUSEUM
B1247
Crockey Hill
Elvington
Bishopthorpe
Sutton upon Derwent
Allerthorpe
Burnby
Copmanthorpe
Acaster Malbis
Naburn
Wheldrake
Thornton
Hayton
Londesborough
Deighton
Pocklington Canal
Storwood
Melbourne
Thorpe le Street
Ouse
Appleton Roebuck
Escrick
LOWER DERWENT VALLEY
Bielby
Shiptonthorpe
Acaster Selby
B1222
East Cottingwith
Everingham
SE
Thorganby
Seaton Ross
Holme Green
A19
B1228
A614
Stillingfleet
Harswell
Rythe
Ellerton
Laytham
Kelfield
Water End
Holme-on-Spalding-Moor
Aughton
Skipwith
North Duffield
A163
Hathorpe
Moor End
Sand Hole
Cawood
Riccall
Foggathorpe
Rascal Moor
A163
Bubwith
Highfield
Wistow
Gribthorpe
B1223
Gunby
Willitoft
THE REAL AEROPLANE MUSEUM
Barlby
Menthorpe
Breighton
Spaldington
SELBY ABBEY
Osgodby
A614
Bursea
South Duffield
Lund
Selby
Cliffe
Foulness
Thorpe Willoughby
A1238
Wressle
B1228
North Howden
Portington
Hive
East Common
Brind
Brayton
Hemingbrough
Cavil
Sandholme
Newsholme
A63
140
141
Eastrington
Scalby
HOWDEN MINSTER
Selby Canal
B1230
Gilberdyke
Barlow
Barmby on the Marsh
A1041
Gateforth
Burn
Long Drax
Howden
M62
Staddlethorpe
A
B
C
D
4
5
6
7
8

Settrington
Whitewall Corner
North Grimston
Langton
Birdsall
Wharram le Street
Duggleby
Kirby Grindalythe
Sledmere
SLEDMERE HOUSE
WHARRAM PERCY MEDIEVAL VILLAGE
Helperthorpe
Butterwick
Weaverthorpe
East Lutton
West Lutton
Octon
Thwing
Octon Cross Roads
Langtoft
Rudston
Cottam
Kilham
BURTON AGNES HALL
BURTON AGNES MANOR HOUSE
Ruston Parva
Lowthorpe
Nafferton
Driffield
Little Driffield
Elmswell
Garton-on-the-Wolds
Thixendale
Fimber
Kirby Underdale
Painsthorpe
Fridaythorpe
Wetwang
YORKSHIRE WOLDS WAY
Huggate
Tibthorpe
Kelleythorpe
Kirkburn
Southburn
Wansford
Skerne
Foston on the Wolds
Bishop Wilton
Great Givendale
Meltonby
Millington
North Dalton
Bainton
Hutton
Hutton Cranswick
Brigham
Rotsea
Kilnwick Percy
Warter
Middleton-on-the-Wolds
Watton
Hempholme
Pocklington
BURNBY HALL GARDENS & MUSEUM TRUST
Nunburnholme
Kilnwick
Lund
Beswick
Burshill
Burnby
Holme on the Wolds
Lockington
Thorpe
Baswick Steer
Hayton
Londesborough
South Dalton
Scorborough
Aike
Thorpe le Street
Shiptonthorpe
Goodmanham
Market Weighton
Etton
Arram
Leconfield
Eske
Everingham
Gardham
Cherry Burton
Routh
Tickton
Harswell
Sancton
Molescroft
Beverley
Weel
Holme-on-Spalding-Moor
Bishop Burton
BEVERLEY FRIARY
MINSTER
Woodmansey
Moor End
North Newbald
North Cliffe
Walkington
Rascal Moor
South Cliffe
South Newbald
Bentley
Thearne
Dunswell
Hotham
High Hunsley
Skidby
Little Weighton
SKIDBY WINDMILL
Bursea
North Cave
Rowley
Inglemire
Kingston upon Hull
Everthorpe
Cottingham
Eppleworth
Riplingham
Portington
Hive
West End
South Cave
Newland
Willerby
Sculcoates
Sandholme
Scalby
Newport
Kirk Ella
East Ella
West Ella
Anlaby
Brantingham
Ellerker
Swanland
Staddlethorpe
Ellerker
THE WOLDS
East Riding of Yorkshire
SE
Foulness
Watton Beck
Leven Canal
Hull
Driffield Canal
A166 A614 A1079 A1035 A164 A1034 A63 M62 A1033 A1174 A1105 B1248 B1253 B1249 B1252 B1251 B1246 B1247 B1230 B1233
160 161 149 141 142
0 1 2 3 miles
0 1 2 3 4 5 km

FLAMBOROUGH HEAD
Flamborough
Grindale
Boynton
Sewerby
SEWERBY HALL AND GARDENS
BONDVILLE MODEL VILLAGE
PRIORY
BAYLE MUSEUM
Bridlington
OLD PENNY MEMORIES
West Hill
Bessingby
Carnaby
Hilderthorpe
Haisthorpe
BRIDLINGTON BAY
PARK ROSE POTTERY AND LEISURE PARK
Burton Agnes
Fraisthorpe
Gransmoor
Barmston
Great Kelk
Lissett
Gembling
Ulrome
SKIPSEA CASTLE
Skipsea
Skipsea Brough
Beeford
North Frodingham
Dunnington
Atwick
Bewholme
North Cliff
Hornsea
FREEPORT HORNSEA
HORNSEA MUSEUM
Hornsea Bridge
Hornsea Mere
Brandesburton
Seaton
Sigglesthorne
Catwick
Goxhill
Rolston
Mappleton
Little Hatfield
Great Hatfield
Great Cowden
Rise
Long Riston
Arnold
Withernwick
Meaux
Skirlaugh
New Ellerby
Marton
West Newton
Aldbrough
East Newton
Old Ellerby
BURTON CONSTABLE HALL
Flinton
Swine
Coniston
Garton
Grimston
Bransholme
Thirtleby
Sproatley
Humbleton
Fitling
Hilston
Sutton on Hull
Ganstead
Bilton
Lelley
Owstwick
Tunstall
Sutton Ings
Stoneferry
Elstronwick
North End
Burton Pidsea
Roos
Summergangs
WILBERFORCE HOUSE
Preston
West End
Waxholme
Marfleet
Salt End
STREETLIFE
THE DEEP
Hedon
Haven Side
Rimswell
Owthorne
Withernsea
TA
A165
A614
A1033
B1253
B1255
B1259
B1249
B1242
B1244
B1243
B1238
B1237
B1239
B1240
B1362
P&R
161
142
143

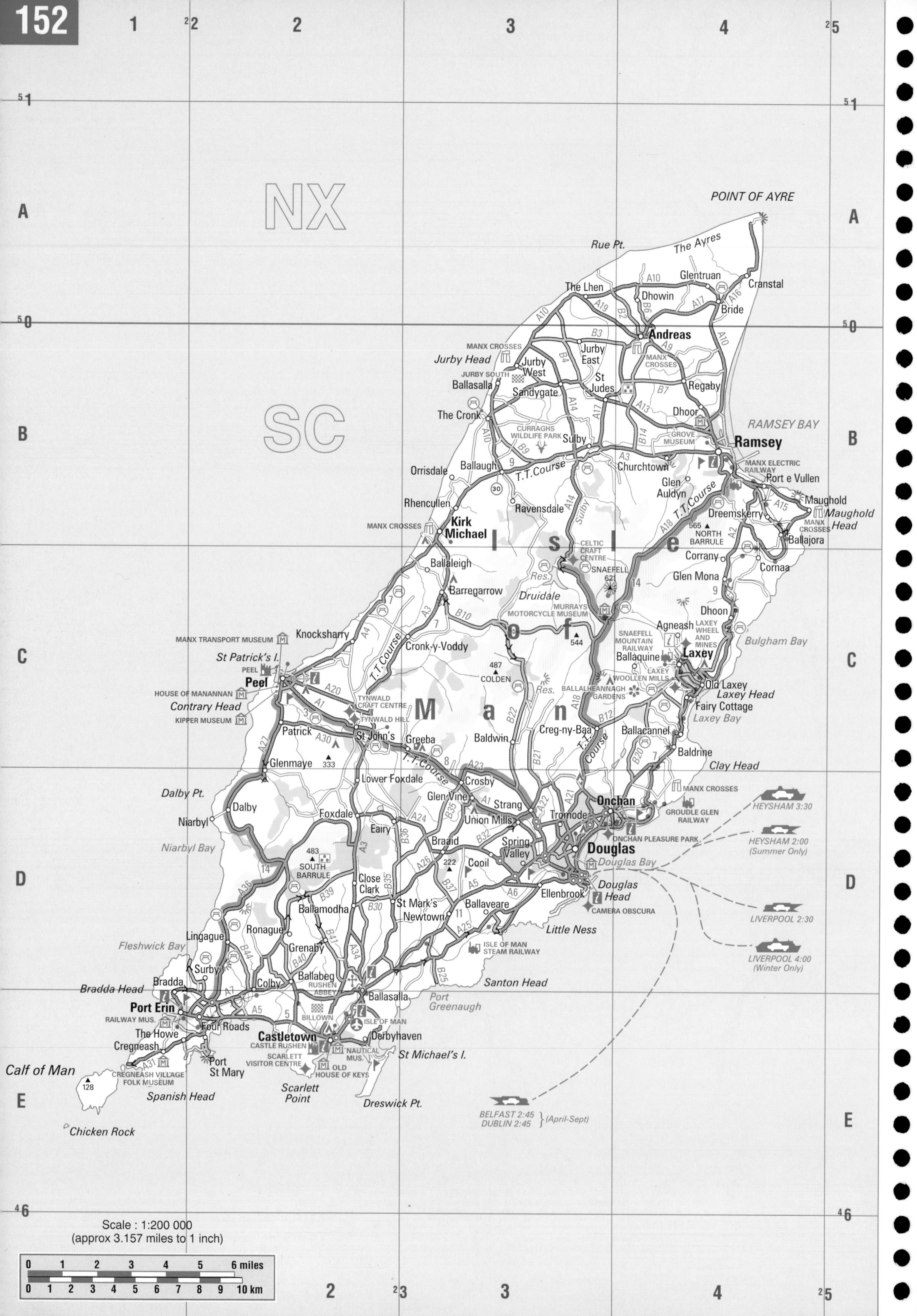
NX
SC
POINT OF AYRE
The Ayres
Rue Pt.
Cranstal
Glentruan
The Lhen
Dhowin
Bride
Andreas
Jurby East
MANX CROSSES
Jurby Head
Jurby West
JURBY SOUTH
Ballasalla
Sandygate
St Judes
Regaby
The Cronk
Dhoor
GROVE MUSEUM
RAMSEY BAY
Ramsey
CURRAGHS WILDLIFE PARK
Sulby
Ballaugh
T.T.Course
Churchtown
MANX ELECTRIC RAILWAY
Port e Vullen
Orrisdale
Glen Auldyn
Maughold
Maughold Head
Rhencullen
Ravensdale
Dreemskerry
Kirk Michael
NORTH BARRULE
Ballajora
Isle
CELTIC CRAFT CENTRE
Corrany
Cornaa
Ballaleigh
SNAEFELL
Glen Mona
Barregarrow
Druidale
Res.
Dhoon
MURRAYS MOTORCYCLE MUSEUM
MANX TRANSPORT MUSEUM
Knocksharry
Agneash
LAXEY WHEEL AND MINES
of
SNAEFELL MOUNTAIN RAILWAY
Bulgham Bay
Cronk-y-Voddy
Laxey
Ballaquine
St Patrick's I.
PEEL
COLDEN
LAXEY WOOLLEN MILLS
Peel
BALLALHEANNAGH GARDENS
Old Laxey
HOUSE OF MANANNAN
Laxey Head
Contrary Head
TYNWALD CRAFT CENTRE
Fairy Cottage
KIPPER MUSEUM
TYNWALD HILL
Man
Laxey Bay
Patrick
St John's
Greeba
Baldwin
Creg-ny-Baa
Ballacannel
Baldrine
Glenmaye
Clay Head
Lower Foxdale
Crosby
MANX CROSSES
Dalby Pt.
Glen Vine
Strang
Onchan
GROUDLE GLEN RAILWAY
HEYSHAM 3:30
Niarbyl
Dalby
Foxdale
Union Mills
Tromode
Eairy
ONCHAN PLEASURE PARK
HEYSHAM 2:00 (Summer Only)
Niarbyl Bay
Braaid
Spring Valley
Douglas
SOUTH BARRULE
Cooil
Douglas Bay
Close Clark
Ellenbrook
Douglas Head
Ballamodha
St Mark's
Ballaveare
CAMERA OBSCURA
Newtown
LIVERPOOL 2:30
Little Ness
Ronague
Lingague
Fleshwick Bay
Grenaby
ISLE OF MAN STEAM RAILWAY
LIVERPOOL 4:00 (Winter Only)
Surby
Ballabeg
RUSHEN ABBEY
Bradda
Colby
Santon Head
Bradda Head
Ballasalla
Port Greenaugh
Port Erin
BILLOWN
RAILWAY MUS.
Four Roads
ISLE OF MAN
The Howe
Castletown
Derbyhaven
CASTLE RUSHEN
NAUTICAL MUS.
St Michael's I.
Cregneash
Port St Mary
SCARLETT VISITOR CENTRE
OLD HOUSE OF KEYS
Calf of Man
CREGNEASH VILLAGE FOLK MUSEUM
Scarlett Point
Spanish Head
Dreswick Pt.
BELFAST 2:45
DUBLIN 2:45
(April-Sept)
Chicken Rock
Scale : 1:200 000
(approx 3.157 miles to 1 inch)
0 1 2 3 4 5 6 miles
0 1 2 3 4 5 6 7 8 9 10 km

FURNESS FELLS
Seascale
Santon Bridge
Eskdale Green
Beckfoot
Boot
Hardknott Pass
Wrynose Pass
Cockley Beck
Eskdale
Holmrook
Drigg
Saltcoats
RAVENGLASS AND ESKDALE RAILWAY & MUS.
Ravenglass
BATH HOUSE
THIRD MILLENNIUM MUNCASTER OWL TRUST WORLD HQ
Broad Oak
Newbiggin
Lane End
Stub Place
Corney
Hycemoor
Selker Bay
Bootle
Black Combe
Whitbeck
Silecroft
Whicham
Kirksanton
Millom
MILLOM FOLK MUSEUM
Haverigg
649 HARTER FELL
Seathwaite Tarn
CONISTON COPPERMINES
CONISTON HOLLY HOW
801 THE OLD MAN OF CONISTON
Bowmanstead
Birker Fell
Devoke Water
Woodend
Hall Dunnerdale
Seathwaite
Ulpha Fell
Duddon
529 CAW
Torver
572 WHITFELL
Ulpha
Hoses
Corney Fell
Broughton Mills
Water Yeat
High Nibthwaite
Blawith
Lower Hawthwaite
Duddon Bridge
Broughton in Furness
Lowick Bridge
Lowick Green
Hallthwaites
DUDDON MOSSES
Foxfield
Grizebeck
Gawthwaite
The Green
The Hill
Kirkby-in-Furness
Beck Side
Penny Bridge
Broughton Beck
Greenodd
Arrad Foot
Mansriggs
Soutergate
LAUREL & HARDY MUS.
Ulverston
Pennington
Swarthmoor
DUDDON SANDS
Askam in Furness
Ireleth
Lindal in Furness
SOUTH LAKES WILD ANIMAL PARK
SANDSCALE HAWS
Great Urswick
Dalton-in-Furness
DALTON CASTLE
Little Urswick
Stainton with Adgarley
Scales
Baycliff
NORTH WALNEY
BARROW (WALNEY ISLAND)
Hawcoat
BOW BRIDGE
Ormsgill
Newton
FURNESS ABBEY
GLEASTON WATERMILL
Barrow-in-Furness
Newbarns
Dendron
Gleaston
Aldingham
North Scale
CUSTOM HO
Newbiggin
Leece
THE DOCK MUSEUM
Vickerstown
Barrow Island
Roosebeck
Biggar
Rampside
Roa Island
Foulney Island
South End
Piel Island
Isle of Walney
South End Point
South Channel
SD
A595
A593
A5092
A5093
A5084
A590
A5087
B5281
B5344
162
163
154
144
A
B
C
D
1
2
3

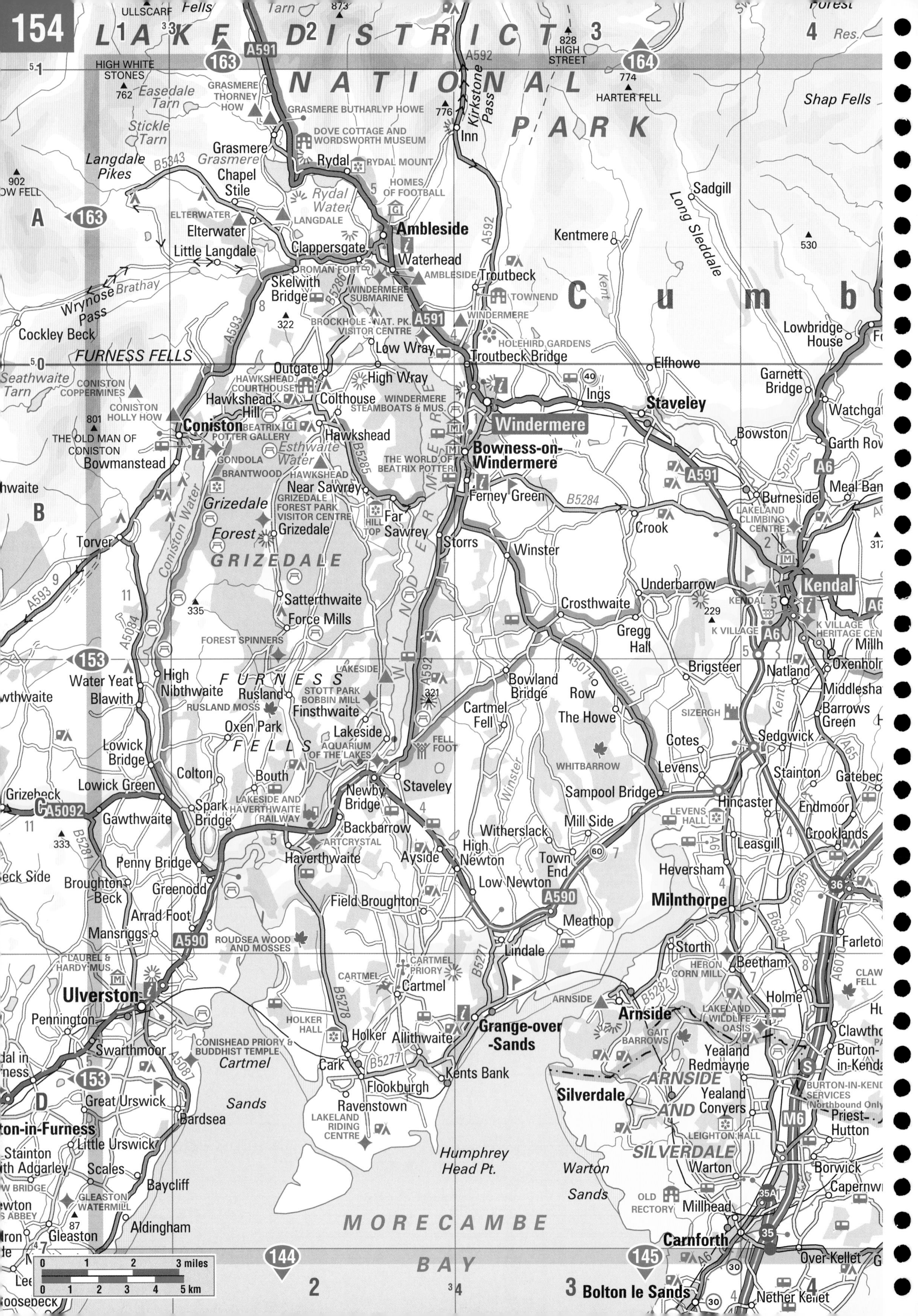
LAKE DISTRICT NATIONAL PARK
Cumb
MORECAMBE BAY
163
164
153
144
145
ULLSCARF
HIGH WHITE STONES
762
Easedale Tarn
Stickle Tarn
GRASMERE THORNEY HOW
GRASMERE BUTHARLYP HOWE
DOVE COTTAGE AND WORDSWORTH MUSEUM
Grasmere
Langdale Pikes
Chapel Stile
Rydal
RYDAL MOUNT
HOMES OF FOOTBALL
Rydal Water
ELTERWATER
Elterwater
LANGDALE
Little Langdale
Ambleside
Clappersgate
Waterhead
ROMAN FORT
AMBLESIDE
Troutbeck
TOWNEND
Skelwith Bridge
WINDERMERE SUBMARINE
Wrynose Pass
Brathay
Cockley Beck
322
BROCKHOLE - NAT. PK. VISITOR CENTRE
WINDERMERE
HOLEHIRD GARDENS
Low Wray
Troutbeck Bridge
FURNESS FELLS
Seathwaite Tarn
CONISTON COPPERMINES
Outgate
HAWKSHEAD COURTHOUSE
High Wray
Hawkshead Hill
Colthouse
WINDERMERE STEAMBOATS & MUS.
CONISTON HOLLY HOW
801
THE OLD MAN OF CONISTON
Coniston
BEATRIX POTTER GALLERY
Hawkshead
Esthwaite Water
Windermere
Bowness-on-Windermere
Bowmanstead
GONDOLA
BRANTWOOD
HAWKSHEAD
THE WORLD OF BEATRIX POTTER
Ferney Green
Near Sawrey
GRIZEDALE FOREST PARK VISITOR CENTRE
Grizedale Forest
GRIZEDALE
Grizedale
HILL TOP
Far Sawrey
Coniston Water
Torver
Storrs
Winster
A593
335
Satterthwaite
Force Mills
FOREST SPINNERS
Water Yeat
Blawith
High Nibthwaite
FURNESS FELLS
Rusland
RUSLAND MOSS
STOTT PARK BOBBIN MILL
Finsthwaite
LAKESIDE
Oxen Park
Lakeside
AQUARIUM OF THE LAKES
FELL FOOT
Lowick Bridge
Colton
Bouth
Staveley
Lowick Green
Grizebeck
Spark Bridge
LAKESIDE AND HAVERTHWAITE RAILWAY
Newby Bridge
Backbarrow
Gawthwaite
333
Penny Bridge
Haverthwaite
ARTCRYSTAL
Ayside
High Newton
Broughton Beck
Greenodd
Low Newton
Arrad Foot
Field Broughton
Mansriggs
ROUDSEA WOOD AND MOSSES
LAUREL & HARDY MUS.
CARTMEL PRIORY
CARTMEL
Cartmel
Lindale
Ulverston
Pennington
HOLKER HALL
Holker
Allithwaite
Grange-over-Sands
Swarthmoor
CONISHEAD PRIORY & BUDDHIST TEMPLE
Cartmel Sands
Cark
Kents Bank
Flookburgh
Great Urswick
Ravenstown
Bardsea
LAKELAND RIDING CENTRE
Little Urswick
Stainton with Adgarley
Scales
Baycliff
Humphrey Head Pt.
GLEASTON WATERMILL
87
Gleaston
Aldingham
Kirkstone Pass
Inn
776
828 HIGH STREET
774 HARTER FELL
Shap Fells
Res.
Sadgill
Long Sleddale
Kentmere
530
Kent
Lowbridge House
Elfhowe
Ings
Staveley
Garnett Bridge
Watchgate
Bowston
Garth Row
Burneside
Meal Bank
B5284
Crook
LAKELAND CLIMBING CENTRE
Underbarrow
229
Kendal
KENDAL
K VILLAGE
K VILLAGE HERITAGE CENTRE
Crosthwaite
Gregg Hall
Gilpin
Brigsteer
Natland
Oxenholme
Millholme
Bowland Bridge
Row
Middleshaw
Cartmel Fell
The Howe
SIZERGH
Barrows Green
Cotes
Sedgwick
WHITBARROW
Levens
Stainton
Gatebeck
Sampool Bridge
Hincaster
Endmoor
Witherslack
Mill Side
LEVENS HALL
Crooklands
Town End
Leasgill
Heversham
Meathop
Milnthorpe
Storth
Beetham
Farleton
HERON CORN MILL
CLAWTHORPE FELL
ARNSIDE
Arnside
Holme
GAIT BARROWS
LAKELAND WILDLIFE OASIS
Clawthorpe
Yealand Redmayne
Burton-in-Kendal
ARNSIDE AND SILVERDALE
Silverdale
Yealand Conyers
BURTON-IN-KENDAL SERVICES (Northbound Only)
Priest Hutton
LEIGHTON HALL
Warton
Borwick
Warton Sands
Capernwray
OLD RECTORY
Millhead
Carnforth
Over Kellet
Bolton le Sands
Nether Kellet
A591
A592
A593
A5084
A5092
A590
A6
M6
B5343
B5286
B5285
B5281
B5278
B5277
B5271
A5074
B5282
B6384
B6385
A65
A6070
0 1 2 3 miles
0 1 2 3 4 5 km

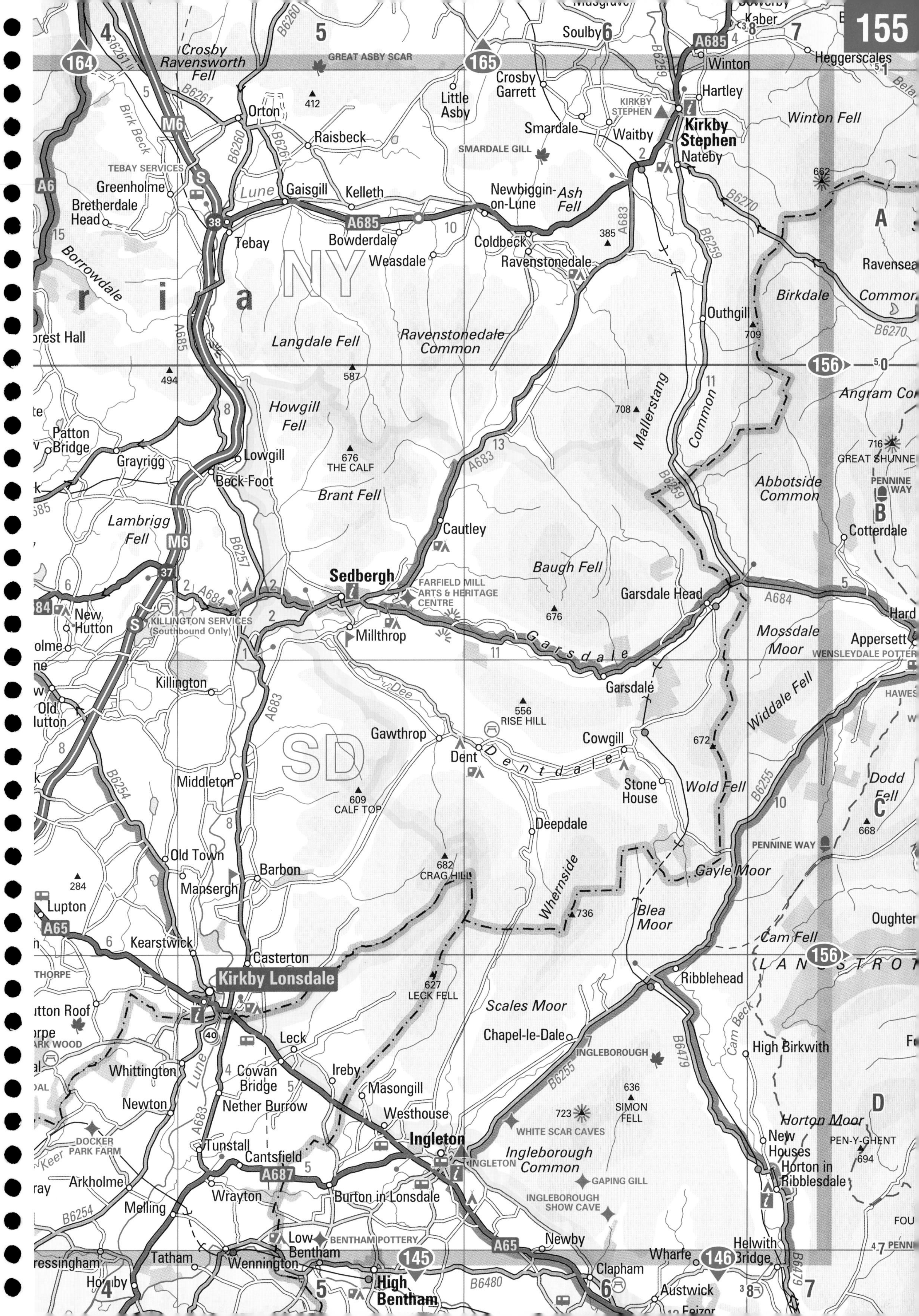

164
165
156
145
146
GREAT ASBY SCAR
Crosby Ravensworth Fell
Soulby
Kaber
Winton
Heggerscales
Crosby Garrett
Little Asby
Orton
412
Birk Beck
Raisbeck
Hartley
KIRKBY STEPHEN
Kirkby Stephen
Winton Fell
Smardale
Waitby
Nateby
SMARDALE GILL
TEBAY SERVICES
Greenholme
Bretherdale Head
Lune
Gaisgill
Kelleth
Newbiggin-on-Lune
Ash Fell
662
Tebay
Bowderdale
Weasdale
Coldbeck
Ravenstonedale
385
Borrowdale
NY
Outhgill
Birkdale
Ravenseat
Langdale Fell
Ravenstonedale Common
709
494
587
Howgill Fell
708
Mallerstang
Common
Angram Common
Patton Bridge
Grayrigg
Lowgill
Beck Foot
676
THE CALF
Brant Fell
716
GREAT SHUNNER
Abbotside Common
PENNINE WAY
Lambrigg Fell
Cautley
Cotterdale
Baugh Fell
Sedbergh
FARFIELD MILL ARTS & HERITAGE CENTRE
Garsdale Head
New Hutton
KILLINGTON SERVICES (Southbound Only)
Milthrop
Garsdale
Mossdale Moor
Appersett
WENSLEYDALE POTTERY
Killington
Old Hutton
Dee
556
RISE HILL
HAWES
Widdale Fell
Gawthrop
Dent
Dentdale
Cowgill
672
SD
Middleton
609
CALF TOP
Stone House
Wold Fell
Dodd Fell
Deepdale
668
Old Town
Barbon
682
CRAG HILL
Whernside
Gayle Moor
284
Mansergh
Lupton
736
Blea Moor
Oughtershaw
Kearstwick
Cam Fell
Casterton
LANGSTROTHDALE
Kirkby Lonsdale
627
LECK FELL
Scales Moor
Ribblehead
Hutton Roof
Chapel-le-Dale
Leck
INGLEBOROUGH
Cam Beck
High Birkwith
Whittington
Cowan Bridge
Ireby
636
SIMON FELL
Masongill
Newton
Nether Burrow
Westhouse
723
WHITE SCAR CAVES
Horton Moor
DOCKER PARK FARM
Tunstall
Ingleton
Ingleborough Common
New Houses
PEN-Y-GHENT
694
Cantsfield
INGLETON
Horton in Ribblesdale
Arkholme
GAPING GILL
Wrayton
Burton in Lonsdale
INGLEBOROUGH SHOW CAVE
Melling
Keer
Low Bentham
BENTHAM POTTERY
Newby
Wharfe
Helwith Bridge
Tatham
Wennington
Clapham
High Bentham
Austwick
Hornby
A685
A683
A684
A65
A687
A6
M6
B6261
B6260
B6259
B6270
B6257
B6254
B6255
B6479
B6480

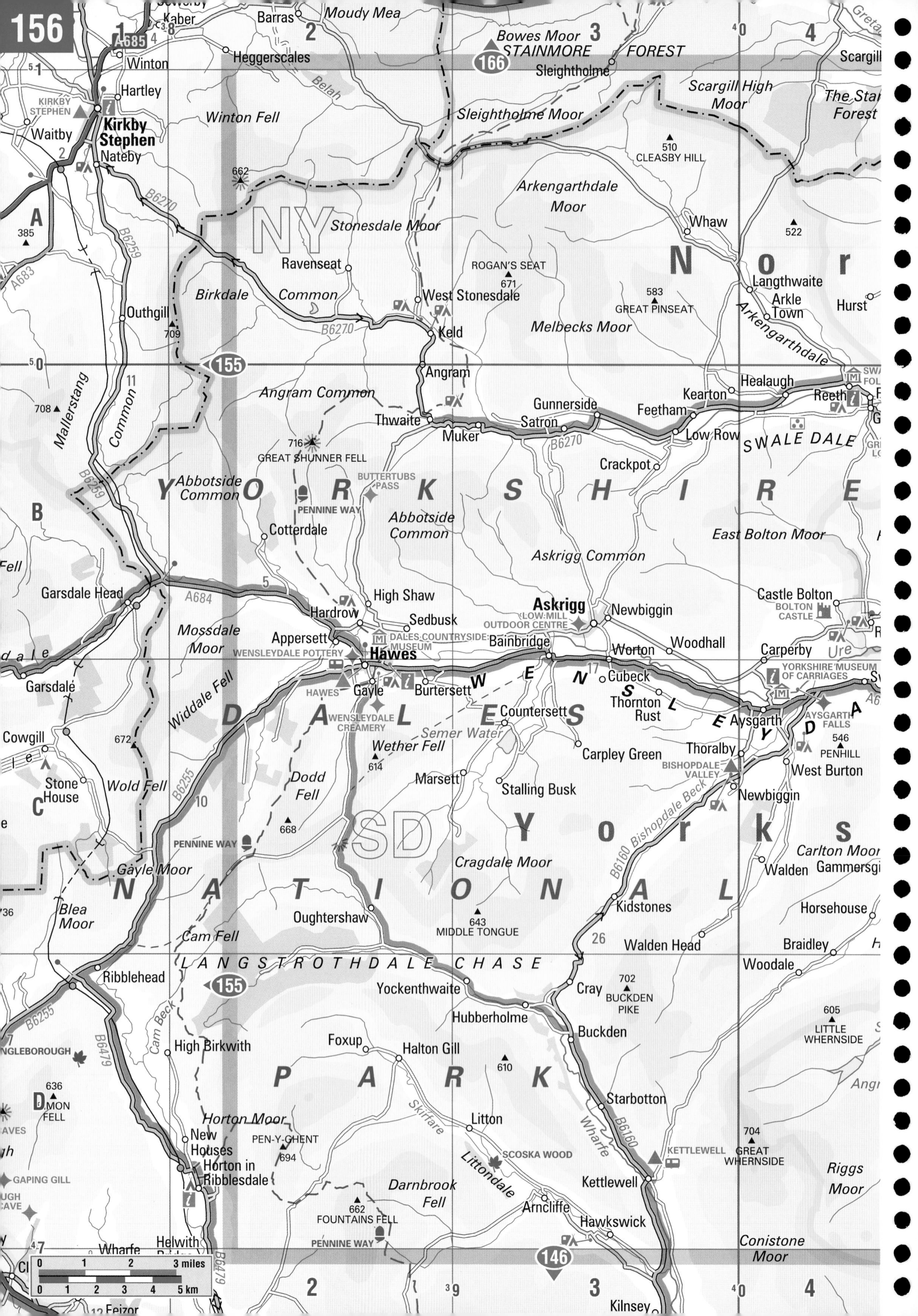

Kirkby Stephen
Winton
Hartley
Waitby
Nateby
Barras
Moudy Mea
Heggerscales
Bowes Moor
STAINMORE FOREST
Sleightholme
Sleightholme Moor
Scargill High Moor
The Stang Forest
Winton Fell
510 CLEASBY HILL
Arkengarthdale Moor
Stonesdale Moor
Whaw
Ravenseat
ROGAN'S SEAT 671
Langthwaite
Arkle Town
Hurst
Birkdale
Common
West Stonesdale
GREAT PINSEAT
Melbecks Moor
Keld
Outhgill
Mallerstang
Common
Angram
Angram Common
Healaugh
Kearton
Reeth
Gunnerside
Feetham
Satron
Thwaite
Muker
Low Row
SWALE DALE
GREAT SHUNNER FELL
Crackpot
Abbotside Common
BUTTERTUBS PASS
PENNINE WAY
YORKSHIRE
Abbotside Common
East Bolton Moor
Cotterdale
Askrigg Common
Garsdale Head
High Shaw
Askrigg
Newbiggin
Castle Bolton
BOLTON CASTLE
Hardrow
Sedbusk
LOW MILL OUTDOOR CENTRE
Mossdale Moor
Appersett
DALES COUNTRYSIDE MUSEUM
Bainbridge
Woodhall
Carperby
WENSLEYDALE POTTERY
Hawes
Worton
Cubeck
YORKSHIRE MUSEUM OF CARRIAGES
Garsdale
HAWES
Gayle
Burtersett
Thornton Rust
Widdale Fell
Countersett
Aysgarth
WENSLEYDALE CREAMERY
AYSGARTH FALLS
Semer Water
Cowgill
Wether Fell
Carpley Green
Thoralby
PENHILL
BISHOPDALE VALLEY
West Burton
Stone House
Wold Fell
Dodd Fell
Marsett
Stalling Busk
Newbiggin
Bishopdale Beck
PENNINE WAY
Yorkshire Dales National Park
Carlton Moor
Gammersgill
Gayle Moor
Cragdale Moor
Walden
Blea Moor
Oughtershaw
Kidstones
Horsehouse
MIDDLE TONGUE
Cam Fell
Walden Head
Braidley
LANGSTROTHDALE CHASE
Woodale
Ribblehead
Yockenthwaite
Cray
BUCKDEN PIKE
Hubberholme
LITTLE WHERNSIDE
Buckden
High Birkwith
Foxup
Halton Gill
Cam Beck
INGLEBOROUGH
Starbotton
Horton Moor
Litton
Skirfare
Wharfe
New Houses
PEN-Y-GHENT
SCOSKA WOOD
KETTLEWELL
GREAT WHERNSIDE
Riggs Moor
Horton in Ribblesdale
Littondale
Kettlewell
GAPING GILL
Darnbrook Fell
FOUNTAINS FELL
Arncliffe
Hawkswick
Wharfe
Helwith
PENNINE WAY
Conistone Moor
Kilnsey
Feizor
0 1 2 3 miles
0 1 2 3 4 5 km

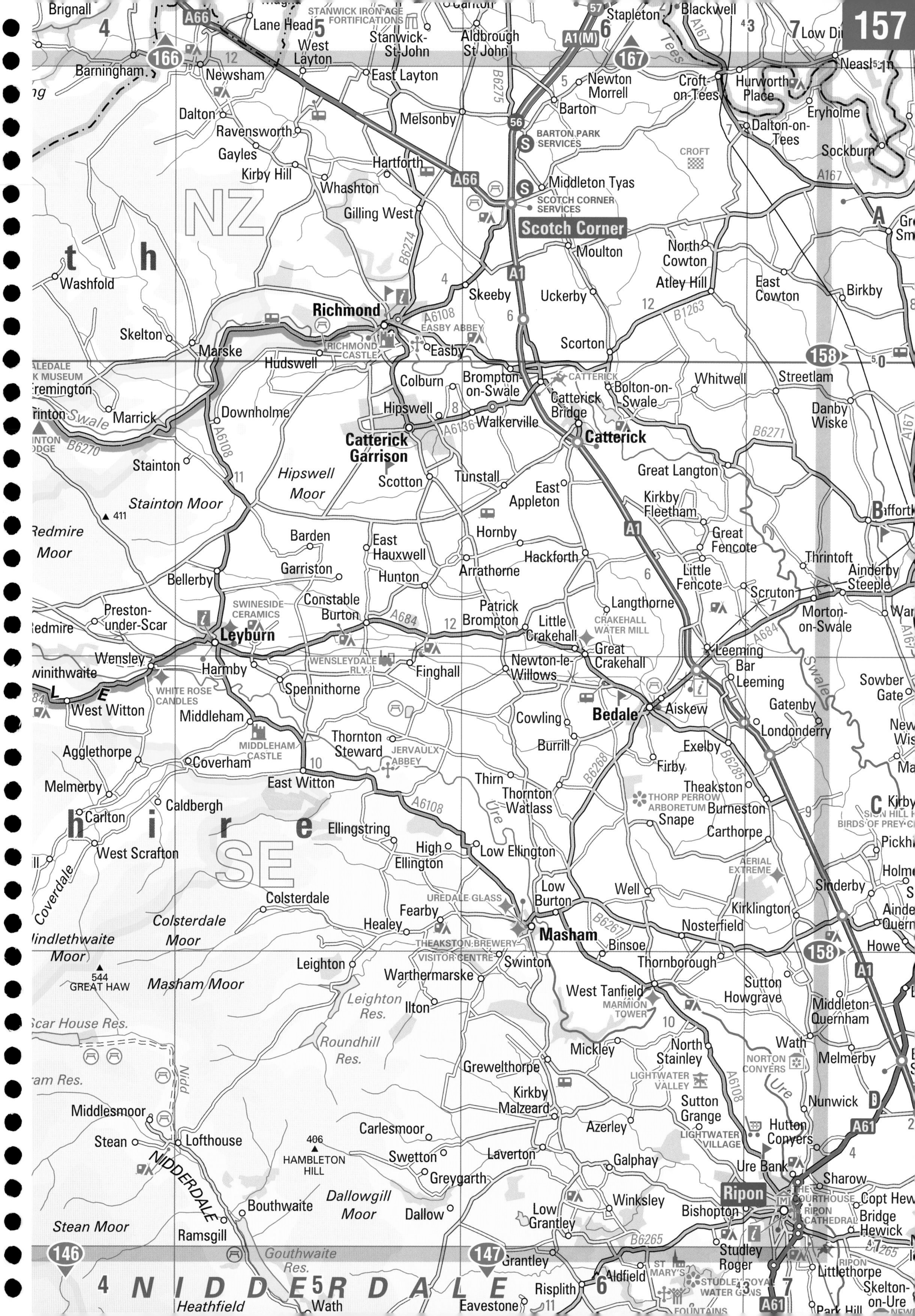

Brignall
Lane Head
West Layton
Stanwick-St-John
STANWICK IRON AGE FORTIFICATIONS
Aldbrough St John
Stapleton
Blackwell
Low Dinsdale
Barningham
Newsham
East Layton
Newton Morrell
Barton
Croft-on-Tees
Hurworth Place
Neasham
Eryholme
Dalton-on-Tees
Sockburn
Dalton
Ravensworth
Melsonby
Gayles
Kirby Hill
Hartforth
Whashton
BARTON PARK SERVICES
CROFT
Middleton Tyas
SCOTCH CORNER SERVICES
Scotch Corner
Gilling West
NZ
Moulton
North Cowton
Atley Hill
East Cowton
Birkby
Washfold
Skeeby
Uckerby
Richmond
EASBY ABBEY
Easby
RICHMOND CASTLE
Skelton
Marske
Hudswell
Scorton
Colburn
Brompton-on-Swale
CATTERICK
Bolton-on-Swale
Whitwell
Streetlam
Danby Wiske
Fremington
Marrick
Downholme
Hipswell
Walkerville
Catterick Bridge
Catterick
Catterick Garrison
Swale
Stainton
Hipswell Moor
Scotton
Tunstall
East Appleton
Great Langton
Kirkby Fleetham
Stainton Moor
Redmire Moor
Barden
East Hauxwell
Hornby
Hackforth
Great Fencote
Little Fencote
Thrintoft
Ainderby Steeple
Garriston
Hunton
Arrathorne
Bellerby
Constable Burton
Patrick Brompton
Langthorne
Scruton
Morton-on-Swale
Preston-under-Scar
Redmire
SWINESIDE CERAMICS
Leyburn
Little Crakehall
CRAKEHALL WATER MILL
Great Crakehall
Leeming
Bar Leeming
Wensley
Harmby
WENSLEYDALE RLY
Finghall
Newton-le-Willows
Sowber Gate
Gatenby
Londonderry
Spennithorne
WHITE ROSE CANDLES
West Witton
Middleham
Cowling
Bedale
Aiskew
Thornton Steward
JERVAULX ABBEY
Burrill
Exelby
MIDDLEHAM CASTLE
Agglethorpe
Coverham
Firby
Melmerby
East Witton
Thirn
Thornton Watlass
Theakston
THORP PERROW ARBORETUM
Burneston
Snape
Carthorpe
Caldbergh
Carlton
Ellingstring
Kirby
SION HILL BIRDS OF PREY
West Scrafton
High Ellington
Low Ellington
SE
Coverdale
AERIAL EXTREME
Sinderby
Holme
Low Burton
Well
Kirklington
Colsterdale
URE DALE GLASS
Fearby
Healey
Masham
Binsoe
Nosterfield
Colsterdale Moor
Windlethwaite Moor
THEAKSTON BREWERY VISITOR CENTRE
Swinton
Thornborough
Howe
Leighton
Warthermarske
544 GREAT HAW
Masham Moor
West Tanfield
Sutton Howgrave
MARMION TOWER
Middleton Quernham
Leighton Res.
Ilton
Scar House Res.
Roundhill Res.
Mickley
North Stainley
Wath
Melmerby
NORTON CONYERS
Grewelthorpe
LIGHTWATER VALLEY
Kirkby Malzeard
Sutton Grange
Nunwick
Middlesmoor
Azerley
Hutton Conyers
LIGHTWATER VILLAGE
Carlesmoor
Stean
Lofthouse
406 HAMBLETON HILL
Swetton
Laverton
Galphay
Ure Bank
Sharow
NIDDERDALE
Greygarth
Ripon
THE COURTHOUSE
Copt Hewick
RIPON CATHEDRAL
Bridge Hewick
Dallowgill Moor
Bouthwaite
Dallow
Low Grantley
Winksley
Bishopton
Stean Moor
Ramsgill
Gouthwaite Res.
Studley Roger
Grantley
ST MARY'S
STUDLEY ROYAL WATER GDNS
RIPON RACECOURSE
Littlethorpe
Aldfield
Risplith
Skelton-on-Ure
NIDDERDALE
Heathfield
Wath
Eavestone
FOUNTAINS
Park Hill

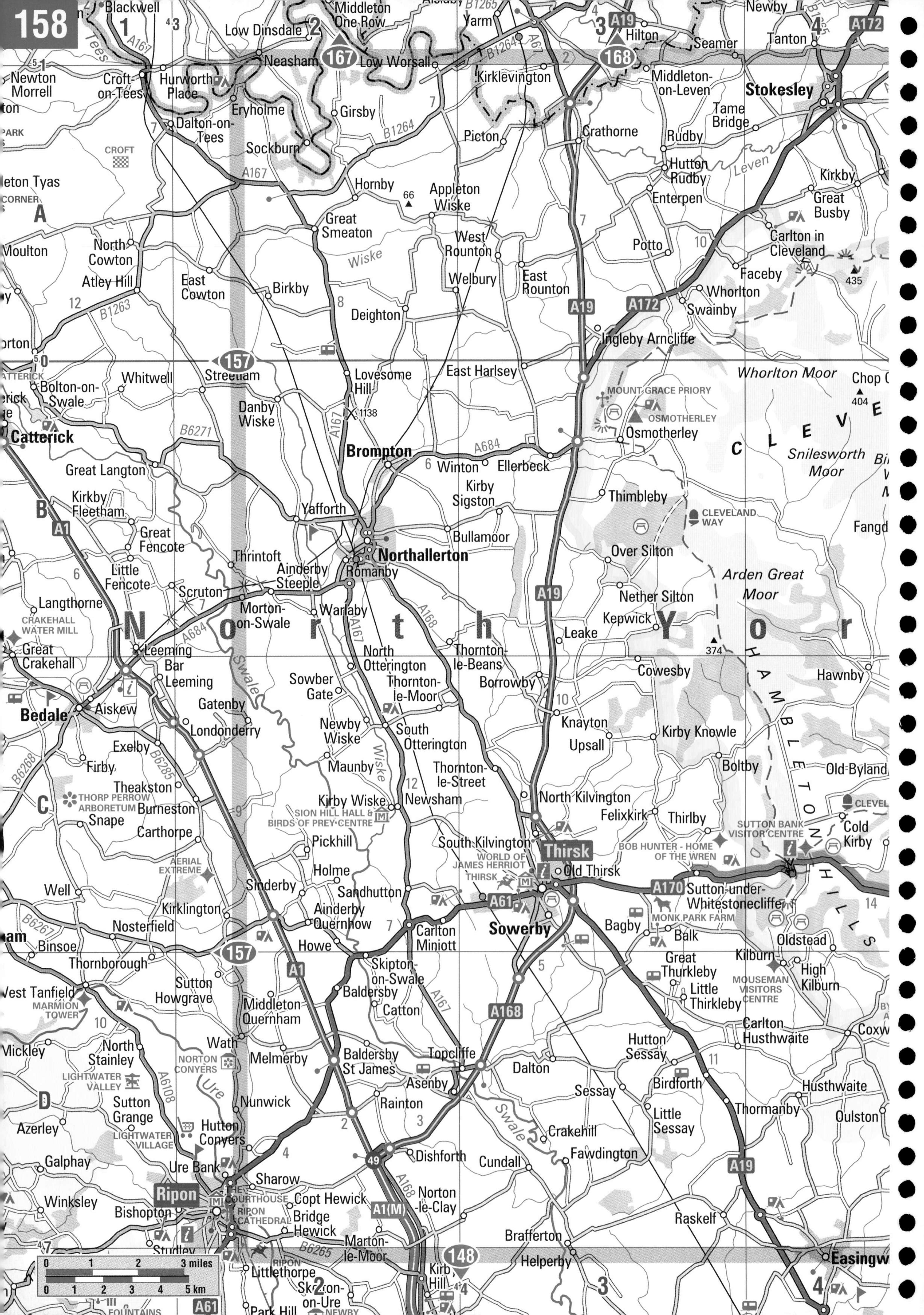
Blackwell
Low Dinsdale
Middleton One Row
Yarm
Newby
Hilton
Seamer
Tanton
Neasham
Low Worsall
Kirklevington
Newton Morrell
Croft-on-Tees
Hurworth Place
Middleton-on-Leven
Stokesley
Eryholme
Girsby
Dalton-on-Tees
Crathorne
Tame Bridge
Picton
Rudby
Sockburn
CROFT
Hutton Rudby
Leven
Kirkby
Hornby
Appleton Wiske
Enterpen
Great Busby
Great Smeaton
West Rounton
Potto
Carlton in Cleveland
Moulton
North Cowton
Wiske
Faceby
Atley Hill
East Cowton
Birkby
Welbury
East Rounton
Whorlton
Swainby
Deighton
Ingleby Arncliffe
Streetlam
Lovesome Hill
East Harlsey
Whorlton Moor
Chop Gate
Bolton-on-Swale
Whitwell
Danby Wiske
MOUNT GRACE PRIORY
OSMOTHERLEY
Osmotherley
Catterick
Brompton
Winton
Ellerbeck
CLEVELAND
Snilesworth Moor
Great Langton
Kirby Sigston
Thimbleby
Kirkby Fleetham
Yafforth
CLEVELAND WAY
Great Fencote
Bullamoor
Northallerton
Over Silton
Thrintoft
Ainderby Steeple
Romanby
Little Fencote
Arden Great Moor
Scruton
Nether Silton
Langthorne
Morton-on-Swale
Warlaby
CRAKEHALL WATER MILL
Kepwick
North Yorkshire
Leake
Great Crakehall
Leeming
North Otterington
Thornton-le-Beans
Bar
Leeming
Swale
Sowber Gate
Thornton-le-Moor
Borrowby
Cowesby
HAMBLETON HILLS
Hawnby
Bedale
Aiskew
Gatenby
Knayton
Londonderry
Newby Wiske
South Otterington
Upsall
Kirby Knowle
Exelby
Firby
Maunby
Thornton-le-Street
Boltby
Old Byland
Theakston
Newsham
North Kilvington
THORP PERROW ARBORETUM
Burneston
Kirby Wiske
Felixkirk
Thirlby
Snape
SION HILL HALL & BIRDS OF PREY CENTRE
SUTTON BANK VISITOR CENTRE
Cold Kirby
Carthorpe
Pickhill
South Kilvington
Thirsk
BOB HUNTER - HOME OF THE WREN
AERIAL EXTREME
WORLD OF JAMES HERRIOT
Holme
THIRSK
Old Thirsk
Well
Sinderby
Sandhutton
Sutton-under-Whitestonecliffe
Kirklington
Ainderby Quernhow
Sowerby
MONK PARK FARM
Nosterfield
Carlton Miniott
Bagby
Balk
Oldstead
Binsoe
Howe
Thornborough
Skipton-on-Swale
Great Thurkleby
Kilburn
High Kilburn
West Tanfield
Sutton Howgrave
Baldersby
Little Thirkleby
MOUSEMAN VISITORS CENTRE
MARMION TOWER
Middleton Quernham
Catton
Carlton Husthwaite
Coxwold
Mickley
North Stainley
Wath
Melmerby
Baldersby St James
Topcliffe
Hutton Sessay
NORTON CONYERS
Dalton
LIGHTWATER VALLEY
Ure
Asenby
Birdforth
Husthwaite
Sutton Grange
Nunwick
Rainton
Sessay
Thormanby
Oulston
Little Sessay
Azerley
Hutton Conyers
LIGHTWATER VILLAGE
Crakehill
Galphay
Ure Bank
Dishforth
Cundall
Fawdington
Sharow
Ripon
THE COURTHOUSE
Copt Hewick
Norton-le-Clay
Winksley
Bishopton
RIPON CATHEDRAL
Bridge Hewick
Raskelf
Brafferton
Studley
Marton-le-Moor
Helperby
Easingwold
RIPON
Littlethorpe
Kirby Hill
Skelton-on-Ure
FOUNTAINS
Park Hill
NEWBY
0 1 2 3 miles
0 1 2 3 4 5 km

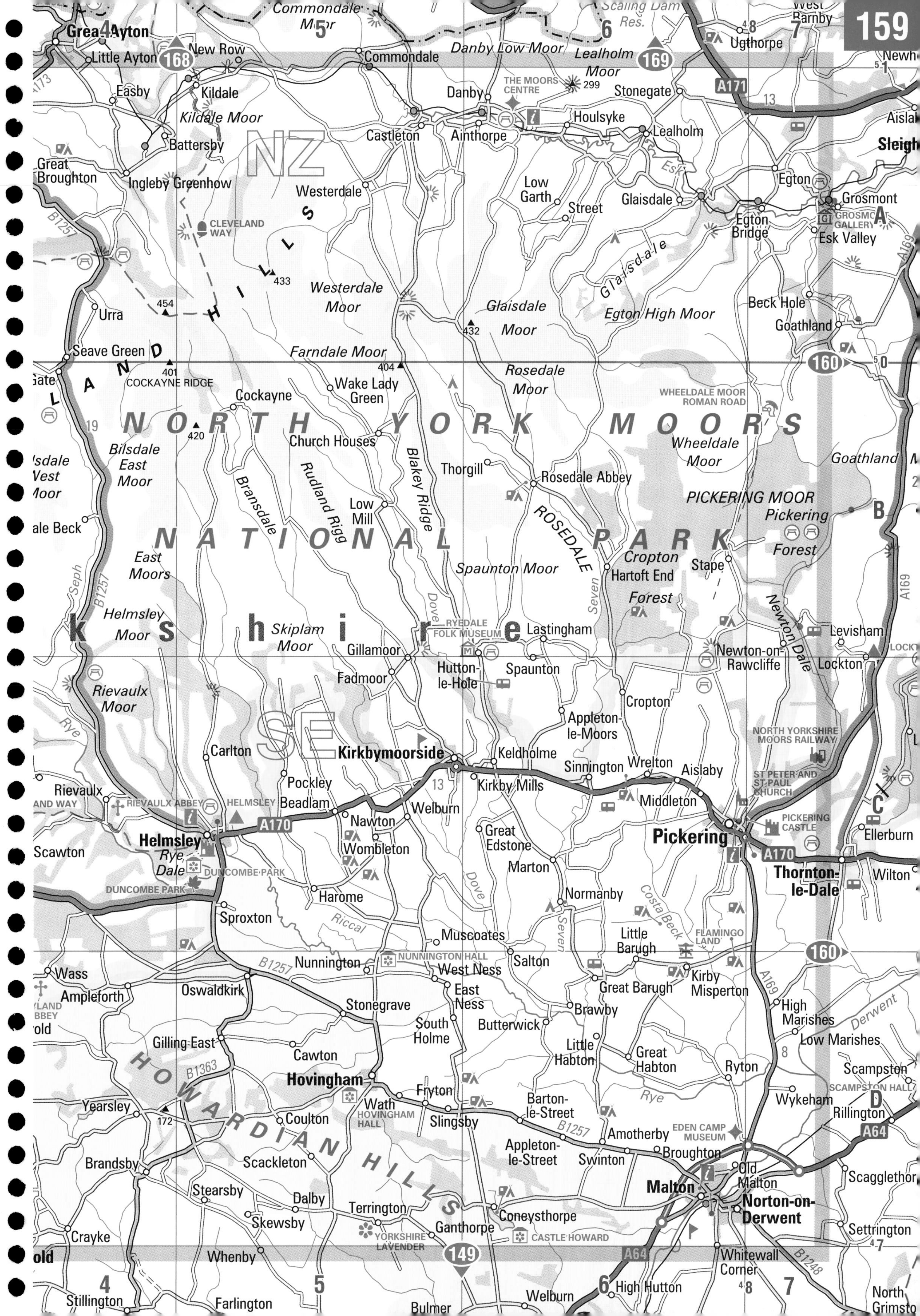

NORTH YORK MOORS NATIONAL PARK
Great Ayton
Little Ayton
New Row
Commondale
Danby Low Moor
Lealholm Moor
Ugthorpe
Easby
Kildale
Kildale Moor
Battersby
Castleton
Danby
Ainthorpe
THE MOORS CENTRE
Houlsyke
Stonegate
Lealholm
Great Broughton
Ingleby Greenhow
Westerdale
Low Garth
Street
Glaisdale
Egton
Grosmont
Egton Bridge
Esk Valley
CLEVELAND WAY
Westerdale Moor
Glaisdale Moor
Egton High Moor
Beck Hole
Goathland
Urra
Seave Green
Farndale Moor
Rosedale Moor
COCKAYNE RIDGE
Cockayne
Wake Lady Green
WHEELDALE MOOR ROMAN ROAD
Church Houses
Wheeldale Moor
Goathland
Bilsdale East Moor
Thorgill
Rosedale Abbey
Bransdale
Rudland Rigg
Blakey Ridge
Low Mill
ROSEDALE
PICKERING MOOR
Pickering Forest
East Moors
Spaunton Moor
Cropton
Hartoft End
Stape
Cropton Forest
Newton Dale
Helmsley Moor
Skiplam Moor
RYEDALE FOLK MUSEUM
Lastingham
Levisham
Gillamoor
Hutton-le-Hole
Spaunton
Newton-on-Rawcliffe
Lockton
Fadmoor
Rievaulx Moor
Cropton
Appleton-le-Moors
NORTH YORKSHIRE MOORS RAILWAY
Carlton
Kirkbymoorside
Keldholme
Sinnington
Wrelton
Aislaby
Pockley
Kirkby Mills
ST PETER AND ST PAUL CHURCH
Rievaulx
RIEVAULX ABBEY
HELMSLEY
Beadlam
Middleton
PICKERING CASTLE
Nawton
Welburn
Great Edstone
Pickering
Ellerburn
Helmsley
Wombleton
Scawton
Rye Dale
DUNCOMBE PARK
Marton
Thornton-le-Dale
Wilton
Normanby
Harome
Sproxton
Costa Beck
Riccal
Muscoates
Little Barugh
FLAMINGO LAND
NUNNINGTON HALL
Nunnington
Salton
Wass
West Ness
Kirby Misperton
Ampleforth
Oswaldkirk
East Ness
Great Barugh
Stonegrave
Brawby
High Marishes
South Holme
Butterwick
Low Marishes
Gilling East
Little Habton
Great Habton
Scampston
Cawton
Ryton
HOWARDIAN HILLS
Hovingham
Fryton
SCAMPSTON HALL
Yearsley
Wath
Barton-le-Street
Wykeham
Rillington
Coulton
HOVINGHAM HALL
Slingsby
Amotherby
EDEN CAMP MUSEUM
Appleton-le-Street
Broughton
Brandsby
Scackleton
Swinton
Old Malton
Scagglethorpe
Stearsby
Malton
Dalby
Norton-on-Derwent
Terrington
Coneysthorpe
Skewsby
Settrington
Crayke
Ganthorpe
YORKSHIRE LAVENDER
CASTLE HOWARD
Whenby
Whitewall Corner
Stillington
Farlington
Bulmer
Welburn
High Hutton
North Grimston

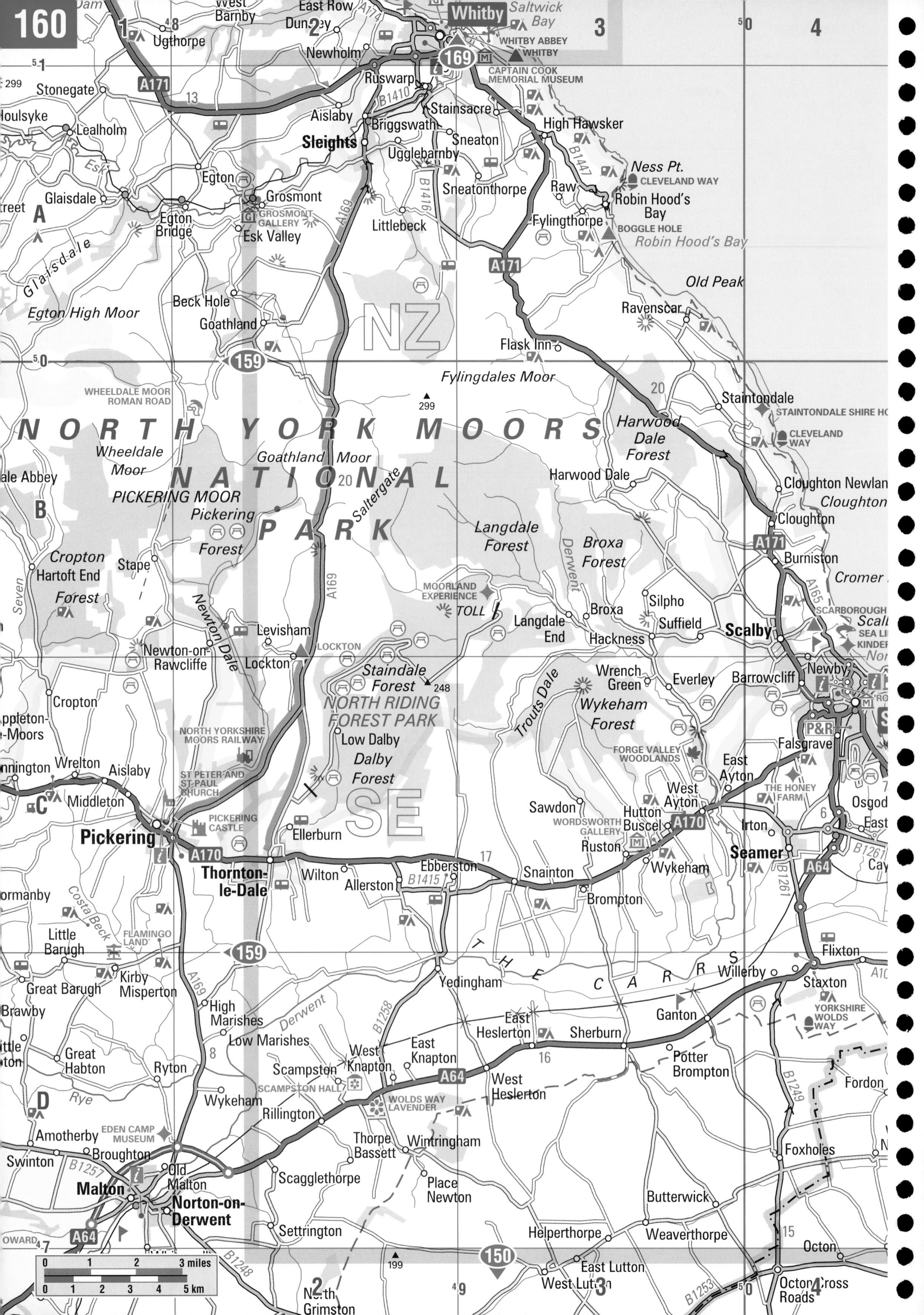

Whitby
Saltwick Bay
WHITBY ABBEY
WHITBY
169
CAPTAIN COOK MEMORIAL MUSEUM
Ugthorpe
West Barnby
East Row
Newholm
Ruswarp
Stonegate
A171
Aislaby
Stainsacre
Briggswath
High Hawsker
Lealholm
Sleights
Sneaton
Ugglebarnby
Egton
Sneatonthorpe
Raw
Ness Pt.
CLEVELAND WAY
Glaisdale
Grosmont
GROSMONT GALLERY
Robin Hood's Bay
Egton Bridge
Esk Valley
Littlebeck
Fylingthorpe
BOGGLE HOLE
Robin Hood's Bay
Glaisdale
Egton High Moor
Beck Hole
Goathland
Old Peak
Ravenscar
NZ
Flask Inn
159
Fylingdales Moor
WHEELDALE MOOR ROMAN ROAD
299
Staintondale
STAINTONDALE SHIRE HORSE
NORTH YORK MOORS NATIONAL PARK
Wheeldale Moor
Goathland Moor
Harwood Dale Forest
CLEVELAND WAY
PICKERING MOOR
Saltergate
Harwood Dale
Cloughton Newlands
Cloughton
Pickering Forest
Langdale Forest
Broxa Forest
Burniston
Cropton
Hartoft End
Stape
Cropton Forest
Cromer
Seven
Newton Dale
A169
MOORLAND EXPERIENCE
TOLL
Silpho
Suffield
Langdale End
Broxa
Hackness
Scalby
SCARBOROUGH
Levisham
LOCKTON
Newton-on-Rawcliffe
Lockton
Staindale Forest
248
NORTH RIDING FOREST PARK
Wrench Green
Everley
Barrowcliff
Newby
Cropton
Trouts Dale
Wykeham Forest
Low Dalby
Dalby Forest
NORTH YORKSHIRE MOORS RAILWAY
FORGE VALLEY WOODLANDS
Falsgrave
P&R
Wrelton
Aislaby
ST PETER AND ST PAUL CHURCH
East Ayton
THE HONEY FARM
West Ayton
Middleton
PICKERING CASTLE
SE
Sawdon
Hutton Buscel
Osgodby
Pickering
Ellerburn
WORDSWORTH GALLERY
A170
Irton
Ruston
Seamer
A170
Thornton-le-Dale
Ebberston
Snainton
Wilton
Allerston
B1415
Wykeham
A64
Brompton
Costa Beck
Little Barugh
FLAMINGO LAND
159
Flixton
THE CARRS
Willerby
Staxton
Great Barugh
Kirby Misperton
Yedingham
Brawby
High Marishes
Derwent
East Heslerton
Sherburn
Ganton
YORKSHIRE WOLDS WAY
Low Marishes
Great Habton
Ryton
Scampston
West Knapton
East Knapton
Potter Brompton
A64
West Heslerton
Fordon
SCAMPSTON HALL
Rye
Wykeham
WOLDS WAY LAVENDER
Rillington
Amotherby
EDEN CAMP MUSEUM
Thorpe Bassett
Wintringham
Foxholes
Broughton
Swinton
Old Malton
Scagglethorpe
Place Newton
Malton
Norton-on-Derwent
Butterwick
Settrington
Helperthorpe
Weaverthorpe
Octon
150
East Lutton
West Lutton
199
North Grimston
Octon Cross Roads
0 1 2 3 miles
0 1 2 3 4 5 km

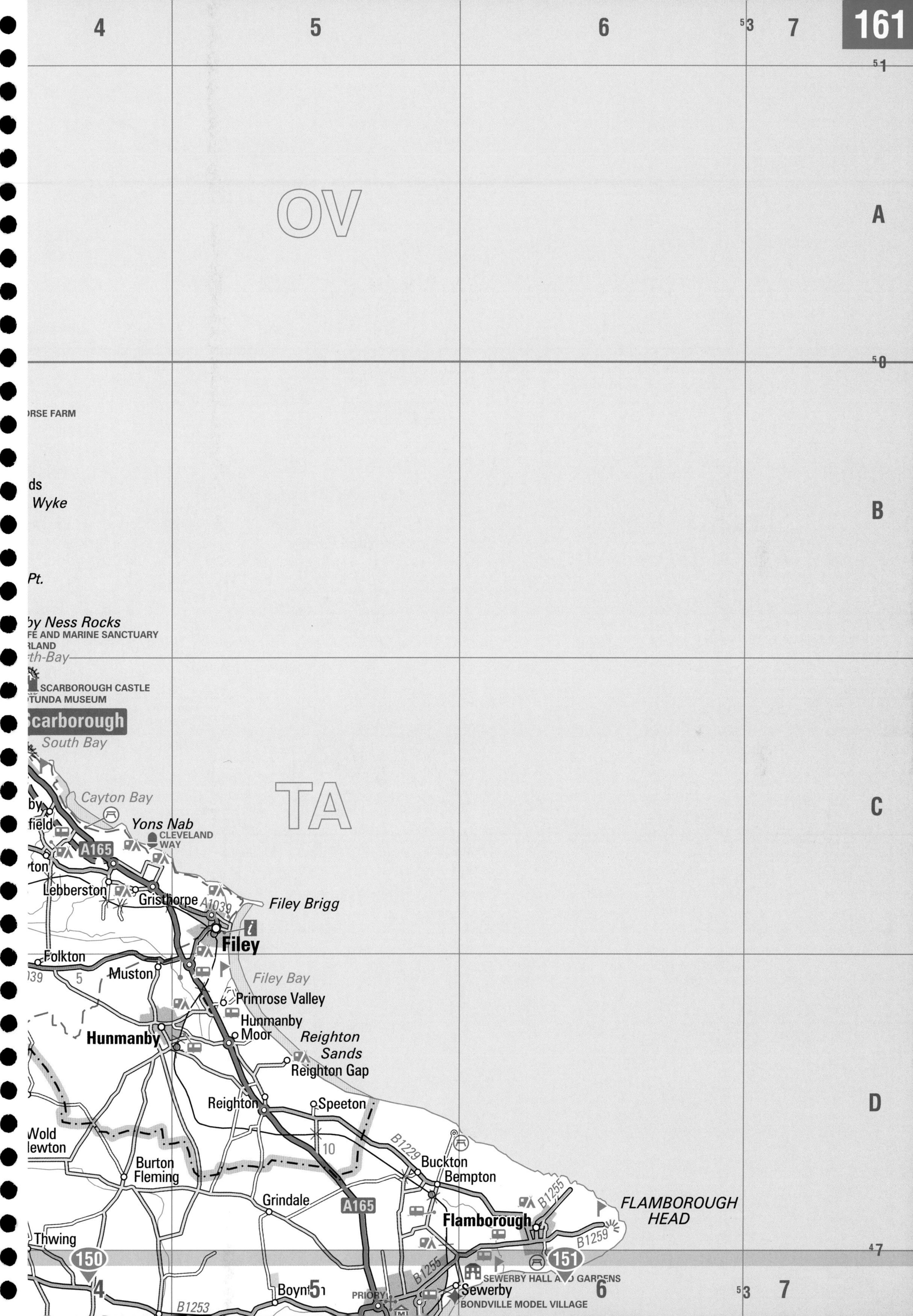

OV
TA
Scarborough
South Bay
SCARBOROUGH CASTLE
Cayton Bay
Yons Nab
CLEVELAND WAY
A165
Lebberston
Gristhorpe
A1039
Filey Brigg
Filey
Folkton
Muston
Filey Bay
Primrose Valley
Hunmanby Moor
Hunmanby
Reighton Sands
Reighton Gap
Reighton
Speeton
B1229
Buckton
Bempton
Burton Fleming
Grindale
Flamborough
B1255
FLAMBOROUGH HEAD
B1259
Thwing
150
151
SEWERBY HALL AND GARDENS
Sewerby
BONDVILLE MODEL VILLAGE
PRIORY
B1253

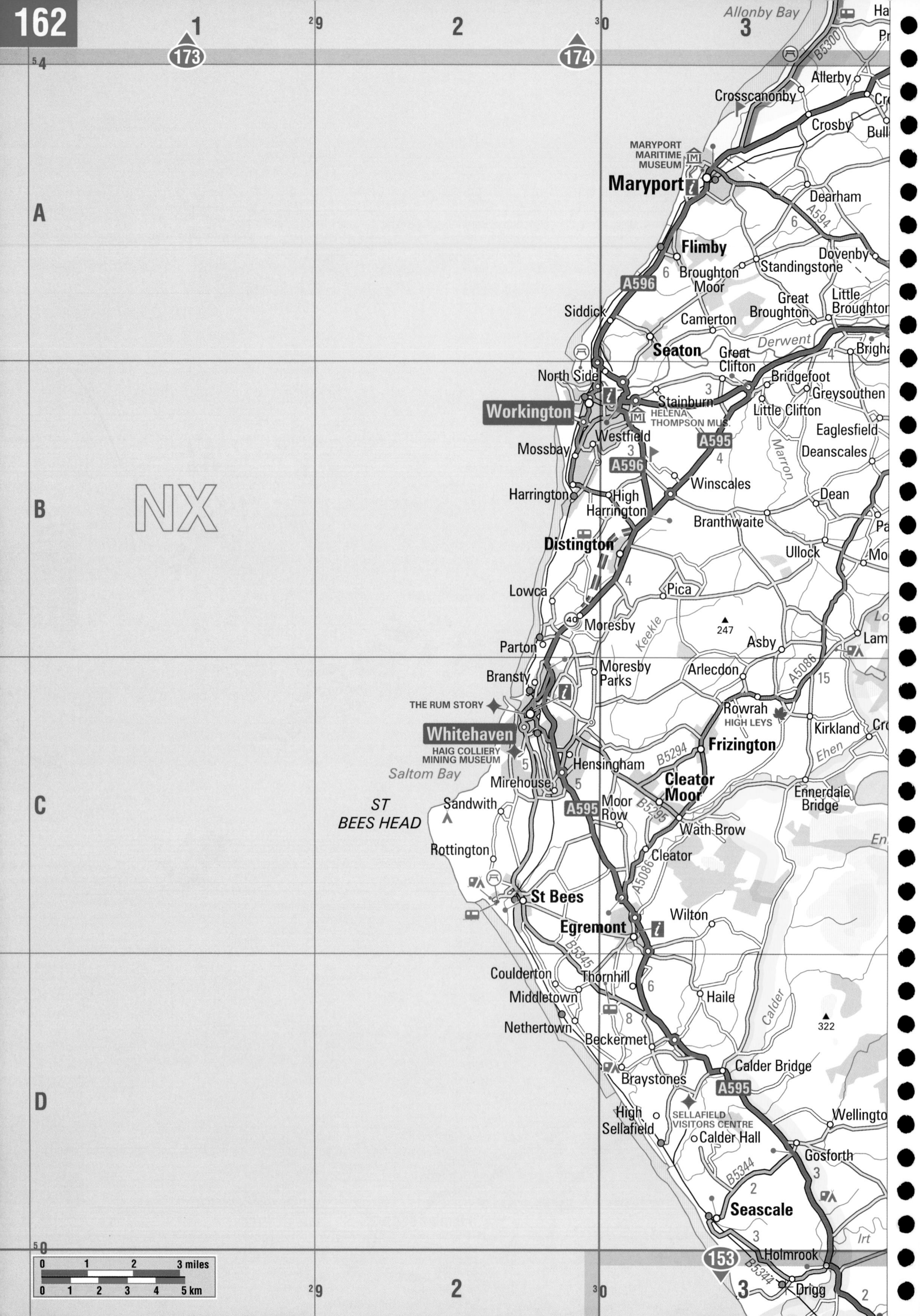

NX
Maryport
MARYPORT MARITIME MUSEUM
Allonby Bay
Allerby
Crosscanonby
Crosby
Dearham
Flimby
Broughton Moor
Dovenby
Standingstone
Great Broughton
Little Broughton
Siddick
Camerton
Seaton
Great Clifton
Derwent
Bridgefoot
Greysouthen
North Side
Workington
Stainburn
HELENA THOMPSON MUS.
Little Clifton
Eaglesfield
Westfield
Mossbay
Deanscales
Marron
Winscales
Harrington
High Harrington
Dean
Branthwaite
Distington
Ullock
Lowca
Pica
Moresby
Keekle
Asby
Parton
Bransty
Moresby Parks
Arlecdon
THE RUM STORY
Rowrah
HIGH LEYS
Kirkland
Whitehaven
HAIG COLLIERY MINING MUSEUM
Frizington
Saltom Bay
Hensingham
Ehen
Cleator Moor
Mirehouse
Ennerdale Bridge
ST BEES HEAD
Sandwith
Moor Row
Wath Brow
Rottington
Cleator
St Bees
Egremont
Wilton
Coulderton
Thornhill
Middletown
Haile
Calder
Nethertown
Beckermet
Calder Bridge
Braystones
High Sellafield
SELLAFIELD VISITORS CENTRE
Calder Hall
Wellington
Gosforth
Seascale
Holmrook
Drigg
Irt
A596
A595
A594
A5086
B5294
B5295
B5345
B5344
B5300
247
322
173
174
153
0 1 2 3 miles
0 1 2 3 4 5 km

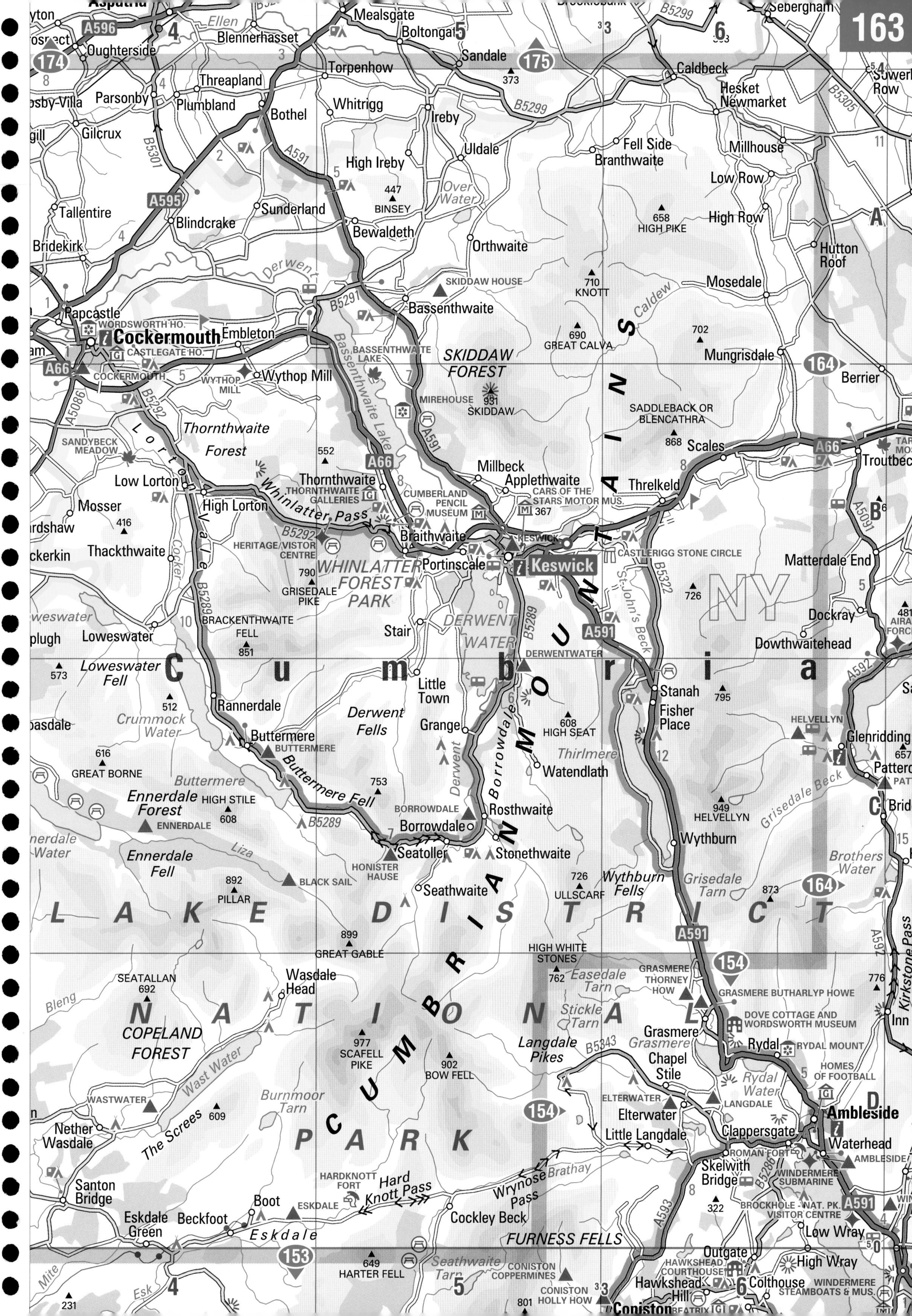
Mealsgate
Boltongate
Blennerhasset
Oughterside
A596
174
Sebergham
B5299
Caldbeck
Sandale
175
Torpenhow
373
Threapland
Parsonby
Plumbland
Whitrigg
Ireby
B5299
Hesket Newmarket
B5305
Sowerby Row
Gilcrux
Bothel
B5301
A591
Uldale
Fell Side
Branthwaite
Millhouse
High Ireby
Over Water
447
BINSEY
Low Row
A595
Tallentire
Blindcrake
Sunderland
Bewaldeth
658
HIGH PIKE
High Row
Bridekirk
Orthwaite
Hutton Roof
Derwent
710
KNOTT
SKIDDAW HOUSE
Mosedale
Papcastle
WORDSWORTH HO.
Cockermouth
Embleton
B5291
Bassenthwaite
Caldew
690
GREAT CALVA
702
Mungrisdale
CASTLEGATE HO.
BASSENTHWAITE LAKE
Bassenthwaite Lake
SKIDDAW FOREST
164
Berrier
A66
COCKERMOUTH
WYTHOP MILL
Wythop Mill
931
SKIDDAW
MIREHOUSE
SADDLEBACK OR BLENCATHRA
A5086
B5292
SANDYBECK MEADOW
Thornthwaite Forest
Lorton
552
A66
A591
868
Scales
A66
Troutbeck
Low Lorton
Thornthwaite
THORNTHWAITE GALLERIES
Millbeck
Applethwaite
Threlkeld
Mosser
High Lorton
Whinlatter Pass
CUMBERLAND PENCIL MUSEUM
CARS OF THE STARS MOTOR MUS.
367
416
B5292
Braithwaite
KESWICK
A5091
Thackthwaite
HERITAGE/VISITOR CENTRE
Portinscale
Keswick
CASTLERIGG STONE CIRCLE
Matterdale End
Cocker
Vale
790
GRISEDALE PIKE
WHINLATTER FOREST PARK
B5289
St. John's Beck
B5322
726
NY
Dockray
Loweswater
Loweswater
10
BRACKENTHWAITE FELL
851
Stair
DERWENT WATER
A591
Dowthwaitehead
Loweswater Fell
573
Cumbria
Little Town
DERWENTWATER
A592
512
Rannerdale
Stanah
795
Crummock Water
Derwent Fells
Grange
608
HIGH SEAT
Fisher Place
HELVELLYN
Glenridding
Buttermere
BUTTERMERE
Borrowdale
Thirlmere
12
616
GREAT BORNE
Derwent
Watendlath
Patterdale
Buttermere Fell
753
Buttermere
Ennerdale Forest
HIGH STILE
608
ENNERDALE
BORROWDALE
Rosthwaite
949
HELVELLYN
Grisedale Beck
B5289
Borrowdale
Ennerdale Water
Seatoller
Stonethwaite
Wythburn
Brothers Water
Ennerdale Fell
Liza
HONISTER HAUSE
726
ULLSCARF
Wythburn Fells
Grisedale Tarn
BLACK SAIL
892
PILLAR
Seathwaite
873
164
LAKE DISTRICT
899
GREAT GABLE
A591
HIGH WHITE STONES
A592
Kirkstone Pass
SEATALLAN
692
Wasdale Head
762
Easedale Tarn
GRASMERE THORNEY HOW
154
776
GRASMERE BUTHARLYP HOWE
Bleng
CUMBRIAN MOUNTAINS
NATIONAL
Stickle Tarn
DOVE COTTAGE AND WORDSWORTH MUSEUM
Inn
COPELAND FOREST
977
SCAFELL PIKE
Langdale Pikes
Grasmere
Grasmere
B5343
Rydal
RYDAL MOUNT
Wast Water
902
BOW FELL
Chapel Stile
HOMES OF FOOTBALL
Rydal Water
WASTWATER
Burnmoor Tarn
ELTERWATER
LANGDALE
Ambleside
154
Elterwater
609
Nether Wasdale
The Screes
PARK
Little Langdale
Clappersgate
Waterhead
ROMAN FORT
AMBLESIDE
Skelwith Bridge
Brathay
WINDERMERE SUBMARINE
Santon Bridge
HARDKNOTT FORT
Hard Knott Pass
Wrynose Pass
B5286
A593
322
BROCKHOLE - NAT. PK. VISITOR CENTRE
A591
Boot
ESKDALE
Eskdale Green
Beckfoot
Cockley Beck
Low Wray
Eskdale
FURNESS FELLS
Outgate
HAWKSHEAD COURTHOUSE
High Wray
153
649
HARTER FELL
Seathwaite Tarn
CONISTON COPPERMINES
Mite
Esk
CONISTON HOLLY HOW
Hawkshead Hill
Colthouse
WINDERMERE STEAMBOATS & MUS.
231
801
Coniston
BEATRIX

Thursby
Dalston
Durdar
Brisco
Cumwhinton
Cumrew
Geltsdale
Cotehill
Hornsby
Newbiggin
Buckabank
Wreay
West Curthwaite
East Curthwaite
Holmwrangle
Croglin
Brackenthwaite
Gaitsgill
Aiketgate
Ainstable
Croglin Water
Scale House
Rosley
Raughton Head
Stockdalewath
SOUTHWAITE SERVICES
Low Hesket
Armathwaite
Welton
Southwaite
High Hesket
HIGH HEAD SCULPTURE VALLEY
Old Town
Ruckcroft
Ivegill
Low Braithwaite
Staffield
High Bankhill
Sebergham
Kirkoswald
Thomas Close
Calthwaite
Inglewood Forest
Caldbeck
Hesket Newmarket
Sowerby Row
Lazonby Fell
Townhead
Lazonby
Glassonby
Hutton End
Fell Side
Branthwaite
Millhouse
New Rent
Plumpton
Brockleymoor
Great Salkeld
Little Salkeld
Low Row
Lamonby
Unthank
HUTTON-IN-THE-FOREST
Skelton
Unthank End
Plumpton Head
Hunsonby
High Row
HIGH PIKE
Ellonby
Winskill
Hutton Roof
Little Blencow
Catterlen
Langwathby
KNOTT
Mosedale
Johnby
Laithes
Edenhall
Caldew
Great Blencow
Newton Reigny
Fair Hill
Penrith
CALVA
Greystoke
Carleton
MAYBURGH HENGE
Mungrisdale
BROUGHAM CASTLE
Berrier
Newbiggin
SADDLEBACK OR BLENCATHRA
Motherby
BECKSTONES ART GALLERY
Eamont Bridge
Scales
Penruddock
Stainton
RHEGED
CLIFTON HALL
TARN MOSS
Troutbeck
DALEMAIN
Sockbridge
LILLIPUT LANE
Clifton
Threlkeld
Hutton
Dacre
Tirril
WETHERIGGS COUNTRY POTTERY
CLIBURN MOSS
Cliburn
LAKELAND BIRD OF PREY CENTRE
Melkinthorpe
CASTLERIGG STONE CIRCLE
Wreay
Pooley Bridge
Askham
Lowther
Hackthorpe
Matterdale End
Longthwaite
Watermillock
Helton
Great Strickland
St John's Beck
Dockray
AIRA FORCE
Knotts
Whale
Dowthwaitehead
ULLSWATER
STREET
Little Strickland
Sleagill
Stanah
Sandwick
Howtown
LOADPOT HILL
Bampton Grange
Fisher Place
HELVELLYN
Bampton
Reagill
Glenridding
Martindale Common
Bampton Common
Rosgill
Thirlmere
Patterdale
PATTERDALE
Dale Head
HELVELLYN
Grisedale Beck
Bridgend
Angle Tarn
Haweswater Reservoir
SHAP ABBEY
Shap
Wythburn
Keld
Hartsop
Brothers Water
Swindale Beck
Ralfland Forest
Wythburn Fells
Grisedale Tarn
LAKE DISTRICT NATIONAL PARK
HIGH STREET
Res.
HARTER FELL
Kirkstone Pass
Shap Fells
DOVE COTTAGE AND
0 1 2 3 miles
0 1 2 3 4 5 km
M6
A6
A66
A595
A591
A5091
A592
A686
B5299
B5305
B5288
B5320
B5322
B6412
B6413
B6261
175
176
163
154

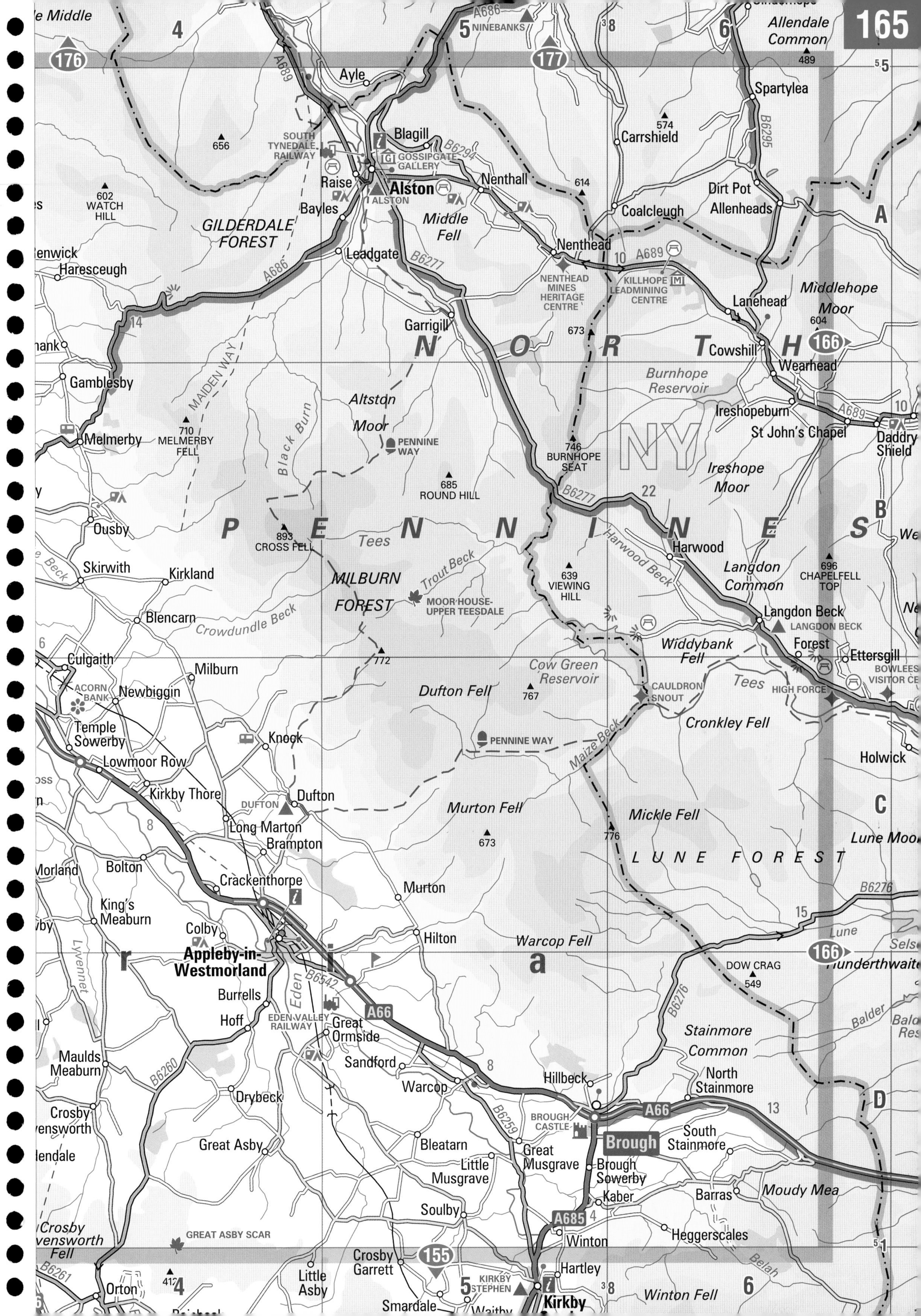
Alston
Nenthead
Garrigill
Allenheads
Cowshill
Wearhead
St John's Chapel
Daddry Shield
Harwood
Langdon Beck
Forest
Ettersgill
Holwick
Melmerby
Gamblesby
Ousby
Skirwith
Kirkland
Blencarn
Culgaith
Milburn
Newbiggin
Temple Sowerby
Knock
Dufton
Kirkby Thore
Long Marton
Brampton
Bolton
Crackenthorpe
Colby
Appleby-in-Westmorland
Murton
Hilton
Burrells
Hoff
Great Ormside
Sandford
Warcop
Hillbeck
North Stainmore
South Stainmore
Brough
Brough Sowerby
Great Musgrave
Little Musgrave
Bleatarn
Kaber
Barras
Soulby
Winton
Hartley
Heggerscales
Crosby Garrett
Little Asby
Great Asby
Drybeck
Maulds Meaburn
King's Meaburn
Orton
Smardale
Kirkby Stephen
PENNINES
NORTH
NY
Cross Fell
Milburn Forest
Dufton Fell
Murton Fell
Mickle Fell
Lune Forest
Warcop Fell
Stainmore Common
Cow Green Reservoir
Burnhope Reservoir
Alston Moor
Gilderdale Forest
Cronkley Fell
Widdybank Fell
Langdon Common
Ireshope Moor
Middlehope Moor
Allendale Common
A66
A686
A689
A685
B6277
B6276
B6259
B6260
B6542
176
177
166
155

Blanchland
Hunstanworth
478 NOOKTON FELL
Spartylea
Muggleswick
Muggleswick Common
Castleside
Allensford
Consett
Leadgate
Templetown
Knitsley
Delves
Horsleyhope
Waskerley
East Butsfield
Cornsay
Satley
HALL HILL FARM
540 BOLT'S LAW
Rookhope
ROOKHOPE NURSERIES
Middlehope Moor
Stanhope Common
516 COLLIER LAW
Tunstall Res.
High Stoop
Lanehead
604
NORTH
Crawleyside
DURHAM DALES CENTRE
Stanhope
Wolsingham Park Moor
Tow Law
WEARDALE
Eastgate
A689
Westgate
St John's Chapel
Daddry Shield
WEARDALE RAILWAY
Frosterley
Wolsingham
Thornley
Hill End
NY
PENNINES
Westernhope Moor
Bollihope Common
Fir Tree
696 CHAPELFELL TOP
Langdon Common
675
Pikeston Fell
Newbiggin Common
487 PAWLAW PIKE
Middleton Common
Redford
Bedburn
Hamsterley
Langdon Beck
LANGDON BECK
Forest
Ettersgill
HIGH FORCE
BOWLEES VISITOR CENTRE
Newbiggin
565
Hamsterley Forest
TEESDALE
Holwick
Middleton-in-Teesdale
Woodland
Woodland Fell
Howle
Morley
Butterknowle
Copley
High Lands
Evenwood
Hill Top
461
Eggleston
Lune Moor
Bowbank
Thringarth
Mickleton
EGGLESTON HALL
Cockfield
Romaldkirk
Grassholme Reservoir
Grassholme
Kinninvie
B6279
Burnt Houses
RABY CASTLE
Hunderthwaite
Hury
Selset Reservoir
Staindrop
DOW CRAG 549
Hunderthwaite Moor
Cotherstone
Stainton
Cleatlam
Hury Reservoir
Little Newsham
Balderhead Reservoir
BALDERSDALE
Clove Lodge
Lartington
BARNARD CASTLE
THE BOWES MUSEUM
Cotherstone Moor
Startforth
Barnard Castle
A67
Westwick
Whorlton
Deep Dale
Deepdale Beck
Boldron
EGGLESTONE ABBEY
ROKEBY PARK
Ovington
Bowes
PENNINE WAY
BOWES CASTLE
Greta Bridge
A66
Gilmonby
Hutton Magna
Moudy Mea
Brignall
Lane Head
Bowes Moor
STAINMORE FOREST
Scargill
Sleightholme
Barningham
Newsham
Scargill High Moor
The Stang Forest
Dalton
0 1 2 3 miles
0 1 2 3 4 5 km

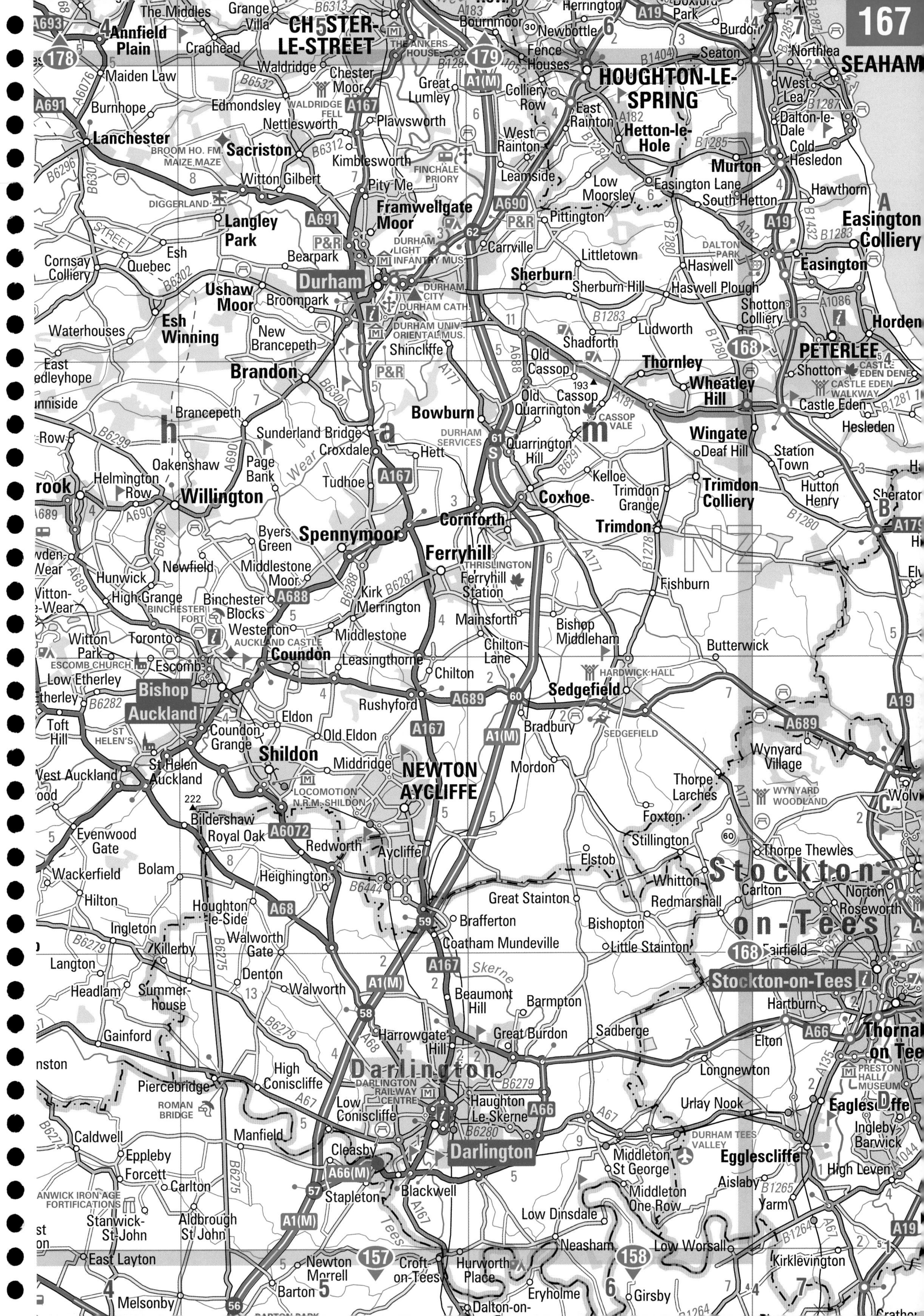

The Middles
Grange Villa
CHESTER-LE-STREET
Annfield Plain
Craghead
178
Maiden Law
Waldridge
Chester Moor
THE ANKERS HOUSE
Bournmoor
179
Herrington
Newbottle
Fence Houses
Burdon
Seaton
Northlea
SEAHAM
HOUGHTON-LE-SPRING
Burnhope
Edmondsley
WALDRIDGE FELL
Great Lumley
Colliery Row
East Rainton
Hetton-le-Hole
West Lea
Dalton-le-Dale
Cold Hesledon
Lanchester
Sacriston
BROOM HO. FM. MAIZE MAZE
Nettlesworth
Plawsworth
Kimblesworth
FINCHALE PRIORY
West Rainton
Leamside
Murton
Witton Gilbert
Pity Me
Framwellgate Moor
Low Moorsley
Easington Lane
South Hetton
Hawthorn
DIGGERLAND
Langley Park
DURHAM LIGHT INFANTRY MUS.
Pittington
Carrville
Easington Colliery
Easington
Cornsay Colliery
Quebec
Esh
Bearpark
Durham
Littletown
DALTON PARK
Haswell
Ushaw Moor
Broompark
DURHAM CITY
DURHAM CATH.
Sherburn
Sherburn Hill
Haswell Plough
Shotton Colliery
Horden
Waterhouses
Esh Winning
New Brancepeth
DURHAM UNIV. ORIENTAL MUS.
Shincliffe
Shadforth
Ludworth
168
PETERLEE
East Hedleyhope
Brandon
Old Cassop
Thornley
Wheatley Hill
Shotton
CASTLE EDEN DENE
CASTLE EDEN WALKWAY
Castle Eden
Hesleden
Inniside
Brancepeth
Bowburn
Old Quarrington
CASSOP VALE
Sunderland Bridge
DURHAM SERVICES
Quarrington Hill
Wingate
Deaf Hill
Station Town
Oakenshaw
Croxdale
Hett
Kelloe
Page Bank
Tudhoe
Coxhoe
Trimdon Grange
Trimdon Colliery
Hutton Henry
Sheraton
Helmington Row
Willington
Wear
Cornforth
Trimdon
Byers Green
Spennymoor
Ferryhill
NZ
Newfield
Middlestone Moor
THRISLINGTON
Ferryhill Station
Fishburn
Hunwick
High Grange
Binchester
BINCHESTER FORT
Blocks
Kirk Merrington
Westerton
Mainsforth
Bishop Middleham
Witton Park
Toronto
AUCKLAND CASTLE
Middlestone
Coundon
Chilton Lane
Butterwick
ESCOMB CHURCH
Escomb
Leasingthorne
Chilton
HARDWICK HALL
Low Etherley
Bishop Auckland
Rushyford
Sedgefield
Toft Hill
ST HELEN'S
Eldon
Coundon Grange
Old Eldon
Bradbury
SEDGEFIELD
Shildon
Middridge
NEWTON AYCLIFFE
Mordon
Wynyard Village
West Auckland
St Helen Auckland
LOCOMOTION N.R.M. SHILDON
Thorpe Larches
WYNYARD WOODLAND
Bildershaw
Foxton
Evenwood Gate
Royal Oak
Redworth
Aycliffe
Stillington
Thorpe Thewles
Bolam
Elstob
Wackerfield
Heighington
Whitton
Stockton-on-Tees
Hilton
Carlton
Norton
Great Stainton
Redmarshall
Roseworth
Houghton-le-Side
Brafferton
Bishopton
Ingleton
Killerby
Walworth Gate
Coatham Mundeville
Little Stainton
Fairfield
Langton
Denton
Skerne
Headlam
Summerhouse
Walworth
Beaumont Hill
Barmpton
Hartburn
Gainford
Harrowgate Hill
Great Burdon
Sadberge
Elton
Thornaby-on-Tees
Darlington
High Coniscliffe
Longnewton
Piercebridge
DARLINGTON RAILWAY CENTRE
PRESTON HALL MUSEUM
ROMAN BRIDGE
Low Coniscliffe
Haughton Le Skerne
Urlay Nook
Eaglescliffe
Caldwell
Manfield
Ingleby Barwick
Eppleby
Cleasby
DURHAM TEES VALLEY
Middleton St George
Egglescliffe
Forcett
Carlton
Blackwell
High Leven
ANWICK IRON AGE FORTIFICATIONS
Stapleton
Middleton One Row
Aislaby
Yarm
Stanwick-St-John
Aldbrough St John
Low Dinsdale
Tees
Neasham
Low Worsall
Kirklevington
East Layton
Newton Morrell
157
Croft-on-Tees
Hurworth Place
158
Barton
Eryholme
Girsby
Melsonby
Dalton-on-Tees
A693
A691
A167
A1(M)
A690
A19
A688
A689
A6072
A68
A66(M)
A66
A67
A177
A181
A182

SEAHAM
179
HOUGHTON-LE-SPRING
Hetton-le-Hole
Murton
Seaton
Northlea
West Lea
Dalton-le-Dale
Cold Hesledon
Hawthorn
Easington Lane
South Hetton
Low Moorsley
Beacon Pt.
Easington Colliery
Easington
Haswell
Haswell Plough
Littletown
DALTON PARK
Shotton Colliery
Horden
PETERLEE
167
Ludworth
Thornley
Wheatley Hill
Shotton
CASTLE EDEN DENE
CASTLE EDEN WALKWAY
Castle Eden
Blackhall Colliery
Blackhall Rocks
High Hesleden
Hesleden
DURHAM COAST
CASSOP VALE
Wingate
Deaf Hill
Station Town
Hart Station
Kelloe
Trimdon Grange
Trimdon Colliery
Trimdon
Hutton Henry
Sheraton
Hart
JACKSONS LANDING
SAINT HILDA'S PARISH CHURCH
HARTLEPOOL'S MARITIME EXPERIENCE
Hartlepool Bay
High Throston
Elwick
West Park
Fishburn
Hartlepool
Dalton Piercy
Rift House
Seaton Carew
Butterwick
HARDWICK HALL
SEDGEFIELD
ROTTERDAM 16:00
ZEEBRUGGE 16:30
Tees Bay
Greatham
ENERGY INFORMATION CENTRE
Graythorp
Wynyard Village
Newton Bewley
Thorpe Larches
WYNYARD WOODLAND
Wolviston
COWPEN BEWLEY
Cowpen Bewley
TEESMOUTH
Salt Scar
REDCAR
Coatham
Foxton
BILLINGHAM ART GALLERY
BILLINGHAM
Stillington
Thorpe Thewles
Dormanstown
KIRKLEATHAM OLD HALL MUSEUM
Marske-by-the-Sea
Stockton-on-Tees
Whitton
Redmarshall
Norton
Roseworth
Haverton Hill
Port Clarence
BILLINGHAM BECK
South Bank
Grangetown
Kirkleatham
Yearby
New Marske
Bishopton
Little Stainton
Fairfield
North Ormesby
Lazenby
Wilton
Upleatham
Middlesbrough
Stockton-on-Tees
DORMAN MUSEUM
Eston
Dunsdale
Skelt
TOCKETTS WATER MILL
Hartburn
Sadberge
Elton
Thornaby on Tees
Middlesbrough
Acklam
NATURES WORLD
Normanby
Park End
Ormesby
ORMESBY HALL
Redcar and
Guisborough
GUISBOROUGH PRIORY
Longnewton
PRESTON HALL MUSEUM
Marton
Hutton Gate
Charltons
Urlay Nook
Eaglescliffe
CAPTAIN COOK BIRTHPLACE
Coulby Newham
Nunthorpe
Cleveland
DURHAM TEES VALLEY
Middleton St George
Egglescliffe
Ingleby Barwick
Stainton
Thornton
Hemlington
Hutton Village
Gisborough Moor
Middleton One Row
Aislaby
Yarm
High Leven
Maltby
Newton under Roseberry
Newby
Great Ayton
Hilton
Seamer
Tanton
Little Ayton
New Row
Low Worsall
Middleton-on-Leven
158
Stokesley
Easby
Kildale
159
Kildale Moor
Tame Bridge
Crathorne
0 1 2 3 miles
0 1 2 3 4 5 km

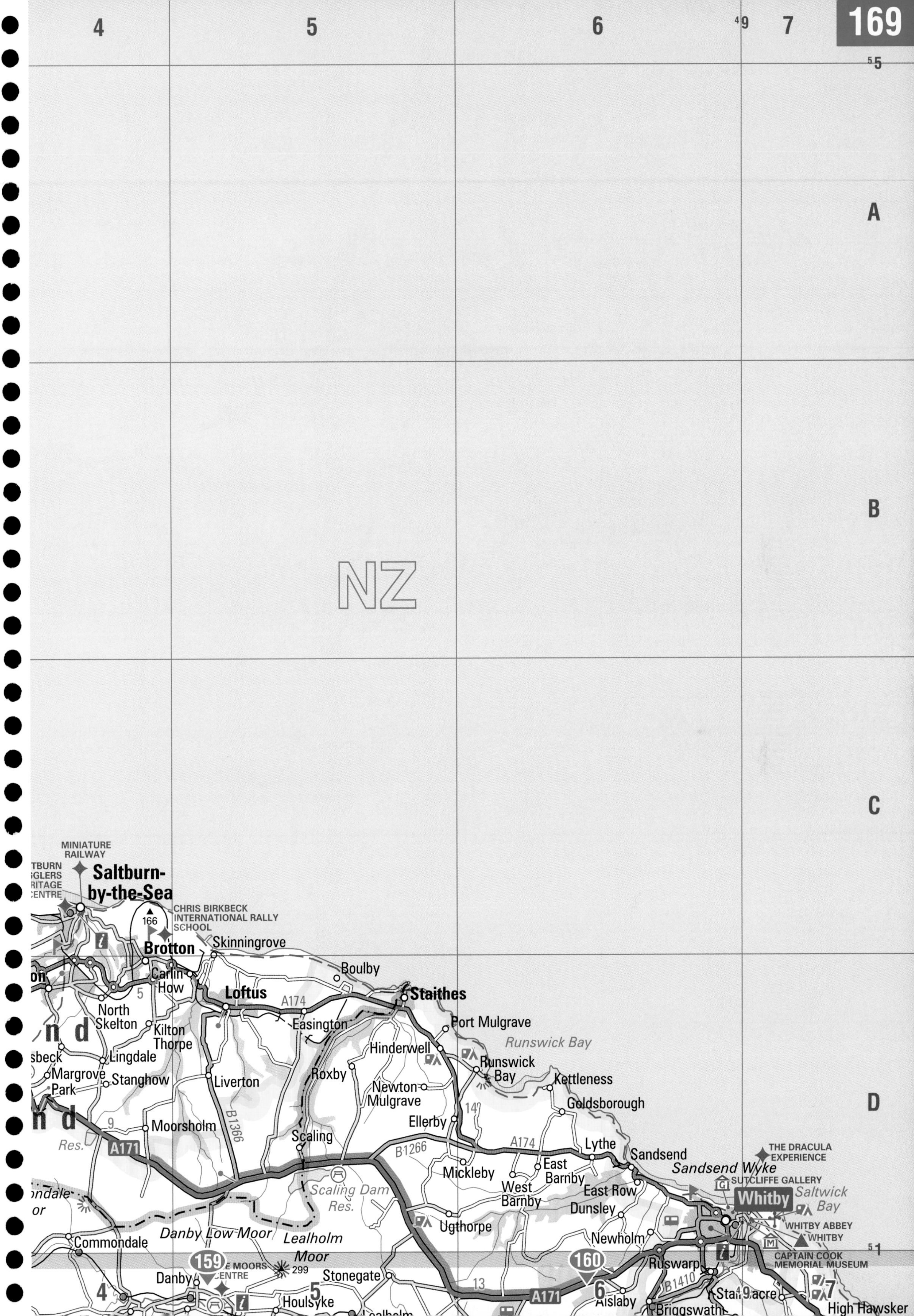
4
5
6
7
A
B
C
D
NZ
MINIATURE RAILWAY
Saltburn-by-the-Sea
CHRIS BIRKBECK INTERNATIONAL RALLY SCHOOL
166
Brotton
Skinningrove
Boulby
Carlin How
Loftus
A174
Staithes
North Skelton
Kilton Thorpe
Easington
Port Mulgrave
Runswick Bay
Hinderwell
Runswick Bay
Lingdale
Margrove Park
Stanghow
Liverton
Roxby
Newton Mulgrave
Kettleness
Goldsborough
Moorsholm
B1366
Ellerby
Scaling
A171
Res.
B1266
A174
Lythe
Sandsend
THE DRACULA EXPERIENCE
Sandsend Wyke
SUTCLIFFE GALLERY
Mickleby
East Barnby
West Barnby
East Row
Dunsley
Scaling Dam Res.
Whitby
Saltwick Bay
Ugthorpe
WHITBY ABBEY
WHITBY
Danby Low Moor
Lealholm Moor
Commondale
Newholm
CAPTAIN COOK MEMORIAL MUSEUM
159
160
299
Ruswarp
Danby
Stonegate
B1410
Houlsyke
A171
Aislaby
Stainsacre
High Hawsker
Briggswath

Barnhills
Portencalzie
North Cairn
South Cairn
Corsewall
Loch Connell
Dounan Bay
Kirkcolm
Cairnryan
Penwhirn Res.
Main Water of Luce
Cross Water of Luce
Mains of Airies
Ervie
Braid Fell
Low Salchrie
The Wig
LOCH RYAN
Knocknain
Leswalt
Slouchnawen Bay
Craigencross
Innermessan
Auchmantle
New Luce
Black Loch
CASTLE KENNEDY GARDENS
White Loch
Glenstockadale
Stranraer
Aird
Castle Kennedy
Broadsea Bay
THE RHINN
CASTLE OF ST. JOHN VISITOR CENTRE
WIGTOWN DISTRICT MUSEUM
Knockglass
Soulseat Loch
GLENWHAN GARDENS
Dunragit
CASTLE OF PARK
Mark
Lochans
Black Hd.
Dunskey Ho.
NW
Torrs Warren
LITTLE WHEELS
Portpatrick
Awhirk
Stoneykirk
Luce Sands
Port of Spittal Bay
Cairngarroch
Sandhead
Cairngarroch Bay
KIRKMADRINE STONES
Sandhead Bay
Money Hd.
Clachanmore
Hole Stone Bay
ARDWELL GDNS.
Ardwell
Ardwell Mains
Chapel Rossan Bay
Ardwell Pt.
Logan Mains
LOGAN BOTANIC GARDEN
Balgowan Pt.
Mull of Logan
LOGAN FISH POND MARINE LIFE CENTRE
Port Nessock or Port Logan Bay
Port Logan
Cairnywellan Hd.
Clanyard Bay
Low Clanyard
Laggantalluch Hd.
Kirkmaiden
Drummore
Cailliness Pt.
Damnaglaur
Crammag Hd.
Maryport
Cairngaan
Port Kemin
MULL OF GAL
A77
A751
A75
A716
A718
B738
B798
B7043
B7077
B7084
B7042
B7065
B7041
0 1 2 3 miles
0 1 2 3 4 5 km

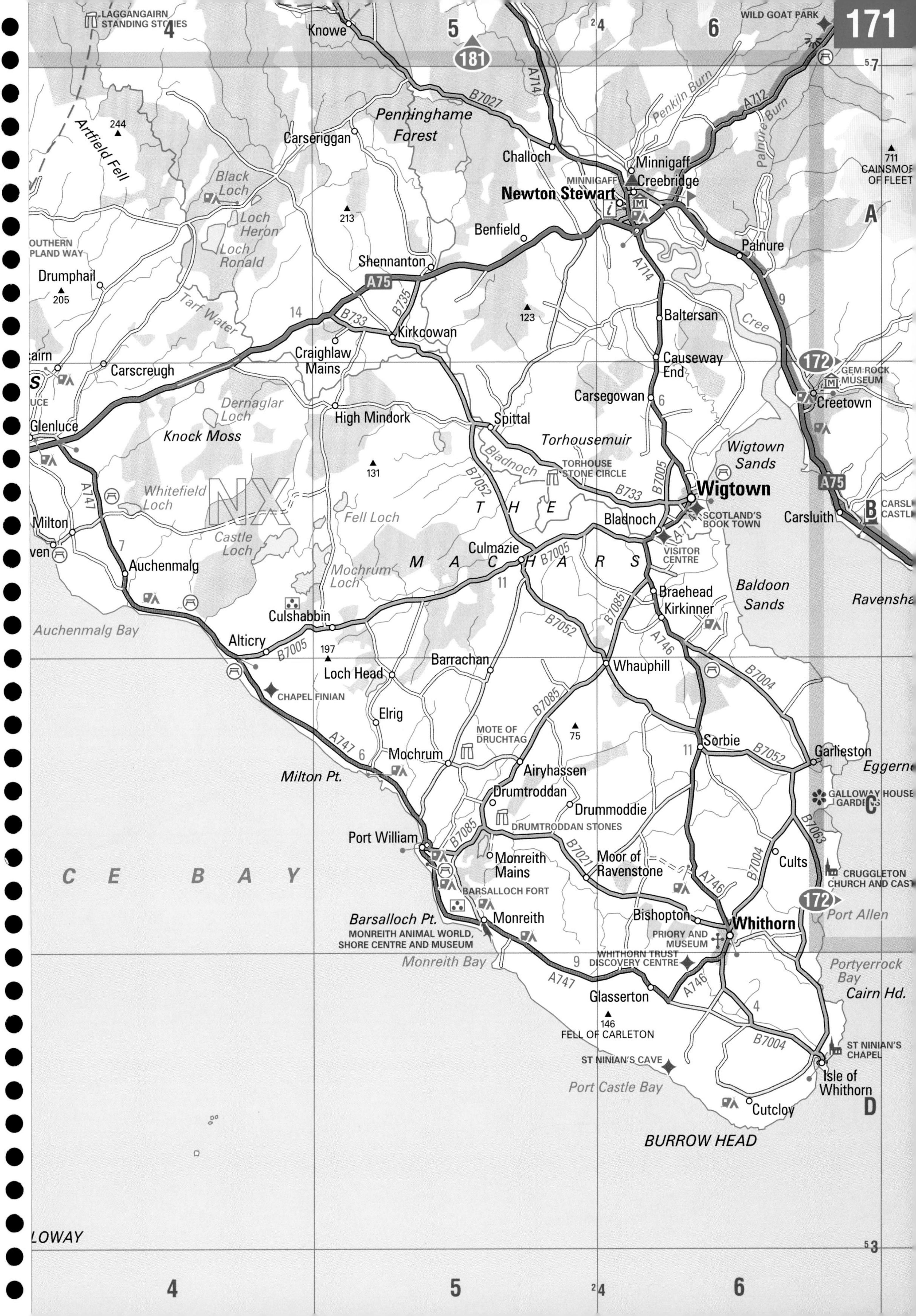

LAGGANGAIRN STANDING STONES
Knowe
181
WILD GOAT PARK
Artfield Fell
244
Penninghame Forest
Carseriggan
Challoch
Minnigaff
Creebridge
Newton Stewart
Penkiln Burn
Palnure Burn
711
CAINSMORE OF FLEET
Black Loch
Loch Heron
Loch Ronald
213
Benfield
Palnure
SOUTHERN UPLAND WAY
Drumphail
205
Shennanton
Tarf Water
Kirkcowan
Craighlaw Mains
123
Baltersan
Cree
Carscreugh
Causeway End
172
GEM ROCK MUSEUM
Creetown
Carsegowan
Dernaglar Loch
High Mindork
Spittal
Glenluce
Knock Moss
Torhousemuir
Wigtown Sands
131
TORHOUSE STONE CIRCLE
Bladnoch
Wigtown
Whitefield Loch
NX
SCOTLAND'S BOOK TOWN
Carsluith
Milton
Fell Loch
THE MACHARS
Castle Loch
Culmazie
VISITOR CENTRE
Auchenmalg
Mochrum Loch
Braehead
Kirkinner
Baldoon Sands
Culshabbin
Auchenmalg Bay
Alticry
197
Barrachan
Whauphill
Loch Head
CHAPEL FINIAN
Elrig
MOTE OF DRUCHTAG
75
Sorbie
Garlieston
Mochrum
Airyhassen
Milton Pt.
Drumtroddan
Drummoddie
GALLOWAY HOUSE GARDENS
DRUMTRODDAN STONES
Port William
Monreith Mains
Moor of Ravenstone
Cults
CRUGGLETON CHURCH AND CASTLE
BARSALLOCH FORT
Port Allen
Barsalloch Pt.
Monreith
Bishopton
Whithorn
MONREITH ANIMAL WORLD, SHORE CENTRE AND MUSEUM
PRIORY AND MUSEUM
WHITHORN TRUST DISCOVERY CENTRE
Monreith Bay
Portyerrock Bay
Glasserton
Cairn Hd.
146
FELL OF CARLETON
ST NINIAN'S CHAPEL
ST NINIAN'S CAVE
Isle of Whithorn
Port Castle Bay
Cutcloy
BURROW HEAD
LOWAY
4
5
6
A
B
C
D

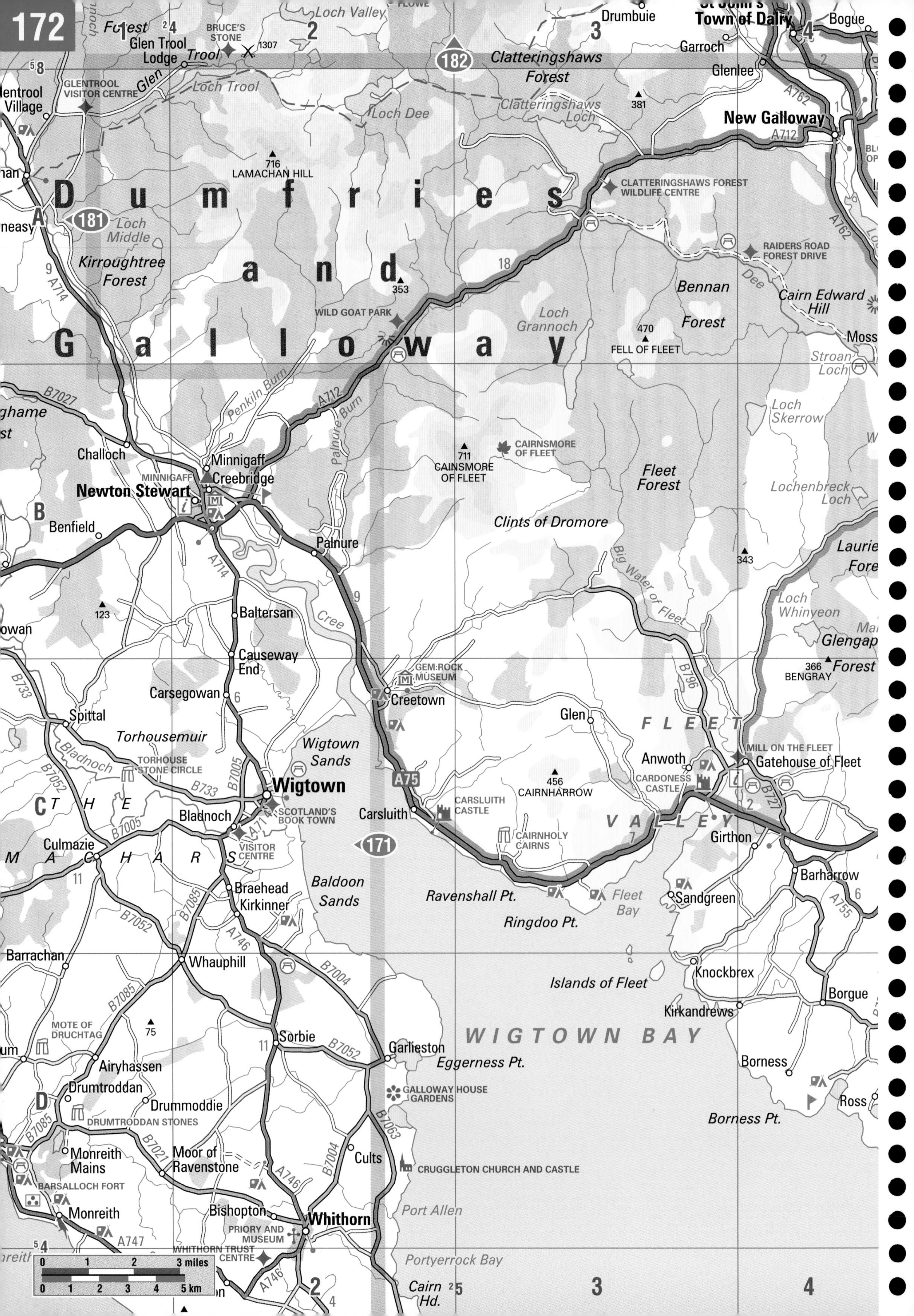
Dumfries and Galloway
Glen Trool Lodge
Loch Trool
Glentrool Visitor Centre
Bruce's Stone
Loch Valley
Loch Dee
Clatteringshaws Forest
Clatteringshaws Loch
Drumbuie
St John's Town of Dalry
Garroch
Glenlee
Bogue
New Galloway
A712
A762
182
716 Lamachan Hill
Clatteringshaws Forest Wildlife Centre
Raiders Road Forest Drive
181
Loch Middle
Kirroughtree Forest
Wild Goat Park
353
Bennan Forest
Cairn Edward Hill
Loch Grannoch
470 Fell of Fleet
Stroan Loch
Loch Skerrow
B7027
Penkiln Burn
Palnure Burn
711 Cairnsmore of Fleet
Cairnsmore of Fleet
Fleet Forest
Lochenbreck Loch
Challoch
Minnigaff
Creebridge
Newton Stewart
Benfield
Palnure
Clints of Dromore
Big Water of Fleet
Laurieston Forest
343
A714
Baltersan
Cree
123
Loch Whinyeon
Glengap Forest
366 Bengray
Causeway End
Carsegowan
Gem:Rock Museum
Creetown
B733
B796
Spittal
Torhousemuir
Glen
Fleet Valley
Bladnoch
Torhouse Stone Circle
Wigtown Sands
Wigtown
Scotland's Book Town
Anworth
Mill on the Fleet
Gatehouse of Fleet
Cardoness Castle
456 Cairnharrow
A75
Carsluith
Carsluith Castle
Cairnholy Cairns
Girthon
B727
B7052
B7005
The Machars
Culmazie
Visitor Centre
171
Baldoon Sands
Braehead
Kirkinner
Ravenshall Pt.
Ringdoo Pt.
Fleet Bay
Sandgreen
Barharrow
A755
A746
Barrachan
Whauphill
B7004
Islands of Fleet
Knockbrex
Borgue
Kirkandrews
B7085
Mote of Druchtag
75
Sorbie
Garlieston
Wigtown Bay
Eggerness Pt.
Borness
Airyhassen
Drumtroddan
Drummoddie
Drumtroddan Stones
Galloway House Gardens
B7063
Ross
Borness Pt.
Monreith Mains
Moor of Ravenstone
B7021
Cults
Cruggleton Church and Castle
Barsalloch Fort
Monreith
Bishopton
Whithorn
Priory and Museum
A747
Whithorn Trust Centre
Port Allen
Portyerrock Bay
Cairn Hd.
0 1 2 3 miles
0 1 2 3 4 5 km

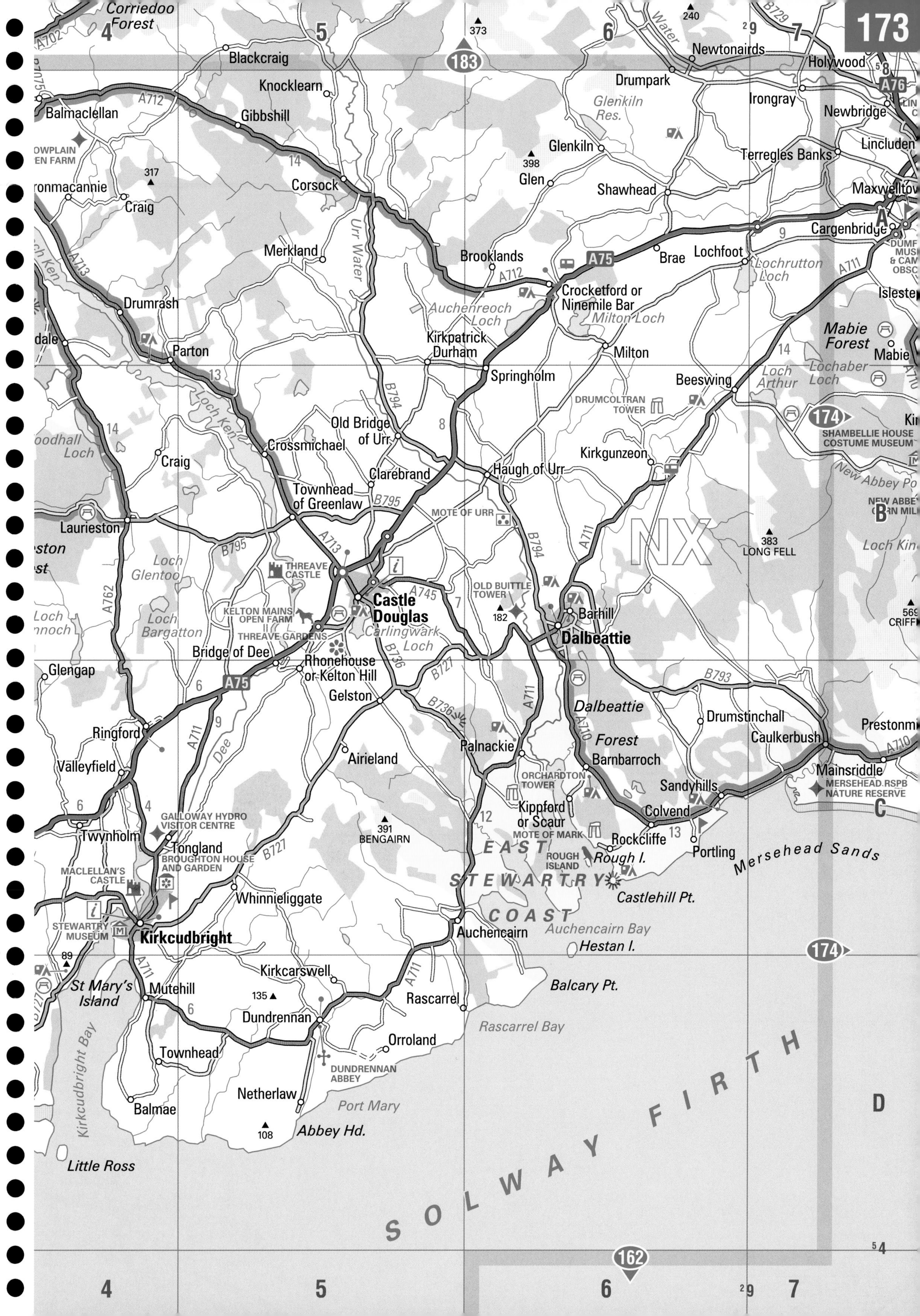

Corriedoo Forest
4
5
6
7
373
240
183
Water
B729
Newtonairds
Holywood
Blackcraig
Knocklearn
Drumpark
Irongray
A76
Newbridge
A702
Balmaclellan
A712
Gibbshill
Glenkiln Res.
Glenkiln
Lincluden
Terregles Banks
317
398
Glen
Shawhead
Maxwelltown
Craig
14
Corsock
Urr Water
Cargenbridge
Merkland
Brooklands
A75
Brae
Lochfoot
9
Lochrutton Loch
A711
A713
A712
Crocketford or Ninemile Bar
Milton Loch
Islesteps
Drumrash
Auchenreoch Loch
Mabie Forest
Mabie
Kirkpatrick Durham
Milton
14
Parton
Springholm
Loch Arthur
Lochaber Loch
13
Beeswing
B794
DRUMCOLTRAN TOWER
Loch Ken
8
174
SHAMBELLIE HOUSE COSTUME MUSEUM
14
Old Bridge of Urr
Crossmichael
Kirkgunzeon
Woodhall Loch
Craig
Haugh of Urr
New Abbey Pow
Clarebrand
Townhead of Greenlaw
B795
MOTE OF URR
NEW ABBEY CORN MILL
B
Laurieston
NX
383 LONG FELL
A711
Loch Kindar
B794
B795
Loch Glentoo
A713
THREAVE CASTLE
i
OLD BUITTLE TOWER
569 CRIFFEL
A745
A762
Castle Douglas
182
Barhill
7
KELTON MAINS OPEN FARM
Loch Bargatton
THREAVE GARDENS
Carlingwark Loch
Dalbeattie
Bridge of Dee
Rhonehouse or Kelton Hill
B736
Glengap
B727
B793
6
A75
Gelston
Dalbeattie Forest
A711
B736
Drumstinchall
Prestonmill
Ringford
9
A710
Caulkerbush
A711
Dee
Palnackie
Airieland
Barnbarroch
A710
Valleyfield
Mainsriddle
ORCHARDTON TOWER
Sandyhills
MERSEHEAD RSPB NATURE RESERVE
6
4
Kippford or Scaur
Colvend
C
GALLOWAY HYDRO VISITOR CENTRE
391 BENGAIRN
12
13
Twynholm
MOTE OF MARK
Rockcliffe
Portling
Tongland
EAST
ROUGH ISLAND
Rough I.
Mersehead Sands
BROUGHTON HOUSE AND GARDEN
B727
MACLELLAN'S CASTLE
STEWARTRY
Castlehill Pt.
Whinnieliggate
COAST
STEWARTRY MUSEUM
Kirkcudbright
Auchencairn
Auchencairn Bay
Hestan I.
174
89
A711
Kirkcarswell
A711
Balcary Pt.
St Mary's Isle
Mutehill
135
6
Rascarrel
Dundrennan
Rascarrel Bay
Orroland
Townhead
Kirkcudbright Bay
DUNDRENNAN ABBEY
D
Netherlaw
Port Mary
Balmae
108
Abbey Hd.
Little Ross
SOLWAY FIRTH
162
4
5
6
7

Newtonairds
Drumpark
Holywood
Kirkton
Tinwald
Locharbriggs
LOCHMABEN CASTLE
Castle Loch
Heck
Heathhall
DUMFRIES AND GALLOWAY AVIATION MUS.
Glenkiln Res.
Irongray
Newbridge
LINCLUDEN COLLEGE
The Grove
Torthorwald
Hightae
Birkshaw Forest
Lincluden
OLD BRIDGE HOUSE MUS.
Terregles Banks
Greystone
RAMMERSCALES HOUSE
Kettleholm
Shawhead
Maxwelltown
Collin
Middleshaw
Dumfries
Greenlea
BURNS HOUSE
Cargenbridge
ROBERT BURNS CENTRE
Racks
Dalton
DUMFRIES MUSEUM & CAMERA OBSCURA
Brae
Lochfoot
Lochrutton Loch
Cleughbrae
Kingholm Quay
Islesteps
Mouswald
Carrutherstown
Milton Loch
Mabie Forest
Mabie
Kelton
Lochar Moss
Lochar Water
Milton
KIRKCONNELL FLOW
Loch Arthur
Lochaber Loch
Beeswing
Glencaple
Bankend
Clarencefield
DRUMCOLTRAN TOWER
RUTHWELL CROSS
Kirkconnell
SHAMBELLIE HOUSE COSTUME MUSEUM
River Nith
Ruthwell
DUNCAN SAVINGS BANK MUSEUM
Kirkgunzeon
Shearington
Blackshaw
Cummertrees
New Abbey
New Abbey Pow
SWEETHEART ABBEY
CAERLAVEROCK CASTLE
Eastpark
NEW ABBEY CORN MILL
NITH
Bowhouse
CAERLAVEROCK
Overton
WILDFOWL AND WETLAND CENTRE
383 LONG FELL
Loch Kindar
Blackshaw Bank
ESTUARY
Drumburn
569 CRIFFELL
Barhill
Dalbeattie
Carsethorn
Kirkbean
ARBIGLAND GARDENS
Drumstinchall
Dalbeattie Forest
Caulkerbush
Prestonmill
Barnbarroch
Mainsriddle
JOHN PAUL JONES BIRTHPLACE MUSEUM
MERSEHEAD RSPB NATURE RESERVE
Skinburness
Sandyhills
Colvend
Southerness
Rockcliffe
Portling
Southerness Pt.
Rough I.
Mersehead Sands
NX
Silloth
Greenrow
Causewayhead
Castlehill Pt.
Blitterlees
Hestan I.
Highlaws
Beckfoot
Pelutho
Newtown
Holme St Cuthbert
Mawbray
Dubmill Pt.
Edderside
New Cowper
West
Allonby
Aspatria
Allonby Bay
Hayton
Prospect
Oughterside
Allerby
Crosscanonby
Crosby Villa
Parsonby
Crosby
SOLWAY FIRTH
SOLWAY COAST
0 1 2 3 miles
0 1 2 3 4 5 km

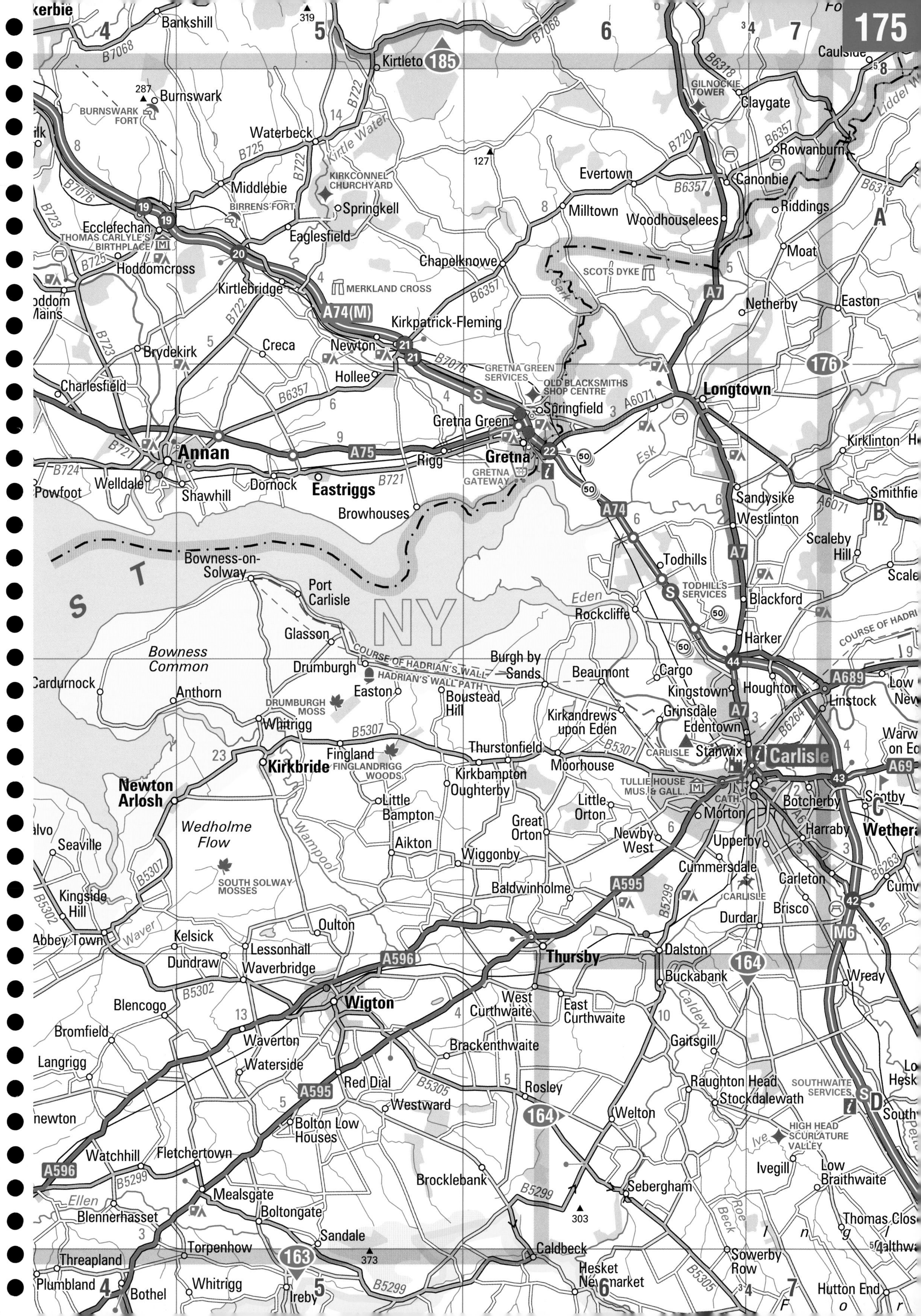
4
5
6
7
Bankshill
319
B7068
Kirtleton
185
B7068
Caulside
8
B6318
GILNOCKIE TOWER
Claygate
Liddel Water
287
Burnswark
BURNSWARK FORT
14
B722
Waterbeck
Kirtle Water
B725
B722
127
B720
B6357
Rowanburn
KIRKCONNEL CHURCHYARD
Middlebie
Evertown
B6357
Canonbie
B6318
B7076
B723
19
19
BIRRENS FORT
Springkell
8
Milltown
Woodhouselees
Riddings
Ecclefechan
THOMAS CARLYLE'S BIRTHPLACE
Eaglesfield
Moat
A
20
B725
Hoddomcross
Chapelknowe
SCOTS DYKE
5
Kirtlebridge
4
MERKLAND CROSS
Sark
A7
Hoddom Mains
B722
B6357
Netherby
Easton
A74(M)
B723
Kirkpatrick-Fleming
Brydekirk
5
Creca
Newton
21
21
B7076
GRETNA GREEN SERVICES
176
Charlesfield
Hollee
OLD BLACKSMITHS SHOP CENTRE
Longtown
B6357
6
4
S
A6071
Springfield
3
Gretna Green
B721
9
Annan
A75
Rigg
Gretna
22
50
Esk
Kirklinton
B724
GRETNA GATEWAY
Powfoot
Welldale
Shawhill
Dornock
Eastriggs
B721
50
Sandysike
Smithfield
Browhouses
A74
6
A6071
Westlinton
B
6
Scaleby
Hill
Bowness-on-Solway
Todhills
A7
Scaleby
S
T
Port Carlisle
TODHILLS SERVICES
S
Blackford
Eden
NY
Rockcliffe
50
COURSE OF HADRIAN'S WALL
Glasson
Harker
50
Bowness Common
COURSE OF HADRIAN'S WALL
Burgh by Sands
Cargo
44
9
Drumburgh
HADRIAN'S WALL PATH
Beaumont
Kingstown
Houghton
A689
Cardurnock
Easton
Low
Anthorn
DRUMBURGH MOSS
Boustead Hill
Kirkandrews upon Eden
Grinsdale
A7
Linstock
Whitrigg
B5307
Edentown
3
B6264
Fingland
Thurstonfield
B5307
CARLISLE
Stanwix
4
Warwick on Eden
23
Kirkbride
FINGLANDRIGG WOODS
Moorhouse
Carlisle
A69
Newton Arlosh
Kirkbampton
Oughterby
TULLIE HOUSE MUS. & GALL.
43
CATH
Botcherby
Sandsby
C
Little Bampton
Little Orton
Morton
Wedholme Flow
Great Orton
Newby West
6
A6
Harraby
Wetheral
Seaville
Aikton
Upperby
3
Wampool
Wiggonby
Cummersdale
B6263
B5307
Carleton
Kingside Hill
SOUTH SOLWAY MOSSES
Baldwinholme
A595
CARLISLE
B5299
Cumwhinton
B5302
Brisco
42
Oulton
Durdar
Abbey Town
Waver
Kelsick
A6
Lessonhall
M6
Dundraw
Thursby
Dalston
164
Waverbridge
A596
Buckabank
Wreay
B5302
Blencogo
Wigton
West Curthwaite
East Curthwaite
13
4
10
Caldew
Bromfield
Waverton
Gaitsgill
Langrigg
Brackenthwaite
Waterside
Raughton Head
SOUTHWAITE SERVICES
Red Dial
B5305
5
Rosley
Stockdalewath
S
D
A595
Westward
5
164
Welton
Southwaite
Newton
Bolton Low Houses
HIGH HEAD SCULPTURE VALLEY
Ive
Watchhill
Fletchertown
Ivegill
Low Braithwaite
A596
B5299
Brocklebank
Ellen
Mealsgate
B5299
Sebergham
Blennerhasset
Boltongate
303
Roe Beck
Thomas Close
3
Sandale
I
n
g
Torpenhow
373
Caldbeck
Sowerby Row
Threapland
163
Hesket Newmarket
Plumbland
4
Bothel
Whitrigg
Ireby
5
B5299
6
B5305
4
7
Hutton End

186
187
185
175
164
165
Dinlabyre
Old Castleton
KIELDER FOREST
LIDDESDALE
BLACK EDGE
JANET ARMSTRONG HOUSE
Newcastleton
Newcastleton or Copshaw Holm
Newcastleton Forest
KIELDER WATER BIRDS OF PREY CENTRE
GLENDHU HILL
Potholm
Langholm
MALCOLM MONUMENT
Tarras Water
Kershope Burn
Tinnisburn Forest
Kershopefoot
Kershope Forest
Black Lyne
White Lyne
Bewcastle Fells
SIGHTY CRAG
Caulside
Liddel Water
GILNOCKIE TOWER
Claygate
Baileyhead
Whitelyne Common
Paddaburn Moor
The Flatt
Blackpool Gate
Rowanburn
Evertown
Canonbie
Crossings
Catlowdy
WHITE PRESTON
Riddings
Woodhouselees
Roughsike
Roadhead
Bewcastle
Haggbeck
Moat
SCOTS DYKE
Spadeadam Forest
Netherby
Easton
Lyne
Stapleton
Spadeadam Farm
Wiley Sike
Longtown
Cumbria
Boltonfellend
Kirkcambeck
West Hall
Gilsland Spa
Esk
Kirklinton
Hethersgill
BIRDOSWALD ROMAN FORT
BIRDOSWALD
Gilsland
HADRIAN'S WALL PATH
King Water
Sandysike
Smithfield
Upper Denton
Westlinton
Banks
Scaleby Hill
Walton
Lanercost
VALLUM
Todhills
TODHILLS SERVICES
Newtown
LANERCOST PRIORY
Low Row
Scaleby
Laversdale
Denton Fell
Blackford
COURSE OF HADRIAN'S WALL
Irthington
Brampton
Rockcliffe
Eden
Milton
Harker
CARLISLE
Beaumont
Cargo
Low Crosby
Hallbankgate
Tindale
Midgeholme
Kingstown
Houghton
Newby East
TALKIN TARN
Farlam
Linstock
Tindale Tarn
Tindale Fells
Halton Lea Gate
Grinsdale
Edentown
Hayton
Talkin
Forest Head
Warwick on Eden
Stanwix
Carlisle
Warwick Bridge
How
Castle Carrock
TULLIE HOUSE MUS. & GALL.
CATH.
Botcherby
Heads Nook
Gelt
COLD FELL
Glendue
Little Orton
Morton
Scotby
Faugh
Wetheral
Great Corby
WETHERAL PRIORY GATEHOUSE
Newby West
Harraby
Upperby
King's Forest of Geltsdale
Cummersdale
Carleton
Cumwhinton
Cumwhitton
Geltsdale Middle
Brisco
Durdar
Eden
Cumrew
Dalston
Cotehill
Hornsby
Wreay
Newbiggin
Holmwrangle
0 1 2 3 miles
0 1 2 3 4 5 km

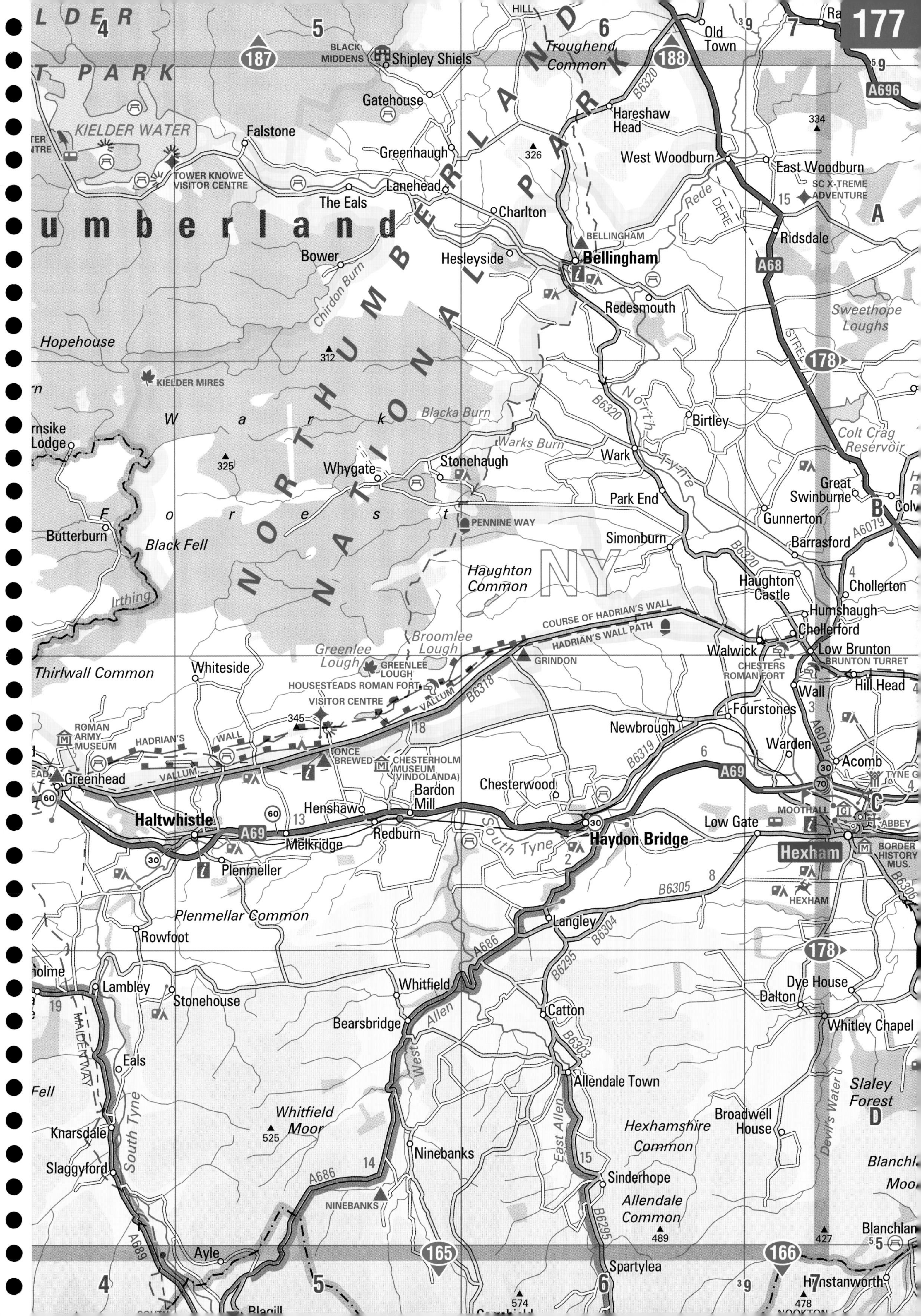

NORTHUMBERLAND NATIONAL PARK
Kielder Water
Tower Knowe Visitor Centre
Falstone
Gatehouse
Greenhaugh
Lanehead
The Eals
Charlton
Bower
Hesleyside
Bellingham
Redesmouth
West Woodburn
East Woodburn
Hareshaw Head
Ridsdale
Hopehouse
Kielder Mires
Wark Forest
Birtley
Wark
Whygate
Stonehaugh
Park End
Pennine Way
Simonburn
Gunnerton
Barrasford
Haughton Castle
Chollerton
Humshaugh
Chollerford
Walwick
Low Brunton
Butterburn
Black Fell
Haughton Common
Broomlee Lough
Greenlee Lough
Course of Hadrian's Wall
Hadrian's Wall Path
Grindon
Chesters Roman Fort
Thirlwall Common
Whiteside
Housesteads Roman Fort
Visitor Centre
Roman Army Museum
Once Brewed
Chesterholm Museum (Vindolanda)
Fourstones
Newbrough
Wall
Warden
Acomb
Greenhead
Haltwhistle
Henshaw
Bardon Mill
Chesterwood
Melkridge
Redburn
Haydon Bridge
Low Gate
Hexham
Plenmeller
Plenmellar Common
Langley
Rowfoot
Lambley
Stonehouse
Whitfield
Bearsbridge
Catton
Dalton
Dye House
Whitley Chapel
Eals
Allendale Town
Whitfield Moor
Hexhamshire Common
Broadwell House
Slaley Forest
Knarsdale
Slaggyford
Ninebanks
Sinderhope
Allendale Common
Ayle
Spartylea
Hunstanworth
Blanchland

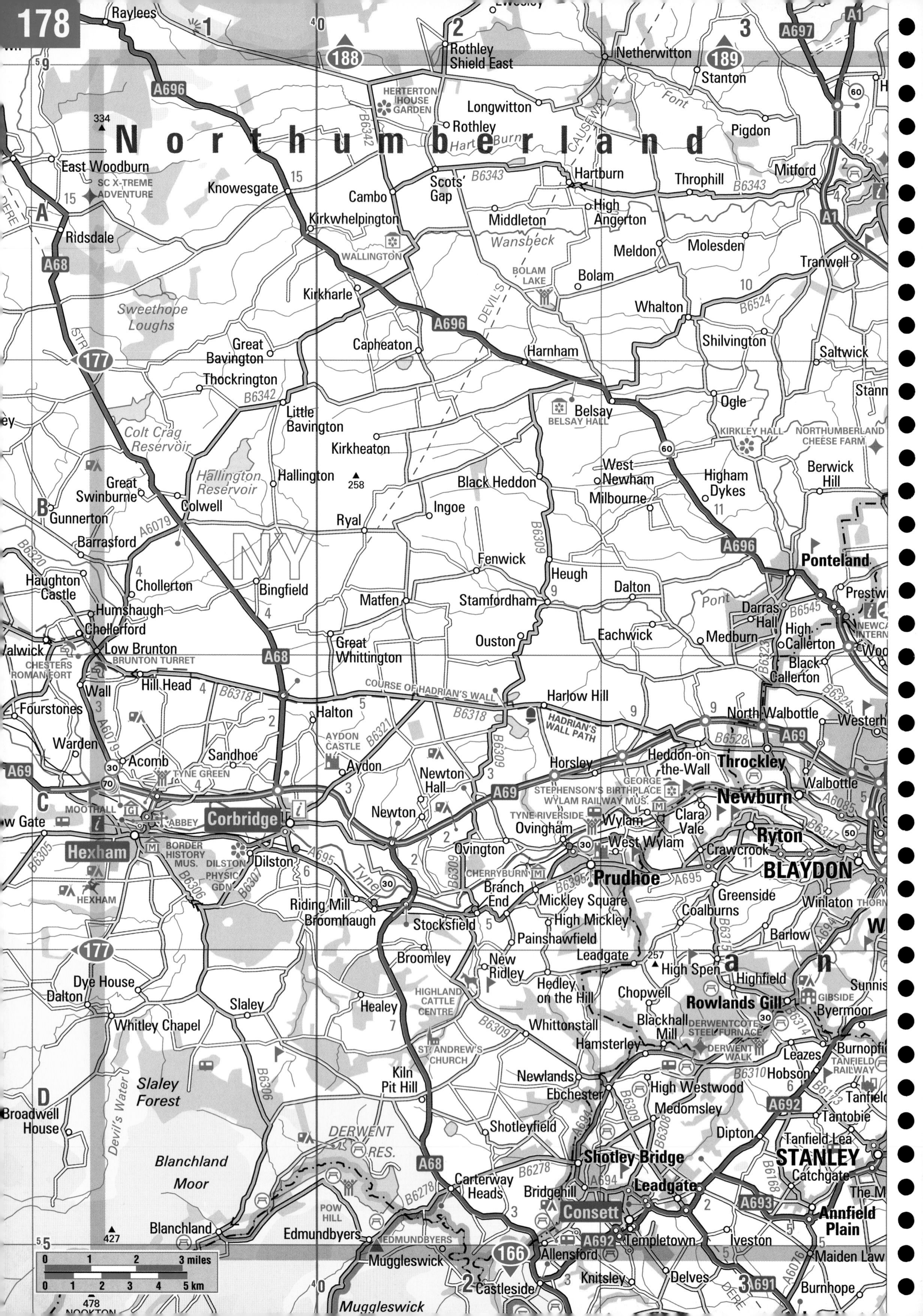
Northumberland
NY
188
189
177
166
A696
A68
A69
A1
A697
A695
A692
A693
A691
A694
A6079
A6085
B6342
B6343
B6524
B6309
B6318
B6321
B6306
B6307
B6305
B6320
B6278
B6310
B6315
B6308
B6168
B6173
B6528
B6545
B6323
B6324
B6314
B6317
B6395
B6076
Raylees
Rothley Shield East
Netherwitton
Stanton
Longwitton
Rothley
Pigdon
HERTERTON HOUSE GARDEN
Hart Burn
Font
East Woodburn
SC X-TREME ADVENTURE
Knowesgate
Cambo
Scots' Gap
Hartburn
Throphill
Mitford
Middleton
High Angerton
Kirkwhelpington
WALLINGTON
Wansbeck
Meldon
Molesden
Tranwell
Ridsdale
BOLAM LAKE
Bolam
Whalton
Kirkharle
Sweethope Loughs
Capheaton
Harnham
Shilvington
Saltwick
Great Bavington
Thockrington
Little Bavington
Kirkheaton
Belsay
BELSAY HALL
Ogle
KIRKLEY HALL
NORTHUMBERLAND CHEESE FARM
Colt Crag Reservoir
Hallington Reservoir
Hallington
Great Swinburne
Colwell
Black Heddon
West Newham
Milbourne
Higham Dykes
Berwick Hill
Gunnerton
Barrasford
Ryal
Ingoe
Fenwick
Heugh
Ponteland
Haughton Castle
Chollerton
Bingfield
Matfen
Stamfordham
Dalton
Pont
Humshaugh
Chollerford
Low Brunton
Great Whittington
Ouston
Eachwick
Medburn
Darras Hall
High Callerton
Black Callerton
CHESTERS ROMAN FORT
BRUNTON TURRET
Wall
Hill Head
COURSE OF HADRIAN'S WALL
Halton
Harlow Hill
North Walbottle
Fourstones
HADRIAN'S WALL PATH
Warden
AYDON CASTLE
Aydon
Acomb
Sandhoe
TYNE GREEN
Horsley
Heddon-on-the-Wall
Throckley
Newton Hall
GEORGE STEPHENSON'S BIRTHPLACE
WYLAM RAILWAY MUS.
Walbottle
Newburn
MOOTHALL
ABBEY
Corbridge
Newton
TYNE RIVERSIDE
Ovingham
Wylam
Clara Vale
Ryton
Hexham
BORDER HISTORY MUS.
DILSTON PHYSIC GDN
Dilston
Ovington
West Wylam
Crawcrook
BLAYDON
HEXHAM
Tyne
CHERRYBURN
Prudhoe
Greenside
Winlaton
Riding Mill
Broomhaugh
Stocksfield
Branch End
Mickley Square
Coalburns
High Mickley
Painshawfield
Barlow
Broomley
New Ridley
Leadgate
High Spen
Highfield
Dye House
Dalton
Slaley
Healey
HIGHLAND CATTLE CENTRE
Hedley on the Hill
Chopwell
Rowlands Gill
GIBSIDE
Byermoor
Whitley Chapel
Whittonstall
Blackhall Mill
DERWENTCOTE STEEL FURNACE
DERWENT WALK
ST ANDREW'S CHURCH
Hamsterley
Leazes
Burnopfield
TANFIELD RAILWAY
Slaley Forest
Kiln Pit Hill
Newlands
High Westwood
Hobson
Tanfield
Ebchester
Medomsley
Tantobie
Broadwell House
Devil's Water
DERWENT RES.
Shotleyfield
Dipton
Tanfield Lea
STANLEY
Catchgate
Blanchland Moor
Shotley Bridge
Leadgate
Carterway Heads
Bridgehill
Consett
Annfield Plain
POW HILL
Blanchland
Edmundbyers
EDMUNDBYERS
Templetown
Iveston
Maiden Law
Muggleswick
Allensford
Knitsley
Delves
Castleside
Burnhope
Muggleswick
Derwent
334
258
257
427
478
0 1 2 3 miles
0 1 2 3 4 5 km

Lynemouth
189
Beacon Pt.
COLLIERY MUSEUM
Woodhorn
Linton
THE SANCTUARY WILDLIFE CENTRE
QUEEN ELIZABETH II
Longhirst
Pegswood
Ashington
Newbiggin-by-the-Sea
Hirst
NORTHUMBRIA CRAFT CENTRE
Bothal
WANSBECK
North Seaton
Morpeth
Stakeford
Guide Post
Scotland Gate
Choppington
West Sleekburn
Cambois
Hepscott
Clifton
Bedlington
Bedlington Station
East Sleekburn
Cowpen
BLYTH
Nedderton
Bebside
Newsham
East Hartford
New Delaval
PLESSEY WOODS
Shankhouse
Nelson Village
New Hartley
Seaton
Seaton Sluice
SEATON DELAVAL HALL
Cramlington
Southfield
East Cramlington
Seaton Delaval
Hartley
ST MARY'S LIGHTHOUSE
St Mary's or Bait I.
NZ
Brenkley
Seaton Burn
Seghill
Holywell
Dinnington
Dudley
Annitsford
Brunswick Village
Wide Open
Burradon
Backworth
Earsdon
WHITLEY BAY
Hazlerigg
NEWCASTLE
Camperdown
Killingworth
Monkseaton
Shiremoor
Cullercoats
BLUE REEF AQUARIUM
TYNEMOUTH CASTLE & PRIORY
STAVANGER 20:45
HAUGESUND 23:00
BERGEN 27:00
AMSTERDAM 15:00
Marden
STEPHENSON RAILWAY MUSEUM
Kenton Bankfoot
Longbenton
THE RISING SUN
Tynemouth
North Shields
ARBEIA ROMAN FORT AND MUSEUM
Gosforth
Kenton
Willington
ROYAL QUAYS
South Shields
SOUTH SHIELDS MUSEUM
Jesmond
WALLSEND
Tyne Tunnel
TOLL
THE LEAS AND MARSDEN ROCK
Marsden Bay
NEWCASTLE UPON TYNE
Heaton
Jarrow
BEDE'S WORLD
ST PAUL'S MONASTERY
Westoe
Harton
Marsden
Byker
SEGEDUNUM FORT
Walker
Scotswood
CASTLE KEEP
NEWCASTLE DISCOVERY
Gateshead
Hebburn
SOUTER LIGHTHOUSE
METROLAND
INTERNATIONAL STADIUM
Hedworth
Whiteleas
Cleadon
Whitburn Colliery
Dunston
Bensham
Boldon Colliery
Pelaw
Whitburn
SHIPLEY ART GAL.
Felling
Boldon
Whickham
Carr Hill
FULWELL WINDMILL
Low Fell
Downhill
Fulwell
Roker
Street Gate
Chowdene
Wrekenton
Hylton Castle
Southwick
Monkwearmouth
NATIONAL GLASS CENTRE
Marley Hill
Lamesley
Springwell
Usworth
Castletown
STATION MUS.
SAINT PETER'S CHURCH
SUNDERLAND MINSTER
Blackfell
OLD HALL
South Hylton
Pallion
Kibblesworth
Birtley
WASHINGTON SERVICES
WASHINGTON
High Barnes
Sunderland
Pennywell
Hendon
Lambton
THE WILDFOWL & WETLANDS TRUST
PENSHAW MON.
BEAMISH
Urpeth
Ouston
New Silksworth
Beamish
Perkinsville
Barley Mow
Rickleton
Fatfield
Penshaw
East Herrington
Tunstall
Ryhope
RYHOPE ENGINES MUS.
Pelton
West Pelton
Grange Villa
Shiney Row
New Herrington
Doxford Park
CHESTER-LE-STREET
Bournmoor
Newbottle
Burdon
Craghead
THE ANKERS HOUSE
Fence Houses
Seaton
Northlea
SEAHAM
Waldridge
Chester Moor
Great Lumley
Colliery Row
HOUGHTON-LE-SPRING
West Lea
Edmondsley
Nettlesworth
Plawsworth
East Rainton
Dalton-le-Dale
A
B
C
D

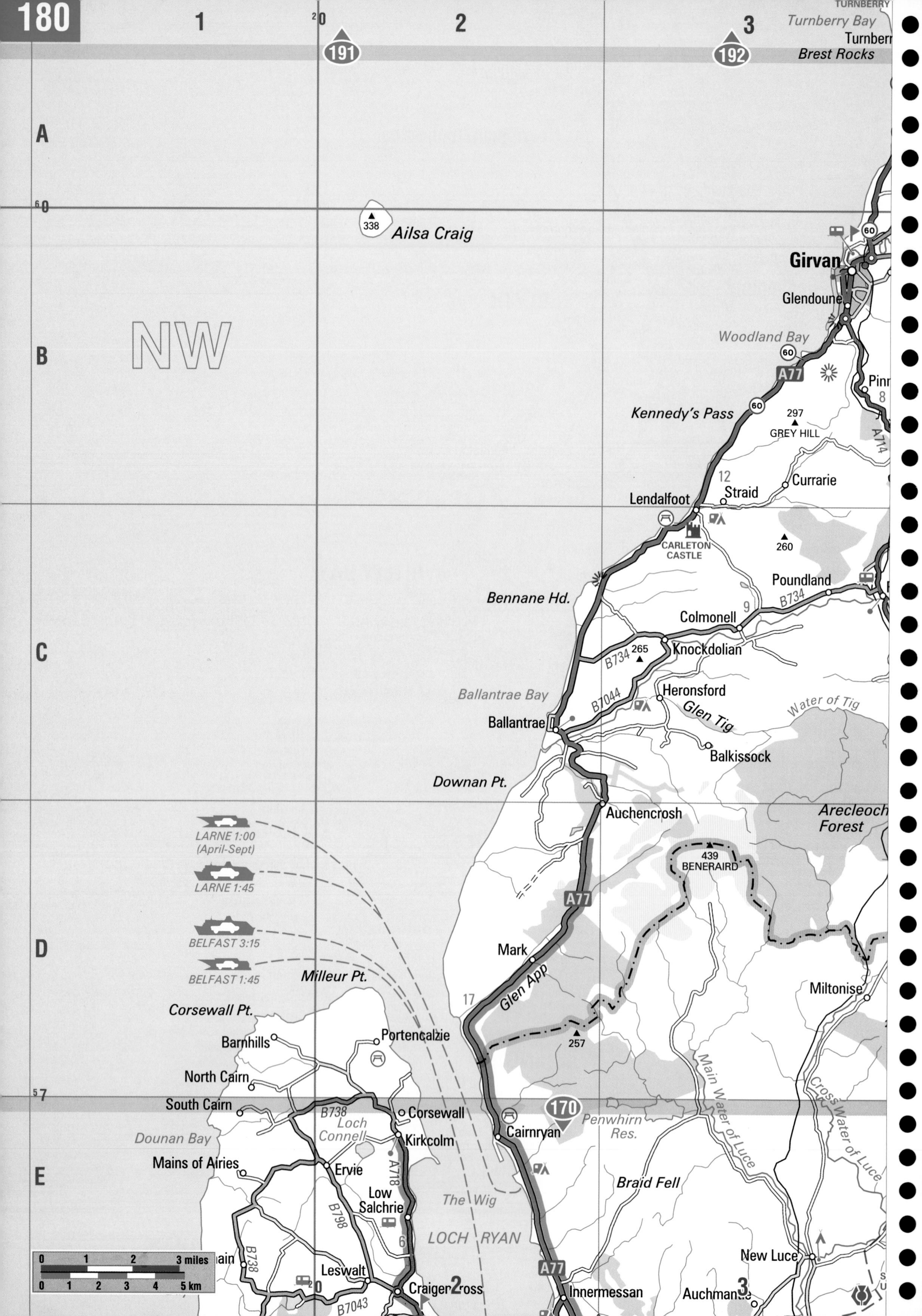

191
192
TURNBERRY
Turnberry Bay
Turnberr
Brest Rocks
Ailsa Craig
338
Girvan
Glendoune
Woodland Bay
A77
Pinn
Kennedy's Pass
297
GREY HILL
A714
Currarie
Straid
Lendalfoot
CARLETON CASTLE
260
Poundland
B734
Bennane Hd.
Colmonell
Knockdolian
B734
265
Ballantrae Bay
Heronsford
B7044
Glen Tig
Water of Tig
Ballantrae
Balkissock
Downan Pt.
Auchencrosh
Arecleoch Forest
439
BENERAIRD
LARNE 1:00 (April-Sept)
LARNE 1:45
BELFAST 3:15
BELFAST 1:45
NW
A77
Mark
Milleur Pt.
Glen App
Miltonise
Corsewall Pt.
Portencalzie
257
Barnhills
North Cairn
South Cairn
Corsewall
B738
Loch Connell
Kirkcolm
170
Cairnryan
Penwhirn Res.
Main Water of Luce
Cross Water of Luce
Dounan Bay
A718
Mains of Airies
Ervie
Braid Fell
Low Salchrie
The Wig
B798
LOCH RYAN
New Luce
B738
Leswalt
A77
Craigencross
B7043
Innermessan
Auchmantle
0 1 2 3 miles
0 1 2 3 4 5 km

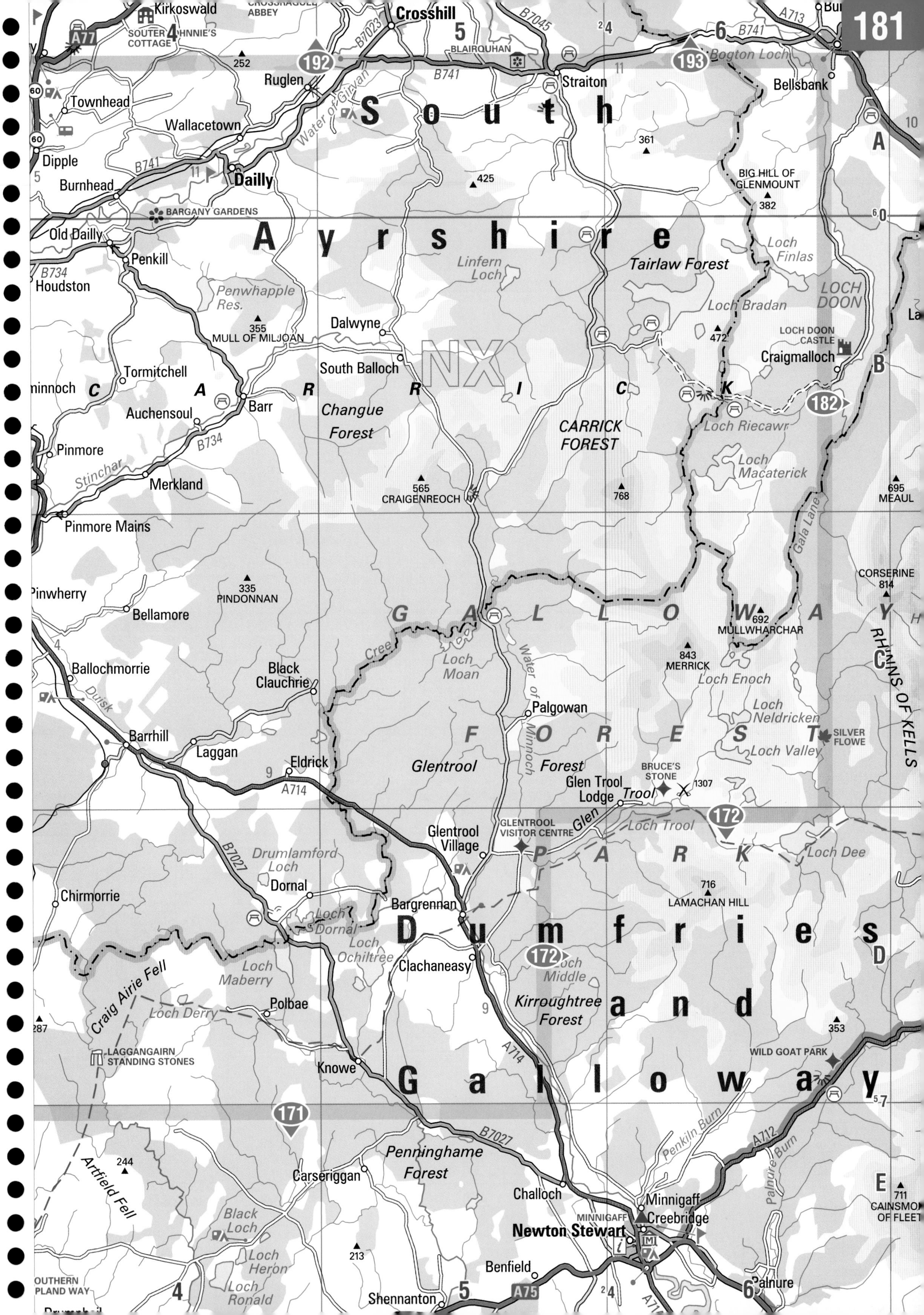
South Ayrshire
Dumfries and Galloway
CARRICK
GALLOWAY FOREST PARK
NX
Kirkoswald
Crosshill
Souter Johnnie's Cottage
Blairquhan
Straiton
Ruglen
Townhead
Wallacetown
Dipple
Dailly
Burnhead
Bargany Gardens
Old Dailly
Penkill
Houstons
Bogton Loch
Bellsbank
Big Hill of Glenmount
Loch Finlas
Tairlaw Forest
Loch Bradan
Loch Doon
Loch Doon Castle
Craigmalloch
Linfern Loch
Penwhapple Res.
Mull of Miljoan
Dalwyne
South Balloch
Tormitchell
Barr
Auchensoul
Changue Forest
Carrick Forest
Loch Riecawr
Loch Macaterick
Pinmore
Merkland
Pinmore Mains
Craigenreoch
Meaul
Gala Lane
Corserine
Pinwherry
Bellamore
Pindonnan
Mullwharchar
Merrick
Loch Moan
Loch Enoch
Rhinns of Kells
Ballochmorrie
Black Clauchrie
Palgowan
Water of Minnoch
Loch Neldricken
Silver Flowe
Loch Valley
Barrhill
Laggan
Eldrick
Glentrool
Forest
Bruce's Stone
Glen Trool Lodge
Loch Trool
Glentrool Visitor Centre
Glentrool Village
Loch Dee
Drumlamford Loch
Dornal
Chirmorrie
Bargrennan
Lamachan Hill
Loch Dornal
Loch Ochiltree
Clachaneasy
Loch Middle
Loch Maberry
Craig Airie Fell
Loch Derry
Polbae
Kirroughtree Forest
Laggangairn Standing Stones
Wild Goat Park
Knowe
Penkiln Burn
Palnure Burn
Artfield Fell
Penninghame Forest
Carseriggan
Challoch
Minnigaff
Creebridge
Newton Stewart
Cairnsmore of Fleet
Black Loch
Loch Heron
Loch Ronald
Benfield
Shennanton
Palnure
Southern Upland Way
A77 A713 B741 B7023 B7045 B734 A714 B7027 A712 A75
192 193 182 172 171

Belston
Trabboch
Ochiltree
Auchinleck
Lugar
Glenmuir
Holmhead
Logan
Masonhill
Coylton
Coalhall
Cumnock
KEIR HARDIE STATUE
MACLAURIN GALLERY & ROZELLE HOUSE
Joppa
Hillhead
BAIRD INSTITUTE MUSEUM
Netherthird
Laigh Glengall
Drongan
Craigens
TAM O'SHANTER EXPERIENCE
Martnaham Loch
Barbieston
Skares
DOON VALLEY RARE BREEDS CENTRE
Sinclairston
Hayhill
Littlemill
Hollybush
Rankinston
Pathhead
Dalrymple
East Ayrshire
Mansfield
Water of Coyle
Connel Park
Bankglen
Nith
New Cumnock
Polnessan
429 KILMEIN HILL
Burnside
Dalleagles
Patna
Burnfoot
Waterside
DOON VALLEY HERITAGE MUSEUM
BENBEOCH 464
Aitkenhead
Loch Spallander Reservoir
Doon
SCOTTISH INDUSTRIAL RAILWAY CENTRE
Burnton
Afton Water
569 ENOCH HILL
Dalmellington
CATHCARTSON VISITOR CENTRE
BLAIRQUHAN
Bogton Loch
Straiton
Bellsbank
Afton Reservoir
South Ayrshire
CAMPBELLS HILL 453
361
425
BIG HILL OF GLENMOUNT 382
Carsphairn Forest
Linfern Loch
Tairlaw Forest
Loch Finlas
LOCH DOON
797 CAIRNSMORE OF CARSPHAIRN
Loch Bradan
472
Lamloch
LOCH DOON CASTLE
Brochloch
Craigmalloch
THE GLENKENS
Garryhorn
Carsphairn
CARRICK FOREST
Loch Riecawr
CAIRN AVEL
Bardennoch
Loch Macaterick
MEAUL 695
768
Dundeugh Forest
Knowehead
GALLOWAY FOREST PARK
Kendoon Loch
Gala Lane
Castlemaddy
Dundeugh
KENDOON
CORSERINE 814
Kendoon
Glenhoul
Loch Harrow
Forrest Lodge
Carsfad Loch
692 MULLWHARCHAR
RHINNS OF KELLS
843 MERRICK
Loch Moan
Loch Enoch
Loch Dungeon
Water of Minnoch
Palgowan
Loch Neldricken
Millquarter
Earlstoun Loch
746
SILVER FLOWE
St John's Town of Dalry
Loch Valley
Drumbuie
Bogue
Forest
BRUCE'S STONE
Glen Trool Lodge
Trool
1307
Garroch
Clatteringshaws Forest
Glenlee
0 1 2 3 miles
0 1 2 3 4 5 km
Loch Dee
Clatteringshaws Loch
381
New Galloway
193
192
181
172
A70
A76
A77
A713
A762
B7036
B7046
B742
B7034
B730
B741
B7045
B729
B7000

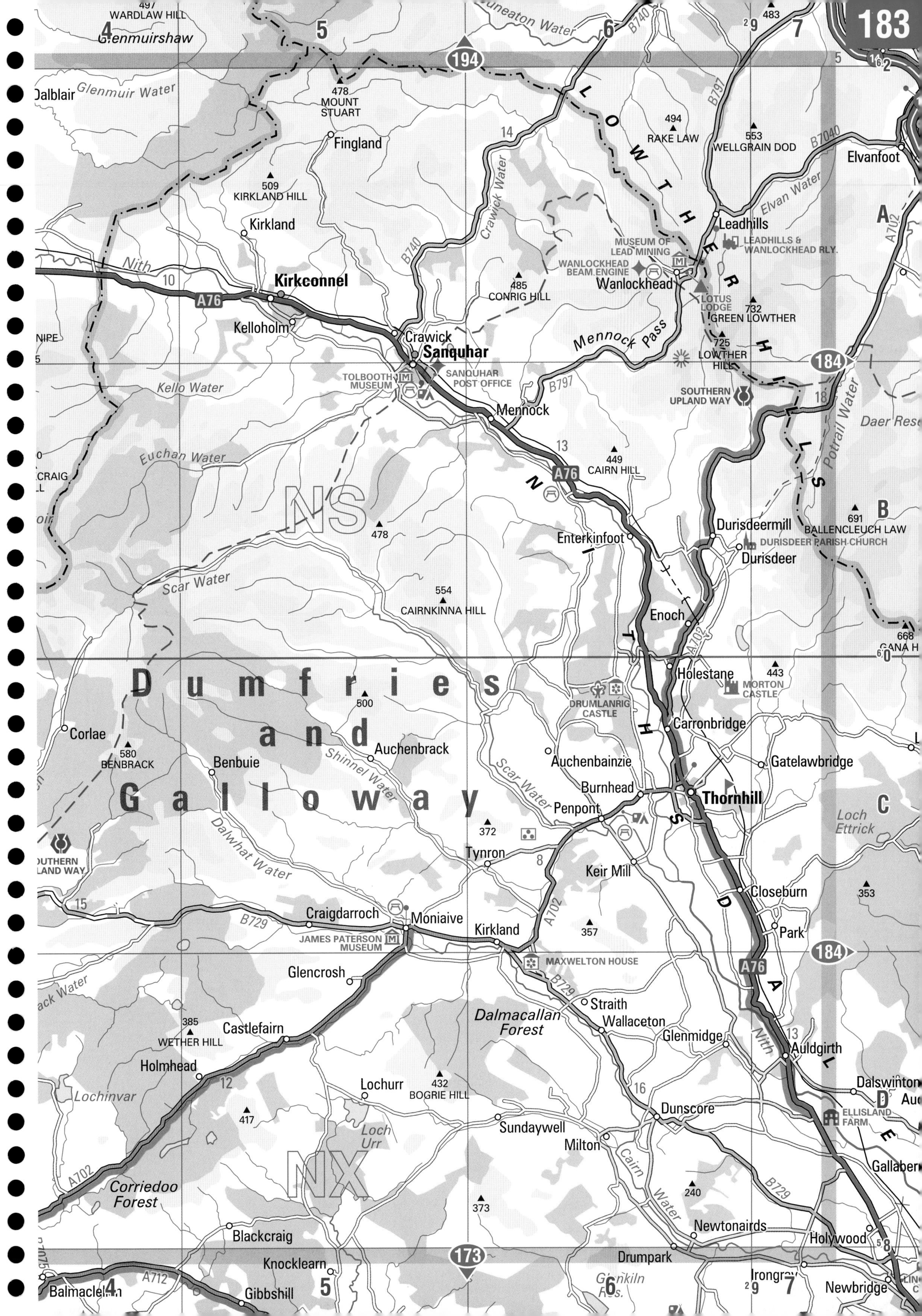

Glenmuirshaw
Dalblair
Glenmuir Water
478 MOUNT STUART
Fingland
509 KIRKLAND HILL
Kirkland
Nith
Kirkconnel
A76
Kelloholm
Kello Water
Euchan Water
Crawick
Sanquhar
TOLBOOTH MUSEUM
SANQUHAR POST OFFICE
Mennock
B740
Crawick Water
485 CONRIG HILL
Mennock Pass
B797
LOWTHER HILLS
494 RAKE LAW
553 WELLGRAIN DOD
Elvanfoot
Elvan Water
B7040
Leadhills
LEADHILLS & WANLOCKHEAD RLY.
MUSEUM OF LEAD MINING
WANLOCKHEAD BEAM ENGINE
Wanlockhead
LOTUS LODGE
732 GREEN LOWTHER
725 LOWTHER HILL
SOUTHERN UPLAND WAY
Daer Rese
Potrail Water
449 CAIRN HILL
NS
478
Enterkinfoot
Durisdeermill
DURISDEER PARISH CHURCH
Durisdeer
691 BALLENCLEUCH LAW
554 CAIRNKINNA HILL
Scar Water
Enoch
A702
668 GANA H
Dumfries and Galloway
500
Holestane
443
MORTON CASTLE
DRUMLANRIG CASTLE
Carronbridge
Corlae
580 BENBRACK
Benbuie
Auchenbrack
Shinnel Water
Auchenbainzie
Gatelawbridge
Burnhead
Thornhill
Penpont
Loch Ettrick
372
Dalwhat Water
Tynron
Keir Mill
NITHSDALE
Closeburn
353
Craigdarroch
Moniaive
JAMES PATERSON MUSEUM
B729
Kirkland
357
Park
MAXWELTON HOUSE
Glencrosh
Straith
Dalmacallan Forest
Wallaceton
385 WETHER HILL
Castlefairn
Glenmidge
Auldgirth
Holmhead
Lochinvar
Lochurr
432 BOGRIE HILL
Dalswinton
ELLISLAND FARM
417
Loch Urr
Sundaywell
Dunscore
Milton
Cairn Water
NX
A702
Corriedoo Forest
373
240
Gallaber
Blackcraig
Newtonairds
Holywood
Drumpark
Knocklearn
A712
Balmaclellan
Gibbshill
Glenkiln Res.
Irongray
Newbridge
194
184
173

LOWTHER HILLS
NITHSDALE
ANNANDALE
Dumfr
NS
NX
Kirkton
Crawford
Glenbreck
Elvanfoot
Leadhills
LEADHILLS & WANLOCKHEAD RLY.
MUSEUM OF LEAD MINING
WANLOCKHEAD BEAM ENGINE
Wanlockhead
LOTUS LODGE
494 RAKE LAW
553 WELLGRAIN DOD
485 CONRIG HILL
732 GREEN LOWTHER
725 LOWTHER HILL
Mennock Pass
SANQUHAR POST OFFICE
SOUTHERN UPLAND WAY
Mennock
449 CAIRN HILL
Enterkinfoot
Durisdeermill
Durisdeer
DURISDEER PARISH CHURCH
691 BALLENCLEUCH LAW
Enoch
668 GANA HILL
Daer Reservoir
Potrail Water
Watermeetings
March
Nether Howecleuch
553 CRAIGMAID
546 CLYDE LAW
Source of River Tweed
DEVIL'S BEEF TUB
Ericstane
Granton
Howslack
Coatsgate
Easter Earshaig
Garpol Water
Kinnelhead
Beattock
Holestane
443
MORTON CASTLE
DRUMLANRIG CASTLE
Carronbridge
512 QUEENSBERRY
Locherben
399
Gatelawbridge
Auchenbainzie
Scar Water
Burnhead
Thornhill
Penpont
Loch Ettrick
Tynron
Keir Mill
Closeburn
353
Forest of Ae
Park
Kirkland
357
MAXWELTON HOUSE
Straith
Wallaceton
Dalmacallan Forest
Glenmidge
Auldgirth
Nith
Ae Village
Water of Ae
Parkgate
Nethermill
Courance
Blackacre
Chapelhill
Johnstonebridge
St Ann's
Lochwood
Kinnel Water
Dalswinton
Auchencairn
Shieldhill
Sundaywell
Dunscore
Milton
Cairn Water
ELLISLAND FARM
Duncow
Gallaberry
Amisfield
Kirkton
Tinwald
240
373
Newtonairds
Holywood
Locharbriggs
Heathhall
DUMFRIES AND GALLOWAY AVIATION MUS.
LINCLUDEN COLLEGE
Irongray
Newbridge
The Grove
Torthorwald
Lochmaben
LOCHMABEN CASTLE
Templand
Millhousebridge
Applegarthtown
A74(M)
A76
A702
A701
A709
B740
B797
B7040
B719
B729
B7020
B7076
183
195
174
0 1 2 3 miles
0 1 2 3 4 5 km

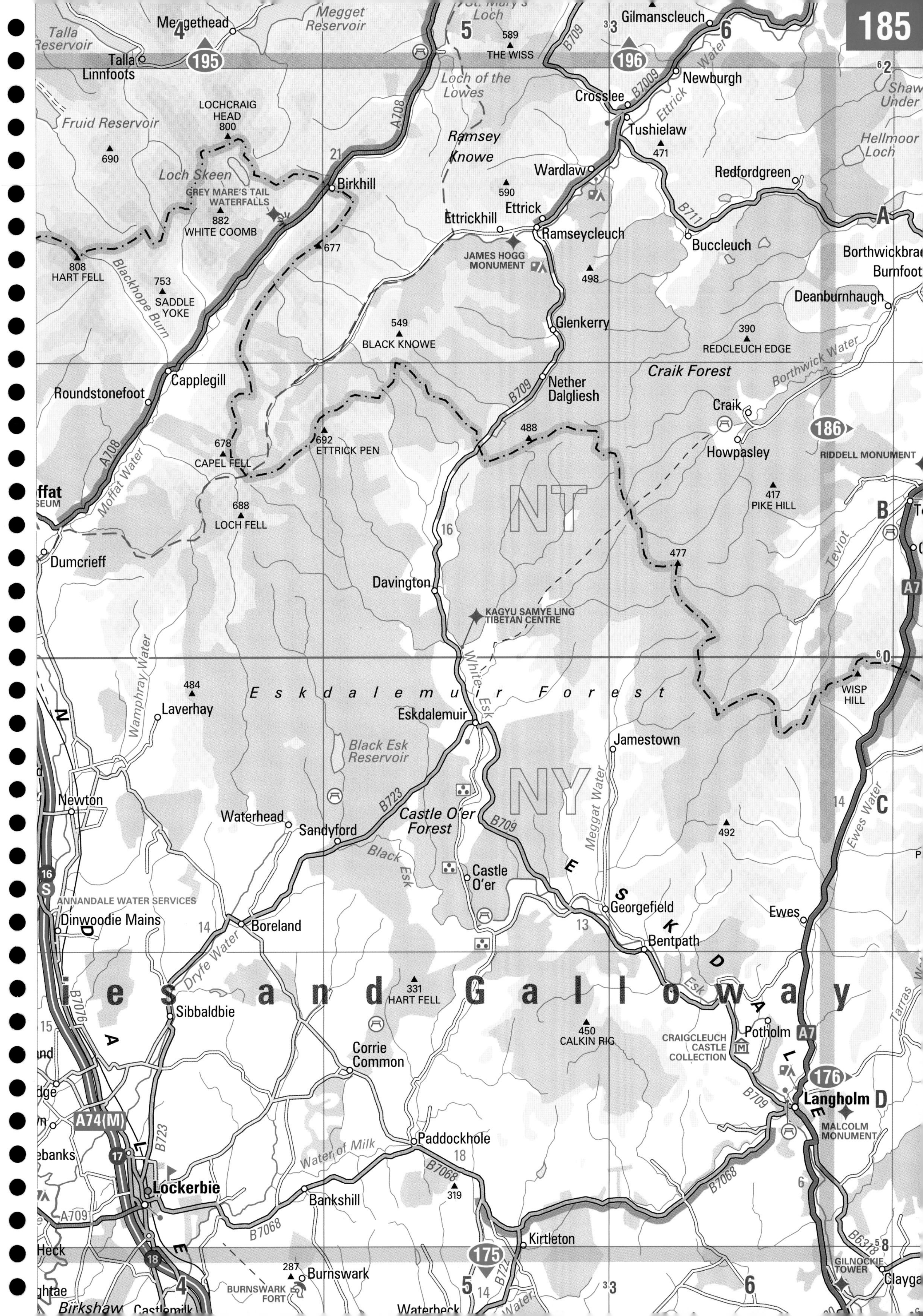
Meggethead
Megget Reservoir
Talla Reservoir
Talla Linnfoots
St. Mary's Loch
THE WISS 589
Gilmanscleuch
Newburgh
Crosslee
Tushielaw
Loch of the Lowes
Fruid Reservoir
LOCHCRAIG HEAD 800
Loch Skeen
GREY MARE'S TAIL WATERFALLS
882 WHITE COOMB
Birkhill
Ramsey Knowe
Wardlaw
Redfordgreen
Ettrick
Ettrickhill
Ramseycleuch
Buccleuch
JAMES HOGG MONUMENT
808 HART FELL
753 SADDLE YOKE
Blackhope Burn
Borthwickbrae
Burnfoot
Deanburnhaugh
Glenkerry
549 BLACK KNOWE
390 REDCLEUCH EDGE
Capplegill
Roundstonefoot
Nether Dalgliesh
Craik Forest
Borthwick Water
Craik
Howpasley
RIDDELL MONUMENT
678 CAPEL FELL
692 ETTRICK PEN
Moffat Water
Moffat
417 PIKE HILL
688 LOCH FELL
NT
Teviot
Dumcrieff
Davington
KAGYU SAMYE LING TIBETAN CENTRE
White Esk
Wamphray Water
484
Laverhay
Eskdalemuir Forest
WISP HILL
Eskdalemuir
Jamestown
Black Esk Reservoir
NY
Meggat Water
Newton
Waterhead
Sandyford
Castle O'er Forest
Black Esk
Castle O'er
ANNANDALE WATER SERVICES
Georgefield
Ewes
Ewes Water
Dinwoodie Mains
Boreland
Bentpath
Dryfe Water
Dumfries and Galloway
331 HART FELL
Sibbaldbie
450 CALKIN RIG
CRAIGCLEUCH CASTLE COLLECTION
Potholm
Corrie Common
ESKDALE
Langholm
MALCOLM MONUMENT
Paddockhole
Water of Milk
Lockerbie
Bankshill
319
Kirtleton
ANNANDALE
Burnswark
BURNSWARK FORT
GILNOCKIE TOWER
Claygate
Birkshaw
Castlemilk
Waterbeck
195
196
186
176
175
A708
B709
B7009
B711
B723
B7076
B7068
B722
B6318
A7
A74(M)
A709

Scottish
Blake Muir
Broadmeadows
BROADMEADOWS
Yarrow
Yarrow Water
FASTHEUGH HILL
Bowhill
BOWHILL HOUSE & COUNTRY PARK
Selkirk
SELKIRK GLASS
Philiphaugh
HALLIWELL'S HOUSE MUSEUM
SIR WALTER SCOTT'S COURTROOM
Midlem
Lindean
WHITLAW MOSSES
SOUTHERN UPLAND WAY
DRYHOPE TOWER
Dryhope
Mountbenger
Yarrow Feus
Sundhope
Ettrickbridge
Kirkhope
Ettrick Forest
Clerklands
Lilliesleaf
BLACK KNOWE HEAD
St. Mary's Loch
Gilmanscleuch
CAVER'S HILL
Akermoor Loch
Woll
Ashkirk
THE WISS
Hassendean
Loch of the Lowes
Newburgh
Crosslee
Ettrick Water
Todrig
Shaws Under Loch
Horsleyhill
Clarilaw
Appletreehall
Ramsey Knowe
Tushielaw
Hellmoor Loch
Ale Water
SMASHA HILL
Wardlaw
Redfordgreen
Borthwickshiels
Burnfoot
Ettrick
Ettrick Hill
Ramseycleuch
Wilton
Hawick
MUSEUM AND SCOTT GALLERY
Roberton
JAMES HOGG MONUMENT
Buccleuch
Borthwickbrae
Burnfoot
DRUMLANRIG'S TOWER
Branxholm Park
Deanburnhaugh
Branxholme
Glenkerry
Newmill
REDCLEUCH EDGE
Craik Forest
Borthwick Water
Nether Dalgliesh
Broadhaugh
Craik
Teviotdale
Northhouse
Dodburn
Howpasley
RIDDELL MONUMENT
Slitrig Water
Allan Water
PIKE HILL
Teviothead
THE PIKE
Priesthaugh
Langburnshiels
Castleweary
Teviot
CALDCLEUCH HEAD
KAGYU SAMYE LING TIBETAN CENTRE
White Esk
WISP HILL
TUDHOPE HILL
Jamestown
Gorrenberry
HERMITAGE CASTLE
Hermitage
Meggat Water
Ewes Water
Newlands
PIKE FELL
ROAN FELL
Steele Road
Castle O'er
Dinlabyre
Eskdale
Georgefield
Ewes
Bentpath
Liddesdale
Old Castleton
Tarras Water
BLACK EDGE
0 1 2 3 miles
0 1 2 3 4 5 km

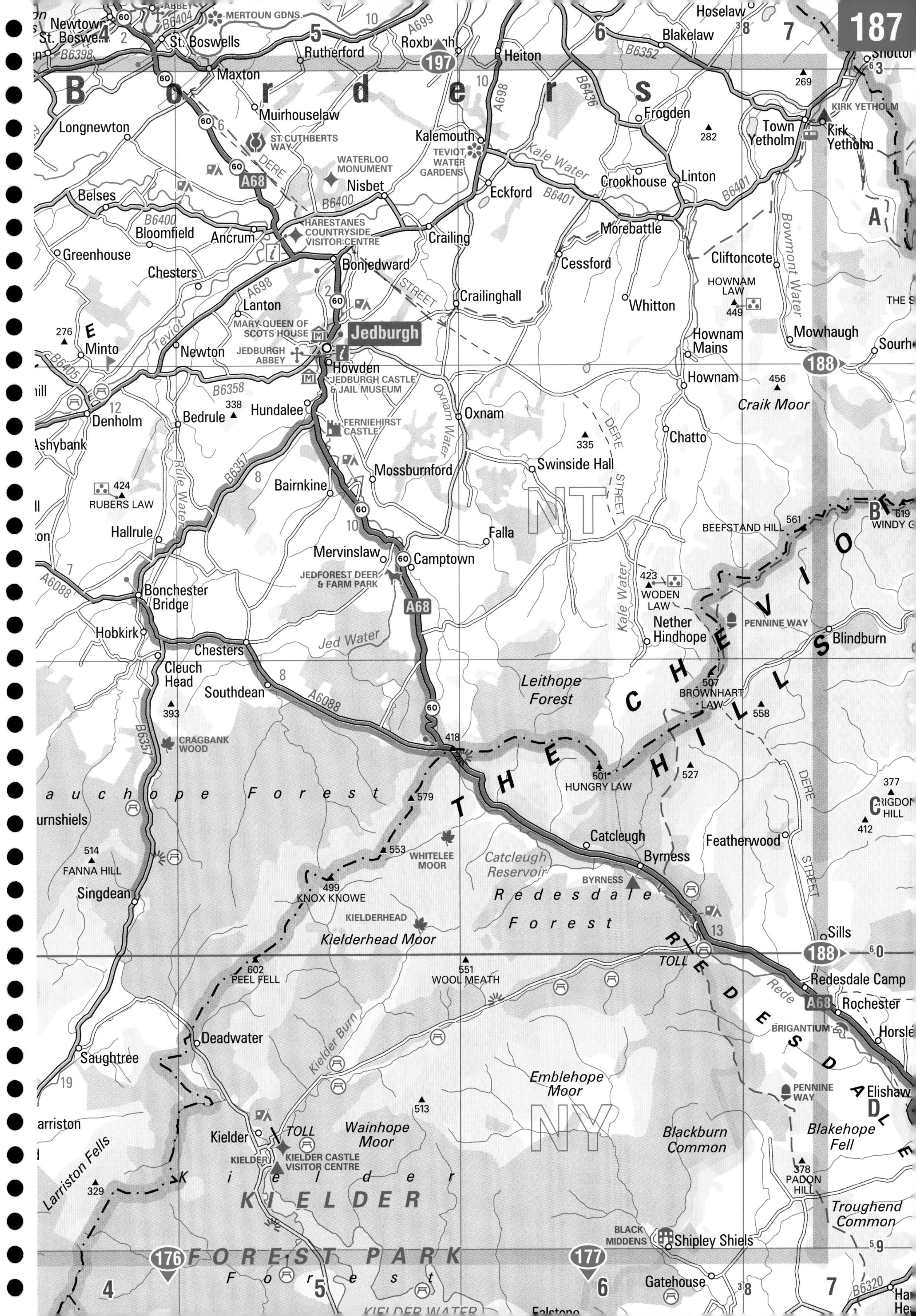
Borders
Newtown St. Boswells
St. Boswells
MERTOUN GDNS.
Rutherford
Roxburgh
Heiton
Hoselaw
Blakelaw
Maxton
Muirhouselaw
Longnewton
ST. CUTHBERTS WAY
WATERLOO MONUMENT
Nisbet
Kalemouth
TEVIOT WATER GARDENS
Eckford
Kale Water
Frogden
Crookhouse
Linton
Town Yetholm
KIRK YETHOLM
Kirk Yetholm
Belses
Bloomfield
Ancrum
HARESTANES COUNTRYSIDE VISITOR CENTRE
Crailing
Morebattle
Cessford
Greenhouse
Chesters
Bonjedward
Cliftoncote
HOWNAM LAW
Bowmont Water
Lanton
MARY QUEEN OF SCOTS HOUSE
Jedburgh
Crailinghall
Whitton
Mowhaugh
Minto
Newton
JEDBURGH ABBEY
Howden
JEDBURGH CASTLE & JAIL MUSEUM
Hownam Mains
Hownam
Craik Moor
Denholm
Bedrule
Hundalee
FERNIEHIRST CASTLE
Oxnam
Oxnam Water
Chatto
Ashybank
Swinside Hall
Mossburnford
Bairnkine
RUBERS LAW
Rule Water
Hallrule
Falla
NT
BEEFSTAND HILL
WINDY GYLE
Mervinslaw
Camptown
JEDFOREST DEER & FARM PARK
WODEN LAW
Kale Water
Bonchester Bridge
Hobkirk
Chesters
Jed Water
Nether Hindhope
PENNINE WAY
Blindburn
Cleuch Head
Southdean
Leithope Forest
BROWNHART LAW
THE CHEVIOT HILLS
CRAGBANK WOOD
HUNGRY LAW
Wauchope Forest
Burnshiels
FANNA HILL
WHITELEE MOOR
Catcleugh
Catcleugh Reservoir
Byrness
Featherwood
BRIGDON HILL
Singdean
KNOX KNOWE
BYRNESS
Redesdale Forest
KIELDERHEAD
Kielderhead Moor
TOLL
Sills
PEEL FELL
WOOL MEATH
Redesdale Camp
Rochester
BRIGANTIUM
Horsley
Deadwater
Kielder Burn
Saughtree
Emblehope Moor
Elishaw
REDESDALE
PENNINE WAY
NY
Larriston
Kielder
TOLL
Wainhope Moor
Blackburn Common
Blakehope Fell
KIELDER
KIELDER CASTLE VISITOR CENTRE
Larriston Fells
PADON HILL
Kielder
KIELDER FOREST PARK
Troughend Common
BLACK MIDDENS
Shipley Shiels
Gatehouse
Falstone
KIELDER WATER
A68
A698
A699
A6088
B6357
B6358
B6400
B6401
B6436
B6352
B6405
B6398
B6404
B6320
DERE STREET
197
188
176
177

Shotton
Westnewton
Lanton
Newtown
West Horton
East Horton
Hazelrigg
Warenton
Kirknewton
Akeld
Weetwood Hall
Kirk Yetholm
Town Yetholm
Hethpool
ST CUTHBERTS WAY
Humbleton
Wooler
Chatton
Greendikes
Earle
Haugh Head
Middleton Hall
Chillingham
CHILLINGHAM CASTLE
CHILLINGHAM WILD CATTLE
Newtown
PENNINE WAY
COLD LAW 452
North Middleton
Lilburn Tower
East Lilburn
Hepburn
South Middleton
Cliftoncote
Bowmont Water
College Burn
THE SCHIL
Langleeford
Ilderton
Roseden
Old Bewick
Mowhaugh
Sourhope
Roddam
Wooperton
New Bewick
Eglingham
AUCHOPE CAIRN
THE CHEVIOT
Harthope Burn
Craik Moor
CHEVIOT HILLS
NT
569 DUNMOOR HILL
NORTHUMBERLAND NATIONAL PARK VISITOR CENTRE
Brandon
Beanley
Greensidehill
Powburn
Breamish
Ingram
Branton
Shill Moor
WINDY GYLE
Glanton
NORTHUMBERLAND NATIONAL PARK
616 CUSHAT LAW
Glanton Pike
Great Ryle
Prendwick
Whittingham
Kidland Forest
Usway Burn
Alnham
Thrunton
Little Ryle
Barrowburn
Blindburn
Yetlington
Scrainwood
Callaly
Thrunton Wood
Biddlestone
Alwin
Netherton
Lorbottle Hall
Shillmoor
Lorbottle
Alwinton
Burradon
High Trewhitt
377 CRIGDON HILL
Linshiels
Cartington
Harbottle
Coquet
Sharperton
DERE STREET
LADY'S WELL
Warton
Snitter
CRAGSIDE
WATTY BELL'S CAIRN 355
Holystone
Flotterton
Rothbury
Caistron
Thropton
CRAGSIDE HOUSE
Hepple
Newtown
Whitton
Sills
Great Tosson
NATIONAL PARK VISITOR CENTRE
Redesdale Camp
Rede
Rochester
NY
440 TOSSON HILL
BRIGANTIUM
Horsley
ROTHBURY FOREST
Otterburn Camp
Forestburn Gate
Elishaw
Harwood Forest
REDESDALE
Blakehope Fell
REDESDALE CHEESE FARM
Otterburn
Elsdon
Fallowlees Burn
Fontburn Res.
Nunnykirk
378 PADON HILL
Ewesley
Troughend Common
Raylees
Old Town
Northumberland
Rothley Shield East
HERTERTON HOUSE GARDEN
Longwitton
Rothley
0 1 2 3 miles
0 1 2 3 4 5 km

NORTHUMBERLAND COAST
Beadnell
Benthall
Beadnell Bay
High Newton-by-the-Sea
Low Newton-by-the-Sea
Embleton Bay
Embleton
Dunstan Steads
Castle Point
DUNSTANBURGH CASTLE
Craster
Dunstan
Howick
Howick Haven
Longhoughton
Boulmer
Boulmer Haven
Alnwick
Alnmouth
Alnmouth Bay
Amble
Coquet I.
Hauxley
Radcliffe
DRURIDGE BAY
Druridge Bay
Widdrington
Cresswell
The Scars
Ellington
Lynemouth
Beacon Pt.
Woodhorn
Ashington
Pegswood
NU
NZ
Bellshill
Adderstone
Lucker
Elford
North Sunderland
Warenford
Newham Hall
Newham
Swinhoe
Fleetham
Newstead
Chathill
Rosebrough
Ellingham
Preston
PRESTON TOWER
Brunton
Brockdam
Brownyside
North Charlton
Doxford
Christon Bank
West Ditchburn
South Charlton
Rock
Rennington
Littlemill
Littlehoughton
Shipley
HULNE ABBEY
Titlington
ALNWICK ABBEY
Denwick
Abberwick
Broome Park
Lemmington Hall
Hawkhill
Lesbury
Bilton
EDLINGHAM CASTLE
Edlingham
High Buston
Shilbottle
Low Buston
Birling
Warkworth
Eastfield Hall
Newton-on-the-Moor
Gloster Hill
Hazon
Swarland Estate
Guyzance
Brainshaugh
North Togston
Swarland
Acklington
Togston
Broomhill
South Broomhill
Longframlington
LONGFRAMLINGTON GARDENS
Felton
West Thirston
East Thirston
Red Row
Weldon
Hesleyhurst
Eshott
West Chevington
Helm
Wingates
Longhorsley
Causey Park Bridge
Stobswood
Widdrington Station
Fenrother
Tritlington
Ulgham
Linton
THE SANCTUARY WILDLIFE CENTRE
Netherwitton
Stanton
Hebron
Longhirst
QUEEN ELIZABETH II
Pigdon
A1
A697
A1068
A189
B1340
B1339
B6347
B6346
B6341
B6345
B6344
B1337
Coquet
Aln
178
179
199
A
B
C
D
4
5
6

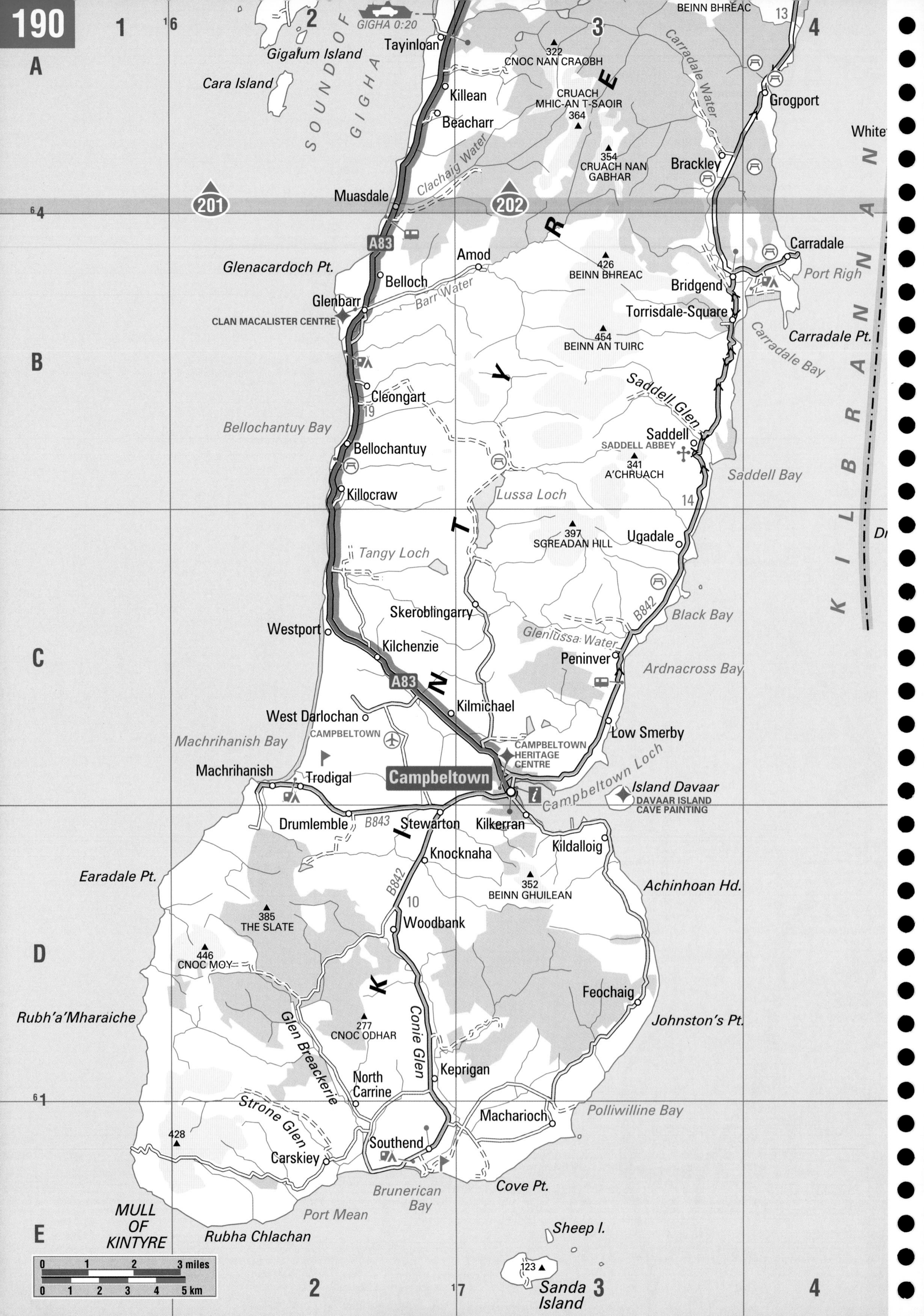

GIGHA 0:20
Gigalum Island
Cara Island
SOUND OF GIGHA
Tayinloan
Killean
Beacharr
Clachaig Water
Muasdale
201
202
322
CNOC NAN CRAOBH
CRUACH MHIC-AN T-SAOIR
364
354
CRUACH NAN GABHAR
BEINN BHREAC
Carradale Water
Grogport
Brackley
White
Carradale
Port Righ
Bridgend
Torrisdale-Square
Carradale Pt.
Carradale Bay
KILBRANNAN
A83
Glenacardoch Pt.
Belloch
Amod
Barr Water
426
BEINN BHREAC
Glenbarr
CLAN MACALISTER CENTRE
454
BEINN AN TUIRC
Cleongart
Saddell Glen
Bellochantuy Bay
Bellochantuy
Saddell
SADDELL ABBEY
341
A'CHRUACH
Saddell Bay
Killocraw
Lussa Loch
KINTYRE
397
SGREADAN HILL
Ugadale
Tangy Loch
Skeroblingarry
B842
Black Bay
Westport
Glenlussa Water
Kilchenzie
Peninver
Ardnacross Bay
Kilmichael
West Darlochan
CAMPBELTOWN
Machrihanish Bay
Low Smerby
CAMPBELTOWN HERITAGE CENTRE
Campbeltown Loch
Machrihanish
Trodigal
Campbeltown
Island Davaar
DAVAAR ISLAND CAVE PAINTING
Drumlemble
B843
Stewarton
Kilkerran
Kildalloig
Knocknaha
Earadale Pt.
352
BEINN GHUILEAN
Achinhoan Hd.
385
THE SLATE
Woodbank
446
CNOC MOY
Feochaig
Rubh'a'Mharaiche
277
CNOC ODHAR
Conie Glen
Glen Breackerie
Johnston's Pt.
Keprigan
North Carrine
Strone Glen
Macharioch
Polliwilline Bay
428
Southend
Carskiey
Cove Pt.
Brunerican Bay
MULL OF KINTYRE
Port Mean
Rubha Chlachan
Sheep I.
123
Sanda Island
0 1 2 3 miles
0 1 2 3 4 5 km

NORTH
ISLE OF ARRAN
ARRAN
Thundergay
MEALL NAN DAMH
573
NORTH SANNOX FARM PARK
A841
Sannox
Sannox Bay
Pirnmill
Loch Tanna
859
Glen Sannox
798
CIR MHÔR
721
BEINN BHARRAIN
Corrie
874
GOAT FELL
BEINN TARSUINN
825
Imachar
202
203
ARDROSSAN 0:55
BRODICK
BRODICK CASTLE
ARRAN AROMATICS VISITOR CENTRE
Glen Iorsa
Glen Rosa
Dougarie
228
Machrie Water
ISLE OF ARRAN HERITAGE MUSEUM
Brodick Bay
Brodick
Strathwhillan
Auchagallon
Glenloig
A'CHRUACH
512
Glen Cloy
B880
Machrie Bay
SOUND
Clauchlands Pt.
Tormore
MACHRIE MOOR STANDING STONES
Blairbeg
Margnaheglish
KING'S CAVE
BALMICHAEL VISITOR CENTRE
Balmichael
503
Lamlash
Lamlash Bay
Holy Island
Cordon
Torbeg
Shiskine
Drumadoon Pt.
314
Kingscross Pt.
Blackwaterfoot
458
TIGHVEIN
Auchencairn
Kingscross
Drumadoon Bay
Kilpatrick
KILPATRICK DUN
Knockenkelly
Whiting Bay
North Kiscadale
South Kiscadale
Glenree
Sliddery Water
Largymore
Brown Hd.
CARN BAN
Corriecravie
GLENASHDALE FALLS
Kilmory Water
Largybeg
Dippen
Sliddery
Lagg
Levencorroch
Dippin Head
Kilmory
SOUTH BANK FARM PARK
Bennan
Kildonan
TORRYLINN CAIRN
Bennan Hd.
Sound of Pladda
Pladda
NR
NS
192
180
4
5
6
7
A
B
C
D
E

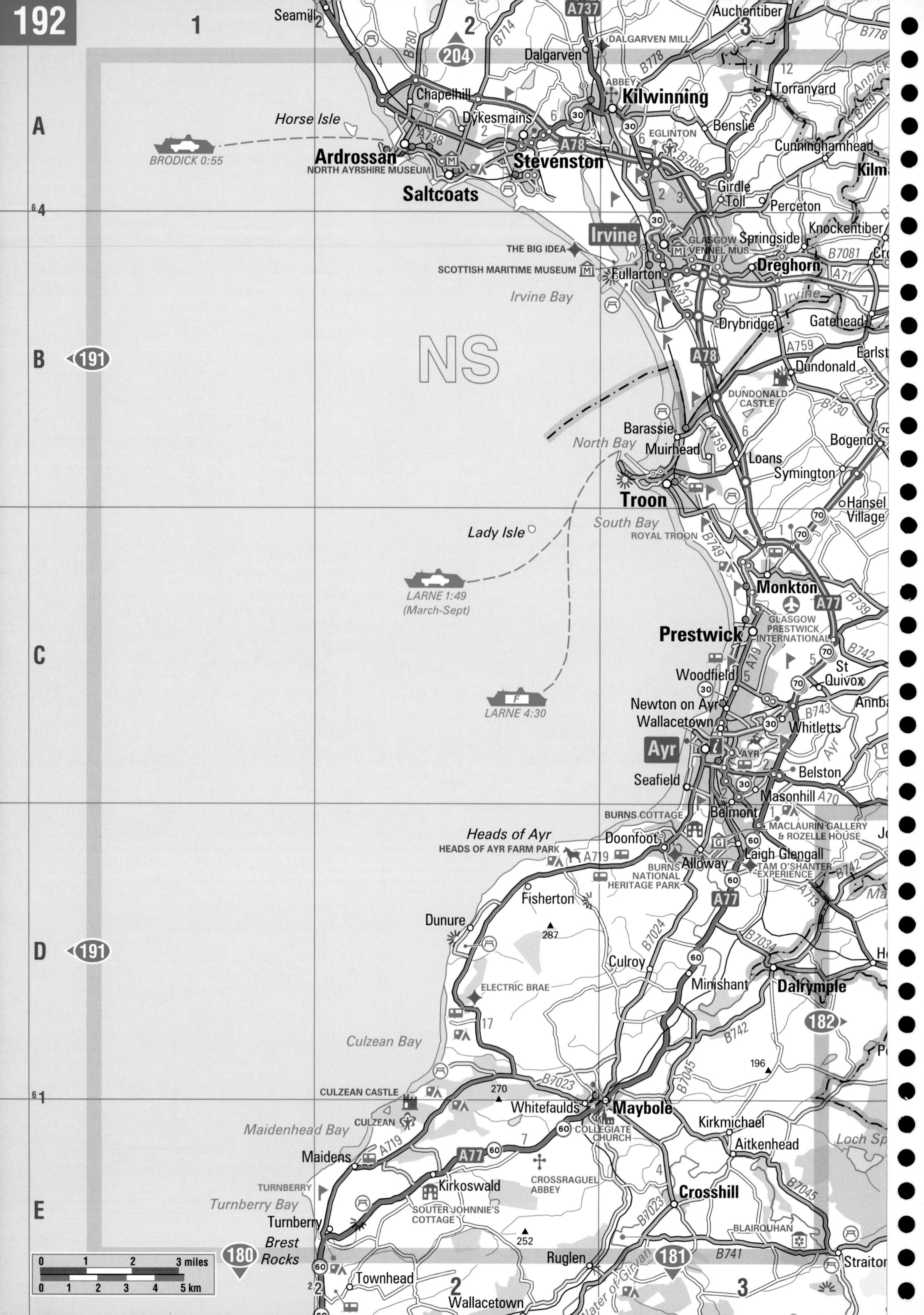

204 191 191 182 180 181

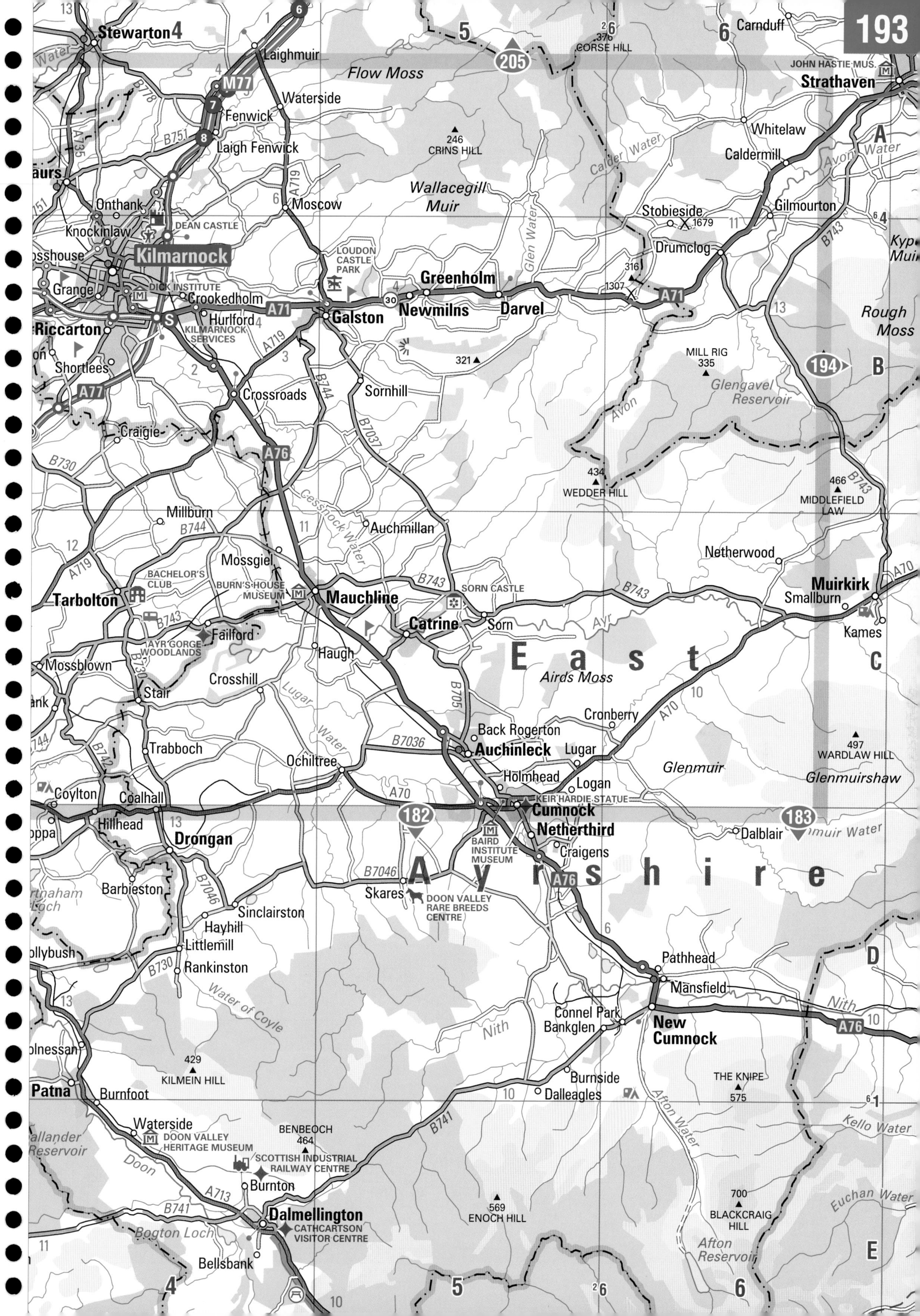
Stewarton
Laighmuir
Flow Moss
CORSE HILL
Carnduff
JOHN HASTIE MUS.
Strathaven
Waterside
Fenwick
Laigh Fenwick
CRINS HILL
Whitelaw
Caldermill
Wallacegill Muir
Moscow
Onthank
DEAN CASTLE
Knockinlaw
Kilmarnock
Stobieside
Gilmourton
Drumclog
LOUDON CASTLE PARK
Greenholm
Grange
DICK INSTITUTE
Crookedholm
Hurlford
Galston
Newmilns
Darvel
Riccarton
KILMARNOCK SERVICES
Rough Moss
MILL RIG
Glengavel Reservoir
Shortlees
Sornhill
Crossroads
Craigie
WEDDER HILL
MIDDLEFIELD LAW
Millburn
Auchmillan
Netherwood
Mossgiel
BACHELOR'S CLUB
BURN'S HOUSE MUSEUM
Tarbolton
Mauchline
SORN CASTLE
Muirkirk
Smallburn
Catrine
Sorn
Failford
AYR GORGE WOODLANDS
Kames
Haugh
East
Airds Moss
Mossblown
Crosshill
Stair
Cronberry
Back Rogerton
Auchinleck
Lugar
Trabboch
Ochiltree
WARDLAW HILL
Glenmuir
Glenmuirshaw
Holmhead
Logan
Coylton
Coalhall
KEIR HARDIE STATUE
Cumnock
Hillhead
Netherthird
Dalblair
Drongan
BAIRD INSTITUTE MUSEUM
Craigens
Barbieston
Ayrshire
Skares
DOON VALLEY RARE BREEDS CENTRE
Sinclairston
Hayhill
Littlemill
Rankinston
Pathhead
Mansfield
Water of Coyle
Connel Park
Bankglen
New Cumnock
Nith
KILMEIN HILL
Patna
Burnfoot
Burnside
Dalleagles
THE KNIPE
Afton Water
Kello Water
Waterside
DOON VALLEY HERITAGE MUSEUM
BENBEOCH
SCOTTISH INDUSTRIAL RAILWAY CENTRE
Burnton
Doon
Dalmellington
CATHCARTSON VISITOR CENTRE
Bogton Loch
ENOCH HILL
BLACKCRAIG HILL
Euchan Water
Afton Reservoir
Bellsbank
M77
A71
A76
A70
A77
A719
B7037
B744
B743
B705
B7036
B7046
B730
B742
B741
A713

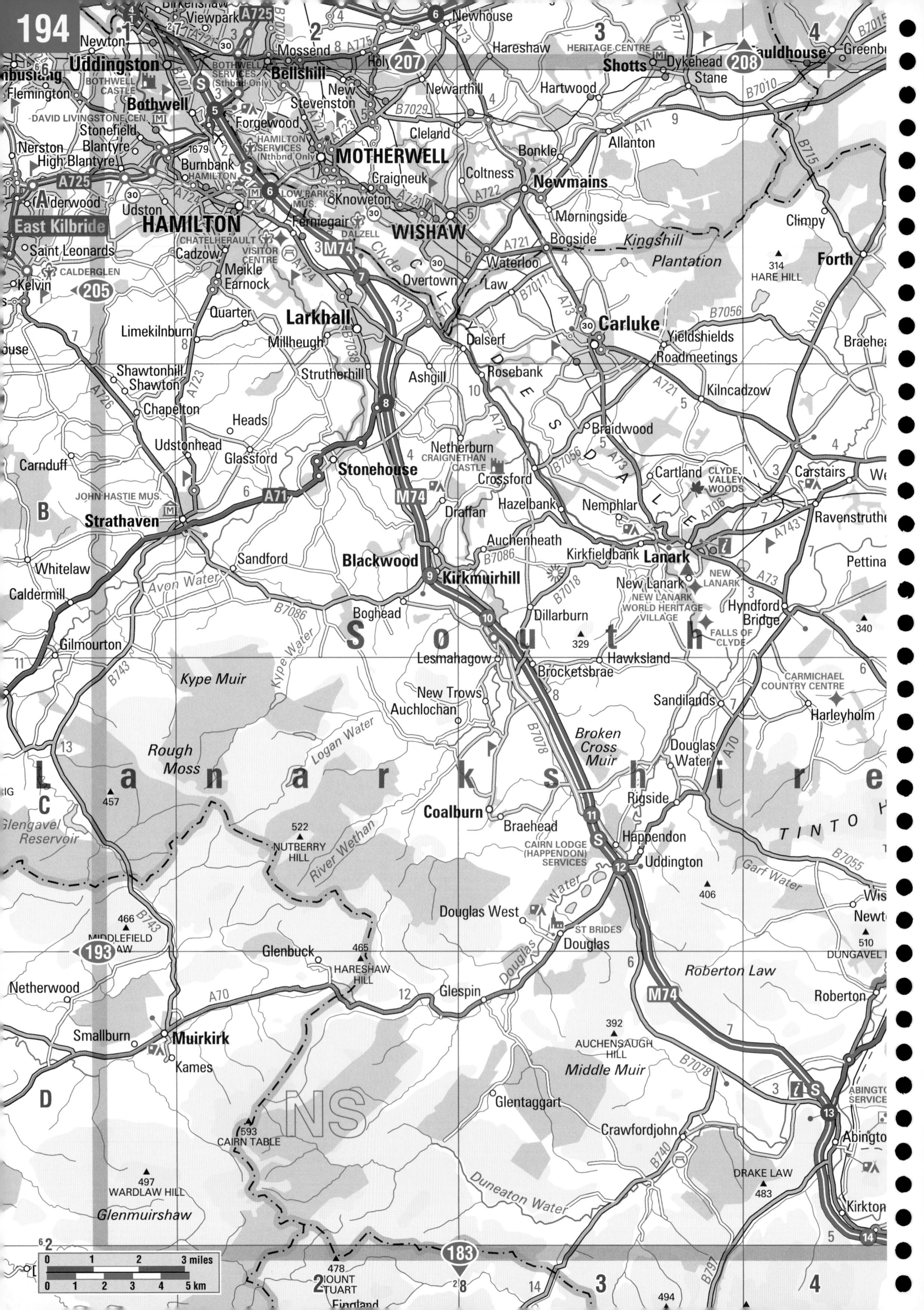
Uddingston
Bothwell
Bellshill
MOTHERWELL
HAMILTON
East Kilbride
WISHAW
Newmains
Shotts
Larkhall
Carluke
Stonehouse
Strathaven
Blackwood
Kirkmuirhill
Lanark
Lesmahagow
Coalburn
Douglas
Muirkirk
Abington
South
Lanarkshire
Kingshill Plantation
Kype Muir
Rough Moss
Broken Cross Muir
Middle Muir
Roberton Law
Glenmuirshaw
CLYDESDALE
NS
207
208
205
193
183

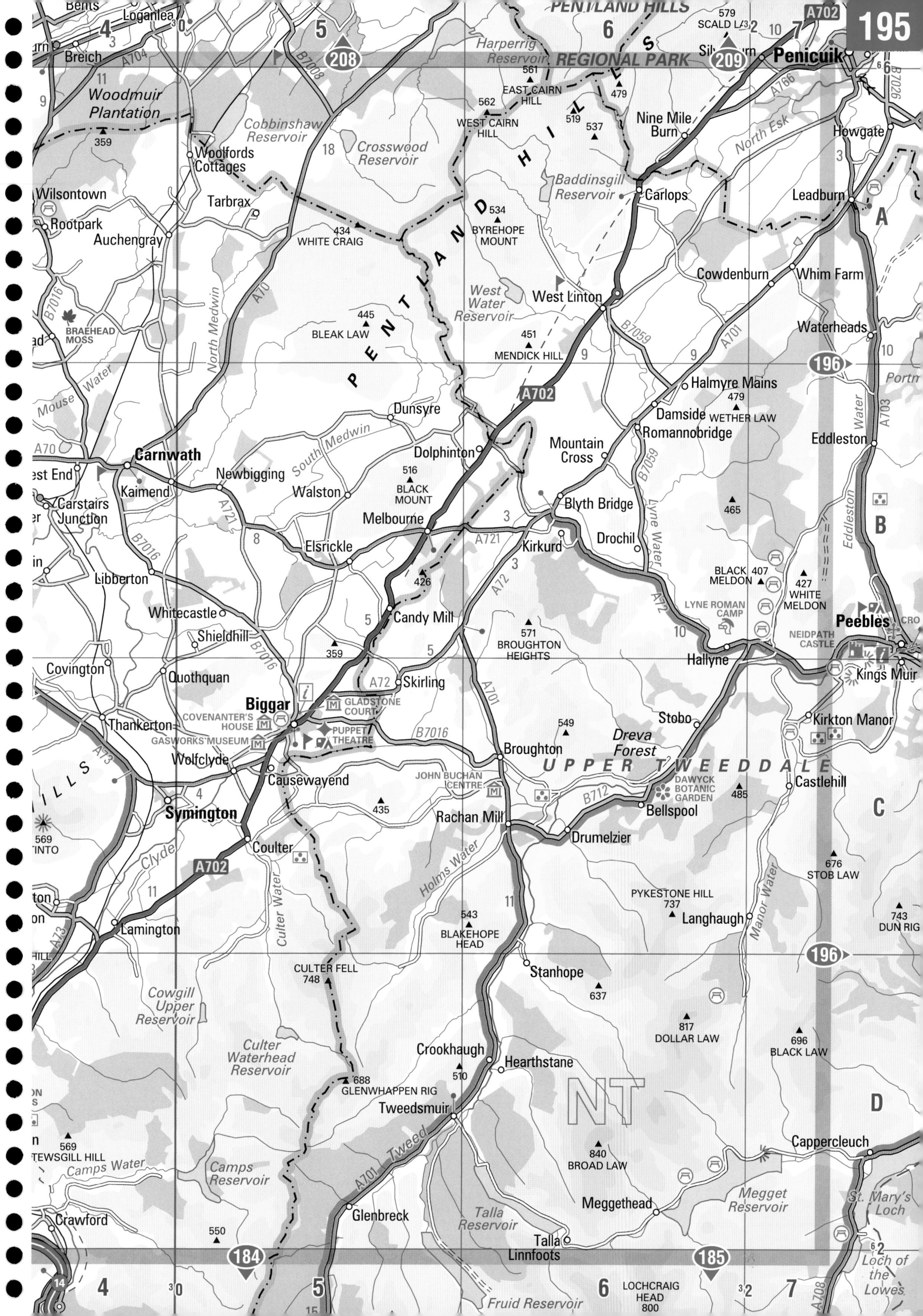

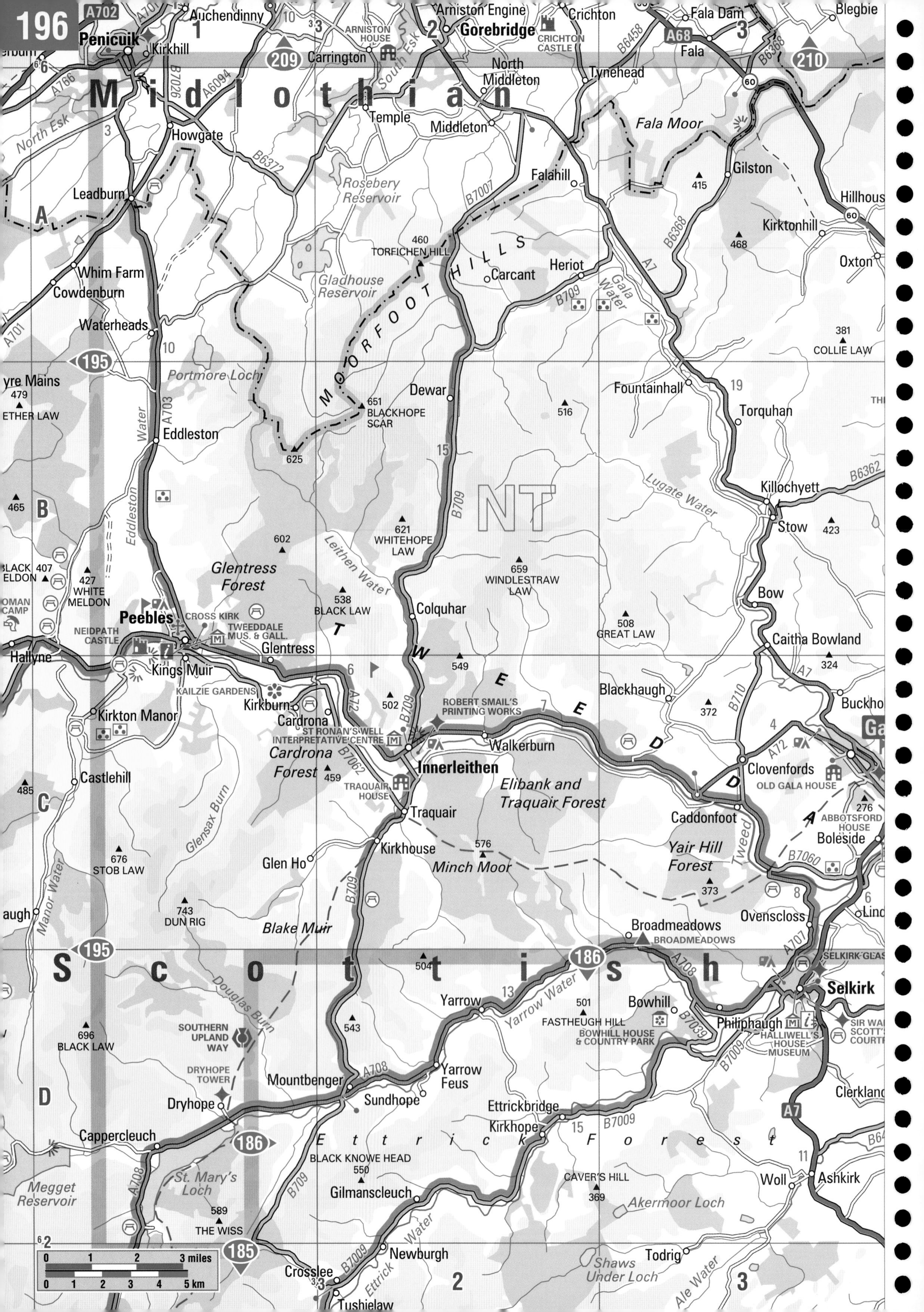
Midlothian
Penicuik
Kirkhill
Auchendinny
Arniston Engine
Gorebridge
Crichton
Crichton Castle
Fala Dam
Fala
Blegbie
Arniston House
Carrington
North Middleton
Tynehead
Temple
Middleton
Fala Moor
Howgate
Leadburn
Rosebery Reservoir
Falahill
Gilston
Hillhouse
Kirktonhill
Oxton
Torfichen Hill
Moorfoot Hills
Carcant
Heriot
Gala Water
Whim Farm
Cowdenburn
Gladhouse Reservoir
Waterheads
Collie Law
Portmore Loch
Dewar
Blackhope Scar
Fountainhall
Torquhan
Eddleston
Eddleston Water
Lugate Water
Killochyett
Stow
Whitehope Law
Windlestraw Law
Glentress Forest
Leithen Water
Black Law
White Meldon
Black Meldon
Colquhar
Bow
Great Law
Peebles
Cross Kirk
Tweeddale Mus. & Gall.
Neidpath Castle
Glentress
Caitha Bowland
Hallyne
Kings Muir
Kailzie Gardens
Kirkburn
Cardrona
Robert Smail's Printing Works
Blackhaugh
Buckholm
Kirkton Manor
St Ronan's Well Interpretative Centre
Walkerburn
Cardrona Forest
Innerleithen
Clovenfords
Old Gala House
Castlehill
Traquair House
Elibank and Traquair Forest
Traquair
Caddonfoot
Abbotsford House
Boleside
Glensax Burn
Kirkhouse
Yair Hill Forest
Stob Law
Glen Ho
Minch Moor
Manor Water
Dun Rig
Blake Muir
Broadmeadows
Ovenscloss
Scottish
Yarrow
Yarrow Water
Fastheugh Hill
Bowhill
Bowhill House & Country Park
Philiphaugh
Halliwell's House Museum
Selkirk
Sir Walter Scott's Courtroom
Black Law
Southern Upland Way
Douglas Burn
Dryhope Tower
Mountbenger
Yarrow Feus
Sundhope
Dryhope
Ettrickbridge
Kirkhope
Clerklands
Cappercleuch
Ettrick Forest
Black Knowe Head
St. Mary's Loch
Megget Reservoir
Gilmanscleuch
Caver's Hill
Akermoor Loch
Woll
Ashkirk
The Wiss
Newburgh
Ettrick Water
Crosslee
Tushielaw
Shaws Under Loch
Todrig
Ale Water
0 1 2 3 miles
0 1 2 3 4 5 km

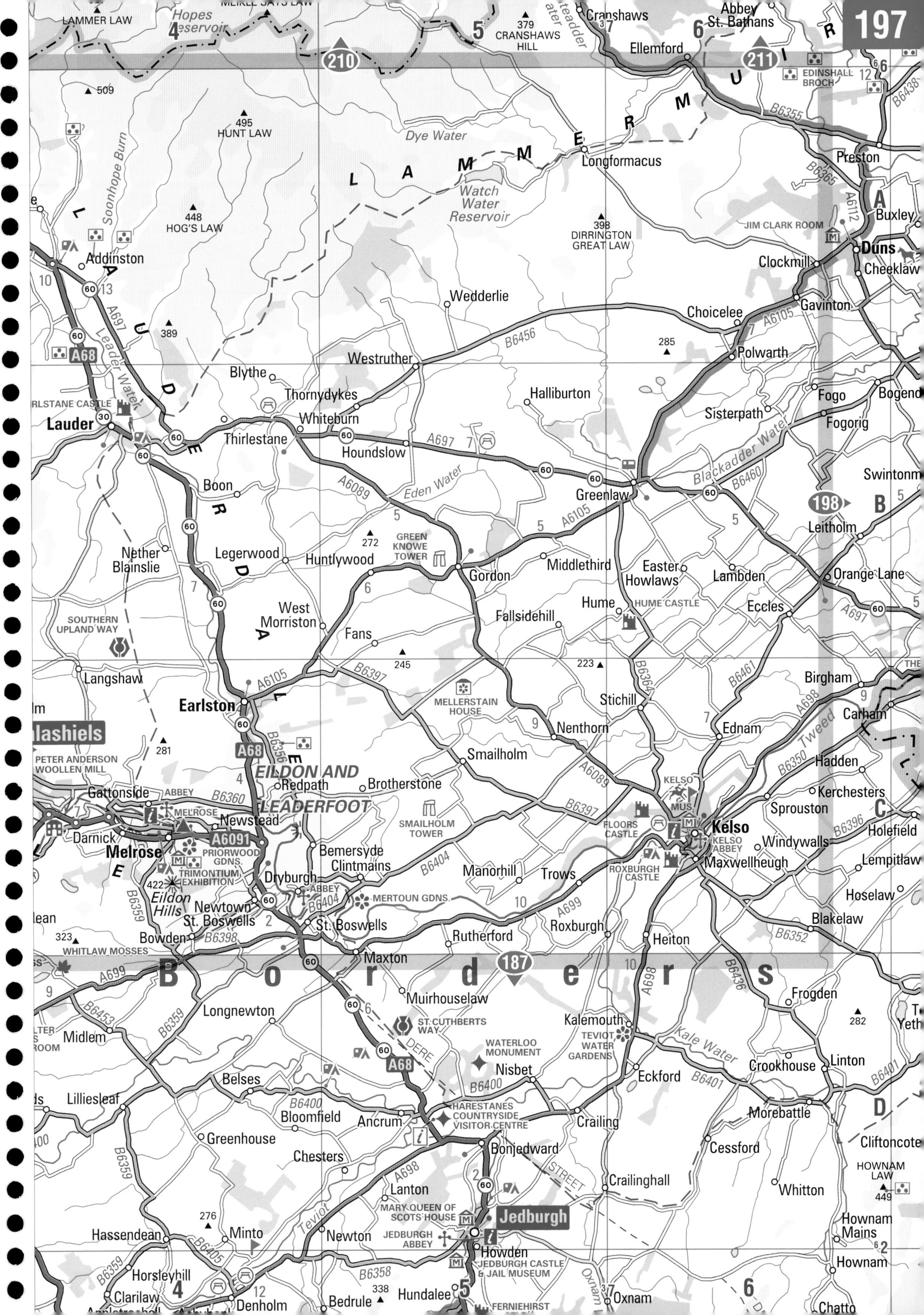
Lammer Law
Hopes Reservoir
Meikle Says Law
379 Cranshaws Hill
Cranshaws
Abbey St. Bathans
Ellemford
210
211
Edinshall Broch
L A M M E R M U I R
509
495 Hunt Law
Dye Water
B6355
Longformacus
Preston
B6365
Soonhope Burn
448 Hog's Law
Watch Water Reservoir
398 Dirrington Great Law
Jim Clark Room
A6112
Buxley
Duns
Addinston
Clockmill
Cheeklaw
L A U D E R D A L E
A697
Leader Water
A68
389
Wedderlie
Choicelee
Gavinton
A6105
B6456
285
Polwarth
Westruther
Blythe
Thornydykes
Halliburton
Fogo
Bogend
Thirlestane Castle
Whiteburn
Sisterpath
Fogorig
Lauder
Thirlestane
Houndslow
A697
Blackadder Water
B6460
Swinton
Boon
A6089
Eden Water
Greenlaw
198
Nether Blainslie
Legerwood
Huntlywood
272
Green Knowe Tower
Gordon
Middlethird
Easter Howlaws
Lambden
Leitholm
Orange Lane
Southern Upland Way
West Morriston
Fans
Hume
Hume Castle
Fallsidehill
Eccles
245
223
B6397
B6364
B6461
Birgham
Langshaw
A6105
Earlston
Mellerstain House
Stichill
Carham
Nenthorn
Ednam
Tweed
Galashiels
281
B6356
Peter Anderson Woollen Mill
Smailholm
A6089
B6350
Hadden
Eildon and Leaderfoot
Redpath
Brotherstone
Kelso
Kerchesters
Gattonside
Abbey
B6360
Sprouston
Melrose
Newstead
Smailholm Tower
Floors Castle
Mus.
Kelso Abbey
Holefield
Darnick
A6091
B6396
Windywalls
Priorwood Gdns.
Bemersyde
Clintmains
B6404
Manorhill
Trows
Roxburgh Castle
Maxwellheugh
Lempitlaw
422
Trimontium Exhibition
Dryburgh
Eildon Hills
Mertoun Gdns.
Hoselaw
B6359
Newtown St. Boswells
St. Boswells
A699
Roxburgh
Blakelaw
323
Whitlaw Mosses
Bowden
B6398
Rutherford
Heiton
B6352
Maxton
187
B o r d e r s
A699
A698
B6436
Frogden
Muirhouselaw
282
Longnewton
B6453
St. Cuthberts Way
Kalemouth
Teviot Water Gardens
Midlem
Waterloo Monument
Kale Water
Linton
Crookhouse
Dere Street
Nisbet
Eckford
B6401
B6400
Belses
Lilliesleaf
B6400
Bloomfield
Ancrum
Harestanes Countryside Visitor Centre
Crailing
Morebattle
Greenhouse
Cessford
Cliftoncote
Chesters
Bonjedward
B6359
A698
Crailinghall
Hownam Law
449
Whitton
Lanton
Mary Queen of Scots House
Jedburgh
276
Teviot
Minto
Hownam Mains
Hassendean
Newton
Jedburgh Abbey
Howden
B6405
Jedburgh Castle & Jail Museum
Hownam
Horsleyhill
B6358
Oxnam Water
Clarilaw
338
Denholm
Bedrule
Hundalee
Oxnam
Ferniehirst
Chatto

Reston
Ayton
Burnmouth
Auchencrow
Prenderguest
EDINSHALL BROCH
Lintlaw
Preston
Chirnside
Lamberton Beach
Lamberton
Chirnsidebridge
Edrom
Foulden
Clappers
Whiteadder Water
FOULDEN TITHE BARN
Buxley
JIM CLARK ROOM
Duns
CRUMSTANE FARM PARK
Allanton
Hutton
Highfields
Berwick-upon-Tweed
Clockmill
Cheeklaw
Blackadder West
Paxton
BARRACKS MUSEUM & RAMPARTS
Tweedmouth
East Ord
TOWER HOUSE POTTERY
Spittal
Gavinton
PAXTON HOUSE
Choicelee
Sinclair's Hill
Fishwick
Loanend
Prior Park
Redshin Cove
Whitsome
UNION SUSPENSION BRIDGE
Polwarth
Horncliffe
Fogo
Bogend
Horndean
Thorntonpark
Murton
Scremerston
Fogorig
Leet Water
Ladykirk
Thornton
NORHAM CASTLE
Swinton
SWINTON KIRK
Norham
West Allerdean
Cheswick
M E R S E
Swintonmill
Shoreswood
Shoresdean
DEVIL'S CAUSEWAY
Simprim
Grindon
Ancroft
Leitholm
Felkington
Berrington
Shellacres
Lambden
Orange Lane
Duddo
Castle Heaton
Bowsden
Eccles
Lennel
Coldstream
TWEED BRIDGE
Cornhill-on-Tweed
HEATHERSLAW LIGHT RAILWAY
ERROL HUT SMITHY AND WOOD WORKSHOP
Barmoor Castle
Barmoor Lane End
West Kyloe
Lowick
Kyloe Hills
THE HIRSEL
Birgham
Etal
HEATHERSLAW CORNMILL
Wark
Carham
LADY WATERFORD HALL
Ednam
East Learmouth
West Learmouth
Crookham
Branxton
Ford
Tweed
Hadden
Pressen
Kerchesters
Sprouston
Holefield
Flodden
Kimmerston
Hetton Steads
Downham
Howtel
KELSO ABBEY
Windywalls
Mindrum
Milfield
Fenton Town
Nesbit
Lempitlaw
Pawston
Kilham
Glen
Doddington
South Hazelrigg
Hoselaw
Lanton
Newtown
West Horton
East Horton
Blakelaw
Shotton
Westnewton
Coupland
Weetwood Hall
Kirknewton
Akeld
Frogden
KIRK YETHOLM
Town Yetholm
Kirk Yetholm
Hethpool
ST CUTHBERTS WAY
Humbleton
Wooler
Chatton
Earle
Haugh Head
Crookhouse
Linton
Middleton Hall
Newtown
Morebattle
PENNINE WAY
COLD LAW
North Middleton
Lilburn Tower
Cliftoncote
Bowmont Water
College Burn
South Middleton
HOWNAM LAW
Whitton
THE SCHIL
Ilderton
Langleeford
Roseden
Mowhaugh
Harthope Burn
Hownam Mains
Sourhope
Roddam
AUCHOPE CAIRN
THE CHEVIOT
Wooperton
Chatto
0 1 2 3 miles
0 1 2 3 4 5 km

NU
NORTHUMBERLAND COAST
Goswick
Beal
Emmanuel Hd.
Holy Island (Lindisfarne)
LINDISFARNE
LINDISFARNE CASTLE
Castle Pt.
Causeway
Holy Island Sands
Holy Island
HERITAGE CENTRE
LINDISFARNE PRIORY
Fenham
Guile Pt.
Fenwick
East Kyloe
Buckton
Elwick
Ross
Budle Bay
Farne Islands
Staple Sound
FARNE ISLANDS
BAMBURGH CASTLE
Inner Sound
Detchant
Middleton
Budle
Bamburgh
North Hazelrigg
Belford
Easington
Waren Mill
Burton
Spindlestone
Glororum
Seahouses
Mousen
Bradford
Elford
North Sunderland
Bellshill
Warenton
Adderstone
Lucker
Newham Hall
Beadnell
Swinhoe
Warenford
Greendikes
Newham
Fleetham
Benthall
Beadnell Bay
Newstead
Rosebrough
Chathill
Chillingham
CHILLINGHAM WILD CATTLE
Ellingham
Preston
High Newton-by-the-Sea
Brunton
Low Newton-by-the-Sea
PRESTON TOWER
Brockdam
Hepburn
Christon Bank
Embleton Bay
Brownyside
North Charlton
Doxford
Embleton
Dunstan Steads
Castle Point
DUNSTANBURGH CASTLE
Old Bewick
West Ditchburn
South Charlton
Harehope
Rock
Craster
New Bewick
Eglingham
Dunstan
Rennington
Beanley
Littlemill
Howick
Breamish
A1
B6353
B1342
B6349
B1341
B1340
B6348
B1339
B6347
B6346
B6341
60
189
211
315
169
101

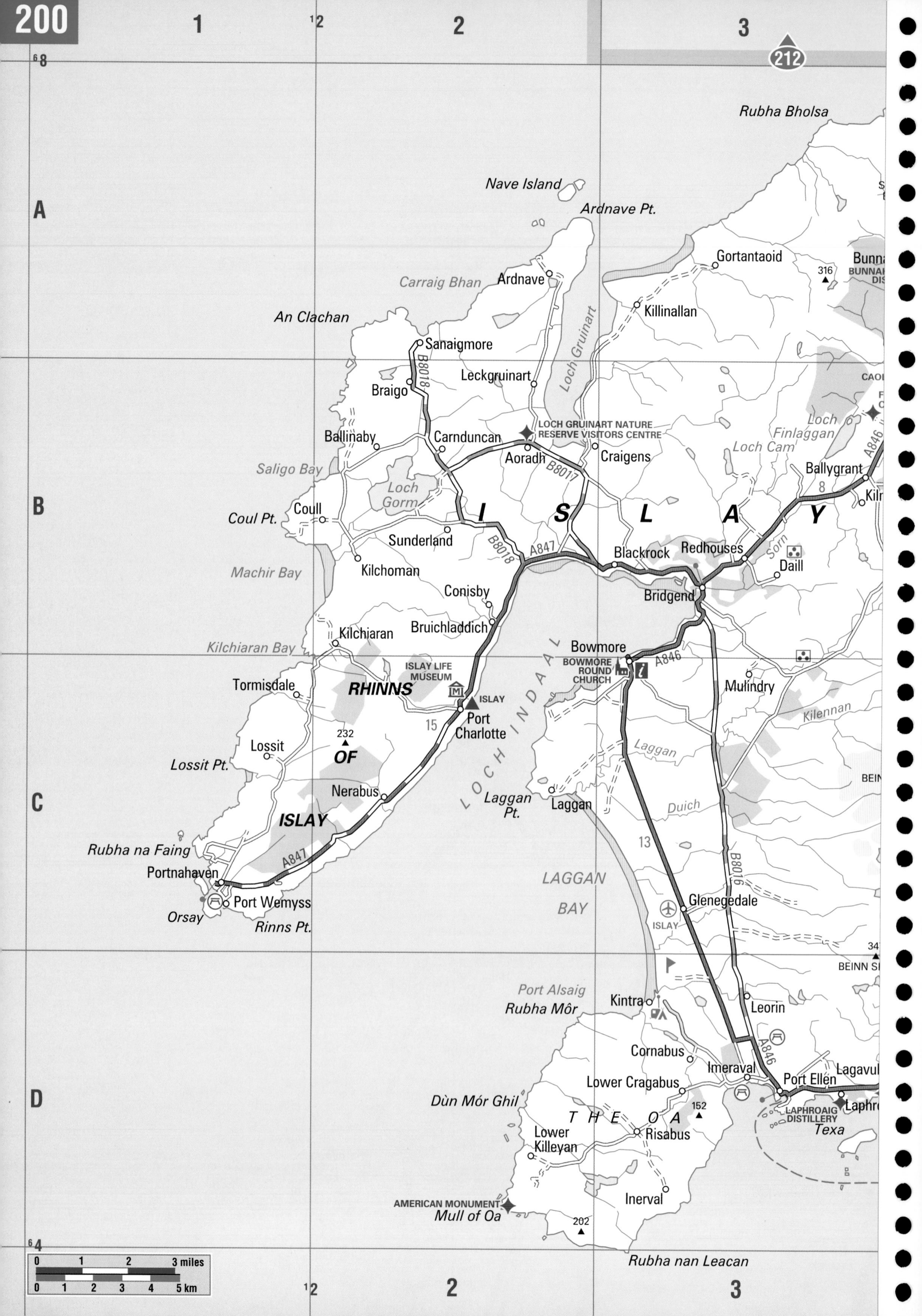
212
Rubha Bholsa
Nave Island
Ardnave Pt.
Ardnave
Carraig Bhan
An Clachan
Gortantaoid
Killinallan
Loch Gruinart
Sanaigmore
Braigo
Leckgruinart
Ballinaby
Carnduncan
LOCH GRUINART NATURE RESERVE VISITORS CENTRE
Aoradh
Craigens
Saligo Bay
Loch Gorm
Coul Pt.
Coull
Sunderland
I S L A Y
Machir Bay
Kilchoman
Blackrock
Redhouses
Daill
Bridgend
Conisby
Bruichladdich
Kilchiaran
Kilchiaran Bay
Bowmore
BOWMORE ROUND CHURCH
ISLAY LIFE MUSEUM
Tormisdale
RHINNS
ISLAY
Port Charlotte
Lossit
OF
Lossit Pt.
Nerabus
LOCH INDAAL
Laggan Pt.
Laggan
Mulindry
Kilennan
Duich
ISLAY
Rubha na Faing
Portnahaven
Port Wemyss
Orsay
Rinns Pt.
LAGGAN BAY
Glenegedale
Loch Finlaggan
Loch Cam
Ballygrant
Port Alsaig
Rubha Môr
Kintra
Leorin
Cornabus
Imeraval
Lower Cragabus
Port Ellen
Lagavul
Dùn Mór Ghil
THE OA
Risabus
Lower Killeyan
LAPHROAIG DISTILLERY
Texa
Inerval
AMERICAN MONUMENT
Mull of Oa
Rubha nan Leacan
3 miles
5 km

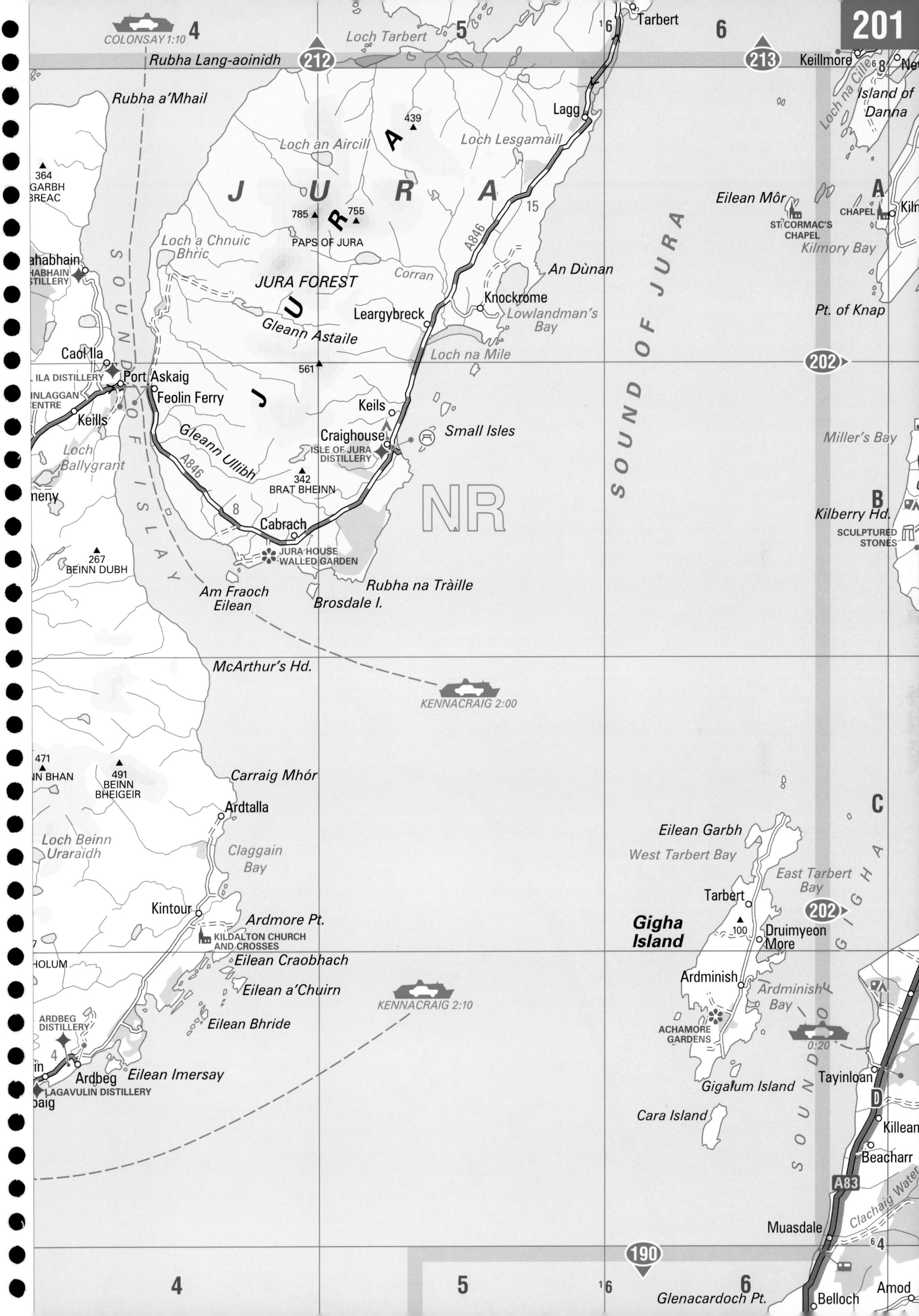

COLONSAY 1:10
4
5
6
Loch Tarbert
Tarbert
Rubha Lang-aoinidh
212
213
Keillmore
Rubha a'Mhail
Island of Danna
Loch na Cille
Lagg
439
Loch an Aircill
Loch Lesgamaill
364
GARBH BREAC
JURA
785
755
PAPS OF JURA
Eilean Mòr
ST CORMAC'S CHAPEL
CHAPEL
A
Kilmory Bay
Loch a Chnuic Bhric
A846
15
Corran
An Dùnan
JURA FOREST
Knockrome
Lowlandman's Bay
Leargybreck
Gleann Astaile
Pt. of Knap
Caol Ila
Loch na Mile
561
202
Port Askaig
Feolin Ferry
Keils
Keills
Craighouse
Small Isles
ISLE OF JURA DISTILLERY
Loch Ballygrant
Gleann Ullibh
Miller's Bay
SOUND OF JURA
342
BRAT BHEINN
SOUND OF ISLAY
NR
B
8
Cabrach
Kilberry Hd.
SCULPTURED STONES
JURA HOUSE WALLED GARDEN
267
BEINN DUBH
Rubha na Tràille
Am Fraoch Eilean
Brosdale I.
McArthur's Hd.
KENNACRAIG 2:00
471
491
BEINN BHEIGEIR
Carraig Mhór
Ardtalla
C
Eilean Garbh
West Tarbert Bay
Loch Beinn Uraraidh
Claggain Bay
East Tarbert Bay
Tarbert
202
Kintour
Ardmore Pt.
100
Gigha Island
Druimyeon More
KILDALTON CHURCH AND CROSSES
Eilean Craobhach
Ardminish
Eilean a'Chuirn
Ardminish Bay
KENNACRAIG 2:10
ARDBEG DISTILLERY
Eilean Bhride
ACHAMORE GARDENS
0:20
4
Ardbeg
Eilean Imersay
Tayinloan
LAGAVULIN DISTILLERY
Gigalum Island
D
Cara Island
Killean
SOUND OF GIGHA
Beacharr
A83
Clachaig Water
Muasdale
4
190
5
6
Amod
Glenacardoch Pt.
Belloch

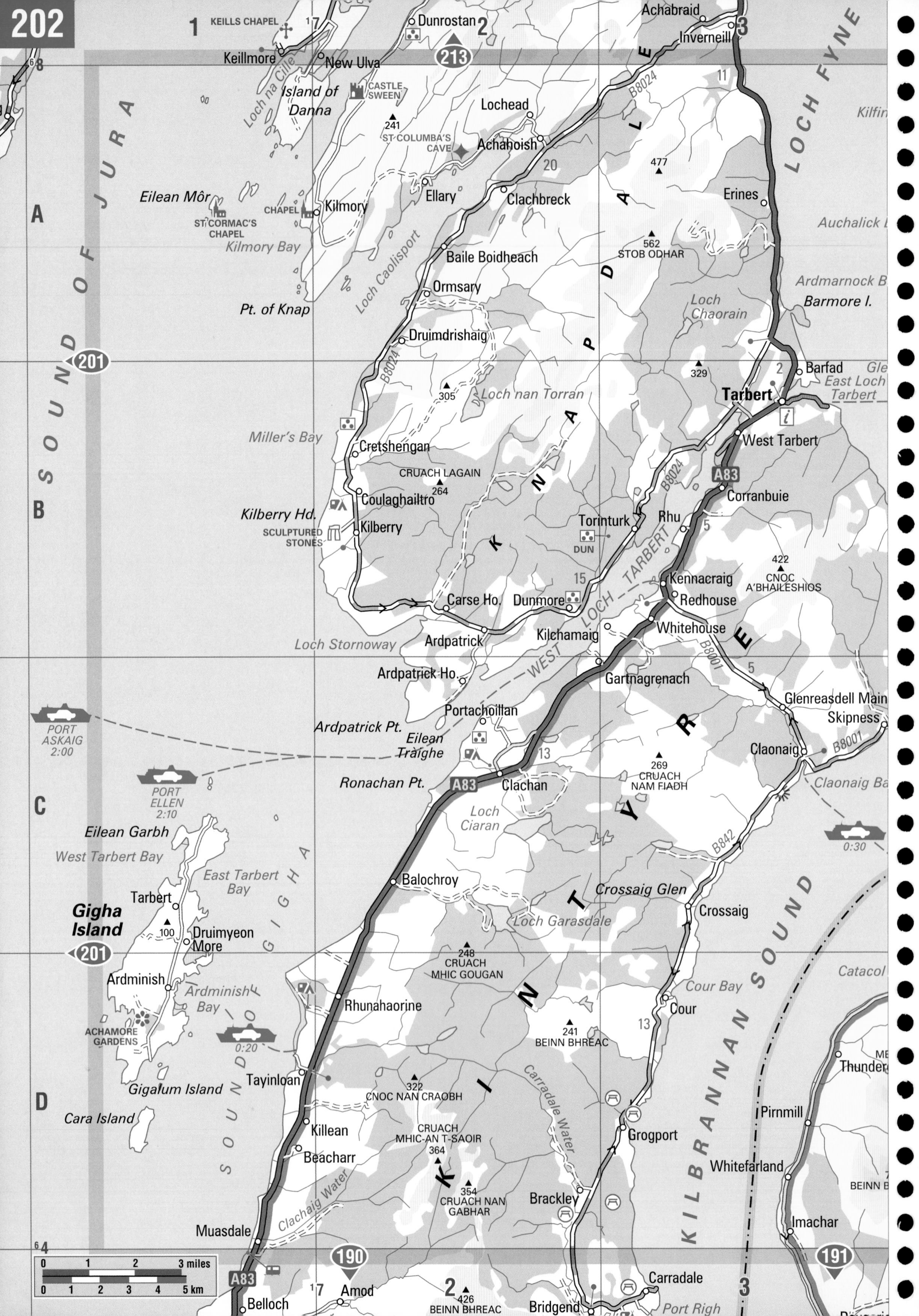

KEILLS CHAPEL
Dunrostan
213
Achabraid
Inverneill
Keillmore
New Ulva
Loch na Cille
Island of Danna
CASTLE SWEEN
Lochead
241
ST COLUMBA'S CAVE
Achahoish
B8024
LOCH FYNE
Kilfin
477
Eilean Mòr
Ellary
Clachbreck
Erines
CHAPEL
Kilmory
ST CORMAC'S CHAPEL
Kilmory Bay
Auchalick
562
STOB ODHAR
Baile Boidheach
Loch Caolisport
Ormsary
Ardmarnock B
Barmore I.
Pt. of Knap
Loch Chaorain
Druimdrishaig
SOUND OF JURA
201
329
Barfad
East Loch Tarbert
305
Loch nan Torran
Tarbert
KNAPDALE
Miller's Bay
West Tarbert
Cretshengan
CRUACH LAGAIN
264
A83
Corranbuie
Coulaghailtro
Kilberry Hd.
Torinturk
Rhu
SCULPTURED STONES
Kilberry
DUN
422
CNOC A'BHAILESHIOS
Kennacraig
Redhouse
Carse Ho.
Dunmore
WEST LOCH TARBERT
Whitehouse
Ardpatrick
Kilchamaig
Loch Stornoway
B8001
Ardpatrick Ho.
Gartnagrenach
Glenreasdell Main
Portachoillan
Skipness
PORT ASKAIG 2:00
Ardpatrick Pt.
Eilean Traighe
Claonaig
269
CRUACH NAM FIADH
PORT ELLEN 2:10
Ronachan Pt.
Clachan
Claonaig Ba
KINTYRE
Loch Ciaran
Eilean Garbh
West Tarbert Bay
B842
0:30
East Tarbert Bay
Balochroy
Crossaig Glen
Crossaig
Tarbert
Gigha Island
100
Druimyeon More
Loch Garasdale
KILBRANNAN SOUND
248
CRUACH MHIC GOUGAN
Catacol
Ardminish
Ardminish Bay
SOUND OF GIGHA
Rhunahaorine
Cour Bay
Cour
ACHAMORE GARDENS
241
BEINN BHREAC
0:20
Thunder
Gigalum Island
Tayinloan
322
CNOC NAN CRAOBH
Carradale Water
Cara Island
CRUACH MHIC-AN T-SAOIR
364
Killean
Grogport
Pirnmill
Beacharr
Whitefarland
354
CRUACH NAN GABHAR
Brackley
BEINN B
Clachaig Water
Muasdale
Imachar
190
191
0 1 2 3 miles
0 1 2 3 4 5 km
A83
Carradale
Amod
426
BEINN BHREAC
Belloch
Bridgend
Port Righ

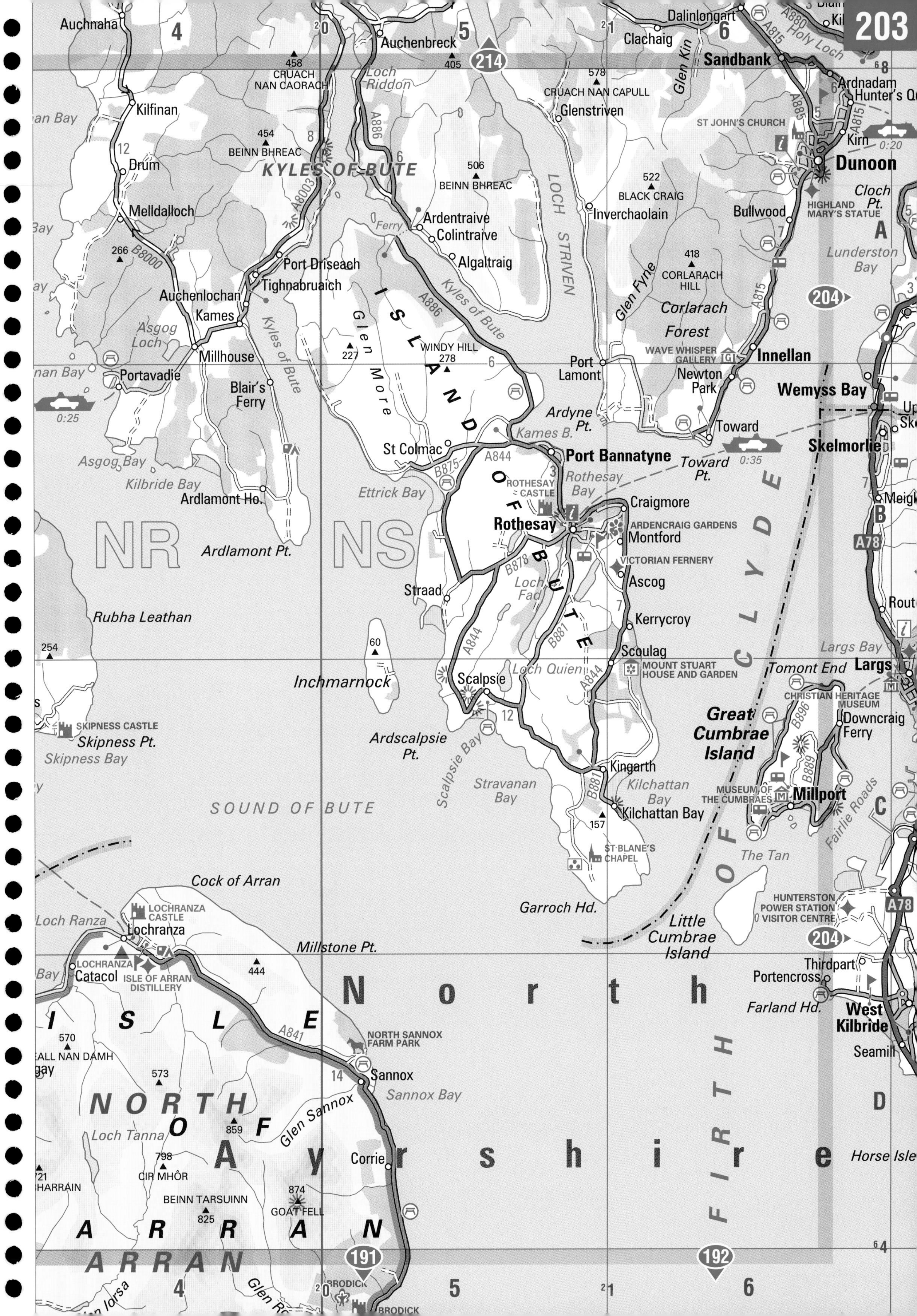
Auchnaha
Auchenbreck
Dalinlongart
Clachaig
Sandbank
Holy Loch
Ardnadam
CRUACH NAN CAORACH
Loch Riddon
CRUACH NAN CAPULL
Glenstriven
Glen Kin
ST JOHN'S CHURCH
Kirn
Dunoon
Kilfinan
BEINN BHREAC
KYLES OF BUTE
Drum
Melldalloch
Ardentraive
Colintraive
Algaltraig
LOCH STRIVEN
Inverchaolain
BLACK CRAIG
Bullwood
HIGHLAND MARY'S STATUE
Cloch Pt.
Lunderston Bay
Port Driseach
Tighnabruaich
Auchenlochan
Kames
Asgog Loch
Millhouse
Portavadie
Blair's Ferry
Kyles of Bute
ISLAND OF BUTE
Glen More
WINDY HILL
CORLARACH HILL
Glen Fyne
Corlarach Forest
WAVE WHISPER GALLERY
Innellan
Port Lamont
Newton Park
Wemyss Bay
Toward
Ardyne Pt.
Kames B.
Port Bannatyne
Toward Pt.
Skelmorlie
St Colmac
Asgog Bay
Kilbride Bay
Ardlamont Ho.
Ettrick Bay
Rothesay Bay
ROTHESAY CASTLE
Rothesay
Craigmore
ARDENCRAIG GARDENS
Montford
VICTORIAN FERNERY
Ascog
NR
NS
Ardlamont Pt.
Straad
Loch Fad
Kerrycroy
Scoulag
MOUNT STUART HOUSE AND GARDEN
Rubha Leathan
Inchmarnock
Scalpsie
Loch Quien
Largs Bay
Largs
Tomont End
CHRISTIAN HERITAGE MUSEUM
Downcraig Ferry
Great Cumbrae Island
FIRTH OF CLYDE
SKIPNESS CASTLE
Skipness Pt.
Skipness Bay
Ardscalpsie Pt.
Scalpsie Bay
Stravanan Bay
Kingarth
Kilchattan Bay
MUSEUM OF THE CUMBRAES
Millport
Fairlie Roads
SOUND OF BUTE
ST BLANE'S CHAPEL
The Tan
Cock of Arran
Garroch Hd.
HUNTERSTON POWER STATION VISITOR CENTRE
Little Cumbrae Island
Loch Ranza
LOCHRANZA CASTLE
Lochranza
Millstone Pt.
Catacol
ISLE OF ARRAN DISTILLERY
Thirdpart
Portencross
Farland Hd.
West Kilbride
North Ayrshire
ISLE OF ARRAN
NORTH SANNOX FARM PARK
Sannox
Sannox Bay
Seamill
NORTH
Loch Tanna
Glen Sannox
Corrie
CIR MHÒR
BEINN TARSUINN
GOAT FELL
Horse Isle
BRODICK
Glen Iorsa

Helensburgh
Dunoon
Gourock
Greenock
PORT GLASGOW
ALEXANDRIA
Kilmacolm
Bridge of Weir
Wemyss Bay
Skelmorlie
Largs
Lochwinnoch
Kilbirnie
Beith
Fairlie
Millport
Great Cumbrae Island
Little Cumbrae Island
West Kilbride
Dalry
Kilwinning
Ardrossan
Saltcoats
Stevenston
Irvine
Dreghorn
FIRTH OF CLYDE
Inverclyde
Renfrewshire
North Ayrshire
CLYDE-MUIRSHIEL REGIONAL PARK
NS

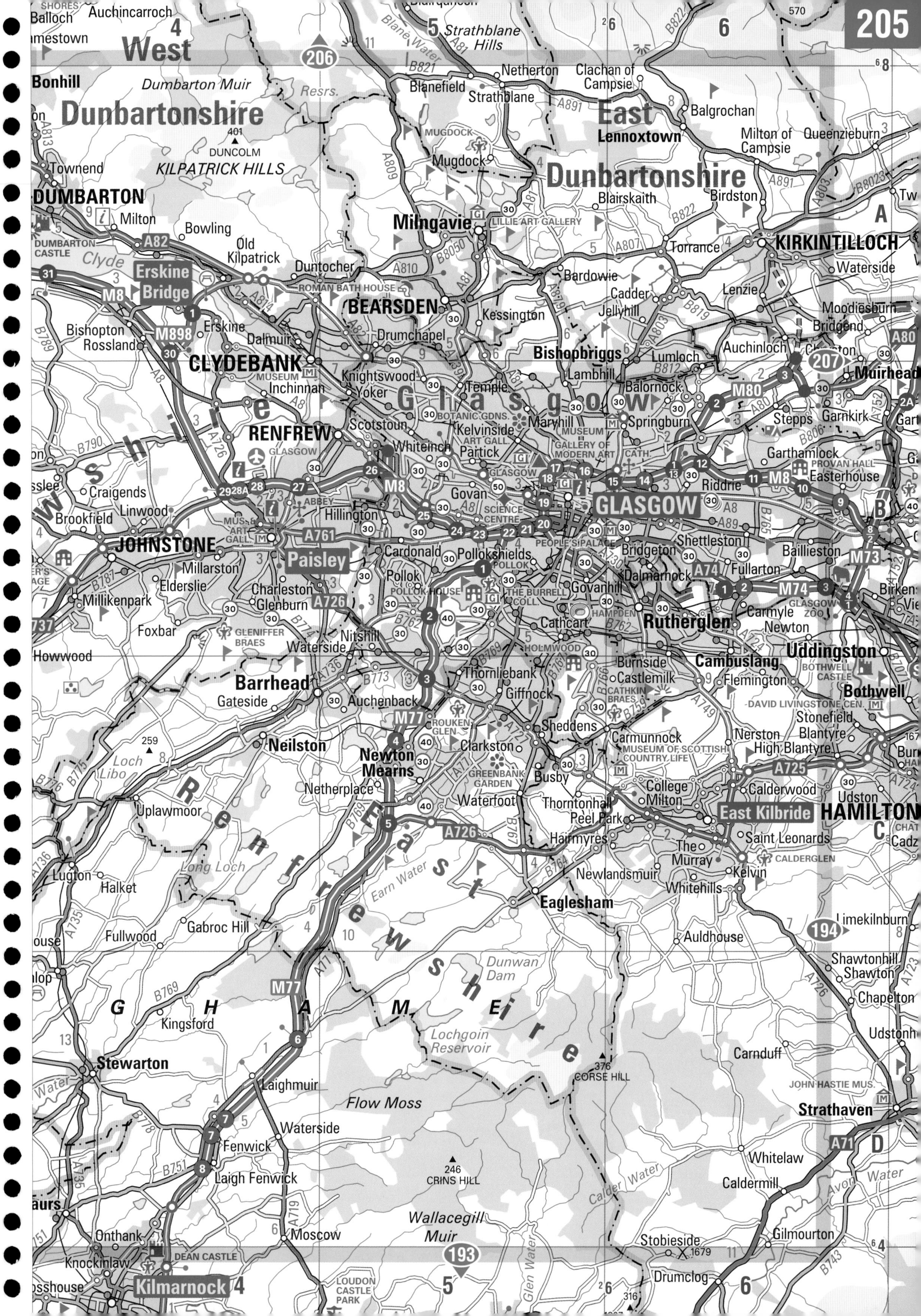
Balloch
Auchincarroch
West
Dunbartonshire
206
Strathblane Hills
Bonhill
Dumbarton Muir
Resrs.
Blanefield
Netherton
Clachan of Campsie
Strathblane
East
Balgrochan
Lennoxtown
Milton of Campsie
Queenzieburn
401
DUNCOLM
KILPATRICK HILLS
MUGDOCK
Mugdock
Dunbartonshire
Townend
DUMBARTON
Milton
Blairskaith
Birdston
LILLIE ART GALLERY
Milngavie
Bowling
Old Kilpatrick
DUMBARTON CASTLE
Clyde
Erskine Bridge
Duntocher
Torrance
KIRKINTILLOCH
Waterside
ROMAN BATH HOUSE
BEARSDEN
Bardowie
Cadder
Jellyhill
Lenzie
Kessington
Moodiesburn
Bridgend
Bishopton
Rossland
Erskine
Dalmuir
Drumchapel
Bishopbriggs
Lumloch
Auchinloch
CLYDEBANK
MUSEUM
Knightswood
Temple
Lambhill
Balornock
207
Muirhead
Inchinnan
Yoker
Glasgow
Stepps
Garnkirk
BOTANIC GDNS.
Maryhill
MUSEUM
Springburn
RENFREW
Scotstoun
Kelvinside
ART GALL.
GALLERY OF MODERN ART
Whiteinch
Partick
CATH.
Garthamlock
PROVAN HALL
GLASGOW
Easterhouse
Riddrie
Craigends
Govan
GLASGOW
Linwood
ABBEY
Hillington
SCIENCE CENTRE
Brookfield
JOHNSTONE
MUS. & ART GALL.
Paisley
PEOPLE'S PALACE
Shettleston
Baillieston
Cardonald
Pollokshields
POLLOK
Bridgeton
Millarston
Dalmarnock
Fullarton
Elderslie
Charleston
Pollok
POLLOK HOUSE
THE BURRELL COLL.
Govanhill
Birkenshaw
Millikenpark
Glenburn
HAMPDEN
Carmyle
GLASGOW ZOO
Newton
Rutherglen
Foxbar
Cathcart
GLENIFFER BRAES
Nitshill
Howwood
Waterside
HOLMWOOD
Burnside
Cambuslang
Uddingston
Castlemilk
BOTHWELL CASTLE
Thornliebank
Flemington
Barrhead
CATHKIN BRAES
Bothwell
Gateside
Auchenback
Giffnock
DAVID LIVINGSTONE CEN.
ROUKEN GLEN
Stonefield
Sheddens
Blantyre
259
Neilston
Carmunnock
Nerston
Clarkston
MUSEUM OF SCOTTISH COUNTRY LIFE
High Blantyre
Loch Libo
Newton Mearns
Busby
GREENBANK GARDEN
College Milton
Calderwood
Netherplace
Waterfoot
Udston
Uplawmoor
Thorntonhall
Peel Park
East Kilbride
HAMILTON
Renfrewshire
East
Hairmyres
The Murray
Saint Leonards
CALDERGLEN
Long Loch
Lugton
Earn Water
Newlandsmuir
Kelvin
Halket
Whitehills
Eaglesham
Limekilnburn
194
Gabroc Hill
Fullwood
Auldhouse
Dunwan Dam
Shawtonhill
Shawton
Chapelton
Kingsford
Lochgoin Reservoir
Udstonhead
376
CORSE HILL
Carnduff
Stewarton
Laighmuir
JOHN HASTIE MUS.
Flow Moss
Strathaven
Waterside
Fenwick
Whitelaw
Laigh Fenwick
246
CRINS HILL
Calder Water
Caldermill
Avon Water
Wallacegill Muir
Onthank
Moscow
Gilmourton
193
Stobieside
Knockinlaw
DEAN CASTLE
Drumclog
Kilmarnock
LOUDON CASTLE PARK
Glen Water
M8
M898
M77
M80
M73
M74
A82
A761
A726
A725
A71
A74
A8
A80

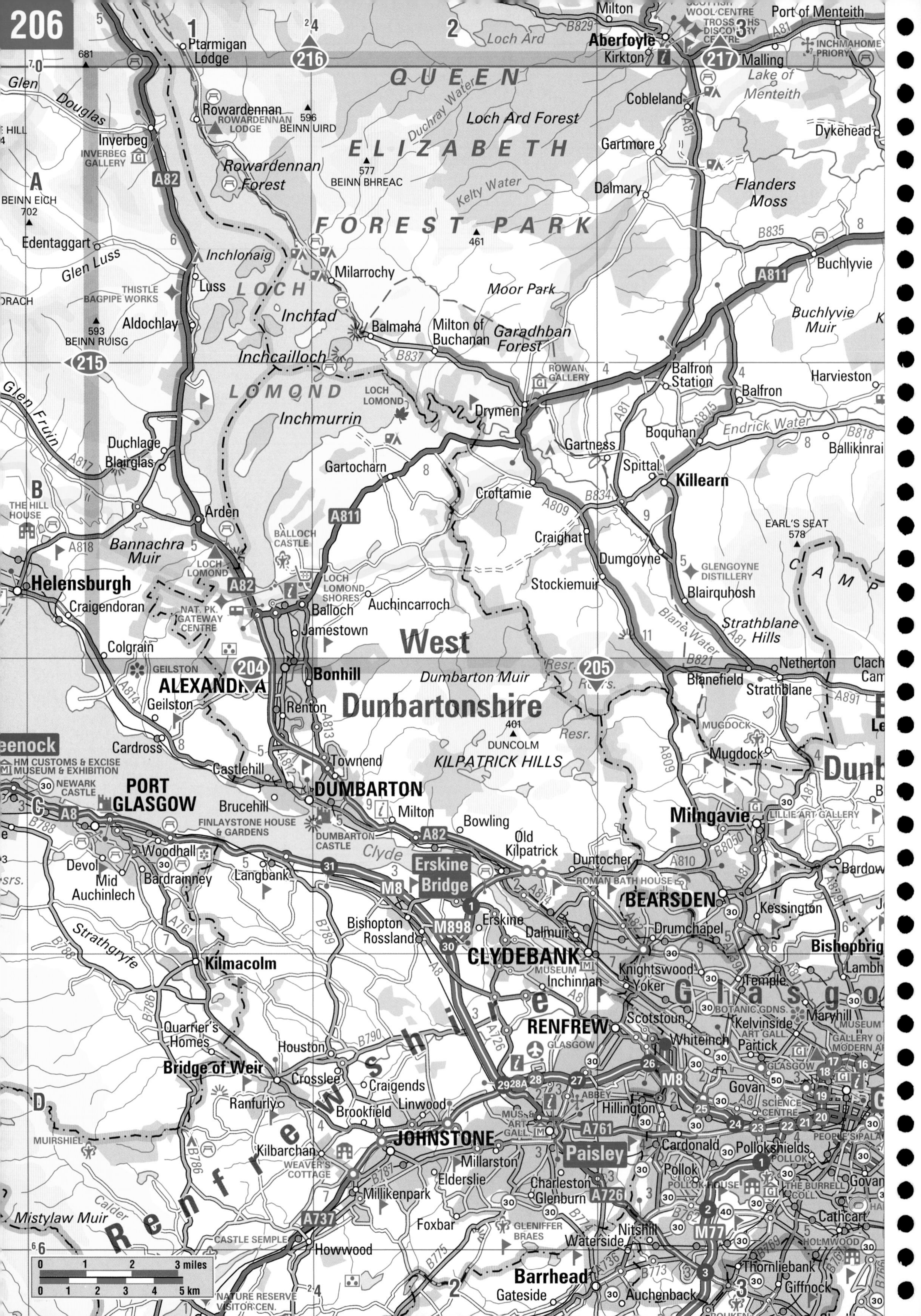
Ptarmigan Lodge
216
Loch Ard
Milton
Aberfoyle
Kirkton
SCOTTISH WOOL CENTRE
217
Port of Menteith
INCHMAHOME PRIORY
Malling
Lake of Menteith
Glen Douglas
QUEEN ELIZABETH FOREST PARK
Rowardennan
ROWARDENNAN LODGE
596 BEINN UIRD
Duchray Water
Loch Ard Forest
Cobleland
Inverbeg
INVERBEG GALLERY
577 BEINN BHREAC
Gartmore
Dykehead
A82
Rowardennan Forest
Kelty Water
Dalmary
Flanders Moss
BEINN EICH 702
Edentaggart
461
B835
Buchlyvie
Inchlonaig
Glen Luss
Luss
LOCH LOMOND
Milarrochy
A811
THISTLE BAGPIPE WORKS
Moor Park
Inchfad
Buchlyvie Muir
Aldochlay
593 BEINN RUISG
Balmaha
Milton of Buchanan
Garadhban Forest
215
Inchcailloch
B837
ROWAN GALLERY
Balfron Station
Balfron
Harvieston
Glen Fruin
LOCH LOMOND
Inchmurrin
Drymen
A875
Endrick Water
B818
Boquhan
Ballikinrain
Duchlage
Blairglas
Gartness
A817
Gartocharn
Spittal
Killearn
Croftamie
B834
A809
THE HILL HOUSE
Arden
A811
Craighat
EARL'S SEAT 578
A818
Bannachra Muir
BALLOCH CASTLE
Dumgoyne
GLENGOYNE DISTILLERY
CAMPSIE FELLS
Helensburgh
LOCH LOMOND
A82
LOCH LOMOND SHORES
Stockiemuir
Craigendoran
NAT. PK. GATEWAY CENTRE
Balloch
Auchincarroch
Blairquhosh
Jamestown
West
Blane Water
Strathblane Hills
Colgrain
GEILSTON
204
Bonhill
Resr.
205
B821
Netherton
Blanefield
Strathblane
ALEXANDRIA
Dumbarton Muir
A814
Geilston
Renton
Dunbartonshire
A891
A813
401 DUNCOLM
Resr.
MUGDOCK
Greenock
Cardross
Mugdock
HM CUSTOMS & EXCISE MUSEUM & EXHIBITION
Castlehill
Townend
KILPATRICK HILLS
A809
NEWARK CASTLE
PORT GLASGOW
A812
DUMBARTON
Brucehill
A8
FINLAYSTONE HOUSE & GARDENS
Milton
Bowling
Milngavie
LILLIE ART GALLERY
B788
DUMBARTON CASTLE
A82
Old Kilpatrick
B8050
Woodhall
Clyde
Erskine Bridge
Duntocher
A810
Devol
Mid Auchinlech
Bardrainney
Langbank
M8
ROMAN BATH HOUSE
Bardowie
BEARSDEN
Kessington
A761
Bishopton
Rossland
M898
Erskine
Dalmuir
Drumchapel
B789
Strathgryfe
B788
CLYDEBANK
Bishopbriggs
Kilmacolm
MUSEUM
Knightswood
Temple
Inchinnan
Yoker
Glasgow
B786
A8
Scotstoun
BOTANIC GDNS.
Maryhill
Kelvinside
Quarrier's Homes
RENFREW
Whiteinch
ART GALL.
Partick
GALLERY OF MODERN ART
Houston
B790
GLASGOW
A726
Bridge of Weir
Crosslee
Renfrewshire
Craigends
M8
GLASGOW
Govan
ABBEY
Ranfurly
Linwood
Hillington
SCIENCE CENTRE
Brookfield
MUS. & ART GALL.
A761
JOHNSTONE
PEOPLE'S PALACE
MUIRSHIEL
Kilbarchan
Paisley
Cardonald
Pollokshields
B786
WEAVER'S COTTAGE
Millarston
POLLOK
B787
Pollok
Elderslie
Charleston
POLLOK HOUSE
THE BURRELL COLL.
Govanhill
Calder
Millikenpark
Glenburn
A726
Mistylaw Muir
A737
Foxbar
GLENIFFER BRAES
B774
Nitshill
M77
Cathcart
CASTLE SEMPLE
Howwood
Waterside
B762
B769
HOLMWOOD
Thornliebank
B773
A736
B775
Barrhead
Giffnock
Gateside
Auchenback
NATURE RESERVE VISITOR CEN.
0 1 2 3 miles
0 1 2 3 4 5 km

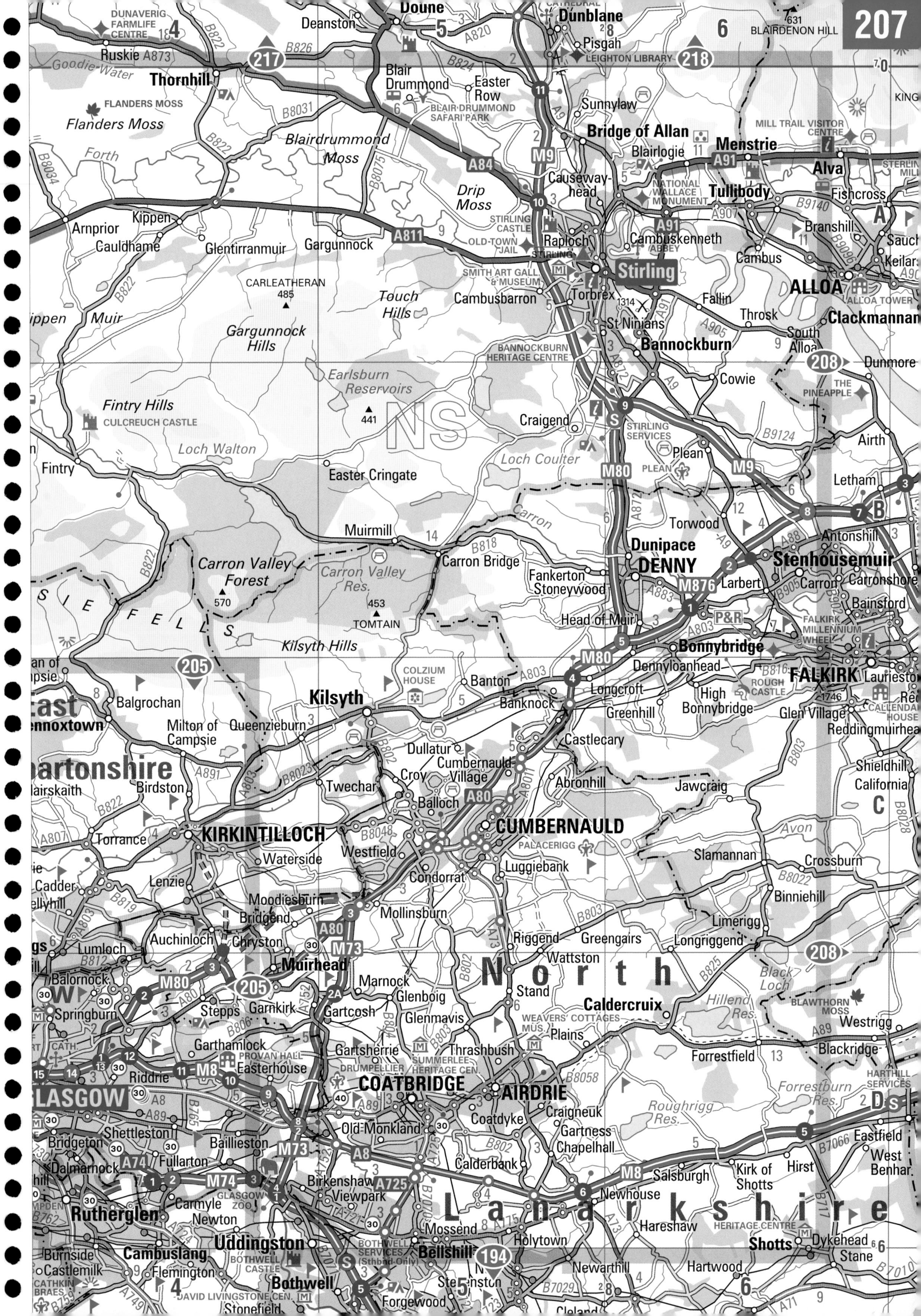
Doune
Deanston
Dunblane
Pisgah
BLAIRDENON HILL
DUNAVERIG FARMLIFE CENTRE
Ruskie
Goodie Water
Thornhill
LEIGHTON LIBRARY
217
218
Blair Drummond
Easter Row
BLAIR DRUMMOND SAFARI PARK
Sunnylaw
FLANDERS MOSS
Flanders Moss
Blairdrummond Moss
Forth
Bridge of Allan
Menstrie
MILL TRAIL VISITOR CENTRE
Blairlogie
Alva
Causewayhead
NATIONAL WALLACE MONUMENT
Tullibody
Fishcross
Drip Moss
Arnprior
Kippen
Cauldhame
Glentirranmuir
Gargunnock
STIRLING CASTLE
OLD TOWN JAIL
Raploch
Cambuskenneth
ABBEY
Branshill
Cambus
SMITH ART GALL & MUSEUM
Stirling
ALLOA
ALLOA TOWER
CARLEATHERAN
485
Touch Hills
Cambusbarron
Torbrex
1314
Fallin
Throsk
Clackmannan
Muir
Gargunnock Hills
St Ninians
Bannockburn
South Alloa
BANNOCKBURN HERITAGE CENTRE
208
Dunmore
Earlsburn Reservoirs
Cowie
THE PINEAPPLE
Fintry Hills
CULCREUCH CASTLE
441
NS
Craigend
STIRLING SERVICES
Airth
Loch Walton
Fintry
Loch Coulter
Plean
PLEAN
Easter Cringate
Letham
Carron
Torwood
Muirmill
Antonshill
Carron Bridge
Dunipace
DENNY
Stenhousemuir
Carron Valley Forest
Carron Valley Res.
Fankerton
Stoneywood
Larbert
Carron
Carronshore
570
453
TOMTAIN
Head of Muir
Bainsford
FALKIRK MILLENNIUM WHEEL
Kilsyth Hills
Bonnybridge
205
COLZIUM HOUSE
Banton
Dennyloanhead
FALKIRK
Laurieston
ROUGH CASTLE
Balgrochan
Kilsyth
Banknock
Longcroft
High Bonnybridge
Milton of Campsie
Queenzieburn
Greenhill
Glen Village
CALLENDAR HOUSE
Reddingmuirhead
Castlecary
Dullatur
Cumbernauld Village
Croy
Twechar
Abronhill
Jawcraig
Shieldhill
California
Birdston
Balloch
Torrance
KIRKINTILLOCH
CUMBERNAULD
Westfield
PALACERIGG
Avon
Waterside
Luggiebank
Slamannan
Crossburn
Lenzie
Condorrat
Binniehill
Moodiesburn
Bridgend
Mollinsburn
Limerigg
Auchinloch
Chryston
Riggend
Greengairs
Longriggend
Lumloch
Muirhead
Wattston
North
Balornock
Marnock
Stand
Black Loch
Springburn
Stepps
Garnkirk
Gartcosh
Glenboig
Caldercruix
Hillend Res.
BLAWTHORN MOSS
Glenmavis
WEAVERS' COTTAGES MUS.
Plains
Westrigg
Garthamlock
PROVAN HALL
Easterhouse
Gartsherrie
SUMMERLEE HERITAGE CEN.
Thrashbush
Forrestfield
Blackridge
Riddrie
DRUMPELLIER
HARTHILL SERVICES
GLASGOW
COATBRIDGE
AIRDRIE
Forrestburn Res.
Roughrigg Res.
Shettleston
Old Monkland
Coatdyke
Craigneuk
Gartness
Eastfield
Bridgeton
Baillieston
Chapelhall
West Benhar
Dalmarnock
Fullarton
Calderbank
Kirk of Shotts
Hirst
Birkenshaw
Salsburgh
Viewpark
Newhouse
Rutherglen
Carmyle
GLASGOW ZOO
Newton
Lanarkshire
Mossend
Hareshaw
HERITAGE CENTRE
Uddingston
Holytown
Shotts
Dykehead
Stane
Burnside
Cambuslang
BOTHWELL SERVICES
Bellshill
194
Castlemilk
Flemington
BOTHWELL CASTLE
Newarthill
Hartwood
CATHKIN BRAES
Bothwell
Stevenston
DAVID LIVINGSTONE CEN.
Forgewood
Stonefield
Cleland

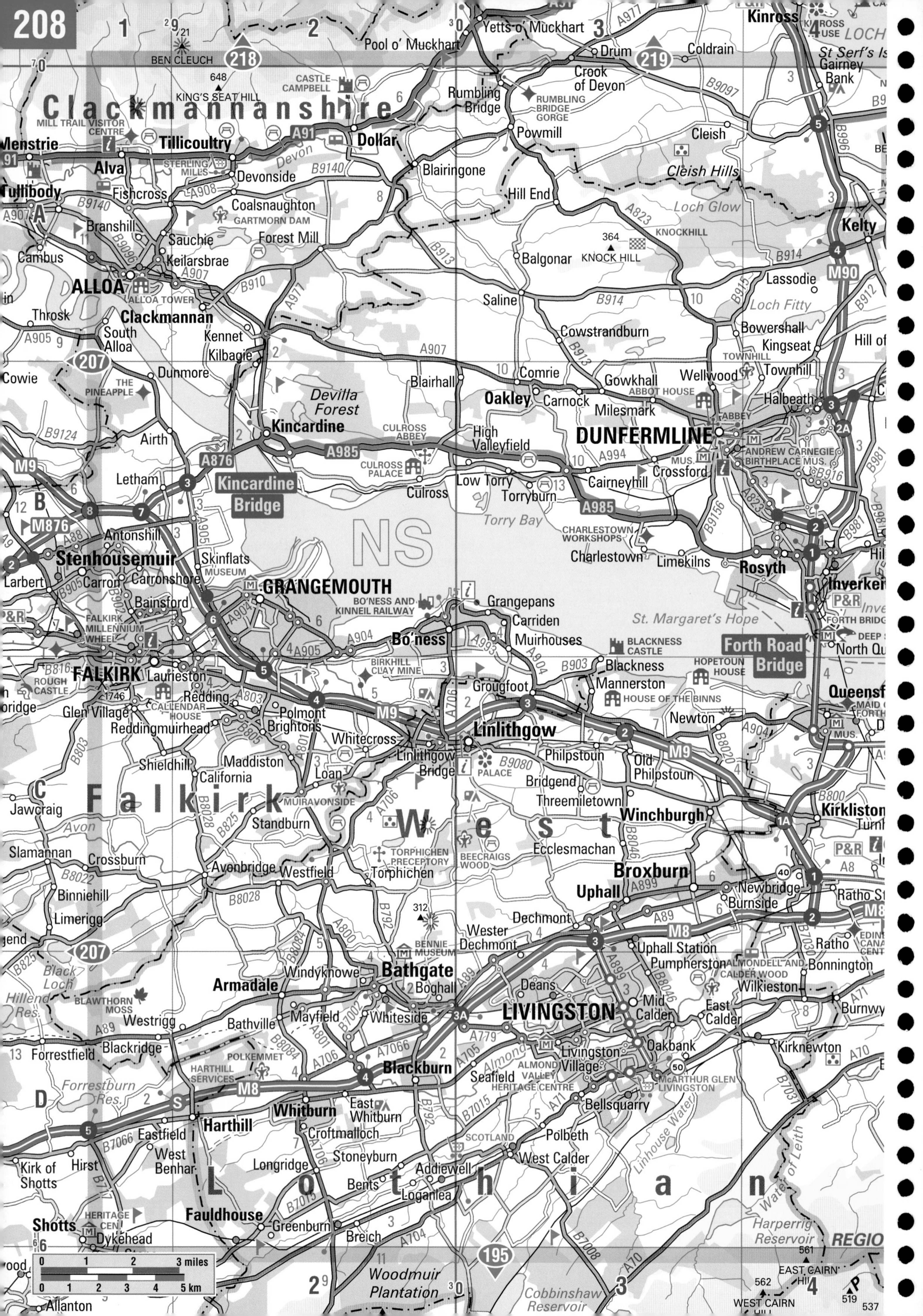
Clackmannanshire
Falkirk
West Lothian
Tillicoultry
Alva
Dollar
ALLOA
Clackmannan
Kincardine
Kincardine Bridge
GRANGEMOUTH
FALKIRK
Stenhousemuir
Bo'ness
Linlithgow
DUNFERMLINE
Rosyth
Forth Road Bridge
Kinross
Kelty
Oakley
Bathgate
Armadale
LIVINGSTON
Broxburn
Uphall
Winchburgh
Blackburn
Whitburn
Harthill
Fauldhouse
Shotts
Kirkliston
Queensferry
NS
BEN CLEUCH
KING'S SEAT HILL
KNOCK HILL
Devilla Forest
Torry Bay
St. Margaret's Hope
Cleish Hills
Loch Glow
Loch Fitty
M9
M8
M90
M876
A985
A876
A91
0
1
2
3 miles
0
1
2
3
4
5 km

GLENROTHES
Leslie
Markinch
Leven
Methil
Buckhaven
East Wemyss
Coaltown of Wemyss
West Wemyss
Dysart
Pathhead
Kirkcaldy
Linktown
Kinghorn
Pettycur
Burntisland
Aberdour
Dalgety Bay
Cowdenbeath
Lochgelly
Lochore
Cardenden
Ballingry
Auchtertool
Balmule
Donibristle
Inchkeith
Inchcolm
Inchmickery
Cramond I.
FIRTH OF FORTH
NT
Largo Bay
Aberlady Bay
Gosford Bay
ZEEBRUGGE 17:30
EDINBURGH
Leith
Newhaven
Granton
Portobello
Joppa
Musselburgh
Prestonpans
Cockenzie and Port Seton
Tranent
Dalkeith
Bonnyrigg and Lasswade
Loanhead
Roslin
Penicuik
Newtongrange
Gorebridge
Currie
Balerno
Edinburgh
Midlothian
PENTLAND HILLS
Nine Mile Burn
Howgate
Temple
Middleton
Fala Moor
Pathhead
Humbie
Pencaitland
Ormiston
Macmerry
Longniddry
Craigielaw

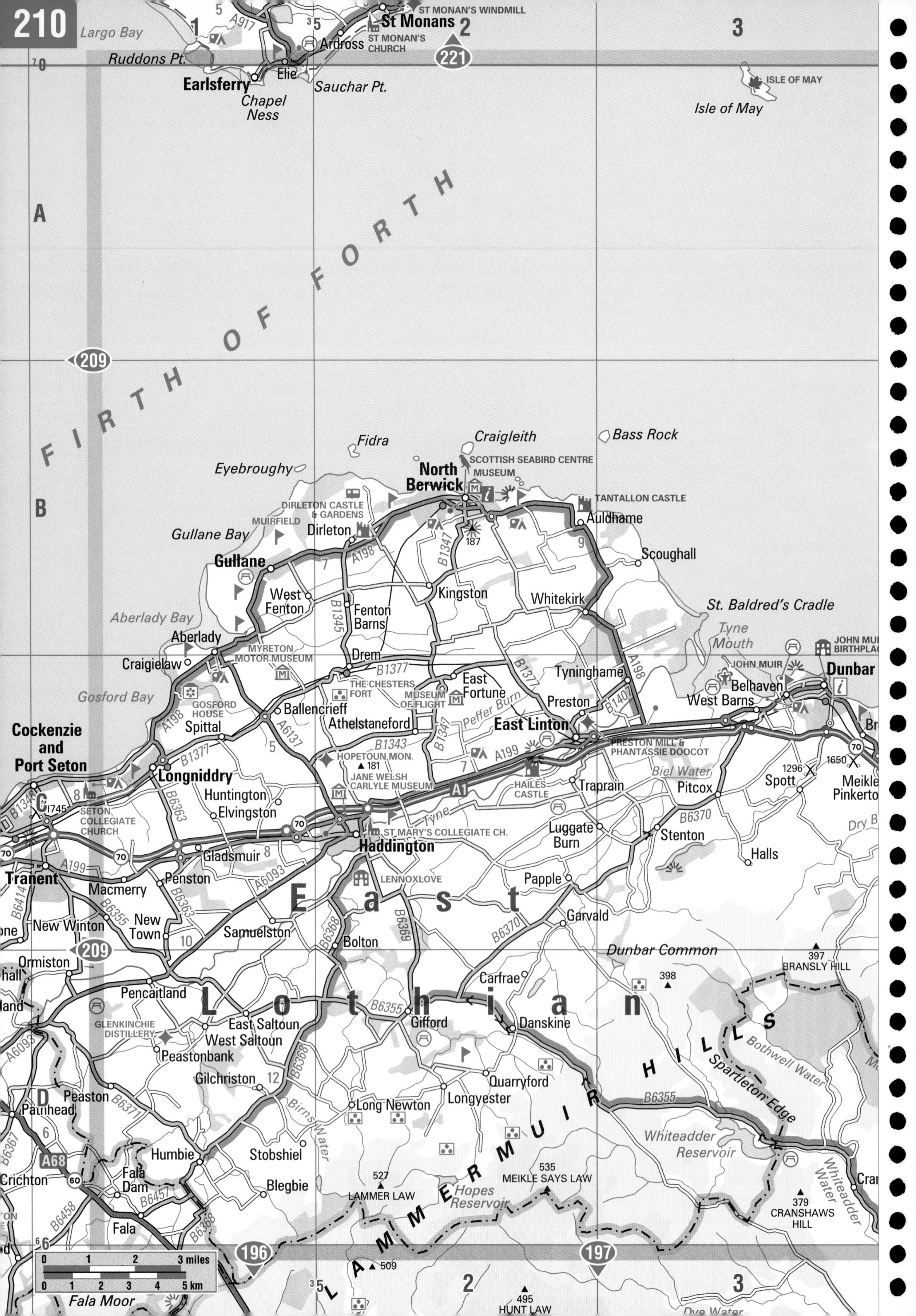

Largo Bay
St Monans
ST MONAN'S WINDMILL
ST MONAN'S CHURCH
Ardross
221
Ruddons Pt.
Elie
Earlsferry
Chapel Ness
Sauchar Pt.
ISLE OF MAY
Isle of May
FIRTH OF FORTH
209
Fidra
Craigleith
Bass Rock
Eyebroughy
SCOTTISH SEABIRD CENTRE
MUSEUM
North Berwick
TANTALLON CASTLE
DIRLETON CASTLE & GARDENS
MUIRFIELD
Dirleton
Auldhame
Gullane Bay
Gullane
Scoughall
West Fenton
Fenton Barns
Kingston
Whitekirk
St. Baldred's Cradle
Aberlady Bay
Aberlady
Tyne Mouth
JOHN MUIR
Craigielaw
MYRETON MOTOR MUSEUM
Drem
Tyninghame
Dunbar
Gosford Bay
GOSFORD HOUSE
THE CHESTERS FORT
MUSEUM OF FLIGHT
East Fortune
Belhaven
West Barns
Ballencrieff
Preston
Cockenzie and Port Seton
Spittal
Athelstaneford
East Linton
PRESTON MILL & PHANTASSIE DOOCOT
HOPETOUN MON.
JANE WELSH CARLYLE MUSEUM
Longniddry
HAILES CASTLE
Traprain
Biel Water
Pitcox
Spott
Meikle Pinkerton
SETON COLLEGIATE CHURCH
Huntington
Elvingston
Luggate Burn
ST. MARY'S COLLEGIATE CH.
Stenton
Haddington
Gladsmuir
Tranent
Penston
Halls
Macmerry
LENNOXLOVE
Papple
East Lothian
New Winton
New Town
Samuelston
Garvald
Bolton
Dunbar Common
Ormiston
BRANSLY HILL
Carfrae
Pencaitland
East Saltoun
Gifford
Danskine
GLENKINCHIE DISTILLERY
West Saltoun
Peastonbank
Bothwell Water
Spartleton Edge
Gilchriston
Quarryford
LAMMERMUIR HILLS
Peaston
Pathhead
Long Newton
Longyester
Whiteadder Reservoir
Humbie
Stobshiel
Birns Water
Crichton
Fala Dam
Blegbie
LAMMER LAW
MEIKLE SAYS LAW
Hopes Reservoir
Fala
CRANSHAWS HILL
Whiteadder Water
Fala Moor
196
197
HUNT LAW
Dye Water

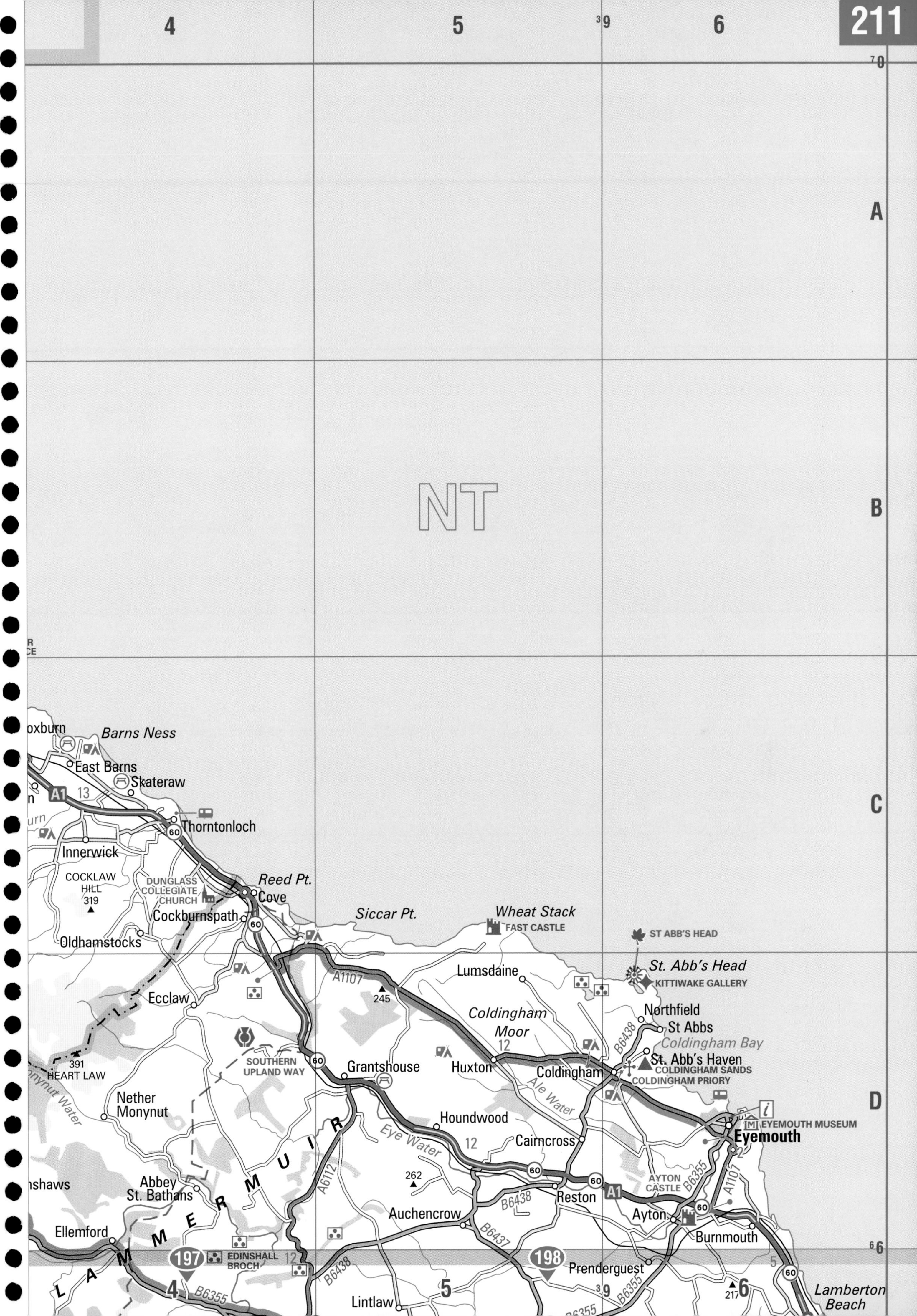
4
5
6
A
B
C
D
NT
Barns Ness
East Barns
Skateraw
Thorntonloch
Innerwick
COCKLAW HILL
319
DUNGLASS COLLEGIATE CHURCH
Reed Pt.
Cove
Cockburnspath
Oldhamstocks
Siccar Pt.
Wheat Stack
FAST CASTLE
ST ABB'S HEAD
St. Abb's Head
KITTIWAKE GALLERY
Lumsdaine
A1107
245
Ecclaw
Coldingham Moor
Northfield
St Abbs
Coldingham Bay
St. Abb's Haven
COLDINGHAM SANDS
COLDINGHAM PRIORY
391
HEART LAW
SOUTHERN UPLAND WAY
Grantshouse
Huxton
Coldingham
Ale Water
B6438
Nether Monynut
Monynut Water
Houndwood
Eye Water
Cairncross
EYEMOUTH MUSEUM
Eyemouth
262
A6112
Abbey St. Bathans
LAMMERMUIR
Auchencrow
B6438
Reston
A1
AYTON CASTLE
B6355
A1107
Ayton
Burnmouth
B6437
Ellemford
197
EDINSHALL BROCH
198
Prenderguest
B6355
217
Lamberton Beach
Lintlaw
B6438

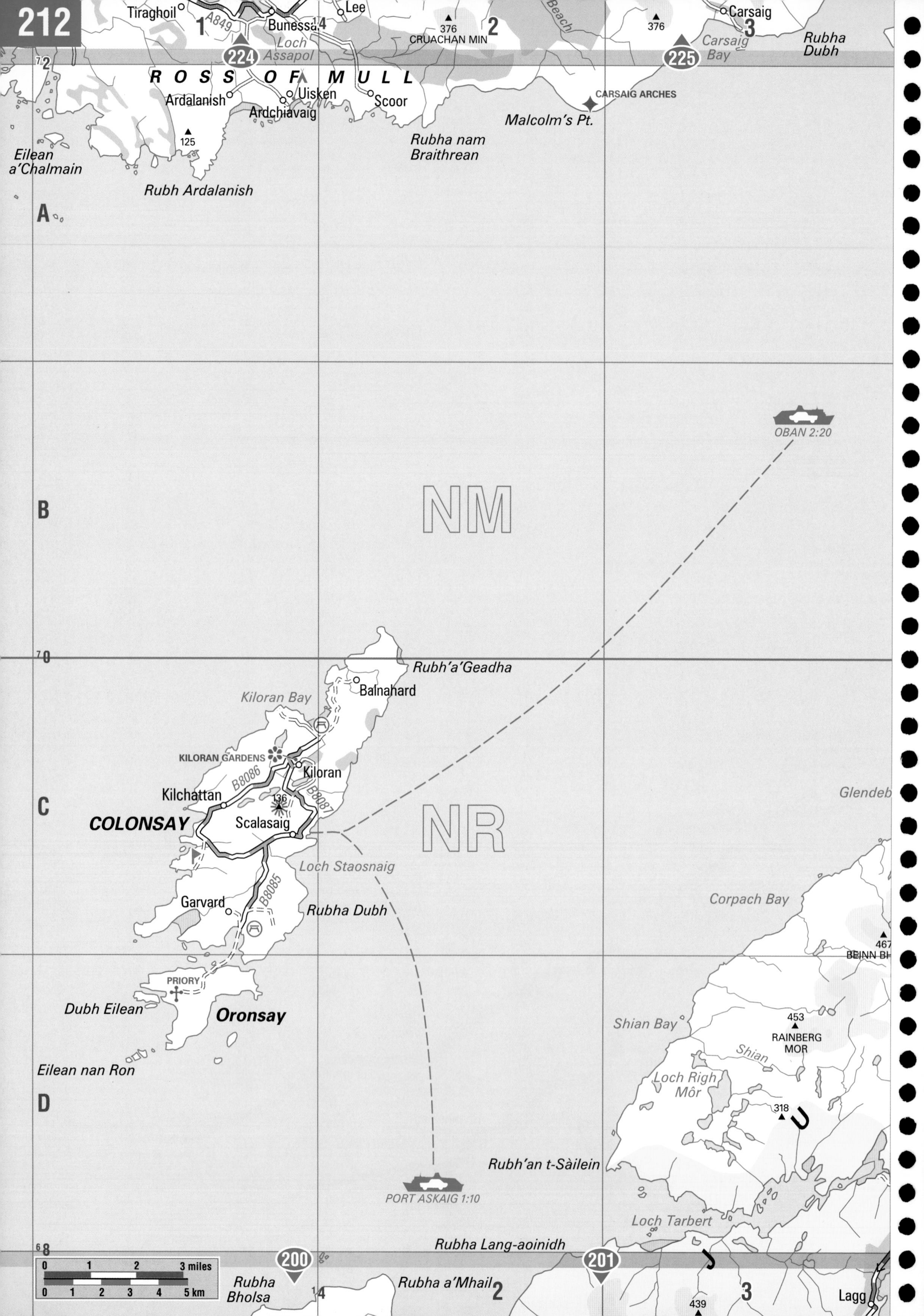
Tiraghoil
A849
Bunessan
Lee
376
CRUACHAN MIN
Beach
376
Carsaig
Carsaig Bay
Rubha Dubh
224
Loch Assapol
225
ROSS OF MULL
Ardalanish
Uisken
Ardchiavaig
Scoor
CARSAIG ARCHES
Malcolm's Pt.
125
Rubha nam Braithrean
Eilean a'Chalmain
Rubh Ardalanish
A
B
NM
OBAN 2:20
Rubh'a'Geadha
Balnahard
Kiloran Bay
KILORAN GARDENS
Kiloran
B8086
B8087
Kilchattan
136
C
COLONSAY
Scalasaig
NR
Glendeb
Loch Staosnaig
Corpach Bay
Garvard
B8085
Rubha Dubh
467
BEINN BH
PRIORY
Dubh Eilean
Oronsay
Shian Bay
453
RAINBERG MOR
Shian
Eilean nan Ron
Loch Righ Mòr
D
318
Rubh'an t-Sàilein
PORT ASKAIG 1:10
Loch Tarbert
Rubha Lang-aoinidh
0 1 2 3 miles
0 1 2 3 4 5 km
200
Rubha Bholsa
201
Rubha a'Mhail
2
3
439
Lagg

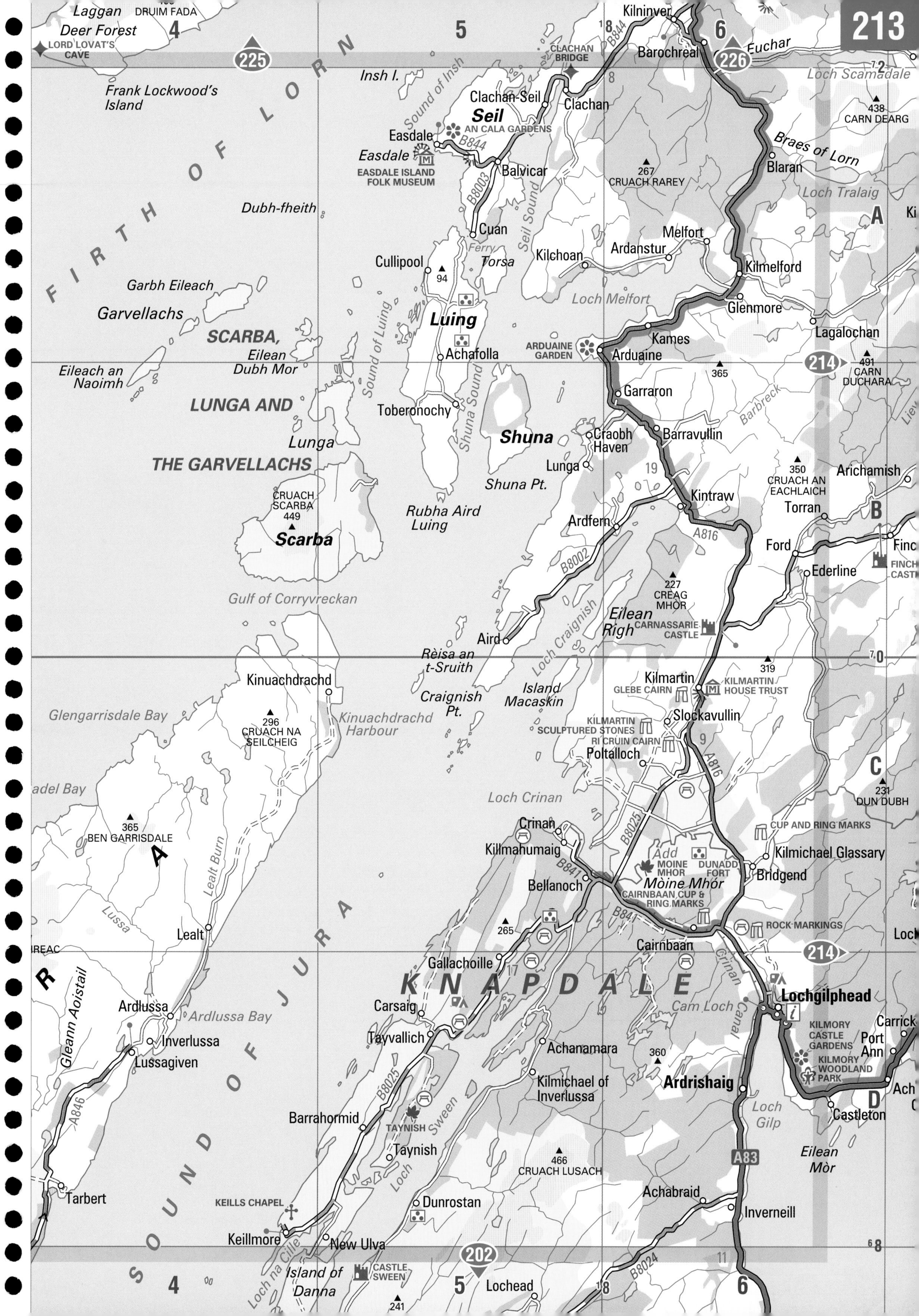
Laggan
DRUIM FADA
Deer Forest
LORD LOVAT'S CAVE
Frank Lockwood's Island
FIRTH OF LORN
Insh I.
Sound of Insh
CLACHAN BRIDGE
Kilninver
Barochreal
Euchar
Loch Scamadale
Clachan-Seil
Clachan
Seil
AN CALA GARDENS
Easdale
EASDALE ISLAND FOLK MUSEUM
Balvicar
438 CARN DEARG
Braes of Lorn
Blaran
267 CRUACH RAREY
Loch Tralaig
Dubh-fheith
Cuan
Seil Sound
Melfort
Ardanstur
Kilchoan
Ferry
Torsa
Cullipool
94
Kilmelford
Garbh Eileach
Garvellachs
Loch Melfort
Glenmore
Luing
Lagalochan
SCARBA, Eilean Dubh Mor
LUNGA AND THE GARVELLACHS
Eileach an Naoimh
Sound of Luing
Achafolla
ARDUAINE GARDEN
Arduaine
Kames
365
491 CARN DUCHARA
Toberonochy
Shuna Sound
Garraron
Barbreck
Shuna
Craobh Haven
Barravullin
Lunga
Shuna Pt.
350 CRUACH AN EACHLAICH
Arichamish
CRUACH SCARBA 449
Scarba
Rubha Aird Luing
Kintraw
Torran
Ardfern
A816
Ford
B8002
Ederline
FINCH CASTLE
227 CREAG MHOR
Gulf of Corryvreckan
Loch Craignish
Eilean Righ
CARNASSARIE CASTLE
Aird
Rèisa an t-Sruith
319
Kinuachdrachd
Kilmartin
GLEBE CAIRN
KILMARTIN HOUSE TRUST
Glengarrisdale Bay
296 CRUACH NA SEILCHEIG
Kinuachdrachd Harbour
Craignish Pt.
Island Macaskin
Slockavullin
KILMARTIN SCULPTURED STONES
RI CRUIN CAIRN
Poltalloch
adel Bay
Loch Crinan
231 DUN DUBH
365 BEN GARRISDALE
Crinan
Killmahumaig
B8025
CUP AND RING MARKS
Kilmichael Glassary
Add
MOINE MHOR
DUNADD FORT
Bridgend
Lealt Burn
Bellanoch
Mòine Mhór
CAIRNBAAN CUP & RING MARKS
Lussa
265
B841
ROCK MARKINGS
Lealt
Cairnbaan
REAC
Gallachoille
Crinan Canal
KNAPDALE
Lochgilphead
SOUND OF JURA
Gleann Aoistail
Carsaig
Cam Loch
Carrick
Ardlussa
Ardlussa Bay
KILMORY CASTLE GARDENS
Port Ann
Inverlussa
Tayvallich
Achanamara
Lussagiven
360
KILMORY WOODLAND PARK
Kilmichael of Inverlussa
Ardrishaig
B8025
Loch Sween
Loch Gilp
Castleton
A846
Barrahormid
TAYNISH
Taynish
466 CRUACH LUSACH
Eilean Mòr
A83
Achabraid
Dunrostan
Tarbert
KEILLS CHAPEL
Inverneill
Keillmore
New Ulva
Loch na Cille
Island of Danna
CASTLE SWEEN
Lochead
B8024
241
A
B
C
D
4
5
6
225
226
214
202

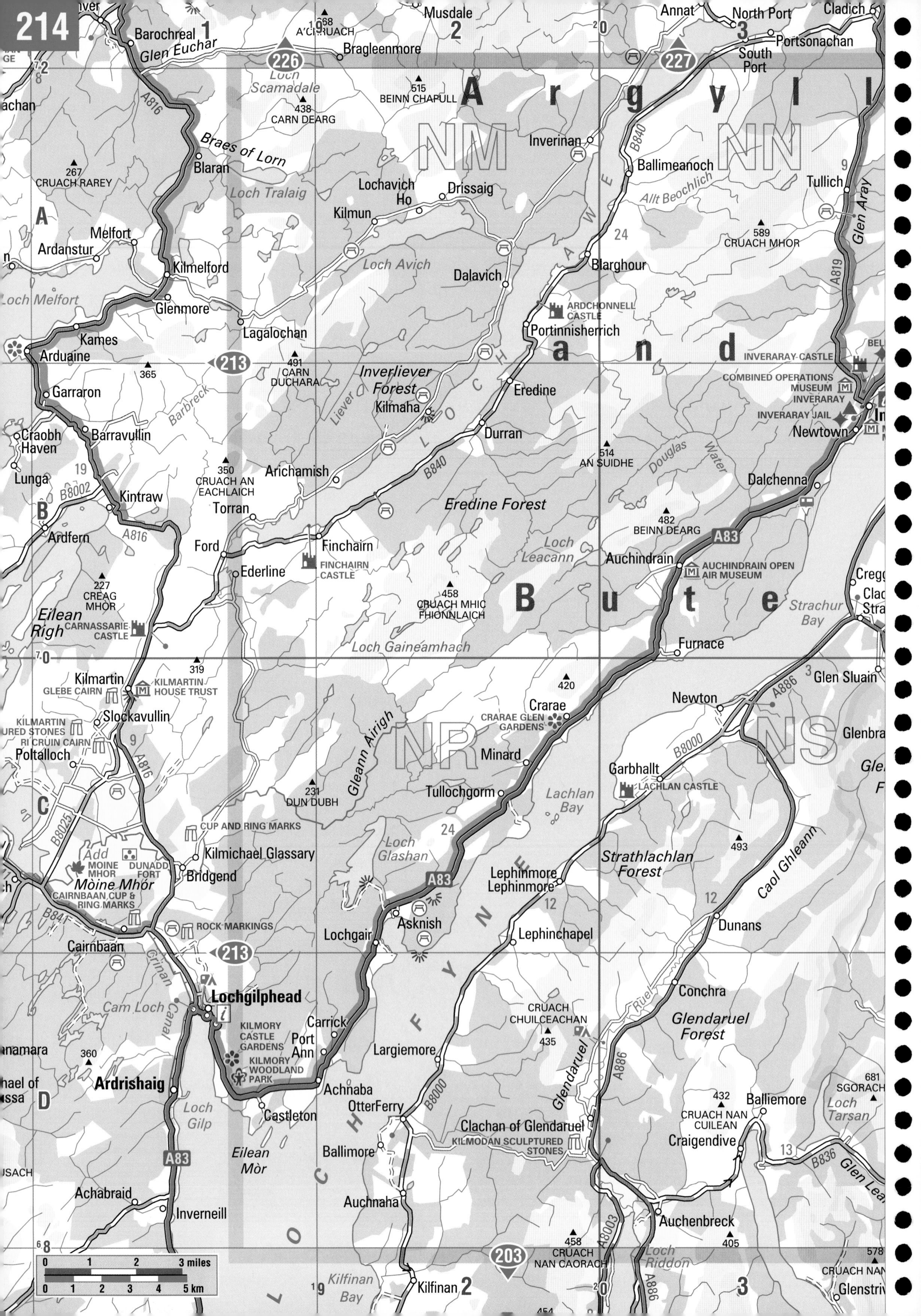
Argyll and Bute
NM
NN
NR
NS
Barochreal
Glen Euchar
Musdale
A' CHRUACH
Bragleenmore
Annat
North Port
Cladich
Portsonachan
South Port
Loch Scamadale
BEINN CHAPULL
CARN DEARG
Braes of Lorn
Blaran
CRUACH RAREY
Loch Tralaig
Lochavich Ho
Drissaig
Kilmun
Inverinan
Ballimeanoch
Allt Beochlich
Tullich
Glen Aray
CRUACH MHOR
Melfort
Ardanstur
Kilmelford
Loch Melfort
Glenmore
Loch Avich
Dalavich
Blarghour
ARDCHONNELL CASTLE
Portinnisherrich
Lagalochan
Kames
Arduaine
CARN DUCHARA
Inverliever Forest
Kilmaha
Liever
Barbreck
Garraron
Eredine
INVERARAY CASTLE
COMBINED OPERATIONS MUSEUM INVERARAY
INVERARAY JAIL
Newtown
Craobh Haven
Barravullin
Lunga
Durran
AN SUIDHE
Douglas Water
Dalchenna
CRUACH AN EACHLAICH
Arichamish
Kintraw
Torran
Eredine Forest
BEINN DEARG
Ardfern
Ford
Finchairn
FINCHAIRN CASTLE
Loch Leacann
Auchindrain
AUCHINDRAIN OPEN AIR MUSEUM
Ederline
CREAG MHOR
CRUACH MHIC FHIONNLAICH
Eilean Righ
CARNASSARIE CASTLE
Strachur Bay
Loch Gaineamhach
Furnace
Kilmartin
GLEBE CAIRN
KILMARTIN HOUSE TRUST
Glen Sluain
Newton
Crarae
CRARAE GLEN GARDENS
KILMARTIN
Slockavullin
RI CRUIN CAIRN
Poltalloch
Gleann Airigh
Minard
Garbhallt
LACHLAN CASTLE
Glenbranter
DUN DUBH
Tullochgorm
Lachlan Bay
CUP AND RING MARKS
Kilmichael Glassary
Loch Glashan
Strathlachlan Forest
Caol Ghleann
MOINE MHOR
DUNADD FORT
Mòine Mhòr
Bridgend
CAIRNBAAN CUP & RING MARKS
Lephinmore
Asknish
Dunans
Lochgair
Lephinchapel
ROCK MARKINGS
Cairnbaan
Crinan Canal
Lochgilphead
Conchra
Ruel
Cam Loch
KILMORY CASTLE GARDENS
Carrick
CRUACH CHUILCEACHAN
Glendaruel Forest
Port Ann
Largiemore
KILMORY WOODLAND PARK
Glendaruel
Ardrishaig
Achnaba
SGORACH
Loch Tarsan
Balliemore
Loch Gilp
OtterFerry
CRUACH NAN CUILEAN
Castleton
Clachan of Glendaruel
KILMODAN SCULPTURED STONES
Craigendive
Eilean Mòr
Ballimore
Glen Lean
Achabraid
Auchnaha
Inverneill
Auchenbreck
CRUACH NAN CAORACH
Loch Riddon
Kilfinan Bay
Kilfinan
Glenstriven
LOCH AWE
LOCH FYNE
0 1 2 3 miles
0 1 2 3 4 5 km

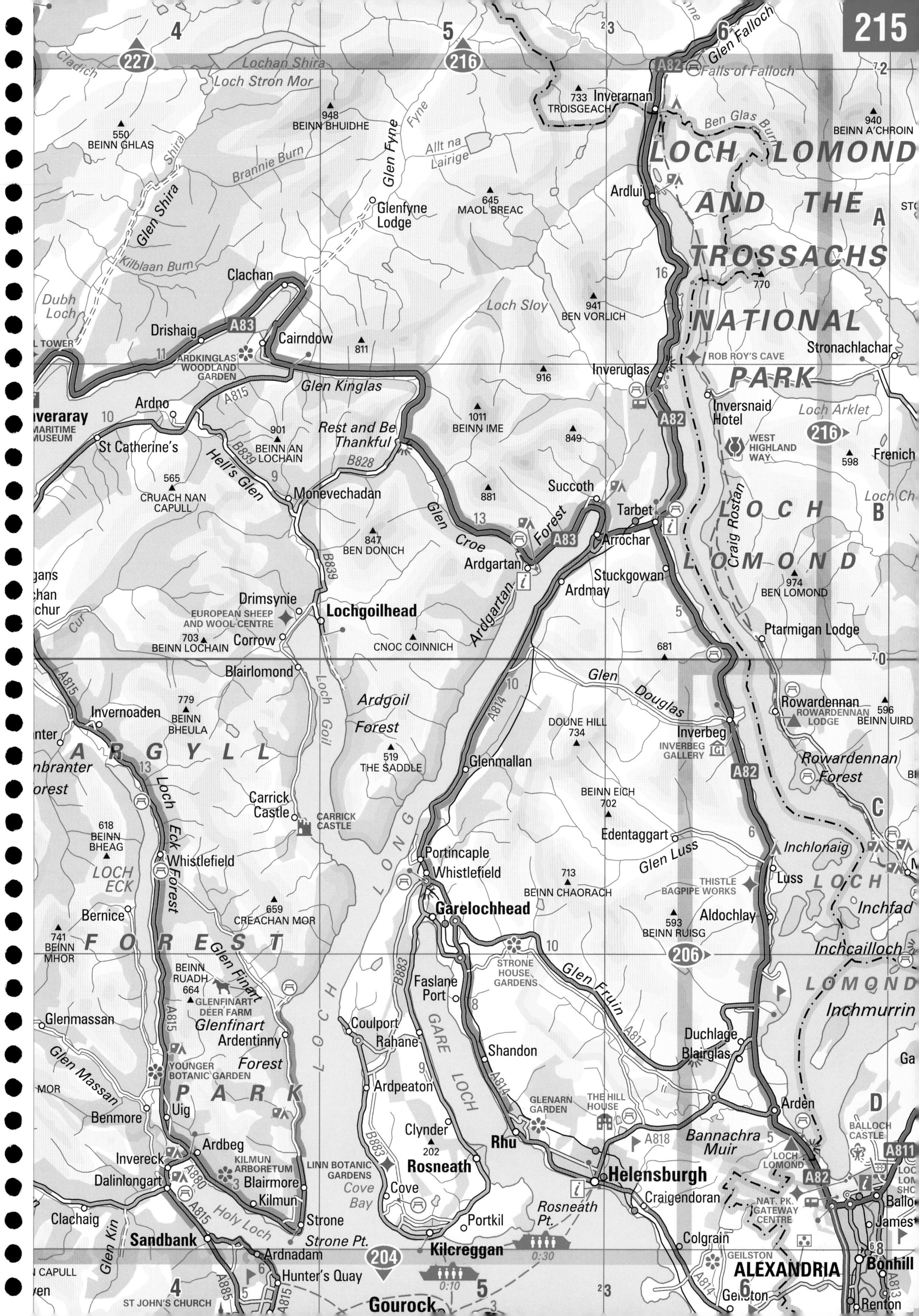
Lochan Shira
Loch Stron Mor
Glen Falloch
Falls of Falloch
Inverarnan
TROISGEACH
BEINN BHUIDHE
BEINN GHLAS
BEINN A'CHROIN
Ben Glas Burn
Glen Fyne
Allt na Lairige
Brannie Burn
Glen Shira
LOCH LOMOND AND THE TROSSACHS NATIONAL PARK
Ardlui
Glenfyne Lodge
MAOL BREAC
Kilblaan Burn
Clachan
Dubh Loch
Loch Sloy
BEN VORLICH
Drishaig
Cairndow
ARDKINGLAS WOODLAND GARDEN
ROB ROY'S CAVE
Stronachlachar
Glen Kinglas
Inveruglas
Ardno
Inveraray
MARITIME MUSEUM
Rest and Be Thankful
BEINN IME
Inversnaid Hotel
Loch Arklet
St Catherine's
BEINN AN LOCHAIN
Hell's Glen
WEST HIGHLAND WAY
Frenich
CRUACH NAN CAPULL
Monevechadan
Succoth
Tarbet
Glen Croe
Forest
Arrochar
LOCH LOMOND
Craig Rostan
BEN DONICH
Ardgartan
Stuckgowan
Ardmay
BEN LOMOND
Drimsynie
EUROPEAN SHEEP AND WOOL CENTRE
Lochgoilhead
Ptarmigan Lodge
BEINN LOCHAIN
Corrow
CNOC COINNICH
Blairlomond
Glen Douglas
Loch Goil
Ardgoil Forest
Rowardennan
ROWARDENNAN LODGE
BEINN UIRD
Invernoaden
BEINN BHEULA
DOUNE HILL
Inverbeg
INVERBEG GALLERY
ARGYLL FOREST PARK
THE SADDLE
Glenmallan
Rowardennan Forest
Loch Eck
Carrick Castle
CARRICK CASTLE
BEINN EICH
Edentaggart
BEINN BHEAG
Portincaple
Whistlefield
Inchlonaig
Glen Luss
Luss
LOCH LONG
BEINN CHAORACH
THISTLE BAGPIPE WORKS
Garelochhead
Bernice
CREACHAN MOR
Aldochlay
BEINN RUISG
Inchfad
BEINN MHOR
Glen Finart
STRONE HOUSE GARDENS
Inchcailloch
Glen Fruin
BEINN RUADH
Faslane Port
GLENFINART DEER FARM
Glenfinart
Glenmassan
Coulport
Rahane
GARE LOCH
Inchmurrin
Ardentinny
Duchlage
Blairglas
Shandon
Glen Massan
YOUNGER BOTANIC GARDEN
Ardpeaton
Arden
Benmore
Uig
GLENARN GARDEN
THE HILL HOUSE
BALLOCH CASTLE
Clynder
Bannachra Muir
Ardbeg
Rhu
Invereck
KILMUN ARBORETUM
LINN BOTANIC GARDENS
Rosneath
LOCH LOMOND
Dalinlongart
Blairmore
Cove Bay
Cove
Helensburgh
Kilmun
Craigendoran
NAT. PK. GATEWAY CENTRE
Balloch
Clachaig
Holy Loch
Strone
Portkil
Rosneath Pt.
Jamestown
Sandbank
Glen Kin
Strone Pt.
Colgrain
Ardnadam
Kilcreggan
GEILSTON
ALEXANDRIA
Bonhill
Hunter's Quay
ST JOHN'S CHURCH
Gourock
Geilston
Renton
A82
A83
A815
A814
A817
A818
A880
A885
A811
A813
B828
B839
B883
227
216
206
204

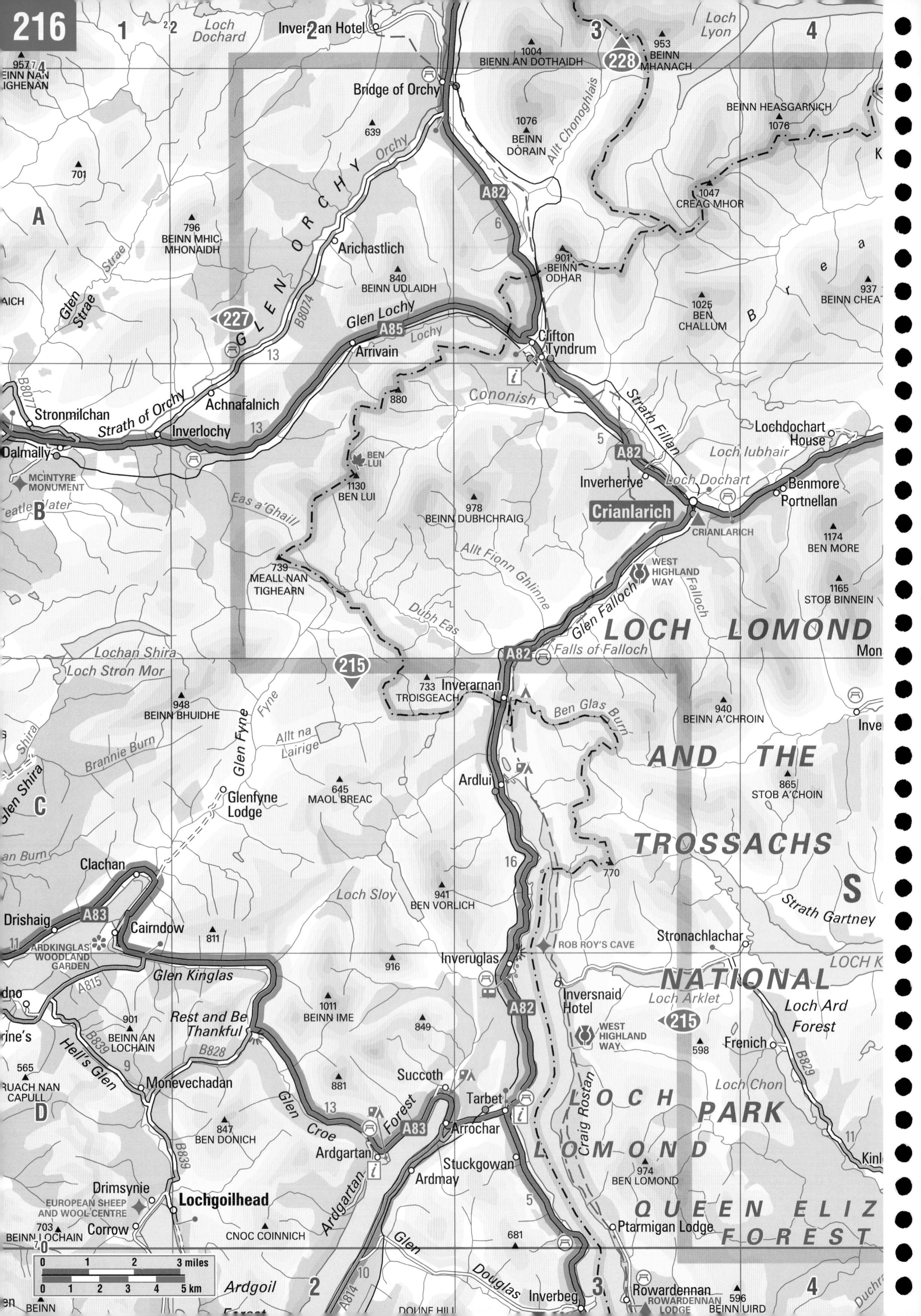
Loch Dochard
Inveroran Hotel
Loch Lyon
1004 BIENN AN DOTHAIDH
228
953 BEINN MHANACH
Bridge of Orchy
BEINN HEASGARNICH 1076
639
1076 BEINN DÒRAIN
Allt Chonoghlais
701
GLEN ORCHY
Orchy
A82
1047 CREAG MHOR
796 BEINN MHIC-MHONAIDH
Arichastlich
901 BEINN ODHAR
840 BEINN UDLAIDH
Glen Strae
Strae
B8074
227
Glen Lochy
A85
Lochy
Arrivain
Clifton
Tyndrum
1025 BEN CHALLUM
937 BEINN CHEAT
Breadalbane
B8077
Stronmilchan
Strath of Orchy
Achnafalnich
Inverlochy
880
Cononish
Strath Fillan
Lochdochart House
Dalmally
Loch Iubhair
MCINTYRE MONUMENT
BEN LUI
1130 BEN LUI
A82
Inverherive
Loch Dochart
Benmore
Portnellan
Eas a'Ghaill
978 BEINN DUBHCHRAIG
Crianlarich
CRIANLARICH
1174 BEN MORE
Allt Fionn Ghlinne
WEST HIGHLAND WAY
739 MEALL NAN TIGHEARN
1165 STOB BINNEIN
Glen Falloch
Falloch
Dubh Eas
LOCH LOMOND AND THE TROSSACHS NATIONAL PARK
Lochan Shira
Falls of Falloch
Loch Stron Mor
215
733 TROISGEACH
Inverarnan
948 BEINN BHUIDHE
Fyne
Ben Glas Burn
940 BEINN A'CHROIN
Glen Shira
Brannie Burn
Allt na Lairige
Glen Fyne
Glenfyne Lodge
645 MAOL BREAC
Ardlui
865 STOB A'CHOIN
Clachan
770
Loch Sloy
941 BEN VORLICH
Strath Gartney
Drishaig
A83
Cairndow
811
ARDKINGLAS WOODLAND GARDEN
ROB ROY'S CAVE
Stronachlachar
Glen Kinglas
916
Inveruglas
A815
Inversnaid Hotel
Loch Arklet
Loch Ard Forest
1011 BEINN IME
A82
215
901 BEINN AN LOCHAIN
Rest and Be Thankful
849
WEST HIGHLAND WAY
598
Frenich
B839
B828
B829
Hell's Glen
565
Monevechadan
Succoth
Glen Croe
881
Tarbet
Loch Chon
847 BEN DONICH
A83
Forest
Arrochar
LOCH LOMOND
Craig Rostan
Ardgartan
Stuckgowan
Ardmay
974 BEN LOMOND
B839
Drimsynie
Lochgoilhead
EUROPEAN SHEEP AND WOOL CENTRE
QUEEN ELIZ FOREST
703 BEINN LOCHAIN
Corrow
CNOC COINNICH
Ardgartan
Ptarmigan Lodge
Glen Douglas
681
0 1 2 3 miles
0 1 2 3 4 5 km
Ardgoil
A814
Inverbeg
Rowardennan
ROWARDENNAN LODGE
596 BEINN UIRD

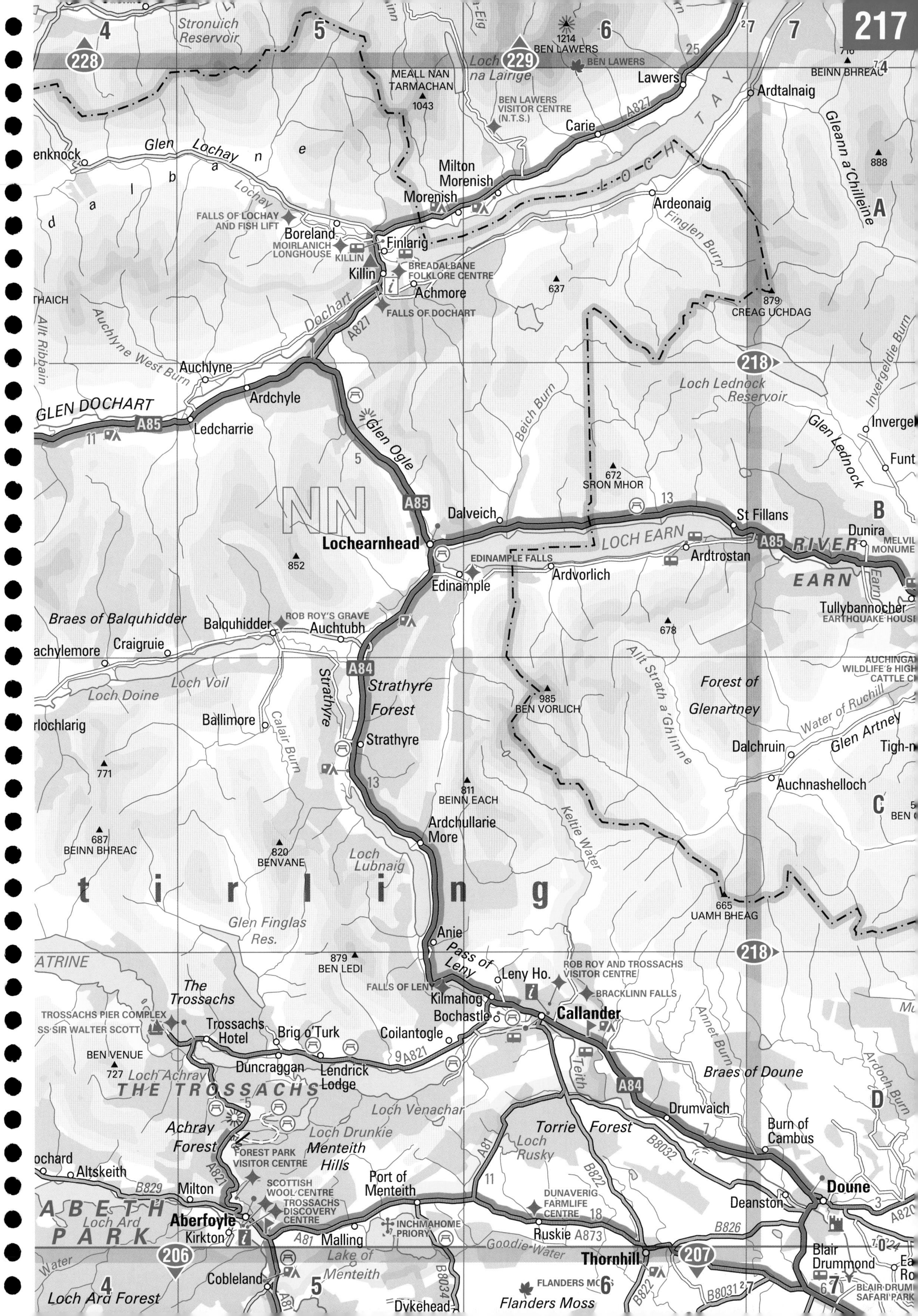

Stronuich Reservoir
228
229
BEN LAWERS
Loch na Lairige
MEALL NAN TARMACHAN
Lawers
Ardtalnaig
BEINN BHREAC
BEN LAWERS VISITOR CENTRE (N.T.S.)
Carie
Glen Lochay
Milton Morenish
Morenish
LOCH TAY
Ardeonaig
Finglen Burn
Gleann a'Chilleine
FALLS OF LOCHAY AND FISH LIFT
Boreland
MOIRLANICH LONGHOUSE
Finlarig
Killin
BREADALBANE FOLKLORE CENTRE
Achmore
FALLS OF DOCHART
CREAG UCHDAG
Dochart
Auchlyne West Burn
Allt Ribbain
Auchlyne
218
Loch Lednock Reservoir
Invergeldie Burn
GLEN DOCHART
A85
Ardchyle
Ledcharrie
Glen Ogle
Beich Burn
Glen Lednock
SRON MHOR
NN
Dalveich
St Fillans
Dunira
Lochearnhead
LOCH EARN
RIVER EARN
EDINAMPLE FALLS
Ardvorlich
Edinample
Ardtrostan
Tullybannocher
EARTHQUAKE HOUSE
Braes of Balquhidder
ROB ROY'S GRAVE
Balquhidder
Auchtubh
Craigruie
Allt Strath a'Ghlinne
A84
Loch Voil
Loch Doine
Strathyre Forest
Strathyre
Forest of Glenartney
BEN VORLICH
Water of Ruchill
Glen Artney
Ballimore
Calair Burn
Dalchruin
Auchnashelloch
BEINN EACH
Keltie Water
Ardchullarie More
BEINN BHREAC
BENVANE
Loch Lubnaig
Stirling
UAMH BHEAG
Glen Finglas Res.
Anie
Pass of Leny
BEN LEDI
Leny Ho.
ROB ROY AND TROSSACHS VISITOR CENTRE
BRACKLINN FALLS
FALLS OF LENY
Kilmahog
Callander
Bochastle
The Trossachs
TROSSACHS PIER COMPLEX
SS SIR WALTER SCOTT
Trossachs Hotel
Brig o'Turk
Coilantogle
A821
BEN VENUE
Loch Achray
Duncraggan
Lendrick Lodge
Annet Burn
Braes of Doune
Ardoch Burn
Teith
THE TROSSACHS
Loch Venachar
Drumvaich
Achray Forest
Loch Drunkie
Torrie Forest
Loch Rusky
Burn of Cambus
FOREST PARK VISITOR CENTRE
Menteith Hills
B8032
Altskeith
Milton
SCOTTISH WOOL CENTRE
TROSSACHS DISCOVERY CENTRE
Port of Menteith
DUNAVERIG FARMLIFE CENTRE
Doune
Deanston
Aberfoyle
Loch Ard
Kirkton
INCHMAHOME PRIORY
Ruskie
B826
Malling
Goodie Water
206
207
Thornhill
Blair Drummond
Lake of Menteith
Cobleland
FLANDERS MOSS
BLAIR DRUMMOND SAFARI PARK
Loch Ard Forest
Dykehead
Flanders Moss

Lawers
Ardtalnaig
Carie
Ardeonaig
Garrow
BEINN BHREAC
Quaich
Loch Freuchie
Glen Quaich
Cablea
Amulree
Corrymuckloch
MEALL NAM FUARAN
Almond
Newton
CREAG UCHDAG
BEN CHONZIE
GLEN ALMOND
MEALL TARSUINN
Loch Lednock Reservoir
Invergeldie
Funtullich
Glen Lednock
Loch Turret Reservoir
Glen Turret
SRON MHOR
St Fillans
LOCH EARN
Ardtrostan
Dunira
MELVILLE MONUMENT
RIVER EARN
Comrie
Lawers
COMRIE CROFT
Ochtertyre
Quoig
Monzie
Monzie Castle
Hosh
Gilmerton
Fowlis Wester
STANDING STONES
Keillour
GLENTURRET DISTILLERY
Crieff
Madderty
Tullybannocher
EARTHQUAKE HOUSE
Ross
Dalginross
Lochlane
CRIEFF VISITORS' CENTRE
STUART CRYSTAL VISITOR CENTRE
The Balloch
AUCHINGARRICH WILDLIFE & HIGHLAND CATTLE CENTRE
Forest of Glenartney
Water of Ruchill
Glen Artney
Culloch
Torlum Wood
DRUMMOND CASTLE GARDENS
OLD CHURCH & TOWER
Muthill
INNERPEFFRAY LIBRARY
Kinkell Bridge
STRATHEARN
Dalchruin
Tigh-na-Blair
Ochtermuthill
Machany Water
Auchnashelloch
BEN CLACH
Langside
Tullibardine
TULLIBARDINE CHAPEL
Auchterarder
Glenlichorn
Knaik
Garrick
Muirton
UAMH BHEAG
BLACKHALL ROMAN CAMPS
Gleneagles Hotel
ARDOCH ROMAN CAMP
GLENEAGLES
Braco
Blackford
Gleneagles House
Bullie Burn
BRACLINN FALLS
Muckle Burn
Greenloaning
Braes of Ogilvie
Glen Eagles
Allan Water
STRATHALLAN
Braes of Doune
Kinbuck
Glendevon Resvrs.
Drumvaich
Balhaldie
Ashfield
Torrie Forest
Burn of Cambus
Sheriff Muir
1715
Doune
CATHEDRAL
Dunblane
Deanston
BLAIRDENON HILL
Pisgah
BEN CLEUCH
LEIGHTON LIBRARY
Blair Drummond
Easter Row
KING'S SEAT HILL
BLAIR DRUMMOND SAFARI PARK
MILL TRAIL VISITOR CENTRE
NN
Perth and Kinross
0 1 2 3 miles
0 1 2 3 4 5 km

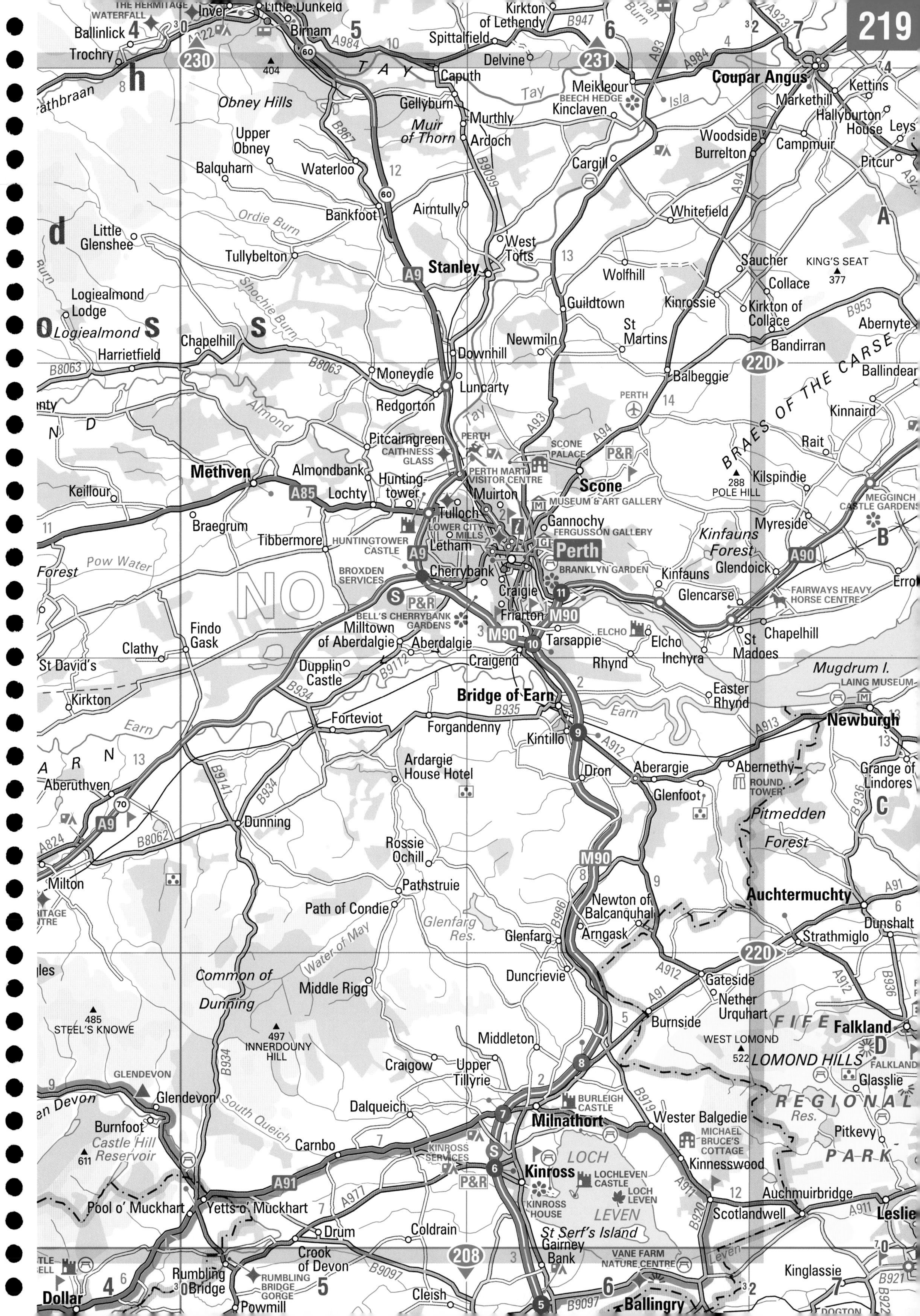
Coupar Angus
Perth
Scone
Stanley
Methven
Bridge of Earn
Newburgh
Auchtermuchty
Falkland
Milnathort
Kinross
Ballingry
Dollar
Leslie
Kinglassie
Strathmiglo
Glenfarg
Dunning
Forteviot
Forgandenny
Aberargie
Abernethy
Luncarty
Redgorton
Almondbank
Tibbermore
Cherrybank
Craigie
Friarton
Kinfauns
Glencarse
Balbeggie
Guildtown
Murthly
Caputh
Birnam
Little Dunkeld
Spittalfield
Kinclaven
Meikleour
Cargill
Burrelton
Woodside
Glendevon
Yetts o' Muckhart
Pool o' Muckhart
Rumbling Bridge
Powmill
Scotlandwell
Kinnesswood
Gateside
LOCH LEVEN
LOMOND HILLS
Obney Hills
BRAES OF THE CARSE

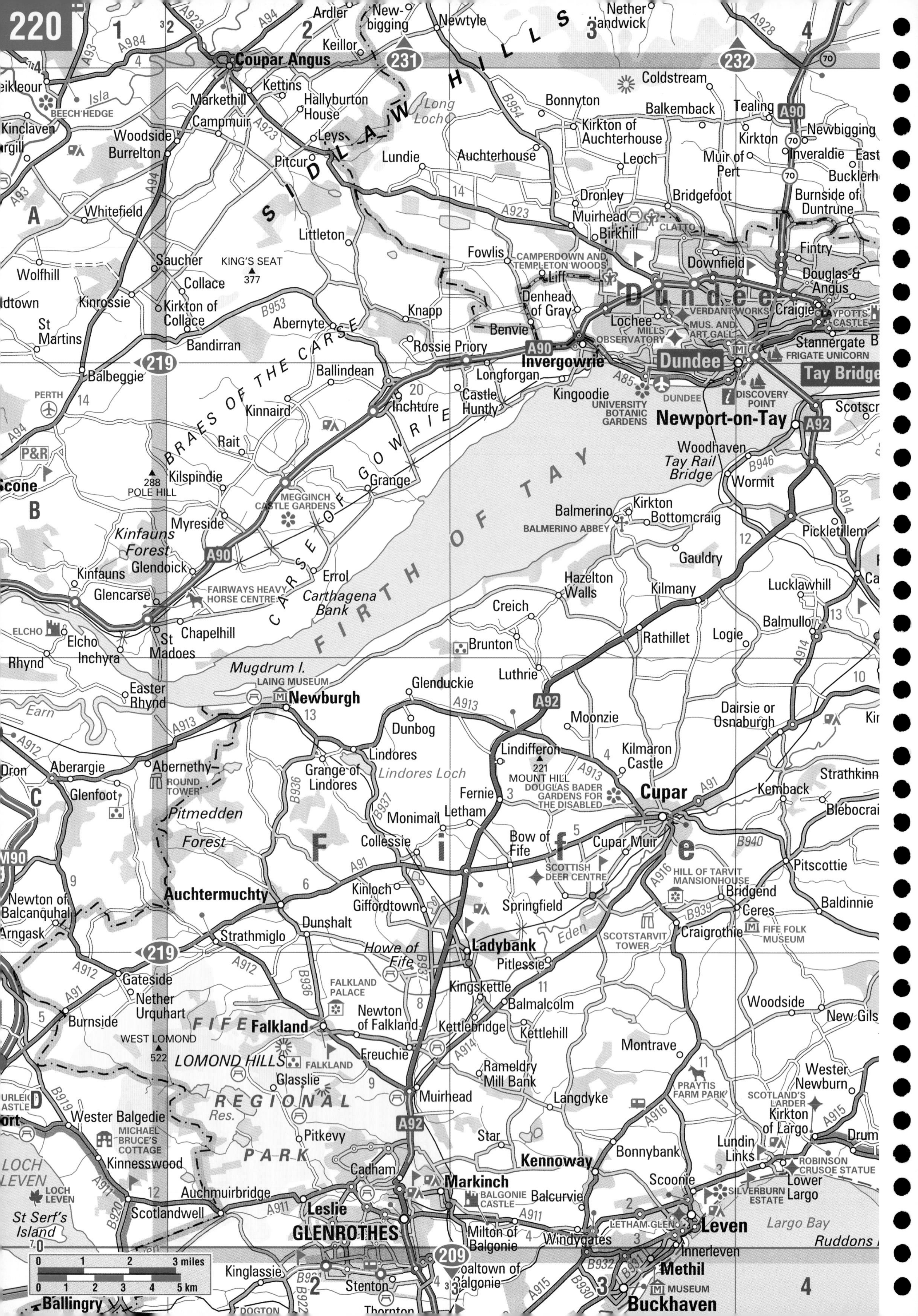
1
2
3
4
Ardler
New-bigging
Newtyle
Nether Handwick
A94
A923
A984
A93
A928
Keillor
231
232
Coupar Angus
70
SIDLAW HILLS
Coldstream
Isla
BEECH HEDGE
Kettins
Markethill
Hallyburton House
Long Loch
B954
Bonnyton
Balkemback
Tealing
A90
Kinclaven
Campmuir
Kirkton of Auchterhouse
Newbigging
Woodside
Leys
Kirkton
Burrelton
Lundie
Auchterhouse
Leoch
Muir of Pert
Inveraldie
East
Pitcur
Bucklerh
14
A
Whitefield
Dronley
Bridgefoot
Burnside of Duntrune
Muirhead
Birkhill
CLATTO
Littleton
Fowlis
CAMPERDOWN AND TEMPLETON WOODS
Fintry
Downfield
Saucher
KING'S SEAT 377
Douglas & Angus
Wolfhill
Collace
Liff
Dundee
Denhead of Gray
Craigie
Kinrossie
Kirkton of Collace
B953
VERDANT WORKS
BROUGHTY CASTLE
St Martins
Abernyte
Knapp
Lochee
MILLS OBSERVATORY
MUS. AND ART GALL.
Benvie
Bandirran
BRAES OF THE CARSE
Rossie Priory
Invergowrie
Stannergate
FRIGATE UNICORN
219
Balbeggie
Ballindean
Longforgan
Tay Bridge
PERTH
20
Castle Huntly
Kingoodie
DUNDEE
DISCOVERY POINT
Inchture
UNIVERSITY BOTANIC GARDENS
Newport-on-Tay
Kinnaird
CARSE OF GOWRIE
A85
A92
Rait
Woodhaven
Tay Rail Bridge
B946
P&R
288 POLE HILL
Kilspindie
Grange
Wormit
Scone
B
MEGGINCH CASTLE GARDENS
FIRTH OF TAY
A914
Balmerino
Kirkton
Bottomcraig
Myreside
BALMERINO ABBEY
Pickletillem
Kinfauns Forest
12
Gauldry
Glendoick
Kinfauns
Errol
Hazelton Walls
Kilmany
Lucklawhill
Glencarse
FAIRWAYS HEAVY HORSE CENTRE
Carthagena Bank
Creich
Balmullo
13
ELCHO
Elcho
Chapelhill
St Madoes
Rathillet
Logie
Brunton
Rhynd
Inchyra
Mugdrum I.
Luthrie
10
Easter Rhynd
LAING MUSEUM
Newburgh
Glenduckie
A913
Earn
Dunbog
Moonzie
Dairsie or Osnaburgh
A912
Lindores
Lindifferon
Kilmaron Castle
Dron
Aberargie
Abernethy
ROUND TOWER
Grange of Lindores
Lindores Loch
221 MOUNT HILL
Strathkinn
C
Glenfoot
B936
DOUGLAS BADER GARDENS FOR THE DISABLED
Fernie
Cupar
A91
Kemback
Blebocrai
Pitmedden Forest
B937
Monimail
Letham
Bow of Fife
Cupar Muir
B940
M90
Collessie
Fife
Pitscottie
SCOTTISH DEER CENTRE
A916
HILL OF TARVIT MANSIONHOUSE
Newton of Balcanquhal
Auchtermuchty
Kinloch
Gifffordtown
Springfield
Bridgend
Ceres
Baldinnie
B939
Arngask
Strathmiglo
Dunshalt
Eden
SCOTSTARVIT TOWER
Craigrothie
FIFE FOLK MUSEUM
Howe of Fife
Ladybank
Pitlessie
Gateside
FALKLAND PALACE
Kingskettle
11
Nether Urquhart
Newton of Falkland
Balmalcolm
Woodside
Burnside
FIFE
Falkland
Kettlebridge
Kettlehill
New Gils
WEST LOMOND 522
Freuchie
Montrave
LOMOND HILLS
FALKLAND
Rameldry Mill Bank
Wester Newburn
Glasslie
PRAYTIS FARM PARK
D
REGIONAL PARK
Muirhead
Langdyke
SCOTLAND'S LARDER
Kirkton of Largo
B919
Wester Balgedie
Res.
A915
MICHAEL BRUCE'S COTTAGE
Pitkevy
Star
Drum
LOCH LEVEN
Kinnesswood
Bonnybank
Lundin Links
ROBINSON CRUSOE STATUE
Cadham
Kennoway
Markinch
Scoonie
Lower Largo
LOCH LEVEN
Auchmuirbridge
BALGONIE CASTLE
Balcurvie
SILVERBURN ESTATE
A911
St Serf's Island
Scotlandwell
Leslie
B920
GLENROTHES
Milton of Balgonie
Windygates
LETHAM GLEN
Leven
Largo Bay
Ruddons
Innerleven
209
Kinglassie
Coaltown of Balgonie
B932
B931
Methil
Stenton
B930
MUSEUM
Ballingry
Thornton
Buckhaven
DOGTON
B922
0 1 2 3 miles
0 1 2 3 4 5 km

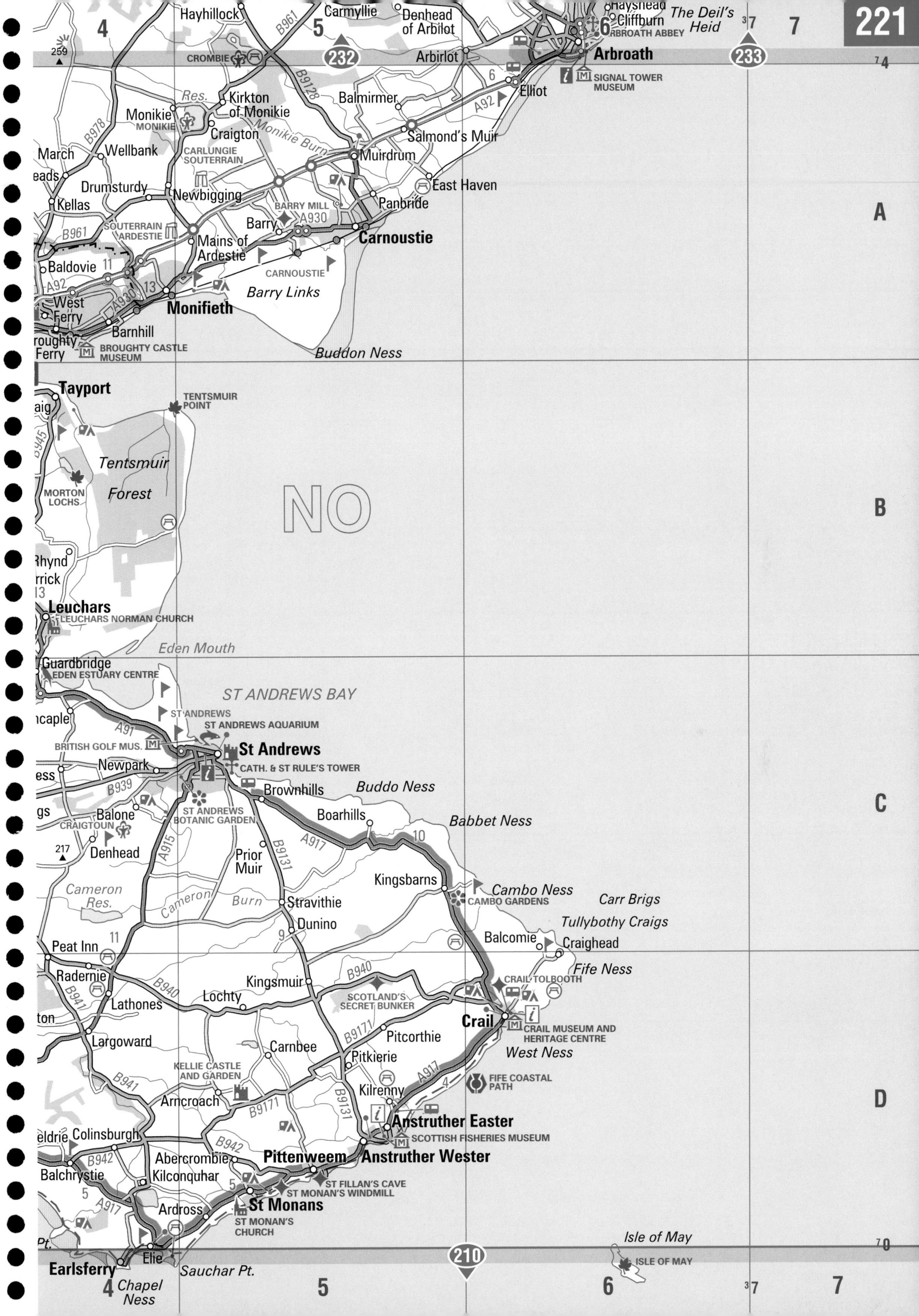
Hayhillock
Carmyllie
Denhead of Arbilot
Hayshead
Cliffburn
The Deil's Heid
ARBROATH ABBEY
Arbroath
SIGNAL TOWER MUSEUM
CROMBIE
Arbirlot
Elliot
Monikie
MONIKIE
Kirkton of Monikie
Craigton
Balmirmer
Salmond's Muir
March
Wellbank
CARLUNGIE SOUTERRAIN
Muirdrum
Drumsturdy
Newbigging
East Haven
Kellas
BARRY MILL
Panbride
SOUTERRAIN ARDESTIE
Barry
Carnoustie
Mains of Ardestie
Baldovie
CARNOUSTIE
West Ferry
Monifieth
Barry Links
Barnhill
Broughty Ferry
BROUGHTY CASTLE MUSEUM
Buddon Ness
Tayport
TENTSMUIR POINT
Tentsmuir Forest
MORTON LOCHS
NO
Leuchars
LEUCHARS NORMAN CHURCH
Eden Mouth
Guardbridge
EDEN ESTUARY CENTRE
ST ANDREWS BAY
ST ANDREWS
ST ANDREWS AQUARIUM
BRITISH GOLF MUS.
St Andrews
CATH. & ST RULE'S TOWER
Newpark
Brownhills
Buddo Ness
ST ANDREWS BOTANIC GARDEN
Balone
CRAIGTOUN
Boarhills
Babbet Ness
Denhead
Prior Muir
Kingsbarns
Cambo Ness
CAMBO GARDENS
Carr Brigs
Cameron Res.
Cameron Burn
Stravithie
Dunino
Tullybothy Craigs
Balcomie
Craighead
Peat Inn
Fife Ness
Radernie
Kingsmuir
CRAIL TOLBOOTH
Lathones
Lochty
SCOTLAND'S SECRET BUNKER
Crail
CRAIL MUSEUM AND HERITAGE CENTRE
Largoward
Pitcorthie
Carnbee
West Ness
Pitkierie
KELLIE CASTLE AND GARDEN
FIFE COASTAL PATH
Kilrenny
Arncroach
Anstruther Easter
SCOTTISH FISHERIES MUSEUM
Colinsburgh
Abercrombie
Pittenweem
Anstruther Wester
Balchrystie
Kilconquhar
ST FILLAN'S CAVE
ST MONAN'S WINDMILL
St Monans
Ardross
ST MONAN'S CHURCH
Isle of May
ISLE OF MAY
Elie
Earlsferry
Sauchar Pt.
Chapel Ness
232
233
210
A B C D
4 5 6 7

1
09
2
286
10
3
4
77
A
B
C
D
73
NL
NM
Hog
Feall Bay
Ari
Calgary Pt.
Gunna
Crossapol Bay
TIREE
Vaul Bay
Salum
Caolas
Rubha Dubh
Vaul
B8069
Ruaig
Balephetrish Bay
Hough Skerries
Balevullin
B8068
Gott Bay
Soa
R. Chraiginis
Kenovay
Kilkenneth
B8068
TIREE
Scarinish
Moss
B8065
Middleton
Heylipol
Heanish
Port Mor
B8065
Crossapol
Rubha Traigh an Duin
Barrapol
Loch a'Phuill
B8067
Hynish Bay
Balemartine
Rinn Thorbhais
Balephuil
141
B8068
Mannal
Balephuil Bay
Hynish
Port Snoig
0 1 2 3 miles
0 1 2 3 4 5 km
2
10
3
4

4
5
6
7
Sanna Point
Sanna
Sanna Bay
Portuairk
Point of Ardnamurchan
ARDNAMURCHAN LIGHTHOUSE
Achosni
B8007
A
Ormsa
Ormsaig
An Acairseid
Cairns of Coll
234
Eilean Mor
Rubha Mor
Sorisdale
Bousd
B8072
Cliad Bay
Arnabost
Gallanach
Grishipoll
B8071
73
COLL
OBAN 2:40
Ballyhaugh
Loch Cliad
104
Arinagour
Totronald
B8070
Loch Eatharna
Eilean Ornsay
Acha
Breachacha Castle
Friesland
Loch Breachacha
Soa
0:55
Ardmore Bay
Glengorm Castle
Quinish Pt.
Mishnish
Quinish
B
Rubha an Aird
Caliach Pt.
Sunipol
Mornish
Penmore Mill
MULL LITTLE THEATRE
Calgary
Dervaig
Calgary Bay
THE OLD BYRE HERITAGE CENTRE
Ensay
342
CARN MOR
Treshnish Pt.
Haunn
Bellart
B8073
Achnac
Rubh a'Chaoil
224
Burg
Kilninian
Achleck
23
C
390
Fanmore
Treshnish Isles
Fladda
LOCH TUATH
Ballygown
EAS FORS WATERFALL
Eilean Dioghlum
Lunga
Gometra
Bearnus
313
Laggan Bay
Ulva
Ulva House
Sound of Ulva
Bac Mor
Little Colonsay
Staffa
STAFFA
FINGAL'S CAVE
INCH KENNETH CHAPEL
Inch Kenneth
D
MACKINNON'S CAVE
Erisgeir
IONA 0:45 (April-Oct)
519
BEINN NA SREINE
ARDMEANACH
224

COLL
Gallanach
Arinagour
Loch Cliad
Loch Eatharna
Eilean Ornsay
Friesland
OBAN 2:40
TIREE 0:55
234
Ardmore Bay
Ardmore Pt.
Quinish Pt.
Glengorm Castle
MULL AND IONA FOLKLORE MUSEUM
Tobermory
Mishnish
'S AIRDE-BEINN
Quinish
Rubha an Aird
Caliach Pt.
Sunipol
Mornish
Penmore Mill
MULL LITTLE THEATRE
Dervaig
Achnadrish
Calgary
Calgary Bay
THE OLD BYRE HERITAGE CENTRE
Loch Frisa
Treshnish Pt.
Ensay
342
CARN MOR
Haunn
Bellart
Achnacraig
Rubh a'Chaoil
223
Burg
Kilninian
Achleck
Fanmore
390
Treshnish Isles
Fladda
Ballygown
LOCH TUATH
EAS FORS WATERFALL
424
BEINN NA DRISE
Eilean Dioghlum
Lunga
Gometra
Laggan Bay
Lagganulva
Bearnus
313
Oskamull
Ulva
Ulva House
Sound of Ulva
Bac Mor
LOCH NA KEAL
Eorsa
Little Colonsay
ISLE OF
INCH KENNETH CHAPEL
Inch Kenneth
Staffa
STAFFA
FINGAL'S CAVE
Balnahard
MACKINNON'S CAVE
561
Erisgeir
Glen Seilisdeir
(April-Oct) 0:45
519
BEINN NA SREINE
ARDMEANACH
Kilfinichen Bay
THE BURG
Eilean Annraidh
MACLEAN'S CROSS
Rubha nan Cearc
LOCH SCRIDAIN
IONA ABBEY AND CATHEDRAL
Loch na Lathaich
Torrans
Kintra
IONA HERITAGE CENTRE
Iona
Baile Mor
ST COLUMBA EXHIBITION & WELCOME CENTRE
Aridhglas
Sound of Iona
Stac an Aoineidh
Fionnphort
Eorabus
A849
Lee
Fidden
Tiraghoil
Bunessan
376
CRUACHAN MIN
Loch Assapol
Erraid
212
ROSS OF MULL
Ardalanish
Uisken
Scoor
Ardchiavaig
Malcolm's Pt.
0 1 2 3 miles
0 1 2 3 4 5 km

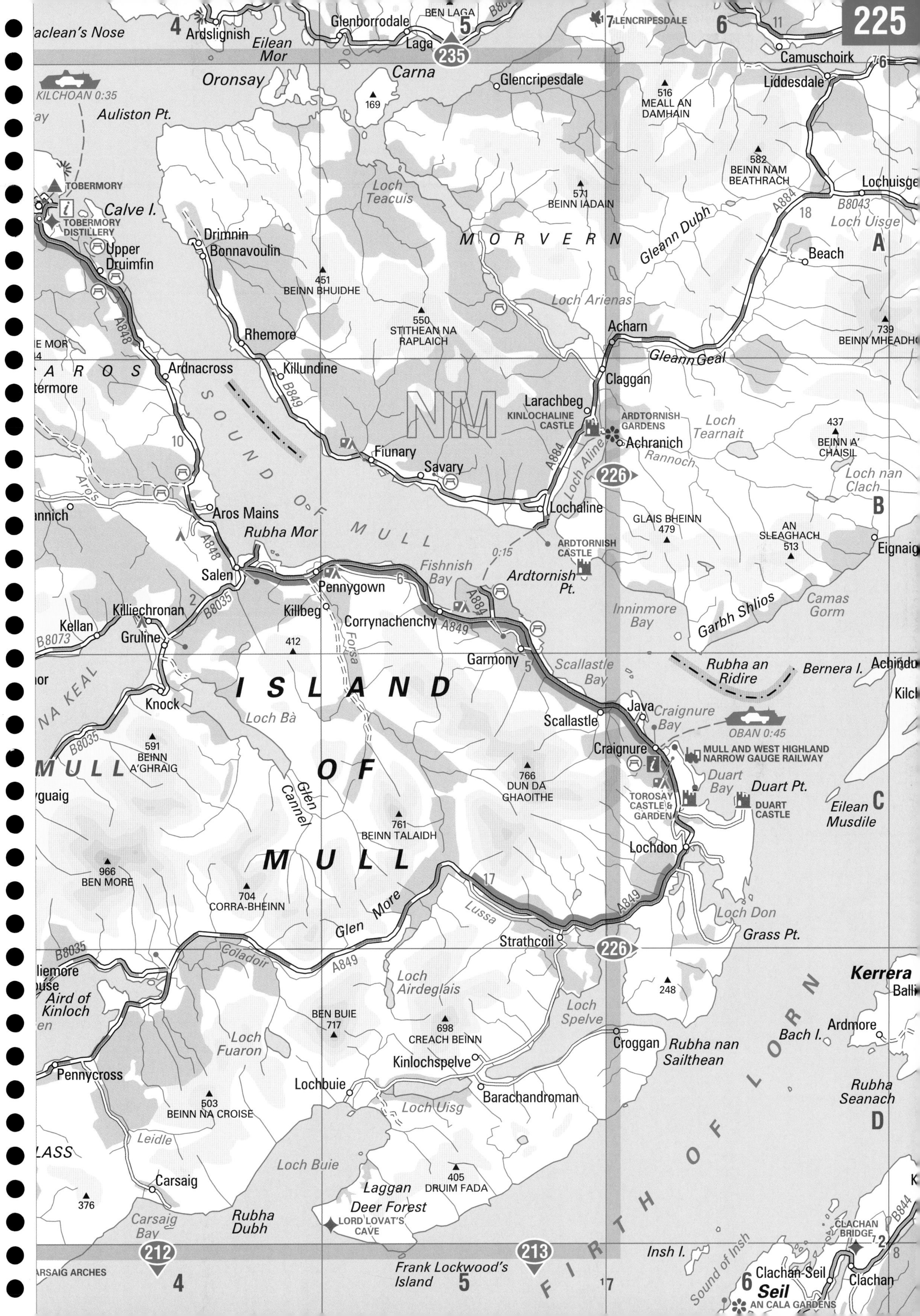
Tobermory
Calve I.
Tobermory Distillery
Upper Druimfin
Drimnin
Bonnavoulin
Rhemore
Ardnacross
Killundine
Sound of Mull
Fiunary
Savary
Aros Mains
Rubha Mor
Salen
Pennygown
Killbeg
Corrynachenchy
Killiechronan
Kellan
Gruline
Garmony
Scallastle
Island of Mull
Knock
Loch Bà
Glen Cannel
Ben More
Corra-Bheinn
Beinn Talaidh
Dun da Ghaoithe
Glen More
Strathcoil
Craignure
Torosay Castle & Garden
Mull and West Highland Narrow Gauge Railway
Duart Castle
Duart Pt.
Lochdon
Loch Don
Grass Pt.
Oban 0:45
Java
Rubha an Ridire
Bernera I.
Morvern
Loch Teacuis
Glencripesdale
Beinn Iadain
Loch Arienas
Acharn
Gleann Geal
Claggan
Larachbeg
Kinlochaline Castle
Ardtornish Gardens
Achranich
Lochaline
Ardtornish Castle
Ardtornish Pt.
Loch Tearnait
Glais Bheinn
Eignaig
Garbh Shlios
Camas Gorm
Liddesdale
Camuschoirk
Lochuisge
Beach
Loch Uisge
Gleann Dubh
Eilean Musdile
Kerrera
Ardmore
Firth of Lorn
Loch Spelve
Croggan
Kinlochspelve
Barachandroman
Lochbuie
Loch Uisg
Loch Buie
Laggan Deer Forest
Lord Lovat's Cave
Carsaig
Carsaig Bay
Rubha Dubh
Pennycross
Frank Lockwood's Island
Insh I.
Clachan-Seil
Clachan
Seil
An Cala Gardens
Glenborrodale
Laga
Ardslignish
Oronsay
Carna
Kilchoan 0:35
Auliston Pt.
NM

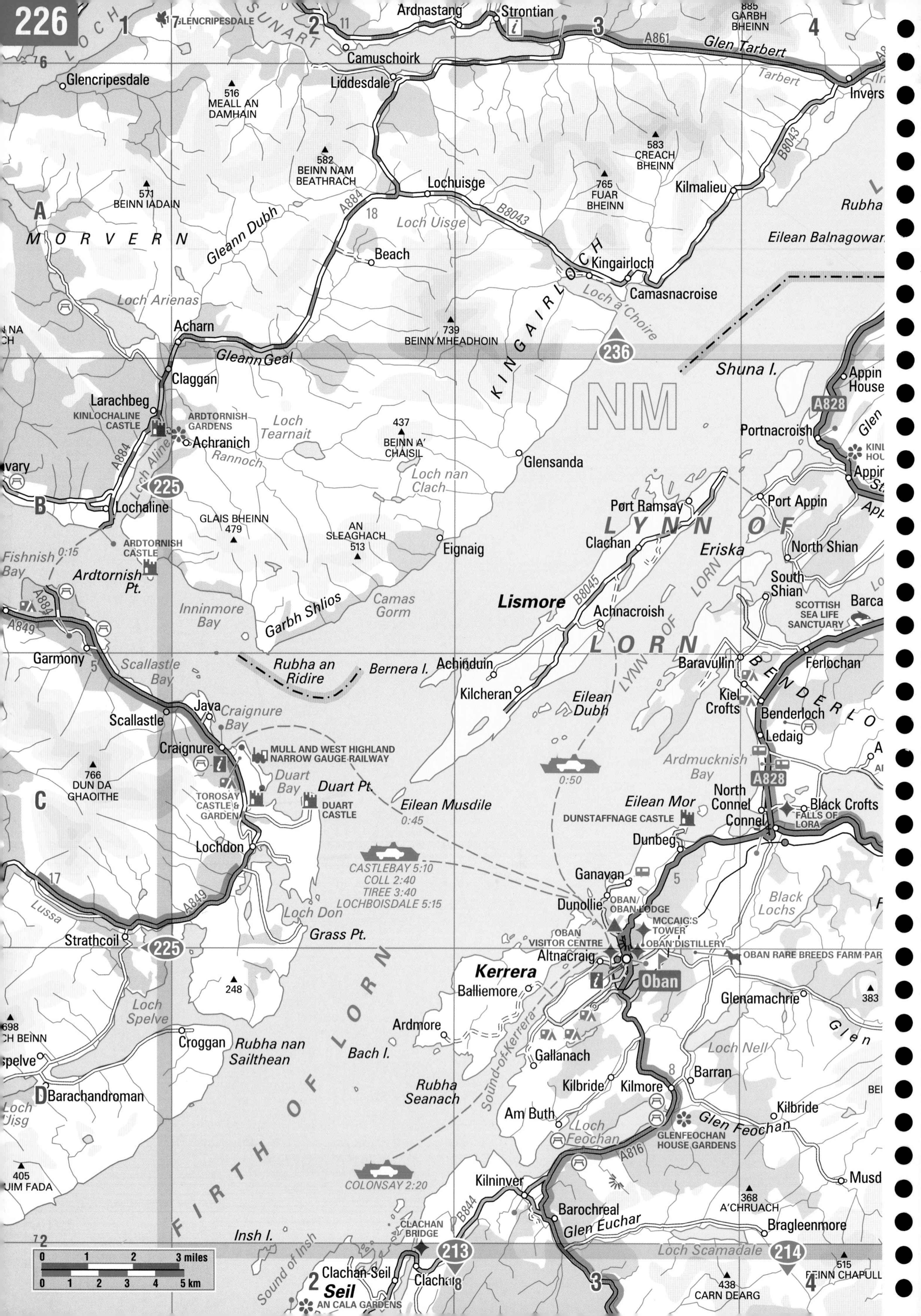
Ardnastang
Strontian
885
GARBH
BHEINN
A861
Glen Tarbert
Camuschoirk
Liddesdale
Glencripesdale
GLENCRIPESDALE
LOCH SUNART
516
MEALL AN
DAMHAIN
583
CREACH
BHEINN
582
BEINN NAM
BEATHRACH
571
BEINN IADAIN
Lochuisge
765
FUAR
BHEINN
Kilmalieu
Inversanda
B8043
Rubha
Eilean Balnagowan
MORVERN
Gleann Dubh
A884
Loch Uisge
Beach
Kingairloch
Camasnacroise
Loch a' Choire
Loch Arienas
Acharn
739
BEINN MHEADHOIN
236
Gleann Geal
Claggan
KINGAIRLOCH
Shuna I.
Appin
House
A828
NM
Larachbeg
KINLOCHALINE
CASTLE
ARDTORNISH
GARDENS
Loch
Tearnait
437
BEINN A'
CHAISIL
Portnacroish
Achranich
Rannoch
Glensanda
Loch nan
Clach
Appin
Loch Aline
225
Lochaline
Port Ramsay
Port Appin
GLAIS BHEINN
479
AN
SLEAGHACH
513
LYNN OF
Clachan
Eriska
North Shian
Eignaig
ARDTORNISH
CASTLE
Fishnish
Bay
0:15
Ardtornish
Pt.
South
Shian
Camas
Gorm
Garbh Shlios
Lismore
B8045
Achnacroish
SCOTTISH
SEA LIFE
SANCTUARY
Barcaldine
Inninmore
Bay
A884
A849
LORN
LYNN OF LORN
Garmony
Scallastle
Bay
Rubha an
Ridire
Bernera I.
Achinduin
Baravullin
Ferlochan
BENDERLOCH
Kilcheran
Eilean
Dubh
Kiel
Crofts
Scallastle
Java
Craignure
Bay
Benderloch
Ledaig
Craignure
MULL AND WEST HIGHLAND
NARROW GAUGE RAILWAY
766
DUN DA
GHAOITHE
Duart
Bay
Duart Pt.
0:50
Ardmucknish
Bay
A828
TOROSAY
CASTLE &
GARDEN
DUART
CASTLE
Eilean Musdile
0:45
Eilean Mor
North
Connel
Black Crofts
DUNSTAFFNAGE CASTLE
FALLS OF
LORA
Connel
Lochdon
Dunbeg
CASTLEBAY 5:10
COLL 2:40
TIREE 3:40
LOCHBOISDALE 5:15
Ganavan
Lussa
A849
Loch Don
Dunollie
OBAN/
OBAN LODGE
Black
Lochs
Strathcoil
225
Grass Pt.
OBAN
VISITOR CENTRE
MCCAIG'S
TOWER
OBAN DISTILLERY
Altnacraig
OBAN RARE BREEDS FARM PARK
Kerrera
Oban
248
Balliemore
Glenamachrie
383
Loch
Spelve
Ardmore
698
BEINN
Croggan
Rubha nan
Sailthean
Bach I.
Sound of Kerrera
Gallanach
Glen
Loch Nell
Barran
Kilbride
Kilmore
Barachandroman
Loch
Uisg
FIRTH OF LORN
Rubha
Seanach
Am Buth
Loch
Feochan
Glen Feochan
Kilbride
GLENFEOCHAN
HOUSE GARDENS
A816
405
UIM FADA
COLONSAY 2:20
Kilninver
Musdale
368
A'CHRUACH
Barochreal
Glen Euchar
Bragleenmore
B844
Insh I.
CLACHAN
BRIDGE
213
Sound of Insh
Loch Scamadale
214
515
BEINN CHAPULL
Clachan-Seil
Seil
Clachan
438
CARN DEARG
AN CALA GARDENS
0 1 2 3 miles
0 1 2 3 4 5 km

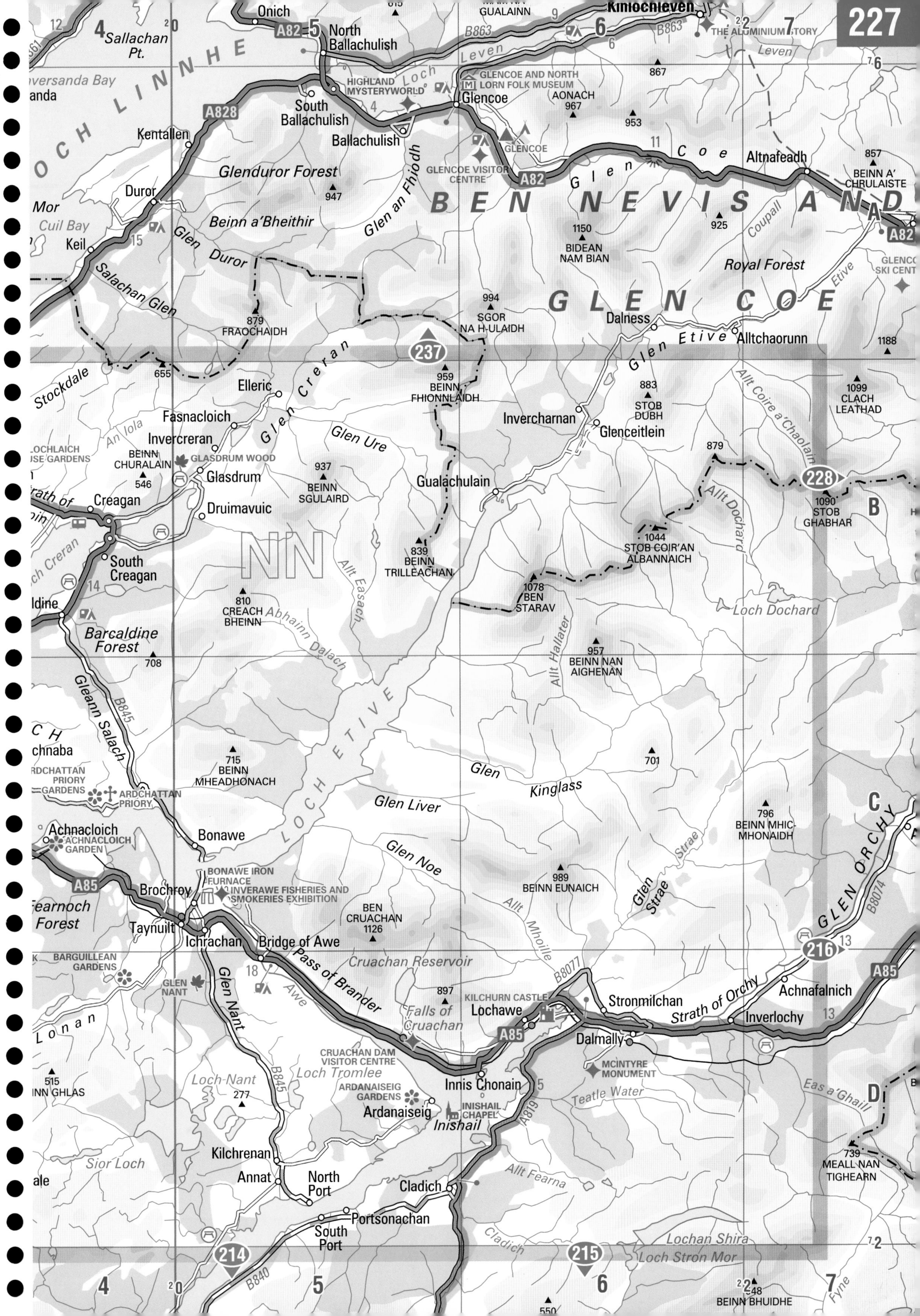
Onich
North Ballachulish
GUALAINN
Kinlochleven
THE ALUMINIUM STORY
Sallachan Pt.
LOCH LINNHE
Leven
HIGHLAND MYSTERYWORLD
GLENCOE AND NORTH LORN FOLK MUSEUM
867
South Ballachulish
Glencoe
AONACH 967
953
Kentallen
Ballachulish
GLENCOE
Glen Coe
Altnafeadh
857 BEINN A' CHRULAISTE
Glenduror Forest
GLENCOE VISITOR CENTRE
947
Glen an Fhiodh
Duror
BEN NEVIS AND
Beinn a'Bheithir
Cuil Bay
Keil
Glen Duror
1150 BIDEAN NAM BIAN
925
Coupall
Royal Forest
Salachan Glen
GLEN COE
994 SGOR NA H-ULAIDH
879 FRAOCHAIDH
Dalness
Glen Etive
Alltchaorunn
1188
237
Glen Creran
655
959 BEINN FHIONNLAIDH
883 STOB DUBH
1099 CLACH LEATHAD
Stockdale
Elleric
Fasnacloich
Invercharnan
Glenceitlein
Allt Coire a'Chaolain
Invercreran
An Iola
Glen Ure
LOCHLAICH HOUSE GARDENS
BEINN CHURALAIN
GLASDRUM WOOD
879
Glasdrum
937 BEINN SGULAIRD
Gualachulain
228
546
Creagan
Druimavuic
1090 STOB GHABHAR
Allt Dochard
NN
839 BEINN TRILLEACHAN
1044 STOB COIR'AN ALBANNAICH
South Creagan
Loch Creran
Allt Easach
810 CREACH BHEINN
1078 BEN STARAV
Loch Dochard
Abhainn Dalach
Allt Hallater
Barcaldine Forest
708
957 BEINN NAN AIGHENAN
Gleann Salach
B845
LOCH ETIVE
715 BEINN MHEADHONACH
701
ARDCHATTAN PRIORY GARDENS
ARDCHATTAN PRIORY
Glen Kinglass
Glen Liver
C
GLEN ORCHY
796 BEINN MHIC-MHONAIDH
Achnacloich
ACHNACLOICH GARDEN
Bonawe
Glen Noe
Strae
BONAWE IRON FURNACE
INVERAWE FISHERIES AND SMOKERIES EXHIBITION
989 BEINN EUNAICH
A85
Brochroy
Fearnoch Forest
BEN CRUACHAN 1126
Glen Strae
Allt Mhoille
B8074
Taynuilt
Ichrachan
Bridge of Awe
216
BARGUILLEAN GARDENS
Cruachan Reservoir
Pass of Brander
GLEN NANT
Glen Nant
Awe
897
KILCHURN CASTLE
Stronmilchan
Strath of Orchy
Achnafalnich
Falls of Cruachan
Lochawe
B8077
Inverlochy
Lonan
Dalmally
CRUACHAN DAM VISITOR CENTRE
MCINTYRE MONUMENT
515 BEINN GHLAS
Loch-Nant
Loch Tromlee
Innis Chonain
Eas a'Ghaill
D
277
ARDANAISEIG GARDENS
INISHAIL CHAPEL
Teatle Water
Ardanaiseig
Inishail
A819
Kilchrenan
Sior Loch
739 MEALL NAN TIGHEARN
Annat
North Port
Cladich
Allt Fearna
Portsonachan
South Port
Cladich
Lochan Shira
214
215
Loch Stron Mor
B840
548 BEINN BHUIDHE
550
Fyne
4
5
6
7

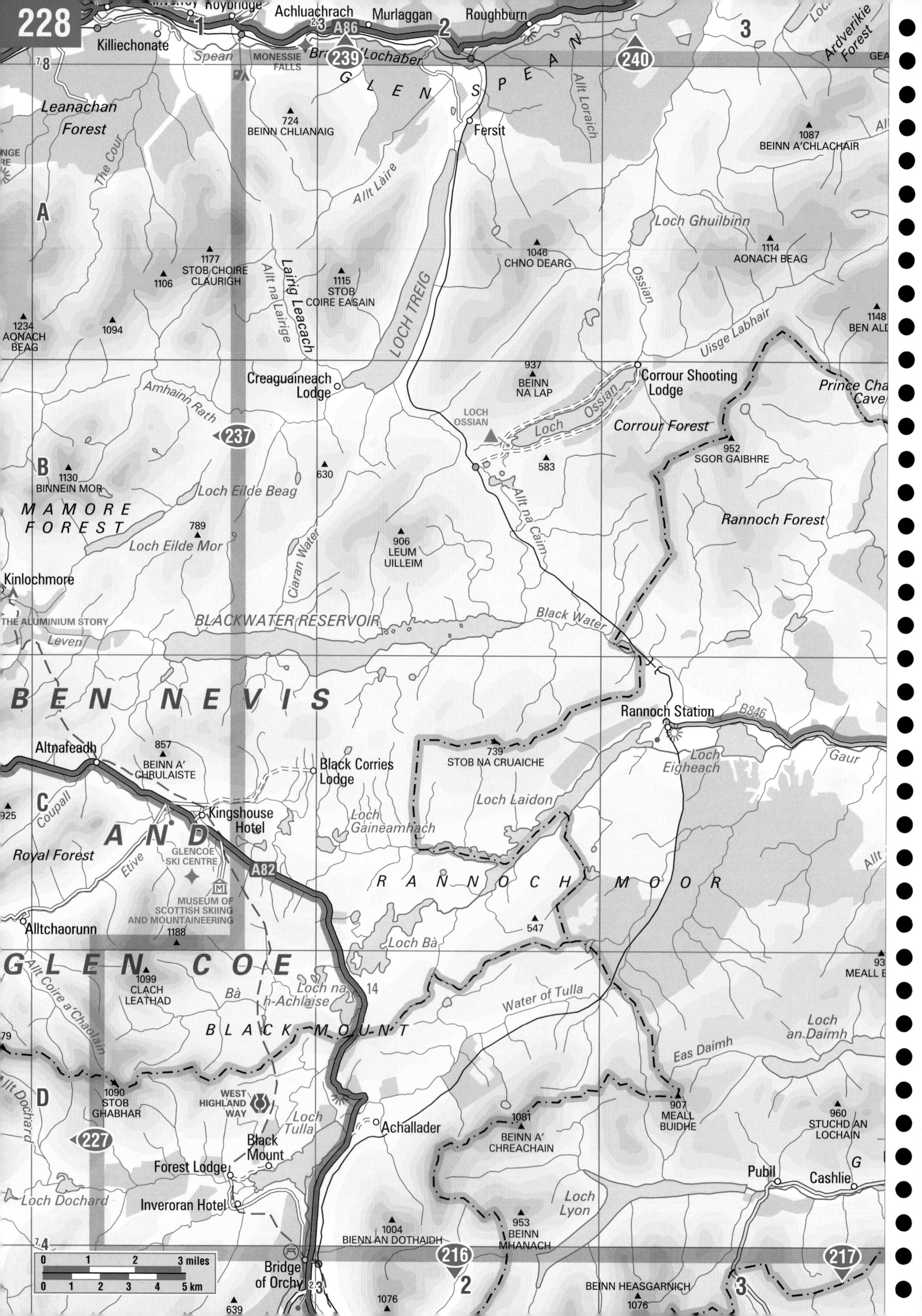

Roybridge
Achluachrach
Murlaggan
Roughburn
Killiechonate
Spean
MONESSIE FALLS
Bridge of Lochaber
A86
239
240
GLEN SPEAN
Ardverikie Forest
Leanachan Forest
The Cour
724 BEINN CHLIANAIG
Fersit
Allt Loraich
1087 BEINN A'CHLACHAIR
Allt Laire
Loch Ghuilbinn
1177 STOB CHOIRE CLAURIGH
1106
Allt na Lairige
Lairig Leacach
1115 STOB COIRE EASAIN
LOCH TREIG
1046 CHNO DEARG
Ossian
1114 AONACH BEAG
1234 AONACH BEAG
1094
Uisge Labhair
1148 BEN ALD
937 BEINN NA LAP
Creaguaineach Lodge
Corrour Shooting Lodge
Prince Charlie's Cave
Amhainn Rath
237
LOCH OSSIAN
Loch Ossian
Corrour Forest
952 SGOR GAIBHRE
630
583
1130 BINNEIN MOR
Loch Eilde Beag
MAMORE FOREST
Allt na Caim
Rannoch Forest
789
Loch Eilde Mor
Ciaran Water
906 LEUM UILLEIM
Kinlochmore
THE ALUMINIUM STORY
BLACKWATER RESERVOIR
Black Water
Leven
BEN NEVIS AND GLEN COE
Rannoch Station
B846
Altnafeadh
857 BEINN A' CHRULAISTE
Black Corries Lodge
739 STOB NA CRUAICHE
Loch Eigheach
Gaur
Loch Laidon
925
Coupall
Kingshouse Hotel
Loch Gaineamhach
Royal Forest
GLENCOE SKI CENTRE
Etive
A82
RANNOCH MOOR
MUSEUM OF SCOTTISH SKIING AND MOUNTAINEERING
Alltchaorunn
1188
547
Loch Bà
1099 CLACH LEATHAD
Allt Coire a'Chaolain
Bà
Loch na h-Achlaise
14
Water of Tulla
MEALL B
BLACK MOUNT
Loch an Daimh
Eas Daimh
Allt Dochard
1090 STOB GHABHAR
WEST HIGHLAND WAY
Loch Tulla
Achallader
1081 BEINN A' CHREACHAIN
907 MEALL BUIDHE
960 STUCHD AN LOCHAIN
227
Black Mount
Forest Lodge
Pubil
Cashlie
Loch Dochard
Inveroran Hotel
Loch Lyon
1004 BIENN AN DOTHAIDH
953 BEINN MHANACH
216
217
0 1 2 3 miles
0 1 2 3 4 5 km
Bridge of Orchy
639
1076
BEINN HEASGARNICH 1076

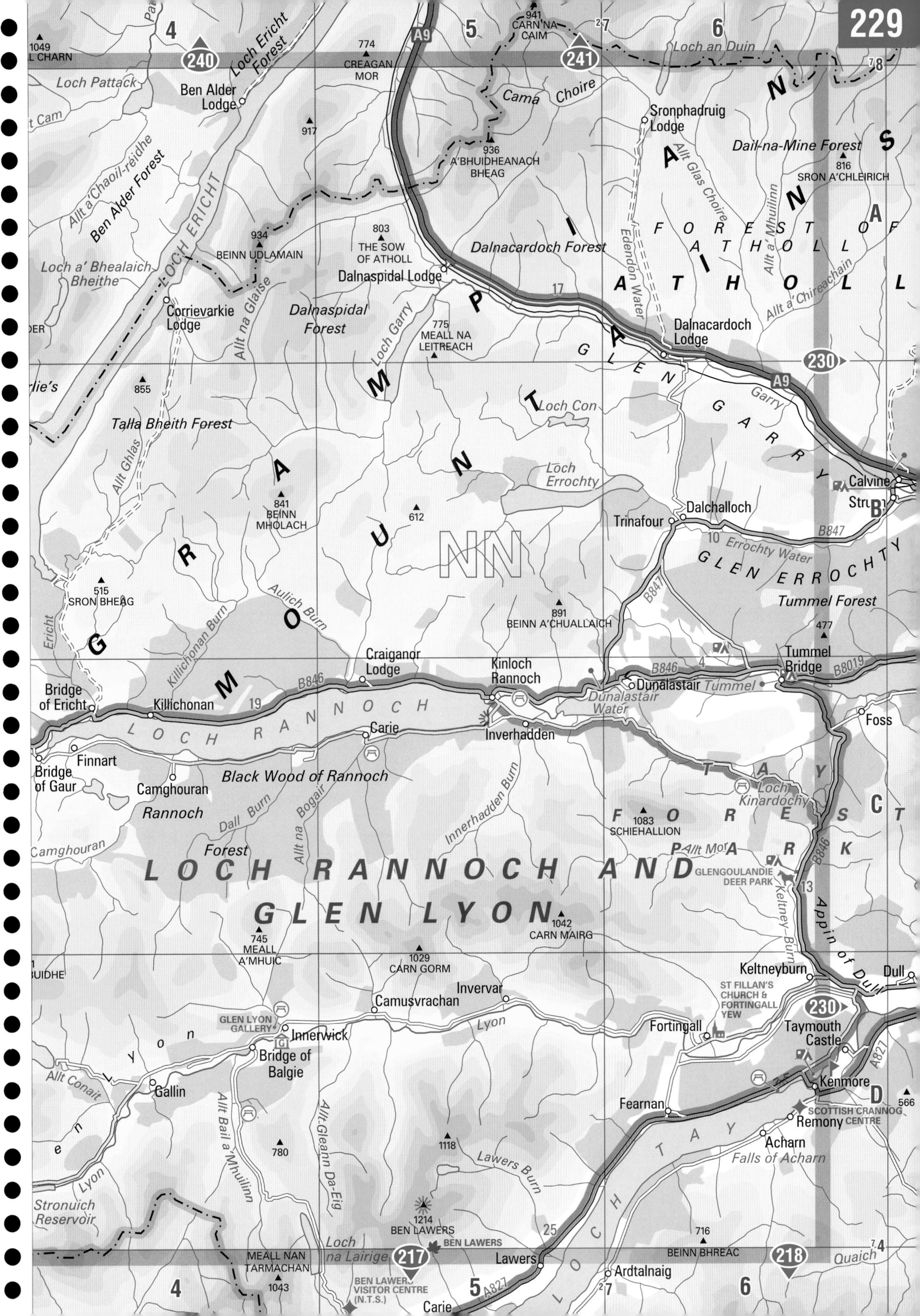

240
241
230
217
218
Loch Ericht Forest
Ben Alder Lodge
Loch Pattack
CREAGAN MOR
CARN NA CAIM
Loch an Duin
Cama Choire
Sronphadruig Lodge
Dail-na-Mine Forest
SRON A'CHLEIRICH
A'BHUIDHEANACH BHEAG
Allt a'Chaoil-reidhe
Ben Alder Forest
LOCH ERICHT
BEINN UDLAMAIN
THE SOW OF ATHOLL
Dalnaspidal Lodge
Dalnacardoch Forest
FOREST OF ATHOLL
Edendon Water
Allt Glas Choire
Allt a' Mhuilinn
Allt a' Chireachain
Loch a' Bhealaich Bheithe
Corrievarkie Lodge
Allt na Glaise
Dalnaspidal Forest
Loch Garry
MEALL NA LEITREACH
Dalnacardoch Lodge
GLEN GARRY
Garry
A9
Talla Bheith Forest
Allt Ghlas
Loch Con
Loch Errochty
Calvine
Dalchalloch
Trinafour
B847
Errochty Water
GLEN ERROCHTY
Tummel Forest
BEINN MHOLACH
NN
GRAMPIAN MOUNTAINS
ATHOLL
SRON BHEAG
Aulich Burn
Killichonan Burn
BEINN A'CHUALLAICH
Craiganor Lodge
Kinloch Rannoch
Tummel Bridge
B8019
B846
Dunalastair
Tummel
Dunalastair Water
Bridge of Ericht
Killichonan
Ericht
LOCH RANNOCH
Carie
Inverhadden
Foss
Finnart
Bridge of Gaur
Camghouran
Black Wood of Rannoch
Rannoch Forest
Dall Burn
Allt na Bogair
Innerhadden Burn
TAY FOREST PARK
Loch Kinardochy
SCHIEHALLION
Allt Mor
GLENGOULANDIE DEER PARK
Keltney Burn
Appin of Dull
LOCH RANNOCH AND GLEN LYON
CARN MAIRG
MEALL A'MHUIC
CARN GORM
Keltneyburn
Dull
ST FILLAN'S CHURCH & FORTINGALL YEW
Camusvrachan
Invervar
GLEN LYON GALLERY
Innerwick
Lyon
Fortingall
Taymouth Castle
Bridge of Balgie
Gallin
Allt Conait
Glen Lyon
A827
Kenmore
Fearnan
SCOTTISH CRANNOG CENTRE
Remony
Acharn
Falls of Acharn
Allt Bail a'Mhuilinn
Allt Gleann Da-Eig
Lawers Burn
LOCH TAY
Stronuich Reservoir
BEN LAWERS
MEALL NAN TARMACHAN
Loch na Lairige
Lawers
Ardtalnaig
BEINN BHREAC
Quaich
BEN LAWERS VISITOR CENTRE (N.T.S.)
Carie

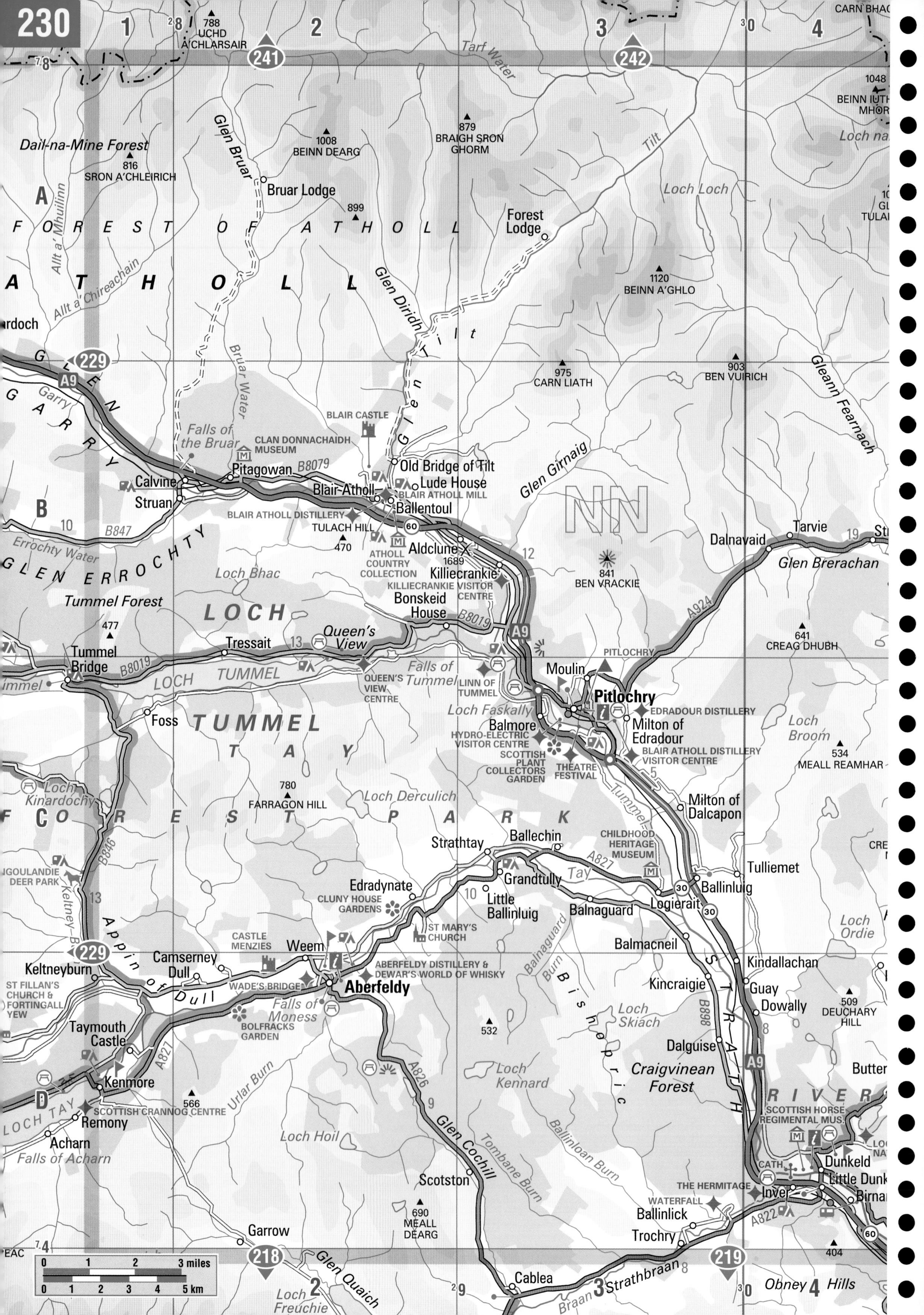

241
242
229
218
219

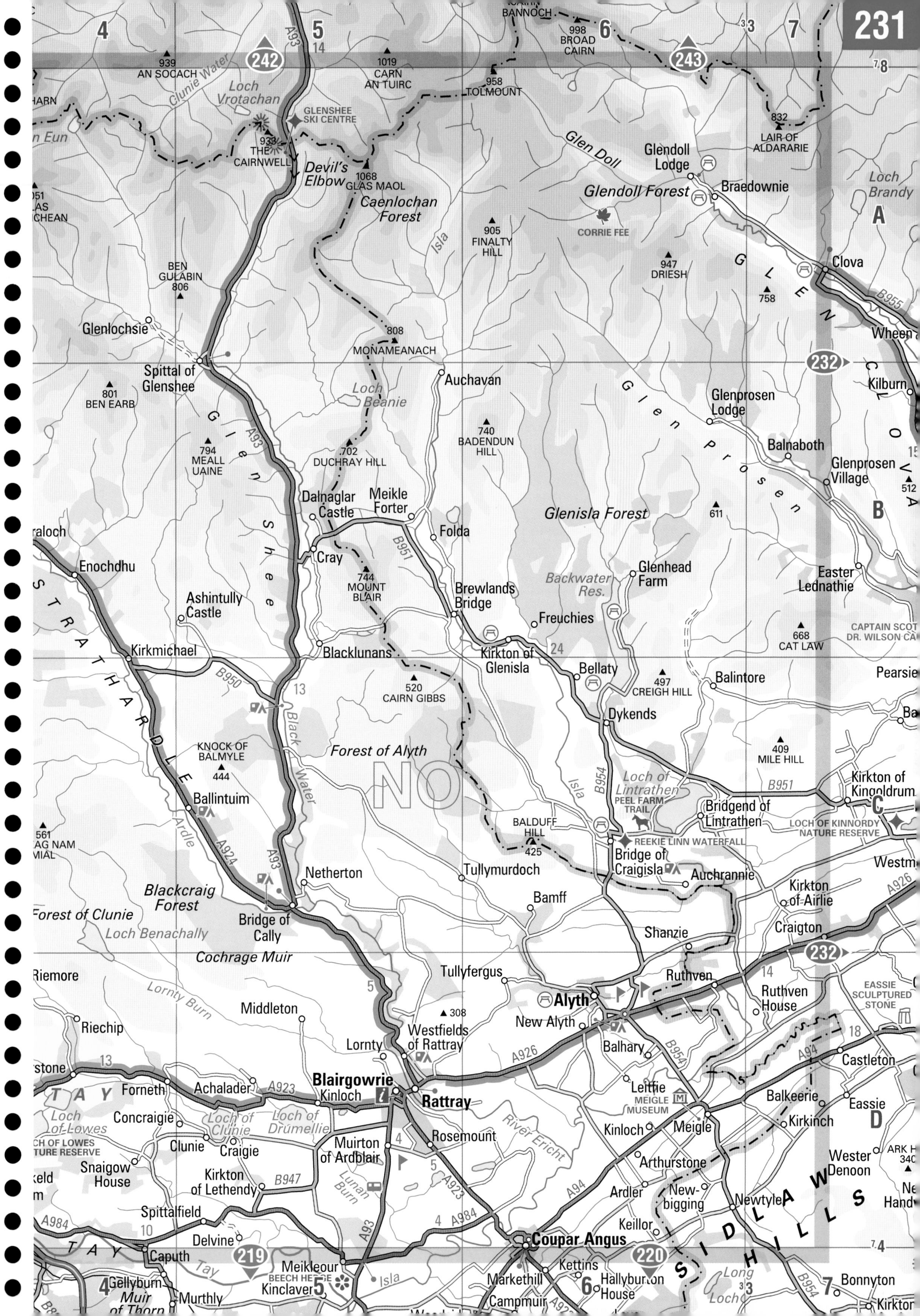
242
243
232
219
220
AN SOCACH
939
Clunie Water
Loch Vrotachan
GLENSHEE SKI CENTRE
933
THE CAIRNWELL
Devil's Elbow
1068
GLAS MAOL
1019
CARN AN TUIRC
958
TOLMOUNT
BANNOCH
998
BROAD CAIRN
832
LAIR OF ALDARARIE
Glen Doll
Glendoll Lodge
Glendoll Forest
Braedownie
CORRIE FEE
Caenlochan Forest
Isla
905
FINALTY HILL
947
DRIESH
Loch Brandy
Clova
GLEN CLOVA
B955
758
Wheen
Kilburn
BEN GULABIN
806
Glenlochsie
808
MONAMEANACH
Spittal of Glenshee
801
BEN EARB
Auchavan
Loch Beanie
740
BADENDUN HILL
Glen Prosen
Glenprosen Lodge
Balnaboth
Glenprosen Village
512
794
MEALL UAINE
Glen Shee
A93
702
DUCHRAY HILL
Dalnaglar Castle
Meikle Forter
Folda
Glenisla Forest
611
Cray
B951
744
MOUNT BLAIR
Enochdhu
Ashintully Castle
Brewlands Bridge
Backwater Res.
Glenhead Farm
Easter Lednathie
Freuchies
668
CAT LAW
CAPTAIN SCOTT DR. WILSON CAIRN
STRATHARDLE
Kirkmichael
Blacklunans
Kirkton of Glenisla
Bellaty
497
CREIGH HILL
Balintore
Pearsie
B950
520
CAIRN GIBBS
Dykends
Black Water
Forest of Alyth
KNOCK OF BALMYLE
444
409
MILE HILL
NO
Loch of Lintrathen
PEEL FARM TRAIL
B954
B951
Kirkton of Kingoldrum
Ballintuim
Bridgend of Lintrathen
LOCH OF KINNORDY NATURE RESERVE
BALDUFF HILL
425
REEKIE LINN WATERFALL
561
Ardle
A924
Bridge of Craigisla
Westmuir
Netherton
Tullymurdoch
Auchrannie
Kirkton of Airlie
A926
Blackcraig Forest
Bamff
Forest of Clunie
Bridge of Cally
Craigton
Loch Benachally
Shanzie
Cochrage Muir
Riemore
Tullyfergus
Ruthven
Ruthven House
EASSIE SCULPTURED STONE
Lornty Burn
Middleton
308
Alyth
New Alyth
Riechip
Westfields of Rattray
Balhary
A94
Castleton
Lornty
A926
Blairgowrie
Kinloch
Rattray
Forneth
Achalader
A923
TAY
Leitfie
MEIGLE MUSEUM
Balkeerie
Eassie
Loch of Lowes
Concraigie
Loch of Clunie
Loch of Drumellie
River Ericht
Kinloch
Meigle
Kirkinch
Clunie
Craigie
Muirton of Ardblair
Rosemount
Arthurstone
Wester Denoon
Snaigow House
Kirkton of Lethendy
B947
Lunan Burn
A923
Ardler
New-bigging
Newtyle
SIDLAW HILLS
Spittalfield
A984
Keillor
Delvine
Coupar Angus
Caputh
Tay
Meikleour
BEECH HEDGE
Isla
Kettins
Markethill
Hallyburton House
Long Loch
Bonnyton
Gellyburn
Muir of Thorn
Murthly
Kinclaver
Campmuir
B954
Kirkton

Glen Lee
696
MONAWEE
Invermark Lodge
Auchronie
243
244
Tarfside
Cairncross
THE RETREAT - GLEN ESK FOLK MUS.
Millden Lodge
Loch Lee
Inchgrundle
Water of Unich
832
LAIR OF ALDARARIE
MUCKLE CAIRN 826
Glen Effock
G L E N
Braedownie
Loch Brandy
Water of Saughs
CRUYS 741
691 WEST KNOCK
North Esk
Auchmull
A n g u s
678 HILL OF WIRREN
E S K
Clova
758
778 WHITE HILL
B955
Wheen
Hunthill Lodge
Dalbog
231
756 FINBRACKS
Witton
Gannochy
Kilburn
Rottal
EDZELL CASTLE AND GARDENS
Balfield
Bridgend
NO
West Water
Dunlappie
440
Tillyarblet
Balnaboth
Glen Prosen
Glenprosen Village
512
C L O V A
545 AULD DARKNEY
BROWN CATERTHUN
WHITE CATERTHUN
Clachnabrain
South Esk
Glenmoy
Kirkton of Menmuir
Tigerton
Inchbare
Newtonmill
Auchnacree
Mains of Balhall
Lochty
Belliehill
Little Brechin
Easter Lednathie
Glenogil
Glenquiech
Ogil
Fern
West Muir
Horniehaugh
668 CAT LAW
CAPTAIN SCOTT & DR. WILSON CAIRN
Dykehead
Newmill of Inshewan
Noran Water
BRECHIN CASTLE CENTRE
A935
Balintore
Pearsie
Cortachy
Memus
Careston Castle
A90
PICTAVIA
CATHEDRAL ROUND TOWER
S T R A T H
South Esk
Tannadice
Balloch
Inverquharity
Murthill
Finavon
Aldbar Castle
409 MILE HILL
Shielhill
Oathlaw
Netherton
Mains of Melgund
Kirkton of Kingoldrum
B951
Northmuir
B957
ABERLEMNO SCULPTURED STONES
Aberlemno
Montreathmont Forest
Kinnordy
Kirriemuir
LOCH OF KINNORDY NATURE RESERVE
BARRIE'S BIRTHPLACE
Carse Gray
B9134
Pitkennedy
252
Turin
Montreathmont Moor
Westmuir
GATEWAY TO THE GLENS MUS.
A926
Mosside
Lunanhead
RESTENNETH PRIORY
Rescobie
B9113
Dubton
Kirkton of Airlie
Mains of Ballindarg
Padanaram
Forfar
Reswallie
Balgavies
Glasterlaw
Craigton
A928
FORFAR LOCH
THE MEFFAN GALLERY & MUSEUM
Burnside
A932
Milldens
Guthrie
Drumgley
B9128
Kingsmuir
Pitmuies
HOUSE OF PITMUIES GARDEN
Leys of Cossans
ST. ORLAND'S STONE
Dunnichen
Letham
Ruthven House
EASSIE SCULPTURED STONE
Dean Water
A94
GLAMIS CASTLE
Caldhame
Lowrie Moor
Idvies
Douglastown
Glamis
Craichie
Castleton
Thornton
Kirkton
B9127
Charleston
ANGUS FOLK MUSEUM
Tulloes
B961
Balkeerie
Eassie
Foffarty
Mosston
Kirkinch
Milton
Gateside
Inverarity
Whigstreet
B978
Greystone
Redford
Wester Denoon
ARK HILL 340
Kirkbuddo
B9127
Nether Handwick
Gallowfauld
Newtyle
A928
Hayhillock
Carmyllie
Denhead of Arbilot
259
CROMBIE
Arbirlot
Coldstream
220
221
0 1 2 3 miles
0 1 2 3 4 5 km
Balkemback
Tealing
A90
Res.
Kirkton of Monikie
Balmirmer
Monikie
MONIKIE
Craigton
Salmond
Kirkton of
Newbigging

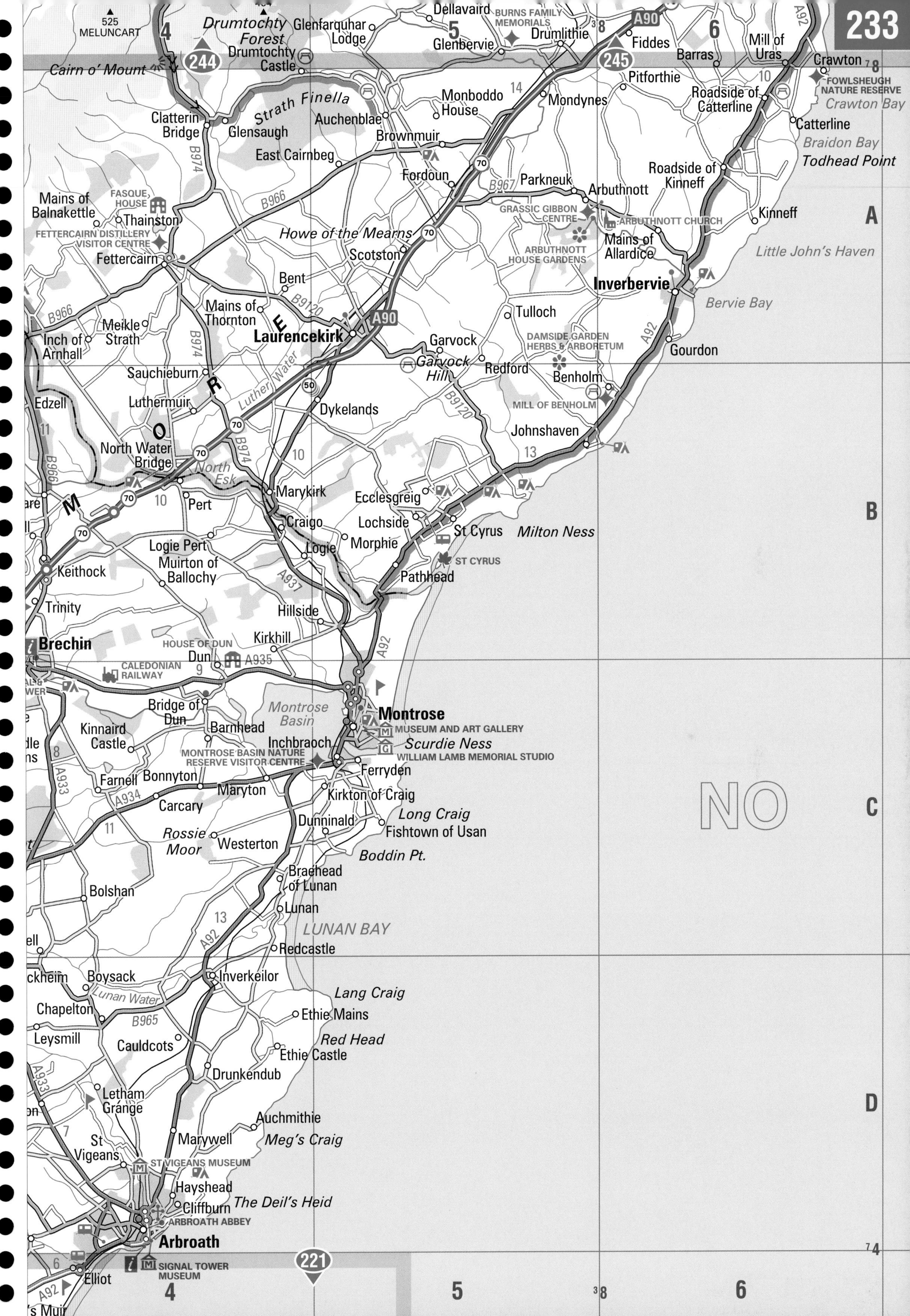
525
MELUNCART
Drumtochty Forest
Glenfarquhar Lodge
Dellavaird
BURNS FAMILY MEMORIALS
Drumlithie
Glenbervie
A90
Fiddes
Mill of Uras
Crawton
FOWLSHEUGH NATURE RESERVE
Crawton Bay
244
Cairn o' Mount
Drumtochty Castle
245
Barras
Pitforthie
Roadside of Catterline
Catterline
Braidon Bay
Todhead Point
Strath Finella
Monboddo House
Mondynes
Clatterin Bridge
Glensaugh
Auchenblae
Brownmuir
B974
East Cairnbeg
Fordoun
Roadside of Kinneff
Parkneuk
Arbuthnott
B967
GRASSIC GIBBON CENTRE
ARBUTHNOTT CHURCH
Kinneff
Mains of Balnakettle
FASQUE HOUSE
Thainston
B966
FETTERCAIRN DISTILLERY VISITOR CENTRE
Fettercairn
Howe of the Mearns
Scotston
ARBUTHNOTT HOUSE GARDENS
Mains of Allardice
Little John's Haven
Inverbervie
Bent
Bervie Bay
Tulloch
Mains of Thornton
B9120
A90
Meikle Strath
Inch of Arnhall
Laurencekirk
Garvock
DAMSIDE GARDEN HERBS & ARBORETUM
A92
Gourdon
Sauchieburn
Luther Water
Garvock Hill
Redford
Benholm
Edzell
Luthermuir
Dykelands
MILL OF BENHOLM
Johnshaven
North Water Bridge
B974
North Esk
Marykirk
Ecclesgreig
Pert
Craigo
Lochside
St Cyrus
Milton Ness
Logie Pert
Morphie
Logie
ST CYRUS
Keithock
Muirton of Ballochy
A937
Pathhead
Trinity
Hillside
Brechin
HOUSE OF DUN
Kirkhill
Dun
A935
CALEDONIAN RAILWAY
Bridge of Dun
Montrose Basin
Montrose
Kinnaird Castle
Barnhead
MUSEUM AND ART GALLERY
Inchbraoch
Scurdie Ness
MONTROSE BASIN NATURE RESERVE VISITOR CENTRE
WILLIAM LAMB MEMORIAL STUDIO
Ferryden
Farnell
Bonnyton
A933
A934
Maryton
Kirkton of Craig
Carcary
NO
Long Craig
Dunninald
Fishtown of Usan
Rossie Moor
Westerton
Boddin Pt.
Braehead of Lunan
Bolshan
Lunan
LUNAN BAY
Redcastle
Boysack
Inverkeilor
Lang Craig
Lunan Water
Chapelton
Ethie Mains
B965
Leysmill
Red Head
Cauldcots
Ethie Castle
Drunkendub
Letham Grange
Auchmithie
St Vigeans
Marywell
Meg's Craig
ST VIGEANS MUSEUM
Hayshead
Cliffburn
The Deil's Heid
ARBROATH ABBEY
Arbroath
221
SIGNAL TOWER MUSEUM
Elliot
A92
A
B
C
D
4
5
6

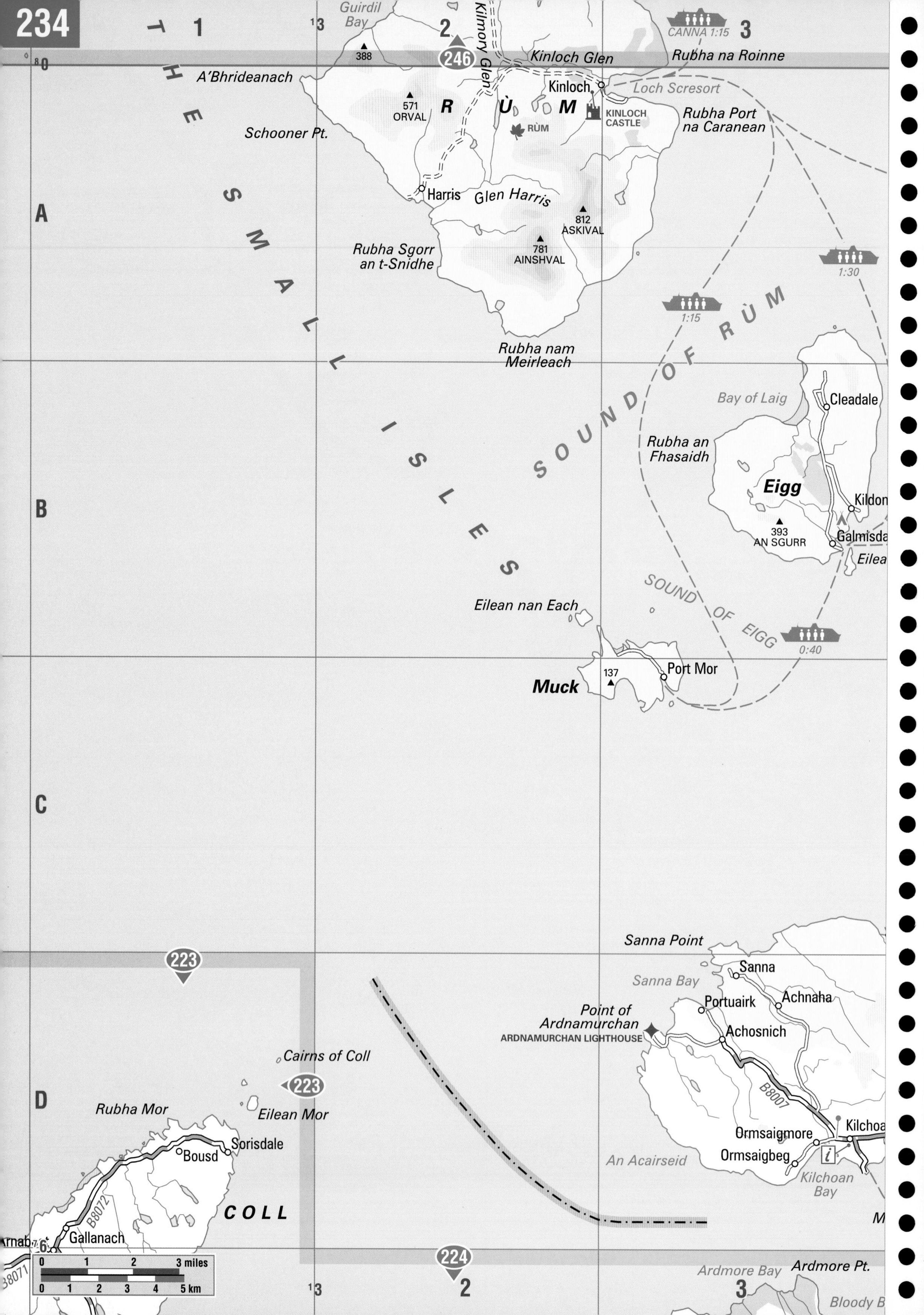
THE SMALL ISLES
RÙM
Guirdil Bay
Kilmory Glen
Kinloch Glen
Rubha na Roinne
CANNA 1:15
A'Bhrideanach
Kinloch
Loch Scresort
571 ORVAL
388
KINLOCH CASTLE
Rubha Port na Caranean
Schooner Pt.
Harris
Glen Harris
812 ASKIVAL
781 AINSHVAL
Rubha Sgorr an t-Snidhe
Rubha nam Meirleach
1:30
1:15
SOUND OF RÙM
Bay of Laig
Cleadale
Rubha an Fhasaidh
Eigg
Kildon
393 AN SGURR
Galmisda
Eilea
SOUND OF EIGG
Eilean nan Each
0:40
137
Port Mor
Muck
Sanna Point
Sanna
Sanna Bay
Portuairk
Achnaha
Point of Ardnamurchan
ARDNAMURCHAN LIGHTHOUSE
Achosnich
B8007
Cairns of Coll
Eilean Mor
Rubha Mor
Sorisdale
Bousd
B8072
COLL
Gallanach
Ormsaigmore
Ormsaigbeg
Kilchoa
An Acairseid
Kilchoan Bay
Ardmore Bay
Ardmore Pt.
Bloody B
246
223
224
0 1 2 3 miles
0 1 2 3 4 5 km

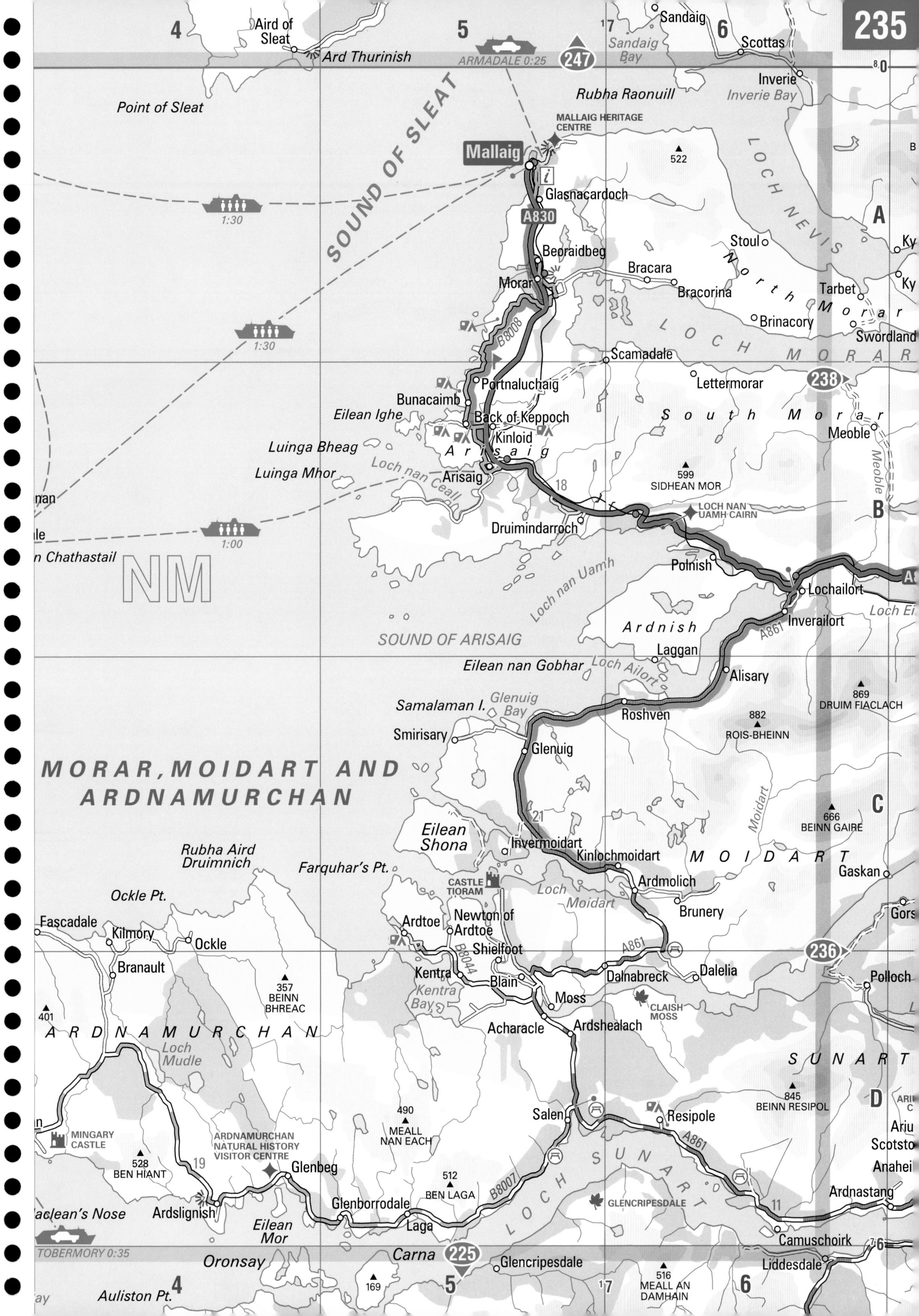
4
5
6
17
Aird of Sleat
Ard Thurinish
Sandaig
Sandaig Bay
Scottas
ARMADALE 0:25
247
Inverie
Inverie Bay
Rubha Raonuill
Point of Sleat
SOUND OF SLEAT
MALLAIG HERITAGE CENTRE
Mallaig
522
LOCH NEVIS
Glasnacardoch
A830
1:30
A
Beoraidbeg
Stoul
Bracara
Morar
Bracorina
North Morar
Tarbet
Brinacory
Swordland
LOCH MORAR
B8008
Scamadale
Portnaluchaig
Lettermorar
238
Bunacaimb
Eilean Ighe
Back of Keppoch
South Morar
Meoble
Kinloid
Luinga Bheag
Arisaig
Loch nan Ceall
Luinga Mhor
599
SIDHEAN MOR
18
LOCH NAN UAMH CAIRN
B
Druimindarroch
1:00
n Chathastail
NM
Polnish
Loch nan Uamh
Lochailort
Loch Ei
Ardnish
Inverailort
A861
SOUND OF ARISAIG
Laggan
Eilean nan Gobhar
Loch Ailort
Alisary
869
DRUIM FIACLACH
Samalaman I.
Glenuig Bay
Roshven
882
ROIS-BHEINN
Smirisary
Glenuig
MORAR, MOIDART AND ARDNAMURCHAN
Moidart
666
BEINN GAIRE
C
21
Eilean Shona
Invermoidart
Kinlochmoidart
MOIDART
Rubha Aird Druimnich
Gaskan
Farquhar's Pt.
CASTLE TIORAM
Ardmolich
Loch Moidart
Ockle Pt.
Brunery
Fascadale
Ardtoe
Newton of Ardtoe
Kilmory
Ockle
Shielfoot
236
Branault
B8044
Kentra
Dalnabreck
Dalelia
Polloch
357
BEINN BHREAC
Blain
Kentra Bay
Moss
CLAISH MOSS
401
ARDNAMURCHAN
Acharacle
Ardshealach
Loch Mudle
SUNART
845
BEINN RESIPOL
D
490
MEALL NAN EACH
Salen
Resipole
MINGARY CASTLE
ARDNAMURCHAN NATURAL HISTORY VISITOR CENTRE
528
BEN HIANT
19
Glenbeg
512
BEN LAGA
B8007
LOCH SUNART
Ardnastang
Maclean's Nose
Ardslignish
Glenborrodale
GLENCRIPESDALE
11
Eilean Mor
Laga
Camuschoirk
TOBERMORY 0:35
Oronsay
Carna
225
Glencripesdale
Liddesdale
169
516
MEALL AN DAMHAIN
Auliston Pt.

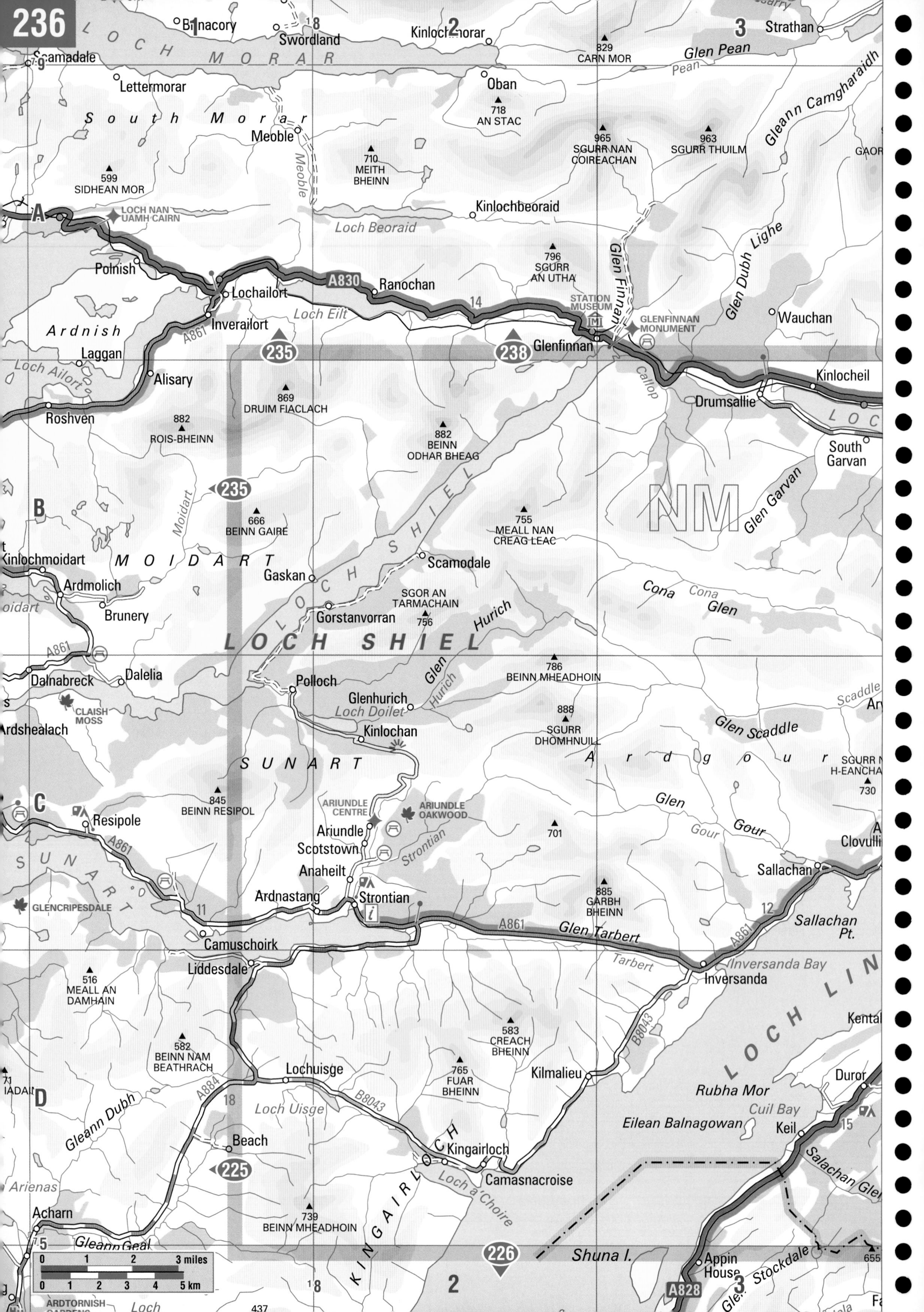
Bunacory
Swordland
Kinlochmorar
Strathan
LOCH MORAR
829 CARN MOR
Glen Pean
Scamadale
Lettermorar
Oban
718 AN STAC
South Morar
Meoble
Gleann Camgharaidh
710 MEITH BHEINN
965 SGURR NAN COIREACHAN
963 SGURR THUILM
599 SIDHEAN MOR
LOCH NAN UAMH CAIRN
Kinlochbeoraid
Loch Beoraid
Polnish
796 SGURR AN UTHA
Glen Dubh Lighe
A830
Ranochan
Lochailort
Glen Finnan
Loch Eilt
STATION MUSEUM
GLENFINNAN MONUMENT
Wauchan
Ardnish
Inverailort
A861
235
238
Glenfinnan
Laggan
Loch Ailort
Alisary
Callop
Kinlocheil
869 DRUIM FIACLACH
Drumsallie
Roshven
882 ROIS-BHEINN
882 BEINN ODHAR BHEAG
South Garvan
NM
Glen Garvan
666 BEINN GAIRE
755 MEALL NAN CREAG LEAC
Kinlochmoidart
MOIDART
Scamodale
Gaskan
Ardmolich
Cona Glen
Brunery
Gorstanvorran
SGOR AN TARMACHAIN 756
LOCH SHIEL
Hurich
Dalnabreck
Dalelia
Polloch
Glen Hurich
786 BEINN MHEADHOIN
CLAISH MOSS
Glenhurich
Loch Doilet
888 SGURR DHOMHNUILL
Ardshealach
Kinlochan
Glen Scaddle
SUNART
Ardgour
SGURR NA H-EANCHAINNE 730
845 BEINN RESIPOL
ARIUNDLE CENTRE
ARIUNDLE OAKWOOD
Glen Gour
Resipole
Ariundle
701
Clovullin
Scotstown
Strontian
Anaheilt
Sallachan
Ardnastang
Strontian
885 GARBH BHEINN
GLENCRIPESDALE
A861
Glen Tarbert
Sallachan Pt.
Camuschoirk
Liddesdale
Inversanda Bay
Inversanda
516 MEALL AN DAMHAIN
LOCH LINNHE
Kentallen
583 CREACH BHEINN
582 BEINN NAM BEATHRACH
B8043
Kilmalieu
Lochuisge
765 FUAR BHEINN
Duror
Rubha Mor
A884
Loch Uisge
Cuil Bay
Gleann Dubh
Eilean Balnagowan
Keil
Beach
Kingairloch
Salachan Glen
225
Camasnacroise
Loch a' Choire
Arienas
Acharn
739 BEINN MHEADHOIN
KINGAIRLOCH
Gleann Geal
226
Shuna I.
Appin House
Glen Stockdale
655
A828
ARDTORNISH GARDENS
0 1 2 3 miles
0 1 2 3 4 5 km

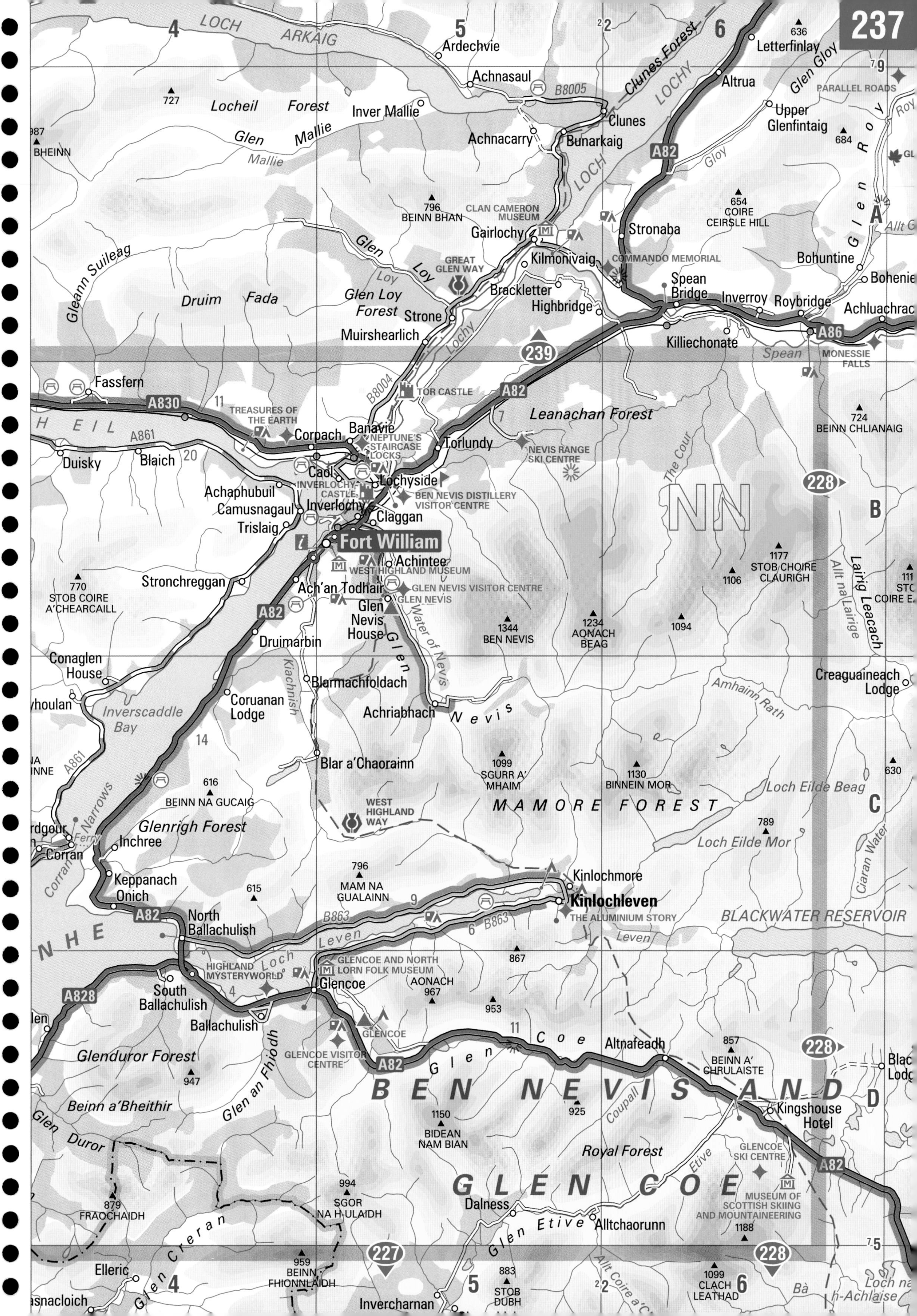
Loch Arkaig
Ardechvie
Letterfinlay
Achnasaul
Clunes Forest
Altrua
Glen Gloy
Parallel Roads
Locheil Forest
Inver Mallie
Clunes
Upper Glenfintaig
Glen Mallie
Achnacarry
Bunarkaig
A82
Loch Lochy
Glen Roy
796 Beinn Bhan
Clan Cameron Museum
654 Coire Ceirsle Hill
Gairlochy
Stronaba
Glenn Suileag
Glen Loy
Kilmonivaig
Commando Memorial
Great Glen Way
Bohuntine
Druim Fada
Glen Loy Forest
Brackletter
Highbridge
Spean Bridge
Inverroy
Roybridge
Bohenie
Achluachrach
Strone
Muirshearlich
Killiechonate
A86
Spean
Monessie Falls
239
Fassfern
A830
Tor Castle
B8004
Treasures of the Earth
Leanachan Forest
724 Beinn Chlianaig
Loch Eil
A861
Corpach
Banavie
Neptune's Staircase Locks
Torlundy
Nevis Range Ski Centre
Duisky
Blaich
Caol
Lochyside
The Cour
228
Achaphubuil
Inverlochy Castle
Ben Nevis Distillery Visitor Centre
Camusnagaul
Inverlochy
Claggan
NN
Trislaig
Fort William
Achintee
West Highland Museum
1177 Stob Choire Claurigh
1106
770 Stob Coire a'Chearcaill
Stronchreggan
Ach'an Todhair
Glen Nevis Visitor Centre
Glen Nevis
Lairig Leacach
Allt na Lairige
Glen Nevis House
Water of Nevis
1344 Ben Nevis
1234 Aonach Beag
1094
Druimarbin
Conaglen House
Kiachnish
Blarmachfoldach
Creaguaineach Lodge
Amhainn Rath
Coruanan Lodge
Inverscaddle Bay
Achriabhach
14
Blar a'Chaorainn
1099 Sgurr a' Mhaim
1130 Binnein Mor
Loch Eilde Beag
630
616 Beinn na Gucaig
Mamore Forest
West Highland Way
789
Corran Narrows
Glenrigh Forest
Inchree
Loch Eilde Mor
Corran
Ciaran Water
Kinlochmore
796 Mam na Gualainn
Keppanach
615
Onich
Kinlochleven
North Ballachulish
B863
The Aluminium Story
Blackwater Reservoir
Leven
Loch Leven
Highland Mysteryworld
Glencoe and North Lorn Folk Museum
867
A828
South Ballachulish
Glencoe
Aonach 967
953
Ballachulish
Glencoe
Glen an Fhiodh
Glencoe Visitor Centre
Glen Coe
Altnafeadh
857 Beinn a' Chrulaiste
Glenduror Forest
947
Ben Nevis and Glen Coe
Beinn a'Bheithir
925
Coupall
Kingshouse Hotel
Glen Duror
1150 Bidean nam Bian
Royal Forest
Glencoe Ski Centre
Etive
994 Sgor na h-Ulaidh
879 Fraochaidh
Dalness
Museum of Scottish Skiing and Mountaineering
Glen Creran
Glen Etive
Alltchaorunn
1188
227
959 Beinn Fhionnlaidh
883 Stob Dubh
1099 Clach Leathad
Allt Coire a'Ch
Elleric
Inverchanan
Bà
Loch na h-Achlaise
4
5
6
A
B
C
D
9
7
11
20
9
6
4
11
2
5

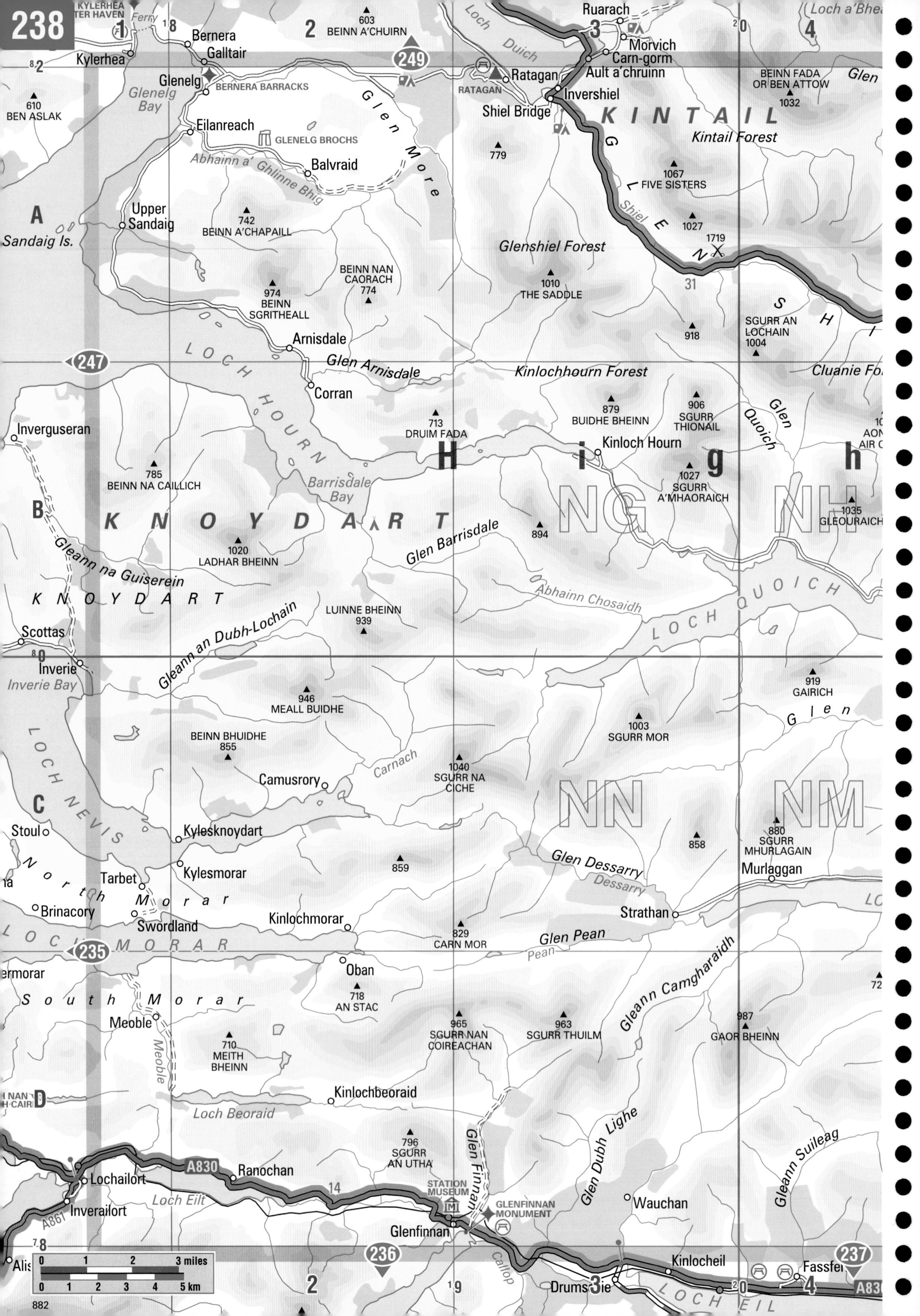
Kylerhea
Ferry
Bernera
Galltair
Glenelg
BERNERA BARRACKS
Glenelg Bay
610
BEN ASLAK
Eilanreach
GLENELG BROCHS
Abhainn a' Ghlinne Bhig
Balvraid
Glen More
603
BEINN A'CHUIRN
249
RATAGAN
Ratagan
Loch Duich
Ruarach
Morvich
Carn-gorm
Ault a'chruinn
Inverhiel
Shiel Bridge
KINTAIL
Kintail Forest
BEINN FADA OR BEN ATTOW
1032
779
1067
FIVE SISTERS
GLEN SHIEL
1027
1719
Glenshiel Forest
1010
THE SADDLE
918
SGURR AN LOCHAIN
1004
Cluanie Fo
Upper Sandaig
Sandaig Is.
742
BEINN A'CHAPAILL
974
BEINN SGRITHEALL
BEINN NAN CAORACH
774
Arnisdale
LOCH HOURN
247
Glen Arnisdale
Corran
Kinlochhourn Forest
713
DRUIM FADA
879
BUIDHE BHEINN
906
SGURR THIONAIL
Glen Quoich
Kinloch Hourn
Highland
1027
SGURR A'MHAORAICH
NG
NH
1035
GLEOURAICH
Inverguseran
785
BEINN NA CAILLICH
Barrisdale Bay
KNOYDART
1020
LADHAR BHEINN
Glen Barrisdale
894
Gleann na Guiserein
Abhainn Chosaidh
LOCH QUOICH
LUINNE BHEINN
939
Gleann an Dubh-Lochain
Scottas
Inverie
Inverie Bay
946
MEALL BUIDHE
919
GAIRICH
Glen
1003
SGURR MOR
BEINN BHUIDHE
855
Carnach
1040
SGURR NA CICHE
Camusrory
LOCH NEVIS
NN
NM
Stoul
Kylesknoydart
Kylesmorar
858
880
SGURR MHURLAGAIN
Tarbet
North Morar
859
Glen Dessarry
Dessarry
Murlaggan
Brinacory
Swordland
Kinlochmorar
Strathan
829
CARN MOR
Glen Pean
Pean
LOCH MORAR
235
Oban
718
AN STAC
Gleann Camgharaidh
South Morar
Meoble
965
SGURR NAN COIREACHAN
963
SGURR THUILM
987
GAOR BHEINN
710
MEITH BHEINN
Kinlochbeoraid
Loch Beoraid
796
SGURR AN UTHA
Glen Finnan
Glen Dubh Lighe
Gleann Suileag
A830
Ranochan
Lochailort
Inverailort
Loch Eilt
A861
STATION MUSEUM
GLENFINNAN MONUMENT
Wauchan
Glenfinnan
236
Callop
Kinlocheil
237
Fassfe
Drumsallie
LOCH EIL
0 1 2 3 miles
0 1 2 3 4 5 km
882

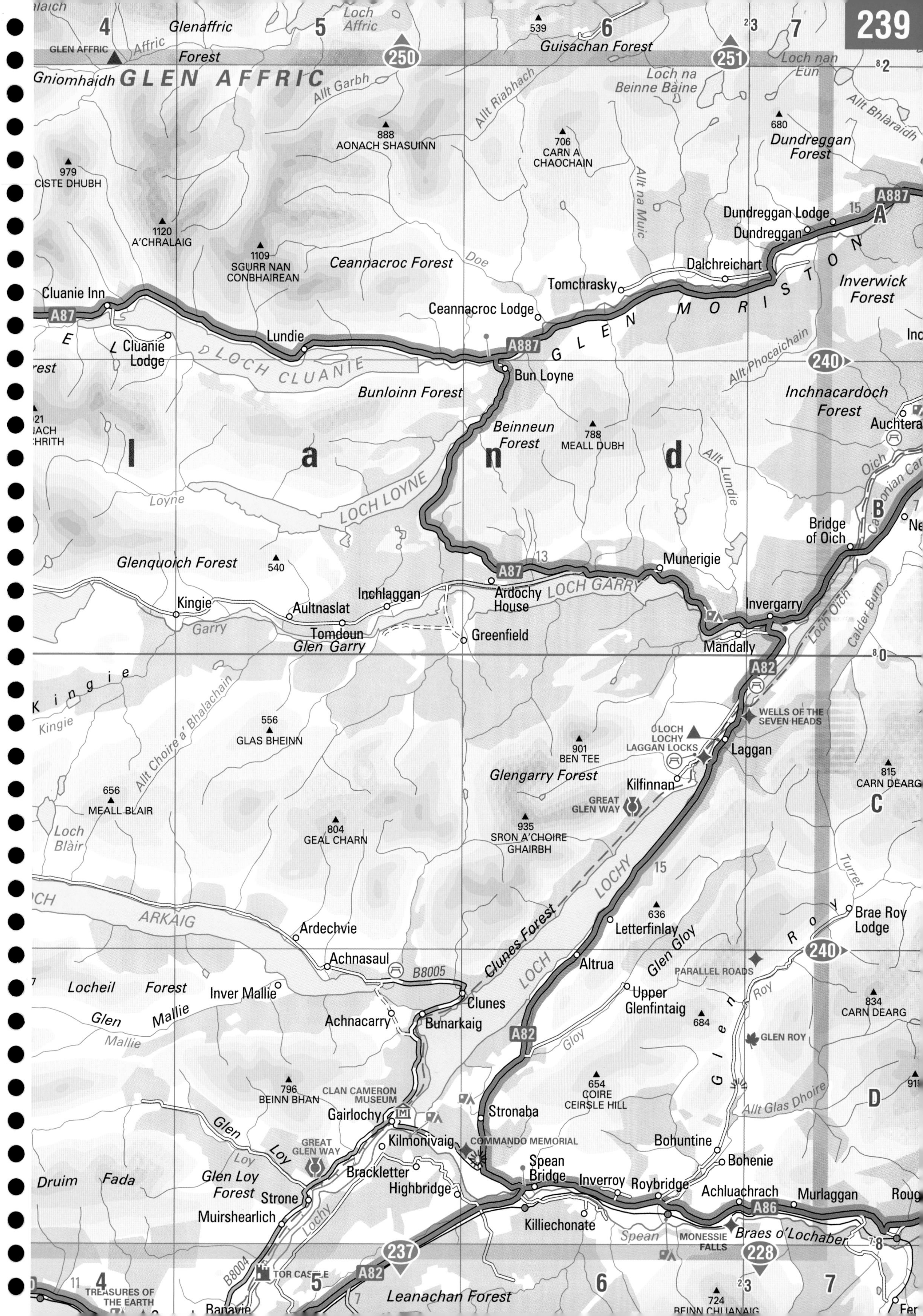
GLEN AFFRIC
Glenaffric
Forest
Loch Affric
Guisachan Forest
Loch na Beinne Bàine
Loch nan Eun
Dundreggan Forest
AONACH SHASUINN
CARN A CHAOCHAIN
CISTE DHUBH
A'CHRALAIG
SGURR NAN CONBHAIREAN
Ceannacroc Forest
Cluanie Inn
Cluanie Lodge
Lundie
LOCH CLUANIE
Ceannacroc Lodge
Tomchrasky
Dalchreichart
Dundreggan
Dundreggan Lodge
GLEN MORISTON
Inverwick Forest
Bun Loyne
Bunloinn Forest
Inchnacardoch Forest
Auchtera
Beinneun Forest
MEALL DUBH
LOCH LOYNE
Glenquoich Forest
Bridge of Oich
Munerigie
Kingie
Aultnaslat
Inchlaggan
Ardochy House
LOCH GARRY
Invergarry
Tomdoun
Glen Garry
Greenfield
Mandally
Loch Oich
Calder Burn
WELLS OF THE SEVEN HEADS
GLAS BHEINN
BEN TEE
LOCH LOCHY
LAGGAN LOCKS
Laggan
Glengarry Forest
Kilfinnan
GREAT GLEN WAY
CARN DEARG
MEALL BLAIR
Loch Blàir
GEAL CHARN
SRON A'CHOIRE GHAIRBH
LOCH LOCHY
LOCH ARKAIG
Ardechvie
Letterfinlay
Brae Roy Lodge
Achnasaul
Clunes Forest
Altrua
Glen Gloy
PARALLEL ROADS
Locheil Forest
Inver Mallie
Clunes
Upper Glenfintaig
Glen Mallie
Achnacarry
Bunarkaig
GLEN ROY
Glen Roy
BEINN BHAN
CLAN CAMERON MUSEUM
COIRE CEIRSLE HILL
Allt Glas Dhoire
Gairlochy
Stronaba
Kilmonivaig
COMMANDO MEMORIAL
Bohuntine
Bohenie
Glen Loy
Brackletter
Spean Bridge
Inverroy
Roybridge
Achluachrach
Murlaggan
Druim Fada
Glen Loy Forest
Strone
Highbridge
Muirshearlich
Killiechonate
MONESSIE FALLS
Braes o'Lochaber
TOR CASTLE
TREASURES OF THE EARTH
Leanachan Forest
BEINN CHLIANAIG
Banavie

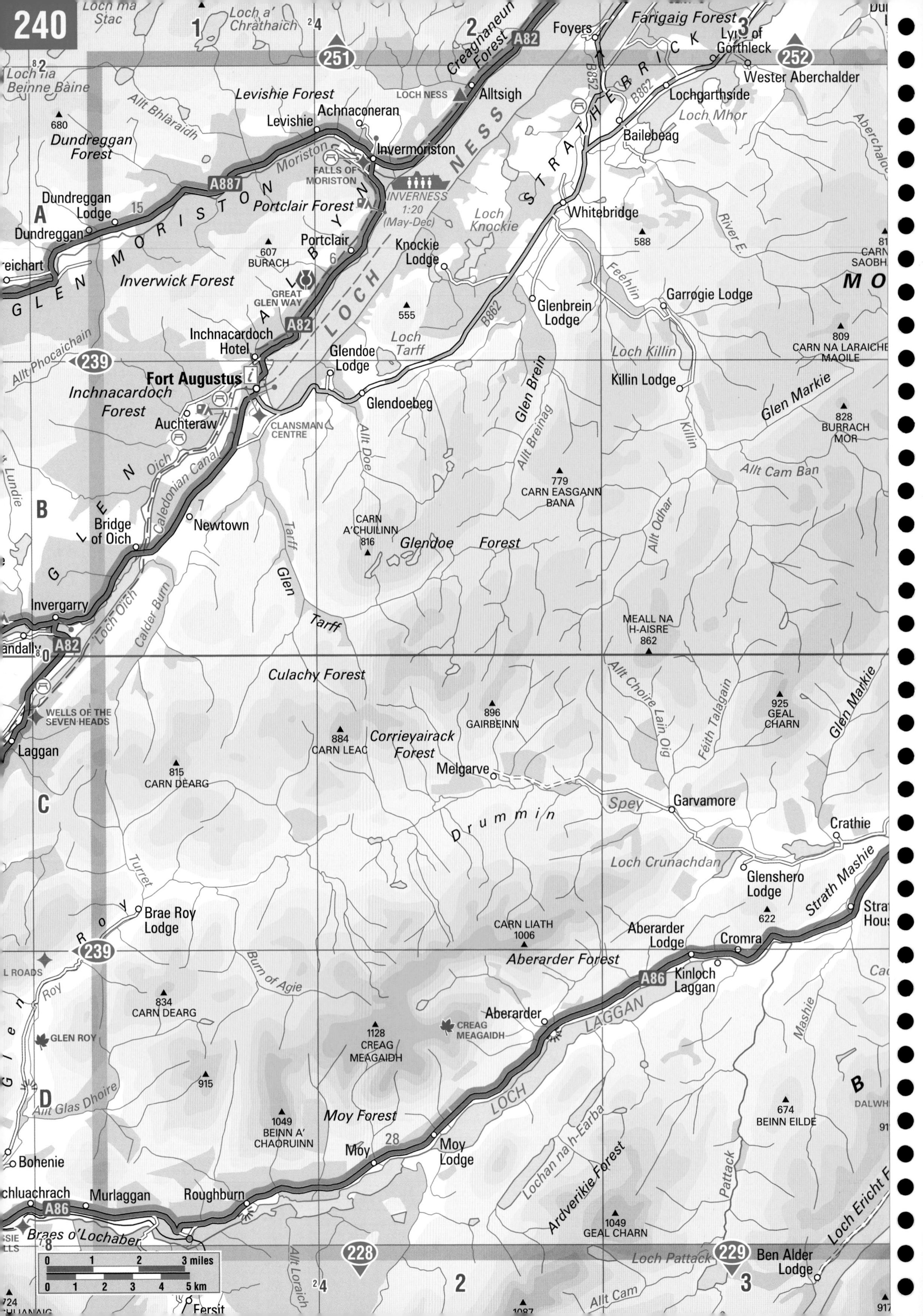

Fort Augustus
Loch Ness
Glen Moriston
Strathherrick
Invermoriston
Foyers
Whitebridge
Glendoe Forest
Culachy Forest
Corrieyairack Forest
Melgarve
Garvamore
Laggan
Invergarry
Bridge of Oich
Newtown
Auchteraw
Inverwick Forest
Inchnacardoch Forest
Levishie Forest
Dundreggan Forest
Portclair Forest
Aberarder Forest
Moy Forest
Ardverikie Forest
Creag Meagaidh
Loch Laggan
Kinloch Laggan
Aberarder
Moy
Roughburn
Murlaggan
Brae Roy Lodge
Loch Pattack
Ben Alder Lodge
A82
A887
A86
B862
B852
251
252
239
228
229
0 1 2 3 miles
0 1 2 3 4 5 km

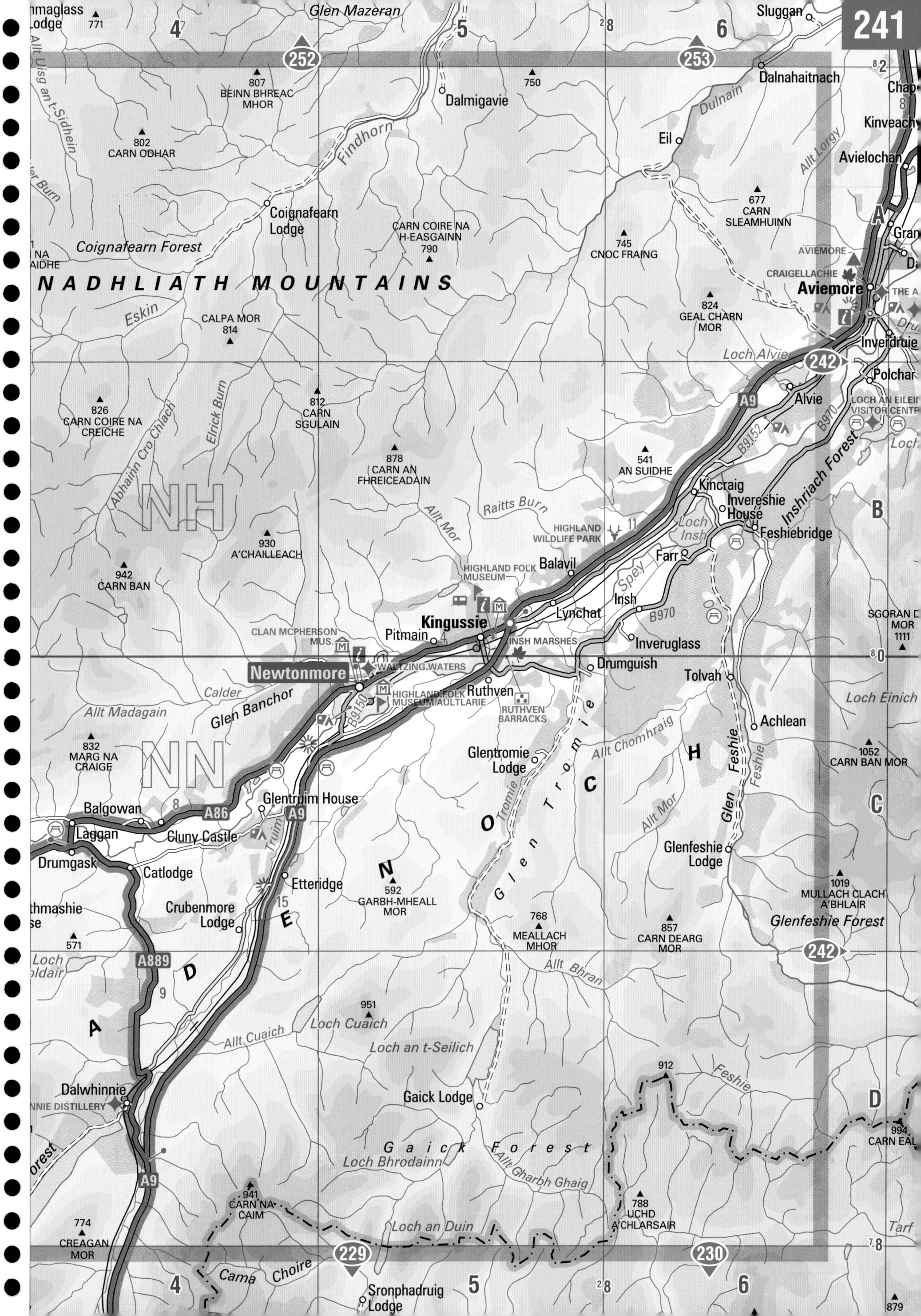
NADHLIATH MOUNTAINS
Glen Mazeran
Dalmigavie
Findhorn
Coignafearn Lodge
Coignafearn Forest
807 BEINN BHREAC MHOR
802 CARN ODHAR
750
CARN COIRE NA H-EASGAINN 790
CALPA MOR 814
Eskin
826 CARN COIRE NA CREICHE
Abhainn Cro Chlach
Elrick Burn
812 CARN SGULAIN
878 CARN AN FHREICEADAIN
930 A'CHAILLEACH
942 CARN BAN
Allt Mor
Raitts Burn
Dalnahaitnach
Dulnain
Eil
Sluggan
677 CARN SLEAMHUINN
745 CNOC FRAING
824 GEAL CHARN MOR
Allt Lorgy
Kinveachy
Avielochan
AVIEMORE
CRAIGELLACHIE
Aviemore
Inverdruie
Polchar
Loch Alvie
Alvie
LOCH AN EILEIN VISITOR CENTRE
B970
B9152
A9
541 AN SUIDHE
Kincraig
Invereshie House
Feshiebridge
Inshriach Forest
HIGHLAND WILDLIFE PARK
Loch Insh
Farr
Spey
Balavil
HIGHLAND FOLK MUSEUM
Lynchat
Insh
Kingussie
Pitmain
CLAN MCPHERSON MUS.
INSH MARSHES
Inveruglass
Drumguish
Tolvah
Newtonmore
WALTZING WATERS
HIGHLAND FOLK MUSEUM/AULTLARIE
Ruthven
RUTHVEN BARRACKS
B9150
Calder
Glen Banchor
Allt Madagain
832 MARG NA CRAIGE
NH
NN
SGORAN DUBH MOR 1111
Loch Einich
Achlean
Allt Chomhraig
Glentromie Lodge
Glen Tromie
Tromie
Feshie
Glen Feshie
1052 CARN BAN MOR
Balgowan
A86
Laggan
Glentruim House
Cluny Castle
Truim
Drumgask
Catlodge
Etteridge
Allt Mor
Glenfeshie Lodge
CAIRNGORMS NATIONAL PARK
592 GARBH-MHEALL MOR
1019 MULLACH CLACH A'BHLAIR
Glenfeshie Forest
Crubenmore Lodge
768 MEALLACH MHOR
857 CARN DEARG MOR
571
Loch Ericht
A889
Allt Bhran
951
Loch Cuaich
Allt Cuaich
Loch an t-Seilich
912
Feshie
Dalwhinnie
DALWHINNIE DISTILLERY
Gaick Lodge
Gaick Forest
Loch Bhrodainn
Allt Gharbh Ghaig
941 CARN NA CAIM
788 UCHD A'CHLARSAIR
994 CARN EALAR
774 CREAGAN MOR
Loch an Duin
Tarf
Cama Choire
Sronphadruig Lodge
879
252
253
242
229
230
4
5
6
A
B
C
D

CAIRNGORMS NATIONAL PARK
THE CAIRNGORM MOUNTAINS
CAIRNGORM MOUNTAINS
GRAMPIAN MOUNTAINS
BRAES OF ABERNETHY
GLEN AVON
Aviemore
Nethy Bridge
Boat of Garten
Coylumbridge
Glenmore Lodge
Braemar
Feshiebridge
Dalnahaitnach
Drumuillie
Cullachie
Birchfield
Chapelton
East Croftmore
Kinveachy
Avielochan
Aundorach
Auchgourish
Granish
Pityoulish
Dalfaber
Inverdruie
Polchar
Alvie
Dell Lodge
Lettoch
Dirdhu
Bridge of Brown
Dorback Lodge
Forest Lodge
Tolvah
Achlean
Glenfeshie Lodge
Allanaquoich
Mar Lodge
Claybokie
Muir
Inverey
Tomintoul
Baddoch
Rothiemurchus
Inshriach Forest
Abernethy Forest
Glen More Forest Park
The Queen's Forest
Forest of Glenavon
Glenfeshie Forest
Forest of Mar
Loch Garten
Loch Morlich
Loch an Eilein
Loch Alvie
Loch Einich
Loch Avon
Loch Etchachan
Loch Vrotachan
Lairig Ghru
Glen Dee
Glen Lui
Glen Ey
Glen Feshie
CAIRN GORM 1245
BEN MACDUI 1309
BRAERIACH 1296
SGORAN DUBH MOR 1111
CARN BAN MOR 1052
MULLACH CLACH A'BHLAIR 1019
BEINN BHROTAIN 1157
DERRY CAIRNGORM 1155
BEINN BHREAC 931
BEINN A'CHAORRUINN 1082
BEN AVON 1171
CARN EAS 1089
CARN NA DROCHAIDE 818
CARN LIATH 818
CARN EALAR 994
AN SGARSOCH 1006
CARN BHAC 920
AN SOCACH 939
BEINN IUTHARN MHOR 1048
CARN EILRIG 742
BYNACK MORE 1090
MEALL A'BHUACHAILLE 810
GEAL CHARN 821
BADDOCH 568
CARN MEADHONACH 588
THE BRUACH 715
CARN SLEAMHUINN 677
LANDMARK FOREST THEME PARK
STRATHSPEY RAILWAY
AUCHGOURISH GDNS
ABERNETHY FOREST NATURE RESERVE
THE AVIEMORE SKI CENTRE
CAIRNGORM WHISKY CENTRE
CAIRNGORM REINDEER CENTRE
ROTHIEMURCHUS ESTATE VISITOR CENTRE
LOCH AN EILEIN VISITOR CENTRE
GLENMORE VISITOR CENTRE
CAIRNGORM CHAIRLIFT, FUNICULAR RLY & SKI CENTRE
TOMINTOUL MUSEUM
KINDROCHIT CASTLE
LINN OF DEE
INVEREY
A9
A95
A939
A93
B970
B9153
B9152
NH NJ NN NO
253 254 241 230 231
0 1 2 3 miles
0 1 2 3 4 5 km

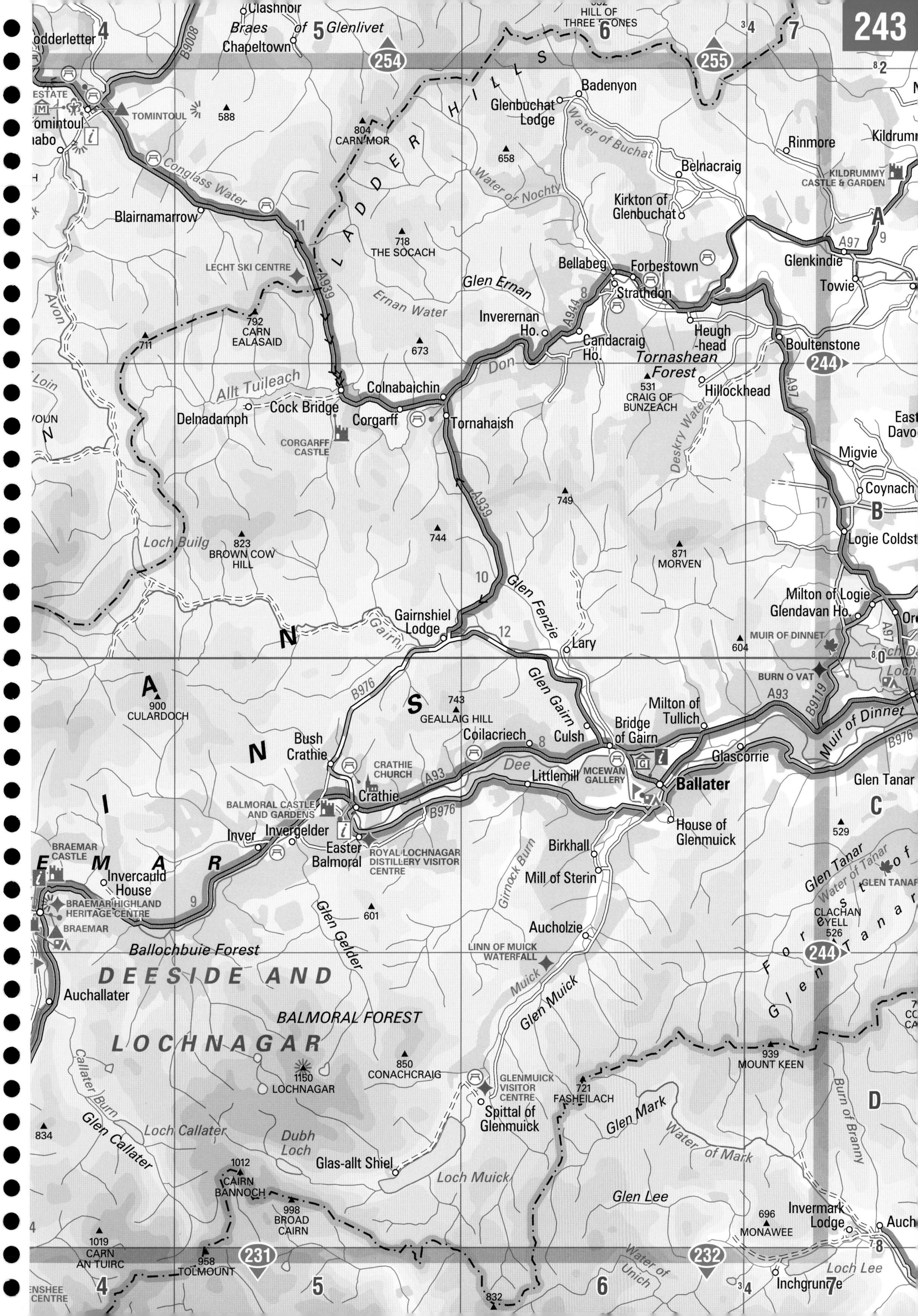

LADDER HILLS
Tomintoul
Glenbuchat Lodge
Badenyon
Water of Buchat
Belnacraig
Kirkton of Glenbuchat
Rinmore
KILDRUMMY CASTLE & GARDEN
Conglass Water
Blairnamarrow
LECHT SKI CENTRE
718 THE SOCACH
Bellabeg
Forbestown
Strathdon
Glenkindie
Towie
Glen Ernan
Ernan Water
Inverernan Ho.
Candacraig Ho.
Heugh-head
Boultenstone
Tornashean Forest
531 CRAIG OF BUNZEACH
Hillockhead
792 CARN EALASAID
Allt Tuileach
Colnabaichin
Delnadamph
Cock Bridge
Corgarff
Tornahaish
CORGARFF CASTLE
Deskry Water
Migvie
Coynach
Logie Coldstone
Loch Builg
823 BROWN COW HILL
744
749
871 MORVEN
Glen Fenzie
Milton of Logie
Glendavan Ho.
Gairnshiel Lodge
Lary
MUIR OF DINNET
BURN O VAT
900 CULARDOCH
743 GEALLAIG HILL
Glen Gairn
Milton of Tullich
Bridge of Gairn
Culsh
Coilacriech
Bush Crathie
CRATHIE CHURCH
Crathie
Littlemill
MCEWAN GALLERY
Ballater
Glascorrie
Muir of Dinnet
Glen Tanar
BALMORAL CASTLE AND GARDENS
Inver
Invergelder
Easter Balmoral
ROYAL LOCHNAGAR DISTILLERY VISITOR CENTRE
House of Glenmuick
Birkhall
Mill of Sterin
BRAEMAR CASTLE
Invercauld House
BRAEMAR HIGHLAND HERITAGE CENTRE
BRAEMAR
Glen Gelder
Girnock Burn
Aucholzie
LINN OF MUICK WATERFALL
CLACHAN YELL 526
GLEN TANAR
Forest of Glen Tanar
Ballochbuie Forest
DEESIDE AND LOCHNAGAR
Auchallater
BALMORAL FOREST
Glen Muick
850 CONACHCRAIG
1150 LOCHNAGAR
GLENMUICK VISITOR CENTRE
Spittal of Glenmuick
721 FASHEILACH
939 MOUNT KEEN
Glen Mark
Water of Mark
Burn of Branny
Glen Callater
Loch Callater
Dubh Loch
Glas-allt Shiel
Loch Muick
Glen Lee
1012 CAIRN BANNOCH
998 BROAD CAIRN
1019 CARN AN TUIRC
958 TOLMOUNT
696 MONAWEE
Invermark Lodge
Loch Lee
Inchgrundle
Water of Unich
254
255
244
231
232

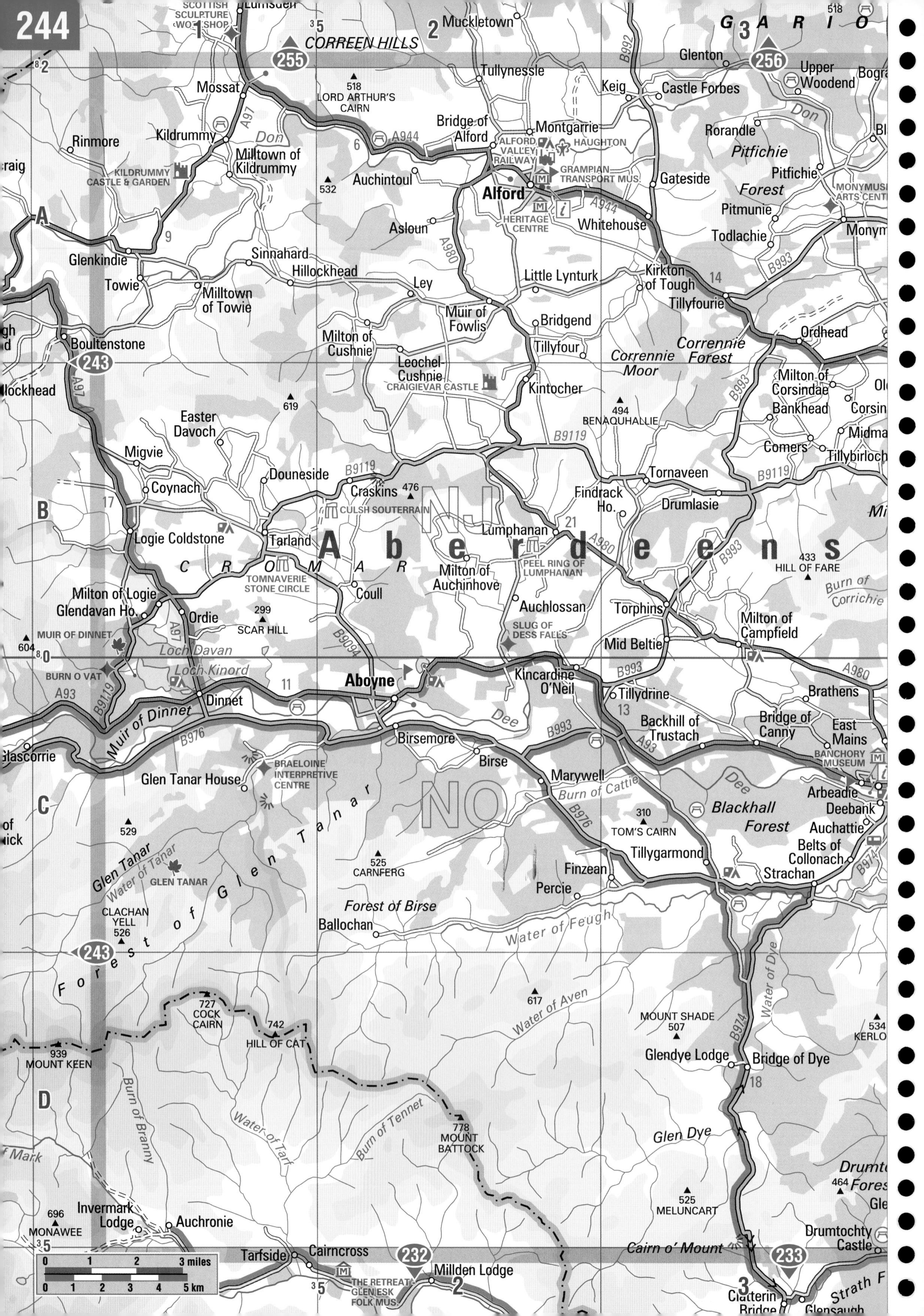
Lumsden
SCOTTISH SCULPTURE WORKSHOP
CORREEN HILLS
255
Muckleton
GARIOCH
256
Glenton
Upper Woodend
Mossat
518
LORD ARTHUR'S CAIRN
Tullynessle
Keig
Castle Forbes
Rinmore
Kildrummy
Don
A944
Bridge of Alford
Montgarrie
ALFORD VALLEY RAILWAY
HAUGHTON
Rorandle
Pitfichie
Milltown of Kildrummy
KILDRUMMY CASTLE & GARDEN
532
Auchintoul
GRAMPIAN TRANSPORT MUS.
Gateside
Pitfichie Forest
MONYMUSK ARTS CENTRE
Alford
HERITAGE CENTRE
Whitehouse
Pitmunie
A
Asloun
A980
Todlachie
Glenkindie
Sinnahard
Hillockhead
Ley
Little Lynturk
Kirkton of Tough
B993
Towie
Milltown of Towie
Muir of Fowlis
Tillyfourie
Bridgend
Ordhead
Boultenstone
243
Milton of Cushnie
Leochel-Cushnie
Tillyfour
Corrennie Moor
Corrennie Forest
CRAIGIEVAR CASTLE
Kintocher
Milton of Corsindae
A97
619
494
BENAQUHALLIE
Bankhead
Corsindae
Easter Davoch
B9119
Midmar
Migvie
Comers
Tillybirloch
Douneside
Tornaveen
Coynach
Craskins
476
NJ
Findrack Ho.
Drumlasie
B
CULSH SOUTERRAIN
Lumphanan
Logie Coldstone
Tarland
Aberdeens
CROMAR
Milton of Auchinhove
PEEL RING OF LUMPHANAN
433
HILL OF FARE
TOMNAVERIE STONE CIRCLE
Coull
Burn of Corrichie
Milton of Logie
Glendavan Ho.
Ordie
Auchlossan
Torphins
Milton of Campfield
299
SCAR HILL
B9094
SLUG OF DESS FALLS
MUIR OF DINNET
604
Mid Beltie
Loch Davan
Loch Kinord
Kincardine O'Neil
B993
A980
BURN O VAT
Aboyne
Brathens
A93
B9119
Dinnet
Tillydrine
Muir of Dinnet
Backhill of Trustach
Bridge of Canny
East Mains
B976
Dee
Birsemore
BANCHORY MUSEUM
Glascorrie
Birse
BRAELOINE INTERPRETIVE CENTRE
Glen Tanar House
Marywell
Burn of Cattie
Dee
Arbeadie
C
NO
Blackhall Forest
Deebank
310
TOM'S CAIRN
Auchattie
529
B976
Belts of Collonach
Glen Tanar
Water of Tanar
GLEN TANAR
525
CARNFERG
Tillygarmond
Finzean
Strachan
B974
Percie
CLACHAN YELL
526
Forest of Birse
Forest of Glen Tanar
Ballochan
Water of Feugh
243
727
COCK CAIRN
617
Water of Aven
Water of Dye
742
HILL OF CAT
MOUNT SHADE
507
534
KERLOCH
939
MOUNT KEEN
Glendye Lodge
Bridge of Dye
D
Burn of Branny
Water of Tarf
Burn of Tennet
778
MOUNT BATTOCK
Glen Dye
Water of Mark
Drumtochty Forest
464
696
MONAWEE
Invermark Lodge
Auchronie
525
MELUNCART
Drumtochty Castle
Cairn o' Mount
Tarfside
Cairncross
232
233
Millden Lodge
THE RETREAT GLEN ESK FOLK MUS.
Clatterin Bridge
Glensaugh
Strath Finella
0 1 2 3 miles
0 1 2 3 4 5 km

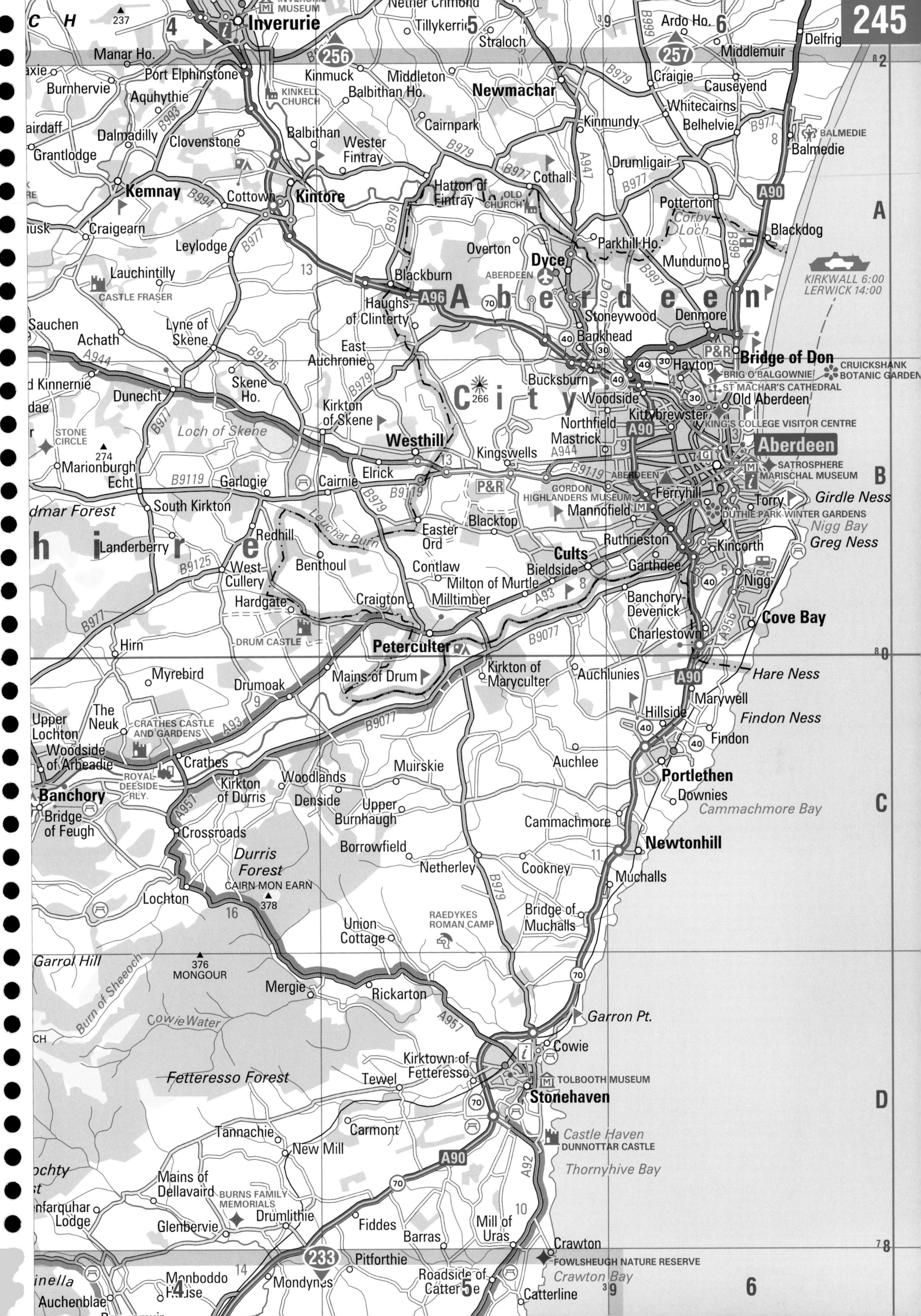
Inverurie
Tillykerrie
Straloch
Ardo Ho.
Delfrig
Manar Ho.
Middlemuir
Port Elphinstone
Kinmuck
Middleton
Craigie
Burnhervie
Aquhythie
KINKELL CHURCH
Balbithan Ho.
Newmachar
Causeyend
Whitecairns
Belhelvie
Dalmadilly
Clovenstone
Balbithan
Wester Fintray
Cairnpark
Kinmundy
BALMEDIE
Balmedie
Grantlodge
Drumligair
Kemnay
Cottown
Kintore
Hatton of Fintray
OLD CHURCH
Cothall
Potterton
Corby Loch
Blackdog
Craigearn
Leylodge
Overton
Dyce
Parkhill Ho.
Mundurno
Lauchintilly
CASTLE FRASER
Blackburn
ABERDEEN
KIRKWALL 6:00
LERWICK 14:00
Haughs of Clinterty
Aberdeen
Stoneywood
Denmore
Sauchen
Achath
Lyne of Skene
Bankhead
East Auchronie
Bridge of Don
Hayton
CRUICKSHANK BOTANIC GARDEN
BRIG O' BALGOWNIE
Kinnernie
Dunecht
Skene Ho.
Bucksburn
ST MACHAR'S CATHEDRAL
City
266
Woodside
Old Aberdeen
Kirkton of Skene
Kittybrewster
Northfield
KING'S COLLEGE VISITOR CENTRE
STONE CIRCLE
Loch of Skene
Mastrick
274
Westhill
Kingswells
Aberdeen
SATROSPHERE
Marionburgh
MARISCHAL MUSEUM
Echt
Garlogie
Cairnie
Elrick
ABERDEEN
GORDON HIGHLANDERS MUSEUM
Ferryhill
Girdle Ness
Torry
South Kirkton
Mannofield
DUTHIE PARK WINTER GARDENS
Nigg Bay
Blacktop
Easter Ord
Ruthrieston
Kincorth
Greg Ness
Redhill
Leuchar Burn
Landerberry
Cults
West Cullery
Benthoul
Contlaw
Bieldside
Garthdee
Milton of Murtle
Nigg
Hardgate
Craigton
Milltimber
Banchory-Devenick
Cove Bay
Hirn
DRUM CASTLE
Peterculter
Charlestown
Myrebird
Drumoak
Mains of Drum
Kirkton of Maryculter
Auchlunies
Hare Ness
Marywell
The Neuk
Upper Lochton
CRATHES CASTLE AND GARDENS
Hillside
Findon Ness
Findon
Woodside of Arbeadie
Crathes
Muirskie
Auchlee
Portlethen
ROYAL DEESIDE RLY.
Kirkton of Durris
Woodlands
Banchory
Bridge of Feugh
Denside
Upper Burnhaugh
Downies
Cammachmore Bay
Crossroads
Cammachmore
Durris Forest
Borrowfield
Newtonhill
Netherley
Cookney
Muchalls
CAIRN MON EARN
378
Lochton
RAEDYKES ROMAN CAMP
Bridge of Muchalls
Union Cottage
Garrol Hill
376
MONGOUR
Burn of Sheeoch
Mergie
Rickarton
Garron Pt.
Cowie Water
Cowie
Kirktown of Fetteresso
Fetteresso Forest
Tewel
TOLBOOTH MUSEUM
Stonehaven
Tannachie
Carmont
Castle Haven
DUNNOTTAR CASTLE
New Mill
Thornyhive Bay
Mains of Dellavaird
BURNS FAMILY MEMORIALS
Lodge
Glenbervie
Drumlithie
Fiddes
Barras
Mill of Uras
Crawton
Pitforthie
FOWLSHEUGH NATURE RESERVE
Monboddo House
Mondynes
Roadside of Catterline
Crawton Bay
Catterline
Auchenblae

488
ABHAL BHEAG
Loch Varkasaig
Balmore
Ose
258
A863
B885
Heatherfield
417
Glenmore
259
Penif
Loch Duagrich
Tungadal
Mugeary
A87
Conorda
Harlosh I.
Tarner I.
Ullinish
Bracadale
Struan
Coillore
Loch Bracadale
Wiay
Idrigill Point
MACLEOD'S MAIDENS
Oronsay
Portnalong
I S L A N
Varragill
Glen Varragill
Upper
BRAES
439
ROINEVAL
Rubha nan Clach
Fiskavaig
Loch Harport
B8009
Fernilea
ARNAVAL
369
TALISKER DISTILLERY
Carbost
Drynoch
A863
Crossal
Gleann Oraid
Merkadale
Drynoch
Talisker Bay
Talisker
Sligachan Hotel
Eynort
Glen Brittle Forest
Eynort
Grula
445
BEINN BHREAC
459
SGURR NAN GILLEAN
964
Glen Sligachan
NG
M I N G I N I S
Loch Eynort
SGURR A'GHREADAIDH
973
Brittle
Glen Brittle
THE CU
GLENBRITTLE
CUILLIN HILLS
Glenbrittle House
Bualintur
992
SGURR ALASDAIR
Loch Coruisk
924
SGURR NAN EAG
Loch Brittle
Rubh an Dunain
Soay Sound
Soay
Mol-chlach
BOAT
PRINCE CHA
Canna
Garrisdale Pt.
A'Chill
Canna Harbour
Sanday
Rubha Shamhnan Insir
Kilmory
Sound of Canna
Guirdil Bay
Kilmory Glen
1:15
MALLAIG 2:30
388
A'Bhrideanach
Kinloch Glen
Rubha na Roinne
234
Kinloch
Loch Scresort
571
ORVAL
R Ù M
KINLOCH CASTLE
RÙM
Rubha Port na Caranean
0 1 2 3 miles
0 1 2 3 4 5 km

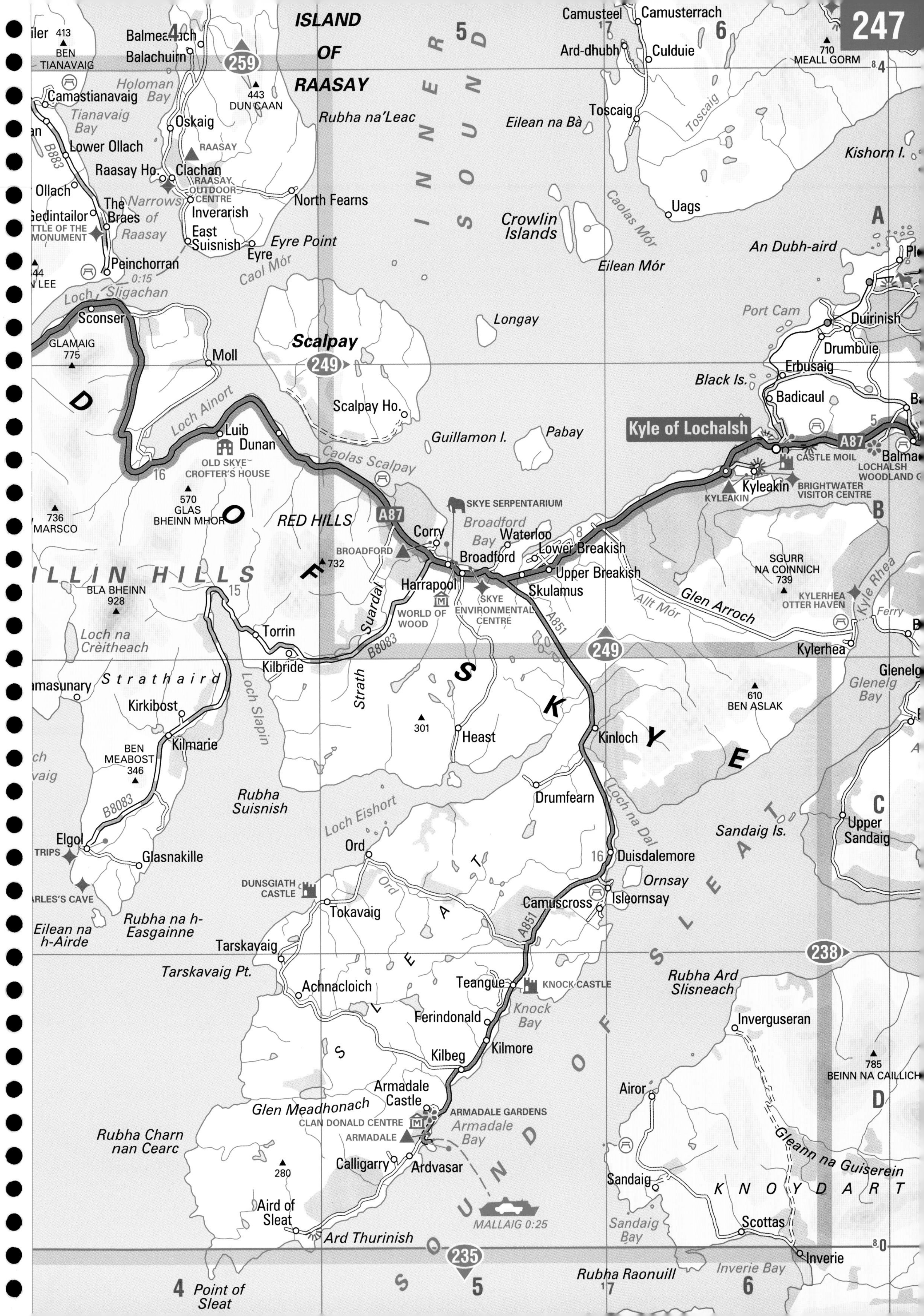
ISLAND
OF
RAASAY
INNER SOUND
Camusteel
Camusterrach
Ard-dhubh
Culduie
MEALL GORM
Balmeanach
Balachuirn
BEN TIANAVAIG
DUN CAAN
Holoman Bay
Camastianavaig
Tianavaig Bay
Oskaig
Rubha na'Leac
Eilean na Bà
Toscaig
Lower Ollach
RAASAY
Raasay Ho.
Clachan
Kishorn I.
Ollach
RAASAY OUTDOOR CENTRE
North Fearns
The Narrows of Raasay
Uags
Gedintailor
Braes
Inverarish
Crowlin Islands
Caolas Mór
East Suisnish
Eyre Point
Eyre
An Dubh-aird
Peinchorran
Caol Mór
Eilean Mór
Loch Sligachan
Sconser
Longay
Port Cam
Duirinish
GLAMAIG
Scalpay
Drumbuie
Moll
Erbusaig
Black Is.
Badicaul
Loch Ainort
Scalpay Ho.
Kyle of Lochalsh
Luib
Guillamon I.
Pabay
A87
Dunan
OLD SKYE CROFTER'S HOUSE
Caolas Scalpay
CASTLE MOIL
LOCHALSH WOODLAND
GLAS BHEINN MHOR
Kyleakin
KYLEAKIN
BRIGHTWATER VISITOR CENTRE
MARSCO
RED HILLS
SKYE SERPENTARIUM
Broadford Bay
Corry
Waterloo
CUILLIN HILLS
BROADFORD
Broadford
Lower Breakish
SGURR NA COINNICH
Upper Breakish
BLA BHEINN
Harrapool
Skulamus
Glen Arroch
Allt Mór
KYLERHEA OTTER HAVEN
Kyle Rhea
Suardal
WORLD OF WOOD
SKYE ENVIRONMENTAL CENTRE
A851
Ferry
Loch na Crèitheach
Torrin
B8083
Kylerhea
Kilbride
Strath
Glenelg
Glenelg Bay
Camasunary
Strathaird
BEN ASLAK
Kirkibost
Loch Slapin
SKYE
Heast
Kinloch
Kilmarie
BEN MEABOST
Rubha Suisnish
Drumfearn
Loch na Dal
Loch Eishort
Upper Sandaig
Elgol
Sandaig Is.
TRIPS
Glasnakille
Ord
Duisdalemore
DUNSGIATH CASTLE
Ornsay
Isleornsay
Camuscross
SPAR CAVE
Tokavaig
Rubha na h-Easgainne
Eilean na h-Airde
Tarskavaig
SLEAT
Tarskavaig Pt.
Rubha Ard Slisneach
Achnacloich
Teangue
KNOCK CASTLE
Knock Bay
Ferindonald
Inverguseran
Kilmore
Kilbeg
BEINN NA CAILLICH
Armadale Castle
Airor
Glen Meadhonach
ARMADALE GARDENS
CLAN DONALD CENTRE
Armadale Bay
Rubha Charn nan Cearc
ARMADALE
Gleann na Guiserein
Calligarry
Ardvasar
Sandaig
KNOYDART
Aird of Sleat
MALLAIG 0:25
Sandaig Bay
Scottas
Ard Thurinish
SOUND OF SLEAT
Inverie
Rubha Raonuill
Inverie Bay
Point of Sleat

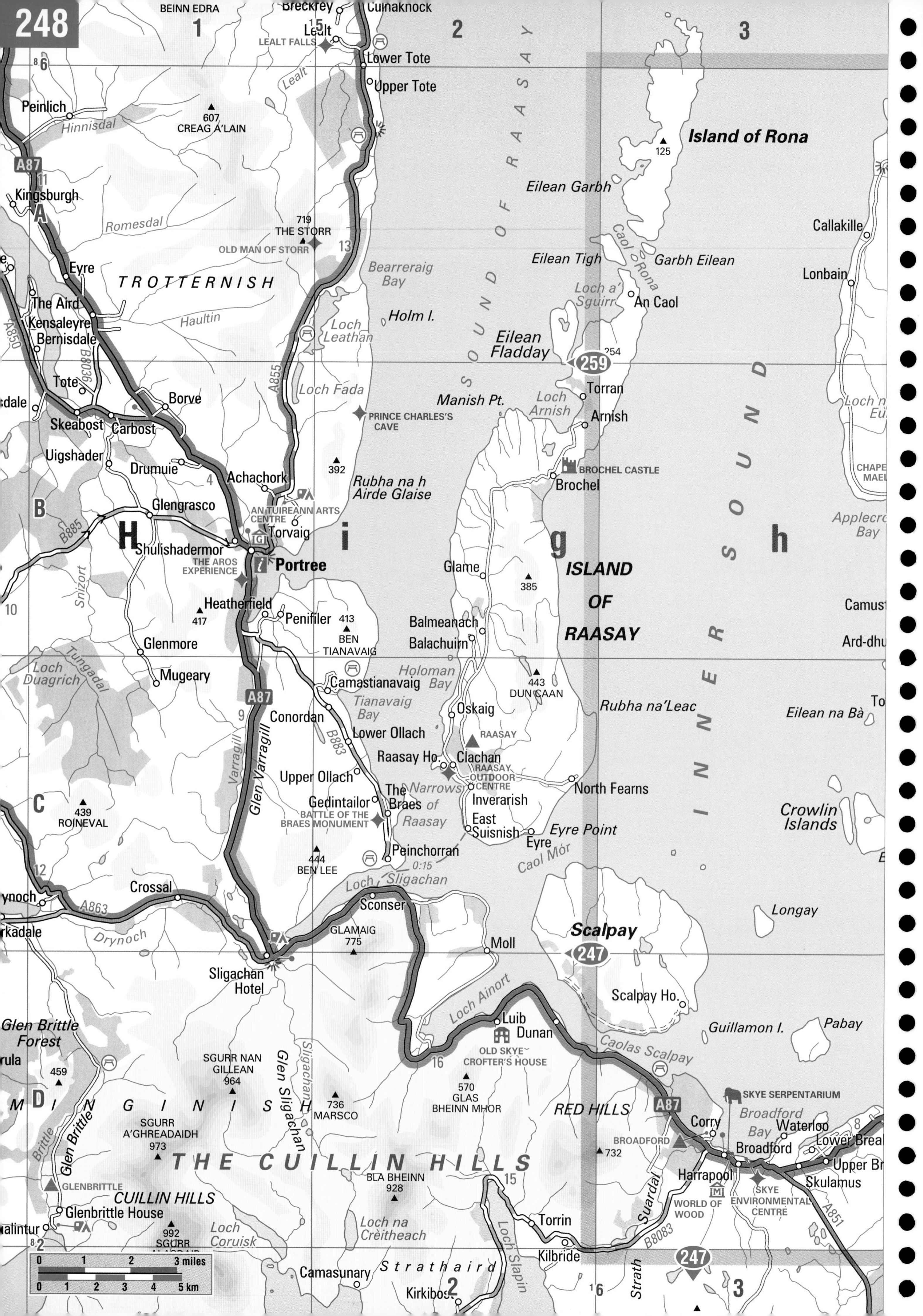
Island of Rona
Eilean Garbh
Eilean Tigh
Garbh Eilean
An Caol
Eilean Fladday
Torran
Arnish
Brochel
BROCHEL CASTLE
ISLAND OF RAASAY
SOUND OF RAASAY
INNER SOUND
Glame
Balmeanach
Balachuirn
Oskaig
Clachan
Raasay Ho.
Inverarish
East Suisnish
Eyre
Eyre Point
North Fearns
Rubha na'Leac
DUN CAAN
Portree
Torvaig
AN TUIREANN ARTS CENTRE
THE AROS EXPERIENCE
Penifiler
BEN TIANAVAIG
Camastianavaig
Conordan
Lower Ollach
Upper Ollach
Gedintailor
The Braes
BATTLE OF THE BRAES MONUMENT
Peinchorran
BEN LEE
Sconser
Sligachan Hotel
GLAMAIG
Moll
Scalpay
Scalpay Ho.
Longay
Crowlin Islands
Guillamon I.
Pabay
Luib
Dunan
OLD SKYE CROFTER'S HOUSE
Caolas Scalpay
Broadford
Broadford Bay
Waterloo
Lower Breakish
Upper Breakish
Skulamus
Corry
Harrapool
SKYE SERPENTARIUM
SKYE ENVIRONMENTAL CENTRE
WORLD OF WOOD
RED HILLS
Torrin
Kilbride
Strath
Suardal
Loch Slapin
Strathaird
Camasunary
Kirkibost
Loch na Crèitheach
Loch Coruisk
BLA BHEINN
GLAS BHEINN MHOR
MARSCO
SGURR NAN GILLEAN
SGURR A'GHREADAIDH
THE CUILLIN HILLS
CUILLIN HILLS
GLENBRITTLE
Glenbrittle House
Glen Brittle
Glen Brittle Forest
MINGINISH
ROINEVAL
Crossal
Drynoch
Glen Varragill
Mugeary
Glenmore
Heatherfield
Loch Duagrich
Shulishadermor
Glengrasco
Achachork
Drumuie
Uigshader
Skeabost
Carbost
Borve
Tote
Bernisdale
Kensaleyre
The Aird
Eyre
TROTTERNISH
Kingsburgh
Peinlich
Hinnisdal
Romesdal
Haultin
CREAG A'LAIN
THE STORR
OLD MAN OF STORR
LEALT FALLS
Lealt
Lower Tote
Upper Tote
Culnaknock
Brecкrey
BEINN EDRA
Bearreraig Bay
Holm I.
Loch Leathan
Loch Fada
PRINCE CHARLES'S CAVE
Rubha na h Airde Glaise
Manish Pt.
Loch Arnish
Holoman Bay
Tianavaig Bay
Narrows of Raasay
Caol Mór
Loch Sligachan
Loch Ainort
Callakille
Lonbain
Applecross Bay
Eilean na Bà
A87
A855
A863
B885
B883
B8083
A851
0 1 2 3 miles
0 1 2 3 4 5 km

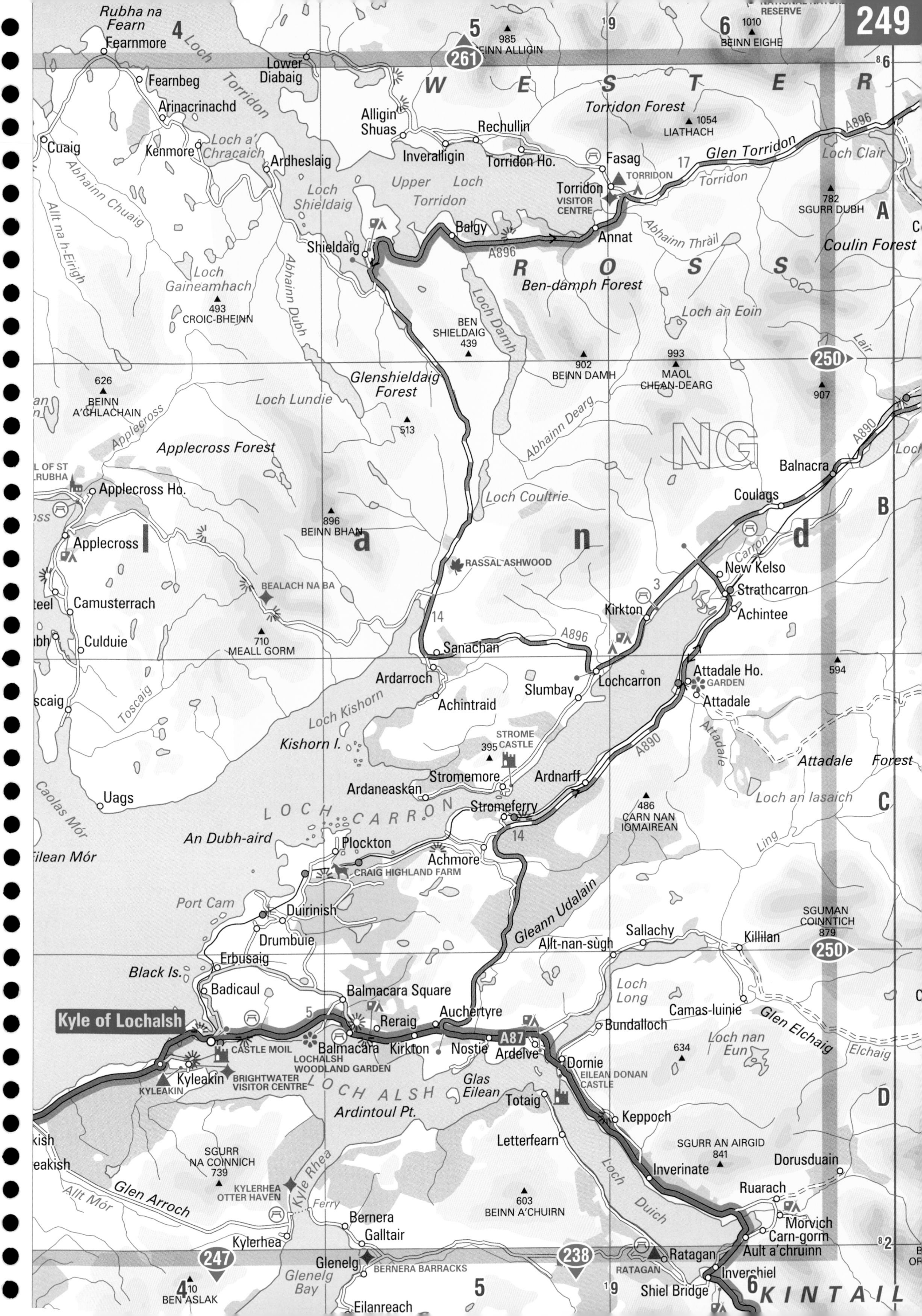

Rubha na Fearn
Fearnmore
Loch Torridon
Fearnbeg
Arinacrinachd
Cuaig
Kenmore
Loch a' Chracaich
Ardheslaig
Lower Diabaig
Alligin Shuas
Inveralligin
Rechullin
Torridon Ho.
Fasag
TORRIDON
Torridon
VISITOR CENTRE
Glen Torridon
Loch Clair
A896
WESTER ROSS
Torridon Forest
1054 LIATHACH
985 BEINN ALLIGIN
1010 BEINN EIGHE
NATIONAL NATURE RESERVE
261
782 SGURR DUBH
Coulin Forest
Upper Loch Torridon
Loch Shieldaig
Shieldaig
Balgy
Annat
Abhainn Thràil
Abhainn Chuaig
Allt na h-Eirigh
Loch Gaineamhach
493 CROIC-BHEINN
Abhainn Dubh
Loch Damh
Ben-damph Forest
Loch an Eoin
BEN SHIELDAIG 439
902 BEINN DAMH
993 MAOL CHEAN-DEARG
250
907
626 BEINN A'CHLACHAIN
Glenshieldaig Forest
Loch Lundie
513
Abhainn Dearg
NG
Applecross
Applecross Forest
Applecross Ho.
Balnacra
A890
Coulags
Loch Coultrie
896 BEINN BHAN
Applecross
Island
RASSAL ASHWOOD
Carron
New Kelso
Strathcarron
Achintee
BEALACH NA BA
Camusterrach
Culduie
710 MEALL GORM
Kirkton
Sanachan
A896
Ardarroch
Achintraid
Slumbay
Lochcarron
Attadale Ho.
GARDEN
Attadale
594
Toscaig
Loch Kishorn
Kishorn I.
STROME CASTLE
395
Attadale Forest
Uags
Caolas Mór
Stromemore
Ardaneaskan
Ardnarff
Stromeferry
486 CARN NAN IOMAIREAN
Loch an Iasaich
LOCH CARRON
An Dubh-aird
Eilean Mór
Plockton
Achmore
CRAIG HIGHLAND FARM
Ling
Port Cam
Duirinish
Drumbuie
Gleann Udalain
SGUMAN COINNTICH 879
Allt-nan-sùgh
Sallachy
Killilan
Erbusaig
Black Is.
Badicaul
Balmacara Square
Loch Long
Camas-luinie
Glen Elchaig
Kyle of Lochalsh
Reraig
Auchertyre
Bundalloch
Loch nan Eun
634
Elchaig
CASTLE MOIL
Balmacara
Kirkton
Nostie
A87
Ardelve
Dornie
LOCHALSH WOODLAND GARDEN
EILEAN DONAN CASTLE
Kyleakin
KYLEAKIN
BRIGHTWATER VISITOR CENTRE
LOCH ALSH
Glas Eilean
Totaig
Ardintoul Pt.
Keppoch
Letterfearn
SGURR AN AIRGID 841
Dorusduain
SGURR NA COINNICH 739
Kyle Rhea
Inverinate
Loch Duich
KYLERHEA OTTER HAVEN
603 BEINN A'CHUIRN
Ruarach
Glen Arroch
Allt Mór
Ferry
Bernera
Galltair
Morvich
Carn-gorm
Ault a'chruinn
Kylerhea
247
238
Ratagan
RATAGAN
Glenelg
BERNERA BARRACKS
Glenelg Bay
Inverchiel
Shiel Bridge
KINTAIL
10 BEN ASLAK
Eilanreach

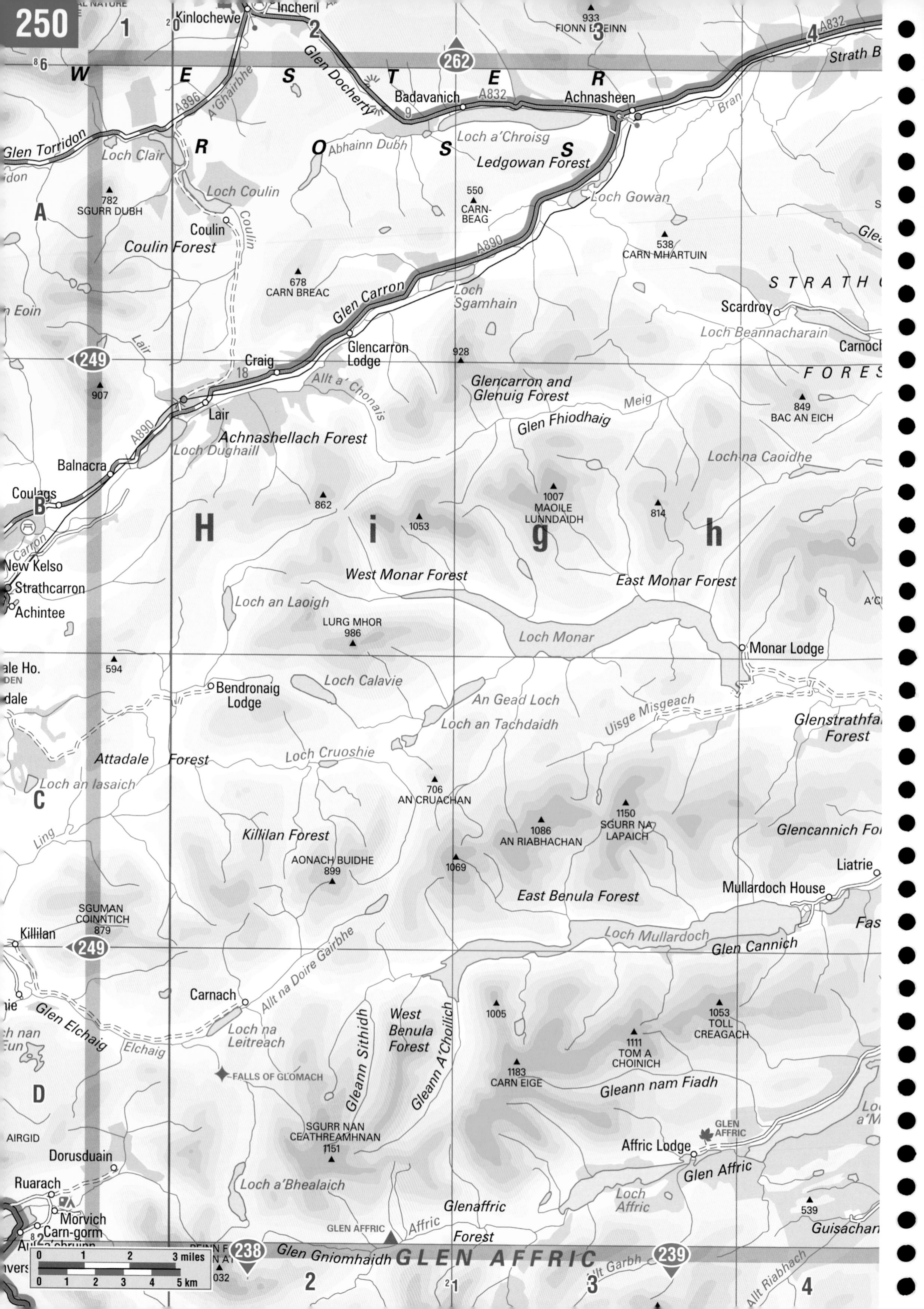
Kinlochewe
Incheril
FIONN BHEINN
933
262
WESTER ROSS
Glen Docherty
Badavanich
A832
Achnasheen
Strath Bran
A896
A'Ghairbhe
Glen Torridon
Loch Clair
Abhainn Dubh
Loch a'Chroisg
Ledgowan Forest
Loch Coulin
782
SGURR DUBH
550
CARN-BEAG
Loch Gowan
Coulin
Coulin Forest
A890
538
CARN MHARTUIN
678
CARN BREAC
Glen Carron
Loch Sgamhain
STRATH
Scardroy
Loch Beannacharain
249
Lair
928
Craig
Glencarron Lodge
FOREST
907
Allt a' Chonais
Glencarron and Glenuig Forest
Meig
849
BAC AN EICH
Glen Fhiodhaig
Lair
Achnashellach Forest
Loch Dughaill
Loch na Caoidhe
Balnacra
Coulags
862
1007
MAOILE LUNNDAIDH
814
1053
Highland
Carron
New Kelso
Strathcarron
Achintee
West Monar Forest
East Monar Forest
Loch an Laoigh
LURG MHOR
986
Loch Monar
Monar Lodge
594
Bendronaig Lodge
Loch Calavie
An Gead Loch
Loch an Tachdaidh
Uisge Misgeach
Glenstrathfarrar Forest
Attadale Forest
Loch Cruoshie
706
AN CRUACHAN
Loch an Iasaich
Ling
1150
SGURR NA LAPAICH
1086
AN RIABHACHAN
Glencannich Forest
Killilan Forest
AONACH BUIDHE
899
1069
Liatrie
East Benula Forest
Mullardoch House
SGUMAN COINNTICH
879
Killilan
Loch Mullardoch
Glen Cannich
Allt na Doire Gairbhe
Carnach
1005
1053
TOLL CREAGACH
Glen Elchaig
Elchaig
Loch na Leitreach
Gleann Sithidh
West Benula Forest
Gleann A'Choilich
1111
TOM A CHOINICH
FALLS OF GLOMACH
1183
CARN EIGE
Gleann nam Fiadh
GLEN AFFRIC
SGURR NAN CEATHREAMHNAN
1151
Affric Lodge
AIRGID
Dorusduain
Glen Affric
Loch Affric
Ruarach
Loch a'Bhealaich
Glenaffric Forest
539
Morvich
Carn-gorm
Affric
GLEN AFFRIC
Guisachan
0 1 2 3 miles
0 1 2 3 4 5 km
238
Glen Gniomhaidh
GLEN AFFRIC
Allt Garbh
239
Allt Riabhach
1 2 3 4
A B C D

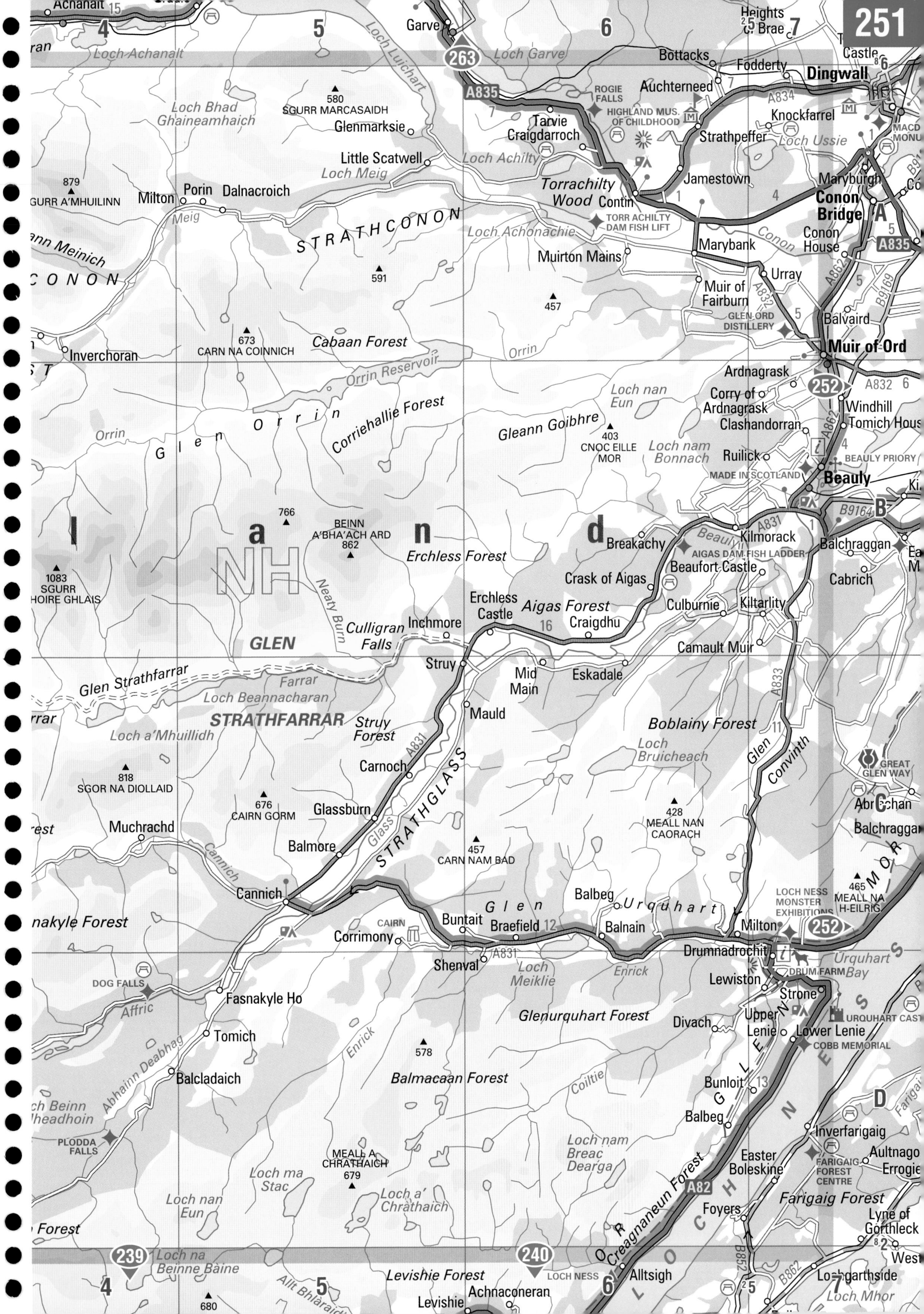
Achanalt
Garve
Heights of Brae
Loch Achanalt
Loch Luichart
263
Loch Garve
Bottacks
Fodderty
Castle
Dingwall
A835
ROGIE FALLS
Auchterneed
A834
HIGHLAND MUS. OF CHILDHOOD
Knockfarrel
Tarvie
Craigdarroch
Strathpeffer
Loch Ussie
Loch Bhad Ghaineamhaich
580
SGURR MARCASAIDH
Glenmarksie
Little Scatwell
Loch Meig
Loch Achilty
Torrachilty Wood
Contin
Jamestown
Maryburgh
Conon Bridge
879
SGURR A'MHUILINN
Milton
Porin
Dalnacroich
Meig
STRATHCONON
Loch Achonachie
TORR ACHILTY DAM FISH LIFT
Marybank
Conon
Conon House
A835
Muirton Mains
Urray
CONON
591
457
Muir of Fairburn
A832
A862
B9169
Balvaird
GLEN ORD DISTILLERY
Inverchoran
673
CARN NA COINNICH
Cabaan Forest
Orrin
Muir of Ord
Orrin Reservoir
Ardnagrask
252
A832
Corry of Ardnagrask
Windhill
Tomich House
Loch nan Eun
Clashandorran
Glen Orrin
Corriehallie Forest
Gleann Goibhre
403
CNOC EILLE MOR
Loch nam Bonnach
Ruilick
BEAULY PRIORY
MADE IN SCOTLAND
Beauly
766
BEINN A'BHA'ACH ARD
862
B9164
Kilmorack
Breakachy
Beauly
AIGAS DAM FISH LADDER
Balchraggan
Erchless Forest
Crask of Aigas
Beaufort Castle
Cabrich
1083
SGURR NA LAPAICH
NH
Neaty Burn
Erchless Castle
Aigas Forest
Culburnie
Kiltarlity
Culligran Falls
Inchmore
Craigdhu
GLEN
Camault Muir
Struy
Mid Main
Eskadale
Glen Strathfarrar
Farrar
Loch Beannacharan
STRATHFARRAR
Struy Forest
Mauld
A833
Boblainy Forest
Loch a'Mhuillidh
Loch Bruicheach
Glen Convinth
A831
818
SGOR NA DIOLLAID
Carnoch
GREAT GLEN WAY
STRATHGLASS
676
CAIRN GORM
Glassburn
428
MEALL NAN CAORACH
Abriachan
Balchraggan
Muchrachd
Glass
Balmore
457
CARN NAM BAD
Cannich
465
MEALL NA H-EILRIG
LOCH NESS MONSTER EXHIBITIONS
Cannich
Balbeg
Glen Urquhart
CAIRN
Buntait
Braefield
Balnain
Milton
Corrimony
Drumnadrochit
Shenval
A831
Loch Meiklie
Enrick
Urquhart Bay
DRUM FARM
DOG FALLS
Lewiston
Fasnakyle Ho
Strone
Affric
Glenurquhart Forest
Upper Lenie
Divach
URQUHART CASTLE
Lower Lenie
Tomich
COBB MEMORIAL
Abhainn Deabhag
Enrick
578
Balcladaich
Balmacaan Forest
Coiltie
Bunloit
Balbeg
Inverfarigaig
PLODDA FALLS
MEALL A CHRATHAICH
679
Loch nam Breac Dearga
Easter Boleskine
FARIGAIG FOREST CENTRE
Aultnagoire
Errogie
Loch ma Stac
Loch a' Chrathaich
A82
Creagnaneun Forest
Farigaig Forest
Loch nan Eun
Foyers
Lyne of Gorthleck
LOCH NESS
239
Loch na Beinne Baine
240
LOCH NESS
Alltsigh
B852
B862
Loch Mhor
Levishie Forest
Achnaconeran
Levishie
Allt Bhlàraidh
680
Whitebridge

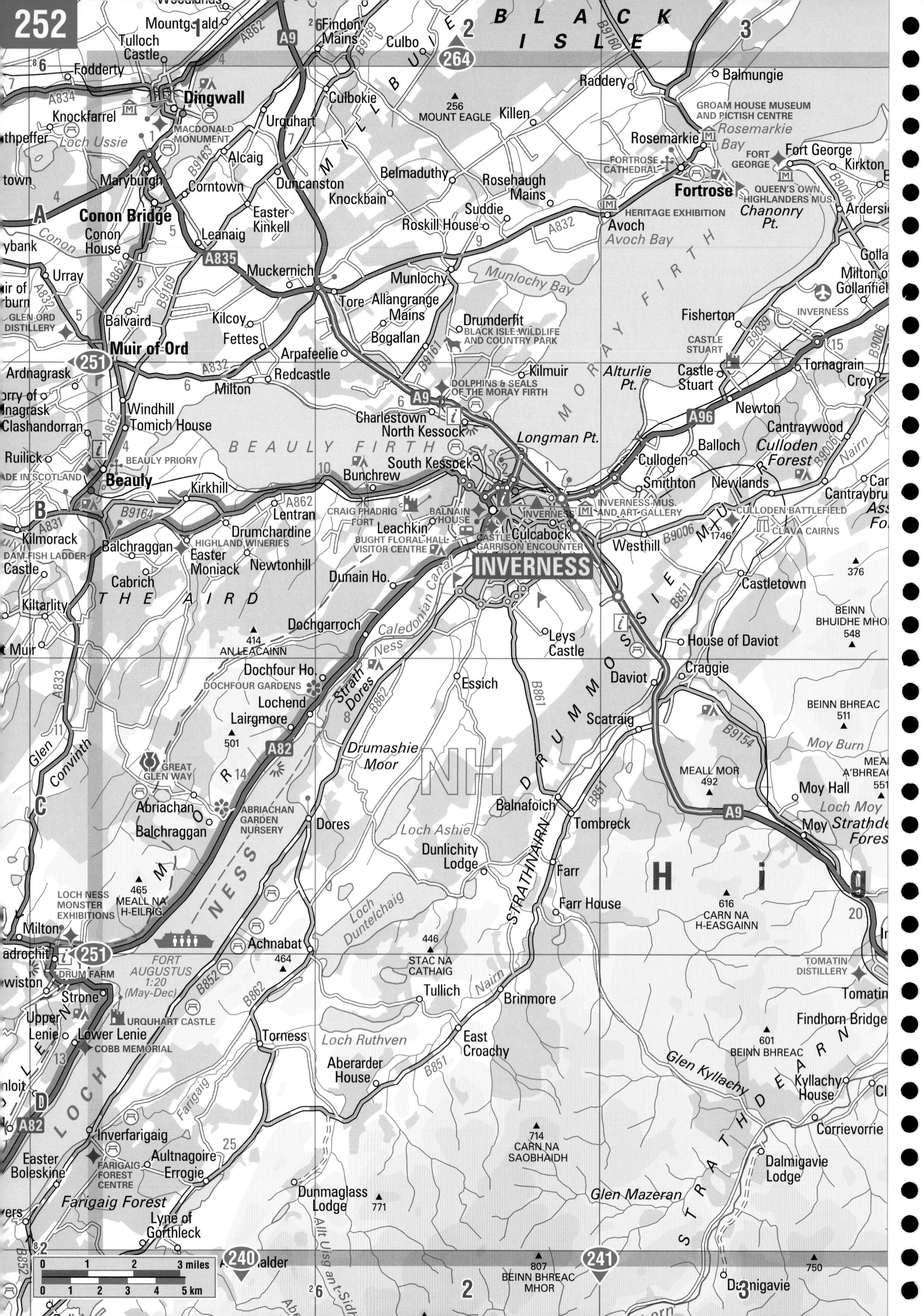
BLACK ISLE
264
Mountgerald
Tulloch Castle
Findon Mains
Culbo
MILLBUIE
Fodderty
Dingwall
Raddery
Balmungie
Knockfarrel
Culbokie
256
MOUNT EAGLE
Killen
GROAM HOUSE MUSEUM AND PICTISH CENTRE
Loch Ussie
MACDONALD MONUMENT
Urquhart
Rosemarkie
Rosemarkie Bay
Alcaig
FORTROSE CATHEDRAL
FORT GEORGE
Fort George
Kirkton
Maryburgh
Corntown
Duncanston
Belmaduthy
Rosehaugh Mains
Fortrose
QUEEN'S OWN HIGHLANDERS MUS.
Knockbain
Conon Bridge
Conon House
Easter Kinkell
Suddie
HERITAGE EXHIBITION
Avoch
Chanonry Pt.
Ardersier
Leanaig
Roskill House
Avoch Bay
A835
Muckernich
Munlochy
Munlochy Bay
Urray
Tore
Allangrange Mains
MORAY FIRTH
Milton of Gollanfield
GLEN ORD DISTILLERY
Balvaird
Kilcoy
Drumderfit
BLACK ISLE WILDLIFE AND COUNTRY PARK
Fisherton
INVERNESS
Fettes
Bogallan
CASTLE STUART
Muir of Ord
Arpafeelie
251
Kilmuir
Alturlie Pt.
Castle Stuart
Tornagrain
Ardnagrask
Redcastle
Croy
Milton
DOLPHINS & SEALS OF THE MORAY FIRTH
Newton
A9
A96
Windhill
Tomich House
Charlestown
North Kessock
Cantraywood
Longman Pt.
Balloch
Culloden Forest
BEAULY FIRTH
Ruilick
BEAULY PRIORY
South Kessock
Culloden
Beauly
Bunchrew
Smithton
Newlands
Cantraybruich
Kirkhill
A862
Lentran
CRAIG PHADRIG FORT
BALNAIN HOUSE
INVERNESS MUS. AND ART GALLERY
CULLODEN BATTLEFIELD
B9164
Drumchardine
Leachkin
CASTLE GARRISON ENCOUNTER
Culcabock
Westhill
1746
CLAVA CAIRNS
Kilmorack
Balchraggan
HIGHLAND WINERIES
BUGHT FLORAL HALL VISITOR CENTRE
Easter Moniack
Newtonhill
INVERNESS
DAM FISH LADDER
376
Cabrich
Dunain Ho.
Castletown
THE AIRD
Caledonian Canal
Kiltarlity
BEINN BHUIDHE MHOR
548
Dochgarroch
414
AN LEACAINN
Leys Castle
House of Daviot
Muir
Dochfour Ho.
Ness
DOCHFOUR GARDENS
Essich
Daviot
Craggie
Lochend
Strath Dores
DRUMMOSSIE MUIR
BEINN BHREAC
511
Lairgmore
Scatraig
501
A82
Drumashie Moor
B9154
Moy Burn
GREAT GLEN WAY
NH
MEALL MOR
492
Glen Convinth
Moy Hall
Abriachan
ABRIACHAN GARDEN NURSERY
Balnafoich
Dores
Tombreck
Loch Moy
Balchraggan
Loch Ashie
Moy
Strathdearn Forest
Dunlichity Lodge
Farr
465
MEALL NA H-EILRIG
LOCH NESS MONSTER EXHIBITIONS
LOCH NESS
Highland
Farr House
616
CARN NA H-EASGAINN
Loch Duntelchaig
STRATHNAIRN
Milton
Achnabat
446
STAC NA CATHAIG
FORT AUGUSTUS 1:20 (May-Dec)
464
TOMATIN DISTILLERY
DRUM FARM
Tomatin
Strone
Tullich
Nairn
Brinmore
Upper Lenie
URQUHART CASTLE
Findhorn Bridge
Lower Lenie
COBB MEMORIAL
Torness
Loch Ruthven
East Croachy
601
BEINN BHREAC
Aberarder House
Glen Kyllachy
Kyllachy House
STRATHDEARN
Farigaig
Inverfarigaig
Corrievorrie
714
CARN NA SAOBHAIDH
Easter Boleskine
FARIGAIG FOREST CENTRE
Aultnagoire
Errogie
Dalmigavie Lodge
Dunmaglass Lodge
771
Glen Mazeran
Farigaig Forest
Lyne of Gorthleck
240
241
807
BEINN BHREAC MHOR
750
Dalmigavie
Allt Uisg an t-Sidhe
0 1 2 3 miles
0 1 2 3 4 5 km

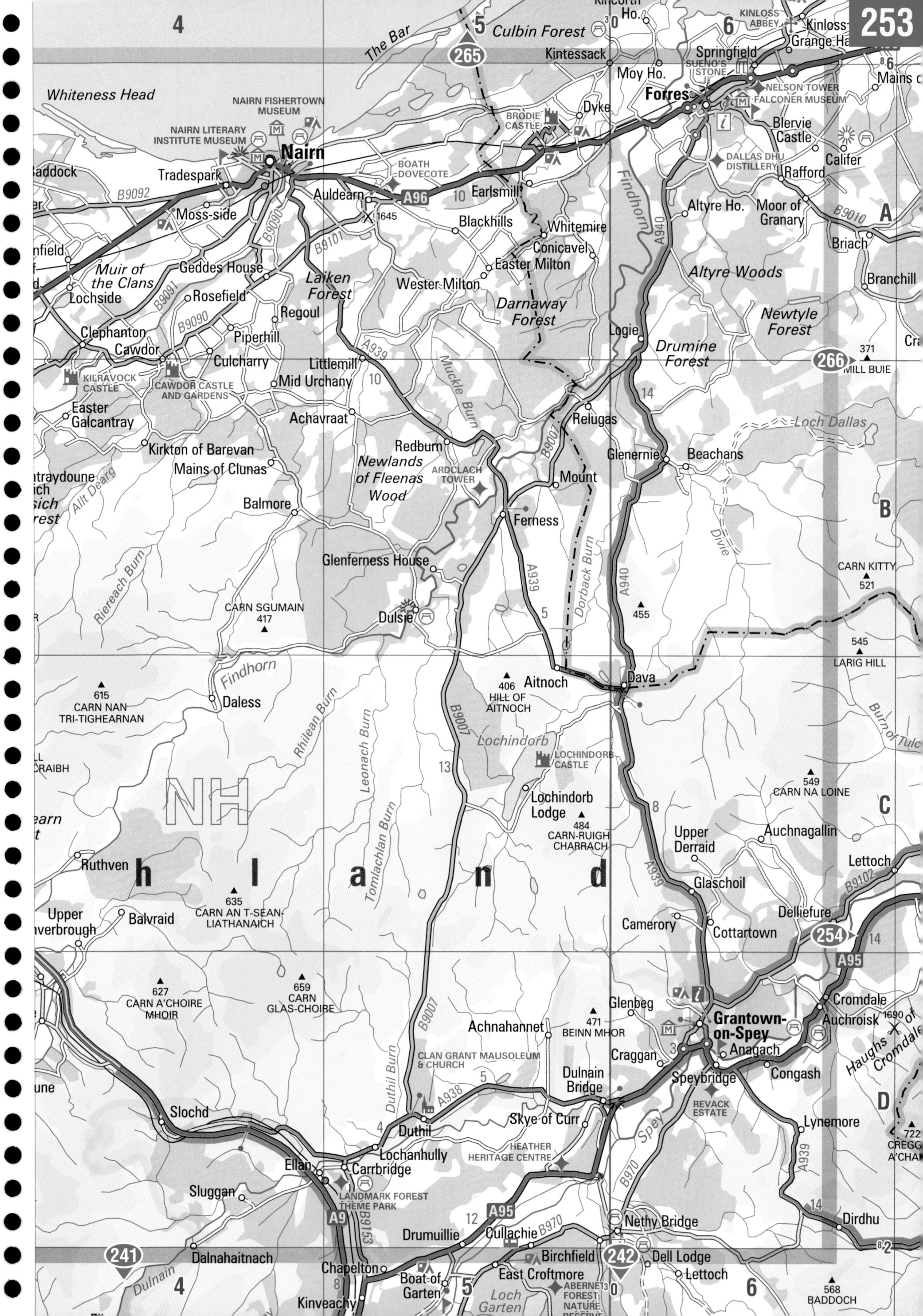
Culbin Forest
The Bar
Whiteness Head
Kintessack
Moy Ho.
Forres
Springfield
SUENO'S STONE
KINLOSS ABBEY
Kinloss
Grange Hall
NELSON TOWER
FALCONER MUSEUM
NAIRN FISHERTOWN MUSEUM
NAIRN LITERARY INSTITUTE MUSEUM
Nairn
BRODIE CASTLE
Dyke
Blervie Castle
Califer
DALLAS DHU DISTILLERY
Rafford
Tradespark
BOATH DOVECOTE
Auldearn
Earlsmill
Moss-side
Blackhills
Whitemire
Altyre Ho.
Moor of Granary
Briach
Conicavel
Easter Milton
Muir of the Clans
Geddes House
Laiken Forest
Wester Milton
Altyre Woods
Branchill
Lochside
Rosefield
Regoul
Darnaway Forest
Newtyle Forest
Clephanton
Cawdor
Piperhill
Logie
Drumine Forest
Culcharry
Littlemill
MILL BUIE
KILRAVOCK CASTLE
CAWDOR CASTLE AND GARDENS
Mid Urchany
Muckle Burn
Relugas
Easter Galcantray
Achavraat
Loch Dallas
Redburn
Kirkton of Barevan
Glenernie
Beachans
Mains of Clunas
Newlands of Fleenas Wood
ARDCLACH TOWER
Mount
Allt Dearg
Balmore
Ferness
Dorback Burn
Divie
Glenferness House
CARN KITTY
Riereach Burn
CARN SGUMAIN
Dulsie
LARIG HILL
Findhorn
Aitnoch
Dava
HILL OF AITNOCH
CARN NAN TRI-TIGHEARNAN
Daless
Rhilean Burn
Leonach Burn
Lochindorb
LOCHINDORB CASTLE
Burn of Tulchan
NH
Lochindorb Lodge
CARN NA LOINE
CARN-RUIGH CHARRACH
Upper Derraid
Auchnagallin
Tomlachlan Burn
Ruthven
Highland
Lettoch
Glaschoil
Upper Inverbrough
Balvraid
CARN AN T-SEAN-LIATHANAICH
Camerory
Delliefure
Cottartown
CARN A'CHOIRE MHOIR
CARN GLAS-CHOIRE
Glenbeg
Cromdale
Achnahannet
BEINN MHOR
Grantown-on-Spey
Auchroisk
Haughs of Cromdale
CLAN GRANT MAUSOLEUM & CHURCH
Craggan
Anagach
Dulnain Bridge
Speybridge
Congash
REVACK ESTATE
Duthil Burn
Slochd
Skye of Curr
Lynemore
Duthil
Spey
HEATHER HERITAGE CENTRE
Lochanhully
Ellan
Carrbridge
Sluggan
LANDMARK FOREST THEME PARK
Nethy Bridge
Dirdhu
Drumuillie
Cullachie
Dalnahaitnach
Birchfield
Dell Lodge
Lettoch
Chapelton
Boat of Garten
East Croftmore
ABERNETHY FOREST NATURE RESERVE
Loch Garten
Kinveachy
Dulnain
BADDOCH
CREGGAN A'CHAIT
A96
A939
A940
A938
A95
A9
B9090
B9091
B9092
B9101
B9007
B9010
B9102
B970
B9153
265
266
254
241
242

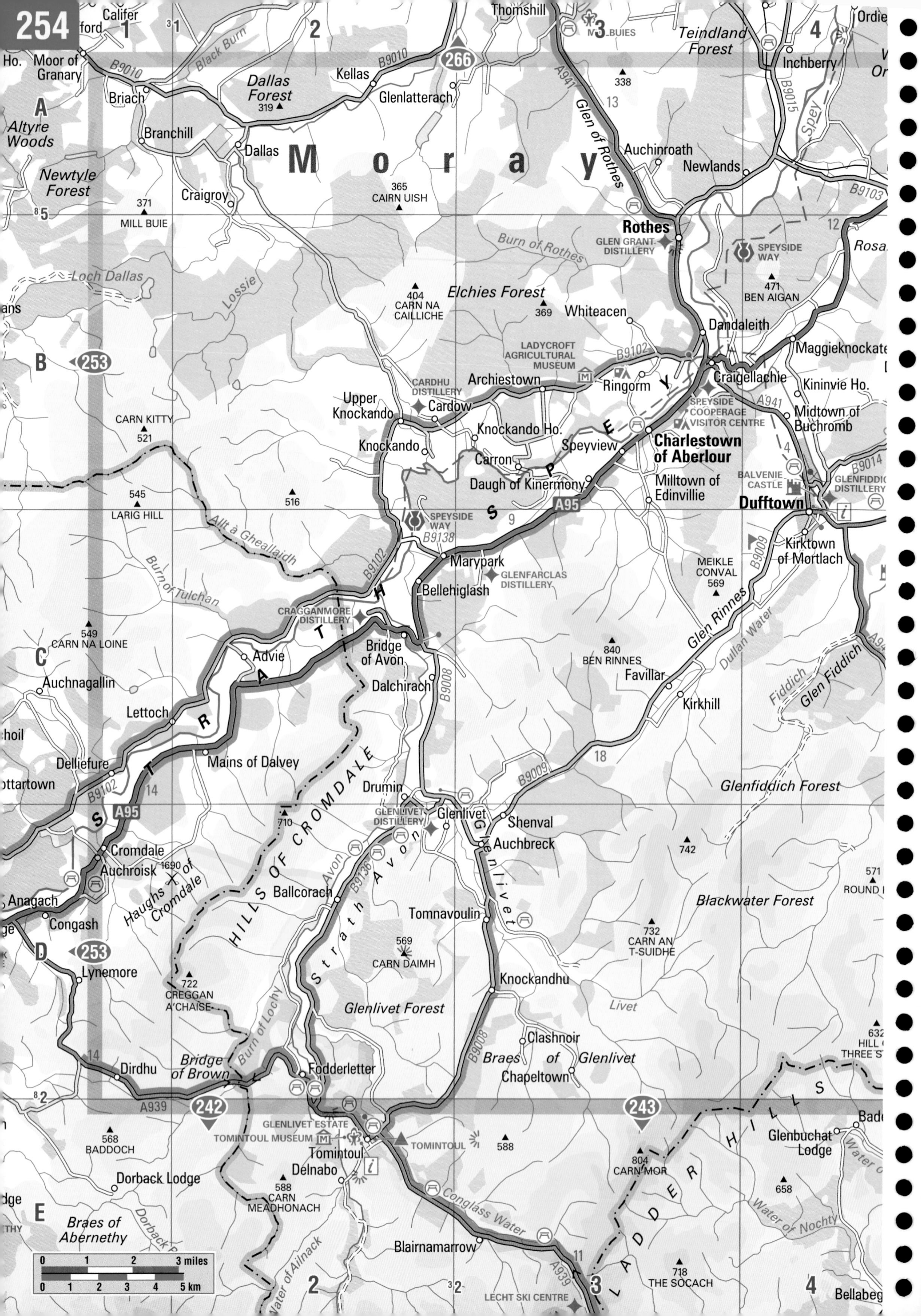
Moray
Rothes
Charlestown of Aberlour
Dufftown
Craigellachie
Dallas
Dallas Forest
Elchies Forest
Archiestown
Knockando
Upper Knockando
Cardow
Marypark
Bellehiglash
Bridge of Avon
Advie
Dalchirach
Lettoch
Mains of Dalvey
Dellefure
Cromdale
Auchroisk
Anagach
Congash
Lynemore
Dirdhu
Bridge of Brown
Fodderletter
Tomintoul
Delnabo
Dorback Lodge
Braes of Abernethy
Blairnamarrow
Glenlivet
Shenval
Auchbreck
Drumin
Tomnavoulin
Knockandhu
Clashnoir
Braes of Glenlivet
Chapeltown
Ballcorach
Glenlivet Forest
Blackwater Forest
Glenfiddich Forest
Kirkhill
Favillar
Glen Rinnes
Kirktown of Mortlach
Milltown of Edinvillie
Midtown of Buchromb
Kininvie Ho.
Maggieknockater
Dandaleith
Whiteacen
Ringorm
Speyview
Daugh of Kinermony
Carron
Knockando Ho.
Auchinroath
Newlands
Inchberry
Teindland Forest
Kellas
Glenlatterach
Briach
Branchill
Craigroy
Moor of Granary
Newtyle Forest
Altyre Woods
Auchnagallin
Glenbuchat Lodge
HILLS OF CROMDALE
LADDER HILLS
STRATH SPEY
Strath Avon
A95
A941
A939
B9102
B9008
B9009
B9136
B9138
B9010
B9015
B9103
B9014
242
243
253
266
LECHT SKI CENTRE
TOMINTOUL MUSEUM
GLENLIVET ESTATE
GLENLIVET DISTILLERY
CRAGGANMORE DISTILLERY
GLENFARCLAS DISTILLERY
CARDHU DISTILLERY
LADYCROFT AGRICULTURAL MUSEUM
SPEYSIDE COOPERAGE VISITOR CENTRE
BALVENIE CASTLE
GLENFIDDICH DISTILLERY
GLEN GRANT DISTILLERY
SPEYSIDE WAY
840 BEN RINNES
569 CARN DAIMH
732 CARN AN T-SUIDHE
804 CARN MOR
718 THE SOCACH
588 CARN MEADHONACH
568 BADDOCH
722 CREGGAN A'CHAISE
549 CARN NA LOINE
545 LARIG HILL
521 CARN KITTY
371 MILL BUIE
365 CAIRN UISH
404 CARN NA CAILLICHE
471 BEN AIGAN
569 MEIKLE CONVAL
0 1 2 3 miles
0 1 2 3 4 5 km

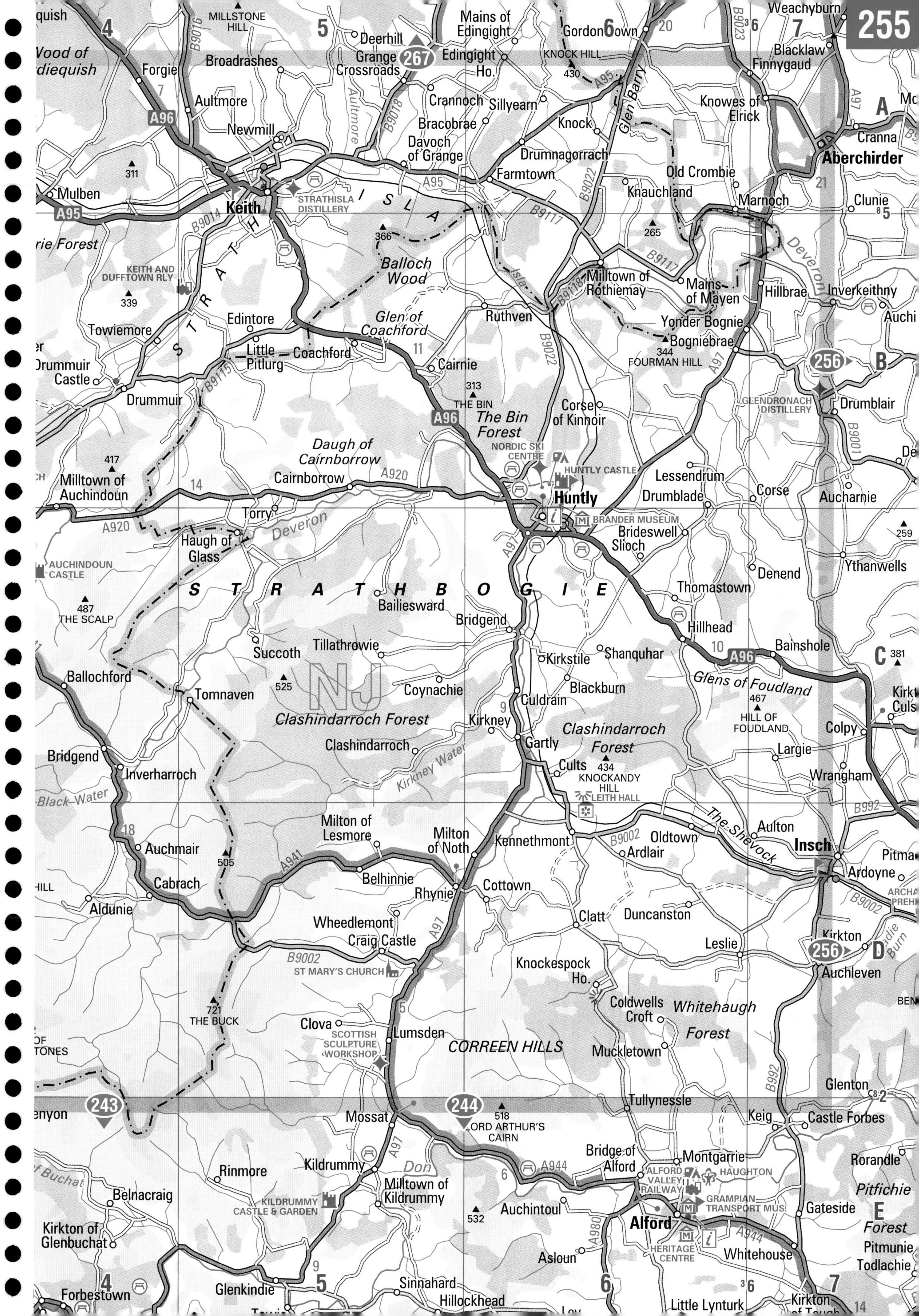
Deerhill
Mains of Edingight
Gordontown
Weachyburn
Broadrashes
Grange Crossroads
267
Edingight Ho.
KNOCK HILL
430
Blacklaw
Finnygaud
Forgie
Wood of Ordiequish
MILLSTONE HILL
Aultmore
Crannoch
Sillyearn
Glen Barry
Knowes of Elrick
A96
Newmill
Bracobrae
Knock
Cranna
Aberchirder
Davoch of Grange
Drumnagorrach
311
Farmtown
Old Crombie
Mulben
A95
STRATHISLA DISTILLERY
Knauchland
Marnoch
Clunie
Keith
B9014
S T R A T H   I S L A
366
B9117
265
Deveron
KEITH AND DUFFTOWN RLY
Balloch Wood
Milltown of Rothiemay
Mains of Mayen
Hillbrae
Inverkeithny
339
Glen of Coachford
Ruthven
Yonder Bognie
Towiemore
Edintore
Bogniebrae
344
FOURMAN HILL
Drummuir Castle
Little Pitlurg
Coachford
Cairnie
256
Drummuir
B9115
313
THE BIN
The Bin Forest
Corse of Kinnoir
GLENDRONACH DISTILLERY
Drumblair
A96
Daugh of Cairnborrow
NORDIC SKI CENTRE
HUNTLY CASTLE
417
Milltown of Auchindoun
Cairnborrow
A920
Lessendrum
Drumblade
Corse
Aucharnie
Huntly
Torry
BRANDER MUSEUM
Brideswell
Slioch
259
Haugh of Glass
Ythanwells
AUCHINDOUN CASTLE
Denend
S T R A T H B O G I E
Thomastown
487
THE SCALP
Bailiesward
Bridgend
Hillhead
Succoth
Tillathrowie
Kirkstile
Shanquhar
Bainshole
381
525
NJ
Ballochford
Tomnaven
Coynachie
Blackburn
Glens of Foudland
467
HILL OF FOUDLAND
Culdrain
Clashindarroch Forest
Kirkney
Clashindarroch Forest
Colpy
Clashindarroch
Gartly
Bridgend
Inverharroch
Kirkney Water
Cults
434
KNOCKANDY HILL
LEITH HALL
Largie
Wrangham
Black Water
Milton of Lesmore
Milton of Noth
Kennethmont
Oldtown
B9002
Ardlair
The Shevock
Aulton
Insch
Auchmair
505
A941
Ardoyne
Cabrach
Belhinnie
Rhynie
Cottown
Aldunie
Clatt
Duncanston
Wheedlemont
Craig Castle
A97
Leslie
Kirkton
256
B9002
ST MARY'S CHURCH
Knockespock Ho.
Auchleven
721
THE BUCK
Coldwells Croft
Whitehaugh Forest
Clova
SCOTTISH SCULPTURE WORKSHOP
Lumsden
CORREEN HILLS
Muckletown
B992
Glenton
243
244
518
LORD ARTHUR'S CAIRN
Tullynessle
Keig
Castle Forbes
Mossat
Bridge of Alford
Montgarrie
Rorandle
Rinmore
Kildrummy
Don
A944
ALFORD VALLEY RAILWAY
HAUGHTON
Pitfichie Forest
Belnacraig
Milltown of Kildrummy
KILDRUMMY CASTLE & GARDEN
532
Auchintoul
GRAMPIAN TRANSPORT MUS.
Gateside
Kirkton of Glenbuchat
A980
Alford
HERITAGE CENTRE
Whitehouse
Pitmunie
Todlachie
Asloun
Forbestown
Glenkindie
Sinnahard
Hillockhead
Little Lynturk
Kirkton
A
B
C
D
E

Aberchirder
Turriff
Cuminestown
New Deer
Fyvie
Methlick
Oldmeldrum
Inverurie
Insch
Kemnay
Kintore
Newmachar
Dyce
Monymusk
Aberdeen
FORMARTINE
GARIOCH
DELGATIE CASTLE
FYVIE CASTLE
HADDO HOUSE AND GARDENS
TOLQUHON CASTLE
LOANHEAD STONE CIRCLE
BENNACHIE
BATTLE OF HARLAW MEMORIAL
INVERURIE MUSEUM
KINKELL CHURCH
ARCHAEOLINK PREHISTORY PARK
MONYMUSK ARTS CENTRE
GLENDRONACH DISTILLERY
Glens of Foudland
HILL OF FOUDLAND
Delgaty Forest
Pitfichie Forest
Deveron
Ythan
Don
Urie
1 2 3 miles
1 2 3 4 5 km

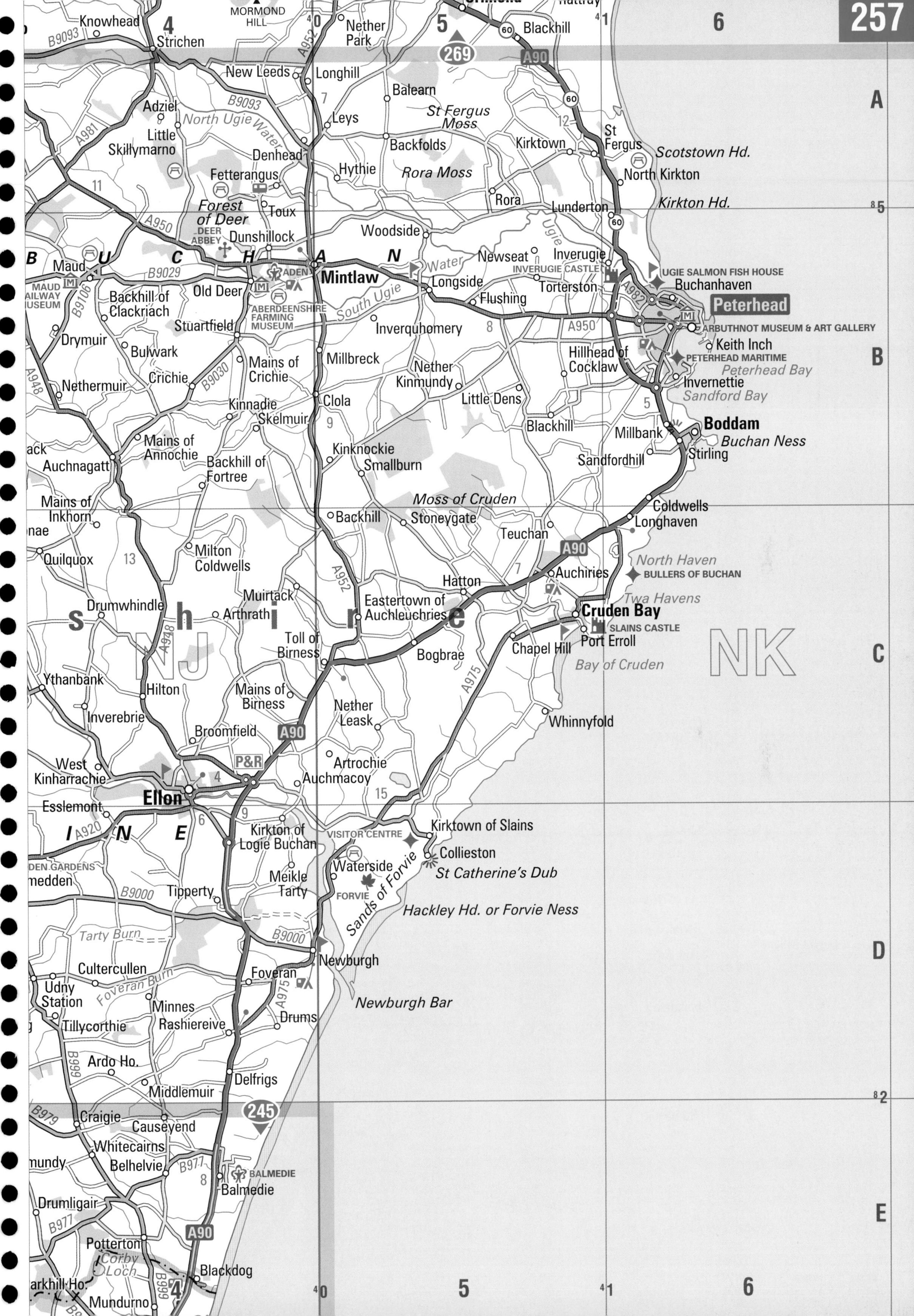

Knowhead
Strichen
MORMOND HILL
Nether Park
Blackhill
269
New Leeds
Longhill
Balearn
Adziel
Little Skillymarno
North Ugie Water
Leys
St Fergus Moss
Denhead
Backfolds
Kirktown
St Fergus
Scotstown Hd.
Fetterangus
Hythie
Rora Moss
North Kirkton
Forest of Deer
Toux
Rora
Kirkton Hd.
Lunderton
Dunshillock
Woodside
DEER ABBEY
Newseat
Inverugie
Maud
Mintlaw
INVERUGIE CASTLE
ADEN
Longside
Torterston
UGIE SALMON FISH HOUSE
Buchanhaven
MAUD RAILWAY MUSEUM
Backhill of Clackriach
Old Deer
Flushing
Peterhead
ABERDEENSHIRE FARMING MUSEUM
South Ugie
Stuartfield
Inverquhomery
ARBUTHNOT MUSEUM & ART GALLERY
Drymuir
Keith Inch
Bulwark
Mains of Crichie
Millbreck
Hillhead of Cocklaw
PETERHEAD MARITIME
Nether Kinmundy
Peterhead Bay
Crichie
Invernettie
Nethermuir
Clola
Little Dens
Sandford Bay
Kinnadie
Skelmuir
Blackhill
Millbank
Boddam
Mains of Annochie
Buchan Ness
Kinknockie
Stirling
Auchnagatt
Backhill of Fortree
Smallburn
Sandfordhill
Moss of Cruden
Mains of Inkhorn
Coldwells
Backhill
Stoneygate
Longhaven
Teuchan
Milton Coldwells
Quilquox
North Haven
Auchiries
BULLERS OF BUCHAN
Hatton
Muirtack
Twa Havens
Eastertown of Auchleuchries
Cruden Bay
Drumwhindle
Arthrath
SLAINS CASTLE
Toll of Birness
Chapel Hill
Port Erroll
Bogbrae
Bay of Cruden
NK
NJ
Ythanbank
Hilton
Mains of Birness
Nether Leask
Inverebrie
Whinnyfold
Broomfield
West Kinharrachie
P&R
Artrochie
Auchmacoy
Ellon
Esslemont
Kirktown of Slains
Kirkton of Logie Buchan
VISITOR CENTRE
Collieston
Waterside
St Catherine's Dub
Meikle Tarty
Tipperty
FORVIE
Sands of Forvie
Hackley Hd. or Forvie Ness
Tarty Burn
Newburgh
Cultercullen
Foveran
Udny Station
Foveran Burn
Minnes
Newburgh Bar
Tillycorthie
Rashiereive
Drums
Ardo Ho.
Delfrigs
Middlemuir
Craigie
245
Causeyend
Whitecairns
Belhelvie
BALMEDIE
Balmedie
Drumligair
Potterton
Corby Loch
Blackdog
Mundurno

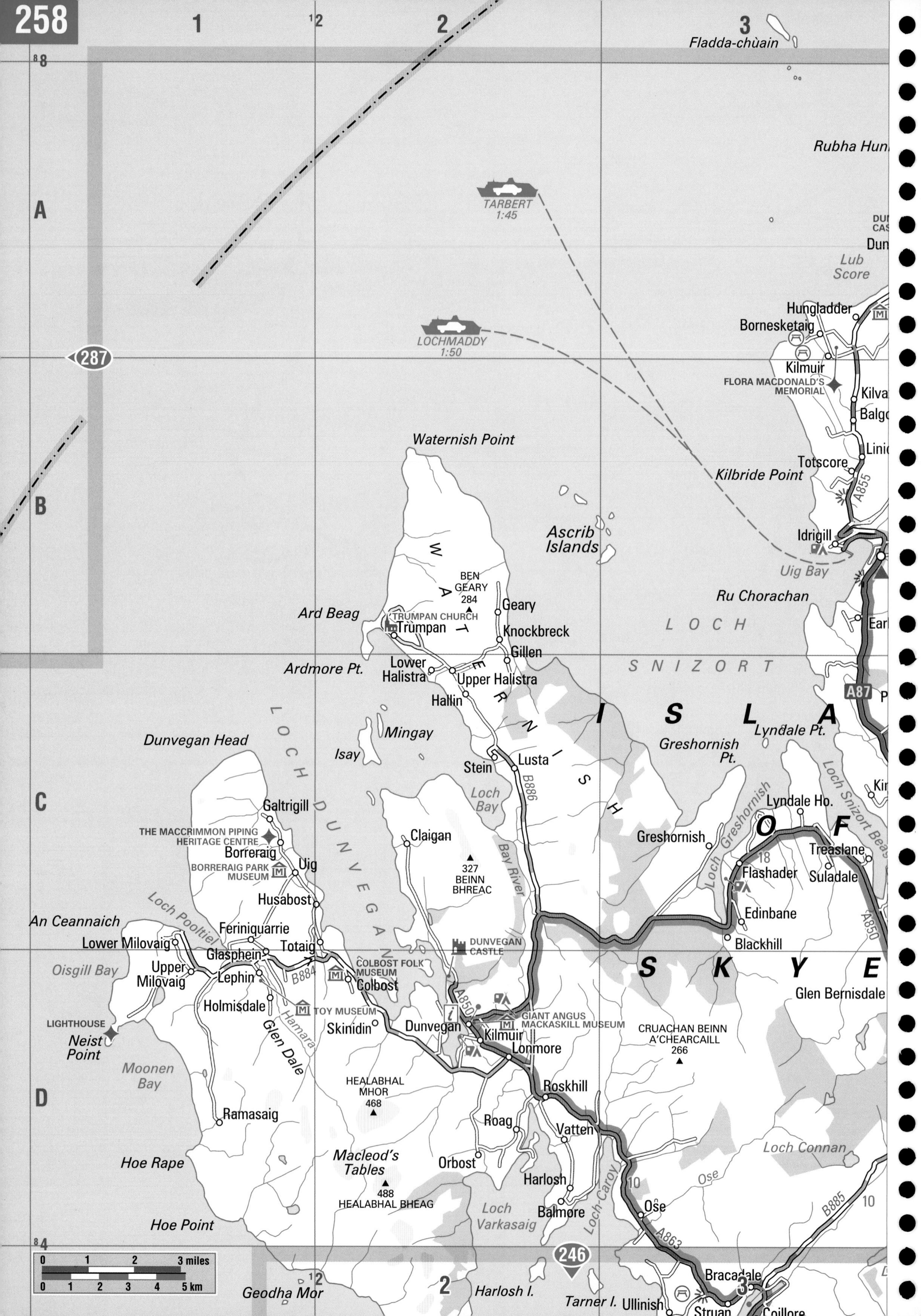
Fladda-chùain
Rubha Hunish
TARBERT 1:45
LOCHMADDY 1:50
287
Lub Score
Hungladder
Bornesketaig
Kilmuir
FLORA MACDONALD'S MEMORIAL
Waternish Point
Totscore
Kilbride Point
Ascrib Islands
Idrigill
Uig Bay
Ru Chorachan
BEN GEARY 284
Geary
Ard Beag
TRUMPAN CHURCH
Trumpan
Knockbreck
Gillen
LOCH SNIZORT
Ardmore Pt.
Lower Halistra
Upper Halistra
Hallin
WATERNISH
ISLE OF SKYE
A87
Lyndale Pt.
Mingay
Isay
Dunvegan Head
Greshornish Pt.
Stein
Lusta
LOCH DUNVEGAN
Loch Bay
B886
Loch Snizort Beag
Lyndale Ho.
Galtrigill
Claigan
Greshornish
Loch Greshornish
THE MACCRIMMON PIPING HERITAGE CENTRE
Borreraig
BORRERAIG PARK MUSEUM
Uig
327 BEINN BHREAC
Bay River
Treaslane
Flashader
Suladale
Husabost
Loch Pooltiel
An Ceannaich
Edinbane
A850
Feriniquarrie
Lower Milovaig
Totaig
DUNVEGAN CASTLE
Blackhill
Glasphein
Oisgill Bay
Upper Milovaig
Lephin
B884
COLBOST FOLK MUSEUM
Colbost
Glen Bernisdale
Holmisdale
TOY MUSEUM
GIANT ANGUS MACKASKILL MUSEUM
LIGHTHOUSE
Neist Point
Hamara
Skinidin
Dunvegan
Kilmuir
CRUACHAN BEINN A'CHEARCAILL 266
Glen Dale
Lonmore
Moonen Bay
HEALABHAL MHOR 468
Roskhill
Ramasaig
Roag
Vatten
Hoe Rape
Macleod's Tables
Orbost
Loch Connan
Harlosh
Loch-Caroy
Ose
488 HEALABHAL BHEAG
B885
Loch Varkasaig
Balmore
A863
Hoe Point
246
Bracadale
Geodha Mor
Harlosh I.
Tarner I.
Ullinish
Struan
Coillore
0 1 2 3 miles
0 1 2 3 4 5 km

4
5
6
260
261
249
248
A
B
C
D
NG
Eilean Trodday
Rubha na h-Aiseig
Balmacqueen
Kilmaluag
MUSEUM OF ISLAND LIFE
Eilean Flodigarry
Flodigarry
MEALL NA SUIRAMACH
543
Staffin I.
Digg
Staffin Bay
Glashvin
THE QUIRAING
Brogaig
Staffin
Stenscholl
TROTTERNISH
Kilt Rock
KILT ROCK & MEALT FALLS
466
BIOD BUIDHE
Elishader
Maligar
Loch Mealt
Valtos
Uig
Conon
Marishader
Garros
Rubha nam Brathairean
Balnaknock
611
BEINN EDRA
Breckrey
Culnaknock
Lealt
LEALT FALLS
Lower Tote
Upper Tote
607
CREAG A'LAIN
Hinnisdal
Island of Rona
125
Eilean Garbh
Romesdal
719
THE STORR
OLD MAN OF STORR
Caol Rona
Eilean Tigh
Garbh Eilean
Callakille
Lonbain
Eyre
TROTTERNISH
Bearreraig Bay
Loch a' Sguirr
An Caol
The Aird
Kensaleyre
Bernisdale
Haultin
Holm I.
Loch Leathan
Eilean Fladday
SOUND OF RAASAY
INNER SOUND
B8036
Tote
A855
Loch Fada
Torran
Manish Pt.
Loch Arnish
Arnish
Loch nan Eun
Borve
Skeabost
Carbost
PRINCE CHARLES'S CAVE
Uigshader
Drumuie
392
Achachork
Rubha na h Airde Glaise
BROCHEL CASTLE
Brochel
CHAPEL OF MAELRUBH
Glengrasco
AN TUIREANN ARTS CENTRE
Torvaig
Applecross Bay
Shulishadermor
THE AROS EXPERIENCE
Portree
Glame
385
ISLAND OF RAASAY
Snizort
Heatherfield
417
Penifiler
413
BEN TIANAVAIG
Balmeanach
Balachuirn
Camusteel
Ard-dhubh
Glenmore
Tungadal
Loch Duagrich
Mugeary
B883
Camastianavaig
Holoman Bay
443
DUN CAAN
A87
Tianavaig Bay
Oskaig
Conordan
Rubha na'Leac
Eilean na Bà

1
2
3
Garbh Eilean
Eilean Mhuire
Eilean an Tighe
Na h-Eileanan Mòra (Shiant Islands)
A
288
288
B
NG
259
Eilean Trodday
Rubha Hunish
Rubha na h-Aiseig
C
DUNTULM CASTLE
20
Balmacqueen
Duntulm
Kilmaluag
MUSEUM OF ISLAND LIFE
Eilean Flodigarry
Flodigarry
MEALL NA SUIRAMACH
543
Staffin I.
259
Digg
Staffin Bay
Kilvaxter
Glashvin
Balgown
THE QUIRAING
Brogaig
Stenscholl
Staffin
Linicro
TROTTERNISH
Kilt Rock
KILT ROCK & MEALT FALLS
A855
466
BIOD BUIDHE
Elishader
D
Maligar
Loch Mealt
Uig
Conon
Valtos
A855
Marishader
Garros
Rubha nam Brathairean
UIG
Balnaknock
611
BEINN EDRA
Breckrey
Culnaknock
Island of Rona
Earlish
Lealt
LEALT FALLS
Lower Tote
Upper Tote
Lealt
0 1 2 3 miles
0 1 2 3 4 5 km
Hinnisdal
607
CREAG A'LAIN
2
3

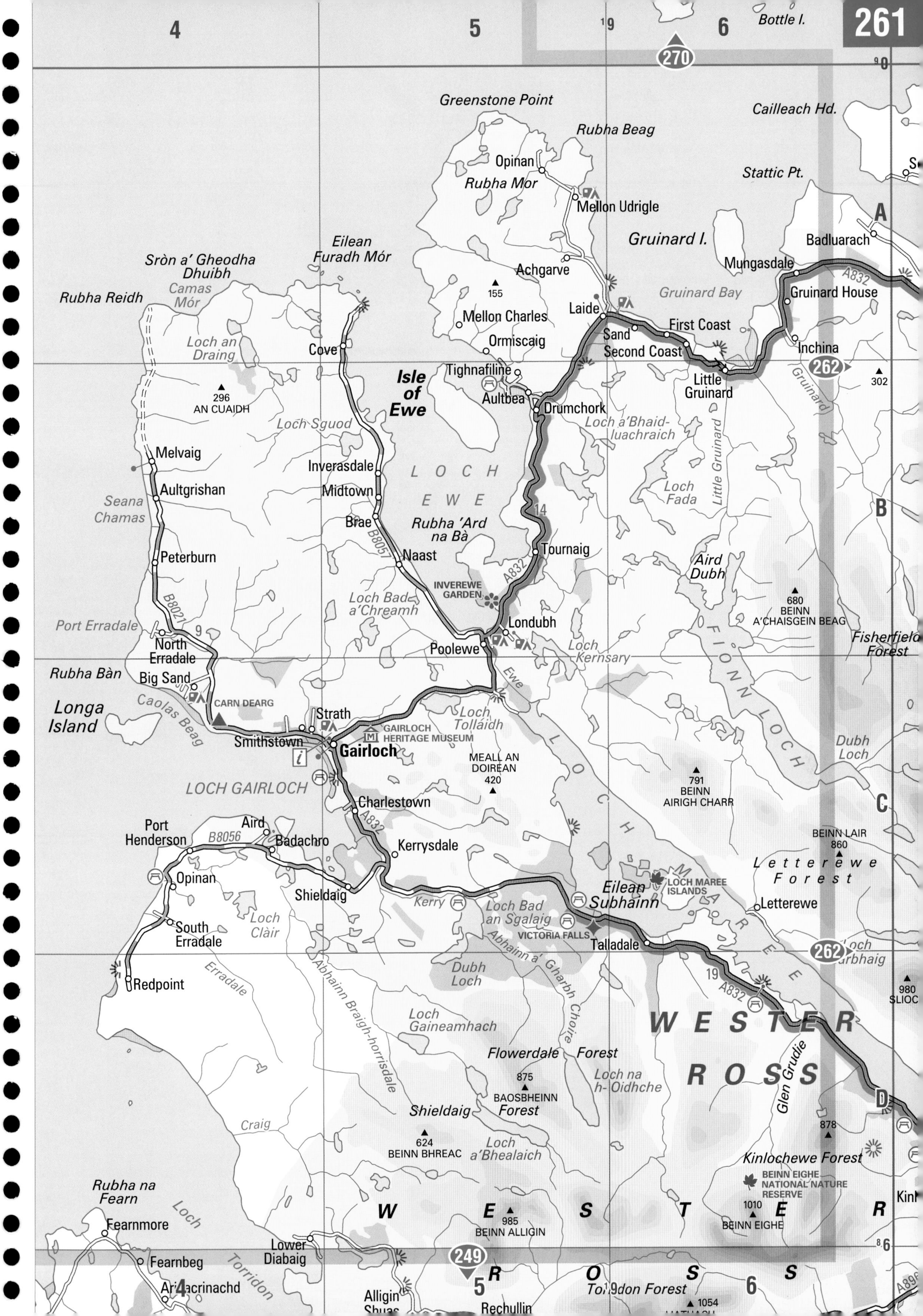

4
5
6
Bottle I.
270
Greenstone Point
Cailleach Hd.
Rubha Beag
Opinan
Rubha Mor
Stattic Pt.
Mellon Udrigle
A
Badluarach
Gruinard I.
Eilean Furadh Mór
Sròn a' Gheodha Dhuibh
Camas Mór
Rubha Reidh
Achgarve
Mungasdale
A832
Gruinard Bay
Gruinard House
155
Mellon Charles
Laide
Sand
First Coast
Second Coast
Inchina
Loch an Draing
Cove
Ormiscaig
Isle of Ewe
Tighnafiline
Aultbea
Drumchork
Little Gruinard
262
302
Gruinard
296
AN CUAIDH
Loch Sguod
Loch a'Bhaid-luachraich
Melvaig
Inverasdale
LOCH EWE
Loch Fada
Little Gruinard
Aultgrishan
Midtown
Seana Chamas
Brae
B8057
Rubha 'Ard na Bà
B
14
Peterburn
Naast
Tournaig
Aird Dubh
INVEREWE GARDEN
Loch Bad a'Chreamh
680
BEINN A'CHAISGEIN BEAG
Port Erradale
B8021
9
Londubh
North Erradale
Poolewe
Loch Kernsary
Fisherfield Forest
Rubha Bàn
Big Sand
Ewe
FIONN LOCH
Longa Island
Caolas Beag
CARN DEARG
Strath
Loch Tolláidh
Smithstown
GAIRLOCH HERITAGE MUSEUM
Gairloch
MEALL AN DOIREAN
420
Dubh Loch
791
BEINN AIRIGH CHARR
LOCH GAIRLOCH
Charlestown
LOCH MAREE
C
Port Henderson
Aird
B8056
Badachro
A832
Kerrysdale
BEINN LAIR
860
Letterewe Forest
Opinan
Shieldaig
Eilean Subhainn
LOCH MAREE ISLANDS
Kerry
Loch Bad an Sgalaig
Letterewe
Loch Clàir
South Erradale
VICTORIA FALLS
Talladale
Abhainn a' Gharbh Choire
Dubh Loch
19
A832
Redpoint
Erradale
Abhainn Braigh-horrisdale
980
SLIOC
Loch Gaineamhach
WESTER ROSS
Flowerdale Forest
Loch na h-Oidhche
875
BAOSBHEINN
Glen Grudie
D
Craig
Shieldaig Forest
624
BEINN BHREAC
Loch a'Bhealaich
878
Kinlochewe Forest
BEINN EIGHE NATIONAL NATURE RESERVE
Rubha na Fearn
Loch
1010
BEINN EIGHE
985
BEINN ALLIGIN
WESTER
Fearnmore
Fearnbeg
Lower Diabaig
249
Torridon
Arinacrinachd
Alligin Shuas
Rechullin
Torridon Forest
ROSS
1054
A896

Carn nan Sgeir
Strathcanaird
Strath Kanaird
Strath nan Lon
270
271
Camas Mór
Isle Martin
Loch Kanaird
A835
415
Allt-Beinn Donuil
Cailleach Hd.
STORNOWAY 2:40
Ardmair
Rhue
Annat Bay
Rhidorroch
Scoraig
Carnach
Rireavach
Stattic Pt.
LITTLE LOCH BROOM
Morefield
Ullapool
Loch Achall
Rhidorroch Ho.
548
ULLAPOOL MUSEUM
ULLAPOOL
Ullapool
LOCHBROOM MUSEUM
Glen Achall
Rhidorroch
635
BEINN GHOBHLACH
Badluarach
Mungasdale
Gruinard House
Durnamuck
Badcaul
A832
Allt na h-Airbhe
Badrallach
558
BEINN EILIDEACH
LECKMELM SHRUBBERY AND ARBORETUM
Leckmelm
Inchina
261
Blarnalearoch
642
MEALL DUBH
302
Gruinard
Camusnagaul
Strath Beag
Rhiroy
Ardessie
767
SAIL MHOR
Ardindrean
Ardcharnich
Dundonnell Hotel
Dundonnell
Eilean Darach
LOCH BROOM
Letters
12
Inverlael Forest
Dundonnell House
Inverlael
LAEL FOREST GARDEN
Strathnasheallag Forest
AN TEALLACH 1062
Lael Forest
Lael
Inverbroom
Loch na Sealga
Strath More
Broom
680
BEINN A'CHAISGEIN BEAG
Dundonnell Forest
Fisherfield Forest
Auchindrean
889
Strath na Sealga
908
BEINN DEARG MHOR
Fain
Braemore
CORRIESHALLOCH GORGE
MEALL LEACACHA
618
Dundonnell
A832
Abhainn Cuileig
Dubh Loch
914
BEINN A' CHLAIDHEIMH
Abhainn Droma
Braemore Forest
Lochdrum
807
Loch a'Bhraoin
BEINN LAIR 860
Letterewe Forest
1019
MULLACH COIRE MHIC FHEARCHAIR
934
1110
SGURR MOR
Letterewe
Lochan Fada
748
GROBAN
999
A'CHAILLEACH
261
Loch Garbhaig
949
MEALL GORM
980
SLIOCH
Abhainn a'Chadh'Bhuidhe
Fannich Forest
WESTER ROSS
BEINN NAN RAMH 711
Fannich Lodge
Glen Grudie
692
Kinlochewe Forest
LOCH FANNICH
Heights of Kinlochewe
Leckie
Strath Chrombuill
878
Taagan
Lochrosque Forest
WESTER ROSS
Kinlochewe Forest
Anancaun
Abhainn Bruachaig
BEINN EIGHE NATIONAL NATURE RESERVE
Incheril
Kinlochewe
933
FIONN BHEINN
A832
1010
BEINN EIGHE
Glen Docherty
Strath Bran
250
0 1 2 3 miles
0 1 2 3 4 5 km
Badavanich
A832
Achnasheen
Bran
1 2 3 4
A B C D

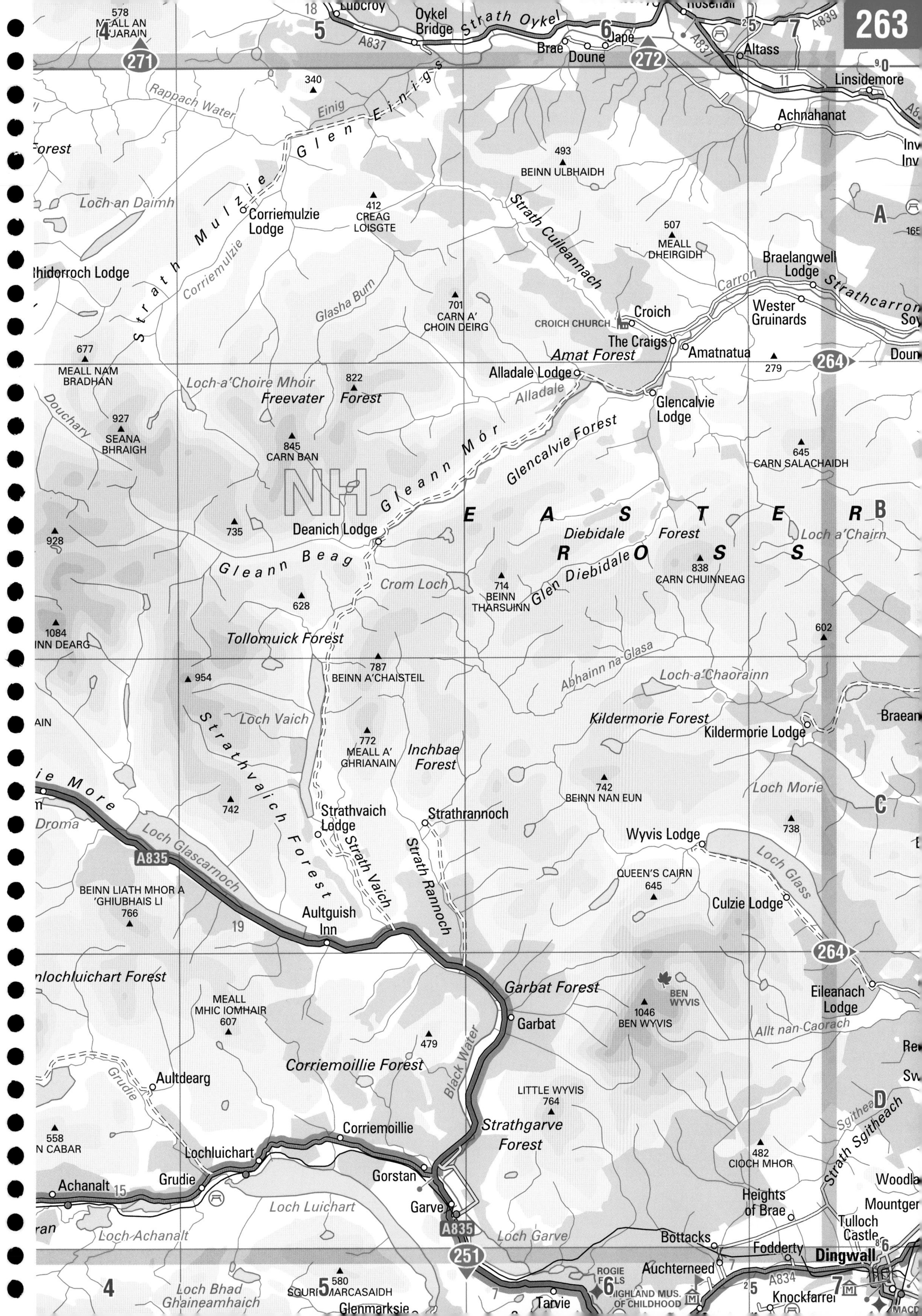
Oykel Bridge
Strath Oykel
Brae
Doune
Altass
Linsidemore
Achnahanat
Rappach Water
Glen Einig
Loch an Daimh
Corriemulzie Lodge
CREAG LOISGTE
BEINN ULBHAIDH
Strath Cuileannach
MEALL DHEIRGIDH
Braelangwell Lodge
Strathcarron
Wester Gruinards
Strath Mulzie
Glasha Burn
CARN A' CHOIN DEIRG
Croich
CROICH CHURCH
The Craigs
Amatnatua
Amat Forest
Alladale Lodge
Glencalvie Lodge
MEALL NAM BRADHAN
Loch a'Choire Mhoir
Freevater Forest
SEANA BHRAIGH
CARN BAN
Gleann Mór
Glencalvie Forest
CARN SALACHAIDH
NH
Deanich Lodge
EASTER ROSS
Diebidale Forest
Loch a'Chairn
Gleann Beag
Crom Loch
BEINN THARSUINN
Glen Diebidale
CARN CHUINNEAG
Tollomuick Forest
BEINN A'CHAISTEIL
Abhainn na Glasa
Loch a'Chaorainn
Loch Vaich
Kildermorie Forest
Kildermorie Lodge
MEALL A' GHRIANAIN
Inchbae Forest
Strathvaich Forest
Loch Morie
BEINN NAN EUN
Strathvaich Lodge
Strathrannoch
Wyvis Lodge
Loch Glascarnoch
A835
Strath Vaich
Strath Rannoch
QUEEN'S CAIRN
Loch Glass
Culzie Lodge
BEINN LIATH MHOR A 'GHIUBHAIS LI
Aultguish Inn
Garbat Forest
BEN WYVIS
Eileanach Lodge
Garbat
Allt nan Caorach
MEALL MHIC IOMHAIR
Corriemoillie Forest
Black Water
Aultdearg
Grudie
LITTLE WYVIS
Strathgarve Forest
Strath Sgitheach
Corriemoillie
Lochluichart
CIOCH MHOR
Achanalt
Grudie
Gorstan
Heights of Brae
Loch Luichart
Garve
Tulloch Castle
Loch Achanalt
Loch Garve
Bottacks
Fodderty
Dingwall
ROGIE FALLS
Auchterneed
Loch Bhad Ghaineamhaich
A834
Knockfarrel
HIGHLAND MUS. OF CHILDHOOD
Tarvie
Glenmarksie

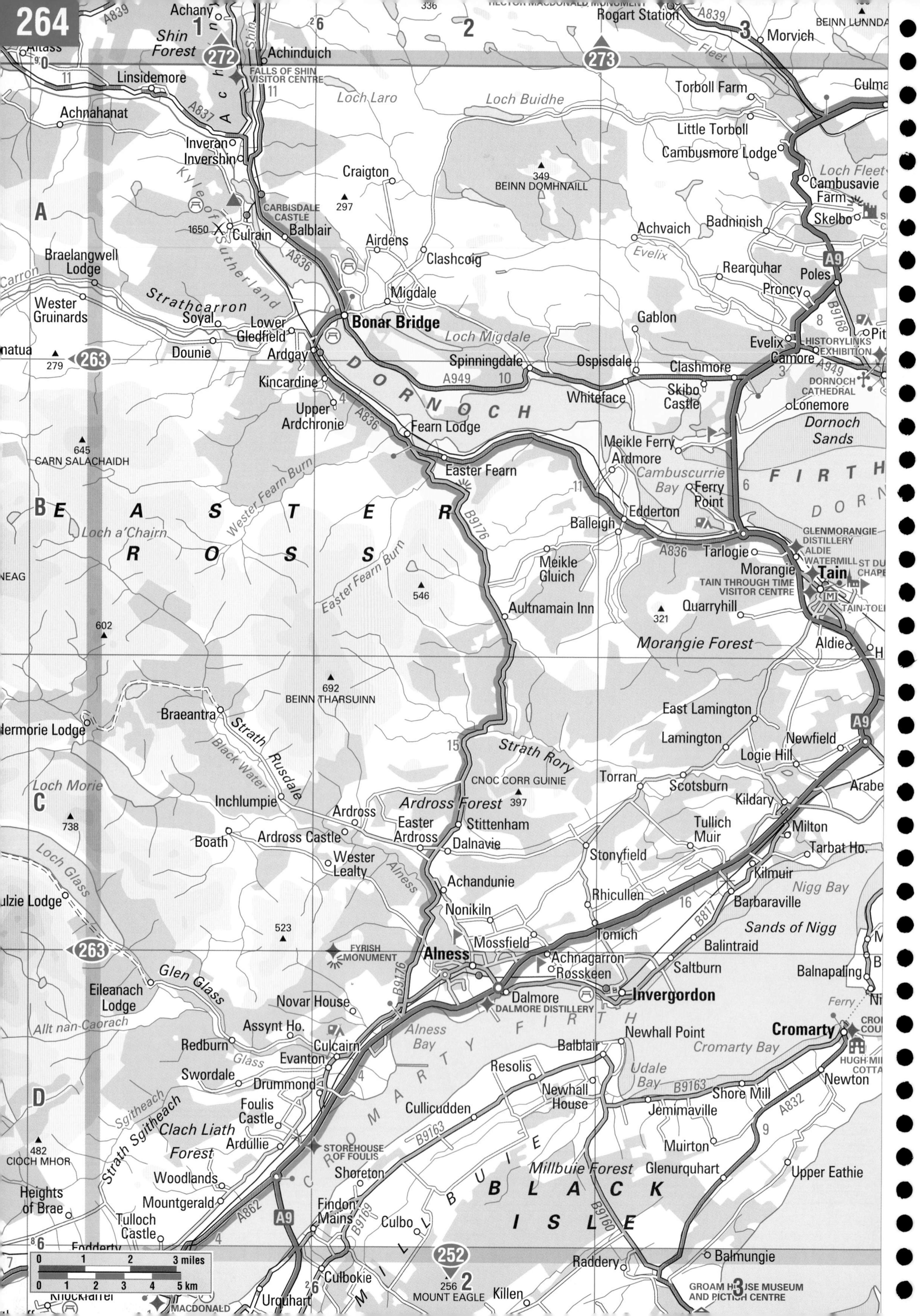
Achany
Shin Forest
Achinduich
Rogart Station
Morvich
Linsidemore
Falls of Shin Visitor Centre
Loch Laro
Loch Buidhe
Torboll Farm
Achnahanat
Little Torboll
Inveran
Invershin
Cambusmore Lodge
Craigton
Beinn Domhnaill
Loch Fleet
Cambusavie Farm
Kyle of Sutherland
Carbisdale Castle
Culrain
Balblair
Achvaich
Badninish
Skelbo
Airdens
Clashcoig
Braelangwell Lodge
Rearquhar
Poles
Proncy
Migdale
Wester Gruinards
Strathcarron
Soyal
Lower Gledfield
Bonar Bridge
Loch Migdale
Gablon
Evelix
Historylinks Exhibition
Dounie
Ardgay
Spinningdale
Ospisdale
Clashmore
Camore
Kincardine
Dornoch Firth
Skibo Castle
Whiteface
Dornoch Cathedral
Lonemore
Upper Ardchronie
Fearn Lodge
Dornoch Sands
Carn Salachaidh
Meikle Ferry
Ardmore
Easter Fearn
Cambuscurrie Bay
Ferry Point
Wester Fearn Burn
Easter Ross
Edderton
Balleigh
Loch a'Chairn
Glenmorangie Distillery
Aldie Watermill
Tarlogie
Meikle Gluich
Morangie
Tain
Easter Fearn Burn
Tain Through Time Visitor Centre
Aultnamain Inn
Quarryhill
Morangie Forest
Aldie
Beinn Tharsuinn
East Lamington
Braeantra
Strath Rusdale
Lamington
Newfield
Strath Rory
Logie Hill
Black Water
Cnoc Corr Guinie
Torran
Scotsburn
Loch Morie
Kildary
Inchlumpie
Ardross Forest
Ardross
Easter Ardross
Stittenham
Tullich Muir
Milton
Boath
Ardross Castle
Dalnavie
Tarbat Ho.
Wester Lealty
Stonyfield
Loch Glass
Kilmuir
Nigg Bay
Achandunie
Rhicullen
Barbaraville
Nonikiln
Sands of Nigg
Tomich
Balintraid
Fyrish Monument
Mossfield
Alness
Achnagarron
Rosskeen
Saltburn
Balnapaling
Glen Glass
Eileanach Lodge
Dalmore
Invergordon
Novar House
Dalmore Distillery
Cromarty Firth
Allt nan Caorach
Assynt Ho.
Alness Bay
Newhall Point
Cromarty
Redburn
Culcairn
Balblair
Cromarty Bay
Evanton
Udale Bay
Swordale
Resolis
Drummond
Newhall House
Shore Mill
Newton
Foulis Castle
Cullicudden
Jemimaville
Clach Liath Forest
Strath Sgitheach
Ardullie
Storehouse of Foulis
Muirton
Cioch Mhor
Millbuie Forest
Glenurquhart
Upper Eathie
Woodlands
Shoreton
Black Isle
Heights of Brae
Mountgerald
Findon Mains
Culbo
Tulloch Castle
Raddery
Balmungie
Culbokie
Mount Eagle
Killen
Urquhart
Groam House Museum and Pictish Centre
0 1 2 3 miles
0 1 2 3 4 5 km

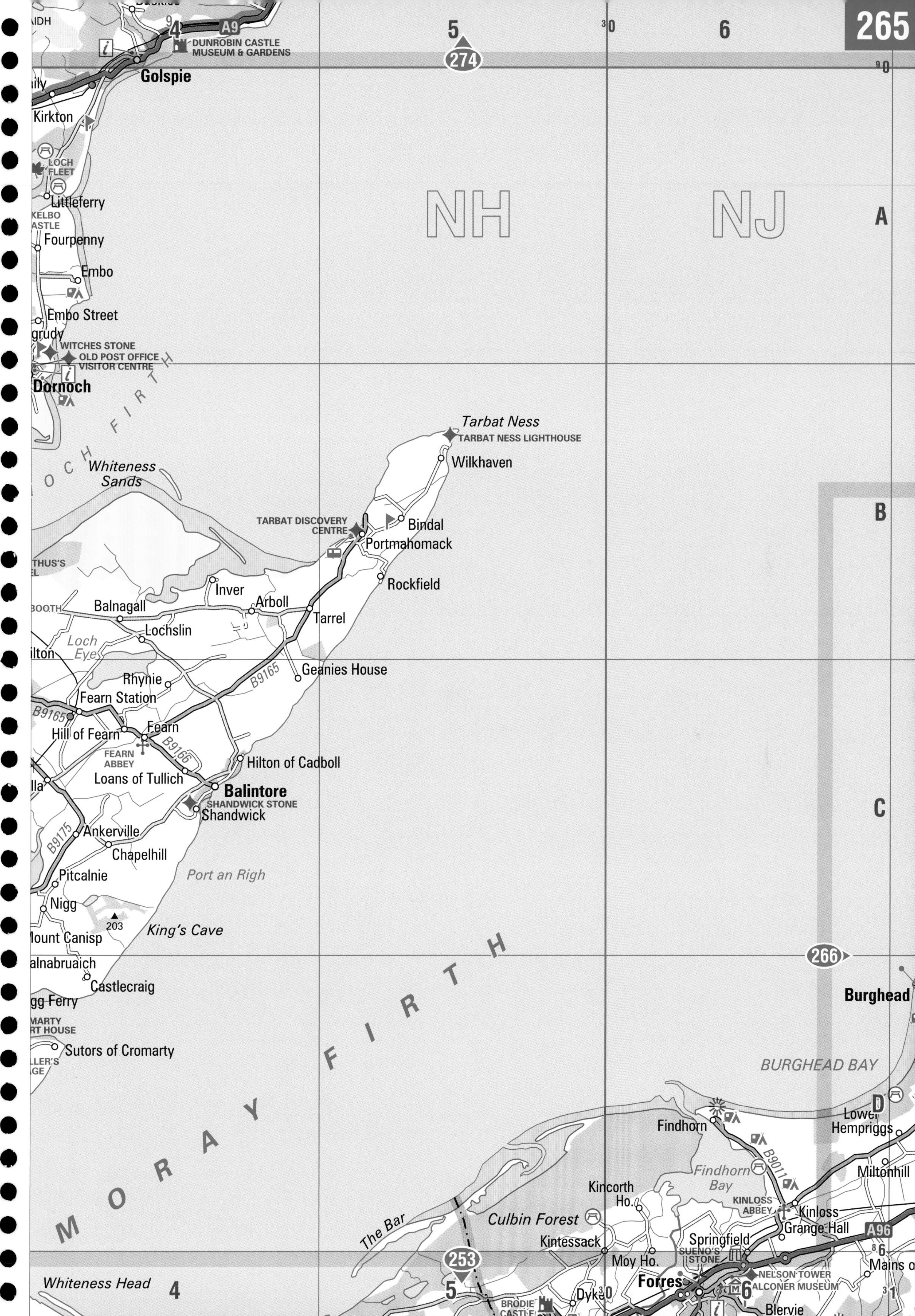

5
6
274
266
253
4
NH
NJ
A
B
C
D
A9
Golspie
DUNROBIN CASTLE MUSEUM & GARDENS
Kirkton
LOCH FLEET
Littleferry
Fourpenny
Embo
Embo Street
WITCHES STONE
OLD POST OFFICE VISITOR CENTRE
Dornoch
Tarbat Ness
TARBAT NESS LIGHTHOUSE
Wilkhaven
Whiteness Sands
TARBAT DISCOVERY CENTRE
Bindal
Portmahomack
Rockfield
Inver
Arboll
Balnagall
Tarrel
Lochslin
Loch Eye
Geanies House
B9165
Rhynie
Fearn Station
Hill of Fearn
Fearn
B9166
FEARN ABBEY
Hilton of Cadboll
Loans of Tullich
Balintore
SHANDWICK STONE
Shandwick
B9175
Ankerville
Chapelhill
Pitcalnie
Port an Righ
Nigg
203
King's Cave
Castlecraig
Sutors of Cromarty
MORAY FIRTH
Burghead
BURGHEAD BAY
Findhorn
Lower Hempriggs
B9011
Findhorn Bay
Miltonhill
Kincorth Ho.
KINLOSS ABBEY
Kinloss
Culbin Forest
The Bar
Grange Hall
A96
Kintessack
Springfield
Moy Ho.
SUENO'S STONE
Mains
Whiteness Head
Forres
NELSON TOWER
FALCONER MUSEUM
Dyke
BRODIE CASTLE
Blervie

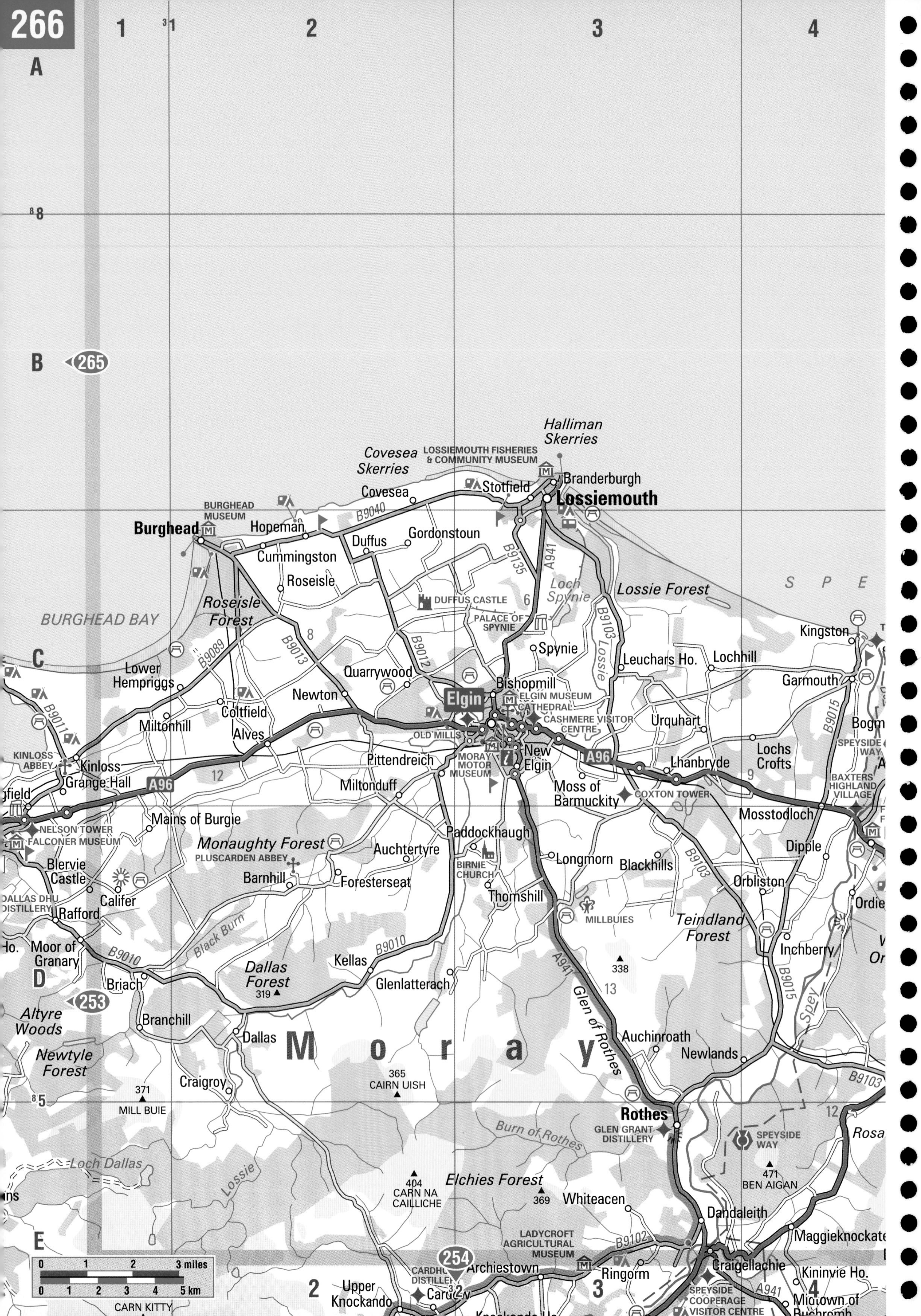

Halliman Skerries
Covesea Skerries
LOSSIEMOUTH FISHERIES & COMMUNITY MUSEUM
Branderburgh
Lossiemouth
Stotfield
Covesea
BURGHEAD MUSEUM
Burghead
Hopeman
Duffus
Gordonstoun
Cummingston
Roseisle
Roseisle Forest
BURGHEAD BAY
DUFFUS CASTLE
PALACE OF SPYNIE
Loch Spynie
Lossie Forest
Spynie
Kingston
Lochhill
Leuchars Ho.
Garmouth
Lower Hempriggs
Quarrywood
Bishopmill
Newton
Elgin
ELGIN MUSEUM
CATHEDRAL
CASHMERE VISITOR CENTRE
Urquhart
Coltfield
Miltonhill
Alves
OLD MILLS
KINLOSS ABBEY
Kinloss
Grange Hall
Pittendreich
MORAY MOTOR MUSEUM
New Elgin
Lhanbryde
Lochs Crofts
SPEYSIDE WAY
BAXTERS HIGHLAND VILLAGE
Miltonduff
Moss of Barmuckity
COXTON TOWER
Mosstodloch
Mains of Burgie
NELSON TOWER
FALCONER MUSEUM
Paddockhaugh
Monaughty Forest
Auchtertyre
PLUSCARDEN ABBEY
BIRNIE CHURCH
Longmorn
Blackhills
Dipple
Blervie Castle
Barnhill
Foresterseat
Orbliston
DALLAS DHU DISTILLERY
Califer
Rafford
Thomshill
MILLBUIES
Teindland Forest
Ordie
Moor of Granary
Black Burn
Inchberry
Dallas Forest
Kellas
Briach
319
Glenlatterach
338
Glen of Rothes
Altyre Woods
Branchill
Dallas
Moray
Auchinroath
Newlands
Newtyle Forest
Craigroy
365 CAIRN UISH
371 MILL BUIE
Rothes
GLEN GRANT DISTILLERY
Burn of Rothes
SPEYSIDE WAY
471 BEN AIGAN
Loch Dallas
Lossie
404 CARN NA CAILLICHE
Elchies Forest
369
Whiteacen
Dandaleith
Maggieknockater
LADYCROFT AGRICULTURAL MUSEUM
Archiestown
Ringorm
Craigellachie
Kininvie Ho.
Upper Knockando
CARDHU DISTILLERY
SPEYSIDE COOPERAGE VISITOR CENTRE
Mid town of Buchromb
CARN KITTY
Spey
A96
A941
B9040
B9089
B9013
B9012
B9135
B9103
B9015
B9010
B9102
B9011
0 1 2 3 miles
0 1 2 3 4 5 km

265
253
254

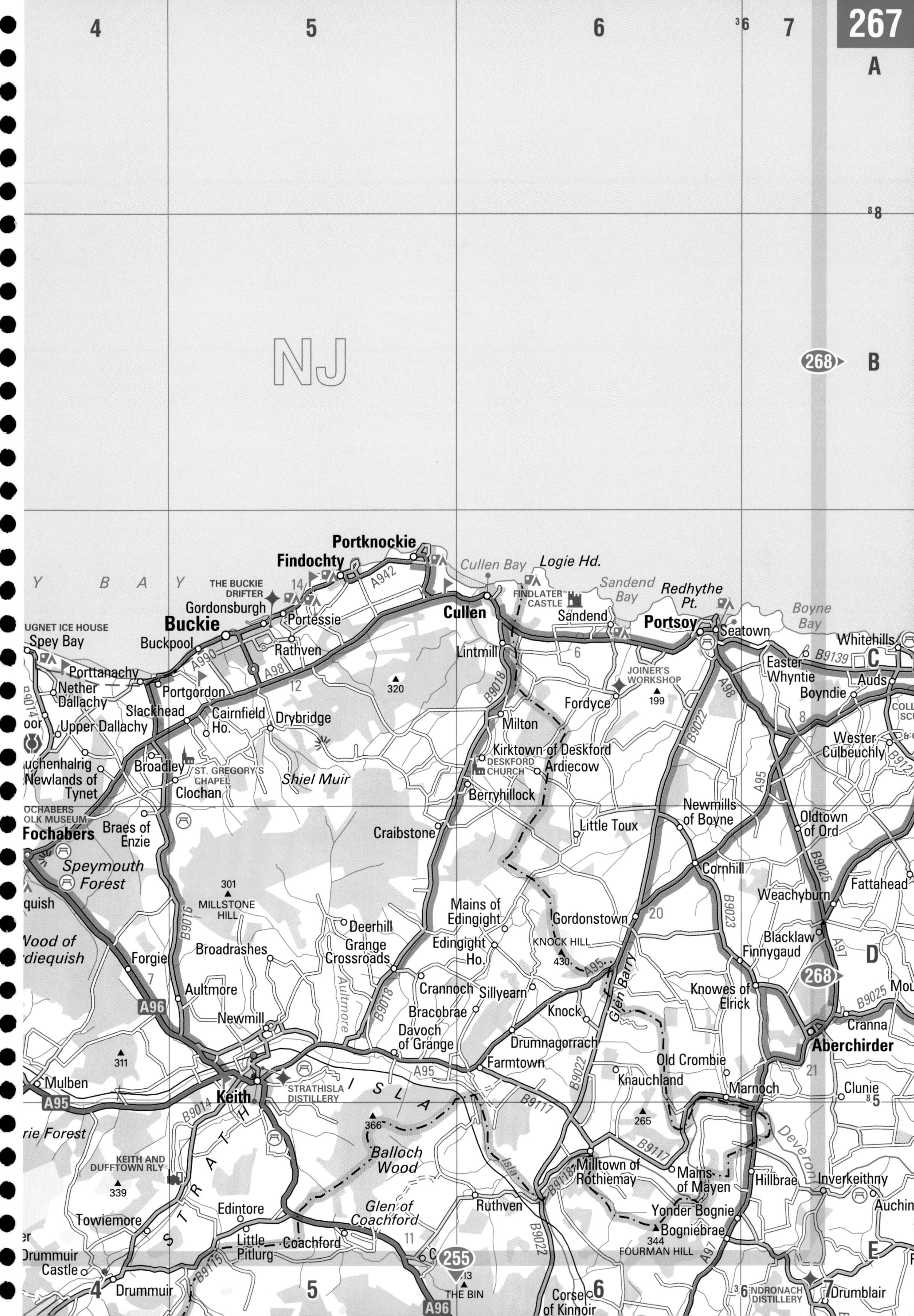
NJ
Portknockie
Findochty
Cullen Bay
Logie Hd.
Sandend Bay
Redhythe Pt.
Boyne Bay
THE BUCKIE DRIFTER
Gordonsburgh
Buckie
Portessie
Cullen
FINDLATER CASTLE
Sandend
Portsoy
Seatown
Whitehills
Spey Bay
Buckpool
Rathven
Lintmill
Easter Whyntie
Porttanachy
Nether Dallachy
Portgordon
Boyndie
Auds
JOINER'S WORKSHOP
Fordyce
Slackhead
Cairnfield Ho.
Drybridge
Milton
Upper Dallachy
Wester Culbeuchly
Kirktown of Deskford
DESKFORD CHURCH
Ardiecow
Broadley
ST. GREGORY'S CHAPEL
Shiel Muir
Newlands of Tynet
Clochan
Berryhillock
Fochabers
Braes of Enzie
Craibstone
Little Toux
Newmills of Boyne
Oldtown of Ord
Speymouth Forest
Cornhill
Fattahead
MILLSTONE HILL
Mains of Edingight
Weachyburn
Deerhill
Gordonstown
Blacklaw
Broadrashes
Grange Crossroads
Edingight Ho.
KNOCK HILL
Finnygaud
Forgie
Glen Barry
Aultmore
Crannoch
Sillyearn
Knowes of Elrick
Bracobrae
Knock
Cranna
Newmill
Davoch of Grange
Drumnagorrach
Aberchirder
Farmtown
Old Crombie
Mulben
Knauchland
Marnoch
Clunie
Keith
STRATHISLA DISTILLERY
ISLA
Balloch Wood
KEITH AND DUFFTOWN RLY
Milltown of Rothiemay
Mains of Mayen
Hillbrae
Inverkeithny
Edintore
Glen of Coachford
Ruthven
Yonder Bognie
Towiemore
Bogniebrae
FOURMAN HILL
Little Pitlurg
Coachford
Drummuir Castle
Drummuir
THE BIN
Corse of Kinnoir
Drumblair
STRATH
268
255

1
2
3
A
B
C
D
E
267
Boyne Bay
Knock Hd.
Boyndie Bay
Seatown
Whitehills
Macduff
MACDUFF MARINE AQUARIUM
Head of Garness
Troup Hd.
Gamrie Bay
Crovie
Gardenstown
Pennan Hd.
Pennan
Quarry Hd
Easter Whyntie
Inverboyndie
Auds
Boyndie
Banff
BANFF MUSEUM
COLLEONARD SCULPTURE GARDEN & GALLERY
DUFF HOUSE
Easter Silverford
West Greenskares
Longmanhill
Dubford
Towie
New Aberdour
Wester Culbeuchly
Doune Park
Montcoffer Ho.
Cushnie
231 WINDYHEADS HILL
Ladysford
Minnonie
Oldtown of Ord
Kirktown of Alvah
Keilhill
Netherbrae
Nether Glasslaw
Mid Cloch
Forbie
Craigmaud
Gorrachie
Greenlaw
King Edward
227 HILL OF FISHRIE
Weachyburn
Fattahead
The Pole of Itlaw
Milltown of Craigston
New Pitsligo
Blacklaw
Finnygaud
Plaidy
Craigston Castle
Fintry
New Byth
Hill of Mountblairy
Muirden
Bonnykelly
Cranna
Garmond
Whitestones
Ironside
Aberchirder
Forglen Ho.
Muiryfold
Balthangie
Oldwhat
Bogton
Deveron
Turriff
DELGATIE CASTLE
Marnoch
Clunie
Carnousie
Mains of Fedderate
Kirkton
Cumineston
Middle Cairncake
Little Colp
Delgaty Forest
Culsh
Mill of Muiresk
Hillbrae
Inverkeithny
Hatton Castle
Howe of Teuchar
New Deer
Auchininna
Darra
Rush-head
Fortrie
Birkenhills
Brownhill
Crofts of Inverthernie
256
Dykeside
Cairnbanno Ho.
Knaven
179
A98
A95
A97
A947
B9139
B9121
B9025
B9023
B9031
B9105
B9027
B9170
B9024
A950
A981
0 1 2 3 miles
0 1 2 3 4 5 km

4
5
6
A
B
C
D
E
NJ
NK
Rosehearty
Fraserburgh
Kinnaird Head
KINNAIRD CASTLE LIGHTHOUSE & SCOTLAND'S LIGHTHOUSE MUSEUM
FRASERBURGH HERITAGE MUSEUM
SANDHAVEN MEAL MILL
PITSLIGO CASTLE
Pittulie
Broadsea
Sandhaven
Peathill
Percyhorner
Pitblae
Fraserburgh Bay
Cairnbulg Pt.
Inverallochy
MAGGIE'S HOOSIE
Coburty
Upper Boyndlie
Mid Ardlaw
Tyrie
Memsie
MEMSIE BURIAL CAIRN
Whitewell
Cairnbulg Castle
Gowanhill
St Combs
Inzie Head
Strathellie
Rathen
Cairness
Loch of Strathbeg
Crimonmogate
LOCH OF STRATHBEG NATURE RESERVE VISITOR CENTRE
Hillhead of Auchentumb
Newburgh
Lonmay
Old Rattray
Rattray Head
Crimond
230
MORMOND HILL
Knowhead
Strichen
Nether Park
Blackhill
New Leeds
Longhill
Balearn
Adziel
North Ugie Water
Little Skillymarno
Leys
St Fergus Moss
Denhead
Backfolds
Kirktown
St Fergus
Scotstown Hd.
Fetterangus
Hythie
Rora Moss
North Kirkton
Forest of Deer
Toux
Rora
Lunderton
Kirkton Hd.
DEER ABBEY
Dunshillock
Woodside
Maud
MAUD RAILWAY MUSEUM
Mintlaw
ADEN
Newseat
Inverugie
INVERUGIE CASTLE
UGIE SALMON FISH HOUSE
Buchanhaven
Backhill of Clackriach
Old Deer
Longside
Torterston
Flushing
Peterhead
ABERDEENSHIRE FARMING MUSEUM
South Ugie
Stuartfield
Inverquhomery
ARBUTHNOT MUSEUM & ART GALLERY
Keith Inch
Drymuir
Bulwark
Mains of Crichie
Millbreck
Hillhead of Cocklaw
PETERHEAD MARITIME
Peterhead Bay
Nethermuir
Crichie
Kinmundy
257
Little Dens
Invernettie
Sandford Bay
Kinnadie
Clola
Skelmuir
A90
A981
A952
A950
A982
A98
A948
B9031
B9032
B9033
B9107
B9093
B9029
B9106
B9030

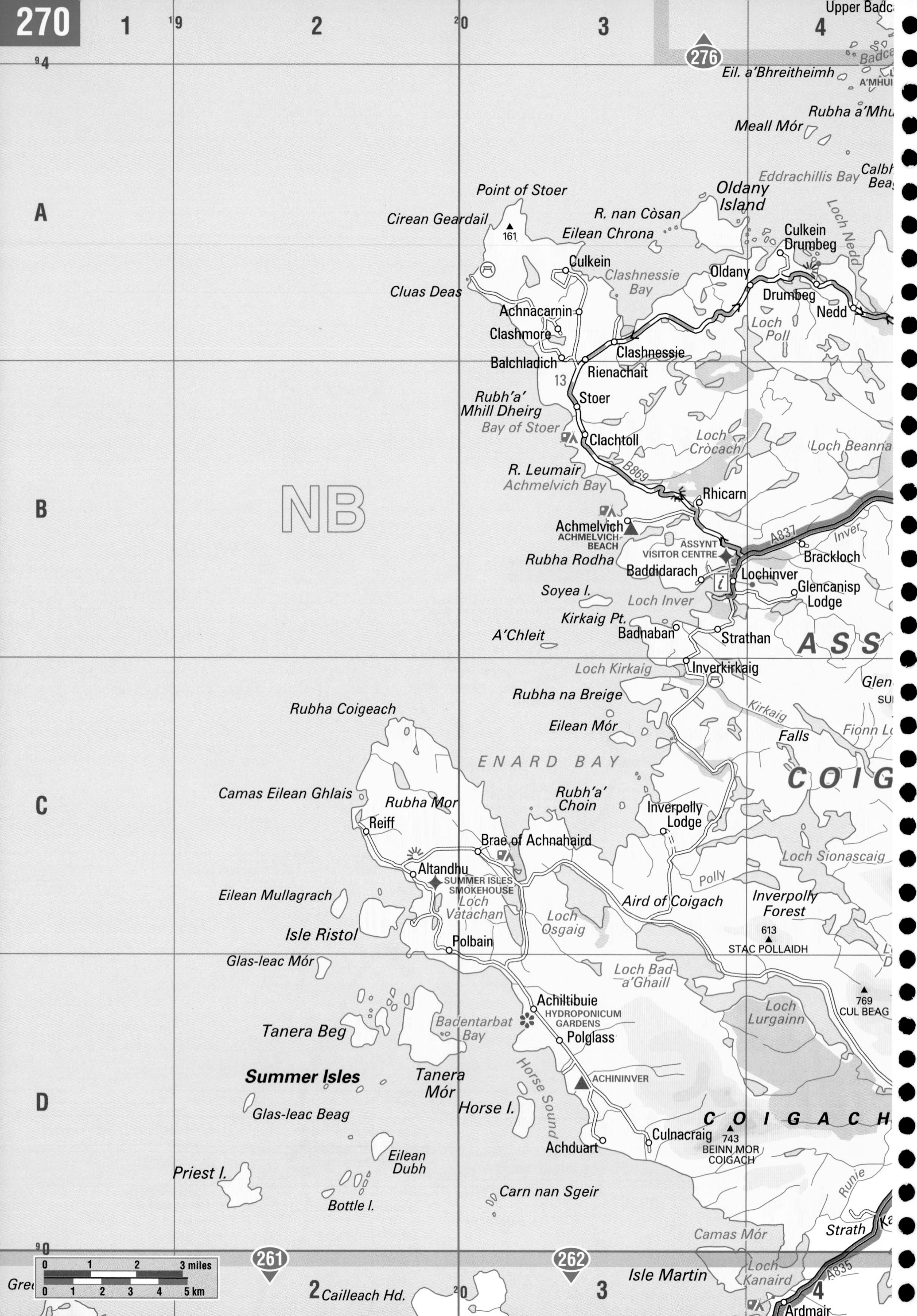

1
2
3
4
276
Upper Badca
Eil. a'Bhreitheimh
Rubha a'Mhu
Meall Mór
Eddrachillis Bay
Point of Stoer
Oldany Island
Cirean Geardail
161
R. nan Còsan
Eilean Chrona
Culkein Drumbeg
Loch Nedd
Culkein
Clashnessie Bay
Oldany
Cluas Deas
Drumbeg
Nedd
Achnacarnin
Loch Poll
Clashmore
Clashnessie
Balchladich
Rienachait
A
13
Rubh'a' Mhill Dheirg
Stoer
Bay of Stoer
Clachtoll
Loch Cròcach
Loch Beanna
R. Leumair
B869
Achmelvich Bay
Rhicarn
NB
B
Achmelvich
ACHMELVICH BEACH
ASSYNT VISITOR CENTRE
A837
Inver
Brackloch
Rubha Rodha
Baddidarach
Lochinver
Glencanisp Lodge
Soyea I.
Loch Inver
Kirkaig Pt.
A'Chleit
Badnaban
Strathan
ASS
Loch Kirkaig
Inverkirkaig
Rubha na Breige
Rubha Coigeach
Kirkaig
Eilean Mór
Falls
Fionn L
ENARD BAY
COIG
Camas Eilean Ghlais
Rubha Mor
Rubh'a' Choin
C
Inverpolly Lodge
Reiff
Brae of Achnahaird
Loch Sionascaig
Altandhu
SUMMER ISLES SMOKEHOUSE
Polly
Eilean Mullagrach
Loch Vatachan
Aird of Coigach
Inverpolly Forest
Loch Osgaig
Isle Ristol
613
STAC POLLAIDH
Polbain
Glas-leac Mór
Loch Bad a'Ghaill
769
CUL BEAG
Achiltibuie
HYDROPONICUM GARDENS
Loch Lurgainn
Badentarbat Bay
Tanera Beg
Polglass
Horse Sound
Summer Isles
Tanera Mór
ACHININVER
D
Horse I.
Glas-leac Beag
COIGACH
Culnacraig
743
BEINN MOR COIGACH
Achduart
Eilean Dubh
Priest I.
Runie
Carn nan Sgeir
Bottle I.
Camas Mór
Strath
261
262
0 1 2 3 miles
0 1 2 3 4 5 km
Isle Martin
Loch Kanaird
A835
2
Cailleach Hd.
3
4
Ardmair

Lower Badcall
BEN STACK
Strath Stack
Gobernuisgach Lodge
BEINN AUSKAIRD
386
276
277
Achfary
332
REAY FOREST
Loch Crocach
Lochmore Lodge
759
A894
Loch More
Calbha Mòr
Loch na Creige Duibhe
Duartmore Forest
Aultanrynie
Loch an Leathaid Bhuain
Allt a' Chraois
Loch a' Chàirn Bhàin
Kylestrome
547
Kinloch
Kylesku
Glendhu Forest
A838
873
BEN HEE
Loch Glendhu
Gleann Dubh
Unapool
B869
34
530
BEINN AIRD DA LOCH
566
Newton
Loch Glencoul
Glen Coul
Gleann Leireag
Loch Merkland
272
Loch an Leothaid
792
BEINN LEOID
Merkland Lodge
808
QUINAG
Loch Dubh a'Chuail
Loch an Eircill
404
A894
EAS COUL AULIN WATERFALL
Lochassynt Lodge
Loch a'Ghriama
776
BEINN UIDHE
740
Corrykinloch
LOCH ASSYNT
NC
Little Assynt
Skiag Bridge
Gorm Loch Mor
Fionn Loch Mor
ARDVRECK CASTLE
Overscaig Hotel
Glen Fiag
Loch Feith an Leòthaid
540
Inchnadamph
Inchnadamph Forest
A837
512
MAOVALLY
INCHNADAMPH
998
BEN MORE ASSYNT
Forest
Stronchrubie
391
846
CANISP
718
BREABAG
MEALL AN AONAICH
715
Loch na Gainimh
Duchally
Strath an Loin
Allt Car
Loanan
Benmore Forest
Loch Awe
Glen Cassley
Loch Veyatie
Cam Loch
Ledbeg
Glen Oykel
Ledmore
BEINN SGEIR
476
HIGHLAND & RARE BREEDS FARM
849
CUL MOR
Elphin
Altnacealgach Hotel
Loch Ailsh
Benmore Lodge
Drumrunie Forest
Knockan
272
Loch Urigill
A837
KNOCKAN CRAG
364
AN STUC
BEINN AN EOIN
554
A835
CROMALT HILLS
Glencass
517
Crom Allt
Drumrunie
Loch Craggie
Loch na Claise Moire
Oykel
Langwell Lodge
Rappach
Kanaird
Strathcanaird
Strath nan Lon
578
MEALL AN FHUARAIN
Lubcroy
Oykel Bridge
Strath Oykel
A837
Invercass
Brae
Oape
Doune
262
263
415
340
Allt-Beinn Donu
Rappach Water
Einig
4
5
6
7
A
B
C
D

1
2
3
A
B
C
D
Gobernuisgach Lodge
277
271
263
Loch Meadie
Loch More
Aultanrynie
Kinloch
A838
34
332
759
Allt a'Chraois
Loch Coire na Saidhe Duibhe
Meadie Burn
Mudale
Altnaharra
A836
B873
Clebrig
Loch a'Ghorm-choire
873
BEN HEE
566
Loch Merkland
Merkland Lodge
792
BEINN LEOID
Loch an Eircill
Loch Dubh a'Chuail
Loch a'Ghriama
Corrykinloch
Loch Fiag
404
473
Strath Vagastie
Klibreck Burn
961
MEALL NAN CON
542
312
CNOC AN ALASKIE
18
Crask Inn
Glen Fiag
Fiag Plantation
Fiag
Loch Gaineamhach
Gorm Loch Mor
Fionn Loch Mor
Overscaig Hotel
Fiag Bridge
Strath Tirry
Tirry
512
MAOVALLY
998
BEN MORE ASSYNT
391
LOCH SHIN
718
MEALL AN AONAICH
715
Duchally
Allt Car
Srath an Lòin
Rhian
Shinness
Benmore Forest
Glen Cassley
Achnairn
Allt a'Bhunn
BEINN SGEIREACH
476
Benmore Lodge
Loch Ailsh
Glen Oykel
Dalchork
Colaboll
364
AN STUC
BEINN AN EOIN
554
Glencassley Castle
Sallachy
Saval
Lairg Lodge
Lairg
Loch na Fuaralaich
Loch Craggie
Loch na Claise Moire
Glenrossal
402
CNOC A'CHOIRE
Grudie Burn
Claonel
Gruids
FERRYCROFT COUNTRYSIDE CENTRE
Oykel Forest
Cassley
Oykel
Invercassley
Rosehall
A839
8
Achany
Glen Achany
B864
Shin Forest
Lubcroy
Oykel Bridge
Strath Oykel
A837
Brae
Doune
Oape
Altnass
Achindu
Linsidemore
FALLS OF SHIN VISITOR CENTRE
11
Achnahanat
Shin
0 1 2 3 miles
0 1 2 3 4 5 km

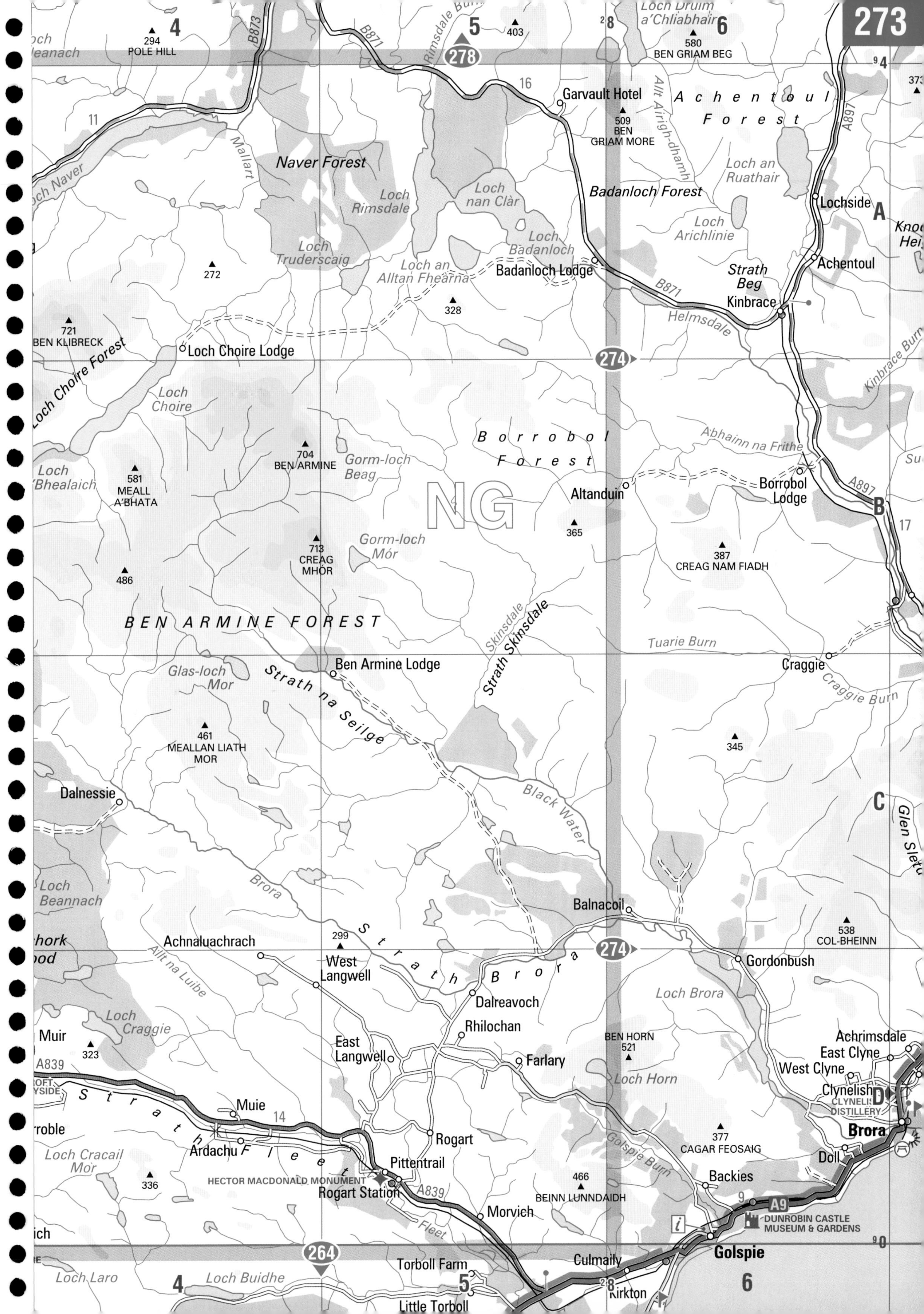

Naver Forest
Loch Rimsdale
Loch nan Clàr
Badanloch Forest
Loch Badanloch
Badanloch Lodge
Garvault Hotel
509 BEN GRIAM MORE
580 BEN GRIAM BEG
Achentoul Forest
Loch an Ruathair
Loch Arichlinie
Lochside
Achentoul
Strath Beg
Kinbrace
Helmsdale
Loch Truderscaig
Loch an Alltan Fhearna
272
328
721 BEN KLIBRECK
294 POLE HILL
403
Loch Choire Lodge
Loch Choire Forest
Loch Choire
704 BEN ARMINE
Gorm-loch Beag
581 MEALL A'BHATA
Loch a'Bhealaich
713 CREAG MHÓR
Gorm-loch Mór
486
Borrobol Forest
Altanduin
Borrobol Lodge
Abhainn na Frithe
365
387 CREAG NAM FIADH
NG
BEN ARMINE FOREST
Ben Armine Lodge
Strath na Seilge
Glas-loch Mor
461 MEALLAN LIATH MOR
Strath Skinsdale
Tuarie Burn
Craggie
Craggie Burn
345
Dalnessie
Black Water
Brora
Loch Beannach
Balnacoil
538 COL-BHEINN
Gordonbush
Achnaluachrach
299 West Langwell
Strath Brora
Loch Brora
Dalreavoch
Rhilochan
East Langwell
Farlary
BEN HORN 521
Loch Horn
Achrimsdale
East Clyne
West Clyne
Clynelish
CLYNELISH DISTILLERY
Brora
Loch Craggie
323
A839
Muie
Strath Fleet
Ardachu
Rogart
Pittentrail
HECTOR MACDONALD MONUMENT
Rogart Station
377 CAGAR FEOSAIG
466 BEINN LUNNDAIDH
Golspie Burn
Backies
Doll
Morvich
A9
DUNROBIN CASTLE MUSEUM & GARDENS
Golspie
Culmaily
Torboll Farm
Little Torboll
Kirkton
Loch Cracail Mor
336
Loch Laro
Loch Buidhe
278
274
264
B871
B873
A897

1
2
3
4
Loch Druim a'Chliabhain
580
BEN GRIAM BEG
279
Rumsdale Water
Loch a' Mhuilinn
Dalnawillan
16
Garvault Hotel
509
BEN GRIAM MORE
Allt Airigh-dhamh
Achentoul Forest
373
348
BEN ALISKY
Glutt Lodge
A897
Loch an Ruathair
Loch nan Clàr
Badanloch Forest
Lochside
438
Knockfin Heights
Glutt Water
A
Loch Arichlinie
Loch Badanloch
Badanloch Lodge
Achentoul
Strath Beg
Kinbrace
B871
318
CNOC LOCH MHADADH
328
Helmsdale
273
Kinbrace Burn
438
CNOC COIRE NA PEARNA
705
MORVEN
Borrobol Forest
Abhainn na Frithe
Suisgill Burn
517
CNOC AN EIREANNAICH
Wag
Altanduin
Borrobol Lodge
A897
NC
Langwell Forest
B
365
17
STRATH OF KILDONAN
Kildonan Burn
387
CREAG NAM FIADH
555
CREAG SCALABSDALE
Kildonan Lodge
BAILE AN ÓR GOLDRUSH SITE
BEINN DUBHAIN
414
Skinsdale
Strath Skinsdale
Tuarie Burn
Craggie
Helmsdale
Torrish
Kilphedir
Craggie Burn
A897
345
ELDRABLE HILL
417
Marrel
HELMSDALE
Navidale
TIMESPAN
West Helmsdale
C
Black Water
628
BEINN DHORAIN
Glen Sletdale
Glen Loth
592
Gartymore
Helmsdale
Portgower
Lothmore
Balnacoil
11
538
COL-BHEINN
Lothbeg
273
Gordonbush
Lothbeg Pt.
A9
Loch Brora
Dalreavoch
Rhilochan
BEN HORN
521
Achrimsdale
East Clyne
Farlary
West Clyne
Loch Horn
Dalchalm
D
Clynelish
CLYNELISH DISTILLERY
377
CAGAR FEOSAIG
Brora
Rogart
Golspie Burn
Doll
466
BEINN LUNNDAIDH
Backies
A839
Morvich
9
DUNROBIN CASTLE MUSEUM & GARDENS
Golspie
265
0 1 2 3 miles
0 1 2 3 4 5 km
Torboll
2
3
4

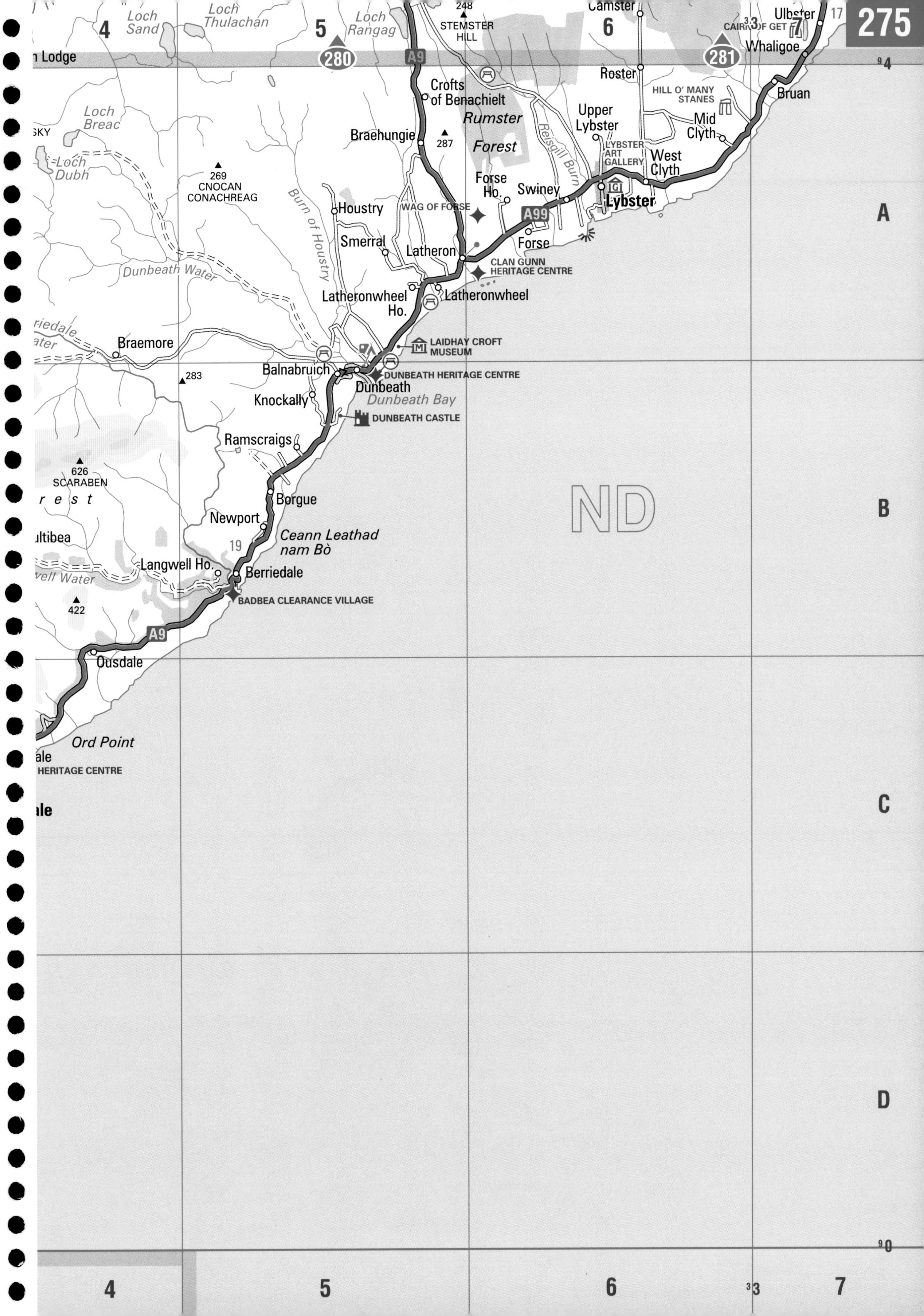
Loch Sand
Loch Thulachan
Loch Rangag
248
STEMSTER HILL
Camster
Ulbster
CAIRN OF GET
Whaligoe
280
281
A9
Roster
Bruan
HILL O' MANY STANES
Crofts of Benachielt
Rumster Forest
Upper Lybster
Mid Clyth
West Clyth
LYBSTER ART GALLERY
Reisgill Burn
Loch Breac
Loch Dubh
Braehungie
287
269
CNOCAN CONACHREAG
Burn of Houstry
Houstry
Forse Ho.
Swiney
Lybster
A99
WAG OF FORSE
Smerral
Latheron
Forse
CLAN GUNN HERITAGE CENTRE
Dunbeath Water
Latheronwheel Ho.
Latheronwheel
Braemore
LAIDHAY CROFT MUSEUM
Balnabruich
283
DUNBEATH HERITAGE CENTRE
Dunbeath
Dunbeath Bay
Knockally
DUNBEATH CASTLE
Ramscraigs
626
SCARABEN
Borgue
Newport
19
Ceann Leathad nam Bò
Langwell Ho.
Berriedale
BADBEA CLEARANCE VILLAGE
422
Ousdale
Ord Point
HERITAGE CENTRE
ND
A
B
C
D
4
5
6
7
94
90
33

1
2
3
4
A
B
C
D
CAPE WRATH
Kearvaig
371
SGRIBHIS-BHEINN
Geodha Ruadh na Fola
Bay of Keisgaig
Kearvaig
Inshore
Loch Keisgaig
Geodha Ruadh
Achiem
457
FASHVEN
Am Balg
423
BEINN DEARG
Loch Airig na Beinn
Sandwood Loch
485
CREAG RIABHACH
Rubh'an Fhir Léithe
Grudie
Loch na Gainimh
Strath Shinary
332
GHLAS BHEINN
Sheigra
Balchrick
Droman
Oldshore Beg
Eilean Roin Mor
Oldshoremore
521
FARRMHEALL
A838
19
Gualin Ho.
Loch Clash
Kinlochbervie
Badcall
B801
Bagh Loch an Roin
Achriesgill
Loch Inchard
Strath Dionard
CRANS
Dionard
L. na Claise Carnaich
Achlyness
Loch Dughaill
Ceathramh Garbh
Rhiconich
Ardmore Pt.
Rubha Ruadh
Ardmore
A838
GANU MOR
908
Foinaven
Fanagmore
Tarbet
NORTH-WEST SUTHERLAND
Loch Laxford
Loch a'Garbh-bhaid Mór
Loch Dionar
Handa Island
Sound of Handa
Foindle
Loch nam Brac
A894
Laxford Bridge
Loch an Easain Uaine
787
ARKLE
Scourie Bay
Laxford
A838
Scourie More
Scourie
Rubh'Aird an t-Sionnaich
Gorm Loch
Lochstack Lodge
719
BEN STACK
Loch Stack
Upper Badcall
Lower Badcall
Strath Stack
BEINN AUSKAIRD
386
Badcall Bay
18
Eil. a'Bhreitheimh
LOCH A'MHUILINN
270
271
Achfary
332
0 1 2 3 miles
0 1 2 3 4 5 km
Loch Crocach
REAY FOREST
Rubha a'Mhucard
A894
Lochmore Lodge
Meall Mór

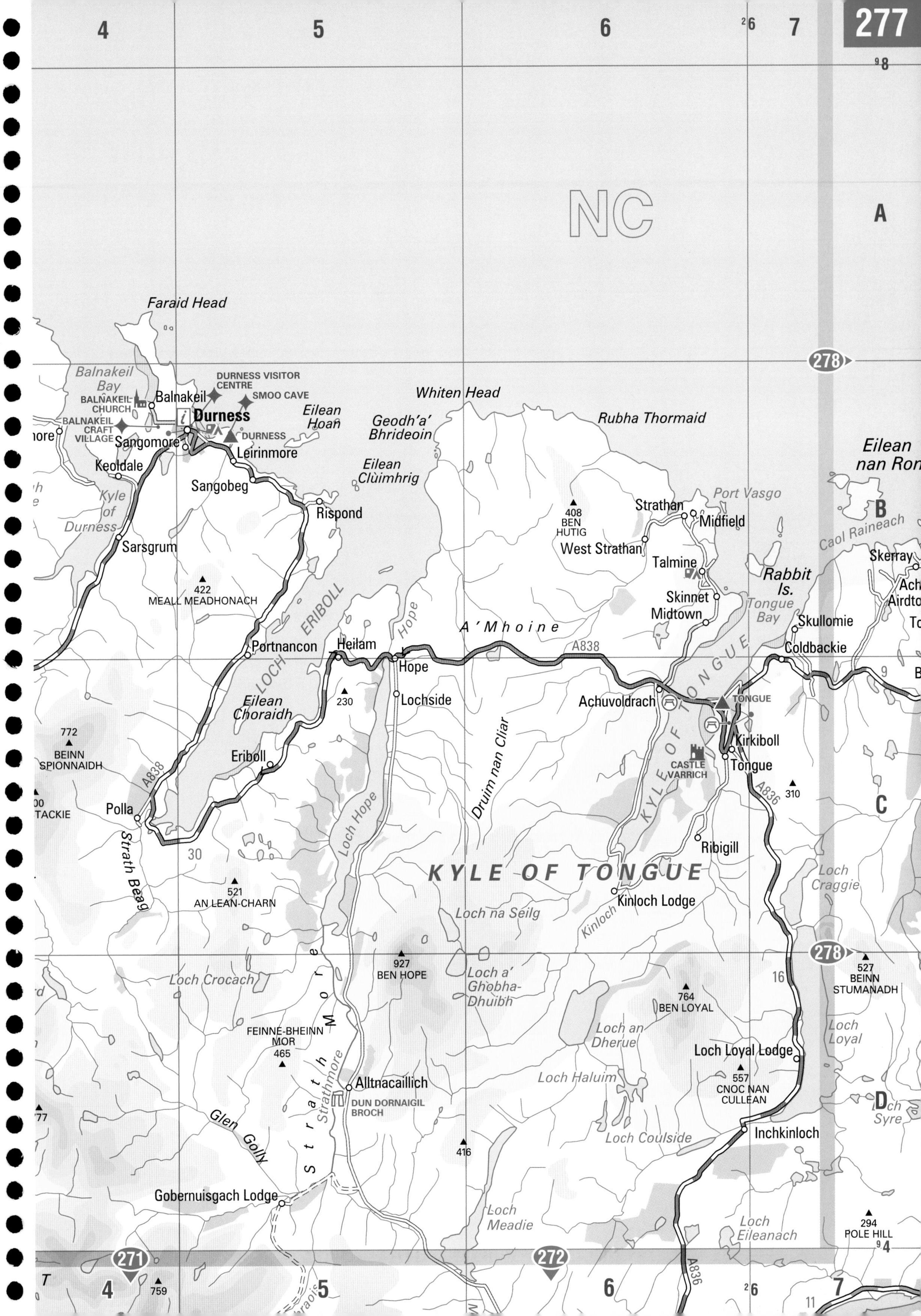

278
278
271
272

1
2
3
A
B
C
D
277
Whiten Head
Rubha Thormaid
Port Vasgo
Eilean nan Ron
Ardmore Pt.
Kirtomy Pt.
Armadale Bay
Farr Pt.
Neave I. or Coombe I.
Caol Raineach
Torrisdale Bay
408 BEN HUTIG
Strathan
Midfield
West Strathan
Talmine
Rabbit Is.
Skerray
Achtoty
Airdtorrisdale
Torrisdale
Farr
STRATHNAVER MUSEUM
Kirtomy
Swordly
Armadale
A836
17
Skinnet
Midtown
Tongue Bay
Skullomie
Bettyhill
Achina
Clachan Burn
Loch Meadie
A'Mhoine
A838
Coldbackie
Invernaver
Borgie
Leckfurin
Achuvoldrach
TONGUE
KYLE OF TONGUE
Kirkiboll
CASTLE VARRICH
Tongue
Loch Buidhe Mor
229
ACHANLOCHY CLEARANCE VILLAGE
Skelpick
Borgie Forest
B871
310
Achagary
Skelpick Burn
Loch Mor na Caorach
Loch nan Clach
Ribigill
Loch Craggie
Kinloch Lodge
Loch na Seilg
Kinloch
STRATHNAVER
Carnachy
Rhifail
527 BEINN STUMANADH
293 BEINN RIFA-GIL
Loch a' Ghobha-Dhuibh
16
764 BEN LOYAL
Loch an Dherue
Loch Loyal
Loch Strathy
Loch Loyal Lodge
Skail
Loch Haluim
557 CNOC NAN CULLEAN
Naver
Langdale
Loch Syre
Syre
Dalvina Lo.
Inchkinloch
416
Loch Coulside
ROSAL CLEARANCE TRAIL
B873
Rimsdale Burn
403
Loch Meadie
Loch Eileanach
294 POLE HILL
273
Garvault
0 1 2 3 miles
0 1 2 3 4 5 km

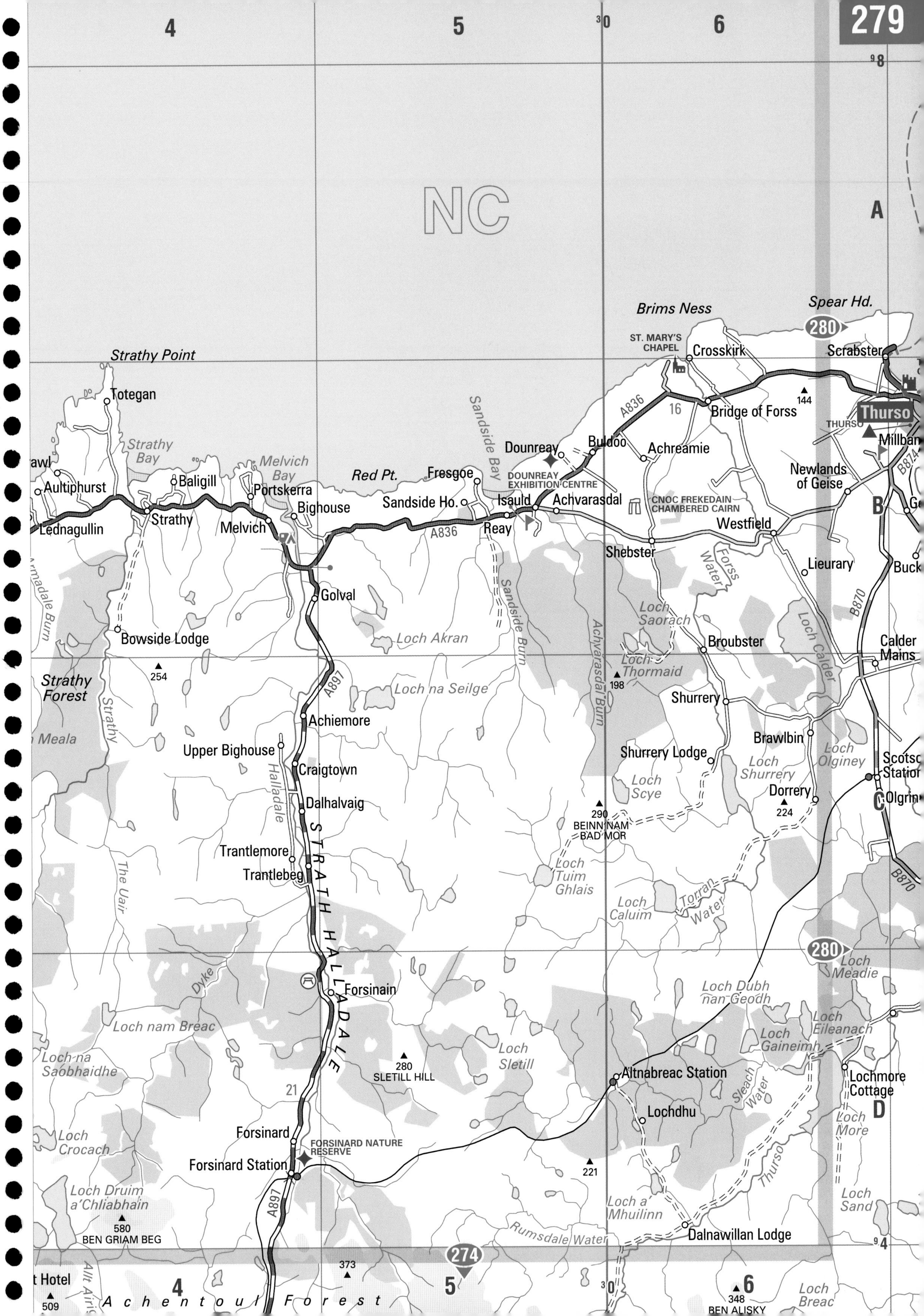

NC
4
5
6
A
B
C
D
Brims Ness
Spear Hd.
280
ST. MARY'S CHAPEL
Crosskirk
Scrabster
Strathy Point
Totegan
A836
16
Bridge of Forss
144
Thurso
THURSO
Millban
Sandside Bay
Dounreay
Buldoo
Achreamie
Newlands of Geise
B874
Strathy Bay
Melvich Bay
Red Pt.
Fresgoe
DOUNREAY EXHIBITION CENTRE
Aultiphurst
Baligill
Portskerra
Sandside Ho.
Isauld
Achvarasdal
CNOC FREKEDAIN CHAMBERED CAIRN
Lednagullin
Strathy
Melvich
Bighouse
A836
Reay
Westfield
Shebster
Forss Water
Lieurary
Buck
Golval
Sandside Burn
Loch Saorach
B870
Loch Calder
Bowside Lodge
Loch Akran
Achvarasdal Burn
Broubster
Calder Mains
254
Loch Thormaid
198
Strathy Forest
A897
Loch na Seilge
Shurrery
Achiemore
Meala
Strathy
Brawlbin
Upper Bighouse
Shurrery Lodge
Loch Olginey
Craigtown
Loch Shurrery
Scotsc Statior
Halladale
Loch Scye
Dorrery
Dalhalvaig
290
224
Olgrin
BEINN NAM BAD MOR
Trantlemore
Trantlebeg
STRATH HALLADALE
The Uair
Loch Tuim Ghlais
B870
Loch Caluim
Torran Water
280
Loch Meadie
Dyke
Forsinain
Loch Dubh nan Geodh
Loch nam Breac
Loch Eileanach
Loch Gaineimh
Loch na Saobhaidhe
280
SLETILL HILL
Loch Sletill
Altnabreac Station
Lochmore Cottage
21
Lochdhu
Sleach Water
Loch Crocach
Forsinard
FORSINARD NATURE RESERVE
Loch More
Forsinard Station
221
Thurso
Loch Druim a'Chliabhain
A897
Loch a' Mhuilinn
Loch Sand
580
BEN GRIAM BEG
Rumsdale Water
Dalnawillan Lodge
274
373
t Hotel
Allt Airi
509
Achentoul Forest
348
BEN ALISKY
Loch Breac

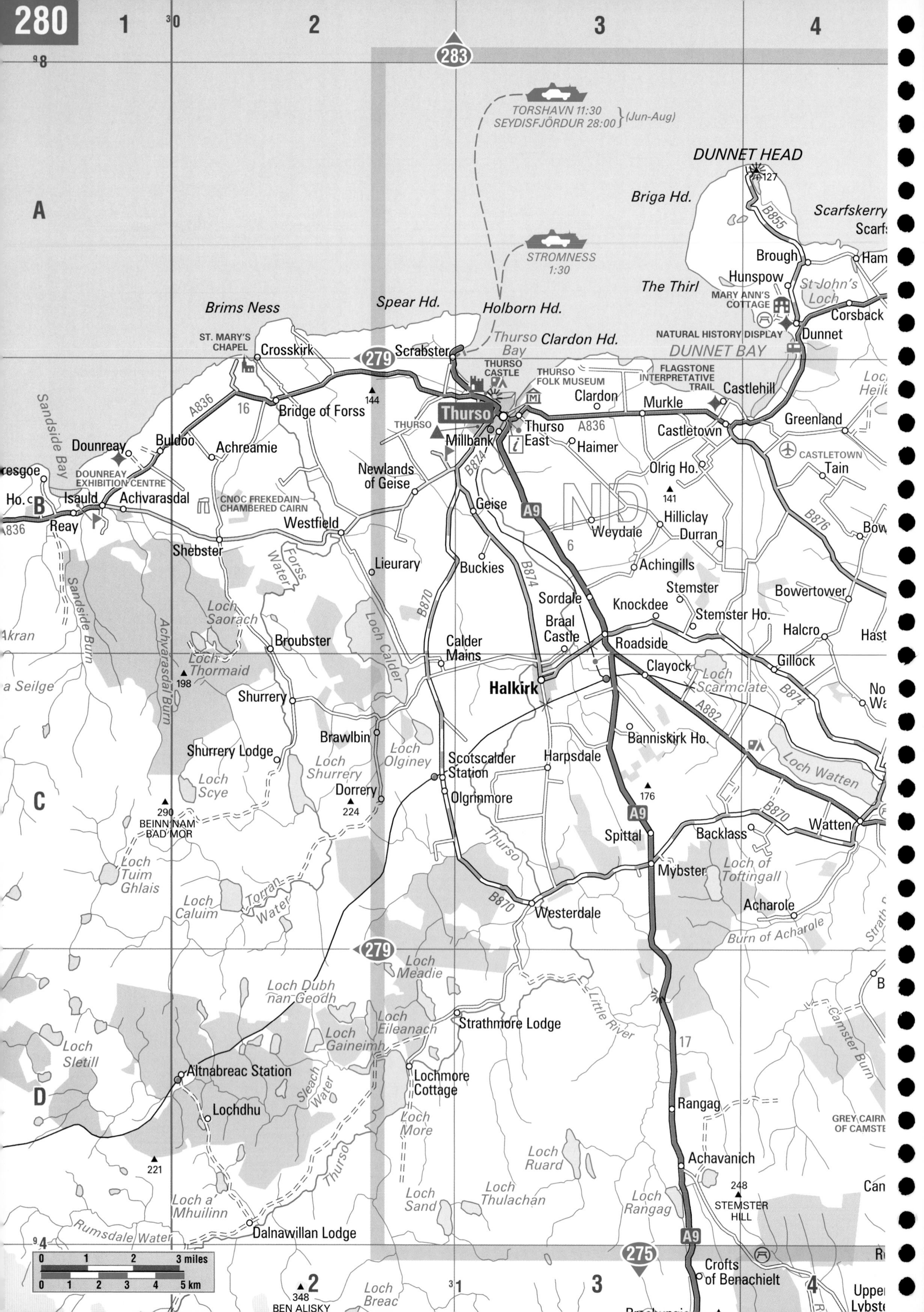

DUNNET HEAD
Briga Hd.
Scarfskerry
Brough
Hunspow
St John's Loch
The Thirl
MARY ANN'S COTTAGE
Corsback
Dunnet
NATURAL HISTORY DISPLAY
DUNNET BAY
FLAGSTONE INTERPRETATIVE TRAIL
Castlehill
Greenland
Castletown
CASTLETOWN
Tain
TORSHAVN 11:30
SEYDISFJÖRDUR 28:00
(Jun-Aug)
STROMNESS 1:30
Holborn Hd.
Spear Hd.
Brims Ness
ST. MARY'S CHAPEL
Crosskirk
Scrabster
Thurso Bay
Clardon Hd.
THURSO CASTLE
THURSO FOLK MUSEUM
Clardon
Murkle
Thurso
Thurso East
Millbank
Haimer
Olrig Ho.
Bridge of Forss
Dounreay
Buldoo
Achreamie
DOUNREAY EXHIBITION CENTRE
Newlands of Geise
Isauld
Reay
Achvarasdal
CNOC FREKEDAIN CHAMBERED CAIRN
Westfield
Geise
Weydale
Hilliclay
Durran
Shebster
Forss Water
Lieurary
Buckies
Achingills
Stemster
Bowertower
Sordale
Knockdee
Stemster Ho.
Halcro
Braal Castle
Roadside
Loch Saorach
Broubster
Calder Mains
Loch Calder
Clayock
Gillock
Loch Thormaid
Halkirk
Loch Scarmclate
Shurrery
Banniskirk Ho.
Brawlbin
Loch Olginey
Scotscalder Station
Harpsdale
Loch Watten
Shurrery Lodge
Loch Shurrery
Loch Scye
Dorrery
Olgrinmore
Watten
Backlass
BEINN NAM BAD MOR
Spittal
Loch Tuim Ghlais
Mybster
Loch of Toftingall
Loch Caluim
Torran Water
Westerdale
Acharole
Burn of Acharole
Loch Meadie
Loch Dubh nan Geodh
Little River
Loch Eileanach
Strathmore Lodge
Loch Gaineimh
Loch Sletill
Altnabreac Station
Lochmore Cottage
Sleach Water
Lochdhu
Rangag
Loch More
GREY CAIRNS OF CAMSTER
Camster Burn
Loch Ruard
Achavanich
STEMSTER HILL
Loch Thulachan
Loch Rangag
Loch a' Mhuilinn
Loch Sand
Dalnawillan Lodge
Rumsdale Water
Thurso
Crofts of Benachielt
BEN ALISKY
Loch Breac
Sandside Bay
Sandside Burn
Achvarasdal Burn
Akran
ND
A836
A9
B874
B870
B855
B876
A882
283
279
275
0 1 2 3 miles
0 1 2 3 4 5 km

Langaton Point
Nethertown
Red Head
Island of Stroma
Mell Head
Uppertown
ST. MARGARETS HOPE 1:00
BURWICK 0:45 (May-Sept)
Muckle Skerry
Pentland Skerries
Men of Mey
St John's Pt.
Boars of Duncansby
Gills Bay
East Mey
CASTLE OF MEY
Rattar
Mey
Gills
Kirkstyle
Huna
DUNCANSBY HEAD
JOHN O'GROATS
Canisbay
John o' Groats
Stacks of Duncansby
A836
A99
Barrock
Inkstack
Brabster
Skirza
Tofts
Skirza Head
Lochend
Gill Burn
Freswick
Freswick Bay
Ness Head
BUCHOLLY CASTLE
Slickly
Reaster
ND
Alterwall
NORTHLANDS VIKING CENTRE
Auckengill
Lyth
LYTH ARTS CENTRE
Sortat
Barrock Ho.
Nybster
Brough Head
Howe
Burn of Lyth
Keiss
KEISS CASTLE
Mireland
Kirk
Loch of Wester
Myrelandhorn
B870
SINCLAIR'S BAY
Killimster
B876
Mains of Watten
CASTLE SINCLAIR
CASTLE GIRNIGOE
Noss Head
Reiss
Winless
Wick
Sealky Head
Ackergill
B874
Bilbster
Staxigoe
Strath
A882
Wick
WICK HERITAGE CENTRE
Papigoe
Stirkoke Ho.
Milton
Broadhaven
Wick Bay
Achairn Burn
Old Wick
Newton
South Hd.
CASTLE OF OLD WICK
Gote O'Tram
Whiterow
Hempriggs House
Tannach
Loch Hempriggs
Helman Hd.
HILL OF OLICLETT
Thrumster
Gansclet
Sarclet
Loch of Yarrows
Sarclet Hd.
Ulbster
CAIRN OF GET
Whaligoe
HILL O' MANY STANES
Bruan
Mid
283
275
A
B
C
D
4
5
6
7

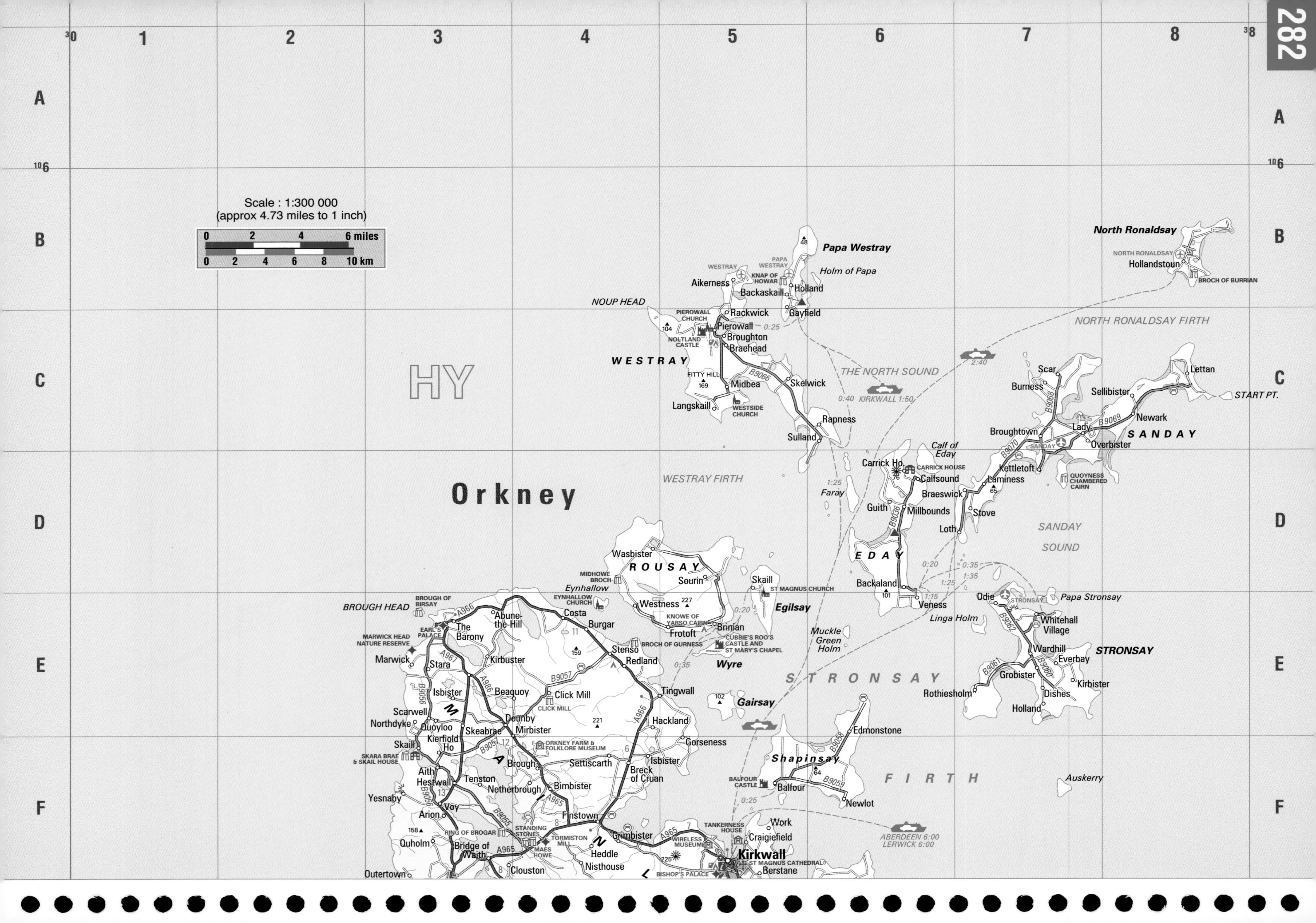
Orkney
HY
Scale : 1:300 000
(approx 4.73 miles to 1 inch)
0 2 4 6 miles
0 2 4 6 8 10 km
North Ronaldsay
Hollandstoun
BROCH OF BURRIAN
NORTH RONALDSAY FIRTH
START PT.
Papa Westray
Holm of Papa
Holland
Gayfield
Backaskaill
KNAP OF HOWAR
Aikerness
NOUP HEAD
WESTRAY
Rackwick
Pierowall
PIEROWALL CHURCH
NOLTLAND CASTLE
Broughton
Braehead
FITTY HILL
Midbea
Skelwick
Langskaill
WESTSIDE CHURCH
Rapness
Sulland
THE NORTH SOUND
KIRKWALL 1:50
WESTRAY FIRTH
Faray
SANDAY
Scar
Burness
Sellibister
Lettan
Newark
Lady
Overbister
Broughtown
Kettletoft
Laminess
QUOYNESS CHAMBERED CAIRN
Stove
SANDAY SOUND
Calf of Eday
Carrick Ho.
CARRICK HOUSE
Calfsound
Braeswick
Guith
Millbounds
Loth
EDAY
Backaland
Veness
Linga Holm
Papa Stronsay
Odie
Whitehall Village
STRONSAY
Wardhill
Everbay
Grobister
Kirbister
Dishes
Rothiesholm
Holland
Auskerry
ROUSAY
Wasbister
Sourin
Westness
MIDHOWE BROCH
Eynhallow
EYNHALLOW CHURCH
KNOWE OF YARSO CAIRN
Frotoft
Brinian
Skaill
ST MAGNUS CHURCH
Egilsay
CUBBIE'S ROO'S CASTLE AND ST MARY'S CHAPEL
Wyre
Muckle Green Holm
STRONSAY FIRTH
Gairsay
Shapinsay
Edmonstone
Balfour
BALFOUR CASTLE
Newlot
ABERDEEN 6:00
LERWICK 6:00
BROUGH HEAD
BROUGH OF BIRSAY
EARL'S PALACE
MARWICK HEAD NATURE RESERVE
Marwick
The Barony
Abune-the-Hill
Costa
Burgar
BROCH OF GURNESS
Stenso
Redland
Tingwall
Kirbuster
Stara
Isbister
Beaquoy
Click Mill
CLICK MILL
Scarwell
Northdyke
Quoyloo
Kierfiold Ho
Dounby
Skeabrae
Mirbister
Hackland
Gorseness
Skaill
SKARA BRAE & SKAIL HOUSE
ORKNEY FARM & FOLKLORE MUSEUM
Brough
Settiscarth
Isbister
Breck of Cruan
Aith
Hestwall
Tenston
Netherbrough
Bimbister
Yesnaby
Arion
Voy
Finstown
RING OF BROGAR
STANDING STONES
MAES HOWE
TORMISTON MILL
Quholm
Bridge of Waith
Grimbister
Heddle
Nisthouse
Clouston
Outertown
WIRELESS MUSEUM
TANKERNESS HOUSE
Work
Craigiefield
Kirkwall
ST MAGNUS CATHEDRAL
BISHOP'S PALACE
Berstane
MAINLAND

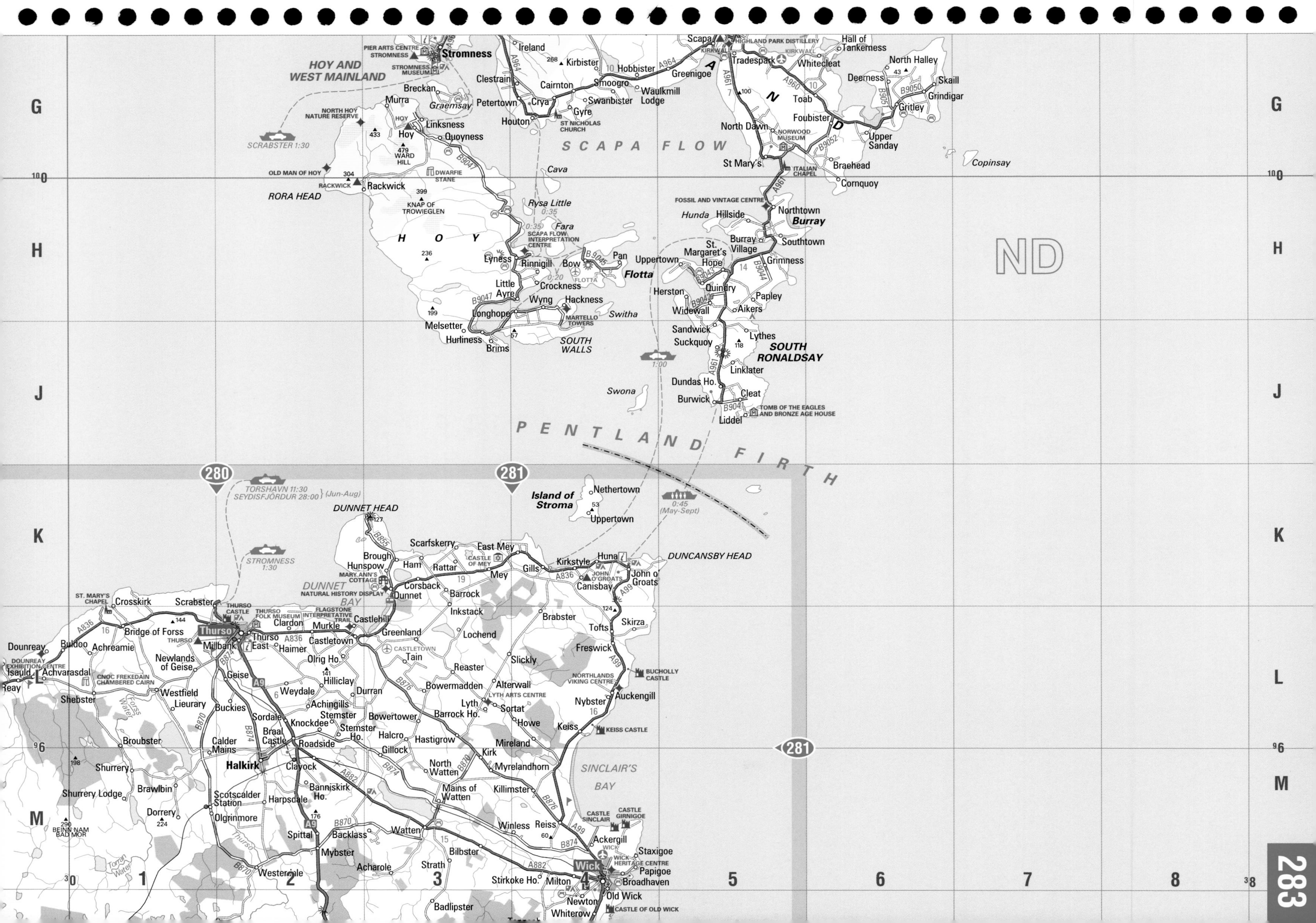
ND
G
H
J
K
L
M
10
96
30
38
1
2
3
4
5
6
7
8
HOY AND WEST MAINLAND
PIER ARTS CENTRE STROMNESS
Stromness
STROMNESS MUSEUM
Ireland
Kirbister
Hobbister
Clestrain
Cairnton
Smoogro
Waulkmill Lodge
Greenigoe
Scapa
HIGHLAND PARK DISTILLERY
Kirkwall
Tradespark
Whitecleat
Hall of Tankerness
North Halley
Deerness
Skaill
Grindigar
Toab
Gritley
Foubister
Upper Sanday
North Dawn
NORWOOD MUSEUM
Braehead
Cornquoy
Copinsay
St Mary's
ITALIAN CHAPEL
Breckan
Murra
Graemsay
Petertown
Crya
Swanbister
Gyre
Houton
ST NICHOLAS CHURCH
NORTH HOY NATURE RESERVE
Linksness
Hoy
Quoyness
WARD HILL
SCRABSTER 1:30
S C A P A F L O W
Cava
DWARFIE STANE
OLD MAN OF HOY
RACKWICK
Rackwick
RORA HEAD
KNAP OF TROWIEGLEN
Rysa Little
Fara
SCAPA FLOW INTERPRETATION CENTRE
H O Y
Lyness
Rinnigill
Bow
Pan
Flotta
Little Ayre
Crockness
Wyng
Hackness
Longhope
Melsetter
Hurliness
Brims
MARTELLO TOWERS
Switha
SOUTH WALLS
FOSSIL AND VINTAGE CENTRE
Hunda
Hillside
Northtown
Burray
Burray Village
Southtown
St. Margaret's Hope
Uppertown
Grimness
Herston
Quindry
Papley
Widewall
Aikers
Sandwick
Suckquoy
Lythes
SOUTH RONALDSAY
Linklater
Swona
Dundas Ho.
Cleat
Burwick
TOMB OF THE EAGLES AND BRONZE AGE HOUSE
Liddel
P E N T L A N D F I R T H
280
281
TORSHAVN 11:30 SEYDISFJÖRDUR 28:00 (Jun-Aug)
Island of Stroma
Nethertown
Uppertown
0:45 (May-Sept)
DUNNET HEAD
STROMNESS 1:30
Scarfskerry
East Mey
CASTLE OF MEY
Brough
Hunspow
Ham
Rattar
Mey
Gills
Kirkstyle
Huna
John o' Groats
DUNCANSBY HEAD
Canisbay
MARY-ANN'S COTTAGE
DUNNET BAY
Corsback
Dunnet
NATURAL HISTORY DISPLAY
Barrock
ST. MARY'S CHAPEL
Crosskirk
Scrabster
THURSO CASTLE
THURSO FOLK MUSEUM
FLAGSTONE INTERPRETATIVE TRAIL
Castlehill
Inkstack
Brabster
Tofts
Skirza
Thurso
Bridge of Forss
Clardon
Murkle
Greenland
Lochend
Freswick
Dounreay
Buldoo
Achreamie
Millbank
East
Haimer
Castletown
CASTLETOWN
Tain
Slickly
DOUNREAY EXHIBITION CENTRE
Newlands of Geise
Olrig Ho.
Reaster
BUCHOLLY CASTLE
Isauld
Achvarasdal
CNOC FREKEDAIN CHAMBERED CAIRN
Geise
Hilliclay
Alterwall
NORTHLANDS VIKING CENTRE
Reay
Westfield
Lieurary
Weydale
Durran
Bowermadden
LYTH ARTS CENTRE
Nybster
Auckengill
Shebster
Forss Water
Buckies
Achingills
Lyth
Sortat
Stemster
Bowertower
Barrock Ho.
Sordale
Knockdee
Stemster Ho.
Howe
Keiss
KEISS CASTLE
Braal Castle
Halcro
Broubster
Calder Mains
Roadside
Hastigrow
Mireland
Gillock
Halkirk
Clayock
North Watten
Kirk
Myrelandhorn
SINCLAIR'S BAY
Shurrery
Banniskirk Ho.
Shurrery Lodge
Brawlbin
Scotscalder Station
Harpsdale
Mains of Watten
Killimster
CASTLE SINCLAIR
CASTLE GIRNIGOE
Dorrery
Olgrinmore
BEINN NAM BAD MÒR
Spittal
Backlass
Watten
Winless
Reiss
Ackergill
Thurso
Mybster
Bilbster
Staxigoe
WICK HERITAGE CENTRE
Torran Water
Westerdale
Acharole
Strath
Wick
Papigoe
Stirkoke Ho.
Milton
Broadhaven
Old Wick
Badlipster
Newton
CASTLE OF OLD WICK
Whiterow
A9
A99
A836
A882
A961
A960
A964
A965
B855
B870
B874
B876
B9041
B9043
B9044
B9045
B9047
B9050
B9051
B9052

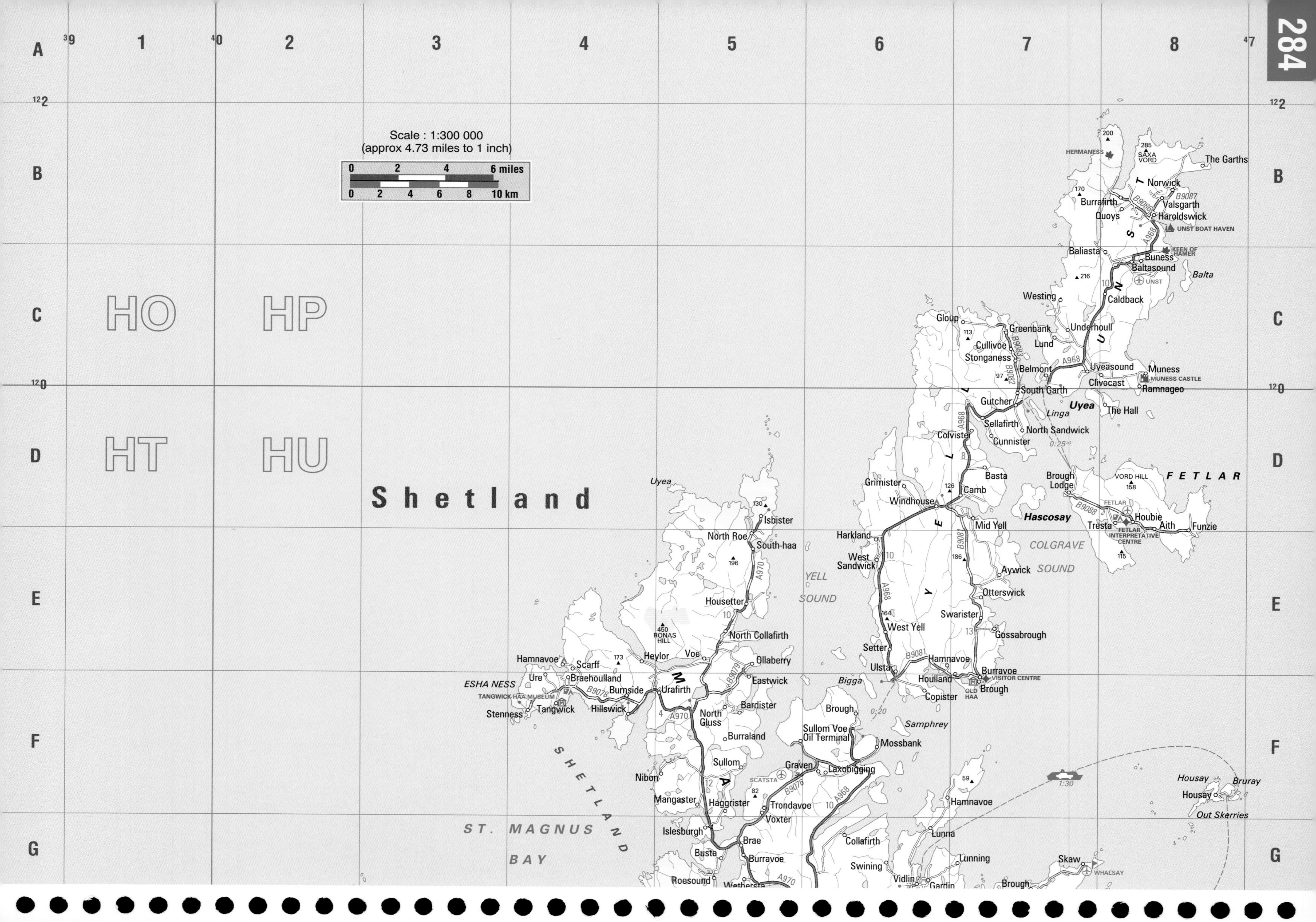
Scale : 1:300 000
(approx 4.73 miles to 1 inch)
0 2 4 6 miles
0 2 4 6 8 10 km
HO
HP
HT
HU
Shetland
FETLAR
UNST
YELL
MAINLAND
Hermaness
Saxa Vord
The Garths
Norwick
Valsgarth
Burrafirth
Quoys
Haroldswick
Unst Boat Haven
Baliasta
Keen of Hamar
Buness
Baltasound
Balta
Unst
Westing
Caldback
Gloup
Greenbank
Underhoull
Cullivoe
Lund
Stonganess
Belmont
Uyeasound
Muness
Muness Castle
Clivocast
Ramnageo
South Garth
Gutcher
Uyea
Linga
The Hall
Sellafirth
North Sandwick
Colvister
Cunnister
Basta
Brough Lodge
Vord Hill
Grimister
Camb
Windhouse
Hascosay
Fetlar
Houbie
Tresta
Aith
Funzie
Fetlar Interpretative Centre
Mid Yell
Colgrave Sound
Harkland
West Sandwick
Aywick
Otterswick
Yell Sound
Swarister
West Yell
Gossabrough
Setter
Hamnavoe
Ulsta
Burravoe
Visitor Centre
Houlland
Brough
Old Haa
Copister
Bigga
Samphrey
Uyea
Isbister
North Roe
South-haa
Ronas Hill
Housetter
North Collafirth
Hamnavoe
Scarff
Heylor
Voe
Ollaberry
Esha Ness
Ure
Braehoulland
Urafirth
Eastwick
Tangwick Haa Museum
Burnside
Bardister
Stenness
Tangwick
Hillswick
North Gluss
Brough
Sullom Voe Oil Terminal
Mossbank
Burraland
Shetland
Sullom
Graven
Laxobigging
Nibon
Scatsta
Hamnavoe
Mangaster
Haggrister
Trondavoe
Voxter
Housay
Bruray
Out Skerries
Islesburgh
Lunna
St. Magnus Bay
Brae
Collafirth
Busta
Burravoe
Lunning
Skaw
Swining
Whalsay
Roesound
Wethersta
Vidlin
Gardin
Brough

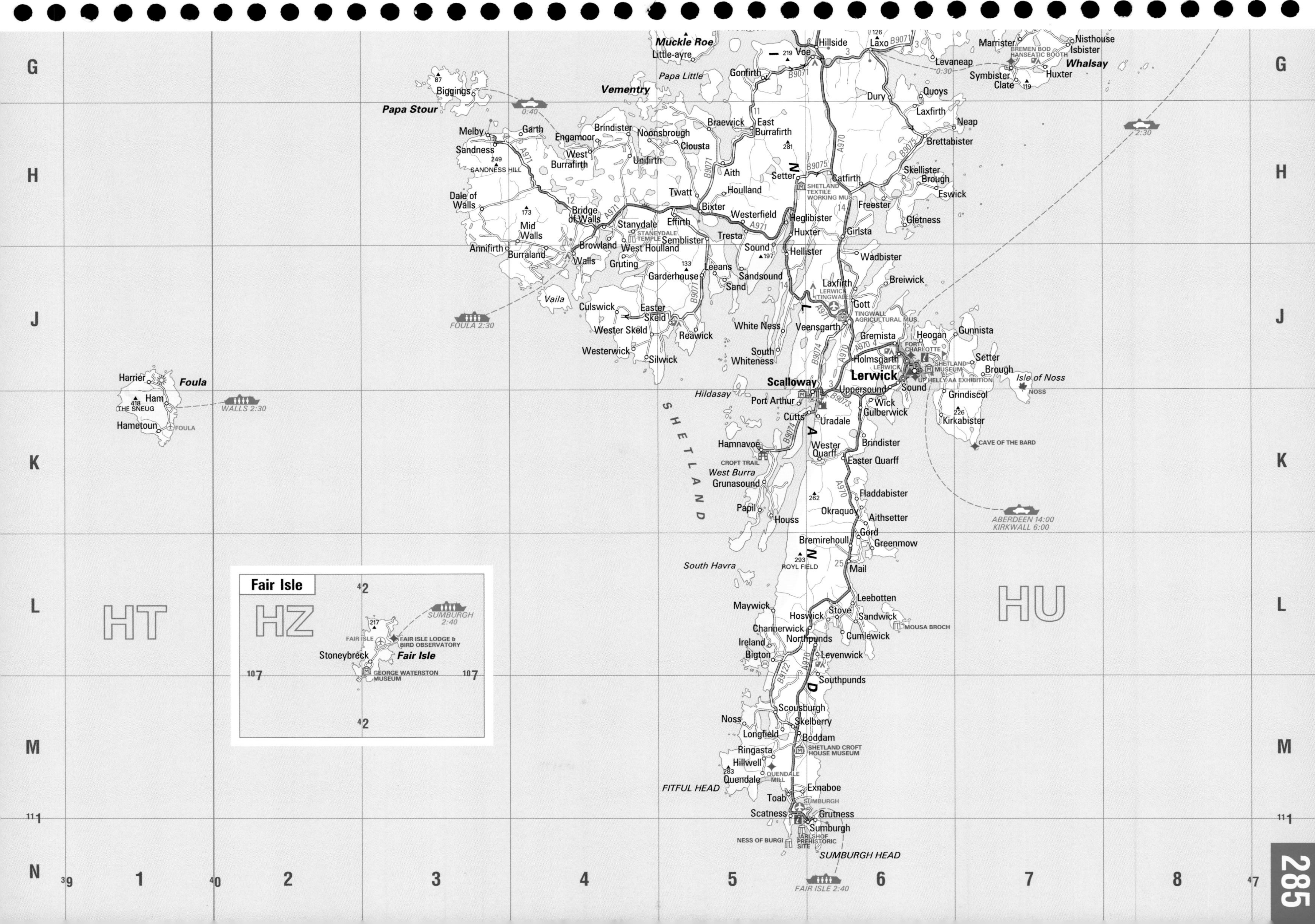
SHETLAND
Lerwick
Scalloway
Muckle Roe
Little-ayre
Papa Little
Vementry
Papa Stour
Biggings
Whalsay
Symbister
Clate
Marrister
Nisthouse
Isbister
Huxter
BREMEN BOD HANSEATIC BOOTH
Levaneap
Hillside
Voe
Laxo
Gonfirth
Dury
Quoys
Laxfirth
Neap
Brettabister
Braewick
East Burrafirth
Melby
Garth
Engamoor
Brindister
Noonsbrough
Clousta
Sandness
SANDNESS HILL
West Burrafirth
Unifirth
Aith
Setter
Catfirth
SHETLAND TEXTILE WORKING MUS.
Skellister
Brough
Eswick
Twatt
Houlland
Freester
Dale of Walls
Bixter
Westerfield
Heglibister
Gletness
Mid Walls
Bridge of Walls
Stanydale
STANEYDALE TEMPLE
Effirth
Semblister
Huxter
Girlsta
Tresta
Annifirth
Burraland
Browland
West Houlland
Sound
Hellister
Walls
Gruting
Wadbister
Garderhouse
Leeans
Sandsound
Sand
Laxfirth
Breiwick
LERWICK TINGWALL
Vaila
Culswick
Easter Skeld
Gott
TINGWALL AGRICULTURAL MUS.
FOULA 2:30
White Ness
Veensgarth
Wester Skeld
Reawick
Gremista
Heogan
Gunnista
FORT CHARLOTTE
Westerwick
Silwick
South Whiteness
Holmsgarth
SHETLAND MUSEUM
Setter
Brough
Harrier
Foula
Isle of Noss
NOSS
Ham
THE SNEUG
WALLS 2:30
Hametoun
FOULA
Hildasay
Uppersound
Sound
UP HELLY AA EXHIBITION
Grindiscol
Port Arthur
Wick
Gulberwick
Kirkabister
Cutts
Uradale
CAVE OF THE BARD
Hamnavoe
Brindister
Wester Quarff
Easter Quarff
CROFT TRAIL
West Burra
Grunasound
Fladdabister
Papil
Houss
Okraquoy
Aithsetter
ABERDEEN 14:00
KIRKWALL 6:00
Gord
Bremirehoull
Greenmow
ROYL FIELD
South Havra
Mail
Fair Isle
HT
HZ
HU
SUMBURGH 2:40
FAIR ISLE
FAIR ISLE LODGE & BIRD OBSERVATORY
Stoneybreck
GEORGE WATERSTON MUSEUM
Maywick
Leebotten
Hoswick
Stove
Sandwick
Channerwick
MOUSA BROCH
Cumlewick
Ireland
Northpunds
Bigton
Levenwick
Southpunds
Scousburgh
Noss
Skelberry
Longfield
Boddam
Ringasta
SHETLAND CROFT HOUSE MUSEUM
Hillwell
QUENDALE MILL
Quendale
FITFUL HEAD
Exnaboe
Toab
SUMBURGH
Scatness
Grutness
Sumburgh
NESS OF BURGI
JARLSHOF PREHISTORIC SITE
SUMBURGH HEAD
FAIR ISLE 2:40
A970
A971
B9071
B9075
B9074
B9073
B9122
G
H
J
K
L
M
N
1
2
3
4
5
6
7
8

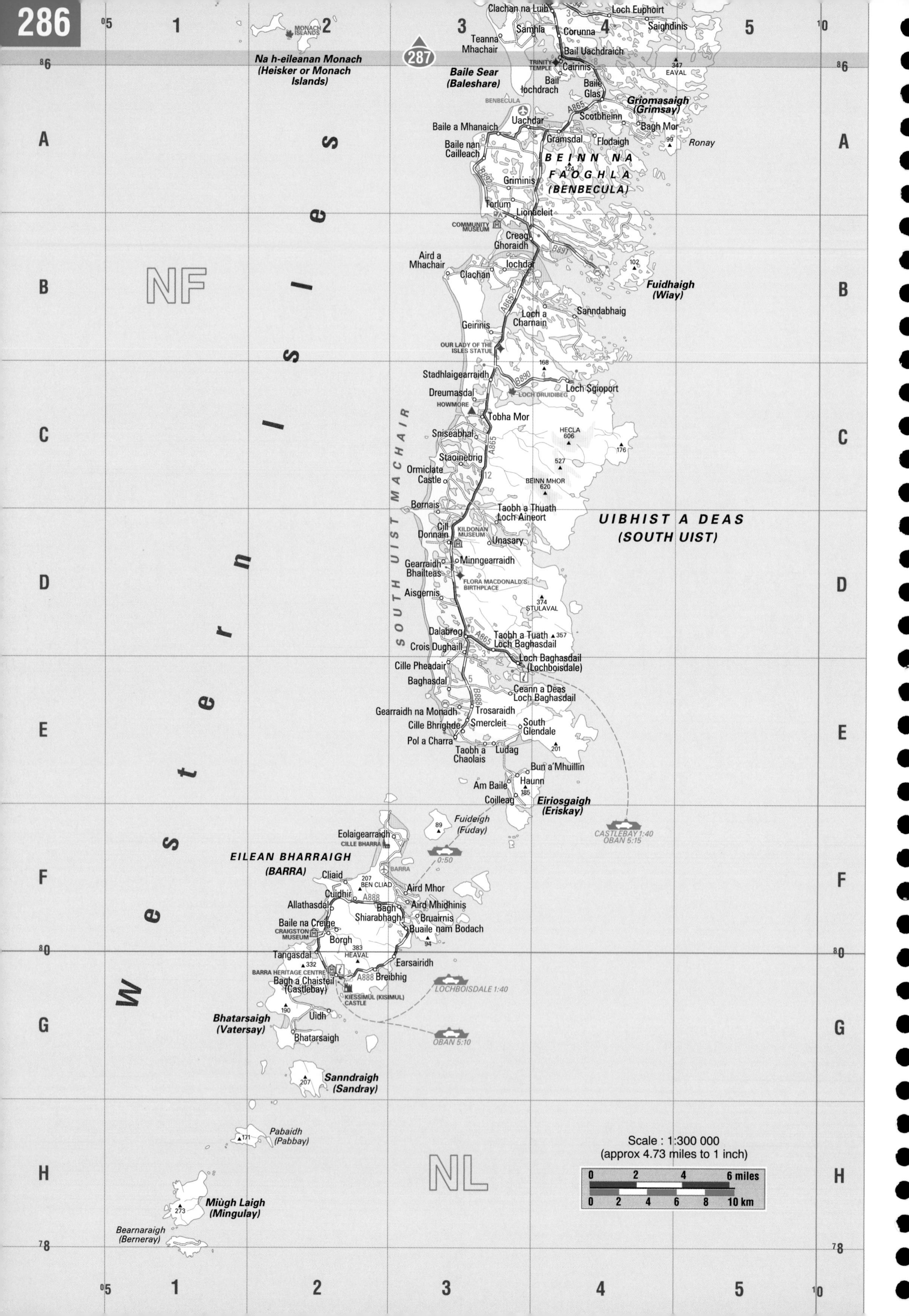
Na h-eileanan Monach
(Heisker or Monach Islands)
NF
Western Isles
Baile Sear
(Baleshare)
Griomasaigh
(Grimsay)
BEINN NA FAOGHLA
(BENBECULA)
Fuidhaigh
(Wiay)
SOUTH UIST MACHAIR
UIBHIST A DEAS
(SOUTH UIST)
Eiriosgaigh
(Eriskay)
Fuideigh
(Fuday)
EILEAN BHARRAIGH
(BARRA)
Bhatarsaigh
(Vatersay)
Sanndraigh
(Sandray)
Pabaidh
(Pabbay)
Miùgh Laigh
(Mingulay)
Bearnaraigh
(Berneray)
NL
Scale : 1:300 000
(approx 4.73 miles to 1 inch)
CASTLEBAY 1:40
OBAN 5:15
LOCHBOISDALE 1:40
OBAN 5:10

Scale : 1:300 000
(approx 4.73 miles to 1 inch)
0 2 4 6 miles
0 2 4 6 8 10 km
St. Kilda
NA
NF
Boreray
ST KILDA
Soay
St Kilda or Hirta
(Hiort)
NB
SOUTH LEWIS,
HARRIS AND
CEANN A TUATH
NA HEARADH
LOCH A SIAR
NORTH UIST
NA HEARADH
(HARRIS)
Tarasaigh
(Taransay)
Scarp
Mealasta Island
Pabaidh
(Pabbay)
Eilean
Bhearnaraigh
(Berneray)
CAOLAS NA HEARADH
UIBHIST A TUATH
(NORTH UIST)
AN CAOLAS MHONACH
Na h-eileanan Monach
(Heisker or Monach
Islands)
Vallay
Baile Sear
(Baleshare)
Griomasaigh
(Grimsay)
NG
Tairbeart
(Tarbert)
An t-Ob
(Leverburgh)
Loch nam Madadh
(Lochmaddy)
Lochportain
Uachdar
Baile a Mhanaich

Scale : 1:300 000
(approx 4.73 miles to 1 inch)
0 2 4 6 miles
0 2 4 6 8 10 km
NB
NG
RUBHA ROBHANAIS
Eòropaidh
Coig Peighinnean
Lional
Port Nis
Suainebost
Tabost
Aird Dhail
Dail bho Dheas
Cros
Dail bho Thuath
Sgiogarstaigh
Gabhsann bho Thuath
Gabhsann bho Dheas
Mealabost Bhuirgh
Cuiashader
Coig Peighinnean Bhuirgh
Bail Àrd Bhuirgh
Siadar
Siadar Iarach
Siadar Uarach
Baile an Truiseil
Barabhas Iarach
Barabhas Uarach
Barabhas
Labost
Bragar
Arnol
Brù
Siabost bho Thuath
Siabost bho Dheas
Pairc Shiaboist
Dail Beag
Dail Mòr
Na Gearrannan
Borghastan
Carlabhagh
Ciribhig
Dun Charlabhaigh
Crothair
Tobson
Great Bernera
Breacleit
Tolastadh a Chaolais
AN CAOLAS
Aird Uig
Cliobh
Bhaltos
Timsgearraidh
Miabhig
Riof
Uigen
Cradhlastadh
Carnais
Cairisiadar
Eadar Dha Fhadhail
Mangurstadh
Tacleit
Barraglom
Circebost
Breasclete
Tobhtarol
Calanais
Crulabhig
Linsiadar
Gearraidh na h-Aibhne
Geisiadar
Einacleite
Islibhig
Breanais
Giosla
EILEAN LEODHAIS
ISLE OF LEWIS
Bail' Ur Tholastaidh
Tolastadh bho Thuath
Gleann Tholàstaidh
Griais
Bac
Col
Col Uarach
Breibhig
BROAD BAY OR LOCH A TUATH
Aird Thunga
Tunga
Port Nan Giùran
Cnoc Amhlaigh
Port Mholair
Grianan
An Gleann Ur
Newmarket
Lacasdal
Stornoway
Sulaisiadar
Aird
Garrabost
EYE PENINSULA
Seisiadar
Mealabost
Aiginis
Pabail Uarach
Sanndabhaig
Tolm
An Cnoc
Suardail
Pabail Iarach
Acha Mor
Loch a' Ghainmhich
ULLAPOOL 2:40
Griomsidar
Liurbost
Ben Casgro
Ranais
Soval Lodge
Crosbost
Lacasaidh
Ceos
Cromor
Baile Ailein
Gearraidh Bhaird
Cearsiadair
Sildinis
Tabost
Cabharstadh
Marbhig
Ceann Tarabhaigh
Airidh a Bhruaich
Ceann Shiphoirt
Calbost
Grabhair
Taobh a' Ghlinne
PARK OR PAIRC
Orasaigh
Leumrabhagh
Eisgean
LOCH LANGABHAT
Aline Lodge
Seaforth I.
Aird a' Mhulaidh
Eilean Iubhard
Huisinis
SOUTH LEWIS, HARRIS AND NORTH UIST
Gobhaig
Abhainn Suidhe
CEANN A TUATH NA HEARADH
Cliasmol
Miabhag
Bun Abhainn Eadarra
Maraig
LOCH A SIAR
Aird Asaig
Reinigeadal
Tarasaigh (Taransay)
Urgha
Tairbeart (Tarbert)
Losgaintir
Paible
Carragraich
Caolas Scalpaigh
Carnach
CAOLAS NAN EILEAN
Na h-Eileanan Mòra (Shiant Islands)
Seilebost
Miabhag
Scalpay
Eilean Scalpaigh (Scalpay)
Borve Lodge
Buirgh
NA HEARADH (HARRIS)
Aird Mhighe
Drinisiadar
Kennacley
Greosabhagh
Plocrapol
Scadabhagh
Sgarasta Mhor
Liceasto
Leac a Li
UIG 1:45
Geocrab
Cliuthar
Beacrabhaic
Caolas Stocinis
Fleoideabhagh
Manais
Aird Mhighe
Cuidhtinis
An t-Ob (Leverburgh)
Fionnsbhagh
Boirseam

Aberdeen

Aberdeen ⇌ C2
Aberdeen College (Gallowgate Centre) . A2
Academy, The B1
Art Gallery 🏛 B1
Arts Centre 🏛 A2
Back Wynd B2
Belmont Cinema 🎥 . . . B1
Belmont St B1
Berry St A2
Blackfriars St B1
Bon-Accord Centre . . . B2
Bon-Accord St C1
Bridge St C1
Broad St B2
Bus Station C2
Car Ferry Terminal C3
Castlegate B3
Cathedral ✝ C1
Central Library B1
College St C2
Commerce St B3
Commercial Quay C3
Constitution St A3
Crown St C1
Denburn Rd B1
East North St A3
Fish Market C3
Galleria, The C1
Gallowgate A2
George St A1
Golden Sq B1
Gordon's College A1
Guild St C2
His Majesty's Theatre 🎭 B1
Hospital 🄷 B1
Information Ctr 🛈 B2
Jamieson Quay C3
John St A1
Justice St B3
King St A3
Lemon Tree, The A2
Loch St A1
Maberly St A1
Marischal College 🏛 . . A2
Maritime Museum & Provost Ross's House 🏛 B2
Market B2
Market St C2/C3
Mercat Cross ✦ B3
Music Hall 🎭 C1
Park St A3
Police Station 🅂 B2
Post Office 🄿🄾 B2/B3
Provost Skene's House 🏠 B2
Queen St B2
Regent Quay B3
St Andrew St A1
St Andrew's Cathedral ✝ B3
St Nicholas Centre . . . B2
St Nicholas St B2
School Hill B1
Spring Garden A1
Town House 🏠 B2
Trinity Centre C2
Trinity Quay B3
Union St B2/C1
Union Terr B1
Upper Kirkgate B2
Virginia St B3
Vue Cinema 🎥 B2
West North St A2
Windmill Brae C1

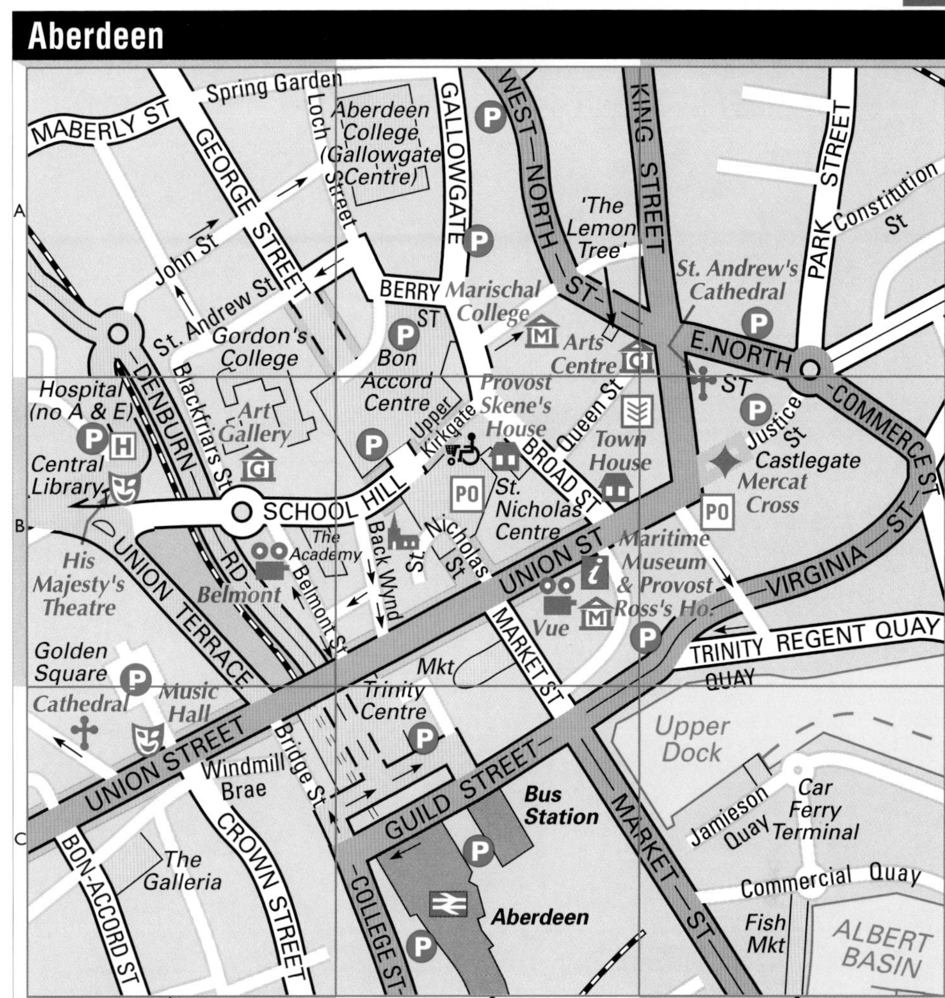

Bath

Aqua Theatre of Glass 🏛 A2
Assembly Rooms and Museum of Costume 🏛 A2
Avon St C2
Barton St B2
Bath Abbey ✝ B2
Bath City College C2
Bath Rugby Club B3
Bath Spa Station ⇌ . . C3
Bennett St A2
Broad Quay C2
Broad St A2
Brock St A1
Building of Bath 🏛 . . . A2
Bus Station C3
Charlotte St B1
Cheap St B2
Circus Mews A1
Corn St C2
Cricket Ground C3
George St A2
Great Pulteney St B3
Green Park C1
Green Park Rd C1
Grove St A3
Guildhall 🏠 B2
Henrietta Gdns A3
Henrietta Mews A3
Henrietta Park A3
Henrietta Rd A3
Henrietta St A3
Henry St C3
Information Ctr 🛈 B3
James St West B1
Jane Austen Centre 🏛 B2
Library B2
Lower Bristol Rd C1
Manvers St C3
Midland Bridge Rd . . . B1
Milk St C2
Milsom St B2
Monmouth Pl B1
Monmouth St B2
New King St B1
No. 1 Royal Crescent 🏛 A1
Norfolk Bldgs B1
North Parade Rd B3
Paragon A2
Police Station 🅂 C3
Post Office 🄿🄾 . B1/B2/C2
Postal Museum 🏛 B2
Pulteney Bridge ✦ . . . B3
Queen Sq B2
Recreation Ground . . . B3
Rivers St A2
Roman Baths & Pump Room ♨ B2
Royal Ave A1
Royal Cr A1
Royal Victoria Park . . . A1
St John's Rd A3
Southgate C2
South Pde C3
Sports & Leisure Centre B3
Spring Gdns C3
Stall St B2
Theatre Royal 🎭 B2
Thermae Bath Spa ✦ . C2
Union St B2
Victoria Art Gallery 🏛 . B3
Walcot St A2/B2
Westgate Bldgs B2
Westgate St B2
William Herschel Museum 🏛 B1

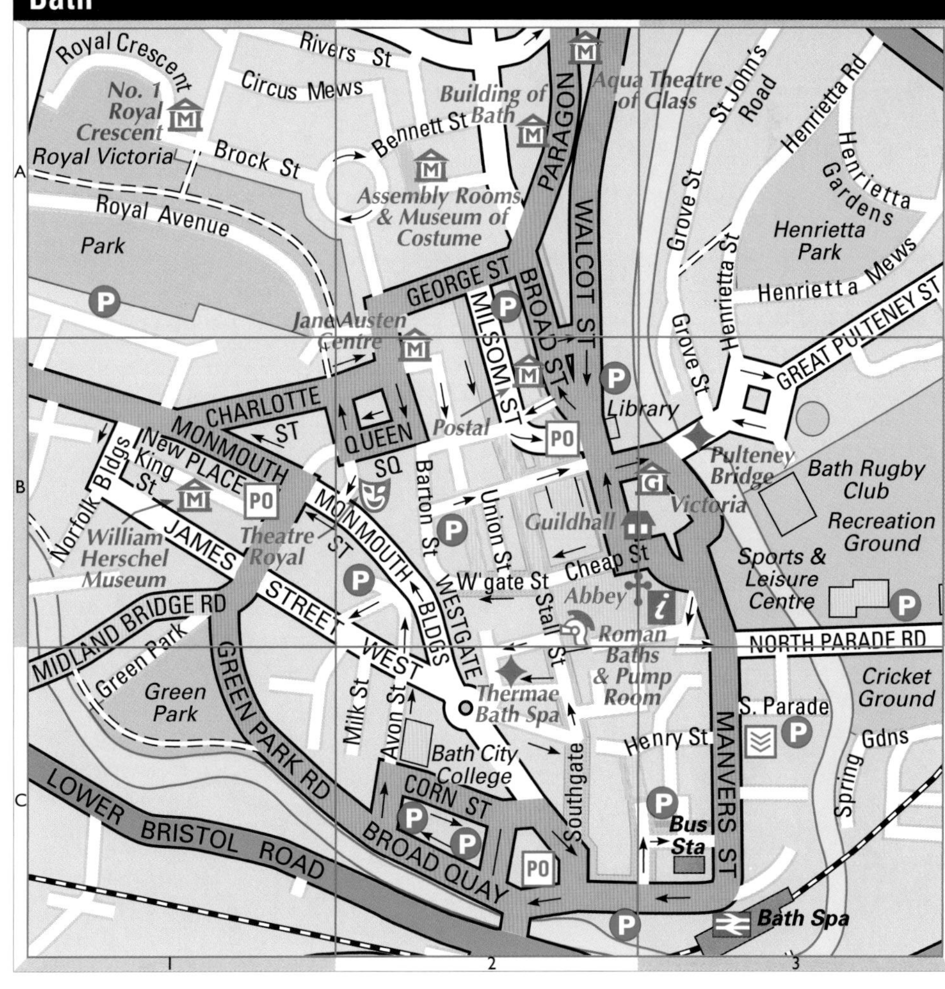

Birmingham approaches

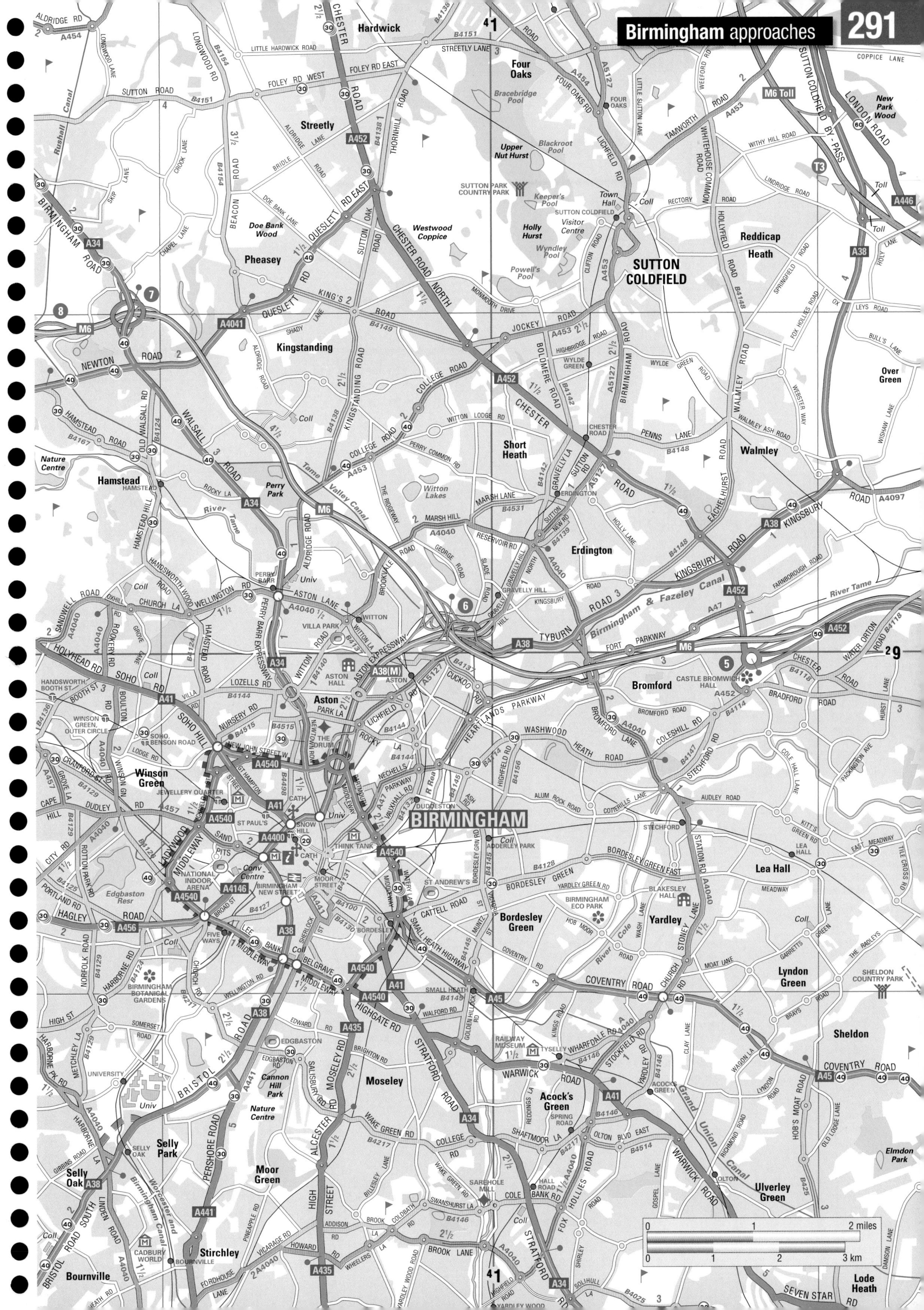
Hardwick
Four Oaks
Streetly
Pheasey
Kingstanding
Sutton Coldfield
Reddicap Heath
Walmley
Over Green
New Park Wood
Hamstead
Perry Park
Short Heath
Erdington
Aston
Bromford
Castle Bromwich Hall
Winson Green
Birmingham
Lea Hall
Bordesley Green
Yardley
Lyndon Green
Sheldon
Moseley
Acock's Green
Selly Park
Selly Oak
Moor Green
Ulverley Green
Stirchley
Bournville
Elmdon Park
Lode Heath
Sutton Park Country Park
Sheldon Country Park
Birmingham Botanical Gardens
Birmingham Eco Park
0 1 2 miles
0 1 2 3 km

Birmingham

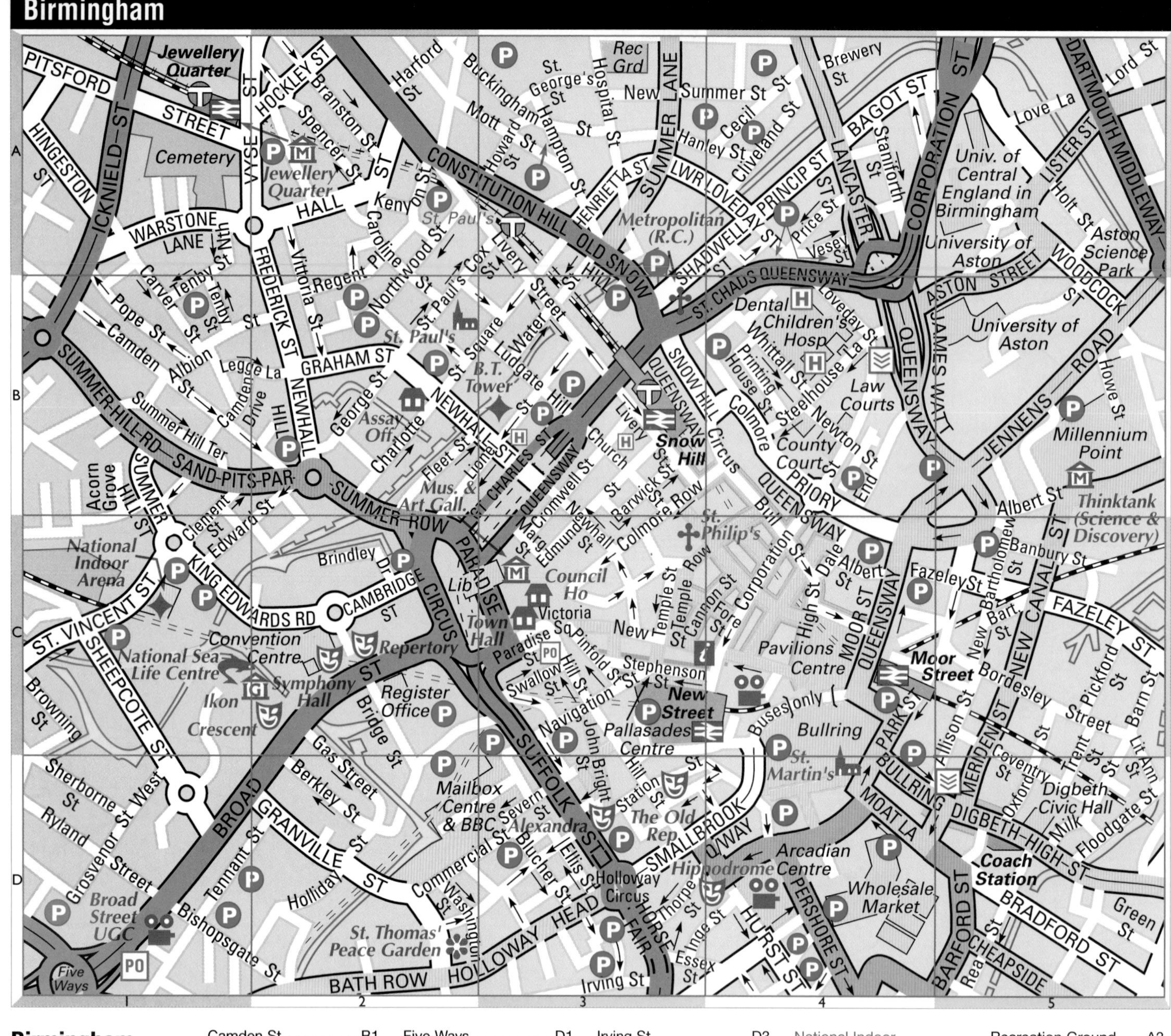

Birmingham

Acorn Gr . . . B1
Albert St . . . B5/C4
Albion St . . . B1
Alexandra Theatre . . . D3
Allison St . . . C5
Arcadian Centre . . . D4
Assay Office . . . B2
Aston Science Park . . . A5
Aston St . . . B5
BT Tower . . . B3
Bagot St . . . A4
Banbury St . . . C5
Barford St . . . D5
Barn St . . . C5
Bartholomew St . . . C5
Barwick St . . . B3
Bath Row . . . D2
Berkley St . . . D2
Bishopsgate St . . . D1
Blucher St . . . D3
Bordesley St . . . C5
Bradford St . . . D5
Branston St . . . A2
Brewery St . . . A4
Bridge St . . . C2
Brindley Dr . . . C2
Broad St . . . C2/D1
Broad Street UGC . . . D1
Browning St . . . C1
Buckingham St . . . A3
Bullring . . . C4/D4
Bull St . . . C4
Cambridge St . . . C2
Camden Dr . . . B1
Camden St . . . B1
Cannon St . . . C3
Caroline St . . . A2
Carver St . . . B1
Cecil St . . . A4
Cemetery . . . A1
Charlotte St . . . B2
Cheapside . . . D5
Children's Hospital . . . B4
Church St . . . B3
Clement St . . . C1
Cliveland St . . . A4
Coach Station . . . D5
Colmore Circus . . . B4
Colmore Row . . . C3
Commercial St . . . D2
Constitution Hill . . . A3
Convention Centre . . . C2
Corporation St . . . A4/B4/C4
Council House . . . C3
County Court . . . B4
Coventry St . . . D5
Cox St . . . A2
Crescent Theatre . . . C2
Cromwell St . . . B3
Dale End . . . C4
Dartmouth Middleway . . . A5
Dental Hospital . . . B4
Digbeth Civic Hall . . . D5
Digbeth High St . . . D5
Edmund St . . . C3
Edward St . . . C1
Ellis St . . . D3
Essex St . . . D3
Fazeley St . . . C5
Five Ways . . . D1
Fleet St . . . B2
Floodgate St . . . D5
Fore St . . . C4
Frederick St . . . B2
Gas St . . . D2
George St . . . B2
Graham St . . . B2
Granville St . . . D2
Great Charles St . . . B3
Green St . . . D5
Grosvenor St West . . . D1
Hall St . . . A2
Hampton St . . . A3
Hanley St . . . A4
Harford St . . . A2
Henrietta St . . . A3
High St . . . C4
Hill St . . . C3/D3
Hingeston St . . . A1
Hippodrome Theatre . . . D4
Hockley St . . . A2
Holliday St . . . D2
Holloway Circus . . . D3
Holloway Head . . . D3
Holt St . . . A5
Horse Fair . . . D3
Hospital St . . . A3
Howard St . . . A3
Howe St . . . B5
Hurst St . . . D4
Icknield St . . . A1
Ikon Gallery . . . C2
Information Ctr . . . C3
Inge St . . . D3
Irving St . . . D3
James Watt Queensway . . . B4
Jennens Rd . . . B5
Jewellery Quarter . . . A1
Jewellery Quarter Museum . . . A2
John Bright St . . . D3
Kenyon St . . . A2
King Edwards Rd . . . C1
Lancaster St . . . A4
Law Courts . . . B4
Legge La . . . B1
Library . . . C2
Lionel St . . . B3
Lister St . . . A5
Little Ann St . . . D5
Livery St . . . B3
Lord St . . . A5
Love La . . . A5
Loveday St . . . B4
Lower Loveday St . . . A4
Ludgate Hill . . . B3
Mailbox Centre & BBC . . . D2
Margaret St . . . C3
Meriden St . . . D5
Metropolitan (R.C.) . . . B3
Milk St . . . D5
Millennium Point . . . B5
Moat La . . . D4
Moor Street . . . C4
Moor St Queensway . . . C4
Mott St . . . A3
Museum & Art Gallery . . . C3
National Indoor Arena . . . C1
National Sea Life Centre . . . C1
Navigation St . . . C3
New Bartholomew St . . . C5
New Canal St . . . C5
New St . . . C3
New Street . . . C3
New Summer St . . . A3
Newhall Hill . . . B2
Newhall St . . . B2/C3
Newton St . . . B4
Northwood St . . . A2
Old Rep Theatre, The . . . D3
Old Snow Hill . . . A3
Oxford St . . . D5
Pallasades Centre . . . C3
Paradise Circus . . . C2
Paradise St . . . C3
Park St . . . C4
Pavilions Centre . . . C4
Pershore St . . . D4
Pickford St . . . C5
Pinfold St . . . C3
Pitsford St . . . A1
Police Station . . . B4/D5
Pope St . . . B1
Post Office . . . C3/D1
Price St . . . A4
Princip St . . . A4
Printing House St . . . B4
Priory Queensway . . . B4
Queensway . . . B3
Rea St . . . D5
Recreation Ground . . . A3
Regent Pl . . . B2
Register Office . . . C2
Repertory Theatre . . . C2
Ryland St . . . D1
St Chads Queensway . . . B4
St George's St . . . A3
St Martin's . . . D4
St Paul's . . . B2
St Paul's Metro station . . . A3
St Paul's Sq . . . B2
St Philip's . . . C3
St Thomas' Peace Garden . . . D2
St Vincent St . . . C1
Sand Pits Pde . . . B1
Severn St . . . D3
Shadwell St . . . A4
Sheepcote St . . . C1
Sherborne St . . . D1
Smallbrook Queensway . . . D3
Snow Hill . . . B3
Snow Hill Queensway . . . B3
Spencer St . . . A2
Staniforth St . . . A4
Station St . . . D3
Steelhouse La . . . B4
Stephenson St . . . C3
Suffolk St . . . D3
Summer Hill Rd . . . B1
Summer Hill St . . . B1
Summer Hill Terr . . . B1
Summer La . . . A3
Summer Row . . . B2
Swallow St . . . C3

Blackpool

Abingdon St A2
Adelaide St B2
Albert Rd B2
Alfred St. A2
Ashton Rd C3
Bank Hey St B1
Belmont Ct C3
Birley St. A2
Blackpool & Fleetwood
Tram B1
Blackpool Tower ✦ . . . B1
Bonny St C1
Caunce St A3
Central Dr C2
Central Pier ✦ C1
Central Pier
(Tram stop) C1
Central Pier
Theatre C1
Chapel St. C1/C2
Charnley Rd B2
Church St A2/A3
Clifton St A1
Clinton Ave C3
Coach Station A2
Cookson St A2
Coronation St B2
Corporation St. A1
Courts C1
Freckleton St. C3
Grosvenor St A3
Hornby Rd. B2/B3
Hounds Hill Shopping
Centre B1
Hull Rd. B2
Ibbison Ct C3
Information Ctr A1
Kent Rd C2
King St. A2
Leamington Rd A3
Lifeboat Station. B1
Lincoln Rd B3
Livingstone Rd C2
Louis Tussaud's
Waxworks C1
Market St. A1
Milbourne St A3
North Pier ✦ A1
North Pier Theatre . . A1
Palatine Rd C2/C3
Park Rd B3/C3
Peter St A3
Police Station C1
Post Office B1/C2
Promenade A1
Queen St A1
Raikes Pde B3
Read's Ave B3/C2
Regent Rd A3/B3
Ribble Rd. C3
Sealife Centre C1
Seaside Way C2
South King St A3/B3
Sutton Pl C3
Talbot Rd A2
Talbot Sq (Tram stop) . A1
Topping St. A2
Tower (Tram stop) B1
Town Hall. A1
Vance Rd B2
Victoria St B1
Winter Gardens Theatre
& Opera House . . . B2
Woolman Rd C3

Blackpool

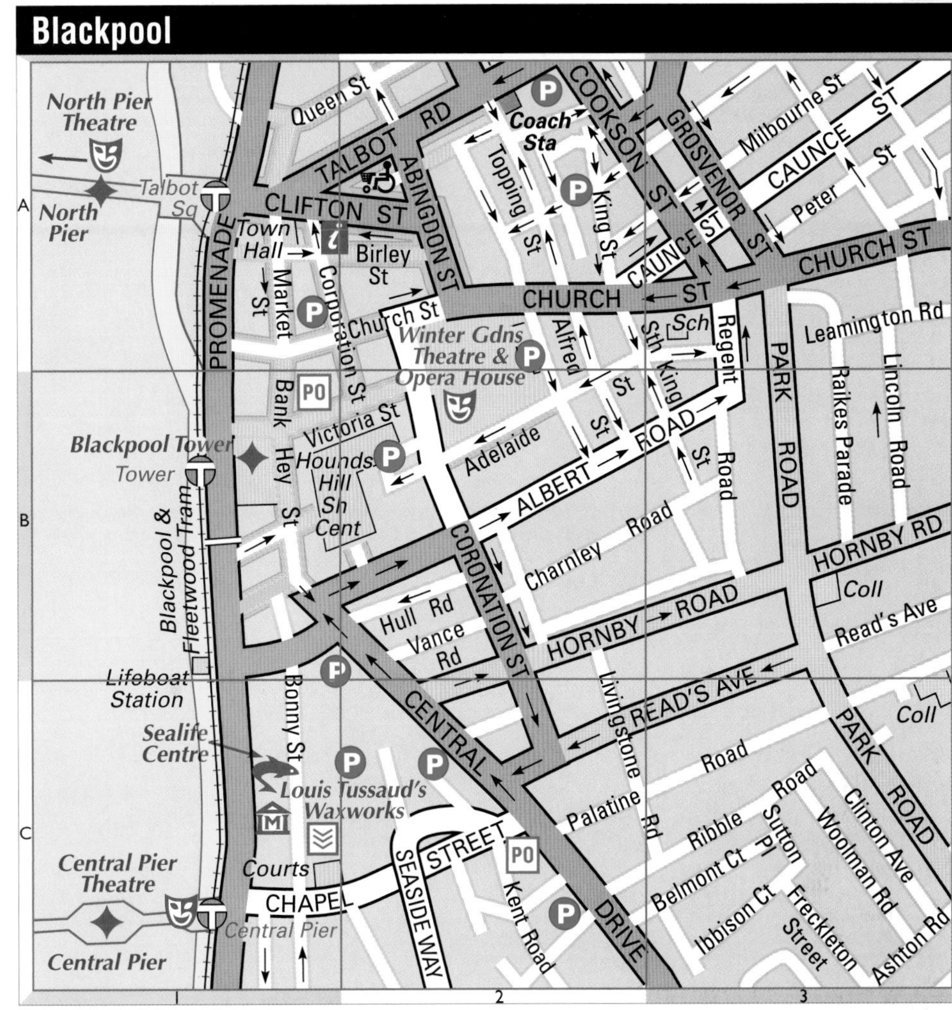

Brighton

Albion St A3
Art Gallery
& Museum B2
Brighton Centre . . . B1
Broad St C3
Cannon Pl B1
Carlton Hill. B3
Church St A1/B2
Churchill Square
Shopping Centre. . . . B1
Clifton Terr. A1
Clock Tower. B1
Dome, The B2
Duke St B1
Duke's La. B1
Dyke Rd. A1
East St. C2
Edward St B3
Frederick St. A2
Fruit & Veg Market
(wholesale) A3
Gardner St. A2
Gloucester Pl. A3
Gloucester Rd A2
Grand Junction Rd . . . C2
Grand Pde. A3
High St B3
Information Ctr C2
John St B3
Law Courts B3
Madeira Dr. C3
Marine Pde C3
Middle St. B1
New Rd B2
North Rd A2
North St. B2
Old Steine B2
Palace Pier ✦ C3
Police Station B3
Post Office . A3/B2/B3
Queen's Rd A1
Regent St A2
Royal Alexandra
Hospital A1
Royal Pavilion B2
St James' St C3
St Nicholas' A1
Sea Life Centre . . . C3
Spring Gdns A2
Sussex Terr A3
Swimming Pool A2
Sydney St A2
The Lanes B2
Theatre Royal B2
Tidy St. A2
Town Hall. C2
University of Brighton . B3
Upper North St A1
Victoria Gdns. B3
Volk's Electric
Railway ✦ C3
West St B1
Western Rd B1

Birmingham continued

Symphony Hall C2
Temple Row. C3
Temple St C3
Tenby St B1
Tenby St North A1
Tennant St. D1
Thinktank (Science
& Discovery) B5
Thorpe St. D3
Town Hall C3
Trent St C5
University of Central
England. A5
University
of Aston. A5/B5
Vesey St A4
Victoria Sq. C3
Vittoria St. B2
Vyse St A1
Warstone La A1
Washington St. D2
Water St. B3
Whittall St B4
Wholesale Market D4
Woodcock St. A5

Brighton

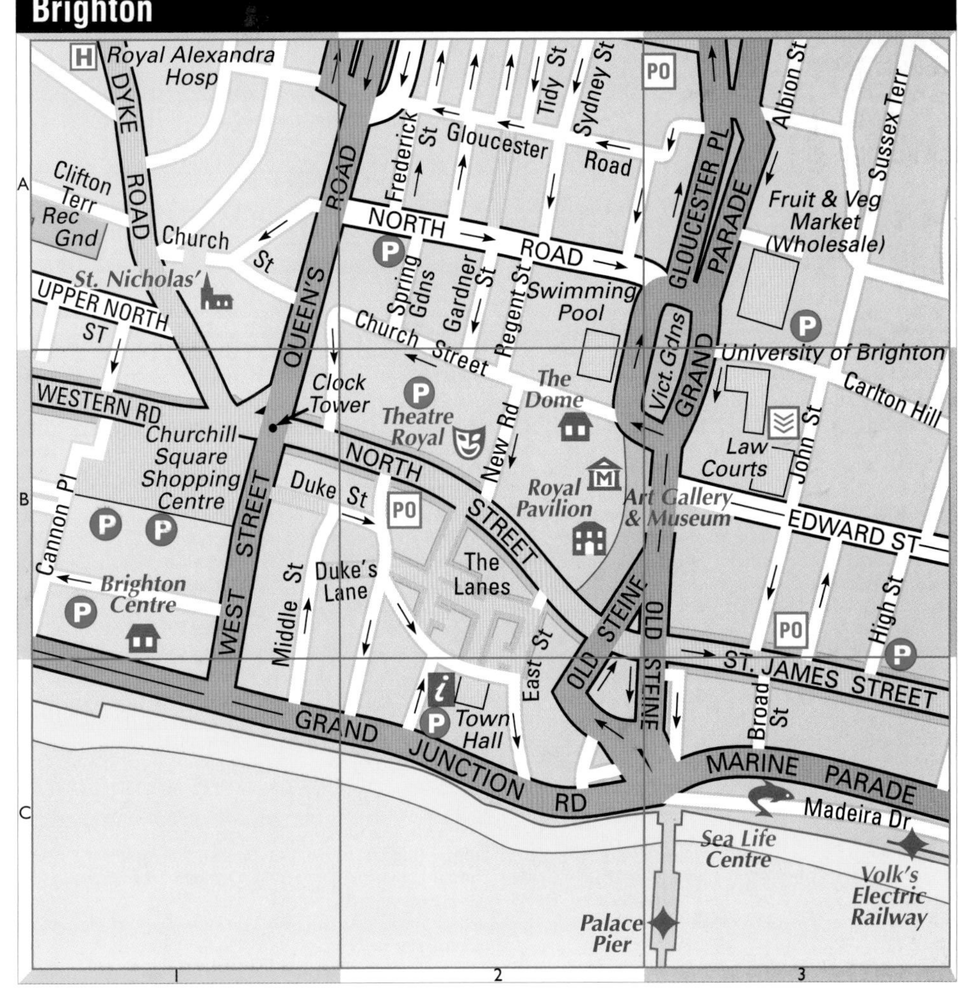

Bristol

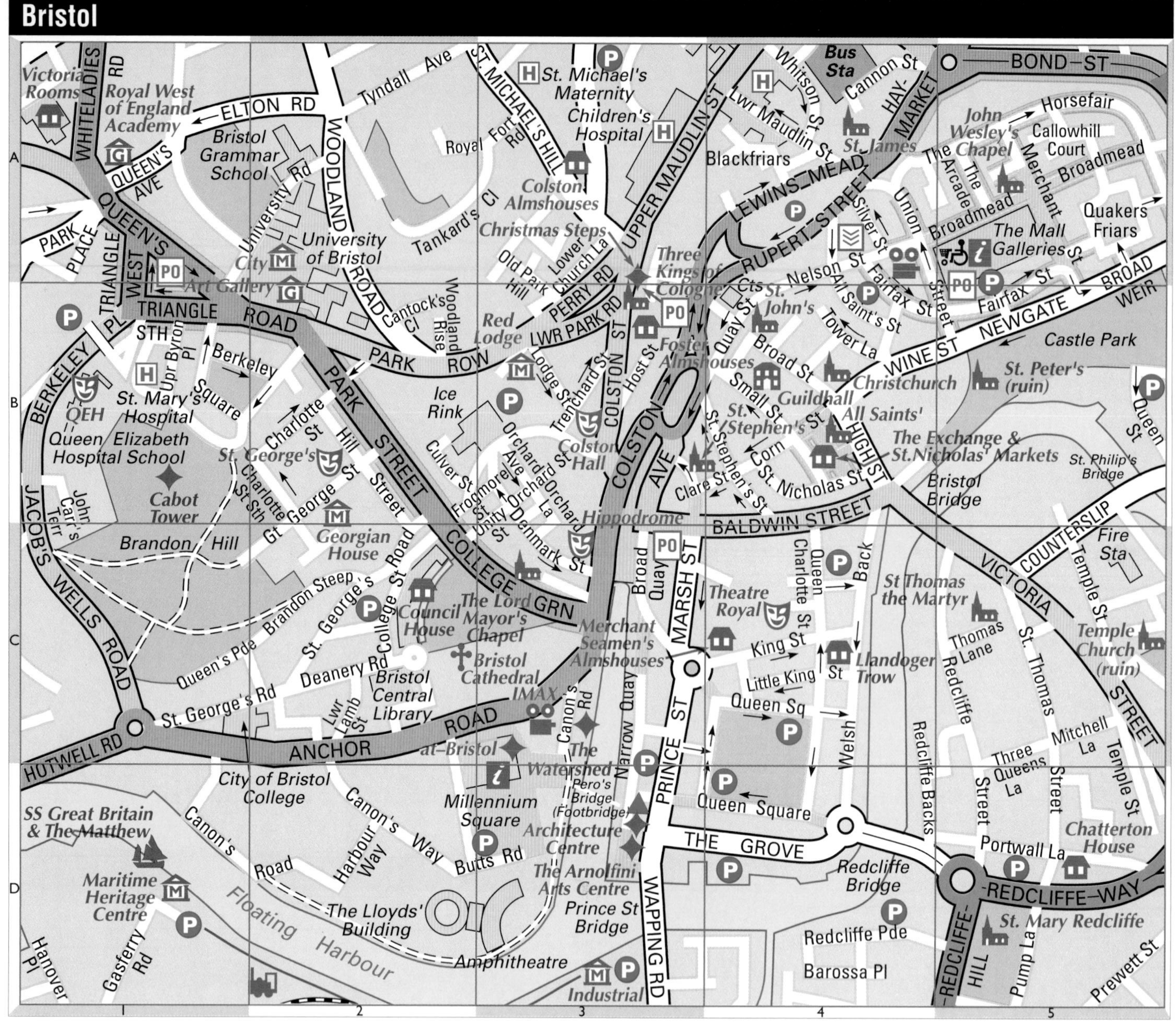

Bristol

All Saint's St B4
All Saints' B4
Amphitheatre D3
Anchor Rd C2
Architecture Centre ✦ D3
Arnolfini Arts Centre, The ✦ D3
Art Gallery B2
at-Bristol ✦ C3
Baldwin St B4
Barossa Pl D4
Berkeley Pl B1
Berkeley Sq B1
Blackfriars A4
Bond St A5
Brandon Hill C1
Brandon Steep C2
Bristol Bridge B4
Bristol Cathedral (CE) ✝ C2
Bristol Central Library C2
Bristol Grammar School A2
Broad Quay C3
Broad St B4
Broad Weir A5
Broadmead A5
Bus Station A4
Butts Rd D3
Cabot Tower ✦ B1
Callowhill Ct A5
Cannon St A4
Canon's Rd C3/D1
Canon's Way D2
Cantock's Cl B2
Castle Park B5
Charlotte St B2
Charlotte St South B2
Chatterton House D5
Children's Hospital A3
Christchurch B4
Christmas Steps ✦ A3
City Museum A2
City of Bristol College C1
Clare St B3
College Green C2/C3
College St C2
Colston Almshouses A3
Colston Ave B3
Colston Hall B3
Colston St B3
Corn St B4
Council House C2
Counterslip C5
Courts B4
Culver St B2
Deanery Rd C2
Denmark St C3
Elton Rd A1/A2
Exchange and St Nicholas' Mkts, The B4
Fairfax St B4/B5
Fire Station C5
Foster Almshouses B3
Frogmore St B2
Gasferry Rd D1
Georgian House B2
Great George St B2
Guildhall B4
Hanover Pl D1
Harbour Way D2
Haymarket A4
High St B4
Hill St B2
Hippodrome C3
Host St B3
Hotwell Rd C1
Ice Rink B2
IMAX Cinema C3
Industrial Museum D3
Information Ctr A5/D3
Jacob's Wells Rd C1
John Carr's Terr B1
John Wesley's Chapel A5
King St C4
Lewins Mead A4
Little King St C4
Llandoger Trow C4
Lloyds' Building, The D2
Lodge St B3
Lord Mayor's Chapel, The C3
Lower Church La A3
Lower Lamb St C2
Lower Maudlin St A4
Lower Park Rd B3
Mall Galleries Shopping Ctr, The A5
Maritime Heritage Centre D1
Marsh St C3
Merchant Seamen's Almshouses C3
Merchant St A5
Millennium Sq D3
Mitchell La C5
Narrow Quay C3
Nelson St A4
Newgate B5
Odeon A4
Old Park Hill A3
Orchard Ave B3
Orchard La B3
Orchard St B3
Park Pl A1
Park Row B2
Park St B2
Pero's Bridge D3
Perry Rd B3
Police Sta A4
Post Office A1/A5/B3/C3
Portwall La D5
Prewett St D5
Prince St C3/D3
Prince St Bridge D3
Pump La D5
QEH Theatre B1
Quakers Friars A5
Quay St B4
Queen Charlotte St C4
Queen Elizabeth Hospital School B1
Queen Sq C4/D4
Queen St B5
Queen's Ave A1
Queen's Parade C1
Queen's Rd A1
Redcliffe Backs C4
Redcliffe Bridge D4
Redcliffe Hill D5
Redcliffe Parade D4
Redcliffe St C5/D5
Redcliffe Way D5
Red Lodge B3
Royal Fort Rd A3
Royal West of England Academy A1
Rupert St A4
St George's B2
St George's Rd C1/C2
St James A4
St John's B4
St Mary Redcliffe D5
St Mary's Hospital B1
St Michael's Hill A3
St Michael's Maternity Hospital A3
St Nicholas St B4
St Peter's (ruin) B5
St Philip's Bridge B5
St Stephen's B3
St Stephen's St B4
St Thomas St C5
St Thomas the Martyr C5
Silver St A4
Small St B4
SS Great Britain and The Matthew D1
Tankard's Cl A2
Temple Church (ruin) C5
Temple St C5/D5
The Arcade A5
The Grove D4
The Horsefair A5
Theatre Royal C4
Thomas La C5
Three Kings of Cologne B3
Three Queens La C5
Tower La B4
Trenchard St B3
Triangle South B1
Triangle West A1
Tyndall Ave A2
Union St A4
Unity St B3
University of Bristol A2
University Rd A2
Upper Maudlin St A3
Upper Byron Pl B1
Victoria Rooms A1
Victoria St C5
Wapping Rd D3
Welsh Back C4
Whiteladies Rd A1
Whitson St A4
Wine St B4
Woodland Rise B2
Woodland Rd A2
YHA ▲ D3

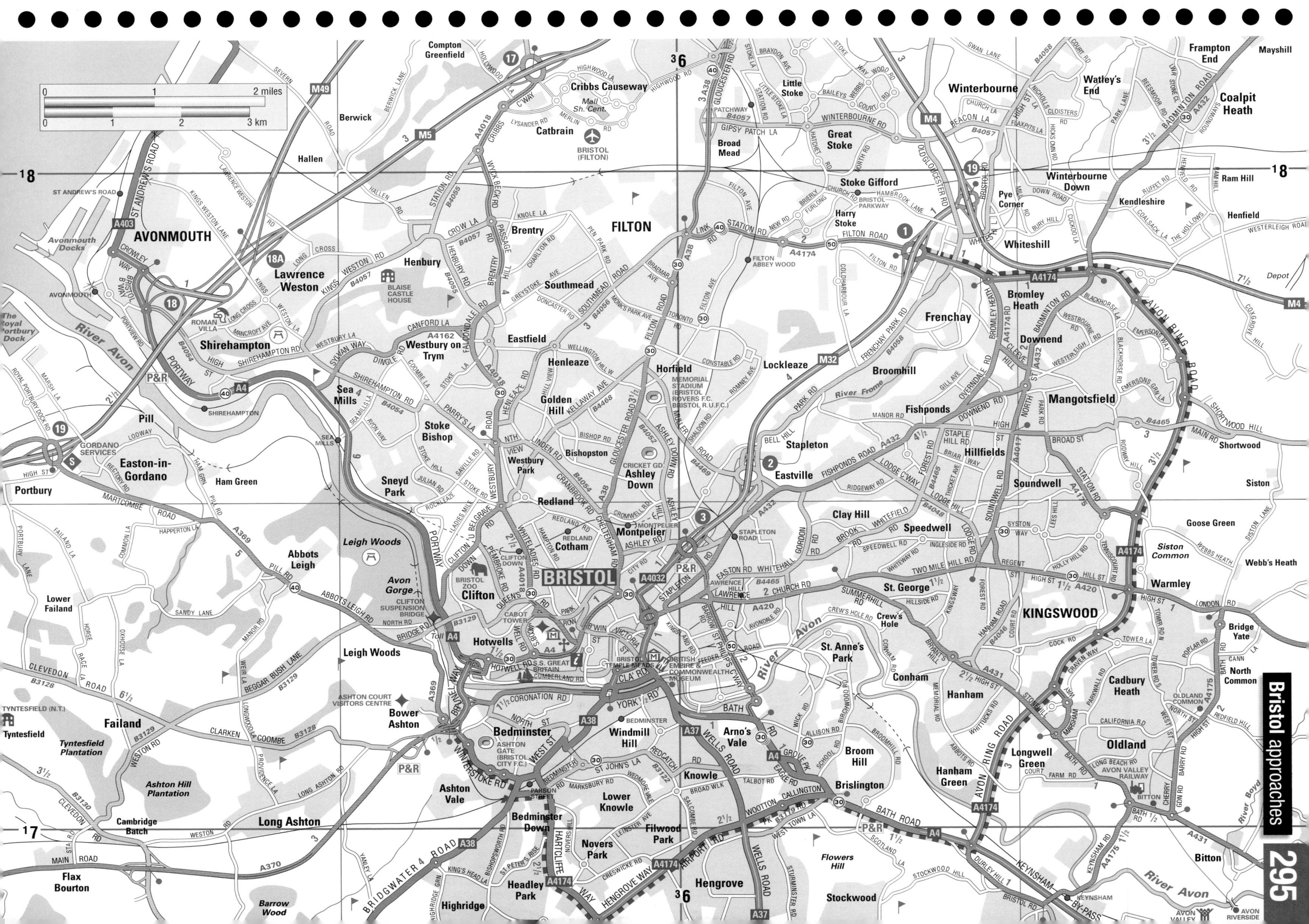
BRISTOL
AVONMOUTH
FILTON
KINGSWOOD
Frampton End
Coalpit Heath
Mayshill
Ram Hill
Henfield
Kendleshire
Watley's End
Winterbourne Down
Winterbourne
Whiteshill
Pye Corner
Bromley Heath
Downend
Mangotsfield
Shortwood
Siston
Webb's Heath
Goose Green
Siston Common
Warmley
Bridge Yate
North Common
Cadbury Heath
Oldland
Bitton
Longwell Green
Hanham
Hanham Green
Conham
Soundwell
Hillfields
Fishponds
Frenchay
Speedwell
St. George
Crew's Hole
Clay Hill
Broomhill
Stoke Gifford
Harry Stoke
Great Stoke
Little Stoke
Broad Mead
Lockleaze
Stapleton
Eastville
St. Anne's Park
Broom Hill
Brislington
Stockwood
Flowers Hill
Arno's Vale
Knowle
Hengrove
Horfield
Ashley Down
Montpelier
Filwood Park
Windmill Hill
Lower Knowle
Novers Park
Cribbs Causeway
Catbrain
Brentry
Southmead
Henleaze
Golden Hill
Bishopston
Redland
Cotham
Eastfield
Westbury Park
Clifton
Hotwells
Bedminster
Bedminster Down
Headley Park
Highridge
Ashton Vale
Compton Greenfield
Henbury
Westbury on Trym
Stoke Bishop
Sneyd Park
Leigh Woods
Bower Ashton
Berwick
Hallen
Lawrence Weston
Sea Mills
Abbots Leigh
Long Ashton
Barrow Wood
Shirehampton
Ham Green
Easton-in-Gordano
Pill
Failand
Lower Failand
Cambridge Batch
Flax Bourton
Portbury
Tyntesfield
Ashton Hill Plantation
Tyntesfield Plantation
River Avon
M4
M5
M32
M49
AVON RING ROAD
WELLS ROAD
BATH ROAD
HARTCLIFFE WAY
BRIDGWATER ROAD
PORTWAY
ST ANDREW'S ROAD
Avonmouth Docks
The Royal Portbury Dock
GORDANO SERVICES
2 miles
3 km

Cambridge

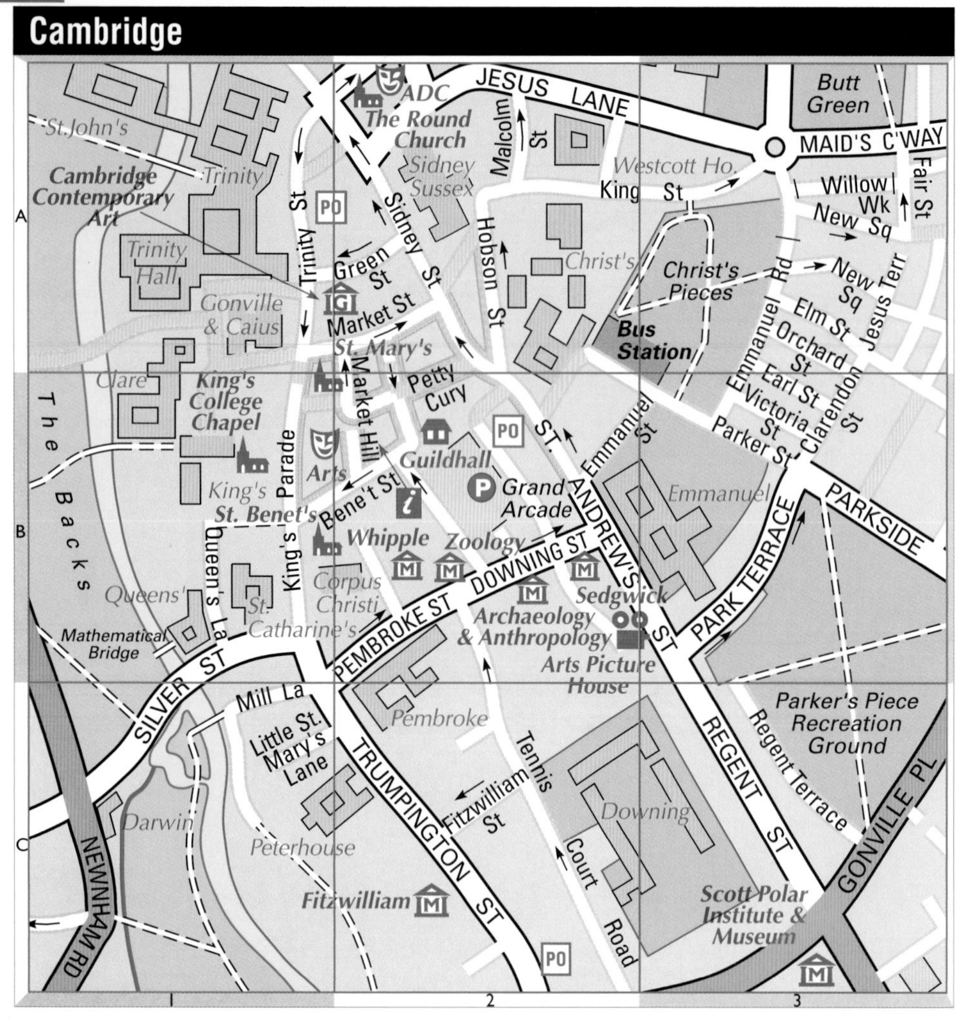

Cambridge

ADC A2
Archaeology & Anthropology B2
Arts Picture House . B2
Arts Theatre B1
Backs, The B1
Bene't St B2
Bus Station A2
Butt Green A3
Cambridge Contemporary Art Gallery A2
Christ's (Coll) A2
Christ's Pieces A3
Clare (Coll) B1
Clarendon St B3
Corpus Christi (Coll) . . B2
Darwin (Coll) C1
Downing (Coll) C2
Downing St B2
Earl St B3
Elm St A3
Emmanuel (Coll) B3
Emmanuel Rd A3
Emmanuel St B2
Fair St A3
Fitzwilliam Museum C2
Fitzwilliam St C2
Gonville & Caius (Coll). A1
Gonville Place C3
Grand Arcade B2
Green St A2
Guildhall B2
Hobson St A2
Information Ctr B2
Jesus La A2
Jesus Terr A3
King St A2
King's (Coll) B1
King's College Chapel B1
King's Parade B1
Little St. Mary's La . . . C1
Maid's Causeway A3
Malcolm St A2
Market Hill B2
Market St A2
Mathematical Bridge . . B1
Mill La C1
New Square A3
Newnham Rd C1
Orchard St A3
Park Terr B3
Parker St B3
Parker's Piece Recreation Ground . . C3
Parkside B3
Pembroke (Coll) C2
Pembroke St B2
Peterhouse (Coll) C1
Petty Cury B2
Post Office . A1/B2/C2
Queens' (Coll) B1
Queen's La B1
Regent St C3
Regent Terr C3
Round Church, The . A2
St Andrew's St B2
St Benet's B1
St Catharine's (Coll) . . B1
St John's (Coll) A1
St Mary's B1
Scott Polar Institute & Museum C3
Sedgwick Museum . B2
Sidney St A2
Sidney Sussex (Coll) . . A2
Silver St C1
Tennis Court Rd C2
Trinity (Coll) A1
Trinity Hall (Coll) A1
Trinity St A1
Trumpington St C2
Victoria St B3
Westcott House (Coll) . A2
Whipple B2
Willow Walk A3
Zoology B2

Canterbury

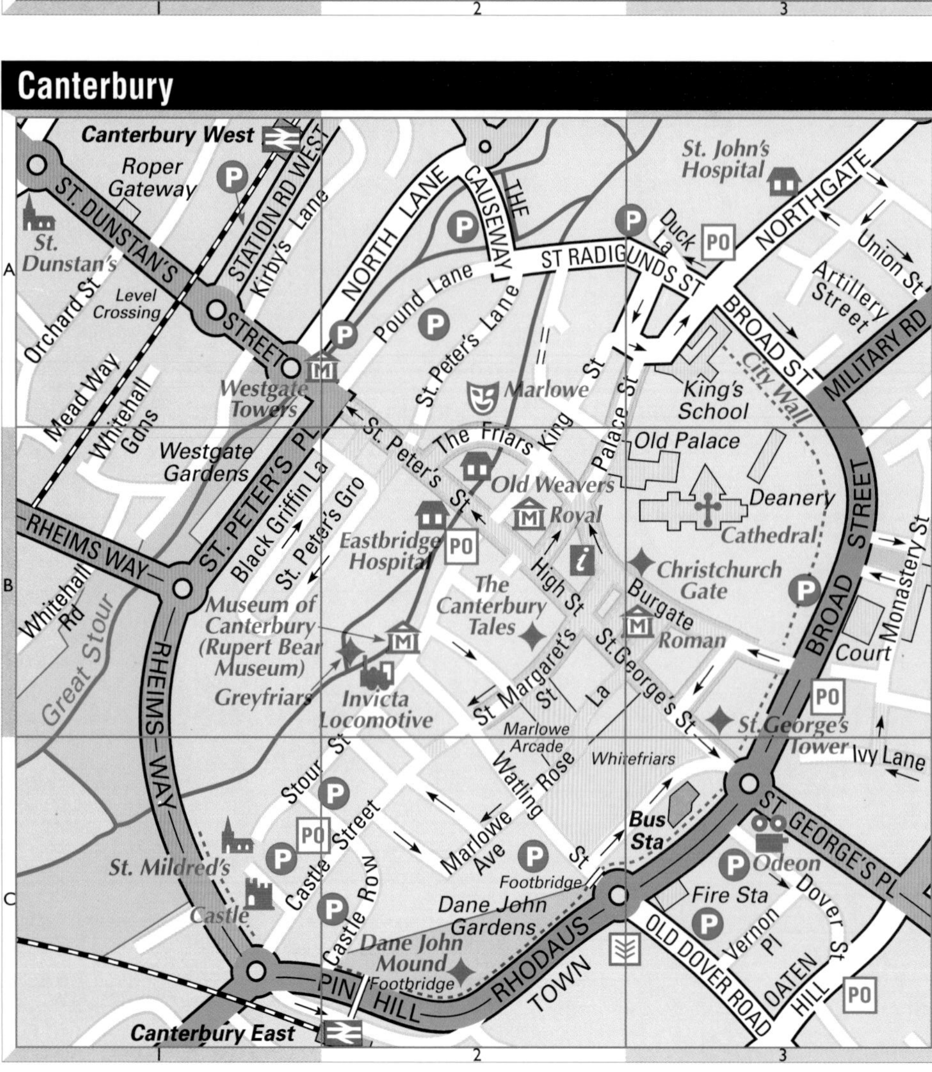

Canterbury

Artillery St A3
Black Griffin La B1
Broad St A3/B3
Burgate B3
Bus Station C3
Canterbury East . . C2
Canterbury Tales, The B2
Canterbury West . . A1
Castle C1
Castle Row C2
Castle St C1
Cathedral B3
Christchurch Gate . . B3
City Wall A3/C2
Court B3
Dane John Gdns C2
Dane John Mound . C2
Deanery B3
Dover St C3
Duck La A3
Eastbridge Hospital . B2
Fire Station C3
Greyfriars B2
High St B2
Information Ctr B2
Invicta Locomotive . B2
Ivy La C3
King St A2
King's School A3
Kirby's La A1
Marlowe Arcade B2
Marlowe Ave C2
Marlowe Theatre . . . A2
Mead Way A1
Military Rd A3
Monastery St B3
Museum of Canterbury (Rupert Bear Museum) B2
North La A2
Northgate A3
Oaten Hill C3
Odeon Cinema C3
Old Dover Rd C3
Old Palace B3
Old Weavers B2
Orchard St A1
Palace St B2
Pin Hill C2
Police Station C2
Post Office A3/B2/B3/C1/C3
Pound La A2
Rheims Way B1
Rhodaus Town C2
Roman Museum . . . B3
Roper Gateway A1
Rose La C2
Royal Museum B2
St Dunstan's A1
St Dunstan's St A1
St George's Pl C3
St George's St B3
St George's Tower . B3
St John's Hospital . A3
St Margaret's St B2
St Mildred's C1
St Peter's Gr B1
St Peter's La A2
St Peter's Pl B1
St Peter's St B2
St Radigunds St A2
Station Rd West A1
Stour St C1
The Causeway A2
The Friars B2
Union St A3
Vernon Pl C3
Watling St C2
Westgate Towers . . A2
Westgate Gdns B1
Whitefriars C3
Whitehall Gdns B1
Whitehall Rd B1

Cardiff / Caerdydd

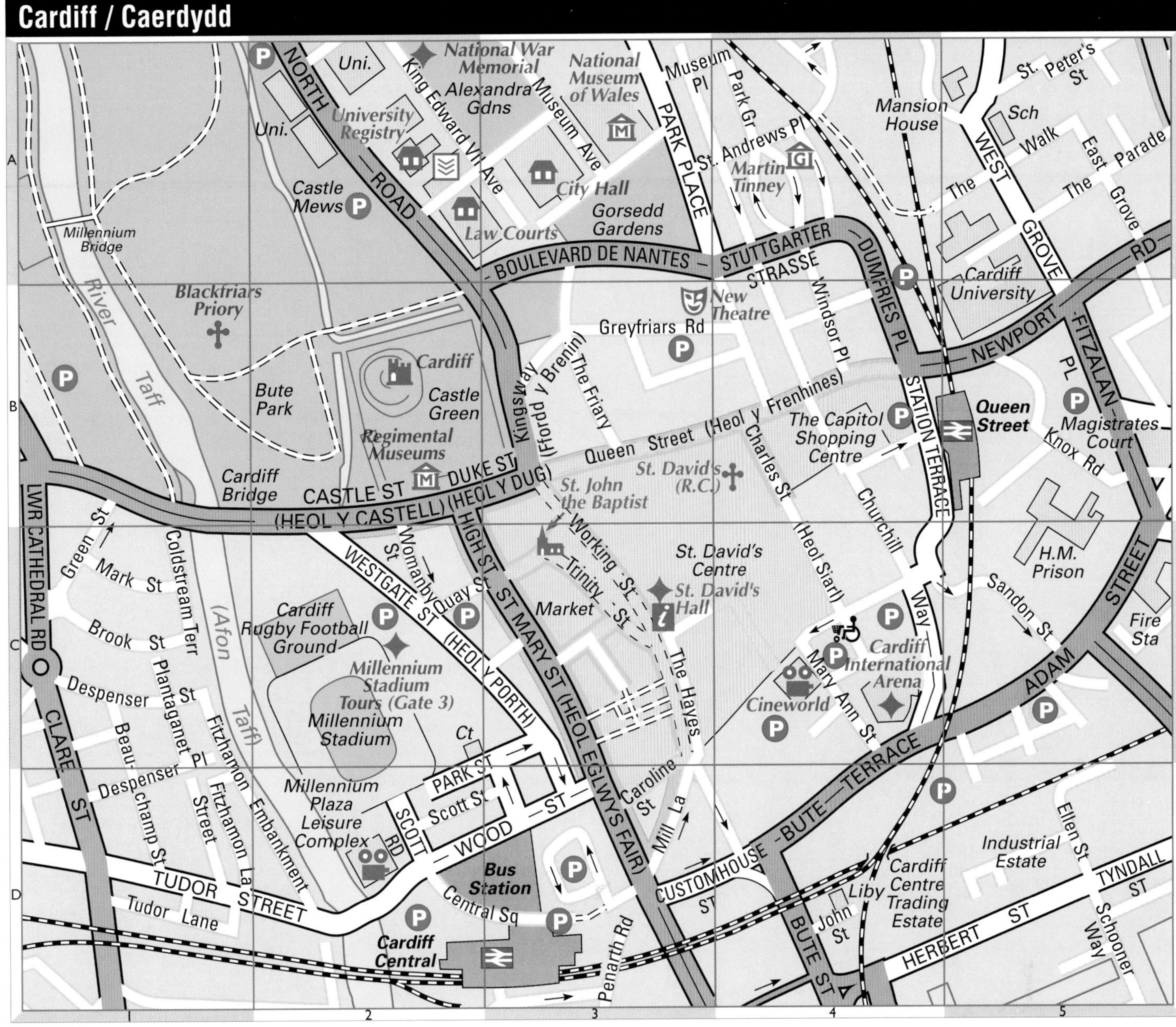

Cardiff/Caerdydd

Adam St C5
Alexandra Gdns. A3
Beauchamp St. D1
Blackfriars Priory ✝ . . . B1
Boulevard De Nantes. A3
Brook St C1
Bus Station D3
Bute Park. B2
Bute St D4
Bute Terr D4
Capitol Shopping Centre, The B4
Cardiff Bridge B1
Cardiff Castle B2
Cardiff Central Station D3
Cardiff Centre Trading Estate D4
Cardiff International Arena ✦ C4
Cardiff Rugby Football Ground C2
Cardiff University. . A2/B5
Caroline St. D3
Castle Green B2
Castle Mews A2
Castle St (Heol y Castell) B2
Central Sq D2
Charles St (Heol Siarl). B4
Churchill Way C4
Cineworld C4
City Hall A3
Clare St D1
Coldstream Terr. C1
Court C2
Customhouse St D3
Despenser Place D1
Despenser St. C1
Duke St (Heol y Dug). . B3
Dumfries Pl B4
East Grove. A5
Ellen St D5
Fire Station C5
Fitzalan Place B5
Fitzhamon Embankment. C1
Fitzhamon La. D1
Gorsedd Gdns. A3
Green St C1
Greyfriars Rd B3
H.M. Prison C5
Herbert St D5
High St C2
Information Ctr C3
John St D4
King Edward VII Ave . . A2
Kingsway (Ffordd y Brenin) B3
Knox Rd B5
Law Courts A2
Library D4
Lower Cathedral Rd . . C1
Magistrates Court B5
Mansion House A5
Mark St C1
Market C3
Martin Tinney A4
Mary Ann St C4
Mill La D3
Millennium Bridge A1
Millennium Plaza Leisure Complex D2
Millennium Stadium. . . C2
Millennium Stadium Tours (Gate 3) ✦ C2
Museum Ave A3
Museum Place. A3
National Museum of Wales A3
National War Memorial ✦ A2
New Theatre B3
Newport Rd. B5
North Rd A2
Park Grove A4
Park Place. A3
Park St. D2
Penarth Rd D3
Plantaganet St. C1
Police Station A2
Quay St C2
Queen St (Heol y Frenhines) . . . B3
Queen St Station . B5
Regimental Museums B2
St Andrews Place A4
St David's ✝ B4
St David's Centre C3
St David's Hall ✦ C3
St John The Baptist C3
St Mary St (Heol Eglwys Fair) . . . C3
St Peter's St A5
Sandon St C5
Schooner Way. D5
Scott Rd D2
Scott St D2
Station Terr B4
Stuttgarter Strasse . . . A4
The Friary B3
The Hayes C3
The Parade A5
The Walk A5
Trinity St C3
Tudor La D1
Tudor St. D1
Tyndall St. D5
Tyndall Street Industrial Estate D5
University Registry . A2
West Gr A5
Westgate St (Heol y Porth) C2
Windsor Place B4
Womanby St C2
Wood St. D3
Working St. C3

CARDIFF
(CAERDYDD)
Church Village
Nantgarw
Watford
Caerphilly Common
The Warren
Coed Coesau-Whips
Llwyncelyn
Park Wood
Coed y Gedrys
Glan-y-llyn
Gwaelod-y-garth
Grath Hill
Taff Vale
Thornhill
PARC CEFN ONN
Cefn Mably Woods
Michaelston-y-Fedw
Castleton
Marshfield
Blacktown
Taff's Well
(Ffynnon-Taf)
CASTELL COCH
Coed-y-Wenallt
Tongwynlais
Soar
Garth Wood
Pentyrch
Morganstown
Radyr
FOREST FARM
Pantmawr
Rhiwbina
Whitchurch
Birchgrove
Llanishen
Llanishen Reservoir
Lisvane
(Llys Faen)
Llanedeyrn
Pentwyn
Cyncoed
Began
St. Mellons
(Llaneirwg)
Llanrumney
Trowbridge
Peterstone Wentlooge
(Llanbedr Gwynllŵg)
Rumney
(Rhymni)
Pwll-Mawr
Newton
Rhymney River
Heath
Roath Park
The Lake
Llandaff North
Gabalfa
Maindy
Llandaff
(Llandaf)
River Taff
Cathays
NATIONAL MUSEUM OF WALES
CARDIFF CASTLE
Roath
Splott
Tremorfa
CARDIFF WEST SERVICES
CARDIFF GATE SERVICES
LLANDAFF CATHEDRAL
Fairwater
St Fagans
(Sain Ffagan)
MUSEUM OF WELSH LIFE
Pontcanna
SOPHIA GDNS
Canton
MILLENNIUM STADIUM
Riverside
CENTRE FOR VISUAL ARTS
St Brides-super-Ely
(Llansanffraid-ar-Elai)
St George's
Ely
(Tre-lai)
Michaelston-super-Ely
Caerau
Drope
River Ely
Saltmead
NINIAN PARK
CARDIFF CENTRAL
Bute E Dock
Roath Dock
Butetown
Grangetown
WALES MILLENNIUM CENTRE
NATIONAL ASSEMBLY
TECHNIQUEST
CARDIFF BAY VISITOR CENTRE
Qn Alexandra Dock
Cardiff Bay Barrage
Culverhouse Cross
Downs
Leckwith
St Nicholas
(Sain Nicolas)
TINKINSWOOD BURIAL CHAMBER
Twyn-yr-odyn
Wallston
St Lythans
Wenvoe
(Gwenfo)
Michaelston-le-Pit
Llandough
M4
A48(M)
A48
A470
A469
A4232
A4119
A4160
A4161
A4054
A4050
A4055
A4234
0 1 2 miles
0 1 2 3 km

Carlisle

Abbey St A1
Annetwell St A1
Bank St B2
Blackfriars St. B2
Botchergate. C3
Bridge St A1
Brunswick St. B3
Bus Station B3
Carlisle (Citadel) Station C2
Castle A1
Castle St A1
Castle Way A1
Cathedral B1
Cecil St B3
Chapel St. A2
Charlotte St. C1
Chatsworth Square . . . A3
Chiswick St B3
Citadel, The. C2
City Walls. A1
Civic Centre. A2
Court B3
Court St. C2
Crosby St B3
Dacre Rd A1
Denton St C1
Devonshire Walk A1
Elm St C2
English St B2
Fire Station A2
Fisher St A2
Georgian Way A2
Guildhall Museum . . B2
Information Ctr B2
James St C2
Junction St C1
King St. C3
Lancaster St C3
Lanes Shopping Centre A2/B2
Laserquest ✦ B2
Library A2/B1
Lime St C2
Lonsdale Rd B3
Lorne Cres. C1
Lorne St. C1
Lowther St. B2
Market Hall A2
Mary St B3
Milbourne St B1
Old Town Hall B2
Peter St A2
Police Station A2
Portland Pl. C3
Portland Sq B3
Post Office A2/B3
Rickergate A2
St Cuthbert's B2
St Cuthbert's La B2
Scotch St. A2
Sheffield St C1
Spencer St B3
Sports Centre A3
Strand Rd A3
Swimming Baths C2
Tait St C3
Tullie House Museum A1
Viaduct Estate Rd B1
Victoria Pl A3
Victoria Viaduct C2
Vue C3
Warwick Rd B3
Water St. C2
West Walls. B1

Carlisle

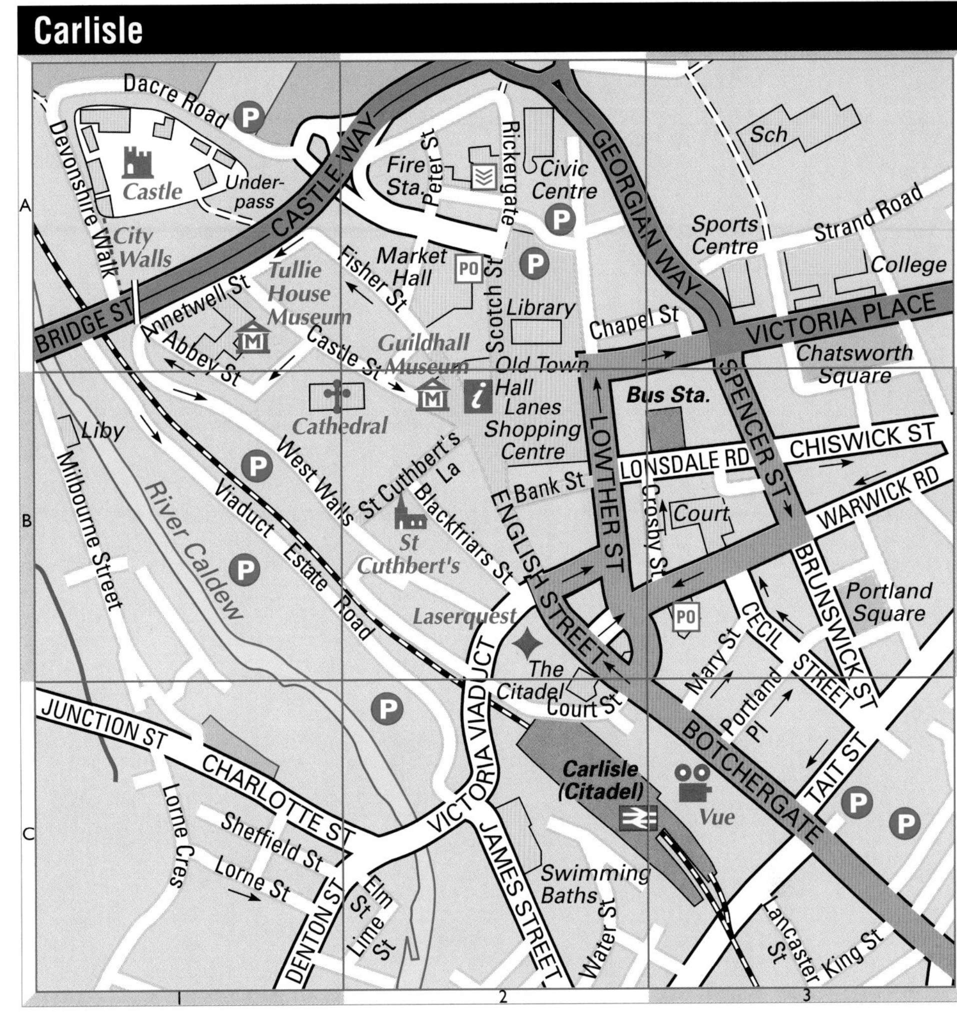

Chester

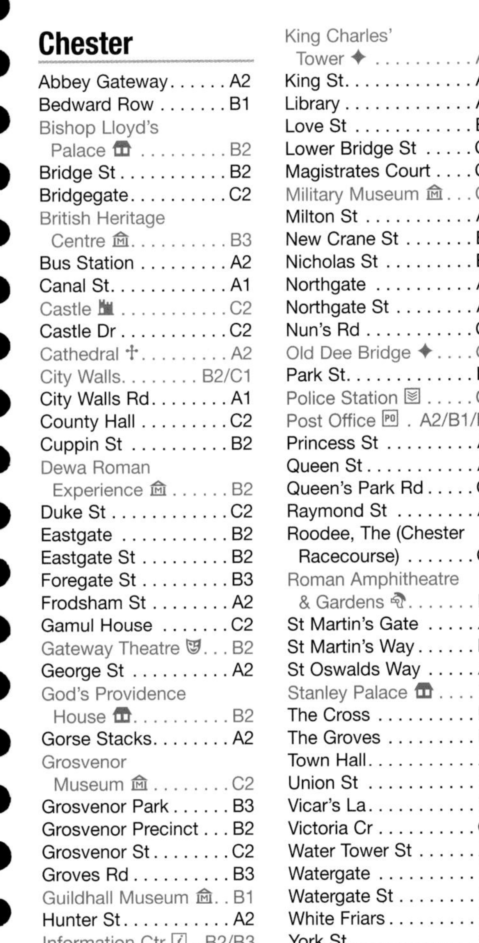

Abbey Gateway. A2
Bedward Row B1
Bishop Lloyd's Palace B2
Bridge St B2
Bridgegate. C2
British Heritage Centre B3
Bus Station A2
Canal St. A1
Castle C2
Castle Dr C2
Cathedral A2
City Walls. B2/C1
City Walls Rd. A1
County Hall C2
Cuppin St B2
Dewa Roman Experience B2
Duke St C2
Eastgate B2
Eastgate St B2
Foregate St B3
Frodsham St A2
Gamul House C2
Gateway Theatre . . . B2
George St A2
God's Providence House B2
Gorse Stacks. A2
Grosvenor Museum C2
Grosvenor Park B3
Grosvenor Precinct . . . B2
Grosvenor St C2
Groves Rd B3
Guildhall Museum . . B1
Hunter St. A2
Information Ctr . B2/B3
King Charles' Tower ✦ A2
King St. A1
Library A2
Love St B3
Lower Bridge St C2
Magistrates Court C2
Military Museum . . . C2
Milton St A3
New Crane St B1
Nicholas St B1
Northgate A2
Northgate St A2
Nun's Rd C1
Old Dee Bridge ✦ C2
Park St. B3
Police Station C1
Post Office . A2/B1/B2
Princess St A1
Queen St A3
Queen's Park Rd C3
Raymond St A1
Roodee, The (Chester Racecourse) C1
Roman Amphitheatre & Gardens B3
St Martin's Gate A1
St Martin's Way B1
St Oswalds Way A3
Stanley Palace B1
The Cross B2
The Groves B3
Town Hall. A2
Union St B3
Vicar's La. B3
Victoria Cr C3
Water Tower St A1
Watergate B1
Watergate St B2
White Friars B2
York St. A3

Chester

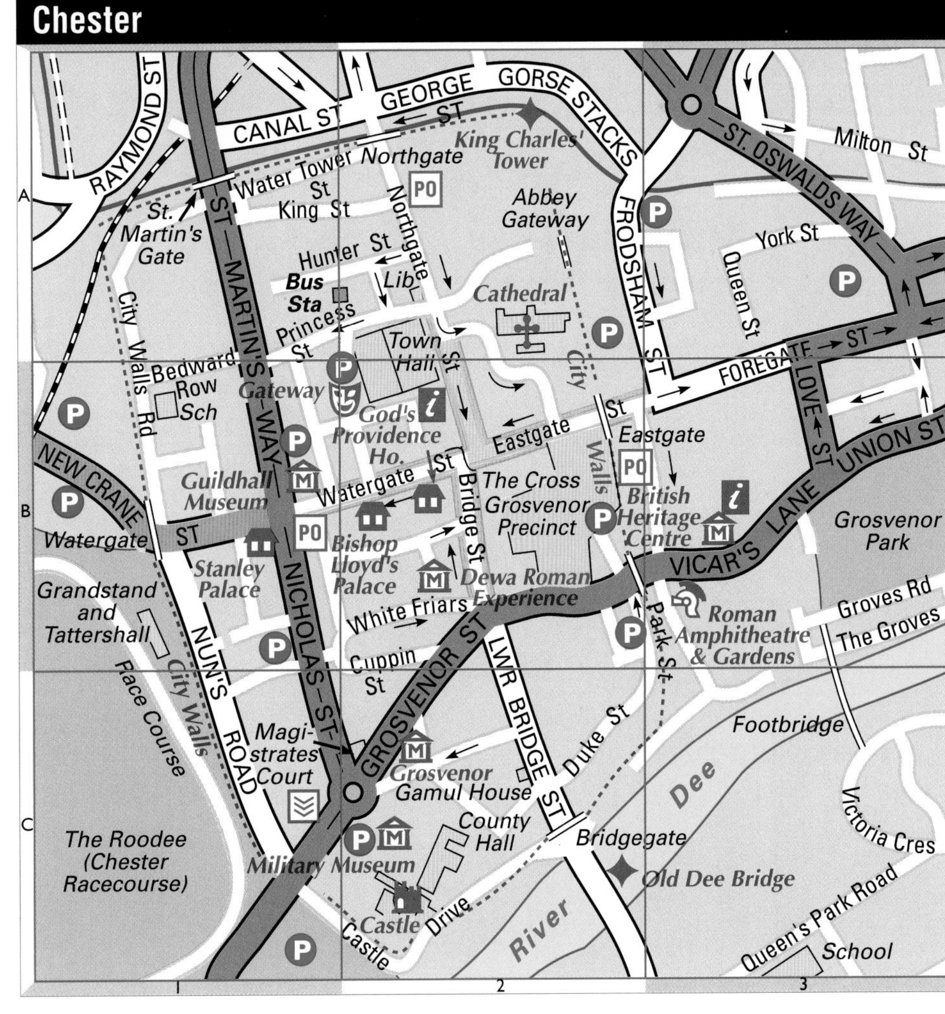

Coventry

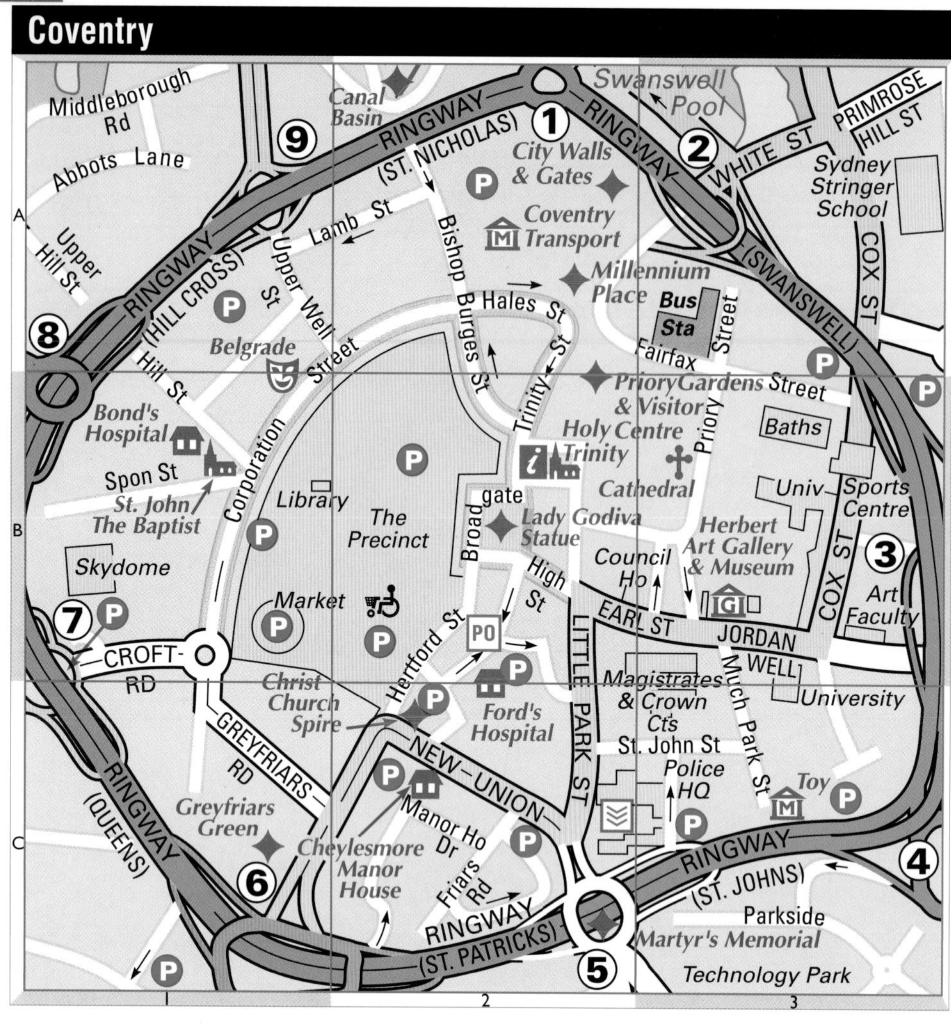

Coventry

Abbots La A1
Art Faculty B3
Baths B3
Belgrade A1
Bishop Burges St A2
Bond's Hospital . . . B1
Broadgate B2
Bus Station A3
Canal Basin ✦ A2
Cheylesmore Manor House C2
Christ Church Spire ✦ C2
City Walls & Gates ✦ . A2
Corporation St. B1
Council House B2
Coventry Cathedral ✝ . B3
Coventry Transport Museum A2
Cox St A3/B3
Croft Rd B1
Earl St B2
Fairfax St A3
Ford's Hospital C2
Friars Rd C2
Greyfriars Green ✦ . . . C1
Greyfriars Rd C1
Hales St A2
Herbert Art Gallery & Museum B3
Hertford St B2
High St B2
Hill St B1
Holy Trinity B2
Information Ctr B2
Jordan Well B3
Lady Godiva Statue ✦ B2
Lamb St A2
Library B1
Little Park St C2
Magistrates & Crown Courts B3
Manor House Dr C2
Market B1
Martyr's Memorial ✦ . . C2
Middleborough Rd . . . A1
Millennium Place ✦ . . . A2
Much Park St C3
New Union C2
Parkside C3
Police HQ C2
Post Office B2
Precinct, The B2
Primrose Hill St A3
Priory Gardens & Visitor Centre ✦ B2
Priory St B3
Ringway (Hill Cross) . . A1
Ringway (Queens) C1
Ringway (St Johns) . . . C3
Ringway (St Nicholas) . A2
Ringway (St Patricks) . C2
Ringway (Swanswell) . . A3
St John St C3
St John The Baptist B1
Skydome B1
Spon St B1
Sports Centre B3
Sydney Stringer School A3
Technology Park C3
Toy Museum C3
Trinity St B2
University B3
Upper Hill St A1
Upper Well St A1
White St A3

Derby

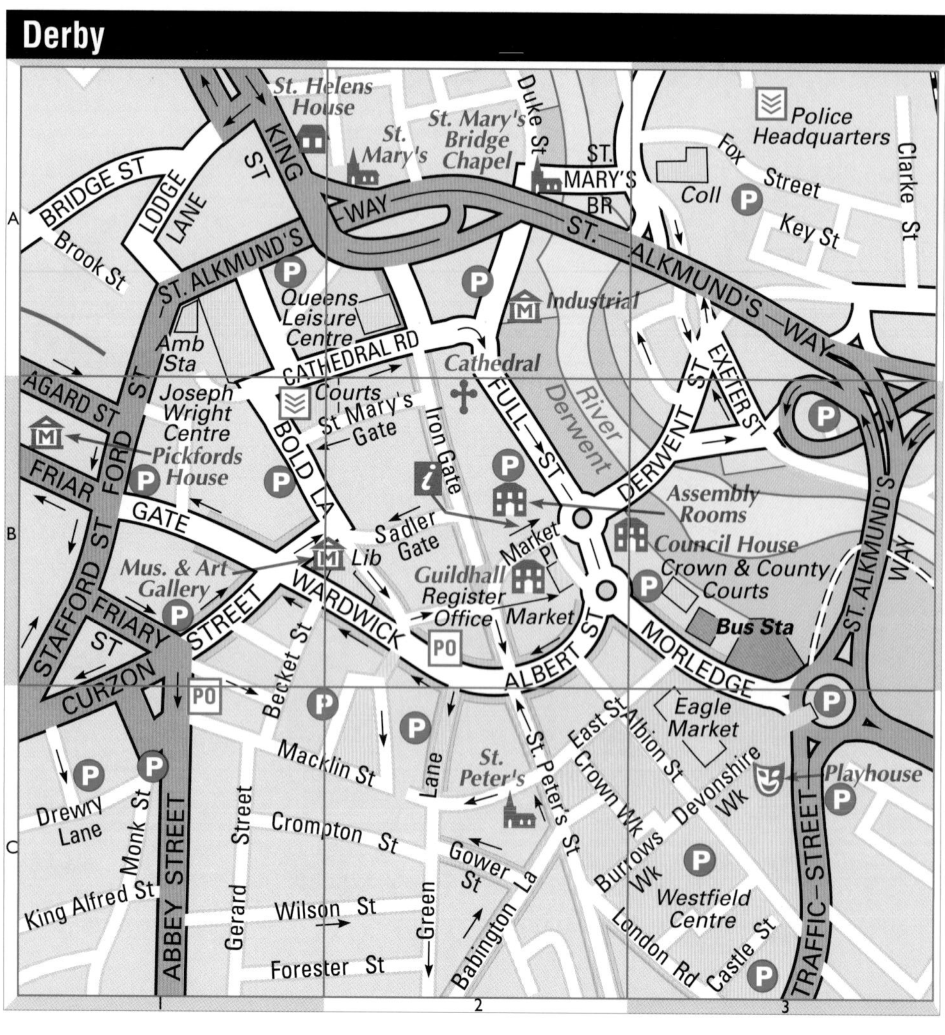

Derby

Abbey St C1
Agard St B1
Albert St B2
Albion St C3
Ambulance Station . . . A1
Assembly Rooms . . B2
Babington La C2
Becket St B1
Bold La B1
Bridge St A1
Brook St A1
Burrows Walk C2
Bus Station B3
Castle St C3
Cathedral ✝ B2
Cathedral Rd A2
Clarke St A3
Council House B3
Crompton St C1
Crown & County Courts B3
Crown Walk C2
Courts B1
Curzon St B1
Derwent St B3
Devonshire Walk C3
Drewry La C1
Duke St A2
Eagle Market C3
East St C2
Exeter St B3
Ford St B1
Forester St C1
Fox St A3
Friar Gate B1
Friary St B1
Full St B2
Gerard St C1
Gower St C2
Green La C2
Guildhall B2
Industrial A2
Information Ctr B2
Iron Gate B2
Joseph Wright Centre . A1
Key St A3
King Alfred St C1
King St A1
Library B2
Lodge La A1
London Rd C3
Macklin St C1
Market B2
Market Pl B2
Monk St C1
Morledge B3
Museum & Art Gallery B2
Pickfords House . . . B1
Playhouse C3
Police HQ A3
Police Station B1
Post Office B2/C1
Queens Leisure Centre A2
Register Office B2
Sadler Gate B2
St Alkmund's Way A1/A3/B3
St Helens House . . A1
St Mary's A2
St Mary's Bridge A2
St Mary's Bridge Chapel A2
St Mary's Gate B2
St Peter's C2
St Peter's St C2
Stafford St B1
Traffic St C3
Wardwick B2
Westfield Centre C3
Wilson St C1

Durham

Alexander Cr B1
Allergate B1
Bowling A2
Bus Station A1
Castle 🏰 B2
Castle Chare A2
Cathedral ✝ B2
Church St C3
Clay La C1
Claypath A3
County Hospital H . . . A1
Crossgate B1
Crossgate Peth B1
Durham Station ⇌ . . . A1
Durham School C1
Elvet Bridge B3
Elvet Court B3
Flass St A1
Framwelgate Bridge . . B2
Gala & Sacred Journey 🎭 A3
Grove St C1
Hallgarth St C3
Hatfield College B3
Hawthorn Terr B1
Heritage Centre 🏛 . . . B3
Information Ctr ℹ A3
John St B1
Kingsgate Bridge B3
Leazes Rd A2/A3
Library A3
Margery La B1
Millburngate A2
Millburngate Bridge . . . A2
Millburngate Centre . . . A2
Museum of Archaeology 🏛 B2
Nevilledale Terr B1
New Elvet B3
New Elvet Bridge B3
North Bailey B3
North Rd A2
Old Elvet B3
Passport Office A2
Pimlico C2
Police Station 🚓 B3
Post Office PO A2
Prebends Bridge C2
Prebends Walk C2
Prince Bishops Shopping Centre B3
Providence Row A3
Quarryheads La C2
Saddler St B3
St Nicholas' ⛪ A3
St Chad's College C3
St Cuthbert's Society . C2
St John's College C2
St Margaret's ⛪ B2
St Mary The Less ⛪ . . C2
St Oswald's ⛪ C3
Silver St B2
South Bailey C2
South St B2
Students' Recreational Centre C3
Sutton St A1
The Avenue B1
Town Hall A2
Treasury Museum 🏛 . . B2
University ✦ B2
University Arts Block . . B3
Walkergate Centre A3
Wharton Park A1

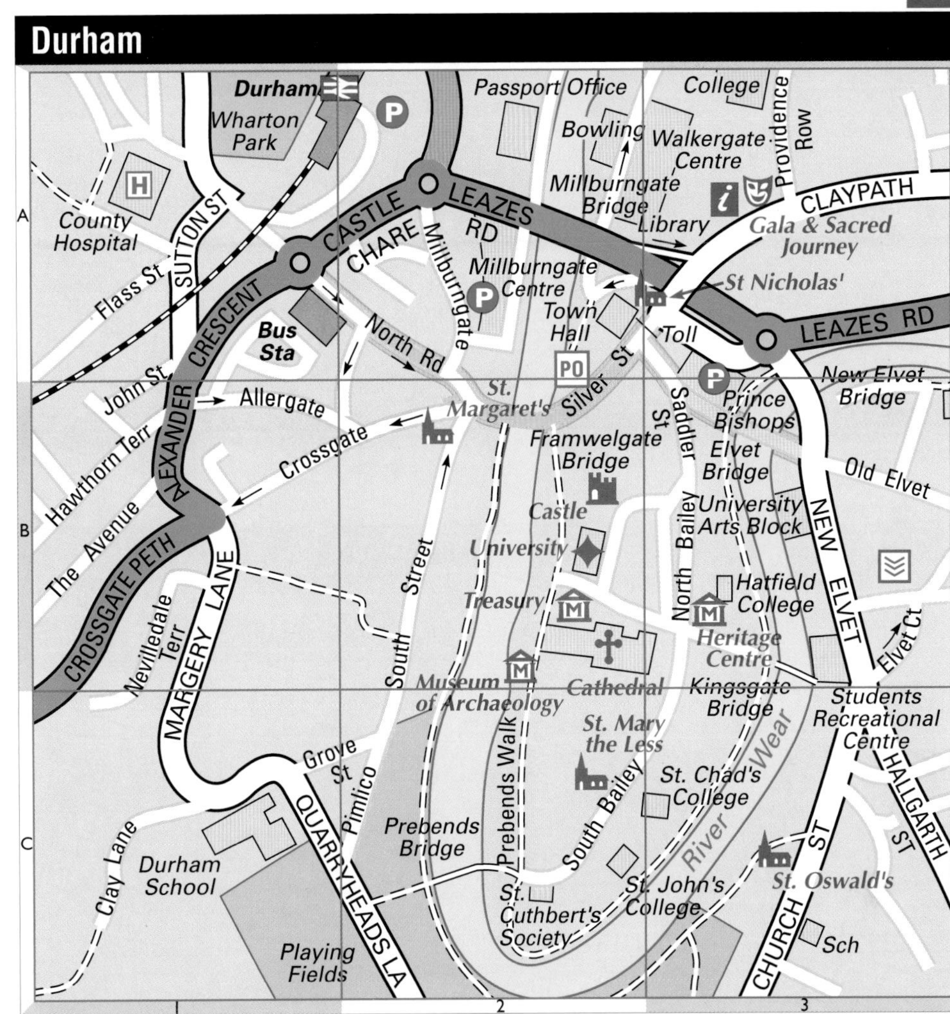

Exeter

Athelstan Rd B3
Bampfylde St A3
Barnfield Hill B3
Barnfield Rd B2/B3
Barnfield Theatre 🎭 . . . B2
Bear St C1
Bedford St B2
Belgrave Rd A3
Blackall Rd A2
Bull Meadow Rd C2
Bus & Coach Sta B3
Castle St B2
Cheeke St A3
Chute St A3
City Wall C2
Civic Centre B3
Clifton Rd A3/B3
Clock Tower A1
Commercial Rd C1
Coombe St C1
Crown Courts C2
Denmark Rd B3
Elmgrove Rd A1
Exeter Central Station ⇌ A1
Fore St C1
Friars Walk C2
Guildhall 🏛 B1
Guildhall Shopping Centre B1
Harlequins Shopping Centre B1
Heavitree Rd B3
High St B1/B2
HM Prison A1
Information Ctr ℹ B3
King William St A2
King St C1
Library B2
Longbrook St A2
Longbrook Terr A2
Magdalen Rd C3
Magdalen St C2
Magistrates & Crown Courts A1
Market C1
Market St C1
Mary Arches St B1
New North Rd A1/A2
North St B1
Northernhay St B1
Odeon 🎥 A3
Mol's Coffee House 🏛 B2
Oxford Rd A3
Paris St B2
Parr St A3
Paul St B1
Post Office PO A3/B2/C1/C3
Preston St C1
Princesshay Shopping Centre . . B2
Queen St A1
Radford Rd C3
Rougemont Castle 🏰 . A2
Rougemont House ✦ . A2
Royal Albert Memorial 🏛 B1
St Leonard's Rd C3
St Mary Steps ⛪ C1
St Nicholas Priory 🏛 . . C1
St Peter's Cathedral ✝ B2
Sidwell St A2/A3
Smythen St C1
South St C1
Southernhay East B2
Southernhay West . . . B2
Spacex 🏛 C1
Spicer Rd B3
Summerland St A3
Swimming Pool B3
Western Way . . A3/C1/C3
Wonford Rd C3
York Rd A2

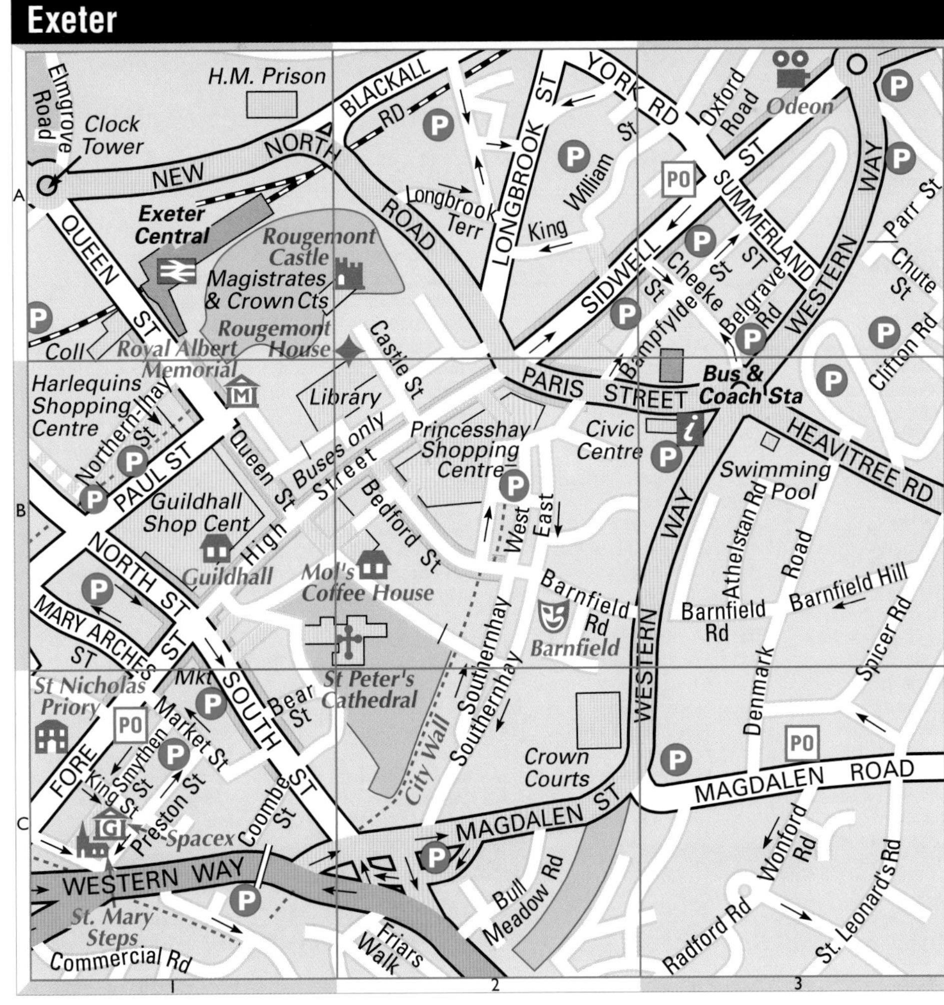

Edinburgh

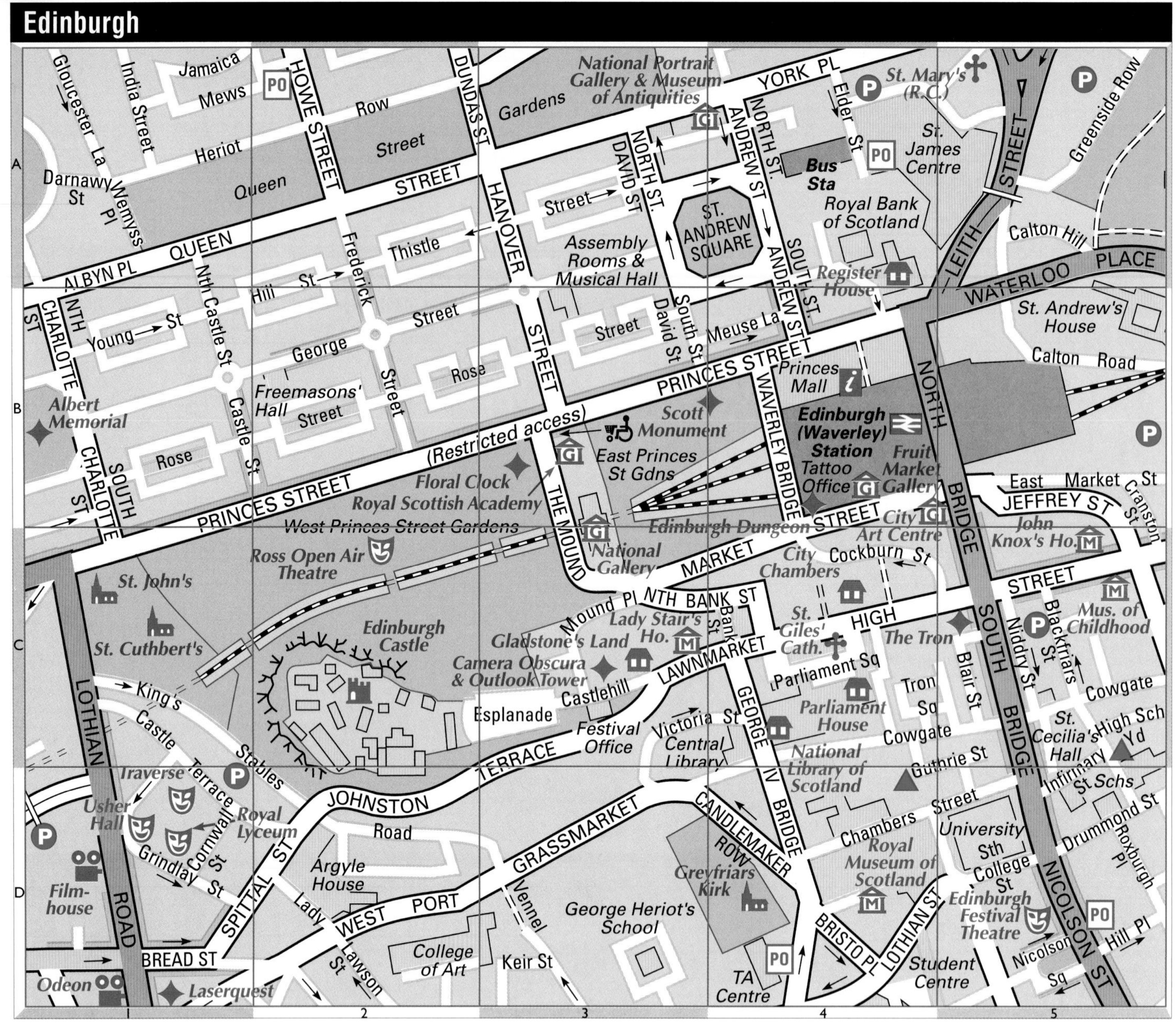

Edinburgh

Albert Memorial ✦ . . . B1
Albyn Pl A1
Argyle House D2
Assembly Rooms & Musical Hall A3
Bank St C4
Blackfriars St C5
Blair St C5
Bread St D1
Bristo Pl D4
Bus Station A4
Calton Hill A5
Calton Rd B5
Camera Obscura & Outlook Tower ✦ . . . C3
Candlemaker Row D4
Castle St B1
Castle Terr C1
Castlehill C3
Central Library C4
Chambers St D4
City Art Centre 🏛 B4
City Chambers 🏛 C4
Cockburn St C4
College of Art D2
Cornwall St D1
Cowgate C4/C5
Cranston St B5
Darnawy St A1
Drummond St D5
Dundas St A2
East Market St B5
East Princes St Gdns . B3
Edinburgh (Waverley) ⇌ B4
Edinburgh Castle 🏰 . . C2
Edinburgh Dungeon ✦ B4
Edinburgh Festival Theatre 🎭 D5
Elder St A4
Esplanade C3
Festival Office C3
Filmhouse 🎥 D1
Floral Clock ✦ B3
Frederick St A2
Freemasons' Hall B2
Fruit Market 🏛 B4
George Heriot's School D3
George IV Bridge C4
George St B2
Gladstone's Land 🏛 . . C3
Gloucester La A1
Grassmarket D3
Greenside Row A5
Greyfriars Kirk ⛪ D4
Grindlay St D1
Guthrie St C4
Hanover St A3
Heriot Row A1/A2
High School Yard C5
High St C4/C5
Hill Pl D5
Hill St B2
Howe St A2
India St A1
Infirmary St D5
Information Ctr ℹ B4
Jamaica Mews A1
Jeffrey St B5
John Knox's House 🏛 C5
Johnston Terr D2
Keir St D3
King's Stables Rd . C1/D2
Lady Lawson St D2
Lady Stair's House 🏛 . C3
Laserquest ✦ D1
Lawnmarket C3
Leith St A5
Lothian Rd C1
Lothian St D4
Market St C4
Meuse La B4
Mound Pl C3
Museum of Childhood 🏛 C5
National Gallery 🏛 . . . C3
National Library of Scotland 🏛 C4
National Portrait Gallery & Museum of Antiquities 🏛 A3
Nicolson Sq D5
Nicolson St D5
Niddry St C5
North Bridge B4
North Bank St C3
North Castle St B1
North Charlotte St B1
North St Andrew St . . . A4
North St David St A3
Odeon 🎥 D1
Parliament House 🏛 . . . C4
Parliament Sq C4
Post Office PO A2/A4/D4/D5
Princes Mall B4
Princes St B2/B3
Queen St A2
Queen Street Gdns . . . A2
Register House 🏛 . . . A4
Rose St B1/B2/B3
Ross Open Air Theatre 🎭 C2
Roxburgh Pl D5
Royal Bank of Scotland A4
Royal Lyceum 🎭 D1
Royal Museum of Scotland 🏛 D4
Royal Scottish Academy 🏛 B3
St Andrew Sq A4
St Andrew's House . . . B5
St Cecilia's Hall C5
St Cuthbert's ⛪ C1
St Giles' ✝ C4
St James Centre A4
St John's ⛪ C1
St Mary's ✝ (R.C.) A5
Scott Monument ✦ . . . B4
South Bridge C5
South Charlotte St B1
South College St D5
South St Andrew St . . . A4
South St David St B3
Spittal St D1
Student Centre D5
TA Centre D4
Tattoo Office B4
The Mound B3
Thistle St A2/A3
Traverse Theatre 🎭 . . . D1
Tron Sq C4
Tron, The ✦ C5
University D5
Usher Hall 🎭 D1
Vennel D3
Victoria St C3
Waterloo Pl A5
Waverley Bridge B4
Wemyss Pl A1
West Port D2
West Princes Street Gdns B2
York Pl A4
Young St B1
Youth Hostel ▲ . . . C5/D4

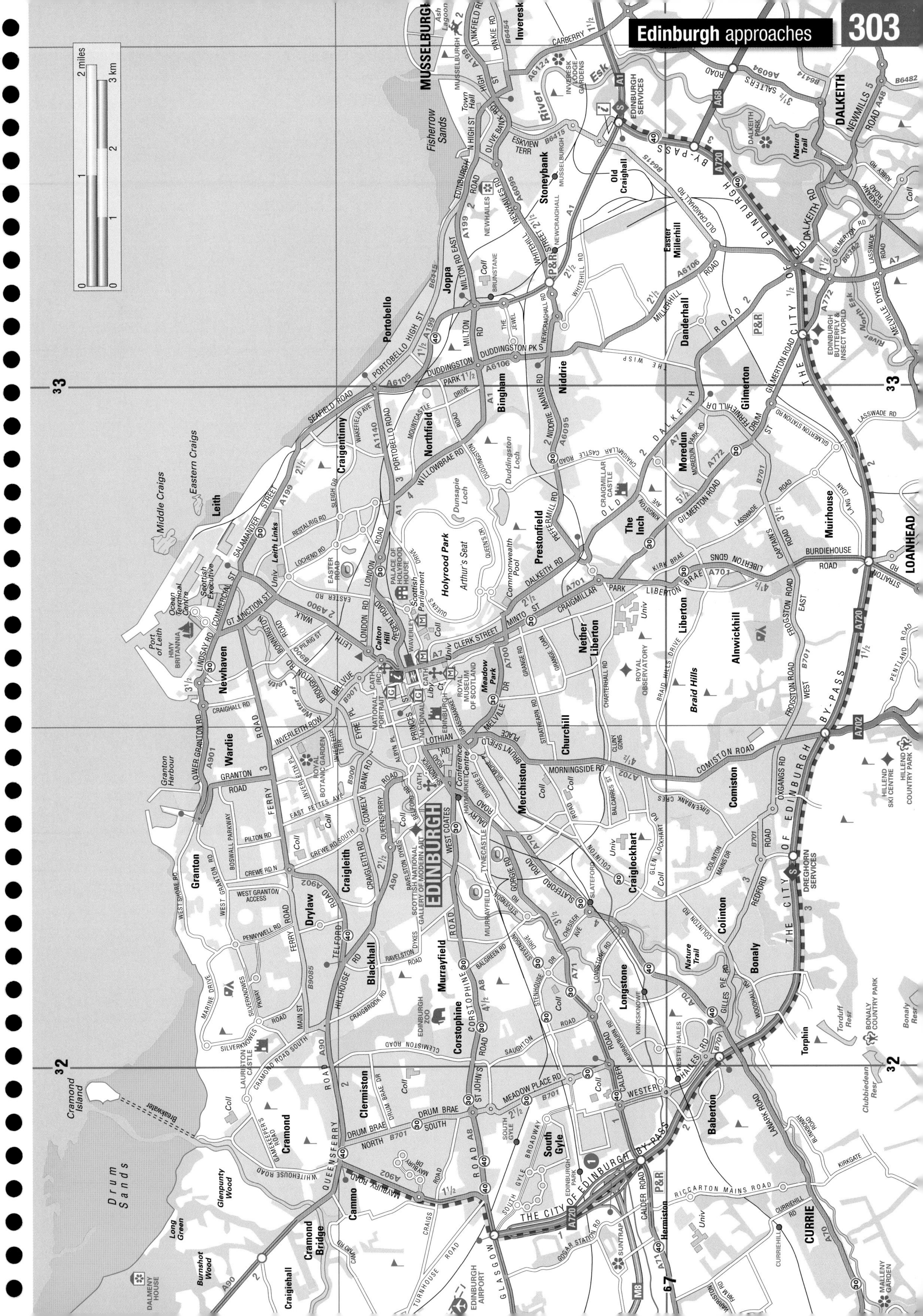

Edinburgh approaches
303
2 miles
3 km
EDINBURGH
MUSSELBURGH
DALKEITH
LOANHEAD
CURRIE
Portobello
Joppa
Leith
Newhaven
Granton
Wardie
Craigentinny
Northfield
Bingham
Niddrie
Stoneybank
Old Craighall
Eastern Millerhill
Danderhall
Gilmerton
Moredun
The Inch
Prestonfield
Nether Liberton
Liberton
Alnwickhill
Muirhouse
Braid Hills
Churchill
Merchiston
Comiston
Craiglockhart
Colinton
Bonaly
Torphin
Longstone
Baberton
Murrayfield
Blackhall
Craigleith
Drylaw
Corstorphine
Clermiston
Cramond
Cammo
Cramond Bridge
Craigiehall
South Gyle
Hermiston
Holyrood Park
Arthur's Seat
Duddingston Loch
Dunsapie Loch
Meadow Park
Royal Observatory
Edinburgh Zoo
Edinburgh Airport
Dalmeny House
Cramond Island
Drum Sands
Fisherrow Sands
Granton Harbour
Port of Leith
Middle Craigs
Eastern Craigs
Glenpunty Wood
Burnshot Wood
Long Green
Hillend Country Park
Bonaly Country Park
Edinburgh Butterfly & Insect World
Dreghorn Services
Edinburgh Services
THE CITY OF EDINBURGH BY-PASS

Glasgow

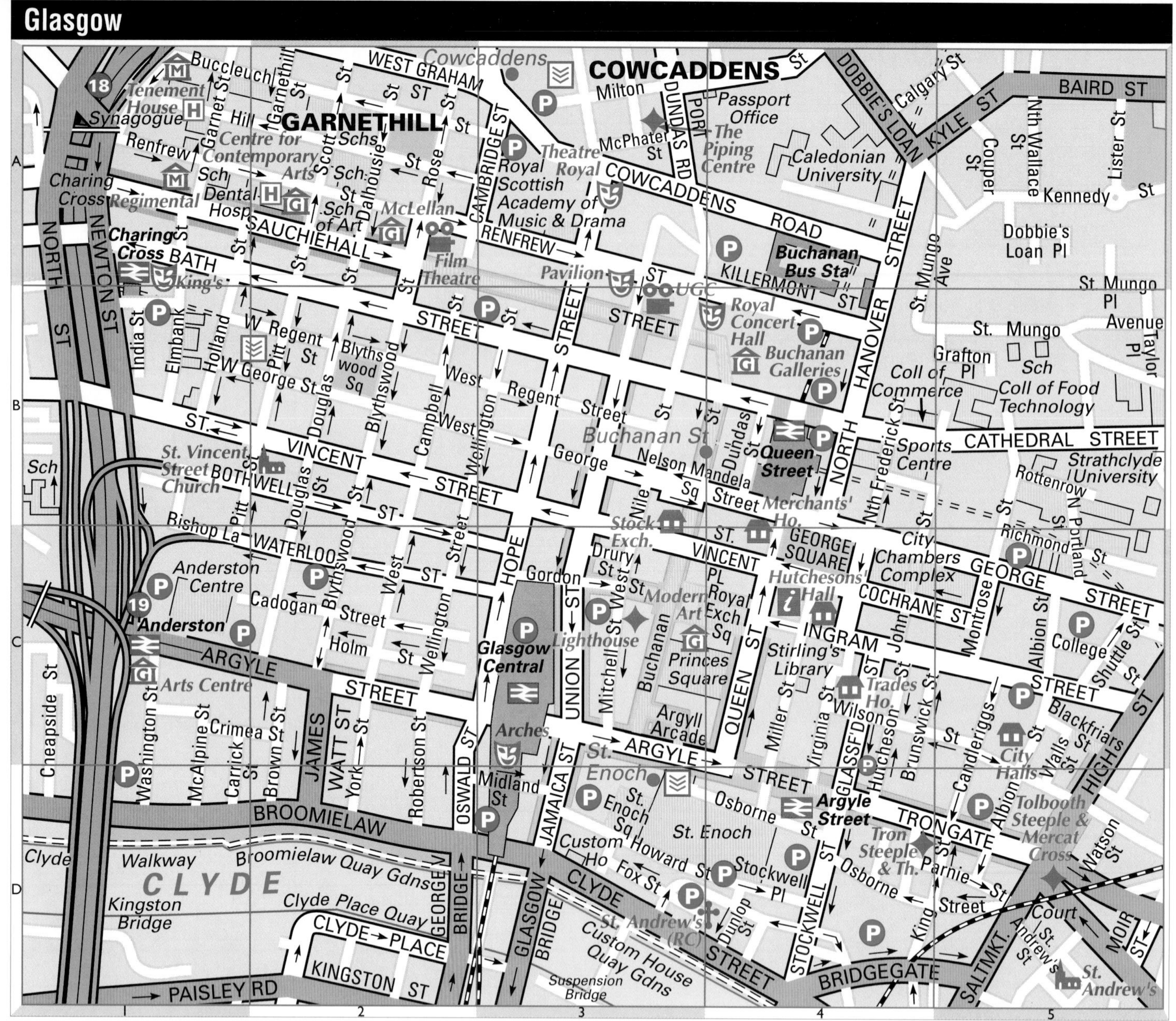

Glasgow

Albion St . . . C5
Anderston Centre . . . C1
Anderston Station ≋ . . . C1
Arches . . . C3
Argyle St . . . C1/C2/C3
Argyle Street Station ≋ . . . D4
Argyll Arcade . . . C3
Arts Centre . . . C1
Baird St . . . A5
Bath St . . . A1/B2
Bishop La . . . C1
Blackfriars St . . . C5
Blythswood Sq . . . B2
Blythswood St . . . B2
Bothwell St . . . B2
Bridgegate . . . D4
Broomielaw . . . D2
Broomielaw Quay Gdns . . . D2
Brown St . . . C2
Brunswick St . . . C4
Buccleuch St . . . A2
Buchanan Bus Station . . . A4
Buchanan Galleries . . . B4
Buchanan St . . . C3
Buchanan St (Metro Station) . . . B3
Cadogan St . . . C2
Caledonian University . . . A4
Calgary St . . . A4
Cambridge St . . . A3
Candleriggs . . . C5
Carrick St . . . C1
Cathedral St . . . B5
Centre for Contemporary Arts . . . A2
Charing Cross Station ≋ . . . A1
Cheapside St . . . C1
City Chambers Complex . . . C4
City Halls . . . C5
Clyde Pl . . . D2
Clyde Place Quay . . . D2
Clyde St . . . D3
Clyde Walkway . . . D1
Cochrane St . . . C4
College of Commerce . . . B4
College of Food Technology . . . B5
College St . . . C5
Couper St . . . A5
Cowcaddens (Metro Station) . . . A3
Cowcaddens Rd . . . A3
Crimea St . . . C1
Custom House . . . D3
Custom House Quay Gdns . . . D3
Dalhousie St . . . A2
Dental Hospital . . . A2
Dobbie's Loan . . . A4
Dobbie's Loan Pl . . . A5
Douglas St . . . B2
Drury St . . . C3
Dundas St . . . B4
Dunlop St . . . D4
Elmbank St . . . B1
Film Theatre . . . A2
Fox St . . . D3
Garnet St . . . A1
Garnethill St . . . A2
George Sq . . . C4
George St . . . C5
George V Bridge . . . D2
Glasgow Bridge . . . D3
Glasgow Central Station ≋ . . . C3
Glassford St . . . C4
Gordon St . . . C3
Grafton Pl . . . B5
High St . . . C5
Hill St . . . A2
Holland St . . . B1
Holm St . . . C2
Hope St . . . B3
Howard St . . . D3
Hutcheson St . . . C4
Hutchesons' Hall . . . C4
India St . . . B1
Information Ctr . . . C4
Ingram St . . . C4/C5
Jamaica St . . . D3
James Watt St . . . C2
John St . . . C4
Kennedy St . . . A5
Killermont St . . . B4
King St . . . D4
King's . . . A1
Kingston Bridge . . . D1
Kingston St . . . D2
Kyle St . . . A5
Lighthouse ✦ . . . C3
Lister St . . . A5
McAlpine St . . . C1
McLellan Gallery . . . A2
McPhater St . . . A3
Merchants' House . . . C4
Midland St . . . D3
Miller St . . . C4
Milton St . . . A3
Mitchell St West . . . C3
Modern Art Gallery . . . C3
Moir St . . . D5
Montrose St . . . C5
Nelson Mandela Sq . . . B3
Newton St . . . A1
Nile St . . . B3
North Frederick St . . . B4
North Hanover St . . . B4
North Portland St . . . C5
North St . . . A1
North Wallace St . . . A5
Osborne St . . . D4/D5
Oswald St . . . D2
Paisley Rd . . . D1
Parnie St . . . D5
Passport Office . . . A4
Pavilion Theatre . . . A3
Piping Centre, The ✦ . . . A3
Pitt St . . . B2
Police Station . . . A3/B2/D3
Port Dundas Rd . . . A3
Princes Square Shopping Centre . . . C4
Queen St . . . C4
Queen Street Station ≋ . . . B4
Regimental Museum . . . A1
Renfrew St . . . A1/A3
Richmond St . . . C5
Robertson St . . . D2
Rose St . . . A2
Rottenrow . . . B5
Royal Concert Hall . . . B4
Royal Exchange Sq . . . C4
Royal Scottish Academy of Music & Drama . . . A3
St Andrew's (R.C.) ✝ . . . D4
St Andrew's . . . D5
St Andrew's St . . . D5
St Enoch (Metro Station) . . . D3
St Enoch Shopping Centre . . . D3
St Enoch Sq . . . D3
St Mungo Ave . . . B5
St Mungo Pl . . . A5
St Vincent Pl . . . C4
St Vincent St . . . B2
St Vincent Street Church . . . B2
Saltmarket . . . D5
Sauchiehall St . . . A2/B3
School of Art . . . A2
Scott St . . . A2
Shuttle St . . . C5
Sports Centre . . . B4
Stirling's Library . . . C4
Stock Exchange . . . B3
Stockwell Pl . . . D4
Stockwell St . . . D4
Strathclyde University . . . B5
Synagogue . . . A1
Taylor Pl . . . B5
Tenement House . . . A1
Theatre Royal . . . A3
Tolbooth Steeple & Mercat Cross ✦ . . . D5
Trades House . . . C4
Tron Steeple & Theatre ✦ . . . D4
Trongate . . . D5
UGC . . . B3
Union St . . . C3
Virginia St . . . C4
Walls St . . . C5
Washington St . . . C1
Waterloo St . . . C2
Watson St . . . D5
Wellington St . . . B3/C2
West Campbell St . . . B2/C2
West George St . . . B2/B3
West Graham St . . . A2
West Regent St . . . B2/B3
Wilson St . . . C4
York St . . . C2

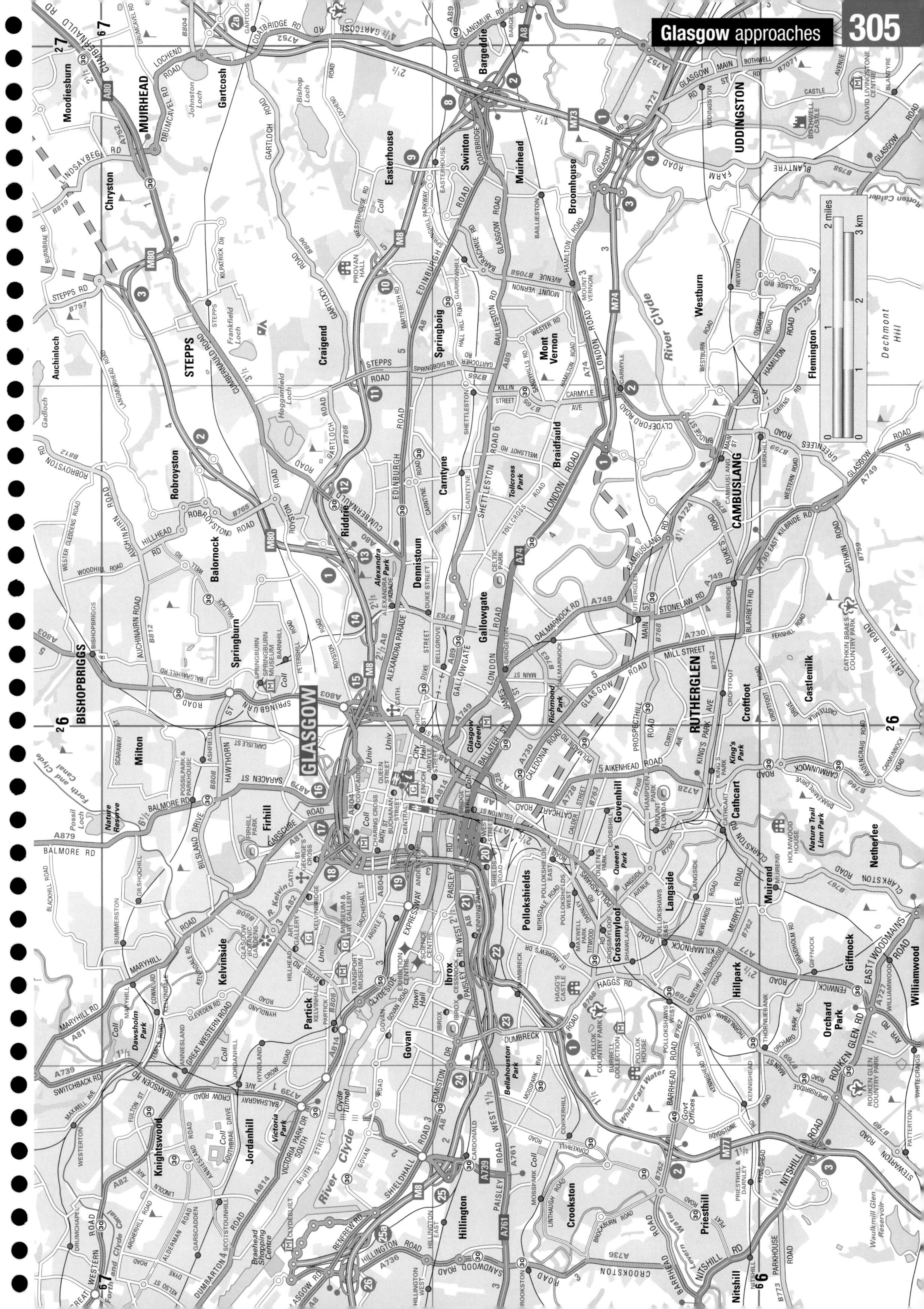
GLASGOW
BISHOPBRIGGS
MUIRHEAD
STEPPS
UDDINGSTON
CAMBUSLANG
RUTHERGLEN
Moodiesburn
Gartcosh
Chryston
Auchinloch
Robroyston
Balornock
Springburn
Milton
Firhill
Kelvinside
Partick
Knightswood
Jordanhill
Govan
Ibrox
Hillington
Crookston
Priesthill
Nitshill
Pollokshields
Crossmyloof
Govanhill
Langside
Cathcart
Muirend
Netherlee
Giffnock
Williamwood
Orchard Park
Hillpark
Castlemilk
Croftfoot
Flemington
Westburn
Broomhouse
Mont Vernon
Braidfauld
Carntyne
Springboig
Easterhouse
Swinton
Bargeddie
Craigend
Riddrie
Dennistoun
Gallowgate
River Clyde
Dechmont Hill

Gloucester

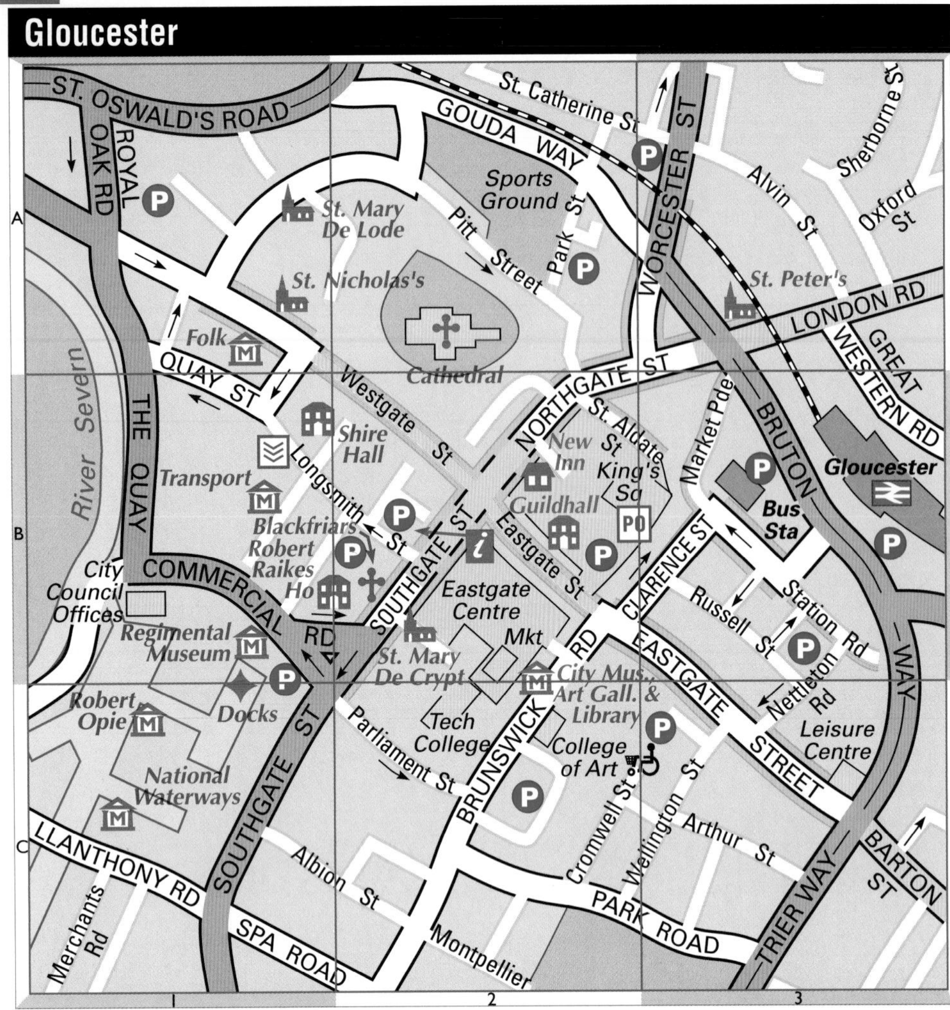

Gloucester

Albion St C1/C2
Alvin St A3
Arthur St C3
Barton St. C3
Blackfriars B2
Brunswick Rd C2
Bruton Way B3
Bus Station B3
City Council Offices. . . B1
City Mus., Art Gall. & Library C2
Clarence St B3
College of Art C2
Commercial Rd B1
Cromwell St. C2
Docks C1
Eastgate Centre. B2
Eastgate St B2/C3
Folk Museum A1
Gloucester Cathedral A2
Gloucester Station B3
Gouda Way A2
Great Western Rd B3
Guildhall B2
Information Ctr B2
King's Sq. B2
Leisure Centre C3
Llanthony Rd. C1
London Rd. A3
Longsmith St. B1
Market. B2
Market Pde B3
Merchants Rd C1
Montpellier. C2
National Waterways C1
Nettleton Rd C3
New Inn B2
Northgate St B2
Oxford St. A3
Park Rd C2/C3
Park St. A2
Parliament St. C2
Pitt St. A2
Police Station B1
Post Office B2
Quay St B1
Regimental B1
Robert Opie C1
Robert Raikes House B2
Royal Oak Rd A1
Russell St B3
St Aldate St B2
St Catherine St A2
St Mary De Crypt . . B2
St Mary De Lode . . . A1
St Nicholas's A1
St Oswald's Rd A1
St Peter's A3
Sherborne St. A3
Shire Hall B1
Southgate St B2/C1
Spa Rd C1
Sports Ground. A2
Station Rd B3
Technical College C2
Transport B1
Trier Way C3
The Quay. B1
Wellington St C3
Westgate St. B2
Worcester St A3

Leicester

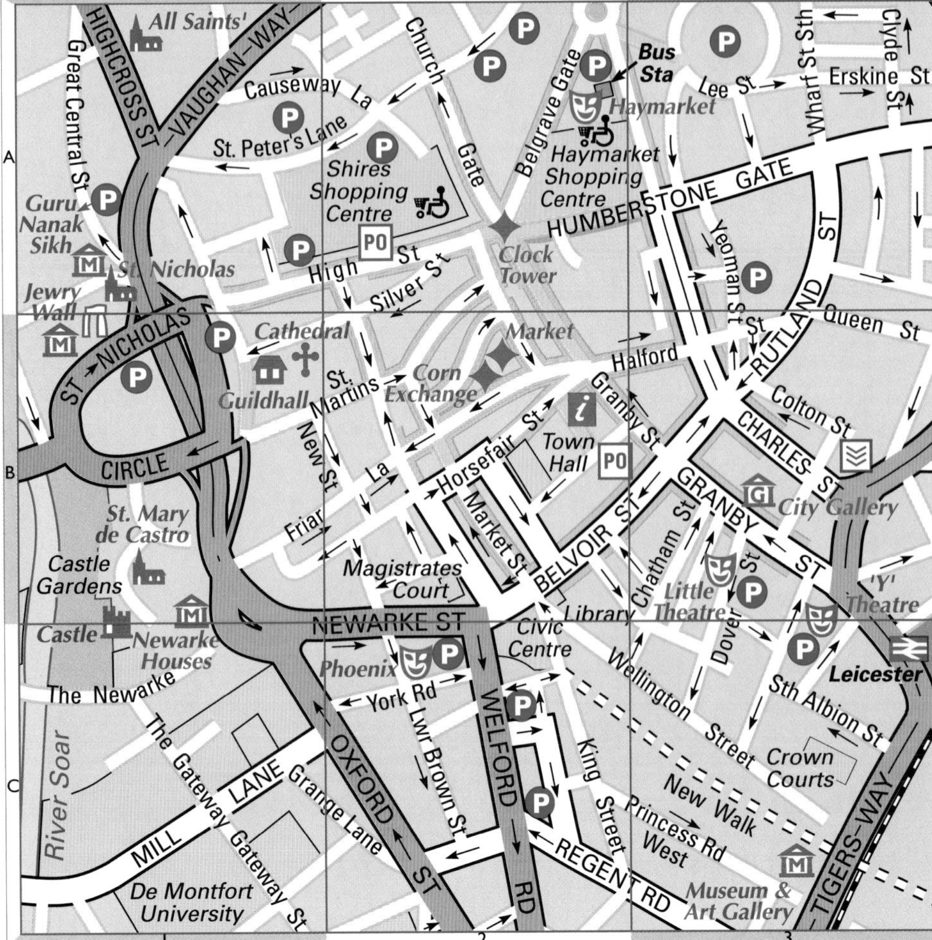

Leicester

All Saints' A1
Belgrave Gate A2
Belvoir St. B2
Bus Station A2
Castle C1
Castle Gardens B1
Cathedral B1
Causeway La. A1
Charles St B3
Chatham St B3
Church Gate A2
City Gallery B3
Civic Centre. C2
Clock Tower A2
Clyde St. A3
Colton St B3
Corn Exchange B2
Crown Courts C3
De Montfort University C1
Dover St C3
Erskine St A3
Friar La B1
Gateway St C1
Granby St B3
Grange La C2
Great Central St A1
Guildhall B1
Guru Nanak Sikh . . A1
Halford St B3
Haymarket A2
Haymarket Shopping Centre A2
High St A2
Highcross St A1
Horsefair St B2
Humberstone Gate A2/A3
Information Ctr B2
Jewry Wall B1
King St. C2
Lee St A3
Leicester Station . . C3
Library B2
Little Theatre B3
Lower Brown St. C2
Magistrates Court B2
Market B2
Market St. B2
Mill La C1
Museum & Art Gallery C3
New St. B2
New Walk C3
Newarke Houses . . . B1
Newarke St B2
Oxford St. C2
Phoenix C2
Police Station B3
Post Office A2/B2
Princess Rd West C3
Queen St B3
Regent Rd C2/C3
Rutland St B3
St Martins B2
St Mary de Castro . . B1
St Nicholas A1
St Nicholas Circle B1
St Peter's La A1
Shires Shopping Ctr . . A2
Silver St A2
South Albion St C3
The Gateway C1
The Newarke C1
Tigers Way. C3
Town Hall. B2
Vaughan Way. A1
Welford Rd. C2
Wellington St C3
Wharf St South A3
'Y' Theatre B3
Yeoman St. A3
York Rd C2

Leeds

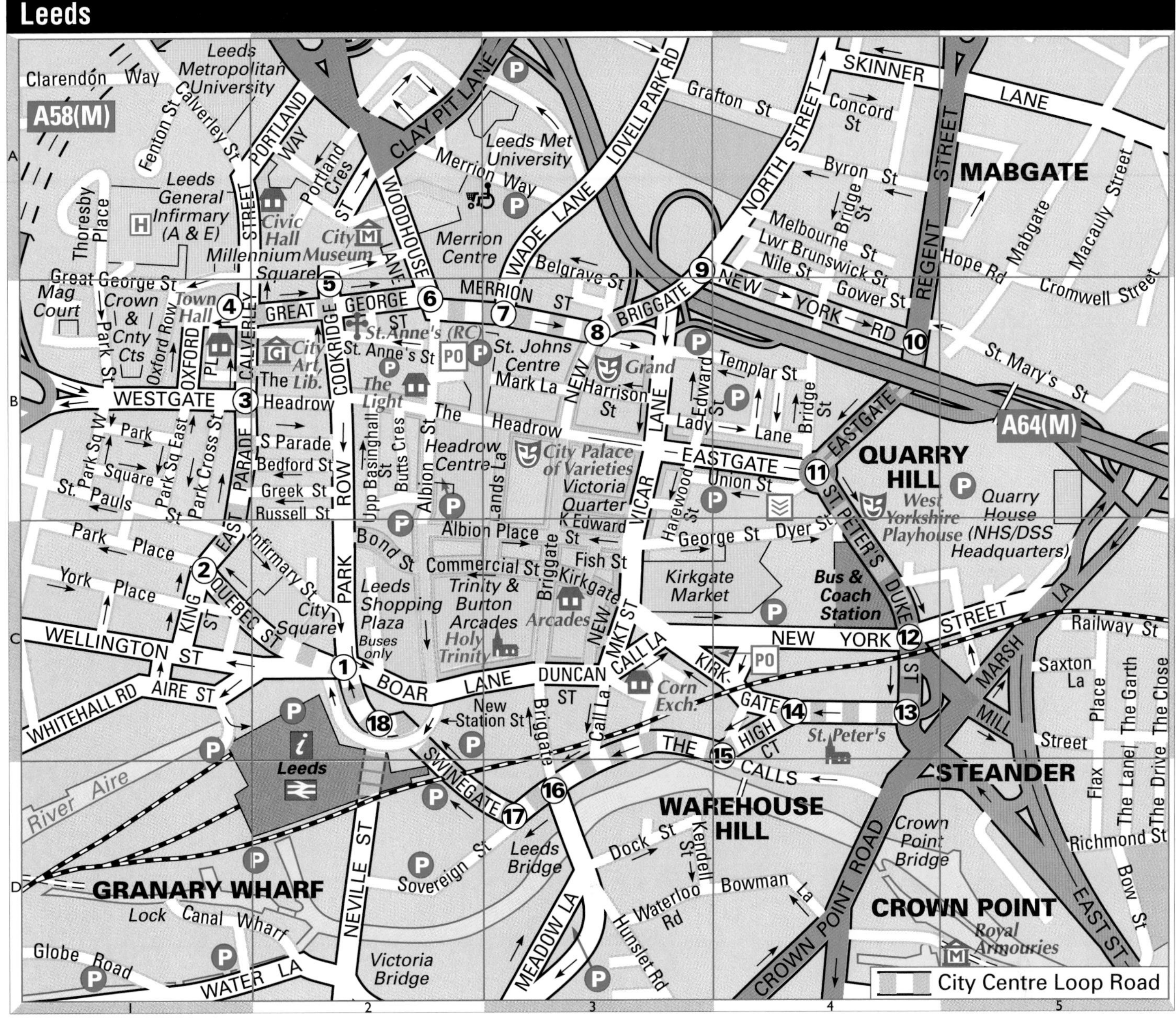

Leeds

Aire St C1
Albion Place C2
Albion St B2
Arcades C3
Bedford St. B2
Belgrave St A3
Boar La C2
Bond St. C2
Bow St. D5
Bowman La. D4
Bridge St A4/B4
Briggate. C3
Bus & Coach Station. . C4
Butts Cres B2
Byron St A4
Call La. C3
Calverley St A1/B1
Canal Wharf. D1
City Art Gallery & Library B2
City Museum A2
City Palace of Varieties B3
City Sq. C2
Civic Hall A2
Clarendon Way A1
Clay Pit La. A2
Commercial St. C2
Concord St A4
Cookridge St. B2
Corn Exchange . . . C3
Cromwell St. B5
Crown & County Courts B1
Crown Point Bridge. . . D4
Crown Point Rd. D4
Dock St D3
Duke St C4
Duncan St C3
Dyer St C4
East Parade. B1
East St. D5
Eastgate B4
Edward St B3
Fenton St. A1
Fish St C3
Flax Place C5
George St C3
Globe Rd. D1
Gower St B4
Grafton St A4
Grand Theatre B3
Great George St . . B1/B2
Greek St B2
Harewood St B3
Harrison St B3
Headrow Centre B2
High Court. C4
Holy Trinity C3
Hope Rd A5
Hunslet Rd. D3
Infirmary St C2
Information Ctr C2
King Edward St C3
Kendell St D3
King St. C1
Kirkgate C3/C4
Kirkgate Market. C3
Lady La B3/B4
Lands La B3
Leeds Bridge. D3
Leeds General Infirmary (A&E) . . . A1
Leeds Metropolitan University A1/A3
Leeds Shopping Plaza C2
Leeds Station D2
Light, The B2
Lovell Park Rd. A3
Lower Brunswick St . . A4
Mabgate A5
Macauly St A5
Magistrates Court B1
Mark La. B3
Marsh La. C5
Meadow La D3
Melbourne St. A4
Merrion Centre A2
Merrion St B3
Merrion Way A2
Mill St C5
Millennium Sq A2
Neville St D2
New Briggate. B3
New Market St C3
New Station St C2
New York Rd B4
New York St. C4
Nile St A4
North St. A4
Oxford Place B1
Oxford Row B1
Park Cross St B1
Park Place. C1
Park Row. C2
Park Sq B1
Park Sq East B1
Park Sq West. B1
Park St. B1
Police Station B4
Portland Cr A2
Portland Way. A2
Post Office B2/C4
Quarry House (NHS/DSS Headquarters) B5
Quebec St C1
Railway St C5
Regent St A4
Richmond St D5
Royal Armouries Museum D5
Russell St B2
St Anne's Cathedral (RC) B2
St Anne's St. B2
St Johns Centre B3
St Mary's St. B5
St Pauls St. B1
St Peter's. B4
St Peter's C4
Saxton La C5
Skinner La. A4/A5
South Parade B2
Sovereign St D2
Swinegate D2
Templar St B4
The Calls D4
The Close C5
The Drive. D5
The Garth C5
The Headrow. B2/B3
The Lane D5
Thoresby Place A1
Town Hall B1
Trinity & Burton Arcades. C2
Union St B4
Upper Basinghall St . . B2
Vicar La B3
Victoria Bridge. D2
Victoria Quarter B3
Wade La A3
Water La D1
Waterloo Rd D3
Wellington St C1
West Yorkshire Playhouse B4
Westgate B1
Whitehall Rd C1
Woodhouse La A2
York Place C1

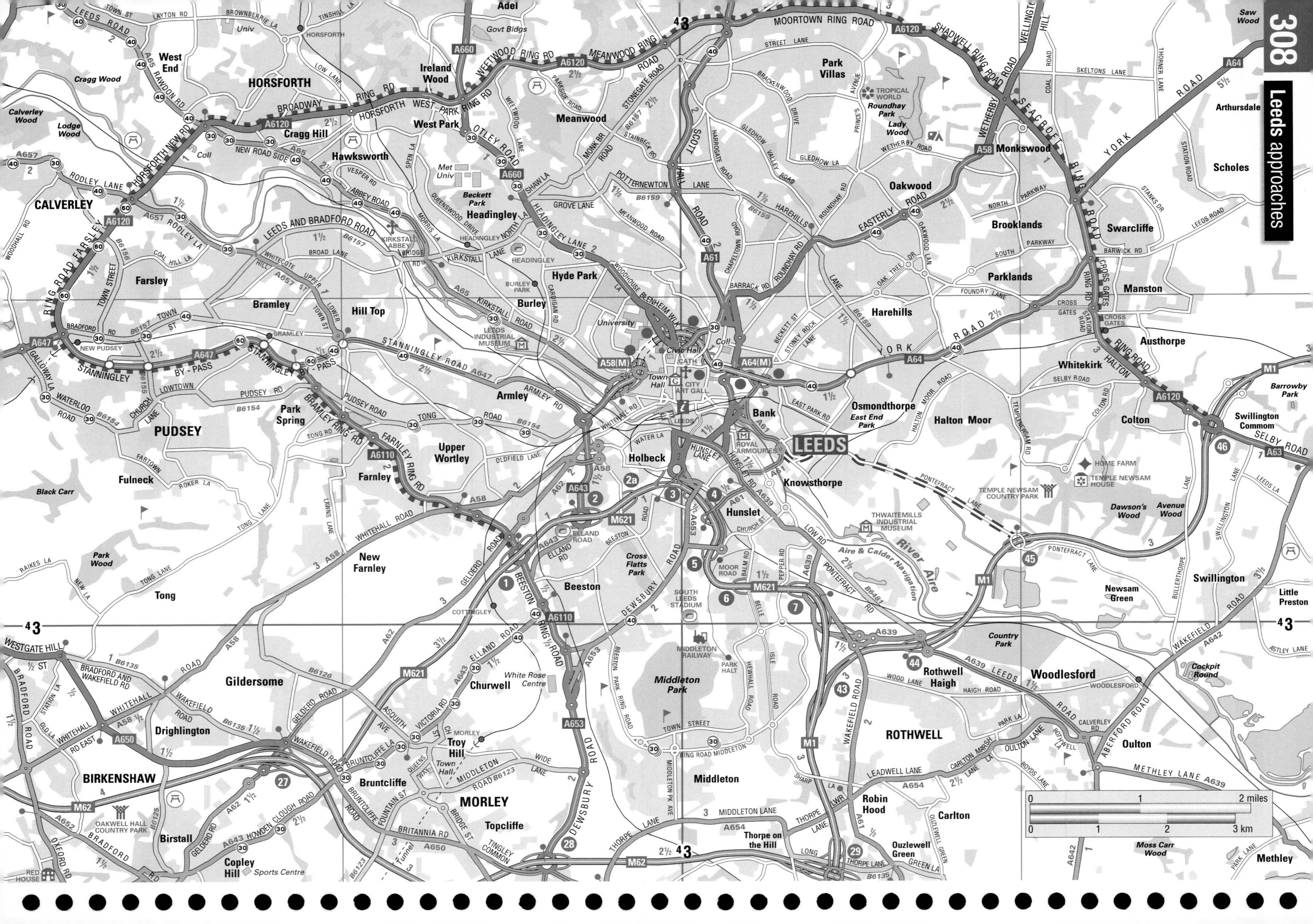
LEEDS
Adel
Govt Bldgs
Saw Wood
Arthursdale
Scholes
West End
HORSFORTH
Ireland Wood
Park Villas
TROPICAL WORLD
Roundhay Park
Lady Wood
Monkswood
Cragg Wood
Calverley Wood
Lodge Wood
Cragg Hill
West Park
Meanwood
Hawksworth
Met Univ
Beckett Park
Headingley
Oakwood
Brooklands
Swarcliffe
CALVERLEY
Farsley
Bramley
Hill Top
Hyde Park
Burley
University
Parklands
Manston
Harehills
Austhorpe
Whitekirk
LEEDS INDUSTRIAL MUSEUM
Civic Hall
Town Hall
CITY ART GALL
Armley
Osmondthorpe
East End Park
Halton Moor
Colton
Barrowby Park
Swillington Common
Park Spring
PUDSEY
Bank
ROYAL ARMOURIES
Upper Wortley
Holbeck
Knowsthorpe
HOME FARM
TEMPLE NEWSAM HOUSE
TEMPLE NEWSAM COUNTRY PARK
Fulneck
Black Carr
Farnley
Hunslet
THWAITEMILLS INDUSTRIAL MUSEUM
Dawson's Wood
Avenue Wood
River Aire
Aire & Calder Navigation
New Farnley
Cross Flatts Park
Park Wood
Tong
Beeston
SOUTH LEEDS STADIUM
Newsam Green
Swillington
Little Preston
Country Park
Gildersome
Churwell
White Rose Centre
MIDDLETON RAILWAY
PARK HALT
Middleton Park
Rothwell Haigh
Woodlesford
Cockpit Round
Drighlington
Troy Hill
ROTHWELL
Oulton
BIRKENSHAW
Town Hall
Bruntcliffe
MORLEY
Middleton
OAKWELL HALL COUNTRY PARK
Birstall
Topcliffe
Tingley Common
Robin Hood
Carlton
Thorpe on the Hill
Oozlewell Green
Moss Carr Wood
Methley
Copley Hill
Sports Centre
RED HOUSE
0 1 2 miles
0 1 2 3 km
MOORTOWN RING ROAD
SHADWELL RING ROAD
WETWOOD RING RD
MEANWOOD RING ROAD
HORSFORTH WEST PARK RING RD
RING ROAD FARSLEY
STANNINGLEY BY-PASS
BRAMLEY RING RD
FARNLEY RING RD
BEESTON RING ROAD
SEACROFT RING ROAD
YORK ROAD
SELBY ROAD
DEWSBURY ROAD
WAKEFIELD ROAD
ABERFORD ROAD
LEEDS AND BRADFORD ROAD
STANNINGLEY ROAD
BRADFORD ROAD
43

Liverpool

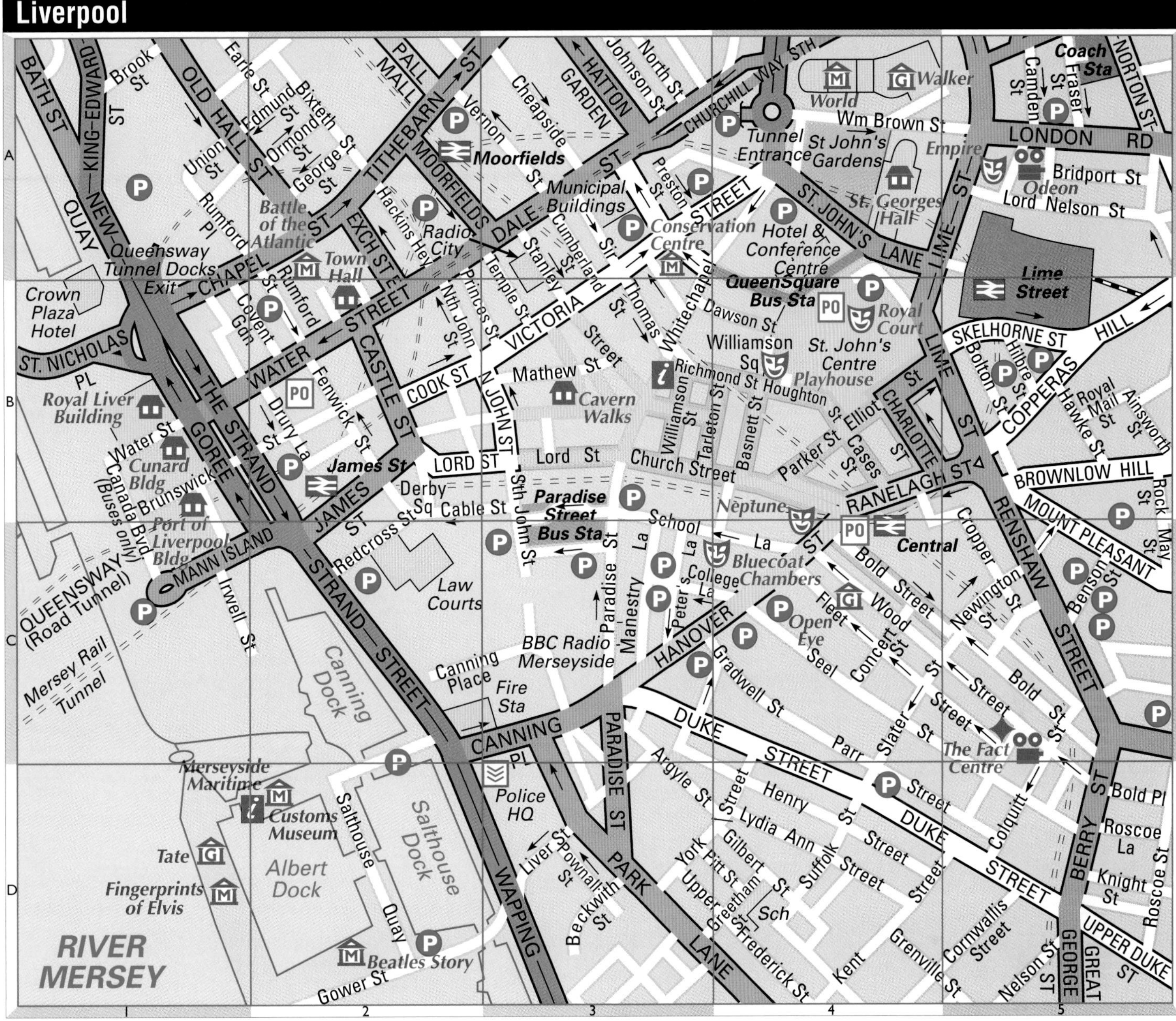

Liverpool

Ainsworth St B5
Argyle St D3
Basnett St B4
Bath St A1
Battle of the Atlantic 🏛 A2
BBC Radio Merseyside C3
Beatles Story 🏛 D2
Beckwith St D3
Benson St C5
Berry St D5
Bixteth St. A2
Bluecoat Chambers 🎭 C4
Bold Place D5
Bold St C4/C5
Bolton St B5
Bridport St. A5
Brook St A1
Brownlow Hill B5
Brunswick St B1
Cable St. B2
Camden St A5
Canada Blvd B1
Canning Place C3
Cases St B4
Castle St B2
Cavern Walks 🏛 B3
Central Station 🚉 . . . C4
Chapel St. A2
Charlotte St. B4
Cheapside A3
Church St B3
Churchill Way South . . A4
Coach Station A5
College La C3
Colquitt St D5
Concert St C4
Conservation Centre 🏛 A3
Cook St B2
Copperas Hill. B5
Cornwallis St. D5
Covent Garden B2
Cropper St. C5
Crown Plaza Hotel. . . . B1
Cumberland St A3
Cunard Building 🏛 . . . B1
Customs Museum 🏛 . D2
Dale St. A3
Dawson St. B4
Derby Sq B2
Drury La. B2
Duke St C3/D4/D5
Earle St A1
Edmund St A2
Elliot St B4
Empire Theatre 🎭 A5
Exchange St East A2
Fact Centre, The ✦ 🎥. C5
Fenwick St. B2
Fingerprints of Elvis 🏛 D1
Fire Station C3
Fleet St C4
Fraser St A5
George St A2
Gilbert St. D4
Goree. B1
Gower St. D2
Gradwell St C4
Great George St D5
Greetham St D4
Grenville St D4
Hackins Hey A2
Hanover St C3
Hatton Garden. A3
Hawke St. B5
Henry St D4
Hilbre St. B5
Houghton St B4
Information Ctr ℹ . B3/D2
Irwell St C1
James St B2
James St Station 🚉 . B2
Johnson St A3
Kent St D4
King Edward St A1
Knight St D5
Law Courts C2
Lime St A5/B5
Lime St Station 🚉. . . . B5
Liver St D3
London Rd. A5
Lord Nelson St A5
Lord St. B2/B3
Lydia Ann St D4
Manestry La. C3
Mann Island. C1
Mathew St. B3
May St. C5
Merseyside Maritime Museum 🏛 D2
Moorfields A2
Moorfields Station 🚉 A2
Mount Pleasant C5
Municipal Buildings . . . A3
Nelson St. D5
Neptune Theatre 🎭 . . . C4
New Quay A1
Newington St. C5
North John St B2/B3
North St. A3
Norton St. A5
Odeon 🎥. A5
Old Hall St. A1
Open Eye Gallery 🏛 . . . C4
Ormond St. A2
Pall Mall. A2
Paradise St C3
Paradise St Bus Station C3
Park La D3
Parker St B4
Parr St. D4
Peter's La C3
Pitt St. D4
Playhouse Theatre 🎭 . B4
Police Headquarters 🏛 D3
Port of Liverpool Building 🏛 B1
Post Office PO . B2/B4/C4
Pownall St D3
Preston St A3
Princes St B2
Queen Square Bus Station B4
Queensway Tunnel (Docks exit) A1
Queensway Tunnel (Entrance) A4
Radio City A3
Ranelagh St. B4
Redcross St. C2
Renshaw St. C5
Richmond St B4
Rock St B5
Roscoe La D5
Roscoe St D5
Royal Court Theatre 🎭 B4
Royal Liver Building 🏛 B1
Royal Mail St. B5
Rumford Place. A1
Rumford St B2
St Georges Hall 🏛 . . . A4
St John's Centre B4
St John's Gdns A4
St John's La A4
St Nicholas Place B1
Salthouse Quay. D2
School La C3
Seel St. C4
Sir Thomas St B3
Skelhorne St B5
Slater St. C4
South John St B3
Stanley St B3
Strand St. C2
Suffolk St. D4
Tarleton St. B3
Tate Gallery 🏛 D1
Temple St B3
The Strand. B1
Tithebarn St. A2
Town Hall 🏛 B2
Union St A1
Upper Duke St. D5
Upper Frederick St . . . D4
Vernon St. A3
Victoria St B3
Walker Art Gallery 🏛. . A4
Wapping D3
Water St. B1/B2
Whitechapel. B3
William Brown St. A4
Williamson Sq B4
Williamson St. B3
Wood St. C4
World Museum 🏛 A4
York St. D3

LIVERPOOL
BIRKENHEAD
BOOTLE
WALLASEY
GARSTON
BEBINGTON
LITHERLAND
AINTREE
KIRKBY
River Mersey
Waterloo
Seaforth
New Brighton
Walton
West Derby
Anfield
Fazakerley
Croxteth
Westvale
Kirkby Park
Melling
Stockbridge Village
Broad Green
Wavertree
Childwall
Edge Hill
Toxteth
Dingle
Aigburth
Otterspool
Allerton
Oxton
Tranmere
Port Sunlight
Spital
Bromborough
Brimstage
Eastham Ferry
Croxteth Country Park
Rimrose Valley Country Park
Aintree Race Course
Sefton Park
Stanley Park
Newsham Park
Wavertree Park
Birkenhead Park
Calderstones Park
Liverpool John Lennon Airport
Speke Hall
Sudley House
Lady Lever Art Gallery
Maritime Museum
Tate Gallery
Albert Dock
Beatles Story
Ferries to Belfast, Douglas & Dublin
Queensway
Kingsway
Ferry
Rail Tunnel
M57
M62
M53
A5036
A59
A580
A5058
A561
A562
A41
A552
0 1 2 miles
0 1 2 3 km

London

London

Abbey St ... C5
Albany St ... A2
Albert Embankment ... D3
Aldersgate St ... A4
Aldwych ... B3
Amwell St ... A3
Apsley House & Wellington Museum ... C1
Baker St ... B1
Banqueting House ... C3
Barbican ... B4
Bath St ... A4
Beech St ... B4
Belgrave Pl ... C1
Belgrave Rd ... D2
Berkeley Sq ... B2
Bermondsey St ... C5
BFI London Imax ... C3
Birdcage Walk ... C2
Bishopsgate ... B5
Black Prince Rd ... D3
Blackfriars ... B4
Blackfriars Bridge ... B4
Blackfriars Rd ... C4
Borough High St ... C4
Borough Rd ... C4
Brill Pl ... A2
British Library ... A2
British Museum ... B3
B.T. Tower ... A2
Brompton Rd ... C1
Brook Dr ... D4
Buckingham Gate ... C2
Buckingham Palace ... C2
Buckingham Palace Rd ... D2
Cabinet War Rooms ... C3
Cannon St ... B5
Carter La ... B4
Central St ... A4
Chancery La ... B3
Charing Cross ... C3
Charing Cross Rd ... B3
Charterhouse St ... B4
Cheapside ... B4
Chelsea Bridge Rd ... D1
Chelsea Royal Hospital ... D1
Chester Rd ... A1
Chiswell St ... B5
City Hall ... C5
City Hospital ... A4
City Rd ... A4/A5
City Thameslink ... B4
Clerkenwell Rd ... A4
Cleveland St ... A2
Commercial St ... A5
Conduit St ... B2
Constitution Hill ... C2
Cuming Museum ... D4
Curzon St ... C1
Davies St ... B1
Dickens House ... A3
Doughty St ... A3
Downing Street ... C3
Drury La ... B3
Dunton Rd ... D5
East Rd ... A5
East St ... D5
Eastcheap ... B5
Ebury Br Rd ... D1
Eccleston St ... D1
Edgware Rd ... B1
Elephant & Castle ... D4
Euston ... A2
Euston Rd ... A2
Eversholt St ... A2
Falmouth Rd ... C4
Farringdon ... A4
Farringdon Rd ... A3
Fenchurch St ... B5
Fleet St ... B4
Flood St ... D1
George St ... B1
Gloucester Pl ... B1
Golden La ... A4
Goswell Rd ... A4
Gower St ... B2
Grange Rd ... D5
Gray's Inn Rd ... A3
Great Dover St ... C5
Great Eastern St ... A5
Great Portland St ... B2
Great St Helen's ... B5
Great Smith St ... D3
Great Suffolk St ... C4
Great Tower St ... B5
Green Park ... C2
Gresham St ... B4
Grosvenor Pl ... C1
Grosvenor Rd ... D2
Grosvenor St ... B1
Guilford St ... A3
Guy's Hospital ... C5
Hackney Rd ... A5
Hampstead Rd ... A2
Harley St ... B1
Haymarket ... C2
Hayward Gallery ... C3
High Holborn ... B3
HMS Belfast ... C5
Holborn Viaduct ... B4
Horseferry Rd ... D2
Houndsditch ... B5
Houses of Parliament ... C3
Hyde Park ... C1
Imperial War Museum ... D4
Information Ctr ... C2/C3
Inner Circle ... A1
Jermyn St ... C2
Judd St ... A3
Kennington La ... D3/D4
Kennington Park Rd ... D4
Kennington Rd ... D4
King's Cross ... A3
King's Rd ... D1
Kingsland Rd ... A5
Kingsway ... B3
Knightsbridge ... C1
Lamb's Conduit St ... A3
Lambeth Bridge ... D3
Lambeth Palace ... D3
Lambeth Palace Rd ... C3
Lambeth Rd ... D3
Lambeth Walk ... D3
Leadenhall St ... B5
Lever St ... A4
Liverpool St ... B5
Lombard St ... B5
London Aquarium ... C3
London Bridge ... C5
London Dungeon ... C5
London Eye ... C3
London Mosque ... A1
London Rd ... C4
London Wall ... B4/B5
London Zoo ... A1
Long Acre ... B3
Long La ... B4
Long La ... C5
Lower Thames St ... B5
Ludgate Hill ... B4
Lupus St ... D2
Madame Tussaud's ... A1
Mansell St ... B5
Marylebone ... A1
Marylebone High St ... B1
Marylebone Rd ... B1
Middlesex St (Petticoat La) ... B5
Midland Rd ... A3
Millbank ... D3
Millennium Bridge ... B4
Minories ... B5
Monument, The ... B5
Moorgate ... B5
Mortimer St ... B2
Mount St ... C1
Museum of London ... B4
National Army Museum ... D1
National Gallery ... B2
National Theatre ... C3
New Bond St ... B2
New Bridge St ... B4
New Cavendish St ... B1
New Kent Rd ... D4
New Oxford St ... B3
New Scotland Yard ... C2
Newgate St ... B4
Newington Butts ... D4
Newman St ... B2
North Audley St ... B1
Old Bond St ... B2
Old Curiosity Shop ... B3
Old Kent Rd ... D5
Old St ... A4/A5
Open Air Theatre ... A1
Ossulston St ... A2
Outer Circle ... A1
Oval Cricket Ground, The ... D3
Oxford St ... B2
Oxford St ... B2
Pall Mall ... C2
Park Cr ... A2
Park La ... C1
Park Rd ... A1
Parliament Sq ... C3
Penton Pl ... D4
Pentonville Rd ... A3
Petty France ... C2
Piccadilly ... C2
Pimlico Rd ... D1
Pitfield St ... A5
Police Station ... A3/B1/B2/B3/B4/B5/C2/C3/D1/D3/D5
Pont St ... D1
Portland Pl ... B2
Post Office ... A2/A3/A4/B2/B3/C2/C3/C4
Queen Elizabeth and Royal Festival Halls ... C3
Queen Mary's Gardens ... A1
Queen Victoria St ... B4
Queen's Gallery ... C2
Queen's Sq ... A3
Regency St ... D2
Regent St ... B2
Regent's Park ... A1
Robert St ... A2
Rochester Row ... D2
Rodney Rd ... D5
Rosebery Ave ... A3
Royal Academy ... B2
Royal College of Physicians ... A2
Royal Hospital Rd ... D1
Russell Sq ... A3
St. Bartholemew's Hospital ... B4
St. George's Cath (R.C.) ... C4
St. George's Rd ... C4
St. George's Sq ... D2
St. James's Palace ... C2
St. James's Park ... C2
St. James's St ... C2
St. John St ... A4
St. Pancras ... A3
St. Pancras International ... A3
St. Paul's Cathedral ... B4
St. Thomas St ... C5
St. Thomas' Hospital ... C3
Seymour Pl ... B1
Seymour St ... B1
Shaftesbury Ave ... B2
Shepherdess Walk ... A4
Skinner St ... A4
Sloane Ave ... D1
Sloane Sq ... D1
Sloane St ... D1
Soane's Museum ... B3
Somerset House ... B3
South Audley St ... C1
South Carriage Dr ... C1
Southwark Bridge ... C4
Southwark Bridge Rd ... C4
Southwark Cathedral ... C5
Southwark St ... C4
Stamford St ... C4
Stanhope St ... A2
Sutherland St ... D2
Tabernacle St ... A5
Tate Britain ... D3
Tate Modern ... C4
Tavistock Pl ... A3
Temple ... B3
The Cut ... C4
The Mall ... C2
The Strand ... B3
Theobalds Rd ... B3
Threadneedle St ... B5
Thurlow St ... D5
Tooley St ... C5
Torrington Pl ... A2
Tottenham Court Rd ... A2
Tower Bridge ... C5
Tower Bridge Rd ... C5
Tower of London ... C5
Trafalgar Sq ... C3
Transport Museum ... B3
Tyers St ... D3
Union St ... C4
University College Hospital ... A2
Upper Thames St ... B4
Upper Woburn Pl ... A2
Vauxhall ... D3
Vauxhall Bridge ... D3
Vauxhall Bridge Rd ... D2
Victoria ... D2
Victoria Coach Station ... D1
Victoria Embankment ... B3/C3
Victoria St ... C2
Wallace Collection ... B1
Walworth Rd ... D4
Wardour St ... B2
Warwick Way ... D2
Waterloo Bridge ... C3
Waterloo ... C3
Waterloo East ... C4
Waterloo Rd ... C4
Wesley's House ... A5
Westminster Abbey ... C3
Westminster Bridge ... B4
Westminster Cathedral (R.C) ... D2
Weston St ... C5
Whitehall ... C3
Wigmore St ... B1
Worship St ... A5
York Rd ... C3

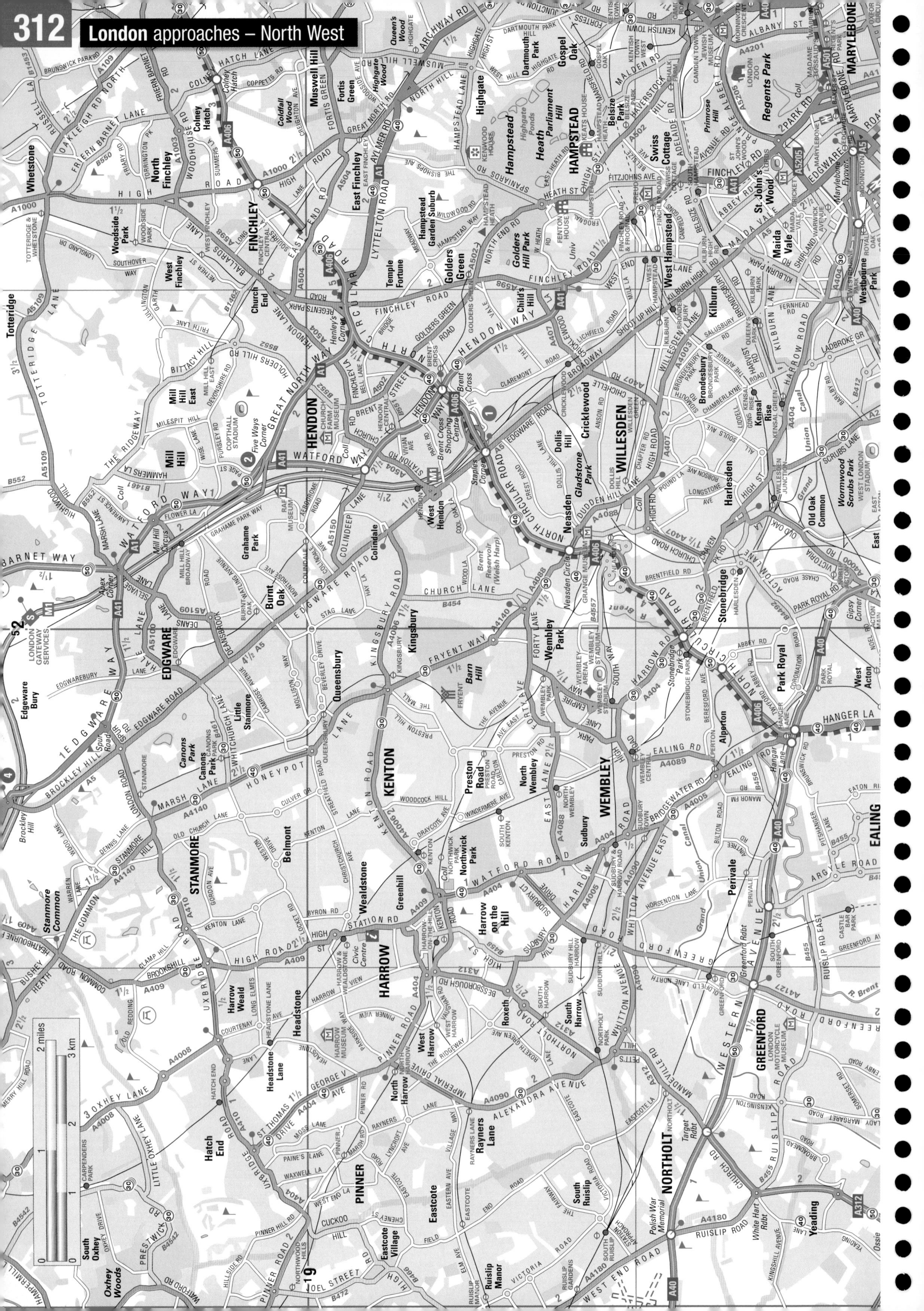

Whetstone
North Finchley
Colney Hatch
Muswell Hill
Fortis Green
Highgate
Hampstead Heath
Parliament Hill
HAMPSTEAD
Gospel Oak
Belsize Park
Swiss Cottage
Primrose Hill
Regents Park
MARYLEBONE
Dartmouth Park
Woodside Park
FINCHLEY
East Finchley
Hampstead Garden Suburb
Golders Green
Golders Hill Park
West Hampstead
St. John's Wood
Maida Vale
West Finchley
Church End
Temple Fortune
Child's Hill
Kilburn
Westbourne Park
Totteridge
Mill Hill East
HENDON
Cricklewood
Brondesbury
Kensal Rise
Mill Hill
Five Ways Corner
Brent Cross
Dollis Hill
WILLESDEN
Gladstone Park
Harlesden
Wormwood Scrubs Park
Old Oak Common
Grahame Park
West Hendon
Colindale
Neasden
Brent Reservoir (Welsh Harp)
Burnt Oak
EDGWARE
Kingsbury
Wembley Park
Stonebridge
Park Royal
West Acton
Edgware Bury
Little Stanmore
Queensbury
Barn Hill
Canons Park
KENTON
Preston Road
North Wembley
WEMBLEY
Alperton
EALING
STANMORE
Belmont
Northwick Park
Sudbury
Perivale
Stanmore Common
Wealdstone
Greenhill
Harrow on the Hill
HARROW
Harrow Weald
Headstone
Roxeth
South Harrow
GREENFORD
West Harrow
North Harrow
Headstone Lane
Hatch End
Rayners Lane
NORTHOLT
PINNER
Eastcote
South Ruislip
Yeading
South Oxhey
Oxhey Woods
Eastcote Village
Ruislip Manor

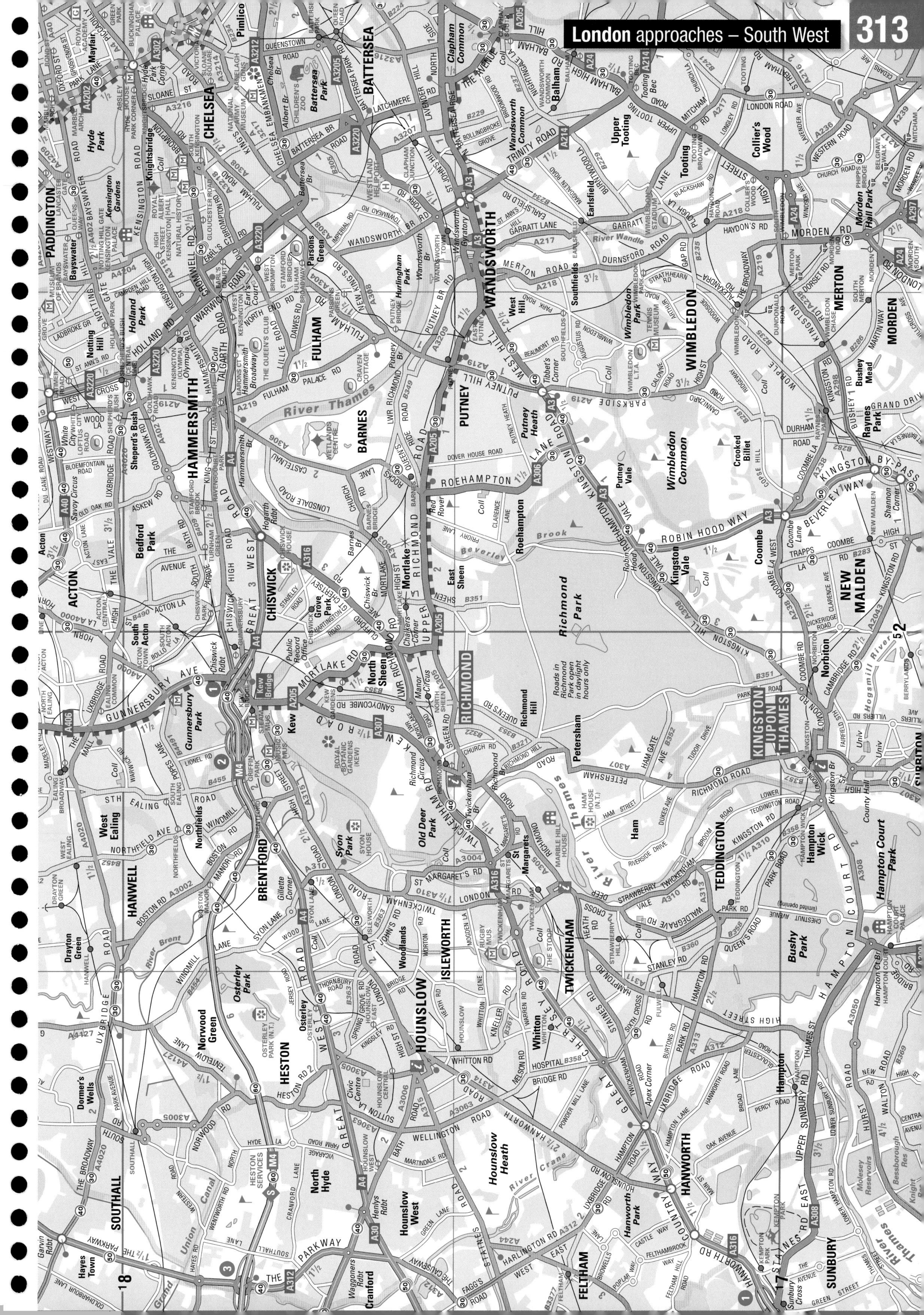
PADDINGTON
CHELSEA
BATTERSEA
HAMMERSMITH
FULHAM
WANDSWORTH
PUTNEY
BARNES
CHISWICK
ACTON
WIMBLEDON
MERTON
MORDEN
NEW MALDEN
KINGSTON UPON THAMES
RICHMOND
TEDDINGTON
TWICKENHAM
ISLEWORTH
HOUNSLOW
BRENTFORD
HANWELL
SOUTHALL
HESTON
HANWORTH
FELTHAM
SUNBURY
Richmond Park
Wimbledon Common
Bushy Park
Hampton Court Park
Hounslow Heath
River Thames
Roads in Richmond Park open in daylight hours only

Southgate
Winchmore Hill
Chingford
Buckhurst Hill
Chigwell
Friday Hill
Palmers Green
Lower Edmonton
Woodford Wells
Grange Hill
Friern Barnet
Edmonton
Chingford Hatch
Highams Park
Hale End
Woodford
Woodford Bridge
Woodford Green
Wood Green
Higham Hill
Clayhall
Fulwell Cross
Muswell Hill
Tottenham
Walthamstow
Snaresbrook
Barkingside
Redbridge
Gants Hill
Newbury Park
Hornsey
Harringay
South Tottenham
Wanstead
Seven Kings
Highgate
Stamford Hill
Upper Clapton
Cranbrook
Archway
Stoke Newington
Clapton
Leytonstone
Hampstead
Lea Bridge
Leyton
Ilford
Loxford
Manor Park
Gospel Oak
Shacklewell
Clapton Park
Kentish Town
Canonbury
Hackney
Stratford
Forest Gate
Little Ilford
Camden Town
Islington
Shoreditch
Dalston
Plashet
Upton
Upton Park
Barking
West Ham
Old Ford
Bow
Bethnal Green
East Ham
Regents Park
Finsbury
Plaistow
Marylebone
Holborn
Spitalfields
Stepney
Beckton
Victoria Park
Wanstead Park
Hackney Marsh
Banbury Reservoir
William Girling Reservoir
Barking Creek
North Circular Road

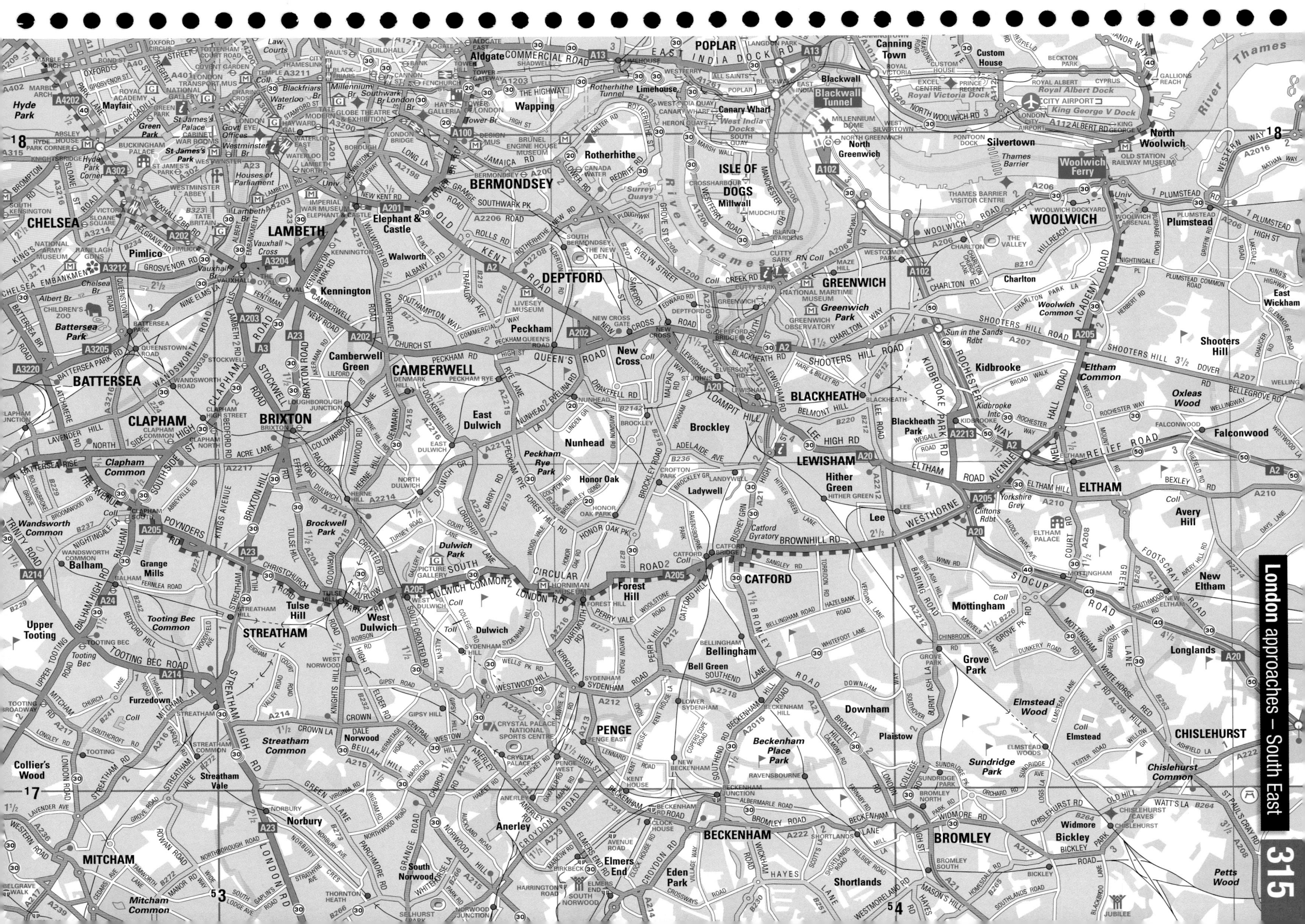
Hyde Park
Mayfair
Green Park
St James's Palace
Houses of Parliament
Aldgate
Wapping
POPLAR
Canning Town
Custom House
Limehouse
Canary Wharf
Blackwall
Blackwall Tunnel
North Greenwich
Silvertown
Thames Barrier
North Woolwich
Woolwich Ferry
CHELSEA
Pimlico
LAMBETH
Elephant & Castle
BERMONDSEY
Rotherhithe
ISLE OF DOGS
Millwall
WOOLWICH
Plumstead
East Wickham
Kennington
Walworth
DEPTFORD
GREENWICH
Greenwich Park
Charlton
Woolwich Common
Battersea Park
BATTERSEA
Camberwell Green
CAMBERWELL
Peckham
New Cross
Shooters Hill
Kidbrooke
Eltham Common
Oxleas Wood
CLAPHAM
BRIXTON
East Dulwich
BLACKHEATH
Blackheath Park
Falconwood
Clapham Common
Nunhead
Peckham Rye Park
Honor Oak
Brockley
LEWISHAM
Hither Green
ELTHAM
Avery Hill
Wandsworth Common
Balham
Grange Mills
Brockwell Park
Dulwich Park
Ladywell
Lee
Upper Tooting
Tooting Bec Common
STREATHAM
Tulse Hill
West Dulwich
Dulwich
Forest Hill
CATFORD
Mottingham
New Eltham
Bellingham
Bell Green
Grove Park
Longlands
Tooting Bec
Furzedown
Streatham Common
Norwood
PENGE
Beckenham Place Park
Downham
Plaistow
Elmstead Wood
Elmstead
CHISLEHURST
Chislehurst Common
Collier's Wood
Streatham Vale
Norbury
Anerley
Sundridge Park
MITCHAM
Mitcham Common
South Norwood
Elmers End
Eden Park
BECKENHAM
Shortlands
BROMLEY
Widmore
Bickley
Petts Wood
River Thames

Manchester

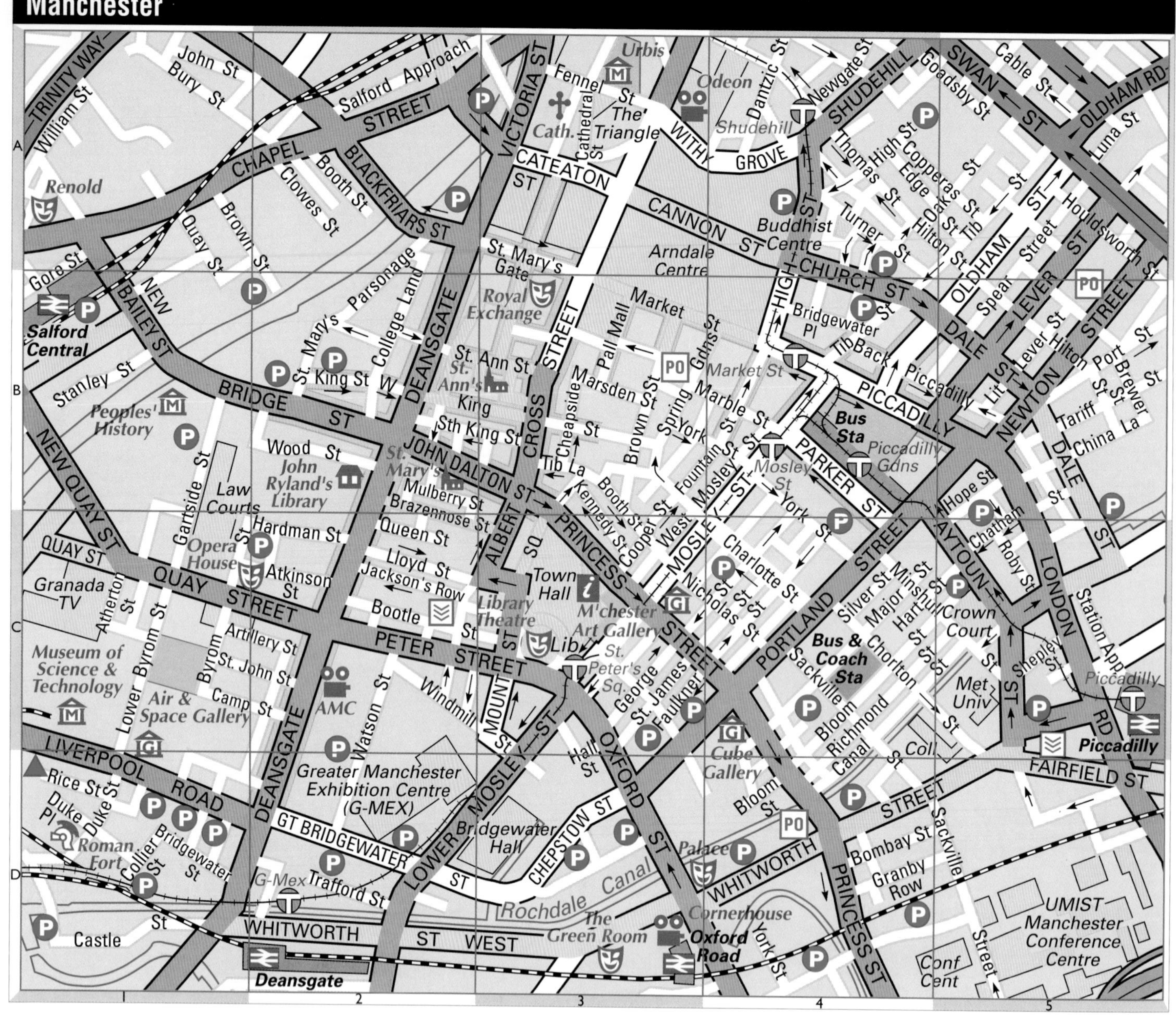

Manchester

Air & Space Gallery ... C1
Albert Sq ... C3
AMC ... C2
Arndale Centre ... A3
Artillery St ... C1
Atherton St ... C1
Atkinson St ... C2
Aytoun St ... C5
Back Piccadilly ... B4
Blackfriars St ... A2
Bloom St ... C4/D4
Bombay St ... D4
Booth St ... A2
Booth St ... B3
Bootle St ... C2
Brazennose St ... B2
Brewer St ... B5
Bridge St ... B1
Bridgewater Hall ... D3
Bridgewater Pl ... B4
Bridgewater St ... D1
Brown St ... A1
Brown St ... B3
Buddhist Centre ... A4
Bury St ... A1
Bus & Coach Station ... C4
Bus Station ... B4
Byrom St ... C1
Cable St ... A5
Camp St ... C1
Canal St ... C4
Cannon St ... A3
Castle St ... D1
Cateaton St ... A3
Cathedral ✝ ... A3
Cathedral St ... A3
Chapel St ... A2
Charlotte St ... C4
Chatham St ... C5
Cheapside ... B3
Chepstow St ... D3
China La ... B5
Chorlton St ... C4
Church St ... A4
Clowes St ... A2
College Land ... B2
Collier St ... D1
Conference Centre ... D5
Cooper St ... C3
Copperas St ... A4
Cornerhouse ... D3
Cross St ... B3
Crown Court ... C5
Cube Gallery ... C4
Dale St ... B5
Dantzic St ... A4
Deansgate ... B2/D2
Deansgate Station ... D2
Duke Pl ... D1
Duke St ... D1
Edge St ... A4
Fairfield St ... D5
Faulkner St ... C3
Fennel St ... A3
Fountain St ... B3
Gartside St ... C1
George St ... C3
G-Mex (Metro Station) ... D2
Goadsby St ... A5
Gore St ... B1
Granada TV Studios ... C1
Granby Row ... D4
Great Bridgewater St ... D2
Greater Manchester Exhibition Centre (G-Mex) ... D2
Green Room, The ... D3
Hall St ... D3
Hardman St ... C2
Hart St ... C4
High St ... A4/B4
Hilton St ... A4/B5
Hope St ... B5
Houldsworth St ... A5
Information Ctr ... C3
Jackson's Row ... C2
John Dalton St ... B2
John Ryland's Library ... B2
John St ... A1
Kennedy St ... B3
King St ... B3
King St West ... B2
Law Courts ... B1
Lever St ... B5
Library ... C3
Library Theatre ... C3
Little Lever St ... B5
Liverpool Rd ... D1
Lloyd St ... C2
London Rd ... C5
Lower Byrom St ... C1
Lower Mosley St ... D2
Luna St ... A5
Major St ... C4
Manchester Art Gallery ... C3
Manchester Metropolitan University ... C5
Marble St ... B4
Market St ... B3
Market St (Metro Station) ... B4
Marsden St ... B3
Minshull St ... C4
Mosley St ... C3
Mosley St (Metro Station) ... B4
Mount St ... C3
Mulberry St ... B2
Museum of Science & Technology ... C1
New Bailey St ... B1
New Quay St ... B1
Newgate St ... A4
Newton St ... B5
Nicholas St ... C3
Oak St ... A4
Odeon ... A3
Oldham Rd ... A5
Oldham St ... B5
Opera House ... C1
Oxford Road ... D3
Oxford St ... D3
Palace Theatre ... D3
Pall Mall ... B3
Parker St ... B4
Peoples' History Museum ... B1
Peter St ... C2
Piccadilly ... B4
Piccadilly (Metro Station) ... C5
Piccadilly Gdns (Metro Station) ... B4
Piccadilly Station ... C5
Police Station ... C2/C5
Port St ... B5
Portland St ... C4
Post Office ... B3/B5/D4
Princess St ... C3/D4
Quay St ... A1
Quay St ... C1
Queen St ... C2
Renold Theatre ... A1
Rice St ... D1
Richmond St ... C4
Roby St ... C5
Roman Fort ... D1
Royal Exchange ... B3
Sackville St ... C4/D5
St Ann St ... B3
St Ann's ... B3
St James St ... C3
St John St ... C1
St Mary's ... B2
St Mary's Gate ... A3
St Mary's Parsonage ... B2
St Peter's Sq (Metro Station) ... C3
Salford Approach ... A2
Salford Central ... B1
Shepley St ... C5
Shudehill ... A4
Shudehill (Metro Station) ... A4
Silver St ... C4
South King St ... B2
Spear St ... A5
Spring Gdns ... B3
Stanley St ... B1
Station Approach ... C5
Swan St ... A5
Tariff St ... B5
Thomas St ... A4
Tib La ... B3
Tib St ... A5/B4
Town Hall ... C3
Trafford St ... D2
Triangle, The ... A3
Trinity Way ... A1
Turner St ... A4
UMIST Manchester Conference Centre ... D5
Urbis Museum ... A3
Victoria St ... A3
Watson St ... C2
West Mosley St ... B4
Whitworth St ... D4
Whitworth St West ... D2
William St ... A1
Windmill St ... C2
Withy Gr ... A3
Wood St ... B2
York St ... B3
York St ... D4

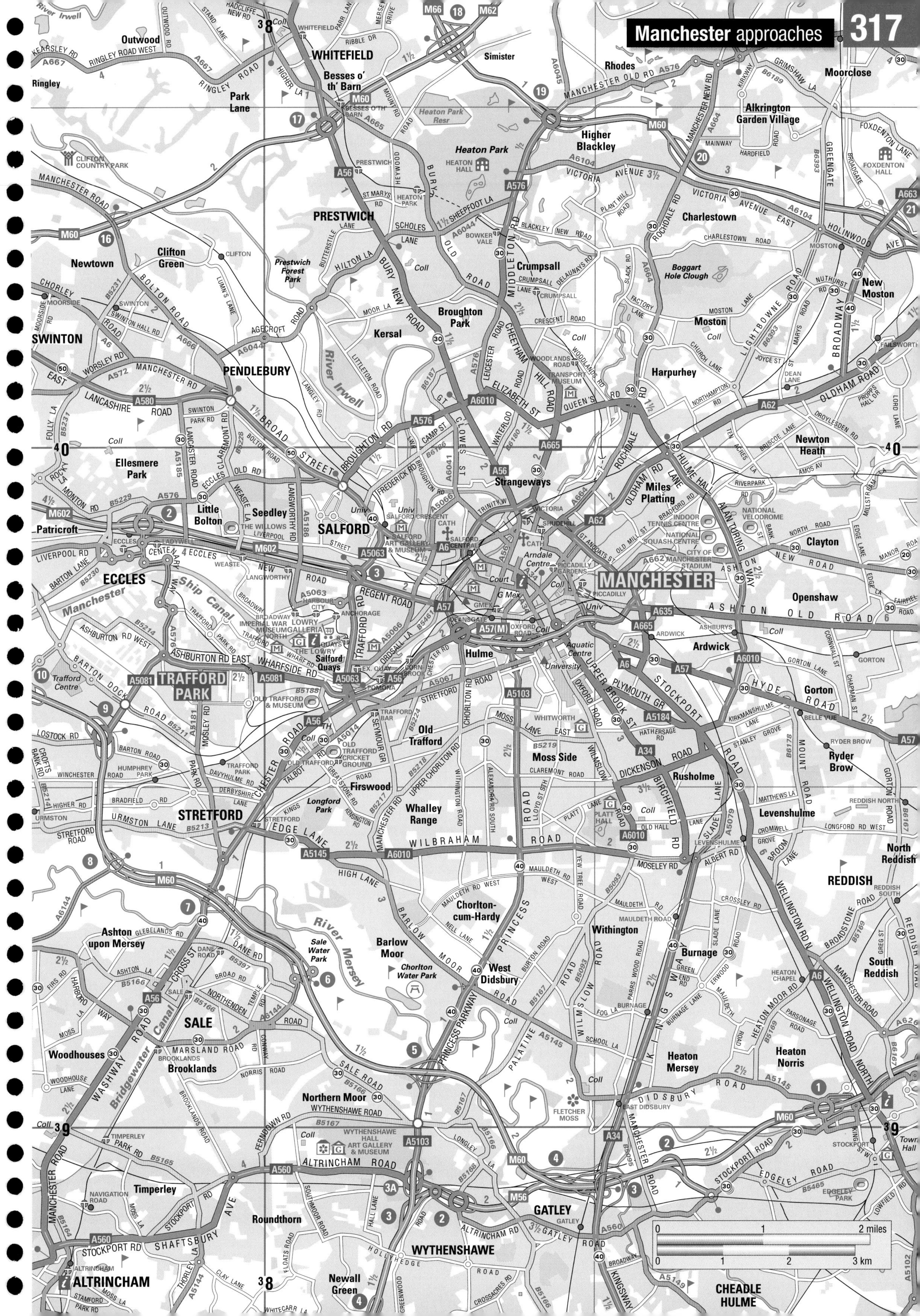
Outwood
WHITEFIELD
Besses o' th' Barn
Simister
Rhodes
Moorclose
Ringley
Park Lane
Heaton Park Resr
Heaton Park
HEATON HALL
Higher Blackley
Alkrington Garden Village
CLIFTON COUNTRY PARK
FOXDENTON HALL
PRESTWICH
Charlestown
Newtown
Clifton Green
Prestwich Forest Park
Crumpsall
Boggart Hole Clough
New Moston
SWINTON
Kersal
Broughton Park
Moston
PENDLEBURY
River Irwell
TRANSPORT MUSEUM
Harpurhey
Ellesmere Park
Newton Heath
Strangeways
Miles Platting
Patricroft
Little Bolton
Seedley
SALFORD
NATIONAL VELODROME
Clayton
ECCLES
MANCHESTER
Manchester Ship Canal
Arndale Centre
PICCADILLY
Openshaw
IMPERIAL WAR MUSEUM NORTH
LOWRY
Salford Quays
G Mex
Hulme
Ardwick
Trafford Centre
TRAFFORD PARK
University
Gorton
Old Trafford
OLD TRAFFORD CRICKET GROUND
Moss Side
Ryder Brow
Firswood
Rusholme
Longford Park
STRETFORD
Whalley Range
Levenshulme
North Reddish
REDDISH
Chorlton-cum-Hardy
Ashton upon Mersey
Barlow Moor
Withington
Sale Water Park
Chorlton Water Park
Burnage
South Reddish
River Mersey
West Didsbury
SALE
Woodhouses
Brooklands
Heaton Mersey
Heaton Norris
Bridgewater Canal
Northern Moor
FLETCHER MOSS
EAST DIDSBURY
WYTHENSHAWE HALL ART GALLERY & MUSEUM
Timperley
Roundthorn
GATLEY
WYTHENSHAWE
ALTRINCHAM
Newall Green
CHEADLE HULME
M60
M62
M66
M602
M56
A57(M)
0 1 2 miles
0 1 2 3 km

Newcastle upon Tyne

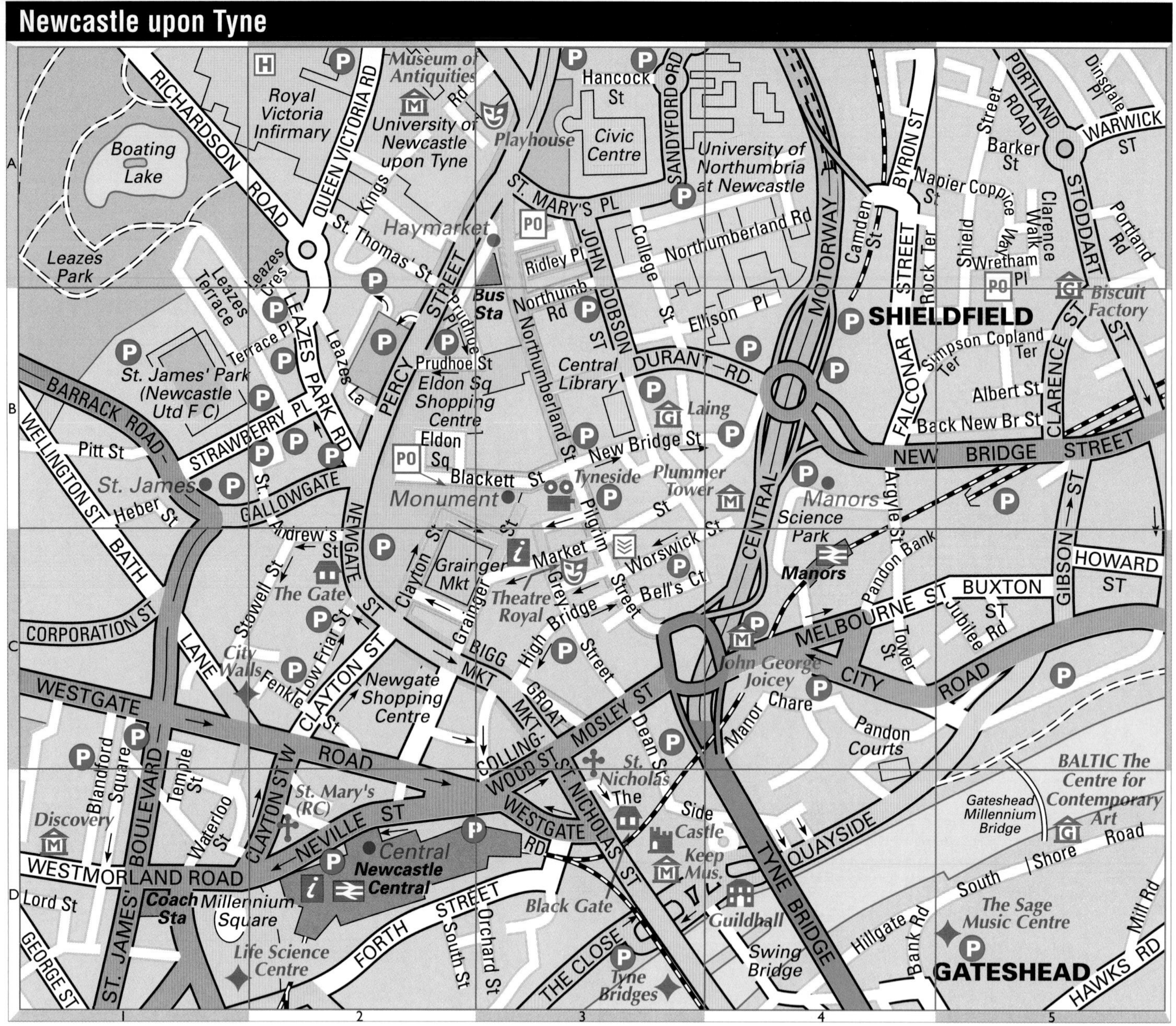

Newcastle upon Tyne

Albert St B5
Argyle St B4
Back New Bridge St . . B5
BALTIC The Centre for Contemporary Art 🏛. D5
Bank Rd. D4
Barker St A5
Barrack Rd B1
Bath La C1
Bell's Court C3
Bigg Market. C3
Biscuit Factory 🏛 B5
Black Gate D3
Blackett St. B2
Blandford Sq D1
Boating Lake A1
Bus Station A3
Buxton St C5
Byron St A4
Camden St A4
Castle D3
Central (metro station). D2
Central Library. B3
Central Motorway B4
City Rd C4/C5
City Walls ✦ C1
Civic Centre. A3
Clarence St B5
Clarence Walk A5
Clayton St C2
Clayton St West. D2
Coach Station D1
College St A3
Collingwood St C3
Copland Terr B5
Coppice Way. A5
Corporation St. C1
Courts C4
Dean St C3
Dinsdale Pl A5
Discovery Museum 🏛. D1
Durant Rd B3
Eldon Sq B2
Eldon Sq Shopping Centre B2
Ellison Pl B3
Falconar St B4
Fenkle St C2
Forth St D2
Gallowgate B2
Gate, The C2
Gateshead Millennium Bridge D5
George St D1
Gibson St C5
Grainger Market C2
Grainger St C2
Grey St C3
Groat Market C3
Guildhall D4
Hancock St A3
Hawks Rd D5
Haymarket (metro station) A3
Heber St B1
High Bridge C3
Hillgate D4
Howard St C5
Information Ctr 🛈 . C3/D2
John Dobson St A3
John George Joicey Museum 🏛 . . C4
Jubilee Rd C5
Keep Museum 🏛 D3
Kings Rd A2
Laing Gallery 🏛 B3
Leazes Cr A2
Leazes La B2
Leazes Park. A1
Leazes Park Rd B2
Leazes Terr B1
Life Science Centre ✦ D2
Lord St. D1
Low Friar St. C2
Manor Chare C4
Manors (metro station). B4
Manors Station . . . C4
Market St. C3
Melbourne St. C4
Mill Rd D5
Millennium Sq D1
Monument (metro station) B3
Mosley St C3
Museum of Antiquities 🏛 A2
Napier St A4
Neville St D2
New Bridge St. . . . B3/B5
Newcastle Central Station D2
Newgate Shopping Centre C2
Newgate St C2
Northumberland Rd. . . A3
Northumberland St . . . B3
Orchard St. D3
Pandon C4
Pandon Bank. C4
Percy St. B2
Pilgrim St. B3
Pitt St. B1
Playhouse Theatre . A3
Plummer Tower 🏛. . . . B4
Police Station C3
Portland Rd A5
Post Office . A3/A5/B2
Prudhoe Pl. B2
Prudhoe St B2
Quayside D4
Queen Victoria Rd A2
Richardson Rd. A1
Ridley Pl A3
Rock Terr. A4
Royal Victoria Infirmary 🄷 A2
Sage Music Centre, The ✦. D5
St Andrew's St. B2
St James (metro station) B1
St James' Blvd D1
St James' Park (Newcastle Utd FC). . B1
St Mary's (RC) ✝ D2
St Mary's Place A3
St Nicholas ✝ C3
St Nicholas St D3
St Thomas' St A2
Sandyford Rd A3
Science Park B4
Shield St A5
Simpson Terr B5
South Shore Rd. D5
South St D2
Stoddart St A5
Stowell St C2
Strawberry Pl. B1
Swing Bridge. D4
Temple St D1
Terrace Pl B1
The Close D3
The Side D3
Theatre Royal C3
Tower St C4
Tyne Bridge D4
Tyne Bridges ✦. D3
Tyneside B3
University of Newcastle upon Tyne A2
University of Northumbria at Newcastle A4
Warwick St A5
Waterloo St D1
Wellington St. B1
Westgate Rd C1/D3
Westmorland Rd D1
Worswick St C3
Wretham Pl A5

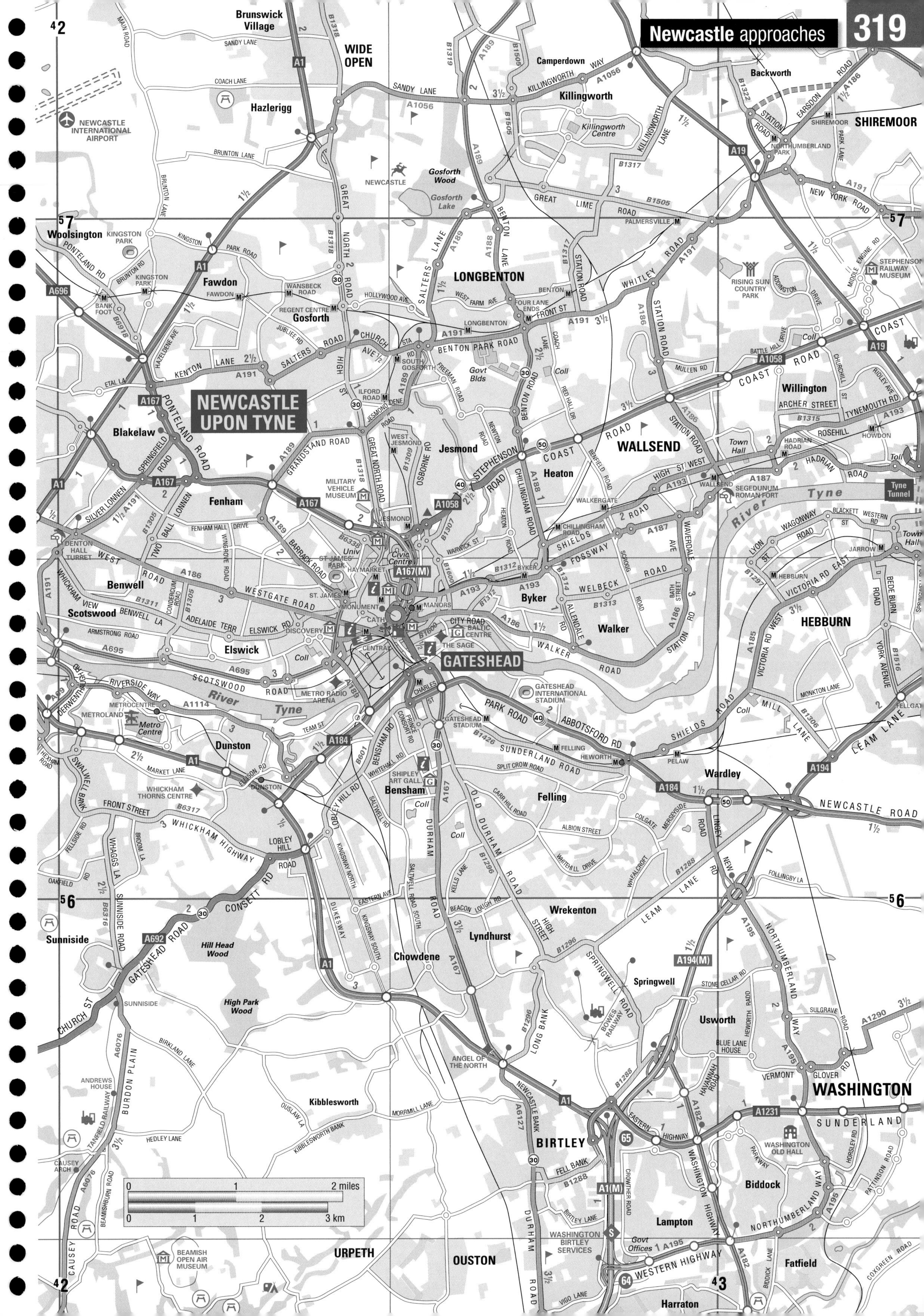
Brunswick Village
WIDE OPEN
Camperdown
Backworth
Killingworth
Killingworth Centre
SHIREMOOR
Hazlerigg
NEWCASTLE INTERNATIONAL AIRPORT
NEWCASTLE
Gosforth Wood
Gosforth Lake
Woolsington
KINGSTON PARK
LONGBENTON
RISING SUN COUNTRY PARK
STEPHENSON RAILWAY MUSEUM
Fawdon
Gosforth
NEWCASTLE UPON TYNE
Blakelaw
Jesmond
Willington
WALLSEND
Heaton
Fenham
MILITARY VEHICLE MUSEUM
Tyne Tunnel
River Tyne
Benwell
Scotswood
Byker
Walker
HEBBURN
Elswick
GATESHEAD
THE SAGE
BALTIC CENTRE
METRO RADIO ARENA
GATESHEAD INTERNATIONAL STADIUM
METROLAND
Metro Centre
Dunston
WHICKHAM THORNS CENTRE
SHIPLEY ART GALL
Bensham
Felling
Wardley
Wrekenton
Sunniside
Hill Head Wood
Lyndhurst
Chowdene
Springwell
High Park Wood
Usworth
ANGEL OF THE NORTH
WASHINGTON
Kibblesworth
BIRTLEY
WASHINGTON OLD HALL
Biddock
BOWES RAILWAY
TANFIELD RAILWAY
Lampton
WASHINGTON BIRTLEY SERVICES
BEAMISH OPEN AIR MUSEUM
URPETH
OUSTON
Fatfield
Harraton
0 1 2 miles
0 1 2 3 km

Norwich

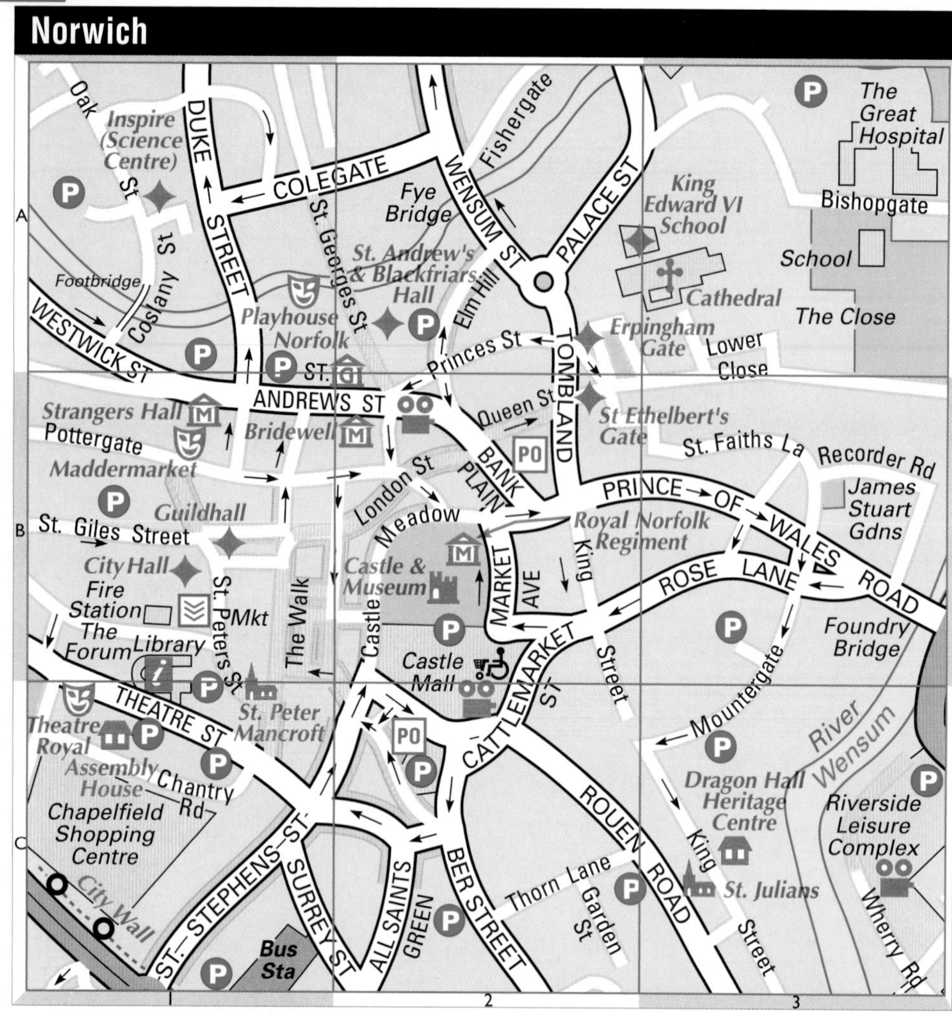

Nottingham

Chaucer St
Trent Univ
GOLDSMITH ST
SHERWOOD ST
Victoria Centre
GLASSHOUSE ST
HUNTINGDON ST
St. Mary's Garden of Rest
Belgrave Centre
TALBOT ST
BURTON ST
Guildhall
Milton St
Rick St
Kent St
BATH ST
Brook Street
Sch
Royal Concert Hall
Theatre Royal
Royal Centre
UPPER PARLIAMENT ST
LOWER PARLIAMENT ST
Playhouse
King St
Clumber St
Lincoln St
George St
Arts
Broad St
Heathcote St
CRANBROOK ST
Albert Hall
MAID MARIAN WAY
Long Row
Old Market Sq
Council Ho.
Pelham St
Carlton St
Goose Gate
St. James St
Sth Pde
Cheapside
VICTORIA ST
Warser Gte
Woolpack La
Row
Mount St
WHEELER GATE
ST. PETER'S GATE
Lace Market
Barker Gate
Park Row
Tales of Robin Hood
Lane
St. Peter's
FLETCHER GATE
St. Mary's Gate
Stoney St
Nott. Arena & Nat. Ice Centre
BELWARD ST
Salutation Inn
Royal Children Inn
Low Pavement
Plumptre St
Friar
Castle Gate
Willoughby Ho.
City of Caves
MIDDLE HILL
HIGH PAVEMENT
BELLAR GATE
Newdigate Ho.
Galleries of Justice
Robin Hood Statue
St. Nicholas
Broad Marsh Precinct
Cliff Road
Castle Museum & Gallery
Castle Rd
Trip to Jerusalem Inn
COLLIN ST
Castle
Brewhouse Yard
Broad Marsh Bus Sta
CANAL ST
Peveril Dr
Hope Dr
CASTLE BOULEVARD
WILFORD ST
Castle Wharf
CARRINGTON ST
Trent St
LONDON ROAD
Station St
STATION STREET
Nottingham Canal
Magistrates Court
Nottingham
Fb

Norwich

All Saints Green C2
Assembly House . . C1
Bank Plain B2
Ber St C2
Bishopgate A3
Bridewell B2
Bus Station C1
Castle Mall B2
Castle Meadow B2
Castle & Museum . . B2
Cathedral A3
Cattlemarket St C2
Chantry Rd C1
Chapelfield Shopping Centre C1
City Hall B1
City Wall C1
Colegate A1
Coslany St A1
Dragon Hall Heritage Centre . . C3
Duke St A1
Elm Hill A2
Erpingham Gate . . . A2
Fire Station B1
Fishergate A2
Foundry Bridge B3
Fye Bridge A2
Garden St C2
Guildhall B1
Information Ctr B1
Inspire (Science Ctr) . A1
James Stuart Gdns . . . B3
King Edward VI Sch . A3
King St B2/B3
Library B1
London St B2
Lower Cl A3
Maddermarket B1
Market B1
Market Ave B2
Mountergate C3
Norfolk B2
Oak St A1
Palace St A2
Police Station B1
Post Office B2/C2
Pottergate B1
Prince of Wales Rd . . . B3
Princes St A2
Queen St B2
Recorder Rd B3
Riverside Leisure Complex C3
Rose La B3
Rouen Rd C2
Royal Norfolk Regiment Museum B2
St Andrew's & Blackfriars Hall . . . A2
St Andrews St B1
St Ethelbert's Gate . B2
St Faiths La B3
St Georges St A2
St Giles St B1
St Julians C3
St Peter Mancroft . . C1
St Peters St B1
St Stephens St C1
Strangers Hall B1
Surrey St C1
The Close A3
The Forum B1
The Great Hospital . . . A3
The Walk B1
Theatre Royal C1
Theatre St C1
Thorn La C2
Tombland A2
Wensum St A2
Westwick St A1
Wherry Rd C3

Nottingham

Albert Hall B1
Arts Theatre A3
Barker Gate B3
Bath St A3
Belgrave Centre A1
Bellar Gate B3
Belward St B3
Brewhouse Yard . . . C1
Broad Marsh Bus Stn . C2
Broad Marsh Precinct . C2
Broad St A3
Brook St A3
Burton St A2
Canal St C2/C3
Carlton St B3
Carrington St C2
Castle C1
Castle Blvd C1
Castle Gate B2
Castle Museum & Gallery C1
Castle Rd C1
Castle Wharf C2
Chaucer St A1
Cheapside B2
City of Caves B2
Cliff Rd C3
Clumber St A2
Collin St C2
Council House B2
Cranbrook St A3
Fletcher Gate B2
Friar La B1
Galleries of Justice . C3
George St A3
Glasshouse St A2
Goldsmith St A1
Goose Gate B3
Guildhall A2
Heathcote St A3
High Pavement B3
Hope Dr C1
Huntingdon St A3
Information Ctr B2
Kent St A3
King St A2
Lincoln St A2
London Rd C3
Long Row B1
Low Pavement B2
Lower Parliament St . . A3
Magistrates Court C2
Maid Marian Way B1
Middle Hill C2
Milton St A2
Mount St B1
National Ice Centre . . . B3
Newdigate House . . . B1
Nottingham C2
Nottingham Arena B3
Park Row B1
Pelham St B2
Peveril Dr C1
Playhouse Theatre . . B1
Plumptre St B3
Police Station A2
Post Office A2/C1
Rick St A3
Robin Hood Statue . C1
Royal Children Inn . . B2
Royal Concert Hall . . A1
St James' St B1
St Mary's Garden of Rest A3
St Mary's Gate B3
St Nicholas C2
St Peter's B2
St Peter's Gate B2
Salutation Inn B1
South Pde B2
South Sherwood St . . . A2
Station St C3
Stoney St B3
Talbot St A1
Tales of Robin Hood . B1
Theatre Royal A2
Trent St C3
Trent University A1
Trip To Jerusalem Inn C1
Upper Parliament St . . A1
Victoria Centre A2
Victoria St B2
Warser Gate B3
Wheeler Gate B2
Wilford St C2
Willoughby House . . B2
Woolpack La B3

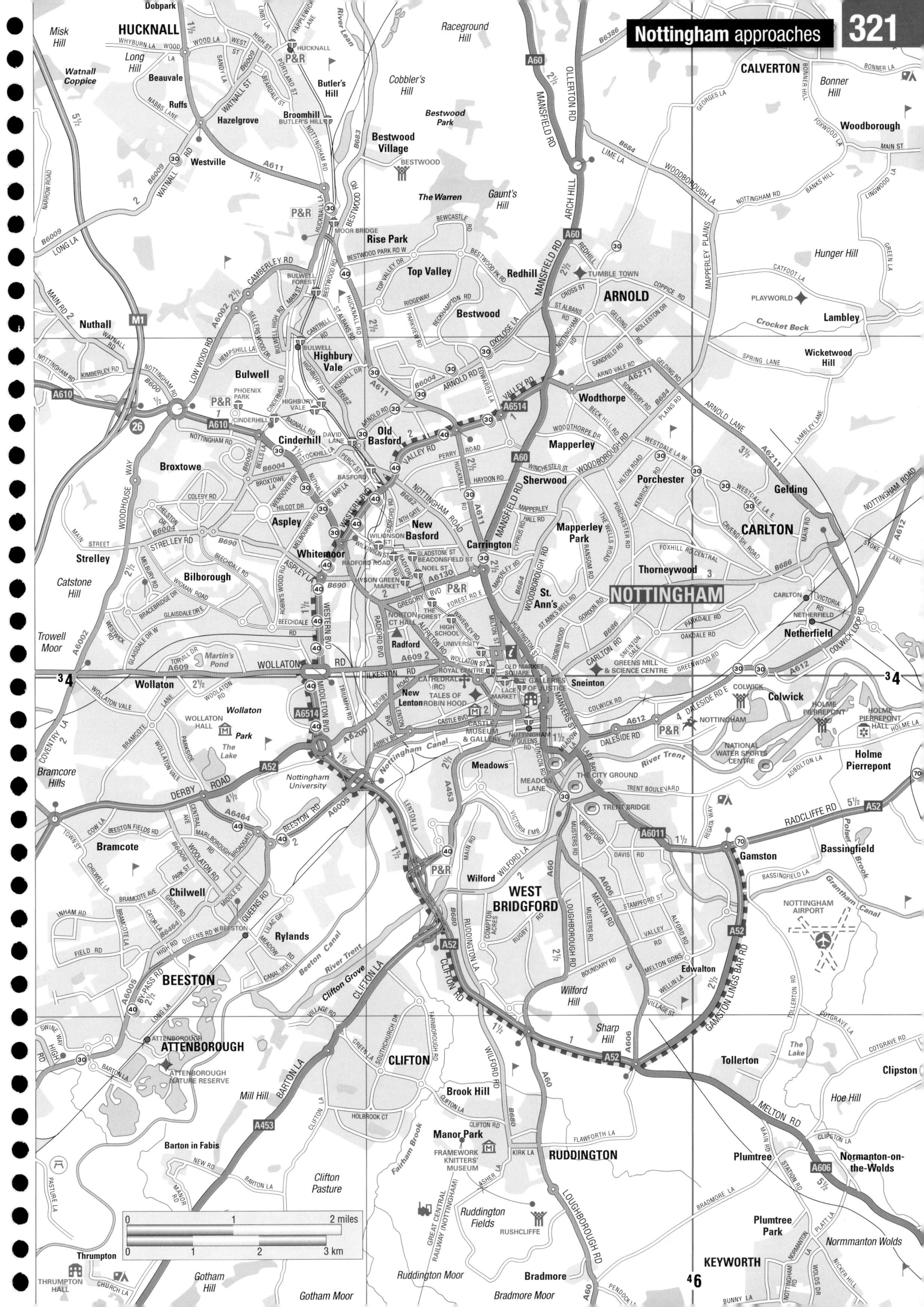

Dobpark
HUCKNALL
Misk Hill
Long Hill
Watnall Coppice
Beauvale
Ruffs
Hazelgrove
Westville
Butler's Hill
Broomhill
Raceground Hill
Cobbler's Hill
Bestwood Park
Bestwood Village
The Warren
Gaunt's Hill
Rise Park
Top Valley
Redhill
Bestwood
ARNOLD
CALVERTON
Bonner Hill
Woodborough
Hunger Hill
PLAYWORLD
Lambley
Crocket Beck
Wicketwood Hill
Nuthall
Bulwell
Highbury Vale
Cinderhill
Old Basford
Broxtowe
Aspley
New Basford
Strelley
Whitemoor
Bilborough
Catstone Hill
Trowell Moor
Carrington
Sherwood
Mapperley
Mapperley Park
Wodthorpe
Porchester
Gelding
CARLTON
Thorneywood
NOTTINGHAM
St. Ann's
Netherfield
Radford
Wollaton
Martin's Pond
Wollaton Park
The Lake
New Lenton
Sneinton
Colwick
Holme Pierrepont
Bramcore Hills
Nottingham University
Meadows
River Trent
NATIONAL WATER SPORTS CENTRE
Bramcote
Chilwell
Wilford
WEST BRIDGFORD
Gamston
Bassingfield
NOTTINGHAM AIRPORT
Grantham Canal
Rylands
Beeston Canal
BEESTON
Edwalton
Wilford Hill
Sharp Hill
ATTENBOROUGH
ATTENBOROUGH NATURE RESERVE
CLIFTON
Tollerton
Clipston
Hoe Hill
Mill Hill
Brook Hill
Barton in Fabis
Manor Park
FRAMEWORK KNITTERS' MUSEUM
RUDDINGTON
Plumtree
Normanton-on-the-Wolds
Clifton Pasture
Ruddington Fields
RUSHCLIFFE
Plumtree Park
Normmanton Wolds
Thrumpton
THRUMPTON HALL
Gotham Hill
Gotham Moor
Ruddington Moor
Bradmore
Bradmore Moor
KEYWORTH
M1
A60
A610
A6514
A611
A52
A453
A606
A6011
A612
0 1 2 miles
0 1 2 3 km

Oxford

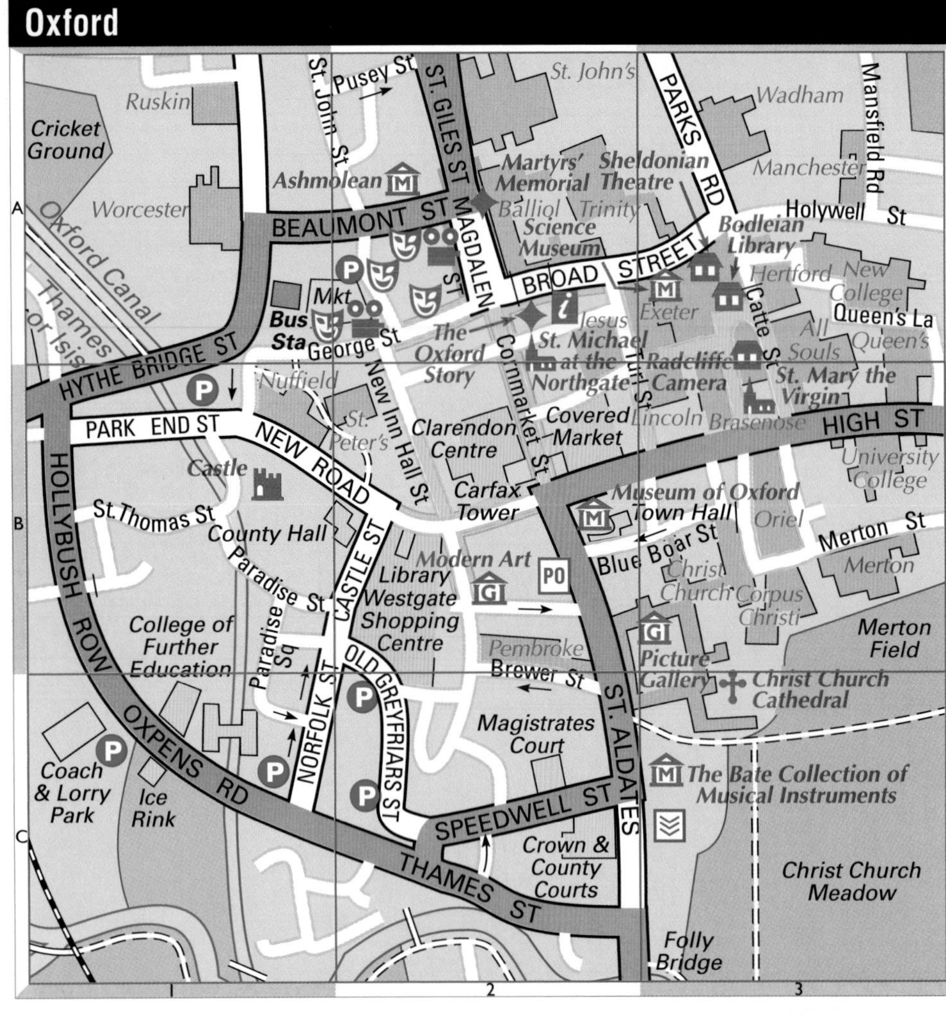

Plymouth

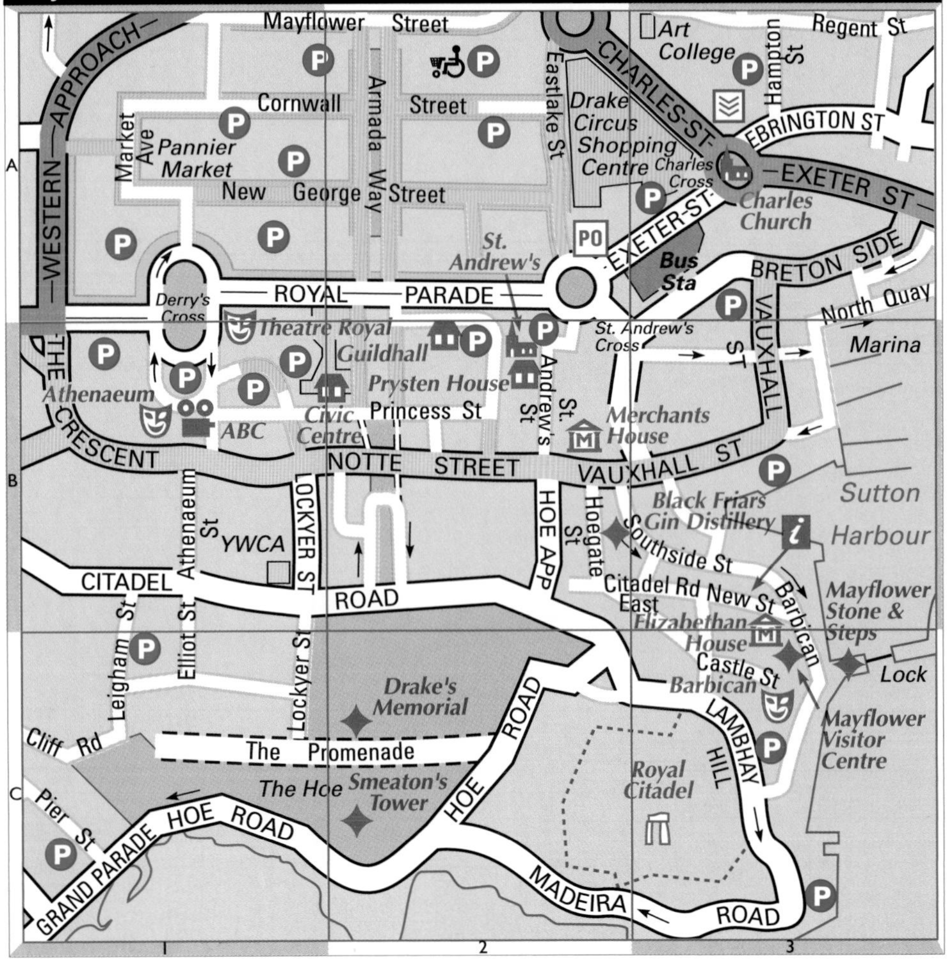

Oxford

All Souls (Coll) A3
Ashmolean Mus . . . A2
Balliol (Coll) A2
Bate Collection, The C3
Beaumont St A1
Blue Boar St B2
Bodleian Library . . . A3
Brasenose (Coll) B3
Brewer St. C2
Broad St A2
Burton-Taylor Theatre A2
Bus Station A1
Carfax Tower B2
Castle B1
Castle St B2
Catte St. A3
Christ Church (Coll) . . . B3
Christ Church Cath . C3
Christ Church Meadow C3
Clarendon Centre B2
Coach & Lorry Park . . . C1
College of Further Education C1
Cornmarket St. B2
Corpus Christi (Coll) . . B3
County Hall B2
Covered Market. B2
Cricket Ground A1
Crown & County Courts C2
Exeter (Coll) A3
Folly Bridge C3
George St A2
Hertford (Coll) A3
High St B3
Hollybush Row B1
Holywell St A3
Hythe Bridge St. B1
Ice Rink C1
Information Ctr A2
Jesus (Coll) A2
Library B2
Lincoln (Coll) B3
Magdalen St A2
Magistrates Court C2
Manchester (Coll) A3
Mansfield Rd A3
Market A1
Martyrs' Memorial ✦. . A2
Merton (Coll) B3
Merton Field B3
Merton St B3
Mus of Modern Art . B2
Museum of Oxford . B2
New College (Coll). . . . A3
New Inn Hall St B2
New Rd B1
New Theatre, The . . A2
Norfolk St C1
Nuffield (Coll). B1
Odeon A2
Old Fire Station A1
Old Greyfriars St C2
Oriel (Coll) B3
Oxford Story, The ✦ . . A2
Oxpens Rd C1
Paradise Sq. B1
Paradise St B1
Park End St B1
Parks Rd A3
Pembroke (Coll). B2
Picture Gallery B3
Playhouse A2
Police Station C3
Post Office B2
Pusey St A2
Queen's (Coll) A3
Queen's La A3
Radcliffe Camera . . A3
Ruskin (Coll) A1
St Aldates C2
St Giles St A2
St John St A1
St John's (Coll) A2
St Mary the Virgin . . B3
St Michael at the Northgate B2
St Peter's (Coll) B2
St Thomas St B1
Science Museum . . A3
Sheldonian Theatre A3
Speedwell St C2
Thames St C2
Town Hall. B2
Trinity (Coll) A2
Turl St A2
University College (Coll) B3
Wadham (Coll). A3
Westgate Shopping Centre B2
Worcester (Coll). A1

Plymouth

ABC B1
Armada Way A2
Art College. A3
Athenaeum St B1
Athenaeum Theatre . B1
Barbican B3
Barbican C3
Black Friars Gin Distillery ✦ B2
Breton Side A3
Bus Station A3
Castle St C3
Charles Church A3
Charles Cross (r'about) A3
Charles St A2
Citadel Rd B1/B2
Citadel Rd East B3
Civic Centre B2
Cliff Rd. C1
Cornwall St A1
Derry's Cross (r'about) A1
Drake Circus Shopping Centre A2
Drake's Memorial ✦ . . C2
Eastlake St A2
Ebrington St A3
Elizabethan House . C3
Elliot St C1
Exeter St A3
Grand Pde. C1
Guildhall B2
Hampton St. A3
Hoe Approach B2
Hoe Rd C1/C2
Hoegate St B2
Information Ctr B3
Lambhay Hill C3
Leigham St C1
Lockyer St. B1
Madeira Rd C2
Marina B3
Market Ave A1
Mayflower St. A1
Mayflower Stone & Steps ✦ C3
Mayflower Visitor Centre ✦. C3
Merchants House . . B2
New George St A1
New St. B3
North Quay A3
Notte St. B2
Pannier Market A1
Pier St C1
Police Station A3
Post Office A2
Princess St B2
Prysten House B2
Regent St A3
Royal Citadel C3
Royal Parade. A1
St Andrew's B2
St Andrew's Cross (r'about). A2
St Andrew's St. B2
Smeaton's Tower ✦ . . C2
Southside St B3
The Crescent. B1
The Hoe. C1
The Promenade C1
Theatre Royal B1
Vauxhall St. B3
Western Approach. . . . A1
YWCA B1

Salisbury

Avon Approach A2
Bedwin St A3
Bishop's Palace . . . C2
Bishops Walk. C2
Blue Boar Row A2
Broad Walk C2
Brown St B3
Bus Station A2
Castle St A2
Catherine St B2
Chapter House C2
Church House B1
Churchill Way East . . . A3
Churchill Way South . . C3
City Hall. A1
Close Wall B2/B3
Court A1
Crane Bridge Rd B1
Crane St B2
Culver St. A3
Culver St South. B3
De Vaux Pl. C2
Dews Rd A1
Exeter St C2
Fisherton St. A1
Friary Estate C3
Friary La C3
Gigant St B3
Greencroft A3
Greencroft St. A3
Guildhall A2
Hall of John Halle . . . B2
High St B2
House of John A'Port A3
Information Ctr A2
Library A2
Maltings, The. A2
Medieval Hall & Discover Salisbury B1
Milford St. A3
Mill Rd B1
Mompesson House (N.T.) B2
New Canal. B2
New St. B2
North Canonry B1
North Gate. B2
North Walk. B2
Old Deanery B2
Playhouse Theatre . A1
Post Office A2/B2
Poultry Cross. A2
Precinct B2
Queen Elizabeth Gardens. B1
Rampart Rd. A3
Regimental Mus . . . B1
St Ann's Gate B2
St Ann St. B3
St Mary's Cathedral ✝. C2
St Thomas A2
Salisbury & South Wiltshire Museum . C1
Salisbury Station . . A1
Salt La. A3
Scots La A2
South Canonry C1
South Gate C2
The Friary C3
West Walk C1
Winchester St A3
Winston Churchill Gdns C3
YHA ▲ A3

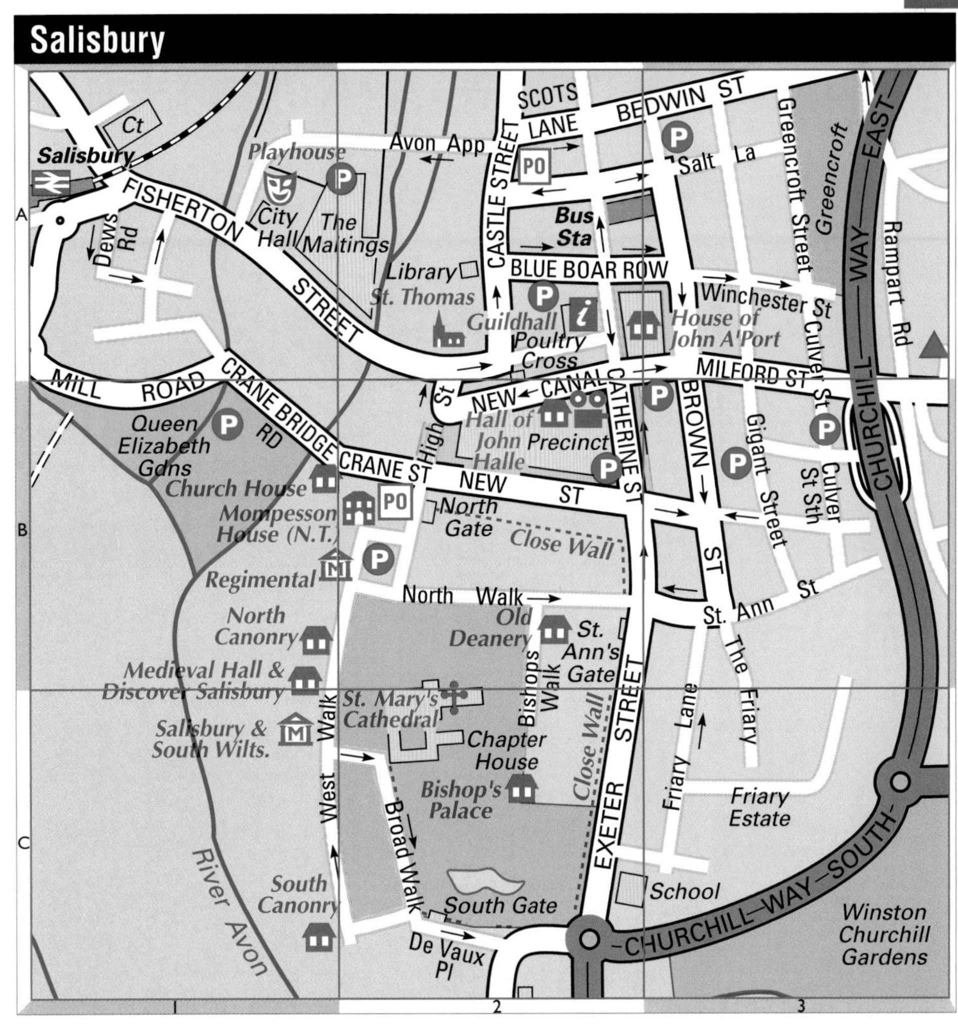

Stratford-upon-Avon

Albany Rd B1
Alcester Rd A1
Arden St A1
Bandstand. B3
Boat Club B3
Brass Rubbing Centre ✦. C2
Bridge St B2
Bridgeway A3
Broad St C1
Broad Walk C1
Bull St C1
Butterfly Farm & Jungle Safari ✦. B3
Bus Station A2
Chapel La B2
Chestnut Walk. B1
Children's Playground . C3
Church St B2
Civic Hall B1
Clopton Bridge ✦ B3
Coach Terminal & Park A3
College La C1
College St C2
Council Offices (District). B2
Council Offices (Town). B2
Cox's Yard ✦. B3
Cricket Ground C3
Ely Gdns B1
Ely St. B2
Foot Ferry C2
Gower Memorial ✦. . . . B3
Great William St A2
Greenhill St B1
Grove Rd B1
Guild St A2
Guildhall & School . B2
Hall's Croft C2
Harvard House B2
High St B2
Holton St. C1
Holy Trinity C2
Information Ctr A3
Judith Shakespeare's House B2
Leisure & Visitor Ctr . . A3
Library A2
Mansell St A1
Masons Court B1
Meer St A2
Narrow La C1
New Place & Nash's House B2
Old Town C2
Payton St. A2
Police Station B1
Post Office A2
Recreation Ground . . . C2
Rother St B1
Ryland St. C2
St Gregory's A3
Sanctus St. C1
Scholars La B1
Seven Meadows Rd . . C1
Shakespeare Centre ✦. A2
Shakespeare Institute . B2
Shakespeare St. A2
Shakespeare's Birthplace ✦. A2
Sheep St B2
Shipston Rd. C3
Southern La. C2
Stratford Healthcare A1
Stratford Hospital . . A1
Stratford Sports Club . C3
The Gallery A3
The Other Place Theatre C2
Town Hall. B2
Town Sq B2
Tramway Bridge B3
Trinity St C2
Tyler St. A2
War Memorial Gdns C2
Warwick Rd. A3
Waterside B2
West St C1
Wood St. B2

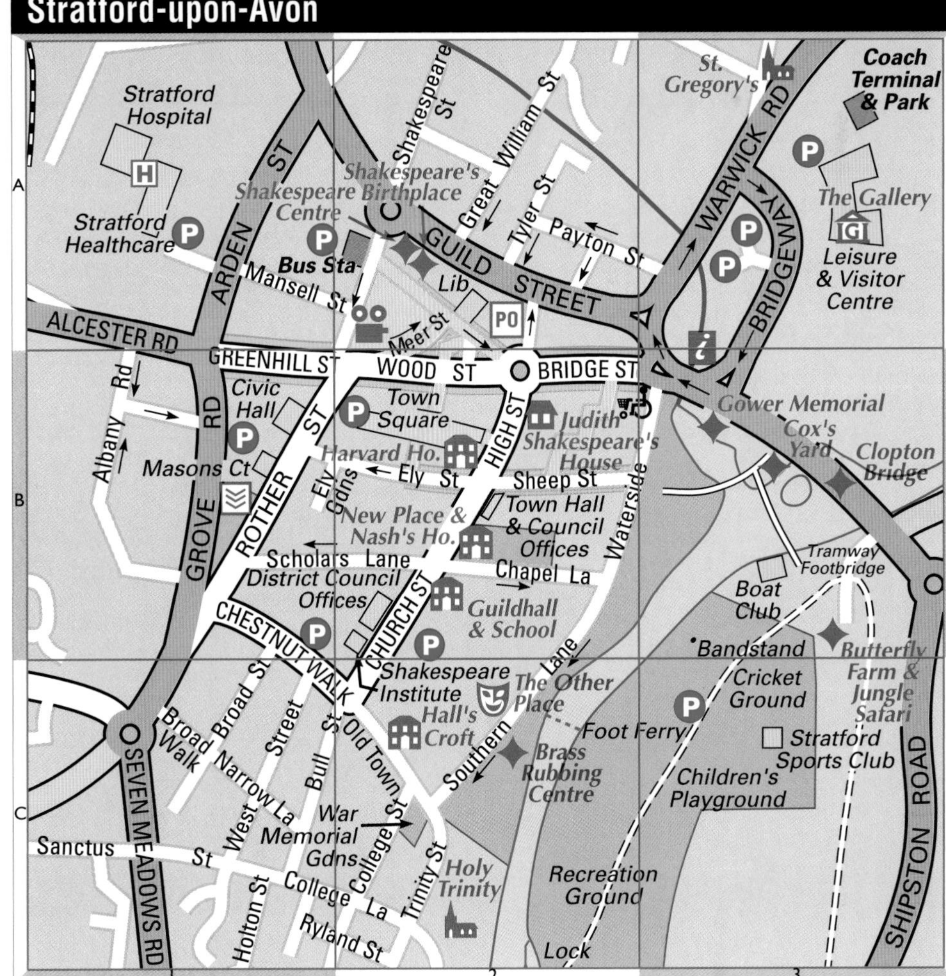

Sheffield

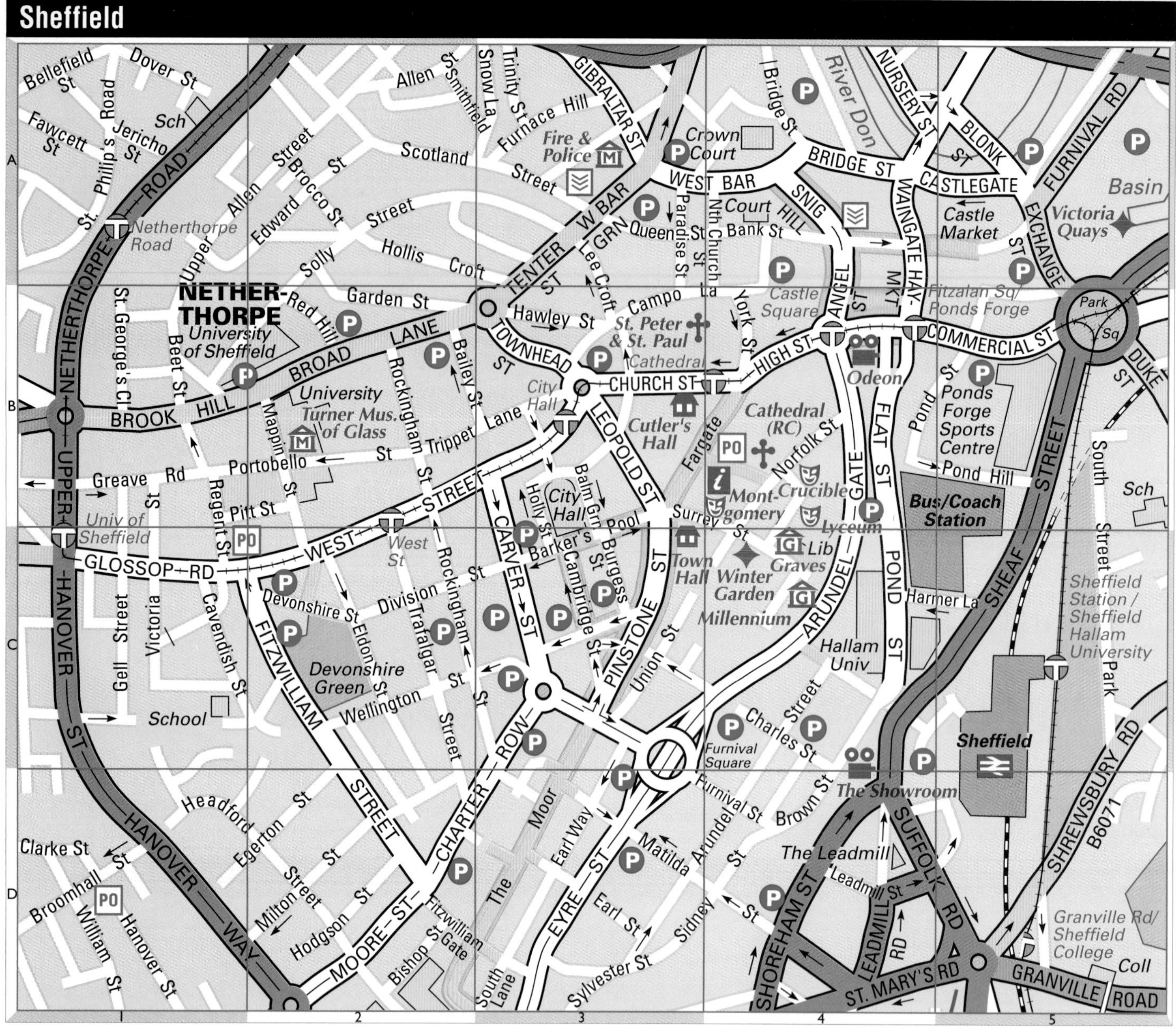

Sheffield

Allen St A2
Angel St. B4
Arundel Gate C4
Arundel St D4
Bailey St B2
Balm Green B3
Bank St A4
Barker's Pool C3
Beet St B1
Bellefield St A1
Bishop St. D2
Blonk St. A5
Bridge St A4
Broad La B2
Brocco St A2
Brook Hill. B1
Broomhall St D1
Brown St D4
Burgess St. C3
Bus/Coach Station . . . B5
Cambridge St C3
Campo La B3
Carver St. C3
Castle Market A5
Castle Square (tram stop). B4
Castlegate A5
Cathedral (RC) ✝. B4
Cathedral (tram stop) . B4
Cavendish St. C1
Charles St C4
Charter Row D2
Church St B3
City Hall. B3
City Hall (tram stop) . . B3
Clarke St D1
Commercial St. B5
Court A4
Crown Court A4
Crucible Theatre . . . B4
Cutler's Hall B3
Devonshire Green C2
Devonshire St C2
Division St C2
Dover St A1
Duke St B5
Earl St D3
Earl Way D3
Edward St A2
Egerton St D2
Eldon St. C2
Exchange St A5
Eyre St. D3
Fargate B3
Fawcett St. A1
Fire & Police A3
Fitzalan Sq / Ponds Forge (tram stop) . . . B4
Fitzwilliam Gate D2
Fitzwilliam St C2
Flat St B4
Furnace Hill A3
Furnival Rd A5
Furnival Sq C4
Furnival St D4
Garden St B2
Gell St C1
Gibraltar St A3
Glossop Rd C1
Granville Rd. D5
Granville Rd / Sheffield College (tram stop) . . D5
Graves Gallery & Museum C4
Greave Rd B1
Hallam University C4
Hanover St D1
Hanover Way. D1
Harmer La C4
Hawley St B3
Haymarket. A4
Headford St. D1
High St B4
Hodgson St D2
Hollis Croft. A2
Holly St B3
Information Ctr B4
Jericho St A1
Leadmill Rd D4
Leadmill St D4
Leadmill, The. D4
Lee Croft A3
Leopold St. B3
Library C4
Lyceum Theatre . . . B4
Mappin St B2
Matilda St D3
Millennium Galleries C4
Milton St D2
Montgomery B4
Moore St D2
Netherthorpe Rd B1
Netherthorpe Rd (tram stop). A1
Norfolk St B4
North Church St A4
Nursery St A4
Odeon B4
Paradise St A3
Park Sq B5
Pinstone St C3
Pitt St. B1
Police Station . . A3/A4
Pond Hill B5
Pond St B4/C4
Ponds Forge Sports Centre B5
Portobello St B2
Post Office . . . B4/C1/D1
Queen St A3
Red Hill B2
Regent St B1
Rockingham St . . . B2/C2
St George's Cl B1
St Mary's Rd D4
St Peter & St Paul Cathedral ✝. B3
St Philip's Rd. A1
Scotland St A2
Sheaf St. C5
Sheffield Station . . C5
Sheffield Station / Sheffield Hallam Uni. (tram stop). C5
Shoreham St D4
Showroom, The D4
Shrewsbury Rd D5
Sidney St. D3
Smithfield A2
Snig Hill. A4
Snow La A3
Solly St A2
South La D3
South Street Park B5
Suffolk Rd D4
Surrey St B3
Sylvester St D3
Tenter St A3
The Moor. D3
Town Hall C3
Townhead St B3
Trafalgar St C2
Trinity St A3
Trippet La B2
Turner Museum of Glass B2
Union St C3
University of Sheffield . B2
University of Sheffield (tram stop). C1
Upper Allen St. A1
Upper Hanover St C1
Victoria Quays ✦. A5
Victoria St C1
Waingate A4
Wellington St. C2
West Bar A3
West Bar Green. A3
West St C2
West St (tram stop) . . . C2
William St D1
Winter Garden ✦. C4
York St. B4

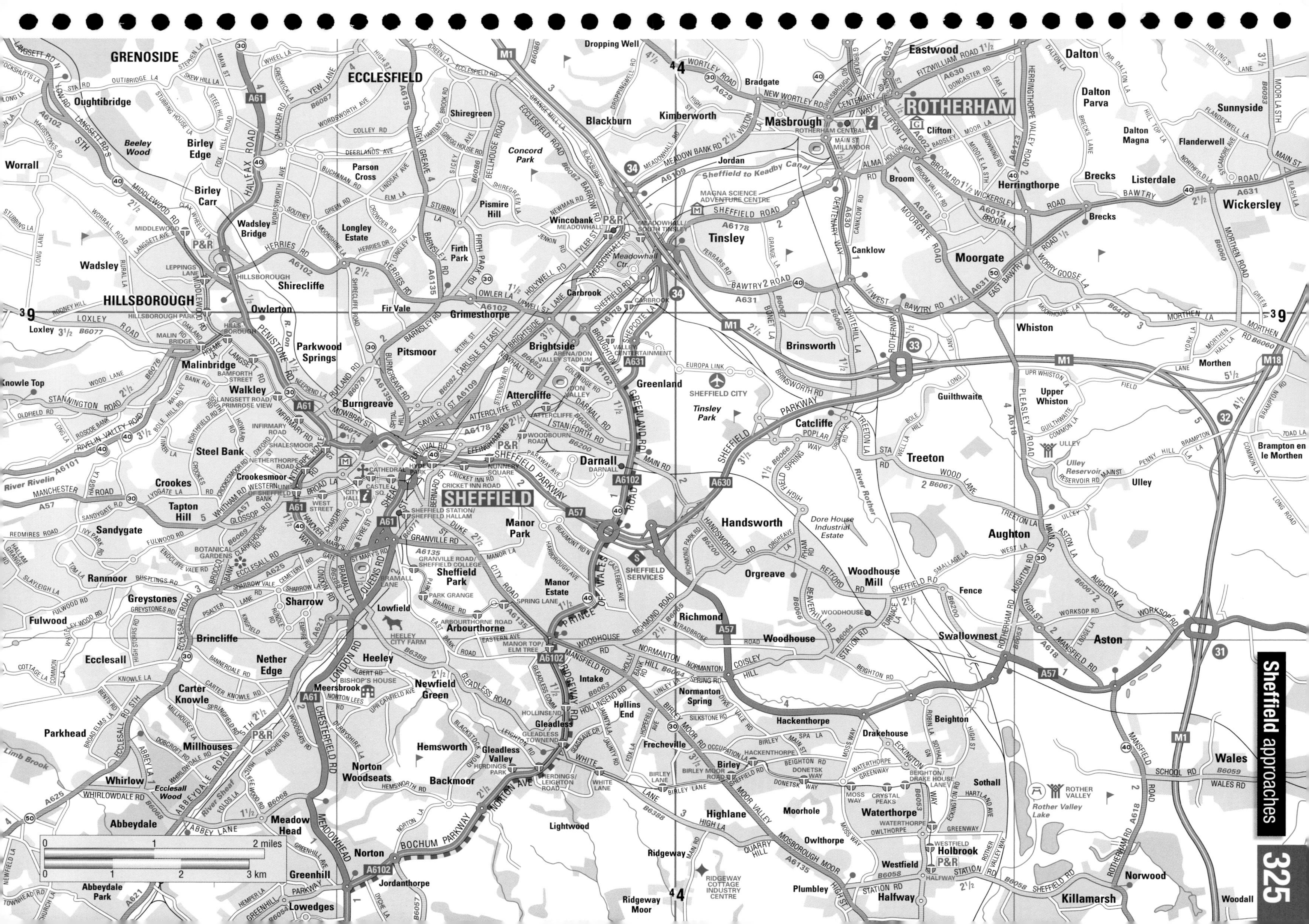

ROTHERHAM
SHEFFIELD
HILLSBOROUGH
ECCLESFIELD
GRENOSIDE
Wickersley
Sunnyside
Flanderwell
Listerdale
Dalton Magna
Dalton Parva
Dalton
Brecks
Herringthorpe
Moorgate
Eastwood
Clifton
Broom
Canklow
Masbrough
Bradgate
Kimberworth
Blackburn
Dropping Well
Jordan
Tinsley
Brinsworth
Whiston
Upper Whiston
Morthen
Brampton en le Morthen
Ulley
Guilthwaite
Treeton
Catcliffe
Aughton
Aston
Swallownest
Fence
Woodhouse Mill
Handsworth
Orgreave
Woodhouse
Richmond
Wales
Norwood
Killamarsh
Woodall
Beighton
Sothall
Holbrook
Drakehouse
Waterthorpe
Westfield
Halfway
Hackenthorpe
Moorhole
Owlthorpe
Plumbley
Birley
Highlane
Ridgeway
Ridgeway Moor
Frecheville
Normanton Spring
Hollins End
Intake
Gleadless
Lightwood
Greenland
Sheffield City
Tinsley Park
Darnall
Attercliffe
Brightside
Carbrook
Wincobank
Concord Park
Pismire Hill
Shiregreen
Firth Park
Grimesthorpe
Pitsmoor
Fir Vale
Burngreave
Parson Cross
Longley Estate
Shirecliffe
Parkwood Springs
Owlerton
Wadsley Bridge
Birley Carr
Birley Edge
Beeley Wood
Oughtibridge
Wadsley
Worrall
Loxley
Knowle Top
Malinbridge
Walkley
Steel Bank
Crookesmoor
Crookes
Tapton Hill
Sandygate
Ranmoor
Greystones
Fulwood
Nether Edge
Sharrow
Brincliffe
Carter Knowle
Ecclesall
Millhouses
Whirlow
Ecclesall Wood
Abbeydale
Abbeydale Park
Parkhead
Heeley
Meersbrook
Newfield Green
Lowfield
Sheffield Park
Arbourthorne
Manor Park
Manor Estate
Hemsworth
Backmoor
Gleadless Valley
Norton Woodseats
Norton
Jordanthorpe
Greenhill
Meadow Head
Lowedges
Rother Valley Lake
Ulley Reservoir
River Rother
R. Don
River Sheaf
River Rivelin
Limb Brook
Dore House Industrial Estate
Magna Science Adventure Centre
Sheffield to Keadby Canal
Sheffield Services
Ridgeway Cottage Industry Centre
Botanical Gardens
Bishop's House
Meadowhall Ctr.
M1
M18
A57
A61
A630
A631
A618
A6135
A6102
A6109
A6178
A625
A621
0 1 2 miles
0 1 2 3 km

Swansea / Abertawe

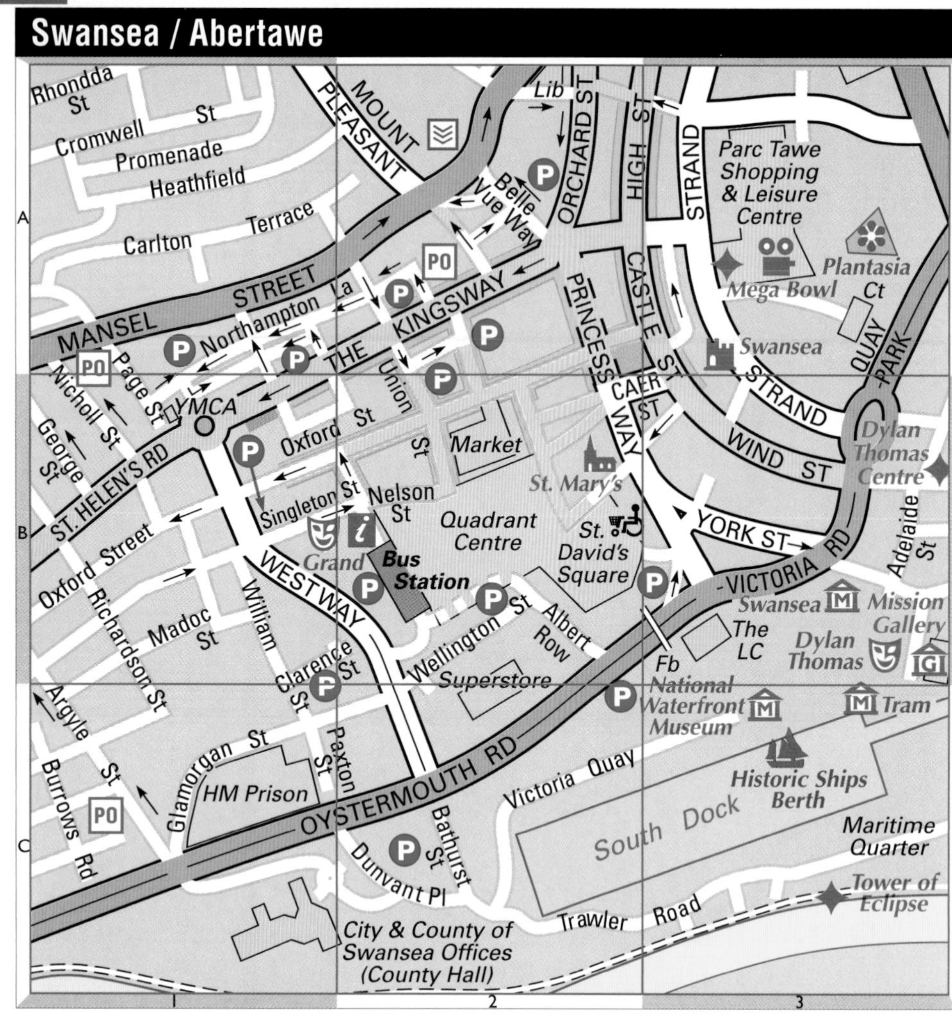

Swansea/ Abertawe

- Adelaide St B3
- Albert Row. B2
- Argyle St C1
- Bathurst St C2
- Belle Vue Way A2
- Burrows Rd C1
- Bus Station B2
- Caer St B2
- Carlton Terr A1
- Castle St A3
- City & County of Swansea Offices (County Hall) C1
- Clarence St B1
- Court A3
- Cromwell St. A1
- Dunvant Pl. C2
- Dylan Thomas Centre ✦. B3
- Dylan Thomas Theatre B3
- George St B1
- Glamorgan St C1
- Grand Theatre B1
- Heathfield A1
- High St A2
- Historic Ships Berth C3
- HM Prison C1
- Information Ctr B2
- Library A2
- LC, The B3
- Madoc St. B1
- Mansel St A1
- Maritime Quarter C3
- Market B2
- Mega Bowl ✦ A3
- Mission Gallery B3
- Mount Pleasant A2
- National Waterfront Museum C3
- Nelson St. B2
- Nicholl St. B1
- Northampton La A1
- Orchard St. A2
- Oxford St. B1
- Oystermouth Rd C2
- Page St B1
- Parc Tawe Shopping & Leisure Centre. A3
- Paxton St. C1
- Plantasia A3
- Police Station A2
- Post Office . A1/A2/C1
- Princess Way. A2
- Promenade A1
- Quadrant Centre B2
- Quay Park A3
- Rhondda St A1
- Richardson St B1
- St David's Sq. B2
- St Helen's Rd B1
- St Mary's B2
- Singleton St. B1
- Strand A3/B3
- Swansea Castle . . . A3
- Swansea Museum . B3
- The Kingsway A2
- Tower of Eclipse ✦ . . . C3
- Tram Museum C3
- Trawler Rd C2
- Union St B2
- Victoria Quay. C2
- Victoria Rd. B3
- Wellington St B2
- Westway B1
- William St B1
- Wind St B3
- YMCA B1
- York St. B3

Winchester

- Archery La. B1
- Beggar's La. A3
- Broadway B3
- Brooks Shopping Centre, The B2
- Bus Station B3
- Butter Cross ✦ B2
- Canon St C1
- Castle Wall C2/C3
- Castle, King Arthur's Round Table B1
- Cathedral ✝. B2
- Chesil St C3
- Chesil Theatre C3
- City Museum B2
- City Offices B3
- City Rd A1
- Clifton Terr. A1
- Close Wall B2/C2
- Colebrook St B2
- College St C2
- Compton Rd C1
- County Council Offices. A1
- Culver Rd C1
- Durngate Pl A3
- Eastgate St B3
- Edgar Rd C1
- Fire Station A3
- Friarsgate B2
- Gordon Rd. A2
- Guildhall B3
- High St B1/B2
- Hyde Abbey Rd. A2
- Information Ctr B2
- Jewry St A2
- Kingsgate Arch C2
- Kingsgate St C2
- Library A1
- Lower Brook St A3
- Magdalen Hill B3
- Market La B2
- Middle Brook St B2
- North Walls A2
- Parchment St A2
- Park Ave A3
- Police Station A3
- Post Office . A1/B2/C2
- River Park Leisure Centre. A2
- Romans' Rd C1
- St Cross Rd. C1
- St George's St. B2
- St James' La B1
- St James Villas C1
- St John's B3
- St John's St. B3
- St Michael's Rd C1
- St Paul's Hill A1
- St Peter St. A2
- St Swithun St C2
- St Thomas St B1
- School of Art A3
- Screen B1
- Southgate St B1
- Staple Gdns A1
- Station Rd A1
- Sussex St A1
- Swan Lane. A1
- Tanner St. B3
- The Square B2
- The Weirs. C3
- Theatre Royal A1
- Tower St A1
- Town Hall. B3
- Union St A3
- Upper Brook St A2
- Wales St A3
- Water Lane B3
- West Gate B1
- Wharf Hill. C3
- Winchester College . . . C2
- Winchester ⇌ A1
- Wolvesey Castle . . . C3

Worcester

Angel Pl A2
Angel St A2
Bridge St B2
Broad St B2
Bromwich Rd C1
Bus Station A2
Carden St B3
Castle St A2
Cathedral ✝ C2
Cathedral Plaza B3
Charles St B3
Citizens' Advice Bureau A3
City Walls Rd B3
College of Technology . B2
College St C3
Commandery 🏛 C3
County Cricket Ground C1
Cripplegate Park B1
Croft Rd A1
Crowngate Centre B2
Deansway B2
Edgar Tower ✦ C3
Farrier St A2
Fire Station B2
Foregate St A2
Foregate St ⇌ A2
Foundry St B3
Friar St B3
Grand Stand Rd A1
Greyfriars 🏛 B3
Guildhall 🏛 B2
High St B2
Huntingdon Hall ♬ . . . B2
Hylton Rd B1
Information Ctr ℹ B2
King's School C2
Kleve Walk C2
Library, Museum & Art Gallery 🏛 A2
Lowesmoor A3
New Rd C1
New St B3
Odeon 🎥 A2
Pheasant St A3
Post Office PO A2/A3
Quay St B2
Queen St A3
Reindeer Court B3
St Martin's Gate B3
St Paul's St B3
Sansome Walk A3
Severn St C3
Shaw St A2
Slingpool Walk C1
South Quay B2
Sports Ground C1
The Butts A2
The Cross A2
The Shambles B3
Tybridge St B1
Worcester Bridge B1
Worcester Library & History Centre A3
Worcester Porcelain Museum 🏛 C3
Worcester Racecourse Pitchcroft A1
Wylds La C3

Worcester

Worcester Racecourse Pitchcroft
Grand Stand
Grand Stand Rd
Footbridge
Castle St
Croft Rd
Library, Museum & Art Gallery
Farrier St
Foregate St
Sansome Wk
Foregate Street
Lowesmoor Wharf
Citizens' Advice Bureau
Lowesmoor
Pheasant St
Odeon
Shaw St
The Butts
Bus Sta
Angel Pl
Angel St
The Cross
Queen St
Worcs. Library & History Centre
Crowngate Centre
Broad St
Martin's Gate
River Severn
Hylton Road
Superstore
Worcester Bridge
Bridge St
Huntingdon Hall
Deansway
High St
The Shambles
Reindeer Court
New St
City Walls Rd
Quay St
South Quay
Guildhall
Fire Sta
Cathedral Plaza
Charles St
Greyfriars
Carden St
Foundry St
St. Paul's St
Friar St
Tybridge St
New Road
Cripplegate Park
College of Technology
County Cricket Ground
Sports Ground
Cathedral
College St
Edgar Tower
Commandery
Wylds La
Bromwich Rd
Slingpool Walk
Kleve Walk
King's School
Worcester Porcelain Museum
Severn St

York

Aldwark B3
Ambulance Station . . . B3
Arc Museum, The 🏛 . . B3
Barley Hall 🏛 B2
Blossom St C1
Bootham A1
Bootham Terr A1
Bridge St C2
Castle Museum 🏛 . . . C3
Castlegate C3
City Art Gallery 🏛 A2
City Wall A2/B1
Clifford St C2
Clifford's Tower 🏛 C3
Coney St B2
Cromwell Rd C2
Crown Court C3
Davygate B2
Deanery Gdns A2
DIG ✦ B3
Fairfax House 🏛 C3
Gillygate A2
Goodramgate B3
Grand Opera House ♬ C2
Guildhall B2
Holy Trinity ⛪ B3
Information Ctr ℹ . A2/B1
Jorvik Viking Centre 🏛 C3
Leeman Rd B1
Lendal B2
Lendal Bridge B1
Library A2
Longfield Terr A1
Lord Mayor's Walk A3
Marygate A1
Merchant Adventurer's Hall 🏛 B3
Merchant Taylors' Hall 🏛 A3
Micklegate C1
Minster, The ✝ A2
Monkgate A3
Museum Gdns ✿ B2
Museum St B2
North St B2
Nunnery La C1
Odeon 🎥 C1
Ouse Bridge B2
Parliament St B3
Piccadilly C3
Police Station ▣ C2
Post Office PO . B2/B3/C1
Priory St C1
Regimental Museum 🏛 C3
Rougier St B1
St Andrewgate B3
St Saviourgate B3
Skeldergate C2
Station Rd C1
Stonegate B2
The Shambles B3
The Stonebow B3
Theatre Royal ♬ A2
Toft Green C1
Tower St C3
Treasurer's House 🏛 . . A3
Trinity La C1
Undercroft Mus 🏛 . . . A2
Victor St C2
York City Screen 🎥 . . . B2
York Dungeon 🏛 C2
York Station ⇌ B1
Yorkshire Museum 🏛 . A2

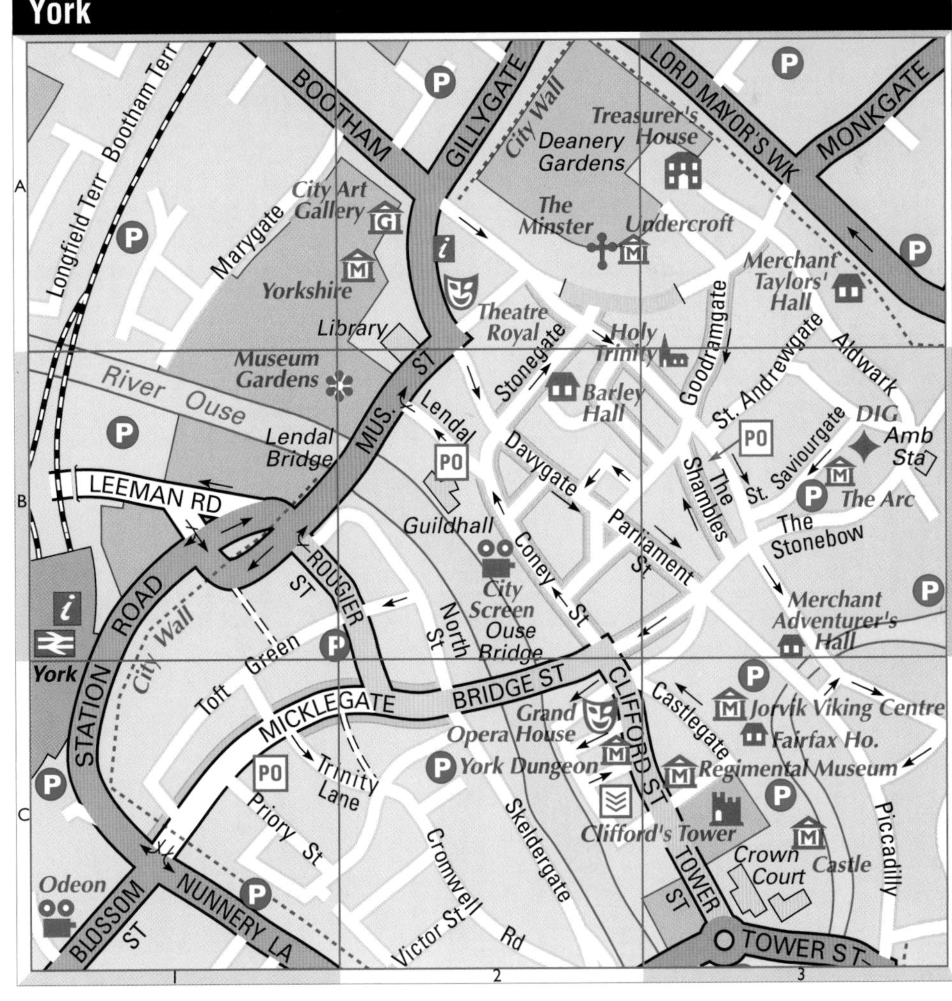

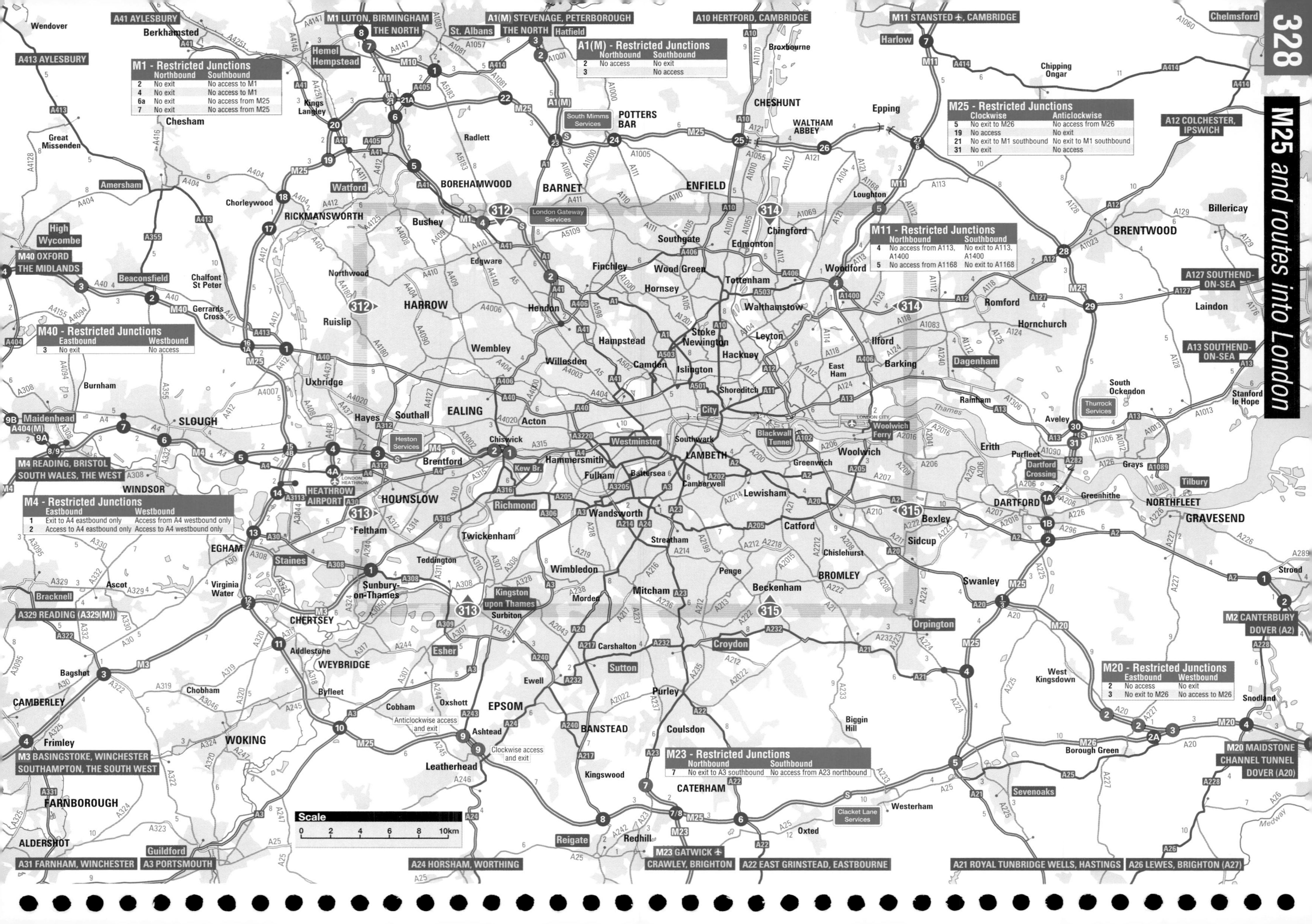
M1 - Restricted Junctions
Northbound | Southbound
2 No exit | No access to M1
4 No exit | No access to M1
6a No exit | No access from M25
7 No exit | No access from M25
A1(M) - Restricted Junctions
Northbound | Southbound
2 No access | No exit
3 No exit | No access
M25 - Restricted Junctions
Clockwise | Anticlockwise
5 No exit to M26 | No access from M26
19 No access | No exit
21 No exit to M1 southbound | No exit to M1 southbound
31 No exit | No access
M11 - Restricted Junctions
Northbound | Southbound
4 No access from A113, A1400 | No exit to A113, A1400
5 No access from A1168 | No exit to A1168
M40 - Restricted Junctions
Eastbound | Westbound
3 No exit | No access
M4 - Restricted Junctions
Eastbound | Westbound
1 Exit to A4 eastbound only | Access from A4 westbound only
2 Access to A4 eastbound only | Access to A4 westbound only
M20 - Restricted Junctions
Eastbound | Westbound
2 No access | No exit
3 No exit to M26 | No access to M26
M23 - Restricted Junctions
Northbound | Southbound
7 No exit to A3 southbound | No access from A23 northbound
Anticlockwise access and exit
Clockwise access and exit
Scale
0 2 4 6 8 10km
A41 AYLESBURY
M1 LUTON, BIRMINGHAM THE NORTH
A1(M) STEVENAGE, PETERBOROUGH THE NORTH
A10 HERTFORD, CAMBRIDGE
M11 STANSTED, CAMBRIDGE
A12 COLCHESTER, IPSWICH
A127 SOUTHEND-ON-SEA
A13 SOUTHEND-ON-SEA
M2 CANTERBURY DOVER (A2)
M20 MAIDSTONE CHANNEL TUNNEL DOVER (A20)
A26 LEWES, BRIGHTON (A27)
A21 ROYAL TUNBRIDGE WELLS, HASTINGS
A22 EAST GRINSTEAD, EASTBOURNE
M23 GATWICK, CRAWLEY, BRIGHTON
A24 HORSHAM, WORTHING
A3 PORTSMOUTH
A31 FARNHAM, WINCHESTER
M3 BASINGSTOKE, WINCHESTER SOUTHAMPTON, THE SOUTH WEST
A329 READING (A329(M))
M4 READING, BRISTOL SOUTH WALES, THE WEST
M40 OXFORD THE MIDLANDS
A413 AYLESBURY

Abbreviations used in the index

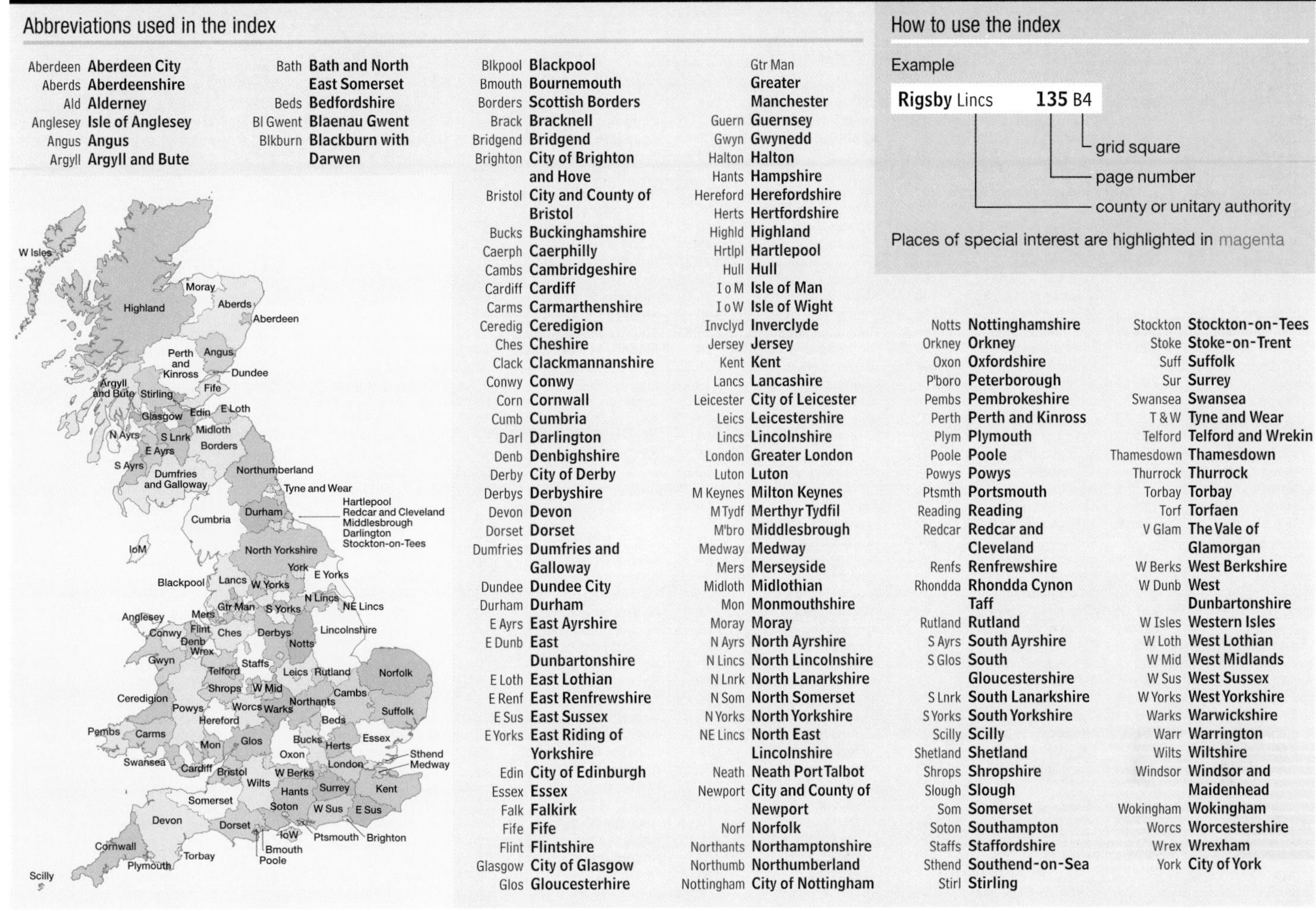

Aberdeen **Aberdeen City**
Aberds **Aberdeenshire**
Ald **Alderney**
Anglesey **Isle of Anglesey**
Angus **Angus**
Argyll **Argyll and Bute**
Bath **Bath and North East Somerset**
Beds **Bedfordshire**
Bl Gwent **Blaenau Gwent**
Blkburn **Blackburn with Darwen**
Blkpool **Blackpool**
Bmouth **Bournemouth**
Borders **Scottish Borders**
Brack **Bracknell**
Bridgend **Bridgend**
Brighton **City of Brighton and Hove**
Bristol **City and County of Bristol**
Bucks **Buckinghamshire**
Caerph **Caerphilly**
Cambs **Cambridgeshire**
Cardiff **Cardiff**
Carms **Carmarthenshire**
Ceredig **Ceredigion**
Ches **Cheshire**
Clack **Clackmannanshire**
Conwy **Conwy**
Corn **Cornwall**
Cumb **Cumbria**
Darl **Darlington**
Denb **Denbighshire**
Derby **City of Derby**
Derbys **Derbyshire**
Devon **Devon**
Dorset **Dorset**
Dumfries **Dumfries and Galloway**
Dundee **Dundee City**
Durham **Durham**
E Ayrs **East Ayrshire**
E Dunb **East Dunbartonshire**
E Loth **East Lothian**
E Renf **East Renfrewshire**
E Sus **East Sussex**
E Yorks **East Riding of Yorkshire**
Edin **City of Edinburgh**
Essex **Essex**
Falk **Falkirk**
Fife **Fife**
Flint **Flintshire**
Glasgow **City of Glasgow**
Glos **Gloucesterhire**
Gtr Man **Greater Manchester**
Guern **Guernsey**
Gwyn **Gwynedd**
Halton **Halton**
Hants **Hampshire**
Hereford **Herefordshire**
Herts **Hertfordshire**
Highld **Highland**
Hrtlpl **Hartlepool**
Hull **Hull**
I o M **Isle of Man**
I o W **Isle of Wight**
Invclyd **Inverclyde**
Jersey **Jersey**
Kent **Kent**
Lancs **Lancashire**
Leicester **City of Leicester**
Leics **Leicestershire**
Lincs **Lincolnshire**
London **Greater London**
Luton **Luton**
M Keynes **Milton Keynes**
M Tydf **Merthyr Tydfil**
M'bro **Middlesbrough**
Medway **Medway**
Mers **Merseyside**
Midloth **Midlothian**
Mon **Monmouthshire**
Moray **Moray**
N Ayrs **North Ayrshire**
N Lincs **North Lincolnshire**
N Lnrk **North Lanarkshire**
N Som **North Somerset**
N Yorks **North Yorkshire**
NE Lincs **North East Lincolnshire**
Neath **Neath Port Talbot**
Newport **City and County of Newport**
Norf **Norfolk**
Northants **Northamptonshire**
Northumb **Northumberland**
Nottingham **City of Nottingham**
Notts **Nottinghamshire**
Orkney **Orkney**
Oxon **Oxfordshire**
P'boro **Peterborough**
Pembs **Pembrokeshire**
Perth **Perth and Kinross**
Plym **Plymouth**
Poole **Poole**
Powys **Powys**
Ptsmth **Portsmouth**
Reading **Reading**
Redcar **Redcar and Cleveland**
Renfs **Renfrewshire**
Rhondda **Rhondda Cynon Taff**
Rutland **Rutland**
S Ayrs **South Ayrshire**
S Glos **South Gloucestershire**
S Lnrk **South Lanarkshire**
S Yorks **South Yorkshire**
Scilly **Scilly**
Shetland **Shetland**
Shrops **Shropshire**
Slough **Slough**
Som **Somerset**
Soton **Southampton**
Staffs **Staffordshire**
Sthend **Southend-on-Sea**
Stirl **Stirling**
Stockton **Stockton-on-Tees**
Stoke **Stoke-on-Trent**
Suff **Suffolk**
Sur **Surrey**
Swansea **Swansea**
T & W **Tyne and Wear**
Telford **Telford and Wrekin**
Thamesdown **Thamesdown**
Thurrock **Thurrock**
Torbay **Torbay**
Torf **Torfaen**
V Glam **The Vale of Glamorgan**
W Berks **West Berkshire**
W Dunb **West Dunbartonshire**
W Isles **Western Isles**
W Loth **West Lothian**
W Mid **West Midlands**
W Sus **West Sussex**
W Yorks **West Yorkshire**
Warks **Warwickshire**
Warr **Warrington**
Wilts **Wiltshire**
Windsor **Windsor and Maidenhead**
Wokingham **Wokingham**
Worcs **Worcestershire**
Wrex **Wrexham**
York **City of York**

How to use the index

Example

Rigsby Lincs **135 B4**

- grid square
- page number
- county or unitary authority

Places of special interest are highlighted in magenta

A

Ab Kettleby Leics **115 C5**
Ab Lench Worcs **80 B3**
Abbas Combe Som **29 C7**
Abberley Worcs **79 A5**
Abberton Essex **71 B4**
Abberton Worcs **80 B2**
Abberwick Northumb **189 B4**
Abbess Roding Essex **69 B5**
Abbey Devon **27 D6**
Abbey-cwm-hir Powys **93 D4**
Abbey Dore Hereford **78 D1**
Abbey Field Essex **70 A3**
Abbey Hulton Stoke **112 A3**
Abbey St Bathans Borders **211 D4**
Abbey Town Cumb **175 C4**
Abbey Village Lancs **137 A5**
Abbey Wood London **50 B1**
Abbeydale S Yorks **130 A3**
Abbeystead Lancs **145 B5**
Abbots Bickington Devon **25 D4**
Abbots Bromley Staffs **113 C4**
Abbots Langley Herts **67 C5**
Abbots Leigh N Som **43 B4**
Abbots Morton Worcs **80 B3**
Abbots Ripton Cambs **100 D4**
Abbots Salford Warks **80 B3**
Abbotsbury Dorset **15 C5**
Abbotsbury Sub Tropical Gardens Dorset **15 C5**
Abbotsford House Borders **197 C4**
Abbotsham Devon **25 C5**
Abbotskerswell Devon **8 A2**
Abbotsley Cambs **84 B4**
Abbotswood Hants **32 C2**
Abbotts Ann Hants **32 A2**
Abcott Shrops **94 D1**
Abdon Shrops **94 C3**
Aber Ceredig **74 D3**
Aber-Arad Carms **73 C6**
Aber-banc Ceredig **73 B6**
Aber Cowarch Gwyn **91 A6**
Aber-Giâr Carms **58 A2**
Aber-gwynfi Neath **40 B3**
Aber-Hirnant Gwyn **109 B4**
Aber-nant Rhondda **41 A5**
Aber-Rhiwlech Gwyn **108 C4**
Aber-Village Powys **60 A3**
Aberaeron Ceredig **74 B3**
Aberaman Rhondda **41 A5**
Aberangell Gwyn **91 A6**
Aberarder Highld **240 D2**
Aberarder House Highld **252 D2**
Aberarder Lodge Highld **240 D3**
Aberargie Perth **219 C6**
Aberarth Ceredig **74 B3**
Aberavon Neath **40 B2**
Aberbeeg Bl Gwent **41 A7**
Abercanaid M Tydf **41 A5**
Abercarn Caerph **41 B7**
Abercastle Pembs **55 A4**
Abercegir Powys **91 B6**
Aberchirder Aberds **268 D1**
Aberconwy House, Conwy Conwy **124 B2**
Abercraf Powys **59 D5**
Abercrombie Fife **221 D5**
Abercych Pembs **73 B5**
Abercynafon Powys **60 B2**
Abercynon Rhondda **41 B5**
Aberdalgie Perth **219 B5**
Aberdâr = Aberdare Rhondda **41 A4**
Aberdare = Aberdâr Rhondda **41 A4**
Aberdaron Gwyn **106 D1**
Aberdaugleddau = Milford Haven Pembs **55 D5**
Aberdeen Aberdeen **245 B6**
Aberdeen Airport Aberdeen **245 A5**
Aberdesach Gwyn **107 A4**
Aberdour Fife **209 B4**
Aberdovey Gwyn **90 C4**
Aberdulais Neath **40 A2**
Aberedw Powys **77 C4**
Abereiddy Pembs **54 A3**
Abererch Gwyn **106 C3**
Aberfan M Tydf **41 A5**
Aberfeldy Perth **230 D2**
Aberffraw Anglesey **122 D3**
Aberffrwd Ceredig **75 A5**
Aberford W Yorks **148 D3**
Aberfoyle Stirl **217 D5**
Abergavenny = Y Fenni Mon **61 B4**
Abergele Conwy **125 B4**
Abergorlech Carms **58 B2**
Abergwaun = Fishguard Pembs **72 C2**
Abergwesyn Powys **76 B2**
Abergwili Carms **58 C1**
Abergwynant Gwyn **91 A4**
Abergwyngregyn Gwyn **123 C6**
Abergynolwyn Gwyn **91 B4**
Aberhonddu = Brecon Powys **60 A2**
Aberhosan Powys **91 C6**
Aberkenfig Bridgend **40 C3**
Aberlady E Loth **210 B1**
Aberlemno Angus **232 C3**
Aberllefenni Gwyn **91 B5**
Abermagwr Ceredig **75 A5**
Abermaw = Barmouth Gwyn **90 A4**
Abermeurig Ceredig **75 C4**
Abermule Powys **93 B5**
Abernaint Powys **109 C6**
Abernant Carms **73 D6**
Abernethy Perth **219 C6**
Abernyte Perth **220 A2**
Aberpennar = Mountain Ash Rhondda **41 B5**
Aberporth Ceredig **73 A5**
Abersoch Gwyn **106 D3**
Abersychan Torf **61 C4**
Abertawe = Swansea Swansea **57 C6**
Aberteifi = Cardigan Ceredig **73 B4**
Aberthin V Glam **41 D5**
Abertillery = Abertyleri Bl Gwent **41 A7**
Abertridwr Caerph **41 C6**
Abertridwr Powys **109 D5**
Abertyleri = Abertillery Bl Gwent **41 A7**
Abertysswg Caerph **60 C3**
Aberuthven Perth **219 C4**
Aberyscir Powys **60 A1**
Aberystwyth Ceredig **90 D3**
Abhainn Suidhe W Isles **287 D5**
Abingdon Oxon **65 D5**
Abinger Common Sur **35 B4**
Abinger Hammer Sur **34 B3**
Abington S Lnrk **194 D4**
Abington Pigotts Cambs **85 C5**
Ablington Glos **64 C2**
Ablington Wilts **31 A5**
Abney Derbys **130 B1**
Aboyne Aberds **244 C2**
Abram Gtr Man **137 C5**
Abriachan Highld **252 C1**
Abridge Essex **69 D4**
Abronhill N Lnrk **207 C5**
Abson S Glos **43 B6**
Abthorpe Northants **82 C3**
Abune-the-Hill Orkney **282 E3**
Aby Lincs **135 B4**
Acaster Malbis York **149 C4**
Acaster Selby N Yorks **149 C4**
Accrington Lancs **137 A6**
Acha Argyll **223 B4**
Acha Mor W Isles **288 E4**
Achabraid Argyll **213 D6**
Achachork Highld **259 D4**
Achafolla Argyll **213 A5**
Achagary Highld **278 C3**
Achahoish Argyll **202 A2**
Achalader Perth **231 D5**
Achallader Argyll **228 D2**
Ach'an Todhair Highld **237 B4**
Achanalt Highld **263 D4**
Achanamara Argyll **213 D5**
Achandunie Highld **264 C2**
Achany Highld **272 D3**
Achaphubuil Highld **237 B4**
Acharacle Highld **235 D5**
Acharn Highld **236 D1**
Acharn Perth **229 D6**
Acharole Highld **280 C4**
Achath Aberds **245 A4**
Achavanich Highld **280 D3**
Achavraat Highld **253 B5**
Achddu Carms **57 B4**
Achduart Highld **270 D3**
Achentoul Highld **274 A2**
Achfary Highld **271 A5**
Achgarve Highld **261 A5**
Achiemore Highld **277 B4**
Achiemore Highld **279 C4**
A'Chill Highld **246 D1**
Achiltibuie Highld **270 D3**
Achina Highld **278 B3**
Achinduich Highld **272 D3**
Achinduin Argyll **226 C3**
Achingills Highld **280 B3**
Achintee Highld **237 B5**
Achintee Highld **249 B6**
Achintraid Highld **249 C5**
Achlean Highld **241 C6**
Achleck Argyll **224 B3**
Achluachrach Highld **239 D6**
Achlyness Highld **276 C3**
Achmelvich Highld **270 B3**
Achmore Highld **249 C5**
Achmore Stirl **217 A5**
Achnaba Argyll **226 C4**
Achnaba Argyll **214 D2**
Achnabat Highld **252 C1**
Achnacarnin Highld **270 A3**
Achnacarry Highld **239 D5**
Achnacloich Argyll **227 C4**
Achnacloich Highld **247 D4**
Achnaconeran Highld **240 A2**
Achnacraig Argyll **224 B3**
Achnacroish Argyll **226 B3**
Achnadrish Argyll **224 A3**
Achnafalnich Argyll **227 D7**
Achnagarron Highld **264 D2**
Achnaha Highld **234 D3**
Achnahanat Highld **263 A7**
Achnahannet Highld **253 D5**
Achnairn Highld **272 C3**
Achnaluachrach Highld **273 D4**
Achnasaul Highld **239 D5**
Achnasheen Highld **250 A3**
Achosnich Highld **234 D3**
Achranich Highld **226 B2**
Achreamie Highld **279 B6**
Achriabhach Highld **237 C5**
Achriesgill Highld **276 C3**
Achrimsdale Highld **274 D3**
Achtoty Highld **278 B2**
Achurch Northants **100 C2**
Achuvoldrach Highld **277 C6**
Achvaich Highld **264 A3**
Achvarasdal Highld **279 B5**
Ackergill Highld **281 C5**
Acklam M'bro **168 D2**
Acklam N Yorks **149 A6**
Ackleton Shrops **95 B5**
Acklington Northumb **189 C5**
Ackton W Yorks **140 A2**
Ackworth Moor Top W Yorks **140 B2**
Acle Norf **121 D6**
Acock's Green W Mid **96 C4**
Acol Kent **53 C5**
Acomb Northumb **178 C1**
Acomb York **149 B4**
Aconbury Hereford **78 D3**
Acre Lancs **137 A6**
Acre Street W Sus **19 B6**
Acrefair Wrex **110 A1**
Acton Ches **127 D6**
Acton Dorset **16 D3**
Acton London **49 A5**
Acton Shrops **93 C7**
Acton Suff **87 C4**
Acton Wrex **126 D3**
Acton Beauchamp Hereford **79 B4**
Acton Bridge Ches **127 B5**
Acton Burnell Shrops **94 A3**
Acton Green Hereford **79 B4**
Acton Pigott Shrops **94 A3**
Acton Round Shrops **95 B4**
Acton Scott Shrops **94 C2**
Acton Trussell Staffs **112 D3**
Acton Turville S Glos **44 A2**
Adbaston Staffs **111 C6**
Adber Dorset **29 C5**
Adderley Shrops **111 A5**
Adderstone Northumb **199 C5**
Addiewell W Loth **208 D2**
Addingham W Yorks **147 C4**
Addington Bucks **66 A2**
Addington London **49 C6**
Addington Kent **37 A4**
Addinston Borders **197 A4**
Addiscombe London **49 C6**
Addlestone Sur **48 C3**
Addlethorpe Lincs **135 C5**
Adel W Yorks **148 D1**
Adeney Telford **111 D6**
Adfa Powys **93 A4**
Adforton Hereford **94 D2**
Adisham Kent **53 D4**
Adlestrop Glos **64 A3**
Adlingfleet E Yorks **141 A6**
Adlington Lancs **137 B5**
Admaston Staffs **112 C4**
Admaston Telford **111 D5**
Admington Warks **81 C5**
Adstock Bucks **83 D4**
Adstone Northants **82 B2**
Adversane W Sus **34 D3**
Advie Highld **254 C2**
Adwalton W Yorks **139 A5**
Adwell Oxon **66 D1**
Adwick le Street S Yorks **140 C3**

Adwick upon Dearne S Yorks 140 C2
Adziel Aberds 269 D4
Ae Village Dumfries 184 D2
Affleck Aberds 256 D3
Affpuddle Dorset 16 B2
Affric Lodge Highld 250 D3
Afon-wen Flint 125 B6
Afton I o W 18 C2
Agglethorpe N Yorks 157 C4
Agneash I o M 152 C4
Aigburth Mers 126 A3
Aiginis W Isles 288 D5
Aike E Yorks 150 C3
Aikerness Orkney 282 B5
Aikers Orkney 283 H5
Aiketgate Cumb 164 A2
Aikton Cumb 175 C5
Ailey Hereford 78 C1
Ailstone Warks 81 B5
Ailsworth P'boro 100 B3
Ainderby Quernhow N Yorks 158 C2
Ainderby Steeple N Yorks 158 B2
Aingers Green Essex 71 A5
Ainsdale Mers 136 B2
Ainsdale-on-Sea Mers 136 B2
Ainstable Cumb 164 A3
Ainsworth Gtr Man 137 B6
Ainthorpe N Yorks 159 A6
Aintree Mers 136 D2
Aintree Racecourse Mers 136 D2
Aird Argyll 213 B5
Aird Dumfries 170 A2
Aird Highld 261 C4
Aird W Isles 288 D6
Aird a Mhachair W Isles 286 B3
Aird a'Mhulaidh W Isles 288 F2
Aird Asaig W Isles 288 G2
Aird Dhail W Isles 288 A5
Aird Mhidhinis W Isles 286 F3
Aird Mhighe W Isles 288 H2
Aird Mhighe W Isles 287 F5
Aird Mhor W Isles 286 F3
Aird of Sleat Highld 247 D4
Aird Thunga W Isles 288 D5
Aird Uig W Isles 287 A5
Airdens Highld 264 A2
Airdrie N Lnrk 207 D5
Airdtorrisdale Highld 278 B2
Airidh a Bhruaich W Isles 288 F3
Airieland Dumfries 173 C5
Airmyn E Yorks 141 A5
Airntully Perth 219 A5
Airor Highld 247 D6
Airth Falk 208 B1
Airton N Yorks 146 B3
Airyhassen Dumfries 171 C5
Aisby Lincs 141 D6
Aisby Lincs 116 B3
Aisgernis W Isles 286 D3
Aiskew N Yorks 157 C6
Aislaby N Yorks 159 C6
Aislaby N Yorks 160 A2
Aislaby Stockton 168 D2
Aisthorpe Lincs 133 A4
Aith Orkney 282 F3
Aith Shetland 285 H5
Aith Shetland 284 D8
Aithsetter Shetland 285 K6
Aitkenhead S Ayrs 192 E3
Aitnoch Highld 253 C5
Akeld Northumb 188 A2
Akeley Bucks 83 D4
Akenham Suff 88 C2
Albaston Corn 11 D5
Alberbury Shrops 110 D2
Albert Dock, Liverpool Mers 126 A3
Albourne W Sus 21 A5
Albrighton Shrops 110 D3
Albrighton Shrops 95 A6
Alburgh Norf 104 C3
Albury Herts 68 A4
Albury Sur 34 B3
Albury End Herts 68 A4
Alby Hill Norf 120 B3
Alcaig Highld 252 A1
Alcaston Shrops 94 C2
Alcester Warks 80 B3
Alciston E Sus 22 B3
Alcombe Som 27 A4
Alcombe Wilts 44 C2
Alconbury Cambs 100 D3
Alconbury Weston Cambs 100 D3
Aldbar Castle Angus 232 C3
Aldborough Norf 120 B3
Aldborough N Yorks 148 A3
Aldbourne Wilts 45 B6
Aldbrough E Yorks 151 D5
Aldbrough St John N Yorks 167 D5
Aldbury Herts 67 B4
Aldcliffe Lancs 145 A4
Aldclune Perth 230 B3
Aldeburgh Suff 89 B5
Aldeby Norf 105 B5
Aldenham Herts 67 D6
Alderbury Wilts 31 C5
Aldercar Derbys 114 A2
Alderford Norf 120 D3
Alderholt Dorset 31 D5
Alderley Glos 62 D3
Alderley Edge Ches 128 B3
Aldermaston W Berks 46 C3
Aldermaston Wharf W Berks 47 C4
Alderminster Warks 81 C5
Alderney Airport Ald 7
Alder's End Hereford 79 C4
Aldersey Green Ches 127 D4
Aldershot Hants 34 A1
Alderton Glos 80 D3
Alderton Northants 83 C4
Alderton Shrops 110 C3
Alderton Suff 88 C4
Alderton Wilts 44 A2
Alderwasley Derbys 130 D3
Aldfield N Yorks 147 A6
Aldford Ches 127 D4
Aldham Essex 70 A3
Aldham Suff 87 C6
Aldie Highld 264 B3
Aldingbourne W Sus 20 B2
Aldingham Cumb 154 D1
Aldington Kent 38 B2
Aldington Worcs 80 C3
Aldington Frith Kent 38 B2
Aldochlay Argyll 206 A1
Aldreth Cambs 101 D6
Aldridge W Mid 96 A3
Aldringham Suff 89 A5
Aldsworth Glos 64 B2
Aldunie Moray 255 D4
Aldwark Derbys 130 D2
Aldwark N Yorks 148 A3
Aldwick W Sus 20 C2
Aldwincle Northants 100 C2
Aldworth W Berks 46 B3
Alexandria W Dunb 206 C1
Alfardisworthy Devon 24 D3
Alfington Devon 13 B6
Alfold Sur 34 C3
Alfold Bars W Sus 34 C3
Alfold Crossways Sur 34 C3
Alford Aberds 244 A2
Alford Lincs 135 B4
Alford Som 29 B6
Alfreton Derbys 131 D4
Alfrick Worcs 79 B5
Alfrick Pound Worcs 79 B5
Alfriston E Sus 22 B3
Algaltraig Argyll 203 A5
Algarkirk Lincs 117 B5
Alhampton Som 29 B6
Aline Lodge W Isles 288 F2
Alisary Highld 235 C6
Alkborough N Lincs 141 A6
Alkerton Oxon 81 C6
Alkham Kent 39 A4
Alkington Shrops 111 B4
Alkmonton Derbys 113 B5
All Cannings Wilts 45 C4
All Saints Church, Godshill I o W 18 C4
All Saints South Elmham Suff 104 C4
All Stretton Shrops 94 B2
Alladale Lodge Highld 263 B6
Allaleigh Devon 8 B2
Allanaquoich Aberds 242 C4
Allangrange Mains Highld 252 A2
Allanton Borders 198 A2
Allanton N Lnrk 194 A3
Allathasdal W Isles 286 F2
Allendale Town Northumb 177 D6
Allenheads Northumb 165 A6
Allens Green Herts 69 B4
Allensford Durham 178 D2
Allensmore Hereford 78 D2
Allenton Derby 114 B1
Aller Som 28 C4
Allerby Cumb 162 A3
Allerford Som 27 A4
Allerston N Yorks 160 C2
Allerthorpe E Yorks 149 C6
Allerton Mers 127 A4
Allerton W Yorks 147 D5
Allerton Bywater W Yorks 140 A2
Allerton Mauleverer N Yorks 148 B3
Allesley W Mid 97 C6
Allestree Derby 114 B1
Allet Corn 4 C2
Allexton Leics 99 A5
Allgreave Ches 129 C4
Allhallows Medway 51 B5
Allhallows-on-Sea Medway 51 B5
Alligin Shuas Highld 249 A5
Allimore Green Staffs 112 D2
Allington Lincs 115 A6
Allington Wilts 31 B6
Allington Wilts 45 C4
Allithwaite Cumb 154 D2
Alloa Clack 208 A1
Allonby Cumb 174 D3
Alloway S Ayrs 192 D3
Allt Carms 57 B5
Allt na h-Airbhe Highld 262 A3
Allt-nan-sùgh Highld 249 D6
Alltchaorunn Highld 237 D5
Alltforgan Powys 109 C4
Alltmawr Powys 77 C4
Alltnacaillich Highld 277 D5
Alltsigh Highld 240 A2
Alltwalis Carms 58 B1
Alltwen Neath 40 A2
Alltyblaca Ceredig 75 D4
Allwood Green Suff 103 D6
Almeley Hereford 78 B1
Almer Dorset 16 B3
Almholme S Yorks 140 C3
Almington Staffs 111 B6
Alminstone Cross Devon 24 C4
Almondbank Perth 219 B5
Almondbury W Yorks 139 B4
Almondsbury S Glos 43 A5
Alne N Yorks 148 A3
Alness Highld 264 D2
Alnham Northumb 188 B2
Alnmouth Northumb 189 B5
Alnwick Northumb 189 B4
Alperton London 49 A4
Alphamstone Essex 87 D4
Alpheton Suff 87 B4
Alphington Devon 13 B4
Alport Derbys 130 C2
Alpraham Ches 127 D5
Alresford Essex 71 A4
Alrewas Staffs 113 D5
Alsager Ches 128 D2
Alsagers Bank Staffs 112 A2
Alsop en le Dale Derbys 129 D6
Alston Cumb 165 A5
Alston Devon 14 A3
Alstone Glos 80 D2
Alstonefield Staffs 129 D6
Alswear Devon 26 C2
Altandhu Highld 270 C2
Altanduin Highld 274 B2
Altarnun Corn 10 C3
Altass Highld 272 D2
Alterwall Highld 281 B4
Altham Lancs 146 D1
Althorne Essex 70 D3
Althorp House, Great Brington Northants 82 A3
Althorpe N Lincs 141 C6
Alticry Dumfries 171 B4
Altnabreac Station Highld 279 D6
Altnacealgach Hotel Highld 271 C5
Altnacraig Argyll 226 D3
Altnafeadh Highld 237 D6
Altnaharra Highld 272 A3
Altofts W Yorks 139 A6
Alton Derbys 130 C3
Alton Hants 33 B6
Alton Staffs 113 A4
Alton Pancras Dorset 15 A7
Alton Priors Wilts 45 C5
Alton Towers Staffs 113 A4
Altrincham Gtr Man 128 A2
Altrua Highld 239 D6
Altskeith Stirl 217 D4
Altyre Ho. Moray 253 A6
Alva Clack 208 A1
Alvanley Ches 127 B4
Alvaston Derby 114 B1
Alvechurch Worcs 96 D3
Alvecote Warks 97 A5
Alvediston Wilts 30 C3
Alveley Shrops 95 C5
Alverdiscott Devon 25 C6
Alverstoke Hants 19 B5
Alverstone I o W 19 C4
Alverton Notts 115 A5
Alves Moray 266 C2
Alvescot Oxon 64 C3
Alveston S Glos 43 A5
Alveston Warks 81 B5
Alvie Highld 241 B6
Alvingham Lincs 143 D5
Alvington Glos 62 C2
Alwalton Cambs 100 B3
Alweston Dorset 29 D6
Alwinton Northumb 188 C2
Alwoodley W Yorks 148 C1
Alyth Perth 231 D6
Am Baile W Isles 286 E3
Am Buth Argyll 226 D3
Amatnatua Highld 263 A6
Amber Hill Lincs 117 A5
Ambergate Derbys 130 D3
Amberley Glos 63 C4
Amberley W Sus 20 A3
Amble Northumb 189 C5
Amblecote W Mid 96 C1
Ambler Thorn W Yorks 138 A3
Ambleside Cumb 154 A2
Ambleston Pembs 55 B6
Ambrosden Oxon 65 B7
Amcotts N Lincs 141 B6
American Air Museum, Duxford Cambs 85 C6
Amersham Bucks 67 D4
Amerton Working Farm, Stowe-by-Chartley Staffs 112 C3
Amesbury Wilts 31 A5
Amington Staffs 97 A5
Amisfield Dumfries 184 D2
Amlwch Anglesey 123 A4
Amlwch Port Anglesey 123 A4
Ammanford = Rhydaman Carms 57 A6
Amod Argyll 190 B3
Amotherby N Yorks 159 D6
Ampfield Hants 32 C3
Ampleforth N Yorks 159 D4
Ampney Crucis Glos 63 C6
Ampney St Mary Glos 64 C1
Ampney St Peter Glos 64 C1
Amport Hants 32 A1
Ampthill Beds 84 D2
Ampton Suff 103 D4
Amroth Pembs 56 B1
Amulree Perth 218 A3
An Caol Highld 248 A3
An Cnoc W Isles 288 D5
An Gleann Ur W Isles 288 D5
An t-Ob = Leverburgh W Isles 287 F5
Anagach Highld 253 D6
Anaheilt Highld 236 C2
Anancaun Highld 262 D2
Ancaster Lincs 116 A2
Anchor Shrops 93 C5
Anchorsholme Blkpool 144 C3
Ancroft Northumb 198 B3
Ancrum Borders 187 A5
Anderby Lincs 135 B5
Anderson Dorset 16 B2
Anderton Ches 127 B6
Andover Hants 32 A2
Andover Down Hants 32 A2
Andoversford Glos 63 B6
Andreas I o M 152 B4
Anfield Mers 136 D2
Angersleigh Som 28 D1
Angle Pembs 55 D4
Angmering W Sus 20 B3
Angram N Yorks 148 C4
Angram N Yorks 156 B2
Anie Stirl 217 C5
Ankerville Highld 265 C4
Anlaby E Yorks 142 A2
Anmer Norf 119 C4
Anna Valley Hants 32 A2
Annan Dumfries 175 B4
Annat Argyll 227 D5
Annat Highld 249 A5
Annbank S Ayrs 193 C4
Anne Hathaway's Cottage, Stratford-upon-Avon Warks 81 B4
Annesley Notts 131 D5
Annesley Woodhouse Notts 131 D4
Annfield Plain Durham 178 D3
Annifirth Shetland 285 J3
Annitsford T & W 179 B4
Annscroft Shrops 94 A2
Ansdell Lancs 136 A2
Ansford Som 29 B6
Ansley Warks 97 B5
Anslow Staffs 113 C6
Anslow Gate Staffs 113 C5
Anstey Herts 85 D6
Anstey Leics 98 A2
Anstruther Easter Fife 221 D5
Anstruther Wester Fife 221 D5
Ansty Hants 33 A6
Ansty Warks 97 C6
Ansty Wilts 30 C3
Ansty W Sus 35 D5
Anthill Common Hants 33 D5
Anthorn Cumb 175 C4
Antingham Norf 121 B4
Anton's Gowt Lincs 117 A5
Antonshill Falk 208 B1
Antony Corn 6 B3
Anwick Lincs 133 D6
Anwoth Dumfries 172 C3
Aoradh Argyll 200 B2
Apes Hall Cambs 102 B1
Apethorpe Northants 100 B2
Apeton Staffs 112 D2
Apley Lincs 133 B6
Apperknowle Derbys 130 B3
Apperley Glos 63 A4
Apperley Bridge W Yorks 147 D5
Appersett N Yorks 156 B2
Appin Argyll 226 B4
Appin House Argyll 226 B4
Appleby N Lincs 142 B1
Appleby-in-Westmorland Cumb 165 C4
Appleby Magna Leics 97 A6
Appleby Parva Leics 97 A6
Applecross Highld 249 B4
Applecross Ho. Highld 249 B4
Appledore Devon 25 B5
Appledore Devon 27 D5
Appledore Kent 38 C1
Appledore Heath Kent 38 B1
Appleford Oxon 65 D6
Applegarthtown Dumfries 185 D4
Appleshaw Hants 32 A2
Applethwaite Cumb 163 B5
Appleton Halton 127 A5
Appleton Oxon 65 C5
Appleton-le-Moors N Yorks 159 C6
Appleton-le-Street N Yorks 159 D6
Appleton Roebuck N Yorks 149 C4
Appleton Thorn Warr 127 A6
Appleton Wiske N Yorks 158 A2
Appletreehall Borders 186 B4
Appletreewick N Yorks 147 A4
Appley Som 27 C5
Appley Bridge Lancs 136 C4
Apse Heath I o W 19 C4
Apsley End Beds 84 D3
Apuldram W Sus 20 B1
Aquhythie Aberds 245 A4
Arabella Highld 265 C4
Arbeadie Aberds 244 C3
Arbeia Roman Fort and Museum T & W 179 C5
Arberth = Narberth Pembs 55 C7
Arbirlot Angus 233 D4
Arboll Highld 265 B4
Arborfield Wokingham 47 C5
Arborfield Cross Wokingham 47 C5
Arborfield Garrison Wokingham 47 C5
Arbour-thorne S Yorks 130 A3
Arbroath Angus 233 D4
Arbuthnott Aberds 233 A5
Archiestown Moray 254 B3
Arclid Ches 128 C2
Ard-dhubh Highld 249 B4
Ardachu Highld 273 D4
Ardalanish Argyll 224 E2
Ardanaiseig Argyll 227 D5
Ardaneaskan Highld 249 C5
Ardanstur Argyll 213 A6
Ardargie House Hotel Perth 219 C5
Ardarroch Highld 249 C5
Ardbeg Argyll 201 D4
Ardbeg Argyll 215 D4
Ardbeg Distillery, Port Ellen Argyll 201 D4
Ardcharnich Highld 262 B3
Ardchiavaig Argyll 224 E2
Ardchullarie More Stirl 217 C5
Ardchyle Stirl 217 B5
Arddleen Powys 110 D1
Ardechvie Highld 239 C5
Ardeley Herts 68 A3
Ardelve Highld 249 D5
Arden Argyll 206 B1
Ardens Grafton Warks 80 B4
Ardentinny Argyll 215 D4
Ardentraive Argyll 203 A5
Ardeonaig Stirl 217 A6
Ardersier Highld 252 A3
Ardessie Highld 262 B2
Ardfern Argyll 213 B6
Ardgartan Argyll 215 B5
Ardgay Highld 264 A1
Ardgour Highld 237 C4
Ardheslaig Highld 249 A4
Ardiecow Moray 267 C6
Ardindrean Highld 262 B3
Ardingly W Sus 35 D6
Ardington Oxon 46 A2
Ardlair Aberds 255 D6
Ardlamont Ho. Argyll 203 B4
Ardleigh Essex 71 A4
Ardler Perth 231 D6
Ardley Oxon 65 A6
Ardlui Argyll 215 A6
Ardlussa Argyll 213 D4
Ardmair Highld 262 A3
Ardmay Argyll 215 B5
Ardminish Argyll 202 D1
Ardmolich Highld 235 C6
Ardmore Argyll 226 D2
Ardmore Highld 276 C3
Ardmore Highld 264 B3
Ardnacross Argyll 225 B4
Ardnadam Argyll 203 A6
Ardnagrask Highld 251 B7
Ardnarff Highld 249 C5
Ardnastang Highld 236 C2
Ardnave Argyll 200 A2
Ardno Argyll 215 B4
Ardo Aberds 256 C3
Ardo Ho. Aberds 257 D4
Ardoch Perth 219 A5
Ardochy House Highld 239 B6
Ardoyne Aberds 256 D1
Ardpatrick Argyll 202 B2
Ardpatrick Ho. Argyll 202 C2
Ardpeaton Argyll 215 D5
Ardrishaig Argyll 213 D6
Ardross Fife 221 D5
Ardross Highld 264 C2
Ardross Castle Highld 264 C2
Ardrossan N Ayrs 204 D2
Ardshealach Highld 235 D5
Ardsley S Yorks 140 C1
Ardslignish Highld 235 D4
Ardtalla Argyll 201 C4
Ardtalnaig Perth 218 A2
Ardtoe Highld 235 C5
Ardtrostan Perth 217 B6
Arduaine Argyll 213 A5
Ardullie Highld 264 D1
Ardvasar Highld 247 D5
Ardvorlich Perth 217 B6
Ardwell Dumfries 170 C3
Ardwell Mains Dumfries 170 C3
Ardwick Gtr Man 138 D1
Areley Kings Worcs 95 D6
Arford Hants 34 C1
Argoed Caerph 41 B6
Argoed Mill Powys 76 A3
Argyll & Sutherland Highlanders Museum (See Stirling Castle) Stirl 207 A5
Arichamish Argyll 214 B2
Arichastlich Argyll 216 A2
Aridhglas Argyll 224 D2
Arileod Argyll 223 B4
Arinacrinachd Highld 249 A4
Arinagour Argyll 223 B5
Arion Orkney 282 F3
Arisaig Highld 235 B5
Ariundle Highld 236 C2
Arkendale N Yorks 148 A2
Arkesden Essex 85 D6
Arkholme Lancs 155 D4
Arkle Town N Yorks 156 A4
Arkley London 68 D2
Arksey S Yorks 140 C3
Arkwright Town Derbys 131 B4
Arle Glos 63 A5
Arlecdon Cumb 162 C3
Arlesey Beds 84 D3
Arleston Telford 111 D5
Arley Ches 128 A1
Arlingham Glos 62 B3
Arlington Devon 25 A7
Arlington E Sus 22 B3
Arlington Glos 64 C2
Arlington Court Devon 25 A7
Armadale Highld 278 B3
Armadale W Loth 208 D2
Armadale Castle Highld 247 D5
Armathwaite Cumb 164 A3
Arminghall Norf 104 A3
Armitage Staffs 113 D4
Armley W Yorks 148 D1
Armscote Warks 81 C5
Armthorpe S Yorks 140 C4
Arnabost Argyll 223 B5
Arncliffe N Yorks 156 D3
Arncroach Fife 221 D5
Arne Dorset 16 C3
Arnesby Leics 98 B3
Arngask Perth 219 C6
Arnisdale Highld 238 A2
Arnish Highld 248 B2
Arniston Engine Midloth 209 D6
Arnol W Isles 288 C4
Arnold E Yorks 151 C4
Arnold Notts 114 A3
Arnolfini Gallery Bristol 43 B4
Arnprior Stirl 207 A4
Arnside Cumb 154 D3
Aros Mains Argyll 225 B4
Arowry Wrex 110 B3
Arpafeelie Highld 252 A2
Arrad Foot Cumb 154 C2
Arram E Yorks 150 C3
Arrathorne N Yorks 157 B6
Arreton I o W 18 C4
Arrington Cambs 85 B5
Arrivain Argyll 216 A2
Arrochar Argyll 215 B5
Arrow Warks 80 B3
Arthington W Yorks 147 C6
Arthingworth Northants 99 C4
Arthog Gwyn 90 A4
Arthrath Aberds 257 C4
Arthurstone Perth 231 D6
Artrochie Aberds 257 C5
Arundel W Sus 20 B3
Arundel Castle W Sus 20 B3
Aryhoulan Highld 237 C4
Asby Cumb 162 B3
Ascog Argyll 203 B6
Ascot Windsor 48 C2
Ascot Racecourse Windsor 48 C2
Ascott Warks 81 D6
Ascott-under-Wychwood Oxon 64 B4
Asenby N Yorks 158 D2
Asfordby Leics 115 D5

Asfordby Hill Leics 115 D5
Asgarby Lincs 116 A4
Asgarby Lincs 134 C3
Ash Kent 50 C2
Ash Kent 53 D4
Ash Som 29 C4
Ash Sur 34 A1
Ash Bullayne Devon 12 A2
Ash Green Warks 97 C6
Ash Magna Shrops 111 B4
Ash Mill Devon 26 C2
Ash Priors Som 27 C6
Ash Street Suff 87 C6
Ash Thomas Devon 27 D5
Ash Vale Sur 34 A1
Ashampstead W Berks 46 B3
Ashbocking Suff 88 B2
Ashbourne Derbys 113 A5
Ashbrittle Som 27 C5
Ashburton Devon 7 A6
Ashbury Devon 11 B6
Ashbury Oxon 45 A6
Ashby N Lincs 141 C7
Ashby by Partney Lincs 135 C4
Ashby cum Fenby NE Lincs 143 C4
Ashby de la Launde Lincs 133 D5
Ashby-de-la-Zouch Leics 114 D1
Ashby Folville Leics 115 D5
Ashby Magna Leics 98 B2
Ashby Parva Leics 98 C2
Ashby Puerorum Lincs 134 B3
Ashby St Ledgers Northants 82 A2
Ashby St Mary Norf 104 A4
Ashchurch Glos 80 D2
Ashcombe Devon 13 D4
Ashcott Som 28 B4
Ashdon Essex 86 C1
Ashe Hants 32 A4
Asheldham Essex 70 C3
Ashen Essex 86 C3
Ashendon Bucks 66 B2
Ashfield Carms 58 C3
Ashfield Stirl 218 D2
Ashfield Suff 88 A3
Ashfield Green Suff 104 D3
Ashfold Crossways W Sus 35 D5
Ashford Devon 25 B6
Ashford Hants 31 D5
Ashford Kent 38 A2
Ashford Sur 48 B3
Ashford Bowdler Shrops 94 D3
Ashford Carbonell Shrops 94 D3
Ashford Hill Hants 46 C3
Ashford in the Water Derbys 130 C1
Ashgill S Lnrk 194 B2
Ashill Devon 27 D5
Ashill Norf 103 A4
Ashill Som 28 D3
Ashingdon Essex 70 D2
Ashington Northumb 179 A4
Ashington Som 29 C5
Ashington W Sus 21 A4
Ashintully Castle Perth 231 B5
Ashkirk Borders 186 A3
Ashlett Hants 18 A3
Ashleworth Glos 63 A4
Ashley Cambs 86 A2
Ashley Ches 128 A2
Ashley Devon 26 D1
Ashley Dorset 17 A5
Ashley Glos 63 D5
Ashley Hants 17 B6
Ashley Hants 32 B2
Ashley Northants 99 B4
Ashley Staffs 111 B6
Ashley Green Bucks 67 C4
Ashley Heath Dorset 17 A5
Ashley Heath Staffs 111 B6
Ashmanhaugh Norf 121 C5
Ashmansworth Hants 46 D2
Ashmansworthy Devon 24 D4
Ashmore Dorset 30 D3
Ashorne Warks 81 B6
Ashover Derbys 130 C3
Ashow Warks 97 D6
Ashprington Devon 8 B2
Ashreigney Devon 26 D1
Ashtead Sur 35 A4
Ashton Ches 127 C5
Ashton Corn 3 C4
Ashton Hants 33 D4
Ashton Hereford 78 A3
Ashton Invclyd 204 A2
Ashton Northants 83 C4
Ashton Northants 100 C2
Ashton Common Wilts 44 D2
Ashton-In-Makerfield Gtr Man 137 D4
Ashton Keynes Wilts 63 D6
Ashton under Hill Worcs 80 D2
Ashton-under-Lyne Gtr Man 138 D2
Ashton upon Mersey Gtr Man 137 D6
Ashurst Hants 32 D2
Ashurst Kent 36 C3
Ashurst W Sus 21 A4
Ashurstwood W Sus 36 C2
Ashwater Devon 11 B4
Ashwell Herts 85 D4
Ashwell Rutland 115 D6
Ashwell Som 28 D3
Ashwellthorpe Norf 104 B2
Ashwick Som 29 A6
Ashwicken Norf 119 D4
Ashybank Borders 186 B4
Askam in Furness Cumb 153 C3
Askern S Yorks 140 B3
Askerswell Dorset 15 B5
Askett Bucks 66 C3
Askham Cumb 164 C3
Askham Notts 132 B2
Askham Bryan York 149 C4
Askham Richard York 148 C4
Asknish Argyll 214 C2
Askrigg N Yorks 156 B3
Askwith N Yorks 147 C5
Aslackby Lincs 116 B3
Aslacton Norf 104 B2
Aslockton Notts 115 B5
Asloun Aberds 244 A2
Aspatria Cumb 174 D4
Aspenden Herts 68 A3
Asperton Lincs 117 B5
Aspley Guise Beds 83 D6
Aspley Heath Beds 83 D6
Aspull Gtr Man 137 C5
Asselby E Yorks 141 A5
Asserby Lincs 135 B4
Assington Suff 87 D5
Assynt Ho. Highld 264 D1
Astbury Ches 128 C3
Astcote Northants 82 B3
Asterley Shrops 94 A1
Asterton Shrops 94 B1
Asthall Oxon 64 B3
Asthall Leigh Oxon 64 B4
Astley Shrops 111 D4
Astley Warks 97 C6
Astley Worcs 79 A5
Astley Abbotts Shrops 95 B5
Astley Bridge Gtr Man 137 B6
Astley Cross Worcs 79 A6
Astley Green Gtr Man 137 D6
Aston Ches 111 A5
Aston Ches 127 B5
Aston Derbys 130 A1
Aston Hereford 94 D2
Aston Herts 68 A2
Aston Oxon 64 C4
Aston Shrops 111 C4
Aston Staffs 111 A6
Aston S Yorks 131 A4
Aston Telford 95 A4
Aston W Mid 96 C3
Aston Wokingham 47 A5
Aston Abbotts Bucks 66 A3
Aston Botterell Shrops 95 C4
Aston-By-Stone Staffs 112 B3
Aston Cantlow Warks 80 B4
Aston Clinton Bucks 66 B3
Aston Crews Hereford 62 A2
Aston Cross Glos 80 D2
Aston End Herts 68 A2
Aston Eyre Shrops 95 B4
Aston Fields Worcs 80 A2
Aston Flamville Leics 98 B1
Aston Ingham Hereford 62 A2
Aston juxta Mondrum Ches 127 D6
Aston le Walls Northants 82 B1
Aston Magna Glos 81 D4
Aston Munslow Shrops 94 C3
Aston on Clun Shrops 94 C1
Aston-on-Trent Derbys 114 C2
Aston Rogers Shrops 94 A1
Aston Rowant Oxon 66 D2
Aston Sandford Bucks 66 C2
Aston Somerville Worcs 80 D3
Aston Subedge Glos 80 C4
Aston Tirrold Oxon 46 A3
Aston Upthorpe Oxon 46 A3
Astrop Northants 82 D2
Astwick Beds 84 D4
Astwood M Keynes 83 C6
Astwood Worcs 79 B6
Astwood Bank Worcs 80 A3
Aswarby Lincs 116 B3
Aswardby Lincs 134 B3
Atch Lench Worcs 80 B3
Atcham Shrops 94 A3
Athelhampton Dorset 16 B1
Athelington Suff 104 D3
Athelney Som 28 C3
Athelstaneford E Loth 210 C2
Atherington Devon 25 C6
Atherstone Warks 97 B6
Atherstone on Stour Warks 81 B5
Atherton Gtr Man 137 C5
Atley Hill N Yorks 157 A6
Atlow Derbys 113 A6
Attadale Highld 249 C6
Attadale Ho. Highld 249 C6
Attenborough Notts 114 B3
Atterby Lincs 142 D1
Attercliffe S Yorks 130 A3
Attleborough Norf 103 B6
Attleborough Warks 97 B6
Attlebridge Norf 120 D3
Atwick E Yorks 151 B4
Atworth Wilts 44 C2
Aubourn Lincs 133 C4
Auchagallon N Ayrs 191 B4
Auchallater Aberds 243 D4
Aucharnie Aberds 256 B1
Auchattie Aberds 244 C3
Auchavan Angus 231 B5
Auchbreck Moray 254 D3
Auchenback E Renf 205 C5
Auchenbainzie Dumfries 183 C6
Auchenblae Aberds 233 A5
Auchenbrack Dumfries 183 C5
Auchenbreck Argyll 214 D3
Auchencairn Dumfries 173 C5
Auchencairn Dumfries 184 D2
Auchencairn N Ayrs 191 C6
Auchencrosh S Ayrs 180 D3
Auchencrow Borders 211 D5
Auchendinny Midloth 209 D5
Auchengray S Lnrk 195 A4
Auchenhalrig Moray 267 C4
Auchenheath S Lnrk 194 B3
Auchenlochan Argyll 203 A4
Auchenmalg Dumfries 171 B4
Auchensoul S Ayrs 181 B4
Auchentiber N Ayrs 204 D3
Auchertyre Highld 249 D5
Auchgourish Highld 242 A2
Auchincarroch W Dunb 206 B2
Auchindrain Argyll 214 B3
Auchindrean Highld 262 B3
Auchininna Aberds 256 B1
Auchinleck E Ayrs 193 C5
Auchinloch N Lnrk 205 A6
Auchinroath Moray 266 D3
Auchintoul Aberds 244 A2
Auchiries Aberds 257 C5
Auchlee Aberds 245 C5
Auchleven Aberds 256 D1
Auchlochan S Lnrk 194 C3
Auchlossan Aberds 244 B2
Auchlunies Aberds 245 C5
Auchlyne Stirl 217 B5
Auchmacoy Aberds 257 C4
Auchmair Moray 255 D4
Auchmantle Dumfries 170 A3
Auchmillan E Ayrs 193 C5
Auchmithie Angus 233 D4
Auchmuirbridge Fife 220 D2
Auchmull Angus 232 A3
Auchnacree Angus 232 B2
Auchnagallin Highld 253 C6
Auchnagatt Aberds 257 B4
Auchnaha Argyll 214 D2
Auchnashelloch Perth 218 C2
Aucholzie Aberds 243 C6
Auchrannie Angus 231 C6
Auchroisk Highld 253 D6
Auchronie Angus 244 D1
Auchterarder Perth 218 C4
Auchteraw Highld 240 B1
Auchterderran Fife 209 A5
Auchterhouse Angus 220 A3
Auchtermuchty Fife 220 C2
Auchterneed Highld 251 A6
Auchtertool Fife 209 A5
Auchtertyre Moray 266 D2
Auchtubh Stirl 217 B5
Auckengill Highld 281 B5
Auckley S Yorks 140 C4
Audenshaw Gtr Man 138 D2
Audlem Ches 111 A5
Audley Staffs 128 D2
Audley End Essex 87 D4
Audley End House Essex 86 D1
Auds Aberds 268 C1
Aughton E Yorks 149 D6
Aughton Lancs 136 C2
Aughton Lancs 145 A5
Aughton S Yorks 131 A4
Aughton Wilts 45 D6
Aughton Park Lancs 136 C3
Auldearn Highld 253 A5
Aulden Hereford 78 B2
Auldgirth Dumfries 183 D7
Auldhame E Loth 210 B2
Auldhouse S Lnrk 205 C6
Ault a'chruinn Highld 249 D6
Aultanrynie Highld 271 A6
Aultbea Highld 261 B5
Aultdearg Highld 263 D4
Aultgrishan Highld 261 B4
Aultguish Inn Highld 263 C5
Aultibea Highld 274 B4
Aultiphurst Highld 279 B4
Aultmore Moray 267 D5
Aultnagoire Highld 252 D1
Aultnamain Inn Highld 264 B2
Aultnaslat Highld 239 B5
Aulton Aberds 255 D7
Aundorach Highld 242 A2
Aunsby Lincs 116 B3
Auquhorthies Aberds 256 D3
Aust S Glos 43 A4
Austendike Lincs 117 C5
Austerfield S Yorks 141 D4
Austrey Warks 97 A5
Austwick N Yorks 146 A1
Authorpe Lincs 135 A4
Authorpe Row Lincs 135 B5
Avebury Wilts 45 C5
Aveley Thurrock 50 A2
Avening Glos 63 D4
Averham Notts 132 D2
Aveton Gifford Devon 7 C5
Avielochan Highld 242 A2
Aviemore Highld 242 A1
Avington Hants 32 B4
Avington W Berks 46 C1
Avoch Highld 252 A3
Avon Hants 17 B5
Avon Dassett Warks 81 C7
Avonbridge Falk 208 C2
Avonmouth Bristol 43 B4
Avonwick Devon 7 B6
Awbridge Hants 32 C2
Awhirk Dumfries 170 B2
Awkley S Glos 43 A4
Awliscombe Devon 13 A6
Awre Glos 62 C3
Awsworth Notts 114 A2
Axbridge Som 42 D3
Axford Hants 33 A5
Axford Wilts 45 C6
Axminster Devon 14 B2
Axmouth Devon 14 B2
Axton Flint 125 A6
Aycliff Kent 39 A5
Aycliffe Durham 167 C5
Aydon Northumb 178 C2
Aylburton Glos 62 C2
Ayle Northumb 165 A5
Aylesbeare Devon 13 B5
Aylesbury Bucks 66 B3
Aylesby NE Lincs 143 C4
Aylesford Kent 37 A5
Aylesham Kent 53 D4
Aylestone Leicester 98 A2
Aylmerton Norf 120 B3
Aylsham Norf 120 C3
Aylton Hereford 79 D4
Aymestrey Hereford 78 A2
Aynho Northants 82 D2
Ayot St Lawrence Herts 68 B1
Ayot St Peter Herts 68 B2
Ayr S Ayrs 192 C3
Ayr Racecourse S Ayrs 192 C3
Aysgarth N Yorks 156 C4
Ayside Cumb 154 C2
Ayston Rutland 99 A5
Aythorpe Roding Essex 69 B5
Ayton Borders 211 D6
Aywick Shetland 284 E7
Azerley N Yorks 157 D6

B

Babbacombe Torbay 8 A3
Babbinswood Shrops 110 B2
Babcary Som 29 C5
Babel Carms 59 B5
Babell Flint 125 B6
Babraham Cambs 85 B7
Babworth Notts 132 A1
Bac W Isles 288 C5
Bachau Anglesey 123 B4
Back of Keppoch Highld 235 B5
Back Rogerton E Ayrs 193 C5
Backaland Orkney 282 D6
Backaskaill Orkney 282 B5
Backbarrow Cumb 154 C2
Backe Carms 56 A2
Backfolds Aberds 269 D5
Backford Ches 127 B4
Backford Cross Ches 126 B3
Backhill Aberds 256 C2
Backhill Aberds 257 C5
Backhill of Clackriach Aberds 257 B4
Backhill of Fortree Aberds 257 B4
Backhill of Trustach Aberds 244 C3
Backies Highld 274 D2
Backlass Highld 280 C4
Backwell N Som 42 C3
Backworth T & W 179 B5
Bacon End Essex 69 B6
Baconsthorpe Norf 120 B3
Bacton Hereford 78 D1
Bacton Norf 121 B5
Bacton Suff 87 A6
Bacton Green Suff 87 A6
Bacup Lancs 138 A1
Badachro Highld 261 C4
Badanloch Lodge Highld 273 A5
Badavanich Highld 250 A3
Badbury Swindon 45 A5
Badby Northants 82 B2
Badcall Highld 276 C3
Badcaul Highld 262 A2
Baddeley Green Stoke 129 D4
Baddesley Clinton Warks 97 D5
Baddesley Clinton Hall Warks 97 D5
Baddesley Ensor Warks 97 B5
Baddidarach Highld 270 B3
Baddoch Aberds 242 D4
Baddock Highld 252 A3
Badenscoth Aberds 256 C2
Badenyon Aberds 243 A6
Badger Shrops 95 B5
Badger's Mount Kent 50 C1
Badgeworth Glos 63 B5
Badgworth Som 42 D2
Badicaul Highld 249 D4
Badingham Suff 88 A4
Badlesmere Kent 52 D2
Badlipster Highld 280 D4
Badluarach Highld 262 A1
Badminton S Glos 44 A2
Badnaban Highld 270 B3
Badninish Highld 264 A3
Badrallach Highld 262 A2
Badsey Worcs 80 C3
Badshot Lea Sur 34 B1
Badsworth W Yorks 140 B2
Badwell Ash Suff 87 A5
Bae Colwyn = Colwyn Bay Conwy 124 B3
Bag Enderby Lincs 134 B3
Bagby N Yorks 158 C3
Bagendon Glos 63 C6
Bagh a Chaisteil = Castlebay W Isles 286 G2
Bagh Mor W Isles 286 A4
Bagh Shiarabhagh W Isles 286 F3
Baghasdal W Isles 286 E3
Bagillt Flint 126 B2
Baginton Warks 97 D6
Baglan Neath 40 B2
Bagley Shrops 110 C3
Bagnall Staffs 129 D4
Bagnor W Berks 46 C2
Bagshot Sur 48 C2
Bagshot Wilts 45 C7
Bagthorpe Norf 119 B4
Bagthorpe Notts 131 D4
Bagworth Leics 98 A1
Bagwy Llydiart Hereford 61 A6
Bail Àrd Bhuirgh W Isles 288 B5
Bail Uachdraich W Isles 287 H3
Baildon W Yorks 147 D5
Baile W Isles 287 F4
Baile a Mhanaich W Isles 286 A3
Baile Ailein W Isles 288 E3
Baile an Truiseil W Isles 288 B4
Baile Boidheach Argyll 202 A2
Baile Glas W Isles 286 A4
Baile Mhartainn W Isles 287 G2
Baile Mhic Phail W Isles 287 G3
Baile Mor Argyll 224 D1
Baile Mor W Isles 287 H2
Baile na Creige W Isles 286 F2
Baile nan Cailleach W Isles 286 A3
Baile Raghaill W Isles 287 G2
Bailebeag Highld 240 A3
Baileyhead Cumb 176 B3
Bailiesward Aberds 255 C5
Baillieston Glasgow 205 B6
Bail'lochdrach W Isles 286 A4
Bail'Ur Tholastaidh W Isles 288 C6
Bainbridge N Yorks 156 B3
Bainsford Falk 208 B1
Bainshole Aberds 255 C7
Bainton E Yorks 150 B2
Bainton P'boro 100 A2
Bairnkine Borders 187 B5
Baker Street Thurrock 50 A3
Baker's End Herts 68 B3
Bakewell Derbys 130 C2
Bala = Y Bala Gwyn 108 B4
Balachuirn Highld 248 B2
Balavil Highld 241 B5
Balbeg Highld 251 D6
Balbeg Highld 251 C6
Balbeggie Perth 219 B6
Balbithan Aberds 245 A4
Balbithan Ho. Aberds 245 A5
Balblair Highld 264 D3
Balblair Highld 264 A1
Balby S Yorks 140 C3
Balchladich Highld 270 A3
Balchraggan Highld 252 C1
Balchraggan Highld 252 B1
Balchrick Highld 276 C2
Balchrystie Fife 221 D4
Balcladaich Highld 251 D4
Balcombe W Sus 35 C6
Balcombe Lane W Sus 35 C6
Balcomie Fife 221 C6
Balcurvie Fife 220 D3
Baldersby N Yorks 158 D2
Baldersby St James N Yorks 158 D2
Balderstone Lancs 145 D6
Balderton Ches 126 C3
Balderton Notts 132 D3
Baldhu Corn 4 C2
Baldinnie Fife 220 C4
Baldock Herts 84 D4
Baldovie Dundee 221 A4
Baldrine I o M 152 C4
Baldslow E Sus 23 A5
Baldwin I o M 152 C3
Baldwinholme Cumb 175 C6
Baldwin's Gate Staffs 112 A1
Bale Norf 120 B2
Balearn Aberds 269 D5
Balemartine Argyll 222 C2
Balephuil Argyll 222 C2
Balerno Edin 209 D4
Balevullin Argyll 222 C2
Balfield Angus 232 B3
Balfour Orkney 282 F5
Balfron Stirl 206 B3
Balfron Station Stirl 206 B3
Balgaveny Aberds 256 B1
Balgavies Angus 232 C3
Balgonar Fife 208 A3
Balgove Aberds 256 C3
Balgowan Highld 241 C4
Balgown Highld 258 B3
Balgrochan E Dunb 205 A6
Balgy Highld 249 A5
Balhaldie Stirl 218 D3
Balhalgardy Aberds 256 D2
Balham London 49 B5
Balhary Perth 231 D6
Baliasta Shetland 284 C8
Baligill Highld 279 B4
Balintore Angus 231 C6
Balintore Highld 265 C4
Balintraid Highld 264 C3
Balk N Yorks 158 C3
Balkeerie Angus 232 D1
Balkemback Angus 220 A3
Balkholme E Yorks 141 A5
Balkissock S Ayrs 180 C3
Ball Shrops 110 C2
Ball Haye Green Staffs 129 D4
Ball Hill Hants 46 C2
Ballabeg I o M 152 D2
Ballacannel I o M 152 C4
Ballachulish Highld 237 D4
Ballajora I o M 152 B4
Ballaleigh I o M 152 C3
Ballamodha I o M 152 D2
Ballantrae S Ayrs 180 C2
Ballaquine I o M 152 C4
Ballards Gore Essex 70 D3
Ballasalla I o M 152 B3
Ballasalla I o M 152 D2
Ballater Aberds 243 C6
Ballaugh I o M 152 B3
Ballaveare I o M 152 D3
Ballcorach Moray 254 D2
Ballechin Perth 230 C3
Balleigh Highld 264 B3
Ballencrieff E Loth 210 C1
Ballentoul Perth 230 B2
Ballidon Derbys 130 D2
Balliemore Argyll 214 D3
Balliemore Argyll 226 D3
Ballikinrain Stirl 206 B3
Ballimeanoch Argyll 214 A3
Ballimore Argyll 214 D2
Ballimore Stirl 217 C5
Ballinaby Argyll 200 B2
Ballindean Perth 220 B2
Ballingdon Suff 87 C4
Ballinger Common Bucks 67 C4
Ballingham Hereford 78 D3
Ballingry Fife 209 A4
Ballinlick Perth 230 D3
Ballinluig Perth 230 C3
Ballintuim Perth 231 C5
Balloch Angus 232 C1
Balloch Highld 252 B3
Balloch N Lnrk 207 C5
Balloch W Dunb 206 B1
Ballochan Aberds 244 C2
Ballochford Moray 255 C4
Ballochmorrie S Ayrs 181 C4
Balls Cross W Sus 34 D2
Balls Green Essex 71 A4
Ballygown Argyll 224 B3
Ballygrant Argyll 200 B3
Ballyhaugh Argyll 223 B4
Balmacara Highld 249 D5
Balmacara Square Highld 249 D5
Balmaclellan Dumfries 173 A4
Balmacneil Perth 230 C3
Balmacqueen Highld 259 A4
Balmae Dumfries 173 D4
Balmaha Stirl 206 A2
Balmalcolm Fife 220 D3
Balmeanach Highld 248 B2
Balmedie Aberds 245 A6
Balmer Heath Shrops 110 B3
Balmerino Fife 220 B3
Balmerlawn Hants 18 A2
Balmichael N Ayrs 191 B5
Balmirmer Angus 221 A5

Balmoral Castle and Gardens Aberds 243 C5
Balmore Highld 258 D2
Balmore Highld 251 C5
Balmore Highld 253 B4
Balmore Perth 230 C3
Balmule Fife 209 B5
Balmullo Fife 220 B4
Balmungie Highld 252 A3
Balnaboth Angus 231 B7
Balnabruaich Highld 264 D3
Balnabruich Highld 275 B5
Balnacoil Highld 274 C2
Balnacra Highld 250 B1
Balnafoich Highld 252 C2
Balnagall Highld 265 B4
Balnaguard Perth 230 C3
Balnahard Argyll 212 C2
Balnahard Argyll 224 C3
Balnain Highld 251 C6
Balnakeil Highld 277 B4
Balnaknock Highld 259 B4
Balnapaling Highld 264 D3
Balne N Yorks 140 B3
Balochroy Argyll 202 C2
Balone Fife 221 C4
Balornock Glasgow 205 B6
Balquharn Perth 219 A5
Balquhidder Stirl 217 B5
Balsall W Mid 97 D5
Balsall Common W Mid 97 D5
Balsall Heath W Mid 96 C3
Balscott Oxon 81 C6
Balsham Cambs 86 B1
Baltasound Shetland 284 C8
Balterley Staffs 128 D2
Baltersan Dumfries 171 A6
Balthangie Aberds 268 D3
Baltonsborough Som 29 B5
Balvaird Highld 252 A1
Balvicar Argyll 213 A5
Balvraid Highld 238 A2
Balvraid Highld 253 C4
Bamber Bridge Lancs 137 A4
Bambers Green Essex 69 A5
Bamburgh Northumb 199 C5
Bamburgh Castle Northumb 199 C5
Bamff Perth 231 C6
Bamford Derbys 130 A2
Bamford Gtr Man 138 B1
Bampton Cumb 164 D3
Bampton Devon 27 C4
Bampton Oxon 64 C4
Bampton Grange Cumb 164 D3
Banavie Highld 237 B5
Banbury Oxon 82 C1
Bancffosfelen Carms 57 A4
Banchory Aberds 244 C3
Banchory-Devenick Aberds 245 B6
Bancycapel Carms 57 A4
Bancyfelin Carms 56 A3
Bancyffordd Carms 73 C7
Bandirran Perth 220 A2
Banff Aberds 268 C1
Bangor Gwyn 123 C5
Bangor-is-y-coed Wrex 110 A2
Bangor on Dee Racecourse Wrex 110 A2
Banham Norf 103 C6
Banham Zoo, Diss Norf 103 C6
Bank Hants 18 A1
Bank Newton N Yorks 146 B3
Bank Street Worcs 79 A4
Bankend Dumfries 174 B3
Bankfoot Perth 219 A5
Bankglen E Ayrs 182 A4
Bankhead Aberdeen 245 A5
Bankhead Aberds 244 B3
Banknock Falk 207 C5
Banks Cumb 176 C3
Banks Lancs 136 A2
Bankshill Dumfries 185 D4
Banningham Norf 120 C4
Banniskirk Ho. Highld 280 C3
Bannister Green Essex 69 A6
Bannockburn Stirl 207 A6
Banstead Sur 35 A5
Bantham Devon 7 C5
Banton N Lnrk 207 C5
Banwell N Som 42 D2
Banyard's Green Suff 104 D3
Bapchild Kent 51 C6
Bar Hill Cambs 85 A5
Barabhas W Isles 288 C4
Barabhas Iarach W Isles 288 C4
Barabhas Uarach W Isles 288 B4
Barachandroman Argyll 225 D5
Barassie S Ayrs 192 B3
Baravullin Argyll 226 C3
Barbaraville Highld 264 C3
Barber Booth Derbys 129 A6
Barbieston S Ayrs 182 A2
Barbon Cumb 155 C5
Barbridge Ches 127 D6
Barbrook Devon 26 A2
Barby Northants 98 D2
Barcaldine Argyll 227 B4
Barcaldine Sea Life Centre Argyll 226 B4
Barcheston Warks 81 D5
Barcombe E Sus 22 A2
Barcombe Cross E Sus 22 A2
Barden N Yorks 157 B5
Barden Scale N Yorks 147 B4
Bardennoch Dumfries 182 C3
Bardfield Saling Essex 69 A6
Bardister Shetland 284 F5
Bardney Lincs 133 C6
Bardon Leics 114 D2
Bardon Mill Northumb 177 C5
Bardowie E Dunb 205 A5
Bardrainney Invclyd 204 A3
Bardsea Cumb 154 D2
Bardsey W Yorks 148 C2
Bardwell Suff 103 D5
Bare Lancs 145 A4
Barfad Argyll 202 B3
Barford Norf 104 A2
Barford Warks 81 A5
Barford St John Oxon 82 D1
Barford St Martin Wilts 31 B4
Barford St Michael Oxon 82 D1
Barfrestone Kent 53 D4
Bargod = Bargoed Caerph 41 B6
Bargoed = Bargod Caerph 41 B6
Bargrennan Dumfries 181 D5
Barham Cambs 100 D3
Barham Kent 53 D4
Barham Suff 88 B2
Barharrow Dumfries 172 C4
Barhill Dumfries 173 B6
Barholm Lincs 116 D3
Barkby Leics 98 A3
Barkestone-le-Vale Leics 115 B5
Barkham Wokingham 47 C5
Barking London 50 A1
Barking Suff 87 B6
Barking Tye Suff 87 B6
Barkingside London 50 A1
Barkisland W Yorks 138 B3
Barkston Lincs 116 A2
Barkston N Yorks 148 D3
Barkway Herts 85 D5
Barlaston Staffs 112 B2
Barlavington W Sus 20 A2
Barlborough Derbys 131 B4
Barlby N Yorks 149 D5
Barlestone Leics 98 A1
Barley Herts 85 D5
Barley Lancs 146 C2
Barley Mow T & W 179 D4
Barleythorpe Rutland 99 A5
Barling Essex 51 A6
Barlow Derbys 130 B3
Barlow N Yorks 140 A4
Barlow T & W 178 C3
Barmby Moor E Yorks 149 C6
Barmby on the Marsh E Yorks 141 A4
Barmer Norf 119 B5
Barmoor Castle Northumb 198 C3
Barmoor Lane End Northumb 198 C4
Barmouth = Abermaw Gwyn 90 A4
Barmpton Darl 167 D6
Barmston E Yorks 151 B4
Barnack P'boro 100 A2
Barnacle Warks 97 C6
Barnard Castle Durham 166 D3
Barnard Gate Oxon 65 B5
Barnardiston Suff 86 C3
Barnbarroch Dumfries 173 C6
Barnburgh S Yorks 140 C2
Barnby Suff 105 C5
Barnby Dun S Yorks 140 C4
Barnby in the Willows Notts 132 D3
Barnby Moor Notts 131 A6
Barnes Street Kent 36 B4
Barnet London 68 D2
Barnetby le Wold N Lincs 142 C2
Barney Norf 120 B1
Barnham Suff 103 D4
Barnham W Sus 20 B2
Barnham Broom Norf 104 A1
Barnhead Angus 233 C4
Barnhill Ches 127 D4
Barnhill Dundee 221 A4
Barnhill Moray 266 D2
Barnhills Dumfries 180 D1
Barningham Durham 166 D3
Barningham Suff 103 D5
Barnoldby le Beck NE Lincs 143 C4
Barnoldswick Lancs 146 C2
Barns Green W Sus 35 D4
Barnsley Glos 64 C1
Barnsley S Yorks 139 C6
Barnstaple Devon 25 B6
Barnston Essex 69 B6
Barnston Mers 126 A2
Barnstone Notts 115 B5
Barnt Green Worcs 96 D3
Barnton Ches 127 B6
Barnton Edin 209 C4
Barnwell All Saints Northants 100 C2
Barnwell St Andrew Northants 100 C2
Barnwood Glos 63 B4
Barochreal Argyll 226 D3
Barons Cross Hereford 78 B2
Barr S Ayrs 181 B4
Barra Airport W Isles 286 F2
Barra Castle Aberds 256 D2
Barrachan Dumfries 171 C5
Barrack Aberds 256 B3
Barraglom W Isles 288 D2
Barrahormid Argyll 213 D5
Barran Argyll 226 D3
Barrapol Argyll 222 C2
Barras Aberds 245 D5
Barras Cumb 165 D6
Barrasford Northumb 177 B7
Barravullin Argyll 213 B6
Barregarrow I o M 152 C3
Barrhead E Renf 205 C4
Barrhill S Ayrs 181 C4
Barrington Cambs 85 C5
Barrington Som 28 D3
Barripper Corn 3 B4
Barrmill N Ayrs 204 C3
Barrock Highld 281 A4
Barrock Ho. Highld 281 B4
Barrow Lancs 146 D1
Barrow Rutland 116 D1
Barrow Suff 86 A3
Barrow Green Kent 51 C6
Barrow Gurney N Som 43 C4
Barrow Haven N Lincs 142 A2
Barrow-in-Furness Cumb 153 D3
Barrow Island Cumb 153 D2
Barrow Nook Lancs 136 C3
Barrow Street Wilts 30 B2
Barrow upon Humber N Lincs 142 A2
Barrow upon Soar Leics 114 D3
Barrow upon Trent Derbys 114 C1
Barroway Drove Norf 102 A1
Barrowburn Northumb 188 B1
Barrowby Lincs 116 B1
Barrowcliff N Yorks 160 C4
Barrowden Rutland 99 A6
Barrowford Lancs 146 D2
Barrows Green Ches 128 D1
Barrows Green Cumb 154 C4
Barrow's Green Mers 127 A5
Barry Angus 221 A5
Barry = Y Barri V Glam 41 E6
Barry Island V Glam 41 E6
Barsby Leics 115 D4
Barsham Suff 105 C4
Barston W Mid 97 D5
Bartestree Hereford 78 C3
Barthol Chapel Aberds 256 C3
Barthomley Ches 128 D2
Bartley Hants 32 D2
Bartley Green W Mid 96 C3
Bartlow Cambs 86 C1
Barton Cambs 85 B6
Barton Ches 127 D4
Barton Glos 64 A2
Barton Lancs 136 C2
Barton Lancs 145 D5
Barton N Yorks 157 A6
Barton Oxon 65 C6
Barton Torbay 8 A3
Barton Warks 80 B4
Barton Bendish Norf 102 A3
Barton Hartshorn Bucks 82 D3
Barton in Fabis Notts 114 B3
Barton in the Beans Leics 97 A6
Barton-le-Clay Beds 84 D2
Barton-le-Street N Yorks 159 D6
Barton-le-Willows N Yorks 149 A6
Barton Mills Suff 102 D3
Barton on Sea Hants 17 B6
Barton on the Heath Warks 81 D5
Barton St David Som 29 B5
Barton Seagrave Northants 99 D5
Barton Stacey Hants 32 A3
Barton Turf Norf 121 C5
Barton-under-Needwood Staffs 113 D5
Barton-upon-Humber N Lincs 142 A2
Barton Waterside N Lincs 142 A2
Barugh S Yorks 139 C6
Barway Cambs 102 D1
Barwell Leics 98 B1
Barwick Herts 68 B3
Barwick Som 29 D5
Barwick in Elmet W Yorks 148 D2
Baschurch Shrops 110 C3
Bascote Warks 81 A7
Basford Green Staffs 129 D4
Bashall Eaves Lancs 145 C6
Bashley Hants 17 B6
Basildon Essex 51 A4
Basingstoke Hants 47 D4
Baslow Derbys 130 B2
Bason Bridge Som 28 A3
Bassaleg Newport 42 A1
Bassenthwaite Cumb 163 A5
Bassett Soton 32 D3
Bassingbourn Cambs 85 C5
Bassingfield Notts 115 B4
Bassingham Lincs 133 C4
Bassingthorpe Lincs 116 C2
Basta Shetland 284 D7
Baston Lincs 116 D4
Bastwick Norf 121 D6
Baswick Steer E Yorks 150 C3
Batchworth Heath Herts 67 D5
Batcombe Dorset 15 A6
Batcombe Som 29 B6
Bate Heath Ches 128 B1
Bateman's, Burwash E Sus 37 D4
Batford Herts 67 B6
Bath Bath 43 C6
Bath Abbey Bath 43 C6
Bath Racecourse Bath 43 C6
Bathampton Bath 44 C1
Bathealton Som 27 C5
Batheaston Bath 44 C1
Bathford Bath 44 C1
Bathgate W Loth 208 D2
Bathley Notts 132 D2
Bathpool Corn 10 D3
Bathpool Som 28 C2
Bathville W Loth 208 D2
Batley W Yorks 139 A5
Batsford Glos 81 D4
Battersby N Yorks 159 A4
Battersea London 49 B5
Battisborough Cross Devon 7 C4
Battisford Suff 87 B6
Battisford Tye Suff 87 B6
Battle E Sus 23 A5
Battle Powys 76 D4
Battle Abbey E Sus 23 A5
Battledown Glos 63 A5
Battlefield Shrops 111 D4
Battlesbridge Essex 70 D1
Battlesden Beds 67 A4
Battlesea Green Suff 104 D3
Battleton Som 27 C4
Battram Leics 98 A1
Battramsley Hants 18 B2
Baughton Worcs 80 C1
Baughurst Hants 46 D3
Baulking Oxon 64 D4
Baumber Lincs 134 B2
Baunton Glos 63 C6
Baverstock Wilts 31 B4
Bawburgh Norf 104 A2
Bawdeswell Norf 120 C2
Bawdrip Som 28 B3
Bawdsey Suff 88 C4
Bawtry S Yorks 141 D4
Baxenden Lancs 137 A6
Baxterley Warks 97 B5
Baybridge Hants 32 C4
Baycliff Cumb 154 D1
Baydon Wilts 45 B6
Bayford Herts 68 C3
Bayford Som 30 C1
Bayles Cumb 165 A5
Baylham Suff 88 B2
Baynard's Green Oxon 65 A6
Bayston Hill Shrops 94 A2
Baythorn End Essex 86 C3
Bayton Worcs 95 D4
Beach Highld 236 D1
Beachampton Bucks 83 D4
Beachamwell Norf 102 A3
Beachans Moray 253 B6
Beacharr Argyll 202 D1
Beachborough Kent 38 B3
Beachley Glos 62 D1
Beacon Devon 14 A1
Beacon End Essex 70 A3
Beacon Hill Sur 34 C1
Beacon's Bottom Bucks 66 D2
Beaconsfield Bucks 67 E4
Beacrabhaic W Isles 288 H2
Beadlam N Yorks 159 C5
Beadlow Beds 84 D3
Beadnell Northumb 189 A5
Beaford Devon 25 D6
Beal Northumb 199 B4
Beal N Yorks 140 A3
Beale Park, Goring W Berks 47 B4
Beamhurst Staffs 113 B4
Beaminster Dorset 15 A4
Beamish Durham 179 D4
Beamish Open Air Museum, Stanley Durham 179 D4
Beamsley N Yorks 147 B4
Bean Kent 50 B2
Beanacre Wilts 44 C3
Beanley Northumb 188 B3
Beaquoy Orkney 282 E4
Bear Cross Bmouth 17 B4
Beardwood Blkburn 137 A5
Beare Green Sur 35 B4
Bearley Warks 81 A4
Bearnus Argyll 224 B2
Bearpark Durham 167 A5
Bearsbridge Northumb 177 D5
Bearsden E Dunb 205 A5
Bearsted Kent 37 A5
Bearstone Shrops 111 B6
Bearwood Hereford 78 B1
Bearwood Poole 17 B4
Bearwood W Mid 96 C3
Beattock Dumfries 184 B3
Beauchamp Roding Essex 69 B5
Beauchief S Yorks 130 A3
Beaufort Bl Gwent 60 B3
Beaufort Castle Highld 251 B7
Beaulieu Hants 18 A2
Beauly Highld 252 B1
Beaumaris Anglesey 123 C6
Beaumaris Castle Anglesey 123 C6
Beaumont Cumb 175 C6
Beaumont Essex 71 A5
Beaumont Hill Darl 167 D5
Beausale Warks 97 D5
Beauworth Hants 33 C4
Beaworthy Devon 11 B5
Beazley End Essex 70 A1
Bebington Mers 126 A3
Bebside Northumb 179 A4
Beccles Suff 105 B5
Becconsall Lancs 136 A3
Beck Foot Cumb 155 B5
Beck Hole N Yorks 159 A7
Beck Row Suff 102 D2
Beck Side Cumb 153 B3
Beckbury Shrops 95 A5
Beckenham London 49 C6
Beckermet Cumb 162 D3
Beckfoot Cumb 163 D4
Beckfoot Cumb 174 D3
Beckford Worcs 80 D2
Beckhampton Wilts 45 C4
Beckingham Lincs 132 D3
Beckingham Notts 141 E5
Beckington Som 44 D2
Beckley E Sus 37 D6
Beckley Hants 17 B6
Beckley Oxon 65 B6
Beckton London 50 A1
Beckwithshaw N Yorks 147 B6
Becontree London 50 A1
Bed-y-coedwr Gwyn 108 C2
Bedale N Yorks 157 C6
Bedburn Durham 166 B4
Bedchester Dorset 30 D2
Beddau Rhondda 41 C5
Beddgelert Gwyn 107 B5
Beddingham E Sus 22 B2
Beddington London 49 C6
Bedfield Suff 88 A3
Bedford Beds 84 B2
Bedgebury Pinetum Kent 37 C5
Bedham W Sus 34 D3
Bedhampton Hants 19 A6
Bedingfield Suff 88 A2
Bedlam N Yorks 147 A6
Bedlington Northumb 179 A4
Bedlington Station Northumb 179 A4
Bedlinog M Tydf 41 A5
Bedminster Bristol 43 B4
Bedmond Herts 67 C5
Bednall Staffs 112 D3
Bedrule Borders 187 B5
Bedstone Shrops 94 D1
Bedwas Caerph 41 C6
Bedworth Warks 97 C6
Bedworth Heath Warks 97 C6
Beeby Leics 98 A3
Beech Hants 33 B5
Beech Staffs 112 B2
Beech Hill Gtr Man 137 C4
Beech Hill W Berks 47 C4
Beechingstoke Wilts 45 D4
Beedon W Berks 46 B2
Beeford E Yorks 151 B4
Beeley Derbys 130 C2
Beelsby NE Lincs 143 C4
Beenham W Berks 46 C3
Beeny Corn 10 B2
Beer Devon 14 C2
Beer Hackett Dorset 29 D6
Beercrocombe Som 28 C3
Beesands Devon 8 C2
Beesby Lincs 135 A4
Beeson Devon 8 C2
Beeston Beds 84 C3
Beeston Ches 127 D5
Beeston Norf 119 D6
Beeston Notts 114 B3
Beeston W Yorks 148 D1
Beeston Castle Ches 127 D5
Beeston Regis Norf 120 A3
Beeswing Dumfries 173 B6
Beetham Cumb 154 D3
Beetley Norf 119 D6
Begbroke Oxon 65 B5
Begelly Pembs 55 D7
Beggar's Bush Powys 77 A6
Beguildy Powys 93 D5
Beighton Norf 105 A4
Beighton S Yorks 131 A4
Beighton Hill Derbys 130 D2
Beith N Ayrs 204 C3
Bekesbourne Kent 52 D3
Bekonscot Model Village, Beaconsfield Bucks 67 D4
Belaugh Norf 121 D4
Belbroughton Worcs 96 D2
Belchamp Otten Essex 87 C4
Belchamp St Paul Essex 86 C3
Belchamp Walter Essex 87 C4
Belchford Lincs 134 B2
Belford Northumb 199 C5
Belhaven E Loth 210 C3
Belhelvie Aberds 245 A6
Belhinnie Aberds 255 D5
Bell Bar Herts 68 C2
Bell Busk N Yorks 146 B3
Bell End Worcs 96 D2
Bell o'th'Hill Ches 111 A4
Bellabeg Aberds 243 A6
Bellamore S Ayrs 181 C4
Bellanoch Argyll 213 C5
Bellaty Angus 231 C6
Belleau Lincs 135 B4
Bellehiglash Moray 254 C2
Bellerby N Yorks 157 B5
Bellever Devon 12 D1
Belliehill Angus 232 B3
Bellingdon Bucks 67 C4
Bellingham Northumb 177 A6
Belloch Argyll 190 B2
Bellochantuy Argyll 190 B2
Bells Yew Green E Sus 36 C4
Bellsbank E Ayrs 182 B2
Bellshill N Lnrk 207 D5
Bellshill Northumb 199 C5
Bellspool Borders 195 C6
Bellsquarry W Loth 208 D3
Belmaduthy Highld 252 A2
Belmesthorpe Rutland 116 D3
Belmont Blkburn 137 B5
Belmont London 49 C5
Belmont S Ayrs 192 C3
Belmont Shetland 284 C7
Belnacraig Aberds 243 A6
Belowda Corn 5 A4
Belper Derbys 114 A1
Belper Lane End Derbys 114 A1
Belsay Northumb 178 B3
Belsay Hall Northumb 178 B2
Belses Borders 187 A4
Belsford Devon 7 B6
Belstead Suff 88 C2
Belston S Ayrs 192 C3
Belstone Devon 11 B7
Belthorn Lancs 137 A6
Beltinge Kent 52 C3
Beltoft N Lincs 141 C6
Belton Leics 114 C2
Belton Lincs 116 B2
Belton N Lincs 141 C5
Belton Norf 105 A5
Belton House, Grantham Lincs 116 B2
Belton in Rutland Rutland 99 A5
Beltring Kent 37 B4
Belts of Collonach Aberds 244 C3
Belvedere London 50 B1
Belvoir Leics 115 B6
Belvoir Leics 115 B6
Bembridge I o W 19 C5
Bemersyde Borders 197 C4
Bemerton Wilts 31 B5
Bempton E Yorks 161 D5
Ben Alder Lodge Highld 229 A4
Ben Armine Lodge Highld 273 C5
Ben Casgro W Isles 288 E5
Benacre Suff 105 C6
Benbecula Airport W Isles 286 A3
Benbuie Dumfries 183 C5
Benderloch Argyll 226 C4
Bendronaig Lodge Highld 250 C2
Benenden Kent 37 C6
Benfield Dumfries 171 A5
Bengate Norf 121 C5
Bengeworth Worcs 80 C3
Benhall Green Suff 89 A4
Benhall Street Suff 89 A4
Benholm Aberds 233 B6
Beningbrough N Yorks 148 B4
Beningbrough Hall N Yorks 148 B4
Benington Herts 68 A2
Benington Lincs 117 A6
Benllech Anglesey 123 B5
Benmore Argyll 215 D4
Benmore Stirl 216 B4
Benmore Lodge Highld 271 C6
Bennacott Corn 10 B3
Bennan N Ayrs 191 C5

Benniworth Lincs 134 A2
Benover Kent 37 B5
Bensham T & W 179 C4
Benslie N Ayrs 204 D3
Benson Oxon 65 D7
Bent Aberds 233 A4
Bent Gate Lancs 137 A6
Benthall Northumb 189 A5
Benthall Shrops 95 A4
Bentham Glos 63 B5
Benthoul Aberdeen 245 B5
Bentlawnt Shrops 94 A1
Bentley E Yorks 150 D3
Bentley Hants 33 A6
Bentley Suff 88 D2
Bentley S Yorks 140 C3
Bentley Warks 97 B5
Bentley Worcs 80 A2
Bentley Heath W Mid 97 D4
Benton Devon 26 B1
Bentpath Dumfries 185 C6
Bents W Loth 208 D2
Bentworth Hants 33 A5
Benvie Dundee 220 A3
Benwick Cambs 101 B5
Beoley Worcs 80 A3
Beoraidbeg Highld 235 A5
Bepton W Sus 20 A1
Berden Essex 69 A4
Bere Alston Devon 6 A3
Bere Ferrers Devon 6 A3
Bere Regis Dorset 16 B2
Berepper Corn 3 C4
Bergh Apton Norf 104 A4
Berinsfield Oxon 65 D6
Berkeley Glos 62 D2
Berkhamsted Herts 67 C4
Berkley Som 30 A2
Berkswell W Mid 97 D5
Bermondsey London 49 B6
Bernera Highld 249 D5
Bernice Argyll 215 C4
Bernisdale Highld 259 C4
Berrick Salome Oxon 65 D7
Berriedale Highld 275 B5
Berrier Cumb 164 C1
Berriew Powys 93 A5
Berrington Northumb 198 B4
Berrington Shrops 94 A3
Berrow Som 42 D2
Berrow Green Worcs 79 B5
Berry Down Cross Devon 25 A6
Berry Hill Glos 62 B1
Berry Hill Pembs 72 B3
Berry Pomeroy Devon 8 A2
Berryhillock Moray 267 C6
Berrynarbor Devon 25 A6
Bersham Wrex 110 A2
Berstane Orkney 282 F5
Berwick E Sus 22 B3
Berwick Bassett Wilts 45 B4
Berwick Hill Northumb 178 B3
Berwick St James Wilts 31 B4
Berwick St John Wilts 30 C3
Berwick St Leonard Wilts 30 B3
Berwick-upon-Tweed Northumb 198 A3
Bescar Lancs 136 B2
Besford Worcs 80 C2
Bessacarr S Yorks 140 C4
Bessels Leigh Oxon 65 C5
Bessingby E Yorks 151 A4
Bessingham Norf 120 B3
Bestbeech Hill E Sus 36 C4
Besthorpe Norf 103 B6
Besthorpe Notts 132 C3
Bestwood Nottingham 114 A3
Bestwood Village Notts 114 A3
Beswick E Yorks 150 C3
Betchworth Sur 35 B5
Beth Shalom Holocaust Centre, Laxton Notts 132 C2
Bethania Ceredig 75 B4
Bethania Gwyn 107 A6
Bethania Gwyn 108 A2
Bethel Anglesey 122 C3
Bethel Gwyn 123 D5
Bethel Gwyn 109 B4
Bethersden Kent 38 A1
Bethesda Gwyn 123 D6
Bethesda Pembs 55 C6
Bethlehem Carms 58 C3
Bethnal Green London 49 A6
Betley Staffs 111 A6
Betsham Kent 50 B3
Betteshanger Kent 53 D5
Bettiscombe Dorset 14 B3
Bettisfield Wrex 110 B3
Betton Shrops 93 A7
Betton Shrops 111 B5
Bettws Bridgend 40 C4
Bettws Mon 61 B4
Bettws Newport 61 D4
Bettws Cedewain Powys 93 B5
Bettws Gwerfil Goch Denb 109 A5
Bettws Ifan Ceredig 73 B6
Bettws Newydd Mon 61 C5
Bettws-y-crwyn Shrops 93 C6
Bettyhill Highld 278 B3
Betws Carms 57 A6
Betws Bledrws Ceredig 75 C4
Betws-Garmon Gwyn 107 A5
Betws-y-Coed Conwy 124 D2
Betws-yn-Rhos Conwy 125 B4
Beulah Ceredig 73 B5
Beulah Powys 76 B3
Bevendean Brighton 21 B6
Bevercotes Notts 132 B1
Beverley E Yorks 150 D3
Beverley Minster E Yorks 150 D3
Beverley Racecourse E Yorks 150 C3
Beverston Glos 63 D4
Bevington Glos 62 D2
Bewaldeth Cumb 163 A5
Bewcastle Cumb 176 B3
Bewdley Worcs 95 D5
Bewerley N Yorks 147 A5
Bewholme E Yorks 151 B4
Bexhill E Sus 23 B5
Bexley London 50 B1
Bexleyheath London 50 B1
Bexwell Norf 102 A2
Beyton Suff 87 A5
Bhaltos W Isles 287 A5
Bhatarsaigh W Isles 286 G2
Bibury Glos 64 C2
Bicester Oxon 65 A6
Bickenhall Som 28 D2
Bickenhill W Mid 97 C4
Bicker Lincs 117 B5
Bickershaw Gtr Man 137 C5
Bickerstaffe Lancs 136 C3
Bickerton Ches 127 D5
Bickerton N Yorks 148 B3
Bickington Devon 12 D2
Bickington Devon 25 B6
Bickleigh Devon 13 A4
Bickleigh Devon 7 A4
Bickleton Devon 25 B6
Bickley London 49 C7
Bickley Moss Ches 111 A4
Bicknacre Essex 70 C1
Bicknoller Som 27 B6
Bicknor Kent 37 A6
Bickton Hants 31 D5
Bicton Shrops 110 D3
Bicton Shrops 93 C6
Bicton Park Gardens Devon 13 C5
Bidborough Kent 36 B3
Biddenden Kent 37 C6
Biddenham Beds 84 C2
Biddestone Wilts 44 B2
Biddisham Som 42 D2
Biddlesden Bucks 82 C3
Biddlestone Northumb 188 C2
Biddulph Staffs 128 D3
Biddulph Moor Staffs 129 D4
Bideford Devon 25 C5
Bidford-on-Avon Warks 80 B4
Bidston Mers 136 D1
Bielby E Yorks 149 C6
Bieldside Aberdeen 245 B5
Bierley I o W 18 D4
Bierley W Yorks 147 D5
Bierton Bucks 66 B3
Big Pit National Mining Museum, Blaenavon Torf 60 C4
Big Sand Highld 261 C4
Bigbury Devon 7 C5
Bigbury on Sea Devon 7 C5
Bigby Lincs 142 C2
Biggar Cumb 153 D2
Biggar S Lnrk 195 C5
Biggin Derbys 129 D6
Biggin Derbys 113 A6
Biggin N Yorks 148 D4
Biggin Hill London 36 A2
Biggings Shetland 285 G3
Biggleswade Beds 84 C3
Bighouse Highld 279 B4
Bighton Hants 33 B5
Bignor W Sus 20 A2
Bigton Shetland 285 L5
Bilberry Corn 5 A5
Bilborough Nottingham 114 A3
Bilbrook Som 27 A5
Bilbrough N Yorks 148 C4
Bilbster Highld 281 C4
Bildershaw Durham 167 C5
Bildeston Suff 87 C5
Billericay Essex 69 D6
Billesdon Leics 99 A4
Billesley Warks 80 B4
Billingborough Lincs 116 B4
Billinge Mers 136 C4
Billingford Norf 120 C2
Billingham Stockton 168 C2
Billinghay Lincs 133 D6
Billingley S Yorks 140 C2
Billingshurst W Sus 34 D3
Billingsley Shrops 95 C5
Billington Beds 67 A4
Billington Lancs 145 D7
Billockby Norf 121 D6
Billown Motor Racing Circuit I o M 152 E2
Billy Row Durham 167 B4
Bilsborrow Lancs 145 D5
Bilsby Lincs 135 B4
Bilsham W Sus 20 B2
Bilsington Kent 38 B2
Bilson Green Glos 62 B2
Bilsthorpe Notts 131 C6
Bilsthorpe Moor Notts 131 D6
Bilston Midloth 209 D5
Bilston W Mid 96 B2
Bilstone Leics 97 A6
Bilting Kent 38 A2
Bilton E Yorks 151 D4
Bilton Northumb 189 B5
Bilton Warks 98 D1
Bilton in Ainsty N Yorks 148 C3
Bimbister Orkney 282 F4
Binbrook Lincs 143 D4
Binchester Blocks Durham 167 B5
Bincombe Dorset 15 C6
Bindal Highld 265 B5
Binegar Som 29 A6
Binfield Brack 47 B6
Binfield Heath Oxon 47 B5
Bingfield Northumb 178 B1
Bingham Notts 115 B5
Bingley W Yorks 147 D5
Bings Heath Shrops 111 D4
Binham Norf 120 B1
Binley Hants 46 D2
Binley W Mid 97 D6
Binley Woods Warks 97 D6
Binniehill Falk 207 C6
Binsoe N Yorks 157 D6
Binstead I o W 19 B4
Binsted Hants 33 A6
Binton Warks 80 B4
Bintree Norf 120 C2
Binweston Shrops 93 A7
Birch Essex 70 B3
Birch Gtr Man 138 C1
Birch Green Essex 70 B3
Birch Heath Ches 127 C5
Birch Hill Ches 127 B5
Birch Vale Derbys 129 A5
Bircham Newton Norf 119 B4
Bircham Tofts Norf 119 B4
Birchanger Essex 69 A5
Birchencliffe W Yorks 139 B4
Bircher Hereford 78 A2
Birchfield Highld 253 D5
Birchgrove Cardiff 41 D6
Birchgrove Swansea 40 B2
Birchington Kent 53 C4
Birchmoor Warks 97 A5
Birchover Derbys 130 C2
Birchwood Lincs 133 C4
Birchwood Warr 137 D5
Bircotes Notts 140 D4
Birdbrook Essex 86 C3
Birdforth N Yorks 158 D3
Birdham W Sus 20 C1
Birdholme Derbys 130 C3
Birdingbury Warks 82 A1
Birdland Park, Bourton-on-the-Water Glos 64 A2
Birdlip Glos 63 B5
Birds Edge W Yorks 139 C5
Birdsall N Yorks 149 A7
Birdsgreen Shrops 95 C5
Birdsmoor Gate Dorset 14 A3
Birdston E Dunb 205 A6
Birdwell S Yorks 139 C6
Birdwood Glos 62 B3
Birgham Borders 198 C1
Birkby N Yorks 158 A2
Birkdale Mers 136 B2
Birkenhead Mers 126 A3
Birkenhills Aberds 256 B2
Birkenshaw N Lnrk 207 D4
Birkenshaw W Yorks 139 A5
Birkhall Aberds 243 C6
Birkhill Angus 220 A3
Birkhill Dumfries 185 A5
Birkholme Lincs 116 C2
Birkin N Yorks 140 A3
Birley Hereford 78 B2
Birling Kent 50 C3
Birling Northumb 189 C5
Birling Gap E Sus 22 C3
Birlingham Worcs 80 C2
Birmingham W Mid 96 C3
Birmingham Botanical Gardens W Mid 96 C3
Birmingham International Airport W Mid 97 C4
Birmingham Museum and Art Gallery W Mid 96 C3
Birmingham Museum of Science and Technology W Mid 96 C3
Birnam Perth 230 D4
Birse Aberds 244 C2
Birsemore Aberds 244 C2
Birstall Leics 98 A2
Birstall W Yorks 139 A5
Birstwith N Yorks 147 B6
Birthorpe Lincs 116 B4
Birtley Hereford 78 A1
Birtley Northumb 177 B6
Birtley T & W 179 D4
Birts Street Worcs 79 D5
Bisbrooke Rutland 99 B5
Biscathorpe Lincs 134 A2
Biscot Luton 67 A5
Bish Mill Devon 26 C2
Bisham Windsor 47 A6
Bishampton Worcs 80 B2
Bishop Auckland Durham 167 C5
Bishop Burton E Yorks 150 D2
Bishop Middleham Durham 167 B6
Bishop Monkton N Yorks 148 A2
Bishop Norton Lincs 142 D1
Bishop Sutton Bath 43 D4
Bishop Thornton N Yorks 147 A6
Bishop Wilton E Yorks 149 B6
Bishopbridge Lincs 142 D2
Bishopbriggs E Dunb 205 B6
Bishopmill Moray 266 C3
Bishops Cannings Wilts 44 C4
Bishop's Castle Shrops 93 C7
Bishop's Caundle Dorset 29 D6
Bishop's Cleeve Glos 63 A5
Bishops Frome Hereford 79 C4
Bishop's Green Essex 69 B6
Bishop's Hull Som 28 C2
Bishop's Itchington Warks 81 B6
Bishops Lydeard Som 27 C6
Bishops Nympton Devon 26 C2
Bishop's Offley Staffs 112 C1
Bishop's Stortford Herts 69 A4
Bishop's Sutton Hants 33 B5
Bishop's Tachbrook Warks 81 A6
Bishops Tawton Devon 25 B6
Bishop's Waltham Hants 33 D4
Bishop's Wood Staffs 95 A6
Bishopsbourne Kent 52 D3
Bishopsteignton Devon 13 D4
Bishopstoke Hants 32 D3
Bishopston Swansea 57 D5
Bishopstone Bucks 66 B3
Bishopstone E Sus 22 B2
Bishopstone Hereford 78 C2
Bishopstone Swindon 45 A6
Bishopstone Wilts 31 C4
Bishopstrow Wilts 30 A2
Bishopswood Som 28 D2
Bishopsworth Bristol 43 C4
Bishopthorpe York 149 C4
Bishopton Darl 167 C6
Bishopton Dumfries 171 C6
Bishopton N Yorks 157 D7
Bishopton Renfs 205 A4
Bishopton Warks 81 B4
Bishton Newport 42 A2
Bisley Glos 63 C5
Bisley Sur 34 A2
Bispham Blkpool 144 C3
Bispham Green Lancs 136 B3
Bissoe Corn 4 C2
Bisterne Close Hants 17 A6
Bitchfield Lincs 116 C2
Bittadon Devon 25 A6
Bittaford Devon 7 B5
Bittering Norf 119 D6
Bitterley Shrops 94 D3
Bitterne Soton 32 D3
Bitteswell Leics 98 C2
Bitton S Glos 43 C5
Bix Oxon 47 A5
Bixter Shetland 285 H5
Blaby Leics 98 B2
Black Bourton Oxon 64 C3
Black Callerton T & W 178 C3
Black Clauchrie S Ayrs 181 C4
Black Corries Lodge Highld 228 C1
Black Crofts Argyll 226 C4
Black Dog Devon 12 A3
Black Heddon Northumb 178 B2
Black Lane Gtr Man 137 C6
Black Marsh Shrops 94 B1
Black Mount Argyll 228 D1
Black Notley Essex 70 A1
Black Pill Swansea 57 C6
Black Tar Pembs 55 D5
Black Torrington Devon 11 A5
Blackacre Dumfries 184 C3
Blackadder West Borders 198 A2
Blackawton Devon 8 B2
Blackborough Devon 13 A5
Blackborough End Norf 118 D3
Blackboys E Sus 36 D3
Blackbrook Derbys 114 A1
Blackbrook Mers 136 D4
Blackbrook Staffs 111 B6
Blackburn Aberds 255 C6
Blackburn Aberds 245 A5
Blackburn Blkburn 137 A5
Blackburn W Loth 208 D2
Blackcraig Dumfries 183 D5
Blackden Heath Ches 128 B2
Blackdog Aberds 245 A6
Blackfell T & W 179 D4
Blackfield Hants 18 A3
Blackford Cumb 175 B6
Blackford Perth 218 D3
Blackford Som 28 A4
Blackford Som 29 C6
Blackfordby Leics 114 D1
Blackgang I o W 18 D3
Blackgang Chine Fantasy I o W 18 D3
Blackhall Colliery Durham 168 B2
Blackhall Mill T & W 178 D3
Blackhall Rocks Durham 168 B2
Blackham E Sus 36 C2
Blackhaugh Borders 196 C3
Blackheath Essex 71 A4
Blackheath Suff 105 D5
Blackheath Sur 34 B3
Blackheath W Mid 96 C2
Blackhill Aberds 257 B5
Blackhill Aberds 269 D5
Blackhill Highld 258 C3
Blackhills Highld 253 A5
Blackhills Moray 266 D3
Blackhorse S Glos 43 B5
Blackland Wilts 44 C4
Blacklaw Aberds 268 D1
Blackley Gtr Man 138 C1
Blacklunans Perth 231 B5
Blackmill Bridgend 40 C4
Blackmoor Hants 33 B6
Blackmoor Gate Devon 26 A1
Blackmore Essex 69 C6
Blackmore End Essex 86 D3
Blackmore End Herts 67 B6
Blackness Falk 208 C3
Blacknest Hants 33 A6
Blacko Lancs 146 C2
Blackpool Blkpool 144 D3
Blackpool Devon 8 C2
Blackpool Pembs 55 C6
Blackpool Airport Lancs 144 D3
Blackpool Gate Cumb 176 B3
Blackpool Pleasure Beach Blkpool 144 D3
Blackpool Sea Life Centre Blkpool 144 D3
Blackpool Tower Blkpool 144 D3
Blackpool Zoo Park Blkpool 144 D3
Blackridge W Loth 208 D1
Blackrock Argyll 200 B3
Blackrock Mon 60 B4
Blackrod Gtr Man 137 B5
Blackshaw Dumfries 174 B3
Blackshaw Head W Yorks 138 A2
Blacksmith's Green Suff 88 A2
Blackstone W Sus 21 A5
Blackthorn Oxon 65 B7
Blackthorpe Suff 87 A5
Blacktoft E Yorks 141 A6
Blacktop Aberdeen 245 B5
Blacktown Newport 42 A1
Blackwall Tunnel London 49 A6
Blackwater Corn 4 C2
Blackwater Hants 34 A1
Blackwater I o W 18 C4
Blackwaterfoot N Ayrs 191 C4
Blackwell Darl 167 D5
Blackwell Derbys 129 B6
Blackwell Derbys 131 D4
Blackwell Warks 81 C5
Blackwell Worcs 96 D2
Blackwell W Sus 36 C1
Blackwood S Lnrk 194 B2
Blackwood = Coed Duon Caerph 41 B6
Blackwood Hill Staffs 129 D4
Blacon Ches 126 C3
Bladnoch Dumfries 171 B6
Bladon Oxon 65 B5
Blaen-gwynfi Neath 40 B3
Blaen-waun Carms 73 D5
Blaen-y-coed Carms 73 D6
Blaen-y-Cwm Denb 109 B5
Blaen-y-cwm Gwyn 108 C2
Blaen-y-cwm Powys 109 C5
Blaenannerch Ceredig 73 B5
Blaenau Ffestiniog Gwyn 108 A2
Blaenavon Torf 61 C4
Blaencelyn Ceredig 73 A6
Blaendyryn Powys 59 B6
Blaenffos Pembs 73 C4
Blaengarw Bridgend 40 B4
Blaengwrach Neath 59 E5
Blaenpennal Ceredig 75 B5
Blaenplwyf Ceredig 75 A4
Blaenporth Ceredig 73 B5
Blaenrhondda Rhondda 40 A4
Blaenycwm Ceredig 92 D2
Blagdon N Som 43 D4
Blagdon Torbay 8 A2
Blagdon Hill Som 28 D2
Blagill Cumb 165 A5
Blaguegate Lancs 136 C3
Blaich Highld 237 B4
Blain Highld 235 D5
Blaina Bl Gwent 60 C4
Blair Atholl Perth 230 B2
Blair Castle, Blair Atholl Perth 230 B2
Blair Drummond Stirl 207 A5
Blair Drummond Safari Park, Dunblane Stirl 207 A5
Blairbeg N Ayrs 191 B6
Blairdaff Aberds 244 A3
Blairglas Argyll 206 B1
Blairgowrie Perth 231 D5
Blairhall Fife 208 B3
Blairingone Perth 208 A2
Blairland N Ayrs 204 D3
Blairlogie Stirl 207 A6
Blairlomond Argyll 215 C4
Blairmore Argyll 215 D4
Blairnamarrow Moray 243 A5
Blairquhosh Stirl 206 B3
Blair's Ferry Argyll 203 B4
Blairskaith E Dunb 205 A5
Blaisdon Glos 62 B3
Blakebrook Worcs 95 D6
Blakedown Worcs 96 D1
Blakelaw Borders 197 C6
Blakeley Staffs 95 B6
Blakeley Lane Staffs 112 A3
Blakemere Hereford 78 C1
Blakeney Glos 62 C2
Blakeney Norf 120 A2
Blakeney Point NNR Norf 120 A2
Blakenhall Ches 111 A6
Blakenhall W Mid 96 B2
Blakeshall Worcs 95 C6
Blakesley Northants 82 B3
Blanchland Northumb 178 D1
Bland Hill N Yorks 147 B6
Blandford Forum Dorset 16 A2
Blandford St Mary Dorset 16 A2
Blanefield Stirl 205 A5
Blankney Lincs 133 C5
Blantyre S Lnrk 194 A1
Blar a'Chaorainn Highld 237 C5
Blaran Argyll 214 A1
Blarghour Argyll 214 A2
Blarmachfoldach Highld 237 C4
Blarnalearoch Highld 262 A3
Blashford Hants 17 A5
Blaston Leics 99 B5
Blatherwycke Northants 99 B6
Blawith Cumb 154 C1
Blaxhall Suff 89 B4
Blaxton S Yorks 141 C4
Blaydon T & W 178 C3
Bleadon N Som 42 D2
Bleak Hey Nook Gtr Man 138 C3
Blean Kent 52 C3
Bleasby Lincs 133 A6
Bleasby Notts 115 A5
Bleasdale Lancs 145 C5
Bleatarn Cumb 165 D5
Blebocraigs Fife 220 C4
Bleddfa Powys 77 A6
Bledington Glos 64 A3
Bledlow Bucks 66 C2
Bledlow Ridge Bucks 66 D2
Blegbie E Loth 210 D1
Blencarn Cumb 165 B4
Blencogo Cumb 175 D4
Blendworth Hants 33 D6
Blenheim Palace, Woodstock Oxon 65 B5
Blenheim Park Norf 119 B5
Blennerhasset Cumb 175 D4
Blervie Castle Moray 253 A6
Bletchingdon Oxon 65 B6
Bletchingley Sur 35 A6
Bletchley M Keynes 83 D5
Bletchley Shrops 111 B5
Bletherston Pembs 55 B6
Bletsoe Beds 84 B2
Blewbury Oxon 46 A3
Blickling Norf 120 C3
Blickling Hall, Aylsham Norf 120 C3
Blidworth Notts 131 D5
Blindburn Northumb 188 B1
Blindcrake Cumb 163 A4
Blindley Heath Sur 35 B6
Blisland Corn 10 D2
Bliss Gate Worcs 95 D5
Blissford Hants 31 D5
Blisworth Northants 83 B4
Blithbury Staffs 113 C4
Blitterlees Cumb 174 C4
Blockley Glos 81 D4
Blofield Norf 104 A4
Blofield Heath Norf 121 D5
Blo'Norton Norf 103 D6
Bloomfield Borders 187 A4
Blore Staffs 113 A5
Blount's Green Staffs 113 B4
Blowick Mers 136 B2
Bloxham Oxon 82 D1
Bloxholm Lincs 133 D5
Bloxwich W Mid 96 A2
Bloxworth Dorset 16 B2
Blubberhouses N Yorks 147 B5
Blue Anchor Som 27 A5
Blue Anchor Swansea 57 C5

Blue Planet Aquarium Ches 127 B4
Blue Row Essex 71 B4
Blundeston Suff 105 B6
Blunham Beds 84 B3
Blunsdon St Andrew Swindon 45 A5
Bluntington Worcs 96 D1
Bluntisham Cambs 101 D5
Blunts Corn 6 A2
Blyborough Lincs 142 D1
Blyford Suff 105 D5
Blymhill Staffs 112 D2
Blyth Notts 131 A6
Blyth Northumb 179 A5
Blyth Bridge Borders 195 B6
Blythburgh Suff 105 D5
Blythe Borders 197 B4
Blythe Bridge Staffs 112 A3
Blyton Lincs 141 D6
Boarhills Fife 221 C5
Boarhunt Hants 19 A5
Boars Head Gtr Man 137 C4
Boars Hill Oxon 65 C5
Boarshead E Sus 36 C3
Boarstall Bucks 66 B1
Boasley Cross Devon 11 B5
Boat of Garten Highld 242 A2
Boath Highld 264 C1
Bobbing Kent 51 C5
Bobbington Staffs 95 B6
Bobbingworth Essex 69 C5
Bocaddon Corn 5 B6
Bochastle Stirl 217 D6
Bocking Essex 70 A1
Bocking Churchstreet Essex 70 A1
Boddam Aberds 257 B6
Boddam Shetland 285 M5
Boddington Glos 63 A4
Bodedern Anglesey 122 B3
Bodelwyddan Denb 125 B5
Bodenham Hereford 78 B3
Bodenham Wilts 31 C5
Bodenham Arboretum and Earth Centre Worcs 95 C6
Bodenham Moor Hereford 78 B3
Bodermid Gwyn 106 D1
Bodewryd Anglesey 122 A3
Bodfari Denb 125 B5
Bodffordd Anglesey 123 C4
Bodham Norf 120 A3
Bodiam E Sus 37 D5
Bodiam Castle E Sus 37 D5
Bodicote Oxon 82 D1
Bodieve Corn 9 D5
Bodinnick Corn 5 B6
Bodle Street Green E Sus 23 A4
Bodmin Corn 5 A5
Bodnant Garden, Colwyn Bay Conwy 124 B3
Bodney Norf 103 B4
Bodorgan Anglesey 122 D3
Bodsham Kent 38 A3
Boduan Gwyn 106 C3
Bodymoor Heath Warks 97 B4
Bogallan Highld 252 A2
Bogbrae Aberds 257 C5
Bogend Borders 198 B1
Bogend S Ayrs 192 B3
Boghall W Loth 208 D2
Boghead S Lnrk 194 B2
Bogmoor Moray 267 C4
Bogniebrae Aberds 255 B6
Bognor Regis W Sus 20 C2
Bograxie Aberds 256 E2
Bogside N Lnrk 194 A3
Bogton Aberds 268 D1
Bogue Dumfries 182 D4
Bohenie Highld 239 D6
Bohortha Corn 4 D3
Bohuntine Highld 239 D6
Boirseam W Isles 287 F5
Bojewyan Corn 2 B1
Bolam Durham 167 C4
Bolam Northumb 178 A2
Bolberry Devon 7 D5
Bold Heath Mers 127 A5
Boldon T & W 179 C5
Boldon Colliery T & W 179 C5
Boldre Hants 18 B2
Boldron Durham 166 D3
Bole Notts 132 A2
Bolehill Derbys 130 D2
Boleside Borders 196 C3
Bolham Devon 27 D4
Bolham Water Devon 27 D6
Bolingey Corn 4 B2
Bollington Ches 129 B4
Bollington Cross Ches 129 B4
Bolney W Sus 35 D5
Bolnhurst Beds 84 B2
Bolshan Angus 233 C4
Bolsover Derbys 131 B4
Bolsterstone S Yorks 139 D5
Bolstone Hereford 78 D3
Boltby N Yorks 158 C3
Bolter End Bucks 66 D2
Bolton Cumb 165 C4
Bolton E Loth 210 C2
Bolton E Yorks 149 B6
Bolton Gtr Man 137 C6
Bolton Northumb 189 B4
Bolton Abbey N Yorks 147 B4
Bolton Abbey, Skipton N Yorks 147 B4
Bolton Bridge N Yorks 147 B4
Bolton-by-Bowland Lancs 146 C1
Bolton Castle, Leyburn N Yorks 156 B4
Bolton le Sands Lancs 145 A4
Bolton Low Houses Cumb 175 D5
Bolton-on-Swale N Yorks 157 B6
Bolton Percy N Yorks 148 C4
Bolton Town End Lancs 145 A4
Bolton upon Dearne S Yorks 140 C2
Boltonfellend Cumb 176 C2
Boltongate Cumb 175 D5
Bolventor Corn 10 D2
Bomere Heath Shrops 110 D3
Bon-y-maen Swansea 57 C6
Bonar Bridge Highld 264 A2
Bonawe Argyll 227 C5
Bonby N Lincs 142 B2
Boncath Pembs 73 C5
Bonchester Bridge Borders 187 B4
Bonchurch I o W 19 D4
Bondleigh Devon 12 A1
Bonehill Devon 12 D2
Bonehill Staffs 97 A4
Bo'ness Falk 208 B2
Bonhill W Dunb 206 C1
Boningale Shrops 95 A6
Bonjedward Borders 187 A5
Bonkle N Lnrk 194 A3
Bonnavoulin Highld 225 A4
Bonnington Edin 208 D4
Bonnington Kent 38 B2
Bonnybank Fife 220 D3
Bonnybridge Falk 207 B6
Bonnykelly Aberds 268 D3
Bonnyrigg and Lasswade Midloth 209 D6
Bonnyton Aberds 256 C1
Bonnyton Angus 220 A3
Bonnyton Angus 233 C4
Bonsall Derbys 130 D2
Bonskeid House Perth 230 B2
Bont Mon 61 B5
Bont-Dolgadfan Powys 91 B6
Bont-goch Ceredig 91 D4
Bont-newydd Conwy 125 B5
Bont Newydd Gwyn 108 A2
Bont Newydd Gwyn 108 C2
Bontddu Gwyn 91 A4
Bonthorpe Lincs 135 B4
Bontnewydd Ceredig 75 B5
Bontnewydd Gwyn 107 A4
Bontuchel Denb 125 D5
Bonvilston V Glam 41 D5
Booker Bucks 66 D3
Boon Borders 197 B4
Boosbeck Redcar 169 D4
Boot Cumb 163 D4
Boot Street Suff 88 C3
Booth W Yorks 138 A3
Booth Wood W Yorks 138 B3
Boothby Graffoe Lincs 133 D4
Boothby Pagnell Lincs 116 B2
Boothen Stoke 112 A2
Boothferry E Yorks 141 A5
Boothville Northants 83 A4
Bootle Cumb 153 B2
Bootle Mers 136 D2
Booton Norf 120 C3
Boquhan Stirl 206 B3
Boraston Shrops 95 D4
Borden Kent 51 C5
Borden W Sus 34 D1
Bordley N Yorks 146 A3
Bordon Hants 33 B7
Bordon Camp Hants 33 B6
Boreham Essex 70 C1
Boreham Wilts 30 A2
Boreham Street E Sus 23 A4
Borehamwood Herts 68 D1
Boreland Dumfries 185 C4
Boreland Stirl 217 A5
Borgh W Isles 286 F2
Borgh W Isles 287 F4
Borghastan W Isles 288 C3
Borgie Highld 278 C2
Borgue Dumfries 172 D4
Borgue Highld 275 B5
Borley Essex 87 C4
Bornais W Isles 286 D3
Bornesketaig Highld 258 A3
Borness Dumfries 172 D4
Borough Green Kent 36 A4
Boroughbridge N Yorks 148 A2
Borras Head Wrex 126 D3
Borreraig Highld 258 C1
Borrobol Lodge Highld 274 B2
Borrowash Derbys 114 B2
Borrowby N Yorks 158 C3
Borrowdale Cumb 163 C5
Borrowfield Aberds 245 C5
Borth Ceredig 90 C4
Borth-y-Gest Gwyn 107 C5
Borthwickbrae Borders 186 B3
Borthwickshiels Borders 186 B3
Borve Highld 259 D4
Borve Lodge W Isles 287 E5
Borwick Lancs 154 D4
Bosavern Corn 2 B1
Bosbury Hereford 79 C4
Boscastle Corn 10 B2
Boscombe Bmouth 17 B5
Boscombe Wilts 31 B6
Boscoppa Corn 5 B5
Bosham W Sus 19 A7
Bosherston Pembs 55 E5
Boskenna Corn 2 C2
Bosley Ches 129 C4
Bossall N Yorks 149 A6
Bossiney Corn 9 C6
Bossingham Kent 38 A3
Bossington Som 26 A3
Bostock Green Ches 127 C6
Boston Lincs 117 A6
Boston Long Hedges Lincs 117 A6
Boston Spa W Yorks 148 C3
Boston West Lincs 117 A5
Boswinger Corn 5 C4
Botallack Corn 2 B1
Botany Bay London 68 D2
Botcherby Cumb 175 C7
Botcheston Leics 98 A1
Botesdale Suff 103 D6
Bothal Northumb 179 A4
Bothamsall Notts 131 B6
Bothel Cumb 163 A4
Bothenhampton Dorset 15 B4
Bothwell S Lnrk 194 A2
Botley Bucks 67 C4
Botley Hants 32 D4
Botley Oxon 65 C5
Botolph Claydon Bucks 66 A2
Botolphs W Sus 21 B4
Bottacks Highld 263 D6
Bottesford Leics 115 B6
Bottesford N Lincs 141 C6
Bottisham Cambs 86 A1
Bottlesford Wilts 45 D5
Bottom Boat W Yorks 139 A6
Bottom House Staffs 129 D5
Bottom of Hutton Lancs 136 A3
Bottom o'th'Moor Gtr Man 137 B5
Bottomcraig Fife 220 B3
Botusfleming Corn 6 A3
Botwnnog Gwyn 106 C2
Bough Beech Kent 36 B2
Boughrood Powys 77 D5
Boughspring Glos 62 D1
Boughton Norf 102 A2
Boughton Notts 131 C6
Boughton Northants 83 A4
Boughton Aluph Kent 38 A2
Boughton Lees Kent 38 A2
Boughton Malherbe Kent 37 B6
Boughton Monchelsea Kent 37 A5
Boughton Street Kent 52 D2
Boulby Redcar 169 D5
Boulden Shrops 94 C3
Boulmer Northumb 189 B5
Boulston Pembs 55 C5
Boultenstone Aberds 243 A7
Boultham Lincs 133 C4
Bourn Cambs 85 B5
Bourne Lincs 116 C3
Bourne End Beds 83 C6
Bourne End Bucks 48 A1
Bourne End Herts 67 C5
Bournemouth Bmouth 17 B4
Bournemouth International Airport Dorset 17 B5
Bournes Green Glos 63 C5
Bournes Green Sthend 51 A6
Bournheath Worcs 96 D2
Bournmoor Durham 179 D5
Bournville W Mid 96 C3
Bourton Dorset 30 B1
Bourton N Som 42 C2
Bourton Oxon 45 A6
Bourton Shrops 94 B3
Bourton on Dunsmore Warks 98 D1
Bourton on the Hill Glos 81 D4
Bourton-on-the-Water Glos 64 A2
Bousd Argyll 223 A5
Boustead Hill Cumb 175 C5
Bouth Cumb 154 C2
Bouthwaite N Yorks 157 D5
Boveney Bucks 48 B2
Boverton V Glam 41 E4
Bovey Tracey Devon 12 D3
Bovingdon Herts 67 C5
Bovingdon Green Bucks 47 A6
Bovingdon Green Herts 67 C5
Bovinger Essex 69 C5
Bovington Camp Dorset 16 C2
Bow Borders 196 B3
Bow Devon 12 A2
Bow Orkney 283 H4
Bow Brickhill M Keynes 83 D6
Bow of Fife Fife 220 C3
Bow Street Ceredig 90 D4
Bowbank Durham 166 C2
Bowburn Durham 167 B6
Bowcombe I o W 18 C3
Bowd Devon 13 B6
Bowden Borders 197 C4
Bowden Devon 8 C2
Bowden Hill Wilts 44 C3
Bowderdale Cumb 155 A5
Bowdon Gtr Man 128 A2
Bower Northumb 177 A5
Bower Hinton Som 29 D4
Bowerchalke Wilts 31 C4
Bowerhill Wilts 44 C3
Bowermadden Highld 280 B4
Bowers Gifford Essex 51 A4
Bowershall Fife 208 A3
Bowertower Highld 280 B4
Bowes Durham 166 D2
Bowgreave Lancs 145 C4
Bowgreen Gtr Man 128 A2
Bowhill Borders 186 A3
Bowhouse Dumfries 174 B3
Bowland Bridge Cumb 154 C3
Bowley Hereford 78 B3
Bowlhead Green Sur 34 C2
Bowling W Dunb 205 A4
Bowling W Yorks 147 D5
Bowling Bank Wrex 110 A2
Bowling Green Worcs 79 B6
Bowmanstead Cumb 154 B2
Bowmore Argyll 200 C3
Bowness-on-Solway Cumb 175 B5
Bowness-on-Windermere Cumb 154 B3
Bowood House and Gardens, Calne Wilts 44 C3
Bowsden Northumb 198 B3
Bowside Lodge Highld 279 B4
Bowston Cumb 154 B3
Bowthorpe Norf 104 A2
Box Glos 63 C4
Box Wilts 44 C2
Box End Beds 84 C2
Boxbush Glos 62 B3
Boxford Suff 87 C5
Boxford W Berks 46 B2
Boxgrove W Sus 20 B2
Boxley Kent 37 A5
Boxmoor Herts 67 C5
Boxted Essex 87 D6
Boxted Suff 87 B4
Boxted Cross Essex 87 D6
Boxted Heath Essex 87 D6
Boxworth Cambs 85 A5
Boxworth End Cambs 85 A5
Boyden Gate Kent 53 C4
Boylestone Derbys 113 B5
Boyndie Aberds 268 C1
Boynton E Yorks 151 A4
Boysack Angus 233 D4
Boyton Corn 10 B4
Boyton Suff 89 C4
Boyton Wilts 30 B3
Boyton Cross Essex 69 C6
Boyton End Suff 86 C3
Bozeat Northants 83 B6
Braaid I o M 152 D3
Braal Castle Highld 280 B3
Brabling Green Suff 88 A3
Brabourne Kent 38 A2
Brabourne Lees Kent 38 A2
Brabster Highld 281 B5
Bracadale Highld 246 A2
Bracara Highld 235 A6
Braceborough Lincs 116 D3
Bracebridge Lincs 133 C4
Bracebridge Heath Lincs 133 C4
Bracebridge Low Fields Lincs 133 C4
Braceby Lincs 116 B3
Bracewell Lancs 146 C2
Brackenfield Derbys 130 D3
Brackenthwaite Cumb 175 D5
Brackenthwaite N Yorks 148 B1
Bracklesham W Sus 19 B7
Brackletter Highld 239 D5
Brackley Argyll 202 D2
Brackley Northants 82 D2
Brackloch Highld 270 B4
Bracknell Brack 47 C6
Braco Perth 218 D3
Bracobrae Moray 267 D6
Bracon Ash Norf 104 B2
Bracorina Highld 235 A6
Bradbourne Derbys 130 D2
Bradbury Durham 167 C6
Bradda I o M 152 E1
Bradden Northants 82 C3
Braddock Corn 5 A6
Bradeley Stoke 128 D3
Bradenham Bucks 66 D3
Bradenham Norf 103 A5
Bradenstoke Wilts 44 B4
Bradfield Essex 88 D2
Bradfield Norf 121 B4
Bradfield W Berks 47 B4
Bradfield Combust Suff 87 B4
Bradfield Green Ches 128 D1
Bradfield Heath Essex 71 A5
Bradfield St Clare Suff 87 B5
Bradfield St George Suff 87 A5
Bradford Corn 10 D2
Bradford Derbys 130 C2
Bradford Devon 11 A5
Bradford Northumb 199 C5
Bradford W Yorks 147 D5
Bradford Abbas Dorset 29 D5
Bradford Cathedral W Yorks 147 D5
Bradford Industrial Museum W Yorks 147 D5
Bradford Leigh Wilts 44 C2
Bradford-on-Avon Wilts 44 C2
Bradford on Tone Som 28 C1
Bradford Peverell Dorset 15 B6
Brading I o W 19 C5
Bradley Derbys 113 A6
Bradley Hants 33 A5
Bradley NE Lincs 143 C4
Bradley Staffs 112 D2
Bradley W Mid 96 B2
Bradley W Yorks 139 A4
Bradley Green Worcs 80 A2
Bradley in the Moors Staffs 113 A4
Bradlow Hereford 79 D5
Bradmore Notts 114 B3
Bradmore W Mid 96 B1
Bradninch Devon 13 A5
Bradnop Staffs 129 D5
Bradpole Dorset 15 B4
Bradshaw Gtr Man 137 B6
Bradshaw W Yorks 138 B3
Bradstone Devon 11 C4
Bradwall Green Ches 128 C2
Bradway S Yorks 130 A3
Bradwell Derbys 129 A6
Bradwell Essex 70 A2
Bradwell M Keynes 83 D5
Bradwell Norf 105 A6
Bradwell Staffs 112 A2
Bradwell Grove Oxon 64 C3
Bradwell on Sea Essex 71 C4
Bradwell Waterside Essex 70 C3
Bradworthy Devon 24 D4
Bradworthy Cross Devon 24 D4
Brae Dumfries 173 A6
Brae Highld 261 B5
Brae Highld 272 D2
Brae Shetland 284 G5
Brae of Achnahaird Highld 270 C3
Brae Roy Lodge Highld 240 C1
Braeantra Highld 264 C1
Braedownie Angus 231 A6
Braefield Highld 251 C6
Braegrum Perth 219 B5
Braehead Dumfries 171 B6
Braehead Orkney 283 G6
Braehead Orkney 282 C5
Braehead S Lnrk 194 C3
Braehead S Lnrk 195 A4
Braehead of Lunan Angus 233 C4
Braehoulland Shetland 284 F4
Braehungie Highld 275 A5
Braelangwell Lodge Highld 263 A7
Braemar Aberds 243 C4
Braemore Highld 275 A4
Braemore Highld 262 C3
Braes of Enzie Moray 267 D4
Braeside Invclyd 204 A2
Braeswick Orkney 282 D7
Braewick Shetland 285 H5
Brafferton Darl 167 C5
Brafferton N Yorks 158 D3
Brafield-on-the-Green Northants 83 B5
Bragar W Isles 288 C3
Bragbury End Herts 68 A2
Bragleenmore Argyll 226 D4
Braichmelyn Gwyn 123 D6
Braid Edin 209 D5
Braides Lancs 144 B4
Braidley N Yorks 156 C4
Braidwood S Lnrk 194 B3
Braigo Argyll 200 B2
Brailsford Derbys 113 A6
Brainshaugh Northumb 189 C5
Braintree Essex 70 A1
Braiseworth Suff 104 D2
Braishfield Hants 32 C2
Braithwaite Cumb 163 B5
Braithwaite S Yorks 140 B4
Braithwaite W Yorks 147 C4
Braithwell S Yorks 140 D3
Bramber W Sus 21 A4
Bramcote Notts 114 B3
Bramcote Warks 97 C7
Bramdean Hants 33 C5
Bramerton Norf 104 A3
Bramfield Herts 68 B2
Bramfield Suff 105 D4
Bramford Suff 88 C2
Bramhall Gtr Man 128 A3
Bramham W Yorks 148 C3
Bramhope W Yorks 147 C6
Bramley Hants 47 D4
Bramley Sur 34 B3
Bramley S Yorks 140 D2
Bramley W Yorks 147 D6
Bramling Kent 53 D4
Brampford Speke Devon 13 B4
Brampton Cambs 100 D4
Brampton Cumb 165 C4
Brampton Cumb 176 C3
Brampton Derbys 130 B3
Brampton Hereford 78 D2
Brampton Lincs 132 B3
Brampton Norf 120 C4
Brampton Suff 105 C5
Brampton S Yorks 140 C2
Brampton Abbotts Hereford 62 A2
Brampton Ash Northants 99 C4
Brampton Bryan Hereford 94 D1
Brampton en le Morthen S Yorks 131 A4
Bramshall Staffs 113 B4
Bramshaw Hants 31 D6
Bramshill Hants 47 C5
Bramshott Hants 34 C1
Bran End Essex 69 A6
Branault Highld 235 D4
Brancaster Norf 119 A4
Brancaster Staithe Norf 119 A4
Brancepeth Durham 167 B5
Branch End Northumb 178 C2
Branchill Moray 266 D1
Brand Green Glos 62 A3
Branderburgh Moray 266 B3
Brandesburton E Yorks 151 C4
Brandeston Suff 88 A3
Brandhill Shrops 94 D2
Brandis Corner Devon 11 A5
Brandiston Norf 120 C3
Brandon Durham 167 B5
Brandon Lincs 116 A2
Brandon Northumb 188 B3
Brandon Suff 102 C3
Brandon Warks 97 D7
Brandon Bank Norf 102 C2
Brandon Creek Norf 102 B2
Brandon Parva Norf 104 A1
Brands Hatch Motor Racing Circuit Kent 50 C2
Brandsby N Yorks 159 D4
Brandy Wharf Lincs 142 D2
Brane Corn 2 C2
Branksome Poole 17 B4
Branksome Park Poole 17 B4
Bransby Lincs 132 B3
Branscombe Devon 14 C1
Bransford Worcs 79 B5
Bransgore Hants 17 B5
Branshill Clack 208 A1
Bransholme Hull 151 D4
Branson's Cross Worcs 96 D3
Branston Leics 115 C6
Branston Lincs 133 C5
Branston Staffs 113 C6
Branston Booths Lincs 133 C5
Branstone I o W 19 C4
Bransty Cumb 162 C2
Brant Broughton Lincs 133 D4
Brantham Suff 88 D2
Branthwaite Cumb 162 B3
Branthwaite Cumb 163 A5
Brantingham E Yorks 142 A1
Branton Northumb 188 B3
Branton S Yorks 140 C4
Branxholm Park Borders 186 B3
Branxholme Borders 186 B3
Branxton Northumb 198 C2
Brassey Green Ches 127 C5
Brassington Derbys 130 D2
Brasted Kent 36 A2
Brasted Chart Kent 36 A2
Brathens Aberds 244 C3
Bratoft Lincs 135 C4
Brattleby Lincs 133 A4
Bratton Telford 111 D5
Bratton Wilts 44 D3
Bratton Clovelly Devon 11 B5
Bratton Fleming Devon 26 B1
Bratton Seymour Som 29 C6
Braughing Herts 68 A3
Braunston Northants 82 A2
Braunston-in-Rutland Rutland 99 A5
Braunstone Town Leics 98 A2
Braunton Devon 25 B5
Brawby N Yorks 159 D6
Brawl Highld 279 B4
Brawlbin Highld 279 C6
Bray Windsor 48 B2
Bray Shop Corn 10 D4
Bray Wick Windsor 48 B1

Braybrooke Northants 99 C4
Braye Ald 7
Brayford Devon 26 B1
Braystones Cumb 162 D3
Braythorn N Yorks 147 C6
Brayton N Yorks 149 D5
Brazacott Corn 10 B3
Breach Kent 51 C5
Breachacha Castle Argyll 223 B4
Breachwood Green Herts 67 A6
Breacleit W Isles 288 D2
Breaden Heath Shrops 110 B3
Breadsall Derbys 114 B1
Breadstone Glos 62 C3
Breage Corn 3 C4
Breakachy Highld 251 B6
Bream Glos 62 C2
Breamore Hants 31 D5
Brean Som 42 D1
Breanais W Isles 287 B4
Brearton N Yorks 148 A2
Breascleit W Isles 288 D3
Breaston Derbys 114 B2
Brechfa Carms 58 B2
Brechin Angus 232 B3
Breck of Cruan Orkney 282 F4
Breckan Orkney 283 G3
Breckrey Highld 259 B5
Brecon = Aberhonddu Powys 60 A2
Brecon Beacons Mountain Centre Powys 60 A1
Bredbury Gtr Man 138 D2
Brede E Sus 23 A6
Bredenbury Hereford 79 B4
Bredfield Suff 88 B3
Bredgar Kent 51 C5
Bredhurst Kent 51 C4
Bredicot Worcs 80 B2
Bredon Worcs 80 D2
Bredon's Norton Worcs 80 D2
Bredwardine Hereford 78 C1
Breedon on the Hill Leics 114 C2
Breibhig W Isles 286 G2
Breibhig W Isles 288 D5
Breich W Loth 208 D2
Breightmet Gtr Man 137 C6
Breighton E Yorks 149 D6
Breinton Hereford 78 D2
Breinton Common Hereford 78 C2
Breiwick Shetland 285 J6
Bremhill Wilts 44 B3
Bremirehoull Shetland 285 L6
Brenchley Kent 37 B4
Brendon Devon 26 A2
Brenkley T & W 179 B4
Brent Eleigh Suff 87 C5
Brent Knoll Som 42 D2
Brent Pelham Herts 85 D6
Brentford London 49 B4
Brentingby Leics 115 D5
Brentwood Essex 69 D5
Brenzett Kent 38 C2
Brereton Staffs 113 D4
Brereton Green Ches 128 C2
Brereton Heath Ches 128 C3
Bressingham Norf 104 C1
Bretby Derbys 113 C6
Bretford Warks 98 D1
Bretforton Worcs 80 C3
Bretherdale Head Cumb 155 A4
Bretherton Lancs 136 A3
Brettabister Shetland 285 H6
Brettenham Norf 103 C5
Brettenham Suff 87 B5
Bretton Derbys 130 B2
Bretton Flint 126 C3
Brewer Street Sur 35 A6
Brewlands Bridge Angus 231 B5
Brewood Staffs 96 A1
Briach Moray 266 D1
Briants Puddle Dorset 16 B2
Brick End Essex 69 A5
Brickendon Herts 68 C3
Bricket Wood Herts 67 C6
Bricklehampton Worcs 80 C2
Bride I o M 152 A4
Bridekirk Cumb 163 A4
Bridell Pembs 73 B4
Bridestowe Devon 11 C6
Brideswell Aberds 255 C6
Bridford Devon 12 C3
Bridfordmills Devon 12 C3
Bridge Kent 52 D3
Bridge End Lincs 116 B4
Bridge Green Essex 85 D6
Bridge Hewick N Yorks 158 D2
Bridge of Alford Aberds 244 A2
Bridge of Allan Stirl 207 A5
Bridge of Avon Moray 254 C2
Bridge of Awe Argyll 227 D5
Bridge of Balgie Perth 229 D4
Bridge of Cally Perth 231 C5
Bridge of Canny Aberds 244 C3
Bridge of Craigisla Angus 231 C6
Bridge of Dee Dumfries 173 C5
Bridge of Don Aberdeen 245 A6
Bridge of Dun Angus 233 C4
Bridge of Dye Aberds 244 D3
Bridge of Earn Perth 219 C6
Bridge of Ericht Perth 229 C4
Bridge of Feugh Aberds 245 C4
Bridge of Forss Highld 279 B6
Bridge of Gairn Aberds 243 C6
Bridge of Gaur Perth 229 C4
Bridge of Muchalls Aberds 245 C5
Bridge of Oich Highld 240 B1
Bridge of Orchy Argyll 216 A2
Bridge of Waith Orkney 282 F3
Bridge of Walls Shetland 285 H4
Bridge of Weir Renfs 204 B3
Bridge Sollers Hereford 78 C2
Bridge Street Suff 87 C4
Bridge Trafford Ches 127 B4
Bridge Yate S Glos 43 B5
Bridgefoot Angus 220 A3
Bridgefoot Cumb 162 B3
Bridgehampton Som 29 C5
Bridgehill Durham 178 D2
Bridgemary Hants 19 A4
Bridgemont Derbys 129 A5
Bridgend Aberds 255 C6
Bridgend Aberds 244 A2
Bridgend Angus 232 B3
Bridgend Argyll 214 C1
Bridgend Argyll 200 B3
Bridgend Argyll 190 B3
Bridgend Cumb 164 D1
Bridgend Fife 220 C3
Bridgend Moray 255 C4
Bridgend N Lnrk 207 C4
Bridgend Pembs 73 B4
Bridgend W Loth 208 C3
Bridgend = Pen-y-bont ar Ogwr Bridgend 40 D4
Bridgend of Lintrathen Angus 231 C6
Bridgerule Devon 10 A3
Bridges Shrops 94 B1
Bridgeton Glasgow 205 B6
Bridgetown Corn 10 C4
Bridgetown Som 27 B4
Bridgham Norf 103 C5
Bridgnorth Shrops 95 B5
Bridgnorth Cliff Railway Shrops 95 B5
Bridgtown Staffs 96 A2
Bridgwater Som 28 B3
Bridlington E Yorks 151 A4
Bridport Dorset 15 B4
Bridstow Hereford 62 A1
Brierfield Lancs 146 D2
Brierley Glos 62 B2
Brierley Hereford 78 B2
Brierley S Yorks 140 B2
Brierley Hill W Mid 96 C2
Briery Hill Bl Gwent 60 C3
Brig o'Turk Stirl 217 D5
Brigg N Lincs 142 C2
Briggswath N Yorks 160 A2
Brigham Cumb 162 A3
Brigham E Yorks 150 B3
Brighouse W Yorks 139 A4
Brighstone I o W 18 C3
Brightgate Derbys 130 D2
Brighthampton Oxon 65 C4
Brightling E Sus 37 D4
Brightlingsea Essex 71 B4
Brighton Brighton 21 B6
Brighton Corn 4 B4
Brighton Hill Hants 33 A5
Brighton Museum and Art Gallery Brighton 21 B6
Brighton Racecourse Brighton 21 B6
Brighton Sea Life Centre Brighton 21 B6
Brightons Falk 208 C2
Brightwalton W Berks 46 B2
Brightwell Suff 88 C3
Brightwell Baldwin Oxon 66 D1
Brightwell cum Sotwell Oxon 65 D6
Brignall Durham 166 D3
Brigsley NE Lincs 143 C4
Brigsteer Cumb 154 C3
Brigstock Northants 99 C6
Brill Bucks 66 B1
Brilley Hereford 77 C6
Brimaston Pembs 55 B5
Brimfield Hereford 78 A3
Brimington Derbys 131 B4
Brimley Devon 12 D2
Brimpsfield Glos 63 B5
Brimpton W Berks 46 C3
Brims Orkney 283 K3
Brimscombe Glos 63 C4
Brimstage Mers 126 A3
Brinacory Highld 235 A6
Brind E Yorks 149 D6
Brindister Shetland 285 H4
Brindister Shetland 285 K6
Brindle Lancs 137 A5
Brindley Ford Staffs 128 D3
Brineton Staffs 112 D2
Bringhurst Leics 99 B5
Brington Cambs 100 D2
Brinian Orkney 282 E5
Briningham Norf 120 B2
Brinkhill Lincs 134 B3
Brinkley Cambs 86 B2
Brinklow Warks 98 D1
Brinkworth Wilts 44 A4
Brinmore Highld 252 D2
Brinscall Lancs 137 A5
Brinsea N Som 42 C3
Brinsley Notts 114 A2
Brinsop Hereford 78 C2
Brinsworth S Yorks 131 A4
Brinton Norf 120 B2
Brisco Cumb 175 C7
Brisley Norf 119 C6
Brislington Bristol 43 B5
Bristol Bristol 43 B4
Bristol City Museum and Art Gallery Bristol 43 B4
Bristol International Airport N Som 43 C4
Bristol Zoo Bristol 43 B4
Briston Norf 120 B2
Britannia Lancs 138 A1
Britford Wilts 31 C5
Brithdir Gwyn 91 A5
British Legion Village Kent 37 A5
British Museum London 49 A5
Briton Ferry Neath 40 B2
Britwell Salome Oxon 66 D1
Brixham Torbay 8 B3
Brixton Devon 7 B4
Brixton London 49 B6
Brixton Deverill Wilts 30 B2
Brixworth Northants 99 D4
Brize Norton Oxon 64 C4
Broad Blunsdon Swindon 64 D2
Broad Campden Glos 81 D4
Broad Chalke Wilts 31 C4
Broad Green Beds 83 C6
Broad Green Essex 70 A2
Broad Green Worcs 79 B5
Broad Haven Pembs 55 C4
Broad Heath Worcs 79 A4
Broad Hill Cambs 102 D1
Broad Hinton Wilts 45 B5
Broad Laying Hants 46 C2
Broad Marston Worcs 80 C4
Broad Oak Carms 58 C2
Broad Oak Cumb 153 A2
Broad Oak Dorset 14 B4
Broad Oak Dorset 30 D1
Broad Oak E Sus 23 A6
Broad Oak E Sus 36 D4
Broad Oak Hereford 61 A6
Broad Oak Mers 136 D4
Broad Street Kent 37 A6
Broad Street Green Essex 70 C2
Broad Town Wilts 45 B4
Broadbottom Gtr Man 138 D2
Broadbridge W Sus 19 A7
Broadbridge Heath W Sus 35 C4
Broadclyst Devon 13 B4
Broadfield Gtr Man 138 B1
Broadfield Lancs 136 A4
Broadfield Pembs 56 B1
Broadfield W Sus 35 C5
Broadford Highld 247 B5
Broadford Bridge W Sus 34 D3
Broadhaugh Borders 186 C3
Broadhaven Highld 281 C5
Broadheath Gtr Man 128 A2
Broadhembury Devon 13 A6
Broadhempston Devon 8 A2
Broadholme Derbys 114 A1
Broadholme Lincs 132 B3
Broadland Row E Sus 23 A6
Broadlay Carms 56 B3
Broadley Lancs 138 B1
Broadley Moray 267 C4
Broadley Common Essex 68 C4
Broadmayne Dorset 16 C1
Broadmeadows Borders 196 C3
Broadmere Hants 33 A5
Broadmoor Pembs 55 D6
Broadoak Kent 52 C3
Broadrashes Moray 267 D5
Broadsea Aberds 269 C4
Broadstairs Kent 53 C5
Broadstone Poole 17 B4
Broadstone Shrops 94 C3
Broadtown Lane Wilts 45 B4
Broadview Gardens, Hadlow Kent 36 B4
Broadwas Worcs 79 B5
Broadwater Herts 68 A2
Broadwater W Sus 21 B4
Broadway Carms 56 B2
Broadway Pembs 55 C4
Broadway Som 28 D3
Broadway Suff 105 D4
Broadway Worcs 80 D3
Broadwell Glos 64 A3
Broadwell Glos 62 B1
Broadwell Oxon 64 C3
Broadwell Warks 82 A1
Broadwell House Northumb 177 D7
Broadwey Dorset 15 C6
Broadwindsor Dorset 14 A4
Broadwood Kelly Devon 11 A7
Broadwoodwidger Devon 11 C5
Brobury Hereford 78 C1
Brochel Highld 248 B2
Brochloch Dumfries 182 C3
Brochroy Argyll 227 C5
Brockamin Worcs 79 B5
Brockbridge Hants 33 D5
Brockdam Northumb 189 A4
Brockdish Norf 104 D3
Brockenhurst Hants 18 A2
Brocketsbrae S Lnrk 194 C3
Brockford Street Suff 88 A2
Brockhall Northants 82 A3
Brockham Sur 35 B4
Brockhampton Glos 63 A6
Brockhampton Hereford 78 D3
Brockhole -National Park Visitor Centre, Windermere Cumb 154 A2
Brockholes W Yorks 139 B4
Brockhurst Derbys 130 C3
Brockhurst Hants 19 A5
Brocklebank Cumb 175 D6
Brocklesby Lincs 142 B3
Brockley N Som 42 C3
Brockley Green Suff 87 B4
Brockleymoor Cumb 164 B2
Brockton Shrops 94 C1
Brockton Shrops 94 B3
Brockton Shrops 93 A7
Brockton Shrops 95 A5
Brockton Telford 111 D6
Brockweir Glos 62 C1
Brockwood Hants 33 C5
Brockworth Glos 63 B4
Brocton Staffs 112 D3
Brodick N Ayrs 191 B6
Brodick Castle N Ayrs 191 B6
Brodsworth S Yorks 140 C3
Brogaig Highld 259 B4
Brogborough Beds 83 D6
Broken Cross Ches 128 B1
Broken Cross Ches 128 B3
Brokenborough Wilts 44 A3
Bromborough Mers 126 A3
Brome Suff 104 D2
Brome Street Suff 104 D2
Bromeswell Suff 88 B4
Bromfield Cumb 175 D4
Bromfield Shrops 94 D2
Bromham Beds 84 B2
Bromham Wilts 44 C3
Bromley London 49 C7
Bromley W Mid 96 C2
Bromley Common London 49 C7
Bromley Green Kent 38 B1
Brompton Medway 51 C4
Brompton N Yorks 158 B2
Brompton N Yorks 160 C3
Brompton-on-Swale N Yorks 157 B6
Brompton Ralph Som 27 B5
Brompton Regis Som 27 B4
Bromsash Hereford 62 A2
Bromsberrow Heath Glos 79 D5
Bromsgrove Worcs 96 D2
Bromyard Hereford 79 B4
Bromyard Downs Hereford 79 B4
Bronaber Gwyn 108 B2
Brongest Ceredig 73 B6
Bronington Wrex 110 B3
Bronllys Powys 77 D5
Bronnant Ceredig 75 B5
Bronte Parsonage Museum, Keighley W Yorks 147 D4
Bronwydd Arms Carms 73 D7
Bronydd Powys 77 C6
Bronygarth Shrops 110 B1
Brook Carms 56 B2
Brook Hants 32 D1
Brook Hants 32 C2
Brook I o W 18 C2
Brook Kent 38 A2
Brook Sur 34 C2
Brook Sur 34 B3
Brook End Beds 84 A2
Brook Hill Hants 31 D6
Brook Street Kent 36 B3
Brook Street Kent 38 B1
Brook Street W Sus 35 D6
Brooke Norf 104 B3
Brooke Rutland 99 A5
Brookenby Lincs 143 D4
Brookend Glos 62 D1
Brookfield Renfs 205 B4
Brookhouse Lancs 145 A5
Brookhouse Green Ches 128 C3
Brookland Kent 38 C1
Brooklands Dumfries 173 A6
Brooklands Gtr Man 137 D6
Brooklands Shrops 111 A4
Brookmans Park Herts 68 C2
Brooks Powys 93 B5
Brooks Green W Sus 35 D4
Brookthorpe Glos 63 B4
Brookville Norf 102 B3
Brookwood Sur 34 A2
Broom Beds 84 C3
Broom S Yorks 140 D2
Broom Warks 80 B3
Broom Worcs 96 D2
Broom Green Norf 120 C1
Broom Hill Dorset 17 A4
Broome Norf 105 B4
Broome Shrops 94 C2
Broome Park Northumb 189 B4
Broomedge Warr 128 A2
Broomer's Corner W Sus 35 D4
Broomfield Aberds 257 C4
Broomfield Essex 69 B7
Broomfield Kent 37 A6
Broomfield Kent 52 C3
Broomfield Som 28 B2
Broomfleet E Yorks 141 A6
Broomhall Ches 111 A5
Broomhall Windsor 48 C2
Broomhaugh Northumb 178 C2
Broomhill Norf 102 A2
Broomhill Northumb 189 C5
Broomhill S Yorks 140 C2
Broomholm Norf 121 B5
Broomley Northumb 178 C2
Broompark Durham 167 A5
Broom's Green Hereford 79 D5
Broomy Lodge Hants 31 D6
Brora Highld 274 D3
Broseley Shrops 95 A4
Brotherhouse Bar Lincs 117 D5
Brotherstone Borders 197 C5
Brothertoft Lincs 117 A5
Brotherton N Yorks 140 A2
Brotton Redcar 169 D4
Broubster Highld 279 B6
Brough Cumb 165 D5
Brough Derbys 130 A1
Brough E Yorks 142 A1
Brough Highld 280 A4
Brough Notts 132 D3
Brough Orkney 282 F4
Brough Shetland 284 F6
Brough Shetland 284 G7
Brough Shetland 284 F7
Brough Shetland 285 J7
Brough Shetland 285 H6
Brough Lodge Shetland 284 D7
Brough Sowerby Cumb 165 D5
Broughall Shrops 111 A4
Broughton Borders 195 C6
Broughton Cambs 101 D4
Broughton Flint 126 C3
Broughton Hants 32 B2
Broughton Lancs 145 D5
Broughton M Keynes 83 C5
Broughton N Lincs 142 C1
Broughton Northants 99 D5
Broughton N Yorks 146 B3
Broughton N Yorks 159 D6
Broughton Orkney 282 C5
Broughton Oxon 81 D7
Broughton V Glam 40 D4
Broughton Astley Leics 98 B2
Broughton Beck Cumb 154 C1
Broughton Common Wilts 44 C2
Broughton Gifford Wilts 44 C2
Broughton Hackett Worcs 80 B2
Broughton in Furness Cumb 153 B3
Broughton Mills Cumb 153 A3
Broughton Moor Cumb 162 A3
Broughton Park Gtr Man 138 C1
Broughton Poggs Oxon 64 C3
Broughtown Orkney 282 C7
Broughty Ferry Dundee 221 A4
Browhouses Dumfries 175 B5
Browland Shetland 285 H4
Brown Candover Hants 33 B4
Brown Edge Lancs 136 B2
Brown Edge Staffs 129 D4
Brown Heath Ches 127 C4
Brownhill Aberds 256 B3
Brownhill Aberds 256 B1
Brownhill Blkburn 145 D6
Brownhill Shrops 110 C3
Brownhills Fife 221 C5
Brownhills W Mid 96 A3
Brownlow Ches 128 C3
Brownlow Heath Ches 128 C3
Brownmuir Aberds 233 A5
Brown's End Glos 79 D5
Brownshill Glos 63 C4
Brownston Devon 7 B6
Brownyside Northumb 189 A4
Broxa N Yorks 160 B3
Broxbourne Herts 68 C3
Broxburn E Loth 210 C3
Broxburn W Loth 208 C3
Broxholme Lincs 133 B4
Broxted Essex 69 A5
Broxton Ches 127 D4
Broxwood Hereford 78 B1
Broyle Side E Sus 22 A2
Brù W Isles 288 C4
Bruairnis W Isles 286 F3
Bruan Highld 275 A7
Bruar Lodge Perth 230 A2
Brucehill W Dunb 206 C1
Bruera Ches 127 C4
Bruern Abbey Oxon 64 A3
Bruichladdich Argyll 200 B2
Bruisyard Suff 88 A4
Brumby N Lincs 141 C6
Brund Staffs 129 C6
Brundall Norf 104 A4
Brundish Suff 88 A3
Brundish Street Suff 104 D3
Brunery Highld 235 C6
Brunshaw Lancs 146 D2
Brunswick Village T & W 179 B4
Bruntcliffe W Yorks 139 A5
Bruntingthorpe Leics 98 B3
Brunton Fife 220 B3
Brunton Northumb 189 A5
Brunton Wilts 45 D6
Brushford Devon 12 A1
Brushford Som 27 C4
Bruton Som 29 B6
Bryanston Dorset 16 A2
Brydekirk Dumfries 175 A4
Bryher Scilly 2 E3
Brymbo Wrex 126 D2
Brympton Som 29 D5
Bryn Carms 57 B5
Bryn Gtr Man 137 C4
Bryn Neath 40 B3
Bryn Shrops 93 C6
Bryn-coch Neath 40 B2
Bryn Du Anglesey 122 C3
Bryn Gates Gtr Man 137 C4
Bryn-glas Conwy 124 C3
Bryn Golau Rhondda 41 C4
Bryn-Iwan Carms 73 C6
Bryn-mawr Gwyn 106 C2
Bryn-nantllech Conwy 125 C4
Bryn-penarth Powys 93 A5
Bryn Rhyd-yr-Arian Conwy 125 C4
Bryn Saith Marchog Denb 125 D5
Bryn Sion Gwyn 91 A6
Bryn-y-gwenin Mon 61 B5
Bryn-y-maen Conwy 124 B3
Bryn-yr-eryr Gwyn 106 B3
Brynamman Carms 59 D4
Brynberian Pembs 72 C4
Brynbryddan Neath 40 B2
Brynbuga = Usk Mon 61 C5
Bryncae Rhondda 41 C4
Bryncethin Bridgend 40 C4
Bryncir Gwyn 107 B4
Bryncroes Gwyn 106 C2
Bryncrug Gwyn 90 B4
Bryneglwys Denb 109 A6
Brynford Flint 126 B1
Bryngwran Anglesey 122 C3
Bryngwyn Ceredig 73 B5
Bryngwyn Mon 61 C5
Bryngwyn Powys 77 C5
Brynhenllan Pembs 72 C3
Brynhoffnant Ceredig 73 A6
Brynithel Bl Gwent 41 A7
Brynmawr Bl Gwent 60 B3
Brynmenyn Bridgend 40 C4
Brynmill Swansea 57 C6
Brynna Rhondda 41 C4
Brynrefail Anglesey 123 B4
Brynrefail Gwyn 123 D5
Brynsadler Rhondda 41 C5
Brynsiencyn Anglesey 123 D4
Brynteg Anglesey 123 B4
Brynteg Ceredig 58 A1
Buaile nam Bodach W Isles 286 F3
Bualintur Highld 246 B3
Buarthmeini Gwyn 108 B3
Bubbenhall Warks 97 D6
Bubwith E Yorks 149 D6
Buccleuch Borders 185 A6
Buchanhaven Aberds 257 B6
Buchanty Perth 218 B4
Buchlyvie Stirl 206 A3
Buckabank Cumb 164 A1
Buckden Cambs 84 A3
Buckden N Yorks 156 D3
Buckenham Norf 105 A4
Buckerell Devon 13 A6
Buckfast Devon 7 A6
Buckfast Abbey, Buckfastleigh Devon 7 A6
Buckfastleigh Devon 7 A6
Buckhaven Fife 209 A6
Buckholm Borders 196 C3
Buckholt Mon 61 B7
Buckhorn Weston Dorset 30 C1
Buckhurst Hill Essex 68 D4
Buckie Moray 267 C5
Buckies Highld 280 B3
Buckingham Bucks 82 D3
Buckingham Palace London 49 B5
Buckland Bucks 66 B3
Buckland Devon 7 C5
Buckland Glos 80 D3
Buckland Hants 18 B2

Buckland Herts 85 D5
Buckland Kent 39 A5
Buckland Oxon 64 D4
Buckland Sur 35 A5
Buckland Abbey Devon 6 A3
Buckland Brewer Devon 25 C5
Buckland Common Bucks 67 C4
Buckland Dinham Som 43 D6
Buckland Filleigh Devon 11 A5
Buckland in the Moor Devon 12 D2
Buckland Monachorum Devon 6 A3
Buckland Newton Dorset 15 A6
Buckland St Mary Som 28 D2
Bucklebury W Berks 46 B3
Bucklegate Lincs 117 B6
Bucklerheads Angus 221 A4
Bucklers Hard Hants 18 B3
Bucklesham Suff 88 C3
Buckley = Bwcle Flint 126 C2
Bucklow Hill Ches 128 A2
Buckminster Leics 116 C1
Bucknall Lincs 133 C6
Bucknall Stoke 112 A3
Bucknell Oxon 65 A6
Bucknell Shrops 94 D1
Buckpool Moray 267 C5
Buck's Cross Devon 24 C4
Bucks Green W Sus 34 C3
Bucks Horn Oak Hants 33 A7
Buck's Mills Devon 25 C4
Bucksburn Aberdeen 245 B5
Buckskin Hants 47 D4
Buckton E Yorks 161 D5
Buckton Hereford 94 D1
Buckton Northumb 199 C4
Buckworth Cambs 100 D3
Budbrooke Warks 81 A5
Budby Notts 131 C6
Budd's Titson Corn 10 A3
Bude Corn 10 A3
Budlake Devon 13 B4
Budle Northumb 199 C5
Budleigh Salterton Devon 13 C5
Budock Water Corn 4 D2
Buerton Ches 111 A5
Buffler's Holt Bucks 82 D3
Bugbrooke Northants 82 B3
Buglawton Ches 128 C3
Bugle Corn 5 B5
Bugley Wilts 30 A2
Bugthorpe E Yorks 149 B6
Buildwas Shrops 95 A4
Builth Road Powys 76 B4
Builth Wells = Llanfair-ym-Muallt Powys 76 B4
Buirgh W Isles 287 E5
Bulby Lincs 116 C3
Bulcote Notts 115 A4
Buldoo Highld 279 B5
Bulford Wilts 31 A5
Bulford Camp Wilts 31 A5
Bulkeley Ches 127 D5
Bulkington Warks 97 C6
Bulkington Wilts 44 D3
Bulkworthy Devon 25 D4
Bull Hill Hants 18 B2
Bullamoor N Yorks 158 B2
Bullbridge Derbys 130 D3
Bullbrook Brack 48 C1
Bulley Glos 62 B3
Bullgill Cumb 162 A3
Bullington Hants 32 A3
Bullington Lincs 133 B5
Bull's Green Herts 68 B2
Bullwood Argyll 203 A6
Bulmer Essex 87 C4
Bulmer N Yorks 149 A5
Bulmer Tye Essex 87 D4
Bulphan Thurrock 50 A3
Bulverhythe E Sus 23 B5
Bulwark Aberds 257 B4
Bulwell Nottingham 114 A3
Bulwick Northants 99 B6
Bumble's Green Essex 68 C4
Bun Abhainn Eadarra W Isles 288 G2
Bun a'Mhuillin W Isles 286 E3
Bun Loyne Highld 239 B6
Bunacaimb Highld 235 B5
Bunarkaig Highld 239 D5
Bunbury Ches 127 D5
Bunbury Heath Ches 127 D5
Bunchrew Highld 252 B2
Bundalloch Highld 249 D5
Buness Shetland 284 C8
Bunessan Argyll 224 D2
Bungay Suff 104 C4
Bunker's Hill Lincs 133 B4
Bunker's Hill Lincs 134 D2
Bunkers Hill Oxon 65 B5
Bunloit Highld 251 D7
Bunnahabhain Argyll 201 A4
Bunny Notts 114 C3
Buntait Highld 251 C5
Buntingford Herts 68 A3
Bunwell Norf 104 B2
Burbage Derbys 129 B5
Burbage Leics 98 B1
Burbage Wilts 45 C6
Burchett's Green Windsor 47 A6
Burcombe Wilts 31 B4
Burcot Oxon 65 D6
Burcott Bucks 66 A3
Burdon T & W 179 D5
Bures Suff 87 D5
Bures Green Suff 87 D5
Burford Ches 127 D6
Burford Oxon 64 B3
Burford Shrops 78 A3
Burg Argyll 224 B2
Burgar Orkney 282 E4
Burgate Hants 31 D5
Burgate Suff 104 D1
Burgess Hill W Sus 21 A6
Burgh Suff 88 B3
Burgh-by-Sands Cumb 175 C6
Burgh Castle Norf 105 A5
Burgh Heath Sur 35 A5
Burgh le Marsh Lincs 135 C5
Burgh Muir Aberds 256 D2
Burgh next Aylsham Norf 120 C4
Burgh on Bain Lincs 134 A2
Burgh St Margaret Norf 121 D6
Burgh St Peter Norf 105 B5
Burghclere Hants 46 C2
Burghead Moray 266 C2
Burghfield W Berks 47 C4
Burghfield Common W Berks 47 C4
Burghfield Hill W Berks 47 C4
Burghill Hereford 78 C2
Burghwallis S Yorks 140 B3
Burham Kent 51 C4
Buriton Hants 33 C6
Burland Ches 127 D6
Burlawn Corn 9 D5
Burleigh Brack 48 C1
Burlescombe Devon 27 D5
Burleston Dorset 16 B1
Burley Hants 17 A6
Burley Rutland 116 D1
Burley W Yorks 148 D1
Burley Gate Hereford 78 C3
Burley in Wharfedale W Yorks 147 C5
Burley Lodge Hants 17 A6
Burley Street Hants 17 A6
Burleydam Ches 111 A5
Burlingjobb Powys 77 B6
Burlow E Sus 22 A3
Burlton Shrops 110 C3
Burmarsh Kent 38 B2
Burmington Warks 81 D5
Burn N Yorks 140 A3
Burn of Cambus Stirl 218 D2
Burnaston Derbys 113 B6
Burnbank S Lnrk 194 A2
Burnby E Yorks 150 C1
Burncross S Yorks 139 D6
Burneside Cumb 154 B4
Burness Orkney 282 C7
Burneston N Yorks 157 C7
Burnett Bath 43 C5
Burnfoot Borders 186 B3
Burnfoot Borders 186 B4
Burnfoot E Ayrs 182 B2
Burnfoot Perth 219 D4
Burnham Bucks 48 A2
Burnham N Lincs 142 B2
Burnham Deepdale Norf 119 A5
Burnham Green Herts 68 B2
Burnham Market Norf 119 A5
Burnham Norton Norf 119 A5
Burnham-on-Crouch Essex 70 D3
Burnham-on-Sea Som 28 A3
Burnham Overy Staithe Norf 119 A5
Burnham Overy Town Norf 119 A5
Burnham Thorpe Norf 119 A5
Burnhead Dumfries 183 C6
Burnhead S Ayrs 181 A4
Burnhervie Aberds 245 A4
Burnhill Green Staffs 95 A5
Burnhope Durham 167 A4
Burnhouse N Ayrs 204 C3
Burniston N Yorks 160 B4
Burnlee W Yorks 139 C4
Burnley Lancs 146 D2
Burnley Lane Lancs 146 D2
Burnmouth Borders 211 D6
Burnopfield Durham 178 D3
Burnsall N Yorks 147 A4
Burnside Angus 232 C3
Burnside E Ayrs 182 A3
Burnside Fife 219 D6
Burnside Shetland 284 F4
Burnside S Lnrk 205 B6
Burnside W Loth 208 C3
Burnside of Duntrune Angus 220 A4
Burnswark Dumfries 175 A4
Burnt Heath Derbys 130 B2
Burnt Houses Durham 166 C4
Burnt Yates N Yorks 147 A6
Burntcommon Sur 34 A3
Burnthouse Corn 4 D2
Burntisland Fife 209 B5
Burnton E Ayrs 182 B2
Burntwood Staffs 96 A3
Burnwynd Edin 208 D4
Burpham Sur 34 A3
Burpham W Sus 20 B3
Burradon Northumb 188 C2
Burradon T & W 179 B4
Burrafirth Shetland 284 B8
Burraland Shetland 284 F5
Burraland Shetland 285 J4
Burras Corn 3 B4
Burravoe Shetland 284 G5
Burravoe Shetland 284 F7
Burray Village Orkney 283 H5
Burrells Cumb 165 D4
Burrelton Perth 220 A2
Burridge Devon 25 B6
Burridge Hants 32 D4
Burrill N Yorks 157 C6
Burringham N Lincs 141 C6
Burrington Devon 26 D1
Burrington Hereford 94 D2
Burrington N Som 42 D3
Burrough Green Cambs 86 B2
Burrough on the Hill Leics 115 D5
Burrow-bridge Som 28 C3
Burrowhill Sur 48 C2
Burry Swansea 57 C4
Burry Green Swansea 57 C4
Burry Port = Porth Tywyn Carms 57 B4
Burscough Lancs 136 B3
Burscough Bridge Lancs 136 B3
Bursea E Yorks 149 D7
Burshill E Yorks 150 C3
Bursledon Hants 18 A3
Burslem Stoke 112 A2
Burstall Suff 88 C1
Burstock Dorset 14 A4
Burston Norf 104 C2
Burston Staffs 112 B3
Burstow Sur 35 B6
Burstwick E Yorks 143 A4
Burtersett N Yorks 156 C2
Burtle Som 28 A3
Burton Ches 126 B3
Burton Ches 127 C5
Burton Dorset 17 B5
Burton Lincs 133 B4
Burton Northumb 199 C5
Burton Pembs 55 D5
Burton Som 28 A1
Burton Wilts 44 B2
Burton Agnes E Yorks 151 A4
Burton Bradstock Dorset 15 C4
Burton Dassett Warks 81 B6
Burton Fleming E Yorks 161 D4
Burton Green W Mid 97 D5
Burton Green Wrex 126 D3
Burton Hastings Warks 97 B7
Burton-in-Kendal Cumb 154 D4
Burton in Lonsdale N Yorks 155 D5
Burton Joyce Notts 115 A4
Burton Latimer Northants 99 D6
Burton Lazars Leics 115 D5
Burton-le-Coggles Lincs 116 C2
Burton Leonard N Yorks 148 A2
Burton on the Wolds Leics 114 C3
Burton Overy Leics 98 B3
Burton Pedwardine Lincs 116 A4
Burton Pidsea E Yorks 151 D5
Burton Salmon N Yorks 140 A2
Burton Stather N Lincs 141 B6
Burton upon Stather N Lincs 141 B6
Burton upon Trent Staffs 113 C6
Burtonwood Warr 137 D4
Burwardsley Ches 127 D5
Burwarton Shrops 95 C4
Burwash E Sus 37 D4
Burwash Common E Sus 36 D4
Burwash Weald E Sus 36 D4
Burwell Cambs 86 A1
Burwell Lincs 134 B3
Burwen Anglesey 123 A4
Burwick Orkney 283 K5
Bury Cambs 101 C4
Bury Gtr Man 137 B7
Bury Som 27 C4
Bury W Sus 20 A3
Bury Green Herts 68 A4
Bury St Edmunds Suff 87 A4
Burythorpe N Yorks 149 A6
Busby E Renf 205 C5
Buscot Oxon 64 D3
Bush Bank Hereford 78 B2
Bush Crathie Aberds 243 C5
Bush Green Norf 104 C3
Bushbury W Mid 96 A2
Bushby Leics 98 A3
Bushey Herts 67 D6
Bushey Heath Herts 67 D6
Bushley Worcs 80 D1
Bushton Wilts 45 B4
Buslingthorpe Lincs 133 A5
Busta Shetland 284 G5
Butcher's Cross E Sus 36 D3
Butcher's Pasture Essex 69 A6
Butcombe N Som 43 C4
Butetown Cardiff 41 D6
Butleigh Som 29 B5
Butleigh Wootton Som 29 B5
Butler's Cross Bucks 66 C3
Butler's End Warks 97 C5
Butlers Marston Warks 81 C6
Butley Suff 89 B4
Butley High Corner Suff 89 C4
Butt Green Ches 127 D6
Butterburn Cumb 177 B4
Buttercrambe N Yorks 149 B6
Butterknowle Durham 166 C4
Butterleigh Devon 13 A4
Buttermere Cumb 163 C4
Buttermere Wilts 46 C1
Buttershaw W Yorks 139 A4
Butterstone Perth 231 D4
Butterton Staffs 129 D5
Butterwick Durham 167 C6
Butterwick Lincs 117 A6
Butterwick N Yorks 159 D6
Butterwick N Yorks 160 D3
Buttington Powys 93 A6
Buttonoak Shrops 95 D5
Butt's Green Hants 32 C2
Buttsash Hants 18 A3
Buxhall Suff 87 B6
Buxhall Fen Street Suff 87 B6
Buxley Borders 198 A2
Buxted E Sus 36 D2
Buxton Derbys 129 B5
Buxton Norf 120 C4
Buxworth Derbys 129 A5
Bwcle = Buckley Flint 126 C2
Bwlch Powys 60 A3
Bwlch-Llan Ceredig 75 C4
Bwlch-y-cibau Powys 109 D6
Bwlch-y-fadfa Ceredig 74 D3
Bwlch-y-ffridd Powys 93 B4
Bwlch-y-sarnau Powys 92 D4
Bwlchgwyn Wrex 126 D2
Bwlchnewydd Carms 73 D6
Bwlchtocyn Gwyn 106 D3
Bwlchyddar Powys 109 C6
Bwlchygroes Pembs 73 C5
Byermoor T & W 178 D3
Byers Green Durham 167 B5
Byfield Northants 82 B2
Byfleet Sur 48 C3
Byford Hereford 78 C1
Bygrave Herts 85 D4
Byker T & W 179 C4
Bylchau Conwy 125 C4
Byley Ches 128 C2
Bynea Carms 57 C5
Byrness Northumb 187 C6
Bythorn Cambs 100 D2
Byton Hereford 78 A1
Byworth W Sus 34 D2

C

Cabharstadh W Isles 288 E4
Cablea Perth 218 A4
Cabourne Lincs 142 C3
Cabrach Argyll 201 B4
Cabrach Moray 255 D4
Cabrich Highld 252 B1
Cabus Lancs 145 C4
Cackle Street E Sus 36 D2
Cadbury Devon 13 A4
Cadbury Barton Devon 26 D1
Cadbury World, Bournville W Mid 96 C3
Cadder E Dunb 205 A6
Caddington Beds 67 B5
Caddonfoot Borders 196 C3
Cade Street E Sus 36 D4
Cadeby Leics 97 A7
Cadeby S Yorks 140 C3
Cadeleigh Devon 13 A4
Cadgwith Corn 3 D5
Cadham Fife 220 D2
Cadishead Gtr Man 137 D6
Cadle Swansea 57 C6
Cadley Lancs 145 D5
Cadley Wilts 45 D6
Cadley Wilts 45 C6
Cadmore End Bucks 66 D2
Cadnam Hants 32 D1
Cadney N Lincs 142 C2
Cadole Flint 126 C2
Cadoxton V Glam 41 E6
Cadoxton-Juxta-Neath Neath 40 B2
Cadshaw Blkburn 137 B6
Cadwell Park Motor Racing Circuit Lincs 134 A2
Cadzow S Lnrk 194 A2
Caeathro Gwyn 123 D4
Caehopkin Powys 59 D5
Caenby Lincs 133 A5
Caenby Corner Lincs 133 A4
Cae'r-bryn Carms 57 A5
Caer Llan Mon 61 C6
Caerau Bridgend 40 B3
Caerau Cardiff 41 D6
Caerdeon Gwyn 90 A4
Caerdydd = Cardiff Cardiff 41 D6
Caerfarchell Pembs 54 B3
Caerffili = Caerphilly Caerph 41 C6
Caerfyrddin = Carmarthen Carms 73 D7
Caergeiliog Anglesey 122 C3
Caergwrle Flint 126 D3
Caergybi = Holyhead Anglesey 122 B2
Caerleon = Caerllion Newport 61 D5
Caerllion = Caerleon Newport 61 D5
Caernarfon Gwyn 123 D4
Caernarfon Castle Gwyn 123 D4
Caerphilly = Caerffili Caerph 41 C6
Caersws Powys 92 B4
Caerwedros Ceredig 73 A6
Caerwent Mon 61 D6
Caerwych Gwyn 107 C6
Caerwys Flint 125 B6
Caethle Gwyn 90 C4
Caim Anglesey 123 B6
Caio Carms 58 B3
Cairinis W Isles 287 H3
Cairisiadar W Isles 287 A5
Cairminis W Isles 287 F5
Cairnbaan Argyll 213 C6
Cairnbanno Ho. Aberds 256 B3
Cairnborrow Aberds 255 B5
Cairnbrogie Aberds 256 D3
Cairnbulg Castle Aberds 269 C5
Cairncross Angus 232 A2
Cairncross Borders 211 D5
Cairndow Argyll 215 A4
Cairness Aberds 269 C5
Cairneyhill Fife 208 B3
Cairnfield Ho. Moray 267 C5
Cairngaan Dumfries 170 D3
Cairngarroch Dumfries 170 C2
Cairnhill Aberds 256 C1
Cairnie Aberds 255 B5
Cairnie Aberds 245 B5
Cairnorrie Aberds 256 B3
Cairnpark Aberds 245 A5
Cairnryan Dumfries 170 A2
Cairnton Orkney 283 G4
Caister-on-Sea Norf 121 D7
Caistor Lincs 142 C3
Caistor St Edmund Norf 104 A3
Caistron Northumb 188 C2
Caitha Bowland Borders 196 B3
Caithness Glass, Perth Perth 219 B5
Calais Street Suff 87 D5
Calanais W Isles 288 D3
Calbost W Isles 288 F5
Calbourne I o W 18 C3
Calceby Lincs 134 B3
Calcot Row W Berks 47 B4
Calcott Kent 52 C3
Caldback Shetland 284 C8
Caldbeck Cumb 163 A6
Caldbergh N Yorks 157 C4
Caldecote Cambs 85 B5
Caldecote Cambs 100 C3
Caldecote Herts 84 D4
Caldecote Northants 82 B3
Caldecott Northants 84 A1
Caldecott Oxon 65 D5
Caldecott Rutland 99 B5
Calder Bridge Cumb 162 D3
Calder Hall Cumb 162 D3
Calder Mains Highld 280 C2
Calder Vale Lancs 145 C5
Calderbank N Lnrk 207 D5
Calderbrook Gtr Man 138 B2
Caldercruix N Lnrk 207 D6
Caldermill S Lnrk 205 D6
Calderwood S Lnrk 205 C6
Caldhame Angus 232 D2
Caldicot Mon 42 A3
Caldwell Derbys 113 D6
Caldwell N Yorks 167 D4
Caldy Mers 126 A2
Caledrhydiau Ceredig 74 C3
Calfsound Orkney 282 D6
Calgary Argyll 224 A2
Califer Moray 266 D1
California Falk 208 C2
California Norf 121 D7
Calke Derbys 114 C1
Callakille Highld 248 A3
Callaly Northumb 188 C3
Callander Stirl 217 D6
Callaughton Shrops 95 B4
Callestick Corn 4 B2
Calligarry Highld 247 D5
Callington Corn 6 A2
Callow Hereford 78 D2
Callow End Worcs 79 C6
Callow Hill Wilts 44 A4
Callow Hill Worcs 95 D5
Callows Grave Worcs 78 A3
Calmore Hants 32 D2
Calmsden Glos 63 C6
Calne Wilts 44 B4
Calow Derbys 131 B4
Calshot Hants 18 A3
Calstock Corn 6 A3
Calstone Wellington Wilts 44 C4
Calthorpe Norf 120 B3
Calthwaite Cumb 164 A2
Calton N Yorks 146 B3
Calton Staffs 129 D6
Calveley Ches 127 D5
Calver Derbys 130 B2
Calver Hill Hereford 78 C1
Calverhall Shrops 111 B5
Calverleigh Devon 27 D4
Calverley W Yorks 147 D6
Calvert Bucks 66 A1
Calverton M Keynes 83 D4
Calverton Notts 115 A4
Calvine Perth 230 B2
Calvo Cumb 174 C4
Cam Glos 62 D3
Camas-luinie Highld 249 D6
Camasnacroise Highld 236 D2
Camastianavaig Highld 247 A4
Camasunary Highld 247 C4
Camault Muir Highld 251 B7
Camb Shetland 284 D7
Camber E Sus 38 D1
Camberley Sur 47 C6
Camberwell London 49 B6
Camblesforth N Yorks 141 A4
Cambo Northumb 178 A2
Cambois Northumb 179 A5
Camborne Corn 3 A4
Cambourne Cambs 85 B5
Cambridge Cambs 85 B6
Cambridge Glos 62 C3
Cambridge Airport Cambs 85 B6
Cambridge Town Sthend 51 A6
Cambus Clack 207 A6
Cambusavie Farm Highld 264 A3
Cambusbarron Stirl 207 A5
Cambuskenneth Stirl 207 A6
Cambuslang S Lnrk 205 B6
Cambusmore Lodge Highld 264 A3
Camden London 49 A5
Camelford Corn 10 C2
Camelot Theme Park, Chorley Lancs 136 B4
Camelsdale W Sus 34 C1
Camerory Highld 253 C6
Camer's Green Worcs 79 D5
Camerton Bath 43 D5
Camerton Cumb 162 A3
Camerton E Yorks 143 A4
Camghouran Perth 229 C4
Cammachmore Aberds 245 C6
Cammeringham Lincs 133 A4
Camore Highld 264 A3
Camp Hill Warks 97 B6
Campbeltown Argyll 190 C3
Campbeltown Airport Argyll 190 C2
Camperdown T & W 179 B4
Campmuir Perth 220 A2
Campsall S Yorks 140 B3
Campsey Ash Suff 88 B4
Campton Beds 84 D3
Camptown Borders 187 B5
Camrose Pembs 55 B5
Camserney Perth 230 D2
Camster Highld 281 D4
Camuschoirk Highld 235 D6
Camuscross Highld 247 C5
Camusnagaul Highld 237 B4
Camusnagaul Highld 262 B2
Camusrory Highld 238 C2
Camusteel Highld 249 B4
Camusterrach Highld 249 B4
Camusvrachan Perth 229 D5
Canada Hants 32 D1
Canadia E Sus 23 A5
Canal Side S Yorks 141 B4
Candacraig Ho. Aberds 243 A6
Candlesby Lincs 135 C4
Candy Mill S Lnrk 195 B5
Cane End Oxon 47 B4
Canewdon Essex 70 D2
Canford Bottom Dorset 17 A4
Canford Cliffs Poole 17 C4
Canford Magna Poole 17 B4
Canham's Green Suff 87 A6
Canholes Derbys 129 B5
Canisbay Highld 281 A5
Cann Dorset 30 C2
Cann Common Dorset 30 C2
Cannard's Grave Som 29 A6
Cannich Highld 251 C5
Cannington Som 28 B2
Cannock Staffs 96 A2
Cannock Wood Staffs 112 D4
Canon Bridge Hereford 78 C2
Canon Frome Hereford 79 C4
Canon Pyon Hereford 78 C2

Canonbie Dumfries 175 A6
Canons Ashby Northants 82 B2
Canonstown Corn 2 B3
Canterbury Kent 52 D3
Canterbury Cathedral Kent 52 D3
Canterbury Tales Kent 52 D3
Cantley Norf 105 A4
Cantley S Yorks 140 C4
Cantlop Shrops 94 A3
Canton Cardiff 41 D6
Cantraybruich Highld 252 B3
Cantraydoune Highld 252 B3
Cantraywood Highld 252 B3
Cantsfield Lancs 155 D5
Canvey Island Essex 51 A4
Canwick Lincs 133 C4
Canworthy Water Corn 10 B3
Caol Highld 237 B5
Caol Ila Argyll 201 A4
Caolas Argyll 222 C3
Caolas Scalpaigh W Isles 288 H3
Caolas Stocinis W Isles 288 H2
Capel Sur 35 B4
Capel Bangor Ceredig 91 D4
Capel Betws Lleucu Ceredig 75 C5
Capel Carmel Gwyn 106 D1
Capel Coch Anglesey 123 B4
Capel Curig Conwy 124 D2
Capel Cynon Ceredig 73 B6
Capel Dewi Ceredig 58 A1
Capel Dewi Ceredig 90 D4
Capel Dewi Carms 58 C1
Capel Garmon Conwy 124 D3
Capel-gwyn Anglesey 122 C3
Capel Gwyn Carms 58 C1
Capel Gwynfe Carms 59 C4
Capel Hendre Carms 57 A5
Capel Hermon Gwyn 108 C2
Capel Isaac Carms 58 C2
Capel Iwan Carms 73 C5
Capel le Ferne Kent 39 B4
Capel Llanilltern Cardiff 41 C5
Capel Mawr Anglesey 123 C4
Capel St Andrew Suff 89 C4
Capel St Mary Suff 88 D1
Capel Seion Ceredig 75 A5
Capel Tygwydd Ceredig 73 B5
Capel Uchaf Gwyn 107 B4
Capel-y-graig Gwyn 123 D5
Capelulo Conwy 124 B2
Capenhurst Ches 126 B3
Capernwray Lancs 154 D4
Capheaton Northumb 178 A2
Cappercleuch Borders 196 D1
Capplegill Dumfries 185 B4
Capton Devon 8 B2
Caputh Perth 219 A5
Car Colston Notts 115 A5
Carbis Bay Corn 2 B3
Carbost Highld 246 A2
Carbost Highld 259 D4
Carbrook S Yorks 130 A3
Carbrooke Norf 103 A5
Carburton Notts 131 B6
Carcant Borders 196 A2
Carcary Angus 233 C4
Carclaze Corn 5 B5
Carcroft S Yorks 140 B3
Cardenden Fife 209 A5
Cardeston Shrops 110 D2
Cardiff = Caerdydd Cardiff 41 D6
Cardiff Bay Barrage Cardiff 41 D6
Cardiff Castle Cardiff 41 D6
Cardiff International Airport V Glam 41 E5
Cardigan = Aberteifi Ceredig 73 B4
Cardington Beds 84 C2
Cardington Shrops 94 B3
Cardinham Corn 5 A6
Cardonald Glasgow 205 B5
Cardow Moray 254 B2
Cardrona Borders 196 C2
Cardross Argyll 206 C1
Cardurnock Cumb 175 C4
Careby Lincs 116 D3
Careston Castle Angus 232 C3
Carew Pembs 55 D6
Carew Cheriton Pembs 55 D6
Carew Newton Pembs 55 D6
Carey Hereford 78 D3
Carfrae E Loth 210 D2
Cargenbridge Dumfries 174 A2
Cargill Perth 219 A6
Cargo Cumb 175 C6
Cargreen Corn 6 A3
Carham Northumb 198 C2
Carhampton Som 27 A5
Carharrack Corn 4 C2
Carie Perth 217 A6
Carie Perth 229 C5
Carines Corn 4 B2
Carisbrooke I o W 18 C3
Carisbrooke Castle I o W 18 C3
Cark Cumb 154 D2
Carlabhagh W Isles 288 C3
Carland Cross Corn 4 B3
Carlby Lincs 116 D3
Carlecotes S Yorks 139 C4
Carlesmoor N Yorks 157 D5
Carleton Cumb 164 C3
Carleton Cumb 176 D2
Carleton Lancs 144 D3
Carleton N Yorks 146 C3
Carleton Forehoe Norf 104 A1
Carleton Rode Norf 104 B2
Carlin How Redcar 169 D5
Carlingcott Bath 43 D5
Carlisle Cumb 175 C7
Carlisle Airport Cumb 176 C2
Carlisle Cathedral Cumb 175 C6
Carlisle Racecourse Cumb 175 C6
Carlops Borders 195 A6
Carlton Beds 83 B6
Carlton Cambs 86 B2
Carlton Leics 97 A6
Carlton Notts 115 A4
Carlton N Yorks 159 C5
Carlton N Yorks 140 A4
Carlton N Yorks 157 C4
Carlton N Yorks 167 D4
Carlton Stockton 167 C6
Carlton Suff 89 A4
Carlton S Yorks 139 B6
Carlton W Yorks 139 A6
Carlton Colville Suff 105 C6
Carlton Curlieu Leics 98 B3
Carlton Husthwaite N Yorks 158 D3
Carlton in Cleveland N Yorks 158 A4
Carlton in Lindrick Notts 131 A5
Carlton le Moorland Lincs 133 D4
Carlton Miniott N Yorks 158 C2
Carlton on Trent Notts 132 C2
Carlton Scroop Lincs 116 A2
Carluke S Lnrk 194 A3
Carmarthen = Caerfyrddin Carms 73 D7
Carmel Anglesey 122 B3
Carmel Carms 57 A5
Carmel Flint 125 B6
Carmel Guern 6
Carmel Gwyn 107 A4
Carmont Aberds 245 D5
Carmunnock Glasgow 205 C6
Carmyle Glasgow 205 B6
Carmyllie Angus 232 D3
Carn-gorm Highld 249 D6
Carnaby E Yorks 151 A4
Carnach Highld 262 A2
Carnach Highld 250 D2
Carnach W Isles 288 H3
Carnachy Highld 278 C3
Càrnais W Isles 287 A5
Carnbee Fife 221 D5
Carnbo Perth 219 D5
Carnbrea Corn 3 A4
Carnduff S Lnrk 205 D6
Carnduncan Argyll 200 B2
Carne Corn 4 D4
Carnforth Lancs 154 D3
Carnhedryn Pembs 54 B4
Carnhell Green Corn 3 B4
Carnkie Corn 4 D2
Carnkie Corn 3 B4
Carno Powys 92 B3
Carnoch Highld 251 C5
Carnoch Highld 251 A4
Carnock Fife 208 B3
Carnon Downs Corn 4 C2
Carnousie Aberds 268 D1
Carnoustie Angus 221 A5
Carnwath S Lnrk 195 B4
Carnyorth Corn 2 B1
Carperby N Yorks 156 C4
Carpley Green N Yorks 156 C3
Carr S Yorks 140 D3
Carr Hill T & W 179 C4
Carradale Argyll 190 B4
Carragraich W Isles 288 H2
Carrbridge Highld 253 D5
Carrefour Selous Jersey 6
Carreg-wen Pembs 73 B5
Carreglefn Anglesey 122 B3
Carrick Argyll 214 D2
Carrick Fife 220 B4
Carrick Castle Argyll 215 C4
Carrick Ho. Orkney 282 D6
Carriden Falk 208 B3
Carrington Gtr Man 137 D6
Carrington Lincs 134 D3
Carrington Midloth 209 D6
Carrog Conwy 108 A2
Carrog Denb 109 A6
Carron Falk 208 B1
Carron Moray 254 B3
Carron Bridge N Lnrk 207 B5
Carronbridge Dumfries 183 C6
Carrshield Northumb 165 A6
Carrutherstown Dumfries 174 A4
Carrville Durham 167 A6
Carsaig Argyll 225 D4
Carsaig Argyll 213 D5
Carscreugh Dumfries 171 B4
Carse Gray Angus 232 C2
Carse Ho. Argyll 202 B2
Carsegowan Dumfries 171 B6
Carseriggan Dumfries 171 A5
Carsethorn Dumfries 174 C2
Carshalton London 49 C5
Carsington Derbys 130 D2
Carskiey Argyll 190 E2
Carsluith Dumfries 171 B6
Carsphairn Dumfries 182 C3
Carstairs S Lnrk 194 B4
Carstairs Junction S Lnrk 195 B4
Carswell Marsh Oxon 64 D4
Carter's Clay Hants 32 C2
Carterton Oxon 64 C3
Carterway Heads Northumb 178 D2
Carthew Corn 5 B5
Carthorpe N Yorks 157 C7
Cartington Northumb 188 C3
Cartland S Lnrk 194 B3
Cartmel Cumb 154 D2
Cartmel Fell Cumb 154 C3
Cartmel Racecourse Cumb 154 D2
Carway Carms 57 B4
Cary Fitzpaine Som 29 C5
Cas-gwent = Chepstow Mon 62 D1
Cascob Powys 77 A6
Cashlie Perth 228 D3
Cashmere Visitor Centre, Elgin Moray 266 C3
Cashmoor Dorset 30 D3
Casnewydd = Newport Newport 42 A2
Cassey Compton Glos 63 B6
Cassington Oxon 65 B5
Cassop Durham 167 B6
Castell Denb 125 C6
Castell Coch Cardiff 41 C6
Castell-Howell Ceredig 74 D3
Castell-Nedd = Neath Neath 40 B2
Castell Newydd Emlyn = Newcastle Emlyn Carms 73 B6
Castell-y-bwch Torf 61 D4
Castellau Rhondda 41 C5
Casterton Cumb 155 D5
Castle Acre Norf 119 D5
Castle Ashby Northants 83 B5
Castle Bolton N Yorks 156 B4
Castle Bromwich W Mid 96 C4
Castle Bytham Lincs 116 D2
Castle Caereinion Powys 93 A5
Castle Camps Cambs 86 C2
Castle Carrock Cumb 176 D3
Castle Cary Som 29 B6
Castle Combe Wilts 44 B2
Castle Combe Motor Racing Circuit Wilts 44 B2
Castle Donington Leics 114 C2
Castle Douglas Dumfries 173 B5
Castle Drogo, Exeter Devon 12 B2
Castle Eaton Swindon 64 D2
Castle Eden Durham 168 B2
Castle Forbes Aberds 244 A3
Castle Frome Hereford 79 C4
Castle Green Sur 48 C2
Castle Gresley Derbys 113 D6
Castle Heaton Northumb 198 B3
Castle Hedingham Essex 86 D3
Castle Hill Kent 37 B4
Castle Howard, Malton N Yorks 159 D6
Castle Huntly Perth 220 B3
Castle Kennedy Dumfries 170 B3
Castle O'er Dumfries 185 C5
Castle Pulverbatch Shrops 94 A2
Castle Rising Norf 118 C3
Castle Stuart Highld 252 B3
Castlebay = Bagh a Chaisteil W Isles 286 G2
Castlebythe Pembs 55 B6
Castlecary N Lnrk 207 C5
Castlecraig Highld 265 D4
Castlefairn Dumfries 183 D5
Castleford W Yorks 140 A2
Castlehill Borders 195 C7
Castlehill Highld 280 B3
Castlehill W Dunb 206 C1
Castlemaddy Dumfries 182 D3
Castlemartin Pembs 55 E5
Castlemilk Dumfries 174 A4
Castlemilk Glasgow 205 C6
Castlemorris Pembs 55 A5
Castlemorton Worcs 79 D5
Castleside Durham 166 A3
Castlethorpe M Keynes 83 C5
Castleton Angus 232 D1
Castleton Argyll 214 D1
Castleton Derbys 129 A6
Castleton Gtr Man 138 B1
Castleton Newport 42 A1
Castleton N Yorks 159 A5
Castletown Ches 127 D4
Castletown Highld 280 B3
Castletown Highld 252 B3
Castletown I o M 152 E2
Castletown T & W 179 D5
Castleweary Borders 186 C3
Castley N Yorks 147 C6
Caston Norf 103 B5
Castor P'boro 100 B3
Catacol N Ayrs 203 D4
Catbrain S Glos 43 A4
Catbrook Mon 61 C7
Catchall Corn 2 C2
Catchems Corner W Mid 97 D5
Catchgate Durham 178 D3
Catcleugh Northumb 187 C6
Catcliffe S Yorks 131 A4
Catcott Som 28 B3
Caterham Sur 35 A6
Catfield Norf 121 C5
Catfirth Shetland 285 H6
Catford London 49 B6
Catforth Lancs 145 D4
Cathays Cardiff 41 D6
Cathcart Glasgow 205 B5
Cathedine Powys 60 A3
Catherington Hants 33 D5
Catherton Shrops 95 D4
Catlodge Highld 241 C4
Catlowdy Cumb 176 B2
Catmore W Berks 46 A2
Caton Lancs 145 A5
Caton Green Lancs 145 A5
Catrine E Ayrs 193 C5
Cat's Ash Newport 61 D5
Catsfield E Sus 23 A5
Catshill Worcs 96 D2
Cattal N Yorks 148 B3
Cattawade Suff 88 D2
Catterall Lancs 145 C4
Catterick N Yorks 157 B6
Catterick Bridge N Yorks 157 B6
Catterick Garrison N Yorks 157 B5
Catterick Racecourse N Yorks 157 B6
Catterlen Cumb 164 B2
Catterline Aberds 233 A6
Catterton N Yorks 148 C4
Catthorpe Leics 98 D2
Cattistock Dorset 15 B5
Catton Northumb 177 D6
Catton N Yorks 158 D2
Catwick E Yorks 151 C4
Catworth Cambs 100 D2
Caudlesprings Norf 103 A5
Caudwell's Mill, Matlock Derbys 130 C2
Caulcott Oxon 65 A6
Cauldcots Angus 233 D4
Cauldhame Stirl 207 A4
Cauldmill Borders 186 B4
Cauldon Staffs 113 A4
Caulkerbush Dumfries 174 C2
Caulside Dumfries 176 A2
Caunsall Worcs 95 C6
Caunton Notts 132 D2
Causeway End Dumfries 171 A6
Causeway Foot W Yorks 147 D4
Causeway-head Stirl 207 A5
Causewayend S Lnrk 195 C5
Causewayhead Cumb 174 C4
Causey Park Bridge Northumb 189 D4
Causeyend Aberds 245 A6
Cautley Cumb 155 B5
Cavendish Suff 87 C4
Cavendish Bridge Leics 114 C2
Cavenham Suff 86 A3
Caversfield Oxon 65 A6
Caversham Reading 47 B5
Caverswall Staffs 112 A3
Cavil E Yorks 149 D6
Cawdor Highld 253 B4
Cawdor Castle and Gardens Highld 253 B4
Cawkwell Lincs 134 B2
Cawood N Yorks 149 D4
Cawsand Corn 6 B3
Cawston Norf 120 C3
Cawthorne S Yorks 139 C5
Cawthorpe Lincs 116 C3
Cawton N Yorks 159 D5
Caxton Cambs 85 B5
Caynham Shrops 94 D3
Caythorpe Lincs 116 A2
Caythorpe Notts 115 A4
Cayton N Yorks 161 C4
Ceann a Bhaigh W Isles 287 H2
Ceann a Deas Loch Baghasdail W Isles 286 E3
Ceann Shiphoirt W Isles 288 F3
Ceann Tarabhaigh W Isles 288 F3
Ceannacroc Lodge Highld 239 A6
Cearsiadair W Isles 288 E4
Cefn Berain Conwy 125 C4
Cefn-brith Conwy 125 D4
Cefn Canol Powys 110 B1
Cefn-coch Conwy 124 C3
Cefn Coch Powys 109 C6
Cefn-coed-y-cymmer M Tydf 60 C2
Cefn Cribbwr Bridgend 40 C3
Cefn Cross Bridgend 40 C3
Cefn-ddwysarn Gwyn 109 B4
Cefn Einion Shrops 93 C6
Cefn-gorwydd Powys 76 C3
Cefn-mawr Wrex 110 A1
Cefn-y-bedd Flint 126 D3
Cefn-y-pant Carms 73 D4
Cefneithin Carms 57 A5
Cei-bach Ceredig 73 A7
Ceinewydd = New Quay Ceredig 73 A6
Ceint Anglesey 123 C4
Cellan Ceredig 75 D5
Cellarhead Staffs 112 A3
Cemaes Anglesey 122 A3
Cemmaes Powys 91 B6
Cemmaes Road Powys 91 B6
Cenarth Carms 73 B5
Cenin Gwyn 107 B4
Central Invclyd 204 A2
Ceos W Isles 288 E4
Ceres Fife 220 C4
Cerne Abbas Dorset 15 A6
Cerney Wick Glos 63 D6
Cerrigceinwen Anglesey 123 C4
Cerrigydrudion Conwy 109 A4
Cessford Borders 187 A6
Ceunant Gwyn 123 D5
Chaceley Glos 79 D6
Chacewater Corn 4 C2
Chackmore Bucks 82 D3
Chacombe Northants 82 C1
Chad Valley W Mid 96 C3
Chadderton Gtr Man 138 C2
Chadderton Fold Gtr Man 138 C1
Chaddesden Derby 114 B1
Chaddesley Corbett Worcs 96 D1
Chaddleworth W Berks 46 B2
Chadlington Oxon 64 A4
Chadshunt Warks 81 B6
Chadwell Leics 115 C5
Chadwell St Mary Thurrock 50 B3
Chadwick End W Mid 97 D5
Chadwick Green Mers 136 D4
Chaffcombe Som 28 D3
Chagford Devon 12 C2
Chailey E Sus 22 A1
Chain Bridge Lincs 117 A6
Chainbridge Cambs 101 A6
Chainhurst Kent 37 B5
Chalbury Dorset 17 A4
Chalbury Common Dorset 17 A4
Chaldon Sur 35 A6
Chaldon Herring Dorset 16 C1
Chale I o W 18 D3
Chale Green I o W 18 D3
Chalfont Common Bucks 67 D5
Chalfont St Giles Bucks 67 D4
Chalfont St Peter Bucks 67 D5
Chalford Glos 63 C4
Chalgrove Oxon 66 D1
Chalk Kent 50 B3
Challacombe Devon 26 A1
Challoch Dumfries 171 A5
Challock Kent 52 D2
Chalton Beds 67 A5
Chalton Hants 33 D6
Chalvington E Sus 22 B3
Chancery Ceredig 75 A4
Chandler's Ford Hants 32 C3
Channel Tunnel Kent 38 B3
Channerwick Shetland 285 L6
Chantry Som 29 A7
Chantry Suff 88 C2
Chapel Fife 209 A5
Chapel Allerton Som 42 D3
Chapel Allerton W Yorks 148 D2
Chapel Amble Corn 9 D5
Chapel Brampton Northants 83 A4
Chapel Chorlton Staffs 112 B2
Chapel-en-le-Frith Derbys 129 A5
Chapel End Warks 97 B6
Chapel Green Warks 97 C5
Chapel Green Warks 82 A1
Chapel Haddlesey N Yorks 140 A3
Chapel Head Cambs 101 C5
Chapel Hill Aberds 257 C5
Chapel Hill Lincs 134 D2
Chapel Hill Mon 62 D1
Chapel Hill N Yorks 148 C2
Chapel Lawn Shrops 93 D7
Chapel-le-Dale N Yorks 155 D6
Chapel Milton Derbys 129 A5
Chapel of Garioch Aberds 256 D2
Chapel Row W Berks 46 C3
Chapel St Leonards Lincs 135 B5
Chapel Stile Cumb 154 A2
Chapelgate Lincs 117 C7
Chapelhall N Lnrk 207 D5
Chapelhill Dumfries 184 C3
Chapelhill Highld 265 C4
Chapelhill N Ayrs 204 D2
Chapelhill Perth 220 B2
Chapelhill Perth 219 A5
Chapelknowe Dumfries 175 A6
Chapelton Angus 233 D4
Chapelton Devon 25 C6
Chapelton Highld 242 A2
Chapelton S Lnrk 194 B1
Chapeltown Blkburn 137 B6
Chapeltown Moray 254 D3
Chapeltown S Yorks 139 D6
Chapmans Well Devon 11 B4
Chapmanslade Wilts 30 A2
Chapmore End Herts 68 B3
Chappel Essex 70 A2
Chard Som 14 A3
Chardstock Devon 14 A3
Charfield S Glos 62 D3
Charford Worcs 80 A2
Charing Kent 38 A1
Charing Cross Dorset 31 D5
Charing Heath Kent 38 A1
Charingworth Glos 81 D5
Charlbury Oxon 65 B4
Charlcombe Bath 43 C6
Charlecote Warks 81 B5
Charlecote Park, Wellesbourne Warks 81 B5
Charles Devon 26 B1
Charles Manning's Amusement Park, Felixstowe Suff 88 D3
Charles Tye Suff 87 B6
Charlesfield Dumfries 175 B4
Charleston Angus 232 D1
Charleston Renfs 205 B4
Charlestown Aberdeen 245 B6
Charlestown Corn 5 B5
Charlestown Derbys 138 D3
Charlestown Dorset 15 D6
Charlestown Fife 208 B3
Charlestown Gtr Man 137 C7
Charlestown Highld 252 B2
Charlestown Highld 261 C5
Charlestown W Yorks 138 A2
Charlestown of Aberlour Moray 254 B3
Charlesworth Derbys 138 D3
Charleton Devon 7 C6
Charlton London 49 B7
Charlton Hants 32 A2
Charlton Herts 68 A1
Charlton Northants 82 D2
Charlton Northumb 177 A6
Charlton Som 43 D5
Charlton Telford 111 D4
Charlton Wilts 30 C3
Charlton Wilts 45 D5
Charlton Wilts 44 A3
Charlton Worcs 80 C3
Charlton W Sus 20 A1
Charlton Abbots Glos 63 A6
Charlton Adam Som 29 C5
Charlton-All-Saints Wilts 31 C5
Charlton Down Dorset 15 B6
Charlton Horethorne Som 29 C6
Charlton Kings Glos 63 A5
Charlton Mackerell Som 29 C5
Charlton Marshall Dorset 16 A2
Charlton Musgrove Som 29 C7
Charlton on Otmoor Oxon 65 B6
Charltons Redcar 168 D4
Charlwood Sur 35 B5
Charlynch Som 28 B2
Charminster Dorset 15 B6
Charmouth Dorset 14 B3
Charndon Bucks 66 A1
Charney Bassett Oxon 65 D4
Charnock Richard Lancs 137 B4
Charsfield Suff 88 B3
Chart Corner Kent 37 A5
Chart Sutton Kent 37 B6
Charter Alley Hants 46 D3
Charterhouse Som 42 D3
Charterville Allotments Oxon 64 B4
Chartham Kent 52 D3
Chartham Hatch Kent 52 D3
Chartridge Bucks 67 C4
Chartwell, Westerham Kent 36 A2
Charvil Wokingham 47 B5
Charwelton Northants 82 B2
Chasetown Staffs 96 A3
Chastleton Oxon 64 A3
Chasty Devon 10 A4
Chatburn Lancs 146 C1
Chatcull Staffs 112 B1
Chatham Medway 51 C4
Chathill Northumb 189 A4
Chatsworth, Bakewell Derbys 130 B2
Chattenden Medway 51 B4
Chatteris Cambs 101 C5
Chattisham Suff 88 C1
Chatto Borders 187 B6
Chatton Northumb 188 A3
Chawleigh Devon 26 D2

Chawley Oxon 65 C5
Chawston Beds 84 B3
Chawton Hants 33 B6
Cheadle Gtr Man 128 A3
Cheadle Staffs 112 A4
Cheadle Heath Gtr Man 128 A3
Cheadle Hulme Gtr Man 128 A3
Cheam London 49 C5
Cheapside Sur 34 A3
Chearsley Bucks 66 B2
Chebsey Staffs 112 C2
Checkendon Oxon 47 A4
Checkley Ches 111 A6
Checkley Hereford 78 D3
Checkley Staffs 112 B4
Chedburgh Suff 86 B3
Cheddar Som 42 D3
Cheddar Showcaves and Gorge Som 42 D3
Cheddington Bucks 67 B4
Cheddleton Staffs 129 D4
Cheddon Fitzpaine Som 28 C2
Chedglow Wilts 63 D5
Chedgrave Norf 105 B4
Chedington Dorset 15 A4
Chediston Suff 105 D4
Chedworth Glos 63 B6
Chedworth Roman Villa Glos 63 B6
Chedzoy Som 28 B3
Cheeklaw Borders 198 A1
Cheeseman's Green Kent 38 B2
Cheglinch Devon 25 A6
Cheldon Devon 26 D2
Chelford Ches 128 B3
Chell Heath Stoke 128 D3
Chellaston Derby 114 B1
Chellington Beds 83 B6
Chelmarsh Shrops 95 C5
Chelmer Village Essex 70 C1
Chelmondiston Suff 88 D3
Chelmorton Derbys 129 C6
Chelmsford Essex 69 C7
Chelsea London 49 B5
Chelsfield London 50 C1
Chelsworth Suff 87 C5
Cheltenham Glos 63 A5
Cheltenham Racecourse Glos 63 A5
Chelveston Northants 84 A1
Chelvey N Som 42 C3
Chelwood Bath 43 C5
Chelwood Common E Sus 36 D2
Chelwood Gate E Sus 36 D2
Chelworth Wilts 63 D5
Chelworth Green Wilts 64 D1
Chemistry Shrops 111 A4
Chenies Bucks 67 D5
Cheny Longville Shrops 94 C2
Chepstow = Cas-gwent Mon 62 D1
Chepstow Racecourse Mon 62 D1
Chequerfield W Yorks 140 A2
Cherhill Wilts 44 B4
Cherington Glos 63 D5
Cherington Warks 81 D5
Cheriton Devon 26 A2
Cheriton Hants 33 C4
Cheriton Kent 38 B3
Cheriton Swansea 57 C4
Cheriton Bishop Devon 12 B2
Cheriton Fitzpaine Devon 12 A3
Cheriton or Stackpole Elidor Pembs 55 E5
Cherrington Telford 111 C5
Cherry Burton E Yorks 150 C2
Cherry Hinton Cambs 85 B6
Cherry Orchard Worcs 79 B6
Cherry Willingham Lincs 133 B5
Cherrybank Perth 219 B6
Chertsey Sur 48 C3
Cheselbourne Dorset 16 B1
Chesham Bucks 67 C4
Chesham Bois Bucks 67 D4
Cheshire Candle Workshops, Burwardsley Ches 127 D5
Cheshunt Herts 68 C3
Cheslyn Hay Staffs 96 A2
Chessington London 49 C4
Chessington World of Adventures London 49 C4
Chester Ches 127 C4
Chester Cathedral Ches 126 C3
Chester-Le-Street Durham 179 D4
Chester Moor Durham 167 A5
Chester Racecourse Ches 126 C3
Chester Zoo Ches 127 B4
Chesterblade Som 29 A6
Chesterfield Derbys 130 B3
Chesters Borders 187 B5
Chesters Borders 187 A5
Chesters Roman Fort Northumb 177 B7
Chesterton Cambs 100 B3
Chesterton Cambs 85 A6
Chesterton Glos 63 C6
Chesterton Oxon 65 A6
Chesterton Shrops 95 B5
Chesterton Staffs 112 A2
Chesterton Warks 81 B6
Chesterwood Northumb 177 C6
Chestfield Kent 52 C3
Cheston Devon 7 B5
Cheswardine Shrops 111 C6
Cheswick Northumb 198 B4
Chetnole Dorset 15 A6
Chettiscombe Devon 27 D4
Chettisham Cambs 102 C1
Chettle Dorset 30 D3
Chetton Shrops 95 B4
Chetwode Bucks 66 A1
Chetwynd Aston Telford 111 D6
Cheveley Cambs 86 A2
Chevening Kent 36 A2
Chevington Suff 86 B3
Chevithorne Devon 27 D4
Chew Magna Bath 43 C4
Chew Stoke Bath 43 C4
Chewton Keynsham Bath 43 C5
Chewton Mendip Som 43 D4
Chicheley M Keynes 83 C6
Chichester W Sus 20 B1
Chichester Cathedral W Sus 20 B1
Chickerell Dorset 15 C6
Chicklade Wilts 30 B3
Chicksgrove Wilts 30 B3
Chidden Hants 33 D5
Chiddingfold Sur 34 C2
Chiddingly E Sus 22 A3
Chiddingstone Kent 36 B2
Chiddingstone Causeway Kent 36 B3
Chiddingstone Hoath Kent 36 B2
Chideock Dorset 14 B4
Chidham W Sus 19 A6
Chidswell W Yorks 139 A5
Chieveley W Berks 46 B2
Chignall St James Essex 69 C6
Chignall Smealy Essex 69 B6
Chigwell Essex 68 D4
Chigwell Row Essex 69 D4
Chilbolton Hants 32 B2
Chilcomb Hants 32 C4
Chilcombe Dorset 15 B5
Chilcompton Som 43 D5
Chilcote Leics 113 D6
Child Okeford Dorset 30 D2
Childer Thornton Ches 126 B3
Childrey Oxon 46 A1
Child's Ercall Shrops 111 C5
Childswickham Worcs 80 D3
Childwall Mers 127 A4
Childwick Green Herts 67 B6
Chilfrome Dorset 15 B5
Chilgrove W Sus 20 A1
Chilham Kent 52 D2
Chilhampton Wilts 31 B4
Chilla Devon 11 A5
Chillaton Devon 11 C5
Chillenden Kent 53 D4
Chillerton I o W 18 C3
Chillesford Suff 89 B4
Chillingham Northumb 188 A3
Chillington Devon 8 C1
Chillington Som 28 D3
Chilmark Wilts 30 B3
Chilson Oxon 64 B4
Chilsworthy Corn 11 D5
Chilsworthy Devon 10 A4
Chilthorne Domer Som 29 D5
Chiltington E Sus 22 A1
Chilton Bucks 66 B1
Chilton Durham 167 C5
Chilton Oxon 46 A2
Chilton Cantelo Som 29 C5
Chilton Foliat Wilts 45 B7
Chilton Lane Durham 167 B6
Chilton Polden Som 28 B3
Chilton Street Suff 86 C3
Chilton Trinity Som 28 B2
Chilvers Coton Warks 97 B6
Chilwell Notts 114 B3
Chilworth Hants 32 D3
Chilworth Sur 34 B3
Chimney Oxon 65 C4
Chineham Hants 47 D4
Chingford London 68 D3
Chinley Derbys 129 A5
Chinley Head Derbys 129 A5
Chinnor Oxon 66 C2
Chipnall Shrops 111 B6
Chippenhall Green Suff 104 D3
Chippenham Cambs 86 A2
Chippenham Wilts 44 B3
Chipperfield Herts 67 C5
Chipping Herts 85 D5
Chipping Lancs 145 C6
Chipping Campden Glos 81 D4
Chipping Hill Essex 70 B2
Chipping Norton Oxon 64 A4
Chipping Ongar Essex 69 C5
Chipping Sodbury S Glos 43 A6
Chipping Warden Northants 82 C1
Chipstable Som 27 C5
Chipstead Kent 36 A2
Chipstead Sur 35 A5
Chirbury Shrops 93 B6
Chirk = Y Waun Wrex 110 B1
Chirk Bank Shrops 110 B1
Chirk Castle Wrex 110 B1
Chirmorrie S Ayrs 181 D4
Chirnside Borders 198 A2
Chirnsidebridge Borders 198 A2
Chirton Wilts 45 D4
Chisbury Wilts 45 C6
Chiselborough Som 29 D4
Chiseldon Swindon 45 B5
Chiserley W Yorks 138 A3
Chislehampton Oxon 65 D6
Chislehurst London 50 B1
Chislet Kent 53 C4
Chiswell Green Herts 67 C6
Chiswick London 49 B5
Chiswick End Cambs 85 C5
Chisworth Derbys 138 D2
Chithurst W Sus 34 D1
Chittering Cambs 101 D6
Chitterne Wilts 30 A3
Chittlehamholt Devon 26 C1
Chittlehampton Devon 26 C1
Chittoe Wilts 44 C3
Chivenor Devon 25 B6
Chobham Sur 48 C2
Choicelee Borders 197 A6
Cholderton Wilts 31 A6
Cholesbury Bucks 67 C4
Chollerford Northumb 177 B7
Chollerton Northumb 178 B1
Cholmondeston Ches 127 C6
Cholsey Oxon 46 A3
Cholstrey Hereford 78 B2
Chop Gate N Yorks 159 B4
Choppington Northumb 179 A4
Chopwell T & W 178 D3
Chorley Ches 127 D5
Chorley Lancs 137 B4
Chorley Shrops 95 C4
Chorley Staffs 113 D4
Chorleywood Herts 67 D5
Chorlton cum Hardy Gtr Man 137 D7
Chorlton Lane Ches 110 A3
Choulton Shrops 94 C1
Chowdene T & W 179 D4
Chowley Ches 127 D4
Chrishall Essex 85 D6
Christ Church Oxford Oxon 65 C6
Christchurch Cambs 101 B6
Christchurch Dorset 17 B5
Christchurch Glos 62 B1
Christchurch Newport 42 A2
Christchurch Priory Dorset 17 B5
Christian Malford Wilts 44 B3
Christleton Ches 127 C4
Christmas Common Oxon 66 D2
Christon N Som 42 D2
Christon Bank Northumb 189 A5
Christow Devon 12 C3
Chryston N Lnrk 207 C4
Chudleigh Devon 12 D3
Chudleigh Knighton Devon 12 D3
Chulmleigh Devon 26 D1
Chunal Derbys 138 D3
Church Lancs 137 A6
Church Aston Telford 111 D6
Church Brampton Northants 83 A4
Church Broughton Derbys 113 B6
Church Crookham Hants 47 D6
Church Eaton Staffs 112 D2
Church End Beds 67 A4
Church End Beds 84 D3
Church End Beds 84 D1
Church End Cambs 100 C4
Church End Cambs 101 A5
Church End E Yorks 150 B3
Church End Essex 86 C1
Church End Essex 69 A7
Church End Hants 47 D4
Church End Lincs 117 B5
Church End Warks 97 B5
Church End Warks 97 B5
Church End Wilts 44 B4
Church Enstone Oxon 65 A4
Church Fenton N Yorks 148 D4
Church Green Devon 14 B1
Church Green Norf 103 B6
Church Gresley Derbys 113 D6
Church Hanborough Oxon 65 B5
Church Hill Ches 127 C6
Church Houses N Yorks 159 B5
Church Knowle Dorset 16 C3
Church Laneham Notts 132 B3
Church Langton Leics 99 B4
Church Lawford Warks 98 D1
Church Lawton Ches 128 D3
Church Leigh Staffs 112 B4
Church Lench Worcs 80 B3
Church Mayfield Staffs 113 A5
Church Minshull Ches 127 C6
Church Norton W Sus 20 C1
Church Preen Shrops 94 B3
Church Pulverbatch Shrops 94 A2
Church Stoke Powys 93 B6
Church Stowe Northants 82 B3
Church Street Kent 51 B4
Church Stretton Shrops 94 B2
Church Town N Lincs 141 C5
Church Town Sur 35 A6
Church Village Rhondda 41 C5
Church Warsop Notts 131 C5
Churcham Glos 62 B3
Churchbank Shrops 93 D7
Churchbridge Staffs 96 A2
Churchdown Glos 63 B4
Churchend Essex 69 A6
Churchend Essex 71 D4
Churchend S Glos 62 D3
Churchfield W Mid 96 B3
Churchgate Street Essex 69 B4
Churchill Devon 25 A6
Churchill Devon 14 A3
Churchill N Som 42 D3
Churchill Oxon 64 A3
Churchill Worcs 96 D1
Churchill Worcs 80 B2
Churchinford Som 28 D2
Churchover Warks 98 C2
Churchstanton Som 28 D1
Churchstow Devon 7 C6
Churchtown Derbys 130 C2
Churchtown I o M 152 B4
Churchtown Lancs 145 C4
Churchtown Mers 136 B2
Churnsike Lodge Northumb 177 B4
Churston Ferrers Torbay 8 B3
Churt Sur 34 C1
Churton Ches 127 D4
Churwell W Yorks 139 A5
Chute Standen Wilts 45 D7
Chwilog Gwyn 107 C4
Chyandour Corn 2 B2
Cilan Uchaf Gwyn 106 D2
Cilcain Flint 126 C1
Cilcennin Ceredig 75 B4
Cilfor Gwyn 107 C6
Cilfrew Neath 40 A2
Cilfynydd Rhondda 41 B5
Cilgerran Pembs 73 B4
Cilgwyn Carms 59 C4
Cilgwyn Gwyn 107 A4
Cilgwyn Pembs 72 C3
Ciliau Aeron Ceredig 74 C3
Cill Donnain W Isles 286 D3
Cille Bhrighde W Isles 286 E3
Cille Pheadair W Isles 286 E3
Cilmery Powys 76 B4
Cilsan Carms 58 C2
Ciltalgarth Gwyn 108 A3
Cilwendeg Pembs 73 C5
Cilybebyll Neath 40 A2
Cilycwm Carms 59 B4
Cimla Neath 40 B2
Cinderford Glos 62 B2
Cippyn Pembs 72 B4
Circebost W Isles 288 D2
Cirencester Glos 63 C6
Ciribhig W Isles 288 C2
City Powys 93 C6
City Dulas Anglesey 123 B4
City of London = London, City of London 49 A6
Clachaig Argyll 215 D4
Clachan Argyll 202 C2
Clachan Argyll 213 A5
Clachan Argyll 226 B3
Clachan Argyll 215 A4
Clachan Highld 248 C2
Clachan W Isles 286 B3
Clachan na Luib W Isles 287 H3
Clachan of Campsie E Dunb 205 A6
Clachan of Glendaruel Argyll 214 D2
Clachan-Seil Argyll 213 A5
Clachan Strachur Argyll 214 B3
Clachaneasy Dumfries 181 D5
Clachanmore Dumfries 170 C2
Clachbreck Argyll 202 A2
Clachnabrain Angus 232 B1
Clachtoll Highld 270 B3
Clackmannan Clack 208 A2
Clacton-on-Sea Essex 71 B5
Cladach Chireboist W Isles 287 H2
Claddach-knockline W Isles 287 H2
Cladich Argyll 227 D5
Claggan Highld 225 B5
Claggan Highld 237 B5
Claigan Highld 258 C2
Claines Worcs 79 B6
Clandown Bath 43 D5
Clanfield Hants 33 D5
Clanfield Oxon 64 C3
Clanville Hants 32 A2
Claonaig Argyll 202 C3
Claonel Highld 272 D3
Clap Hill Kent 38 B2
Clapgate Dorset 17 A4
Clapgate Herts 68 A4
Clapham Beds 84 B2
Clapham London 49 B5
Clapham N Yorks 146 A1
Clapham W Sus 20 B3
Clappers Borders 198 A3
Clappersgate Cumb 154 A2
Clapton Som 14 A4
Clapton-in-Gordano N Som 42 B3
Clapton-on-the-Hill Glos 64 B2
Clapworthy Devon 26 C1
Clara Vale T & W 178 C3
Clarach Ceredig 90 D4
Clarbeston Pembs 55 B6
Clarbeston Road Pembs 55 B6
Clarborough Notts 132 A2
Clardon Highld 280 B3
Clare Suff 86 C3
Clarebrand Dumfries 173 B5
Claremont Landscape Garden, Esher Sur 48 C4
Clarencefield Dumfries 174 B3
Clarilaw Borders 186 B4
Clark's Green Sur 35 C4
Clarkston E Renf 205 C5
Clashandorran Highld 251 B7
Clashcoig Highld 264 A2
Clashindarroch Aberds 255 C5
Clashmore Highld 270 A3
Clashmore Highld 264 B3
Clashnessie Highld 270 A3
Clashnoir Moray 254 D3
Clate Shetland 285 G7
Clathy Perth 219 C4
Clatt Aberds 255 D6
Clatter Powys 92 B3
Clatterford I o W 18 C3
Clatterin Bridge Aberds 233 A4
Clatworthy Som 27 B5
Claughton Lancs 145 C5
Claughton Lancs 145 A5
Claughton Mers 126 A3
Claverdon Warks 81 A4
Claverham N Som 42 C3
Clavering Essex 85 D6
Claverley Shrops 95 B5
Claverton Bath 44 C1
Clawdd-newydd Denb 125 D5
Clawthorpe Cumb 154 D4
Clawton Devon 11 B4
Claxby Lincs 142 D3
Claxby Lincs 135 B4
Claxton Norf 104 A4
Claxton N Yorks 149 A5
Clay Common Suff 105 C5
Clay Coton Northants 98 D2
Clay Cross Derbys 130 C3
Clay Hill W Berks 46 B3
Clay Lake Lincs 117 C5
Claybokie Aberds 242 D3
Claybrooke Magna Leics 98 C1
Claybrooke Parva Leics 98 C1
Claydon Oxon 82 B1
Claydon Suff 88 B2
Claygate Dumfries 175 A6
Claygate Kent 37 B5
Claygate Sur 49 C4
Claygate Cross Kent 36 A4
Clayhanger Devon 27 C5
Clayhanger W Mid 96 A3
Clayhidon Devon 27 D6
Clayhill E Sus 37 D6
Clayhill Hants 18 A2
Clayock Highld 280 C3
Claypole Lincs 115 A6
Clayton Staffs 112 A2
Clayton S Yorks 140 C2
Clayton W Sus 21 A5
Clayton W Yorks 147 D5
Clayton Green Lancs 137 A4
Clayton-le-Moors Lancs 146 D1
Clayton-le-Woods Lancs 137 A4
Clayton West W Yorks 139 B5
Clayworth Notts 132 A2
Cleadale Highld 234 B3
Cleadon T & W 179 C5
Clearbrook Devon 7 A4
Clearwell Glos 62 C1
Cleasby N Yorks 167 D5
Cleat Orkney 283 K5
Cleatlam Durham 166 D4
Cleator Cumb 162 C3
Cleator Moor Cumb 162 C3
Clebrig Highld 272 A3
Cleckheaton W Yorks 139 A4
Clee St Margaret Shrops 94 C3
Cleedownton Shrops 94 C3
Cleehill Shrops 94 D3
Cleethorpes NE Lincs 143 C5
Cleeton St Mary Shrops 95 D4
Cleeve N Som 42 C3
Cleeve Hill Glos 63 A5
Cleeve Prior Worcs 80 C3
Clegyrnant Powys 91 B7
Clehonger Hereford 78 D2
Cleish Perth 208 A3
Cleland N Lnrk 194 A3
Clench Common Wilts 45 C5
Clenchwarton Norf 118 C2
Clent Worcs 96 D2
Cleobury Mortimer Shrops 95 D4
Cleobury North Shrops 95 C4
Cleongart Argyll 190 B2
Clephanton Highld 253 A4
Clerklands Borders 186 A4
Clestrain Orkney 283 G4
Cleuch Head Borders 187 B4
Cleughbrae Dumfries 174 A3
Clevancy Wilts 45 B4
Clevedon N Som 42 B3
Cleveley Oxon 65 A4
Cleveleys Lancs 144 C3
Cleverton Wilts 44 A3
Clevis Bridgend 40 D3
Clewer Som 42 D3
Cley next the Sea Norf 120 A2
Claid W Isles 286 F2
Cliasmol W Isles 287 D5
Cliburn Cumb 164 C3
Click Mill Orkney 282 E4
Cliddesden Hants 33 A5
Cliff End E Sus 23 A6
Cliffburn Angus 233 D4
Cliffe Medway 51 B4
Cliffe N Yorks 149 D5
Cliffe Woods Medway 51 B4
Clifford Hereford 77 C6
Clifford W Yorks 148 C3
Clifford Chambers Warks 81 B4
Clifford's Mesne Glos 62 A3
Cliffsend Kent 53 C5
Clifton Beds 84 D3
Clifton Bristol 43 B4
Clifton Cumb 164 C3
Clifton Derbys 113 A5
Clifton Lancs 145 D4
Clifton Nottingham 114 B3
Clifton Northumb 179 A4
Clifton N Yorks 147 C5
Clifton Oxon 82 D1
Clifton Stirl 216 A3
Clifton S Yorks 140 D3
Clifton Worcs 79 C6
Clifton York 149 B4
Clifton Campville Staffs 113 D6
Clifton Green Gtr Man 137 C6
Clifton Hampden Oxon 65 D6
Clifton Reynes M Keynes 83 B6
Clifton upon Dunsmore Warks 98 D2
Clifton upon Teme Worcs 79 A5
Cliftoncote Borders 187 A7
Cliftonville Kent 53 B5
Climaen gwyn Neath 59 E4
Climping W Sus 20 B3
Climpy S Lnrk 194 A4
Clink Som 30 A1
Clint N Yorks 147 B6
Clint Green Norf 120 D2
Clintmains Borders 197 C5
Cliobh W Isles 287 A5
Clippesby Norf 121 D6
Clipsham Rutland 116 D2
Clipston Northants 99 C4
Clipstone Notts 131 C5
Clitheroe Lancs 146 C1
Cliuthar W Isles 288 H2
Clive Shrops 111 C4
Clivocast Shetland 284 C8
Clixby Lincs 142 C3
Clocaenog Denb 125 D5
Clochan Moray 267 C5
Clock Face Mers 136 D4
Clockmill Borders 197 A6
Cloddiau Powys 93 A6
Clodock Hereford 61 A5
Clola Aberds 257 B5
Clophill Beds 84 D2
Clopton Northants 100 C2
Clopton Suff 88 B3
Clopton Corner Suff 88 B3
Clopton Green Suff 86 B3
Close Clark I o M 152 D2
Closeburn Dumfries 183 C6
Closworth Som 29 D5
Clothall Herts 85 D4
Clotton Ches 127 C5
Clough Foot W Yorks 138 A2
Cloughton N Yorks 160 B4
Cloughton Newlands N Yorks 160 B4
Clousta Shetland 285 H5
Clouston Orkney 282 F3
Clova Aberds 255 D5
Clova Angus 232 A1
Clove Lodge Durham 166 D2
Clovelly Devon 24 C4
Clovelly Village Devon 24 C4
Clovenfords Borders 196 C3
Clovenstone Aberds 245 A4
Clovullin Highld 237 C4
Clow Bridge Lancs 137 A7
Clowne Derbys 131 B4
Clows Top Worcs 95 D5

Cloy Wrex 110 A2
Cluanie Inn Highld 239 A4
Cluanie Lodge Highld 239 A4
Clun Shrops 93 C7
Clunbury Shrops 94 C1
Clunderwen Carms 55 C7
Clune Highld 252 D3
Clunes Highld 239 D6
Clungunford Shrops 94 D1
Clunie Aberds 268 D1
Clunie Perth 231 D5
Clunton Shrops 94 C1
Cluny Fife 209 A5
Cluny Castle Highld 241 C4
Clutton Bath 43 D5
Clutton Ches 127 D4
Clwt-grugoer Conwy 125 C4
Clwt-y-bont Gwyn 123 D5
Clydach Mon 60 B4
Clydach Swansea 40 A1
Clydach Vale Rhondda 41 B4
Clydebank W Dunb 205 A4
Clydey Pembs 73 C5
Clyffe Pypard Wilts 45 B4
Clynder Argyll 215 D5
Clyne Neath 40 A3
Clynelish Highld 274 D2
Clynnog-fawr Gwyn 107 A4
Clyro Powys 77 C6
Clyst Honiton Devon 13 B4
Clyst Hydon Devon 13 A5
Clyst St George Devon 13 C4
Clyst St Lawrence Devon 13 A5
Clyst St Mary Devon 13 B4
Cnoc Amhlaigh W Isles 288 D6
Cnwch-coch Ceredig 75 A5
Coachford Aberds 255 B5
Coad's Green Corn 10 D3
Coal Aston Derbys 130 B3
Coalbrookdale Telford 95 A4
Coalbrookvale Bl Gwent 60 C3
Coalburn S Lnrk 194 C3
Coalburns T & W 178 C3
Coalcleugh Northumb 165 A6
Coaley Glos 62 C3
Coalhall E Ayrs 182 A2
Coalhill Essex 70 D1
Coalpit Heath S Glos 43 A5
Coalport Telford 95 A4
Coalsnaughton Clack 208 A2
Coaltown of Balgonie Fife 209 A5
Coaltown of Wemyss Fife 209 A6
Coalville Leics 114 D2
Coalway Glos 62 B1
Coat Som 29 C4
Coatbridge N Lnrk 207 D5
Coatdyke N Lnrk 207 D5
Coate Swindon 45 A5
Coate Wilts 44 C4
Coates Cambs 101 B5
Coates Glos 63 C5
Coates Lancs 146 C2
Coates Notts 132 A3
Coates W Sus 20 A2
Coatham Redcar 168 C3
Coatham Mundeville Darl 167 C5
Coatsgate Dumfries 184 B3
Cobbaton Devon 25 C7
Cobbler's Green Norf 104 B3
Coberley Glos 63 B5
Cobham Kent 50 C3
Cobham Sur 48 C4
Cobholm Island Norf 105 A6
Cobleland Stirl 206 A3
Cobnash Hereford 78 A2
Coburty Aberds 269 C4
Cock Bank Wrex 110 A2
Cock Bridge Aberds 243 B5
Cock Clarks Essex 70 C2
Cockayne N Yorks 159 B5
Cockayne Hatley Cambs 85 C4
Cockburnspath Borders 211 C4
Cockenzie and Port Seton E Loth 209 C7
Cockerham Lancs 145 B4
Cockermouth Cumb 163 A4
Cockernhoe Green Herts 67 A6
Cockfield Durham 166 C4
Cockfield Suff 87 B5
Cockfosters London 68 D2
Cocking W Sus 20 A1
Cockington Torbay 8 A2
Cocklake Som 28 A4
Cockley Beck Cumb 163 D5
Cockley Cley Norf 102 A3
Cockshutt Shrops 110 C3
Cockthorpe Norf 120 A1
Cockwood Devon 13 C4
Cockyard Hereford 78 D2
Codda Corn 10 D2
Coddenham Suff 88 B2
Coddington Ches 127 D4
Coddington Hereford 79 C5
Coddington Notts 132 D3
Codford St Mary Wilts 30 B3
Codford St Peter Wilts 30 B3
Codicote Herts 68 B2
Codmore Hill W Sus 34 D3
Codnor Derbys 114 A2
Codrington S Glos 43 B6
Codsall Staffs 95 A6
Codsall Wood Staffs 95 A6
Coed Duon = Blackwood Caerph 41 B6
Coed Mawr Gwyn 123 C5
Coed Morgan Mon 61 B5
Coed-Talon Flint 126 D2
Coed-y-bryn Ceredig 73 B6
Coed-y-paen Mon 61 D5
Coed-yr-ynys Powys 60 A3
Coed Ystumgwern Gwyn 107 D5
Coedely Rhondda 41 C5
Coedkernew Newport 42 A1
Coedpoeth Wrex 126 D2
Coedway Powys 110 D2
Coelbren Powys 59 D5
Coffinswell Devon 8 A2
Cofton Hackett Worcs 96 D3
Cogan V Glam 41 D6
Cogenhoe Northants 83 A5
Cogges Oxon 65 C4
Coggeshall Essex 70 A2
Coggeshall Hamlet Essex 70 A2
Coggins Mill E Sus 36 D3
Coig Peighinnean W Isles 288 A6
Coig Peighinnean Bhuirgh W Isles 288 B5
Coignafearn Lodge Highld 241 A4
Coilacriech Aberds 243 C6
Coilantogle Stirl 217 D5
Coilleag W Isles 286 E3
Coillore Highld 246 A2
Coity Bridgend 40 C4
Col W Isles 288 C5
Col Uarach W Isles 288 D5
Colaboll Highld 272 C3
Colan Corn 4 A3
Colaton Raleigh Devon 13 C5
Colbost Highld 258 D2
Colburn N Yorks 157 B5
Colby Cumb 165 C4
Colby I o M 152 D2
Colby Norf 120 B4
Colchester Essex 71 A4
Colchester Zoo Essex 70 A3
Colcot V Glam 41 E6
Cold Ash W Berks 46 C3
Cold Ashby Northants 98 D3
Cold Ashton S Glos 43 B6
Cold Aston Glos 64 B2
Cold Blow Pembs 55 C7
Cold Brayfield M Keynes 83 B6
Cold Hanworth Lincs 133 A5
Cold Harbour Lincs 116 B2
Cold Hatton Telford 111 C5
Cold Hesledon Durham 168 A2
Cold Higham Northants 82 B3
Cold Kirby N Yorks 158 C4
Cold Newton Leics 99 A4
Cold Northcott Corn 10 C3
Cold Norton Essex 70 C2
Cold Overton Leics 115 D6
Coldbackie Highld 277 C7
Coldbeck Cumb 155 A6
Coldblow London 50 B2
Coldean Brighton 21 B6
Coldeast Devon 12 D3
Colden W Yorks 138 A2
Colden Common Hants 32 C3
Coldfair Green Suff 89 A5
Coldham Cambs 101 A6
Coldharbour Glos 62 C1
Coldharbour Kent 36 A3
Coldharbour Sur 35 B4
Coldingham Borders 211 D6
Coldrain Perth 219 D5
Coldred Kent 39 A4
Coldridge Devon 12 A1
Coldstream Angus 220 A3
Coldstream Borders 198 C2
Coldwaltham W Sus 20 A3
Coldwells Aberds 257 B6
Coldwells Croft Aberds 255 D6
Coldyeld Shrops 94 B1
Cole Som 29 B6
Cole Green Herts 68 B2
Cole Henley Hants 46 D2
Colebatch Shrops 93 C7
Colebrook Devon 13 A5
Colebrooke Devon 12 B2
Coleby Lincs 133 C4
Coleby N Lincs 141 B6
Coleford Devon 12 A2
Coleford Glos 62 B1
Coleford Som 29 A6
Colehill Dorset 17 A4
Coleman's Hatch E Sus 36 C2
Colemere Shrops 110 B3
Colemore Hants 33 B6
Coleorton Leics 114 D2
Colerne Wilts 44 B2
Cole's Green Suff 88 A3
Coles Green Suff 88 C1
Colesbourne Glos 63 B5
Colesden Beds 84 B3
Coleshill Bucks 67 D4
Coleshill Oxon 64 D3
Coleshill Warks 97 C5
Colestocks Devon 13 A5
Colgate W Sus 35 C5
Colgrain Argyll 206 B1
Colinsburgh Fife 221 D4
Colinton Edin 209 D5
Colintraive Argyll 203 A5
Colkirk Norf 119 C6
Collace Perth 220 A2
Collafirth Shetland 284 G6
Collaton St Mary Torbay 8 B2
College Milton S Lnrk 205 C6
Collessie Fife 220 C2
Collier Row London 69 D5
Collier Street Kent 37 B5
Collier's End Herts 68 A3
Collier's Green Kent 37 C5
Colliery Row T & W 167 A6
Collieston Aberds 257 D5
Collin Dumfries 174 A3
Collingbourne Ducis Wilts 45 D6
Collingbourne Kingston Wilts 45 D6
Collingham Notts 132 C3
Collingham W Yorks 148 C2
Collington Hereford 79 A4
Collingtree Northants 83 B4
Collins Green Warr 137 D4
Colliston Angus 233 D4
Collycroft Warks 97 C6
Collynie Aberds 256 C3
Collyweston Northants 100 A1
Colmonell S Ayrs 180 C3
Colmworth Beds 84 B3
Coln Rogers Glos 64 C1
Coln St Aldwyn's Glos 64 C2
Coln St Dennis Glos 64 B1
Colnabaichin Aberds 243 B5
Colnbrook Slough 48 B3
Colne Cambs 101 D5
Colne Lancs 146 C2
Colne Edge Lancs 146 C2
Colne Engaine Essex 87 D4
Colney Norf 104 A2
Colney Heath Herts 68 C2
Colney Street Herts 67 C6
Colpy Aberds 256 C1
Colquhar Borders 196 B2
Colsterdale N Yorks 157 C5
Colsterworth Lincs 116 C2
Colston Bassett Notts 115 B4
Coltfield Moray 266 C2
Colthouse Cumb 154 B2
Coltishall Norf 121 D4
Coltness N Lnrk 194 A3
Colton Cumb 154 C2
Colton Norf 104 A2
Colton N Yorks 148 C4
Colton Staffs 113 C4
Colton W Yorks 148 D2
Colva Powys 77 B6
Colvend Dumfries 173 C6
Colvister Shetland 284 D7
Colwall Green Hereford 79 C5
Colwall Stone Hereford 79 C5
Colwell Northumb 178 B1
Colwich Staffs 112 C4
Colwick Notts 115 A4
Colwinston V Glam 40 D4
Colworth W Sus 20 B2
Colwyn Bay = Bae Colwyn Conwy 124 B3
Colyford Devon 14 B2
Colyton Devon 14 B2
Combe Hereford 78 A1
Combe Oxon 65 B5
Combe W Berks 46 C1
Combe Common Sur 34 C2
Combe Down Bath 43 C6
Combe Florey Som 27 B6
Combe Hay Bath 43 D6
Combe Martin Devon 25 A6
Combe Moor Hereford 78 A1
Combe Raleigh Devon 13 A6
Combe St Nicholas Som 28 D3
Combeinteignhead Devon 13 D4
Comberbach Ches 127 B6
Comberton Cambs 85 B5
Comberton Hereford 78 A2
Combpyne Devon 14 B2
Combridge Staffs 113 B4
Combrook Warks 81 B6
Combs Derbys 129 B5
Combs Suff 87 B6
Combs Ford Suff 87 B6
Combwich Som 28 A2
Comers Aberds 244 B3
Comins Coch Ceredig 90 D4
Commercial End Cambs 86 A1
Commins Capel Betws Ceredig 75 C5
Commins Coch Powys 91 B6
Common Edge Blkpool 144 D3
Common Side Derbys 130 B3
Commondale N Yorks 169 D4
Commonmoor Corn 6 A1
Commonside Ches 127 B5
Compstall Gtr Man 138 D2
Compton Devon 8 A2
Compton Hants 32 C3
Compton Sur 34 B1
Compton Sur 34 B2
Compton W Berks 46 B3
Compton Wilts 45 D5
Compton W Sus 33 D6
Compton Abbas Dorset 30 D2
Compton Abdale Glos 63 B6
Compton Acres Poole 17 C4
Compton Bassett Wilts 44 B4
Compton Beauchamp Oxon 45 A6
Compton Bishop Som 42 D2
Compton Chamberlayne Wilts 31 C4
Compton Dando Bath 43 C5
Compton Dundon Som 29 B4
Compton Martin Bath 43 D4
Compton Pauncefoot Som 29 C6
Compton Valence Dorset 15 B5
Comrie Fife 208 B3
Comrie Perth 218 B2
Conaglen House Highld 237 C4
Conchra Argyll 214 D3
Concraigie Perth 231 D5
Conder Green Lancs 145 B4
Conderton Worcs 80 D2
Condicote Glos 64 A2
Condorrat N Lnrk 207 C5
Condover Shrops 94 A2
Coney Weston Suff 103 D5
Coneyhurst W Sus 35 D4
Coneysthorpe N Yorks 159 D6
Coneythorpe N Yorks 148 B2
Conford Hants 33 B7
Congash Highld 253 D6
Congdon's Shop Corn 10 D3
Congerstone Leics 97 A6
Congham Norf 119 C4
Congl-y-wal Gwyn 108 A2
Congleton Ches 128 C3
Congresbury N Som 42 C3
Congreve Staffs 112 D3
Conicavel Moray 253 A5
Coningsby Lincs 134 D2
Conington Cambs 100 C3
Conington Cambs 85 A5
Conisbrough S Yorks 140 D3
Conisby Argyll 200 B2
Conisholme Lincs 143 D6
Coniston Cumb 154 B2
Coniston E Yorks 151 D4
Coniston Cold N Yorks 146 B3
Conistone N Yorks 146 A3
Connah's Quay Flint 126 C2
Connel Argyll 226 C4
Connel Park E Ayrs 182 A4
Connor Downs Corn 2 B3
Conon Bridge Highld 252 A1
Conon House Highld 252 A1
Cononley N Yorks 146 C3
Conordan Highld 247 A4
Consall Staffs 112 A3
Consett Durham 178 D3
Constable Burton N Yorks 157 B5
Constantine Corn 3 C5
Constantine Bay Corn 9 D4
Contin Highld 251 A6
Contlaw Aberdeen 245 B5
Conwy Conwy 124 B2
Conwy Castle Conwy 124 B2
Conyer Kent 51 C6
Conyers Green Suff 87 A4
Cooden E Sus 23 B5
Cooil I o M 152 D3
Cookbury Devon 11 A5
Cookham Windsor 48 A1
Cookham Dean Windsor 47 A6
Cookham Rise Windsor 48 A1
Cookhill Worcs 80 B3
Cookley Suff 104 D4
Cookley Worcs 95 C6
Cookley Green Oxon 66 D1
Cookney Aberds 245 C5
Cookridge W Yorks 147 C6
Cooksbridge E Sus 22 A2
Cooksmill Green Essex 69 C6
Coolham W Sus 35 D4
Cooling Medway 51 B4
Coombe Corn 24 D3
Coombe Corn 4 B4
Coombe Hants 33 C5
Coombe Wilts 45 D5
Coombe Bissett Wilts 31 C5
Coombe Hill Glos 63 A4
Coombe Keynes Dorset 16 C2
Coombes W Sus 21 B4
Coopersale Common Essex 69 C4
Cootham W Sus 20 A3
Copdock Suff 88 C2
Copford Green Essex 70 A3
Copgrove N Yorks 148 A2
Copister Shetland 284 F6
Cople Beds 84 C3
Copley Durham 166 C3
Coplow Dale Derbys 129 B6
Copmanthorpe York 149 C4
Coppathorne Corn 10 A3
Coppenhall Staffs 112 D3
Coppenhall Moss Ches 128 D2
Copperhouse Corn 2 B3
Coppingford Cambs 100 C3
Copplestone Devon 12 A2
Coppull Lancs 137 B4
Coppull Moor Lancs 137 B4
Copsale W Sus 35 D4
Copshaw Holm = Newcastleton Borders 176 A2
Copster Green Lancs 145 D6
Copston Magna Warks 98 C1
Copt Heath W Mid 97 D4
Copt Hewick N Yorks 158 D2
Copt Oak Leics 114 D2
Copthorne Shrops 110 D3
Copthorne W Sus 35 C6
Copy's Green Norf 119 B6
Copythorne Hants 32 D2
Corbets Tey London 50 A2
Corbridge Northumb 178 C1
Corby Northants 99 C5
Corby Glen Lincs 116 C2
Cordon N Ayrs 191 B6
Coreley Shrops 95 D4
Cores End Bucks 48 A2
Corfe Som 28 D2
Corfe Castle Dorset 16 C3
Corfe Castle Dorset 16 C3
Corfe Mullen Dorset 16 B3
Corfton Shrops 94 C2
Corgarff Aberds 243 B5
Corhampton Hants 33 C5
Corlae Dumfries 183 C4
Corley Warks 97 C6
Corley Ash Warks 97 C5
Corley Moor Warks 97 C5
Cornaa I o M 152 C4
Cornabus Argyll 200 D3
Cornel Conwy 124 C2
Corner Row Lancs 144 D4
Corney Cumb 153 A2
Cornforth Durham 167 B6
Cornhill Aberds 267 D6
Cornhill-on-Tweed Northumb 198 C2
Cornholme W Yorks 138 A2
Cornish Cyder Farm, Truro Corn 4 B2
Cornish Hall End Essex 86 D2
Cornquoy Orkney 283 H6
Cornsay Durham 166 A4
Cornsay Colliery Durham 167 A4
Corntown Highld 252 A1
Corntown V Glam 40 D4
Cornwell Oxon 64 A3
Cornwood Devon 7 B5
Cornworthy Devon 8 B2
Corpach Highld 237 B4
Corpusty Norf 120 B3
Corran Highld 237 C4
Corran Highld 238 B2
Corranbuie Argyll 202 B3
Corrany I o M 152 C4
Corrie N Ayrs 203 D5
Corrie Common Dumfries 185 D5
Corriecravie N Ayrs 191 C5
Corriemoillie Highld 263 D5
Corriemulzie Lodge Highld 263 A5
Corrievarkie Lodge Perth 229 A4
Corrievorrie Highld 252 D3
Corrimony Highld 251 C5
Corringham Lincs 141 D6
Corringham Thurrock 51 A4
Corris Gwyn 91 B5
Corris Uchaf Gwyn 91 B5
Corrour Shooting Lodge Highld 228 B3
Corrow Argyll 215 B4
Corry Highld 247 B5
Corry of Ardnagrask Highld 251 B7
Corrykinloch Highld 271 B6
Corrymuckloch Perth 218 A3
Corrynachenchy Argyll 225 B5
Cors-y-Gedol Gwyn 107 D5
Corsback Highld 280 A4
Corscombe Dorset 15 A5
Corse Aberds 255 B7
Corse Glos 62 A3
Corse Lawn Worcs 79 D6
Corse of Kinnoir Aberds 255 B6
Corsewall Dumfries 170 A2
Corsham Wilts 44 B2
Corsindae Aberds 244 B3
Corsley Wilts 30 A2
Corsley Heath Wilts 30 A2
Corsock Dumfries 173 A5
Corston Bath 43 C5
Corston Wilts 44 A3
Corstorphine Edin 209 C4
Cortachy Angus 232 C1
Corton Suff 105 B6
Corton Wilts 30 A3
Corton Denham Som 29 C6
Coruanan Lodge Highld 237 C4
Corunna W Isles 287 H3
Corwen Denb 109 A5
Coryton Devon 11 C5
Coryton Thurrock 51 A4
Cosby Leics 98 B2
Coseley W Mid 96 B2
Cosgrove Northants 83 C4
Cosham Ptsmth 19 A5
Cosheston Pembs 55 D6
Cossall Notts 114 A2
Cossington Leics 115 D4
Cossington Som 28 A3
Costa Orkney 282 E4
Costessey Norf 120 D3
Costock Notts 114 C3
Coston Leics 115 C6
Cote Oxon 64 C4
Cotebrook Ches 127 C5
Cotehele House Corn 6 A3
Cotehill Cumb 176 D2
Cotes Cumb 154 C3
Cotes Leics 114 C3
Cotes Staffs 112 B2
Cotesbach Leics 98 C2
Cotgrave Notts 115 B4
Cothall Aberds 245 A5
Cotham Notts 115 A5
Cothelstone Som 28 B1
Cotherstone Durham 166 D3
Cothill Oxon 65 D5
Cotleigh Devon 14 A2
Cotmanhay Derbys 114 A2
Cotmaton Devon 13 C6
Coton Cambs 85 B6
Coton Northants 98 D3
Coton Staffs 112 C2
Coton Staffs 112 B3
Coton Clanford Staffs 112 C2
Coton Hill Shrops 110 D3
Coton Hill Staffs 112 B3
Coton in the Elms Derbys 113 D6
Cotswold Wild Life Park, Burford Oxon 64 C3
Cott Devon 8 A1
Cottam E Yorks 150 A2
Cottam Lancs 145 D5
Cottam Notts 132 B3
Cottartown Highld 253 C6
Cottenham Cambs 85 A6
Cotterdale N Yorks 156 B2
Cottered Herts 68 A3
Cotteridge W Mid 96 D3
Cotterstock Northants 100 B2
Cottesbrooke Northants 99 D4
Cottesmore Rutland 116 D2
Cotteylands Devon 27 D4
Cottingham E Yorks 150 D3
Cottingham Northants 99 B5
Cottingley W Yorks 147 D5
Cottisford Oxon 82 D2
Cotton Staffs 113 A4
Cotton Suff 87 A6
Cotton End Beds 84 C2
Cottown Aberds 255 D6
Cottown Aberds 245 A4
Cottown Aberds 256 B3
Cotwalton Staffs 112 B3
Couch's Mill Corn 5 B6
Coughton Hereford 62 A1
Coughton Warks 80 A3
Coulaghailtro Argyll 202 B2
Coulags Highld 249 B6
Coulby Newham M'bro 168 D3
Coulderton Cumb 162 D2
Coulin Highld 250 A2
Coull Aberds 244 B2
Coull Argyll 200 B2
Coulport Argyll 215 D5
Coulsdon London 35 A5
Coulston Wilts 44 D3
Coulter S Lnrk 195 C5
Coulton N Yorks 159 D5
Cound Shrops 94 A3
Coundon Durham 167 C5
Coundon W Mid 97 C6
Coundon Grange Durham 167 C5
Countersett N Yorks 156 C3
Countess Wilts 31 A5
Countess Wear Devon 13 C4
Countesthorpe Leics 98 B2
Countisbury Devon 26 A2
County Oak W Sus 35 C5
Coup Green Lancs 137 A4
Coupar Angus Perth 231 D6
Coupland Northumb 198 C3
Cour Argyll 202 D3
Courance Dumfries 184 C3
Court-at-Street Kent 38 B2
Court Henry Carms 58 C2
Courteenhall Northants 83 B4
Courtsend Essex 71 D4
Courtway Som 28 B2
Cousland Midloth 209 D6
Cousley Wood E Sus 37 C4
Cove Argyll 215 D5
Cove Borders 211 C4
Cove Devon 27 D4

Cove Hants 34 A1
Cove Highld 261 A5
Cove Bay Aberdeen 245 B6
Cove Bottom Suff 105 D5
Covehithe Suff 105 C6
Coven Staffs 96 A2
Coveney Cambs 101 C6
Covenham St Bartholomew Lincs 143 D5
Covenham St Mary Lincs 143 D5
Coventry W Mid 97 D6
Coventry Airport Warks 97 D6
Coventry Cathedral W Mid 97 D6
Coverack Corn 3 D5
Coverham N Yorks 157 C5
Covesea Moray 266 B2
Covington Cambs 100 D2
Covington S Lnrk 195 C4
Cow Ark Lancs 145 C6
Cowan Bridge Lancs 155 D5
Cowbeech E Sus 22 A4
Cowbit Lincs 117 D5
Cowbridge Lincs 117 A6
Cowbridge Som 27 A4
Cowbridge = Y Bont-Faen V Glam 41 D4
Cowdale Derbys 129 B5
Cowden Kent 36 B2
Cowdenbeath Fife 209 A4
Cowdenburn Borders 195 A7
Cowers Lane Derbys 113 A7
Cowes I o W 18 B3
Cowesby N Yorks 158 C3
Cowfold W Sus 35 D5
Cowgill Cumb 155 C6
Cowie Aberds 245 D5
Cowie Stirl 207 B6
Cowley Devon 13 B4
Cowley Glos 63 B5
Cowley London 48 A3
Cowley Oxon 65 C6
Cowleymoor Devon 27 D4
Cowling Lancs 137 B4
Cowling N Yorks 146 C3
Cowling N Yorks 157 C6
Cowlinge Suff 86 B3
Cowpe Lancs 138 A1
Cowpen Northumb 179 A4
Cowpen Bewley Stockton 168 C2
Cowplain Hants 33 D5
Cowshill Durham 165 A6
Cowslip Green N Som 42 C3
Cowstrandburn Fife 208 A3
Cowthorpe N Yorks 148 B3
Cox Common Suff 105 C4
Cox Green Windsor 48 B1
Cox Moor Notts 131 D5
Coxbank Ches 111 A5
Coxbench Derbys 114 A1
Coxford Norf 119 C5
Coxford Soton 32 D2
Coxheath Kent 37 A5
Coxhill Kent 39 A4
Coxhoe Durham 167 B6
Coxley Som 29 A5
Coxwold N Yorks 158 D4
Coychurch Bridgend 40 D4
Coylton S Ayrs 193 C4
Coylumbridge Highld 242 A2
Coynach Aberds 244 B1
Coynachie Aberds 255 C5
Coytrahen Bridgend 40 C3
Crabadon Devon 7 B6
Crabbs Cross Worcs 80 A3
Crabtree W Sus 35 D5
Crackenthorpe Cumb 165 C4
Crackington Haven Corn 10 B2
Crackley Warks 97 D5
Crackleybank Shrops 111 D6
Crackpot N Yorks 156 B3
Cracoe N Yorks 146 A3
Craddock Devon 27 D5
Cradhlastadh W Isles 287 A5
Cradley Hereford 79 C5
Cradley Heath W Mid 96 C2
Crafthole Corn 6 B2
Cragg Vale W Yorks 138 A3
Craggan Highld 253 D6
Craggie Highld 274 C2
Craggie Highld 252 C3
Craghead Durham 179 D4
Crai Powys 59 C5
Craibstone Moray 267 D5
Craichie Angus 232 D3
Craig Dumfries 173 A4
Craig Dumfries 173 B4
Craig Highld 250 B2
Craig Castle Aberds 255 D5
Craig-cefn-parc Swansea 40 A1
Craig Penllyn V Glam 41 D4
Craig-y-don Conwy 124 A2
Craig-y-nos Powys 59 D5
Craiganor Lodge Perth 229 C5
Craigdam Aberds 256 C3
Craigdarroch Dumfries 183 C5
Craigdarroch Highld 251 A6
Craigdhu Highld 251 B6
Craigearn Aberds 245 A4
Craigellachie Moray 254 B3
Craigencross Dumfries 170 A2
Craigend Perth 219 B6
Craigend Stirl 207 B5
Craigendive Argyll 214 D3
Craigendoran Argyll 215 D6
Craigends Renfs 205 B4
Craigens Argyll 200 B2
Craigens E Ayrs 182 A3
Craighat Stirl 206 B2
Craighead Fife 221 D6
Craighlaw Mains Dumfries 171 A5
Craighouse Argyll 201 B5
Craigie Aberds 245 A6
Craigie Dundee 220 A4
Craigie Perth 219 B6
Craigie Perth 231 D5
Craigie S Ayrs 193 B4
Craigiefield Orkney 282 F5
Craigielaw E Loth 210 C1
Craiglockhart Edin 209 C5
Craigmalloch E Ayrs 182 C2
Craigmaud Aberds 268 D3
Craigmillar Edin 209 C5
Craigmore Argyll 203 B6
Craignant Shrops 110 B1
Craigneuk N Lnrk 194 A2
Craigneuk N Lnrk 207 D5
Craignure Argyll 225 C6
Craigo Angus 233 B4
Craigow Perth 219 D5
Craigrothie Fife 220 C3
Craigroy Moray 266 D2
Craigruie Stirl 217 B4
Craigston Castle Aberds 268 D2
Craigton Aberdeen 245 B5
Craigton Angus 232 C1
Craigton Angus 221 A5
Craigton Highld 264 A2
Craigtown Highld 279 C4
Craik Borders 185 B6
Crail Fife 221 D6
Crailing Borders 187 A5
Crailinghall Borders 187 A5
Craiselound N Lincs 141 D5
Crakehill N Yorks 158 D3
Crakemarsh Staffs 113 B4
Crambe N Yorks 149 A6
Cramlington Northumb 179 B4
Cramond Edin 209 C4
Cramond Bridge Edin 209 C4
Cranage Ches 128 C2
Cranberry Staffs 112 B2
Cranborne Dorset 31 D4
Cranbourne Brack 48 B2
Cranbrook Kent 37 C5
Cranbrook Common Kent 37 C5
Crane Moor S Yorks 139 C6
Crane's Corner Norf 119 D6
Cranfield Beds 83 C6
Cranford London 48 B4
Cranford St Andrew Northants 99 D6
Cranford St John Northants 99 D6
Cranham Glos 63 B4
Cranham London 50 A2
Crank Mers 136 D4
Crank Wood Gtr Man 137 C5
Cranleigh Sur 34 C3
Cranley Suff 104 D2
Cranmer Green Suff 103 D6
Cranmore I o W 18 C2
Cranna Aberds 268 D1
Crannich Argyll 225 B4
Crannoch Moray 267 D5
Cranoe Leics 99 B4
Cransford Suff 88 A4
Cranshaws Borders 210 D3
Cranstal I o M 152 A4
Crantock Corn 4 A2
Cranwell Lincs 116 A3
Cranwich Norf 102 B3
Cranworth Norf 103 A5
Craobh Haven Argyll 213 B5
Crapstone Devon 7 A4
Crarae Argyll 214 C2
Crask Inn Highld 272 B3
Crask of Aigas Highld 251 B6
Craskins Aberds 244 B2
Craster Northumb 189 B5
Craswall Hereford 77 D6
Cratfield Suff 104 D4
Crathes Aberds 245 C4
Crathes Castle and Gardens Aberds 245 C4
Crathie Aberds 243 C5
Crathie Highld 240 C3
Crathorne N Yorks 158 A3
Craven Arms Shrops 94 C2
Crawcrook T & W 178 C3
Crawford Lancs 136 C3
Crawford S Lnrk 195 D4
Crawfordjohn S Lnrk 194 D3
Crawick Dumfries 183 A5
Crawley Hants 32 B3
Crawley Oxon 64 B4
Crawley W Sus 35 C5
Crawley Down W Sus 35 C6
Crawleyside Durham 166 A2
Crawshawbooth Lancs 137 A7
Crawton Aberds 233 A6
Cray N Yorks 156 D3
Cray Perth 231 B5
Crayford London 50 B2
Crayke N Yorks 159 D4
Crays Hill Essex 69 D7
Cray's Pond Oxon 47 A4
Creacombe Devon 26 D3
Creag Ghoraidh W Isles 286 B3
Creagan Argyll 227 B4
Creaguaineach Lodge Highld 228 B2
Creaksea Essex 70 D3
Creaton Northants 99 D4
Creca Dumfries 175 A5
Credenhill Hereford 78 C2
Crediton Devon 12 A3
Creebridge Dumfries 171 A6
Creech Heathfield Som 28 C2
Creech St Michael Som 28 C2
Creed Corn 4 C4
Creekmouth London 50 A1
Creeting Bottoms Suff 88 B2
Creeting St Mary Suff 88 B1
Creeton Lincs 116 C3
Creetown Dumfries 171 B6
Creg-ny-Baa I o M 152 C3
Creggans Argyll 214 B3
Cregneash I o M 152 E1
Cregrina Powys 77 B5
Creich Fife 220 B3
Creigiau Cardiff 41 C5
Cremyll Corn 6 B3
Creslow Bucks 66 A3
Cressage Shrops 94 A3
Cressbrook Derbys 129 B6
Cresselly Pembs 55 D6
Cressing Essex 70 A1
Cresswell Northumb 189 D5
Cresswell Staffs 112 B3
Cresswell Quay Pembs 55 D6
Creswell Derbys 131 B5
Cretingham Suff 88 A3
Cretshengan Argyll 202 B2
Crewe Ches 127 D4
Crewe Ches 128 D2
Crewgreen Powys 110 D2
Crewkerne Som 14 A4
Crianlarich Stirl 216 B3
Cribyn Ceredig 75 C4
Criccieth Gwyn 107 C4
Crich Derbys 130 D3
Crichie Aberds 257 B4
Crichton Midloth 209 D6
Crick Mon 61 D6
Crick Northants 98 D2
Crickadarn Powys 77 C4
Cricket Malherbie Som 28 D3
Cricket St Thomas Som 14 A3
Crickheath Shrops 110 C1
Crickhowell Powys 60 B4
Cricklade Wilts 64 D2
Cricklewood London 49 A5
Cridling Stubbs N Yorks 140 A3
Crieff Perth 218 B3
Crieff Visitors' Centre Perth 218 B3
Criggion Powys 110 D1
Crigglestone W Yorks 139 B6
Crimond Aberds 269 D5
Crimonmogate Aberds 269 D5
Crimplesham Norf 102 A2
Crinan Argyll 213 C5
Cringleford Norf 104 A2
Cringles W Yorks 147 C4
Crinow Pembs 56 A1
Cripplesease Corn 2 B3
Cripplestyle Dorset 31 D4
Cripp's Corner E Sus 37 D5
Croasdale Cumb 162 C3
Crock Street Som 28 D3
Crockenhill Kent 50 C2
Crockernwell Devon 12 B2
Crockerton Wilts 30 A2
Crocketford or Ninemile Bar Dumfries 173 A6
Crockey Hill York 149 C5
Crockham Hill Kent 36 A2
Crockleford Heath Essex 71 A4
Crockness Orkney 283 H4
Croes-goch Pembs 54 A4
Croes-lan Ceredig 73 B6
Croes-y-mwyalch Torf 61 D5
Croeserw Neath 40 B3
Croesor Gwyn 107 B6
Croesyceiliog Carms 57 A4
Croesyceiliog Torf 61 D5
Croesywaun Gwyn 107 A5
Croft Leics 98 B2
Croft Lincs 135 C5
Croft Pembs 73 B4
Croft Warr 137 D5
Croft Motor Racing Circuit N Yorks 157 A6
Croft-on-Tees N Yorks 157 A6
Croftamie Stirl 206 B2
Croftmalloch W Loth 208 D2
Crofton Wilts 45 C6
Crofton W Yorks 140 B1
Crofts of Benachielt Highld 275 A5
Crofts of Haddo Aberds 256 C3
Crofts of Inverthernie Aberds 256 B2
Crofts of Meikle Ardo Aberds 256 B3
Crofty Swansea 57 C5
Croggan Argyll 225 D6
Croglin Cumb 164 A3
Croich Highld 263 A6
Crois Dughaill W Isles 286 D3
Cromarty Highld 264 D3
Cromblet Aberds 256 C2
Cromdale Highld 253 D6
Cromer Herts 68 A2
Cromer Norf 120 A4
Cromford Derbys 130 D2
Cromhall S Glos 62 D2
Cromhall Common S Glos 43 A5
Cromor W Isles 288 E5
Cromra Highld 240 C3
Cromwell Notts 132 C2
Cronberry E Ayrs 193 C6
Crondall Hants 33 A6
Cronk-y-Voddy I o M 152 C3
Cronton Mers 127 A4
Crook Cumb 154 B3
Crook Durham 167 B4
Crook of Devon Perth 219 D5
Crookedholm E Ayrs 193 B4
Crookes S Yorks 130 A3
Crookham Northumb 198 C3
Crookham W Berks 46 C3
Crookham Village Hants 47 D5
Crookhaugh Borders 195 D6
Crookhouse Borders 187 A6
Crooklands Cumb 154 C4
Croome Park, Pershore Worcs 80 C1
Cropredy Oxon 82 C1
Cropston Leics 114 D3
Cropthorne Worcs 80 C2
Cropton N Yorks 159 C6
Cropwell Bishop Notts 115 B4
Cropwell Butler Notts 115 B4
Cros W Isles 288 A6
Crosbost W Isles 288 E4
Crosby Cumb 162 A3
Crosby I o M 152 D3
Crosby N Lincs 141 B6
Crosby Garrett Cumb 155 A6
Crosby Ravensworth Cumb 165 D4
Crosby Villa Cumb 162 A3
Croscombe Som 29 A5
Cross Som 42 D3
Cross Ash Mon 61 B6
Cross-at-Hand Kent 37 B5
Cross Green Devon 11 C4
Cross Green Suff 87 B5
Cross Green Suff 87 B4
Cross Green Warks 81 B6
Cross Hands Carms 57 A5
Cross-hands Carms 73 D4
Cross Hands Pembs 55 C6
Cross Hill Derbys 114 A2
Cross Houses Shrops 94 A3
Cross in Hand E Sus 36 D3
Cross in Hand Leics 98 C2
Cross Inn Ceredig 73 A6
Cross Inn Ceredig 75 B4
Cross Inn Rhondda 41 C5
Cross Keys Kent 36 A3
Cross Lane Head Shrops 95 B5
Cross Lanes Corn 3 C4
Cross Lanes N Yorks 148 A4
Cross Lanes Wrex 110 A2
Cross Oak Powys 60 A3
Cross of Jackston Aberds 256 C2
Cross o'th'hands Derbys 113 A6
Cross Street Suff 104 D2
Crossaig Argyll 202 C3
Crossal Highld 246 A3
Crossapol Argyll 222 C2
Crossburn Falk 207 C6
Crossbush W Sus 20 B3
Crosscanonby Cumb 162 A3
Crossdale Street Norf 120 B4
Crossens Mers 136 B2
Crossflatts W Yorks 147 C5
Crossford Fife 208 B3
Crossford S Lnrk 194 B3
Crossgate Lincs 117 C5
Crossgatehall E Loth 209 D6
Crossgates Fife 208 B4
Crossgates Powys 77 A4
Crossgill Lancs 145 A5
Crosshill E Ayrs 193 C4
Crosshill Fife 209 A4
Crosshill S Ayrs 192 E3
Crosshouse E Ayrs 192 B3
Crossings Cumb 176 B3
Crosskeys Caerph 41 B7
Crosskirk Highld 279 A6
Crosslanes Shrops 110 D2
Crosslee Borders 185 A6
Crosslee Renfs 205 B4
Crossmichael Dumfries 173 B5
Crossmoor Lancs 144 D4
Crossroads Aberds 245 C4
Crossroads E Ayrs 193 B4
Crossway Hereford 79 D4
Crossway Mon 61 B6
Crossway Powys 77 B4
Crossway Green Worcs 79 A6
Crossways Dorset 16 C1
Crosswell Pembs 72 C4
Crosswood Ceredig 75 A5
Crosthwaite Cumb 154 B3
Croston Lancs 136 B3
Crostwick Norf 121 D4
Crostwight Norf 121 C5
Crothair W Isles 288 D2
Crouch Kent 36 A4
Crouch Hill Dorset 29 D7
Crouch House Green Kent 36 B2
Croucheston Wilts 31 C4
Croughton Northants 82 D2
Crovie Aberds 268 C3
Crow Edge S Yorks 139 C4
Crow Hill Hereford 62 A2
Crowan Corn 3 B4
Crowborough E Sus 36 C3
Crowcombe Som 27 B6
Crowdecote Derbys 129 C6
Crowden Derbys 138 D3
Crowell Oxon 66 D2
Crowfield Northants 82 C3
Crowfield Suff 88 B2
Crowhurst E Sus 23 A5
Crowhurst Sur 36 B1
Crowhurst Lane End Sur 36 B1
Crowland Lincs 117 D5
Crowlas Corn 2 B3
Crowle N Lincs 141 B5
Crowle Worcs 80 B2
Crowmarsh Gifford Oxon 47 A4
Crown Corner Suff 104 D3
Crownhill Plym 6 B3
Crownland Suff 103 E6
Crownthorpe Norf 104 A1
Crowntown Corn 3 B4
Crows-an-wra Corn 2 C1
Crowshill Norf 103 A5
Crowsnest Shrops 94 A1
Crowthorne Brack 47 C6
Crowton Ches 127 B5
Croxall Staffs 113 D5
Croxby Lincs 142 D3
Croxdale Durham 167 B5
Croxden Staffs 113 B4
Croxley Green Herts 67 D5
Croxton Cambs 84 A4
Croxton N Lincs 142 B2
Croxton Norf 103 C4
Croxton Staffs 112 B1
Croxton Kerrial Leics 115 C6
Croxtonbank Staffs 112 B1
Croy Highld 252 B3
Croy N Lnrk 207 C5
Croyde Devon 25 B5
Croydon Cambs 85 C5
Croydon London 49 C6
Crubenmore Lodge Highld 241 C4
Cruckmeole Shrops 94 A2
Cruckton Shrops 110 D3
Cruden Bay Aberds 257 C5
Crudgington Telford 111 D5
Crudwell Wilts 63 D5
Crug Powys 93 D5
Crugmeer Corn 9 D5
Crugybar Carms 58 B3
Crulabhig W Isles 288 D2
Crumlin = Crymlyn Caerph 41 B7
Crumpsall Gtr Man 138 C1
Crundale Kent 38 A2
Crundale Pembs 55 C5
Cruwys Morchard Devon 26 D3
Crux Easton Hants 46 D2
Crwbin Carms 57 A4
Crya Orkney 283 G4
Cryers Hill Bucks 66 D3
Crymlyn Gwyn 123 C6
Crymlyn = Crumlin Caerph 41 B7
Crymych Pembs 73 C4
Crynant Neath 40 A2
Crynfryn Ceredig 75 B4
Crystal Palace National Sports Centre London 49 B6
Cuaig Highld 249 A4
Cuan Argyll 213 A5
Cubbington Warks 81 A6
Cubeck N Yorks 156 C3
Cubert Corn 4 B2
Cubley S Yorks 139 C5
Cubley Common Derbys 113 B5
Cublington Bucks 66 A3
Cublington Hereford 78 D2
Cuckfield W Sus 35 D6
Cucklington Som 30 C1
Cuckney Notts 131 B5
Cuckoo Hill Notts 141 D5
Cuddesdon Oxon 65 C7
Cuddington Bucks 66 B2
Cuddington Ches 127 B6
Cuddington Heath Ches 110 A3
Cuddy Hill Lancs 145 D4
Cudham London 36 A2
Cudliptown Devon 11 D6
Cudworth Som 28 D3
Cudworth S Yorks 140 C1
Cuffley Herts 68 C3
Cuiashader W Isles 288 B6
Cuidhir W Isles 286 F2
Cuidhtinis W Isles 287 F5
Culbo Highld 264 D2
Culbokie Highld 252 A2
Culburnie Highld 251 B6
Culcabock Highld 252 B2
Culcairn Highld 264 D2
Culcharry Highld 253 A4
Culcheth Warr 137 D5
Culdrain Aberds 255 C6
Culduie Highld 249 B4
Culford Suff 103 D4
Culgaith Cumb 165 C4
Culham Oxon 65 D6
Culkein Highld 270 A3
Culkein Drumbeg Highld 270 A4
Culkerton Glos 63 D5
Cullachie Highld 253 D5
Cullen Moray 267 C6
Cullercoats T & W 179 B5
Cullicudden Highld 264 D2
Cullingworth W Yorks 147 D4
Cullipool Argyll 213 A5
Cullivoe Shetland 284 C7
Culloch Perth 218 C2
Culloden Highld 252 B3
Culloden Battlefield, Inverness Highld 252 B3
Cullompton Devon 13 A5
Culmaily Highld 265 A4
Culmazie Dumfries 171 B5
Culmington Shrops 94 C2
Culmstock Devon 27 D6
Culnacraig Highld 270 D3
Culnaknock Highld 259 B5
Culpho Suff 88 C3
Culrain Highld 264 A1
Culross Fife 208 B2
Culroy S Ayrs 192 D3
Culsh Aberds 256 B3
Culsh Aberds 243 C6
Culshabbin Dumfries 171 B5
Culswick Shetland 285 J4
Cultercullen Aberds 257 D4
Cults Aberdeen 245 B5
Cults Aberds 255 C6
Cults Dumfries 171 C6
Culverstone Green Kent 50 C3
Culverthorpe Lincs 116 A3
Culworth Northants 82 C2
Culzean Castle, Maybole S Ayrs 192 E2
Culzie Lodge Highld 263 C7
Cumbernauld N Lnrk 207 C5
Cumbernauld Village N Lnrk 207 C5
Cumberworth Lincs 135 B5
Cuminestown Aberds 268 D3
Cumlewick Shetland 285 L6
Cummersdale Cumb 175 C6
Cummertrees Dumfries 174 B4
Cummingston Moray 266 C2
Cumnock E Ayrs 193 C5
Cumnor Oxon 65 C5
Cumrew Cumb 176 D3
Cumwhinton Cumb 176 D2
Cumwhitton Cumb 176 D3
Cundall N Yorks 158 D3
Cunninghamhead N Ayrs 204 D3
Cunnister Shetland 284 D7
Cupar Fife 220 C3
Cupar Muir Fife 220 C3
Cupernham Hants 32 C2
Curbar Derbys 130 B2
Curbridge Hants 32 D4
Curbridge Oxon 64 C4
Curdridge Hants 32 D4
Curdworth Warks 97 B4
Curland Som 28 D2
Curlew Green Suff 89 A4
Currarie S Ayrs 180 B3
Curridge W Berks 46 B2
Currie Edin 209 D4
Curry Mallet Som 28 C3
Curry Rivel Som 28 C3
Curtisden Green Kent 37 B5
Curtisknowle Devon 7 B6
Cury Corn 3 C4
Cushnie Aberds 268 C2
Cushuish Som 28 B1
Cusop Hereford 77 C6
Cutcloy Dumfries 171 D6
Cutcombe Som 27 B4
Cutgate Gtr Man 138 B1
Cutiau Gwyn 90 A4
Cutlers Green Essex 86 D1
Cutnall Green Worcs 80 A1
Cutsdean Glos 80 D3
Cutthorpe Derbys 130 B3
Cutts Shetland 285 K6

Cutty Sark, Greenwich London 49 B6
Cuxham Oxon 66 D1
Cuxton Medway 51 C4
Cuxwold Lincs 142 C3
Cwm Bl Gwent 60 C3
Cwm Denb 125 B5
Cwm Swansea 40 B1
Cwm-byr Carms 58 B3
Cwm-Cewydd Gwyn 91 A6
Cwm-cou Ceredig 73 B5
Cwm-Dulais Swansea 57 B6
Cwm-felin-fach Caerph 41 B6
Cwm Ffrwd-oer Torf 61 C4
Cwm-hesgen Gwyn 108 C2
Cwm-hwnt Rhondda 59 E6
Cwm Irfon Powys 76 C2
Cwm-Llinau Powys 91 B6
Cwm-mawr Carms 57 A5
Cwm-parc Rhondda 40 B4
Cwm Penmachno Conwy 108 A2
Cwm-y-glo Carms 57 A5
Cwm-y-glo Gwyn 123 D5
Cwmafan Neath 40 B2
Cwmaman Rhondda 41 B5
Cwmann Carms 75 D4
Cwmavon Torf 61 C4
Cwmbach Carms 73 D5
Cwmbach Carms 57 B4
Cwmbach Powys 76 B4
Cwmbach Powys 77 D5
Cwmbâch Rhondda 41 A5
Cwmbelan Powys 92 C3
Cwmbran = Cwmbrân Torf 61 D4
Cwmbrân = Cwmbran Torf 61 D4
Cwmbrwyno Ceredig 91 D5
Cwmcarn Caerph 41 B7
Cwmcarvan Mon 61 C6
Cwmcych Pembs 73 C5
Cwmdare Rhondda 41 A4
Cwmderwen Powys 92 A3
Cwmdu Carms 58 B3
Cwmdu Powys 60 A3
Cwmdu Swansea 57 C6
Cwmduad Carms 73 C6
Cwmdwr Carms 59 B4
Cwmfelin Bridgend 40 C3
Cwmfelin M Tydf 41 A5
Cwmfelin Boeth Carms 56 A1
Cwmfelin Mynach Carms 73 D5
Cwmffrwd Carms 57 A4
Cwmgiedd Powys 59 D4
Cwmgors Neath 59 D4
Cwmgwili Carms 57 A5
Cwmgwrach Neath 40 A3
Cwmhiraeth Carms 73 C6
Cwmifor Carms 58 C3
Cwmisfael Carms 57 A4
Cwmllynfell Neath 59 D4
Cwmorgan Carms 73 C5
Cwmpengraig Carms 73 C6
Cwmrhos Powys 60 A3
Cwmsychpant Ceredig 74 D3
Cwmtillery Bl Gwent 60 C4
Cwmwysg Powys 59 C5
Cwmyoy Mon 61 A4
Cwmystwyth Ceredig 92 D1
Cwrt Gwyn 91 B4
Cwrt-newydd Ceredig 74 D3
Cwrt-y-cadno Carms 58 A3
Cwrt-y-gollen Powys 60 B4
Cydweli = Kidwelly Carms 57 B4
Cyffordd Llandudno = Llandudno Junction Conwy 124 B2
Cyffylliog Denb 125 D5
Cyfronydd Powys 93 A5
Cymer Neath 40 B3
Cyncoed Cardiff 41 C6
Cynghordy Carms 59 A5
Cynheidre Carms 57 B4
Cynwyd Denb 109 A5
Cynwyl Elfed Carms 73 D6
Cywarch Gwyn 91 A6

D

Dacre Cumb 164 C2
Dacre N Yorks 147 A5
Dacre Banks N Yorks 147 A5
Daddry Shield Durham 166 B1
Dadford Bucks 82 D3
Dadlington Leics 97 B7
Dafarn Faig Gwyn 107 B4
Dafen Carms 57 B5
Daffy Green Norf 103 A5
Dagenham London 50 A1
Daglingworth Glos 63 C5
Dagnall Bucks 67 B4
Dail Beag W Isles 288 C3
Dail bho Dheas W Isles 288 A5
Dail bho Thuath W Isles 288 A5
Dail Mor W Isles 288 C3
Daill Argyll 200 B3
Dailly S Ayrs 181 A4
Dairsie or Osnaburgh Fife 220 C4
Daisy Hill Gtr Man 137 C5
Dalabrog W Isles 286 D3
Dalavich Argyll 214 A2
Dalbeattie Dumfries 173 B6
Dalblair E Ayrs 182 A4
Dalbog Angus 232 A3
Dalbury Derbys 113 B6
Dalby I o M 152 D2
Dalby N Yorks 159 D5
Dalchalloch Perth 229 B6
Dalchalm Highld 274 D3
Dalchenna Argyll 214 B3
Dalchirach Moray 254 C2
Dalchork Highld 272 C3
Dalchreichart Highld 239 A6
Dalchruin Perth 218 C2
Dalderby Lincs 134 C2
Dale Pembs 54 D4
Dale Abbey Derbys 114 B2
Dale Head Cumb 164 D2
Dale of Walls Shetland 285 H3
Dalelia Highld 235 D6
Daless Highld 253 C4
Dalfaber Highld 242 A2
Dalgarven N Ayrs 204 D2
Dalgety Bay Fife 209 B4
Dalginross Perth 218 B2
Dalguise Perth 230 D3
Dalhalvaig Highld 279 C4
Dalham Suff 86 A3
Dalinlongart Argyll 215 D4
Dalkeith Midloth 209 D6
Dallam Warr 137 D4
Dallas Moray 266 D2
Dalleagles E Ayrs 182 A3
Dallinghoo Suff 88 B3
Dallington E Sus 23 A4
Dallington Northants 83 A4
Dallow N Yorks 157 D5
Dalmadilly Aberds 245 A4
Dalmally Argyll 227 D6
Dalmarnock Glasgow 205 B6
Dalmary Stirl 206 A3
Dalmellington E Ayrs 182 B2
Dalmeny Edin 208 C4
Dalmigavie Highld 241 A5
Dalmigavie Lodge Highld 252 D3
Dalmore Highld 264 D2
Dalmuir W Dunb 205 A4
Dalnabreck Highld 235 D5
Dalnacardoch Lodge Perth 229 A6
Dalnacroich Highld 251 A5
Dalnaglar Castle Perth 231 B5
Dalnahaitnach Highld 253 D4
Dalnaspidal Lodge Perth 229 A5
Dalnavaid Perth 230 B4
Dalnavie Highld 264 C2
Dalnawillan Lodge Highld 279 D6
Dalness Highld 237 D5
Dalnessie Highld 273 C4
Dalqueich Perth 219 D5
Dalreavoch Highld 273 D5
Dalry N Ayrs 204 D2
Dalrymple E Ayrs 192 D3
Dalserf S Lnrk 194 A3
Dalston Cumb 175 C6
Dalswinton Dumfries 184 D2
Dalton Dumfries 174 A4
Dalton Lancs 136 C3
Dalton Northumb 177 D7
Dalton Northumb 178 B3
Dalton N Yorks 158 D3
Dalton N Yorks 157 A5
Dalton S Yorks 140 D2
Dalton-in-Furness Cumb 153 C3
Dalton-le-Dale Durham 168 A2
Dalton-on-Tees N Yorks 157 A6
Dalton Piercy Hrtlpl 168 B2
Dalveich Stirl 217 B6
Dalvina Lodge Highld 278 D2
Dalwhinnie Highld 241 D4
Dalwood Devon 14 A2
Dalwyne S Ayrs 181 B5
Dam Green Norf 103 C6
Dam Side Lancs 144 C4
Damerham Hants 31 D5
Damgate Norf 105 A5
Damnaglaur Dumfries 170 D3
Damside Borders 195 B6
Danbury Essex 70 C1
Danby N Yorks 159 A6
Danby Wiske N Yorks 158 B2
Dandaleith Moray 254 B3
Danderhall Midloth 209 D6
Dane End Herts 68 A3
Danebridge Ches 129 C4
Danehill E Sus 36 D2
Danemoor Green Norf 103 A6
Danesford Shrops 95 B5
Daneshill Hants 47 D4
Dangerous Corner Lancs 136 B4
Danskine E Loth 210 D2
Darcy Lever Gtr Man 137 C6
Darenth Kent 50 B2
Daresbury Halton 127 A5
Darfield S Yorks 140 C2
Darfoulds Notts 131 B5
Dargate Kent 52 C2
Darite Corn 6 A1
Darlaston W Mid 96 B2
Darley N Yorks 147 B6
Darley Bridge Derbys 130 C2
Darley Head N Yorks 147 B5
Darley Moor Motor Racing Circuit Derbys 113 A5
Darlingscott Warks 81 C5
Darlington Darl 167 D5
Darliston Shrops 111 B4
Darlton Notts 132 B2
Darnall S Yorks 130 A3
Darnick Borders 197 C4
Darowen Powys 91 B6
Darra Aberds 256 B2
Darracott Devon 25 B5
Darras Hall Northumb 178 B3
Darrington W Yorks 140 A2
Darsham Suff 89 A5
Dartford Kent 50 B2
Dartford Crossing Kent 50 B2
Dartington Devon 8 A1
Dartington Cider Press Centre Devon 8 A1
Dartington Crystal Devon 25 D5
Dartmeet Devon 12 D1
Dartmouth Devon 8 B2
Darton S Yorks 139 C6
Darvel E Ayrs 193 B5
Darwell Hole E Sus 23 A4
Darwen Blkburn 137 A5
Datchet Windsor 48 B2
Datchworth Herts 68 B2
Datchworth Green Herts 68 B2
Daubhill Gtr Man 137 C6
Daugh of Kinermony Moray 254 B3
Dauntsey Wilts 44 A3
Dava Moray 253 C6
Davenham Ches 127 B6
Davenport Green Ches 128 B3
Daventry Northants 82 A2
David's Well Powys 93 D4
Davidson's Mains Edin 209 C5
Davidstow Corn 10 C2
Davington Dumfries 185 B5
Daviot Aberds 256 D2
Daviot Highld 252 C3
Davoch of Grange Moray 267 D5
Davyhulme Gtr Man 137 D6
Dawley Telford 95 A4
Dawlish Devon 13 D4
Dawlish Warren Devon 13 D4
Dawn Conwy 124 B3
Daws Heath Essex 51 A5
Daw's House Corn 10 C4
Dawsmere Lincs 118 B1
Dayhills Staffs 112 B3
Daylesford Glos 64 A3
Ddôl-Cownwy Powys 109 D5
Ddrydwy Anglesey 122 C3
Deadwater Northumb 187 D5
Deaf Hill Durham 167 B6
Deal Kent 53 D5
Deal Hall Essex 71 D4
Dean Cumb 162 B3
Dean Devon 7 A6
Dean Devon 25 A6
Dean Dorset 30 D3
Dean Hants 33 D4
Dean Som 29 A6
Dean Prior Devon 7 A6
Dean Row Ches 128 A3
Deanburnhaugh Borders 186 B2
Deane Gtr Man 137 C5
Deane Hants 46 D3
Deanich Lodge Highld 263 B5
Deanland Dorset 30 D3
Deans W Loth 208 D3
Deanscales Cumb 162 B3
Deanshanger Northants 83 D4
Deanston Stirl 218 D2
Dearham Cumb 162 A3
Debach Suff 88 B3
Debden Essex 86 D1
Debden Essex 68 D4
Debden Cross Essex 86 D1
Debenham Suff 88 A2
Dechmont W Loth 208 C3
Deddington Oxon 82 D1
Dedham Essex 87 D6
Dedham Heath Essex 87 D6
Deebank Aberds 244 C3
Deene Northants 99 B6
Deenethorpe Northants 99 B6
Deep Sea World, North Queensferry Fife 208 B4
Deepcar S Yorks 139 D5
Deepcut Sur 34 A2
Deepdale Cumb 155 C6
Deeping Gate Lincs 100 A3
Deeping St James Lincs 100 A3
Deeping St Nicholas Lincs 117 D5
Deerhill Moray 267 D5
Deerhurst Glos 63 A4
Deerness Orkney 283 G6
Defford Worcs 80 C2
Defynnog Powys 59 C6
Deganwy Conwy 124 B2
Deighton N Yorks 158 A2
Deighton W Yorks 139 B4
Deighton York 149 C5
Deiniolen Gwyn 123 D5
Delabole Corn 9 C6
Delamere Ches 127 C5
Delfrigs Aberds 257 D4
Dell Lodge Highld 242 A3
Delliefure Highld 254 C1
Delnabo Moray 243 A4
Delnadamph Aberds 243 B5
Delph Gtr Man 138 C2
Delves Durham 166 A4
Delvine Perth 231 D5
Dembleby Lincs 116 B3
Denaby Main S Yorks 140 D2
Denbigh = Dinbych Denb 125 C5
Denbury Devon 8 A2
Denby Derbys 114 A1
Denby Dale W Yorks 139 C5
Denchworth Oxon 65 D4
Dendron Cumb 153 C3
Denel End Beds 84 D2
Denend Aberds 255 C7
Denford Northants 100 D1
Dengie Essex 70 C3
Denham Bucks 48 A3
Denham Suff 86 A3
Denham Suff 104 D2
Denham Green Bucks 48 A3
Denham Street Suff 104 D2
Denhead Aberds 269 D4
Denhead Fife 221 C4
Denhead of Arbilot Angus 232 D3
Denhead of Gray Dundee 220 A3
Denholm Borders 187 B4
Denholme W Yorks 147 D4
Denholme Clough W Yorks 147 D4
Denio Gwyn 106 C3
Denmead Hants 33 D5
Denmore Aberdeen 245 A6
Denmoss Aberds 256 B1
Dennington Suff 88 A3
Denny Falk 207 B6
Denny Lodge Hants 18 A2
Dennyloanhead Falk 207 B6
Denshaw Gtr Man 138 B2
Denside Aberds 245 C5
Densole Kent 39 A4
Denston Suff 86 B3
Denstone Staffs 113 A5
Dent Cumb 155 C6
Denton Cambs 100 C3
Denton Darl 167 D5
Denton E Sus 22 B2
Denton Gtr Man 138 D2
Denton Kent 39 A4
Denton Lincs 115 B6
Denton Norf 104 C3
Denton Northants 83 B5
Denton N Yorks 147 C5
Denton Oxon 65 C6
Denton's Green Mers 136 D3
Denver Norf 102 A2
Denwick Northumb 189 B5
Deopham Norf 103 A6
Deopham Green Norf 103 B6
Depden Suff 86 B3
Depden Green Suff 86 B3
Deptford London 49 B6
Deptford Wilts 31 B4
Derby Derby 114 B1
Derbyhaven I o M 152 E2
Dereham Norf 120 D1
Deri Caerph 41 A6
Derril Devon 10 A4
Derringstone Kent 39 A4
Derrington Staffs 112 C2
Derriton Devon 10 A4
Derry Hill Wilts 44 B3
Derryguaig Argyll 224 C3
Derrythorpe N Lincs 141 C6
Dersingham Norf 118 B3
Dervaig Argyll 224 A3
Derwen Denb 125 D5
Derwenlas Powys 91 C5
Desborough Northants 99 C5
Desford Leics 98 A1
Detchant Northumb 199 C4
Detling Kent 37 A5
Deuddwr Powys 110 D1
Devauden Mon 61 D6
Devil's Bridge Ceredig 75 A6
Devizes Wilts 44 C4
Devol Invclyd 204 A3
Devon & Exeter Racecourse Devon 13 C4
Devonport Plym 6 B3
Devonside Clack 208 A2
Devoran Corn 4 D2
Dewar Borders 196 B2
Dewlish Dorset 16 B1
Dewsbury W Yorks 139 A5
Dewsbury Moor W Yorks 139 A5
Dewshall Court Hereford 78 D2
Dhoon I o M 152 C4
Dhoor I o M 152 B4
Dhowin I o M 152 A4
Dial Post W Sus 21 A4
Dibden Hants 18 A3
Dibden Purlieu Hants 18 A3
Dickleburgh Norf 104 C2
Didbrook Glos 80 D3
Didcot Oxon 46 A3
Diddington Cambs 84 A3
Diddlebury Shrops 94 C3
Didley Hereford 78 D2
Didling W Sus 20 A1
Didmarton Glos 44 A2
Didsbury Gtr Man 138 D1
Didworthy Devon 7 A5
Digby Lincs 133 D5
Digg Highld 259 B4
Diggerland, Cullompton Devon 13 A5
Diggerland, Langley Park Durham 167 A5
Diggle Gtr Man 138 C3
Digmoor Lancs 136 C3
Digswell Park Herts 68 B2
Dihewyd Ceredig 74 C3
Dilham Norf 121 C5
Dilhorne Staffs 112 A3
Dillarburn S Lnrk 194 B3
Dillington Cambs 84 A3
Dilston Northumb 178 C1
Dilton Marsh Wilts 30 A2
Dilwyn Hereford 78 B2
Dinas Carms 73 C5
Dinas Gwyn 106 C2
Dinas Cross Pembs 72 C3
Dinas Dinlle Gwyn 107 A4
Dinas-Mawddwy Gwyn 91 A6
Dinas Powys V Glam 41 D6
Dinbych = Denbigh Denb 125 C5
Dinbych-y-Pysgod = Tenby Pembs 56 B1
Dinder Som 29 A5
Dinedor Hereford 78 D3
Dingestow Mon 61 B6
Dingle Mers 126 A3
Dingleden Kent 37 C6
Dingley Northants 99 C4
Dingwall Highld 252 A1
Dinlabyre Borders 186 D4
Dinmael Conwy 109 A5
Dinnet Aberds 244 C1
Dinnington Som 28 D4
Dinnington S Yorks 131 A5
Dinnington T & W 179 B4
Dinorwic Gwyn 123 D5
Dinton Bucks 66 B2
Dinton Wilts 31 B4
Dinwoodie Mains Dumfries 185 C4
Dinworthy Devon 24 D4
Dippen N Ayrs 191 C6
Dippenhall Sur 33 A7
Dipple Moray 266 D4
Dipple S Ayrs 181 A4
Diptford Devon 7 B6
Dipton Durham 178 D3
Dirdhu Highld 254 D1
Dirleton E Loth 210 B2
Dirt Pot Northumb 165 A6
Discoed Powys 77 A6
Discovery Point Dundee 220 B4
Diseworth Leics 114 C2
Dishes Orkney 282 E7
Dishforth N Yorks 158 D2
Disley Ches 129 A4
Diss Norf 104 D2
Disserth Powys 76 B4
Distington Cumb 162 B3
Ditchampton Wilts 31 B4
Ditcheat Som 29 B6
Ditchingham Norf 104 B4
Ditchling E Sus 21 A6
Ditherington Shrops 111 D4
Dittisham Devon 8 B2
Ditton Halton 127 A4
Ditton Kent 37 A5
Ditton Green Cambs 86 B2
Ditton Priors Shrops 95 C4
Divach Highld 251 D6
Divlyn Carms 59 B4
Dixton Glos 80 D2
Dixton Mon 61 B7
Dobcross Gtr Man 138 C2
Dobwalls Corn 5 A7
Doc Penfro = Pembroke Dock Pembs 55 D5
Doccombe Devon 12 C2
Dochfour Ho. Highld 252 C2
Dochgarroch Highld 252 B2
Docking Norf 119 B4
Docklow Hereford 78 B3
Dockray Cumb 164 C1
Dockroyd W Yorks 147 D4
Dodburn Borders 186 C3
Doddinghurst Essex 69 D5
Doddington Cambs 101 B5
Doddington Kent 51 D6
Doddington Lincs 133 B4
Doddington Northumb 198 C3
Doddington Shrops 95 D4
Doddiscombsleigh Devon 12 C3
Dodford Northants 82 A3
Dodford Worcs 96 D2
Dodington S Glos 43 A6
Dodleston Ches 126 C3
Dods Leigh Staffs 112 B4
Dodworth S Yorks 139 C6
Doe Green Warr 127 A5
Doe Lea Derbys 131 C4
Dog Village Devon 13 B4
Dogdyke Lincs 134 D2
Dogmersfield Hants 47 D5
Dogridge Wilts 45 A4
Dogsthorpe P'boro 100 A3
Dol-fôr Powys 91 B6
Dôl-y-Bont Ceredig 90 D4
Dol-y-cannau Powys 77 C6
Dolanog Powys 109 D5
Dolau Powys 77 A5
Dolau Rhondda 41 C4
Dolbenmaen Gwyn 107 B5
Dolfach Powys 91 B7
Dolfor Powys 93 C5
Dolgarrog Conwy 124 C2
Dolgellau Gwyn 91 A5
Dolgran Carms 58 B1
Dolhendre Gwyn 108 B3
Doll Highld 274 D2
Dollar Clack 208 A2
Dolley Green Powys 77 A6
Dollwen Ceredig 91 D4
Dolphin Flint 126 B1
Dolphinholme Lancs 145 B5
Dolphinton S Lnrk 195 B6
Dolton Devon 25 D6
Dolwen Conwy 124 B3
Dolwen Powys 92 A3
Dolwyd Conwy 124 B3
Dolwyddelan Conwy 124 D2
Dolyhir Powys 77 B6
Doncaster S Yorks 140 C3
Doncaster Racecourse S Yorks 140 C4
Dones Green Ches 127 B6
Donhead St Andrew Wilts 30 C3
Donhead St Mary Wilts 30 C3
Donibristle Fife 209 B4
Donington Lincs 117 B5
Donington on Bain Lincs 134 A2
Donington Park Motor Racing Circuit Leics 114 C2
Donington South Ing Lincs 117 B5
Donisthorpe Leics 113 D7
Donkey Town Sur 48 C2
Donnington Glos 64 A2
Donnington Hereford 79 D5
Donnington Shrops 94 A3
Donnington Telford 111 D6
Donnington W Berks 46 C2
Donnington W Sus 20 B1
Donnington Wood Telford 111 D6
Donyatt Som 28 D3
Doonfoot S Ayrs 192 D3
Dorback Lodge Highld 242 A3
Dorchester Dorset 15 B6
Dorchester Oxon 65 D6
Dorchester Abbey, Wallingford Oxon 65 D6
Dordon Warks 97 A5
Dore S Yorks 130 A3
Dores Highld 252 C1
Dorking Sur 35 B4
Dormansland Sur 36 B2
Dormanstown Redcar 168 C3
Dormington Hereford 78 C3
Dormston Worcs 80 B2
Dornal S Ayrs 181 D4
Dorney Bucks 48 B2
Dornie Highld 249 D5
Dornoch Highld 264 B3
Dornock Dumfries 175 B5
Dorrery Highld 279 C6
Dorridge W Mid 97 D4
Dorrington Lincs 133 D5
Dorrington Shrops 94 A2
Dorsington Warks 80 C4
Dorstone Hereford 77 C7
Dorton Bucks 66 B1
Dorusduain Highld 250 D1
Dosthill Staffs 97 B5
Dottery Dorset 15 B4
Doublebois Corn 5 A6
Dougarie N Ayrs 191 B4
Doughton Glos 63 D4
Douglas I o M 152 D3
Douglas S Lnrk 194 C3
Douglas & Angus Dundee 220 A4
Douglas Water S Lnrk 194 C3
Douglas West S Lnrk 194 C3
Douglastown Angus 232 D2
Doulting Som 29 A6
Dounby Orkney 282 E3
Doune Highld 272 D2
Doune Stirl 218 D2
Doune Park Aberds 268 C2
Douneside Aberds 244 B1

Dounie Highld 264 A1
Dounreay Highld 279 B5
Dousland Devon 7 A4
Dovaston Shrops 110 C2
Dove Cottage and Wordsworth Museum Cumb 154 A2
Dove Holes Derbys 129 B5
Dovenby Cumb 162 A3
Dover Kent 39 A5
Dover Castle Kent 39 A5
Dovercourt Essex 88 D3
Doverdale Worcs 79 A6
Doveridge Derbys 113 B5
Doversgreen Sur 35 B5
Dowally Perth 230 D4
Dowbridge Lancs 144 D4
Dowdeswell Glos 63 B5
Dowlais M Tydf 60 C2
Dowland Devon 25 D6
Dowlish Wake Som 28 D3
Down Ampney Glos 64 D2
Down Hatherley Glos 63 A4
Down St Mary Devon 12 A2
Down Thomas Devon 7 B4
Downcraig Ferry N Ayrs 204 C1
Downderry Corn 6 B2
Downe London 50 C1
Downend I o W 18 C4
Downend S Glos 43 B5
Downend W Berks 46 B2
Downfield Dundee 220 A3
Downgate Corn 11 D4
Downham Essex 70 D1
Downham Lancs 146 C1
Downham Northumb 198 C2
Downham Market Norf 102 A2
Downhead Som 29 A6
Downhill Perth 219 A5
Downhill T & W 179 D5
Downholland Cross Lancs 136 C2
Downholme N Yorks 157 B5
Downies Aberds 245 C6
Downley Bucks 66 D3
Downside Som 29 A6
Downside Sur 35 A4
Downton Hants 17 B6
Downton Wilts 31 C5
Downton on the Rock Hereford 94 D2
Dowsby Lincs 116 C4
Dowsdale Lincs 117 D5
Dowthwaitehead Cumb 163 B6
Doxey Staffs 112 C3
Doxford Northumb 189 A4
Doxford Park T & W 179 D5
Doynton S Glos 43 B6
Draffan S Lnrk 194 B2
Dragonby N Lincs 141 B7
Drakeland Corner Devon 7 B4
Drakemyre N Ayrs 204 C2
Drake's Broughton Worcs 80 C2
Drakes Cross Worcs 96 D3
Drakewalls Corn 11 D5
Draughton Northants 99 D4
Draughton N Yorks 147 B4
Drax N Yorks 141 A4
Draycote Warks 98 D1
Draycott Derbys 114 B2
Draycott Glos 81 D4
Draycott Som 42 D3
Draycott in the Clay Staffs 113 C5
Draycott in the Moors Staffs 112 A3
Drayford Devon 26 D2
Drayton Leics 99 B5
Drayton Lincs 117 B5
Drayton Norf 120 D3
Drayton Oxon 82 C1
Drayton Oxon 65 D5
Drayton Ptsmth 19 A5
Drayton Som 28 C4
Drayton Worcs 96 D2
Drayton Bassett Staffs 97 A4
Drayton Beauchamp Bucks 67 B4
Drayton Manor Park, Tamworth Staffs 97 A4
Drayton Parslow Bucks 66 A3
Drayton St Leonard Oxon 65 D6
Dre-fach Ceredig 75 D4
Dre-fach Carms 57 A6
Dreamland Theme Park, Margate Kent 53 B5
Drebley N Yorks 147 B4
Dreemskerry I o M 152 B4
Dreenhill Pembs 55 C5
Drefach Carms 73 C6
Drefach Carms 57 A5
Drefelin Carms 73 C6
Dreghorn N Ayrs 192 B3
Drellingore Kent 39 A4
Drem E Loth 210 C2
Dresden Stoke 112 A3
Dreumasdal W Isles 286 C3
Drewsteignton Devon 12 B2
Driby Lincs 134 B3
Driffield E Yorks 150 B3
Driffield Glos 63 D6
Drigg Cumb 153 A1
Drighlington W Yorks 139 A5
Drimnin Highld 225 A4
Drimpton Dorset 14 A4
Drimsynie Argyll 215 B4
Drinisiadar W Isles 288 H2
Drinkstone Suff 87 A5
Drinkstone Green Suff 87 A5
Drishaig Argyll 215 A4
Drissaig Argyll 214 A2
Drochil Borders 195 B6
Drointon Staffs 112 C4
Droitwich Spa Worcs 80 A1
Droman Highld 276 C2
Dron Perth 219 C6
Dronfield Derbys 130 B3
Dronfield Woodhouse Derbys 130 B3
Drongan E Ayrs 182 A2
Dronley Angus 220 A3
Droxford Hants 33 D5
Droylsden Gtr Man 138 D2
Druid Denb 109 A5
Druidston Pembs 55 C4
Druimarbin Highld 237 B4
Druimavuic Argyll 227 B5
Druimdrishaig Argyll 202 A2
Druimindarroch Highld 235 B5
Druimyeon More Argyll 202 C1
Drum Argyll 203 A4
Drum Perth 219 D5
Drumbeg Highld 270 A4
Drumblade Aberds 255 B6
Drumblair Aberds 256 B1
Drumbuie Dumfries 182 D3
Drumbuie Highld 249 C4
Drumburgh Cumb 175 C5
Drumburn Dumfries 174 B2
Drumchapel Glasgow 205 A5
Drumchardine Highld 252 B1
Drumchork Highld 261 B5
Drumclog S Lnrk 193 B6
Drumderfit Highld 252 A2
Drumeldrie Fife 220 D4
Drumelzier Borders 195 C6
Drumfearn Highld 247 C5
Drumgask Highld 241 C4
Drumgley Angus 232 C2
Drumguish Highld 241 C5
Drumin Moray 254 C2
Drumlasie Aberds 244 B3
Drumlemble Argyll 190 D2
Drumligair Aberds 245 A6
Drumlithie Aberds 245 D4
Drummoddie Dumfries 171 C5
Drummond Highld 264 D2
Drummore Dumfries 170 D3
Drummuir Moray 255 B4
Drummuir Castle Moray 255 B4
Drumnadrochit Highld 251 D7
Drumnagorrach Moray 267 D6
Drumoak Aberds 245 C4
Drumpark Dumfries 183 D6
Drumphail Dumfries 171 A4
Drumrash Dumfries 173 A4
Drumrunie Highld 271 D4
Drums Aberds 257 D4
Drumsallie Highld 236 B3
Drumstinchall Dumfries 173 C6
Drumsturdy Angus 221 A4
Drumtochty Castle Aberds 244 E3
Drumtroddan Dumfries 171 C5
Drumuie Highld 259 D4
Drumuillie Highld 253 D5
Drumvaich Stirl 217 D6
Drumwhindle Aberds 257 C4
Drunkendub Angus 233 D4
Drury Flint 126 C2
Drury Square Norf 119 D6
Drusillas Park, Polegate E Sus 22 B3
Dry Doddington Lincs 115 A6
Dry Drayton Cambs 85 A5
Drybeck Cumb 165 D4
Drybridge Moray 267 C5
Drybridge N Ayrs 192 B3
Drybrook Glos 62 B2
Dryburgh Borders 197 C4
Dryhope Borders 196 D1
Drylaw Edin 209 C5
Drym Corn 3 B4
Drymen Stirl 206 B2
Drymuir Aberds 257 B4
Drynoch Highld 246 A3
Dryslwyn Carms 58 C2
Dryton Shrops 94 A3
Dubford Aberds 268 C3
Dubton Angus 232 C3
Duchally Highld 271 C6
Duchlage Argyll 206 B1
Duck Corner Suff 89 C4
Duckington Ches 127 D4
Ducklington Oxon 65 C4
Duckmanton Derbys 131 B4
Duck's Cross Beds 84 B3
Duddenhoe End Essex 85 D6
Duddingston Edin 209 C5
Duddington Northants 100 A1
Duddleswell E Sus 36 D2
Duddo Northumb 198 B3
Duddon Ches 127 C5
Duddon Bridge Cumb 153 B3
Dudleston Shrops 110 B2
Dudleston Heath Shrops 110 B2
Dudley T & W 179 B4
Dudley W Mid 96 B2
Dudley Port W Mid 96 B2
Dudley Zoological Gardens W Mid 96 B2
Duffield Derbys 114 A1
Duffryn Newport 42 A1
Duffryn Neath 40 B3
Dufftown Moray 254 C4
Duffus Moray 266 C2
Dufton Cumb 165 C4
Duggleby N Yorks 150 A1
Duirinish Highld 249 C4
Duisdalemore Highld 247 C6
Duisky Highld 237 B4
Dukestown Bl Gwent 60 B3
Dukinfield Gtr Man 138 D2
Dulas Anglesey 123 B4
Dulcote Som 29 A5
Dulford Devon 13 A5
Dull Perth 230 D2
Dullatur N Lnrk 207 C5
Dullingham Cambs 86 B2
Dulnain Bridge Highld 253 D5
Duloe Beds 84 A3
Duloe Corn 6 B1
Dulsie Highld 253 B5
Dulverton Som 27 C4
Dulwich London 49 B6
Dumbarton W Dunb 205 A4
Dumbleton Glos 80 D3
Dumcrieff Dumfries 185 B4
Dumfries Dumfries 174 A2
Dumgoyne Stirl 206 B3
Dummer Hants 33 A4
Dumpford W Sus 34 D1
Dumpton Kent 53 C5
Dun Angus 233 C4
Dun Charlabhaigh W Isles 288 C2
Dunain Ho. Highld 252 B2
Dunalastair Perth 229 C6
Dunan Highld 247 B4
Dunans Argyll 214 C3
Dunball Som 28 A3
Dunbar E Loth 210 C3
Dunbeath Highld 275 B5
Dunbeg Argyll 226 C3
Dunblane Stirl 218 D2
Dunbog Fife 220 C2
Duncanston Aberds 255 D6
Duncanston Highld 252 A1
Dunchurch Warks 98 D1
Duncote Northants 82 B3
Duncow Dumfries 184 D2
Duncraggan Stirl 217 D5
Duncrievie Perth 219 D6
Duncton W Sus 20 A2
Dundas Ho. Orkney 283 K5
Dundee Dundee 220 A4
Dundee Airport Dundee 220 B3
Dundeugh Dumfries 182 D3
Dundon Som 29 B4
Dundonald S Ayrs 192 B3
Dundonnell Highld 262 B2
Dundonnell Hotel Highld 262 B2
Dundonnell House Highld 262 B3
Dundraw Cumb 175 D5
Dundreggan Highld 239 A7
Dundreggan Lodge Highld 240 A1
Dundrennan Dumfries 173 D5
Dundry N Som 43 C4
Dunecht Aberds 245 B4
Dunfermline Fife 208 B3
Dunfield Glos 64 D2
Dunford Bridge S Yorks 139 C4
Dungworth S Yorks 130 A2
Dunham Notts 132 B3
Dunham Massey Gtr Man 128 A2
Dunham-on-the-Hill Ches 127 B4
Dunham Town Gtr Man 128 A2
Dunhampton Worcs 79 A6
Dunholme Lincs 133 B5
Dunino Fife 221 C5
Dunipace Falk 207 B6
Dunira Perth 218 B2
Dunkeld Perth 230 D4
Dunkerton Bath 43 D6
Dunkeswell Devon 13 A6
Dunkeswick N Yorks 148 C2
Dunkirk Kent 52 D2
Dunkirk Norf 120 C4
Dunk's Green Kent 36 A4
Dunlappie Angus 232 B3
Dunley Hants 46 D2
Dunley Worcs 79 A5
Dunlichity Lodge Highld 252 C2
Dunlop E Ayrs 205 D4
Dunmaglass Lodge Highld 252 D1
Dunmore Argyll 202 B2
Dunmore Falk 208 B1
Dunnet Highld 280 A4
Dunnichen Angus 232 D3
Dunninald Angus 233 C5
Dunning Perth 219 C5
Dunnington E Yorks 151 B4
Dunnington Warks 80 B3
Dunnington York 149 B5
Dunnockshaw Lancs 137 A7
Dunollie Argyll 226 C3
Dunoon Argyll 203 A6
Dunragit Dumfries 170 B3
Dunrobin Castle Museum & Gardens Highld 274 D2
Dunrostan Argyll 213 D5
Duns Borders 198 A1
Duns Tew Oxon 65 A5
Dunsby Lincs 116 C4
Dunscore Dumfries 183 D6
Dunscroft S Yorks 141 C4
Dunsdale Redcar 168 D4
Dunsden Green Oxon 47 B5
Dunsfold Sur 34 C3
Dunsford Devon 12 C3
Dunshalt Fife 220 C2
Dunshillock Aberds 257 B4
Dunskey Ho. Dumfries 170 B2
Dunsley N Yorks 169 D6
Dunsmore Bucks 66 C3
Dunsop Bridge Lancs 145 B6
Dunstable Beds 67 A5
Dunstall Staffs 113 C5
Dunstall Common Worcs 80 C1
Dunstall Green Suff 86 A3
Dunstan Northumb 189 B5
Dunstan Steads Northumb 189 A5
Dunster Som 27 A4
Dunster Castle, Minehead Som 27 A4
Duntisbourne Lincs 133 C5
Dunston Norf 104 A3
Dunston Staffs 112 D3
Dunston T & W 179 C4
Dunsville S Yorks 140 C4
Dunswell E Yorks 150 D3
Dunsyre S Lnrk 195 B5
Dunterton Devon 11 D4
Duntisbourne Abbots Glos 63 C5
Duntisbourne Leer Glos 63 C5
Duntisbourne Rouse Glos 63 C5
Duntish Dorset 15 A6
Duntocher W Dunb 205 A4
Dunton Beds 84 C4
Dunton Bucks 66 A3
Dunton Norf 119 B5
Dunton Bassett Leics 98 B2
Dunton Green Kent 36 A3
Dunton Wayletts Essex 69 D6
Duntulm Highld 259 A4
Dunure S Ayrs 192 D2
Dunvant Swansea 57 C5
Dunvegan Highld 258 D2
Dunvegan Castle Highld 258 C2
Dunwich Suff 105 D5
Dunwood Staffs 129 D4
Dupplin Castle Perth 219 C5
Durdar Cumb 175 C7
Durgates E Sus 36 C4
Durham Durham 167 A5
Durham Cathedral Durham 167 A5
Durham Tees Valley Airport Stockton 167 D6
Durisdeer Dumfries 183 B6
Durisdeermill Dumfries 183 B6
Durkar W Yorks 139 B6
Durleigh Som 28 B2
Durley Hants 32 D4
Durley Wilts 45 C6
Durnamuck Highld 262 A2
Durness Highld 277 B5
Durno Aberds 256 D2
Duror Highld 236 D3
Durran Argyll 214 B2
Durran Highld 280 B3
Durrington Wilts 31 A5
Durrington W Sus 21 B4
Dursley Glos 62 D3
Durston Som 28 C2
Durweston Dorset 16 A2
Dury Shetland 285 G6
Duston Northants 83 A4
Duthil Highld 253 D5
Dutlas Powys 93 D6
Duton Hill Essex 69 A6
Dutson Corn 10 C4
Dutton Ches 127 B5
Duxford Cambs 85 C6
Duxford Oxon 65 D4
Duxford Airfield (Imperial War Museum), Sawston Cambs 85 C6
Dwygyfylchi Conwy 124 B2
Dwyran Anglesey 123 D4
Dyce Aberdeen 245 A5
Dye House Northumb 178 D1
Dyffryn Bridgend 40 B3
Dyffryn Carms 73 D6
Dyffryn Pembs 72 C2
Dyffryn Ardudwy Gwyn 107 D5
Dyffryn Castell Ceredig 91 D5
Dyffryn Ceidrych Carms 59 C4
Dyffryn Cellwen Neath 59 E5
Dyke Lincs 116 C4
Dyke Moray 253 A5
Dykehead Angus 232 B1
Dykehead N Lnrk 207 E6
Dykehead Stirl 206 A3
Dykelands Aberds 233 B5
Dykends Angus 231 C6
Dykeside Aberds 256 B2
Dykesmains N Ayrs 204 D2
Dylife Powys 91 C6
Dymchurch Kent 38 C2
Dymock Glos 79 D5
Dyrham S Glos 43 B6
Dyrham Park S Glos 43 B6
Dysart Fife 209 A6
Dyserth Denb 125 B5

E

Eachwick Northumb 178 B3
Eadar Dha Fhadhail W Isles 287 A5
Eagland Hill Lancs 144 C4
Eagle Lincs 132 C3
Eagle Barnsdale Lincs 132 C3
Eagle Moor Lincs 132 C3
Eaglescliffe Stockton 168 D2
Eaglesfield Cumb 162 B3
Eaglesfield Dumfries 175 A5
Eaglesham E Renf 205 C5
Eaglethorpe Northants 100 B2
Eairy I o M 152 D2
Eakley Lanes M Keynes 83 B5
Eakring Notts 132 C1
Ealand N Lincs 141 B5
Ealing London 49 A4
Eals Northumb 177 D4
Eamont Bridge Cumb 164 C3
Earby Lancs 146 C3
Earcroft Blkburn 137 A5
Eardington Shrops 95 B5
Eardisland Hereford 78 B2
Eardisley Hereford 77 C7
Eardiston Shrops 110 C2
Eardiston Worcs 79 A4
Earith Cambs 101 D5
Earl Shilton Leics 98 B1
Earl Soham Suff 88 A3
Earl Sterndale Derbys 129 C5
Earl Stonham Suff 88 B2
Earle Northumb 188 A2
Earley Wokingham 47 B5
Earlham Norf 104 A3
Earlish Highld 258 B3
Earls Barton Northants 83 A5
Earls Colne Essex 70 A2
Earl's Croome Worcs 79 C6
Earl's Green Suff 87 A6
Earlsdon W Mid 97 D6
Earlsferry Fife 221 E4
Earlsfield Lincs 116 B2
Earlsford Aberds 256 C3
Earlsheaton W Yorks 139 A5
Earlsmill Moray 253 A5
Earlston Borders 197 C4
Earlston E Ayrs 193 B4
Earlswood Mon 61 D6
Earlswood Sur 35 B5
Earlswood Warks 96 D4
Earnley W Sus 19 B7
Earsairidh W Isles 286 G3
Earsdon T & W 179 B5
Earsham Norf 104 C4
Earswick York 149 B5
Eartham W Sus 20 B2
Easby N Yorks 159 A4
Easby N Yorks 157 A5
Easdale Argyll 213 A5
Easebourne W Sus 34 D1
Easenhall Warks 98 D1
Eashing Sur 34 B2
Easington Bucks 66 B1
Easington Durham 168 A2
Easington E Yorks 143 B5
Easington Northumb 199 C5
Easington Oxon 82 D1
Easington Oxon 66 D1
Easington Redcar 169 D5
Easington Colliery Durham 168 A2
Easington Lane T & W 167 A6
Easingwold N Yorks 148 A4
Easole Street Kent 53 D4
Eassie Angus 232 D1
East Aberthaw V Glam 41 E5
East Adderbury Oxon 82 D1
East Allington Devon 7 C6
East Anstey Devon 26 C3
East Appleton N Yorks 157 B6
East Ardsley W Yorks 139 A6
East Ashling W Sus 19 A7
East Auchronie Aberds 245 B5
East Ayton N Yorks 160 C3
East Bank Bl Gwent 60 C4
East Barkwith Lincs 133 A6
East Barming Kent 37 A5
East Barnby N Yorks 169 D6
East Barnet London 68 D2
East Barns E Loth 211 C4
East Barsham Norf 119 B6
East Beckham Norf 120 B3
East Bedfont London 48 B3
East Bergholt Suff 87 D6
East Bilney Norf 119 D6
East Blatchington E Sus 22 B2
East Boldre Hants 18 A2
East Brent Som 42 D2
East Bridgford Notts 115 A4
East Buckland Devon 26 B1
East Budleigh Devon 13 C5
East Burrafirth Shetland 285 H5
East Burton Dorset 16 C2
East Butsfield Durham 166 A4
East Butterwick N Lincs 141 C6
East Cairnbeg Aberds 233 A5
East Calder W Loth 208 D3
East Carleton Norf 104 A2
East Carlton Northants 99 C5
East Carlton W Yorks 147 C6
East Chaldon Dorset 16 C1
East Challow Oxon 46 A1
East Chiltington E Sus 21 A6
East Chinnock Som 29 D4
East Chisenbury Wilts 45 D5
East Clandon Sur 34 A3
East Claydon Bucks 66 A2
East Clyne Highld 274 D2
East Coker Som 29 D5
East Combe Som 27 B6
East Common N Yorks 149 D5
East Compton Som 29 A6
East Cottingwith E Yorks 149 C6
East Cowes I o W 18 B4
East Cowick E Yorks 141 A4
East Cowton N Yorks 157 A7
East Cramlington Northumb 179 B4
East Cranmore Som 29 A6
East Creech Dorset 16 C3
East Croachy Highld 252 D2
East Croftmore Highld 242 A2
East Curthwaite Cumb 164 A1
East Dean E Sus 22 C3
East Dean Hants 31 C6
East Dean W Sus 20 A2
East Down Devon 25 A7
East Drayton Notts 132 B2
East Ella Hull 142 A2
East End Dorset 16 B3
East End E Yorks 143 A4
East End Hants 18 B2
East End Hants 33 C5
East End Hants 46 C2
East End Herts 69 A4
East End Kent 37 C6
East End N Som 42 B3
East End Oxon 65 B4
East Farleigh Kent 37 A5
East Farndon Northants 99 C4
East Ferry Lincs 141 D6
East Fortune E Loth 210 C2
East Garston W Berks 46 B1
East Ginge Oxon 46 A2
East Goscote Leics 115 D4
East Grafton Wilts 45 C6
East Grimstead Wilts 31 C6
East Grinstead W Sus 36 C1
East Guldeford E Sus 38 C1
East Haddon Northants 82 A3
East Hagbourne Oxon 46 A3
East Halton N Lincs 142 B3
East Ham London 50 A1
East Hanney Oxon 65 D5
East Hanningfield Essex 70 C1
East Hardwick W Yorks 140 B2
East Harling Norf 103 C5
East Harlsey N Yorks 158 B3
East Harnham Wilts 31 C5
East Harptree Bath 43 D4
East Hartford Northumb 179 B4
East Harting W Sus 33 D6
East Hatley Cambs 85 B4
East Hauxwell N Yorks 157 B5
East Haven Angus 221 A5
East Heckington Lincs 117 A4
East Hedleyhope Durham 167 A4
East Hendred Oxon 46 A2
East Herrington T & W 179 D5
East Heslerton N Yorks 160 D3
East Hoathly E Sus 22 A3
East Horrington Som 29 A5
East Horsley Sur 34 A3
East Horton Northumb 198 C4
East Huntspill Som 28 A3
East Hyde Beds 67 B6
East Ilkerton Devon 26 A2
East Ilsley W Berks 46 A2
East Keal Lincs 134 C3
East Kennett Wilts 45 C5
East Keswick W Yorks 148 C2
East Kilbride S Lnrk 205 C6
East Kirkby Lincs 134 C3

East Knapton N Yorks 160 D2
East Knighton Dorset 16 C2
East Knoyle Wilts 30 B2
East Kyloe Northumb 199 C4
East Lambrook Som 28 D4
East Lamington Highld 264 C3
East Langdon Kent 39 A5
East Langton Leics 99 B4
East Langwell Highld 273 D5
East Lavant W Sus 20 B1
East Lavington W Sus 20 A2
East Layton N Yorks 157 A5
East Leake Notts 114 C3
East Learmouth Northumb 198 C2
East Leigh Devon 12 A1
East Lexham Norf 119 D5
East Lilburn Northumb 188 A3
East Linton E Loth 210 C2
East Liss Hants 33 C6
East Looe Corn 6 B1
East Lound N Lincs 141 D5
East Lulworth Dorset 16 C2
East Lutton N Yorks 150 A2
East Lydford Som 29 B5
East Mains Aberds 244 C3
East Malling Kent 37 A5
East March Angus 220 A4
East Marden W Sus 33 D7
East Markham Notts 132 B2
East Marton N Yorks 146 B3
East Meon Hants 33 C5
East Mere Devon 27 D4
East Mersea Essex 71 B4
East Mey Highld 281 A5
East Molesey Sur 49 C4
East Morden Dorset 16 B3
East Morton W Yorks 147 C4
East Ness N Yorks 159 D5
East Newton E Yorks 151 D5
East Norton Leics 99 A4
East Nynehead Som 27 C6
East Oakley Hants 46 D3
East Ogwell Devon 12 D3
East Orchard Dorset 30 D2
East Ord Northumb 198 A3
East Panson Devon 11 B4
East Peckham Kent 37 B4
East Pennard Som 29 B5
East Perry Cambs 84 A3
East Portlemouth Devon 7 D6
East Prawle Devon 8 D1
East Preston W Sus 20 B3
East Putford Devon 25 D4
East Quantoxhead Som 27 A6
East Rainton T & W 167 A6
East Ravendale NE Lincs 143 D4
East Raynham Norf 119 C5
East Rhidorroch Lodge Highld 262 A4
East Rigton W Yorks 148 C2
East Rounton N Yorks 158 A3
East Row N Yorks 169 D6
East Rudham Norf 119 C5
East Runton Norf 120 A3
East Ruston Norf 121 C5
East Saltoun E Loth 210 D1
East Sleekburn Northumb 179 A4
East Somerton Norf 121 D6
East Stockwith Lincs 141 D5
East Stoke Dorset 16 C2
East Stoke Notts 115 A5
East Stour Dorset 30 C2
East Stourmouth Kent 53 C4
East Stowford Devon 26 C1
East Stratton Hants 32 B4
East Studdal Kent 39 A5
East Suisnish Highld 248 C2
East Taphouse Corn 5 A6
East-the-Water Devon 25 C5
East Thirston Northumb 189 D4
East Tilbury Thurrock 50 B3
East Tisted Hants 33 B6
East Torrington Lincs 133 A6
East Tuddenham Norf 120 D2
East Tytherley Hants 32 C1
East Tytherton Wilts 44 B3
East Village Devon 12 A3
East Wall Shrops 94 B3
East Walton Norf 119 D4
East Wellow Hants 32 C2
East Wemyss Fife 209 A6
East Whitburn W Loth 208 D2
East Williamston Pembs 55 D6
East Winch Norf 118 D3
East Winterslow Wilts 31 B6
East Wittering W Sus 19 B6
East Witton N Yorks 157 C5
East Woodburn Northumb 177 A7
East Woodhay Hants 46 C2
East Worldham Hants 33 B6
East Worlington Devon 26 D2
East Worthing W Sus 21 B4
Eastbourne E Sus 22 C4
Eastbridge Suff 89 A5
Eastburn W Yorks 147 C4
Eastbury Herts 67 D5
Eastbury W Berks 46 B1
Eastby N Yorks 147 B4
Eastchurch Kent 52 B1
Eastcombe Glos 63 C4
Eastcote London 48 A4
Eastcote Northants 82 B3
Eastcote W Mid 97 D4
Eastcott Corn 24 D3
Eastcott Wilts 44 D4
Eastcourt Wilts 63 D5
Eastcourt Wilts 45 C6
Easter Ardross Highld 264 C2
Easter Balmoral Aberds 243 C5
Easter Boleskine Highld 251 D7
Easter Compton S Glos 43 A4
Easter Cringate Stirl 207 B5
Easter Davoch Aberds 244 B1
Easter Earshaig Dumfries 184 B3
Easter Fearn Highld 264 B2
Easter Galcantray Highld 253 B4
Easter Howgate Midloth 209 D5
Easter Howlaws Borders 197 B6
Easter Kinkell Highld 252 A1
Easter Lednathie Angus 232 B1
Easter Milton Highld 253 A5
Easter Moniack Highld 252 B1
Easter Ord Aberds 245 B5
Easter Quarff Shetland 285 K6
Easter Rhynd Perth 219 C6
Easter Row Stirl 207 A5
Easter Silverford Aberds 268 C2
Easter Skeld Shetland 285 J5
Easter Whyntie Aberds 267 C7
Eastergate W Sus 20 B2
Easterhouse Glasgow 207 D4
Eastern Green W Mid 97 C5
Easterton Wilts 44 D4
Eastertown Som 42 D2
Eastertown of Auchleuchries Aberds 257 C5
Eastfield N Lnrk 208 D1
Eastfield N Yorks 160 C4
Eastfield Hall Northumb 189 C5
Eastgate Durham 166 B2
Eastgate Norf 120 C3
Eastham Mers 126 A3
Eastham Ferry Mers 126 A3
Easthampstead Brack 47 C6
Eastheath Wokingham 47 C6
Easthope Shrops 94 B3
Easthorpe Essex 70 A3
Easthorpe Leics 115 B6
Easthorpe Notts 132 D2
Easthouses Midloth 209 D6
Eastington Devon 12 A2
Eastington Glos 62 C3
Eastington Glos 64 B2
Eastleach Martin Glos 64 C3
Eastleach Turville Glos 64 C2
Eastleigh Devon 25 C5
Eastleigh Hants 32 D3
Eastling Kent 51 D6
Eastmoor Derbys 130 B3
Eastmoor Norf 102 A3
Eastney Ptsmth 19 B5
Eastnor Hereford 79 D5
Eastoft N Lincs 141 B6
Eastoke Hants 19 B6
Easton Cambs 100 D3
Easton Cumb 175 C5
Easton Cumb 176 B2
Easton Devon 12 C2
Easton Dorset 15 D6
Easton Hants 32 B4
Easton Lincs 116 C2
Easton Norf 120 D3
Easton Som 29 A5
Easton Suff 88 B3
Easton Wilts 44 B2
Easton Grey Wilts 44 A2
Easton-in-Gordano N Som 43 B4
Easton Maudit Northants 83 B5
Easton on the Hill Northants 100 A2
Easton Royal Wilts 45 C6
Eastpark Dumfries 174 B3
Eastrea Cambs 101 B4
Eastriggs Dumfries 175 B5
Eastrington E Yorks 141 A5
Eastry Kent 53 D5
Eastville Bristol 43 B5
Eastville Lincs 135 D4
Eastwell Leics 115 C5
Eastwick Herts 68 B4
Eastwick Shetland 284 F5
Eastwood Notts 114 A2
Eastwood Sthend 51 A5
Eastwood W Yorks 138 A2
Eathorpe Warks 81 A6
Eaton Ches 127 C5
Eaton Ches 128 C3
Eaton Leics 115 C5
Eaton Norf 104 A3
Eaton Notts 132 B2
Eaton Oxon 65 C5
Eaton Shrops 94 C1
Eaton Shrops 94 C3
Eaton Bishop Hereford 78 D2
Eaton Bray Beds 67 A4
Eaton Constantine Shrops 94 A3
Eaton Green Beds 67 A4
Eaton Hastings Oxon 64 D3
Eaton on Tern Shrops 111 C5
Eaton Socon Cambs 84 B3
Eavestone N Yorks 147 A6
Ebberston N Yorks 160 C2
Ebbesbourne Wake Wilts 30 C3
Ebbw Vale = Glyn Ebwy Bl Gwent 60 C3
Ebchester Durham 178 D3
Ebford Devon 13 C4
Ebley Glos 63 C4
Ebnal Ches 110 A3
Ebrington Glos 81 D4
Ecchinswell Hants 46 D2
Ecclaw Borders 211 D4
Ecclefechan Dumfries 175 A4
Eccles Borders 197 B6
Eccles Gtr Man 137 D6
Eccles Kent 51 C4
Eccles on Sea Norf 121 C6
Eccles Road Norf 103 B6
Ecclesall S Yorks 130 A3
Ecclesfield S Yorks 139 D6
Ecclesgreig Aberds 233 B5
Eccleshall Staffs 112 C2
Eccleshill W Yorks 147 D5
Ecclesmachan W Loth 208 C3
Eccleston Ches 127 C4
Eccleston Lancs 136 B4
Eccleston Mers 136 D3
Eccleston Park Mers 136 D3
Eccup W Yorks 148 C1
Echt Aberds 245 B4
Eckford Borders 187 A6
Eckington Derbys 131 B4
Eckington Worcs 80 C2
Ecton Northants 83 A5
Edale Derbys 129 A6
Edburton W Sus 21 A5
Edderside Cumb 174 D3
Edderton Highld 264 B3
Eddistone Devon 24 C3
Eddleston Borders 196 B1
Eden Camp Museum, Malton N Yorks 159 D6
Eden Park London 49 C6
Edenbridge Kent 36 B2
Edenfield Lancs 137 B6
Edenhall Cumb 164 B3
Edenham Lincs 116 C3
Edensor Derbys 130 C2
Edentaggart Argyll 215 C6
Edenthorpe S Yorks 140 C4
Edentown Cumb 175 C6
Ederline Argyll 214 B1
Edern Gwyn 106 C2
Edgarley Som 29 B5
Edgbaston W Mid 96 C3
Edgcott Bucks 66 A1
Edgcott Som 26 B3
Edge Shrops 94 A1
Edge End Glos 62 B1
Edge Green Ches 127 D4
Edge Hill Mers 136 E2
Edgebolton Shrops 111 C4
Edgefield Norf 120 B2
Edgefield Street Norf 120 B2
Edgeside Lancs 138 A1
Edgeworth Glos 63 C5
Edgmond Telford 111 D6
Edgmond Marsh Telford 111 C6
Edgton Shrops 94 C1
Edgware London 68 D1
Edgworth Blkburn 137 B6
Edinample Stirl 217 B5
Edinbane Highld 258 C3
Edinburgh Edin 209 C5
Edinburgh Airport Edin 209 C4
Edinburgh Castle Edin 209 C5
Edinburgh Crystal Visitor Centre, Penicuik Midloth 209 D5
Edinburgh Zoo Edin 209 C5
Edingale Staffs 113 D6
Edingight Ho. Moray 267 D6
Edingley Notts 131 D6
Edingthorpe Norf 121 B5
Edingthorpe Green Norf 121 B5
Edington Som 28 B3
Edington Wilts 44 D3
Edintore Moray 255 B5
Edith Weston Rutland 99 A6
Edithmead Som 28 A3
Edlesborough Bucks 67 B4
Edlingham Northumb 189 C4
Edlington Lincs 134 B2
Edmondsham Dorset 31 D4
Edmondsley Durham 167 A5
Edmondthorpe Leics 115 D6
Edmonstone Orkney 282 E6
Edmonton London 68 D3
Edmundbyers Durham 178 D2
Ednam Borders 197 C6
Ednaston Derbys 113 A6
Edradynate Perth 230 C2
Edrom Borders 198 A2
Edstaston Shrops 111 B4
Edstone Warks 81 A4
Edvin Loach Hereford 79 B4
Edwalton Notts 114 B3
Edwardstone Suff 87 C5
Edwinsford Carms 58 B3
Edwinstowe Notts 131 C6
Edworth Beds 84 C4
Edwyn Ralph Hereford 79 B4
Edzell Angus 232 B3
Efail Isaf Rhondda 41 C5
Efailnewydd Gwyn 106 C3
Efailwen Carms 72 D4
Efenechtyd Denb 125 D6
Effingham Sur 35 A4
Effirth Shetland 285 H5
Efford Devon 12 A3
Egdon Worcs 80 B2
Egerton Gtr Man 137 B6
Egerton Kent 37 B7
Egerton Forstal Kent 37 B6
Eggborough N Yorks 140 A3
Eggbuckland Plym 7 B4
Eggington Beds 67 A4
Egginton Derbys 113 C6
Egglescliffe Stockton 168 D2
Eggleston Durham 166 C2
Egham Sur 48 B3
Egleton Rutland 99 A5
Eglingham Northumb 189 B4
Egloshayle Corn 9 D6
Egloskerry Corn 10 C3
Eglwys-Brewis V Glam 41 E5
Eglwys Cross Wrex 110 A3
Eglwys Fach Ceredig 91 C4
Eglwysbach Conwy 124 B3
Eglwyswen Pembs 73 C4
Eglwyswrw Pembs 72 C4
Egmanton Notts 132 C2
Egremont Cumb 162 C3
Egremont Mers 136 D2
Egton N Yorks 159 A7
Egton Bridge N Yorks 159 A7
Eight Ash Green Essex 70 A3
Eignaig Highld 226 B2
Eil Highld 241 A6
Eilanreach Highld 238 A2
Eilean Darach Highld 262 B3
Eileanach Lodge Highld 264 D1
Einacleite W Isles 288 E2
Eisgean W Isles 288 F4
Eisingrug Gwyn 107 C6
Elan Village Powys 76 A3
Elberton S Glos 43 A5
Elburton Plym 7 B4
Elcho Perth 219 B6
Elcombe Swindon 45 A5
Eldernell Cambs 101 B5
Eldersfield Worcs 79 D6
Elderslie Renfs 205 B4
Eldon Durham 167 C5
Eldrick S Ayrs 181 C4
Eldroth N Yorks 146 A1
Eldwick W Yorks 147 C5
Elfhowe Cumb 154 B3
Elford Northumb 199 C5
Elford Staffs 113 D5
Elgin Moray 266 C3
Elgol Highld 247 C4
Elham Kent 38 A3
Elie Fife 221 D4
Elim Anglesey 122 B3
Eling Hants 32 D2
Elishader Highld 259 B5
Elishaw Northumb 188 D1
Elkesley Notts 132 B1
Elkstone Glos 63 B5
Ellan Highld 253 D4
Elland W Yorks 139 A4
Ellary Argyll 202 A2
Ellastone Staffs 113 A5
Ellemford Borders 211 D4
Ellenbrook I o M 152 D3
Ellenhall Staffs 112 C2
Ellen's Green Sur 34 C3
Ellerbeck N Yorks 158 B3
Ellerburn N Yorks 160 C2
Ellerby N Yorks 169 D5
Ellerdine Heath Telford 111 C5
Ellerhayes Devon 13 A4
Elleric Argyll 227 B5
Ellerker E Yorks 141 A7
Ellerton E Yorks 149 D6
Ellerton Shrops 111 C6
Ellesborough Bucks 66 C3
Ellesmere Shrops 110 B3
Ellesmere Port Ches 127 B4
Ellingham Norf 105 B4
Ellingham Northumb 189 A4
Ellingstring N Yorks 157 C5
Ellington Cambs 100 D3
Ellington Northumb 189 D5
Elliot Angus 221 A6
Ellisfield Hants 33 A5
Ellistown Leics 114 D2
Ellon Aberds 257 C4
Ellonby Cumb 164 B2
Ellough Suff 105 C5
Elloughton E Yorks 142 A1
Ellwood Glos 62 C1
Elm Cambs 101 A6
Elm Hill Dorset 30 C2
Elm Park London 50 A2
Elmbridge Worcs 80 A2
Elmdon Essex 85 D6
Elmdon W Mid 97 C4
Elmdon Heath W Mid 97 C4
Elmers End London 49 C6
Elmesthorpe Leics 98 B1
Elmfield I o W 19 B5
Elmhurst Staffs 113 D5
Elmley Castle Worcs 80 C2
Elmley Lovett Worcs 79 A6
Elmore Glos 62 B3
Elmore Back Glos 62 B3
Elmscott Devon 24 C3
Elmsett Suff 87 C6
Elmstead Market Essex 71 A4
Elmsted Kent 38 A3
Elmstone Kent 53 C4
Elmstone Hardwicke Glos 63 A5
Elmswell E Yorks 150 B2
Elmswell Suff 87 A5
Elmton Derbys 131 B5
Elphin Highld 271 C5
Elphinstone E Loth 209 C6
Elrick Aberds 245 B5
Elrig Dumfries 171 C5
Elsdon Northumb 188 D2
Elsecar S Yorks 140 D1
Elsenham Essex 69 A5
Elsfield Oxon 65 B6
Elsham N Lincs 142 B2
Elsing Norf 120 D2
Elslack N Yorks 146 C3
Elson Shrops 110 B2
Elsrickle S Lnrk 195 B5
Elstead Sur 34 B2
Elsted W Sus 33 D7
Elsthorpe Lincs 116 C3
Elstob Durham 167 C6
Elston Notts 115 A5
Elston Wilts 31 A4
Elstone Devon 26 D1
Elstow Beds 84 C2
Elstree Herts 68 D1
Elstronwick E Yorks 151 D5
Elswick Lancs 144 D4
Elsworth Cambs 85 A5
Elterwater Cumb 154 A2
Eltham London 50 B1
Eltisley Cambs 85 B4
Elton Cambs 100 B2
Elton Ches 127 B4
Elton Derbys 130 C2
Elton Glos 62 B3
Elton Hereford 94 D2
Elton Notts 115 B5
Elton Stockton 168 D2
Elton Green Ches 127 B4
Elvanfoot S Lnrk 184 A2
Elvaston Derbys 114 B2
Elveden Suff 103 D4
Elvingston E Loth 210 C1
Elvington Kent 53 D4
Elvington York 149 C5
Elwick Hrtlpl 168 B2
Elwick Northumb 199 C5
Elworth Ches 128 C2
Elworthy Som 27 B5
Ely Cambs 102 C1
Ely Cardiff 41 D6
Ely Cathedral and Museum Cambs 102 C1
Emberton M Keynes 83 C5
Embleton Cumb 163 A4
Embleton Northumb 189 A5
Embo Highld 265 A4
Embo Street Highld 265 A4
Emborough Som 43 D5
Embsay N Yorks 147 B4
Emery Down Hants 18 A1
Emley W Yorks 139 B5
Emmbrook Wokingham 47 C5
Emmer Green Reading 47 B5
Emmington Oxon 66 C2
Emneth Norf 101 A6
Emneth Hungate Norf 101 A7
Empingham Rutland 99 A6
Empshott Hants 33 B6
Emstrey Shrops 111 D4
Emsworth Hants 19 A6
Enborne W Berks 46 C2
Enchmarsh Shrops 94 B3
Enderby Leics 98 B2
Endmoor Cumb 154 C4
Endon Staffs 129 D4
Endon Bank Staffs 129 D4
Enfield London 68 D3
Enfield Wash London 68 D3
Enford Wilts 45 D5
Engamoor Shetland 285 H4
Engine Common S Glos 43 A5
Englefield W Berks 47 B4
Englefield Green Sur 48 B2
Englesea-brook Ches 128 D2
English Bicknor Glos 62 B1
English Frankton Shrops 110 C3
Englishcombe Bath 43 C6
Enham Alamein Hants 32 A2
Enmore Som 28 B2
Ennerdale Bridge Cumb 162 C3
Enoch Dumfries 183 B6
Enochdhu Perth 231 B4
Ensay Argyll 224 B2
Ensbury Bmouth 17 B4
Ensdon Shrops 110 D3
Ensis Devon 25 C6
Enstone Oxon 65 A4
Enterkinfoot Dumfries 183 B6
Enterpen N Yorks 158 A3
Enville Staffs 95 C6
Eolaigearraidh W Isles 286 F3
Eorabus Argyll 224 D2
Eòropaidh W Isles 288 A6
Epperstone Notts 115 A4
Epping Essex 69 C4
Epping Green Essex 68 C4
Epping Green Herts 68 C2
Epping Upland Essex 68 C4
Eppleby N Yorks 167 D4
Eppleworth E Yorks 150 D3
Epsom Sur 49 C5
Epsom Racecourse Sur 35 A5
Epwell Oxon 81 C6
Epworth N Lincs 141 C5
Epworth Turbary N Lincs 141 C5
Erbistock Wrex 110 A2
Erbusaig Highld 249 D4
Erchless Castle Highld 251 B6
Erddig Wrex 110 A2
Erdington W Mid 96 B4
Eredine Argyll 214 B2
Eriboll Highld 277 C5
Ericstane Dumfries 184 A3
Eridge Green E Sus 36 C3
Erines Argyll 202 A3
Eriswell Suff 102 D3
Erith London 50 B2
Erlestoke Wilts 44 D3
Ermine Lincs 133 B4
Ermington Devon 7 B5
Erpingham Norf 120 B3
Errogie Highld 252 D1
Errol Perth 220 B2
Erskine Renfs 205 A4
Erskine Bridge Renfs 205 A4
Ervie Dumfries 170 A2
Erwarton Suff 88 D3
Erwood Powys 77 C4
Eryholme N Yorks 157 A7
Eryrys Denb 126 D2
Escomb Durham 167 C4
Escrick N Yorks 149 C5
Esgairdawe Carms 58 A3
Esgairgeiliog Powys 91 B5
Esh Durham 167 A4
Esh Winning Durham 167 A4
Esher Sur 48 C4
Esholt W Yorks 147 C5
Eshott Northumb 189 D5
Eshton N Yorks 146 B3
Esk Valley N Yorks 159 A7
Eskadale Highld 251 C6
Eskbank Midloth 209 D6
Eskdale Green Cumb 163 D4
Eskdalemuir Dumfries 185 C5
Eske E Yorks 150 C3
Eskham Lincs 143 D5
Esprick Lancs 144 D4
Essendine Rutland 116 D3
Essendon Herts 68 C2
Essich Highld 252 C2
Essington Staffs 96 A2
Esslemont Aberds 257 D4
Eston Redcar 168 D3
Eswick Shetland 285 H6
Etal Northumb 198 C3
Etchilhampton Wilts 44 C4
Etchingham E Sus 37 D5
Etchinghill Kent 38 B3
Etchinghill Staffs 112 D4
Ethie Castle Angus 233 D4
Ethie Mains Angus 233 D4
Etling Green Norf 120 D2
Eton Windsor 48 B2
Eton Wick Windsor 48 B2
Etteridge Highld 241 C4
Ettersgill Durham 166 C1
Ettingshall W Mid 96 B2
Ettington Warks 81 C5
Etton E Yorks 150 C2
Etton P'boro 100 A3
Ettrick Borders 185 A5
Ettrickbridge Borders 186 A2
Ettrickhill Borders 185 A5
Etwall Derbys 113 B6
Eureka!, Halifax W Yorks 138 A3
Euston Suff 103 D4
Euximoor Drove Cambs 101 B6
Euxton Lancs 137 B4
Evanstown Bridgend 41 C4
Evanton Highld 264 D2
Evedon Lincs 116 A3
Evelix Highld 264 A3
Evenjobb Powys 77 A6
Evenley Northants 82 D2
Evenlode Glos 64 A3
Evenwood Durham 167 C4
Evenwood Gate Durham 167 C4
Everbay Orkney 282 E7
Evercreech Som 29 B6
Everdon Northants 82 B2

Everingham E Yorks 149 C7
Everleigh Wilts 45 D6
Everley N Yorks 160 C3
Eversholt Beds 84 D1
Evershot Dorset 15 A5
Eversley Hants 47 C5
Eversley Cross Hants 47 C5
Everthorpe E Yorks 150 D2
Everton Beds 84 B4
Everton Hants 18 B1
Everton Mers 136 D2
Everton Notts 141 D4
Evertown Dumfries 175 A6
Evesbatch Hereford 79 C4
Evesham Worcs 80 C3
Evington Leicester 98 A3
Ewden Village S Yorks 139 D5
Ewell Sur 49 C5
Ewell Minnis Kent 39 A4
Ewelme Oxon 66 D1
Ewen Glos 63 D6
Ewenny V Glam 40 D4
Ewerby Lincs 116 A4
Ewerby Thorpe Lincs 116 A4
Ewes Dumfries 185 C6
Ewesley Northumb 188 D3
Ewhurst Sur 34 B3
Ewhurst Green E Sus 37 D5
Ewhurst Green Sur 34 C3
Ewloe Flint 126 C3
Ewloe Green Flint 126 C2
Ewood Blkburn 137 A5
Eworthy Devon 11 B5
Ewshot Hants 33 A7
Ewyas Harold Hereford 61 A5
Exbourne Devon 11 A7
Exbury Hants 18 B3
Exbury Gardens, Fawley Hants 18 A3
Exebridge Som 27 C4
Exelby N Yorks 157 C6
Exeter Devon 13 B4
Exeter Cathedral Devon 13 B4
Exeter International Airport Devon 13 B4
Exford Som 26 B3
Exhall Warks 80 B4
Exley Head W Yorks 147 D4
Exminster Devon 13 C4
Exmouth Devon 13 C5
Exnaboe Shetland 285 M5
Exning Suff 86 A2
Explosion, Gosport Hants 19 A5
Exton Devon 13 C4
Exton Hants 33 C5
Exton Rutland 116 D2
Exton Som 27 B4
Exwick Devon 13 B4
Eyam Derbys 130 B2
Eydon Northants 82 B2
Eye Hereford 78 A2
Eye P'boro 100 A4
Eye Suff 104 D2
Eye Green P'boro 100 A4
Eyemouth Borders 211 D6
Eyeworth Beds 85 C4
Eyhorne Street Kent 37 A6
Eyke Suff 88 B4
Eynesbury Cambs 84 B3
Eynort Highld 246 B2
Eynsford Kent 50 C2
Eynsham Oxon 65 C5
Eype Dorset 14 B4
Eyre Highld 259 C4
Eyre Highld 248 C2
Eythorne Kent 39 A4
Eyton Hereford 78 A2
Eyton Shrops 94 C1
Eyton Wrex 110 A2
Eyton upon the Weald Moors Telford 111 D5

F

Faccombe Hants 46 D1
Faceby N Yorks 158 A3
Facit Lancs 138 B1
Faddiley Ches 127 D5
Fadmoor N Yorks 159 C5
Faerdre Swansea 40 A1
Failand N Som 43 B4
Failford S Ayrs 193 C4
Failsworth Gtr Man 138 C1
Fain Highld 262 C3
Fair Green Norf 118 D3
Fair Hill Cumb 164 B3
Fair Oak Hants 32 D3
Fair Oak Green Hants 47 C4
Fairbourne Gwyn 90 A4
Fairburn N Yorks 140 A2
Fairfield Derbys 129 B5
Fairfield Stockton 168 D2
Fairfield Worcs 80 C3
Fairfield Worcs 96 D2
Fairford Glos 64 C2
Fairhaven Lancs 136 A2
Fairlie N Ayrs 204 C2
Fairlight E Sus 23 A6
Fairlight Cove E Sus 23 A6
Fairmile Devon 13 B5
Fairmilehead Edin 209 D5
Fairoak Staffs 111 B6
Fairseat Kent 50 C3
Fairstead Essex 70 B1
Fairstead Norf 118 D3
Fairwarp E Sus 36 D2
Fairy Cottage I o M 152 C4
Fairy Cross Devon 25 C5
Fakenham Norf 119 C6
Fakenham Magna Suff 103 D5
Fakenham Racecourse Norf 119 C6
Fala Midloth 210 D1
Fala Dam Midloth 210 D1
Falahill Borders 196 A2
Falcon Hereford 79 D4
Faldingworth Lincs 133 A5
Falfield S Glos 62 D2
Falkenham Suff 88 D3
Falkirk Falk 208 C1
Falkland Fife 220 D2
Falkland Palace Fife 220 D2
Falla Borders 187 B6
Fallgate Derbys 130 C3
Fallin Stirl 207 A6
Fallowfield Gtr Man 138 D1
Fallsidehill Borders 197 B5
Falmer E Sus 21 B6
Falmouth Corn 4 D3
Falsgrave N Yorks 160 C4
Falstone Northumb 177 A5
Fanagmore Highld 276 D2
Fangdale Beck N Yorks 159 B4
Fangfoss E Yorks 149 B6
Fankerton Falk 207 B5
Fanmore Argyll 224 B3
Fannich Lodge Highld 262 D4
Fans Borders 197 B5
Far Bank S Yorks 140 B4
Far Bletchley M Keynes 83 D5
Far Cotton Northants 83 B4
Far Forest Worcs 95 D5
Far Laund Derbys 114 A1
Far Sawrey Cumb 154 B2
Farcet Cambs 100 B4
Farden Shrops 94 D3
Fareham Hants 19 A4
Farewell Staffs 113 D4
Farforth Lincs 134 B3
Faringdon Oxon 64 D3
Farington Lancs 136 A4
Farlam Cumb 176 D3
Farlary Highld 273 D5
Farleigh N Som 42 C3
Farleigh Sur 49 C6
Farleigh Hungerford Som 44 D2
Farleigh Wallop Hants 33 A5
Farlesthorpe Lincs 135 B4
Farleton Cumb 154 C4
Farleton Lancs 145 A5
Farley Shrops 94 A1
Farley Staffs 113 A4
Farley Wilts 31 C6
Farley Green Sur 34 B3
Farley Hill Luton 67 A5
Farley Hill Wokingham 47 C5
Farleys End Glos 62 B3
Farlington N Yorks 149 A5
Farlow Shrops 95 C4
Farmborough Bath 43 C5
Farmcote Glos 63 A6
Farmcote Shrops 95 B5
Farmington Glos 64 B2
Farmoor Oxon 65 C5
Farmtown Moray 267 D6
Farnborough London 50 C1
Farnborough Hants 34 A1
Farnborough Warks 82 C1
Farnborough W Berks 46 A2
Farnborough Green Hants 34 A1
Farncombe Sur 34 B2
Farndish Beds 83 A6
Farndon Ches 127 D4
Farndon Notts 132 D2
Farnell Angus 233 C4
Farnham Dorset 30 D3
Farnham Essex 69 A4
Farnham N Yorks 148 A2
Farnham Suff 89 A4
Farnham Sur 34 B1
Farnham Common Bucks 48 A2
Farnham Green Essex 69 A4
Farnham Royal Bucks 48 A2
Farnhill N Yorks 147 C4
Farningham Kent 50 C2
Farnley N Yorks 147 C6
Farnley W Yorks 147 D6
Farnley Tyas W Yorks 139 B4
Farnsfield Notts 131 D6
Farnworth Gtr Man 137 C6
Farnworth Halton 127 A5
Farr Highld 252 C2
Farr Highld 241 B6
Farr Highld 278 B3
Farr House Highld 252 C2
Farringdon Devon 13 B5
Farrington Gurney Bath 43 D5
Farsley W Yorks 147 D6
Farthinghoe Northants 82 D2
Farthingloe Kent 39 A4
Farthingstone Northants 82 B3
Fartown W Yorks 139 B4
Farway Devon 14 B1
Fasag Highld 249 A5
Fascadale Highld 235 C4
Faslane Port Argyll 215 D5
Fasnacloich Argyll 227 B5
Fasnakyle Ho. Highld 251 D5
Fassfern Highld 237 B4
Fatfield T & W 179 D5
Fattahead Aberds 268 D1
Faugh Cumb 176 D3
Fauldhouse W Loth 208 D2
Faulkbourne Essex 70 B1
Faulkland Som 43 D6
Fauls Shrops 111 B4
Faversham Kent 52 C2
Favillar Moray 254 C3
Fawdington N Yorks 158 D3
Fawfieldhead Staffs 129 C5
Fawkham Green Kent 50 C2
Fawler Oxon 65 B4
Fawley Bucks 47 A5
Fawley Hants 18 A3
Fawley W Berks 46 A1
Fawley Chapel Hereford 62 A1
Faxfleet E Yorks 141 A6
Faygate W Sus 35 C5
Fazakerley Mers 136 D2
Fazeley Staffs 97 A5
Fearby N Yorks 157 C5
Fearn Highld 265 C4
Fearn Lodge Highld 264 B2
Fearn Station Highld 265 C4
Fearnan Perth 229 D6
Fearnbeg Highld 249 A4
Fearnhead Warr 137 D5
Fearnmore Highld 261 D4
Featherstone Staffs 96 A2
Featherstone W Yorks 140 A2
Featherwood Northumb 187 C7
Feckenham Worcs 80 A3
Feering Essex 70 A2
Feetham N Yorks 156 B3
Feizor N Yorks 146 A1
Felbridge Sur 35 C6
Felbrigg Norf 120 B4
Felcourt Sur 36 B1
Felden Herts 67 C5
Felin-Crai Powys 59 C5
Felindre Ceredig 75 C4
Felindre Carms 58 C2
Felindre Carms 58 B3
Felindre Carms 59 C4
Felindre Carms 73 C6
Felindre Powys 93 C5
Felindre Swansea 57 B6
Felindre Farchog Pembs 72 C4
Felinfach Ceredig 75 C4
Felinfach Powys 77 D4
Felinfoel Carms 57 B5
Felingwm isaf Carms 58 C2
Felingwm uchaf Carms 58 C2
Felinwynt Ceredig 73 A5
Felixkirk N Yorks 158 C3
Felixstowe Suff 88 D3
Felixstowe Ferry Suff 88 D4
Felkington Northumb 198 B3
Felkirk W Yorks 140 B1
Fell Side Cumb 163 A6
Felling T & W 179 C4
Felmersham Beds 84 B1
Felmingham Norf 120 C4
Felpham W Sus 20 C2
Felsham Suff 87 B5
Felsted Essex 69 A6
Feltham London 48 B4
Felthorpe Norf 120 D3
Felton Hereford 78 C3
Felton Northumb 189 C4
Felton N Som 43 C4
Felton Butler Shrops 110 D2
Feltwell Norf 102 B3
Fen Ditton Cambs 85 A6
Fen Drayton Cambs 85 A5
Fen End W Mid 97 D5
Fen Side Lincs 134 D3
Fenay Bridge W Yorks 139 B4
Fence Lancs 146 D2
Fence Houses T & W 179 D5
Fengate Norf 120 C3
Fengate P'boro 100 B4
Fenham Northumb 199 B4
Fenhouses Lincs 117 A5
Feniscliffe Blkburn 137 A5
Feniscowles Blkburn 137 A5
Feniton Devon 13 B6
Fenlake Beds 84 C2
Fenny Bentley Derbys 130 D6
Fenny Bridges Devon 13 B6
Fenny Compton Warks 81 B7
Fenny Drayton Leics 97 B6
Fenny Stratford M Keynes 83 D5
Fenrother Northumb 189 D4
Fenstanton Cambs 85 A5
Fenton Cambs 101 D5
Fenton Lincs 132 D3
Fenton Lincs 132 B3
Fenton Stoke 112 A2
Fenton Mains E Loth 210 B2
Fenton Town Northumb 198 C3
Fenwick E Ayrs 205 D4
Fenwick Northumb 178 B2
Fenwick Northumb 199 B4
Fenwick S Yorks 140 B3
Feochaig Argyll 190 D3
Feock Corn 4 D3
Feolin Ferry Argyll 201 B4
Ferens Art Gallery, Hull Hull 142 A2
Ferindonald Highld 247 D5
Feriniquarrie Highld 258 C1
Ferlochan Argyll 226 B4
Fern Angus 232 B2
Ferndale Rhondda 41 B5
Ferndown Dorset 17 A4
Ferness Highld 253 B5
Ferney Green Cumb 154 B3
Fernham Oxon 64 D3
Fernhill Heath Worcs 79 B6
Fernhurst W Sus 34 D1
Fernie Fife 220 C3
Ferniegair S Lnrk 194 A2
Fernilea Highld 246 A2
Fernilee Derbys 129 B5
Ferrensby N Yorks 148 A2
Ferring W Sus 20 B3
Ferry Hill Cambs 101 C5
Ferry Point Highld 264 B3
Ferrybridge W Yorks 140 A2
Ferryden Angus 233 C5
Ferryhill Aberdeen 245 B6
Ferryhill Durham 167 B5
Ferryhill Station Durham 167 B6
Ferryside Carms 56 A3
Fersfield Norf 103 C6
Fersit Highld 228 A2
Ferwig Ceredig 73 B4
Feshiebridge Highld 241 B6
Festival Park Visitor Centre, Ebbw Vale Bl Gwent 60 C3
Fetcham Sur 35 A4
Fetlar Airport Shetland 284 D8
Fetterangus Aberds 269 D4
Fettercairn Aberds 233 A4
Fettes Highld 252 A1
Fewcott Oxon 65 A6
Fewston N Yorks 147 B5
Ffair-Rhos Ceredig 75 B6
Ffairfach Carms 58 C3
Ffaldybrenin Carms 58 A3
Ffarmers Carms 58 A3
Ffawyddog Powys 60 B4
Ffestiniog Railway, Porthmadog Gwyn 107 B6
Fforest Carms 57 B5
Fforest-fâch Swansea 57 C6
Ffos-y-ffin Ceredig 74 B3
Ffostrasol Ceredig 73 B6
Ffridd-Uchaf Gwyn 107 A5
Ffrith Flint 126 D2
Ffrwd Gwyn 107 A4
Ffynnon ddrain Carms 73 D7
Ffynnon-oer Ceredig 75 C4
Ffynnongroyw Flint 125 A6
Fidden Argyll 224 D2
Fiddes Aberds 245 D5
Fiddington Glos 80 D2
Fiddington Som 28 A2
Fiddleford Dorset 30 D2
Fiddlers Hamlet Essex 69 C4
Field Staffs 112 B4
Field Broughton Cumb 154 C2
Field Dalling Norf 120 B2
Field Head Leics 98 A1
Fifehead Magdalen Dorset 30 C1
Fifehead Neville Dorset 30 D1
Fifield Oxon 64 B3
Fifield Wilts 45 D5
Fifield Windsor 48 B2
Fifield Bavant Wilts 31 C4
Figheldean Wilts 31 A5
Filands Wilts 44 A3
Filby Norf 121 D6
Filey N Yorks 161 C5
Filgrave M Keynes 83 C5
Filkins Oxon 64 C3
Filleigh Devon 26 C1
Filleigh Devon 26 D2
Fillingham Lincs 133 A4
Fillongley Warks 97 C5
Filton S Glos 43 B5
Fimber E Yorks 150 A1
Finavon Angus 232 C2
Finchairn Argyll 214 B2
Fincham Norf 102 A2
Finchampstead Wokingham 47 C5
Finchdean Hants 33 D6
Finchingfield Essex 86 D2
Finchley London 68 D2
Findern Derbys 113 B7
Findhorn Moray 265 D6
Findhorn Bridge Highld 253 D4
Findo Gask Perth 219 B5
Findochty Moray 267 C5
Findon Aberds 245 C6
Findon W Sus 21 B4
Findon Mains Highld 264 D2
Findrack Ho. Aberds 244 B3
Finedon Northants 99 D6
Fingal Street Suff 88 A3
Fingask Aberds 256 D2
Fingerpost Worcs 95 D5
Fingest Bucks 66 D2
Finghall N Yorks 157 C5
Fingland Cumb 175 C5
Fingland Dumfries 183 A5
Finglesham Kent 53 D5
Fingringhoe Essex 71 A4
Finlarig Stirl 217 A5
Finmere Oxon 82 D3
Finnart Perth 229 C4
Finningham Suff 87 A6
Finningley S Yorks 141 D4
Finnygaud Aberds 267 D6
Finsbury London 49 A6
Finstall Worcs 80 A2
Finsthwaite Cumb 154 C2
Finstock Oxon 65 B4
Finstown Orkney 282 F4
Fintry Aberds 268 D2
Fintry Dundee 220 A4
Fintry Stirl 207 B4
Finzean Aberds 244 C3
Fionnphort Argyll 224 D2
Fionnsbhagh W Isles 287 F5
Fir Tree Durham 166 B4
Firbeck S Yorks 131 A5
Firby N Yorks 157 C6
Firby N Yorks 149 A6
Firgrove Gtr Man 138 B2
Firsby Lincs 135 C4
Firsdown Wilts 31 B6
First Coast Highld 261 A6
Fishbourne I o W 19 B4
Fishbourne W Sus 20 B1
Fishbourne Palace W Sus 20 B1
Fishburn Durham 167 B6
Fishcross Clack 208 A1
Fisher Place Cumb 163 C6
Fisherford Aberds 256 C1
Fisher's Pond Hants 32 C3
Fisherstreet W Sus 34 C2
Fisherton Highld 252 A3
Fisherton S Ayrs 192 D2
Fishguard = Abergwaun Pembs 72 C2
Fishlake S Yorks 141 B4
Fishleigh Barton Devon 25 C6
Fishponds Bristol 43 B5
Fishpool Glos 62 A2
Fishtoft Lincs 117 A6
Fishtoft Drove Lincs 117 A6
Fishtown of Usan Angus 233 C5
Fishwick Borders 198 A3
Fiskavaig Highld 246 A2
Fiskerton Lincs 133 B5
Fiskerton Notts 132 D2
Fitling E Yorks 151 D5
Fittleton Wilts 31 A5
Fittleworth W Sus 20 A3
Fitton End Cambs 118 D1
Fitz Shrops 110 D3
Fitzhead Som 27 C6
Fitzwilliam W Yorks 140 B2
Fitzwilliam Museum, Cambridge Cambs 85 B6
Fiunary Highld 225 B5
Five Acres Glos 62 B1
Five Ashes E Sus 36 D3
Five Oak Green Kent 36 B4
Five Oaks Jersey 6
Five Oaks W Sus 34 D3
Five Roads Carms 57 B4
Fivecrosses Ches 127 B5
Fivehead Som 28 C3
Flack's Green Essex 70 B1
Flackwell Heath Bucks 48 A1
Fladbury Worcs 80 C2
Fladdabister Shetland 285 K6
Flagg Derbys 129 C6
Flambards Experience, Helston Corn 3 C4
Flamborough E Yorks 161 D6
Flamingo Land, Pickering N Yorks 159 D6
Flamstead Herts 67 B5
Flamstead End Herts 68 C3
Flansham W Sus 20 B2
Flanshaw W Yorks 139 A6
Flasby N Yorks 146 B3
Flash Staffs 129 C5
Flashader Highld 258 C3
Flask Inn N Yorks 160 A3
Flaunden Herts 67 C5
Flawborough Notts 115 A5
Flawith N Yorks 148 A3
Flax Bourton N Som 43 C4
Flaxby N Yorks 148 B2
Flaxholme Derbys 114 A1
Flaxley Glos 62 B2
Flaxpool Som 27 B6
Flaxton N Yorks 149 A5
Fleckney Leics 98 B3
Flecknoe Warks 82 A2
Fledborough Notts 132 B3
Fleet Hants 47 D6
Fleet Hants 19 A6
Fleet Lincs 117 C6
Fleet Air Arm Museum, Yeovil Som 29 C5
Fleet Hargate Lincs 117 C6
Fleetham Northumb 189 A4
Fleetlands Hants 19 A4
Fleetville Herts 67 C6
Fleetwood Lancs 144 C3
Flemingston V Glam 41 D5
Flemington S Lnrk 205 C6
Flempton Suff 87 A4
Fleoideabhagh W Isles 287 F5
Fletchertown Cumb 175 D5
Fletching E Sus 36 D2
Flexbury Corn 10 A3
Flexford Sur 34 B2
Flimby Cumb 162 A3
Flimwell E Sus 37 C5
Flint = Y Fflint Flint 126 B2
Flint Mountain Flint 126 B2
Flintham Notts 115 A5
Flinton E Yorks 151 D5
Flintsham Hereford 77 B7
Flitcham Norf 119 C4
Flitton Beds 84 D2
Flitwick Beds 84 D2
Flixborough N Lincs 141 B6
Flixborough Stather N Lincs 141 B6
Flixton Gtr Man 137 D6
Flixton N Yorks 160 D4
Flixton Suff 104 C4
Flockton W Yorks 139 B5
Flodaigh W Isles 286 A4
Flodden Northumb 198 C3
Flodigarry Highld 259 A4
Flood's Ferry Cambs 101 B5
Flookburgh Cumb 154 D2
Florden Norf 104 B2
Flore Northants 82 A3
Flotterton Northumb 188 C2
Flowton Suff 88 C1
Flush House W Yorks 139 C4
Flushing Aberds 257 B5
Flushing Corn 4 D3
Flyford Flavell Worcs 80 B2
Foals Green Suff 104 D3
Fobbing Thurrock 51 A4
Fochabers Moray 266 D4
Fochriw Caerph 60 C3
Fockerby N Lincs 141 B6
Fodderletter Moray 254 D2
Fodderty Highld 251 A7
Foel Powys 109 D4
Foel-gastell Carms 57 A5
Foffarty Angus 232 D2
Foggathorpe E Yorks 149 D6
Fogo Borders 197 B6
Fogorig Borders 198 B1
Foindle Highld 276 D2
Folda Angus 231 B5
Fole Staffs 112 B4
Foleshill W Mid 97 C6
Folke Dorset 29 D6
Folkestone Kent 39 B4
Folkestone Racecourse Kent 38 B3
Folkingham Lincs 116 B3
Folkington E Sus 22 B3
Folksworth Cambs 100 C3
Folkton N Yorks 161 D4
Folla Rule Aberds 256 C2
Follifoot N Yorks 148 B2
Folly Gate Devon 11 B6
Fonthill Bishop Wilts 30 B3
Fonthill Gifford Wilts 30 B3
Fontmell Magna Dorset 30 D2
Fontwell W Sus 20 B2
Fontwell Park Racecourse W Sus 20 B2
Foolow Derbys 130 B1
Foots Cray London 50 B1
Forbestown Aberds 243 A6
Force Mills Cumb 154 B2
Forcett N Yorks 167 D4
Ford Argyll 214 B1
Ford Bucks 66 C2
Ford Devon 25 C5
Ford Glos 64 A1
Ford Northumb 198 C3
Ford Shrops 110 D3
Ford Staffs 129 D5
Ford Wilts 44 B2
Ford W Sus 20 B2
Ford End Essex 69 B6
Ford Street Som 27 D6
Fordcombe Kent 36 B3
Fordell Fife 209 B4
Forden Powys 93 A6
Forder Green Devon 8 A1
Fordham Cambs 102 D2
Fordham Essex 70 A3
Fordham Norf 102 B2
Fordhouses W Mid 96 A2
Fordingbridge Hants 31 D5

Fordon E Yorks 160 D4
Fordoun Aberds 233 A5
Ford's Green Suff 87 A6
Fordstreet Essex 70 A3
Fordwells Oxon 64 B4
Fordwich Kent 52 D3
Fordyce Aberds 267 C6
Forebridge Staffs 112 C3
Forest Durham 165 B6
Forest Becks Lancs 146 B1
Forest Gate London 49 A7
Forest Green Sur 35 B4
Forest Hall Cumb 154 A4
Forest Head Cumb 176 D3
Forest Hill Oxon 65 C6
Forest Lane Head N Yorks 148 B2
Forest Lodge Argyll 228 D1
Forest Lodge Highld 242 A3
Forest Lodge Perth 230 A3
Forest Mill Clack 208 A2
Forest Row E Sus 36 C2
Forest Town Notts 131 C5
Forestburn Gate Northumb 188 D3
Foresterseat Moray 266 D2
Forestside W Sus 33 D6
Forfar Angus 232 C2
Forgandenny Perth 219 C5
Forge Powys 91 C5
Forge Side Torf 60 C4
Forgewood N Lnrk 194 A2
Forgie Moray 267 D4
Forglen Ho. Aberds 268 D1
Formby Mers 136 C2
Forncett End Norf 104 B2
Forncett St Mary Norf 104 B2
Forncett St Peter Norf 104 B2
Forneth Perth 231 D4
Fornham All Saints Suff 87 A4
Fornham St Martin Suff 87 A4
Forres Moray 253 A6
Forrest Lodge Dumfries 182 D3
Forrestfield N Lnrk 207 D6
Forsbrook Staffs 112 A3
Forse Highld 275 A6
Forse Ho. Highld 275 A6
Forsinain Highld 279 D5
Forsinard Highld 279 D4
Forsinard Station Highld 279 D4
Forston Dorset 15 B6
Fort Augustus Highld 240 B1
Fort George Guern 6
Fort George Highld 252 A3
Fort Victoria Country Park & Marine Aquarium I o W 18 C2
Fort William Highld 237 B5
Forteviot Perth 219 C5
Forth S Lnrk 194 A4
Forth Road Bridge Fife 208 C4
Forthampton Glos 79 D6
Fortingall Perth 229 D6
Forton Hants 32 A3
Forton Lancs 145 B4
Forton Shrops 110 D3
Forton Som 14 A3
Forton Staffs 111 C6
Forton Heath Shrops 110 D3
Fortrie Aberds 256 B1
Fortrose Highld 252 A3
Fortuneswell Dorset 15 D6
Forty Green Bucks 67 D4
Forty Hill London 68 D3
Forward Green Suff 88 B1
Fosbury Wilts 45 D7
Fosdyke Lincs 117 B6
Foss Perth 230 C1
Foss Cross Glos 63 C6
Fossebridge Glos 64 B1
Foster Street Essex 69 C4
Fosterhouses S Yorks 141 B4
Foston Derbys 113 B5
Foston Lincs 115 A6
Foston N Yorks 149 A5
Foston on the Wolds E Yorks 151 B4
Fotherby Lincs 143 D5
Fotheringhay Northants 100 B2
Foubister Orkney 283 G6
Foul Mile E Sus 22 A4
Foulby W Yorks 140 B1
Foulden Borders 198 A3
Foulden Norf 102 B3
Foulis Castle Highld 264 D1
Foulridge Lancs 146 C2
Foulsham Norf 120 C2
Fountainhall Borders 196 B3
Fountains Abbey, Ripon N Yorks 147 A6
Four Ashes Staffs 95 C6
Four Ashes Suff 103 D6
Four Crosses Powys 93 A4
Four Crosses Powys 110 D1
Four Crosses Wrex 126 D2
Four Elms Kent 36 B2
Four Forks Som 28 B2
Four Gotes Cambs 118 D1
Four Lane Ends Ches 127 C5
Four Lanes Corn 3 B4
Four Marks Hants 33 B5
Four Mile Bridge Anglesey 122 C2
Four Oaks E Sus 37 D6
Four Oaks W Mid 97 C5
Four Oaks W Mid 96 B4
Four Roads Carms 57 B4
Four Roads I o M 152 E2
Four Throws Kent 37 D5
Fourlane Ends Derbys 130 D3
Fourlanes End Ches 128 D3
Fourpenny Highld 265 A4
Fourstones Northumb 177 C6
Fovant Wilts 31 C4
Foveran Aberds 257 D4
Fowey Corn 5 B6
Fowley Common Warr 137 D5
Fowlis Angus 220 A3
Fowlis Wester Perth 218 B4
Fowlmere Cambs 85 C6
Fownhope Hereford 78 D3
Fox Corner Sur 34 A2
Fox Lane Hants 34 A1
Fox Street Essex 71 A4
Foxbar Renfs 205 B4
Foxcombe Hill Oxon 65 C5
Foxdale I o M 152 D2
Foxearth Essex 87 C4
Foxfield Cumb 153 B3
Foxham Wilts 44 B3
Foxhole Corn 5 B4
Foxhole Swansea 57 C6
Foxholes N Yorks 160 D4
Foxhunt Green E Sus 22 A3
Foxley Norf 120 C2
Foxley Wilts 44 A2
Foxt Staffs 112 A4
Foxton Cambs 85 C6
Foxton Durham 167 C6
Foxton Leics 99 B4
Foxton Canal Locks Leics 98 C3
Foxup N Yorks 156 D2
Foxwist Green Ches 127 C6
Foxwood Shrops 95 D4
Foy Hereford 62 A1
Foyers Highld 251 D6
Fraddam Corn 2 B3
Fraddon Corn 4 B4
Fradley Staffs 113 D5
Fradswell Staffs 112 B3
Fraisthorpe E Yorks 151 A4
Framfield E Sus 36 D2
Framingham Earl Norf 104 A3
Framingham Pigot Norf 104 A3
Framlingham Suff 88 A3
Framlingham Castle Suff 88 A3
Frampton Dorset 15 B6
Frampton Lincs 117 B6
Frampton Cotterell S Glos 43 A5
Frampton Mansell Glos 63 C5
Frampton on Severn Glos 62 C3
Frampton West End Lincs 117 A5
Framsden Suff 88 B2
Framwellgate Moor Durham 167 A5
Franche Worcs 95 D6
Frankby Mers 126 A2
Frankley Worcs 96 C2
Frank's Bridge Powys 77 B5
Frankton Warks 98 D1
Frant E Sus 36 C3
Fraserburgh Aberds 269 C4
Frating Green Essex 71 A4
Fratton Ptsmth 19 B5
Freathy Corn 6 B3
Freckenham Suff 102 D2
Freckleton Lancs 136 A3
Freeby Leics 115 C6
Freehay Staffs 112 A4
Freeland Oxon 65 B5
Freeport Hornsea Outlet Village E Yorks 151 C5
Freester Shetland 285 H6
Freethorpe Norf 105 A5
Freiston Lincs 117 A6
Fremington Devon 25 B6
Fremington N Yorks 156 B4
Frenchay S Glos 43 B5
Frenchbeer Devon 12 C1
Frenich Stirl 216 D4
Frensham Sur 34 B1
Fresgoe Highld 279 B5
Freshfield Mers 136 C1
Freshford Bath 44 C1
Freshwater I o W 18 C2
Freshwater Bay I o W 18 C2
Freshwater East Pembs 55 E6
Fressingfield Suff 104 D3
Freston Suff 88 D2
Freswick Highld 281 B5
Fretherne Glos 62 C3
Frettenham Norf 120 D4
Freuchie Fife 220 D2
Freuchies Angus 231 B6
Freystrop Pembs 55 C5
Friar's Gate E Sus 36 C2
Friarton Perth 219 B6
Friday Bridge Cambs 101 A6
Friday Street E Sus 22 B4
Fridaythorpe E Yorks 150 B1
Friern Barnet London 68 D2
Friesland Argyll 223 B4
Friesthorpe Lincs 133 A5
Frieston Lincs 116 A2
Frieth Bucks 66 D2
Frilford Oxon 65 D5
Frilsham W Berks 46 B3
Frimley Sur 34 A1
Frimley Green Sur 34 A1
Frindsbury Medway 51 B4
Fring Norf 119 B4
Fringford Oxon 65 A7
Frinsted Kent 37 A6
Frinton-on-Sea Essex 71 A6
Friockheim Angus 232 D3
Friog Gwyn 90 A4
Frisby on the Wreake Leics 115 D4
Friskney Lincs 135 D4
Friskney Eaudike Lincs 135 D4
Friskney Tofts Lincs 135 D4
Friston E Sus 22 C3
Friston Suff 89 A5
Fritchley Derbys 130 D3
Frith Bank Lincs 117 A6
Frith Common Worcs 79 A4
Fritham Hants 31 D6
Frithelstock Devon 25 D5
Frithelstock Stone Devon 25 D5
Frithville Lincs 134 D3
Frittenden Kent 37 B6
Frittiscombe Devon 8 C2
Fritton Norf 104 B3
Fritton Norf 105 A5
Fritwell Oxon 65 A6
Frizinghall W Yorks 147 D5
Frizington Cumb 162 C3
Frocester Glos 62 C3
Frodesley Shrops 94 A3
Frodingham N Lincs 141 B6
Frodsham Ches 127 B5
Frogden Borders 187 A6
Froggatt Derbys 130 B2
Froghall Staffs 112 A4
Frogmore Devon 7 C6
Frogmore Hants 34 A1
Frognall Lincs 117 D4
Frogshail Norf 121 B4
Frolesworth Leics 98 B2
Frome Som 30 A1
Frome St Quintin Dorset 15 A5
Fromes Hill Hereford 79 C4
Fron Denb 125 C5
Fron Gwyn 107 A5
Fron Gwyn 106 C3
Fron Powys 77 A4
Fron Powys 93 A6
Fron Powys 93 B5
Froncysyllte Wrex 110 A1
Frongoch Gwyn 108 B4
Frostenden Suff 105 C5
Frosterley Durham 166 B3
Frotoft Orkney 282 E5
Froxfield Wilts 45 C6
Froxfield Green Hants 33 C6
Froyle Hants 33 A6
Fryerning Essex 69 C6
Fryton N Yorks 159 D5
Fulbeck Lincs 133 D4
Fulbourn Cambs 85 B7
Fulbrook Oxon 64 B3
Fulford Som 28 C2
Fulford Staffs 112 B3
Fulford York 149 C5
Fulham London 49 B5
Fulking W Sus 21 A5
Full Sutton E Yorks 149 B6
Fullarton Glasgow 205 B6
Fullarton N Ayrs 192 B3
Fuller Street Essex 70 B1
Fuller's Moor Ches 127 D4
Fullerton Hants 32 B2
Fulletby Lincs 134 B2
Fullwood E Ayrs 205 C4
Fulmer Bucks 48 A2
Fulmodestone Norf 120 B1
Fulnetby Lincs 133 B5
Fulstow Lincs 143 D5
Fulwell T & W 179 D5
Fulwood Lancs 145 D5
Fulwood S Yorks 130 A3
Fundenhall Norf 104 B2
Fundenhall Street Norf 104 B2
Funtington W Sus 19 A6
Funtley Hants 19 A4
Funtullich Perth 218 B2
Funzie Shetland 284 D8
Furley Devon 14 A2
Furnace Argyll 214 B3
Furnace Carms 57 B5
Furnace End Warks 97 B5
Furneaux Pelham Herts 68 A4
Furness Vale Derbys 129 A5
Furze Platt Windsor 48 A1
Furzehill Devon 26 A2
Fyfett Som 28 D2
Fyfield Essex 69 C5
Fyfield Glos 64 C3
Fyfield Hants 32 A1
Fyfield Oxon 65 D5
Fyfield Wilts 45 C5
Fylingthorpe N Yorks 160 A3
Fyvie Aberds 256 C2

G

Gabhsann bho Dheas W Isles 288 B5
Gabhsann bho Thuath W Isles 288 B5
Gablon Highld 264 A3
Gabroc Hill E Ayrs 205 C4
Gaddesby Leics 115 D4
Gadebridge Herts 67 C5
Gaer Powys 60 A3
Gaerllwyd Mon 61 D6
Gaerwen Anglesey 123 C4
Gagingwell Oxon 65 A5
Gaick Lodge Highld 241 D5
Gailey Staffs 112 D3
Gainford Durham 167 D4
Gainsborough Lincs 141 D6
Gainsborough Suff 88 C2
Gainsford End Essex 86 D3
Gairloch Highld 261 C5
Gairlochy Highld 239 D5
Gairney Bank Perth 208 A4
Gairnshiel Lodge Aberds 243 B5
Gaisgill Cumb 155 A5
Gaitsgill Cumb 164 A1
Galashiels Borders 196 C3
Galgate Lancs 145 B4
Galhampton Som 29 C6
Gallaberry Dumfries 184 D2
Gallachoille Argyll 213 D5
Gallanach Argyll 226 D3
Gallanach Argyll 223 A5
Gallantry Bank Ches 127 D5
Gallatown Fife 209 A5
Galley Common Warks 97 B6
Galley Hill Cambs 85 A5
Galleyend Essex 69 C7
Galleywood Essex 69 C7
Gallin Perth 229 D4
Gallowfauld Angus 232 D2
Gallows Green Staffs 113 A4
Galltair Highld 249 D5
Galmisdale Highld 234 B3
Galmpton Devon 7 C5
Galmpton Torbay 8 B2
Galphay N Yorks 157 D6
Galston E Ayrs 193 B5
Galtrigill Highld 258 C1
Gamblesby Cumb 165 B4
Gamesley Derbys 138 D3
Gamlingay Cambs 84 B4
Gammersgill N Yorks 157 C4
Gamston Notts 132 B2
Ganarew Hereford 62 B1
Ganavan Argyll 226 C3
Gang Corn 6 A2
Ganllwyd Gwyn 108 C2
Gannochy Angus 232 A3
Gannochy Perth 219 B6
Gansclet Highld 281 D5
Ganstead E Yorks 151 D4
Ganthorpe N Yorks 159 D5
Ganton N Yorks 160 D3
Garbat Highld 263 D6
Garbhallt Argyll 214 C3
Garboldisham Norf 103 C6
Garden City Flint 126 C3
Garden Village Wrex 126 D3
Garden Village W Yorks 148 D3
Gardenstown Aberds 268 C2
Garderhouse Shetland 285 J5
Gardham E Yorks 150 C2
Gardin Shetland 284 G6
Gare Hill Som 30 A1
Garelochhead Argyll 215 C5
Garford Oxon 65 D5
Garforth W Yorks 148 D3
Gargrave N Yorks 146 B3
Gargunnock Stirl 207 A5
Garlic Street Norf 104 C3
Garlieston Dumfries 171 C6
Garlinge Green Kent 52 D3
Garlogie Aberds 245 B4
Garmond Aberds 268 D3
Garmony Argyll 225 B5
Garmouth Moray 266 C4
Garn-yr-erw Torf 60 B4
Garnant Carms 58 D3
Garndiffaith Torf 61 C4
Garndolbenmaen Gwyn 107 B4
Garnedd Conwy 124 D2
Garnett Bridge Cumb 154 B4
Garnfadryn Gwyn 106 C2
Garnkirk N Lnrk 207 D4
Garnlydan Bl Gwent 60 B3
Garnswllt Swansea 57 B6
Garrabost W Isles 288 D6
Garraron Argyll 213 B6
Garras Corn 3 C5
Garreg Gwyn 107 B6
Garrick Perth 218 C3
Garrigill Cumb 165 A5
Garriston N Yorks 157 B5
Garroch Dumfries 182 D3
Garrogie Lodge Highld 240 A3
Garros Highld 259 B4
Garrow Perth 230 D2
Garryhorn Dumfries 182 C3
Garsdale Cumb 155 C6
Garsdale Head Cumb 155 B6
Garsdon Wilts 44 A3
Garshall Green Staffs 112 B3
Garsington Oxon 65 C6
Garstang Lancs 145 C4
Garston Mers 127 A4
Garswood Mers 137 D4
Gartcosh N Lnrk 207 D4
Garth Bridgend 40 B3
Garth Gwyn 123 C5
Garth Powys 76 C3
Garth Shetland 285 H4
Garth Wrex 110 A1
Garth Row Cumb 154 B4
Garthamlock Glasgow 205 B6
Garthbrengy Powys 76 D4
Garthdee Aberdeen 245 B6
Gartheli Ceredig 75 C4
Garthmyl Powys 93 B5
Garthorpe Leics 115 C6
Garthorpe N Lincs 141 B6
Gartly Aberds 255 C6
Gartmore Stirl 206 A3
Gartnagrenach Argyll 202 C2
Gartness N Lnrk 207 D5
Gartness Stirl 206 B3
Gartocharn W Dunb 206 B2
Garton E Yorks 151 D5
Garton-on-the-Wolds E Yorks 150 B2
Gartsherrie N Lnrk 207 D5
Gartymore Highld 274 C4
Garvald E Loth 210 C2
Garvamore Highld 240 C3
Garvard Argyll 212 C1
Garvault Hotel Highld 273 A5
Garve Highld 263 D5
Garvestone Norf 103 A6
Garvock Aberds 233 A5
Garvock Invclyd 204 A2
Garway Hereford 61 A6
Garway Hill Hereford 61 A6
Gaskan Highld 236 B1
Gastard Wilts 44 C2
Gasthorpe Norf 103 C5
Gatcombe I o W 18 C3
Gate Burton Lincs 132 A3
Gate Helmsley N Yorks 149 B5
Gateacre Mers 127 A4
Gatebeck Cumb 154 C4
Gateford Notts 131 A5
Gateforth N Yorks 140 A3
Gatehead E Ayrs 192 B3
Gatehouse Northumb 177 A5
Gatehouse of Fleet Dumfries 172 C4
Gatelawbridge Dumfries 183 C7
Gateley Norf 119 C6
Gatenby N Yorks 158 C2
Gateshead T & W 179 C4
Gateshead International Stadium T & W 179 C4
Gatesheath Ches 127 C4
Gateside Aberds 244 A3
Gateside Angus 232 D2
Gateside E Renf 205 C4
Gateside Fife 219 D6
Gateside N Ayrs 204 C3
Gathurst Gtr Man 136 C4
Gatley Gtr Man 128 A3
Gattonside Borders 197 C4
Gatwick Airport W Sus 35 B5
Gaufron Powys 76 A3
Gaulby Leics 98 A3
Gauldry Fife 220 B3
Gaunt's Common Dorset 17 A4
Gautby Lincs 134 B1
Gavinton Borders 197 A6
Gawber S Yorks 139 C6
Gawcott Bucks 82 D3
Gawsworth Ches 128 C3
Gawthorpe W Yorks 139 A5
Gawthrop Cumb 155 C5
Gawthwaite Cumb 153 B3
Gay Street W Sus 34 D3
Gaydon Warks 81 B6
Gayfield Orkney 282 B5
Gayhurst M Keynes 83 C5
Gayle N Yorks 156 C2
Gayles N Yorks 157 A5
Gayton Mers 126 A2
Gayton Norf 119 D4
Gayton Northants 83 B4
Gayton Staffs 112 C3
Gayton le Marsh Lincs 135 A4
Gayton le Wold Lincs 134 A2
Gayton Thorpe Norf 119 D4
Gaywood Norf 118 C3
Gazeley Suff 86 A3
Geanies House Highld 265 C4
Gearraidh Bhailteas W Isles 286 D3
Gearraidh Bhaird W Isles 288 E4
Gearraidh na h-Aibhne W Isles 288 D3
Gearraidh na Monadh W Isles 286 E3
Geary Highld 258 B2
Geddes House Highld 253 A4
Gedding Suff 87 B5
Geddington Northants 99 C5
Gedintailor Highld 247 A4
Gedling Notts 115 A4
Gedney Lincs 117 C7
Gedney Broadgate Lincs 117 C7
Gedney Drove End Lincs 118 C1
Gedney Dyke Lincs 117 C7
Gedney Hill Lincs 117 D6
Gee Cross Gtr Man 138 D2
Geilston Argyll 206 C1
Geirinis W Isles 286 B3
Geise Highld 280 B3
Geisiadar W Isles 288 D2
Geldeston Norf 105 B4
Gell Conwy 124 C3
Gelli Pembs 55 C6
Gelli Rhondda 41 B4
Gellideg M Tydf 60 C2
Gellifor Denb 125 C6
Gelligaer Caerph 41 B6
Gellilydan Gwyn 107 C6
Gellinudd Neath 40 A2
Gellyburn Perth 219 A5
Gellywen Carms 73 D5
Gelston Dumfries 173 C5
Gelston Lincs 116 A2
Gembling E Yorks 151 B4
Gentleshaw Staffs 113 D4
Geocrab W Isles 288 H2
George Green Bucks 48 A3
George Nympton Devon 26 C2
Georgefield Dumfries 185 C5
Georgeham Devon 25 B5
Georgetown Bl Gwent 60 C3
Gerlan Gwyn 123 D6
Germansweek Devon 11 B5
Germoe Corn 2 C3
Gerrans Corn 4 D3
Gerrards Cross Bucks 48 A3
Gestingthorpe Essex 87 D4
Geuffordd Powys 109 D7
Gib Hill Ches 127 B6
Gibbet Hill Warks 98 C2
Gibbshill Dumfries 173 A5
Gidea Park London 50 A2
Gidleigh Devon 12 C1
Giffnock E Renf 205 C5
Gifford E Loth 210 D2
Giffordland N Ayrs 204 D2
Giffordtown Fife 220 C2
Giggleswick N Yorks 146 A2
Gilberdyke E Yorks 141 A6
Gilchriston E Loth 210 D1
Gilcrux Cumb 163 A4
Gildersome W Yorks 139 A5
Gildingwells S Yorks 131 A5
Gileston V Glam 41 E5
Gilfach Caerph 41 B6
Gilfach Goch Rhondda 41 C4
Gilfachrheda Ceredig 73 A7
Gillamoor N Yorks 159 C5
Gillar's Green Mers 136 D3
Gillen Highld 258 C2
Gilling East N Yorks 159 D5
Gilling West N Yorks 157 A5
Gillingham Dorset 30 C2
Gillingham Medway 51 C4
Gillingham Norf 105 B5
Gillock Highld 280 C4
Gillow Heath Staffs 128 D3
Gills Highld 281 A5
Gill's Green Kent 37 C5
Gilmanscleuch Borders 196 D2
Gilmerton Edin 209 D5
Gilmerton Perth 218 B3
Gilmonby Durham 166 D2
Gilmorton Leics 98 C2
Gilmourton S Lnrk 205 D6
Gilsland Cumb 176 C4
Gilsland Spa Cumb 176 C4
Gilston Borders 196 A3
Gilston Herts 68 B4
Gilwern Mon 60 B4
Gimingham Norf 121 B4
Giosla W Isles 288 E2
Gipping Suff 87 A6
Gipsey Bridge Lincs 117 A5
Girdle Toll N Ayrs 204 D3
Girlsta Shetland 285 H6
Girsby N Yorks 158 A2
Girtford Beds 84 B3
Girthon Dumfries 172 C4
Girton Cambs 85 A6
Girton Notts 132 C3
Girvan S Ayrs 180 B3
Gisburn Lancs 146 C2
Gisleham Suff 105 C6
Gislingham Suff 104 D1
Gissing Norf 104 C2

Gittisham Devon 13 B6
Gladestry Powys 77 B6
Gladsmuir E Loth 210 C1
Glais Swansea 40 A2
Glaisdale N Yorks 159 A6
Glame Highld 248 B2
Glamis Angus 232 D1
Glamis Castle Angus 232 D1
Glan Adda Gwyn 123 C5
Glan-Conwy Conwy 124 D3
Glan Conwy Conwy 124 B3
Glan-Duar Carms 58 A2
Glan-Dwyfach Gwyn 107 B4
Glan Gors Anglesey 123 C4
Glan-rhyd Gwyn 107 A4
Glan-traeth Anglesey 122 C2
Glan-y-don Flint 125 B6
Glan-y-nant Powys 92 C3
Glan-y-wern Gwyn 107 C6
Glan-yr-afon Anglesey 123 B6
Glan-yr-afon Gwyn 108 A4
Glan-yr-afon Gwyn 109 A5
Glanaman Carms 57 A6
Glandford Norf 120 A2
Glandwr Pembs 73 D4
Glandy Cross Carms 72 D4
Glandyfi Ceredig 91 C4
Glangrwyney Powys 60 B4
Glanmule Powys 93 B5
Glanrafon Ceredig 90 D4
Glanrhyd Gwyn 106 C2
Glanrhyd Pembs 72 B4
Glanton Northumb 188 B3
Glanton Pike Northumb 188 B3
Glanvilles Wootton Dorset 15 A6
Glapthorn Northants 100 B2
Glapwell Derbys 131 C4
Glas-allt Shiel Aberds 243 D5
Glasbury Powys 77 D5
Glaschoil Highld 253 C6
Glascoed Denb 125 B4
Glascoed Mon 61 C5
Glascoed Powys 109 D6
Glascorrie Aberds 243 C6
Glascote Staffs 97 A5
Glascwm Powys 77 B5
Glasdrum Argyll 227 B5
Glasfryn Conwy 125 D4
Glasgow Glasgow 205 B5
Glasgow Airport Renfs 205 B4
Glasgow Art Gallery & Museum Glasgow 205 B5
Glasgow Botanic Gardens Glasgow 205 B5
Glasgow Cathedral Glasgow 205 B6
Glasgow Prestwick International Airport S Ayrs 192 C3
Glashvin Highld 259 B4
Glasinfryn Gwyn 123 D5
Glasnacardoch Highld 235 A5
Glasnakille Highld 247 C4
Glasphein Highld 258 D1
Glaspwll Powys 91 C5
Glassburn Highld 251 C5
Glasserton Dumfries 171 D6
Glassford S Lnrk 194 B2
Glasshouse Hill Glos 62 A3
Glasshouses N Yorks 147 A5
Glasslie Fife 220 D2
Glasson Cumb 175 B5
Glasson Lancs 144 B4
Glassonby Cumb 164 B3
Glasterlaw Angus 232 C3
Glaston Rutland 99 A5
Glastonbury Som 29 B5
Glastonbury Abbey Som 29 B4
Glatton Cambs 100 C3
Glazebrook Warr 137 D5
Glazebury Warr 137 D5
Glazeley Shrops 95 C5
Gleadless S Yorks 130 A3
Gleadsmoss Ches 128 C3
Gleann Tholàstaidh W Isles 288 C6
Gleaston Cumb 153 C3
Gleiniant Powys 92 B3
Glemsford Suff 87 C4
Glen Dumfries 172 C3
Glen Dumfries 173 A6
Glen Auldyn I o M 152 B4
Glen Bernisdale Highld 259 D4
Glen Ho. Borders 176 A2
Glen Mona I o M 152 C4
Glen Nevis House Highld 237 B5
Glen Parva Leics 98 B2
Glen Sluain Argyll 214 C3
Glen Tanar House Aberds 244 C1
Glen Trool Lodge Dumfries 181 C6
Glen Village Falk 208 C1
Glen Vine I o M 152 D3
Glenamachrie Argyll 226 D4
Glenbarr Argyll 190 B2
Glenbeg Highld 235 D4
Glenbeg Highld 253 D6
Glenbervie Aberds 245 D4
Glenboig N Lnrk 207 D5
Glenborrodale Highld 235 D5
Glenbranter Argyll 215 C4
Glenbreck Borders 195 D5
Glenbrein Lodge Highld 240 A2
Glenbrittle House Highld 246 B3
Glenbuchat Lodge Aberds 243 A6
Glenbuck E Ayrs 194 D2
Glenburn Renfs 205 B4
Glencalvie Lodge Highld 263 B6
Glencanisp Lodge Highld 270 B4
Glencaple Dumfries 174 B2
Glencarron Lodge Highld 250 A2
Glencarse Perth 219 B6
Glencassley Castle Highld 272 D2
Glenceitlein Highld 227 B6
Glencoe Highld 237 D4
Glencraig Fife 209 A4
Glencripesdale Highld 225 A5
Glencrosh Dumfries 183 D5
Glendavan Ho. Aberds 244 B1
Glendevon Perth 219 D4
Glendoe Lodge Highld 240 B2
Glendoebeg Highld 240 B2
Glendoick Perth 220 B2
Glendoll Lodge Angus 231 A6
Glendoune S Ayrs 180 B3
Glenduckie Fife 220 C2
Glendye Lodge Aberds 244 D3
Gleneagles Hotel Perth 218 C4
Gleneagles House Perth 218 D4
Glenegedale Argyll 200 C3
Glenelg Highld 238 A2
Glenernie Moray 253 B6
Glenfarg Perth 219 C6
Glenfarquhar Lodge Aberds 245 D4
Glenferness House Highld 253 B5
Glenfeshie Lodge Highld 241 C6
Glenfiddich Distillery, Dufftown Moray 254 B4
Glenfield Leics 98 A2
Glenfinnan Highld 238 D3
Glenfoot Perth 219 C6
Glenfyne Lodge Argyll 215 A5
Glengap Dumfries 173 C4
Glengarnock N Ayrs 204 C3
Glengorm Castle Argyll 224 A3
Glengrasco Highld 259 D4
Glenhead Farm Angus 231 B6
Glenhoul Dumfries 182 D4
Glenhurich Highld 236 C2
Glenkerry Borders 185 A5
Glenkiln Dumfries 173 A6
Glenkindie Aberds 244 A1
Glenlatterach Moray 266 D2
Glenlee Dumfries 182 D4
Glenlichorn Perth 218 C2
Glenlivet Moray 254 D2
Glenlochsie Perth 231 A4
Glenloig N Ayrs 191 B5
Glenluce Dumfries 171 B4
Glenmallan Argyll 215 C5
Glenmarksie Highld 251 A5
Glenmassan Argyll 215 D4
Glenmavis N Lnrk 207 D5
Glenmaye I o M 152 D2
Glenmidge Dumfries 183 D6
Glenmore Argyll 213 A6
Glenmore Highld 259 D4
Glenmore Lodge Highld 242 B2
Glenmoy Angus 232 B2
Glenogil Angus 232 B2
Glenprosen Lodge Angus 231 B6
Glenprosen Village Angus 232 B1
Glenquiech Angus 232 B2
Glenreasdell Mains Argyll 202 C3
Glenree N Ayrs 191 C5
Glenridding Cumb 164 D1
Glenrossal Highld 272 D2
Glenrothes Fife 220 D2
Glensanda Highld 226 B3
Glensaugh Aberds 233 A4
Glenshero Lodge Highld 240 C3
Glenstockadale Dumfries 170 A2
Glenstriven Argyll 203 A5
Glentaggart S Lnrk 194 D3
Glentham Lincs 142 D2
Glentirranmuir Stirl 207 A4
Glenton Aberds 256 D1
Glentress Borders 196 C1
Glentromie Lodge Highld 241 C5
Glentrool Village Dumfries 181 D5
Glentruan I o M 152 A4
Glentruim House Highld 241 C4
Glenturret Distillery, Crieff Perth 218 B3
Glentworth Lincs 133 A4
Glenuig Highld 235 C5
Glenurquhart Highld 264 D3
Glespin S Lnrk 194 D3
Gletness Shetland 285 H6
Glewstone Hereford 62 A1
Glinton P'boro 100 A3
Glooston Leics 99 B4
Glororum Northumb 199 C5
Glossop Derbys 138 D3
Gloster Hill Northumb 189 C5
Gloucester Glos 63 B4
Gloucester Cathedral Glos 63 B4
Gloucestershire Airport Glos 63 A4
Gloup Shetland 284 C7
Glusburn N Yorks 147 C4
Glutt Lodge Highld 274 A3
Glutton Bridge Derbys 129 C5
Glympton Oxon 65 A5
Glyn-Ceiriog Wrex 109 B7
Glyn-cywarch Gwyn 107 C6
Glyn Ebwy = Ebbw Vale Bl Gwent 60 C3
Glyn-neath = Glynedd Neath 59 E5
Glynarthen Ceredig 73 B6
Glynbrochan Powys 92 C3
Glyncoch Rhondda 41 B5
Glyncorrwg Neath 40 B3
Glynde E Sus 22 B2
Glyndebourne E Sus 22 A2
Glyndyfrdwy Denb 109 A6
Glynedd = Glyn-neath Neath 59 E5
Glynogwr Bridgend 41 C4
Glyntaff Rhondda 41 C5
Glyntawe Powys 59 D5
Gnosall Staffs 112 C2
Gnosall Heath Staffs 112 C2
Goadby Leics 99 B4
Goadby Marwood Leics 115 C5
Goat Lees Kent 38 A2
Goatacre Wilts 44 B4
Goathill Dorset 29 D6
Goathland N Yorks 160 A2
Goathurst Som 28 B2
Gobernuisgach Lodge Highld 277 D5
Gobhaig W Isles 287 D5
Gobowen Shrops 110 B2
Godalming Sur 34 B2
Godley Gtr Man 138 D2
Godmanchester Cambs 100 D4
Godmanstone Dorset 15 B6
Godmersham Kent 52 D2
Godney Som 29 A4
Godolphin Cross Corn 3 B4
Godre'r-graig Neath 59 E4
Godshill Hants 31 D5
Godshill I o W 18 C4
Godstone Sur 35 A6
Godstone Farm Sur 35 A6
Godwinscroft Hants 17 B5
Goetre Mon 61 C5
Goferydd Anglesey 122 B2
Goff's Oak Herts 68 C3
Gogar Edin 209 C4
Goginan Ceredig 91 D4
Golan Gwyn 107 B5
Golant Corn 5 B6
Golberdon Corn 10 D4
Golborne Gtr Man 137 D5
Golcar W Yorks 139 B4
Gold Hill Norf 102 B1
Goldcliff Newport 42 A2
Golden Cross E Sus 22 A3
Golden Green Kent 36 B4
Golden Grove Carms 57 A5
Golden Hill Hants 17 B6
Golden Pot Hants 33 A6
Golden Valley Glos 63 A5
Goldenhill Stoke 128 D3
Golders Green London 49 A5
Goldhanger Essex 70 C3
Golding Shrops 94 A3
Goldington Beds 84 B2
Goldsborough N Yorks 148 B2
Goldsborough N Yorks 169 D6
Goldsithney Corn 2 B3
Goldsworthy Devon 25 C4
Goldthorpe S Yorks 140 C2
Gollanfield Highld 253 A4
Golspie Highld 274 D2
Golval Highld 279 B4
Gomeldon Wilts 31 B5
Gomersal W Yorks 139 A5
Gomshall Sur 34 B3
Gonalston Notts 115 A4
Gonfirth Shetland 285 G5
Good Easter Essex 69 B6
Gooderstone Norf 102 A3
Goodleigh Devon 25 B7
Goodmanham E Yorks 150 C1
Goodnestone Kent 52 C2
Goodnestone Kent 53 D4
Goodrich Hereford 62 B1
Goodrington Torbay 8 B2
Goodshaw Lancs 137 A7
Goodwick = Wdig Pembs 72 C2
Goodwood Racecourse W Sus 20 A1
Goodworth Clatford Hants 32 A2
Goole E Yorks 141 A5
Goonbell Corn 4 C2
Goonhavern Corn 4 B2
Goose Eye W Yorks 147 C4
Goose Green Gtr Man 137 C4
Goose Green Norf 104 C2
Goose Green W Sus 21 A4
Gooseham Corn 24 D3
Goosey Oxon 65 D4
Goosnargh Lancs 145 D5
Goostrey Ches 128 B2
Gorcott Hill Warks 80 A3
Gord Shetland 285 L6
Gordon Borders 197 B5
Gordonbush Highld 274 D2
Gordonsburgh Moray 267 C5
Gordonstoun Moray 266 C2
Gordonstown Aberds 267 D6
Gordonstown Aberds 256 C2
Gore Kent 53 D5
Gore Cross Wilts 44 D4
Gore Pit Essex 70 B2
Gorebridge Midloth 209 D6
Gorefield Cambs 117 D7
Gorey Jersey 6
Gorgie Edin 209 C5
Goring Oxon 47 A4
Goring-by-Sea W Sus 21 B4
Goring Heath Oxon 47 B4
Gorleston-on-Sea Norf 105 A6
Gornalwood W Mid 96 B2
Gorrachie Aberds 268 D2
Gorran Churchtown Corn 5 C4
Gorran Haven Corn 5 C5
Gorrenberry Borders 186 D3
Gors Ceredig 75 A5
Gorse Hill Swindon 45 A5
Gorsedd Flint 125 B6
Gorseinon Swansea 57 C5
Gorseness Orkney 282 F5
Gorsgoch Ceredig 74 C3
Gorslas Carms 57 A5
Gorsley Glos 62 A2
Gorstan Highld 263 D5
Gorstanvorran Highld 236 B2
Gorsteyhill Staffs 128 D2
Gorsty Hill Staffs 113 C5
Gortantaoid Argyll 200 A3
Gorton Gtr Man 138 D1
Gosbeck Suff 88 B2
Gosberton Lincs 117 B5
Gosberton Clough Lincs 117 C4
Gosfield Essex 70 A1
Gosford Hereford 78 A3
Gosforth Cumb 162 D3
Gosforth T & W 179 C4
Gosmore Herts 68 A1
Gosport Hants 19 B5
Gossabrough Shetland 284 E7
Gossington Glos 62 C3
Goswick Northumb 199 B4
Gotham Notts 114 B3
Gotherington Glos 63 A5
Gott Shetland 285 J6
Goudhurst Kent 37 C5
Goulceby Lincs 134 B2
Gourdas Aberds 256 B2
Gourdon Aberds 233 A6
Gourock Invclyd 204 A2
Govan Glasgow 205 B5
Govanhill Glasgow 205 B5
Goveton Devon 7 C6
Govilon Mon 61 B4
Gowanhill Aberds 269 C5
Gowdall E Yorks 140 A4
Gowerton Swansea 57 C5
Gowkhall Fife 208 B3
Gowthorpe E Yorks 149 B6
Goxhill E Yorks 151 C4
Goxhill N Lincs 142 A3
Goxhill Haven N Lincs 142 A3
Goytre Neath 40 C2
Grabhair W Isles 288 F4
Graby Lincs 116 C3
Grade Corn 3 D5
Graffham W Sus 20 A2
Grafham Cambs 84 A3
Grafham Sur 34 B3
Grafton Hereford 78 D2
Grafton N Yorks 148 A3
Grafton Oxon 64 C3
Grafton Shrops 110 D3
Grafton Worcs 78 A3
Grafton Flyford Worcs 80 B2
Grafton Regis Northants 83 C4
Grafton Underwood Northants 99 C6
Grafty Green Kent 37 B6
Graianrhyd Denb 126 D2
Graig Conwy 124 B3
Graig Denb 125 B5
Graig-fechan Denb 125 D6
Grain Medway 51 B5
Grainsby Lincs 143 D4
Grainthorpe Lincs 143 D5
Grampound Corn 4 C4
Grampound Road Corn 4 B4
Gramsdal W Isles 286 A4
Granborough Bucks 66 A2
Granby Notts 115 B5
Grandborough Warks 82 A1
Grandtully Perth 230 C3
Grange Cumb 163 C5
Grange E Ayrs 193 B4
Grange Medway 51 C4
Grange Mers 126 A2
Grange Perth 220 B2
Grange Crossroads Moray 267 D5
Grange Hall Moray 265 D6
Grange Hill Essex 68 D4
Grange Moor W Yorks 139 B5
Grange of Lindores Fife 220 C2
Grange-over-Sands Cumb 154 D3
Grange Villa Durham 179 D4
Grangemill Derbys 130 D2
Grangemouth Falk 208 B2
Grangepans Falk 208 B3
Grangetown Cardiff 41 D6
Grangetown Redcar 168 C3
Granish Highld 242 A2
Gransmoor E Yorks 151 B4
Granston Pembs 55 A4
Grantchester Cambs 85 B6
Grantham Lincs 116 B2
Grantley N Yorks 147 A6
Grantlodge Aberds 245 A4
Granton Dumfries 184 B3
Granton Edin 209 C5
Grantown-on-Spey Highld 253 D6
Grantshouse Borders 211 D5
Grappenhall Warr 127 A6
Grasby Lincs 142 C2
Grasmere Cumb 154 A2
Grasscroft Gtr Man 138 C2
Grassendale Mers 126 A3
Grassholme Durham 166 C2
Grassington N Yorks 147 A4
Grassmoor Derbys 131 C4
Grassthorpe Notts 132 C2
Grateley Hants 32 A1
Gratwich Staffs 112 B4
Graveley Cambs 84 A4
Graveley Herts 68 A2
Gravelly Hill W Mid 96 B4
Gravels Shrops 94 A1
Graven Shetland 284 F6
Graveney Kent 52 C2
Gravesend Herts 68 A4
Gravesend Kent 50 B3
Grayingham Lincs 142 D1
Grayrigg Cumb 155 B4
Grays Thurrock 50 B3
Grayshott Hants 34 C1
Grayswood Sur 34 C2
Graythorp Hrtlpl 168 C3
Grazeley Wokingham 47 C4
Greasbrough S Yorks 140 D2
Greasby Mers 126 A2
Great Abington Cambs 86 C1
Great Addington Northants 99 D6
Great Alne Warks 80 B4
Great Altcar Lancs 136 C2
Great Amwell Herts 68 B3
Great Asby Cumb 165 D4
Great Ashfield Suff 87 A5
Great Ayton N Yorks 168 D3
Great Baddow Essex 70 C1
Great Bardfield Essex 86 D2
Great Barford Beds 84 B3
Great Barr W Mid 96 B3
Great Barrington Glos 64 B3
Great Barrow Ches 127 C4
Great Barton Suff 87 A4
Great Barugh N Yorks 159 D6
Great Bavington Northumb 178 A1
Great Bealings Suff 88 C3
Great Bedwyn Wilts 45 C6
Great Bentley Essex 71 A5
Great Billing Northants 83 A5
Great Bircham Norf 119 B4
Great Blakenham Suff 88 B2
Great Blencow Cumb 164 B2
Great Bolas Telford 111 C5
Great Bookham Sur 35 A4
Great Bourton Oxon 82 C1
Great Bowden Leics 99 C4
Great Bradley Suff 86 B2
Great Braxted Essex 70 B2
Great Bricett Suff 87 B6
Great Brickhill Bucks 83 D6
Great Bridge W Mid 96 B2
Great Bridgeford Staffs 112 C2
Great Brington Northants 82 A3
Great Bromley Essex 71 A4
Great Broughton Cumb 162 A3
Great Broughton N Yorks 158 A4
Great Budworth Ches 127 B6
Great Burdon Darl 167 D6
Great Burgh Sur 35 A5
Great Burstead Essex 69 D6
Great Busby N Yorks 158 A4
Great Canfield Essex 69 B5
Great Carlton Lincs 135 A4
Great Casterton Rutland 100 A2
Great Chart Kent 38 A1
Great Chatwell Staffs 112 D1
Great Chesterford Essex 85 C7
Great Cheverell Wilts 44 D3
Great Chishill Cambs 85 D6
Great Clacton Essex 71 B5
Great Cliff W Yorks 139 B6
Great Clifton Cumb 162 B3
Great Coates NE Lincs 143 C4
Great Comberton Worcs 80 C2
Great Corby Cumb 176 D2
Great Cornard Suff 87 C4
Great Cowden E Yorks 151 C5
Great Coxwell Oxon 64 D3
Great Crakehall N Yorks 157 B6
Great Cransley Northants 99 D5
Great Cressingham Norf 103 A4
Great Crosby Mers 136 D2
Great Cubley Derbys 113 B5
Great Dalby Leics 115 D5
Great Denham Beds 84 C2
Great Doddington Northants 83 A5
Great Dunham Norf 119 D5
Great Dunmow Essex 69 A6
Great Durnford Wilts 31 B5
Great Easton Essex 69 A6
Great Easton Leics 99 B5
Great Eccleston Lancs 144 C4
Great Edstone N Yorks 159 C6
Great Ellingham Norf 103 B6
Great Elm Som 30 A1
Great Eversden Cambs 85 B5
Great Fencote N Yorks 157 B6
Great Finborough Suff 87 B6
Great Fransham Norf 119 D5
Great Gaddesden Herts 67 B5
Great Gidding Cambs 100 C3
Great Givendale E Yorks 149 B7
Great Glemham Suff 88 A4
Great Glen Leics 98 B3
Great Gonerby Lincs 116 B1
Great Gransden Cambs 85 B4
Great Green Norf 104 C3
Great Green Suff 87 B5
Great Habton N Yorks 159 D6
Great Hale Lincs 116 A4
Great Hallingbury Essex 69 B5
Great Hampden Bucks 66 C3
Great Harrowden Northants 99 D5
Great Harwood Lancs 146 D1
Great Haseley Oxon 66 C1
Great Hatfield E Yorks 151 C4
Great Haywood Staffs 112 C3
Great Heath W Mid 97 C6
Great Heck N Yorks 140 A3
Great Henny Essex 87 D4
Great Hinton Wilts 44 D3
Great Hockham Norf 103 B5
Great Holland Essex 71 B6
Great Horkesley Essex 87 D5
Great Hormead Herts 68 A3
Great Horton W Yorks 147 D5
Great Horwood Bucks 83 D4
Great Houghton Northants 83 B4
Great Houghton S Yorks 140 C2
Great Hucklow Derbys 130 B1
Great Kelk E Yorks 151 B4
Great Kimble Bucks 66 C3
Great Kingshill Bucks 66 D3
Great Langton N Yorks 157 B6
Great Leighs Essex 70 B1
Great Leighs Racecourse Essex 70 B1
Great Lever Gtr Man 137 C6
Great Limber Lincs 142 C3
Great Linford M Keynes 83 C5
Great Livermere Suff 103 D4
Great Longstone Derbys 130 B2
Great Lumley Durham 167 A5
Great Lyth Shrops 94 A2
Great Malvern Worcs 79 C5
Great Maplestead Essex 87 D4
Great Marton Blkpool 144 D3
Great Massingham Norf 119 C4
Great Melton Norf 104 A2
Great Milton Oxon 66 C1
Great Missenden Bucks 66 C3
Great Mitton Lancs 145 D7
Great Mongeham Kent 53 D5
Great Moulton Norf 104 B2
Great Munden Herts 68 A3
Great Musgrave Cumb 165 D5
Great Ness Shrops 110 D2
Great Notley Essex 70 A1
Great Oakley Essex 71 A5
Great Oakley Northants 99 C5
Great Offley Herts 67 A6
Great Orme Tramway, Llandudno Conwy 124 A2
Great Ormside Cumb 165 D5
Great Orton Cumb 175 C6
Great Ouseburn N Yorks 148 A3
Great Oxendon Northants 99 C4
Great Oxney Green Essex 69 C6
Great Palgrave Norf 119 D5
Great Parndon Essex 68 C4
Great Paxton Cambs 84 A4
Great Plumpton Lancs 144 D3
Great Plumstead Norf 121 D5
Great Ponton Lincs 116 B2
Great Preston W Yorks 140 A2
Great Raveley Cambs 101 C4

Great Rissington Glos 64 B2
Great Rollright Oxon 81 D6
Great Ryburgh Norf 119 C6
Great Ryle Northumb 188 B3
Great Ryton Shrops 94 A2
Great Saling Essex 69 A7
Great Salkeld Cumb 164 B3
Great Sampford Essex 86 D2
Great Sankey Warr 127 A5
Great Saxham Suff 86 A3
Great Shefford W Berks 46 B1
Great Shelford Cambs 85 B6
Great Smeaton N Yorks 158 A2
Great Snoring Norf 119 B6
Great Somerford Wilts 44 A3
Great Stainton Darl 167 C6
Great Stambridge Essex 70 D2
Great Staughton Cambs 84 A3
Great Steeping Lincs 135 C4
Great Stonar Kent 53 D5
Great Strickland Cumb 164 C3
Great Stukeley Cambs 100 D4
Great Sturton Lincs 134 B2
Great Sutton Ches 126 B3
Great Sutton Shrops 94 C3
Great Swinburne Northumb 178 B1
Great Tew Oxon 65 A4
Great Tey Essex 70 A2
Great Thurkleby N Yorks 158 D3
Great Thurlow Suff 86 B2
Great Torrington Devon 25 D5
Great Tosson Northumb 188 C3
Great Totham Essex 70 B2
Great Totham Essex 70 B2
Great Tows Lincs 143 D4
Great Urswick Cumb 153 C3
Great Wakering Essex 51 A6
Great Waldingfield Suff 87 C5
Great Walsingham Norf 119 B6
Great Waltham Essex 69 B6
Great Warley Essex 69 D5
Great Washbourne Glos 80 D2
Great Weldon Northants 99 C6
Great Welnetham Suff 87 B4
Great Wenham Suff 87 D6
Great Whittington Northumb 178 B2
Great Wigborough Essex 70 B3
Great Wilbraham Cambs 86 B1
Great Wishford Wilts 31 B4
Great Witcombe Glos 63 B5
Great Witley Worcs 79 A5
Great Wolford Warks 81 D5
Great Wratting Suff 86 C2
Great Wymondley Herts 68 A2
Great Wyrley Staffs 96 A2
Great Wytheford Shrops 111 D4
Great Yarmouth Norf 105 A6
Great Yarmouth Sea Life Centre Norf 105 A6
Great Yeldham Essex 86 D3
Greater Doward Hereford 62 B1
Greatford Lincs 116 D3
Greatgate Staffs 113 A4
Greatham Hants 33 B6
Greatham Hrtlpl 168 C2
Greatham W Sus 20 A3
Greatstone on Sea Kent 38 C2
Greatworth Northants 82 C2
Greave Lancs 138 A1
Greeba I o M 152 C3
Green Denb 125 C5
Green End Beds 84 B3
Green Hammerton N Yorks 148 B3
Green Lane Powys 93 B5
Green Ore Som 43 D4
Green St Green London 50 C1
Green Street Herts 68 D1
Greenbank Shetland 284 C7
Greenburn W Loth 208 D2
Greendikes Northumb 188 A3
Greenfield Beds 84 D2
Greenfield Flint 126 B1
Greenfield Gtr Man 138 C2
Greenfield Highld 239 B6
Greenfield Oxon 66 D2
Greenford London 48 A4
Greengairs N Lnrk 207 C5
Greenham W Berks 46 C2
Greenhaugh Northumb 177 A5
Greenhead Northumb 177 C4
Greenhill Falk 207 C6
Greenhill London 49 A4
Greenhill Kent 52 C3
Greenhill Leics 114 D2
Greenhills N Ayrs 204 C3
Greenhithe Kent 50 B2
Greenholm E Ayrs 193 B5
Greenholme Cumb 155 A4
Greenhouse Borders 187 A4
Greenhow Hill N Yorks 147 A5
Greenigoe Orkney 283 G5
Greenland Highld 280 B4
Greenlands Bucks 47 A5
Greenlaw Aberds 268 D1
Greenlaw Borders 197 B6
Greenlea Dumfries 174 A3
Greenloaning Perth 218 D3
Greenmeadow Community Farm, Pontnewydd Torf 61 D4
Greenmount Gtr Man 137 B6
Greenmow Shetland 285 L6
Greenock Invclyd 204 A2
Greenock West Invclyd 204 A2
Greenodd Cumb 154 C2
Greenrow Cumb 174 C4
Greens Norton Northants 82 C3
Greenside T & W 178 C3
Greensidehill Northumb 188 B2
Greenstead Green Essex 70 A2
Greensted Essex 69 C5
Greensted Church, Chipping Ongar Essex 69 C5
Greenwich London 49 B6
Greet Glos 80 D3
Greete Shrops 94 D3
Greetham Lincs 134 B3
Greetham Rutland 116 D2
Greetland W Yorks 138 A3
Gregg Hall Cumb 154 B3
Gregson Lane Lancs 137 A4
Greinetobht W Isles 287 G3
Greinton Som 28 B4
Gremista Shetland 285 J6
Grenaby I o M 152 D2
Grendon Northants 83 A5
Grendon Warks 97 A5
Grendon Common Warks 97 B5
Grendon Green Hereford 78 B3
Grendon Underwood Bucks 66 A1
Grenofen Devon 11 D5
Grenoside S Yorks 139 D6
Greosabhagh W Isles 288 H2
Gresford Wrex 126 D3
Gresham Norf 120 B3
Greshornish Highld 258 C3
Gressenhall Norf 119 D6
Gressingham Lancs 145 A5
Gresty Green Ches 128 D2
Greta Bridge Durham 166 D3
Gretna Dumfries 175 B6
Gretna Green Dumfries 175 B6
Gretton Glos 80 D3
Gretton Northants 99 B5
Gretton Shrops 94 B3
Grewelthorpe N Yorks 157 D6
Grey Green N Lincs 141 C5
Greygarth N Yorks 157 D5
Greynor Carms 57 B5
Greysouthen Cumb 162 B3
Greystoke Cumb 164 B2
Greystone Angus 232 D3
Greystone Dumfries 174 A2
Greywell Hants 47 D5
Griais W Isles 288 C5
Grianan W Isles 288 D5
Gribthorpe E Yorks 149 D6
Gridley Corner Devon 11 B4
Griff Warks 97 C6
Griffithstown Torf 61 D4
Grimbister Orkney 282 F4
Grimblethorpe Lincs 134 A2
Grimeford Village Lancs 137 B5
Grimethorpe S Yorks 140 C2
Griminis W Isles 286 A3
Grimister Shetland 284 D6
Grimley Worcs 79 A6
Grimness Orkney 283 H5
Grimoldby Lincs 134 A3
Grimpo Shrops 110 C2
Grimsargh Lancs 145 D5
Grimsbury Oxon 82 C1
Grimsby NE Lincs 143 B4
Grimscote Northants 82 B3
Grimscott Corn 10 A3
Grimsthorpe Lincs 116 C3
Grimston E Yorks 151 D5
Grimston Leics 115 C4
Grimston Norf 119 C4
Grimston York 149 B5
Grimstone Dorset 15 B6
Grinacombe Moor Devon 11 B5
Grindale E Yorks 161 D5
Grindigar Orkney 283 G6
Grindiscol Shetland 285 K6
Grindle Shrops 95 A5
Grindleford Derbys 130 B2
Grindleton Lancs 146 C1
Grindley Staffs 112 C4
Grindley Brook Shrops 111 A4
Grindlow Derbys 130 B1
Grindon Northumb 198 B3
Grindon Staffs 129 D5
Grindonmoor Gate Staffs 129 D5
Gringley on the Hill Notts 141 D5
Grinsdale Cumb 175 C6
Grinshill Shrops 111 C4
Grinton N Yorks 156 B4
Griomsidar W Isles 288 E4
Grishipoll Argyll 223 B4
Grisling Common E Sus 36 D2
Gristhorpe N Yorks 161 C4
Griston Norf 103 B5
Gritley Orkney 283 G6
Grittenham Wilts 44 A4
Grittleton Wilts 44 A2
Grizebeck Cumb 153 B3
Grizedale Cumb 154 B2
Grobister Orkney 282 E7
Groby Leics 98 A2
Groes Conwy 125 C5
Groes Neath 40 C2
Groes-faen Rhondda 41 C5
Groes-lwyd Powys 109 D7
Groesffordd Marli Denb 125 B5
Groeslon Gwyn 123 D5
Groeslon Gwyn 107 A4
Grogport Argyll 202 D3
Gromford Suff 89 B4
Gronant Flint 125 A5
Groombridge E Sus 36 C3
Grosmont Mon 61 A6
Grosmont N Yorks 160 A2
Grosvenor Museum, Chester Ches 127 C4
Groton Suff 87 C5
Groudle Glen Railway I o M 152 D4
Grougfoot Falk 208 C3
Grouville Jersey 6
Grove Dorset 15 D7
Grove Kent 53 C4
Grove Notts 132 B2
Grove Oxon 65 D5
Grove Park London 49 B7
Grove Vale W Mid 96 B3
Grovesend Swansea 57 B5
Grudie Highld 263 D5
Gruids Highld 272 D3
Gruinard House Highld 261 A6
Grula Highld 246 B2
Gruline Argyll 225 B4
Grunasound Shetland 285 K5
Grundisburgh Suff 88 B3
Grunsagill Lancs 146 B1
Gruting Shetland 285 J4
Grutness Shetland 285 N6
Gualachulain Highld 227 B6
Gualin Ho. Highld 276 C4
Guardbridge Fife 221 C4
Guarlford Worcs 79 C6
Guay Perth 230 D4
Guernsey Airport Guern 6
Guestling Green E Sus 23 A6
Guestling Thorn E Sus 23 A6
Guestwick Norf 120 C2
Guestwick Green Norf 120 C2
Guide Blkburn 137 A6
Guide Post Northumb 179 A4
Guilden Morden Cambs 85 C4
Guilden Sutton Ches 127 C4
Guildford Sur 34 B2
Guildtown Perth 219 A6
Guilsborough Northants 98 D3
Guilsfield Powys 109 D7
Guilton Kent 53 D4
Guineaford Devon 25 B6
Guisborough Redcar 168 D4
Guiseley W Yorks 147 C5
Guist Norf 120 C1
Guith Orkney 282 D6
Guiting Power Glos 64 A1
Gulberwick Shetland 285 K6
Gullane E Loth 210 B1
Gulval Corn 2 B2
Gulworthy Devon 11 D5
Gumfreston Pembs 55 D7
Gumley Leics 98 B3
Gummow's Shop Corn 4 B3
Gun Hill E Sus 22 A3
Gunby E Yorks 149 D6
Gunby Lincs 116 C2
Gundleton Hants 33 B5
Gunn Devon 26 B1
Gunnerside N Yorks 156 B3
Gunnerton Northumb 177 B7
Gunness N Lincs 141 B6
Gunnislake Corn 11 D5
Gunnista Shetland 285 J7
Gunthorpe Norf 120 B2
Gunthorpe Notts 115 A4
Gunthorpe P'boro 100 A3
Gunville I o W 18 C3
Gunwalloe Corn 3 C4
Gurnard I o W 18 B3
Gurnett Ches 129 B4
Gurney Slade Som 29 A6
Gurnos Powys 59 E4
Gussage All Saints Dorset 31 D4
Gussage St Michael Dorset 30 D3
Guston Kent 39 A5
Gutcher Shetland 284 D7
Guthrie Angus 232 C3
Guyhirn Cambs 101 A5
Guyhirn Gull Cambs 101 A5
Guy's Head Lincs 118 C1
Guy's Marsh Dorset 30 C2
Guyzance Northumb 189 C5
Gwaenysgor Flint 125 A5
Gwalchmai Anglesey 122 C3
Gwaun-Cae-Gurwen Neath 59 D4
Gwaun-Leision Neath 59 D4
Gwbert Ceredig 73 B4
Gweek Corn 3 C5
Gwehelog Mon 61 C5
Gwenddwr Powys 77 C4
Gwennap Corn 4 D2
Gwenter Corn 3 D5
Gwernaffield Flint 126 C2
Gwernesney Mon 61 C6
Gwernogle Carms 58 B2
Gwernymynydd Flint 126 C2
Gwersyllt Wrex 126 D3
Gwespyr Flint 125 A6
Gwithian Corn 2 A3
Gwredog Anglesey 123 B4
Gwyddelwern Denb 109 A5
Gwyddgrug Carms 58 B1
Gwydyr Uchaf Conwy 124 C2
Gwynfryn Wrex 126 D2
Gwystre Powys 77 A4
Gwytherin Conwy 124 C3
Gyfelia Wrex 110 A2
Gyffin Conwy 124 B2
Gyre Orkney 283 G4
Gyrn-goch Gwyn 107 B4

H

Habberley Shrops 94 A1
Habergham Lancs 146 D2
Habrough NE Lincs 142 B3
Haceby Lincs 116 B3
Hacheston Suff 88 B4
Hackbridge London 49 C5
Hackenthorpe S Yorks 131 A4
Hackford Norf 103 A6
Hackforth N Yorks 157 B6
Hackland Orkney 282 E4
Hackleton Northants 83 B5
Hackness N Yorks 160 B3
Hackness Orkney 283 H4
Hackney London 49 A6
Hackthorn Lincs 133 A4
Hackthorpe Cumb 164 C3
Haconby Lincs 116 C4
Hacton London 50 A2
Hadden Borders 198 C1
Haddenham Bucks 66 C2
Haddenham Cambs 101 D6
Haddington E Loth 210 C2
Haddington Lincs 133 C4
Haddiscoe Norf 105 B5
Haddon Cambs 100 B3
Haddon Ches 129 C4
Haddon Hall Derbys 130 C2
Hade Edge W Yorks 139 C4
Hademore Staffs 97 A4
Hadfield Derbys 138 D3
Hadham Cross Herts 68 B4
Hadham Ford Herts 68 A4
Hadleigh Essex 51 A5
Hadleigh Suff 87 C6
Hadley Telford 111 D5
Hadley End Staffs 113 C5
Hadlow Kent 36 B4
Hadlow Down E Sus 36 D3
Hadnall Shrops 111 D4
Hadstock Essex 86 C1
Hady Derbys 130 B3
Hadzor Worcs 80 A2
Haffenden Quarter Kent 37 B6
Hafod-Dinbych Conwy 124 D3
Hafod-lom Conwy 124 B3
Haggate Lancs 146 D2
Haggbeck Cumb 176 B2
Haggerston Northumb 198 B4
Haggrister Shetland 284 F5
Hagley Hereford 78 C3
Hagley Worcs 96 C2
Hagworthingham Lincs 134 C3
Haigh Gtr Man 137 C5
Haigh S Yorks 139 B5
Haigh Moor W Yorks 139 A5
Haighton Green Lancs 145 D5
Hail Weston Cambs 84 A3
Haile Cumb 162 D3
Hailes Glos 80 D3
Hailey Herts 68 B3
Hailey Oxon 65 B4
Hailsham E Sus 22 B3
Haimer Highld 280 B3
Hainault London 69 D4
Hainford Norf 120 D4
Hainton Lincs 134 A1
Hairmyres S Lnrk 205 C6
Haisthorpe E Yorks 151 A4
Hakin Pembs 55 D4
Halam Notts 132 D1
Halbeath Fife 208 B4
Halberton Devon 27 D5
Halcro Highld 280 B4
Hale Gtr Man 128 A2
Hale Halton 127 A4
Hale Hants 31 D5
Hale Bank Halton 127 A4
Hale Street Kent 37 B4
Halebarns Gtr Man 128 A2
Hales Norf 105 B4
Hales Staffs 111 B6
Hales Place Kent 52 D3
Halesfield Telford 95 A5
Halesgate Lincs 117 C6
Halesowen W Mid 96 C2
Halesworth Suff 105 D4
Halewood Mers 127 A4
Halford Shrops 94 C2
Halford Warks 81 C5
Halfpenny Furze Carms 56 A2
Halfpenny Green Staffs 95 B6
Halfway Carms 58 B3
Halfway Carms 59 B5
Halfway W Berks 46 C2
Halfway Bridge W Sus 34 D2
Halfway House Shrops 110 D2
Halfway Houses Kent 51 B6
Halifax W Yorks 138 A3
Halket E Ayrs 205 C4
Halkirk Highld 280 C3
Halkyn Flint 126 B2
Hall Dunnerdale Cumb 153 A3
Hall Green W Mid 96 C4
Hall Green W Yorks 139 B6
Hall Grove Herts 68 B2
Hall of Tankerness Orkney 283 G6
Hall of the Forest Shrops 93 C6
Halland E Sus 22 A2
Hallaton Leics 99 B4
Hallatrow Bath 43 D5
Hallbankgate Cumb 176 D3
Hallen S Glos 43 A4
Halliburton Borders 197 B5
Hallin Highld 258 C2
Halling Medway 51 C4
Hallington Lincs 134 A3
Hallington Northumb 178 B1
Halliwell Gtr Man 137 B6
Halloughton Notts 132 D1
Hallow Worcs 79 B6
Hallrule Borders 187 B4
Halls E Loth 210 C3
Hall's Green Herts 68 A2
Hallthwaites Cumb 153 B2
Hallworthy Corn 10 C2
Hallyburton House Perth 220 A2
Hallyne Borders 195 B6
Halmer End Staffs 112 A1
Halmore Glos 62 C2
Halmyre Mains Borders 195 B6
Halnaker W Sus 20 B2
Halsall Lancs 136 B2
Halse Northants 82 C2
Halse Som 27 C6
Halsetown Corn 2 B3
Halsham E Yorks 143 A4
Halsinger Devon 25 B6
Halstead Essex 87 D4
Halstead Kent 50 C1
Halstead Leics 99 A4
Halstock Dorset 15 A5
Haltham Lincs 134 C2
Haltoft End Lincs 117 A6
Halton Bucks 66 B3
Halton Halton 127 A5
Halton Lancs 145 A5
Halton Northumb 178 C1
Halton Wrex 110 B2
Halton W Yorks 148 D2
Halton East N Yorks 147 B4
Halton Gill N Yorks 156 D2
Halton Holegate Lincs 135 C4
Halton Lea Gate Northumb 176 D4
Halton West N Yorks 146 B2
Haltwhistle Northumb 177 C5
Halvergate Norf 105 A5
Halwell Devon 8 B1
Halwill Devon 11 B5
Halwill Junction Devon 11 A5
Ham Devon 14 A2
Ham Glos 62 D2
Ham London 49 B4
Ham Highld 280 A4
Ham Kent 53 D5
Ham Shetland 285 K1
Ham Wilts 46 C1
Ham Common Dorset 30 C2
Ham Green Hereford 79 C5
Ham Green Kent 37 D6
Ham Green Kent 51 C5
Ham Green N Som 43 B4
Ham Green Worcs 80 A3
Ham Street Som 29 B5
Hamble-le-Rice Hants 18 A3
Hambleden Bucks 47 A5
Hambledon Hants 33 D5
Hambledon Sur 34 C2
Hambleton Lancs 144 C3
Hambleton N Yorks 149 D4
Hambridge Som 28 C3
Hambrook S Glos 43 B5
Hambrook W Sus 19 A6
Hameringham Lincs 134 C3
Hamerton Cambs 100 D3
Hametoun Shetland 285 K1
Hamilton S Lnrk 194 A2
Hamilton Park Racecourse S Lnrk 194 A2
Hammer W Sus 34 C1
Hammerpot W Sus 20 B3
Hammersmith London 49 B5
Hammerwich Staffs 96 A3
Hammerwood E Sus 36 C2
Hammond Street Herts 68 C3
Hammoon Dorset 30 D2
Hamnavoe Shetland 284 E4
Hamnavoe Shetland 285 K5
Hamnavoe Shetland 284 E6
Hamnavoe Shetland 284 F6
Hampden National Stadium Glasgow 205 B5
Hampden Park E Sus 22 B4
Hamperden End Essex 86 D1
Hampnett Glos 64 B1
Hampole S Yorks 140 B3
Hampreston Dorset 17 B4
Hampstead London 49 A5
Hampstead Norreys W Berks 46 B3
Hampsthwaite N Yorks 147 B6
Hampton London 48 C4
Hampton Shrops 95 C5
Hampton Worcs 80 C3
Hampton Bishop Hereford 78 D3
Hampton Court Palace, Teddington London 49 C4
Hampton Heath Ches 110 A3
Hampton in Arden W Mid 97 C5
Hampton Loade Shrops 95 C5
Hampton Lovett Worcs 80 A1
Hampton Lucy Warks 81 B5
Hampton on the Hill Warks 81 A5
Hampton Poyle Oxon 65 B6
Hamrow Norf 119 C6
Hamsey E Sus 22 A2
Hamsey Green Sur 35 A6
Hamstall Ridware Staffs 113 D5
Hamstead I o W 18 B2
Hamstead W Mid 96 B3
Hamstead Marshall W Berks 46 C2
Hamsterley Durham 166 B4
Hamsterley Durham 178 D3
Hamstreet Kent 38 B2
Hamworthy Poole 16 B3
Hanbury Staffs 113 C5
Hanbury Worcs 80 A2
Hanbury Woodend Staffs 113 C5
Hanby Lincs 116 B3
Hanchurch Staffs 112 A2
Handbridge Ches 127 C4
Handcross W Sus 35 D5
Handforth Ches 128 A3
Handley Ches 127 D4
Handsacre Staffs 113 D4
Handsworth S Yorks 131 A4
Handsworth W Mid 96 B3
Handy Cross Devon 25 C5
Hanford Stoke 112 A2
Hanging Langford Wilts 31 B4
Hangleton W Sus 20 B3
Hanham S Glos 43 B5
Hankelow Ches 111 A5
Hankerton Wilts 63 D5
Hankham E Sus 22 B4
Hanley Stoke 112 A2
Hanley Castle Worcs 79 C6
Hanley Child Worcs 79 A4
Hanley Swan Worcs 79 C6
Hanley William Worcs 79 A4
Hanlith N Yorks 146 A3
Hanmer Wrex 110 B3
Hannah Lincs 135 B5
Hannington Hants 46 D3
Hannington Northants 99 D5
Hannington Swindon 64 D2
Hannington Wick Swindon 64 D2
Hansel Village S Ayrs 192 B3
Hanslope M Keynes 83 C5
Hanthorpe Lincs 116 C3
Hanwell London 49 A4
Hanwell Oxon 82 C1
Hanwood Shrops 94 A2
Hanworth London 48 B4
Hanworth Norf 120 B3
Happendon S Lnrk 194 C3
Happisburgh Norf 121 B5
Happisburgh Common Norf 121 C5
Hapsford Ches 127 B4
Hapton Lancs 146 D1
Hapton Norf 104 B2
Harberton Devon 8 B1
Harbertonford Devon 8 B1
Harbledown Kent 52 D3
Harborne W Mid 96 C3
Harborough Magna Warks 98 D1
Harbottle Northumb 188 C2
Harbour Park, Littlehampton W Sus 20 C3
Harbury Warks 81 B6
Harby Leics 115 B5
Harby Notts 132 B3
Harcombe Devon 13 B6
Harden W Mid 96 A3
Harden W Yorks 147 D4

Hardenhuish Wilts 44 B3
Hardgate Aberds 245 B4
Hardham W Sus 20 A3
Hardingham Norf 103 A6
Hardingstone Northants 83 B4
Hardington Som 43 D6
Hardington Mandeville Som 29 D5
Hardington Marsh Som 15 A5
Hardley Hants 18 A3
Hardley Street Norf 105 A4
Hardmead M Keynes 83 C6
Hardrow N Yorks 156 B2
Hardstoft Derbys 131 C4
Hardway Hants 19 A5
Hardway Som 29 B7
Hardwick Bucks 66 B3
Hardwick Cambs 85 B5
Hardwick Norf 118 D3
Hardwick Norf 104 C3
Hardwick Notts 131 B6
Hardwick Northants 83 A5
Hardwick Oxon 65 C4
Hardwick Oxon 65 A6
Hardwick W Mid 96 B3
Hardwick Hall Derbys 131 C4
Hardwicke Glos 62 B3
Hardwicke Glos 63 A5
Hardwicke Hereford 77 C6
Hardy's Green Essex 70 A3
Hare Green Essex 71 A4
Hare Hatch Wokingham 47 B6
Hare Street Herts 68 A3
Hareby Lincs 134 C3
Hareden Lancs 145 B6
Harefield London 67 D5
Harehills W Yorks 148 D2
Harehope Northumb 188 A3
Harescеugh Cumb 165 A4
Harescombe Glos 63 B4
Haresfield Glos 63 B4
Hareshaw N Lnrk 207 D6
Hareshaw Head Northumb 177 A6
Harewood W Yorks 148 C2
Harewood End Hereford 62 A1
Harewood House, Wetherby W Yorks 148 C2
Harford Carms 58 A3
Harford Devon 7 B5
Hargate Norf 104 B2
Hargatewall Derbys 129 B6
Hargrave Ches 127 C4
Hargrave Northants 100 D2
Hargrave Suff 86 B3
Harker Cumb 175 B6
Harkland Shetland 284 E6
Harkstead Suff 88 D2
Harlaston Staffs 113 D6
Harlaw Ho. Aberds 256 D2
Harlaxton Lincs 116 B1
Harle Syke Lancs 146 D2
Harlech Gwyn 107 C5
Harlech Castle Gwyn 107 C5
Harlequin Notts 115 B4
Harlescott Shrops 111 D4
Harlesden London 49 A5
Harleston Devon 8 C1
Harleston Norf 104 C3
Harleston Suff 87 B6
Harlestone Northants 83 A4
Harley Shrops 94 A3
Harley S Yorks 139 D6
Harleyholm S Lnrk 194 C4
Harlington Beds 84 D2
Harlington London 48 B3
Harlington S Yorks 140 C2
Harlosh Highld 258 D2
Harlow Essex 69 B4
Harlow Carr RHS Garden, Harrogate N Yorks 148 B1
Harlow Hill Northumb 178 C2
Harlow Hill N Yorks 148 B1
Harlthorpe E Yorks 149 D6
Harlton Cambs 85 B5
Harman's Cross Dorset 16 C3
Harmby N Yorks 157 C5
Harmer Green Herts 68 B2
Harmer Hill Shrops 110 C3
Harmondsworth London 48 B3
Harmston Lincs 133 C4
Harnham Northumb 178 B2
Harnhill Glos 63 C6
Harold Hill London 69 D5
Harold Wood London 69 D5
Haroldston West Pembs 55 C4
Haroldswick Shetland 284 B8
Harome N Yorks 159 C5
Harpenden Herts 67 B6
Harpford Devon 13 B5
Harpham E Yorks 150 A3
Harpley Norf 119 C4
Harpley Worcs 79 A4
Harpole Northants 82 A3
Harpsdale Highld 280 C3
Harpsden Oxon 47 A5
Harpswell Lincs 133 A4
Harpur Hill Derbys 129 B5
Harpurhey Gtr Man 138 C1
Harraby Cumb 175 C7
Harrapool Highld 247 B5
Harrier Shetland 285 J1
Harrietfield Perth 219 B4
Harrietsham Kent 37 A6
Harrington Cumb 162 B2
Harrington Lincs 134 B3
Harrington Northants 99 C4
Harringworth Northants 99 B6
Harris Highld 234 A2
Harris Museum, Preston Lancs 136 A4
Harrogate N Yorks 148 B2
Harrold Beds 83 B6
Harrow London 49 A4
Harrow on the Hill London 49 A4
Harrow Street Suff 87 D5
Harrow Weald London 67 D6
Harrowbarrow Corn 6 A2
Harrowden Beds 84 C2
Harrowgate Hill Darl 167 D5
Harston Cambs 85 B6
Harston Leics 115 B6
Harswell E Yorks 150 C1
Hart Hrtlpl 168 B2
Hart Common Gtr Man 137 C5
Hart Hill Luton 67 A6
Hart Station Hrtlpl 168 B2
Hartburn Northumb 178 A2
Hartburn Stockton 168 D2
Hartest Suff 87 B4
Hartfield E Sus 36 C2
Hartford Cambs 101 D4
Hartford Ches 127 B6
Hartford End Essex 69 B6
Hartfordbridge Hants 47 D5
Hartforth N Yorks 157 A5
Harthill Ches 127 D5
Harthill N Lnrk 208 D2
Harthill S Yorks 131 A4
Hartington Derbys 129 C6
Hartland Devon 24 C3
Hartlebury Worcs 95 D6
Hartlepool Hrtlpl 168 B3
Hartlepool's Maritime Experience Hrtlpl 168 B3
Hartley Cumb 155 A6
Hartley Kent 50 C3
Hartley Kent 37 C5
Hartley Northumb 179 B5
Hartley Westpall Hants 47 D4
Hartley Wintney Hants 47 D5
Hartlip Kent 51 C5
Hartoft End N Yorks 159 B6
Harton N Yorks 149 A6
Harton Shrops 94 C2
Harton T & W 179 C5
Hartpury Glos 62 A3
Hartshead W Yorks 139 A4
Hartshill Warks 97 B6
Hartshorne Derbys 113 C7
Hartsop Cumb 164 D2
Hartwell Northants 83 B4
Hartwood N Lnrk 194 A3
Harvieston Stirl 206 B3
Harvington Worcs 80 C3
Harvington Cross Worcs 80 C3
Harwell Oxon 46 A2
Harwich Essex 88 D3
Harwood Durham 165 B6
Harwood Gtr Man 137 B6
Harwood Dale N Yorks 160 B3
Harworth Notts 140 D4
Hasbury W Mid 96 C2
Hascombe Sur 34 B2
Haselbech Northants 99 D4
Haselbury Plucknett Som 29 D4
Haseley Warks 81 A5
Haselor Warks 80 B4
Hasfield Glos 63 A4
Hasguard Pembs 55 D4
Haskayne Lancs 136 C2
Hasketon Suff 88 B3
Hasland Derbys 130 C3
Haslemere Sur 34 C2
Haslingden Lancs 137 A6
Haslingfield Cambs 85 B6
Haslington Ches 128 D2
Hassall Ches 128 D2
Hassall Green Ches 128 D2
Hassell Street Kent 38 A2
Hassendean Borders 186 A4
Hassingham Norf 105 A4
Hassocks W Sus 21 A5
Hassop Derbys 130 B2
Hastigrow Highld 281 B4
Hastingleigh Kent 38 A2
Hastings E Sus 23 B6
Hastings Castle E Sus 23 A6
Hastings Sea Life Centre E Sus 23 B6
Hastingwood Essex 69 C4
Hastoe Herts 67 C4
Haswell Durham 167 A6
Haswell Plough Durham 167 A6
Hatch Beds 84 C3
Hatch Hants 47 D4
Hatch Wilts 30 C3
Hatch Beauchamp Som 28 C3
Hatch End London 67 D6
Hatch Green Som 28 D3
Hatchet Gate Hants 18 A2
Hatching Green Herts 67 B6
Hatchmere Ches 127 B5
Hatcliffe NE Lincs 143 C4
Hatfield Hereford 78 B3
Hatfield Herts 68 C2
Hatfield S Yorks 141 C4
Hatfield Worcs 80 B1
Hatfield Broad Oak Essex 69 B5
Hatfield Garden Village Herts 68 C2
Hatfield Heath Essex 69 B5
Hatfield House Herts 68 C2
Hatfield Hyde Herts 68 B2
Hatfield Peverel Essex 70 B1
Hatfield Woodhouse S Yorks 141 C4
Hatford Oxon 64 D4
Hatherden Hants 46 D1
Hatherleigh Devon 11 A6
Hathern Leics 114 C2
Hatherop Glos 64 C2
Hathersage Derbys 130 A2
Hathershaw Gtr Man 138 C2
Hatherton Ches 111 A5
Hatherton Staffs 112 D3
Hatley St George Cambs 85 B4
Hatt Corn 6 A2
Hattingley Hants 33 B5
Hatton Aberds 257 C5
Hatton Derbys 113 C6
Hatton Lincs 134 B1
Hatton Shrops 94 B2
Hatton Warks 81 A5
Hatton Warr 127 A5
Hatton Castle Aberds 256 B2
Hatton Country World Warks 81 A5
Hatton Heath Ches 127 C4
Hatton of Fintray Aberds 245 A5
Hattoncrook Aberds 256 D3
Haugh E Ayrs 193 C4
Haugh Gtr Man 138 B2
Haugh Lincs 135 B4
Haugh Head Northumb 188 A3
Haugh of Glass Moray 255 C5
Haugh of Urr Dumfries 173 B6
Haugham Lincs 134 A3
Haughley Suff 87 A6
Haughley Green Suff 87 A6
Haughs of Clinterty Aberdeen 245 A5
Haughton Notts 132 B1
Haughton Shrops 95 B4
Haughton Shrops 110 C2
Haughton Shrops 111 D4
Haughton Shrops 95 A5
Haughton Staffs 112 C2
Haughton Castle Northumb 177 B7
Haughton Green Gtr Man 138 D2
Haughton Le Skerne Darl 167 D6
Haughton Moss Ches 127 D5
Haultwick Herts 68 A3
Haunn Argyll 224 B2
Haunn W Isles 286 E3
Haunton Staffs 113 D6
Hauxley Northumb 189 C5
Hauxton Cambs 85 B6
Havant Hants 19 A6
Haven Hereford 78 B2
Haven Bank Lincs 134 D2
Haven Side E Yorks 142 A3
Havenstreet I o W 19 B4
Havercroft W Yorks 140 B1
Haverfordwest = Hwlffordd Pembs 55 C5
Haverhill Suff 86 C2
Haverigg Cumb 153 C2
Havering-atte-Bower London 69 D5
Haveringland Norf 120 C3
Haversham M Keynes 83 C5
Haverthwaite Cumb 154 C2
Haverton Hill Stockton 168 C2
Hawarden = Penarlâg Flint 126 C3
Hawcoat Cumb 153 C3
Hawen Ceredig 73 B6
Hawes N Yorks 156 C2
Hawes Side Blkpool 144 D3
Hawes'Green Norf 104 B3
Hawford Worcs 79 A6
Hawick Borders 186 B4
Hawk Green Gtr Man 129 A4
Hawkchurch Devon 14 A3
Hawkedon Suff 86 B3
Hawkenbury Kent 37 B6
Hawkenbury Kent 36 C3
Hawkeridge Wilts 44 D2
Hawkerland Devon 13 C5
Hawkes End W Mid 97 C6
Hawkesbury S Glos 43 A6
Hawkesbury Warks 97 C6
Hawkesbury Upton S Glos 44 A1
Hawkhill Northumb 189 B5
Hawkhurst Kent 37 C5
Hawkinge Kent 39 B4
Hawkley Hants 33 C6
Hawkridge Som 26 B3
Hawkshead Cumb 154 B2
Hawkshead Hill Cumb 154 B2
Hawksland S Lnrk 194 C3
Hawkswick N Yorks 156 D3
Hawksworth Notts 115 A5
Hawksworth W Yorks 147 C5
Hawksworth W Yorks 147 D6
Hawkwell Essex 70 D2
Hawley Hants 34 A1
Hawley Kent 50 B2
Hawling Glos 63 A6
Hawnby N Yorks 158 C4
Haworth W Yorks 147 D4
Hawstead Suff 87 B4
Hawthorn Durham 168 A2
Hawthorn Rhondda 41 C6
Hawthorn Wilts 44 C2
Hawthorn Hill Brack 48 B1
Hawthorn Hill Lincs 134 D2
Hawthorpe Lincs 116 C3
Hawton Notts 132 D2
Haxby York 149 B5
Haxey N Lincs 141 C5
Hay Green Norf 118 D2
Hay-on-Wye = Y Gelli Gandryll Powys 77 C6
Hay Street Herts 68 A3
Haydock Mers 137 D4
Haydock Park Racecourse Mers 137 D4
Haydon Dorset 29 D6
Haydon Bridge Northumb 177 C6
Haydon Wick Swindon 45 A5
Haye Corn 6 A2
Hayes London 49 C7
Hayes London 48 A4
Hayfield Derbys 129 A5
Hayfield Fife 209 A5
Hayhill E Ayrs 182 A2
Hayhillock Angus 232 D3
Hayle Corn 2 B3
Haynes Beds 84 C2
Haynes Church End Beds 84 C2
Hayscastle Pembs 55 B4
Hayscastle Cross Pembs 55 B5
Hayshead Angus 233 D4
Hayton Aberdeen 245 B6
Hayton Cumb 174 D4
Hayton Cumb 176 D3
Hayton E Yorks 149 C7
Hayton Notts 132 A2
Hayton's Bent Shrops 94 C3
Haytor Vale Devon 12 D2
Haywards Heath W Sus 35 D6
Haywood S Yorks 140 B3
Haywood Oaks Notts 131 D6
Hazel Grove Gtr Man 129 A4
Hazel Street Kent 37 C4
Hazelbank S Lnrk 194 B3
Hazelbury Bryan Dorset 16 A1
Hazeley Hants 47 D5
Hazelhurst Gtr Man 138 C2
Hazelslade Staffs 112 D4
Hazelton Glos 64 B1
Hazelton Walls Fife 220 B3
Hazelwood Derbys 114 A1
Hazlemere Bucks 66 D3
Hazlerigg T & W 179 B4
Hazlewood N Yorks 147 B4
Hazon Northumb 189 C4
Heacham Norf 118 B3
Head of Muir Falk 207 B6
Headbourne Worthy Hants 32 B3
Headbrook Hereford 77 B7
Headcorn Kent 37 B6
Headingley W Yorks 148 D1
Headington Oxon 65 C6
Headlam Durham 167 D4
Headless Cross Worcs 80 A3
Headley Hants 46 C3
Headley Hants 33 B7
Headley Sur 35 A5
Headon Notts 132 B2
Heads S Lnrk 194 B2
Heads Nook Cumb 176 D2
Heage Derbys 130 D3
Healaugh N Yorks 148 C3
Healaugh N Yorks 156 B4
Heald Green Gtr Man 128 A3
Heale Devon 26 A1
Heale Som 29 A6
Healey Gtr Man 138 B1
Healey Northumb 178 D2
Healey N Yorks 157 C5
Healing NE Lincs 143 B4
Heamoor Corn 2 B2
Heanish Argyll 222 C3
Heanor Derbys 114 A2
Heanton Punchardon Devon 25 B6
Heapham Lincs 132 A3
Heart of the National Forest Leics 113 D7
Hearthstane Borders 195 D6
Heasley Mill Devon 26 B2
Heast Highld 247 C5
Heath Cardiff 41 D6
Heath Derbys 131 C4
Heath and Reach Beds 67 A4
Heath End Hants 46 C3
Heath End Sur 34 B1
Heath End Warks 81 A5
Heath Hayes Staffs 112 D4
Heath Hill Shrops 111 D6
Heath House Som 28 A4
Heath Town W Mid 96 B2
Heathcote Derbys 129 C6
Heather Leics 114 D1
Heatherfield Highld 259 D4
Heathfield Devon 12 D3
Heathfield E Sus 36 D3
Heathfield Som 27 C6
Heathhall Dumfries 174 A2
Heathrow Airport London 48 B3
Heathstock Devon 14 A2
Heathton Shrops 95 B6
Heatley Warr 128 A2
Heaton Lancs 144 A4
Heaton Staffs 129 C4
Heaton T & W 179 C4
Heaton W Yorks 147 D5
Heaton Moor Gtr Man 138 D1
Heaverham Kent 36 A3
Heaviley Gtr Man 129 A4
Heavitree Devon 13 B4
Hebburn T & W 179 C5
Hebden N Yorks 147 A4
Hebden Bridge W Yorks 138 A2
Hebron Anglesey 123 B4
Hebron Carms 73 D4
Hebron Northumb 178 A3
Heck Dumfries 184 D3
Heckfield Hants 47 C5
Heckfield Green Suff 104 D2
Heckfordbridge Essex 70 A3
Heckington Lincs 116 A4
Heckmondwike W Yorks 139 A5
Heddington Wilts 44 C3
Heddle Orkney 282 F4
Heddon-on-the-Wall Northumb 178 C3
Hedenham Norf 104 B4
Hedge End Hants 32 D3
Hedgerley Bucks 48 A2
Hedging Som 28 C3
Hedley on the Hill Northumb 178 D2
Hednesford Staffs 112 D3
Hedon E Yorks 142 A3
Hedsor Bucks 48 A2
Hedworth T & W 179 C5
Heeley City Farm, Sheffield S Yorks 130 A3
Hegdon Hill Hereford 78 B3
Heggerscales Cumb 165 D6
Heglibister Shetland 285 H5
Heighington Darl 167 C5
Heighington Lincs 133 C5
Heights of Brae Highld 263 D7
Heights of Kinlochewe Highld 262 D2
Heilam Highld 277 B5
Heiton Borders 197 C6
Hele Devon 25 A6
Hele Devon 13 A4
Helensburgh Argyll 215 D5
Helford Corn 3 C5
Helford Passage Corn 3 C5
Helhoughton Norf 119 C5
Helions Bumpstead Essex 86 C2
Hellaby S Yorks 140 D3
Helland Corn 10 D1
Hellesdon Norf 120 D4
Hellidon Northants 82 B2
Hellifield N Yorks 146 B2
Hellingly E Sus 22 A3
Hellington Norf 104 A4
Hellister Shetland 285 J5
Helm Northumb 189 D4
Helmdon Northants 82 C2
Helmingham Suff 88 B2
Helmington Row Durham 167 B4
Helmsdale Highld 274 C4
Helmshore Lancs 137 A6
Helmsley N Yorks 159 C5
Helperby N Yorks 148 A3
Helperthorpe N Yorks 160 D3
Helpringham Lincs 116 A4
Helpston P'boro 100 A3
Helsby Ches 127 B4
Helsey Lincs 135 B5
Helston Corn 3 C4
Helstone Corn 10 C1
Helton Cumb 164 C3
Helwith Bridge N Yorks 146 A2
Hemblington Norf 121 D5
Hemel Hempstead Herts 67 C5
Hemingbrough N Yorks 149 D5
Hemingby Lincs 134 B2
Hemingford Abbots Cambs 101 D4
Hemingford Grey Cambs 101 D4
Hemingstone Suff 88 B2
Hemington Leics 114 C2
Hemington Northants 100 C2
Hemington Som 43 D6
Hemley Suff 88 C3
Hemlington M'bro 168 D3
Hemp Green Suff 89 A4
Hempholme E Yorks 150 B3
Hempnall Norf 104 B3
Hempnall Green Norf 104 B3
Hempriggs House Highld 281 D5
Hempstead Essex 86 D2
Hempstead Medway 51 C4
Hempstead Norf 120 B3
Hempstead Norf 121 C6
Hempsted Glos 63 B4
Hempton Norf 119 C6
Hempton Oxon 82 D1
Hemsby Norf 121 D6
Hemswell Lincs 142 D1
Hemswell Cliff Lincs 133 A4
Hemsworth W Yorks 140 B2
Hemyock Devon 27 D6
Hen-feddau fawr Pembs 73 C5
Henbury Bristol 43 B4
Henbury Ches 128 B3
Hendon London 49 A5
Hendon T & W 179 D6
Hendre Flint 126 C1
Hendre-ddu Conwy 124 C3
Hendreforgan Rhondda 41 C4
Hendy Carms 57 B5
Heneglwys Anglesey 123 C4
Henfield W Sus 21 A5
Henford Devon 11 B4
Henghurst Kent 38 B1
Hengoed Caerph 41 B6
Hengoed Powys 77 B6
Hengoed Shrops 110 B1
Hengrave Suff 87 A4
Henham Essex 69 A5
Heniarth Powys 93 A5
Henlade Som 28 C2
Henley Shrops 94 D3
Henley Som 28 B4
Henley Suff 88 B2
Henley W Sus 34 D1
Henley-in-Arden Warks 81 A4
Henley-on-Thames Oxon 47 A5
Henley's Down E Sus 23 A5
Henllan Ceredig 73 B6
Henllan Denb 125 C5
Henllan Amgoed Carms 73 D4
Henllys Torf 61 D4
Henlow Beds 84 D3
Hennock Devon 12 C3
Henny Street Essex 87 D4
Henryd Conwy 124 B2
Henry's Moat Pembs 55 B6
Hensall N Yorks 140 A3
Henshaw Northumb 177 C5
Hensingham Cumb 162 C2
Henstead Suff 105 C5
Henstridge Som 30 D1
Henstridge Ash Som 29 C7
Henstridge Marsh Som 30 C1
Henton Oxon 66 C2
Henton Som 29 A4
Henwood Corn 10 D3
Heogan Shetland 285 J6
Heol-las Swansea 40 B1
Heol Senni Powys 59 C6
Heol-y-Cyw Bridgend 40 C4
Hepburn Northumb 188 A3
Hepple Northumb 188 C2
Hepscott Northumb 179 A4
Heptonstall W Yorks 138 A2
Hepworth Suff 103 D5
Hepworth W Yorks 139 C4
Herbrandston Pembs 55 D4
Hereford Hereford 78 C3
Hereford Cathedral Hereford 78 D3
Hereford Racecourse Hereford 78 C3
Heriot Borders 196 A2
Heritage Motor Centre, Gaydon Warks 81 B6
Hermiston Edin 209 C4
Hermitage Borders 186 D4
Hermitage Dorset 15 A6
Hermitage W Berks 46 B3
Hermitage W Sus 19 A6
Hermon Anglesey 122 D3
Hermon Carms 73 C6
Hermon Carms 58 C3
Hermon Pembs 73 C5
Herne Kent 52 C3
Herne Bay Kent 52 C3
Herner Devon 25 C6
Hernhill Kent 52 C2
Herodsfoot Corn 5 A7
Herongate Essex 69 D6
Heronsford S Ayrs 180 C3
Herriard Hants 33 A5
Herringfleet Suff 105 B5
Herringswell Suff 102 D3
Hersden Kent 53 C4
Hersham Corn 10 A3
Hersham Sur 48 C4
Herstmonceux E Sus 22 A4
Herston Orkney 283 H5

Hertford Herts 68 B3
Hertford Heath Herts 68 B3
Hertingfordbury Herts 68 B3
Hesket Newmarket Cumb 163 A6
Hesketh Bank Lancs 136 A3
Hesketh Lane Lancs 145 C6
Heskin Green Lancs 136 B4
Hesleden Durham 168 B2
Hesleyside Northumb 177 A6
Heslington York 149 B5
Hessay York 148 B4
Hessenford Corn 6 B2
Hessett Suff 87 A5
Hessle E Yorks 142 A2
Hest Bank Lancs 145 A4
Heston London 48 B4
Hestwall Orkney 282 F3
Heswall Mers 126 A2
Hethe Oxon 65 A6
Hethersett Norf 104 A2
Hethersgill Cumb 176 C2
Hethpool Northumb 188 A1
Hett Durham 167 B5
Hetton N Yorks 146 B3
Hetton-le-Hole T & W 167 A6
Hetton Steads Northumb 198 C4
Heugh Northumb 178 B2
Heugh-head Aberds 243 A6
Heveningham Suff 104 D4
Hever Kent 36 B2
Hever Castle and Gardens Kent 36 B2
Heversham Cumb 154 C3
Hevingham Norf 120 C3
Hewas Water Corn 5 C4
Hewelsfield Glos 62 C1
Hewish N Som 42 C3
Hewish Som 14 A4
Heworth York 149 B5
Hexham Northumb 178 C1
Hexham Abbey Northumb 178 C1
Hexham Racecourse Northumb 177 C7
Hextable Kent 50 B2
Hexton Herts 84 D3
Hexworthy Devon 12 D1
Hey Lancs 146 C2
Heybridge Essex 69 D6
Heybridge Essex 70 C2
Heybridge Basin Essex 70 C2
Heybrook Bay Devon 7 C4
Heydon Cambs 85 C6
Heydon Norf 120 C3
Heydour Lincs 116 B3
Heylipol Argyll 222 C2
Heylor Shetland 284 E4
Heysham Lancs 144 A4
Heyshott W Sus 20 A1
Heyside Gtr Man 138 C2
Heytesbury Wilts 30 A3
Heythrop Oxon 64 A4
Heywood Gtr Man 138 B1
Heywood Wilts 44 D2
Hibaldstow N Lincs 142 C1
Hickleton S Yorks 140 C2
Hickling Norf 121 C6
Hickling Notts 115 C4
Hickling Green Norf 121 C6
Hickling Heath Norf 121 C6
Hickstead W Sus 35 D5
Hidcote Boyce Glos 81 C4
Hidcote Manor Garden, Moreton-in-Marsh Glos 81 C4
High Ackworth W Yorks 140 B2
High Angerton Northumb 178 A2
High Bankhill Cumb 164 A3
High Barnes T & W 179 D5
High Beach Essex 68 D4
High Bentham N Yorks 145 A6
High Bickington Devon 25 C7
High Birkwith N Yorks 155 D6
High Blantyre S Lnrk 194 A1
High Bonnybridge Falk 207 C6
High Bradfield S Yorks 139 D5
High Bray Devon 26 B1
High Brooms Kent 36 B3
High Bullen Devon 25 C6
High Buston Northumb 189 C5
High Callerton Northumb 178 B3
High Catton E Yorks 149 B6
High Cogges Oxon 65 C4
High Coniscliffe Darl 167 D5
High Cross Hants 33 C6
High Cross Herts 68 B3
High Easter Essex 69 B6
High Eggborough N Yorks 140 A3
High Ellington N Yorks 157 C5
High Ercall Telford 111 D4
High Etherley Durham 167 C4
High Garrett Essex 70 A1
High Grange Durham 167 B4
High Green Norf 104 A2
High Green S Yorks 139 D6
High Green Worcs 80 C1
High Halden Kent 37 C6
High Halstow Medway 51 B4
High Ham Som 28 B4
High Harrington Cumb 162 B3
High Hatton Shrops 111 C5
High Hawsker N Yorks 160 A3
High Hesket Cumb 164 A2
High Hesleden Durham 168 B2
High Hoyland S Yorks 139 B5
High Hunsley E Yorks 150 D2
High Hurstwood E Sus 36 D2
High Hutton N Yorks 149 A6
High Ireby Cumb 163 A5
High Kelling Norf 120 A3
High Kilburn N Yorks 158 D4
High Lands Durham 166 C4
High Lane Gtr Man 129 A4
High Lane Hereford 79 A4
High Laver Essex 69 C5
High Legh Ches 128 A2
High Leven Stockton 168 D2
High Littleton Bath 43 D5
High Lorton Cumb 163 B4
High Marishes N Yorks 159 D7
High Marnham Notts 132 B3
High Melton S Yorks 140 C3
High Mickley Northumb 178 C2
High Mindork Dumfries 171 B5
High Moorland Visitor Centre, Princetown Devon 11 D6
High Newton Cumb 154 C3
High Newton-by-the-Sea Northumb 189 A5
High Nibthwaite Cumb 154 C1
High Offley Staffs 112 C1
High Ongar Essex 69 C5
High Onn Staffs 112 D2
High Roding Essex 69 B6
High Row Cumb 163 A6
High Salvington W Sus 21 B4
High Sellafield Cumb 162 D3
High Shaw N Yorks 156 B2
High Spen T & W 178 D3
High Stoop Durham 166 A4
High Street Corn 5 B4
High Street Kent 37 C5
High Street Suff 89 B5
High Street Suff 105 D5
High Street Suff 87 C4
High Street Green Suff 87 B6
High Throston Hrtlpl 168 B2
High Toynton Lincs 134 C2
High Trewhitt Northumb 188 C3
High Valleyfield Fife 208 B3
High Westwood Durham 178 D3
High Wray Cumb 154 B2
High Wych Herts 69 B4
High Wycombe Bucks 66 D3
Higham Derbys 130 D3
Higham Kent 51 B4
Higham Lancs 146 D2
Higham Suff 87 D6
Higham Suff 86 A3
Higham Dykes Northumb 178 B3
Higham Ferrers Northants 83 A6
Higham Gobion Beds 84 D3
Higham on the Hill Leics 97 B6
Higham Wood Kent 36 B3
Highampton Devon 11 A5
Highbridge Highld 239 D5
Highbridge Som 28 A3
Highbrook W Sus 35 C6
Highburton W Yorks 139 B4
Highbury Som 29 A6
Highclere Hants 46 C2
Highcliffe Dorset 17 B6
Higher Ansty Dorset 16 A1
Higher Ashton Devon 12 C3
Higher Ballam Lancs 144 D3
Higher Bartle Lancs 145 D5
Higher Boscaswell Corn 2 B1
Higher Burwardsley Ches 127 D5
Higher Clovelly Devon 24 C4
Higher End Gtr Man 136 C4
Higher Kinnerton Flint 126 C3
Higher Penwortham Lancs 136 A4
Higher Town Scilly 2 E4
Higher Walreddon Devon 11 D5
Higher Walton Lancs 137 A4
Higher Walton Warr 127 A5
Higher Wheelton Lancs 137 A5
Higher Whitley Ches 127 A6
Higher Wincham Ches 128 B1
Higher Wych Ches 110 A3
Highfield E Yorks 149 D6
Highfield Gtr Man 137 C6
Highfield N Ayrs 204 C3
Highfield Oxon 65 A6
Highfield S Yorks 130 A3
Highfield T & W 178 D3
Highfields Cambs 85 B5
Highfields Northumb 198 A3
Highgate London 49 A5
Highland Folk Museum, Aultlairie Highld 241 C5
Highland Folk Museum, Kingussie Highld 241 B5
Highlane Ches 128 C3
Highlane Derbys 131 A4
Highlaws Cumb 174 D4
Highleadon Glos 62 A3
Highleigh W Sus 20 C1
Highley Shrops 95 C5
Highmoor Cross Oxon 47 A5
Highmoor Hill Mon 42 A3
Highnam Glos 62 B3
Highnam Green Glos 62 A3
Highsted Kent 51 C6
Highstreet Green Essex 86 D3
Hightae Dumfries 174 A3
Hightown Ches 128 C3
Hightown Mers 136 C2
Hightown Green Suff 87 B5
Highway Wilts 44 B4
Highweek Devon 12 D3
Highworth Swindon 64 D3
Hilborough Norf 103 A4
Hilcote Derbys 131 D4
Hilcott Wilts 45 D5
Hilden Park Kent 36 B3
Hildenborough Kent 36 B3
Hildersham Cambs 86 C1
Hilderstone Staffs 112 B3
Hilderthorpe E Yorks 151 A4
Hilfield Dorset 15 A6
Hilgay Norf 102 B2
Hill Pembs 55 D7
Hill S Glos 62 D2
Hill W Mid 96 B4
Hill Brow W Sus 33 C6
Hill Dale Lancs 136 B3
Hill Dyke Lincs 117 A6
Hill End Durham 166 B3
Hill End Fife 208 A3
Hill End N Yorks 147 B4
Hill Head Hants 18 A4
Hill Head Northumb 178 C1
Hill Mountain Pembs 55 D5
Hill of Beath Fife 209 A4
Hill of Fearn Highld 265 C4
Hill of Mountblairy Aberds 268 D1
Hill Ridware Staffs 113 D4
Hill Top Durham 166 C2
Hill Top Hants 18 A3
Hill Top W Mid 96 B2
Hill Top W Yorks 139 B6
Hill Top, Sawrey Cumb 154 B2
Hill View Dorset 16 B3
Hillam N Yorks 140 A3
Hillbeck Cumb 165 D5
Hillborough Kent 53 C4
Hillbrae Aberds 256 D2
Hillbrae Aberds 255 B7
Hillbutts Dorset 16 A3
Hillclifflane Derbys 113 A6
Hillcommon Som 27 C6
Hillend Fife 208 B4
Hillerton Devon 12 B2
Hillesden Bucks 66 A1
Hillesley Glos 43 A6
Hillfarance Som 27 C6
Hillhead Aberds 255 C6
Hillhead Devon 8 B3
Hillhead S Ayrs 182 A2
Hillhead of Auchentumb Aberds 269 D4
Hillhead of Cocklaw Aberds 257 B5
Hillhouse Borders 197 A4
Hilliclay Highld 280 B3
Hillier Gardens and Arboretum Hants 32 C2
Hillingdon London 48 A3
Hillington Glasgow 205 B5
Hillington Norf 119 C4
Hillmorton Warks 98 D2
Hillockhead Aberds 244 A1
Hillockhead Aberds 243 B6
Hillside Aberds 245 C6
Hillside Angus 233 B5
Hillside Mers 136 B2
Hillside Orkney 283 H5
Hillside Shetland 285 G6
Hillswick Shetland 284 F4
Hillway I o W 19 C5
Hillwell Shetland 285 M5
Hilmarton Wilts 44 B4
Hilperton Wilts 44 D2
Hilsea Ptsmth 19 A5
Hilston E Yorks 151 D5
Hilton Aberds 257 C4
Hilton Cambs 85 A4
Hilton Cumb 165 C5
Hilton Derbys 113 B6
Hilton Dorset 16 A1
Hilton Durham 167 C4
Hilton Highld 264 B3
Hilton Shrops 95 B5
Hilton Stockton 168 D2
Hilton of Cadboll Highld 265 C4
Himbleton Worcs 80 B2
Himley Staffs 96 B1
Hincaster Cumb 154 C4
Hinckley Leics 98 B1
Hinderclay Suff 103 D6
Hinderton Ches 126 B3
Hinderwell N Yorks 169 D5
Hindford Shrops 110 B2
Hindhead Sur 34 C1
Hindley Gtr Man 137 C5
Hindley Green Gtr Man 137 C5
Hindlip Worcs 80 B1
Hindolveston Norf 120 C2
Hindon Wilts 30 B3
Hindringham Norf 120 B1
Hingham Norf 103 A6
Hinstock Shrops 111 C5
Hintlesham Suff 88 C1
Hinton Hants 17 B6
Hinton Hereford 78 D1
Hinton Northants 82 B2
Hinton Shrops 94 A2
Hinton S Glos 43 B6
Hinton Ampner Hants 33 C4
Hinton Blewett Bath 43 D4
Hinton Charterhouse Bath 43 D6
Hinton-in-the-Hedges Northants 82 D2
Hinton Martell Dorset 17 A4
Hinton on the Green Worcs 80 C3
Hinton Parva Swindon 45 A6
Hinton St George Som 28 D4
Hinton St Mary Dorset 30 D1
Hinton Waldrist Oxon 65 D4
Hints Shrops 95 D4
Hints Staffs 97 A4
Hinwick Beds 83 A6
Hinxhill Kent 38 A2
Hinxton Cambs 85 C6
Hinxworth Herts 84 C4
Hipperholme W Yorks 139 A4
Hipswell N Yorks 157 B5
Hirael Gwyn 123 C5
Hiraeth Carms 73 D4
Hirn Aberds 245 B4
Hirnant Powys 109 C5
Hirst N Lnrk 207 D6
Hirst Northumb 179 A4
Hirst Courtney N Yorks 140 A4
Hirwaen Denb 125 C6
Hirwaun Rhondda 59 E6
Hiscott Devon 25 C6
Histon Cambs 85 A6
Historic Royal Dockyard Ptsmth 19 A5
Hitcham Suff 87 B5
Hitchin Herts 68 A1
Hither Green London 49 B6
Hittisleigh Devon 12 B2
Hive E Yorks 149 D7
Hixon Staffs 112 C4
HMS Victory Ptsmth 19 A5
HMY Britannia Edin 209 C5
Hoaden Kent 53 D4
Hoaldalbert Mon 61 A5
Hoar Cross Staffs 113 C5
Hoarwithy Hereford 62 A1
Hoath Kent 53 C4
Hobarris Shrops 93 D7
Hobbister Orkney 283 G4
Hobkirk Borders 187 B4
Hobson Durham 178 D3
Hoby Leics 115 D4
Hockering Norf 120 D2
Hockerton Notts 132 D2
Hockley Essex 70 D2
Hockley Heath W Mid 97 D4
Hockliffe Beds 67 A4
Hockwold cum Wilton Norf 102 C3
Hockworthy Devon 27 D5
Hoddesdon Herts 68 C3
Hoddlesden Blkburn 137 A6
Hoddom Mains Dumfries 175 A4
Hoddomcross Dumfries 175 A4
Hodgeston Pembs 55 E6
Hodley Powys 93 B5
Hodnet Shrops 111 C5
Hodthorpe Derbys 131 B5
Hoe Hants 33 D4
Hoe Norf 120 D1
Hoe Gate Hants 33 D5
Hoff Cumb 165 D4
Hog Patch Sur 34 B1
Hoggard's Green Suff 87 B4
Hoggeston Bucks 66 A3
Hogha Gearraidh W Isles 287 G2
Hoghton Lancs 137 A5
Hognaston Derbys 130 D2
Hogsthorpe Lincs 135 B5
Holbeach Lincs 117 C6
Holbeach Bank Lincs 117 C6
Holbeach Clough Lincs 117 C6
Holbeach Drove Lincs 117 D6
Holbeach Hurn Lincs 117 C6
Holbeach St Johns Lincs 117 D6
Holbeach St Marks Lincs 117 B6
Holbeach St Matthew Lincs 117 B7
Holbeck Notts 131 B5
Holbeck W Yorks 148 D1
Holbeck Woodhouse Notts 131 B5
Holberrow Green Worcs 80 B3
Holbeton Devon 7 B5
Holborn London 49 A6
Holbrook Derbys 114 A1
Holbrook Suff 88 D2
Holbrook S Yorks 131 A4
Holburn Northumb 198 C4
Holbury Hants 18 A3
Holcombe Devon 13 D4
Holcombe Som 29 A6
Holcombe Rogus Devon 27 D5
Holcot Northants 83 A4
Holden Lancs 146 C1
Holdenby Northants 82 A3
Holdenhurst Bmouth 17 B5
Holdgate Shrops 94 C3
Holdingham Lincs 116 A3
Holditch Dorset 14 A3
Hole-in-the-Wall Hereford 62 A2
Holefield Borders 198 C2
Holehouses Ches 128 B2
Holemoor Devon 11 A5
Holestane Dumfries 183 C6
Holford Som 27 A6
Holgate York 149 B4
Holker Cumb 154 D2
Holkham Norf 119 A5
Hollacombe Devon 11 A4
Holland Orkney 282 B5
Holland Orkney 282 E7
Holland Fen Lincs 117 A5
Holland-on-Sea Essex 71 B6
Hollandstoun Orkney 282 B8
Hollee Dumfries 175 B5
Hollesley Suff 89 C4
Hollicombe Torbay 8 A2
Hollingbourne Kent 37 A6
Hollington Derbys 113 B6
Hollington E Sus 23 A5
Hollington Staffs 113 B4
Hollington Grove Derbys 113 B6
Hollingworth Gtr Man 138 D3
Hollins Gtr Man 137 C7
Hollins Green Warr 137 D5
Hollins Lane Lancs 145 B4
Hollinsclough Staffs 129 C5
Hollinwood Gtr Man 138 C2
Hollinwood Shrops 111 B4
Hollocombe Devon 26 D1
Hollow Meadows S Yorks 130 A2
Holloway Derbys 130 D3
Hollowell Northants 98 D3
Holly End Norf 101 A6
Holly Green Worcs 79 C6
Hollybush Caerph 41 A6
Hollybush E Ayrs 182 A1
Hollybush Worcs 79 D5
Hollym E Yorks 143 A5
Hollywood Worcs 96 D3
Holmbridge W Yorks 139 C4
Holmbury St Mary Sur 35 B4
Holmbush Corn 5 B5
Holmcroft Staffs 112 C3
Holme Cambs 100 C3
Holme Cumb 154 D4
Holme Notts 132 D3
Holme N Yorks 158 C2
Holme W Yorks 139 C4
Holme Chapel Lancs 138 A1
Holme Green N Yorks 149 C4
Holme Hale Norf 103 A4
Holme Lacy Hereford 78 D3
Holme Marsh Hereford 78 B1
Holme next the Sea Norf 119 A4
Holme-on-Spalding-Moor E Yorks 149 D7
Holme on the Wolds E Yorks 150 C2
Holme Pierrepont Notts 115 B4
Holme St Cuthbert Cumb 174 D4
Holme Wood W Yorks 147 D5
Holmer Hereford 78 C3
Holmer Green Bucks 67 D4
Holmes Chapel Ches 128 C2
Holmesfield Derbys 130 B3
Holmeswood Lancs 136 B3
Holmewood Derbys 131 C4
Holmfirth W Yorks 139 C4
Holmhead Dumfries 183 D5
Holmhead E Ayrs 193 C5
Holmisdale Highld 258 D1
Holmpton E Yorks 143 A5
Holmrook Cumb 153 A1
Holmsgarth Shetland 285 J6
Holmwrangle Cumb 164 A3
Holne Devon 7 A6
Holnest Dorset 15 A6
Holsworthy Devon 10 A4
Holsworthy Beacon Devon 11 A4
Holt Dorset 17 A4
Holt Norf 120 B2
Holt Wilts 44 C2
Holt Worcs 79 A6
Holt Wrex 127 D4
Holt End Hants 33 B5
Holt End Worcs 80 A3
Holt Fleet Worcs 79 A6
Holt Heath Worcs 79 A6
Holt Park W Yorks 147 C6
Holtby York 149 B5
Holton Oxon 65 C7
Holton Som 29 C6
Holton Suff 105 D4
Holton cum Beckering Lincs 133 A6
Holton Heath Dorset 16 B3
Holton le Clay Lincs 143 C4
Holton le Moor Lincs 142 D2
Holton St Mary Suff 87 D6
Holwell Dorset 29 D7
Holwell Herts 84 D3
Holwell Leics 115 C5
Holwell Oxon 64 C3
Holwick Durham 166 C2
Holworth Dorset 16 C1
Holy Cross Worcs 96 D2
Holy Island Northumb 199 B5
Holybourne Hants 33 A6
Holyhead = Caergybi Anglesey 122 B2
Holymoorside Derbys 130 C3
Holyport Windsor 48 B1
Holystone Northumb 188 C2
Holytown N Lnrk 207 D5
Holywell Cambs 101 D5
Holywell Corn 4 B2
Holywell Dorset 15 A5
Holywell E Sus 22 C3
Holywell Northumb 179 B5
Holywell = Treffynnon Flint 126 B1
Holywell Bay Fun Park, Newquay Corn 4 B2
Holywell Green W Yorks 138 B3
Holywell Lake Som 27 C6
Holywell Row Suff 102 D3
Holywood Dumfries 184 D2
Hom Green Hereford 62 A1
Homer Shrops 95 A4
Homersfield Suff 104 C3
Homington Wilts 31 C5
Honey Hill Kent 52 C3
Honey Street Wilts 45 C5
Honey Tye Suff 87 D5
Honeyborough Pembs 55 D5
Honeybourne Worcs 80 C4
Honeychurch Devon 12 A1
Honiley Warks 97 D5
Honing Norf 121 C5
Honingham Norf 120 D3
Honington Lincs 116 A2
Honington Suff 103 D5
Honington Warks 81 C5
Honiton Devon 13 A6
Honley W Yorks 139 B4
Hoo Green Ches 128 A2
Hoo St Werburgh Medway 51 B4
Hood Green S Yorks 139 C6
Hooe E Sus 23 B4
Hooe Plym 7 B4
Hooe Common E Sus 23 A4
Hook E Yorks 141 A5
Hook London 49 C4
Hook Hants 47 D5
Hook Pembs 55 C5
Hook Wilts 45 A4
Hook Green Kent 37 C4
Hook Green Kent 50 C3
Hook Norton Oxon 81 D6
Hooke Dorset 15 B5
Hookgate Staffs 111 B6
Hookway Devon 12 B3
Hookwood Sur 35 B5
Hoole Ches 127 C4
Hooley Sur 35 A5
Hoop Mon 61 C7
Hooton Ches 126 B3
Hooton Levitt S Yorks 140 D3
Hooton Pagnell S Yorks 140 C2
Hooton Roberts S Yorks 140 D2
Hop Pole Lincs 117 D4
Hope Derbys 129 A6
Hope Devon 7 D5
Hope Highld 277 C5
Hope Powys 93 A6
Hope Shrops 94 A1
Hope Staffs 129 D6
Hope = Yr Hôb Flint 126 D3
Hope Bagot Shrops 94 D3
Hope Bowdler Shrops 94 B2
Hope End Green Essex 69 A5
Hope Green Ches 129 A4
Hope Mansell Hereford 62 B2
Hope under Dinmore Hereford 78 B3
Hopeman Moray 266 C2
Hope's Green Essex 51 A4
Hopesay Shrops 94 C1
Hopley's Green Hereford 78 B1
Hopperton N Yorks 148 B3
Hopstone Shrops 95 B5
Hopton Shrops 110 C2
Hopton Shrops 111 C4
Hopton Staffs 112 C3
Hopton Suff 103 D5
Hopton Cangeford Shrops 94 C3

Hopton Castle Shrops 94 D1
Hopton on Sea Norf 105 A6
Hopton Wafers Shrops 95 D4
Hoptonheath Shrops 94 D1
Hopwas Staffs 97 A4
Hopwood Gtr Man 138 C1
Hopwood Worcs 96 D3
Horam E Sus 22 A3
Horbling Lincs 116 B4
Horbury W Yorks 139 B5
Horcott Glos 64 C2
Horden Durham 168 A2
Horderley Shrops 94 C2
Hordle Hants 17 B6
Hordley Shrops 110 B2
Horeb Ceredig 73 B6
Horeb Carms 57 B4
Horeb Carms 58 C2
Horfield Bristol 43 B5
Horham Suff 104 D3
Horkesley Heath Essex 70 A3
Horkstow N Lincs 142 B1
Horley Oxon 81 C7
Horley Sur 35 B5
Hornblotton Green Som 29 B5
Hornby Lancs 145 A5
Hornby N Yorks 157 B6
Hornby N Yorks 158 A2
Horncastle Lincs 134 C2
Hornchurch London 50 A2
Horncliffe Northumb 198 B3
Horndean Borders 198 B2
Horndean Hants 33 D6
Horndon Devon 11 D6
Horndon on the Hill Thurrock 50 A3
Horne Sur 35 B6
Horniehaugh Angus 232 B2
Horning Norf 121 D5
Horninghold Leics 99 B5
Horninglow Staffs 113 C6
Horningsea Cambs 85 A6
Horningsham Wilts 30 A2
Horningtoft Norf 119 C6
Horns Corner Kent 37 D5
Horns Cross Devon 25 C4
Horns Cross E Sus 37 D6
Hornsby Cumb 176 D3
Hornsea E Yorks 151 C5
Hornsea Bridge E Yorks 151 C5
Hornsey London 49 A6
Hornton Oxon 81 C6
Horrabridge Devon 7 A4
Horringer Suff 87 A4
Horringford I o W 18 C4
Horse Bridge Staffs 129 D4
Horsebridge Devon 11 D5
Horsebridge Hants 32 B2
Horsebrook Staffs 112 D2
Horsehay Telford 95 A4
Horseheath Cambs 86 C2
Horsehouse N Yorks 156 C4
Horsell Sur 34 A2
Horseman's Green Wrex 110 A3
Horseway Cambs 101 C6
Horsey Norf 121 C6
Horsford Norf 120 D3
Horsforth W Yorks 147 D6
Horsham Worcs 79 B5
Horsham W Sus 35 C4
Horsham St Faith Norf 120 D4
Horsington Lincs 134 C1
Horsington Som 29 C7
Horsley Derbys 114 A1
Horsley Glos 63 D4
Horsley Northumb 178 C2
Horsley Northumb 188 D1
Horsley Cross Essex 71 A5
Horsley Woodhouse Derbys 114 A1
Horsleycross Street Essex 71 A5
Horsleyhill Borders 186 B4
Horsleyhope Durham 166 A3
Horsmonden Kent 37 B4
Horspath Oxon 65 C6
Horstead Norf 121 D4
Horsted Keynes W Sus 36 D1
Horton Bucks 67 B4
Horton Dorset 17 A4
Horton Lancs 146 B2
Horton Northants 83 B5
Horton Shrops 110 C3
Horton S Glos 43 A6
Horton Som 28 D3
Horton Staffs 129 D4
Horton Swansea 57 D4
Horton Wilts 45 C4
Horton Windsor 48 B3
Horton-cum-Studley Oxon 65 B6
Horton Green Ches 110 A3
Horton Heath Hants 32 D3
Horton in Ribblesdale N Yorks 155 D7
Horton Kirby Kent 50 C2
Hortonlane Shrops 110 D3
Horwich Gtr Man 137 B5
Horwich End Derbys 129 A5
Horwood Devon 25 C6
Hose Leics 115 C5
Hoselaw Borders 198 C2
Hoses Cumb 153 A3
Hosh Perth 218 B3
Hosta W Isles 287 G2
Hoswick Shetland 285 L6
Hotham E Yorks 150 D1
Hothfield Kent 38 A1
Hoton Leics 114 C3
Houbie Shetland 284 D8
Houdston S Ayrs 181 B3
Hough Ches 128 D2
Hough Ches 128 B3
Hough Green Halton 127 A4
Hough-on-the-Hill Lincs 116 A2
Hougham Lincs 116 A1
Houghton Cambs 101 D4
Houghton Cumb 175 C7
Houghton Hants 32 B2
Houghton Pembs 55 D5
Houghton W Sus 20 A3
Houghton Conquest Beds 84 C2
Houghton Green E Sus 37 D7
Houghton Green Warr 137 D5
Houghton-le-Side Darl 167 C5
Houghton-Le-Spring T & W 167 A6
Houghton on the Hill Leics 98 A3
Houghton Regis Beds 67 A5
Houghton St Giles Norf 119 B6
Houlland Shetland 285 H5
Houlland Shetland 284 F7
Houlsyke N Yorks 159 A6
Hound Hants 18 A3
Hound Green Hants 47 D5
Houndslow Borders 197 B5
Houndwood Borders 211 D5
Hounslow London 48 B4
Hounslow Green Essex 69 B6
Housay Shetland 284 F8
House of Daviot Highld 252 B3
House of Glenmuick Aberds 243 C6
Housesteads Roman Fort Northumb 177 C5
Housetter Shetland 284 E5
Houss Shetland 285 K5
Houston Renfs 205 B4
Houstry Highld 275 A5
Houton Orkney 283 G4
Hove Brighton 21 B5
Hoveringham Notts 115 A4
Hoveton Norf 121 D5
Hovingham N Yorks 159 D5
How Cumb 176 D3
How Caple Hereford 79 D4
How End Beds 84 C2
How Green Kent 36 B2
Howbrook S Yorks 139 D6
Howden Borders 187 A5
Howden E Yorks 141 A5
Howden-le-Wear Durham 167 B4
Howe Highld 281 B5
Howe Norf 104 A3
Howe N Yorks 158 C2
Howe Bridge Gtr Man 137 C5
Howe Green Essex 70 C1
Howe of Teuchar Aberds 256 B2
Howe Street Essex 69 B6
Howe Street Essex 86 D2
Howell Lincs 116 A4
Howey Powys 77 B4
Howgate Midloth 196 A1
Howick Northumb 189 B5
Howle Durham 166 C3
Howle Telford 111 C5
Howlett End Essex 86 D1
Howley Som 14 A2
Hownam Borders 187 B6
Hownam Mains Borders 187 A6
Howpasley Borders 185 B6
Howsham N Lincs 142 C2
Howsham N Yorks 149 A6
Howslack Dumfries 184 B3
Howtel Northumb 198 C2
Howton Hereford 61 A6
Howtown Cumb 164 D2
Howwood Renfs 204 B3
Hoxne Suff 104 D2
Hoy Orkney 283 G3
Hoylake Mers 126 A2
Hoyland S Yorks 139 C6
Hoylandswaine S Yorks 139 C5
Hubberholme N Yorks 156 D3
Hubbert's Bridge Lincs 117 A5
Huby N Yorks 147 C6
Huby N Yorks 149 A4
Hucclecote Glos 63 B4
Hucking Kent 37 A6
Hucknall Notts 114 A3
Huddersfield W Yorks 139 B4
Huddington Worcs 80 B2
Hudswell N Yorks 157 A5
Huggate E Yorks 150 B1
Hugglescote Leics 114 D2
Hugh Town Scilly 2 E4
Hughenden Valley Bucks 66 D3
Hughley Shrops 94 B3
Huish Devon 25 D6
Huish Wilts 45 C5
Huish Champflower Som 27 C5
Huish Episcopi Som 28 C4
Huisinis W Isles 287 C4
Hulcott Bucks 66 B3
Hulland Derbys 113 A6
Hulland Ward Derbys 113 A6
Hullavington Wilts 44 A2
Hullbridge Essex 70 D2
Hulme Gtr Man 138 D1
Hulme End Staffs 129 D6
Hulme Walfield Ches 128 C3
Hulver Street Suff 105 C5
Hulverstone I o W 18 C2
Humber Hereford 78 B3
Humber Bridge E Yorks 142 A2
Humberside International Airport N Lincs 142 B2
Humberston NE Lincs 143 C5
Humbie E Loth 210 D1
Humbleton E Yorks 151 D5
Humbleton Northumb 188 A2
Humby Lincs 116 B3
Hume Borders 197 B6
Humshaugh Northumb 177 B7
Huna Highld 281 A5
Huncoat Lancs 146 D1
Huncote Leics 98 B2
Hundalee Borders 187 B5
Hunderthwaite Durham 166 C2
Hundle Houses Lincs 134 D2
Hundleby Lincs 134 C3
Hundleton Pembs 55 D5
Hundon Suff 86 C3
Hundred Acres Hants 33 D4
Hundred End Lancs 136 A3
Hundred House Powys 77 B5
Hungarton Leics 98 A3
Hungerford Hants 31 D5
Hungerford W Berks 46 C1
Hungerford Newtown W Berks 46 B1
Hungerton Lincs 116 C1
Hungladder Highld 258 A3
Hunmanby N Yorks 161 D4
Hunmanby Moor N Yorks 161 D5
Hunningham Warks 81 A6
Hunny Hill I o W 18 C3
Hunsdon Herts 68 B4
Hunsingore N Yorks 148 B3
Hunslet W Yorks 148 D2
Hunsonby Cumb 164 B3
Hunspow Highld 280 A4
Hunstanton Norf 118 A3
Hunstanworth Durham 166 A2
Hunsterson Ches 111 A5
Hunston Suff 87 A5
Hunston W Sus 20 B1
Hunstrete Bath 43 C5
Hunt End Worcs 80 A3
Hunter's Quay Argyll 203 A6
Hunthill Lodge Angus 232 A2
Hunting-tower Perth 219 B5
Huntingdon Cambs 100 D4
Huntingdon Racecourse Cambs 100 D4
Huntingfield Suff 104 D4
Huntingford Dorset 30 B2
Huntington E Loth 210 C1
Huntington Hereford 77 B6
Huntington Staffs 112 D3
Huntington York 149 B5
Huntley Glos 62 B3
Huntly Aberds 255 C6
Huntlywood Borders 197 B5
Hunton Kent 37 B5
Hunton N Yorks 157 B5
Hunt's Corner Norf 103 C6
Hunt's Cross Mers 127 A4
Huntsham Devon 27 C5
Huntspill Som 28 A3
Huntworth Som 28 B3
Hunwick Durham 167 B4
Hunworth Norf 120 B2
Hurdsfield Ches 129 B4
Hurley Warks 97 B5
Hurley Windsor 47 A6
Hurlford E Ayrs 193 B4
Hurliness Orkney 283 K3
Hurn Dorset 17 B5
Hurn's End Lincs 118 A1
Hursley Hants 32 C3
Hurst N Yorks 156 A4
Hurst Som 29 D4
Hurst Wokingham 47 B5
Hurst Green E Sus 37 D5
Hurst Green Lancs 145 D6
Hurst Wickham W Sus 21 A5
Hurstbourne Priors Hants 32 A3
Hurstbourne Tarrant Hants 46 D1
Hurstpierpoint W Sus 21 A5
Hurstwood Lancs 146 D2
Hurtmore Sur 34 B2
Hurworth Place Darl 157 A6
Hury Durham 166 D2
Husabost Highld 258 C2
Husbands Bosworth Leics 98 C3
Husborne Crawley Beds 83 D6
Husthwaite N Yorks 158 D4
Hutchwns Bridgend 40 D3
Huthwaite Notts 131 D4
Huttoft Lincs 135 B5
Hutton Borders 198 A3
Hutton Cumb 164 C2
Hutton E Yorks 150 B3
Hutton Essex 69 D6
Hutton Lancs 136 A3
Hutton N Som 42 D2
Hutton Buscel N Yorks 160 C3
Hutton Conyers N Yorks 158 D2
Hutton Cranswick E Yorks 150 B3
Hutton End Cumb 164 B2
Hutton Gate Redcar 168 D3
Hutton Henry Durham 168 B2
Hutton-le-Hole N Yorks 159 B6
Hutton Magna Durham 166 D4
Hutton Roof Cumb 163 A6
Hutton Roof Cumb 155 D4
Hutton Rudby N Yorks 158 A3
Hutton Sessay N Yorks 158 D3
Hutton Village Redcar 168 D3
Hutton Wandesley N Yorks 148 B4
Huxley Ches 127 C5
Huxter Shetland 285 H5
Huxter Shetland 285 G7
Huxton Borders 211 D5
Huyton Mers 136 D3
Hwlffordd = Haverfordwest Pembs 55 C5
Hycemoor Cumb 153 B1
Hyde Glos 63 C4
Hyde Gtr Man 138 D2
Hyde Hants 31 D5
Hyde Heath Bucks 67 C4
Hyde Park S Yorks 140 C3
Hydestile Sur 34 B2
Hylton Castle T & W 179 D5
Hyndford Bridge S Lnrk 194 B4
Hynish Argyll 222 D2
Hyssington Powys 93 B7
Hythe Hants 18 A3
Hythe Kent 38 B3
Hythe End Windsor 48 B3
Hythie Aberds 269 D5

I

Ibberton Dorset 16 A1
Ible Derbys 130 D2
Ibsley Hants 17 A5
Ibstock Leics 114 D2
Ibstone Bucks 66 D2
Ibthorpe Hants 46 D1
Ibworth Hants 46 D3
Ichrachan Argyll 227 C5
Ickburgh Norf 103 B4
Ickenham London 48 A3
Ickford Bucks 66 C1
Ickham Kent 53 D4
Ickleford Herts 84 D3
Icklesham E Sus 23 A6
Ickleton Cambs 85 C6
Icklingham Suff 102 D3
Ickwell Green Beds 84 C3
Ickworth House Suff 87 A4
Icomb Glos 64 A3
Idbury Oxon 64 B3
Iddesleigh Devon 11 A6
Ide Devon 12 B3
Ide Hill Kent 36 A2
Ideford Devon 12 D3
Iden E Sus 37 D7
Iden Green Kent 37 C6
Iden Green Kent 37 C5
Idle W Yorks 147 D5
Idlicote Warks 81 C5
Idmiston Wilts 31 B5
Idole Carms 57 A4
Idridgehay Derbys 113 A6
Idrigill Highld 258 B3
Idstone Oxon 45 A6
Idvies Angus 232 D3
Iffley Oxon 65 C6
Ifield W Sus 35 C5
Ifold W Sus 34 C3
Iford E Sus 22 B2
Ifton Heath Shrops 110 B2
Ightfield Shrops 111 B4
Ightham Kent 36 A3
Ightham Mote, Sevenoaks Kent 49 B6
Iken Suff 89 B5
Ilam Staffs 129 D6
Ilchester Som 29 C5
Ilderton Northumb 188 A3
Ilford London 50 A1
Ilfracombe Devon 25 A6
Ilkeston Derbys 114 A2
Ilketshall St Andrew Suff 105 C4
Ilketshall St Lawrence Suff 105 C4
Ilketshall St Margaret Suff 104 C4
Ilkley W Yorks 147 C5
Illey W Mid 96 C2
Illingworth W Yorks 138 A3
Illogan Corn 3 A4
Illston on the Hill Leics 99 B4
Ilmer Bucks 66 C2
Ilmington Warks 81 C5
Ilminster Som 28 D3
Ilsington Devon 12 D2
Ilston Swansea 57 C5
Ilton N Yorks 157 D5
Ilton Som 28 D3
Imachar N Ayrs 202 D3
Imeraval Argyll 200 D3
Immingham NE Lincs 142 B3
Imperial War Museum London 49 B6
Imperial War Museum North Gtr Man 137 D7
Impington Cambs 85 A6
Ince Ches 127 B4
Ince Blundell Mers 136 C2
Ince in Makerfield Gtr Man 137 C4
Inch of Arnhall Aberds 233 A4
Inchbare Angus 233 B4
Inchberry Moray 266 D4
Inchbraoch Angus 233 C5
Incheril Highld 262 D2
Inchgrundle Angus 232 A2
Inchina Highld 261 A6
Inchinnan Renfs 205 B4
Inchkinloch Highld 277 D6
Inchlaggan Highld 239 B5
Inchlumpie Highld 264 C1
Inchmore Highld 251 B5
Inchnacardoch Hotel Highld 240 A1
Inchnadamph Highld 271 B5
Inchree Highld 237 C4
Inchture Perth 220 B2
Inchyra Perth 219 B6
Indian Queens Corn 4 B4
Inerval Argyll 200 D3
Ingatestone Essex 69 D6
Ingbirchworth S Yorks 139 C5
Ingestre Staffs 112 C3
Ingham Lincs 133 A4
Ingham Norf 121 C5
Ingham Suff 103 D4
Ingham Corner Norf 121 C5
Ingleborough Norf 118 D1
Ingleby Derbys 114 C1
Ingleby Lincs 132 B3
Ingleby Arncliffe N Yorks 158 A3
Ingleby Barwick Stockton 168 D2
Ingleby Greenhow N Yorks 159 A4
Inglemire Hull 150 D3
Inglesbatch Bath 43 C6
Inglesham Swindon 64 D3
Ingleton Durham 167 C4
Ingleton N Yorks 155 D5
Inglewhite Lancs 145 C5
Ingliston Edin 208 C4
Ingoe Northumb 178 B2
Ingol Lancs 145 D5
Ingoldisthorpe Norf 118 B3
Ingoldmells Lincs 135 C5
Ingoldsby Lincs 116 B3
Ingon Warks 81 B5
Ingram Northumb 188 B3
Ingrave Essex 69 D6
Ingrow W Yorks 147 D4
Ings Cumb 154 B3
Ingst S Glos 43 A4
Ingworth Norf 120 C3
Inham's End Cambs 101 B4
Inkberrow Worcs 80 B3
Inkpen W Berks 46 C1
Inkstack Highld 281 A4
Inn Cumb 154 A3
Innellan Argyll 203 A6
Innerleithen Borders 196 C2
Innerleven Fife 220 D3
Innermessan Dumfries 170 A2
Innerwick E Loth 211 C4
Innerwick Perth 229 D4
Innis Chonain Argyll 227 D6
Insch Aberds 256 D1
Insh Highld 241 B6
Inshore Highld 276 B4
Inskip Lancs 145 D4
Instoneville S Yorks 140 B3
Instow Devon 25 B5
Intake S Yorks 140 C3
Inver Aberds 243 C5
Inver Highld 265 B4
Inver Perth 230 D4
Inver Mallie Highld 239 D5
Inverailort Highld 235 B6
Inveraldie Angus 220 A4
Inveralligin Highld 249 A5
Inverallochy Aberds 269 C5
Inveran Highld 264 A1
Inveraray Argyll 214 B3
Inveraray Jail Argyll 214 B3
Inverarish Highld 248 C2
Inverarity Angus 232 D2
Inverarnan Stirl 215 A6
Inverasdale Highld 261 B5
Inverbeg Argyll 206 A1
Inverbervie Aberds 233 A6
Inverboyndie Aberds 268 C1
Inverbroom Highld 262 B3
Invercassley Highld 272 D2
Invercauld House Aberds 243 C4
Inverchaolain Argyll 203 A5
Invercharnan Highld 227 B6
Inverchoran Highld 251 A4
Invercreran Argyll 227 B5
Inverdruie Highld 242 A2
Inverebrie Aberds 257 C4
Invereck Argyll 215 D4
Inverernan Ho. Aberds 243 A6
Invereshie House Highld 241 B6
Inveresk E Loth 209 C6
Inverewe Gardens, Gairloch Highld 261 B5
Inverey Aberds 242 D3
Inverfarigaig Highld 251 D7
Invergarry Highld 239 B7
Invergelder Aberds 243 C5
Invergeldie Perth 218 B2
Invergordon Highld 264 D3
Invergowrie Perth 220 A3
Inverguseran Highld 247 D6
Inverhadden Perth 229 C5
Inverharroch Moray 255 C4
Inverherive Stirl 216 B3
Inverie Highld 247 E6
Inverinan Argyll 214 A2
Inverinate Highld 249 D6
Inverkeilor Angus 233 D4
Inverkeithing Fife 208 B4
Inverkeithny Aberds 256 B1
Inverkip Invclyd 204 A2
Inverkirkaig Highld 270 C3
Inverlael Highld 262 B3
Inverlochlarig Stirl 216 C4
Inverlochy Argyll 227 D6
Inverlochy Highld 237 B5
Inverlussa Argyll 213 D4
Invermark Lodge Angus 244 D1
Invermoidart Highld 235 C5
Invermoriston Highld 240 A2
Invernaver Highld 278 B3
Inverneill Argyll 213 D6
Inverness Highld 252 B2
Inverness Airport Highld 252 A3
Invernettie Aberds 257 B6
Invernoaden Argyll 215 C4
Inveroran Hotel Argyll 228 D1
Inverpolly Lodge Highld 270 C3
Inverquharity Angus 232 C2
Inverquhomery Aberds 257 B5
Inverroy Highld 239 D6
Inversanda Highld 236 D3
Invershiel Highld 238 A3
Invershin Highld 264 A1
Inversnaid Hotel Stirl 215 B6
Inverugie Aberds 257 B6
Inveruglas Argyll 215 B6
Inveruglass Highld 241 B6
Inverurie Aberds 256 D2
Invervar Perth 229 D5
Inverythan Aberds 256 B2
Inwardleigh Devon 11 B6
Inworth Essex 70 B2
Iochdar W Isles 286 B3
Iona Abbey and Cathedral Argyll 224 D1
Iping W Sus 34 D1
Ipplepen Devon 8 A2
Ipsden Oxon 47 A4
Ipsley Worcs 80 A3
Ipstones Staffs 129 D5
Ipswich Suff 88 C2
Irby Mers 126 A2
Irby in the Marsh Lincs 135 C4
Irby upon Humber NE Lincs 142 C3
Irchester Northants 83 A6
Ireby Cumb 163 A5
Ireby Lancs 155 D5
Ireland Orkney 283 G4
Ireland Shetland 285 L5
Ireland's Cross Shrops 111 A6
Ireleth Cumb 153 C3
Ireshopeburn Durham 165 B6
Irlam Gtr Man 137 D6
Irnham Lincs 116 C3
Iron Acton S Glos 43 A5
Iron Cross Warks 80 B3
Ironbridge Telford 95 A4
Ironbridge Gorge Museum, Telford Shrops 95 A4
Irongray Dumfries 173 A7
Ironmacannie Dumfries 173 A4
Ironside Aberds 268 D3
Ironville Derbys 131 D4
Irstead Norf 121 C5
Irthington Cumb 176 C2

Irthlingborough Northants 99 D6
Irton N Yorks 160 C4
Irvine N Ayrs 192 B3
Isauld Highld 279 B5
Isbister Orkney 282 E3
Isbister Orkney 282 F4
Isbister Shetland 284 D5
Isbister Shetland 285 G7
Isfield E Sus 22 A2
Isham Northants 99 D5
Islay Airport Argyll 200 C3
Isle Abbotts Som 28 C3
Isle Brewers Som 28 C3
Isle of Man Airport I o M 152 E2
Isle of Man Steam Railway I o M 152 E1
Isle of Whithorn Dumfries 171 D6
Isleham Cambs 102 D2
Isleornsay Highld 247 C6
Islesburgh Shetland 284 G5
Islesteps Dumfries 174 A2
Isleworth London 49 B4
Isley Walton Leics 114 C2
Islibhig W Isles 287 B4
Islington London 49 A6
Islip Northants 100 D1
Islip Oxon 65 B6
Istead Rise Kent 50 C3
Isycoed Wrex 127 D4
Itchen Soton 32 D3
Itchen Abbas Hants 32 B4
Itchen Stoke Hants 33 B4
Itchingfield W Sus 35 D4
Itchington S Glos 43 A5
Itteringham Norf 120 B3
Itton Devon 12 B1
Itton Common Mon 61 D6
Ivegill Cumb 164 A2
Iver Bucks 48 A3
Iver Heath Bucks 48 A3
Iveston Durham 178 D3
Ivinghoe Bucks 67 B4
Ivinghoe Aston Bucks 67 B4
Ivington Hereford 78 B2
Ivington Green Hereford 78 B2
Ivy Chimneys Essex 68 C4
Ivy Cross Dorset 30 C2
Ivy Hatch Kent 36 A3
Ivybridge Devon 7 B5
Ivychurch Kent 38 C2
Iwade Kent 51 C6
Iwerne Courtney or Shroton Dorset 30 D2
Iwerne Minster Dorset 30 D2
Ixworth Suff 103 D5
Ixworth Thorpe Suff 103 D5

J

Jack Hill N Yorks 147 B6
Jack in the Green Devon 13 B5
Jacksdale Notts 131 D4
Jackstown Aberds 256 C2
Jacobstow Corn 10 B2
Jacobstowe Devon 11 A6
Jameston Pembs 55 E6
Jamestown Dumfries 185 C6
Jamestown Highld 251 A6
Jamestown W Dunb 206 B1
Jarlshof Prehistoric Site Shetland 285 N5
Jarrow T & W 179 C5
Jarvis Brook E Sus 36 D3
Jasper's Green Essex 69 A7
Java Argyll 225 C6
Jawcraig Falk 207 C6
Jaywick Essex 71 B5
Jealott's Hill Brack 47 B6
Jedburgh Borders 187 A5
Jeffreyston Pembs 55 D6
Jellyhill E Dunb 205 A6
Jemimaville Highld 264 D3
Jersey Airport Jersey 6
Jersey Farm Herts 67 C6
Jersey Zoo & Wildlife Park Jersey 6
Jesmond T & W 179 C4
Jevington E Sus 22 B3
Jockey End Herts 67 B5
Jodrell Bank Visitor Centre, Holmes Chapel Ches 128 B2
John o'Groats Highld 281 A5
Johnby Cumb 164 B2
John's Cross E Sus 37 D5
Johnshaven Aberds 233 B5
Johnston Pembs 55 C5
Johnstone Renfs 205 B4
Johnstonebridge Dumfries 184 C3
Johnstown Carms 57 A4
Johnstown Wrex 110 A2
Joppa Edin 209 C6
Joppa S Ayrs 182 A2
Jordans Bucks 67 D4
Jordanthorpe S Yorks 130 A3
Jorvik Centre York 149 B5
Judges Lodging, Presteigne Powys 77 A7
Jump S Yorks 140 C1
Jumpers Green Dorset 17 B5
Juniper Green Edin 209 D4
Jurby East I o M 152 B3
Jurby South Motor Racing Circuit I o M 152 B3
Jurby West I o M 152 B3

K

Kaber Cumb 165 D5
Kaimend S Lnrk 195 B4
Kaimes Edin 209 D5
Kalemouth Borders 187 A6
Kames Argyll 203 A4
Kames Argyll 213 A6
Kames E Ayrs 194 D1
Kea Corn 4 C3
Keadby N Lincs 141 B6
Keal Cotes Lincs 134 C3
Kearsley Gtr Man 137 C6
Kearstwick Cumb 155 C5
Kearton N Yorks 156 B3
Kearvaig Highld 276 A3
Keasden N Yorks 145 A7
Keckwick Halton 127 A5
Keddington Lincs 134 A3
Kedington Suff 86 C3
Kedleston Derbys 113 A7
Kedleston Hall Derbys 113 A7
Keelby Lincs 142 B3
Keele Staffs 112 A2
Keeley Green Beds 84 C2
Keeston Pembs 55 C5
Keevil Wilts 44 D3
Kegworth Leics 114 C2
Kehelland Corn 3 A4
Keig Aberds 244 A3
Keighley W Yorks 147 C4
Keighley and Worth Valley Railway W Yorks 147 D4
Keil Highld 236 D3
Keilarsbrae Clack 208 A1
Keilhill Aberds 268 D2
Keillmore Argyll 213 D4
Keillor Perth 231 D6
Keillour Perth 219 B4
Keills Argyll 201 B4
Keils Argyll 201 B5
Keinton Mandeville Som 29 B5
Keir Mill Dumfries 183 C6
Keisby Lincs 116 C3
Keiss Highld 281 B5
Keith Moray 267 D5
Keith Inch Aberds 257 B6
Keithock Angus 233 B4
Kelbrook Lancs 146 C3
Kelby Lincs 116 A3
Keld Cumb 164 D3
Keld N Yorks 156 A2
Keldholme N Yorks 159 C6
Kelfield N Lincs 141 C6
Kelfield N Yorks 149 D4
Kelham Notts 132 D2
Kellan Argyll 225 B4
Kellas Angus 221 A4
Kellas Moray 266 D2
Kellaton Devon 8 D2
Kelleth Cumb 155 A5
Kelleythorpe E Yorks 150 B2
Kelling Norf 120 A2
Kellingley N Yorks 140 A3
Kellington N Yorks 140 A3
Kelloe Durham 167 B6
Kelloholm Dumfries 183 A5
Kelly Devon 11 C4
Kelly Bray Corn 11 D4
Kelmarsh Northants 99 D4
Kelmscot Oxon 64 D3
Kelsale Suff 89 A4
Kelsall Ches 127 C5
Kelsall Hill Ches 127 C5
Kelshall Herts 85 D5
Kelsick Cumb 175 C4
Kelso Borders 197 C6
Kelso Racecourse Borders 197 C6
Kelstedge Derbys 130 C3
Kelstern Lincs 143 D4
Kelston Bath 43 C6
Keltneyburn Perth 229 D6
Kelton Dumfries 174 A2
Kelty Fife 208 A4
Kelvedon Essex 70 B2
Kelvedon Hatch Essex 69 D5
Kelvin S Lnrk 205 C6
Kelvinside Glasgow 205 B5
Kelynack Corn 2 B1
Kemback Fife 220 C4
Kemberton Shrops 95 A5
Kemble Glos 63 D5
Kemerton Worcs 80 D2
Kemeys Commander Mon 61 C5
Kemnay Aberds 245 A4
Kemp Town Brighton 21 B6
Kempley Glos 62 A2
Kemps Green Warks 96 D4
Kempsey Worcs 79 C6
Kempsford Glos 64 D2
Kempshott Hants 47 D4
Kempston Beds 84 C2
Kempston Hardwick Beds 84 C2
Kempton Shrops 94 C1
Kempton Park Racecourse Sur 48 B4
Kemsing Kent 36 A3
Kemsley Kent 51 C6
Kenardington Kent 38 B1
Kenchester Hereford 78 C2
Kencot Oxon 64 C3
Kendal Cumb 154 B4
Kendoon Dumfries 182 D4
Kendray S Yorks 139 C6
Kenfig Bridgend 40 C3
Kenfig Hill Bridgend 40 C3
Kenilworth Warks 97 D5
Kenilworth Castle Warks 97 D5
Kenknock Stirl 217 A4
Kenley London 35 A6
Kenley Shrops 94 A3
Kenmore Highld 249 A4
Kenmore Perth 230 D1
Kenn Devon 13 C4
Kenn N Som 42 C3
Kennacley W Isles 288 H2
Kennacraig Argyll 202 B3
Kennerleigh Devon 12 A3
Kennet Clack 208 A2
Kennethmont Aberds 255 D6
Kennett Cambs 86 A2
Kennford Devon 13 C4
Kenninghall Norf 103 C6
Kenninghall Heath Norf 103 C6
Kennington Kent 38 A2
Kennington Oxon 65 C6
Kennoway Fife 220 D3
Kenny Hill Suff 102 D2
Kennythorpe N Yorks 149 A6
Kenovay Argyll 222 C2
Kensaleyre Highld 259 C4
Kensington London 49 B5
Kensworth Beds 67 B5
Kensworth Common Beds 67 B5
Kent International Airport Kent 53 C5
Kent Street E Sus 23 A5
Kent Street Kent 37 A4
Kent Street W Sus 35 D5
Kentallen Highld 237 D4
Kentchurch Hereford 61 A6
Kentford Suff 86 A3
Kentisbeare Devon 13 A5
Kentisbury Devon 25 A7
Kentisbury Ford Devon 25 A7
Kentmere Cumb 154 A3
Kenton Devon 13 C4
Kenton Suff 88 A2
Kenton T & W 179 C4
Kenton Bankfoot T & W 179 C4
Kentra Highld 235 D5
Kents Bank Cumb 154 D2
Kent's Green Glos 62 A3
Kent's Oak Hants 32 C2
Kenwick Shrops 110 B3
Kenwyn Corn 4 C3
Keoldale Highld 277 B4
Keppanach Highld 237 C4
Keppoch Highld 249 D6
Keprigan Argyll 190 D2
Kepwick N Yorks 158 B3
Kerchesters Borders 197 C6
Keresley W Mid 97 C6
Kernborough Devon 8 C1
Kerne Bridge Hereford 62 B1
Kerris Corn 2 C2
Kerry Powys 93 C5
Kerrycroy Argyll 203 B6
Kerry's Gate Hereford 78 D1
Kerrysdale Highld 261 C5
Kersall Notts 132 C2
Kersey Suff 87 C6
Kershopefoot Cumb 176 A2
Kersoe Worcs 80 D2
Kerswell Devon 13 A5
Kerswell Green Worcs 79 C6
Kesgrave Suff 88 C3
Kessingland Suff 105 C6
Kessingland Beach Suff 105 C6
Kessington E Dunb 205 A5
Kestle Corn 5 C4
Kestle Mill Corn 4 B3
Keston London 49 C7
Keswick Cumb 163 B5
Keswick Norf 104 A3
Keswick Norf 121 B5
Ketley Telford 111 D5
Ketley Bank Telford 111 D5
Ketsby Lincs 134 B3
Kettering Northants 99 D5
Ketteringham Norf 104 A2
Kettins Perth 220 A2
Kettlebaston Suff 87 B5
Kettlebridge Fife 220 D3
Kettleburgh Suff 88 A3
Kettlehill Fife 220 D3
Kettleholm Dumfries 174 A4
Kettleness N Yorks 169 D6
Kettleshulme Ches 129 B4
Kettlesing Bottom N Yorks 147 B6
Kettlesing Head N Yorks 147 B6
Kettlestone Norf 119 B6
Kettlethorpe Lincs 132 B3
Kettletoft Orkney 282 D7
Kettlewell N Yorks 156 D3
Ketton Rutland 100 A1
Kew London 49 B4
Kew Br. London 49 B4
Kew Gardens London 49 B4
Kewstoke N Som 42 C2
Kexbrough S Yorks 139 C6
Kexby Lincs 132 A3
Kexby York 149 B6
Key Green Ches 128 C3
Keyham Leics 98 A3
Keyhaven Hants 18 B2
Keyingham E Yorks 143 A4
Keymer W Sus 21 A6
Keynsham Bath 43 C5
Keysoe Beds 84 A2
Keysoe Row Beds 84 A2
Keyston Cambs 100 D2
Keyworth Notts 115 B4
Kibblesworth T & W 179 D4
Kibworth Beauchamp Leics 98 B3
Kibworth Harcourt Leics 98 B3
Kidbrooke London 49 B7
Kiddemore Green Staffs 95 A6
Kidderminster Worcs 95 D6
Kiddington Oxon 65 A5
Kidlington Oxon 65 B5
Kidmore End Oxon 47 B4
Kidsgrove Staffs 128 D3
Kidstones N Yorks 156 C3
Kidwelly = Cydweli Carms 57 B4
Kiel Crofts Argyll 226 C4
Kielder Northumb 187 D5
Kielder Castle Visitor Centre Northumb 187 D5
Kierfiold Ho. Orkney 282 F3
Kilbagie Clack 208 B2
Kilbarchan Renfs 205 B4
Kilbeg Highld 247 D5
Kilberry Argyll 202 B2
Kilbirnie N Ayrs 204 C3
Kilbride Argyll 226 D3
Kilbride Argyll 226 D4
Kilbride Highld 247 B4
Kilburn Angus 232 B1
Kilburn Derbys 114 A1
Kilburn London 49 A5
Kilburn N Yorks 158 D4
Kilby Leics 98 B3
Kilchamaig Argyll 202 B3
Kilchattan Argyll 212 C1
Kilchattan Bay Argyll 203 C6
Kilchenzie Argyll 190 C2
Kilcheran Argyll 226 C3
Kilchiaran Argyll 200 B2
Kilchoan Argyll 213 A5
Kilchoan Highld 234 D3
Kilchoman Argyll 200 B2
Kilchrenan Argyll 227 D5
Kilconquhar Fife 221 D4
Kilcot Glos 62 A2
Kilcoy Highld 252 A1
Kilcreggan Argyll 215 D5
Kildale N Yorks 159 A5
Kildalloig Argyll 190 D3
Kildary Highld 264 C3
Kildermorie Lodge Highld 263 C7
Kildonan N Ayrs 191 C6
Kildonan Lodge Highld 274 B3
Kildonnan Highld 234 B3
Kildrummy Aberds 244 A1
Kildwick N Yorks 147 C4
Kilfinan Argyll 203 A4
Kilfinnan Highld 239 C6
Kilgetty Pembs 56 B1
Kilgwrrwg Common Mon 61 D6
Kilham E Yorks 150 A3
Kilham Northumb 198 C2
Kilkenneth Argyll 222 C2
Kilkerran Argyll 190 D3
Kilkhampton Corn 24 D3
Killamarsh Derbys 131 A4
Killay Swansea 57 C6
Killbeg Argyll 225 B5
Killean Argyll 202 D1
Killearn Stirl 206 B3
Killen Highld 252 A2
Killerby Darl 167 D4
Killerton House, Exeter Devon 13 A4
Killichonan Perth 229 C4
Killiechonate Highld 239 D6
Killiechronan Argyll 225 B4
Killiecrankie Perth 230 B3
Killiemor Argyll 224 C3
Killiemore House Argyll 224 D3
Killilan Highld 249 C6
Killimster Highld 281 C5
Killin Stirl 217 A5
Killin Lodge Highld 240 B3
Killinallan Argyll 200 A3
Killinghall N Yorks 148 B1
Killington Cumb 155 C5
Killingworth T & W 179 B4
Killmahumaig Argyll 213 C5
Killochyett Borders 196 B3
Killocraw Argyll 190 B2
Killundine Highld 225 B4
Kilmacolm Invclyd 204 B3
Kilmaha Argyll 214 B2
Kilmahog Stirl 217 D6
Kilmalieu Highld 236 D2
Kilmaluag Highld 259 A4
Kilmany Fife 220 B3
Kilmarie Highld 247 C4
Kilmarnock E Ayrs 193 B4
Kilmaron Castle Fife 220 C3
Kilmartin Argyll 213 C6
Kilmaurs E Ayrs 205 D4
Kilmelford Argyll 213 A6
Kilmeny Argyll 200 B3
Kilmersdon Som 43 D5
Kilmeston Hants 33 C4
Kilmichael Argyll 190 C2
Kilmichael Glassary Argyll 214 C1
Kilmichael of Inverlussa Argyll 213 D5
Kilmington Devon 14 B2
Kilmington Wilts 30 B1
Kilmonivaig Highld 239 D5
Kilmorack Highld 251 B6
Kilmore Argyll 226 D3
Kilmore Highld 247 D5
Kilmory Argyll 202 A2
Kilmory Highld 235 C4
Kilmory Highld 246 D2
Kilmory N Ayrs 191 C5
Kilmuir Highld 258 D2
Kilmuir Highld 252 B2
Kilmuir Highld 264 C3
Kilmuir Highld 258 A3
Kilmun Argyll 215 D4
Kilmun Argyll 214 A2
Kiln Pit Hill Northumb 178 D2
Kilncadzow S Lnrk 194 B3
Kilndown Kent 37 C5
Kilnhurst S Yorks 140 D2
Kilninian Argyll 224 B2
Kilninver Argyll 226 D3
Kilnsea E Yorks 143 B6
Kilnsey N Yorks 146 A3
Kilnwick E Yorks 150 C2
Kilnwick Percy E Yorks 149 B1
Kiloran Argyll 212 C1
Kilpatrick N Ayrs 191 C5
Kilpeck Hereford 78 D2
Kilphedir Highld 274 C3
Kilpin E Yorks 141 A5
Kilpin Pike E Yorks 141 A5
Kilrenny Fife 221 D5
Kilsby Northants 98 D2
Kilspindie Perth 220 B2
Kilsyth N Lnrk 207 C5
Kiltarlity Highld 251 B7
Kilton Notts 131 B5
Kilton Som 27 A6
Kilton Thorpe Redcar 169 D4
Kilvaxter Highld 258 B3
Kilve Som 27 A6
Kilvington Notts 115 A5
Kilwinning N Ayrs 204 D3
Kimber worth S Yorks 140 D2
Kimberley Norf 103 A6
Kimberley Notts 114 A3
Kimble Wick Bucks 66 C3
Kimblesworth Durham 167 A5
Kimbolton Cambs 84 A2
Kimbolton Hereford 78 A3
Kimcote Leics 98 C2
Kimmeridge Dorset 16 D3
Kimmerston Northumb 198 C3
Kimpton Hants 32 A1
Kimpton Herts 68 B1
Kinbrace Highld 274 A2
Kinbuck Stirl 218 D2
Kincaple Fife 221 C4
Kincardine Fife 208 B2
Kincardine Highld 264 B2
Kincardine Bridge Fife 208 B2
Kincardine O'Neil Aberds 244 C2
Kinclaven Perth 219 A6
Kincorth Aberdeen 245 B6
Kincorth Ho. Moray 265 D6
Kincraig Highld 241 B6
Kincraigie Perth 230 D3
Kindallachan Perth 230 D3
Kinderland, Scarborough N Yorks 160 B4
Kineton Glos 64 A1
Kineton Warks 81 B6
Kinfauns Perth 219 B6
King Edward Aberds 268 D2
King Sterndale Derbys 129 B5
Kingairloch Highld 236 D2
Kingarth Argyll 203 C5
Kingcoed Mon 61 C6
Kingerby Lincs 142 D2
Kingham Oxon 64 A3
Kingholm Quay Dumfries 174 A2
Kinghorn Fife 209 B5
Kingie Highld 239 B5
Kinglassie Fife 209 A5
Kingoodie Perth 220 B3
King's Acre Hereford 78 C2
King's Bromley Staffs 113 D5
King's Caple Hereford 62 A1
King's Cliffe Northants 100 B2
Kings College Chapel, Cambridge Cambs 85 B6
King's Coughton Warks 80 B3
King's Heath W Mid 96 C3
Kings Hedges Cambs 85 A6
Kings Langley Herts 67 C5
King's Lynn Norf 118 C3
King's Meaburn Cumb 165 C4
King's Mills Wrex 110 A2
Kings Muir Borders 196 C1
King's Newnham Warks 98 D1
King's Newton Derbys 114 C1
King's Norton Leics 98 A3
King's Norton W Mid 96 D3
King's Nympton Devon 26 D1
King's Pyon Hereford 78 B2
King's Ripton Cambs 101 D4
King's Somborne Hants 32 B2
King's Stag Dorset 30 D1
King's Stanley Glos 63 C4
King's Sutton Northants 82 D1
King's Thorn Hereford 78 D3
King's Walden Herts 67 A6
Kings Worthy Hants 32 B3
Kingsand Corn 6 B3
Kingsbarns Fife 221 C5
Kingsbridge Devon 7 C6
Kingsbridge Som 27 B4
Kingsburgh Highld 258 C3
Kingsbury London 49 A5
Kingsbury Warks 97 B5
Kingsbury Episcopi Som 28 C4
Kingsclere Hants 46 D3
Kingscote Glos 63 D4
Kingscott Devon 25 D6
Kingscross N Ayrs 191 C6
Kingsdon Som 29 C5
Kingsdown Kent 39 A5
Kingseat Fife 208 A4
Kingsey Bucks 66 C2
Kingsfold W Sus 35 C4
Kingsford E Ayrs 205 D4
Kingsford Worcs 95 C6
Kingsforth N Lincs 142 B2
Kingsgate Kent 53 B5
Kingsheanton Devon 25 B6
Kingshouse Hotel Highld 237 D6
Kingside Hill Cumb 175 C4
Kingskerswell Devon 8 A2
Kingskettle Fife 220 D3
Kingsland Anglesey 122 B2
Kingsland Hereford 78 A2
Kingsley Ches 127 B5
Kingsley Hants 33 B6
Kingsley Staffs 112 A4
Kingsley Green W Sus 34 C1
Kingsley Holt Staffs 112 A4
Kingsley Park Northants 83 A4
Kingsmuir Angus 232 D2
Kingsmuir Fife 221 D5
Kingsnorth Kent 38 B2
Kingstanding W Mid 96 B3
Kingsteignton Devon 12 D3
Kingsthorpe Northants 83 A4
Kingston Cambs 85 B5
Kingston Devon 7 C5
Kingston Dorset 16 A1
Kingston Dorset 16 D3
Kingston E Loth 210 B2
Kingston Hants 17 A5
Kingston I o W 18 C3
Kingston Kent 52 D3
Kingston Moray 266 C4
Kingston Bagpuize Oxon 65 D5
Kingston Blount Oxon 66 D2
Kingston by Sea W Sus 21 B5
Kingston Deverill Wilts 30 B2
Kingston Gorse W Sus 20 B3
Kingston Lacy, Wimborne Minster Dorset 16 A3
Kingston Lisle Oxon 45 A7
Kingston Maurward Dorset 15 B7
Kingston near Lewes E Sus 22 B1
Kingston on Soar Notts 114 C3
Kingston Russell Dorset 15 B5
Kingston St Mary Som 28 C2
Kingston Seymour N Som 42 C3
Kingston Upon Hull Hull 142 A2
Kingston upon Thames London 49 C4
Kingston Vale London 49 B5
Kingstone Hereford 78 D2
Kingstone Som 28 D3
Kingstone Staffs 113 C4

Kingstown Cumb 175 C6
Kingswear Devon 8 B2
Kingswells Aberdeen 245 B5
Kingswinford W Mid 96 C1
Kingswood Bucks 66 B1
Kingswood Glos 62 D3
Kingswood Hereford 77 B6
Kingswood Kent 37 A6
Kingswood Powys 93 A6
Kingswood S Glos 43 B5
Kingswood Sur 35 A5
Kingswood Warks 97 D4
Kingthorpe Lincs 133 B6
Kington Hereford 77 B6
Kington Worcs 80 B2
Kington Langley Wilts 44 B3
Kington Magna Dorset 30 C1
Kington St Michael Wilts 44 B3
Kingussie Highld 241 B5
Kingweston Som 29 B5
Kininvie Ho. Moray 254 B4
Kinkell Bridge Perth 218 C4
Kinknockie Aberds 257 B5
Kinlet Shrops 95 C5
Kinloch Fife 220 C2
Kinloch Highld 234 A2
Kinloch Highld 271 A6
Kinloch Highld 247 C5
Kinloch Perth 231 D5
Kinloch Perth 231 D6
Kinloch Hourn Highld 238 B3
Kinloch Laggan Highld 240 D3
Kinloch Lodge Highld 277 C6
Kinloch Rannoch Perth 229 C5
Kinlochan Highld 236 C2
Kinlochard Stirl 217 D4
Kinlochbeoraid Highld 238 D2
Kinlochbervie Highld 276 C3
Kinlocheil Highld 236 B3
Kinlochewe Highld 262 D2
Kinlochleven Highld 237 C5
Kinlochmoidart Highld 235 C6
Kinlochmorar Highld 238 C2
Kinlochmore Highld 237 C5
Kinlochspelve Argyll 225 D5
Kinloid Highld 235 B5
Kinloss Moray 265 D6
Kinmel Bay Conwy 125 A4
Kinmuck Aberds 256 E3
Kinmundy Aberds 245 A5
Kinnadie Aberds 257 B4
Kinnaird Perth 220 B2
Kinnaird Castle Angus 233 C4
Kinneff Aberds 233 A6
Kinnelhead Dumfries 184 B3
Kinnell Angus 233 C4
Kinnerley Shrops 110 C2
Kinnersley Hereford 78 C1
Kinnersley Worcs 79 C6
Kinnerton Powys 77 A6
Kinnesswood Perth 219 D6
Kinninvie Durham 166 C3
Kinnordy Angus 232 C1
Kinoulton Notts 115 B4
Kinross Perth 219 D6
Kinrossie Perth 219 A6
Kinsbourne Green Herts 67 B6
Kinsey Heath Ches 111 A5
Kinsham Hereford 78 A1
Kinsham Worcs 80 D2
Kinsley W Yorks 140 B2
Kinson Bmouth 17 B4
Kintbury W Berks 46 C1
Kintessack Moray 265 D5
Kintillo Perth 219 C6
Kintocher Aberds 244 B2
Kinton Hereford 94 D2
Kinton Shrops 110 D2
Kintore Aberds 245 A4
Kintour Argyll 201 C4
Kintra Argyll 224 D2
Kintra Argyll 200 D3
Kintraw Argyll 213 B6
Kinuachdrachd Argyll 213 C5
Kinveachy Highld 242 A2
Kinver Staffs 95 C6
Kippax W Yorks 148 D3
Kippen Stirl 207 A4
Kippford or Scaur Dumfries 173 C6
Kirbister Orkney 283 G4
Kirbister Orkney 282 E7
Kirbuster Orkney 282 E3
Kirby Bedon Norf 104 A3
Kirby Bellars Leics 115 D5
Kirby Cane Norf 105 B4
Kirby Cross Essex 71 A6
Kirby Grindalythe N Yorks 150 A2
Kirby Hill N Yorks 148 A2
Kirby Hill N Yorks 157 A5
Kirby Knowle N Yorks 158 C3
Kirby-le-Soken Essex 71 A6
Kirby Misperton N Yorks 159 D6
Kirby Muxloe Leics 98 A2
Kirby Row Norf 105 B4
Kirby Sigston N Yorks 158 B3
Kirby Underdale E Yorks 149 B7
Kirby Wiske N Yorks 158 C2
Kirdford W Sus 34 D3
Kirk Highld 281 C4
Kirk Bramwith S Yorks 140 B4
Kirk Deighton N Yorks 148 B2
Kirk Ella E Yorks 142 A2
Kirk Hallam Derbys 114 A2
Kirk Hammerton N Yorks 148 B3
Kirk Ireton Derbys 130 D2
Kirk Langley Derbys 113 B6
Kirk Merrington Durham 167 B5
Kirk Michael I o M 152 B3
Kirk of Shotts N Lnrk 207 D6
Kirk Sandall S Yorks 140 C4
Kirk Smeaton N Yorks 140 B3
Kirk Yetholm Borders 188 A1
Kirkabister Shetland 285 K6
Kirkandrews Dumfries 172 D4
Kirkandrews upon Eden Cumb 175 C6
Kirkbampton Cumb 175 C6
Kirkbean Dumfries 174 C2
Kirkbride Cumb 175 C5
Kirkbuddo Angus 232 D3
Kirkburn Borders 196 C1
Kirkburn E Yorks 150 B2
Kirkburton W Yorks 139 B4
Kirkby Lincs 142 D2
Kirkby Mers 136 D3
Kirkby N Yorks 158 A4
Kirkby Fleetham N Yorks 157 B6
Kirkby Green Lincs 133 D5
Kirkby In Ashfield Notts 131 D5
Kirkby-in-Furness Cumb 153 B3
Kirkby la Thorpe Lincs 116 A4
Kirkby Lonsdale Cumb 155 D5
Kirkby Malham N Yorks 146 A2
Kirkby Mallory Leics 98 A1
Kirkby Malzeard N Yorks 157 D6
Kirkby Mills N Yorks 159 C6
Kirkby on Bain Lincs 134 C2
Kirkby Overblow N Yorks 148 C2
Kirkby Stephen Cumb 155 A6
Kirkby Thore Cumb 165 C4
Kirkby Underwood Lincs 116 C3
Kirkby Wharfe N Yorks 148 C4
Kirkbymoorside N Yorks 159 C5
Kirkcaldy Fife 209 A5
Kirkcambeck Cumb 176 C3
Kirkcarswell Dumfries 173 D5
Kirkcolm Dumfries 170 A2
Kirkconnel Dumfries 183 A5
Kirkconnell Dumfries 174 B2
Kirkcowan Dumfries 171 A5
Kirkcudbright Dumfries 173 C4
Kirkdale Mers 136 D2
Kirkfieldbank S Lnrk 194 B3
Kirkgunzeon Dumfries 173 B6
Kirkham Lancs 144 D4
Kirkham N Yorks 149 A6
Kirkhamgate W Yorks 139 A5
Kirkharle Northumb 178 A2
Kirkheaton Northumb 178 B2
Kirkheaton W Yorks 139 B4
Kirkhill Angus 233 B4
Kirkhill Highld 252 B1
Kirkhill Midloth 209 D5
Kirkhill Moray 254 C3
Kirkhope Borders 186 A2
Kirkhouse Borders 196 C2
Kirkiboll Highld 277 C6
Kirkibost Highld 247 C4
Kirkinch Angus 231 D7
Kirkinner Dumfries 171 B6
Kirkintilloch E Dunb 205 A6
Kirkland Cumb 162 C3
Kirkland Cumb 165 B4
Kirkland Dumfries 183 C6
Kirkland Dumfries 183 A5
Kirkleatham Redcar 168 C3
Kirklevington Stockton 158 A3
Kirkley Suff 105 B6
Kirklington Notts 132 D1
Kirklington N Yorks 157 C7
Kirklinton Cumb 176 C2
Kirkliston Edin 208 C4
Kirkmaiden Dumfries 170 D3
Kirkmichael Perth 231 C4
Kirkmichael S Ayrs 192 E3
Kirkmuirhill S Lnrk 194 B2
Kirknewton Northumb 198 C3
Kirknewton W Loth 208 D4
Kirkney Aberds 255 C6
Kirkoswald Cumb 164 A3
Kirkoswald S Ayrs 192 E2
Kirkpatrick Durham Dumfries 173 A5
Kirkpatrick-Fleming Dumfries 175 A5
Kirksanton Cumb 153 B2
Kirkstall W Yorks 147 D6
Kirkstead Lincs 134 C1
Kirkstile Aberds 255 C6
Kirkstyle Highld 281 A5
Kirkton Aberds 256 D1
Kirkton Aberds 268 E1
Kirkton Angus 232 D2
Kirkton Angus 220 A4
Kirkton Borders 186 B4
Kirkton Dumfries 184 D2
Kirkton Fife 220 B3
Kirkton Highld 249 D5
Kirkton Highld 249 B6
Kirkton Highld 265 A4
Kirkton Highld 252 A3
Kirkton Perth 219 C4
Kirkton S Lnrk 194 D4
Kirkton Stirl 217 D5
Kirkton Manor Borders 195 C7
Kirkton of Airlie Angus 231 C7
Kirkton of Auchterhouse Angus 220 A3
Kirkton of Auchterless Aberds 256 B2
Kirkton of Barevan Highld 253 B4
Kirkton of Bourtie Aberds 256 D3
Kirkton of Collace Perth 219 A6
Kirkton of Craig Angus 233 C5
Kirkton of Culsalmond Aberds 256 C1
Kirkton of Durris Aberds 245 C4
Kirkton of Glenbuchat Aberds 243 A6
Kirkton of Glenisla Angus 231 B6
Kirkton of Kingoldrum Angus 232 C1
Kirkton of Largo Fife 220 D4
Kirkton of Lethendy Perth 231 D5
Kirkton of Logie Buchan Aberds 257 D4
Kirkton of Maryculter Aberds 245 C5
Kirkton of Menmuir Angus 232 B3
Kirkton of Monikie Angus 221 A5
Kirkton of Oyne Aberds 256 D1
Kirkton of Rayne Aberds 256 D1
Kirkton of Skene Aberds 245 B5
Kirkton of Tough Aberds 244 A3
Kirktonhill Borders 196 A3
Kirktown Aberds 269 D5
Kirktown of Alvah Aberds 268 C1
Kirktown of Deskford Moray 267 C6
Kirktown of Fetteresso Aberds 245 D5
Kirktown of Mortlach Moray 254 C4
Kirktown of Slains Aberds 257 D5
Kirkurd Borders 195 B6
Kirkwall Orkney 282 F5
Kirkwall Airport Orkney 283 G5
Kirkwhelpington Northumb 178 A1
Kirmington N Lincs 142 B3
Kirmond le Mire Lincs 142 D3
Kirn Argyll 203 A6
Kirriemuir Angus 232 C1
Kirstead Green Norf 104 B3
Kirtlebridge Dumfries 175 A5
Kirtleton Dumfries 185 D5
Kirtling Cambs 86 B2
Kirtling Green Cambs 86 B2
Kirtlington Oxon 65 B5
Kirtomy Highld 278 B3
Kirton Lincs 117 B6
Kirton Notts 132 C1
Kirton Suff 88 D3
Kirton End Lincs 117 A5
Kirton Holme Lincs 117 A5
Kirton in Lindsey N Lincs 142 D1
Kislingbury Northants 82 B3
Kites Hardwick Warks 82 A1
Kittisford Som 27 C5
Kittle Swansea 57 D5
Kitt's Green W Mid 97 C4
Kitt's Moss Gtr Man 128 A3
Kittybrewster Aberdeen 245 B6
Kitwood Hants 33 B5
Kivernoll Hereford 78 D2
Kiveton Park S Yorks 131 A4
Knaith Lincs 132 A3
Knaith Park Lincs 132 A3
Knap Corner Dorset 30 C2
Knaphill Sur 34 A2
Knapp Perth 220 A2
Knapp Som 28 C3
Knapthorpe Notts 132 D2
Knapton Norf 121 B5
Knapton York 149 B4
Knapton Green Hereford 78 B2
Knapwell Cambs 85 A5
Knaresborough N Yorks 148 B2
Knarsdale Northumb 177 D4
Knauchland Moray 267 D6
Knaven Aberds 256 B3
Knayton N Yorks 158 C3
Knebworth Herts 68 A2
Knebworth House, Stevenage Herts 68 A2
Knedlington E Yorks 141 A5
Kneesall Notts 132 C2
Kneesworth Cambs 85 C5
Kneeton Notts 115 A5
Knelston Swansea 57 D4
Knenhall Staffs 112 B3
Knettishall Suff 103 C5
Knightacott Devon 26 B1
Knightcote Warks 81 B6
Knightley Dale Staffs 112 C2
Knighton Devon 7 C4
Knighton Leicester 98 A2
Knighton Staffs 111 C6
Knighton Staffs 111 A6
Knighton = Tref-y-Clawdd Powys 93 D6
Knightshayes Court Devon 27 D4
Knightswood Glasgow 205 B5
Knightwick Worcs 79 B5
Knill Hereford 77 A6
Knipton Leics 115 B6
Knitsley Durham 166 A4
Kniveton Derbys 130 D2
Knock Argyll 225 C4
Knock Cumb 165 C4
Knock Moray 267 D6
Knockally Highld 275 B5
Knockan Highld 271 C5
Knockandhu Moray 254 D3
Knockando Moray 254 B2
Knockando Ho. Moray 254 B3
Knockbain Highld 252 A2
Knockbreck Highld 258 B2
Knockbrex Dumfries 172 D3
Knockdee Highld 280 B3
Knockdolian S Ayrs 180 C3
Knockenkelly N Ayrs 191 C6
Knockentiber E Ayrs 192 B3
Knockespock Ho. Aberds 255 D6
Knockfarrel Highld 251 A7
Knockglass Dumfries 170 B2
Knockhill Motor Racing Circuit Fife 208 A3
Knockholt Kent 36 A2
Knockholt Pound Kent 36 A2
Knockie Lodge Highld 240 A2
Knockin Shrops 110 C2
Knockinlaw E Ayrs 193 B4
Knocklearn Dumfries 173 A5
Knocknaha Argyll 190 D2
Knocknain Dumfries 170 A1
Knockrome Argyll 201 A5
Knocksharry I o M 152 C2
Knodishall Suff 89 A5
Knole House & Gardens Kent 36 A3
Knolls Green Ches 128 B3
Knolton Wrex 110 B2
Knolton Bryn Wrex 110 B2
Knook Wilts 30 A3
Knossington Leics 99 A5
Knott End-on-Sea Lancs 144 C3
Knotting Beds 84 A2
Knotting Green Beds 84 A2
Knottingley W Yorks 140 A3
Knotts Cumb 164 C2
Knotts Lancs 146 B1
Knotty Ash Mers 136 D3
Knotty Green Bucks 67 D4
Knowbury Shrops 94 D3
Knowe Dumfries 181 D5
Knowehead Dumfries 182 C4
Knowes of Elrick Aberds 267 D7
Knowesgate Northumb 178 A1
Knoweton N Lnrk 194 A2
Knowhead Aberds 269 D4
Knowl Hill Windsor 47 B6
Knowle Bristol 43 B5
Knowle Devon 12 A2
Knowle Devon 13 C5
Knowle Devon 25 B5
Knowle Shrops 94 D3
Knowle W Mid 97 D4
Knowle Green Lancs 145 D6
Knowle Park W Yorks 147 C4
Knowlton Dorset 31 D4
Knowlton Kent 53 D4
Knowsley Mers 136 D3
Knowsley Safari Park Mers 136 D3
Knowstone Devon 26 C3
Knox Bridge Kent 37 B5
Knucklas Powys 93 D6
Knuston Northants 83 A6
Knutsford Ches 128 B2
Knutton Staffs 112 A2
Knypersley Staffs 128 D3
Kuggar Corn 3 D5
Kyle of Lochalsh Highld 249 D4
Kyleakin Highld 247 B6
Kylerhea Highld 247 B6
Kylesknoydart Highld 238 C2
Kylesku Highld 271 A5
Kylesmorar Highld 238 C2
Kylestrome Highld 271 A5
Kyllachy House Highld 252 D3
Kynaston Shrops 110 C2
Kynnersley Telford 111 D5
Kyre Magna Worcs 79 A4

L

La Fontenelle Guern 6
La Planque Guern 6
Labost W Isles 288 C3
Lacasaidh W Isles 288 E4
Lacasdal W Isles 288 D5
Laceby NE Lincs 143 C4
Lacey Green Bucks 66 D3
Lach Dennis Ches 128 B2
Lackford Suff 102 D3
Lacock Wilts 44 C3
Ladbroke Warks 81 B7
Laddingford Kent 37 B4
Lade Bank Lincs 134 D3
Ladock Corn 4 B3
Lady Orkney 282 C7
Ladybank Fife 220 C3
Ladykirk Borders 198 B2
Ladysford Aberds 269 C4
Laga Highld 235 D5
Lagalochan Argyll 214 A1
Lagavulin Argyll 201 D4
Lagg Argyll 201 A5
Lagg N Ayrs 191 C5
Laggan Argyll 200 C2
Laggan Highld 239 C6
Laggan Highld 241 C4
Laggan Highld 235 C6
Laggan S Ayrs 181 C4
Lagganulva Argyll 224 B3
Laide Highld 261 A5
Laigh Fenwick E Ayrs 205 D4
Laigh Glengall S Ayrs 192 D3
Laighmuir E Ayrs 205 D4
Laindon Essex 50 A3
Lair Highld 250 B2
Lairg Highld 272 D3
Lairg Lodge Highld 272 D3
Lairg Muir Highld 272 D3
Lairgmore Highld 252 C1
Laisterdyke W Yorks 147 D5
Laithes Cumb 164 B2
Lake I o W 19 C4
Lake Wilts 31 B5
Lakenham Norf 104 A3
Lakenheath Suff 102 C3
Lakesend Norf 101 B7
Lakeside Cumb 154 C2
Lakeside and Haverthwaite Railway Cumb 153 B2
Laleham Sur 48 C3
Laleston Bridgend 40 D3
Lamarsh Essex 87 D4
Lamas Norf 120 C4
Lambden Borders 197 B6
Lamberhurst Kent 37 C4
Lamberhurst Quarter Kent 37 C4
Lamberton Borders 198 A3
Lambeth London 49 B6
Lambhill Glasgow 205 B5
Lambley Notts 115 A4
Lambley Northumb 177 D4
Lamborough Hill Oxon 65 C5
Lambourn W Berks 46 B1
Lambourne End Essex 69 D4
Lambs Green W Sus 35 C5
Lambston Pembs 55 C5
Lambton T & W 179 D4
Lamerton Devon 11 D5
Lamesley T & W 179 D4
Laminess Orkney 282 D7
Lamington Highld 264 C3
Lamington S Lnrk 195 C4
Lamlash N Ayrs 191 B6
Lamloch Dumfries 182 C3
Lamonby Cumb 164 B2
Lamorna Corn 2 C2
Lamorran Corn 4 C3
Lampardbrook Suff 88 A3
Lampeter = Llanbedr Pont Steffan Ceredig 75 D4
Lampeter Velfrey Pembs 56 A1
Lamphey Pembs 55 D6
Lamplugh Cumb 162 B3
Lamport Northants 99 D4
Lamyatt Som 29 B6
Lana Devon 10 B4
Lanark S Lnrk 194 B3
Lancaster Lancs 145 A4
Lancaster Leisure Park Lancs 145 A4
Lanchester Durham 167 A4
Lancing W Sus 21 B4
Landbeach Cambs 85 A6
Landcross Devon 25 C5
Landerberry Aberds 245 B4
Landford Wilts 31 D6
Landford Manor Wilts 31 C6
Landimore Swansea 57 C4
Landkey Devon 25 B6
Landore Swansea 57 C6
Landrake Corn 6 A2
Land's End Corn 2 C1
Land's End Airport Corn 2 C1
Landscove Devon 8 A1
Landshipping Pembs 55 C6
Landshipping Quay Pembs 55 C6
Landulph Corn 6 A3
Landwade Suff 86 A2
Lane Corn 4 A3
Lane End Bucks 66 D3
Lane End Cumb 153 A2
Lane End Dorset 16 B2
Lane End Hants 33 C4
Lane End I o W 19 C5
Lane End Lancs 146 C2
Lane Ends Lancs 146 D1
Lane Ends Lancs 146 B1
Lane Ends N Yorks 146 C3
Lane Head Derbys 129 B6
Lane Head Durham 166 D4
Lane Head Gtr Man 137 D5
Lane Head W Yorks 139 C4
Lane Side Lancs 137 A6
Laneast Corn 10 C3
Laneham Notts 132 B3
Lanehead Durham 165 A6
Lanehead Northumb 177 A5
Lanercost Cumb 176 C3
Laneshaw Bridge Lancs 146 C3
Lanfach Caerph 41 B7
Langar Notts 115 B5
Langbank Renfs 204 A3
Langbar N Yorks 147 B4
Langburnshiels Borders 186 C4
Langcliffe N Yorks 146 A2
Langdale Highld 278 D2
Langdale End N Yorks 160 B3
Langdon Corn 10 C4
Langdon Beck Durham 165 B6
Langdon Hills Essex 50 A3
Langdyke Fife 220 D3
Langenhoe Essex 71 B4
Langford Beds 84 C3
Langford Devon 13 A5
Langford Essex 70 C2
Langford Notts 132 D3
Langford Oxon 64 C3
Langford Budville Som 27 C6
Langham Essex 87 D6
Langham Norf 120 A2
Langham Rutland 115 D6
Langham Suff 103 E5
Langhaugh Borders 195 C7
Langho Lancs 145 D7
Langholm Dumfries 185 D6
Langleeford Northumb 188 A2
Langley Ches 129 B4
Langley Hants 18 A3
Langley Herts 68 A2
Langley Kent 37 A6
Langley Northumb 177 C6
Langley Slough 48 B3
Langley Warks 81 A4
Langley W Sus 33 C7
Langley Burrell Wilts 44 B3
Langley Common Derbys 113 B6
Langley Heath Kent 37 A6
Langley Lower Green Essex 85 D6
Langley Marsh Som 27 C5
Langley Park Durham 167 A5
Langley Street Norf 105 A4
Langley Upper Green Essex 85 D6
Langney E Sus 22 B4
Langold Notts 131 A5
Langore Corn 10 C4
Langport Som 28 C4
Langrick Lincs 117 A5
Langridge Bath 43 C6
Langridge Ford Devon 25 C6
Langrigg Cumb 175 D4
Langrish Hants 33 C6
Langsett S Yorks 139 C5
Langshaw Borders 197 C4
Langside Perth 218 C2
Langskaill Orkney 282 C5
Langstone Hants 19 A6
Langstone Newport 61 D5
Langthorne N Yorks 157 B6
Langthorpe N Yorks 148 A2
Langthwaite N Yorks 156 A4
Langtoft E Yorks 150 A3
Langtoft Lincs 116 D4
Langton Durham 167 D4
Langton Lincs 134 C2
Langton Lincs 134 B3
Langton N Yorks 149 A6
Langton by Wragby Lincs 133 B6
Langton Green Kent 36 C3
Langton Green Suff 104 D2
Langton Herring Dorset 15 C6
Langton Matravers Dorset 17 D4
Langtree Devon 25 D5
Langwathby Cumb 164 B3
Langwell Ho. Highld 275 B5
Langwell Lodge Highld 271 D4
Langwith Derbys 131 C5
Langwith Junction Derbys 131 C5
Langworth Lincs 133 B5
Lanhydrock House, Bodmin Corn 5 A5
Lanivet Corn 5 A5
Lanlivery Corn 5 B5

Lanner Corn 4 D2
Lanreath Corn 5 B6
Lansallos Corn 5 B6
Lansdown Glos 63 A5
Lanteglos Highway Corn 5 B6
Lanton Borders 187 A5
Lanton Northumb 198 C3
Lapford Devon 12 A2
Laphroaig Argyll 200 D3
Lapley Staffs 112 D2
Lapworth Warks 97 D4
Larachbeg Highld 225 B5
Larbert Falk 207 B6
Larden Green Ches 127 D5
Largie Aberds 255 C7
Largiemore Argyll 214 D2
Largoward Fife 221 D4
Largs N Ayrs 204 C2
Largybeg N Ayrs 191 C6
Largymore N Ayrs 191 C6
Larkfield Invclyd 204 A2
Larkhall S Lnrk 194 A2
Larkhill Wilts 31 A5
Larling Norf 103 C5
Larriston Borders 186 D4
Lartington Durham 166 D3
Lary Aberds 243 B6
Lasham Hants 33 A5
Lashenden Kent 37 B6
Lassington Glos 62 A3
Lassodie Fife 208 A4
Lastingham N Yorks 159 B6
Latcham Som 29 A4
Latchford Herts 68 A3
Latchford Warr 127 A6
Latchingdon Essex 70 C2
Latchley Corn 11 D5
Lately Common Warr 137 D5
Lathbury M Keynes 83 C5
Latheron Highld 275 A5
Latheronwheel Highld 275 A5
Latheronwheel Ho. Highld 275 A5
Lathones Fife 221 D4
Latimer Bucks 67 D5
Latteridge S Glos 43 A5
Lattiford Som 29 C6
Latton Wilts 64 D1
Latton Bush Essex 69 C4
Lauchintilly Aberds 245 A4
Lauder Borders 197 B4
Laugharne Carms 56 A3
Laughterton Lincs 132 B3
Laughton E Sus 22 A3
Laughton Leics 98 C3
Laughton Lincs 116 B3
Laughton Lincs 141 D6
Laughton Common S Yorks 131 A5
Laughton en le Morthen S Yorks 131 A5
Launcells Corn 10 A3
Launceston Corn 10 C4
Launton Oxon 65 A7
Laurencekirk Aberds 233 A5
Laurieston Dumfries 173 B4
Laurieston Falk 208 C2
Lavendon M Keynes 83 B6
Lavenham Suff 87 C5
Laverhay Dumfries 185 C4
Laversdale Cumb 176 C2
Laverstock Wilts 31 B5
Laverstoke Hants 32 A3
Laverton Glos 80 D3
Laverton N Yorks 157 D6
Laverton Som 44 D1
Lavister Wrex 126 D3
Law S Lnrk 194 A3
Lawers Perth 217 A6
Lawers Perth 218 B2
Lawford Essex 88 D1
Lawhitton Corn 11 C4
Lawkland N Yorks 146 A1
Lawley Telford 95 A4
Lawnhead Staffs 112 C2
Lawrenny Pembs 55 D6
Lawshall Suff 87 B4
Lawton Hereford 78 B2
Laxey I o M 152 C4
Laxey Wheel and Mines I o M 152 C4
Laxfield Suff 104 D3
Laxfirth Shetland 285 J6
Laxfirth Shetland 285 H6
Laxford Bridge Highld 276 D3
Laxo Shetland 285 G6
Laxobigging Shetland 284 F6
Laxton E Yorks 141 A5
Laxton Notts 132 C2
Laxton Northants 99 B6
Laycock W Yorks 147 C4
Layer Breton Essex 70 B3
Layer de la Haye Essex 70 B3
Layer Marney Essex 70 B3
Layham Suff 87 C6
Laylands Green W Berks 46 C1
Laytham E Yorks 149 D6
Layton Blkpool 144 D3
Lazenby Redcar 168 C3
Lazonby Cumb 164 B3
Le Planel Guern 6
Le Villocq Guern 6
Lea Derbys 130 D3
Lea Hereford 62 A2
Lea Lincs 132 A3
Lea Shrops 94 C1
Lea Shrops 94 A2
Lea Wilts 44 A3
Lea Marston Warks 97 B5
Lea Town Lancs 145 D4
Leabrooks Derbys 131 D4
Leac a Li W Isles 288 H2
Leachkin Highld 252 B2
Leadburn Midloth 196 A1
Leaden Roding Essex 69 B5
Leadenham Lincs 133 D4
Leadgate Cumb 165 A5
Leadgate Durham 178 D3
Leadgate Northumb 178 D3
Leadhills S Lnrk 183 A6
Leafield Oxon 64 B4
Leagrave Luton 67 A5
Leake N Yorks 158 B3
Leake Commonside Lincs 134 D3
Lealholm N Yorks 159 A6
Lealt Argyll 213 C4
Lealt Highld 259 B5
Leamington Hastings Warks 82 A1
Leamonsley Staffs 96 A4
Leamside Durham 167 A6
Leanaig Highld 252 A1
Leargybreck Argyll 201 A5
Leasgill Cumb 154 C3
Leasingham Lincs 116 A3
Leasingthorne Durham 167 C5
Leasowe Mers 136 D1
Leatherhead Sur 35 A4
Leatherhead Common Sur 35 A4
Leathley N Yorks 147 C6
Leaton Shrops 110 D3
Leaveland Kent 52 D2
Leavening N Yorks 149 A6
Leaves Green London 49 C7
Leazes Durham 178 D3
Lebberston N Yorks 161 C4
Lechlade-on-Thames Glos 64 D3
Leck Lancs 155 D5
Leckford Hants 32 B2
Leckfurin Highld 278 C3
Leckgruinart Argyll 200 B2
Leckhampstead Bucks 83 D4
Leckhampstead W Berks 46 B2
Leckhampstead Thicket W Berks 46 B2
Leckhampton Glos 63 B5
Leckie Highld 262 D2
Leckmelm Highld 262 A3
Leckwith V Glam 41 D6
Leconfield E Yorks 150 C3
Ledaig Argyll 226 C4
Ledburn Bucks 67 A4
Ledbury Hereford 79 D5
Ledcharrie Stirl 217 B5
Ledgemoor Hereford 78 B2
Ledicot Hereford 78 A2
Ledmore Highld 271 C5
Lednagullin Highld 278 B3
Ledsham Ches 126 B3
Ledsham W Yorks 140 A2
Ledston W Yorks 140 A2
Ledston Luck W Yorks 148 D3
Ledwell Oxon 65 A5
Lee Argyll 224 D3
Lee Devon 25 A5
Lee Hants 32 D2
Lee Lancs 145 B5
Lee Shrops 110 B3
Lee Brockhurst Shrops 111 C4
Lee Clump Bucks 67 C4
Lee Mill Devon 7 B5
Lee Moor Devon 7 A4
Lee-on-the-Solent Hants 19 A4
Leeans Shetland 285 J5
Leebotten Shetland 285 L6
Leebotwood Shrops 94 B2
Leece Cumb 153 D3
Leechpool Pembs 55 C5
Leeds Kent 37 A6
Leeds W Yorks 148 D1
Leeds Bradford International Airport W Yorks 147 C6
Leeds Castle Kent 37 A6
Leeds City Art Gallery W Yorks 148 D1
Leedstown Corn 3 B4
Leek Staffs 129 D4
Leek Wootton Warks 81 A5
Leekbrook Staffs 129 D4
Leeming N Yorks 157 C6
Leeming Bar N Yorks 157 B6
Lees Derbys 113 B6
Lees Gtr Man 138 C2
Lees W Yorks 147 D4
Leeswood Flint 126 C2
Legbourne Lincs 134 A3
Legerwood Borders 197 B4
Legoland Windsor 48 B2
Legsby Lincs 133 A6
Leicester Leicester 98 A2
Leicester Forest East Leics 98 A2
Leicester Racecourse Leics 98 A3
Leigh Dorset 15 A6
Leigh Glos 63 A4
Leigh Gtr Man 137 C5
Leigh Kent 36 B3
Leigh Shrops 94 A1
Leigh Sur 35 B5
Leigh Wilts 63 D6
Leigh Worcs 79 B5
Leigh Beck Essex 51 A5
Leigh Common Som 30 C1
Leigh Delamere Wilts 44 B2
Leigh Green Kent 37 C7
Leigh on Sea Sthend 51 A5
Leigh Park Hants 19 A6
Leigh Sinton Worcs 79 B5
Leigh upon Mendip Som 29 A6
Leigh Woods N Som 43 B4
Leighswood W Mid 96 A3
Leighterton Glos 63 D4
Leighton N Yorks 157 D5
Leighton Powys 93 A6
Leighton Shrops 95 A4
Leighton Som 29 A7
Leighton Bromswold Cambs 100 D3
Leighton Buzzard Beds 67 A4
Leinthall Earls Hereford 78 A2
Leinthall Starkes Hereford 78 A2
Leintwardine Hereford 94 D2
Leire Leics 98 B2
Leirinmore Highld 277 B5
Leiston Suff 89 A5
Leitfie Perth 231 D6
Leith Edin 209 C5
Leitholm Borders 198 B1
Lelant Corn 2 B3
Lelley E Yorks 151 D5
Lem Hill Worcs 95 D5
Lemmington Hall Northumb 189 B4
Lempitlaw Borders 198 C1
Lenchwick Worcs 80 C3
Lendalfoot S Ayrs 180 C3
Lendrick Lodge Stirl 217 D5
Lenham Kent 37 A6
Lenham Heath Kent 37 B7
Lennel Borders 198 B2
Lennoxtown E Dunb 205 A6
Lenton Lincs 116 B3
Lenton Nottingham 114 B3
Lentran Highld 252 B1
Lenwade Norf 120 D2
Leny Ho. Stirl 217 D6
Lenzie E Dunb 205 A6
Leoch Angus 220 A3
Leochel-Cushnie Aberds 244 A2
Leominster Hereford 78 B2
Leonard Stanley Glos 63 C4
Leonardslee Gardens W Sus 35 D5
Leorin Argyll 200 D3
Lepe Hants 18 B3
Lephin Highld 258 D1
Lephinchapel Argyll 214 C2
Lephinmore Argyll 214 C2
Leppington N Yorks 149 A6
Lepton W Yorks 139 B5
Lerryn Corn 5 B6
Lerwick Shetland 285 J6
Lerwick (Tingwall) Airport Shetland 285 J6
Lesbury Northumb 189 B5
Leslie Aberds 255 D6
Leslie Fife 220 D2
Lesmahagow S Lnrk 194 C3
Lesnewth Corn 10 B2
Lessendrum Aberds 255 B6
Lessingham Norf 121 C5
Lessonhall Cumb 175 C5
Leswalt Dumfries 170 A2
Letchmore Heath Herts 67 D6
Letchworth Herts 84 D4
Letcombe Bassett Oxon 46 A1
Letcombe Regis Oxon 46 A1
Letham Angus 232 D3
Letham Falk 208 B1
Letham Fife 220 C3
Letham Perth 219 B5
Letham Grange Angus 233 D4
Lethenty Aberds 256 B3
Letheringham Suff 88 B3
Letheringsett Norf 120 B2
Lettaford Devon 12 C2
Lettan Orkney 282 C8
Letterewe Highld 261 C6
Letterfearn Highld 249 D5
Letterfinlay Highld 239 C6
Lettermorar Highld 235 B6
Lettermore Argyll 224 B3
Letters Highld 262 B3
Letterston Pembs 55 B5
Lettoch Highld 242 A3
Lettoch Highld 254 C1
Letton Hereford 78 C1
Letton Hereford 94 D1
Letton Green Norf 103 A5
Letty Green Herts 68 B2
Letwell S Yorks 131 A5
Leuchars Fife 221 B4
Leuchars Ho. Moray 266 C3
Leumrabhagh W Isles 288 F4
Levan Invclyd 204 A2
Levaneap Shetland 285 G6
Levedale Staffs 112 D2
Leven E Yorks 151 C4
Leven Fife 220 D3
Levencorroch N Ayrs 191 C6
Levens Cumb 154 C3
Levens Green Herts 68 A3
Levenshulme Gtr Man 138 D1
Levenwick Shetland 285 L6
Leverburgh = An t-Ob W Isles 287 F5
Leverington Cambs 118 D1
Leverton Lincs 117 A7
Leverton Highgate Lincs 117 A7
Leverton Lucasgate Lincs 117 A7
Leverton Outgate Lincs 117 A7
Levington Suff 88 D3
Levisham N Yorks 160 B2
Levishie Highld 240 A2
Lew Oxon 64 C4
Lewannick Corn 10 C3
Lewdown Devon 11 C5
Lewes E Sus 22 A2
Leweston Pembs 55 B5
Lewisham London 49 B6
Lewiston Highld 251 D7
Lewistown Bridgend 40 C4
Lewknor Oxon 66 D2
Leworthy Devon 10 A4
Leworthy Devon 26 B1
Lewtrenchard Devon 11 C5
Lexden Essex 70 A3
Ley Aberds 244 A2
Ley Corn 5 A6
Leybourne Kent 37 A4
Leyburn N Yorks 157 B5
Leyfields Staffs 97 A5
Leyhill Bucks 67 C4
Leyland Lancs 136 A4
Leylodge Aberds 245 A4
Leymoor W Yorks 139 B4
Leys Aberds 269 D5
Leys Perth 220 A2
Leys Castle Highld 252 B2
Leys of Cossans Angus 232 D1
Leysdown-on-Sea Kent 52 B2
Leysmill Angus 233 D4
Leysters Pole Hereford 78 A3
Leyton London 49 A6
Leytonstone London 49 A6
Lezant Corn 11 D4
Leziate Norf 118 D3
Lhanbryde Moray 266 C3
Liatrie Highld 250 C4
Libanus Powys 60 A1
Libberton S Lnrk 195 B4
Liberton Edin 209 D5
Liceasto W Isles 288 H2
Lichfield Staffs 96 A4
Lichfield Cathedral Staffs 113 D5
Lickey Worcs 96 D2
Lickey End Worcs 96 D2
Lickfold W Sus 34 D2
Liddel Orkney 283 K5
Liddesdale Highld 236 D1
Liddington Swindon 45 A6
Lidgate Suff 86 B3
Lidget S Yorks 141 C4
Lidget Green W Yorks 147 D5
Lidgett Notts 131 C6
Lidlington Beds 84 D1
Lidstone Oxon 65 A4
Lieurary Highld 279 B6
Liff Angus 220 A3
Lifton Devon 11 C4
Liftondown Devon 11 C4
Lighthorne Warks 81 B6
Lightwater Sur 48 C2
Lightwater Valley N Yorks 157 D6
Lightwood Stoke 112 A3
Lightwood Green Ches 111 A5
Lightwood Green Wrex 110 A2
Lilbourne Northants 98 D2
Lilburn Tower Northumb 188 A3
Lilleshall Telford 111 D6
Lilley Herts 67 A6
Lilley W Berks 46 B2
Lilliesleaf Borders 186 A4
Lillingstone Dayrell Bucks 83 D4
Lillingstone Lovell Bucks 83 C4
Lillington Dorset 29 D6
Lillington Warks 81 A6
Lilliput Poole 17 B4
Lilstock Som 27 A6
Lilyhurst Shrops 111 D6
Limbury Luton 67 A5
Limebrook Hereford 78 A1
Limefield Gtr Man 137 B7
Limekilnburn S Lnrk 194 A2
Limekilns Fife 208 B3
Limerigg Falk 207 C6
Limerstone I o W 18 C3
Limington Som 29 C5
Limpenhoe Norf 105 A4
Limpley Stoke Wilts 44 C1
Limpsfield Sur 36 A2
Limpsfield Chart Sur 36 A2
Linby Notts 131 D5
Linchmere W Sus 34 C1
Lincluden Dumfries 174 A2
Lincoln Lincs 133 B4
Lincoln Castle Lincs 133 B4
Lincoln Cathedral Lincs 133 B4
Lincomb Worcs 79 A6
Lincombe Devon 7 B6
Lindal in Furness Cumb 153 C3
Lindale Cumb 154 C3
Lindean Borders 196 C3
Lindfield W Sus 35 D6
Lindford Hants 33 B7
Lindifferon Fife 220 C3
Lindisfarne Priory, Holy Island Northumb 199 B5
Lindley W Yorks 139 B4
Lindley Green N Yorks 147 C6
Lindores Fife 220 C2
Lindridge Worcs 79 A4
Lindsell Essex 69 A6
Lindsey Suff 87 C5
Linford Hants 17 A5
Linford Thurrock 50 B3
Lingague I o M 152 D2
Lingards Wood W Yorks 138 B3
Lingbob W Yorks 147 D4
Lingdale Redcar 169 D4
Lingen Hereford 78 A1
Lingfield Sur 36 B1
Lingfield Park Racecourse Sur 36 B1
Lingreabhagh W Isles 287 F5
Lingwood Norf 105 A4
Linicro Highld 258 B3
Linkenholt Hants 46 D1
Linkhill Kent 37 D6
Linkinhorne Corn 10 D4
Linklater Orkney 283 K5
Linksness Orkney 283 G3
Linktown Fife 209 A5
Linley Shrops 94 B1
Linley Green Hereford 79 B4
Linlithgow W Loth 208 C3
Linlithgow Bridge W Loth 208 C2
Linshiels Northumb 188 C1
Linsiadar W Isles 288 D3
Linsidemore Highld 264 A1
Linslade Beds 67 A4
Linstead Parva Suff 104 D4
Linstock Cumb 176 D2
Linthwaite W Yorks 139 B4
Lintlaw Borders 198 A2
Lintmill Moray 267 C6
Linton Borders 187 A6
Linton Cambs 86 C1
Linton Derbys 113 D6
Linton Hereford 62 A2
Linton Kent 37 B5
Linton Northumb 189 D5
Linton N Yorks 146 A3
Linton W Yorks 148 C2
Linton-on-Ouse N Yorks 148 A3
Linwood Hants 17 A5
Linwood Lincs 133 A6
Linwood Renfs 205 B4
Lionacleit W Isles 286 B3
Lional W Isles 288 A6
Liphook Hants 34 C1
Liscard Mers 136 D2
Liscombe Som 26 B3
Liskeard Corn 6 A1
L'Islet Guern 6
Liss Hants 33 C6
Liss Forest Hants 33 C6
Lissett E Yorks 151 B4
Lissington Lincs 133 A6
Lisvane Cardiff 41 C6
Liswerry Newport 42 A2
Litcham Norf 119 D5
Litchborough Northants 82 B3
Litchfield Hants 46 D2
Litherland Mers 136 D2
Litlington Cambs 85 C5
Litlington E Sus 22 B3
Little Abington Cambs 86 C1
Little Addington Northants 99 D6
Little Alne Warks 80 A4
Little Altcar Mers 136 C2
Little Asby Cumb 155 A5
Little Assynt Highld 271 B4
Little Aston Staffs 96 A3
Little Atherfield I o W 18 C3
Little Ayre Orkney 283 H4
Little-ayre Shetland 285 G5
Little Ayton N Yorks 168 D3
Little Baddow Essex 70 C1
Little Badminton S Glos 44 A2
Little Ballinluig Perth 230 C3
Little Bampton Cumb 175 C5
Little Bardfield Essex 86 D2
Little Barford Beds 84 B3
Little Barningham Norf 120 B3
Little Barrington Glos 64 B3
Little Barrow Ches 127 B4
Little Barugh N Yorks 159 D6
Little Bavington Northumb 178 B1
Little Bealings Suff 88 C3
Little Bedwyn Wilts 45 C6
Little Bentley Essex 71 A5
Little Berkhamsted Herts 68 C2
Little Billing Northants 83 A5
Little Birch Hereford 78 D3
Little Blakenham Suff 88 C2
Little Blencow Cumb 164 B2
Little Bollington Ches 128 A2
Little Bookham Sur 35 A4
Little Bowden Leics 99 C4
Little Bradley Suff 86 B2
Little Brampton Shrops 94 C1
Little Brechin Angus 232 B3
Little Brickhill M Keynes 83 D6
Little Brington Northants 82 A3
Little Bromley Essex 71 A4
Little Broughton Cumb 162 A3
Little Budworth Ches 127 C5
Little Burstead Essex 69 D6
Little Bytham Lincs 116 D3
Little Carlton Lincs 134 A3
Little Carlton Notts 132 D2
Little Casterton Rutland 100 A2
Little Cawthorpe Lincs 134 A3
Little Chalfont Bucks 67 D4
Little Chart Kent 38 A1
Little Chesterford Essex 85 C7
Little Cheverell Wilts 44 D3
Little Chishill Cambs 85 D6
Little Clacton Essex 71 B5
Little Clifton Cumb 162 B3
Little Colp Aberds 256 B2
Little Comberton Worcs 80 C2
Little Common E Sus 23 B5
Little Compton Warks 81 D5
Little Cornard Suff 87 D4
Little Cowarne Hereford 79 B4
Little Coxwell Oxon 64 D3
Little Crakehall N Yorks 157 B6
Little Cressingham Norf 103 A4
Little Crosby Mers 136 C2
Little Dalby Leics 115 D5
Little Dawley Telford 95 A4
Little Dens Aberds 257 B5
Little Dewchurch Hereford 78 D3
Little Downham Cambs 101 C7
Little Driffield E Yorks 150 B3
Little Dunham Norf 119 D5
Little Dunkeld Perth 230 D4
Little Dunmow Essex 69 A6
Little Easton Essex 69 A6
Little Eaton Derbys 114 A1
Little Eccleston Lancs 144 C4
Little Ellingham Norf 103 B6
Little End Essex 69 C5
Little Eversden Cambs 85 B5
Little Faringdon Oxon 64 C3
Little Fencote N Yorks 157 B6
Little Fenton N Yorks 148 D4
Little Finborough Suff 87 B6
Little Fransham Norf 119 D6
Little Gaddesden Herts 67 B4
Little Gidding Cambs 100 C3
Little Glemham Suff 88 B4
Little Glenshee Perth 219 A4
Little Gransden Cambs 85 B4
Little Green Som 29 A7
Little Grimsby Lincs 143 D5
Little Gruinard Highld 261 B6
Little Habton N Yorks 159 D6
Little Hadham Herts 68 A4
Little Hale Lincs 116 A4
Little Hallingbury Essex 69 B4
Little Hampden Bucks 66 C3
Little Harrowden Northants 99 D5
Little Haseley Oxon 66 C1
Little Hatfield E Yorks 151 C4
Little Hautbois Norf 121 C4
Little Haven Pembs 55 C4
Little Hay Staffs 96 A4
Little Hayfield Derbys 129 A5
Little Haywood Staffs 112 C4
Little Heath W Mid 97 C6
Little Hereford Hereford 78 A3
Little Horkesley Essex 87 D5
Little Horsted E Sus 22 A2
Little Horton W Yorks 147 D5
Little Horwood Bucks 83 D4
Little Houghton Northants 83 B5
Little Houghton S Yorks 140 C2

Little Hucklow Derbys 129 B6
Little Hulton Gtr Man 137 C6
Little Humber E Yorks 142 A3
Little Hungerford W Berks 46 B3
Little Irchester Northants 83 A6
Little Kimble Bucks 66 C3
Little Kineton Warks 81 B6
Little Kingshill Bucks 66 D3
Little Langdale Cumb 154 A2
Little Langford Wilts 31 B4
Little Laver Essex 69 C5
Little Leigh Ches 127 B6
Little Leighs Essex 69 B7
Little Lever Gtr Man 137 C6
Little London Bucks 66 B1
Little London E Sus 22 A3
Little London Hants 32 A2
Little London Hants 47 D4
Little London Lincs 117 C5
Little London Lincs 118 C1
Little London Norf 120 C3
Little London Powys 92 C4
Little Longstone Derbys 130 B1
Little Lynturk Aberds 244 A2
Little Malvern Worcs 79 C5
Little Maplestead Essex 87 D4
Little Marcle Hereford 79 D4
Little Marlow Bucks 47 A6
Little Marsden Lancs 146 D2
Little Massingham Norf 119 C4
Little Melton Norf 104 A2
Little Mill Mon 61 C5
Little Milton Oxon 65 C7
Little Missenden Bucks 67 D4
Little Musgrave Cumb 165 D5
Little Ness Shrops 110 D3
Little Neston Ches 126 B2
Little Newcastle Pembs 55 B5
Little Newsham Durham 166 D4
Little Oakley Essex 71 A6
Little Oakley Northants 99 C5
Little Orton Cumb 175 C6
Little Ouseburn N Yorks 148 A3
Little Paxton Cambs 84 A3
Little Petherick Corn 9 D5
Little Pitlurg Moray 255 B5
Little Plumpton Lancs 144 D3
Little Plumstead Norf 121 D5
Little Ponton Lincs 116 B2
Little Raveley Cambs 101 D4
Little Reedness E Yorks 141 A6
Little Ribston N Yorks 148 B2
Little Rissington Glos 64 B2
Little Ryburgh Norf 119 C6
Little Ryle Northumb 188 B3
Little Salkeld Cumb 164 B3
Little Sampford Essex 86 D2
Little Sandhurst Brack 47 C6
Little Saxham Suff 86 A3
Little Scatwell Highld 251 A5
Little Sessay N Yorks 158 D3
Little Shelford Cambs 85 B6
Little Singleton Lancs 144 D3
Little Skillymarno Aberds 269 D4
Little Smeaton N Yorks 140 B3
Little Snoring Norf 119 B6
Little Sodbury S Glos 43 A6
Little Somborne Hants 32 B2
Little Somerford Wilts 44 A3
Little Stainforth N Yorks 146 A2
Little Stainton Darl 167 C6
Little Stanney Ches 127 B4
Little Staughton Beds 84 A3
Little Steeping Lincs 135 C4
Little Stoke Staffs 112 B3
Little Stonham Suff 88 A2
Little Stretton Leics 98 A3
Little Stretton Shrops 94 B2
Little Strickland Cumb 164 D3
Little Stukeley Cambs 100 D4
Little Sutton Ches 126 B3
Little Tew Oxon 65 A4
Little Thetford Cambs 102 D1
Little Thirkleby N Yorks 158 D3
Little Thurlow Suff 86 B2
Little Thurrock Thurrock 50 B3
Little Torboll Highld 264 A3
Little Torrington Devon 25 D5
Little Totham Essex 70 B2
Little Toux Aberds 267 D6
Little Town Cumb 163 C5
Little Town Lancs 145 D6
Little Urswick Cumb 153 C3
Little Wakering Essex 51 A6
Little Walden Essex 86 C1
Little Waldingfield Suff 87 C5
Little Walsingham Norf 119 B6
Little Waltham Essex 69 B7
Little Warley Essex 69 D6
Little Weighton E Yorks 150 D2
Little Weldon Northants 99 C6
Little Welnetham Suff 87 A4
Little Wenlock Telford 95 A4
Little Whittingham Green Suff 104 D3
Little Wilbraham Cambs 86 B1
Little Wishford Wilts 31 B4
Little Witley Worcs 79 A5
Little Wittenham Oxon 65 D6
Little Wolford Warks 81 D5
Little Wratting Suff 86 C2
Little Wymington Beds 83 A6
Little Wymondley Herts 68 A2
Little Wyrley Staffs 96 A3
Little Yeldham Essex 86 D3
Littlebeck N Yorks 160 A2
Littleborough Gtr Man 138 B2
Littleborough Notts 132 A3
Littlebourne Kent 53 D4
Littlebredy Dorset 15 C5
Littlebury Essex 85 D7
Littlebury Green Essex 85 D6
Littledean Glos 62 B2
Littleferry Highld 265 A4
Littleham Devon 13 C5
Littleham Devon 25 C5
Littlehampton W Sus 20 B3
Littlehempston Devon 8 A2
Littlehoughton Northumb 189 B5
Littlemill Aberds 243 C6
Littlemill E Ayrs 182 A2
Littlemill Highld 253 A5
Littlemill Northumb 189 B5
Littlemoor Dorset 15 C6
Littlemore Oxon 65 C6
Littleover Derby 114 B1
Littleport Cambs 102 C1
Littlestone on Sea Kent 38 C2
Littlethorpe Leics 98 B2
Littlethorpe N Yorks 148 A2
Littleton Ches 127 C4
Littleton Hants 32 B3
Littleton Perth 220 A2
Littleton Som 29 B4
Littleton Sur 48 C3
Littleton Sur 34 B2
Littleton Drew Wilts 44 A2
Littleton-on-Severn S Glos 43 A4
Littleton Pannell Wilts 44 D4
Littletown Durham 167 A6
Littlewick Green Windsor 47 B6
Littleworth Beds 84 C2
Littleworth Glos 63 C4
Littleworth Oxon 64 D4
Littleworth Staffs 112 D4
Littleworth Worcs 80 B1
Litton Derbys 129 B6
Litton N Yorks 156 D3
Litton Som 43 D4
Litton Cheney Dorset 15 B5
Liurbost W Isles 288 E4
Liverpool Mers 136 D2
Liverpool Airport Mers 127 A4
Liverpool Cathedral (C of E) Mers 126 A3
Liverpool Cathedral (RC) Mers 136 D2
Liverpool John Lennon Airport Mers 127 A4
Liversedge W Yorks 139 A5
Liverton Devon 12 D3
Liverton Redcar 169 D5
Livingston W Loth 208 D3
Livingston Village W Loth 208 D3
Lixwm Flint 125 B6
Lizard Corn 3 D5
Llaingoch Anglesey 122 B2
Llaithddu Powys 93 C4
Llan Powys 91 B6
Llan Ffestiniog Gwyn 108 A2
Llan-y-pwll Wrex 126 D3
Llanaber Gwyn 90 A4
Llanaelhaearn Gwyn 106 B3
Llanafan Ceredig 75 A5
Llanafan-fawr Powys 76 B3
Llanallgo Anglesey 123 B4
Llanandras = Presteigne Powys 77 A7
Llanarmon Gwyn 107 C4
Llanarmon Dyffryn Ceiriog Wrex 109 B6
Llanarmon-yn-Ial Denb 126 D1
Llanarth Ceredig 73 A7
Llanarth Mon 61 B5
Llanarthne Carms 58 C2
Llanasa Flint 125 A6
Llanbabo Anglesey 122 B3
Llanbadarn Fawr Ceredig 90 D4
Llanbadarn Fynydd Powys 93 D5
Llanbadarn-y-Garreg Powys 77 C5
Llanbadoc Mon 61 C5
Llanbadrig Anglesey 122 A3
Llanbeder Newport 61 D5
Llanbedr Gwyn 107 D5
Llanbedr Powys 77 C5
Llanbedr Powys 60 A4
Llanbedr-Dyffryn-Clwyd Denb 125 D6
Llanbedr Pont Steffan = Lampeter Ceredig 75 D4
Llanbedr-y-cennin Conwy 124 C2
Llanbedrgoch Anglesey 123 B5
Llanbedrog Gwyn 106 C3
Llanberis Gwyn 123 D5
Llanbethêry V Glam 41 E5
Llanbister Powys 93 D5
Llanblethian V Glam 41 D4
Llanboidy Carms 73 D5
Llanbradach Caerph 41 B6
Llanbrynmair Powys 91 B6
Llancarfan V Glam 41 D5
Llancayo Mon 61 C5
Llancloudy Hereford 61 A6
Llancynfelyn Ceredig 90 C4
Llandaff Cardiff 41 D6
Llandanwg Gwyn 107 D5
Llandarcy Neath 40 B2
Llandawke Carms 56 A2
Llanddaniel Fab Anglesey 123 C4
Llanddarog Carms 57 A5
Llanddeiniol Ceredig 75 A4
Llanddeiniolen Gwyn 123 D5
Llandderfel Gwyn 109 B4
Llanddeusant Anglesey 122 B3
Llanddeusant Carms 59 C4
Llanddew Powys 77 D4
Llanddewi Swansea 57 D4
Llanddewi-Brefi Ceredig 75 C5
Llanddewi Rhydderch Mon 61 B5
Llanddewi Velfrey Pembs 56 A1
Llanddewi'r Cwm Powys 76 C4
Llanddoged Conwy 124 C3
Llanddona Anglesey 123 C5
Llanddowror Carms 56 A2
Llanddulas Conwy 125 B4
Llanddwywe Gwyn 107 D5
Llanddyfynan Anglesey 123 C5
Llandefaelog Fach Powys 76 D4
Llandefaelog-tre'r-graig Powys 77 E5
Llandefalle Powys 77 D5
Llandegai Gwyn 123 C5
Llandegfan Anglesey 123 C5
Llandegla Denb 126 D1
Llandegley Powys 77 A5
Llandegveth Mon 61 D5
Llandegwning Gwyn 106 C2
Llandeilo Carms 58 C3
Llandeilo Graban Powys 77 C4
Llandeilo'r Fan Powys 59 B5
Llandeloy Pembs 55 B4
Llandenny Mon 61 C6
Llandevenny Mon 42 A3
Llandewednock Corn 3 D5
Llandewi Ystradenny Powys 77 A5
Llandinabo Hereford 61 A7
Llandinam Powys 92 C4
Llandissilio Pembs 55 B7
Llandogo Mon 62 C1
Llandough V Glam 41 D4
Llandough V Glam 41 D6
Llandovery = Llanymddyfri Carms 59 B4
Llandow V Glam 40 D4
Llandre Ceredig 90 D4
Llandre Carms 58 A3
Llandrillo Denb 109 B5
Llandrillo-yn-Rhos Conwy 124 A3
Llandrindod = Llandrindod Wells Powys 77 A4
Llandrindod Wells = Llandrindod Powys 77 A4
Llandrinio Powys 110 D1
Llandudno Conwy 124 A2
Llandudno Junction = Cyffordd Llandudno Conwy 124 B2
Llandwrog Gwyn 107 A4
Llandybie Carms 57 A6
Llandyfaelog Carms 57 A4
Llandyfan Carms 57 A6
Llandyfriog Ceredig 73 B6
Llandyfrydog Anglesey 123 B4
Llandygwydd Ceredig 73 B5
Llandynan Denb 109 A6
Llandyrnog Denb 125 C6
Llandysilio Powys 110 D1
Llandyssil Powys 93 B5
Llandysul Ceredig 73 B7
Llanedeyrn Cardiff 41 C7
Llanedi Carms 57 B5
Llaneglwys Powys 77 D4
Llanegryn Gwyn 90 B3
Llanegwad Carms 58 C2
Llaneilian Anglesey 123 A4
Llanelian-yn-Rhos Conwy 124 B3
Llanelidan Denb 125 D6
Llanelieu Powys 77 D5
Llanellen Mon 61 B5
Llanelli Carms 57 C5
Llanelltyd Gwyn 91 A5
Llanelly Mon 60 B4
Llanelly Hill Mon 60 B4
Llanelwedd Powys 76 B4
Llanelwy = St Asaph Denb 125 B5
Llanenddwyn Gwyn 107 D5
Llanengan Gwyn 106 D2
Llanerchymedd Anglesey 123 B4
Llanerfyl Powys 92 A4
Llanfachraeth Anglesey 122 B3
Llanfachreth Gwyn 108 C2
Llanfaelog Anglesey 122 C3
Llanfaelrhys Gwyn 106 D2
Llanfaenor Mon 61 B6
Llanfaes Anglesey 123 C6
Llanfaes Powys 60 A2
Llanfaethlu Anglesey 122 B3
Llanfaglan Gwyn 123 D4
Llanfair Gwyn 107 D5
Llanfair-ar-y-bryn Carms 59 B5
Llanfair Caereinion Powys 93 A5
Llanfair Clydogau Ceredig 75 C5
Llanfair-Dyffryn-Clwyd Denb 125 D6
Llanfair Kilgheddin Mon 61 C5
Llanfair-Nant-Gwyn Pembs 73 C4
Llanfair Talhaiarn Conwy 125 B4
Llanfair Waterdine Shrops 93 D6
Llanfair-ym-Muallt = Builth Wells Powys 76 B4
Llanfairfechan Conwy 124 B1
Llanfairpwll-gwyngyll Anglesey 123 C5
Llanfairyneubwll Anglesey 122 C3
Llanfairynghornwy Anglesey 122 A3
Llanfallteg Carms 56 A1
Llanfaredd Powys 77 B4
Llanfarian Ceredig 75 A4
Llanfechain Powys 109 C6
Llanfechan Powys 76 B3
Llanfechell Anglesey 122 A3
Llanfendigaid Gwyn 90 B3
Llanferres Denb 126 C1
Llanfflewyn Anglesey 122 B3
Llanfihangel-ar-arth Carms 58 B1
Llanfihangel-Crucorney Mon 61 A5
Llanfihangel Glyn Myfyr Conwy 109 A4
Llanfihangel Nant Bran Powys 59 B6
Llanfihangel-nant-Melan Powys 77 B5
Llanfihangel Rhydithon Powys 77 A5
Llanfihangel Rogiet Mon 42 A3
Llanfihangel Tal-y-llyn Powys 60 A3
Llanfihangel-uwch-Gwili Carms 58 C1
Llanfihangel-y-Creuddyn Ceredig 75 A5
Llanfihangel-y-pennant Gwyn 107 B5
Llanfihangel-y-pennant Gwyn 91 B4
Llanfihangel-y-traethau Gwyn 107 C5
Llanfihangel-yn-Ngwynfa Powys 109 D5
Llanfihangel yn Nhowyn Anglesey 122 C3
Llanfilo Powys 77 D5
Llanfoist Mon 61 B4
Llanfor Gwyn 108 B4
Llanfrechfa Torf 61 D5
Llanfrothen Gwyn 107 B6
Llanfrynach Powys 60 A2
Llanfwrog Anglesey 122 B3
Llanfwrog Denb 125 D6
Llanfyllin Powys 109 D6
Llanfynydd Carms 58 C2
Llanfynydd Flint 126 D2
Llanfyrnach Pembs 73 C5
Llangadfan Powys 109 D5
Llangadog Carms 59 C4
Llangadwaladr Anglesey 122 D3
Llangadwaladr Powys 109 B6
Llangaffo Anglesey 123 D4
Llangain Carms 56 A3
Llangammarch Wells Powys 76 C3
Llangan V Glam 41 D4
Llangarron Hereford 62 A1
Llangasty Talyllyn Powys 60 A3
Llangathen Carms 58 C2
Llangattock Powys 60 B4
Llangattock Lingoed Mon 61 A5
Llangattock nigh Usk Mon 61 C5
Llangattock-Vibon-Avel Mon 61 B6
Llangedwyn Powys 109 C6
Llangefni Anglesey 123 C4
Llangeinor Bridgend 40 C4
Llangeitho Ceredig 75 C5
Llangeler Carms 73 C6
Llangelynin Gwyn 90 B3
Llangendeirne Carms 57 A4
Llangennech Carms 57 B5
Llangennith Swansea 57 C4
Llangenny Powys 60 B4
Llangernyw Conwy 124 C3
Llangian Gwyn 106 D2
Llanglydwen Carms 73 D4
Llangoed Anglesey 123 C6
Llangoedmor Ceredig 73 B4
Llangollen Denb 109 A7
Llangolman Pembs 55 B7
Llangors Powys 60 A3
Llangovan Mon 61 C6
Llangower Gwyn 108 B4
Llangrannog Ceredig 73 A6
Llangristiolus Anglesey 123 C4
Llangrove Hereford 62 B1
Llangua Mon 61 A5
Llangunllo Powys 93 D6
Llangunnor Carms 57 A4
Llangurig Powys 92 D3
Llangwm Conwy 109 A4
Llangwm Mon 61 C6
Llangwm Pembs 55 D5
Llangwnnadl Gwyn 106 C2
Llangwyfan Denb 125 C6
Llangwyfan-isaf Anglesey 122 D3
Llangwyllog Anglesey 123 C4
Llangwyryfon Ceredig 75 A4
Llangybi Ceredig 75 C5
Llangybi Gwyn 107 B4
Llangybi Mon 61 D5
Llangyfelach Swansea 57 C6
Llangynhafal Denb 125 C6
Llangynidr Powys 60 B3
Llangynin Carms 56 A2
Llangynog Carms 56 A3
Llangynog Powys 109 C5
Llangynwyd Bridgend 40 C3
Llanhamlach Powys 60 A2
Llanharan Rhondda 41 C5
Llanharry Rhondda 41 C5
Llanhennock Mon 61 D5
Llanhiledd = Llanhilleth Bl Gwent 41 A7
Llanhilleth = Llanhiledd Bl Gwent 41 A7
Llanidloes Powys 92 C3
Llaniestyn Gwyn 106 C2
Llanifyny Powys 91 D6
Llanigon Powys 77 D6
Llanilar Ceredig 75 A5
Llanilid Rhondda 41 C4
Llanilltud Fawr = Llantwit Major V Glam 41 E4
Llanishen Cardiff 41 C6
Llanishen Mon 61 C6
Llanllawddog Carms 58 C1
Llanllechid Gwyn 123 D6
Llanllowell Mon 61 D5
Llanllugan Powys 93 A4
Llanllwch Carms 56 A3
Llanllwchaiarn Powys 93 B5
Llanllwni Carms 58 B1
Llanllyfni Gwyn 107 A4
Llanmadoc Swansea 57 C4
Llanmaes V Glam 41 E4
Llanmartin Newport 42 A2
Llanmihangel V Glam 41 D4
Llanmorlais Swansea 57 C5
Llannefydd Conwy 125 B4
Llannon Carms 57 B5
Llannor Gwyn 106 C3
Llanon Ceredig 75 B4
Llanover Mon 61 C5
Llanpumsaint Carms 73 D7
Llanreithan Pembs 55 B4
Llanrhaeadr Denb 125 C5
Llanrhaeadr-ym-Mochnant Powys 109 C6
Llanrhian Pembs 54 A4
Llanrhidian Swansea 57 C4
Llanrhos Conwy 124 A2
Llanrhyddlad Anglesey 122 B3
Llanrhystud Ceredig 75 B4
Llanrosser Hereford 77 D6
Llanrothal Hereford 61 B6
Llanrug Gwyn 123 D5
Llanrumney Cardiff 41 C7
Llanrwst Conwy 124 C3
Llansadurnen Carms 56 A2
Llansadwrn Anglesey 123 C5
Llansadwrn Carms 58 B3
Llansaint Carms 56 B3
Llansamlet Swansea 40 B1
Llansannan Conwy 125 C4
Llansannor V Glam 41 D4
Llansantffraed Ceredig 75 B4
Llansantffraed Powys 60 A3
Llansantffraed Cwmdeuddwr Powys 76 A3
Llansantffraed-in-Elvel Powys 77 B4
Llansantffraid-ym-Mechain Powys 109 C7
Llansawel Carms 58 B3
Llansilin Powys 109 C7
Llansoy Mon 61 C6
Llanspyddid Powys 60 A2
Llanstadwell Pembs 55 D5
Llansteffan Carms 56 A3
Llanstephan Powys 77 C5
Llantarnam Torf 61 D5
Llanteg Pembs 56 A1
Llanthony Mon 61 A4
Llantilio Crossenny Mon 61 B5
Llantilio Pertholey Mon 61 B5
Llantood Pembs 73 B4
Llantrisant Anglesey 122 B3
Llantrisant Mon 61 D5
Llantrisant Rhondda 41 C5
Llantrithyd V Glam 41 D5
Llantwit Fardre Rhondda 41 C5
Llantwit Major = Llanilltud Fawr V Glam 41 E4
Llanuwchllyn Gwyn 108 B3
Llanvaches Newport 61 D6
Llanvair Discoed Mon 61 D6
Llanvapley Mon 61 B5
Llanvetherine Mon 61 B5
Llanveynoe Hereford 77 D7
Llanvihangel Gobion Mon 61 C5
Llanvihangel-Ystern-Llewern Mon 61 B6
Llanwarne Hereford 61 A7
Llanwddyn Powys 109 D5
Llanwenog Ceredig 74 D3
Llanwern Newport 42 A2
Llanwinio Carms 73 D5
Llanwnda Gwyn 107 A4
Llanwnda Pembs 72 C2
Llanwnnen Ceredig 75 D4
Llanwnog Powys 92 B4
Llanwrda Carms 59 B4
Llanwrin Powys 91 B5
Llanwrthwl Powys 76 A3
Llanwrtud = Llanwrtyd Wells Powys 76 C2
Llanwrtyd Powys 76 C2
Llanwrtyd Wells = Llanwrtud Powys 76 C2
Llanwyddelan Powys 93 A4
Llanyblodwel Shrops 110 C1
Llanybri Carms 56 A3
Llanybydder Carms 58 A2
Llanycefn Pembs 55 B6
Llanychaer Pembs 72 C2
Llanycil Gwyn 108 B4
Llanycrwys Carms 75 D5
Llanymawddwy Gwyn 91 A7
Llanymddyfri = Llandovery Carms 59 B4
Llanymynech Powys 110 C1
Llanynghenedl Anglesey 122 B3
Llanynys Denb 125 C6
Llanyre Powys 76 A4
Llanystumdwy Gwyn 107 C4
Llanywern Powys 60 A3
Llawhaden Pembs 55 C6
Llawnt Shrops 110 B1
Llawr Dref Gwyn 106 D2
Llawryglyn Powys 92 B3
Llay Wrex 126 D3
Llechcynfarwy Anglesey 122 B3
Llecheiddior Gwyn 107 B4
Llechfaen Powys 60 A2
Llechryd Caerph 60 C3
Llechryd Ceredig 73 B5
Llechrydau Powys 110 B1
Llechwedd Slate Caverns, Blaenau Ffestiniog Gwyn 108 A2
Lledrod Ceredig 75 A5
Llenmerewig Powys 93 B5
Llethrid Swansea 57 C5
Llidiad Nenog Carms 58 B2
Llidiardau Gwyn 108 B3
Llidiart-y-parc Denb 109 A6
Llithfaen Gwyn 106 B3
Llong Flint 126 C2
Llowes Powys 77 C5
Llundain-fach Ceredig 75 C4
Llwydcoed Rhondda 41 A4
Llwyn Shrops 93 C6
Llwyn-du Mon 61 B4
Llwyn-hendy Carms 57 C5
Llwyn-têg Carms 57 B5
Llwyn-y-brain Carms 56 A1
Llwyn-y-groes Ceredig 75 C4
Llwyncelyn Ceredig 74 C3
Llwyndafydd Ceredig 73 A6
Llwynderw Powys 93 A6
Llwyndyrys Gwyn 106 B3
Llwyngwril Gwyn 90 B3
Llwynmawr Wrex 110 B1
Llwynypia Rhondda 41 B4
Llynclys Shrops 110 C1
Llynfaes Anglesey 123 C4
Llys-y-frân Pembs 55 B6
Llysfaen Conwy 124 B3
Llyswen Powys 77 D5
Llysworney V Glam 41 D4
Llywel Powys 59 B5
Loan Falk 208 C2
Loanend Northumb 198 A3
Loanhead Midloth 209 D5
Loans S Ayrs 192 B3
Loans of Tullich Highld 265 C4
Lobb Devon 25 B5
Loch a Charnain W Isles 286 B4

Loch a'Ghainmhich W Isles 288 E3
Loch Baghasdail = Lochboisdale W Isles 286 E3
Loch Choire Lodge Highld 273 A4
Loch Euphoirt W Isles 287 H3
Loch Head Dumfries 171 C5
Loch Loyal Lodge Highld 277 D7
Loch nam Madadh = Lochmaddy W Isles 287 H4
Loch Ness Monster Exhibition, Drumnadrochit Highld 252 C1
Loch Sgioport W Isles 286 C4
Lochailort Highld 235 B6
Lochaline Highld 225 B5
Lochanhully Highld 253 D5
Lochans Dumfries 170 B2
Locharbriggs Dumfries 184 D2
Lochassynt Lodge Highld 271 B4
Lochavich Ho. Argyll 214 A2
Lochawe Argyll 227 D6
Lochboisdale = Loch Baghasdail W Isles 286 E3
Lochbuie Argyll 225 D5
Lochcarron Highld 249 C5
Lochdhu Highld 279 D6
Lochdochart House Stirl 216 B4
Lochdon Argyll 225 C6
Lochdrum Highld 263 C4
Lochead Argyll 202 A2
Lochearnhead Stirl 217 B5
Lochee Dundee 220 A3
Lochend Highld 252 C1
Lochend Highld 281 B4
Locherben Dumfries 184 C2
Lochfoot Dumfries 173 A6
Lochgair Argyll 214 C2
Lochgarthside Highld 240 A3
Lochgelly Fife 209 A4
Lochgilphead Argyll 214 D1
Lochgoilhead Argyll 215 B5
Lochhill Moray 266 C3
Lochindorb Lodge Highld 253 C5
Lochinver Highld 270 B3
Lochlane Perth 218 B3
Lochluichart Highld 263 D5
Lochmaben Dumfries 184 D3
Lochmaddy = Loch nam Madadh W Isles 287 H4
Lochmore Cottage Highld 280 D2
Lochmore Lodge Highld 271 A5
Lochore Fife 209 A4
Lochportain W Isles 287 G4
Lochranza N Ayrs 203 C4
Lochs Crofts Moray 266 C4
Lochside Aberds 233 B5
Lochside Highld 277 C5
Lochside Highld 274 A2
Lochside Highld 253 A4
Lochslin Highld 265 B4
Lochstack Lodge Highld 276 D3
Lochton Aberds 245 C4
Lochty Angus 232 B3
Lochty Fife 221 D5
Lochty Perth 219 B5
Lochuisge Highld 236 D1
Lochurr Dumfries 183 D5
Lochwinnoch Renfs 204 C3
Lochwood Dumfries 184 C3
Lochyside Highld 237 B5
Lockengate Corn 5 A5
Lockerbie Dumfries 185 D4
Lockeridge Wilts 45 C5
Lockerley Hants 32 C1
Locking N Som 42 D2
Lockinge Oxon 46 A2
Lockington E Yorks 150 C2
Lockington Leics 114 C2
Lockleywood Shrops 111 C5
Locks Heath Hants 18 A4
Lockton N Yorks 160 B2
Lockwood W Yorks 139 B4
Locomotion Museum, Shildon Durham 167 C5
Loddington Leics 99 A4
Loddington Northants 99 D5
Loddiswell Devon 7 C6
Loddon Norf 105 B4
Lode Cambs 86 A1
Loders Dorset 15 B4
Lodsworth W Sus 34 D2
Lofthouse N Yorks 157 D5
Lofthouse W Yorks 139 A6
Loftus Redcar 169 D5
Logan E Ayrs 193 C5
Logan Mains Dumfries 170 C2
Loganlea W Loth 208 D2
Loggerheads Staffs 111 B6
Logie Angus 233 B4
Logie Fife 220 B4
Logie Moray 253 A6
Logie Coldstone Aberds 244 B1
Logie Hill Highld 264 C3
Logie Newton Aberds 256 C1
Logie Pert Angus 233 B4
Logiealmond Lodge Perth 219 A4
Logierait Perth 230 C3
Login Carms 73 D4
Lolworth Cambs 85 A5
Lonbain Highld 248 A3
Londesborough E Yorks 150 C1
London, City of = City of London London 49 A6
London City Airport London 50 A1
London Colney Herts 68 C1
London Gatwick Airport W Sus 35 B5
London Heathrow Airport London 48 B3
London Luton Airport Luton 67 A6
London Stansted Airport Essex 69 A5
London Zoo London 49 A5
Londonderry N Yorks 157 C7
Londonthorpe Lincs 116 B2
Londubh Highld 261 B5
Lonemore Highld 264 B3
Long Ashton N Som 43 B4
Long Bennington Lincs 115 A6
Long Bredy Dorset 15 B5
Long Buckby Northants 82 A3
Long Clawson Leics 115 C5
Long Common Hants 32 D4
Long Compton Staffs 112 C2
Long Compton Warks 81 D5
Long Crendon Bucks 66 C1
Long Crichel Dorset 30 D3
Long Ditton Sur 49 C4
Long Drax N Yorks 141 A4
Long Duckmanton Derbys 131 B4
Long Eaton Derbys 114 B2
Long Green Worcs 79 D6
Long Hanborough Oxon 65 B5
Long Itchington Warks 81 A7
Long Lawford Warks 98 D1
Long Load Som 29 C4
Long Marston Herts 66 B3
Long Marston N Yorks 148 B4
Long Marston Warks 81 C4
Long Marton Cumb 165 C4
Long Melford Suff 87 C4
Long Newnton Glos 63 D5
Long Newton E Loth 210 D2
Long Preston N Yorks 146 B2
Long Riston E Yorks 151 C4
Long Sight Gtr Man 138 C2
Long Stratton Norf 104 B2
Long Street M Keynes 83 C4
Long Sutton Hants 33 A6
Long Sutton Lincs 118 C1
Long Sutton Som 29 C4
Long Thurlow Suff 87 A6
Long Whatton Leics 114 C2
Long Wittenham Oxon 65 D6
Longbar N Ayrs 204 C3
Longbenton T & W 179 C4
Longborough Glos 64 A2
Longbridge Warks 81 A5
Longbridge W Mid 96 D3
Longbridge Deverill Wilts 30 A2
Longburton Dorset 29 D6
Longcliffe Derbys 130 D2
Longcot Oxon 64 D3
Longcroft Falk 207 C5
Longden Shrops 94 A2
Longdon Staffs 113 D4
Longdon Worcs 79 D6
Longdon Green Staffs 113 D4
Longdon on Tern Telford 111 D5
Longdown Devon 12 B3
Longdowns Corn 4 D2
Longfield Kent 50 C3
Longfield Shetland 285 M5
Longford Derbys 113 B6
Longford Glos 63 A4
Longford London 48 B3
Longford Shrops 111 B5
Longford Telford 111 D6
Longford W Mid 97 C6
Longfordlane Derbys 113 B6
Longforgan Perth 220 B3
Longformacus Borders 197 A5
Longframlington Northumb 189 C4
Longham Dorset 17 B4
Longham Norf 119 D6
Longhaven Aberds 257 C6
Longhill Aberds 269 D4
Longhirst Northumb 179 A4
Longhope Glos 62 B2
Longhope Orkney 283 H4
Longhorsley Northumb 189 D4
Longhoughton Northumb 189 B5
Longlane Derbys 113 B6
Longlane W Berks 46 B2
Longleat, Warminster Wilts 30 A2
Longlevens Glos 63 A4
Longley W Yorks 139 C4
Longley Green Worcs 79 B5
Longmanhill Aberds 268 C2
Longmoor Camp Hants 33 B6
Longmorn Moray 266 D3
Longnewton Borders 187 A4
Longnewton Stockton 167 D6
Longney Glos 62 B3
Longniddry E Loth 210 C1
Longnor Shrops 94 A2
Longnor Staffs 129 C5
Longparish Hants 32 A3
Longport Stoke 112 A2
Longridge Lancs 145 D6
Longridge Staffs 112 D3
Longridge W Loth 208 D2
Longriggend N Lnrk 207 C6
Longsdon Staffs 129 D4
Longshaw Gtr Man 136 C4
Longside Aberds 257 B5
Longstanton Cambs 85 A5
Longstock Hants 32 B2
Longstone Pembs 56 B1
Longstowe Cambs 85 B5
Longthorpe P'boro 100 B3
Longthwaite Cumb 164 C2
Longton Lancs 136 A3
Longton Stoke 112 A3
Longtown Cumb 175 B6
Longtown Hereford 61 A5
Longview Mers 136 D3
Longville in the Dale Shrops 94 B3
Longwick Bucks 66 C2
Longwitton Northumb 178 A2
Longwood Shrops 95 A4
Longworth Oxon 65 D4
Longyester E Loth 210 D2
Lonmay Aberds 269 D5
Lonmore Highld 258 D2
Looe Corn 6 B1
Loose Kent 37 A5
Loosley Row Bucks 66 C3
Lopcombe Corner Wilts 31 B6
Lopen Som 28 D4
Loppington Shrops 110 C3
Lopwell Devon 6 A3
Lorbottle Northumb 188 C3
Lorbottle Hall Northumb 188 C3
Lord's Cricket Ground London 49 A5
Lornty Perth 231 D5
Loscoe Derbys 114 A2
Losgaintir W Isles 287 E5
Lossiemouth Moray 266 B3
Lossit Argyll 200 C1
Lostford Shrops 111 B5
Lostock Gralam Ches 128 B1
Lostock Green Ches 128 B1
Lostock Hall Lancs 136 A4
Lostock Junction Gtr Man 137 C5
Lostwithiel Corn 5 B6
Loth Orkney 282 D7
Lothbeg Highld 274 C3
Lothersdale N Yorks 146 C3
Lothmore Highld 274 C3
Loudwater Bucks 67 D4
Loughborough Leics 114 D3
Loughor Swansea 57 C5
Loughton Essex 68 D4
Loughton M Keynes 83 D5
Loughton Shrops 95 C4
Louis Tussaud's Waxworks Blkpool 144 D3
Lound Lincs 116 D3
Lound Notts 132 A1
Lound Suff 105 B6
Lount Leics 114 D1
Louth Lincs 134 A3
Love Clough Lancs 137 A7
Lovedean Hants 33 D5
Lover Wilts 31 C6
Loversall S Yorks 140 D3
Loves Green Essex 69 C6
Lovesome Hill N Yorks 158 B2
Loveston Pembs 55 D6
Lovington Som 29 B5
Low Ackworth W Yorks 140 B2
Low Barlings Lincs 133 B5
Low Bentham N Yorks 145 A6
Low Bradfield S Yorks 139 D5
Low Bradley N Yorks 147 C4
Low Braithwaite Cumb 164 A2
Low Brunton Northumb 177 B7
Low Burnham N Lincs 141 C5
Low Burton N Yorks 157 C6
Low Buston Northumb 189 C5
Low Catton E Yorks 149 B6
Low Clanyard Dumfries 170 D3
Low Coniscliffe Darl 167 D5
Low Crosby Cumb 176 D2
Low Dalby N Yorks 160 C2
Low Dinsdale Darl 167 D6
Low Ellington N Yorks 157 C6
Low Etherley Durham 167 C4
Low Fell T & W 179 D4
Low Fulney Lincs 117 C5
Low Garth N Yorks 159 A6
Low Gate Northumb 177 C7
Low Grantley N Yorks 157 D6
Low Habberley Worcs 95 D6
Low Ham Som 28 C4
Low Hesket Cumb 164 A2
Low Hesleyhurst Northumb 188 D3
Low Hutton N Yorks 149 A6
Low Laithe N Yorks 147 A5
Low Leighton Derbys 129 A5
Low Lorton Cumb 163 B4
Low Marishes N Yorks 159 D7
Low Marnham Notts 132 C3
Low Mill N Yorks 159 B5
Low Moor Lancs 146 C1
Low Moor W Yorks 139 A4
Low Moorsley T & W 167 A6
Low Newton Cumb 154 C3
Low Newton-by-the-Sea Northumb 189 A5
Low Row Cumb 163 A6
Low Row Cumb 176 C3
Low Row N Yorks 156 B3
Low Salchrie Dumfries 170 A2
Low Smerby Argyll 190 C3
Low Torry Fife 208 B3
Low Worsall N Yorks 158 A2
Low Wray Cumb 154 A2
Lowbridge House Cumb 154 A4
Lowca Cumb 162 B2
Lowdham Notts 115 A4
Lowe Shrops 111 B4
Lowe Hill Staffs 129 D4
Lower Aisholt Som 28 B2
Lower Arncott Oxon 65 B7
Lower Ashton Devon 12 C3
Lower Assendon Oxon 47 A5
Lower Badcall Highld 276 D2
Lower Bartle Lancs 145 D4
Lower Basildon W Berks 47 B4
Lower Beeding W Sus 35 D5
Lower Benefield Northants 100 C1
Lower Boddington Northants 82 B1
Lower Brailes Warks 81 D6
Lower Breakish Highld 247 B5
Lower Broadheath Worcs 79 B6
Lower Bullingham Hereford 78 D3
Lower Cam Glos 62 C3
Lower Chapel Powys 76 D4
Lower Chute Wilts 45 D7
Lower Cragabus Argyll 200 D3
Lower Crossings Derbys 129 A5
Lower Cumberworth W Yorks 139 C5
Lower Cwm-twrch Powys 59 D4
Lower Darwen Blkburn 137 A5
Lower Dean Beds 84 A2
Lower Diabaig Highld 261 D4
Lower Dicker E Sus 22 A3
Lower Dinchope Shrops 94 C2
Lower Down Shrops 94 C1
Lower Drift Corn 2 C2
Lower Dunsforth N Yorks 148 A3
Lower Egleton Hereford 79 C4
Lower Elkstone Staffs 129 D5
Lower End Beds 67 A4
Lower Everleigh Wilts 45 D5
Lower Farringdon Hants 33 B6
Lower Foxdale I o M 152 D2
Lower Frankton Shrops 110 B2
Lower Froyle Hants 33 A6
Lower Gledfield Highld 264 A1
Lower Green Norf 120 B1
Lower Hacheston Suff 88 B4
Lower Halistra Highld 258 C2
Lower Halstow Kent 51 C5
Lower Hardres Kent 52 D3
Lower Hawthwaite Cumb 153 B3
Lower Heath Ches 128 C3
Lower Hempriggs Moray 266 C2
Lower Hergest Hereford 77 B6
Lower Heyford Oxon 65 A5
Lower Higham Kent 51 B4
Lower Holbrook Suff 88 D2
Lower Hordley Shrops 110 C2
Lower Horsebridge E Sus 22 A3
Lower Killeyan Argyll 200 D2
Lower Kingswood Sur 35 A5
Lower Kinnerton Ches 126 C3
Lower Langford N Som 42 C3
Lower Largo Fife 220 D4
Lower Leigh Staffs 112 B4
Lower Lemington Glos 81 D5
Lower Lenie Highld 251 D7
Lower Lydbrook Glos 62 B1
Lower Lye Hereford 78 A2
Lower Machen Newport 42 A1
Lower Maes-coed Hereford 78 D1
Lower Mayland Essex 70 C3
Lower Midway Derbys 113 C7
Lower Milovaig Highld 258 C1
Lower Moor Worcs 80 C2
Lower Nazeing Essex 68 C3
Lower Netchwood Shrops 95 B4
Lower Ollach Highld 247 A4
Lower Penarth V Glam 41 D6
Lower Penn Staffs 95 B6
Lower Pennington Hants 18 B2
Lower Peover Ches 128 B2
Lower Pexhill Ches 128 B3
Lower Place Gtr Man 138 B2
Lower Quinton Warks 81 C4
Lower Rochford Worcs 79 A4
Lower Seagry Wilts 44 A3
Lower Shelton Beds 84 C1
Lower Shiplake Oxon 47 B5
Lower Shuckburgh Warks 82 A1
Lower Slaughter Glos 64 A2
Lower Stanton St Quintin Wilts 44 A3
Lower Stoke Medway 51 B5
Lower Stondon Beds 84 D3
Lower Stow Bedon Norf 103 B5
Lower Street Norf 121 B4
Lower Street Norf 121 D5
Lower Strensham Worcs 80 C2
Lower Stretton Warr 127 A6
Lower Sundon Beds 67 A5
Lower Swanwick Hants 18 A3
Lower Swell Glos 64 A2
Lower Tean Staffs 112 B4
Lower Thurlton Norf 105 B5
Lower Tote Highld 259 B5
Lower Town Pembs 72 C2
Lower Tysoe Warks 81 C6
Lower Upham Hants 32 D4
Lower Vexford Som 27 B6
Lower Weare Som 42 D3
Lower Welson Hereford 77 B6
Lower Whitley Ches 127 B6
Lower Wield Hants 33 A5
Lower Winchendon Bucks 66 B2
Lower Withington Ches 128 C3
Lower Woodend Bucks 47 A6
Lower Woodford Wilts 31 B5
Lower Wyche Worcs 79 C5
Lowesby Leics 99 A4
Lowestoft Suff 105 B6
Loweswater Cumb 163 B4
Lowford Hants 32 D3
Lowgill Cumb 155 B5
Lowgill Lancs 145 A6
Lowick Northants 100 C1
Lowick Northumb 198 C4
Lowick Bridge Cumb 154 C1
Lowick Green Cumb 154 C1
Lowlands Torf 61 D4
Lowmoor Row Cumb 165 C4
Lownie Moor Angus 232 D2
Lowsonford Warks 81 A4
Lowther Cumb 164 C3
Lowthorpe E Yorks 150 A3
Lowton Gtr Man 137 D5
Lowton Common Gtr Man 137 D5
Loxbeare Devon 27 D4
Loxhill Sur 34 C3
Loxhore Devon 25 B7
Loxley Warks 81 B5
Loxton N Som 42 D2
Loxwood W Sus 34 C3
Lubcroy Highld 271 D6
Lubenham Leics 99 C4
Luccombe Som 27 A4
Luccombe Village I o W 19 D4
Lucker Northumb 199 C5
Luckett Corn 11 D4
Luckington Wilts 44 A2
Lucklawhill Fife 220 B4
Luckwell Bridge Som 27 B4
Lucton Hereford 78 A2
Ludag W Isles 286 E3
Ludborough Lincs 143 D4
Ludchurch Pembs 56 A1
Luddenden W Yorks 138 A3
Luddenden Foot W Yorks 138 A3
Luddesdown Kent 50 C3
Luddington N Lincs 141 B6
Luddington Warks 81 B4
Luddington in the Brook Northants 100 C3
Lude House Perth 230 B2
Ludford Lincs 134 A2
Ludford Shrops 94 D3
Ludgershall Bucks 66 B1
Ludgershall Wilts 45 D6
Ludgvan Corn 2 B3
Ludham Norf 121 D5
Ludlow Shrops 94 D3
Ludlow Racecourse Shrops 94 D2
Ludwell Wilts 30 C3
Ludworth Durham 167 A6
Luffincott Devon 10 B4
Lugar E Ayrs 193 C5
Lugg Green Hereford 78 A2
Luggate Burn E Loth 210 C3
Luggiebank N Lnrk 207 C5
Lugton E Ayrs 205 C4
Lugwardine Hereford 78 C3
Luib Highld 247 B4
Lulham Hereford 78 C2
Lullenden Sur 36 B2
Lullington Derbys 113 D6
Lullington Som 44 D1
Lulsgate Bottom N Som 43 C4
Lulsley Worcs 79 B5
Lulworth Castle Dorset 16 C2
Lumb W Yorks 138 A3
Lumby N Yorks 148 D3
Lumloch E Dunb 205 B6
Lumphanan Aberds 244 B2
Lumphinnans Fife 209 A4
Lumsdaine Borders 211 D5
Lumsden Aberds 255 D5
Lunan Angus 233 C4
Lunanhead Angus 232 C2
Luncarty Perth 219 B5
Lund E Yorks 150 C2
Lund N Yorks 149 D5
Lund Shetland 284 C7
Lunderton Aberds 269 E6
Lundie Angus 220 A2
Lundie Highld 239 A5
Lundin Links Fife 220 D4
Lunga Argyll 213 B5
Lunna Shetland 284 G6
Lunning Shetland 284 G7
Lunnon Swansea 57 D5
Lunsford's Cross E Sus 23 A5
Lunt Mers 136 C2
Luntley Hereford 78 B1
Luppitt Devon 13 A6
Lupset W Yorks 139 B6
Lupton Cumb 155 C4
Lurgashall W Sus 34 D2
Lusby Lincs 134 C3
Luson Devon 7 C5
Luss Argyll 206 A1
Lussagiven Argyll 213 D4
Lusta Highld 258 C2
Lustleigh Devon 12 C2
Luston Hereford 78 A2
Luthermuir Aberds 233 B4
Luthrie Fife 220 C3
Luton Devon 13 D4
Luton Luton 67 A5
Luton Medway 51 C4
Lutterworth Leics 98 C2
Lutton Devon 7 B4
Lutton Lincs 118 C1
Lutton Northants 100 C3
Lutworthy Devon 26 D2
Luxborough Som 27 B4
Luxulyan Corn 5 B5
Lybster Highld 275 A6
Lydbury North Shrops 94 C1
Lydcott Devon 26 B1
Lydd Kent 38 C2
Lydd on Sea Kent 38 C2
Lydden Kent 39 A4
Lydden Motor Racing Circuit Kent 39 A4
Lyddington Rutland 99 B5
Lyde Green Hants 47 D5
Lydeard St Lawrence Som 27 B6
Lydford Devon 11 C6
Lydford-on-Fosse Som 29 B5
Lydgate W Yorks 138 A2
Lydham Shrops 94 B1
Lydiard Green Wilts 45 A4
Lydiard Millicent Wilts 45 A4
Lydiate Mers 136 C2
Lydlinch Dorset 30 D1
Lydney Glos 62 C2
Lydstep Pembs 55 E6
Lye W Mid 96 C2
Lye Green Bucks 67 C4
Lye Green E Sus 36 C3
Lyford Oxon 65 D4
Lymbridge Green Kent 38 A3
Lyme Park, Disley Ches 129 A4
Lyme Regis Dorset 14 B3
Lyminge Kent 38 A3
Lymington Hants 18 B2
Lyminster W Sus 20 B3
Lymm Warr 128 A1
Lymore Hants 18 B1
Lympne Kent 38 B3
Lympsham Som 42 D2
Lympstone Devon 13 C4
Lynchat Highld 241 B5
Lyndale Ho. Highld 258 C3
Lyndhurst Hants 18 A2
Lyndon Rutland 99 A6
Lyne Sur 48 C3
Lyne Down Hereford 79 D4
Lyne of Gorthleck Highld 252 D1
Lyne of Skene Aberds 245 A4
Lyneal Shrops 110 B3
Lyneham Oxon 64 A3
Lyneham Wilts 44 B4
Lynemore Highld 253 D6
Lynemouth Northumb 189 D5
Lyness Orkney 283 H4
Lyng Norf 120 D2
Lyng Som 28 C3
Lynmouth Devon 26 A2
Lynsted Kent 51 C6
Lynton Devon 26 A2
Lynton & Lynmouth Cliff Railway Devon 26 A2
Lyon's Gate Dorset 15 A6
Lyonshall Hereford 78 B1

Lytchett Matravers Dorset 16 B3
Lytchett Minster Dorset 16 B3
Lyth Highld 281 B4
Lytham Lancs 136 A2
Lytham St Anne's Lancs 136 A2
Lythe N Yorks 169 D6
Lythes Orkney 283 K5

M

Mabe Burnthouse Corn 4 D2
Mabie Dumfries 174 A2
Mablethorpe Lincs 135 A5
Macclesfield Ches 129 B4
Macclesfield Forest Ches 129 B4
Macduff Aberds 268 C2
Mace Green Suff 88 C2
Macharioch Argyll 190 E3
Machen Caerph 41 C7
Machrihanish Argyll 190 C2
Machynlleth Powys 91 B5
Machynys Carms 57 C5
Mackerel's Common W Sus 34 D3
Mackworth Derbys 113 B7
Macmerry E Loth 210 C1
Madame Tussaud's London 49 A5
Madderty Perth 219 B4
Maddiston Falk 208 C2
Madehurst W Sus 20 A2
Madeley Staffs 111 A6
Madeley Telford 95 A4
Madeley Heath Staffs 112 A1
Madeley Park Staffs 112 A1
Madingley Cambs 85 A5
Madley Hereford 78 D2
Madresfield Worcs 79 C6
Madron Corn 2 B2
Maen-y-groes Ceredig 73 A6
Maenaddwyn Anglesey 123 B4
Maenclochog Pembs 55 B6
Maendy V Glam 41 D5
Maentwrog Gwyn 107 B6
Maer Staffs 112 B1
Maerdy Conwy 109 A5
Maerdy Rhondda 41 B4
Maes-Treylow Powys 77 A6
Maesbrook Shrops 110 C1
Maesbury Shrops 110 C2
Maesbury Marsh Shrops 110 C2
Maesgwyn-Isaf Powys 109 D6
Maesgwynne Carms 73 D5
Maeshafn Denb 126 C2
Maesllyn Ceredig 73 B6
Maesmynis Powys 76 C4
Maesteg Bridgend 40 B3
Maestir Ceredig 75 D4
Maesy cwmmer Caerph 41 B6
Maesybont Carms 57 A5
Maesycrugiau Carms 58 A1
Maesymeillion Ceredig 73 B7
Magdalen Laver Essex 69 C5
Maggieknockater Moray 254 B4
Magham Down E Sus 22 A4
Maghull Mers 136 C2
Magna Science Adventure Centre, Rotherham S Yorks 140 D2
Magor Mon 42 A3
Magpie Green Suff 104 D1
Maiden Bradley Wilts 30 B2
Maiden Law Durham 167 A4
Maiden Newton Dorset 15 B5
Maiden Wells Pembs 55 E5
Maidencombe Torbay 8 A3
Maidenhall Suff 88 C2
Maidenhead Windsor 48 A1
Maidens S Ayrs 192 E2
Maiden's Green Brack 48 B1
Maidensgrave Suff 88 C3
Maidenwell Corn 10 D2
Maidenwell Lincs 134 B3
Maidford Northants 82 B3
Maids Moreton Bucks 83 D4
Maidstone Kent 37 A5
Maidwell Northants 99 D4
Mail Shetland 285 L6
Main Powys 109 D6
Maindee Newport 42 A2
Mains of Airies Dumfries 170 A1
Mains of Allardice Aberds 233 A6
Mains of Annochie Aberds 257 B4
Mains of Ardestie Angus 221 A5
Mains of Balhall Angus 232 B3
Mains of Ballindarg Angus 232 C2
Mains of Balnakettle Aberds 233 A4
Mains of Birness Aberds 257 C4
Mains of Burgie Moray 266 D1
Mains of Clunas Highld 253 B4
Mains of Crichie Aberds 257 B4
Mains of Dalvey Highld 254 C2
Mains of Dellavaird Aberds 245 D4
Mains of Drum Aberds 245 C5
Mains of Edingight Moray 267 D6
Mains of Fedderate Aberds 268 E3
Mains of Inkhorn Aberds 257 C4
Mains of Mayen Moray 255 B6
Mains of Melgund Angus 232 C3
Mains of Thornton Aberds 233 A4
Mains of Watten Highld 281 C4
Mainsforth Durham 167 B6
Mainsriddle Dumfries 174 C2
Mainstone Shrops 93 C6
Maisemore Glos 63 A4
Malacleit W Isles 287 G2
Malborough Devon 7 D6
Malcoff Derbys 129 A5
Maldon Essex 70 C2
Malham N Yorks 146 A3
Maligar Highld 259 B4
Mallaig Highld 235 A5
Malleny Mills Edin 209 D4
Malling Stirl 217 D5
Mallory Park Motor Racing Circuit Leics 98 A1
Malltraeth Anglesey 123 D4
Mallwyd Gwyn 91 A6
Malmesbury Wilts 44 A3
Malmsmead Devon 26 A2
Malpas Ches 110 A3
Malpas Corn 4 C3
Malpas Newport 61 D5
Malswick Glos 62 A3
Maltby Stockton 168 D2
Maltby S Yorks 140 D3
Maltby le Marsh Lincs 135 A4
Malting Green Essex 70 A3
Maltman's Hill Kent 37 B7
Malton N Yorks 159 D6
Malvern Link Worcs 79 C5
Malvern Wells Worcs 79 C5
Mamble Worcs 95 D4
Man-moel Caerph 41 A6
Manaccan Corn 3 C5
Manafon Powys 93 A5
Manais W Isles 287 F6
Manar Ho. Aberds 256 D2
Manaton Devon 12 C2
Manby Lincs 134 A3
Mancetter Warks 97 B6
Manchester Gtr Man 138 D1
Manchester Airport Gtr Man 128 A3
Manchester National Velodrome Gtr Man 138 D1
Mancot Flint 126 C3
Mandally Highld 239 B6
Manea Cambs 101 C6
Manfield N Yorks 167 D5
Mangaster Shetland 284 F5
Mangotsfield S Glos 43 B5
Mangurstadh W Isles 287 A5
Mankinholes W Yorks 138 A2
Manley Ches 127 B5
Mannal Argyll 222 C2
Mannerston W Loth 208 C3
Manningford Bohune Wilts 45 D5
Manningford Bruce Wilts 45 D5
Manningham W Yorks 147 D5
Mannings Heath W Sus 35 D5
Mannington Dorset 17 A4
Manningtree Essex 88 D1
Mannofield Aberdeen 245 B6
Manor Estate S Yorks 130 A3
Manor Park London 50 A1
Manorbier Pembs 55 E6
Manordeilo Carms 58 C3
Manorhill Borders 197 C5
Manorowen Pembs 72 C2
Mansel Lacy Hereford 78 C2
Manselfield Swansea 57 D5
Mansell Gamage Hereford 78 C1
Mansergh Cumb 155 C5
Mansfield E Ayrs 182 A4
Mansfield Notts 131 C5
Mansfield Woodhouse Notts 131 C5
Mansriggs Cumb 154 C1
Manston Dorset 30 D2
Manston Kent 53 C5
Manston W Yorks 148 D2
Manswood Dorset 16 A3
Manthorpe Lincs 116 D3
Manthorpe Lincs 116 B2
Manton N Lincs 142 C1
Manton Notts 131 B5
Manton Rutland 99 A5
Manton Wilts 45 C5
Manuden Essex 69 A4
Manx Electric Railway I o M 152 B4
Maperton Som 29 C6
Maple Cross Herts 67 D5
Maplebeck Notts 132 C2
Mapledurham Oxon 47 B4
Mapledurwell Hants 47 D4
Maplehurst W Sus 35 D4
Maplescombe Kent 50 C2
Mapleton Derbys 113 A5
Mapleton E Yorks 151 C5
Mapperley Derbys 114 A2
Mapperley Park Nottingham 114 A3
Mapperton Dorset 15 B5
Mappleborough Green Warks 80 A3
Mappowder Dorset 16 A1
Mar Lodge Aberds 242 C3
Maraig W Isles 288 G2
Marazanvose Corn 4 B3
Marazion Corn 2 B3
Marbhig W Isles 288 F5
Marbury Ches 111 A4
March Cambs 101 B6
March S Lnrk 184 A2
Marcham Oxon 65 D5
Marchamley Shrops 111 C4
Marchington Staffs 113 B5
Marchington Woodlands Staffs 113 C5
Marchroes Gwyn 106 D3
Marchwiel Wrex 110 A2
Marchwood Hants 32 D2
Marcross V Glam 40 E4
Marden Hereford 78 C3
Marden Kent 37 B5
Marden T & W 179 B5
Marden Wilts 45 D4
Marden Beech Kent 37 B5
Marden Thorn Kent 37 B5
Mardy Mon 61 B5
Marefield Leics 99 A4
Mareham le Fen Lincs 134 C2
Mareham on the Hill Lincs 134 C2
Marehay Derbys 114 A1
Marehill W Sus 20 A3
Maresfield E Sus 36 D2
Marfleet Hull 142 A3
Marford Wrex 126 D3
Margam Neath 40 C2
Margaret Marsh Dorset 30 D2
Margaret Roding Essex 69 B5
Margaretting Essex 69 C6
Margate Kent 53 B5
Margnaheglish N Ayrs 191 B6
Margrove Park Redcar 169 D4
Marham Norf 119 D4
Marhamchurch Corn 10 A3
Marholm P'boro 100 A3
Mariandyrys Anglesey 123 B6
Marianglas Anglesey 123 B5
Mariansleigh Devon 26 C2
Marionburgh Aberds 245 B4
Marishader Highld 259 B4
Maritime and Industrial Museum Swansea 57 C6
Marjoriebanks Dumfries 184 D3
Mark Dumfries 170 B3
Mark S Ayrs 180 D2
Mark Som 28 A3
Mark Causeway Som 28 A3
Mark Cross E Sus 22 A2
Mark Cross E Sus 36 C3
Markbeech Kent 36 B2
Markby Lincs 135 B4
Market Bosworth Leics 97 A7
Market Deeping Lincs 116 E4
Market Drayton Shrops 111 B5
Market Harborough Leics 99 C4
Market Lavington Wilts 44 D4
Market Overton Rutland 116 D1
Market Rasen Lincs 133 A6
Market Rasen Racecourse Lincs 133 A6
Market Stainton Lincs 134 B2
Market Warsop Notts 131 C5
Market Weighton E Yorks 150 C1
Market Weston Suff 103 D5
Markethill Perth 220 A2
Markfield Leics 114 D2
Markham Caerph 41 A6
Markham Moor Notts 132 B2
Markinch Fife 220 D2
Markington N Yorks 148 A1
Marks Tey Essex 70 A3
Marksbury Bath 43 C5
Markyate Herts 67 B5
Marland Gtr Man 138 B1
Marlborough Wilts 45 C5
Marlbrook Hereford 78 B3
Marlbrook Worcs 96 D2
Marlcliff Warks 80 B3
Marldon Devon 8 A2
Marlesford Suff 88 B4
Marley Green Ches 111 A4
Marley Hill T & W 179 D4
Marley Mount Hants 17 B6
Marlingford Norf 104 A2
Marloes Pembs 54 D3
Marlow Bucks 47 A6
Marlow Hereford 94 D2
Marlow Bottom Bucks 47 A6
Marlpit Hill Kent 36 B2
Marlpool Derbys 114 A2
Marnhull Dorset 30 D1
Marnoch Aberds 267 D6
Marnock N Lnrk 207 D5
Marple Gtr Man 129 A4
Marple Bridge Gtr Man 129 A4
Marr S Yorks 140 C3
Marrel Highld 274 C4
Marrick N Yorks 157 B4
Marrister Shetland 285 G7
Marros Carms 56 B2
Marsden T & W 179 C5
Marsden W Yorks 138 B3
Marsett N Yorks 156 C3
Marsh Devon 28 D2
Marsh W Yorks 147 D4
Marsh Baldon Oxon 65 D6
Marsh Gibbon Bucks 66 A1
Marsh Green Devon 13 B5
Marsh Green Kent 36 B2
Marsh Green Staffs 128 D3
Marsh Lane Derbys 131 B4
Marsh Street Som 27 A4
Marshall's Heath Herts 67 B6
Marshalsea Dorset 14 A3
Marshalswick Herts 67 C6
Marsham Norf 120 C3
Marshaw Lancs 145 B5
Marshborough Kent 53 D5
Marshbrook Shrops 94 C2
Marshchapel Lincs 143 D5
Marshfield Newport 42 A1
Marshfield S Glos 44 B1
Marshgate Corn 10 B2
Marshland St James Norf 101 A7
Marshside Mers 136 B2
Marshwood Dorset 14 B3
Marske N Yorks 157 A5
Marske-by-the-Sea Redcar 168 C4
Marston Ches 127 B6
Marston Hereford 78 B1
Marston Lincs 116 A1
Marston Oxon 65 C6
Marston Staffs 112 D2
Marston Staffs 112 C3
Marston Warks 97 B5
Marston Wilts 44 D3
Marston Doles Warks 82 B1
Marston Green W Mid 97 C4
Marston Magna Som 29 C5
Marston Meysey Wilts 64 D2
Marston Montgomery Derbys 113 B5
Marston Moretaine Beds 84 C1
Marston on Dove Derbys 113 C6
Marston St Lawrence Northants 82 C2
Marston Stannett Hereford 78 B3
Marston Trussell Northants 98 C3
Marstow Hereford 62 B1
Marsworth Bucks 67 B4
Marten Wilts 45 D6
Marthall Ches 128 B3
Martham Norf 121 D6
Martin Hants 31 D4
Martin Kent 39 A5
Martin Lincs 133 D6
Martin Lincs 134 C2
Martin Dales Lincs 134 C1
Martin Drove End Hants 31 C4
Martin Hussingtree Worcs 80 A1
Martin Mill Kent 39 A5
Martinhoe Devon 26 A1
Martinhoe Cross Devon 26 A1
Martinscroft Warr 127 A6
Martinstown Dorset 15 C6
Martlesham Suff 88 C3
Martlesham Heath Suff 88 C3
Martletwy Pembs 55 C6
Martley Worcs 79 B5
Martock Som 29 D4
Marton Ches 128 C3
Marton E Yorks 151 D4
Marton Lincs 132 A3
Marton M'bro 168 D3
Marton N Yorks 148 A3
Marton N Yorks 159 C6
Marton Shrops 93 A6
Marton Shrops 110 C3
Marton Warks 81 A7
Marton-le-Moor N Yorks 158 D2
Martyr Worthy Hants 32 B4
Martyr's Green Sur 34 A3
Marwell Zoo, Bishop's Waltham Hants 32 C4
Marwick Orkney 282 E3
Marwood Devon 25 B6
Mary Arden's House, Stratford-upon-Avon Warks 81 B4
Mary Rose Ptsmth 19 A5
Mary Tavy Devon 11 D6
Marybank Highld 251 A6
Maryburgh Highld 252 A1
Maryhill Glasgow 205 B5
Marykirk Aberds 233 B4
Marylebone Gtr Man 137 C4
Marypark Moray 254 C2
Maryport Cumb 162 A3
Maryport Dumfries 170 D3
Maryton Angus 233 C4
Marywell Aberds 244 C2
Marywell Aberds 245 C6
Marywell Angus 233 D4
Masham N Yorks 157 C6
Mashbury Essex 69 B6
Masongill N Yorks 155 D5
Masonhill S Ayrs 192 C3
Mastin Moor Derbys 131 B4
Mastrick Aberdeen 245 B5
Matching Essex 69 B5
Matching Green Essex 69 B5
Matching Tye Essex 69 B5
Matfen Northumb 178 B2
Matfield Kent 37 B4
Mathern Mon 62 D1
Mathon Hereford 79 C5
Mathry Pembs 55 A4
Matlaske Norf 120 B3
Matlock Derbys 130 C2
Matlock Bath Derbys 130 D2
Matson Glos 63 B4
Matterdale End Cumb 164 C1
Mattersey Notts 132 A1
Mattersey Thorpe Notts 132 A1
Mattingley Hants 47 D5
Mattishall Norf 120 D2
Mattishall Burgh Norf 120 D2
Mauchline E Ayrs 193 C4
Maud Aberds 257 B4
Maugersbury Glos 64 A3
Maughold I o M 152 B4
Mauld Highld 251 C6
Maulden Beds 84 D2
Maulds Meaburn Cumb 165 D4
Maunby N Yorks 158 C2
Maund Bryan Hereford 78 B3
Maundown Som 27 C5
Mautby Norf 121 D6
Mavis Enderby Lincs 134 C3
Maw Green Ches 128 D2
Mawbray Cumb 174 D3
Mawdesley Lancs 136 B3
Mawdlam Bridgend 40 C3
Mawgan Corn 3 C5
Mawla Corn 4 C2
Mawnan Corn 3 C5
Mawnan Smith Corn 3 C5
Mawsley Northants 99 D5
Maxey P'boro 100 A3
Maxstoke Warks 97 C5
Maxton Borders 197 C5
Maxton Kent 39 A5
Maxwellheugh Borders 197 C6
Maxwelltown Dumfries 174 A2
Maxworthy Corn 10 B3
May Bank Staffs 112 A2
Mayals Swansea 57 C6
Maybole S Ayrs 192 E3
Mayfield E Sus 36 D3
Mayfield Midloth 209 D6
Mayfield Staffs 113 A5
Mayfield W Loth 208 D2
Mayford Sur 34 A2
Mayland Essex 70 C3
Maynard's Green E Sus 22 A3
Maypole Mon 61 B6
Maypole Scilly 2 E4
Maypole Green Essex 70 A3
Maypole Green Norf 105 B5
Maypole Green Suff 88 A3
Maywick Shetland 285 L5
Meadle Bucks 66 C3
Meadowtown Shrops 93 A7
Meaford Staffs 112 B2
Meal Bank Cumb 154 B4
Mealabost W Isles 288 D5
Mealabost Bhuirgh W Isles 288 B5
Mealsgate Cumb 175 D5
Meanwood W Yorks 148 D1
Mearbeck N Yorks 146 A2
Meare Som 29 A4
Meare Green Som 28 C3
Mears Ashby Northants 83 A5
Measham Leics 114 D1
Meath Green Sur 35 B5
Meathop Cumb 154 C3
Meaux E Yorks 150 D3
Meavy Devon 7 A4
Medbourne Leics 99 B4
Medburn Northumb 178 B3
Meddon Devon 24 D3
Meden Vale Notts 131 C5
Medlam Lincs 134 D3
Medmenham Bucks 47 A6
Medomsley Durham 178 D3
Medstead Hants 33 B5
Meer End W Mid 97 D5
Meerbrook Staffs 129 C4
Meers Bridge Lincs 135 A4
Meesden Herts 85 D6
Meeth Devon 11 A6
Meggethead Borders 195 D6
Meidrim Carms 73 D5
Meifod Denb 125 D5
Meifod Powys 109 D6
Meigle N Ayrs 204 B1
Meigle Perth 231 D6
Meikle Earnock S Lnrk 194 A2
Meikle Ferry Highld 264 B3
Meikle Forter Angus 231 B5
Meikle Gluich Highld 264 B2
Meikle Pinkerton E Loth 211 C4
Meikle Strath Aberds 233 A4
Meikle Tarty Aberds 257 D4
Meikle Wartle Aberds 256 C2
Meikleour Perth 219 A6
Meinciau Carms 57 A4
Meir Stoke 112 A3
Meir Heath Staffs 112 A3
Melbourn Cambs 85 C5
Melbourne Derbys 114 C1
Melbourne E Yorks 149 C6
Melbourne S Lnrk 195 B5
Melbury Abbas Dorset 30 C2
Melbury Bubb Dorset 15 A5
Melbury Osmond Dorset 15 A5
Melbury Sampford Dorset 15 A5
Melby Shetland 285 H3
Melchbourne Beds 84 A2
Melcombe Bingham Dorset 16 A1
Melcombe Regis Dorset 15 C6
Meldon Devon 11 B6
Meldon Northumb 178 A3
Meldreth Cambs 85 C5
Meldrum Ho. Aberds 256 D3
Melfort Argyll 213 A6
Melgarve Highld 240 C2
Meliden Denb 125 A5
Melin-y-coed Conwy 124 C3
Melin-y-ddôl Powys 93 A4
Melin-y-grug Powys 93 A4
Melin-y-Wig Denb 109 A5
Melinbyrhedyn Powys 91 C6
Melincourt Neath 40 A3
Melkinthorpe Cumb 164 C3
Melkridge Northumb 177 C5
Melksham Wilts 44 C3
Melldalloch Argyll 203 A4
Melling Lancs 155 D4
Melling Mers 136 C2
Melling Mount Mers 136 C3
Mellis Suff 104 D2
Mellon Charles Highld 261 A5
Mellon Udrigle Highld 261 A5
Mellor Gtr Man 129 A4
Mellor Lancs 145 D6
Mellor Brook Lancs 145 D6
Mells Som 30 A1
Melmerby Cumb 165 B4
Melmerby N Yorks 158 D2
Melmerby N Yorks 157 C4
Melplash Dorset 15 B4
Melrose Borders 197 C4
Melsetter Orkney 283 K3
Melsonby N Yorks 157 A5
Meltham W Yorks 138 B4
Melton Suff 88 B3
Melton Constable Norf 120 B2
Melton Mowbray Leics 115 D5
Melton Ross N Lincs 142 B2
Meltonby E Yorks 149 B6
Melvaig Highld 261 B4
Melverley Shrops 110 D2
Melverley Green Shrops 110 D2
Melvich Highld 279 B4
Membury Devon 14 A2
Memsie Aberds 269 C4
Memus Angus 232 C2
Menabilly Corn 5 B5
Menai Bridge = Porthaethwy Anglesey 123 C5
Mendham Suff 104 C3
Mendlesham Suff 88 A2
Mendlesham Green Suff 88 A1
Menheniot Corn 6 A1
Mennock Dumfries 183 B6
Menston W Yorks 147 C5
Menstrie Clack 207 A6
Menthorpe N Yorks 149 D5
Mentmore Bucks 67 B4
Meoble Highld 238 D1
Meole Brace Shrops 110 D3
Meols Mers 136 D1
Meonstoke Hants 33 D5
Meopham Kent 50 C3
Meopham Station Kent 50 C3
Mepal Cambs 101 C6
Meppershall Beds 84 D3
Merbach Hereford 77 C7
Mere Ches 128 A2
Mere Wilts 30 B2
Mere Brow Lancs 136 B3
Mere Green W Mid 96 B4
Mereclough Lancs 146 D2
Mereside Blkpool 144 D3
Mereworth Kent 37 A4
Mergie Aberds 245 D4
Meriden W Mid 97 C5
Merkadale Highld 246 A2
Merkland Dumfries 173 A5
Merkland S Ayrs 181 B4

Merkland Lodge Highld 271 B7
Merley Poole 17 B4
Merlin's Bridge Pembs 55 C5
Merrington Shrops 110 C3
Merrion Pembs 55 E5
Merriott Som 28 D4
Merrivale Devon 11 D6
Merrow Sur 34 A3
Merrymeet Corn 6 A1
Merseyside Maritime Museum Mers 136 D2
Mersham Kent 38 B2
Merstham Sur 35 A5
Merston W Sus 20 B1
Merstone I o W 18 C4
Merther Corn 4 C3
Merthyr Carms 73 D6
Merthyr Cynog Powys 76 D3
Merthyr-Dyfan V Glam 41 E6
Merthyr Mawr Bridgend 40 D3
Merthyr Tudful = Merthyr Tydfil M Tydf 60 C2
Merthyr Tydfil = Merthyr Tudful M Tydf 60 C2
Merthyr Vale M Tydf 41 B5
Merton Devon 25 D6
Merton London 49 B5
Merton Norf 103 B5
Merton Oxon 65 B6
Mervinslaw Borders 187 B5
Meshaw Devon 26 D2
Messing Essex 70 B2
Messingham N Lincs 141 C6
Metfield Suff 104 C3
Metheringham Lincs 133 C5
Methil Fife 209 A6
Methlem Gwyn 106 C1
Methley W Yorks 140 A1
Methlick Aberds 256 C3
Methven Perth 219 B5
Methwold Norf 102 B3
Methwold Hythe Norf 102 B3
Metroland, Gateshead T & W 179 C4
Mettingham Suff 105 C4
Mevagissey Corn 5 C5
Mewith Head N Yorks 145 A7
Mexborough S Yorks 140 C2
Mey Highld 281 A4
Meysey Hampton Glos 64 D2
Miabhag W Isles 288 H2
Miabhag W Isles 287 D5
Miabhig W Isles 287 A5
Michaelchurch Hereford 61 A7
Michaelchurch Escley Hereford 77 D7
Michaelchurch on Arrow Powys 77 B6
Michaelston-le-Pit V Glam 41 D6
Michaelston-y-Fedw Newport 42 A1
Michaelstow Corn 10 D1
Michealston-super-Ely Cardiff 41 D6
Micheldever Hants 32 B4
Michelmersh Hants 32 C2
Mickfield Suff 88 A2
Mickle Trafford Ches 127 C4
Micklebring S Yorks 140 D3
Mickleby N Yorks 169 D6
Mickleham Sur 35 A4
Mickleover Derby 113 B7
Micklethwaite W Yorks 147 C5
Mickleton Durham 166 C2
Mickleton Glos 81 C4
Mickletown W Yorks 140 A1
Mickley N Yorks 157 D6
Mickley Square Northumb 178 C2
Mid Ardlaw Aberds 269 C4
Mid Auchinlech Invclyd 204 A3
Mid Beltie Aberds 244 B3
Mid Calder W Loth 208 D3
Mid Cloch Forbie Aberds 268 D2
Mid Clyth Highld 275 A6
Mid-Hants Railway (Watercress Line), New Alresford Hants 33 B4
Mid Lavant W Sus 20 B1
Mid Main Highld 251 C6
Mid Urchany Highld 253 B4
Mid Walls Shetland 285 H4
Mid Yell Shetland 284 D7
Midbea Orkney 282 C5
Middle Assendon Oxon 47 A5
Middle Aston Oxon 65 A5
Middle Barton Oxon 65 A5
Middle Cairncake Aberds 256 B3
Middle Claydon Bucks 66 A2
Middle Drums Angus 232 C3
Middle Handley Derbys 131 B4
Middle Littleton Worcs 80 C3
Middle Maes-coed Hereford 78 D1
Middle Mill Pembs 54 B4
Middle Rasen Lincs 133 A5
Middle Rigg Perth 219 D5
Middle Tysoe Warks 81 C6
Middle Wallop Hants 32 B1
Middle Winterslow Wilts 31 B6
Middle Woodford Wilts 31 B5
Middlebie Dumfries 175 A5
Middleforth Green Lancs 136 A4
Middleham N Yorks 157 C5
Middlehope Shrops 94 C2
Middlemarsh Dorset 15 A6
Middlemuir Aberds 257 D4
Middlesbrough M'bro 168 C2
Middleshaw Cumb 155 C4
Middleshaw Dumfries 174 A4
Middlesmoor N Yorks 157 D4
Middlestone Durham 167 B5
Middlestone Moor Durham 167 B5
Middlestown W Yorks 139 B5
Middlethird Borders 197 B5
Middleton Aberds 245 A5
Middleton Argyll 222 C2
Middleton Cumb 155 C5
Middleton Derbys 130 D2
Middleton Derbys 130 C1
Middleton Essex 87 D4
Middleton Gtr Man 138 C1
Middleton Hants 32 A3
Middleton Hereford 78 A3
Middleton Lancs 144 B4
Middleton Midloth 196 A2
Middleton Norf 118 D3
Middleton Northants 99 C5
Middleton Northumb 178 A2
Middleton Northumb 199 C5
Middleton N Yorks 159 C6
Middleton Perth 219 D6
Middleton Perth 231 D5
Middleton Shrops 94 D3
Middleton Shrops 93 B6
Middleton Shrops 110 C2
Middleton Suff 89 A5
Middleton Swansea 57 D4
Middleton Warks 97 B4
Middleton W Yorks 139 A5
Middleton W Yorks 147 C5
Middleton Cheney Northants 82 C1
Middleton Green Staffs 112 B3
Middleton Hall Northumb 188 A2
Middleton-in-Teesdale Durham 166 C2
Middleton Moor Suff 89 A5
Middleton-on-Leven N Yorks 158 A3
Middleton-on-Sea W Sus 20 B2
Middleton on the Hill Hereford 78 A3
Middleton-on-the-Wolds E Yorks 150 C2
Middleton One Row Darl 167 D6
Middleton Priors Shrops 95 B4
Middleton Quernham N Yorks 158 D2
Middleton Railway, Hunslet W Yorks 139 A6
Middleton St George Darl 167 D6
Middleton Scriven Shrops 95 C4
Middleton Stoney Oxon 65 A6
Middleton Tyas N Yorks 157 A6
Middletown Cumb 162 D2
Middletown Powys 110 D2
Middlewich Ches 128 C1
Middlewood Green Suff 88 A1
Middlezoy Som 28 B3
Middridge Durham 167 C5
Midfield Highld 277 B6
Midge Hall Lancs 136 A4
Midgeholme Cumb 176 D4
Midgham W Berks 46 C3
Midgley W Yorks 138 A3
Midgley W Yorks 139 B5
Midhopestones S Yorks 139 D5
Midhurst W Sus 34 D1
Midlem Borders 186 A4
Midmar Aberds 244 B3
Midsomer Norton Bath 43 D5
Midton Invclyd 204 A2
Midtown Highld 277 B6
Midtown Highld 261 B5
Midtown of Buchromb Moray 254 B4
Midville Lincs 134 D3
Midway Ches 129 A4
Migdale Highld 264 A2
Migvie Aberds 244 B1
Milarrochy Stirl 206 A2
Milborne Port Som 29 D6
Milborne St Andrew Dorset 16 B2
Milborne Wick Som 29 C6
Milbourne Northumb 178 B3
Milburn Cumb 165 C4
Milbury Heath S Glos 62 D2
Milcombe Oxon 81 D7
Milden Suff 87 C5
Mildenhall Suff 102 D3
Mildenhall Wilts 45 C6
Mile Cross Norf 120 D4
Mile Elm Wilts 44 C3
Mile End Essex 70 A3
Mile End Glos 62 B1
Mile Oak Brighton 21 B5
Milebrook Powys 93 D7
Milebush Kent 37 B5
Mileham Norf 119 D6
Milesmark Fife 208 B3
Milestones, Basingstoke Hants 47 D4
Milfield Northumb 198 C3
Milford Derbys 114 A1
Milford Devon 24 C3
Milford Powys 93 B4
Milford Staffs 112 C3
Milford Sur 34 B2
Milford Wilts 31 C5
Milford Haven = Aberdaugleddau Pembs 55 D5
Milford on Sea Hants 18 B1
Milkwall Glos 62 C1
Milkwell Wilts 30 C3
Mill Bank W Yorks 138 A3
Mill Common Suff 105 C5
Mill End Bucks 47 A5
Mill End Herts 85 D5
Mill Green Essex 69 C6
Mill Green Norf 104 C2
Mill Green Suff 87 C5
Mill Hill London 68 D2
Mill Lane Hants 47 D5
Mill of Kingoodie Aberds 256 D3
Mill of Muiresk Aberds 256 B1
Mill of Sterin Aberds 243 C6
Mill of Uras Aberds 245 D5
Mill Place N Lincs 142 C1
Mill Side Cumb 154 C3
Mill Street Norf 120 D2
Milland W Sus 34 D1
Millarston Renfs 205 B4
Millbank Aberds 257 B6
Millbank Highld 280 B3
Millbeck Cumb 163 B5
Millbounds Orkney 282 D6
Millbreck Aberds 257 B5
Millbridge Sur 34 B1
Millbrook Beds 84 D2
Millbrook Corn 6 B3
Millbrook Soton 32 D2
Millburn S Ayrs 193 C4
Millcombe Devon 8 C2
Millcorner E Sus 37 D6
Milldale Staffs 129 D6
Millden Lodge Angus 232 A3
Milldens Angus 232 C3
Millennium Stadium Cardiff 41 D6
Millerhill Midloth 209 D6
Miller's Dale Derbys 129 B6
Miller's Green Derbys 130 D2
Millgreen Shrops 111 C5
Millhalf Hereford 77 C6
Millhayes Devon 14 A2
Millhead Lancs 154 D3
Millheugh S Lnrk 194 A2
Millholme Cumb 155 B4
Millhouse Argyll 203 A4
Millhouse Cumb 163 A6
Millhouse Green S Yorks 139 C5
Millhousebridge Dumfries 185 D4
Millhouses S Yorks 130 A3
Millikenpark Renfs 205 B4
Millin Cross Pembs 55 C5
Millington E Yorks 150 B1
Millmeece Staffs 112 B2
Millom Cumb 153 B2
Millook Corn 10 B2
Millpool Corn 10 D2
Millport N Ayrs 204 C1
Millquarter Dumfries 182 D4
Millthorpe Lincs 116 B4
Millthrop Cumb 155 B5
Milltimber Aberdeen 245 B5
Milltown Corn 5 B6
Milltown Derbys 130 C3
Milltown Devon 25 B6
Milltown Dumfries 175 A6
Milltown of Aberdalgie Perth 219 B5
Milltown of Auchindoun Moray 255 B4
Milltown of Craigston Aberds 268 D2
Milltown of Edinvillie Moray 254 B3
Milltown of Kildrummy Aberds 244 A1
Milltown of Rothiemay Moray 255 B6
Milltown of Towie Aberds 244 A1
Milnathort Perth 219 D6
Milner's Heath Ches 127 C4
Milngavie E Dunb 205 A5
Milnrow Gtr Man 138 B2
Milnshaw Lancs 137 A6
Milnthorpe Cumb 154 C3
Milo Carms 57 A5
Milson Shrops 95 D4
Milstead Kent 37 A7
Milston Wilts 31 A5
Milton Angus 232 D1
Milton Cambs 85 A6
Milton Cumb 176 C3
Milton Derbys 113 C7
Milton Dumfries 171 B4
Milton Dumfries 173 A6
Milton Dumfries 183 D6
Milton Highld 251 A5
Milton Highld 251 C6
Milton Highld 252 B1
Milton Highld 281 C5
Milton Highld 264 C3
Milton Moray 267 C6
Milton Notts 132 B2
Milton N Som 42 C2
Milton Oxon 82 D1
Milton Oxon 65 D5
Milton Pembs 55 D6
Milton Perth 219 C4
Milton Ptsmth 19 B5
Milton Stirl 217 D5
Milton Stoke 129 D4
Milton W Dunb 205 A4
Milton Abbas Dorset 16 A2
Milton Abbot Devon 11 D5
Milton Bridge Midloth 209 D5
Milton Bryan Beds 83 D6
Milton Clevedon Som 29 B6
Milton Coldwells Aberds 257 C4
Milton Combe Devon 6 A3
Milton Damerel Devon 25 D4
Milton End Glos 64 C2
Milton Ernest Beds 84 B2
Milton Green Ches 127 D4
Milton Hill Oxon 65 D5
Milton Keynes M Keynes 83 D5
Milton Keynes Village M Keynes 83 D5
Milton Lilbourne Wilts 45 C5
Milton Malsor Northants 83 B4
Milton Morenish Perth 217 A6
Milton of Auchinhove Aberds 244 B2
Milton of Balgonie Fife 220 D3
Milton of Buchanan Stirl 206 A2
Milton of Campfield Aberds 244 B3
Milton of Campsie E Dunb 205 A6
Milton of Corsindae Aberds 244 B3
Milton of Cushnie Aberds 244 A2
Milton of Dalcapon Perth 230 C3
Milton of Edradour Perth 230 C3
Milton of Gollanfield Highld 252 A3
Milton of Lesmore Aberds 255 D5
Milton of Logie Aberds 244 B1
Milton of Murtle Aberdeen 245 B5
Milton of Noth Aberds 255 D6
Milton of Tullich Aberds 243 C6
Milton on Stour Dorset 30 C1
Milton Regis Kent 51 C6
Milton under Wychwood Oxon 64 B3
Miltonduff Moray 266 C2
Miltonhill Moray 266 C1
Miltonise Dumfries 180 D3
Milverton Som 27 C6
Milverton Warks 81 A6
Milwich Staffs 112 B3
Minard Argyll 214 C2
Minchinhampton Glos 63 C4
Mindrum Northumb 198 C2
Minehead Som 27 A4
Minera Wrex 126 D2
Minesmere RSPB Nature Reserve Suff 89 A5
Minety Wilts 63 D6
Minffordd Gwyn 107 C5
Minffordd Gwyn 91 A5
Minffordd Gwyn 123 C5
Miningsby Lincs 134 C3
Minions Corn 10 D3
Minishant S Ayrs 192 D3
Minllyn Gwyn 91 A6
Minnes Aberds 257 D4
Minngearraidh W Isles 286 D3
Minnigaff Dumfries 171 A6
Minnonie Aberds 268 C2
Minskip N Yorks 148 A2
Minstead Hants 32 D1
Minsted W Sus 34 D1
Minster Kent 51 B6
Minster Kent 53 C5
Minster Lovell Oxon 64 B4
Minsterley Shrops 94 A1
Minsterworth Glos 62 B3
Minterne Magna Dorset 15 A6
Minting Lincs 134 B1
Mintlaw Aberds 257 B5
Minto Borders 187 A4
Minton Shrops 94 B2
Minwear Pembs 55 C6
Minworth W Mid 97 B4
Mirbister Orkney 282 E4
Mirehouse Cumb 162 C2
Mireland Highld 281 B5
Mirfield W Yorks 139 B5
Miserden Glos 63 C5
Miskin Rhondda 41 C5
Misson Notts 141 D4
Misterton Leics 98 C2
Misterton Notts 141 D5
Misterton Som 15 A4
Mistley Essex 88 D2
Mitcham London 49 C5
Mitchel Troy Mon 61 B6
Mitcheldean Glos 62 B2
Mitchell Corn 4 B3
Mitcheltroy Common Mon 61 C6
Mitford Northumb 178 A3
Mithian Corn 4 B2
Mitton Staffs 112 D2
Mixbury Oxon 82 D3
Moat Cumb 175 A7
Moats Tye Suff 87 B6
Mobberley Ches 128 B2
Mobberley Staffs 112 A4
Moccas Hereford 78 C1
Mochdre Conwy 124 B3
Mochdre Powys 93 C4
Mochrum Dumfries 171 C5
Mockbeggar Hants 17 A5
Mockerkin Cumb 162 B3
Modbury Devon 7 B5
Moddershall Staffs 112 B3
Model Village, Babbacombe Devon 8 A3
Moelfre Anglesey 123 B5
Moelfre Powys 109 C6
Moffat Dumfries 184 B3
Moggerhanger Beds 84 C3
Moira Leics 113 D7
Mol-chlach Highld 246 C3
Molash Kent 52 D2
Mold = Yr Wyddgrug Flint 126 C2
Moldgreen W Yorks 139 B4
Molehill Green Essex 69 A5
Molescroft E Yorks 150 C3
Molesden Northumb 178 A3
Molesworth Cambs 100 D2
Moll Highld 247 A4
Molland Devon 26 C3
Mollington Ches 126 B3
Mollington Oxon 82 C1
Mollinsburn N Lnrk 207 C5
Monachty Ceredig 75 B4
Monachylemore Stirl 217 C4
Monar Lodge Highld 250 B4
Monaughty Powys 77 A6
Monboddo House Aberds 233 A5
Mondynes Aberds 233 A5
Monevechadan Argyll 215 B4
Monewden Suff 88 B3
Moneydie Perth 219 B5
Moniaive Dumfries 183 C5
Monifieth Angus 221 A4
Monikie Angus 221 A4
Monimail Fife 220 C2
Monington Pembs 72 B4
Monk Bretton S Yorks 139 C6
Monk Fryston N Yorks 140 A3
Monk Sherborne Hants 47 D4
Monk Soham Suff 88 A3
Monk Street Essex 69 A6
Monken Hadley London 68 D2
Monkhopton Shrops 95 B4
Monkland Hereford 78 B2
Monkleigh Devon 25 C5
Monknash V Glam 40 D4
Monkokehampton Devon 11 A6
Monks Eleigh Suff 87 C5
Monk's Gate W Sus 35 D5
Monks Heath Ches 128 B3
Monks Kirby Warks 98 C1
Monks Risborough Bucks 66 C3
Monkseaton T & W 179 B5
Monkshill Aberds 256 B2
Monksilver Som 27 B5
Monkspath W Mid 96 D4
Monkswood Mon 61 C5
Monkton Devon 14 A1
Monkton Kent 53 C4
Monkton Pembs 55 D5
Monkton S Ayrs 192 C3
Monkton Combe Bath 44 C1
Monkton Deverill Wilts 30 B2
Monkton Farleigh Wilts 44 C2
Monkton Heathfield Som 28 C2
Monkton Up Wimborne Dorset 31 D4
Monkwearmouth T & W 179 D5
Monkwood Hants 33 B5
Monmouth = Trefynwy Mon 61 B7
Monmouth Cap Mon 61 A5
Monnington on Wye Hereford 78 C1
Monreith Dumfries 171 C5
Monreith Mains Dumfries 171 C5
Mont Saint Guern 6
Montacute Som 29 D4
Montacute House Som 29 D5
Montcoffer Ho. Aberds 268 C1
Montford Argyll 203 B6
Montford Shrops 110 D3
Montford Bridge Shrops 110 D3
Montgarrie Aberds 244 A2
Montgomery = Trefaldwyn Powys 93 B6
Montrave Fife 220 D3
Montrose Angus 233 C5
Montsale Essex 71 D4
Monxton Hants 32 A2
Monyash Derbys 129 C6
Monymusk Aberds 244 A3
Monzie Perth 218 B3
Monzie Castle Perth 218 B3
Moodiesburn N Lnrk 207 C4
Moonzie Fife 220 C3
Moor Allerton W Yorks 148 D1
Moor Crichel Dorset 16 A3
Moor End E Yorks 149 D7
Moor End York 149 B5
Moor Monkton N Yorks 148 B4
Moor of Granary Moray 253 A6
Moor of Ravenstone Dumfries 171 C5
Moor Row Cumb 162 C3
Moor Street Kent 51 C5
Moorby Lincs 134 C2
Moordown Bmouth 17 B4
Moore Halton 127 A5
Moorend Glos 62 C3
Moorends S Yorks 141 B4
Moorgate S Yorks 140 D2
Moorgreen Notts 114 A2
Moorhall Derbys 130 B3
Moorhampton Hereford 78 C1
Moorhead W Yorks 147 D5
Moorhouse Cumb 175 C6
Moorhouse Notts 132 C2
Moorlinch Som 28 B3
Moorsholm Redcar 169 D4
Moorside Gtr Man 138 C2
Moorthorpe W Yorks 140 B2
Moortown Hants 17 A5
Moortown I o W 18 C3
Moortown Lincs 142 D2
Morangie Highld 264 B3
Morar Highld 235 A5
Morborne Cambs 100 B3
Morchard Bishop Devon 12 A2
Morcombelake Dorset 14 B4
Morcott Rutland 99 A6
Morda Shrops 110 C1
Morden Dorset 16 B3
Morden London 49 C5
Mordiford Hereford 78 D3
Mordon Durham 167 C6
More Shrops 94 B1
Morebath Devon 27 C4
Morebattle Borders 187 A6
Morecambe Lancs 144 A4
Morefield Highld 262 A3
Moreleigh Devon 7 B6
Morenish Perth 217 A5
Moresby Cumb 162 B2
Moresby Parks Cumb 162 C2
Morestead Hants 32 C4
Moreton Dorset 16 C2
Moreton Essex 69 C5
Moreton Mers 136 D1
Moreton Oxon 66 C1
Moreton Staffs 112 D1
Moreton Corbet Shrops 111 C4
Moreton-in-Marsh Glos 81 D5
Moreton Jeffries Hereford 79 C4
Moreton Morrell Warks 81 B6
Moreton on Lugg Hereford 78 C3
Moreton Pinkney Northants 82 C2
Moreton Say Shrops 111 B5
Moreton Valence Glos 62 C3
Moretonhampstead Devon 12 C2
Morfa Carms 57 A5
Morfa Carms 57 C5
Morfa Bach Carms 56 A3
Morfa Bychan Gwyn 107 C5
Morfa Dinlle Gwyn 107 A4
Morfa Glas Neath 59 E5
Morfa Nefyn Gwyn 106 B2
Morfydd Denb 109 A6
Morgan's Vale Wilts 31 C5
Moriah Ceredig 75 A5
Morland Cumb 164 C3
Morley Derbys 114 A1
Morley Durham 166 C4
Morley W Yorks 139 A5
Morley Green Ches 128 A3
Morley St Botolph Norf 104 B1
Morningside Edin 209 C5
Morningside N Lnrk 194 A3
Morningthorpe Norf 104 B3
Morpeth Northumb 179 A4
Morphie Aberds 233 B5

Morrey Staffs 113 D5
Morris Green Essex 86 D3
Morriston Swansea 57 C6
Morston Norf 120 A2
Mortehoe Devon 25 A5
Mortimer W Berks 47 C4
Mortimer West End Hants 47 C4
Mortimer's Cross Hereford 78 A2
Mortlake London 49 B5
Morton Cumb 175 C6
Morton Derbys 131 C4
Morton Lincs 116 C3
Morton Lincs 141 D6
Morton Lincs 132 C3
Morton Norf 120 D3
Morton Notts 132 D2
Morton Shrops 110 C1
Morton S Glos 62 D2
Morton Bagot Warks 80 A4
Morton-on-Swale N Yorks 157 B7
Morvah Corn 2 B2
Morval Corn 6 B1
Morvich Highld 249 D6
Morvich Highld 273 D5
Morville Shrops 95 B4
Morville Heath Shrops 95 B4
Morwenstow Corn 24 D3
Mosborough S Yorks 131 A4
Moscow E Ayrs 205 D4
Mosedale Cumb 163 A6
Moseley W Mid 96 C3
Moseley W Mid 96 B2
Moseley Worcs 79 B6
Mosquito Aircraft Museum, London Colney Herts 68 C1
Moss Argyll 222 C2
Moss Highld 235 D5
Moss S Yorks 140 B3
Moss Wrex 126 D3
Moss Bank Mers 136 D4
Moss Edge Lancs 144 C4
Moss End Brack 47 B6
Moss of Barmuckity Moray 266 C3
Moss Pit Staffs 112 C3
Moss-side Highld 253 A4
Moss Side Lancs 144 D3
Mossat Aberds 244 A1
Mossbank Shetland 284 F6
Mossbay Cumb 162 B2
Mossblown S Ayrs 193 C4
Mossbrow Gtr Man 128 A2
Mossburnford Borders 187 B5
Mossdale Dumfries 173 A4
Mossend N Lnrk 207 D5
Mosser Cumb 163 B4
Mossfield Highld 264 C2
Mossgiel E Ayrs 193 C4
Mosside Angus 232 C2
Mossley Ches 128 C3
Mossley Gtr Man 138 C2
Mossley Hill Mers 126 A3
Mosstodloch Moray 266 D4
Mosston Angus 232 D3
Mossy Lea Lancs 136 B4
Mosterton Dorset 15 A4
Moston Gtr Man 138 C1
Moston Shrops 111 C4
Moston Green Ches 128 C2
Mostyn Flint 125 A6
Mostyn Quay Flint 125 A6
Motcombe Dorset 30 C2
Mothecombe Devon 7 C5
Motherby Cumb 164 C2
Motherwell N Lnrk 194 A2
Mottingham London 49 B7
Mottisfont Hants 32 C2
Mottisfont Abbey Garden Hants 32 C2
Mottistone I o W 18 C3
Mottram in Longdendale Gtr Man 138 D2
Mottram St Andrew Ches 128 B3
Mouilpied Guern 6
Mouldsworth Ches 127 B5
Moulin Perth 230 C3
Moulsecoomb Brighton 21 B6
Moulsford Oxon 46 A3
Moulsoe M Keynes 83 C6
Moulton Ches 127 C6
Moulton Lincs 117 C6
Moulton Northants 83 A4
Moulton N Yorks 157 A6
Moulton Suff 86 A2
Moulton V Glam 41 D5
Moulton Chapel Lincs 117 D5
Moulton Eaugate Lincs 117 D6
Moulton St Mary Norf 105 A4
Moulton Seas End Lincs 117 C6
Mounie Castle Aberds 256 D2
Mount Corn 4 B2
Mount Corn 5 A6
Mount Highld 253 B5
Mount Bures Essex 87 D5
Mount Canisp Highld 264 C3
Mount Hawke Corn 4 C2
Mount Pleasant Ches 128 D3
Mount Pleasant Derbys 114 A1
Mount Pleasant Derbys 113 D6
Mount Pleasant Flint 126 B2
Mount Pleasant Hants 18 B1
Mount Pleasant W Yorks 139 A5
Mount Sorrel Wilts 31 C4
Mount Tabor W Yorks 138 A3
Mountain W Yorks 147 D4
Mountain Ash = Aberpennar Rhondda 41 B5
Mountain Cross Borders 195 B6
Mountain Water Pembs 55 B5
Mountbenger Borders 196 D2
Mountfield E Sus 37 D5
Mountgerald Highld 264 D1
Mountjoy Corn 4 A3
Mountnessing Essex 69 D6
Mounton Mon 61 D7
Mountsorrel Leics 114 D3
Mousehole Corn 2 C2
Mousen Northumb 199 C5
Mouswald Dumfries 174 A3
Mow Cop Ches 128 D3
Mowhaugh Borders 187 A7
Mowsley Leics 98 C3
Moxley W Mid 96 B2
Moy Highld 240 D2
Moy Highld 252 C3
Moy Hall Highld 252 C3
Moy Ho. Moray 265 D6
Moy Lodge Highld 240 D2
Moyles Court Hants 17 A5
Moylgrove Pembs 72 B4
Muasdale Argyll 202 D1
Much Birch Hereford 78 D3
Much Cowarne Hereford 79 C4
Much Dewchurch Hereford 78 D2
Much Hadham Herts 68 B4
Much Hoole Lancs 136 A3
Much Marcle Hereford 79 D4
Much Wenlock Shrops 95 A4
Muchalls Aberds 245 C6
Muchelney Som 28 C4
Muchlarnick Corn 5 B7
Muchrachd Highld 251 C4
Muckernich Highld 252 A1
Mucking Thurrock 50 A3
Muckleford Dorset 15 B6
Mucklestone Staffs 111 B6
Muckleton Shrops 111 C4
Muckletown Aberds 255 D6
Muckley Corner Staffs 96 A3
Muckton Lincs 134 A3
Mudale Highld 272 A3
Muddiford Devon 25 B6
Mudeford Dorset 17 B5
Mudford Som 29 D5
Mudgley Som 28 A4
Mugdock Stirl 205 A5
Mugeary Highld 246 A3
Mugginton Derbys 113 A6
Muggleswick Durham 166 A3
Muie Highld 273 D4
Muir Aberds 242 D3
Muir of Fairburn Highld 251 A6
Muir of Fowlis Aberds 244 A2
Muir of Ord Highld 252 A1
Muir of Pert Angus 220 A4
Muirden Aberds 268 D2
Muirdrum Angus 221 A5
Muirhead Angus 220 A3
Muirhead Fife 220 D2
Muirhead N Lnrk 207 D4
Muirhead S Ayrs 192 B3
Muirhouselaw Borders 187 A5
Muirhouses Falk 208 B3
Muirkirk E Ayrs 194 D1
Muirmill Stirl 207 B5
Muirshearlich Highld 239 D5
Muirskie Aberds 245 C5
Muirtack Aberds 257 C4
Muirton Highld 264 D3
Muirton Perth 219 B6
Muirton Perth 218 C4
Muirton Mains Highld 251 A6
Muirton of Ardblair Perth 231 D5
Muirton of Ballochy Angus 233 B4
Muiryfold Aberds 268 D2
Muker N Yorks 156 B3
Mulbarton Norf 104 A2
Mulben Moray 267 D4
Mulindry Argyll 200 C3
Mullardoch House Highld 250 C4
Mullion Corn 3 D4
Mullion Cove Corn 3 D4
Mumby Lincs 135 B5
Muncaster Owl Trust World HQ Cumb 153 A2
Munderfield Row Hereford 79 B4
Munderfield Stocks Hereford 79 B4
Mundesley Norf 121 B5
Mundford Norf 103 B4
Mundham Norf 104 B4
Mundon Essex 70 C2
Mundurno Aberdeen 245 A6
Munerigie Highld 239 B6
Muness Shetland 284 C8
Mungasdale Highld 261 A6
Mungrisdale Cumb 163 A6
Munlochy Highld 252 A2
Munsley Hereford 79 C4
Munslow Shrops 94 C3
Murchington Devon 12 C1
Murcott Oxon 65 B6
Murkle Highld 280 B3
Murlaggan Highld 238 C4
Murlaggan Highld 239 D7
Murra Orkney 283 G3
Murrayfield Edin 209 C5
Murrayfield Stadium Edin 209 C5
Murrays Motorcycle Museum I o M 152 C3
Murrow Cambs 101 A5
Mursley Bucks 66 A3
Murthill Angus 232 C2
Murthly Perth 219 A5
Murton Cumb 165 C5
Murton Durham 167 A6
Murton Northumb 198 B3
Murton York 149 B5
Musbury Devon 14 B2
Muscoates N Yorks 159 C5
Musdale Argyll 226 D4
Museum of Childhood, Bethnal Green London 49 A6
Museum of the Broads, Sutton Norf 121 C5
Musselburgh E Loth 209 C6
Musselburgh Racecourse E Loth 209 C6
Muston Leics 115 B6
Muston N Yorks 161 D4
Mustow Green Worcs 95 D6
Mutehill Dumfries 173 D4
Mutford Suff 105 C5
Muthill Perth 218 C3
Mutterton Devon 13 A5
Muxton Telford 111 D6
Mybster Highld 280 C3
Myddfai Carms 59 C4
Myddle Shrops 110 C3
Mydroilyn Ceredig 74 C3
Myerscough Lancs 145 D4
Mylor Bridge Corn 4 D3
Mynachlog-ddu Pembs 72 C4
Myndtown Shrops 94 C1
Mynydd Bach Ceredig 75 A6
Mynydd-bach Mon 61 D6
Mynydd Bodafon Anglesey 123 B4
Mynydd-isa Flint 126 C2
Mynyddygarreg Carms 57 B4
Mynytho Gwyn 106 C3
Myrebird Aberds 245 C4
Myrelandhorn Highld 281 C4
Myreside Perth 220 B2
Myrtle Hill Carms 59 B4
Mytchett Sur 34 A1
Mytholm W Yorks 138 A2
Mytholmroyd W Yorks 138 A3
Myton-on-Swale N Yorks 148 A3
Mytton Shrops 110 D3

N

Na Gearrannan W Isles 288 C2
Naast Highld 261 B5
Naburn York 149 C4
Nackington Kent 52 D3
Nacton Suff 88 C3
Nafferton E Yorks 150 B3
Nailbridge Glos 62 B2
Nailsbourne Som 28 C2
Nailsea N Som 42 B3
Nailstone Leics 97 A7
Nailsworth Glos 63 D4
Nairn Highld 253 A4
Nalderswood Sur 35 B5
Nancegollan Corn 3 B4
Nancledra Corn 2 B2
Nanhoron Gwyn 106 C2
Nannau Gwyn 108 C2
Nannerch Flint 125 C6
Nanpantan Leics 114 D3
Nanpean Corn 5 B4
Nanstallon Corn 5 A5
Nant-ddu Powys 60 B2
Nant-glas Powys 76 A3
Nant Peris Gwyn 107 A6
Nant Uchaf Denb 125 D5
Nant-y-Bai Carms 59 A4
Nant-y-cafn Neath 59 E5
Nant-y-derry Mon 61 C5
Nant-y-ffin Carms 58 B2
Nant-y-moel Bridgend 40 B4
Nant-y-pandy Conwy 124 B1
Nanternis Ceredig 73 A6
Nantgaredig Carms 58 C1
Nantgarw Rhondda 41 C6
Nantglyn Denb 125 C5
Nantgwyn Powys 92 D3
Nantlle Gwyn 107 A5
Nantmawr Shrops 110 C1
Nantmel Powys 76 A4
Nantmor Gwyn 107 B6
Nantwich Ches 127 D6
Nantycaws Carms 57 A4
Nantyffyllon Bridgend 40 B3
Nantyglo Bl Gwent 60 B3
Naphill Bucks 66 D3
Nappa N Yorks 146 B2
Napton on the Hill Warks 82 A1
Narberth = Arberth Pembs 55 C7
Narborough Leics 98 B2
Narborough Norf 119 D4
Nasareth Gwyn 107 A4
Naseby Northants 98 D3
Nash Bucks 83 D4
Nash Hereford 77 A7
Nash Newport 42 A2
Nash Shrops 95 D4
Nash Lee Bucks 66 C3
Nassington Northants 100 B2
Nasty Herts 68 A3
Nateby Cumb 155 A6
Nateby Lancs 145 C4
National Agricultural Centre, Stoneleigh Warks 97 D6
National Botanic Garden of Wales Carms 57 A5
National Cycle Collection, Llandrindod Wells Powys 77 A4
National Exhibition Centre, Birmingham W Mid 97 C4
National Fishing Heritage Centre, Grimsby NE Lincs 143 C4
National Gallery London 49 B5
National Hockey Stadium M Keynes 83 D5
National Ice Centre Nottingham 114 B3
National Maritime Museum London 49 B6
National Maritime Museum, Falmouth Corn 4 D3
National Motor Museum, Beaulieu Hants 18 A2
National Museum of Photography, Bradford W Yorks 147 D5
National Museum of Wales Cardiff 41 D6
National Portrait Gallery (See National Gallery) London 49 A5
National Railway Museum York 149 B4
National Seal Sanctuary, Gweek Corn 3 C5
National Space Science Centre Leics 98 A2
National Squash Centre Gtr Man 138 D1
Natland Cumb 154 C4
Natural History Museum London 49 B5
Natureland Seal Sanctuary, Skegness Lincs 135 C5
Naughton Suff 87 C6
Naunton Glos 64 A2
Naunton Worcs 80 D1
Naunton Beauchamp Worcs 80 B2
Navenby Lincs 133 D4
Navestock Heath Essex 69 D5
Navestock Side Essex 69 D5
Navidale Highld 274 C4
Nawton N Yorks 159 C5
Nayland Suff 87 D5
Nazeing Essex 68 C4
Neacroft Hants 17 B5
Neal's Green Warks 97 C6
Neap Shetland 285 H7
Near Sawrey Cumb 154 B2
Neasham Darl 167 D6
Neath = Castell-Nedd Neath 40 B2
Neath Abbey Neath 40 B2
Neatishead Norf 121 C5
Nebo Anglesey 123 A4
Nebo Ceredig 75 B4
Nebo Conwy 124 D3
Nebo Gwyn 107 A4
Necton Norf 103 A4
Nedd Highld 270 A4
Nedderton Northumb 179 A4
Nedging Tye Suff 87 C6
Needham Norf 104 C3
Needham Market Suff 88 B1
Needingworth Cambs 101 D5
Needwood Staffs 113 C5
Neen Savage Shrops 95 D4
Neen Sollars Shrops 95 D4
Neenton Shrops 95 C4
Nefyn Gwyn 106 B3
Neilston E Renf 205 C4
Neinthirion Powys 92 A3
Neithrop Oxon 82 C1
Nelly Andrews Green Powys 93 A6
Nelson Caerph 41 B6
Nelson Lancs 146 D2
Nelson Village Northumb 179 B4
Nemphlar S Lnrk 194 B3
Nempnett Thrubwell Bath 43 C4
Nene Terrace Lincs 101 A4
Nenthall Cumb 165 A5
Nenthead Cumb 165 A5
Nenthorn Borders 197 C5
Nerabus Argyll 200 C2
Nercwys Flint 126 C2
Nerston S Lnrk 205 C6
Nesbit Northumb 198 C3
Ness Ches 126 B3
Ness Gardens, Connah's Quay Ches 126 B3
Nesscliffe Shrops 110 D2
Neston Ches 126 B2
Neston Wilts 44 C2
Nether Alderley Ches 128 B3
Nether Blainslie Borders 197 B4
Nether Booth Derbys 129 A6
Nether Broughton Leics 115 C4
Nether Burrow Lancs 155 D5
Nether Cerne Dorset 15 B6
Nether Compton Dorset 29 D5
Nether Crimond Aberds 256 D3
Nether Dalgliesh Borders 185 B5
Nether Dallachy Moray 267 C4
Nether Exe Devon 13 A4
Nether Glasslaw Aberds 268 D3
Nether Handwick Angus 232 D1
Nether Haugh S Yorks 140 D2
Nether Heage Derbys 130 D3
Nether Heyford Northants 82 B3
Nether Hindhope Borders 187 B6
Nether Howecleuch S Lnrk 184 A3
Nether Kellet Lancs 145 A5
Nether Kinmundy Aberds 257 B5
Nether Langwith Notts 131 B5
Nether Leask Aberds 257 C5
Nether Lenshie Aberds 256 B1
Nether Monynut Borders 211 D4
Nether Padley Derbys 130 B2
Nether Park Aberds 269 D5
Nether Poppleton York 149 B4
Nether Silton N Yorks 158 B3
Nether Stowey Som 28 B1
Nether Urquhart Fife 219 D6
Nether Wallop Hants 32 B2
Nether Wasdale Cumb 163 D4
Nether Whitacre Warks 97 B5
Nether Worton Oxon 82 D1
Netheravon Wilts 31 A5
Netherbrae Aberds 268 D2
Netherbrough Orkney 282 F4
Netherburn S Lnrk 194 B3
Netherbury Dorset 15 B4
Netherby Cumb 175 A6
Netherby N Yorks 148 C2
Nethercote Warks 82 A2
Nethercott Devon 25 B5
Netherend Glos 62 C1
Netherfield E Sus 23 A5
Netherhampton Wilts 31 C5
Netherlaw Dumfries 173 D5
Netherley Aberds 245 C5
Netherley Mers 127 A4
Nethermill Dumfries 184 D3
Nethermuir Aberds 257 B4
Netherplace E Renf 205 C5
Netherseal Derbys 113 D6
Netherthird E Ayrs 182 A3
Netherthong W Yorks 139 C4
Netherthorpe S Yorks 131 A5
Netherton Angus 232 C3
Netherton Devon 12 D3
Netherton Hants 46 D1
Netherton Mers 136 C2
Netherton Northumb 188 C2
Netherton Oxon 65 D5
Netherton Perth 231 C5
Netherton Stirl 205 A5
Netherton W Mid 96 C2
Netherton Worcs 80 C2
Netherton W Yorks 139 B4
Netherton W Yorks 139 B5
Nethertown Cumb 162 D2
Nethertown Highld 281 A5
Netherwitton Northumb 189 D4
Netherwood E Ayrs 193 C6
Nethy Bridge Highld 253 D6
Netley Hants 18 A3
Netley Marsh Hants 32 D2
Netteswell Essex 69 B4
Nettlebed Oxon 47 A5
Nettlebridge Som 29 A6
Nettlecombe Dorset 15 B5
Nettleden Herts 67 B5
Nettleham Lincs 133 B5
Nettlestead Kent 37 A4
Nettlestead Green Kent 37 A4
Nettlestone I o W 19 B5
Nettlesworth Durham 167 A5
Nettleton Lincs 142 C3
Nettleton Wilts 44 B2
Neuadd Carms 58 C3
Nevendon Essex 70 D1
Nevern Pembs 72 B3
Nevis Range Ski Centre, Torlundy Highld 237 B5
New Abbey Dumfries 174 B2
New Aberdour Aberds 268 C3
New Addington London 49 C6
New Alresford Hants 33 B4
New Alyth Perth 231 D6
New Arley Warks 97 C5
New Ash Green Kent 50 C3
New Barn Kent 50 C3
New Barnetby N Lincs 142 B2
New Barton Northants 83 A5
New Bewick Northumb 188 A3
New-bigging Angus 231 D6
New Bilton Warks 98 D1
New Bolingbroke Lincs 134 D3
New Boultham Lincs 133 B4
New Bradwell M Keynes 83 C5
New Brancepeth Durham 167 A5
New Bridge Wrex 110 A1
New Brighton Flint 126 C2
New Brighton Mers 136 D2
New Brinsley Notts 131 D4
New Broughton Wrex 126 D3
New Buckenham Norf 104 B1
New Byth Aberds 268 D3
New Catton Norf 120 D4
New Cheriton Hants 33 C4
New Costessey Norf 120 D3
New Cowper Cumb 174 D4
New Cross Ceredig 75 A5
New Cross London 49 B6
New Cumnock E Ayrs 182 A4
New Deer Aberds 256 B3
New Delaval Northumb 179 B4
New Duston Northants 83 A4
New Earswick York 149 B5
New Edlington S Yorks 140 D3
New Elgin Moray 266 C3
New Ellerby E Yorks 151 D4
New Eltham London 50 B1
New End Worcs 80 B3
New Farnley W Yorks 147 D6
New Ferry Mers 126 A3
New Fryston W Yorks 140 A2
New Galloway Dumfries 172 A4
New Gilston Fife 220 D4
New Grimsby Scilly 2 E3
New Hainford Norf 120 D4
New Hartley Northumb 179 B5
New Haw Sur 48 C3
New Hedges Pembs 56 B1
New Herrington T & W 179 D5
New Hinksey Oxon 65 C6
New Holkham Norf 119 B5
New Holland N Lincs 142 A2
New Houghton Derbys 131 C4
New Houghton Norf 119 C4
New Houses N Yorks 155 D7
New Humberstone Leicester 98 A3
New Hutton Cumb 155 B4
New Hythe Kent 37 A5
New Inn Carms 58 B1
New Inn Mon 61 C6
New Inn Pembs 55 A6
New Inn Torf 61 D5
New Invention Shrops 93 D6
New Invention W Mid 96 A2
New Kelso Highld 249 B6
New Kingston Notts 114 C3
New Lanark S Lnrk 194 B3
New Lanark Village & Visitor Centre, Lanark S Lnrk 194 B3
New Lane Lancs 136 B3
New Lane End Warr 137 D5
New Leake Lincs 135 D4
New Leeds Aberds 269 D4
New Longton Lancs 136 A4
New Luce Dumfries 170 A3
New Malden London 49 C5
New Marske Redcar 168 C4
New Marton Shrops 110 B2
New Micklefield W Yorks 148 D3
New Mill Aberds 245 D4
New Mill Herts 67 B4
New Mill Wilts 45 C5
New Mill W Yorks 139 C4
New Mills Ches 128 A2
New Mills Corn 4 B3
New Mills Derbys 129 A4
New Mills Powys 93 A4
New Milton Hants 17 B6
New Moat Pembs 55 B6
New Ollerton Notts 131 C6
New Oscott W Mid 96 B3
New Park N Yorks 148 B1
New Pitsligo Aberds 268 D3

New Pleasurewood Hills Leisure Park, Lowestoft Suff 105 B6
New Polzeath Corn 9 D5
New Quay = Ceinewydd Ceredig 73 A6
New Rackheath Norf 121 D4
New Radnor Powys 77 A6
New Rent Cumb 164 B2
New Ridley Northumb 178 D2
New Road Side N Yorks 146 C3
New Romney Kent 38 C2
New Rossington S Yorks 140 D4
New Row Ceredig 75 A6
New Row Lancs 145 D6
New Row N Yorks 168 D4
New Sarum Wilts 31 B5
New Silksworth T & W 179 D5
New Stevenston N Lnrk 194 A2
New Street Staffs 129 D5
New Street Lane Shrops 111 B5
New Swanage Dorset 17 C4
New Totley S Yorks 130 B3
New Town E Loth 210 C1
New Tredegar = Tredegar Newydd Caerph 41 A6
New Trows S Lnrk 194 C3
New Ulva Argyll 213 D5
New Walsoken Cambs 101 A6
New Waltham NE Lincs 143 C4
New Whittington Derbys 130 B3
New Wimpole Cambs 85 C5
New Winton E Loth 210 C1
New Yatt Oxon 65 B4
New York Lincs 134 D2
New York N Yorks 147 A5
Newall W Yorks 147 C5
Newark Orkney 282 C8
Newark P'boro 100 A4
Newark Castle Notts 132 D2
Newark-on-Trent Notts 132 D2
Newarthill N Lnrk 194 A2
Newbarns Cumb 153 C3
Newbattle Midloth 209 D6
Newbiggin Cumb 153 A1
Newbiggin Cumb 153 D3
Newbiggin Cumb 164 C2
Newbiggin Cumb 164 A3
Newbiggin Cumb 165 C4
Newbiggin Durham 166 C2
Newbiggin N Yorks 156 B3
Newbiggin N Yorks 156 C3
Newbiggin-by-the-Sea Northumb 179 A5
Newbiggin-on-Lune Cumb 155 A6
Newbigging Angus 220 A4
Newbigging Angus 221 A4
Newbigging S Lnrk 195 B5
Newbold Derbys 130 B3
Newbold Leics 114 D2
Newbold on Avon Warks 98 D1
Newbold on Stour Warks 81 C5
Newbold Pacey Warks 81 B5
Newbold Verdon Leics 98 A1
Newborough Anglesey 123 D4
Newborough P'boro 100 A4
Newborough Staffs 113 C5
Newbottle Northants 82 D2
Newbottle T & W 179 D5
Newbourne Suff 88 C3
Newbridge Caerph 41 B7
Newbridge Ceredig 75 C4
Newbridge Corn 2 B2
Newbridge Corn 6 A2
Newbridge Dumfries 174 A2
Newbridge Edin 208 C4
Newbridge Hants 32 D1
Newbridge I o W 18 C3
Newbridge Pembs 55 A5
Newbridge Green Worcs 79 D6
Newbridge-on-Usk Mon 61 D5
Newbridge on Wye Powys 76 B4
Newbrough Northumb 177 C6
Newbuildings Devon 12 A2
Newburgh Aberds 257 D4
Newburgh Aberds 269 D4
Newburgh Borders 185 A6
Newburgh Fife 220 C2
Newburgh Lancs 136 B3
Newburn T & W 178 C3
Newbury W Berks 46 C2
Newbury Park London 50 A1
Newbury Racecourse W Berks 46 C2
Newby Cumb 164 C3
Newby Lancs 146 C2
Newby N Yorks 155 D6
Newby N Yorks 168 D3
Newby N Yorks 160 B4
Newby Bridge Cumb 154 C2
Newby East Cumb 176 D2
Newby Hall, Ripon N Yorks 148 A2
Newby West Cumb 175 C6
Newby Wiske N Yorks 158 C2
Newcastle Mon 61 B6
Newcastle Shrops 93 C6
Newcastle Discovery T & W 179 C4
Newcastle Emlyn = Castell Newydd Emlyn Carms 73 B6
Newcastle International Airport T & W 178 B3
Newcastle Racecourse T & W 179 B4
Newcastle-under-Lyme Staffs 112 A2
Newcastle Upon Tyne T & W 179 C4
Newcastleton = Copshaw Holm Borders 176 A2
Newchapel Pembs 73 C5
Newchapel Powys 92 C3
Newchapel Staffs 128 D3
Newchapel Sur 35 B6
Newchurch Carms 73 D6
Newchurch I o W 19 C4
Newchurch Kent 38 B2
Newchurch Lancs 146 D2
Newchurch Mon 61 D6
Newchurch Powys 77 B6
Newchurch Staffs 113 C5
Newcott Devon 14 A2
Newcraighall Edin 209 C6
Newdigate Sur 35 B4
Newell Green Brack 48 B1
Newenden Kent 37 D6
Newent Glos 62 A3
Newerne Glos 62 C2
Newfield Durham 167 B5
Newfield Highld 264 C3
Newford Scilly 2 E4
Newfound Hants 46 D3
Newgale Pembs 54 B4
Newgate Norf 120 A2
Newgate Street Herts 68 C3
Newhall Ches 111 A5
Newhall Derbys 113 C6
Newhall House Highld 264 D2
Newhall Point Highld 264 D3
Newham Northumb 189 A4
Newham Hall Northumb 189 A4
Newhaven Derbys 129 D6
Newhaven Edin 209 C5
Newhaven E Sus 22 B2
Newhey Gtr Man 138 B2
Newholm N Yorks 169 D6
Newhouse N Lnrk 207 D5
Newick E Sus 36 D2
Newingreen Kent 38 B3
Newington Kent 51 C5
Newington Kent 38 B3
Newington Kent 53 C5
Newington Notts 141 D4
Newington Oxon 65 D7
Newington Shrops 94 C2
Newland Glos 62 C1
Newland Hull 150 D3
Newland N Yorks 141 A4
Newland Worcs 79 C5
Newlandrig Midloth 209 D6
Newlands Borders 186 D4
Newlands Highld 252 B3
Newlands Moray 266 D4
Newlands Northumb 178 D2
Newland's Corner Sur 34 B3
Newlands of Geise Highld 280 B2
Newlands of Tynet Moray 267 C4
Newlands Park Anglesey 122 B2
Newlandsmuir S Lnrk 205 C6
Newlot Orkney 282 F6
Newlyn Corn 2 C2
Newmachar Aberds 245 A5
Newmains N Lnrk 194 A3
Newmarket Suff 86 A2
Newmarket W Isles 288 D5
Newmarket Racecourse Suff 86 A2
Newmill Borders 186 B3
Newmill Corn 2 B2
Newmill Moray 267 D5
Newmill of Inshewan Angus 232 B2
Newmills of Boyne Aberds 267 D6
Newmiln Perth 219 A6
Newmilns E Ayrs 193 B5
Newnham Cambs 85 B6
Newnham Glos 62 B2
Newnham Hants 47 D5
Newnham Herts 84 D4
Newnham Kent 51 D6
Newnham Northants 82 B2
Newnham Bridge Worcs 79 A4
Newpark Fife 221 C4
Newport Devon 25 B6
Newport E Yorks 150 D1
Newport Essex 85 D7
Newport Highld 275 B5
Newport I o W 18 C4
Newport Norf 121 D7
Newport Telford 111 D6
Newport = Casnewydd Newport 42 A2
Newport = Trefdraeth Pembs 72 C3
Newport Museum & Art Gallery Newport 42 A2
Newport-on-Tay Fife 220 B4
Newport Pagnell M Keynes 83 C5
Newpound Common W Sus 34 D3
Newquay Corn 4 A3
Newquay Airport Corn 4 A3
Newquay Sea Life Centre Corn 4 A2
Newsbank Ches 128 C3
Newseat Aberds 256 C2
Newseat Aberds 257 B5
Newsham Northumb 179 B5
Newsham N Yorks 166 D4
Newsham N Yorks 158 C2
Newsholme E Yorks 141 A5
Newsholme Lancs 146 B2
Newsome W Yorks 139 B4
Newstead Borders 197 C4
Newstead Notts 131 D5
Newstead Northumb 189 A4
Newstead Abbey, Kirkby in Ashfield Notts 131 D5
Newthorpe N Yorks 148 D3
Newton Argyll 214 C3
Newton Borders 187 A5
Newton Bridgend 40 D3
Newton Cambs 85 C6
Newton Cambs 118 D1
Newton Cardiff 42 B1
Newton Ches 127 D5
Newton Ches 127 C4
Newton Ches 127 B5
Newton Cumb 153 C3
Newton Derbys 131 D4
Newton Dorset 30 D1
Newton Dumfries 185 C4
Newton Dumfries 175 A5
Newton Gtr Man 138 D2
Newton Hereford 78 D1
Newton Hereford 78 B3
Newton Highld 264 D3
Newton Highld 271 A5
Newton Highld 281 D5
Newton Highld 252 B3
Newton Lancs 144 D4
Newton Lancs 145 B6
Newton Lancs 155 D4
Newton Lincs 116 B3
Newton Moray 266 C2
Newton Norf 119 D5
Newton Notts 115 A4
Newton Northants 99 C5
Newton Northumb 178 C2
Newton Perth 218 A3
Newton S Lnrk 205 B6
Newton S Lnrk 194 C4
Newton Staffs 112 C4
Newton Suff 87 C5
Newton Swansea 57 D6
Newton S Yorks 140 C3
Newton Warks 98 D2
Newton Wilts 31 C6
Newton W Loth 208 C3
Newton Abbot Devon 12 D3
Newton Abbot Racecourse Devon 12 D3
Newton Arlosh Cumb 175 C4
Newton Aycliffe Durham 167 C5
Newton Bewley Hrtlpl 168 C2
Newton Blossomville M Keynes 83 B6
Newton Bromswold Northants 84 A1
Newton Burgoland Leics 97 A6
Newton by Toft Lincs 133 A5
Newton Ferrers Devon 7 C4
Newton Flotman Norf 104 B3
Newton Hall Northumb 178 C2
Newton Harcourt Leics 98 B3
Newton Heath Gtr Man 138 C1
Newton Ho. Aberds 256 D1
Newton Kyme N Yorks 148 C3
Newton-le-Willows Mers 137 D4
Newton-le-Willows N Yorks 157 C6
Newton Longville Bucks 83 D5
Newton Mearns E Renf 205 C5
Newton Morrell N Yorks 157 A6
Newton Mulgrave N Yorks 169 D5
Newton of Ardtoe Highld 235 C5
Newton of Balcanquhal Perth 219 C6
Newton of Falkland Fife 220 D2
Newton on Ayr S Ayrs 192 C3
Newton on Ouse N Yorks 148 B4
Newton-on-Rawcliffe N Yorks 159 B7
Newton-on-the-Moor Northumb 189 C4
Newton on Trent Lincs 132 B3
Newton Park Argyll 203 B6
Newton Poppleford Devon 13 C5
Newton Purcell Oxon 82 D3
Newton Regis Warks 97 A5
Newton Reigny Cumb 164 B2
Newton St Cyres Devon 12 B3
Newton St Faith Norf 120 D4
Newton St Loe Bath 43 C6
Newton St Petrock Devon 25 D5
Newton Solney Derbys 113 C6
Newton Stacey Hants 32 A3
Newton Stewart Dumfries 171 A6
Newton Tony Wilts 31 A6
Newton Tracey Devon 25 C6
Newton under Roseberry Redcar 168 D3
Newton upon Derwent E Yorks 149 C6
Newton Valence Hants 33 B6
Newtonairds Dumfries 183 D6
Newtongrange Midloth 209 D6
Newtonhill Aberds 245 C6
Newtonhill Highld 252 B1
Newtonmill Angus 233 B4
Newtonmore Highld 241 C5
Newtown Argyll 214 B3
Newtown Ches 127 B5
Newtown Corn 3 C5
Newtown Cumb 174 D3
Newtown Cumb 176 C3
Newtown Derbys 129 A4
Newtown Devon 26 C2
Newtown Glos 62 C2
Newtown Glos 80 D2
Newtown Hants 31 D6
Newtown Hants 32 C2
Newtown Hants 33 D5
Newtown Hants 46 C2
Newtown Hants 32 D4
Newtown Hants 18 A3
Newtown Hereford 79 C4
Newtown Highld 240 B1
Newtown I o M 152 D3
Newtown I o W 18 B3
Newtown Northumb 188 C3
Newtown Northumb 188 A3
Newtown Northumb 198 C3
Newtown Poole 17 B4
Newtown Shrops 110 B3
Newtown Staffs 129 C4
Newtown Staffs 129 C5
Newtown Wilts 30 C3
Newtown = Y Drenewydd Powys 93 B5
Newtown Linford Leics 98 A2
Newtown St Boswells Borders 197 C4
Newtown Unthank Leics 98 A1
Newtyle Angus 231 D6
Neyland Pembs 55 D5
Niarbyl I o M 152 D2
Nibley S Glos 43 A5
Nibley Green Glos 62 D3
Nibon Shetland 284 F5
Nicholashayne Devon 27 D6
Nicholaston Swansea 57 D5
Nidd N Yorks 148 A2
Nigg Aberdeen 245 B6
Nigg Highld 265 C4
Nigg Ferry Highld 264 D3
Nightcott Som 26 C3
Nilig Denb 125 D5
Nine Ashes Essex 69 C5
Nine Mile Burn Midloth 195 A6
Nine Wells Pembs 54 B3
Ninebanks Northumb 177 D5
Ninfield E Sus 23 A5
Ningwood I o W 18 C2
Nisbet Borders 187 A5
Nisthouse Orkney 282 F4
Nisthouse Shetland 285 G7
Niton I o W 18 D4
Nitshill Glasgow 205 B5
No Man's Heath Ches 111 A4
No Man's Heath Warks 97 A5
Noak Hill London 69 D5
Noblethorpe S Yorks 139 C5
Nobottle Northants 82 A3
Nocton Lincs 133 C5
Noke Oxon 65 B6
Nolton Pembs 55 C4
Nolton Haven Pembs 55 C4
Nomansland Devon 26 D3
Nomansland Wilts 31 D6
Noneley Shrops 110 C3
Nonikiln Highld 264 C2
Nonington Kent 53 D4
Noonsbrough Shetland 285 H4
Norbreck Blkpool 144 C3
Norbridge Hereford 79 C5
Norbury Ches 111 A4
Norbury Derbys 113 A5
Norbury Shrops 94 B1
Norbury Staffs 112 C1
Nordelph Norf 102 A1
Norden Gtr Man 138 B1
Norden Heath Dorset 16 C3
Nordley Shrops 95 B4
Norham Northumb 198 B3
Norley Ches 127 B5
Norleywood Hants 18 B2
Norman Cross Cambs 100 B3
Normanby N Lincs 141 B6
Normanby N Yorks 159 C6
Normanby Redcar 168 D3
Normanby-by-Spital Lincs 133 A5
Normanby by Stow Lincs 132 A3
Normanby le Wold Lincs 142 D3
Normandy Sur 34 A2
Norman's Bay E Sus 23 B4
Norman's Green Devon 13 A5
Normanstone Suff 105 B6
Normanton Derby 114 B1
Normanton Leics 115 A6
Normanton Lincs 116 A2
Normanton Notts 132 D2
Normanton Rutland 99 A6
Normanton W Yorks 140 A1
Normanton le Heath Leics 114 D1
Normanton on Soar Notts 114 C3
Normanton-on-the-Wolds Notts 115 B4
Normanton on Trent Notts 132 C2
Normoss Lancs 144 D3
Norney Sur 34 B2
Norrington Common Wilts 44 C2
Norris Green Mers 136 D2
Norris Hill Leics 114 D1
North Anston S Yorks 131 A5
North Aston Oxon 65 A5
North Baddesley Hants 32 D2
North Ballachulish Highld 237 C4
North Barrow Som 29 C6
North Barsham Norf 119 B6
North Benfleet Essex 51 A4
North Bersted W Sus 20 B2
North Berwick E Loth 210 B2
North Boarhunt Hants 33 D5
North Bovey Devon 12 C2
North Bradley Wilts 44 D2
North Brentor Devon 11 C5
North Brewham Som 29 B7
North Buckland Devon 25 A5
North Burlingham Norf 121 D5
North Cadbury Som 29 C6
North Cairn Dumfries 180 D1
North Carlton Lincs 133 B4
North Carrine Argyll 190 E2
North Cave E Yorks 150 D1
North Cerney Glos 63 C6
North Charford Wilts 31 D5
North Charlton Northumb 189 A4
North Cheriton Som 29 C6
North Cliff E Yorks 151 C5
North Cliffe E Yorks 150 D1
North Clifton Notts 132 B3
North Cockerington Lincs 143 D5
North Coker Som 29 D5
North Collafirth Shetland 284 E5
North Common E Sus 36 D1
North Connel Argyll 226 C4
North Cornelly Bridgend 40 C3
North Cotes Lincs 143 C5
North Cove Suff 105 C5
North Cowton N Yorks 157 A6
North Crawley M Keynes 83 C6
North Cray London 50 B1
North Creake Norf 119 B5
North Curry Som 28 C3
North Dalton E Yorks 150 B2
North Dawn Orkney 283 G5
North Deighton N Yorks 148 B2
North Duffield N Yorks 149 D5
North Elkington Lincs 143 D4
North Elmham Norf 120 C1
North Elmshall W Yorks 140 B2
North End Bucks 66 A3
North End E Yorks 151 D5
North End Essex 69 B6
North End Hants 46 C2
North End Lincs 117 A5
North End N Som 42 C3
North End Ptsmth 19 A5
North End Som 28 C2
North End W Sus 21 B4
North Erradale Highld 261 B4
North Fambridge Essex 70 D2
North Fearns Highld 248 C2
North Featherstone W Yorks 140 A2
North Ferriby E Yorks 142 A1
North Frodingham E Yorks 151 B4
North Gluss Shetland 284 F5
North Gorley Hants 31 D5
North Green Norf 104 C3
North Green Suff 89 A4
North Greetwell Lincs 133 B5
North Grimston N Yorks 150 A1
North Halley Orkney 283 G6
North Halling Medway 51 C4
North Hayling Hants 19 A6
North Hazelrigg Northumb 199 C4
North Heasley Devon 26 B2
North Heath W Sus 34 D3
North Hill Cambs 101 D6
North Hill Corn 10 D3
North Hinksey Oxon 65 C5
North Holmwood Sur 35 B4
North Howden E Yorks 149 D6
North Huish Devon 7 B6
North Hykeham Lincs 133 C4
North Johnston Pembs 55 C5
North Kelsey Lincs 142 C2
North Kelsey Moor Lincs 142 C2
North Kessock Highld 252 B2
North Killingholme N Lincs 142 B3
North Kilvington N Yorks 158 C3
North Kilworth Leics 98 C3
North Kirkton Aberds 269 D6
North Kiscadale N Ayrs 191 C6
North Kyme Lincs 133 D6
North Lancing W Sus 21 B4
North Lee Bucks 66 C3
North Leigh Oxon 65 B4
North Leverton with Habblesthorpe Notts 132 A2
North Littleton Worcs 80 C3
North Lopham Norf 103 C6
North Luffenham Rutland 99 A6
North Marden W Sus 33 D7
North Marston Bucks 66 A2
North Middleton Midloth 196 A2
North Middleton Northumb 188 A3
North Molton Devon 26 C2
North Moreton Oxon 46 A3
North Mundham W Sus 20 B1
North Muskham Notts 132 D2
North Newbald E Yorks 150 D2
North Newington Oxon 81 D7
North Newnton Wilts 45 D5
North Newton Som 28 B2
North Nibley Glos 62 D3
North Norfolk Railway, Sheringham Norf 120 A3
North Oakley Hants 46 D3
North Ockendon London 50 A2
North Ormesby M'bro 168 C3
North Ormsby Lincs 143 D4
North Otterington N Yorks 158 C2
North Owersby Lincs 142 D2
North Perrott Som 15 A4
North Petherton Som 28 B2
North Petherwin Corn 10 C3
North Pickenham Norf 103 A4
North Piddle Worcs 80 B2
North Poorton Dorset 15 B5
North Port Argyll 227 D5
North Queensferry Fife 208 B4
North Radworthy Devon 26 B2
North Rauceby Lincs 116 A3
North Reston Lincs 134 A3
North Rigton N Yorks 148 C1
North Rode Ches 128 C3
North Roe Shetland 284 E5
North Ronaldsay Airport Orkney 282 B8
North Runcton Norf 118 D3
North Sandwick Shetland 284 D7
North Scale Cumb 153 D2
North Scarle Lincs 132 C3
North Seaton Northumb 179 A4
North Shian Argyll 226 B4
North Shields T & W 179 C5
North Shoebury Sthend 51 A6
North Shore Blkpool 144 D3
North Side Cumb 162 B3
North Side P'boro 101 B4
North Skelton Redcar 169 D4
North Somercotes Lincs 143 D6
North Stainley N Yorks 157 D6
North Stainmore Cumb 165 D6
North Stifford Thurrock 50 A3
North Stoke Bath 43 C6
North Stoke Oxon 47 A4
North Stoke W Sus 20 A3
North Street Hants 33 B5
North Street Kent 52 D2
North Street Medway 51 B5
North Street W Berks 47 B4
North Sunderland Northumb 199 C6
North Tamerton Corn 10 B4
North Tawton Devon 12 A1
North Thoresby Lincs 143 D4
North Tidworth Wilts 31 A6
North Togston Northumb 189 C5
North Tuddenham Norf 120 D2
North Walbottle T & W 178 C3
North Walsham Norf 121 B4
North Waltham Hants 33 A4
North Warnborough Hants 47 D5
North Water Bridge Angus 233 B4

North Watten Highld 280 C4
North Weald Bassett Essex 69 C4
North Wheatley Notts 132 A2
North Whilborough Devon 8 A2
North Wick Bath 43 C4
North Willingham Lincs 133 A6
North Wingfield Derbys 131 C4
North Witham Lincs 116 C2
North Woolwich London 50 B1
North Wootton Dorset 29 D6
North Wootton Norf 118 C3
North Wootton Som 29 A5
North Wraxall Wilts 44 B2
North Wroughton Swindon 45 A5
North Yorkshire Moors Railway, Pickering N Yorks 160 C2
Northacre Norf 103 B5
Northallerton N Yorks 158 B2
Northam Devon 25 C5
Northam Soton 32 D3
Northampton Northants 83 A4
Northaw Herts 68 C2
Northbeck Lincs 116 A3
Northborough P'boro 100 A3
Northbourne Kent 53 D5
Northbridge Street E Sus 37 D5
Northchapel W Sus 34 D2
Northchurch Herts 67 C4
Northcott Devon 10 B4
Northdown Kent 53 B5
Northdyke Orkney 282 E3
Northend Bath 44 C1
Northend Bucks 66 D2
Northend Warks 81 B6
Northenden Gtr Man 137 D7
Northfield Aberdeen 245 B6
Northfield Borders 211 D6
Northfield E Yorks 142 A2
Northfield W Mid 96 D3
Northfields Lincs 100 A2
Northfleet Kent 50 B3
Northgate Lincs 117 C4
Northhouse Borders 186 C3
Northiam E Sus 37 D6
Northill Beds 84 C3
Northington Hants 33 B4
Northlands Lincs 134 D3
Northlea Durham 179 D6
Northleach Glos 64 B2
Northleigh Devon 14 B1
Northlew Devon 11 B6
Northmoor Oxon 65 C5
Northmoor Green or Moorland Som 28 B3
Northmuir Angus 232 C1
Northney Hants 19 A6
Northolt London 48 A4
Northop Flint 126 C2
Northop Hall Flint 126 C2
Northorpe Lincs 116 D3
Northorpe Lincs 117 B5
Northorpe Lincs 141 D6
Northover Som 29 B4
Northover Som 29 C5
Northowram W Yorks 139 A4
Northport Dorset 16 C3
Northpunds Shetland 285 L6
Northrepps Norf 120 B4
Northtown Orkney 283 H5
Northumbria Craft Centre, Morpeth Northumb 178 A3
Northway Glos 80 D2
Northwich Ches 127 B6
Northwick S Glos 43 A4
Northwold Norf 102 B3
Northwood Derbys 130 C2
Northwood London 67 D5
Northwood I o W 18 B3
Northwood Kent 53 C5
Northwood Shrops 110 B3
Northwood Green Glos 62 B3
Norton E Sus 22 B2
Norton Glos 63 A4
Norton Halton 127 A5
Norton Herts 84 D4
Norton I o W 18 C2
Norton Mon 61 B6
Norton Notts 131 B5
Norton Northants 82 A3
Norton Powys 77 A7
Norton Shrops 94 C2
Norton Shrops 94 A3
Norton Shrops 95 A5
Norton Stockton 168 C2
Norton Suff 87 A5
Norton S Yorks 140 B3
Norton Wilts 44 A2
Norton Worcs 80 B1
Norton Worcs 80 C3
Norton W Sus 20 C1
Norton W Sus 20 B2
Norton Bavant Wilts 30 A3
Norton Bridge Staffs 112 B2
Norton Canes Staffs 96 A3
Norton Canon Hereford 78 C1
Norton Corner Norf 120 C2
Norton Disney Lincs 132 D3
Norton East Staffs 96 A3
Norton Ferris Wilts 30 B1
Norton Fitzwarren Som 28 C1
Norton Green I o W 18 C2
Norton Hawkfield Bath 43 C4
Norton Heath Essex 69 C6
Norton in Hales Shrops 111 B6
Norton-in-the-Moors Stoke 128 D3
Norton-Juxta-Twycross Leics 97 A6
Norton-le-Clay N Yorks 158 D3
Norton Lindsey Warks 81 A5
Norton Malreward Bath 43 C5
Norton Mandeville Essex 69 C5
Norton-on-Derwent N Yorks 159 D6
Norton St Philip Som 43 D6
Norton sub Hamdon Som 29 D4
Norton Woodseats S Yorks 130 A3
Norwell Notts 132 C2
Norwell Woodhouse Notts 132 C2
Norwich Norf 104 A3
Norwich Castle Museum Norf 104 A3
Norwich Cathedral Norf 104 A3
Norwich International Airport Norf 120 D4
Norwick Shetland 284 B8
Norwood Derbys 131 A4
Norwood Hill Sur 35 B5
Norwoodside Cambs 101 B6
Noseley Leics 99 B4
Noss Shetland 285 M5
Noss Mayo Devon 7 C4
Nosterfield N Yorks 157 C6
Nostie Highld 249 D5
Notgrove Glos 64 A2
Nothe Fort, Weymouth Dorset 15 D6
Nottage Bridgend 40 D3
Nottingham Nottingham 114 B3
Nottingham Castle Museum Nottingham 114 B3
Nottingham East Midlands Airport Leics 114 C2
Nottingham Racecourse Nottingham 114 B3
Nottington Dorset 15 C6
Notton Wilts 44 C3
Notton W Yorks 139 B6
Nounsley Essex 70 B1
Noutard's Green Worcs 79 A5
Novar House Highld 264 D2
Nox Shrops 110 D3
Nuffield Oxon 47 A4
Nun Hills Lancs 138 A1
Nun Monkton N Yorks 148 B4
Nunburnholme E Yorks 150 C1
Nuncargate Notts 131 D5
Nuneaton Warks 97 B6
Nuneham Courtenay Oxon 65 D6
Nunney Som 30 A1
Nunnington N Yorks 159 D5
Nunnykirk Northumb 188 D3
Nunsthorpe NE Lincs 143 C4
Nunthorpe M'bro 168 D3
Nunthorpe York 149 B5
Nunton Wilts 31 C5
Nunwick N Yorks 157 D7
Nupend Glos 62 C3
Nursling Hants 32 D2
Nursted Hants 33 C6
Nutbourne W Sus 20 A3
Nutbourne W Sus 19 A6
Nutfield Sur 35 A6
Nuthall Notts 114 A3
Nuthampstead Herts 85 D6
Nuthurst W Sus 35 D4
Nutley E Sus 36 D2
Nutley Hants 33 A5
Nutwell S Yorks 140 C4
Nybster Highld 281 B5
Nyetimber W Sus 20 C1
Nyewood W Sus 33 C7
Nymans Garden, Crawley W Sus 35 D5
Nymet Rowland Devon 12 A2
Nymet Tracey Devon 12 A2
Nympsfield Glos 63 C4
Nynehead Som 27 C6
Nyton W Sus 20 B2

O

Oad Street Kent 51 C5
Oadby Leics 98 A3
Oak Cross Devon 11 B6
Oakamoor Staffs 113 A4
Oakbank W Loth 208 D3
Oakdale Caerph 41 B6
Oake Som 27 C6
Oaken Staffs 95 A6
Oakenclough Lancs 145 C5
Oakengates Telford 111 D6
Oakenholt Flint 126 B2
Oakenshaw Durham 167 B5
Oakenshaw W Yorks 139 A4
Oakerthorpe Derbys 130 D3
Oakes W Yorks 139 B4
Oakfield Torf 61 D5
Oakford Ceredig 74 C3
Oakford Devon 27 C4
Oakfordbridge Devon 27 C4
Oakgrove Ches 129 C4
Oakham Rutland 99 A5
Oakhanger Hants 33 B6
Oakhill Som 29 A6
Oakhurst Kent 36 A3
Oakington Cambs 85 A6
Oaklands Herts 68 B2
Oaklands Powys 76 B4
Oakle Street Glos 62 B3
Oakley Beds 84 B2
Oakley Bucks 66 B1
Oakley Fife 208 B3
Oakley Hants 46 D3
Oakley Oxon 66 C2
Oakley Poole 17 B4
Oakley Suff 104 D2
Oakley Green Windsor 48 B2
Oakley Park Powys 92 C3
Oakmere Ches 127 C5
Oakridge Glos 63 C5
Oakridge Hants 47 D4
Oaks Shrops 94 A2
Oaks Green Derbys 113 B5
Oaksey Wilts 63 D5
Oakthorpe Leics 113 D7
Oakwood Adventure Park, Narberth Pembs 55 C6
Oakwoodhill Sur 35 C4
Oakworth W Yorks 147 D4
Oape Highld 272 D2
Oare Kent 52 C2
Oare Som 26 A3
Oare W Berks 46 B3
Oare Wilts 45 C5
Oasby Lincs 116 B3
Oathlaw Angus 232 C2
Oatlands N Yorks 148 B2
Oban Argyll 226 D3
Oban Highld 238 D2
Oborne Dorset 29 D6
Obthorpe Lincs 116 D3
Occlestone Green Ches 128 C1
Occold Suff 104 D2
Ochiltree E Ayrs 193 C5
Ochtermuthill Perth 218 C3
Ochtertyre Perth 218 B3
Ockbrook Derbys 114 B2
Ockham Sur 34 A3
Ockle Highld 235 C4
Ockley Sur 35 C4
Ocle Pychard Hereford 78 C3
Octon E Yorks 150 A3
Octon Cross Roads E Yorks 150 A3
Odcombe Som 29 D5
Odd Down Bath 43 C6
Oddendale Cumb 164 D3
Odder Lincs 133 B4
Oddingley Worcs 80 B2
Oddington Glos 64 A3
Oddington Oxon 65 B6
Odell Beds 83 B6
Odie Orkney 282 E7
Odiham Hants 47 D5
Odstock Wilts 31 C5
Odstone Leics 97 A6
Offchurch Warks 81 A6
Offenham Worcs 80 C3
Offham E Sus 22 A1
Offham Kent 37 A4
Offham W Sus 20 B3
Offord Cluny Cambs 84 A4
Offord Darcy Cambs 84 A4
Offton Suff 87 C6
Offwell Devon 14 B1
Ogbourne Maizey Wilts 45 B5
Ogbourne St Andrew Wilts 45 B5
Ogbourne St George Wilts 45 B6
Ogil Angus 232 B2
Ogle Northumb 178 B3
Ogmore V Glam 40 D3
Ogmore-by-Sea V Glam 40 D3
Ogmore Vale Bridgend 40 B4
Okeford Fitzpaine Dorset 30 D2
Okehampton Devon 11 B6
Okehampton Camp Devon 11 B6
Okraquoy Shetland 285 K6
Old Northants 99 D4
Old Aberdeen Aberdeen 245 B6
Old Alresford Hants 33 B4
Old Arley Warks 97 B5
Old Basford Nottingham 114 A3
Old Basing Hants 47 D4
Old Bewick Northumb 188 A3
Old Blacksmith's Shop Centre, Gretna Green Dumfries 175 B6
Old Bolingbroke Lincs 134 C3
Old Bramhope W Yorks 147 C6
Old Brampton Derbys 130 B3
Old Bridge of Tilt Perth 230 B2
Old Bridge of Urr Dumfries 173 B5
Old Buckenham Norf 103 B6
Old Burghclere Hants 46 D2
Old Byland N Yorks 159 C4
Old Cassop Durham 167 B6
Old Castleton Borders 186 D4
Old Catton Norf 120 D4
Old Clee NE Lincs 143 C4
Old Cleeve Som 27 A5
Old Clipstone Notts 131 C6
Old Colwyn Conwy 124 B3
Old Coulsdon London 35 A6
Old Crombie Aberds 267 D6
Old Dailly S Ayrs 181 B4
Old Dalby Leics 115 C4
Old Deer Aberds 257 B4
Old Denaby S Yorks 140 D2
Old Edlington S Yorks 140 D3
Old Eldon Durham 167 C5
Old Ellerby E Yorks 151 D4
Old Felixstowe Suff 88 D4
Old Fletton P'boro 100 B3
Old Glossop Derbys 138 D3
Old Goole E Yorks 141 A5
Old Hall Powys 91 D7
Old Heath Essex 71 A4
Old Heathfield E Sus 36 D3
Old Hill W Mid 96 C2
Old House, Rochford Essex 70 D2
Old Hunstanton Norf 118 A3
Old Hurst Cambs 101 D4
Old Hutton Cumb 155 C4
Old Kea Corn 4 C3
Old Kilpatrick W Dunb 205 A4
Old Kinnernie Aberds 245 B4
Old Knebworth Herts 68 A2
Old Langho Lancs 145 D7
Old Laxey I o M 152 C4
Old Leake Lincs 135 D4
Old Malton N Yorks 159 D6
Old Micklefield W Yorks 148 D3
Old Milton Hants 17 B6
Old Milverton Warks 81 A5
Old Monkland N Lnrk 207 D5
Old Netley Hants 18 A3
Old Philpstoun W Loth 208 C3
Old Quarrington Durham 167 B6
Old Radnor Powys 77 B6
Old Rattray Aberds 269 D5
Old Rayne Aberds 256 D1
Old Romney Kent 38 C2
Old Sarum, Salisbury Wilts 31 B5
Old Sodbury S Glos 43 A6
Old Somerby Lincs 116 B2
Old Stratford Northants 83 C4
Old Thirsk N Yorks 158 C3
Old Town Cumb 164 A2
Old Town Cumb 155 C4
Old Town Northumb 188 D1
Old Town Scilly 2 E4
Old Trafford Gtr Man 137 D7
Old Tupton Derbys 130 C3
Old Warden Beds 84 C3
Old Weston Cambs 100 D2
Old Whittington Derbys 130 B3
Old Wick Highld 281 C5
Old Windsor Windsor 48 B2
Old Wives Lees Kent 52 D2
Old Woking Sur 34 A3
Old Woodhall Lincs 134 C2
Oldany Highld 270 A4
Oldberrow Warks 80 A4
Oldborough Devon 12 A2
Oldbury Shrops 95 B5
Oldbury Warks 97 B6
Oldbury W Mid 96 C2
Oldbury-on-Severn S Glos 62 D2
Oldbury on the Hill Glos 44 A2
Oldcastle Bridgend 40 D4
Oldcastle Mon 61 A5
Oldcotes Notts 131 A5
Oldfallow Staffs 112 D3
Oldfield Worcs 79 A6
Oldford Som 44 D1
Oldham Gtr Man 138 C2
Oldhamstocks E Loth 211 C4
Oldland S Glos 43 B5
Oldmeldrum Aberds 256 D3
Oldshore Beg Highld 276 C2
Oldshoremore Highld 276 C3
Oldstead N Yorks 158 C4
Oldtown Aberds 255 D6
Oldtown of Ord Aberds 267 D7
Oldway Swansea 57 D5
Oldways End Devon 26 C3
Oldwhat Aberds 268 D3
Olgrinmore Highld 280 C2
Oliver's Battery Hants 32 C3
Ollaberry Shetland 284 E5
Ollerton Ches 128 B2
Ollerton Notts 131 C6
Ollerton Shrops 111 C5
Olmarch Ceredig 75 C5
Olney M Keynes 83 B5
Olrig Ho. Highld 280 B3
Olton W Mid 96 C4
Olveston S Glos 43 A5
Olwen Ceredig 75 D4
Ombersley Worcs 79 A6
Ompton Notts 132 C1
Onchan I o M 152 D3
Onecote Staffs 129 D5
Onen Mon 61 B6
Ongar Hill Norf 118 C2
Ongar Street Hereford 78 A1
Onibury Shrops 94 D2
Onich Highld 237 C4
Onllwyn Neath 59 D5
Onneley Staffs 111 A6
Onslow Village Sur 34 B2
Onthank E Ayrs 205 D4
Openwoodgate Derbys 114 A1
Opinan Highld 261 A5
Opinan Highld 261 C4
Orange Lane Borders 198 B1
Orange Row Norf 118 C2
Orasaigh W Isles 288 F4
Orbliston Moray 266 D4
Orbost Highld 258 D2
Orby Lincs 135 C4
Orchard Hill Devon 25 C5
Orchard Portman Som 28 C2
Orcheston Wilts 31 A4
Orcop Hereford 61 A6
Orcop Hill Hereford 61 A6
Ord Highld 247 C5
Ordhead Aberds 244 A3
Ordie Aberds 244 B1
Ordiequish Moray 266 D4
Ordsall Notts 132 A1
Ore E Sus 23 A6
Oreton Shrops 95 C4
Orford Suff 89 C5
Orford Warr 137 D5
Orgreave Staffs 113 D5
Orlestone Kent 38 B1
Orleton Hereford 78 A2
Orleton Worcs 79 A4
Orlingbury Northants 99 D5
Ormesby Redcar 168 D3
Ormesby St Margaret Norf 121 D6
Ormesby St Michael Norf 121 D6
Ormiclate Castle W Isles 286 C3
Ormiscaig Highld 261 A5
Ormiston E Loth 209 D7
Ormsaigbeg Highld 234 D3
Ormsaigmore Highld 234 D3
Ormsary Argyll 202 A2
Ormsgill Cumb 153 C2
Ormskirk Lancs 136 C3
Orpington London 50 C1
Orrell Gtr Man 136 C4
Orrell Mers 136 D2
Orrisdale I o M 152 B3
Orroland Dumfries 173 D5
Orsett Thurrock 50 A3
Orslow Staffs 112 D2
Orston Notts 115 A5
Orthwaite Cumb 163 A5
Ortner Lancs 145 B5
Orton Cumb 155 A5
Orton Northants 99 D5
Orton Longueville P'boro 100 B3
Orton-on-the-Hill Leics 97 A6
Orton Waterville P'boro 100 B3
Orwell Cambs 85 B5
Osbaldeston Lancs 145 D6
Osbaldwick York 149 B5
Osbaston Shrops 110 C2
Osborne House I o W 18 B4
Osbournby Lincs 116 B3
Oscroft Ches 127 C5
Ose Highld 258 D3
Osgathorpe Leics 114 D2
Osgodby Lincs 142 D2
Osgodby N Yorks 149 D5
Osgodby N Yorks 161 C4
Oskaig Highld 248 C2
Oskamull Argyll 224 B3
Osmaston Derbys 113 A6
Osmaston Derby 114 B1
Osmington Dorset 16 C1
Osmington Mills Dorset 16 C1
Osmotherley N Yorks 158 B3
Ospisdale Highld 264 B3
Ospringe Kent 52 C2
Ossett W Yorks 139 A5
Ossington Notts 132 C2
Ostend Essex 70 D3
Oswaldkirk N Yorks 159 D5
Oswaldtwistle Lancs 137 A6
Oswestry Shrops 110 C1
Otford Kent 36 A3
Otham Kent 37 A5
Othery Som 28 B3
Otley Suff 88 B3
Otley W Yorks 147 C6
Otter Ferry Argyll 214 D2
Otterbourne Hants 32 C3
Otterburn Northumb 188 D1
Otterburn N Yorks 146 B2
Otterburn Camp Northumb 188 D1
Otterham Corn 10 B2
Otterhampton Som 28 A2
Ottershaw Sur 48 C3
Otterswick Shetland 284 E7
Otterton Devon 13 C5
Ottery St Mary Devon 13 B6
Ottinge Kent 38 A3
Ottringham E Yorks 143 A4
Oughterby Cumb 175 C5
Oughtershaw N Yorks 156 C2
Oughterside Cumb 174 D4
Oughtibridge S Yorks 139 D6
Oughtrington Warr 128 A1
Oulston N Yorks 158 D4
Oulton Cumb 175 C5
Oulton Norf 120 C3
Oulton Staffs 112 B3
Oulton Suff 105 B6
Oulton W Yorks 139 A6
Oulton Broad Suff 105 B6
Oulton Park Motor Racing Circuit Ches 127 C5
Oulton Street Norf 120 C3
Oundle Northants 100 C2
Ousby Cumb 165 B4
Ousdale Highld 275 B4
Ousden Suff 86 B3
Ousefleet E Yorks 141 A6
Ouston Durham 179 D4
Ouston Northumb 178 B2
Out Newton E Yorks 143 A5
Out Rawcliffe Lancs 144 C4
Outertown Orkney 282 F3
Outgate Cumb 154 B2
Outhgill Cumb 155 A6
Outlane W Yorks 138 B3
Outwell Norf 101 A7
Outwick Hants 31 D5
Outwood Sur 35 B6
Outwood W Yorks 139 A6
Outwoods Staffs 112 D1
Ovenden W Yorks 138 A3
Ovenscloss Borders 196 C3
Over Cambs 101 D5
Over Ches 127 C6
Over S Glos 43 A4
Over Compton Dorset 29 D5
Over Green W Mid 97 B4
Over Haddon Derbys 130 C2
Over Hulton Gtr Man 137 C5
Over Kellet Lancs 154 D4
Over Kiddington Oxon 65 A5
Over Knutsford Ches 128 B2
Over Monnow Mon 61 B7
Over Norton Oxon 64 A4
Over Peover Ches 128 B2
Over Silton N Yorks 158 B3
Over Stowey Som 28 B1
Over Stratton Som 28 D4
Over Tabley Ches 128 A2
Over Wallop Hants 32 B1
Over Whitacre Warks 97 B5
Over Worton Oxon 65 A5
Overbister Orkney 282 C7
Overbury Worcs 80 D2
Overcombe Dorset 15 C6
Overgreen Derbys 130 B3
Overleigh Som 29 B4
Overley Green Warks 80 B3
Overpool Ches 126 B3
Overscaig Hotel Highld 271 B7
Overseal Derbys 113 D6
Oversland Kent 52 D2
Overstone Northants 83 A5
Overstrand Norf 120 A4
Overthorpe Northants 82 C1
Overton Aberdeen 245 A5
Overton Ches 127 B5
Overton Dumfries 174 B2
Overton Hants 32 A4
Overton Lancs 144 B4
Overton N Yorks 149 B4
Overton Shrops 94 D3
Overton Swansea 57 D4
Overton W Yorks 139 B5
Overton = Owrtyn Wrex 110 A2
Overton Bridge Wrex 110 A2
Overtown N Lnrk 194 A3
Oving Bucks 66 A2
Oving W Sus 20 B2
Ovingdean Brighton 21 B6
Ovingham Northumb 178 C2
Ovington Durham 166 D4
Ovington Essex 86 C3
Ovington Hants 33 B4
Ovington Norf 103 A5
Ovington Northumb 178 C2
Ower Hants 32 D2
Owermoigne Dorset 16 C1
Owlbury Shrops 93 B7
Owler Bar Derbys 130 B2
Owlerton S Yorks 130 A3
Owl's Green Suff 88 A3
Owlswick Bucks 66 C2
Owmby Lincs 142 C2

Owmby-by-Spital Lincs 133 A5
Owrtyn = Overton Wrex 110 A2
Owslebury Hants 32 C4
Owston Leics 99 A4
Owston S Yorks 140 B3
Owston Ferry N Lincs 141 C6
Owstwick E Yorks 151 D5
Owthorne E Yorks 143 A5
Owthorpe Notts 115 B4
Oxborough Norf 102 A3
Oxburgh Hall Norf 102 A3
Oxcombe Lincs 134 B3
Oxen Park Cumb 154 C2
Oxenholme Cumb 154 C4
Oxenhope W Yorks 147 D4
Oxenton Glos 80 D2
Oxenwood Wilts 45 D7
Oxford Oxon 65 C6
Oxford University Botanic Garden Oxon 65 C6
Oxhey Herts 67 D6
Oxhill Warks 81 C6
Oxley W Mid 96 A2
Oxley Green Essex 70 B3
Oxley's Green E Sus 37 D4
Oxnam Borders 187 B6
Oxshott Sur 48 C4
Oxspring S Yorks 139 C5
Oxted Sur 36 A1
Oxton Borders 196 A3
Oxton Notts 131 D6
Oxwich Swansea 57 D4
Oxwick Norf 119 C6
Oykel Bridge Highld 271 D6
Oyne Aberds 256 D1

P

Pabail Iarach W Isles 288 D6
Pabail Uarach W Isles 288 D6
Pace Gate N Yorks 147 B5
Packington Leics 114 D1
Padanaram Angus 232 C2
Padbury Bucks 83 D4
Paddington London 49 A5
Paddlesworth Kent 38 B3
Paddock Wood Kent 37 B4
Paddockhaugh Moray 266 D3
Paddockhole Dumfries 185 D5
Padfield Derbys 138 D3
Padiham Lancs 146 D1
Padog Conwy 124 D3
Padside N Yorks 147 B5
Padstow Corn 9 D5
Padworth W Berks 47 C4
Page Bank Durham 167 B5
Pagelsham Eastend Essex 70 D3
Pagham W Sus 20 C1
Paglesham Churchend Essex 70 D3
Paibeil W Isles 287 H2
Paible W Isles 287 E5
Paignton Torbay 8 A2
Paignton & Dartmouth Steam Railway Devon 8 A2
Paignton Zoo Torbay 8 B2
Pailton Warks 98 C1
Painscastle Powys 77 C5
Painshawfield Northumb 178 C2
Painsthorpe E Yorks 149 B7
Painswick Glos 63 C4
Pairc Shiaboist W Isles 288 C3
Paisley Renfs 205 B4
Pakefield Suff 105 B6
Pakenham Suff 87 A5
Palace House, Beaulieu Hants 18 A2
Palace of Holyroodhouse Edin 209 C5
Pale Gwyn 109 B4
Palestine Hants 31 A6
Paley Street Windsor 47 B6
Palfrey W Mid 96 B3
Palgowan Dumfries 181 C5
Palgrave Suff 104 D2
Pallion T & W 179 D5
Palmarsh Kent 38 B3
Palnackie Dumfries 173 C6
Palnure Dumfries 171 A6
Palterton Derbys 131 C4
Pamber End Hants 47 D4
Pamber Green Hants 47 D4
Pamber Heath Hants 47 C4
Pamphill Dorset 16 A3
Pampisford Cambs 85 C6
Pan Orkney 283 H4
Panbride Angus 221 A5
Pancrasweek Devon 10 A3
Pandy Gwyn 90 B4
Pandy Mon 61 A5
Pandy Powys 91 B7
Pandy Wrex 109 B6
Pandy Tudur Conwy 124 C3
Panfield Essex 70 A1
Pangbourne W Berks 47 B4
Pannal N Yorks 148 B2
Panshanger Herts 68 B2
Pant Shrops 110 C1
Pant-glas Carms 58 C2
Pant-glas Gwyn 107 B4
Pant-glâs Powys 91 C5
Pant-glas Shrops 110 B1
Pant Mawr Powys 91 D6
Pant-teg Carms 58 C1
Pant-y-Caws Carms 73 D4
Pant-y-dwr Powys 92 D3
Pant-y-ffridd Powys 93 A5
Pant-y-Wacco Flint 125 B6
Pant-yr-awel Bridgend 40 C4
Pantgwyn Ceredig 73 B5
Pantgwyn Carms 58 C2
Pantlasau Swansea 57 C6
Panton Lincs 134 B1
Pantperthog Gwyn 91 B5
Pantyffynnon Carms 57 A6
Pantymwyn Flint 126 C1
Panxworth Norf 121 D5
Papa Westray Airport Orkney 282 B5
Papcastle Cumb 163 A4
Papigoe Highld 281 C5
Papil Shetland 285 K5
Papley Orkney 283 H5
Papple E Loth 210 C2
Papplewick Notts 131 D5
Papworth Everard Cambs 85 A4
Papworth St Agnes Cambs 85 A4
Par Corn 5 B5
Paradise Wildlife Park, Broxbourne Herts 68 C3
Parbold Lancs 136 B3
Parbrook Som 29 B5
Parbrook W Sus 34 D3
Parc Gwyn 108 B3
Parc-Seymour Newport 61 D6
Parc-y-rhôs Carms 75 D4
Parcllyn Ceredig 73 A5
Pardshaw Cumb 162 B3
Parham Suff 88 A4
Park Dumfries 183 C7
Park Corner Oxon 47 A4
Park Corner Windsor 47 A6
Park End M'bro 168 D3
Park End Northumb 177 B6
Park Gate Hants 18 A4
Park Hill Notts 132 D1
Park Hill N Yorks 148 A2
Park Rose Pottery and Leisure Park, Bridlington E Yorks 151 A4
Park Street W Sus 35 C4
Parkend Glos 62 C2
Parkeston Essex 88 D3
Parkgate Ches 126 B2
Parkgate Dumfries 184 D3
Parkgate Kent 37 C6
Parkgate Sur 35 B5
Parkham Devon 25 C4
Parkham Ash Devon 25 C4
Parkhill Ho. Aberds 245 A5
Parkhouse Mon 61 C6
Parkhouse Green Derbys 131 C4
Parkhurst I o W 18 B3
Parkmill Swansea 57 D5
Parkneuk Aberds 233 A5
Parkstone Poole 17 B4
Parley Cross Dorset 17 B4
Parracombe Devon 26 A1
Parrog Pembs 72 C3
Parsley Hay Derbys 129 C6
Parson Cross S Yorks 139 D6
Parson Drove Cambs 101 A5
Parsonage Green Essex 69 C7
Parsonby Cumb 163 A4
Parson's Heath Essex 71 A4
Partick Glasgow 205 B5
Partington Gtr Man 137 D6
Partney Lincs 135 C4
Parton Cumb 162 B2
Parton Dumfries 173 A4
Parton Glos 63 A4
Partridge Green W Sus 21 A4
Parwich Derbys 130 D1
Passenham Northants 83 D4
Paston Norf 121 B5
Patchacott Devon 11 B5
Patcham Brighton 21 B6
Patching W Sus 20 B3
Patchole Devon 25 A7
Patchway S Glos 43 A5
Pateley Bridge N Yorks 147 A5
Paternoster Heath Essex 70 B3
Path of Condie Perth 219 C5
Pathe Som 28 B3
Pathhead Aberds 233 B5
Pathhead E Ayrs 182 A4
Pathhead Fife 209 A5
Pathhead Midloth 209 D6
Pathstruie Perth 219 C5
Patna E Ayrs 182 A2
Patney Wilts 45 D4
Patrick I o M 152 C2
Patrick Brompton N Yorks 157 B6
Patrington E Yorks 143 A5
Patrixbourne Kent 52 D3
Patterdale Cumb 164 D1
Pattingham Staffs 95 B6
Pattishall Northants 82 B3
Pattiswick Green Essex 70 A2
Patton Bridge Cumb 155 B4
Paul Corn 2 C2
Paulerspury Northants 83 C4
Paull E Yorks 142 A3
Paulton Bath 43 D5
Paultons Park, Totton Hants 32 D2
Pavenham Beds 84 B1
Pawlett Som 28 A3
Pawston Northumb 198 C2
Paxford Glos 81 D4
Paxton Borders 198 A3
Payhembury Devon 13 A5
Paythorne Lancs 146 B2
Peacehaven E Sus 22 B2
Peak Dale Derbys 129 B5
Peak Forest Derbys 129 B6
Peakirk P'boro 100 A3
Pearsie Angus 232 C1
Pease Pottage W Sus 35 C5
Peasedown St John Bath 43 D6
Peasemore W Berks 46 B2
Peasenhall Suff 89 A4
Peaslake Sur 34 B3
Peasley Cross Mers 136 D4
Peasmarsh E Sus 37 D6
Peaston E Loth 210 D1
Peastonbank E Loth 210 D1
Peat Inn Fife 221 D4
Peathill Aberds 269 C4
Peatling Magna Leics 98 B2
Peatling Parva Leics 98 C2
Peaton Shrops 94 C3
Peats Corner Suff 88 A2
Pebmarsh Essex 87 D4
Pebworth Worcs 80 C4
Pecket Well W Yorks 138 A2
Peckforton Ches 127 D5
Peckham London 49 B6
Peckleton Leics 98 A1
Pedlinge Kent 38 B3
Pedmore W Mid 96 C2
Pedwell Som 28 B4
Peebles Borders 196 B1
Peel I o M 152 C2
Peel Common Hants 19 A4
Peel Park S Lnrk 205 C6
Peening Quarter Kent 37 D6
Pegsdon Beds 84 D3
Pegswood Northumb 179 A4
Pegwell Kent 53 C5
Peinchorran Highld 247 A4
Peinlich Highld 259 C4
Pelaw T & W 179 C4
Pelcomb Bridge Pembs 55 C5
Pelcomb Cross Pembs 55 C5
Peldon Essex 70 B3
Pellon W Yorks 138 A3
Pelsall W Mid 96 A3
Pelton Durham 179 D4
Pelutho Cumb 174 D4
Pelynt Corn 5 B7
Pemberton Gtr Man 137 C4
Pembrey Carms 57 B4
Pembrey Motor Racing Circuit Carms 57 B4
Pembridge Hereford 78 B1
Pembroke = Penfro Pembs 55 D5
Pembroke Castle Pembs 55 D5
Pembroke Dock = Doc Penfro Pembs 55 D5
Pembury Kent 36 B4
Pen-bont Rhydybeddau Ceredig 91 D4
Pen-clawdd Swansea 57 C5
Pen-ffordd Pembs 55 B6
Pen-groes-oped Mon 61 C5
Pen-llyn Anglesey 122 B3
Pen-lon Anglesey 123 D4
Pen-sarn Gwyn 107 B4
Pen-sarn Gwyn 107 D5
Pen-twyn Mon 61 C7
Pen-y-banc Carms 58 C3
Pen-y-bont Carms 73 D6
Pen-y-bont Gwyn 91 B5
Pen-y-bont Gwyn 107 D6
Pen-y-bont Powys 109 C7
Pen-y-bont ar Ogwr = Bridgend Bridgend 40 D4
Pen-y-bryn Gwyn 91 A4
Pen-y-bryn Pembs 73 B4
Pen-y-cae Powys 59 D5
Pen-y-cae-mawr Mon 61 D6
Pen-y-cefn Flint 125 B6
Pen-y-clawdd Mon 61 C6
Pen-y-coedcae Rhondda 41 C5
Pen-y-fai Bridgend 40 C3
Pen-y-garn Ceredig 90 D4
Pen-y-garn Carms 58 B2
Pen-y-garnedd Anglesey 123 C5
Pen-y-gop Conwy 108 A4
Pen-y-graig Gwyn 106 C1
Pen-y-groes Carms 57 A5
Pen-y-groeslon Gwyn 106 C2
Pen-y-Gwryd Hotel Gwyn 107 A6
Pen-y-stryt Denb 126 D1
Pen-yr-heol Mon 61 B6
Pen-yr-Heolgerrig M Tydf 60 C2
Penallt Mon 61 B7
Penally Pembs 55 E7
Penalt Hereford 62 A1
Penare Corn 5 C4
Penarlâg = Hawarden Flint 126 C3
Penarth V Glam 41 D6
Penbryn Ceredig 73 A5
Pencader Carms 58 B1
Pencaenewydd Gwyn 107 B4
Pencaitland E Loth 210 D1
Pencarnisiog Anglesey 122 C3
Pencarreg Carms 75 D4
Pencelli Powys 60 A2
Pencoed Bridgend 41 C4
Pencombe Hereford 78 B3
Pencoyd Hereford 61 A7
Pencraig Hereford 62 A1
Pencraig Powys 109 C5
Pendeen Corn 2 B1
Pendennis Castle Corn 4 D3
Penderyn Rhondda 59 E6
Pendine Carms 56 B2
Pendlebury Gtr Man 137 C6
Pendleton Lancs 146 D1
Pendock Worcs 79 D5
Pendoggett Corn 9 D6
Pendomer Som 29 D5
Pendoylan V Glam 41 D5
Pendre Bridgend 40 C4
Penegoes Powys 91 B5
Penfro = Pembroke Pembs 55 D5
Pengam Caerph 41 B6
Penge London 49 B6
Pengenffordd Powys 77 D5
Pengorffwysfa Anglesey 123 A4
Pengover Green Corn 6 A1
Penhale Corn 3 D4
Penhale Corn 4 B4
Penhalvaen Corn 4 D2
Penhill Swindon 45 A5
Penhow Newport 61 D6
Penhurst E Sus 23 A4
Peniarth Gwyn 90 B4
Penicuik Midloth 209 D5
Peniel Carms 58 C1
Peniel Denb 125 C5
Penifiler Highld 259 D4
Peninver Argyll 190 C3
Penisarwaun Gwyn 123 D5
Penistone S Yorks 139 C5
Penjerrick Corn 4 D2
Penketh Warr 127 A5
Penkill S Ayrs 181 B4
Penkridge Staffs 112 D3
Penley Wrex 110 B3
Penllergaer Swansea 57 C6
Penllyn V Glam 41 D4
Penmachno Conwy 124 D2
Penmaen Swansea 57 D5
Penmaenan Conwy 124 B2
Penmaenmawr Conwy 124 B2
Penmaenpool Gwyn 91 A4
Penmark V Glam 41 E5
Penmarth Corn 4 D2
Penmon Anglesey 123 B6
Penmore Mill Argyll 224 A3
Penmorfa Ceredig 73 A6
Penmorfa Gwyn 107 B5
Penmynydd Anglesey 123 C5
Penn Bucks 67 D4
Penn W Mid 96 B1
Penn Street Bucks 67 D4
Pennal Gwyn 91 B5
Pennan Aberds 268 C3
Pennant Ceredig 75 B4
Pennant Denb 109 B5
Pennant Denb 125 D5
Pennant Powys 91 C6
Pennant Melangell Powys 109 C5
Pennar Pembs 55 D5
Pennard Swansea 57 D5
Pennerley Shrops 94 B1
Pennington Cumb 153 C3
Pennington Gtr Man 137 D5
Pennington Hants 18 B2
Penny Bridge Cumb 154 C2
Pennycross Argyll 225 D4
Pennygate Norf 121 C5
Pennygown Argyll 225 B4
Pennymoor Devon 26 D3
Pennywell T & W 179 D5
Penparc Ceredig 73 B5
Penparc Pembs 55 A4
Penparcau Ceredig 90 D3
Penperlleni Mon 61 C5
Penpillick Corn 5 B5
Penpol Corn 4 D3
Penpoll Corn 5 B6
Penpont Dumfries 183 C6
Penpont Powys 59 C6
Penrherber Carms 73 C5
Penrhiw goch Carms 57 A5
Penrhiw-llan Ceredig 73 B6
Penrhiw-pâl Ceredig 73 B6
Penrhiwceiber Rhondda 41 B5
Penrhos Gwyn 106 C3
Penrhôs Mon 61 B6
Penrhos Powys 59 D4
Penrhosfeilw Anglesey 122 B2
Penrhyn Bay Conwy 124 A3
Penrhyn Castle Gwyn 123 C6
Penrhyn-coch Ceredig 90 D4
Penrhyndeudraeth Gwyn 107 C6
Penrhynside Conwy 124 A3
Penrice Swansea 57 D4
Penrith Cumb 164 B3
Penrose Corn 9 D4
Penruddock Cumb 164 C2
Penryn Corn 4 D2
Pensarn Carms 57 A4
Pensarn Conwy 125 B4
Pensax Worcs 79 A5
Pensby Mers 126 A2
Penselwood Som 30 B1
Pensford Bath 43 C5
Penshaw T & W 179 D5
Penshurst Kent 36 B3
Pensilva Corn 6 A1
Penston E Loth 210 C1
Pentewan Corn 5 C5
Pentir Gwyn 123 D5
Pentire Corn 4 A2
Pentlow Essex 87 C4
Pentney Norf 119 D4
Penton Mewsey Hants 32 A2
Pentraeth Anglesey 123 C5
Pentre Carms 57 A5
Pentre Powys 93 C4
Pentre Powys 93 B6
Pentre Rhondda 41 B4
Pentre Shrops 110 D2
Pentre Wrex 110 A1
Pentre Wrex 109 B6
Pentre-bâch Ceredig 75 D4
Pentre-bach Powys 59 B6
Pentre Berw Anglesey 123 C4
Pentre-bont Conwy 124 D2
Pentre-celyn Denb 125 D6
Pentre-Celyn Powys 91 B6
Pentre-chwyth Swansea 57 C6
Pentre-cwrt Carms 73 C6
Pentre Dolau-Honddu Powys 76 C3
Pentre-dwr Swansea 40 B1
Pentre-galar Pembs 73 C4
Pentre-Gwenlais Carms 57 A6
Pentre Gwynfryn Gwyn 107 D5
Pentre Halkyn Flint 126 B2
Pentre-Isaf Conwy 124 C3
Pentre Llanrhaeadr Denb 125 C5
Pentre-llwyn-llŵyd Powys 76 B3
Pentre-llyn Ceredig 75 A5
Pentre-llyn cymmer Conwy 125 D4
Pentre Meyrick V Glam 41 D4
Pentre-poeth Newport 42 A1
Pentre-rhew Ceredig 75 C5
Pentre-tafarn-y-fedw Conwy 124 C3
Pentre-ty-gwyn Carms 59 B5
Pentrebach M Tydf 41 A5
Pentrebach Swansea 57 B6
Pentrebeirdd Powys 109 D6
Pentrecagal Carms 73 B6
Pentredwr Denb 109 A6
Pentrefelin Ceredig 75 D5
Pentrefelin Carms 58 C2
Pentrefelin Conwy 124 B3
Pentrefelin Gwyn 107 C5
Pentrefoelas Conwy 124 D3
Pentregat Ceredig 73 A6
Pentreheyling Shrops 93 B6
Pentre'r Felin Conwy 124 C3
Pentre'r-felin Powys 59 B6
Pentrich Derbys 130 D3
Pentridge Dorset 31 D4
Pentyrch Cardiff 41 C6
Penuchadre V Glam 40 D3
Penuwch Ceredig 75 B4
Penwithick Corn 5 B5
Penwyllt Powys 59 D5
Penybanc Carms 57 A6
Penybont Powys 77 A5
Penybontfawr Powys 109 C5
Penycae Wrex 110 A1
Penycwm Pembs 54 B4
Penyffordd Flint 126 C3
Penyffridd Gwyn 107 A5
Penygarnedd Powys 109 C6
Penygraig Rhondda 41 B4
Penygroes Gwyn 107 A4
Penygroes Pembs 73 C4
Penyrheol Caerph 41 C6
Penysarn Anglesey 123 A4
Penywaun Rhondda 41 A4
Penzance Corn 2 B2
Penzance Heliport Corn 2 B2
People's Palace Glasgow 205 B6
Peopleton Worcs 80 B2
Peover Heath Ches 128 B2
Peper Harow Sur 34 B2
Perceton N Ayrs 204 D3
Percie Aberds 244 C2
Percyhorner Aberds 269 C4
Periton Som 27 A4
Perivale London 49 A4
Perkinsville Durham 179 D4
Perlethorpe Notts 131 B6
Perranarworthal Corn 4 D2
Perranporth Corn 4 B2
Perranuthnoe Corn 2 C3
Perranzabuloe Corn 4 B2
Perry Barr W Mid 96 B3
Perry Green Herts 68 B4
Perry Green Wilts 44 A3
Perry Street Kent 50 B3
Perryfoot Derbys 129 A6
Pershall Staffs 112 B2
Pershore Worcs 80 C2
Pert Angus 233 B4
Pertenhall Beds 84 A2
Perth Perth 219 B6
Perth Racecourse Perth 219 B6
Perthy Shrops 110 B2
Perton Staffs 95 B6
Pertwood Wilts 30 B2
Peter Tavy Devon 11 D6
Peterborough P'boro 100 B3
Peterborough Cathedral P'boro 100 B3
Peterburn Highld 261 B4
Peterchurch Hereford 78 D1
Peterculter Aberdeen 245 B5
Peterhead Aberds 257 B6
Peterlee Durham 168 A2
Peter's Green Herts 67 B6
Peters Marland Devon 25 D5
Petersfield Hants 33 C6
Peterston super-Ely V Glam 41 D5
Peterstone Wentlooge Newport 42 A1
Peterstow Hereford 62 A1
Petertown Orkney 283 G4
Petham Kent 52 D3
Petrockstow Devon 11 A6
Pett E Sus 23 A6
Pettaugh Suff 88 B2
Petteridge Kent 37 B4
Pettinain S Lnrk 195 B4
Pettistree Suff 88 B3
Petton Devon 27 C5
Petton Shrops 110 C3
Petts Wood London 50 C1
Petty Aberds 256 C2
Pettycur Fife 209 B5
Pettymuick Aberds 257 D4
Petworth W Sus 34 D2
Petworth House W Sus 34 D2
Pevensey E Sus 22 B4
Pevensey Bay E Sus 23 B4
Pewsey Wilts 45 C5
Philham Devon 24 C3
Philiphaugh Borders 186 A3
Phillack Corn 2 B3
Philleigh Corn 4 D3
Philpstoun W Loth 208 C3
Phocle Green Hereford 62 A2
Phoenix Green Hants 47 D5
Pica Cumb 162 B3
Piccotts End Herts 67 C5
Pickering N Yorks 159 C6
Picket Piece Hants 32 A2
Picket Post Hants 17 A5
Pickhill N Yorks 158 C2
Picklescott Shrops 94 B2
Pickletillem Fife 220 B4
Pickmere Ches 128 B1
Pickney Som 28 C1
Pickstock Telford 111 C6
Pickwell Devon 25 A5
Pickwell Leics 115 D5
Pickworth Lincs 116 B3
Pickworth Rutland 116 D2
Picton Ches 127 B4
Picton Flint 125 A6
Picton N Yorks 158 A3
Piddinghoe E Sus 22 B2
Piddington Northants 83 B5
Piddington Oxon 66 B1
Piddlehinton Dorset 15 B7
Piddletrenthide Dorset 15 B7
Pidley Cambs 101 D5
Piece Hall Art Gallery, Halifax W Yorks 138 A3
Piercebridge Darl 167 D5
Pierowall Orkney 282 C5
Pigdon Northumb 178 A3
Pikehall Derbys 130 D1
Pilgrims Hatch Essex 69 D5
Pilham Lincs 141 D6
Pill N Som 43 B4
Pillaton Corn 6 A2
Pillerton Hersey Warks 81 C6
Pillerton Priors Warks 81 C5
Pilleth Powys 77 A6
Pilley Hants 18 B2

Pilley S Yorks 139 C6
Pilling Lancs 144 C4
Pilling Lane Lancs 144 C3
Pillowell Glos 62 C2
Pillwell Dorset 30 D1
Pilning S Glos 43 A4
Pilsbury Derbys 129 C6
Pilsdon Dorset 14 B4
Pilsgate P'boro 100 A2
Pilsley Derbys 130 B2
Pilsley Derbys 131 C4
Pilton Devon 25 B6
Pilton Northants 100 C2
Pilton Rutland 99 A6
Pilton Som 29 A5
Pilton Green Swansea 57 D4
Pimperne Dorset 16 A3
Pin Mill Suff 88 D3
Pinchbeck Lincs 117 C5
Pinchbeck Bars Lincs 117 C4
Pinchbeck West Lincs 117 C5
Pincheon Green S Yorks 141 B4
Pinehurst Swindon 45 A5
Pinfold Lancs 136 B2
Pinged Carms 57 B4
Pinhoe Devon 13 B4
Pinkneys Green Windsor 47 A6
Pinley W Mid 97 D6
Pinminnoch S Ayrs 180 B3
Pinmore S Ayrs 181 B4
Pinmore Mains S Ayrs 181 B4
Pinner London 48 A4
Pinvin Worcs 80 C2
Pinwherry S Ayrs 180 C3
Pinxton Derbys 131 D4
Pipe and Lyde Hereford 78 C3
Pipe Gate Shrops 111 A6
Piperhill Highld 253 A4
Piper's Pool Corn 10 C3
Pipewell Northants 99 C5
Pippacott Devon 25 B6
Pipton Powys 77 D5
Pirbright Sur 34 A2
Pirnmill N Ayrs 202 D3
Pirton Herts 84 D3
Pirton Worcs 80 C1
Pisgah Ceredig 75 A5
Pisgah Stirl 218 D2
Pishill Oxon 47 A5
Pistyll Gwyn 106 B3
Pitagowan Perth 230 B2
Pitblae Aberds 269 C4
Pitcairngreen Perth 219 B5
Pitcalnie Highld 265 C4
Pitcaple Aberds 256 D2
Pitch Green Bucks 66 C2
Pitch Place Sur 34 A2
Pitchcombe Glos 63 C4
Pitchcott Bucks 66 A2
Pitchford Shrops 94 A3
Pitcombe Som 29 B6
Pitcorthie Fife 221 D5
Pitcox E Loth 210 C3
Pitcur Perth 220 A2
Pitfichie Aberds 244 A3
Pitforthie Aberds 233 A6
Pitgrudy Highld 264 A3
Pitkennedy Angus 232 C3
Pitkevy Fife 220 D2
Pitkierie Fife 221 D5
Pitlessie Fife 220 D3
Pitlochry Perth 230 C3
Pitmachie Aberds 256 D1
Pitmain Highld 241 B5
Pitmedden Aberds 256 D3
Pitminster Som 28 D2
Pitmuies Angus 232 D3
Pitmunie Aberds 244 A3
Pitney Som 29 C4
Pitscottie Fife 220 C4
Pitsea Essex 51 A4
Pitsford Northants 83 A4
Pitsmoor S Yorks 130 A3
Pitstone Bucks 67 B4
Pitstone Green Bucks 67 B4
Pitt Rivers Museum (See University Museum) Oxon 65 C6
Pittendreich Moray 266 C2
Pittentrail Highld 273 D5
Pittenweem Fife 221 D5
Pittington Durham 167 A6
Pittodrie Aberds 256 D1
Pitton Wilts 31 B6
Pittswood Kent 36 B4
Pittulie Aberds 269 C4
Pity Me Durham 167 A5
Pityme Corn 9 D5
Pityoulish Highld 242 A2
Pixey Green Suff 104 D3
Pixham Sur 35 A4
Pixley Hereford 79 D4
Place Newton N Yorks 160 D2
Plaidy Aberds 268 D2
Plains N Lnrk 207 D5
Plaish Shrops 94 B3
Plaistow W Sus 34 C3
Plaitford Hants 32 D1
Plank Lane Gtr Man 137 D5
Plas-canol Gwyn 90 A3
Plas Gogerddan Ceredig 90 D4
Plas Llwyngwern Powys 91 B5
Plas Mawr, Conwy Conwy 124 B2
Plas Nantyr Wrex 109 B6
Plas-yn-Cefn Denb 125 B5
Plastow Green Hants 46 C3
Platt Kent 36 A4
Platt Bridge Gtr Man 137 C5
Platts Common S Yorks 139 C6
Plawsworth Durham 167 A5
Plaxtol Kent 36 A4
Play Hatch Oxon 47 B5
Playden E Sus 37 D7
Playford Suff 88 C3
Playing Place Corn 4 C3
Playley Green Glos 79 D5
Plealey Shrops 94 A2
Plean Stirl 207 B6
Pleasington Blkburn 137 A5
Pleasley Derbys 131 C5
Pleasure Island Theme Park NE Lincs 143 C5
Pleckgate Blkburn 145 D6
Plenmeller Northumb 177 C5
Pleshey Essex 69 B6
Plockton Highld 249 C5
Plocrapol W Isles 288 H2
Ploughfield Hereford 78 C1
Plowden Shrops 94 C1
Ploxgreen Shrops 94 A1
Pluckley Kent 38 A1
Pluckley Thorne Kent 37 B7
Plumbland Cumb 163 A4
Plumley Ches 128 B2
Plumpton Cumb 164 B2
Plumpton E Sus 21 A6
Plumpton Green E Sus 21 A6
Plumpton Head Cumb 164 B3
Plumpton Racecourse E Sus 21 A6
Plumstead London 50 B1
Plumstead Norf 120 B3
Plumtree Notts 115 B4
Plungar Leics 115 B5
Plush Dorset 15 A7
Plwmp Ceredig 73 A6
Plymouth Plym 6 B3
Plymouth City Airport Plym 7 A4
Plympton Plym 7 B4
Plymstock Plym 7 B4
Plymtree Devon 13 A5
Pockley N Yorks 159 C5
Pocklington E Yorks 149 C7
Pode Hole Lincs 117 C5
Podimore Som 29 C5
Podington Beds 83 A6
Podmore Staffs 112 B1
Point Clear Essex 71 B4
Pointon Lincs 116 B4
Pokesdown Bmouth 17 B5
Pol a Charra W Isles 286 E3
Polbae Dumfries 181 D4
Polbain Highld 270 C2
Polbathic Corn 6 B2
Polbeth W Loth 208 D3
Polchar Highld 242 B1
Pole Elm Worcs 79 C6
Polebrook Northants 100 C2
Polegate E Sus 22 B3
Poles Highld 264 A3
Polesden Lacey, Dorking Sur 35 A4
Polesworth Warks 97 A5
Polgigga Corn 2 C1
Polglass Highld 270 D3
Polgooth Corn 5 B4
Poling W Sus 20 B3
Polkerris Corn 5 B5
Polla Highld 277 C4
Pollington E Yorks 140 B4
Polloch Highld 236 C1
Pollok Glasgow 205 B5
Pollok House Glasgow 205 B5
Pollokshields Glasgow 205 B5
Polmassick Corn 5 C4
Polmont Falk 208 C2
Polnessan E Ayrs 182 A2
Polnish Highld 235 B6
Polperro Corn 5 B7
Polruan Corn 5 B6
Polsham Som 29 A5
Polstead Suff 87 D5
Poltalloch Argyll 213 C6
Poltimore Devon 13 B4
Polton Midloth 209 D5
Polwarth Borders 197 A6
Polyphant Corn 10 C3
Polzeath Corn 9 D5
Ponders End London 68 D3
Pondersbridge Cambs 101 B4
Pondtail Hants 34 A1
Ponsanooth Corn 4 D2
Ponsworthy Devon 12 D2
Pont Aber Carms 59 C4
Pont Aber-Geirw Gwyn 108 C2
Pont-ar-gothi Carms 58 C2
Pont ar Hydfer Powys 59 C5
Pont-ar-llechau Carms 59 C4
Pont Cwm Pydew Denb 109 B5
Pont Cyfyng Conwy 124 D2
Pont Cysyllte Wrex 110 A1
Pont Dolydd Prysor Gwyn 108 B2
Pont-faen Powys 76 D3
Pont Fronwydd Gwyn 108 C3
Pont-gareg Pembs 72 B4
Pont-Henri Carms 57 B4
Pont-Llogel Powys 109 D5
Pont Pen-y-benglog Gwyn 123 D6
Pont Rhyd-goch Conwy 124 C1
Pont-Rhyd-sarn Gwyn 108 C3
Pont Rhyd-y-cyff Bridgend 40 C3
Pont-rhyd-y-groes Ceredig 75 A6
Pont-rug Gwyn 123 D5
Pont Senni = Sennybridge Powys 59 C6
Pont-siân Ceredig 74 D3
Pont-y-gwaith Rhondda 41 B5
Pont-y-pant Conwy 124 D2
Pont y Pennant Gwyn 108 C4
Pont-y-Pŵl = Pontypool Torf 61 C4
Pont yclun Rhondda 41 C5
Pont yr Afon-Gam Gwyn 108 A2
Pont-yr-hafod Pembs 55 B5
Pontamman Carms 57 A6
Pontantwn Carms 57 A4
Pontardawe Neath 40 A2
Pontarddulais Swansea 57 B5
Pontarsais Carms 58 C1
Pontblyddyn Flint 126 C2
Pontbren Araeth Carms 58 C3
Pontbren Llwyd Rhondda 59 E6
Pontefract W Yorks 140 A2
Pontefract Racecourse W Yorks 140 A2
Ponteland Northumb 178 B3
Ponterwyd Ceredig 91 D5
Pontesbury Shrops 94 A1
Pontfadog Wrex 110 B1
Pontfaen Pembs 55 A6
Pontgarreg Ceredig 73 A6
Ponthir Torf 61 D5
Ponthirwaun Ceredig 73 B5
Pontllanfraith Caerph 41 B6
Pontlliw Swansea 57 B6
Pontllyfni Gwyn 107 A4
Pontlottyn Caerph 60 C3
Pontneddfechan Powys 59 E6
Pontnewydd Torf 61 D4
Pontrhydfendigaid Ceredig 75 B6
Pontrhydyfen Neath 40 B2
Pontrilas Hereford 61 A5
Pontrobert Powys 109 D6
Ponts Green E Sus 23 A4
Pontshill Hereford 62 A2
Pontsticill M Tydf 60 B2
Pontwgan Conwy 124 B2
Pontyates Carms 57 B4
Pontyberem Carms 57 A5
Pontycymer Bridgend 40 B4
Pontyglasier Pembs 72 C4
Pontypool = Pont-y-Pŵl Torf 61 C4
Pontypridd Rhondda 41 C5
Pontywaun Caerph 41 B7
Pooksgreen Hants 32 D2
Pool Corn 3 A4
Pool W Yorks 147 C6
Pool o'Muckhart Clack 219 D5
Pool Quay Powys 110 D1
Poole Poole 17 B4
Poole Keynes Glos 63 D5
Poolend Staffs 129 D4
Poolewe Highld 261 B5
Pooley Bridge Cumb 164 C2
Poolfold Staffs 128 D3
Poolhill Glos 62 A3
Poolsbrook Derbys 131 B4
Pootings Kent 36 B2
Pope Hill Pembs 55 C5
Popeswood Brack 47 C6
Popham Hants 33 A4
Poplar London 49 A6
Popley Hants 47 D4
Porchester Notts 114 A3
Porchfield I o W 18 B3
Porin Highld 251 A5
Poringland Norf 104 A3
Porkellis Corn 3 B4
Porlock Som 26 A3
Porlock Weir Som 26 A3
Port Ann Argyll 214 D2
Port Appin Argyll 226 B4
Port Arthur Shetland 285 K5
Port Askaig Argyll 201 B4
Port Bannatyne Argyll 203 B5
Port Carlisle Cumb 175 B5
Port Charlotte Argyll 200 C2
Port Clarence Stockton 168 C2
Port Driseach Argyll 203 A4
Port e Vullen I o M 152 B4
Port Ellen Argyll 200 D3
Port Elphinstone Aberds 256 E2
Port Erin I o M 152 E1
Port Erroll Aberds 257 C5
Port-Eynon Swansea 57 D4
Port Gaverne Corn 9 C6
Port Glasgow Invclyd 204 A3
Port Henderson Highld 261 C4
Port Isaac Corn 9 C5
Port Lamont Argyll 203 A5
Port Lion Pembs 55 D5
Port Logan Dumfries 170 C2
Port Mholair W Isles 288 D6
Port Mor Highld 234 C3
Port Mulgrave N Yorks 169 D5
Port Nan Giùran W Isles 288 D6
Port nan Long W Isles 287 G3
Port Nis W Isles 288 A6
Port of Menteith Stirl 217 D5
Port Quin Corn 9 C5
Port Ramsay Argyll 226 B3
Port St Mary I o M 152 E2
Port Sunlight Mers 126 A3
Port Talbot Neath 40 B2
Port Tennant Swansea 57 C6
Port Wemyss Argyll 200 C1
Port William Dumfries 171 C5
Portachoillan Argyll 202 C2
Portavadie Argyll 203 B4
Portbury N Som 43 B4
Portchester Hants 19 A5
Portclair Highld 240 A2
Portencalzie Dumfries 180 D2
Portencross N Ayrs 204 D1
Portesham Dorset 15 C6
Portessie Moray 267 C5
Portfield Gate Pembs 55 C5
Portgate Devon 11 C5
Portgordon Moray 267 C4
Portgower Highld 274 C4
Porth Corn 4 A3
Porth Rhondda 41 B5
Porth Navas Corn 3 C5
Porth Tywyn = Burry Port Carms 57 B4
Porth-y-waen Shrops 110 C1
Porthaethwy = Menai Bridge Anglesey 123 C5
Porthallow Corn 3 C5
Porthallow Corn 6 B1
Porthcawl Bridgend 40 D3
Porthcothan Corn 9 D4
Porthcurno Corn 2 C1
Porthgain Pembs 54 A4
Porthill Shrops 110 D3
Porthkerry V Glam 41 E5
Porthleven Corn 3 C4
Porthllechog Anglesey 123 A4
Porthmadog Gwyn 107 C5
Porthmeor Corn 2 B2
Portholland Corn 5 C4
Porthoustock Corn 3 C6
Porthpean Corn 5 B5
Porthtowan Corn 3 A4
Porthyrhyd Carms 57 A5
Porthyrhyd Carms 59 B4
Portincaple Argyll 215 C5
Portington E Yorks 149 D6
Portinnisherrich Argyll 214 A2
Portinscale Cumb 163 B5
Portishead N Som 42 B3
Portkil Argyll 215 D5
Portknockie Moray 267 C5
Portlethen Aberds 245 C6
Portling Dumfries 173 C6
Portloe Corn 4 D4
Portmahomack Highld 265 B5
Portmeirion Gwyn 107 C5
Portmeirion Village Gwyn 107 C5
Portmellon Corn 5 C5
Portmore Hants 18 B2
Portnacroish Argyll 226 B4
Portnahaven Argyll 200 C1
Portnalong Highld 246 A2
Portnaluchaig Highld 235 B5
Portnancon Highld 277 B5
Portnellan Stirl 216 B4
Portobello Edin 209 C6
Porton Wilts 31 B5
Portpatrick Dumfries 170 B2
Portreath Corn 3 A4
Portree Highld 259 D4
Portscatho Corn 4 D3
Portsea Ptsmth 19 A5
Portskerra Highld 279 B4
Portskewett Mon 43 A4
Portslade Brighton 21 B5
Portslade-by-Sea Brighton 21 B5
Portsmouth Ptsmth 19 A5
Portsmouth W Yorks 138 A2
Portsmouth Sea Life Centre Ptsmth 19 B5
Portsonachan Argyll 227 D5
Portsoy Aberds 267 C6
Portswood Soton 32 D3
Porttanachy Moray 267 C4
Portuairk Highld 234 D3
Portway Hereford 78 D2
Portway Worcs 96 D3
Portwrinkle Corn 6 B2
Poslingford Suff 86 C3
Postbridge Devon 12 D1
Postcombe Oxon 66 D2
Postling Kent 38 B3
Postwick Norf 104 A3
Potholm Dumfries 185 D6
Potsgrove Beds 67 A4
Pott Row Norf 119 C4
Pott Shrigley Ches 129 B4
Potten End Herts 67 C5
Potter Brompton N Yorks 160 D3
Potter Heigham Norf 121 D6
Potter Street Essex 69 C4
Potterhanworth Lincs 133 C5
Potterhanworth Booths Lincs 133 C5
Potteries Museum & Art Gallery, Stoke-on-Trent Stoke 112 A2
Potterne Wilts 44 D3
Potterne Wick Wilts 44 D4
Potternewton W Yorks 148 D2
Potters Bar Herts 68 C2
Potter's Cross Staffs 95 C6
Potterspury Northants 83 C4
Potterton Aberds 245 A6
Potterton W Yorks 148 D3
Potto N Yorks 158 A3
Potton Beds 84 C4
Poughill Corn 10 A3
Poughill Devon 12 A3
Poulshot Wilts 44 D3
Poulton Glos 64 C2
Poulton Mers 136 D2
Poulton-le-Fylde Lancs 144 D3
Pound Bank Worcs 95 D5
Pound Green E Sus 36 D3
Pound Green I o W 18 C2
Pound Green Worcs 95 D5
Pound Hill W Sus 35 C5
Poundfield E Sus 36 C3
Poundland S Ayrs 180 C3
Poundon Bucks 66 A1
Poundsgate Devon 12 D2
Poundstock Corn 10 B3
Powburn Northumb 188 B3
Powderham Devon 13 C4
Powderham Castle Devon 13 C4
Powerstock Dorset 15 B5
Powfoot Dumfries 174 B4
Powick Worcs 79 B6
Powis Castle, Welshpool Powys 93 A6
Powmill Perth 208 A3
Poxwell Dorset 16 C1
Poyle Slough 48 B3
Poynings W Sus 21 A5
Poyntington Dorset 29 D6
Poynton Ches 129 A4
Poynton Green Telford 111 D4
Poystreet Green Suff 87 B5
Praa Sands Corn 2 C3
Pratt's Bottom London 50 C1
Praze Corn 2 B3
Praze-an-Beeble Corn 3 B4
Predannack Wollas Corn 3 D4
Prees Shrops 111 B4
Prees Green Shrops 111 B4
Prees Heath Shrops 111 B4
Prees Higher Heath Shrops 111 B4
Prees Lower Heath Shrops 111 B4
Preesall Lancs 144 C3
Preesgweene Shrops 110 B1
Prenderguest Borders 198 A3
Prendwick Northumb 188 B3
Prengwyn Ceredig 73 B7
Prenteg Gwyn 107 B5
Prenton Mers 126 A3
Prescot Mers 136 D3
Prescott Shrops 110 C3
Pressen Northumb 198 C2
Prestatyn Denb 125 A5
Prestbury Ches 129 B4
Prestbury Glos 63 A5
Presteigne = Llanandras Powys 77 A7
Presthope Shrops 94 B3
Prestleigh Som 29 A6
Preston Borders 198 A1
Preston Brighton 21 B6
Preston Devon 12 D3
Preston Dorset 15 C7
Preston E Loth 210 C2
Preston E Yorks 151 D4
Preston Glos 63 C6
Preston Glos 79 D4
Preston Herts 68 A1
Preston Kent 52 C2
Preston Kent 53 C4
Preston Lancs 136 A4
Preston Northumb 189 A4
Preston Rutland 99 A5
Preston Shrops 111 D4
Preston Wilts 44 B4
Preston Wilts 45 B6
Preston Bagot Warks 81 A4
Preston Bissett Bucks 66 A1
Preston Bowyer Som 27 C6
Preston Brockhurst Shrops 111 C4
Preston Brook Halton 127 A5
Preston Candover Hants 33 A5
Preston Capes Northants 82 B2
Preston Crowmarsh Oxon 65 D7
Preston Gubbals Shrops 110 D3
Preston Hall Museum, Stockton-on-Tees Stockton 168 D2
Preston on Stour Warks 81 C5
Preston on the Hill Halton 127 A5
Preston on Wye Hereford 78 C1
Preston Plucknett Som 29 D5
Preston St Mary Suff 87 B5
Preston-under-Scar N Yorks 157 B4
Preston upon the Weald Moors Telford 111 D5
Preston Wynne Hereford 78 C3
Prestonmill Dumfries 174 C2
Prestonpans E Loth 209 C6
Prestwich Gtr Man 137 C7
Prestwick Northumb 178 B3
Prestwick S Ayrs 192 C3
Prestwood Bucks 66 C3
Price Town Bridgend 40 B4
Prickwillow Cambs 102 C1
Priddy Som 43 D4
Priest Hutton Lancs 154 D4
Priest Weston Shrops 93 B6
Priesthaugh Borders 186 C3
Primethorpe Leics 98 B2
Primrose Green Norf 120 D2
Primrose Valley N Yorks 161 D5
Primrosehill Herts 67 C5
Princes Gate Pembs 56 A1
Princes Risborough Bucks 66 C3
Princethorpe Warks 97 D7
Princetown Caerph 60 B3
Princetown Devon 11 D6
Prinknash Abbey, Gloucester Glos 63 B4
Prion Denb 125 C5
Prior Muir Fife 221 C5
Prior Park Northumb 198 A3
Priors Frome Hereford 78 D3
Priors Hardwick Warks 82 B1
Priors Marston Warks 82 B1
Priorslee Telford 111 D6
Priory Church, Lancaster Lancs 145 A4
Priory Wood Hereford 77 C6
Priston Bath 43 C5
Pristow Green Norf 104 C2
Prittlewell Sthend 51 A5
Privett Hants 33 C5
Prixford Devon 25 B6
Probus Corn 4 C3
Proncy Highld 264 A3
Prospect Cumb 174 D4
Prudhoe Northumb 178 C2
Ptarmigan Lodge Stirl 215 B6
Pubil Perth 228 D3
Puckeridge Herts 68 A3
Puckington Som 28 D3
Pucklechurch S Glos 43 B5
Pucknall Hants 32 C2
Puckrup Glos 80 D1
Puddinglake Ches 128 C2
Puddington Ches 126 B3
Puddington Devon 26 D3
Puddledock Norf 103 B6
Puddletown Dorset 16 B1
Pudleston Hereford 78 B3
Pudsey W Yorks 147 D6
Pulborough W Sus 20 A3
Puleston Telford 111 C6
Pulford Ches 126 D3
Pulham Dorset 15 A7
Pulham Market Norf 104 C2
Pulham St Mary Norf 104 C3
Pulloxhill Beds 84 D2
Pumpherston W Loth 208 D3
Pumsaint Carms 58 A3
Puncheston Pembs 55 B6
Puncknowle Dorset 15 C5
Punnett's Town E Sus 36 D4
Purbrook Hants 19 A5
Purewell Dorset 17 B5
Purfleet Thurrock 50 B2
Puriton Som 28 A3
Purleigh Essex 70 C2
Purley London 49 C6
Purley W Berks 47 B4
Purlogue Shrops 93 D6
Purls Bridge Cambs 101 C6
Purse Caundle Dorset 29 D6
Purslow Shrops 94 C1
Purston Jaglin W Yorks 140 B2
Purton Glos 62 C2
Purton Glos 62 C2
Purton Wilts 45 A4
Purton Stoke Wilts 64 D1

Pury End Northants 83 C4
Pusey Oxon 65 D4
Putley Hereford 79 D4
Putney London 49 B5
Putsborough Devon 25 A5
Puttenham Herts 66 B3
Puttenham Sur 34 B2
Puxton N Som 42 C3
Pwll Carms 57 B4
Pwll-glas Denb 125 D6
Pwll-trap Carms 56 A2
Pwll-y-glaw Neath 40 B2
Pwllcrochan Pembs 55 D5
Pwllgloyw Powys 76 D4
Pwllheli Gwyn 106 C3
Pwllmeyric Mon 61 D7
Pye Corner Newport 42 A2
Pye Green Staffs 112 D3
Pyecombe W Sus 21 A5
Pyewipe NE Lincs 143 B4
Pyle I o W 18 D3
Pyle = Y Pîl Bridgend 40 C3
Pylle Som 29 B6
Pymoor Cambs 101 C6
Pyrford Sur 34 A3
Pyrton Oxon 66 D1
Pytchley Northants 99 D5
Pyworthy Devon 10 A4

Q

Quabbs Shrops 93 C6
Quadring Lincs 117 B5
Quainton Bucks 66 B2
Quarley Hants 31 A6
Quarndon Derbys 114 A1
Quarrier's Homes Invclyd 204 B3
Quarrington Lincs 116 A3
Quarrington Hill Durham 167 B6
Quarry Bank W Mid 96 C2
Quarry Bank Mill, Wilmslow Ches 128 A3
Quarryford E Loth 210 D2
Quarryhill Highld 264 B3
Quarrywood Moray 266 C2
Quarter S Lnrk 194 A2
Quatford Shrops 95 B5
Quatt Shrops 95 C5
Quebec Durham 167 A4
Quedgeley Glos 63 B4
Queen Adelaide Cambs 102 C1
Queen Camel Som 29 C5
Queen Charlton Bath 43 C5
Queen Dart Devon 26 D3
Queen Oak Dorset 30 B1
Queen Street Kent 37 B4
Queen Street Wilts 44 A4
Queenborough Kent 51 B6
Queenhill Worcs 79 D6
Queen's Head Shrops 110 C2
Queen's Park Beds 84 C2
Queen's Park Northants 83 A4
Queen's View Centre, Loch Tummel Perth 230 C2
Queensbury W Yorks 147 D5
Queensferry Edin 208 C4
Queensferry Flint 126 C3
Queenstown Blkpool 144 D3
Queenzieburn N Lnrk 207 C4
Quemerford Wilts 44 C4
Quendale Shetland 285 M5
Quendon Essex 85 D7
Queniborough Leics 115 D4
Quenington Glos 64 C2
Quernmore Lancs 145 B5
Quethiock Corn 6 A2
Quholm Orkney 282 F3
Quicks Green W Berks 46 B3
Quidenham Norf 103 C6
Quidhampton Hants 46 D3
Quidhampton Wilts 31 B5
Quilquox Aberds 257 C4
Quina Brook Shrops 111 B4
Quindry Orkney 283 H5
Quinton Northants 83 B4
Quinton W Mid 96 C2
Quintrell Downs Corn 4 A3
Quixhill Staffs 113 A5
Quoditch Devon 11 B5
Quoig Perth 218 B3
Quorndon Leics 114 D3
Quothquan S Lnrk 195 C4
Quoyloo Orkney 282 E3
Quoyness Orkney 283 G3
Quoys Shetland 284 B8
Quoys Shetland 285 G6

R

Raasay Ho. Highld 248 C2
Rabbit's Cross Kent 37 B5
Raby Mers 126 B3
Rachan Mill Borders 195 C6
Rachub Gwyn 123 D6
Rackenford Devon 26 D3
Rackham W Sus 20 A3
Rackheath Norf 121 D4
Racks Dumfries 174 A3
Rackwick Orkney 283 H3
Rackwick Orkney 282 C5
Radbourne Derbys 113 B6
Radcliffe Gtr Man 137 C6
Radcliffe Northumb 189 C5
Radcliffe on Trent Notts 115 B4
Radclive Bucks 82 D3
Radcot Oxon 64 D3
Raddery Highld 252 A3
Radernie Fife 221 D4
Radford Semele Warks 81 A6
Radipole Dorset 15 C6
Radlett Herts 67 D6
Radley Oxon 65 D6
Radmanthwaite Notts 131 C5
Radmoor Shrops 111 C5
Radmore Green Ches 127 D5
Radnage Bucks 66 D2
Radstock Bath 43 D5
Radstone Northants 82 C2
Radway Warks 81 C6
Radway Green Ches 128 D2
Radwell Beds 84 B2
Radwell Herts 84 D4
Radwinter Essex 86 D2
Radyr Cardiff 41 C6
RAF Museum, Cosford Shrops 95 A5
RAF Museum, Hendon London 49 A5
Rafford Moray 253 A6
Ragdale Leics 115 D4
Raglan Mon 61 C6
Ragley Hall Warks 80 B3
Ragnall Notts 132 B3
Rahane Argyll 215 D5
Rainford Mers 136 C3
Rainford Junction Mers 136 C3
Rainham London 50 A2
Rainham Medway 51 C5
Rainhill Mers 136 D3
Rainhill Stoops Mers 136 D4
Rainow Ches 129 B4
Rainton N Yorks 158 D2
Rainworth Notts 131 D5
Raisbeck Cumb 155 A5
Raise Cumb 165 A5
Rait Perth 220 B2
Raithby Lincs 134 A3
Raithby Lincs 134 C3
Rake W Sus 33 C7
Rakewood Gtr Man 138 B2
Ram Carms 75 D4
Ram Lane Kent 38 A1
Ramasaig Highld 258 D1
Rame Corn 4 D2
Rame Corn 6 C3
Rameldry Mill Bank Fife 220 D3
Ramnageo Shetland 284 C8
Rampisham Dorset 15 A5
Rampside Cumb 153 D3
Rampton Cambs 85 A6
Rampton Notts 132 B2
Ramsbottom Gtr Man 137 B6
Ramsbury Wilts 45 B6
Ramscraigs Highld 275 B5
Ramsdean Hants 33 C6
Ramsdell Hants 46 D3
Ramsden Oxon 65 B4
Ramsden Bellhouse Essex 69 D7
Ramsden Heath Essex 69 D7
Ramsey Cambs 101 C4
Ramsey Essex 88 D3
Ramsey I o M 152 B4
Ramsey Forty Foot Cambs 101 C5
Ramsey Heights Cambs 101 C4
Ramsey Island Essex 70 C3
Ramsey Mereside Cambs 101 C4
Ramsey St Mary's Cambs 101 C4
Ramseycleuch Borders 185 A5
Ramsgate Kent 53 C5
Ramsgill N Yorks 157 D5
Ramshorn Staffs 113 A4
Ramsnest Common Sur 34 C2
Ranais W Isles 288 E5
Ranby Lincs 134 B2
Ranby Notts 131 A6
Rand Lincs 133 B6
Randwick Glos 63 C4
Ranfurly Renfs 204 B3
Rangag Highld 280 D3
Rangemore Staffs 113 C5
Rangeworthy S Glos 43 A5
Rankinston E Ayrs 182 A2
Ranmoor S Yorks 130 A3
Ranmore Common Sur 35 A4
Rannerdale Cumb 163 C4
Rannoch Station Perth 228 C3
Ranochan Highld 238 D2
Ranskill Notts 131 A6
Ranton Staffs 112 C2
Ranworth Norf 121 D5
Raploch Stirl 207 A5
Rapness Orkney 282 C6
Rascal Moor E Yorks 149 D7
Rascarrel Dumfries 173 D5
Rashiereive Aberds 257 D4
Raskelf N Yorks 158 D3
Rassau Bl Gwent 60 B3
Rastrick W Yorks 139 A4
Ratagan Highld 238 A3
Ratby Leics 98 A2
Ratcliffe Culey Leics 97 B6
Ratcliffe on Soar Leics 114 C2
Ratcliffe on the Wreake Leics 115 D4
Rathen Aberds 269 C5
Rathillet Fife 220 B3
Rathmell N Yorks 146 B2
Ratho Edin 208 C4
Ratho Station Edin 208 C4
Rathven Moray 267 C5
Ratley Warks 81 C6
Ratlinghope Shrops 94 B2
Rattar Highld 281 A4
Ratten Row Lancs 144 C4
Rattery Devon 7 A6
Rattlesden Suff 87 B5
Rattray Perth 231 D5
Raughton Head Cumb 164 A1
Raunds Northants 100 D1
Ravenfield S Yorks 140 D2
Ravenglass Cumb 153 A1
Ravenglass and Eskdale Railway & Museum Cumb 153 A1
Raveningham Norf 105 B4
Ravenscar N Yorks 160 A3
Ravenscraig Invclyd 204 A2
Ravensdale I o M 152 B3
Ravensden Beds 84 B2
Ravenseat N Yorks 156 A2
Ravenshead Notts 131 D5
Ravensmoor Ches 127 D6
Ravensthorpe Northants 98 D3
Ravensthorpe W Yorks 139 A5
Ravenstone Leics 114 D2
Ravenstone M Keynes 83 B5
Ravenstonedale Cumb 155 A6
Ravenstown Cumb 154 D2
Ravenstruther S Lnrk 194 B4
Ravensworth N Yorks 157 A5
Raw N Yorks 160 A3
Rawcliffe E Yorks 141 A4
Rawcliffe York 149 B4
Rawcliffe Bridge E Yorks 141 A4
Rawdon W Yorks 147 D6
Rawmarsh S Yorks 140 D2
Rawreth Essex 70 D1
Rawridge Devon 14 A2
Rawtenstall Lancs 137 A7
Raxton Aberds 256 C3
Raydon Suff 87 D6
Raylees Northumb 188 D2
Rayleigh Essex 70 D2
Rayne Essex 70 A1
Rayners Lane London 48 A4
Raynes Park London 49 C5
Reach Cambs 86 A1
Read Lancs 146 D1
Reading Reading 47 B5
Reading Street Kent 37 C7
Reagill Cumb 165 D4
Rearquhar Highld 264 A3
Rearsby Leics 115 D4
Reaster Highld 281 B4
Reawick Shetland 285 J5
Reay Highld 279 B5
Rechullin Highld 249 A5
Reculver Kent 53 C4
Red Dial Cumb 175 D5
Red Hill Worcs 79 B6
Red House Glass Cone, Wordsley W Mid 96 C1
Red Houses Jersey 6
Red Lodge Suff 102 D2
Red Rail Hereford 62 A1
Red Rock Gtr Man 137 C4
Red Roses Carms 56 A2
Red Row Northumb 189 D5
Red Street Staffs 128 D3
Red Wharf Bay Anglesey 123 B5
Redberth Pembs 55 D6
Redbourn Herts 67 B6
Redbourne N Lincs 142 D1
Redbrook Glos 62 B1
Redbrook Wrex 111 A4
Redburn Highld 264 D1
Redburn Highld 253 B5
Redburn Northumb 177 C5
Redcar Redcar 168 C4
Redcar Racecourse Redcar 168 C4
Redcastle Angus 233 C4
Redcastle Highld 252 B1
Redcliff Bay N Som 42 B3
Redding Falk 208 C2
Reddingmuirhead Falk 208 C2
Reddish Gtr Man 138 D1
Redditch Worcs 80 A3
Rede Suff 87 B4
Redenhall Norf 104 C3
Redesdale Camp Northumb 187 D7
Redesmouth Northumb 177 A6
Redford Aberds 233 A5
Redford Angus 232 D3
Redford Durham 166 B3
Redfordgreen Borders 185 A6
Redgorton Perth 219 B5
Redgrave Suff 103 D6
Redhill Aberds 256 C1
Redhill Aberds 245 B4
Redhill N Som 42 C3
Redhill Sur 35 A5
Redhouse Argyll 202 B3
Redhouses Argyll 200 B3
Redisham Suff 105 C5
Redland Bristol 43 B4
Redland Orkney 282 E4
Redlingfield Suff 104 D2
Redlynch Som 29 B7
Redlynch Wilts 31 C6
Redmarley D'Abitot Glos 79 D5
Redmarshall Stockton 167 C6
Redmile Leics 115 B5
Redmire N Yorks 156 B4
Redmoor Corn 5 A5
Rednal Shrops 110 C2
Redpath Borders 197 C4
Redpoint Highld 261 D4
Redruth Corn 3 A4
Redvales Gtr Man 137 C7
Redwick Newport 42 A3
Redwick S Glos 43 A4
Redworth Darl 167 C5
Reed Herts 85 D5
Reedham Norf 105 A5
Reedness E Yorks 141 A5
Reeds Beck Lincs 134 C2
Reepham Lincs 133 B5
Reepham Norf 120 C2
Reeth N Yorks 156 B4
Regaby I o M 152 B4
Regoul Highld 253 A4
Reiff Highld 270 C2
Reigate Sur 35 A5
Reighton N Yorks 161 D5
Reighton Gap N Yorks 161 D5
Reinigeadal W Isles 288 G3
Reiss Highld 281 C5
Rejerrah Corn 4 B2
Releath Corn 3 B4
Relubbus Corn 2 B3
Relugas Moray 253 B5
Remenham Wokingham 47 A5
Remenham Hill Wokingham 47 A5
Remony Perth 229 D6
Rempstone Notts 114 C3
Rendcomb Glos 63 C6
Rendham Suff 88 A4
Rendlesham Suff 88 B4
Renfrew Renfs 205 B5
Renhold Beds 84 B2
Renishaw Derbys 131 B4
Rennington Northumb 189 B5
Renton W Dunb 206 C1
Renwick Cumb 164 A3
Repps Norf 121 D6
Repton Derbys 113 C7
Reraig Highld 249 D5
Rescobie Angus 232 C3
Resipole Highld 235 D6
Resolis Highld 264 D2
Resolven Neath 40 A3
Reston Borders 211 D5
Reswallie Angus 232 C3
Retew Corn 4 B4
Retford Notts 132 A2
Rettendon Essex 70 D1
Rettendon Place Essex 70 D1
Revesby Lincs 134 C2
Revesby Bridge Lincs 134 C3
Rew Street I o W 18 B3
Rewe Devon 13 B4
Reydon Suff 105 D5
Reydon Smear Suff 105 D5
Reymerston Norf 103 A6
Reynalton Pembs 55 D6
Reynoldston Swansea 57 C4
Rezare Corn 11 D4
Rhaeadr Gwy = Rhayader Powys 76 A3
Rhandirmwyn Carms 59 A4
Rhayader = Rhaeadr Gwy Powys 76 A3
Rhedyn Gwyn 106 C2
Rhemore Highld 225 A4
Rhencullen I o M 152 B3
Rhes-y-cae Flint 126 B1
Rhewl Denb 125 C6
Rhewl Denb 109 A6
Rhian Highld 272 C3
Rhicarn Highld 270 B3
Rhiconich Highld 276 C3
Rhicullen Highld 264 C2
Rhidorroch Ho. Highld 262 A3
Rhifail Highld 278 D3
Rhigos Rhondda 59 E6
Rhilochan Highld 273 D5
Rhiroy Highld 262 B3
Rhisga = Risca Caerph 60 D4
Rhiw Gwyn 106 D2
Rhiwabon = Ruabon Wrex 110 A2
Rhiwbina Cardiff 41 C6
Rhiwbryfdir Gwyn 107 B6
Rhiwderin Newport 42 A1
Rhiwlas Gwyn 123 D5
Rhiwlas Gwyn 108 B4
Rhiwlas Powys 109 B6
Rhodes Gtr Man 138 C1
Rhodes Minnis Kent 38 A3
Rhodesia Notts 131 B5
Rhodiad Pembs 54 B3
Rhondda Rhondda 41 B4
Rhonehouse or Kelton Hill Dumfries 173 C5
Rhoose = Y Rhws V Glam 41 E5
Rhôs Carms 73 C6
Rhôs Neath 40 A2
Rhos-fawr Gwyn 106 C3
Rhos-goch Powys 77 C5
Rhos-hill Pembs 73 B4
Rhos-on-Sea Conwy 124 A3
Rhos-y-brithdir Powys 109 C6
Rhos-y-garth Ceredig 75 A5
Rhos-y-gwaliau Gwyn 108 B4
Rhos-y-llan Gwyn 106 C2
Rhos-y-Madoc Wrex 110 A2
Rhos-y-meirch Powys 77 A6
Rhosaman Carms 59 D4
Rhosbeirio Anglesey 122 A3
Rhoscefnhir Anglesey 123 C5
Rhoscolyn Anglesey 122 C2
Rhoscrowther Pembs 55 D5
Rhosesmor Flint 126 C2
Rhosgadfan Gwyn 107 A5
Rhosgoch Anglesey 123 B4
Rhoshirwaun Gwyn 106 D1
Rhoslan Gwyn 107 B4
Rhoslefain Gwyn 90 B3
Rhosllanerchrugog Wrex 110 A1
Rhosmaen Carms 58 C3
Rhosmeirch Anglesey 123 C4
Rhosneigr Anglesey 122 C3
Rhosnesni Wrex 126 D3
Rhosrobin Wrex 126 D3
Rhossili Swansea 57 D4
Rhosson Pembs 54 B3
Rhostryfan Gwyn 107 A4
Rhostyllen Wrex 110 A2
Rhosybol Anglesey 123 B4
RHS Garden, Wisley Sur 34 A3
Rhu Argyll 202 B3
Rhu Argyll 215 D5
Rhualt Denb 125 B5
Rhuddall Heath Ches 127 C5
Rhuddlan Ceredig 58 A1
Rhuddlan Denb 125 B5
Rhue Highld 262 A2
Rhulen Powys 77 B5
Rhunahaorine Argyll 202 D2
Rhuthun = Ruthin Denb 125 D6
Rhyd Gwyn 107 B6
Rhyd Powys 92 A3
Rhyd-Ddu Gwyn 107 A5
Rhyd-moel-ddu Powys 93 D4
Rhyd-Rosser Ceredig 75 B4
Rhyd-uchaf Gwyn 108 B4
Rhyd-wen Gwyn 91 A5
Rhyd-y-clafdy Gwyn 106 C3
Rhŷd-y-foel Conwy 125 B4
Rhyd-y-fro Neath 59 E4
Rhyd-y-gwin Swansea 57 B6
Rhyd-y-meirch Mon 61 C5
Rhyd-y-meudwy Denb 125 D6
Rhyd-y-pandy Swansea 57 B6
Rhyd-y-sarn Gwyn 107 B6
Rhyd-yr-onen Gwyn 90 B4
Rhydaman = Ammanford Carms 57 A6
Rhydargaeau Carms 58 C1
Rhydcymerau Carms 58 B2
Rhydd Worcs 79 C6
Rhydding Neath 40 B2
Rhydfudr Ceredig 75 B4
Rhydlewis Ceredig 73 B6
Rhydlios Gwyn 106 C1
Rhydlydan Conwy 124 D3
Rhydness Powys 77 C5
Rhydowen Ceredig 74 D3
Rhydspence Hereford 77 C6
Rhydtalog Flint 126 D2
Rhydwyn Anglesey 122 B3
Rhydycroesau Shrops 110 B1
Rhydyfelin Ceredig 75 A4
Rhydyfelin Rhondda 41 C5
Rhydymain Gwyn 108 C3
Rhydymwyn Flint 126 C2
Rhyl = Y Rhyl Denb 125 A5
Rhymney = Rhymni Caerph 60 C3
Rhymni = Rhymney Caerph 60 C3
Rhynd Fife 221 B4
Rhynd Perth 219 B6
Rhynie Aberds 255 D5
Rhynie Highld 265 C4
Ribbesford Worcs 95 D5
Ribblehead N Yorks 155 D6
Ribbleton Lancs 145 D5
Ribchester Lancs 145 D6
Ribigill Highld 277 C6
Riby Lincs 142 C3
Riby Cross Roads Lincs 142 C3
Riccall N Yorks 149 D5
Riccarton E Ayrs 193 B4
Richards Castle Hereford 78 A2
Richings Park Bucks 48 B3
Richmond London 49 B4
Richmond N Yorks 157 A5
Rickarton Aberds 245 D5
Rickinghall Suff 103 D6
Rickleton T & W 179 D4
Rickling Essex 85 D6
Rickmansworth Herts 67 D5
Riddings Cumb 175 A7
Riddings Derbys 131 D4
Riddlecombe Devon 25 D7
Riddlesden W Yorks 147 C4
Riddrie Glasgow 205 B6
Ridge Dorset 16 C3
Ridge Hants 32 D2
Ridge Wilts 30 B3
Ridge Green Sur 35 B6
Ridge Lane Warks 97 B5
Ridgebourne Powys 77 A4
Ridgehill N Som 43 C4
Ridgeway Cross Hereford 79 C5
Ridgewell Essex 86 C3
Ridgewood E Sus 22 A2
Ridgmont Beds 84 D1
Riding Mill Northumb 178 C2
Ridleywood Wrex 127 D4
Ridlington Norf 121 B5
Ridlington Rutland 99 A5
Ridsdale Northumb 177 A7
Riechip Perth 231 D4
Riemore Perth 230 D4
Rienachait Highld 270 A3
Rievaulx N Yorks 159 C4
Rievaulx Abbey N Yorks 159 C4
Rift House Hrtlpl 168 B2
Rigg Dumfries 175 B5
Riggend N Lnrk 207 C5
Rigsby Lincs 135 B4
Rigside S Lnrk 194 C3
Riley Green Lancs 137 A5
Rileyhill Staffs 113 D5
Rilla Mill Corn 10 D3
Rillington N Yorks 160 D2
Rimington Lancs 146 C2
Rimpton Som 29 C6
Rimswell E Yorks 143 A5
Rinaston Pembs 55 B5
Ringasta Shetland 285 M5
Ringford Dumfries 173 C4
Ringinglow S Yorks 130 A2
Ringland Norf 120 D3
Ringles Cross E Sus 36 D2
Ringmer E Sus 22 A2
Ringmore Devon 7 C5
Ringorm Moray 254 B3
Ring's End Cambs 101 A5
Ringsfield Suff 105 C5
Ringsfield Corner Suff 105 C5
Ringshall Herts 67 B4
Ringshall Suff 87 B6
Ringshall Stocks Suff 87 B6
Ringstead Norf 119 A4
Ringstead Northants 100 D1
Ringwood Hants 17 A5
Ringwould Kent 39 A5
Rinmore Aberds 243 A7
Rinnigill Orkney 283 H4
Rinsey Corn 2 C3
Riof W Isles 288 D2
Ripe E Sus 22 A3
Ripley Derbys 130 D3
Ripley Hants 17 B5
Ripley N Yorks 148 A1
Ripley Sur 34 A3
Riplingham E Yorks 150 D2
Ripon N Yorks 157 D7
Ripon Cathedral N Yorks 157 D7
Ripon Racecourse N Yorks 148 A2
Rippingale Lincs 116 C3
Ripple Kent 39 A5
Ripple Worcs 79 D6
Ripponden W Yorks 138 B3
Rireavach Highld 262 A2
Risabus Argyll 200 D3
Risbury Hereford 78 B3
Risby Suff 86 A3
Risca = Rhisga Caerph 60 D4
Rise E Yorks 151 C4
Riseden E Sus 36 C4
Risegate Lincs 117 C5
Riseholme Lincs 133 B4
Riseley Beds 84 A2
Riseley Wokingham 47 C5
Rishangles Suff 88 A2
Rishton Lancs 146 D1
Rishworth W Yorks 138 B3
Rising Bridge Lancs 137 A6
Risley Derbys 114 B2
Risley Warr 137 D5
Risplith N Yorks 147 A6
Rispond Highld 277 B5

Rivar Wilts 45 C7
Rivenhall End Essex 70 B2
River Bank Cambs 86 A1
Riverhead Kent 36 A3
Rivington Lancs 137 B5
Roa Island Cumb 153 D3
Roachill Devon 26 C3
Road Green Norf 104 B3
Roade Northants 83 B4
Roadhead Cumb 176 B3
Roadmeetings S Lnrk 194 B3
Roadside Highld 280 B3
Roadside of Catterline Aberds 233 A6
Roadside of Kinneff Aberds 233 A6
Roadwater Som 27 B5
Roag Highld 258 D2
Roath Cardiff 41 D6
Rob Roy and Trossachs Visitor Centre, Callander Stirl 217 D6
Robert Burns Centre, Dumfries Dumfries 174 A2
Roberton Borders 186 B3
Roberton S Lnrk 194 D4
Robertsbridge E Sus 37 D5
Robertown W Yorks 139 A4
Robeston Cross Pembs 55 D4
Robeston Wathen Pembs 55 C6
Robin Hood W Yorks 139 A6
Robin Hood Doncaster Sheffield International Airport S Yorks 141 D4
Robin Hood's Bay N Yorks 160 A3
Roborough Devon 25 D6
Roborough Devon 7 A4
Roby Mers 136 D3
Roby Mill Lancs 136 C4
Rocester Staffs 113 B5
Roch Pembs 55 B4
Roch Gate Pembs 55 B4
Rochdale Gtr Man 138 B1
Roche Corn 5 A4
Rochester Medway 51 C4
Rochester Northumb 188 D1
Rochester Castle Medway 51 C4
Rochester Cathedral Medway 51 C4
Rochford Essex 70 D2
Rock Corn 9 D5
Rock Northumb 189 A5
Rock Worcs 95 D5
Rock W Sus 21 A4
Rock Ferry Mers 126 A3
Rockbeare Devon 13 B5
Rockbourne Hants 31 D5
Rockcliffe Cumb 175 B6
Rockcliffe Dumfries 173 C6
Rockfield Highld 265 B5
Rockfield Mon 61 B6
Rockford Hants 17 A5
Rockhampton S Glos 62 D2
Rockingham Northants 99 B5
Rockingham Motor Speedway Northants 99 B6
Rockland All Saints Norf 103 B5
Rockland St Mary Norf 104 A4
Rockland St Peter Norf 103 B5
Rockley Wilts 45 B5
Rockwell End Bucks 47 A5
Rockwell Green Som 27 C6
Rodborough Glos 63 C4
Rodbourne Swindon 45 A5
Rodbourne Wilts 44 A3
Rodbourne Cheney Swindon 45 A5
Rodd Hereford 77 A7
Roddam Northumb 188 A3
Rodden Dorset 15 C6
Rode Som 44 D2
Rode Heath Ches 128 D3
Rodeheath Ches 128 C3
Roden Telford 111 D4
Rodhuish Som 27 B5
Rodington Telford 111 D4
Rodley Glos 62 B3
Rodley W Yorks 147 D6
Rodmarton Glos 63 D5
Rodmell E Sus 22 B2
Rodmersham Kent 51 C6
Rodney Stoke Som 42 D3
Rodsley Derbys 113 A6
Rodway Som 28 B2
Rodwell Dorset 15 D6
Roe Green Herts 85 D5
Roecliffe N Yorks 148 A2
Roehampton London 49 B5
Roesound Shetland 284 G5
Roffey W Sus 35 C4
Rogart Highld 273 D5
Rogart Station Highld 273 D5
Rogate W Sus 33 C7
Rogerstone Newport 42 A1
Roghadal W Isles 287 F5
Rogiet Mon 42 A3
Rogue's Alley Cambs 101 A5
Roke Oxon 66 D1
Roker T & W 179 D6
Rollesby Norf 121 D6
Rolleston Leics 99 A4
Rolleston Notts 132 D2
Rolleston-on-Dove Staffs 113 C6
Rolston E Yorks 151 C5
Rolvenden Kent 37 C6
Rolvenden Layne Kent 37 C6
Romaldkirk Durham 166 C2
Roman Baths & Pump Room, Bath Bath 43 C6
Romanby N Yorks 158 B2
Romannobridge Borders 195 B6
Romansleigh Devon 26 C2
Romford London 50 A2
Romiley Gtr Man 138 D2
Romney, Hythe and Dymchurch Light Railway Kent 38 B3
Romsey Hants 32 C2
Romsey Town Cambs 85 B6
Romsley Shrops 95 C5
Romsley Worcs 96 D2
Ronague I o M 152 D2
Rookhope Durham 166 A2
Rookley I o W 18 C4
Rooks Bridge Som 42 D2
Roos E Yorks 151 D5
Roosebeck Cumb 153 D3
Rootham's Green Beds 84 B3
Rootpark S Lnrk 195 A4
Ropley Hants 33 B5
Ropley Dean Hants 33 B5
Ropsley Lincs 116 B2
Rora Aberds 269 D5
Rorandle Aberds 244 A3
Rorrington Shrops 93 A7
Roscroggan Corn 3 A4
Rose Corn 4 B2
Rose Ash Devon 26 C2
Rose Green W Sus 20 C2
Rose Grove Lancs 146 D2
Rose Hill E Sus 22 A2
Rose Hill Lancs 146 D2
Rose Hill Suff 88 C2
Roseacre Kent 37 A5
Roseacre Lancs 144 D4
Rosebank S Lnrk 194 B3
Rosebrough Northumb 189 A4
Rosebush Pembs 55 B6
Rosecare Corn 10 B2
Rosedale Abbey N Yorks 159 B6
Roseden Northumb 188 A3
Rosefield Highld 253 A4
Rosehall Highld 272 D2
Rosehaugh Mains Highld 252 A2
Rosehearty Aberds 269 C4
Rosehill Shrops 111 B5
Roseisle Moray 266 C2
Roselands E Sus 22 B4
Rosemarket Pembs 55 D5
Rosemarkie Highld 252 A3
Rosemary Lane Devon 27 D6
Rosemount Perth 231 D5
Rosenannon Corn 5 A4
Rosewell Midloth 209 D5
Roseworth Stockton 168 C2
Roseworthy Corn 3 B4
Rosgill Cumb 164 D3
Roshven Highld 235 C6
Roskhill Highld 258 D2
Roskill House Highld 252 A2
Rosley Cumb 175 D6
Roslin Midloth 209 D5
Rosliston Derbys 113 D6
Rosneath Argyll 215 D5
Ross Dumfries 172 D4
Ross Northumb 199 C5
Ross Perth 218 B2
Ross-on-Wye Hereford 62 A2
Rossett Wrex 126 D3
Rossett Green N Yorks 148 B2
Rossie Ochill Perth 219 C5
Rossie Priory Perth 220 A2
Rossington S Yorks 140 D4
Rosskeen Highld 264 D2
Rossland Renfs 205 A4
Roster Highld 281 E4
Rostherne Ches 128 A2
Rosthwaite Cumb 163 C5
Roston Derbys 113 A5
Rosyth Fife 208 B4
Rothbury Northumb 188 C3
Rotherby Leics 115 D4
Rotherfield E Sus 36 D3
Rotherfield Greys Oxon 47 A5
Rotherfield Peppard Oxon 47 A5
Rotherham S Yorks 140 D2
Rothersthorpe Northants 83 B4
Rotherwick Hants 47 D5
Rothes Moray 254 B3
Rothesay Argyll 203 B5
Rothiebrisbane Aberds 256 C2
Rothiemurchus Estate Visitor Centre Highld 242 A2
Rothienorman Aberds 256 C2
Rothiesholm Orkney 282 E7
Rothley Leics 114 D3
Rothley Northumb 178 A2
Rothley Shield East Northumb 188 D3
Rothmaise Aberds 256 C1
Rothwell Lincs 142 D3
Rothwell Northants 99 C5
Rothwell W Yorks 139 A6
Rothwell Haigh W Yorks 139 A6
Rotsea E Yorks 150 B3
Rottal Angus 232 B1
Rotten End Suff 89 A4
Rottingdean Brighton 21 B6
Rottington Cumb 162 C2
Rotunda, Folkestone Kent 39 B4
Roud I o W 18 C4
Rough Close Staffs 112 B3
Rough Common Kent 52 D3
Rougham Norf 119 C5
Rougham Suff 87 A5
Rougham Green Suff 87 A5
Roughburn Highld 240 D1
Roughlee Lancs 146 C2
Roughley W Mid 96 B4
Roughsike Cumb 176 B3
Roughton Lincs 134 C2
Roughton Norf 120 B4
Roughton Shrops 95 B5
Roughton Moor Lincs 134 C2
Roundhay W Yorks 148 D2
Roundstonefoot Dumfries 185 B4
Roundstreet Common W Sus 34 D3
Roundway Wilts 44 C4
Rous Lench Worcs 80 B3
Rousdon Devon 14 B2
Routenburn N Ayrs 204 B1
Routh E Yorks 150 C3
Row Corn 10 D1
Row Cumb 154 C3
Row Heath Essex 71 B5
Rowanburn Dumfries 175 A7
Rowardennan Stirl 206 A1
Rowde Wilts 44 C3
Rowen Conwy 124 B2
Rowfoot Northumb 177 C4
Rowhedge Essex 71 A4
Rowhook W Sus 35 C4
Rowington Warks 81 A5
Rowland Derbys 130 B2
Rowlands Castle Hants 33 D6
Rowlands Gill T & W 178 D3
Rowledge Sur 33 A7
Rowlestone Hereford 61 A5
Rowley E Yorks 150 D2
Rowley Shrops 93 A7
Rowley Hill W Yorks 139 B4
Rowley Regis W Mid 96 C2
Rowly Sur 34 B3
Rowney Green Worcs 96 D3
Rownhams Hants 32 D2
Rowrah Cumb 162 C3
Rowsham Bucks 66 B3
Rowsley Derbys 130 C2
Rowstock Oxon 46 A2
Rowston Lincs 133 D5
Rowton Ches 127 C4
Rowton Shrops 110 D2
Rowton Telford 111 D5
Roxburgh Borders 197 C6
Roxby N Lincs 141 B7
Roxby N Yorks 169 D5
Roxton Beds 84 B3
Roxwell Essex 69 C6
Royal Botanic Gardens Edin 209 C5
Royal Leamington Spa Warks 81 A6
Royal Museum of Scotland Edin 209 C5
Royal Oak Darl 167 C5
Royal Oak Lancs 136 C3
Royal Pavilion, Brighton Brighton 21 B6
Royal Tunbridge Wells Kent 36 C3
Royal Welch Fusiliers Regimental Museum (See Caernarfon Castle) Gwyn 123 D4
Royal Worcester Porcelain, Worcester Worcs 79 B6
Roybridge Highld 239 D6
Roydhouse W Yorks 139 B5
Roydon Essex 68 C4
Roydon Norf 119 C4
Roydon Norf 104 C1
Roydon Hamlet Essex 68 C4
Royston Herts 85 C5
Royston S Yorks 139 B6
Royton Gtr Man 138 C2
Rozel Jersey 6
Ruabon = Rhiwabon Wrex 110 A2
Ruaig Argyll 222 C3
Ruan Lanihorne Corn 4 C3
Ruan Minor Corn 3 D5
Ruarach Highld 249 D6
Ruardean Glos 62 B2
Ruardean Woodside Glos 62 B2
Rubery Worcs 96 D2
Ruckcroft Cumb 164 A3
Ruckhall Hereford 78 D2
Ruckinge Kent 38 B2
Ruckland Lincs 134 B3
Ruckley Shrops 94 A3
Rudbaxton Pembs 55 B5
Rudby N Yorks 158 A3
Ruddington Notts 114 B3
Rudford Glos 62 A3
Rudge Shrops 95 B6
Rudge Som 44 D2
Rudgeway S Glos 43 A5
Rudgwick W Sus 34 C3
Rudhall Hereford 62 A2
Rudheath Ches 128 B1
Rudley Green Essex 70 C2
Rudry Caerph 41 C6
Rudston E Yorks 150 A3
Rudyard Staffs 129 D4
Rufford Lancs 136 B3
Rufforth York 148 B4
Rugby Warks 98 D2
Rugeley Staffs 112 D4
Ruglen S Ayrs 181 A4
Ruilick Highld 251 B7
Ruishton Som 28 C2
Ruisigearraidh W Isles 287 F4
Ruislip London 48 A3
Ruislip Common London 48 A3
Rumbling Bridge Perth 208 A3
Rumburgh Suff 104 C4
Rumford Corn 9 D4
Rumney Cardiff 41 D7
Runcorn Halton 127 A5
Runcton W Sus 20 B1
Runcton Holme Norf 102 A2
Rundlestone Devon 11 D6
Runfold Sur 34 B1
Runhall Norf 103 A6
Runham Norf 105 A6
Runham Norf 121 D6
Runnington Som 27 C6
Runsell Green Essex 70 C1
Runswick Bay N Yorks 169 D6
Runwell Essex 70 D1
Ruscombe Wokingham 47 B5
Rush Green London 50 A2
Rush-head Aberds 256 B3
Rushall Hereford 79 D4
Rushall Norf 104 C2
Rushall Wilts 45 D5
Rushall W Mid 96 A3
Rushbrooke Suff 87 A4
Rushbury Shrops 94 B3
Rushden Herts 85 D5
Rushden Northants 83 A6
Rushenden Kent 51 B6
Rushford Norf 103 C5
Rushlake Green E Sus 22 A4
Rushmere Suff 105 C5
Rushmere St Andrew Suff 88 C3
Rushmoor Sur 34 B1
Rushock Worcs 96 D1
Rusholme Gtr Man 138 D1
Rushton Ches 127 C5
Rushton Northants 99 C5
Rushton Shrops 95 A4
Rushton Spencer Staffs 129 C4
Rushwick Worcs 79 B6
Rushyford Durham 167 C5
Ruskie Stirl 217 D6
Ruskington Lincs 133 D5
Rusland Cumb 154 C2
Rusper W Sus 35 C5
Ruspidge Glos 62 B2
Russell's Water Oxon 47 A5
Russel's Green Suff 104 D3
Rusthall Kent 36 C3
Rustington W Sus 20 B3
Ruston N Yorks 160 C3
Ruston Parva E Yorks 150 A3
Ruswarp N Yorks 160 A2
Rutherford Borders 197 C5
Rutherglen S Lnrk 205 B6
Ruthernbridge Corn 5 A5
Ruthin = Rhuthun Denb 125 D6
Ruthin Craft Centre Denb 125 D6
Ruthrieston Aberdeen 245 B6
Ruthven Aberds 255 B6
Ruthven Angus 231 D6
Ruthven Highld 253 C4
Ruthven Highld 241 C5
Ruthven House Angus 231 D7
Ruthvoes Corn 4 A4
Ruthwell Dumfries 174 B3
Ruyton-XI-Towns Shrops 110 C2
Ryal Northumb 178 B2
Ryal Fold Blkburn 137 A5
Ryall Dorset 14 B4
Ryarsh Kent 37 A4
Rydal Cumb 154 A2
Ryde I o W 19 B4
Rye E Sus 37 D7
Rye Foreign E Sus 37 D6
Rye Harbour E Sus 38 D1
Rye Park Herts 68 B3
Rye Street Worcs 79 D5
Ryecroft Gate Staffs 129 C4
Ryehill E Yorks 143 A4
Ryhall Rutland 116 D3
Ryhill W Yorks 140 B1
Ryhope T & W 179 D6
Rylstone N Yorks 146 B3
Ryme Intrinseca Dorset 29 D5
Ryther N Yorks 149 D4
Ryton Glos 79 D5
Ryton N Yorks 159 D6
Ryton Shrops 95 A5
Ryton T & W 178 C3
Ryton-on-Dunsmore Warks 97 D6

S

Sabden Lancs 146 D1
Sacombe Herts 68 B3
Sacriston Durham 167 A5
Sadberge Darl 167 D6
Saddell Argyll 190 B3
Saddington Leics 98 B3
Saddle Bow Norf 118 D3
Saddlescombe W Sus 21 A5
Sadgill Cumb 154 A3
Saffron Walden Essex 86 D1
Sageston Pembs 55 D6
Saham Hills Norf 103 A5
Saham Toney Norf 103 A5
Saighdinis W Isles 287 H3
Saighton Ches 127 C4
St Abbs Borders 211 D6
St Abb's Haven Borders 211 D6
St Agnes Corn 4 B2
St Agnes Scilly 2 F3
St Albans Herts 67 C6
St Alban's Abbey Herts 67 C6
St Allen Corn 4 B3
St Andrews Fife 221 C5
St Andrew's Major V Glam 41 D6
St Anne Ald 7
St Annes Lancs 136 A2
St Ann's Dumfries 184 C3
St Ann's Chapel Corn 11 D5
St Ann's Chapel Devon 7 C5
St Anthony Corn 3 C5
St Anthony's Hill E Sus 22 B4
St Arvans Mon 61 D7
St Asaph = Llanelwy Denb 125 B5
St Athan V Glam 41 E5
St Aubin Jersey 6
St Austell Corn 5 B5
St Bees Cumb 162 C2
St Blazey Corn 5 B5
St Boswells Borders 197 C4
St Brelade Jersey 6
St Breock Corn 9 D5
St Breward Corn 10 D1
St Briavels Glos 62 C1
St Bride's Pembs 54 C3
St Brides Major V Glam 40 D3
St Bride's Netherwent Mon 42 A3
St Brides super Ely V Glam 41 D5
St Brides Wentlooge Newport 42 A1
St Budeaux Plym 6 B3
St Buryan Corn 2 C2
St Catherine Bath 44 B1
St Catherine's Argyll 215 B4
St Clears = Sanclêr Carms 56 A2
St Cleer Corn 6 A1
St Clement Corn 4 C3
St Clements Jersey 6
St Clement's Caves, Hastings E Sus 23 A6
St Clether Corn 10 C3
St Colmac Argyll 203 B5
St Columb Major Corn 4 A4
St Columb Minor Corn 4 A3
St Columb Road Corn 4 B4
St Combs Aberds 269 C5
St Cross South Elmham Suff 104 C3
St Cyrus Aberds 233 B5
St David's Perth 218 B4
St David's = Tyddewi Pembs 54 B3
St Day Corn 4 C2
St Dennis Corn 4 B4
St Devereux Hereford 78 D2
St Dogmaels Pembs 73 B4
St Dogwells Pembs 55 B5
St Dominick Corn 6 A3
St Donat's V Glam 40 E4
St Edith's Wilts 44 C3
St Endellion Corn 9 D5
St Enoder Corn 4 B3
St Erme Corn 4 B3
St Erney Corn 6 B2
St Erth Corn 2 B3
St Ervan Corn 9 D4
St Eval Corn 4 A3
St Ewe Corn 5 C4
St Fagans Cardiff 41 D6
St Fagans Museum of Welsh Life Cardiff 41 D6
St Fergus Aberds 269 D5
St Fillans Perth 217 B6
St Florence Pembs 55 D6
St Genny's Corn 10 B2
St George Conwy 125 B4
St George's V Glam 41 D5
St Germans Corn 6 B2
St Giles Lincs 133 B4
St Giles Cathedral Edin 209 C5
St Giles in the Wood Devon 25 D6
St Giles on the Heath Devon 11 B4
St Harmon Powys 92 D3
St Helen Auckland Durham 167 C4
St Helena Warks 97 A5
St Helen's E Sus 23 A6
St Helens I o W 19 C5
St Helens Mers 136 D4
St Helier London 49 C5
St Helier Jersey 6
St Hilary Corn 2 B3
St Hilary V Glam 41 D5
Saint Hill W Sus 36 C1
St Illtyd Bl Gwent 41 A7
St Ippollitts Herts 68 A1
St Ishmael's Pembs 54 D4
St Issey Corn 9 D5
St Ive Corn 6 A2
St Ives Cambs 101 D5
St Ives Corn 2 A3
St Ives Dorset 17 A5
St James South Elmham Suff 104 C4
St Jidgey Corn 9 E5
St John Corn 6 B3
St John's I o M 152 C2
St John's Jersey 6
St John's Sur 34 A2
St John's Worcs 79 B6
St John's Chapel Durham 166 B1
St John's Fen End Norf 118 D2
St John's Highway Norf 118 D2
St John's Town of Dalry Dumfries 182 D4
St Judes I o M 152 B3
St Just Corn 2 B1
St Just in Roseland Corn 4 D3
St Just In Roseland Corn 4 D3
St Katherine's Aberds 256 C2
St Keverne Corn 3 C5
St Kew Corn 9 D6
St Kew Highway Corn 9 D6
St Keyne Corn 6 A1
St Lawrence Corn 5 A5
St Lawrence Essex 70 C3
St Lawrence I o W 18 D4
St Leonard's Bucks 67 C4
St Leonards Dorset 17 A5
St Leonards E Sus 23 B5
Saint Leonards S Lnrk 205 C4
St Levan Corn 2 C1
St Lythans V Glam 41 D6
St Mabyn Corn 9 D6
St Madoes Perth 219 B6
St Margaret South Elmham Suff 104 C4
St Margaret's Hereford 78 D1
St Margarets Herts 68 B3
St Margaret's at Cliffe Kent 39 A5
St Margaret's Hope Orkney 283 H5
St Mark's I o M 152 D2
St Martin Corn 6 B1
St Martins Corn 3 C5
St Martin's Jersey 6
St Martins Perth 219 A6
St Martin's Shrops 110 B2
St Mary Bourne Hants 46 D2
St Mary Church V Glam 41 D5
St Mary Cray London 50 C1
St Mary Hill V Glam 41 D4
St Mary Hoo Medway 51 B5
St Mary in the Marsh Kent 38 C2
St Mary's Jersey 6
St Mary's Orkney 283 G5
St Mary's Bay Kent 38 C2
St Mary's Church Warks 81 A5
St Maughans Mon 61 B6
St Mawes Corn 4 D3
St Mawgan Corn 4 A3
St Mellion Corn 6 A2
St Mellons Cardiff 42 A1
St Merryn Corn 9 D4
St Mewan Corn 5 B4
St Michael Caerhays Corn 5 C4
St Michael Penkevil Corn 4 C3
St Michael South Elmham Suff 104 C4
St Michael's Kent 37 C6
St Michaels Worcs 78 A3
St Michael's Mount, Penzance Corn 2 C3

St Michael's on Wyre Lancs 145 C4
St Minver Corn 9 D5
St Monans Fife 221 D5
St Neot Corn 5 A6
St Neots Cambs 84 A3
St Newlyn East Corn 4 B3
St Nicholas Pembs 72 C1
St Nicholas V Glam 41 D5
St Nicholas at Wade Kent 53 C4
St Ninians Stirl 207 A5
St Osyth Essex 71 B5
St Osyth Heath Essex 71 B5
St Ouens Jersey 6
St Owens Cross Hereford 62 A1
St Paul's Cathedral London 49 A6
St Paul's Cray London 50 C1
St Paul's Walden Herts 68 A1
St Peter Port Guern 6
St Peter's Jersey 6
St Peter's Kent 53 C5
St Petrox Pembs 55 E5
St Pinnock Corn 5 A7
St Quivox S Ayrs 192 C3
St Ruan Corn 3 D5
St Sampson Guern 6
St Stephen Corn 4 B4
St Stephen's Corn 10 C4
St Stephens Corn 6 B3
St Stephens Herts 67 C6
St Teath Corn 9 C6
St Thomas Devon 13 B4
St Tudy Corn 9 D6
St Twynnells Pembs 55 E5
St Veep Corn 5 B6
St Vigeans Angus 233 D4
St Wenn Corn 5 A4
St Weonards Hereford 61 A6
Saintbury Glos 80 D4
Salcombe Devon 7 D6
Salcombe Regis Devon 13 C6
Salcott Essex 70 B3
Sale Gtr Man 137 D6
Sale Green Worcs 80 B2
Saleby Lincs 135 B4
Salehurst E Sus 37 D5
Salem Ceredig 91 D4
Salem Carms 58 C3
Salen Argyll 225 B4
Salen Highld 235 D5
Salesbury Lancs 145 D6
Salford Beds 83 D6
Salford Gtr Man 137 D7
Salford Oxon 64 A3
Salford Priors Warks 80 B3
Salfords Sur 35 B5
Salhouse Norf 121 D5
Saline Fife 208 A3
Salisbury Wilts 31 C5
Salisbury Cathedral Wilts 31 C5
Salisbury Racecourse Wilts 31 C4
Sallachan Highld 236 C3
Sallachy Highld 249 C6
Sallachy Highld 272 D3
Salle Norf 120 C3
Salmonby Lincs 134 B3
Salmond's Muir Angus 221 A5
Salperton Glos 64 A1
Salph End Beds 84 B2
Salsburgh N Lnrk 207 D6
Salt Staffs 112 C3
Salt End E Yorks 142 A3
Saltaire W Yorks 147 D5
Saltaire 1853 Gallery W Yorks 147 D5
Saltash Corn 6 B3
Saltburn Highld 264 D3
Saltburn-by-the-Sea Redcar 169 C4
Saltby Leics 115 C6
Saltcoats Cumb 153 A1
Saltcoats N Ayrs 204 D2
Saltdean Brighton 22 B1
Salter Lancs 145 A6
Salterforth Lancs 146 C2
Salterswall Ches 127 C6
Saltfleet Lincs 143 D6
Saltfleetby All Saints Lincs 143 D6
Saltfleetby St Clements Lincs 143 D6
Saltfleetby St Peter Lincs 135 A4
Saltford Bath 43 C5
Salthouse Norf 120 A2
Saltmarshe E Yorks 141 A5
Saltney Flint 126 C3
Salton N Yorks 159 D6
Saltwick Northumb 178 B3
Saltwood Kent 38 B3
Salum Argyll 222 C3
Salvington W Sus 21 B4
Salwarpe Worcs 80 A1
Salwayash Dorset 15 B4
Sambourne Warks 80 A3
Sambrook Telford 111 C6
Samhla W Isles 287 H2
Samlesbury Lancs 145 D5
Samlesbury Bottoms Lancs 137 A5
Sammy Miller's Motorcycle Museum Hants 17 B6
Sampford Arundel Som 27 D6
Sampford Brett Som 27 A5
Sampford Courtenay Devon 12 A1
Sampford Peverell Devon 27 D5
Sampford Spiney Devon 11 D6
Sampool Bridge Cumb 154 C3
Samuelston E Loth 210 C1
Sanachan Highld 249 B5
Sanaigmore Argyll 200 A2
Sanclêr = St Clears Carms 56 A2
Sancreed Corn 2 C2
Sancton E Yorks 150 D2
Sand Highld 261 A6
Sand Shetland 285 J5
Sand Hole E Yorks 149 D7
Sand Hutton N Yorks 149 B5
Sandaig Highld 247 D6
Sandal Magna W Yorks 139 B6
Sandale Cumb 175 D5
Sanday Airport Orkney 282 C7
Sandbach Ches 128 C2
Sandbank Argyll 215 D4
Sandbanks Poole 17 C4
Sandend Aberds 267 C6
Sanderstead London 49 C6
Sandfields Glos 63 A5
Sandford Cumb 165 D5
Sandford Devon 12 A3
Sandford Dorset 16 C3
Sandford I o W 18 C4
Sandford N Som 42 D3
Sandford Shrops 111 B4
Sandford S Lnrk 194 B2
Sandford on Thames Oxon 65 C6
Sandford Orcas Dorset 29 C6
Sandford St Martin Oxon 65 A5
Sandfordhill Aberds 257 B6
Sandgate Kent 38 B3
Sandgreen Dumfries 172 C3
Sandhaven Aberds 269 C4
Sandhead Dumfries 170 C2
Sandhills Sur 34 C2
Sandhoe Northumb 178 C1
Sandholme E Yorks 150 D1
Sandholme Lincs 117 B6
Sandhurst Brack 47 C6
Sandhurst Glos 63 A4
Sandhurst Kent 37 D5
Sandhurst Cross Kent 37 D5
Sandhutton N Yorks 158 C2
Sandiacre Derbys 114 B2
Sandilands Lincs 135 A5
Sandilands S Lnrk 194 C3
Sandiway Ches 127 B6
Sandleheath Hants 31 D5
Sandling Kent 37 A5
Sandlow Green Ches 128 C2
Sandness Shetland 285 H3
Sandon Essex 70 C1
Sandon Herts 85 D5
Sandon Staffs 112 B3
Sandown I o W 19 C4
Sandown Park Racecourse Sur 48 C4
Sandplace Corn 6 B1
Sandridge Herts 67 B6
Sandridge Wilts 44 C3
Sandringham Norf 118 C3
Sandsend N Yorks 169 D6
Sandside Ho. Highld 279 B5
Sandsound Shetland 285 J5
Sandtoft N Lincs 141 C5
Sandway Kent 37 A6
Sandwell W Mid 96 C3
Sandwich Kent 53 D5
Sandwick Cumb 164 D2
Sandwick Orkney 283 K5
Sandwick Shetland 285 L6
Sandwith Cumb 162 C2
Sandy Beds 84 C3
Sandy Carms 57 B4
Sandy Bank Lincs 134 D2
Sandy Haven Pembs 55 D4
Sandy Lane Wilts 44 C3
Sandy Lane Wrex 110 A2
Sandycroft Flint 126 C3
Sandyford Dumfries 185 C5
Sandyford Stoke 128 D3
Sandygate I o M 152 B3
Sandyhills Dumfries 173 C6
Sandylands Lancs 144 A4
Sandypark Devon 12 C2
Sandysike Cumb 175 B6
Sangobeg Highld 277 B5
Sangomore Highld 277 B5
Sanna Highld 234 D3
Sanndabhaig W Isles 288 D5
Sanndabhaig W Isles 286 B4
Sannox N Ayrs 203 D5
Sanquhar Dumfries 183 B5
Santa Pod Raceway Beds 83 A6
Santon N Lincs 142 B1
Santon Bridge Cumb 163 D4
Santon Downham Suff 103 C4
Sapcote Leics 98 B1
Sapey Common Hereford 79 A5
Sapiston Suff 103 D5
Sapley Cambs 100 D4
Sapperton Glos 63 C5
Sapperton Lincs 116 B3
Saracen's Head Lincs 117 C6
Sarclet Highld 281 D5
Sardis Carms 57 B5
Sarn Bridgend 40 C4
Sarn Powys 93 B6
Sarn Bach Gwyn 106 D3
Sarn Meyllteyrn Gwyn 106 C2
Sarnau Ceredig 73 A6
Sarnau Carms 56 A3
Sarnau Gwyn 109 B4
Sarnau Powys 76 D4
Sarnau Powys 110 D1
Sarnesfield Hereford 78 B1
Saron Carms 73 C6
Saron Carms 57 A6
Saron Denb 125 C5
Saron Gwyn 107 A4
Saron Gwyn 123 D5
Sarratt Herts 67 D5
Sarre Kent 53 C4
Sarsden Oxon 64 A3
Sarsgrum Highld 277 B4
Satley Durham 166 A4
Satron N Yorks 156 B3
Satterleigh Devon 26 C1
Satterthwaite Cumb 154 B2
Satwell Oxon 47 A5
Sauchen Aberds 244 A3
Saucher Perth 219 A6
Sauchie Clack 208 A1
Sauchieburn Aberds 233 B4
Saughall Ches 126 B3
Saughtree Borders 187 D4
Saul Glos 62 C3
Saundby Notts 132 A2
Saundersfoot Pembs 56 B1
Saunderton Bucks 66 C2
Saunton Devon 25 B5
Sausthorpe Lincs 134 C3
Saval Highld 272 D3
Savary Highld 225 B5
Savile Park W Yorks 138 A3
Sawbridge Warks 82 A2
Sawbridgeworth Herts 69 B4
Sawdon N Yorks 160 C3
Sawley Derbys 114 B2
Sawley Lancs 146 C1
Sawley N Yorks 147 A6
Sawston Cambs 85 C6
Sawtry Cambs 100 C3
Saxby Leics 115 D6
Saxby Lincs 133 A5
Saxby All Saints N Lincs 142 B1
Saxelbye Leics 115 C5
Saxham Street Suff 88 A1
Saxilby Lincs 132 B3
Saxlingham Norf 120 B2
Saxlingham Green Norf 104 B3
Saxlingham Nethergate Norf 104 B3
Saxlingham Thorpe Norf 104 B3
Saxmundham Suff 89 A4
Saxon Street Cambs 86 B2
Saxondale Notts 115 B4
Saxtead Suff 88 A3
Saxtead Green Suff 88 A3
Saxthorpe Norf 120 B3
Saxton N Yorks 148 D3
Sayers Common W Sus 21 A5
Scackleton N Yorks 159 D5
Scadabhagh W Isles 288 H2
Scaftworth Notts 141 D4
Scagglethorpe N Yorks 160 D2
Scaitcliffe Lancs 137 A6
Scalasaig Argyll 212 C1
Scalby E Yorks 141 A6
Scalby N Yorks 160 B4
Scaldwell Northants 99 D4
Scale Houses Cumb 164 A3
Scaleby Cumb 176 C2
Scaleby Hill Cumb 176 C2
Scales Cumb 153 C3
Scales Cumb 163 B6
Scales Lancs 145 D4
Scalford Leics 115 C5
Scaling N Yorks 169 D5
Scallastle Argyll 225 C5
Scalloway Shetland 285 K6
Scalpay W Isles 288 H3
Scalpay Ho. Highld 247 B5
Scalpsie Argyll 203 C5
Scamadale Highld 235 A6
Scamblesby Lincs 134 B2
Scamodale Highld 236 B2
Scampston N Yorks 160 D2
Scampton Lincs 133 B4
Scapa Orkney 283 G5
Scapegoat Hill W Yorks 138 B3
Scar Orkney 282 C7
Scarborough N Yorks 160 C4
Scarborough Sea Life Centre N Yorks 160 B4
Scarcliffe Derbys 131 C4
Scarcroft W Yorks 148 C2
Scarcroft Hill W Yorks 148 C2
Scardroy Highld 250 A4
Scarff Shetland 284 E4
Scarfskerry Highld 281 A4
Scargill Durham 166 D3
Scarinish Argyll 222 C3
Scarisbrick Lancs 136 B2
Scarning Norf 119 D6
Scarrington Notts 115 A5
Scartho NE Lincs 143 C4
Scarwell Orkney 282 E3
Scatness Shetland 285 M5
Scatraig Highld 252 C3
Scawby N Lincs 142 C1
Scawsby S Yorks 140 C3
Scawton N Yorks 158 C4
Scayne's Hill W Sus 35 D6
Scethrog Powys 60 A3
Scholar Green Ches 128 D3
Scholes W Yorks 139 C4
Scholes W Yorks 139 A4
Scholes W Yorks 148 D2
School Green Ches 127 C6
Science & Industry Museum, Manchester Gtr Man 138 D1
Science Centre Glasgow 205 B5
Science Museum London 49 B5
Scleddau Pembs 55 A5
Sco Ruston Norf 121 C4
Scofton Notts 131 A6
Scole Norf 104 D2
Scolpaig W Isles 287 G2
Scone Perth 219 B6
Scone Palace, Perth Perth 219 B6
Sconser Highld 247 A4
Scoonie Fife 220 D3
Scoor Argyll 224 E3
Scopwick Lincs 133 D5
Scoraig Highld 262 A2
Scorborough E Yorks 150 C3
Scorrier Corn 4 C2
Scorton Lancs 145 C5
Scorton N Yorks 157 A6
Scotbheinn W Isles 286 A4
Scotby Cumb 176 D2
Scotch Corner N Yorks 157 A6
Scotforth Lancs 145 B4
Scothern Lincs 133 B5
Scotland Gate Northumb 179 A4
Scotlandwell Perth 219 D6
Scotney Castle Garden Kent 37 C4
Scotsburn Highld 264 C3
Scotscalder Station Highld 280 C2
Scotscraig Fife 220 B4
Scots'Gap Northumb 178 A2
Scotston Aberds 233 A5
Scotston Perth 230 D3
Scotstoun Glasgow 205 B5
Scotstown Highld 236 C2
Scotswood T & W 178 C3
Scottas Highld 247 D6
Scotter Lincs 141 C6
Scotterthorpe Lincs 141 C6
Scottlethorpe Lincs 116 C3
Scotton Lincs 141 D6
Scotton N Yorks 157 B5
Scotton N Yorks 148 B2
Scottow Norf 121 C4
Scoughall E Loth 210 B3
Scoulag Argyll 203 C6
Scoulton Norf 103 A5
Scourie Highld 276 D2
Scourie More Highld 276 D2
Scousburgh Shetland 285 M5
Scrabster Highld 280 B2
Scrafield Lincs 134 C3
Scrainwood Northumb 188 C2
Scrane End Lincs 117 A6
Scraptoft Leics 98 A3
Scratby Norf 121 D7
Scrayingham N Yorks 149 A6
Scredington Lincs 116 A3
Scremby Lincs 135 C4
Scremerston Northumb 198 B4
Screveton Notts 115 A5
Scrivelsby Lincs 134 C2
Scriven N Yorks 148 B2
Scrooby Notts 141 D4
Scropton Derbys 113 B5
Scrub Hill Lincs 134 D2
Scruton N Yorks 157 B6
Sculcoates Hull 150 D3
Sculthorpe Norf 119 B5
Scunthorpe N Lincs 141 B6
Scurlage Swansea 57 D4
Sea Palling Norf 121 C6
Sea Zoo Anglesey 123 D4
Seaborough Dorset 14 A4
Seacombe Mers 136 D2
Seacroft Lincs 135 C5
Seacroft W Yorks 148 D2
Seadyke Lincs 117 B6
Seafield S Ayrs 192 C3
Seafield W Loth 208 D3
Seaford E Sus 22 C2
Seaforth Mers 136 D2
Seagrave Leics 115 D4
Seaham Durham 168 A2
Seahouses Northumb 199 C6
Seal Kent 36 A3
Sealand Flint 126 C3
Seale Sur 34 B1
Seamer N Yorks 168 D2
Seamer N Yorks 160 C4
Seamill N Ayrs 204 D2
Searby Lincs 142 C2
Seasalter Kent 52 C2
Seascale Cumb 162 D3
Seathorne Lincs 135 C5
Seathwaite Cumb 153 A3
Seathwaite Cumb 163 C5
Seatoller Cumb 163 C5
Seaton Corn 6 B2
Seaton Cumb 162 A3
Seaton Devon 14 C2
Seaton Durham 179 D5
Seaton E Yorks 151 C4
Seaton Northumb 179 B5
Seaton Rutland 99 B6
Seaton Burn T & W 179 B4
Seaton Carew Hrtlpl 168 C3
Seaton Delaval Northumb 179 B5
Seaton Ross E Yorks 149 C6
Seaton Sluice Northumb 179 B5
Seatown Aberds 267 C6
Seatown Dorset 14 B4
Seave Green N Yorks 159 A4
Seaview I o W 19 B5
Seaville Cumb 175 C4
Seavington St Mary Som 28 D3
Seavington St Michael Som 28 D4
Sebergham Cumb 164 A1
Seckington Warks 97 A5
Second Coast Highld 261 A6
Sedbergh Cumb 155 B5
Sedbury Glos 62 D1
Sedbusk N Yorks 156 B2
Sedgeberrow Worcs 80 D3
Sedgebrook Lincs 115 B6
Sedgefield Durham 167 C6
Sedgefield Racecourse Durham 167 C6
Sedgeford Norf 119 B4
Sedgehill Wilts 30 C2
Sedgley W Mid 96 B2
Sedgwick Cumb 154 C4
Sedlescombe E Sus 23 A5
Sedlescombe Street E Sus 23 A5
Seend Wilts 44 C3
Seend Cleeve Wilts 44 C3
Seer Green Bucks 67 D4
Seething Norf 104 B4
Sefton Mers 136 C2
Seghill Northumb 179 B4
Seifton Shrops 94 C2
Seighford Staffs 112 C2
Seilebost W Isles 287 E5
Seion Gwyn 123 D5
Seisdon Staffs 95 B6
Seisiadar W Isles 288 D6
Selattyn Shrops 110 B1
Selborne Hants 33 B6
Selby N Yorks 149 D5
Selham W Sus 34 D2
Selhurst London 49 C6
Selkirk Borders 186 A3
Selkirk Glass Borders 186 A3
Sellack Hereford 62 A1
Sellafirth Shetland 284 D7
Sellibister Orkney 282 C8
Sellindge Kent 38 B2
Sellindge Lees Kent 38 B3
Selling Kent 52 D2
Sells Green Wilts 44 C3
Selly Oak W Mid 96 C3
Selmeston E Sus 22 B3
Selsdon London 49 C6
Selsey W Sus 20 C1
Selsfield Common W Sus 35 C6
Selsted Kent 39 A4
Selston Notts 131 D4
Selworthy Som 27 A4
Semblister Shetland 285 H5
Semer Suff 87 C5
Semington Wilts 44 C2
Semley Wilts 30 C2
Send Sur 34 A3
Send Marsh Sur 34 A3
Senghenydd Caerph 41 B6
Sennen Corn 2 C1
Sennen Cove Corn 2 C1
Sennybridge = Pont Senni Powys 59 C6
Serlby Notts 131 A6
Sessay N Yorks 158 D3
Setchey Norf 118 D3
Setley Hants 18 A2
Setter Shetland 285 H5
Setter Shetland 284 E6
Setter Shetland 285 J7
Settiscarth Orkney 282 F4
Settle N Yorks 146 A2
Settrington N Yorks 160 D2
Seven Kings London 50 A1
Seven Sisters Neath 59 E5
Sevenhampton Glos 63 A6
Sevenoaks Kent 36 A3
Sevenoaks Weald Kent 36 A3
Severn Beach S Glos 43 A4
Severn Bridges Visitor Centre S Glos 43 A4
Severn Stoke Worcs 79 C6
Severn Valley Railway Worcs 95 D5
Severnhampton Swindon 64 D3
Sevington Kent 38 A2
Sewards End Essex 86 D1
Sewardstone Essex 68 D3
Sewardstonebury Essex 68 D3
Sewerby E Yorks 151 A4
Sewerby Hall and Gardens, Bridlington E Yorks 151 A5
Seworgan Corn 4 D2
Sewstern Leics 116 C1
Sezincote Glos 81 D4
Sgarasta Mhor W Isles 287 E5
Sgiogarstaigh W Isles 288 A6
Shabbington Bucks 66 C1
Shackerstone Leics 97 A6
Shackleford Sur 34 B2
Shade W Yorks 138 A2
Shadforth Durham 167 A6
Shadingfield Suff 105 C5
Shadoxhurst Kent 38 B1
Shadsworth Blkburn 137 A6
Shadwell Norf 103 C5
Shadwell W Yorks 148 D2
Shaftesbury Dorset 30 C2
Shafton S Yorks 140 B1
Shakespeare's Birthplace, Stratford-upon-Avon Warks 81 B5
Shalbourne Wilts 45 C7
Shalcombe I o W 18 C2
Shalden Hants 33 A5
Shaldon Devon 13 D4
Shalfleet I o W 18 C3
Shalford Essex 69 A7
Shalford Sur 34 B3
Shalford Green Essex 69 A7
Shallowford Devon 26 A2
Shalmsford Street Kent 52 D2
Shalstone Bucks 82 D3
Shamley Green Sur 34 B3
Shandon Argyll 215 D5
Shandwick Highld 265 C4
Shangton Leics 99 B4
Shankhouse Northumb 179 B4
Shanklin I o W 19 C4
Shanklin Chine I o W 19 C4
Shanquhar Aberds 255 C6
Shanzie Perth 231 C6
Shap Cumb 164 D3
Shapwick Dorset 16 A3
Shapwick Som 28 B4
Shardlow Derbys 114 B2
Shareshill Staffs 96 A2
Sharlston W Yorks 140 B1
Sharlston Common W Yorks 140 B1
Sharnbrook Beds 84 B1
Sharnford Leics 98 B1
Sharoe Green Lancs 145 D5
Sharow N Yorks 158 D2
Sharp Street Norf 121 C5
Sharpenhoe Beds 84 D2
Sharperton Northumb 188 C2
Sharpness Glos 62 C2
Sharpthorne W Sus 35 C6
Sharrington Norf 120 B2
Shatterford Worcs 95 C5
Shaugh Prior Devon 7 A4
Shavington Ches 128 D2
Shaw Gtr Man 138 C2
Shaw W Berks 46 C2
Shaw Wilts 44 C2
Shaw Green Lancs 136 B4
Shaw Mills N Yorks 147 A6
Shawbury Shrops 111 C4
Shawdon Hall Northumb 188 B3
Shawell Leics 98 C2
Shawford Hants 32 C3
Shawforth Lancs 138 A1
Shawhead Dumfries 173 A6
Shawhill Dumfries 175 B5
Shawton S Lnrk 194 B1
Shawtonhill S Lnrk 194 B1
Shear Cross Wilts 30 A2
Shearington Dumfries 174 B3
Shearsby Leics 98 B3
Shebbear Devon 11 A5
Shebdon Staffs 111 C6
Shebster Highld 279 B6

Sheddens E Renf 205 C5
Shedfield Hants 33 D4
Sheen Staffs 129 C6
Sheepscar W Yorks 148 D2
Sheepscombe Glos 63 B4
Sheepstor Devon 7 A4
Sheepwash Devon 11 A5
Sheepway N Som 42 B3
Sheepy Magna Leics 97 A6
Sheepy Parva Leics 97 A6
Sheering Essex 69 B5
Sheerness Kent 51 B6
Sheet Hants 33 C6
Sheffield S Yorks 130 A3
Sheffield Bottom W Berks 47 C4
Sheffield Green E Sus 36 D2
Sheffield Park, Uckfield E Sus 36 D2
Shefford Beds 84 D3
Shefford Woodlands W Berks 46 B1
Sheigra Highld 276 B2
Sheinton Shrops 95 A4
Shelderton Shrops 94 D2
Sheldon Derbys 129 C6
Sheldon Devon 13 A6
Sheldon W Mid 97 C4
Sheldwich Kent 52 D2
Shelf W Yorks 139 A4
Shelfanger Norf 104 C2
Shelfield Warks 80 A4
Shelfield W Mid 96 A3
Shelford Notts 115 A4
Shellacres Northumb 198 B2
Shelley Essex 69 C5
Shelley Suff 87 D6
Shelley W Yorks 139 B5
Shellingford Oxon 64 D4
Shellow Bowells Essex 69 C6
Shelsley Beauchamp Worcs 79 A5
Shelsley Walsh Worcs 79 A5
Shelthorpe Leics 114 D3
Shelton Beds 84 A2
Shelton Norf 104 B3
Shelton Notts 115 A5
Shelton Shrops 110 D3
Shelton Green Norf 104 B3
Shelve Shrops 94 B1
Shelwick Hereford 78 C3
Shenfield Essex 69 D6
Shenington Oxon 81 C6
Shenley Herts 68 C1
Shenley Brook End M Keynes 83 D5
Shenley Church End M Keynes 83 D5
Shenleybury Herts 68 C1
Shenmore Hereford 78 D1
Shennanton Dumfries 171 A5
Shenstone Staffs 96 A4
Shenstone Worcs 95 D6
Shenton Leics 97 A6
Shenval Highld 251 D6
Shenval Moray 254 D3
Shepeau Stow Lincs 117 D6
Shephall Herts 68 A2
Shepherd's Green Oxon 47 A5
Shepherd's Port Norf 118 B3
Shepherdswell Kent 39 A4
Shepley W Yorks 139 C4
Shepperdine S Glos 62 D2
Shepperton Sur 48 C3
Shepreth Cambs 85 C5
Shepshed Leics 114 D2
Shepton Beauchamp Som 28 D4
Shepton Mallet Som 29 A6
Shepton Montague Som 29 B6
Shepway Kent 37 A5
Sheraton Durham 168 B2
Sherborne Dorset 29 D6
Sherborne Glos 64 B2
Sherborne St John Hants 47 D4
Sherbourne Warks 81 A5
Sherburn Durham 167 A6
Sherburn N Yorks 160 D3
Sherburn Hill Durham 167 A6
Sherburn in Elmet N Yorks 148 D3
Shere Sur 34 B3
Shereford Norf 119 C5
Sherfield English Hants 32 C1
Sherfield on Loddon Hants 47 D4
Sherford Devon 8 C1
Sheriff Hutton N Yorks 149 A5
Sheriffhales Shrops 111 D6
Sheringham Norf 120 A3
Sherington M Keynes 83 C5
Shernal Green Worcs 80 A2
Shernborne Norf 119 B4
Sherrington Wilts 30 B3
Sherston Wilts 44 A2
Sherwood Green Devon 25 C6
Shettleston Glasgow 205 B6
Shevington Gtr Man 136 C4
Shevington Moor Gtr Man 136 B4
Shevington Vale Gtr Man 136 C4
Sheviock Corn 6 B2
Shide I o W 18 C3
Shiel Bridge Highld 238 A3
Shieldaig Highld 249 A5
Shieldaig Highld 261 C5
Shieldhill Dumfries 184 D3
Shieldhill Falk 208 C1
Shieldhill S Lnrk 195 B5
Shielfoot Highld 235 D5
Shielhill Angus 232 C2
Shielhill Invclyd 204 A2
Shifford Oxon 65 C4
Shifnal Shrops 95 A5
Shilbottle Northumb 189 C4
Shildon Durham 167 C5
Shillingford Devon 27 C4
Shillingford Oxon 65 D6
Shillingford St George Devon 13 C4
Shillingstone Dorset 30 D2
Shillington Beds 84 D3
Shillmoor Northumb 188 C1
Shilton Oxon 64 C3
Shilton Warks 97 C7
Shilvington Northumb 178 A3
Shimpling Norf 104 C2
Shimpling Suff 87 B4
Shimpling Street Suff 87 B4
Shincliffe Durham 167 A5
Shiney Row T & W 179 D5
Shinfield Wokingham 47 C5
Shingham Norf 102 A3
Shingle Street Suff 89 C4
Shinner's Bridge Devon 8 A1
Shinness Highld 272 C3
Shipbourne Kent 36 A3
Shipdham Norf 103 A5
Shipham Som 42 D3
Shiphay Torbay 8 A2
Shiplake Oxon 47 B5
Shipley Derbys 114 A2
Shipley Northumb 189 B4
Shipley Shrops 95 B6
Shipley W Sus 35 D4
Shipley W Yorks 147 D5
Shipley Shiels Northumb 187 D6
Shipmeadow Suff 105 C4
Shippea Hill Station Cambs 102 C2
Shippon Oxon 65 D5
Shipston-on-Stour Warks 81 C5
Shipton Glos 63 B6
Shipton N Yorks 149 B4
Shipton Shrops 94 B3
Shipton Bellinger Hants 31 A6
Shipton Gorge Dorset 15 B4
Shipton Green W Sus 19 A7
Shipton Moyne Glos 44 A2
Shipton on Cherwell Oxon 65 B5
Shipton Solers Glos 63 B6
Shipton-under-Wychwood Oxon 64 B3
Shiptonthorpe E Yorks 150 C1
Shirburn Oxon 66 D1
Shirdley Hill Lancs 136 B2
Shire Horse Centre, Stratford-upon-Avon Warks 81 B5
Shirebrook Derbys 131 C5
Shiregreen S Yorks 139 D6
Shirehampton Bristol 43 B4
Shiremoor T & W 179 B5
Shirenewton Mon 61 D6
Shireoaks Notts 131 A5
Shirkoak Kent 38 B1
Shirl Heath Hereford 78 B2
Shirland Derbys 130 D3
Shirley Derbys 113 A6
Shirley London 49 C6
Shirley Soton 32 D3
Shirley W Mid 96 D4
Shirrell Heath Hants 33 D4
Shirwell Devon 25 B6
Shirwell Cross Devon 25 B6
Shiskine N Ayrs 191 C5
Shobdon Hereford 78 A2
Shobnall Staffs 113 C6
Shobrooke Devon 12 A3
Shoby Leics 115 D4
Shocklach Ches 110 A3
Shoeburyness Sthend 51 A6
Sholden Kent 53 D5
Sholing Soton 32 D3
Shoot Hill Shrops 110 D3
Shop Corn 24 D3
Shop Corn 9 D4
Shop Corner Suff 88 D3
Shore Mill Highld 264 D3
Shoreditch London 49 A6
Shoreham Kent 50 C2
Shoreham Airport W Sus 21 B5
Shoreham-By-Sea W Sus 21 B5
Shoresdean Northumb 198 B3
Shoreswood Northumb 198 B3
Shoreton Highld 264 D2
Shorncote Glos 63 D6
Shorne Kent 50 B3
Short Heath W Mid 96 A2
Shortacombe Devon 11 C6
Shortgate E Sus 22 A2
Shortlanesend Corn 4 C3
Shortlees E Ayrs 193 B4
Shortstown Beds 84 C2
Shorwell I o W 18 C3
Shoscombe Bath 43 D6
Shotatton Shrops 110 C2
Shotesham Norf 104 B3
Shotgate Essex 70 D1
Shotley Suff 88 D3
Shotley Bridge Durham 178 D2
Shotley Gate Suff 88 D3
Shotleyfield Northumb 178 D2
Shottenden Kent 52 D2
Shottermill Sur 34 C1
Shottery Warks 81 B4
Shotteswell Warks 81 C7
Shottisham Suff 88 C4
Shottle Derbys 113 A7
Shottlegate Derbys 113 A7
Shotton Durham 168 B2
Shotton Flint 126 C3
Shotton Northumb 198 C2
Shotton Colliery Durham 167 A6
Shotts N Lnrk 207 D6
Shotwick Ches 126 B3
Shouldham Norf 102 A2
Shouldham Thorpe Norf 102 A2
Shoulton Worcs 79 B6
Shover's Green E Sus 37 C4
Shrawardine Shrops 110 D3
Shrawley Worcs 79 A6
Shrewley Common Warks 81 A5
Shrewsbury Shrops 110 D3
Shrewton Wilts 31 A4
Shripney W Sus 20 B2
Shrivenham Oxon 45 A6
Shropham Norf 103 B5
Shrub End Essex 70 A3
Shucknall Hereford 78 C3
Shudy Camps Cambs 86 C2
Shulishadermor Highld 259 D4
Shurdington Glos 63 B5
Shurlock Row Windsor 47 B6
Shurrery Highld 279 C6
Shurrery Lodge Highld 279 C6
Shurton Som 28 A2
Shustoke Warks 97 B5
Shute Devon 14 B2
Shute Devon 12 A3
Shutford Oxon 81 C6
Shuthonger Glos 80 D1
Shutlanger Northants 83 B4
Shuttington Warks 97 A5
Shuttlewood Derbys 131 B4
Siabost bho Dheas W Isles 288 C3
Siabost bho Thuath W Isles 288 C3
Siadar W Isles 288 B4
Siadar Iarach W Isles 288 B4
Siadar Uarach W Isles 288 B4
Sibbaldbie Dumfries 185 D4
Sibbertoft Northants 98 C3
Sibdon Carwood Shrops 94 C2
Sibford Ferris Oxon 81 D6
Sibford Gower Oxon 81 D6
Sible Hedingham Essex 86 D3
Sibsey Lincs 134 D3
Sibson Cambs 100 B2
Sibson Leics 97 A6
Sibthorpe Notts 115 A5
Sibton Suff 89 A4
Sibton Green Suff 105 D4
Sicklesmere Suff 87 A4
Sicklinghall N Yorks 148 C2
Sid Devon 13 C6
Sidbury Devon 13 B6
Sidbury Shrops 95 C4
Sidcot N Som 42 D3
Sidcup London 50 B1
Siddick Cumb 162 A3
Siddington Ches 128 B3
Siddington Glos 63 D6
Sidemoor Worcs 96 D2
Sidestrand Norf 121 B4
Sidford Devon 13 B6
Sidlesham W Sus 20 C1
Sidley E Sus 23 B5
Sidlow Sur 35 B5
Sidmouth Devon 13 C6
Sigford Devon 12 D2
Sigglesthorne E Yorks 151 C4
Sighthill Edin 209 C4
Sigingstone V Glam 41 D4
Signet Oxon 64 B3
Silchester Hants 47 C4
Sildinis W Isles 288 F3
Sileby Leics 114 D3
Silecroft Cumb 153 B2
Silfield Norf 104 B2
Silian Ceredig 75 C4
Silk Willoughby Lincs 116 A3
Silkstone S Yorks 139 C5
Silkstone Common S Yorks 139 C5
Silloth Cumb 174 C4
Sills Northumb 188 C1
Sillyearn Moray 267 D6
Siloh Carms 59 B4
Silpho N Yorks 160 B3
Silsden W Yorks 147 C4
Silsoe Beds 84 D2
Silver End Essex 70 B2
Silverburn Midloth 209 D5
Silverdale Lancs 154 D3
Silverdale Staffs 112 A2
Silvergate Norf 120 C3
Silverhill E Sus 23 A5
Silverley's Green Suff 104 D3
Silverstone Northants 82 C3
Silverstone Motor Racing Circuit Northants 82 C3
Silverton Devon 13 A4
Silvington Shrops 95 D4
Silwick Shetland 285 J4
Simmondley Derbys 138 D3
Simonburn Northumb 177 B6
Simonsbath Som 26 B2
Simonstone Lancs 146 D1
Simprim Borders 198 B2
Simpson M Keynes 83 D5
Simpson Cross Pembs 55 C4
Sinclair's Hill Borders 198 A2
Sinclairston E Ayrs 182 A2
Sinderby N Yorks 158 C2
Sinderhope Northumb 177 D6
Sindlesham Wokingham 47 C5
Singdean Borders 187 C4
Singleborough Bucks 83 D4
Singleton Lancs 144 D3
Singleton W Sus 20 A1
Singlewell Kent 50 B3
Sinkhurst Green Kent 37 B6
Sinnahard Aberds 244 A1
Sinnington N Yorks 159 C6
Sinton Green Worcs 79 A6
Sipson London 48 B3
Sirhowy Bl Gwent 60 B3
Sisland Norf 104 B4
Sissinghurst Kent 37 C5
Sissinghurst, Cranbrook Kent 37 C6
Sisterpath Borders 197 B6
Siston S Glos 43 B5
Sithney Corn 3 C4
Sittingbourne Kent 51 C5
Six Ashes Staffs 95 C5
Six Hills Leics 115 C4
Six Mile Bottom Cambs 86 B1
Sixhills Lincs 133 A6
Sixpenny Handley Dorset 30 D3
Sizewell Suff 89 A5
Skail Highld 278 D3
Skaill Orkney 282 F3
Skaill Orkney 282 D5
Skaill Orkney 283 G6
Skara Brae Orkney 282 F3
Skares E Ayrs 182 A3
Skateraw E Loth 211 C4
Skaw Shetland 284 G7
Skeabost Highld 259 D4
Skeabrae Orkney 282 E3
Skeeby N Yorks 157 A6
Skeffington Leics 99 A4
Skeffling E Yorks 143 B5
Skegby Notts 131 C4
Skegness Lincs 135 C5
Skelberry Shetland 285 M5
Skelbo Highld 264 A3
Skelbrooke S Yorks 140 B3
Skeldyke Lincs 117 B6
Skellingthorpe Lincs 133 B4
Skellister Shetland 285 H6
Skellow S Yorks 140 B3
Skelmanthorpe W Yorks 139 B5
Skelmersdale Lancs 136 C3
Skelmonae Aberds 256 C3
Skelmorlie N Ayrs 204 B1
Skelmuir Aberds 257 B4
Skelpick Highld 278 C3
Skelton Cumb 164 B2
Skelton E Yorks 141 A5
Skelton N Yorks 157 A4
Skelton Redcar 169 D4
Skelton York 149 B4
Skelton-on-Ure N Yorks 148 A2
Skelwick Orkney 282 C5
Skelwith Bridge Cumb 154 A2
Skendleby Lincs 135 C4
Skene Ho. Aberds 245 B4
Skenfrith Mon 61 A6
Skerne E Yorks 150 B3
Skeroblingarry Argyll 190 C3
Skerray Highld 278 B2
Skerton Lancs 145 A4
Sketchley Leics 98 B1
Sketty Swansea 57 C6
Skewen Neath 40 B2
Skewsby N Yorks 159 D5
Skeyton Norf 120 C4
Skiag Bridge Highld 271 B5
Skibo Castle Highld 264 B3
Skidbrooke Lincs 143 D6
Skidbrooke North End Lincs 143 D6
Skidby E Yorks 150 D3
Skilgate Som 27 C4
Skillington Lincs 116 C1
Skinburness Cumb 174 C4
Skinflats Falk 208 B2
Skinidin Highld 258 D2
Skinnet Highld 277 B6
Skinningrove Redcar 169 C5
Skipness Argyll 202 C3
Skippool Lancs 144 C3
Skipsea E Yorks 151 B4
Skipsea Brough E Yorks 151 B4
Skipton N Yorks 146 B3
Skipton-on-Swale N Yorks 158 D2
Skipwith N Yorks 149 D5
Skirbeck Lincs 117 A6
Skirbeck Quarter Lincs 117 A6
Skirlaugh E Yorks 151 D4
Skirling Borders 195 C5
Skirmett Bucks 47 A5
Skirpenbeck E Yorks 149 B6
Skirwith Cumb 165 B4
Skirza Highld 281 B5
Skulamus Highld 247 B5
Skullomie Highld 277 B7
Skyborry Green Shrops 93 D6
Skye of Curr Highld 253 D5
Skyreholme N Yorks 147 A4
Slackhall Derbys 129 A5
Slackhead Moray 267 C5
Slad Glos 63 C4
Slade Devon 25 A6
Slade Pembs 55 C5
Slade Green London 50 B2
Slaggyford Northumb 177 D4
Slaidburn Lancs 145 B7
Slaithwaite W Yorks 138 B3
Slaley Northumb 178 D1
Slamannan Falk 207 C6
Slapton Bucks 67 A4
Slapton Devon 8 C2
Slapton Northants 82 C3
Slatepit Dale Derbys 130 C3
Slattocks Gtr Man 138 C1
Slaugham W Sus 35 D5
Slaughterford Wilts 44 B2
Slawston Leics 99 B4
Sleaford Hants 33 B7
Sleaford Lincs 116 A3
Sleagill Cumb 164 D3
Sleapford Telford 111 D5
Sledge Green Worcs 79 D6
Sledmere E Yorks 150 A2
Sleightholme Durham 166 D2
Sleights N Yorks 160 A2
Slepe Dorset 16 B3
Slickly Highld 281 B4
Sliddery N Ayrs 191 C5
Sligachan Hotel Highld 246 B3
Slimbridge Glos 62 C3
Slimbridge Wildfowl & Wetlands Centre, Frampton on Severn Glos 62 C3
Slindon Staffs 112 B2
Slindon W Sus 20 B2
Slinfold W Sus 35 C4
Sling Gwyn 123 D6
Slingsby N Yorks 159 D5
Slioch Aberds 255 C6
Slip End Beds 67 B5
Slip End Herts 85 D4
Slipton Northants 99 D6
Slitting Mill Staffs 112 D4
Slochd Highld 253 D4
Slockavullin Argyll 213 C6
Sloley Norf 121 C4
Sloothby Lincs 135 B4
Slough Slough 48 B2
Slough Green W Sus 35 D5
Sluggan Highld 253 D4
Slumbay Highld 249 C5
Slyfield Sur 34 A2
Slyne Lancs 145 A4
Smailholm Borders 197 C5
Small Dole W Sus 21 A5
Small Hythe Kent 37 C6
Smallbridge Gtr Man 138 B2
Smallburgh Norf 121 C5
Smallburn Aberds 257 B5
Smallburn E Ayrs 194 D1
Smalley Derbys 114 A2
Smallfield Sur 35 B6
Smallridge Devon 14 A3
Smannell Hants 32 A2
Smardale Cumb 155 A6
Smarden Kent 37 B6
Smarden Bell Kent 37 B6
Smeatharpe Devon 28 D1
Smeeth Kent 38 B2
Smeeton Westerby Leics 98 B3
Smercleit W Isles 286 E3
Smerral Highld 275 A5
Smethwick W Mid 96 C3
Smirisary Highld 235 C5
Smisby Derbys 114 D1
Smith Green Lancs 145 B4
Smithfield Cumb 176 C2
Smithincott Devon 27 D5
Smith's Green Essex 69 A5
Smithstown Highld 261 C4
Smithton Highld 252 B3
Smithy Green Ches 128 B2
Smockington Leics 98 C1
Smoogro Orkney 283 G4
Smythe's Green Essex 70 B3
Snaefell Mountain Railway I o M 152 C4
Snaigow House Perth 231 D4
Snailbeach Shrops 94 A1
Snailwell Cambs 86 A2
Snainton N Yorks 160 C3
Snaith E Yorks 140 A4
Snape N Yorks 157 C6
Snape Suff 89 B4
Snape Green Lancs 136 B2
Snarestone Leics 97 A6
Snarford Lincs 133 A5
Snargate Kent 38 C1
Snave Kent 38 C2
Snead Powys 93 B7
Sneath Common Norf 104 C2
Sneaton N Yorks 160 A2
Sneatonthorpe N Yorks 160 A3
Snelland Lincs 133 A5
Snelston Derbys 113 A5
Snetterton Motor Racing Circuit Norf 103 C6
Snettisham Norf 118 B3
Snibston Discovery Park, Coalville Leics 114 D2
Sniseabhal W Isles 286 C3
Snitter Northumb 188 C3
Snitterby Lincs 142 D1
Snitterfield Warks 81 B5
Snitton Shrops 94 D3
Snodhill Hereford 77 C7
Snodland Kent 51 C3
Snowden Hill S Yorks 139 C5
Snowdon Mountain Railway, Llanberis Gwyn 107 A6
Snowdown Kent 53 D4
Snowshill Glos 80 D3
Snowshill Manor Glos 80 D3
Snydale W Yorks 140 B2
Soar Anglesey 122 C3
Soar Carms 58 C3
Soar Devon 7 D6
Soar-y-Mynydd Ceredig 76 B1
Soberton Hants 33 D5
Soberton Heath Hants 33 D5
Sockbridge Cumb 164 C3
Sockburn Darl 158 A2
Soham Cambs 102 D1
Soham Cotes Cambs 102 D1
Solas W Isles 287 G3
Soldon Cross Devon 24 D4
Soldridge Hants 33 B5
Sole Street Kent 50 C3
Sole Street Kent 38 A2
Solihull W Mid 97 D4
Sollers Dilwyn Hereford 78 B2
Sollers Hope Hereford 79 D4
Sollom Lancs 136 B3
Solva Pembs 54 B3
Somerby Leics 115 D5
Somerby Lincs 142 C2
Somercotes Derbys 131 D4
Somerford Dorset 17 B5
Somerford Keynes Glos 63 D6
Somerley W Sus 19 B7
Somerleyton Suff 105 B5
Somersal Herbert Derbys 113 B5
Somersby Lincs 134 B3
Somersham Cambs 101 D5
Somersham Suff 88 C1
Somerton Oxon 65 A5
Somerton Som 29 C4
Sompting W Sus 21 B4
Sonning Wokingham 47 B5
Sonning Common Oxon 47 A5
Sonning Eye Oxon 47 B5
Sontley Wrex 110 A2
Sopley Hants 17 B5
Sopwell Herts 67 C6
Sopworth Wilts 44 A2
Sorbie Dumfries 171 C6
Sordale Highld 280 B3
Sorisdale Argyll 223 A5
Sorn E Ayrs 193 C5
Sornhill E Ayrs 193 B5
Sortat Highld 281 B4
Sotby Lincs 134 B2
Sots Hole Lincs 133 C6
Sotterley Suff 105 C5
Soudley Shrops 111 C6
Soughton Flint 126 C2
Soulbury Bucks 66 A3
Soulby Cumb 165 D5
Souldern Oxon 82 D2
Souldrop Beds 84 A1
Sound Ches 111 A5
Sound Shetland 285 H5
Sound Shetland 285 J6
Sound Heath Ches 111 A5
Soundwell S Glos 43 B5

Sourhope Borders 188 A1
Sourin Orkney 282 D5
Sourton Devon 11 B6
Soutergate Cumb 153 B3
South Acre Norf 119 D5
South Allington Devon 8 D1
South Alloa Falk 208 A1
South Ambersham W Sus 34 D2
South Anston S Yorks 131 A5
South Ascot Windsor 48 C2
South Ballachulish Highld 237 D4
South Balloch S Ayrs 181 B5
South Bank Redcar 168 C3
South Barrow Som 29 C6
South Beach Gwyn 106 C3
South Benfleet Essex 51 A4
South Bersted W Sus 20 B2
South Brent Devon 7 F2
South Brewham Som 29 B7
South Broomhill Northumb 189 D5
South Burlingham Norf 105 A4
South Cadbury Som 29 C6
South Cairn Dumfries 170 A1
South Carlton Lincs 133 B4
South Cave E Yorks 150 D2
South Cerney Glos 63 D6
South Chard Som 14 A3
South Charlton Northumb 189 A4
South Cheriton Som 29 C6
South Cliffe E Yorks 150 D1
South Clifton Notts 132 B3
South Cockerington Lincs 134 A3
South Cornelly Bridgend 40 C3
South Cove Suff 105 C5
South Creagan Argyll 227 B4
South Creake Norf 119 B5
South Croxton Leics 115 D4
South Croydon London 49 C6
South Dalton E Yorks 150 C2
South Darenth Kent 50 C2
South Duffield N Yorks 149 D5
South Elkington Lincs 134 A2
South Elmsall W Yorks 140 B2
South End Bucks 66 A3
South End Cumb 153 D3
South End N Lincs 142 A3
South Erradale Highld 261 C4
South Fambridge Essex 70 D2
South Fawley W Berks 46 A1
South Ferriby N Lincs 142 A1
South Garth Shetland 284 D7
South Garvan Highld 236 B3
South Glendale W Isles 286 E3
South Godstone Sur 35 B6
South Gorley Hants 31 D5
South Green Essex 69 D6
South Green Kent 51 C5
South-haa Shetland 284 E5
South Ham Hants 47 D4
South Hanningfield Essex 70 D1
South Harting W Sus 33 D6
South Hatfield Herts 68 C2
South Hayling Hants 19 B6
South Hazelrigg Northumb 199 C4
South Heath Bucks 67 C4
South Heighton E Sus 22 B2
South Hetton Durham 167 A6
South Hiendley W Yorks 140 B1
South Hill Corn 10 D4
South Hinksey Oxon 65 C6
South Hole Devon 24 C3
South Holme N Yorks 159 D5
South Holmwood Sur 35 B4
South Hornchurch London 50 A2
South Hykeham Lincs 133 C4
South Hylton T & W 179 D5
South Kelsey Lincs 142 D2
South Kessock Highld 252 B2
South Killingholme N Lincs 142 B3
South Kilvington N Yorks 158 C3
South Kilworth Leics 98 C3
South Kirkby W Yorks 140 B2
South Kirkton Aberds 245 B4
South Kiscadale N Ayrs 191 C6
South Kyme Lincs 117 A4
South Lancing W Sus 21 B4
South Leigh Oxon 65 C4
South Leverton Notts 132 A2
South Littleton Worcs 80 C3
South Lopham Norf 103 C6
South Luffenham Rutland 99 A6
South Malling E Sus 22 A2
South Marston Swindon 45 A5
South Middleton Northumb 188 A2
South Milford N Yorks 148 D3
South Millbrex Aberds 256 B3
South Milton Devon 7 C6
South Mimms Herts 68 C2
South Molton Devon 26 C2
South Moreton Oxon 46 A3
South Mundham W Sus 20 B1
South Muskham Notts 132 D2
South Newbald E Yorks 150 D2
South Newington Oxon 81 D7
South Newton Wilts 31 B4
South Normanton Derbys 131 D4
South Norwood London 49 C6
South Nutfield Sur 35 B6
South Ockendon Thurrock 50 A2
South Ormsby Lincs 134 B3
South Otterington N Yorks 158 C2
South Owersby Lincs 142 D2
South Oxhey Herts 67 D6
South Perrott Dorset 15 A4
South Petherton Som 28 D4
South Petherwin Corn 10 C4
South Pickenham Norf 103 A4
South Pool Devon 7 C6
South Port Argyll 227 D5
South Radworthy Devon 26 B2
South Rauceby Lincs 116 A3
South Raynham Norf 119 C5
South Reston Lincs 135 A4
South Runcton Norf 102 A2
South Scarle Notts 132 C3
South Shian Argyll 226 B4
South Shields T & W 179 C5
South Shields Museum T & W 179 C5
South Shore Blkpool 144 D3
South Somercotes Lincs 143 D6
South Stainley N Yorks 148 A2
South Stainmore Cumb 165 D6
South Stifford Thurrock 50 B3
South Stoke Oxon 46 A3
South Stoke W Sus 20 B3
South Street E Sus 22 A1
South Street London 36 A2
South Street Kent 52 C3
South Street Kent 52 D2
South Tawton Devon 12 B1
South Thoresby Lincs 135 B4
South Tidworth Wilts 31 A6
South Town Hants 33 B5
South View Hants 47 D4
South Walsham Norf 121 D5
South Warnborough Hants 33 A6
South Weald Essex 69 D5
South Weston Oxon 66 D2
South Wheatley Corn 10 B3
South Wheatley Notts 132 A2
South Whiteness Shetland 285 J5
South Widcombe Bath 43 D4
South Wigston Leics 98 B2
South Willingham Lincs 134 A1
South Wingfield Derbys 130 D3
South Witham Lincs 116 D2
South Wonston Hants 32 B3
South Woodham Ferrers Essex 70 D2
South Wootton Norf 118 C3
South Wraxall Wilts 44 C2
South Zeal Devon 12 B1
Southall London 48 A4
Southam Glos 63 A5
Southam Warks 81 A7
Southampton Soton 32 D3
Southampton International Airport Hants 32 D3
Southborough Kent 36 B3
Southbourne Bmouth 17 B5
Southbourne W Sus 19 A6
Southburgh Norf 103 A5
Southburn E Yorks 150 B2
Southchurch Sthend 51 A6
Southcott Wilts 45 D5
Southcourt Bucks 66 B3
Southdean Borders 187 C5
Southdene Mers 136 D3
Southease E Sus 22 B2
Southend Argyll 190 E2
Southend W Berks 46 B3
Southend Wilts 45 B5
Southend Airport Essex 51 A5
Southend-on-Sea Sthend 51 A5
Southend Sea Life Centre Essex 51 A5
Southernden Kent 37 B6
Southerndown V Glam 40 D3
Southerness Dumfries 174 C2
Southery Norf 102 B2
Southfield Northumb 179 B4
Southfleet Kent 50 B3
Southgate Ceredig 75 A4
Southgate London 68 D2
Southgate Norf 120 C3
Southgate Swansea 57 D5
Southill Beds 84 C3
Southleigh Devon 14 B2
Southminster Essex 70 D3
Southmoor Oxon 65 D4
Southoe Cambs 84 A3
Southolt Suff 88 A2
Southorpe P'boro 100 A2
Southowram W Yorks 139 A4
Southport Mers 136 B2
Southpunds Shetland 285 L6
Southrepps Norf 121 B4
Southrey Lincs 133 C6
Southrop Glos 64 C2
Southrope Hants 33 A5
Southsea Ptsmth 19 B5
Southstoke Bath 43 C6
Southtown Norf 105 A6
Southtown Orkney 283 H5
Southwaite Cumb 164 A2
Southwark London 49 B6
Southwater W Sus 35 D4
Southwater Street W Sus 35 D4
Southway Som 29 A5
Southwell Dorset 15 D6
Southwell Notts 132 D1
Southwell Minster Notts 132 D2
Southwell Racecourse Notts 132 D2
Southwick Hants 19 A5
Southwick Northants 100 B2
Southwick T & W 179 D5
Southwick Wilts 44 D2
Southwick W Sus 21 B5
Southwold Suff 105 D6
Southwood Norf 105 A4
Southwood Som 29 B5
Soval Lodge W Isles 288 E4
Sowber Gate N Yorks 158 C2
Sowerby N Yorks 158 C3
Sowerby W Yorks 138 A3
Sowerby Bridge W Yorks 138 A3
Sowerby Row Cumb 164 B1
Sowood W Yorks 138 B3
Sowton Devon 13 B4
Soyal Highld 264 A1
Spa Common Norf 121 B4
Spacey Houses N Yorks 148 B2
Spadeadam Farm Cumb 176 B3
Spalding Lincs 117 C5
Spaldington E Yorks 149 D6
Spaldwick Cambs 100 D3
Spalford Notts 132 C3
Spanby Lincs 116 B3
Sparham Norf 120 D2
Spark Bridge Cumb 154 C2
Sparkford Som 29 C6
Sparkhill W Mid 96 C3
Sparkwell Devon 7 B4
Sparrow Green Norf 119 D6
Sparrowpit Derbys 129 A5
Sparsholt Hants 32 B3
Sparsholt Oxon 46 A1
Spartylea Northumb 165 A6
Spaunton N Yorks 159 C6
Spaxton Som 28 B2
Spean Bridge Highld 239 D6
Spear Hill W Sus 21 A4
Speen Bucks 66 D3
Speen W Berks 46 C2
Speeton N Yorks 161 D5
Speke Mers 127 A4
Speke Hall Mers 127 A4
Speldhurst Kent 36 B3
Spellbrook Herts 69 B4
Spelsbury Oxon 64 A4
Spelter Bridgend 40 B3
Spencers Wood Wokingham 47 C5
Spennithorne N Yorks 157 C5
Spennymoor Durham 167 B5
Spetchley Worcs 80 B1
Spetisbury Dorset 16 A3
Spexhall Suff 105 C4
Spey Bay Moray 267 C4
Speybridge Highld 253 D6
Speyview Moray 254 B3
Spilsby Lincs 135 C4
Spindlestone Northumb 199 C5
Spinkhill Derbys 131 B4
Spinningdale Highld 264 B2
Spirit of the West, St Columb Major Corn 4 A4
Spirthill Wilts 44 B3
Spital Hill S Yorks 140 D4
Spital in the Street Lincs 133 A4
Spitfire and Hurricane Memorial, Manston Kent 53 C5
Spithurst E Sus 22 A2
Spittal Dumfries 171 B5
Spittal E Loth 210 C1
Spittal Highld 280 C3
Spittal Northumb 198 A4
Spittal Pembs 55 B5
Spittal Stirl 206 B3
Spittal of Glenmuick Aberds 243 D6
Spittal of Glenshee Perth 231 A5
Spittalfield Perth 231 D5
Spixworth Norf 120 D4
Splayne's Green E Sus 36 D2
Spofforth N Yorks 148 B2
Spon End W Mid 97 D6
Spon Green Flint 126 C2
Spondon Derby 114 B2
Spooner Row Norf 104 B1
Sporle Norf 119 D5
Spott E Loth 210 C3
Spratton Northants 99 D4
Spreakley Sur 34 B1
Spreyton Devon 12 B2
Spridlington Lincs 133 A5
Spring Vale S Yorks 139 C5
Spring Valley I o M 152 D3
Springburn Glasgow 205 B6
Springfield Dumfries 175 B6
Springfield Essex 69 C7
Springfield Fife 220 C3
Springfield Moray 253 A6
Springfield W Mid 96 C3
Springhill Staffs 96 A2
Springholm Dumfries 173 B6
Springkell Dumfries 175 A5
Springside N Ayrs 192 B3
Springthorpe Lincs 132 A3
Springwell T & W 179 D4
Sproatley E Yorks 151 D4
Sproston Green Ches 128 C2
Sprotbrough S Yorks 140 C3
Sproughton Suff 88 C2
Sprouston Borders 197 C6
Sprowston Norf 120 D4
Sproxton Leics 115 C6
Sproxton N Yorks 159 C5
Spurstow Ches 127 D5
Spynie Moray 266 C3
Squires Gate Blkpool 144 D3
Srannda W Isles 287 F5
Sronphadruig Lodge Perth 229 A6
SS Great Britain Bristol 43 B4
Stableford Shrops 95 B5
Stableford Staffs 112 B2
Stacey Bank S Yorks 139 D5
Stackhouse N Yorks 146 A2
Stackpole Pembs 55 E5
Staddiscombe Devon 7 B4
Staddlethorpe E Yorks 141 A6
Stadhampton Oxon 65 D7
Stadhlaigearraidh W Isles 286 C3
Staffield Cumb 164 A3
Staffin Highld 259 B4
Stafford Staffs 112 C3
Stagsden Beds 84 C1
Stainburn Cumb 162 B3
Stainburn N Yorks 147 C6
Stainby Lincs 116 C2
Staincross S Yorks 139 B6
Staindrop Durham 166 C4
Staines Sur 48 B3
Stainfield Lincs 116 C3
Stainfield Lincs 133 B6
Stainforth N Yorks 146 A2
Stainforth S Yorks 140 B4
Staining Lancs 144 D3
Stainland W Yorks 138 B3
Stainsacre N Yorks 160 A3
Stainsby Derbys 131 C4
Stainton Cumb 154 C4
Stainton Cumb 164 C2
Stainton Durham 166 D3
Stainton M'bro 168 D2
Stainton N Yorks 157 B5
Stainton S Yorks 140 D3
Stainton by Langworth Lincs 133 B5
Stainton le Vale Lincs 142 D3
Stainton with Adgarley Cumb 153 C3
Staintondale N Yorks 160 B3
Stair Cumb 163 B5
Stair E Ayrs 193 C4
Stairhaven Dumfries 171 B4
Staithes N Yorks 169 D5
Stake Pool Lancs 144 C4
Stakeford Northumb 179 A4
Stalbridge Dorset 30 D1
Stalbridge Weston Dorset 29 D7
Stalham Norf 121 C5
Stalham Green Norf 121 C5
Stalisfield Green Kent 51 D6
Stalling Busk N Yorks 156 C3
Stallingborough NE Lincs 142 B3
Stalmine Lancs 144 C3
Stalybridge Gtr Man 138 D2
Stambourne Essex 86 D3
Stambourne Green Essex 86 D3
Stamford Lincs 100 A2
Stamford Bridge Ches 127 C4
Stamford Bridge E Yorks 149 B6
Stamfordham Northumb 178 B2
Stanah Cumb 163 C6
Stanborough Herts 68 B2
Stanbridge Beds 67 A4
Stanbridge Dorset 17 A4
Stanbrook Worcs 79 C6
Stanbury W Yorks 147 D4
Stand Gtr Man 137 C6
Stand N Lnrk 207 D5
Standburn Falk 208 C2
Standeford Staffs 96 A2
Standen Kent 37 B6
Standen, East Grinstead W Sus 36 C1
Standford Hants 33 B7
Standingstone Cumb 162 A3
Standish Gtr Man 137 B4
Standlake Oxon 65 C4
Standon Hants 32 C3
Standon Herts 68 A3
Standon Staffs 112 B2
Stane N Lnrk 194 A3
Stanfield Norf 119 C6
Stanford Beds 84 C3
Stanford Kent 38 B3
Stanford Bishop Hereford 79 B4
Stanford Bridge Worcs 79 A5
Stanford Dingley W Berks 46 B3
Stanford in the Vale Oxon 64 D4
Stanford-le-Hope Thurrock 50 A3
Stanford on Avon Northants 98 D2
Stanford on Soar Notts 114 C3
Stanford on Teme Worcs 79 A5
Stanford Rivers Essex 69 C5
Stanfree Derbys 131 B4
Stanghow Redcar 169 D4
Stanground P'boro 100 B4
Stanhoe Norf 119 B5
Stanhope Borders 195 D6
Stanhope Durham 166 B2
Stanion Northants 99 C6
Stanley Derbys 114 A2
Stanley Durham 178 D3
Stanley Lancs 136 C3
Stanley Perth 219 A6
Stanley Staffs 129 D4
Stanley W Yorks 139 A6
Stanley Common Derbys 114 A2
Stanley Gate Lancs 136 C3
Stanley Hill Hereford 79 C4
Stanlow Ches 127 B4
Stanmer Brighton 21 B6
Stanmore London 67 D6
Stanmore Hants 32 C3
Stanmore W Berks 46 B2
Stannergate Dundee 220 A4
Stanningley W Yorks 147 D6
Stannington Northumb 179 B4
Stannington S Yorks 130 A3
Stansbatch Hereford 78 A1
Stansfield Suff 86 B3
Stanstead Suff 87 C4
Stanstead Abbotts Herts 68 B3
Stansted Kent 50 C3
Stansted Airport Essex 69 A5
Stansted Mountfitchet Essex 69 A5
Stanton Glos 80 D3
Stanton Mon 61 A5
Stanton Northumb 178 A3
Stanton Staffs 113 A5
Stanton Suff 103 D5
Stanton by Bridge Derbys 114 C1
Stanton-by-Dale Derbys 114 B2
Stanton Drew Bath 43 C4
Stanton Fitzwarren Swindon 64 D2
Stanton Harcourt Oxon 65 C5
Stanton Hill Notts 131 C4
Stanton in Peak Derbys 130 C2
Stanton Lacy Shrops 94 D2
Stanton Long Shrops 94 B3
Stanton-on-the-Wolds Notts 115 B4
Stanton Prior Bath 43 C5
Stanton St Bernard Wilts 45 C4
Stanton St John Oxon 65 C6
Stanton St Quintin Wilts 44 B3
Stanton Street Suff 87 A5
Stanton under Bardon Leics 114 D2
Stanton upon Hine Heath Shrops 111 C4
Stanton Wick Bath 43 C5
Stanwardine in the Fields Shrops 110 C3
Stanwardine in the Wood Shrops 110 C3
Stanway Essex 70 A3
Stanway Glos 80 D3
Stanway Green Suff 104 D3
Stanwell Sur 48 B3
Stanwell Moor Sur 48 B3
Stanwick Northants 100 D1
Stanwick-St-John N Yorks 167 D4
Stanwix Cumb 175 C7
Stanydale Shetland 285 H4
Staoinebrig W Isles 286 C3
Stape N Yorks 159 B6
Stapehill Dorset 17 A4
Stapeley Ches 111 A5
Stapeley Water Gardens, Nantwich Ches 127 D6
Stapenhill Staffs 113 C6
Staple Kent 53 D4
Staple Som 27 A6
Staple Cross E Sus 37 D5
Staple Fitzpaine Som 28 D2
Staplefield W Sus 35 D5
Stapleford Cambs 85 B6
Stapleford Herts 68 B3
Stapleford Leics 115 D6
Stapleford Lincs 132 D3
Stapleford Notts 114 B2
Stapleford Wilts 31 B4
Stapleford Abbotts Essex 69 D5
Stapleford Tawney Essex 69 D5
Staplegrove Som 28 C2
Staplehay Som 28 C2
Staplehurst Kent 37 B5
Staplers I o W 18 C4
Stapleton Bristol 43 B5
Stapleton Cumb 176 B3
Stapleton Hereford 78 A1
Stapleton Leics 98 B1
Stapleton N Yorks 167 D5
Stapleton Shrops 94 A2
Stapleton Som 29 C4
Stapley Som 28 D1
Staploe Beds 84 A3
Staplow Hereford 79 C4
Star Fife 220 D3
Star Pembs 73 C5
Star Som 42 D3
Stara Orkney 282 E3
Starbeck N Yorks 148 B2
Starbotton N Yorks 156 D3
Starcross Devon 13 C4
Stareton Warks 97 D6
Starkholmes Derbys 130 D3
Starlings Green Essex 85 D6
Starston Norf 104 C3
Startforth Durham 166 D3
Startley Wilts 44 A3
Stathe Som 28 C3
Stathern Leics 115 B5
Station Town Durham 168 B2
Staughton Green Cambs 84 A3
Staughton Highway Cambs 84 A3
Staunton Glos 62 B1
Staunton Glos 62 A3
Staunton in the Vale Notts 115 A6
Staunton on Arrow Hereford 78 A1
Staunton on Wye Hereford 78 C1
Staveley Cumb 154 C2
Staveley Cumb 154 B3
Staveley Derbys 131 B4
Staveley N Yorks 148 A2
Staverton Devon 8 A1
Staverton Glos 63 A4
Staverton Northants 82 A2
Staverton Wilts 44 C2
Staverton Bridge Glos 63 A4
Stawell Som 28 B3
Staxigoe Highld 281 C5
Staxton N Yorks 160 D4
Staylittle Powys 91 C6
Staynall Lancs 144 C3
Staythorpe Notts 132 D2
Stean N Yorks 157 D4
Stearsby N Yorks 159 D5
Steart Som 28 A2
Stebbing Essex 69 A6
Stebbing Green Essex 69 A6
Stedham W Sus 34 D1
Steele Road Borders 186 D4
Steen's Bridge Hereford 78 B3
Steep Hants 33 C6
Steep Marsh Hants 33 C6
Steeple Dorset 16 C3
Steeple Essex 70 C3
Steeple Ashton Wilts 44 D3
Steeple Aston Oxon 65 A5
Steeple Barton Oxon 65 A5
Steeple Bumpstead Essex 86 C2
Steeple Claydon Bucks 66 A1
Steeple Gidding Cambs 100 C3
Steeple Langford Wilts 31 B4
Steeple Morden Cambs 85 C4
Steeton W Yorks 147 C4
Stein Highld 258 C2
Steinmanhill Aberds 256 B2
Stelling Minnis Kent 38 A3
Stemster Highld 280 B3
Stemster Ho. Highld 280 B3
Stenalees Corn 5 B5
Stenhousemuir Falk 207 B6
Stenigot Lincs 134 A2
Stenness Shetland 284 F4
Stenscholl Highld 259 B4
Stenso Orkney 282 E4
Stenson Derbys 114 C1
Stenton E Loth 210 C3
Stenton Fife 209 A5
Stenwith Lincs 115 B6
Stepaside Pembs 56 B1
Stepping Hill Gtr Man 129 A4
Steppingley Beds 84 D2
Stepps N Lnrk 205 B6
Sternfield Suff 89 A4
Sterridge Devon 25 A6
Stert Wilts 44 D4
Stetchworth Cambs 86 B2
Stevenage Herts 68 A2
Stevenston N Ayrs 204 D2
Steventon Hants 32 A4
Steventon Oxon 65 D5

Stevington Beds 84 B1
Stewartby Beds 84 C2
Stewarton Argyll 190 D2
Stewarton E Ayrs 205 D4
Stewkley Bucks 66 A3
Stewton Lincs 134 A3
Steyne Cross I o W 19 C5
Steyning W Sus 21 A4
Steynton Pembs 55 D5
Stibb Corn 24 D3
Stibb Cross Devon 25 D5
Stibb Green Wilts 45 C6
Stibbard Norf 120 C1
Stibbington Cambs 100 B2
Stichill Borders 197 C6
Sticker Corn 5 B4
Stickford Lincs 134 D3
Sticklepath Devon 12 B1
Stickney Lincs 134 D3
Stiffkey Norf 119 A6
Stifford's Bridge Hereford 79 C5
Stillingfleet N Yorks 149 C4
Stillington N Yorks 149 A4
Stillington Stockton 167 C6
Stilton Cambs 100 C3
Stinchcombe Glos 62 D3
Stinsford Dorset 15 B7
Stirchley Telford 95 A5
Stirkoke Ho. Highld 281 C5
Stirling Aberds 257 B6
Stirling Stirl 207 A5
Stirling Castle Stirl 207 A5
Stisted Essex 70 A1
Stithians Corn 4 D2
Stittenham Highld 264 C2
Stivichall W Mid 97 D6
Stixwould Lincs 134 C1
Stoak Ches 127 B4
Stobieside S Lnrk 193 B6
Stobo Borders 195 C6
Stoborough Dorset 16 C3
Stoborough Green Dorset 16 C3
Stobshiel E Loth 210 D1
Stobswood Northumb 189 D5
Stock Essex 69 D6
Stock Green Worcs 80 B2
Stock Wood Worcs 80 B3
Stockbridge Hants 32 B2
Stockbury Kent 51 C5
Stockcross W Berks 46 C2
Stockdalewath Cumb 164 A1
Stockerston Leics 99 B5
Stockheath Hants 19 A6
Stockiemuir Stirl 206 B3
Stocking Pelham Herts 69 A4
Stockingford Warks 97 B6
Stockland Devon 14 A2
Stockland Bristol Som 28 A2
Stockleigh English Devon 12 A3
Stockleigh Pomeroy Devon 12 A3
Stockley Wilts 44 C4
Stocklinch Som 28 D3
Stockport Gtr Man 138 D1
Stocksbridge S Yorks 139 D5
Stocksfield Northumb 178 C2
Stockton Hereford 78 A3
Stockton Norf 105 B4
Stockton Shrops 93 A6
Stockton Shrops 95 B5
Stockton Warks 82 A1
Stockton Wilts 30 B3
Stockton Heath Warr 127 A6
Stockton-on-Tees Stockton 168 D2
Stockton on Teme Worcs 79 A5
Stockton on the Forest York 149 B5
Stockwood Park Museum, Luton Luton 67 B5
Stodmarsh Kent 53 C4
Stody Norf 120 B2
Stoer Highld 270 B3
Stoford Som 29 D5
Stoford Wilts 31 B4
Stogumber Som 27 B5
Stogursey Som 28 A2
Stoke Devon 24 C3
Stoke Hants 46 D2
Stoke Hants 19 A6
Stoke Medway 51 B5
Stoke Suff 88 C2
Stoke Abbott Dorset 15 A4
Stoke Albany Northants 99 C5
Stoke Ash Suff 104 D2
Stoke Bardolph Notts 115 A4
Stoke Bliss Worcs 79 A4
Stoke Bruerne Northants 83 C4
Stoke by Clare Suff 86 C3
Stoke-by-Nayland Suff 87 D5
Stoke Canon Devon 13 B4
Stoke Charity Hants 32 B3
Stoke Climsland Corn 11 D4
Stoke D'Abernon Sur 35 A4
Stoke Doyle Northants 100 C2
Stoke Dry Rutland 99 B5
Stoke Farthing Wilts 31 C4
Stoke Ferry Norf 102 B3
Stoke Fleming Devon 8 C2
Stoke Gabriel Devon 8 B2
Stoke Gifford S Glos 43 B5
Stoke Golding Leics 97 B6
Stoke Goldington M Keynes 83 C5
Stoke Green Bucks 48 A2
Stoke Hammond Bucks 66 A3
Stoke Heath Shrops 111 C5
Stoke Holy Cross Norf 104 A3
Stoke Lacy Hereford 79 C4
Stoke Lyne Oxon 65 A6
Stoke Mandeville Bucks 66 B3
Stoke Newington London 49 A6
Stoke on Tern Shrops 111 C5
Stoke-on-Trent Stoke 112 A2
Stoke Orchard Glos 63 A5
Stoke Poges Bucks 48 A2
Stoke Prior Hereford 78 B3
Stoke Prior Worcs 80 A2
Stoke Rivers Devon 26 B1
Stoke Rochford Lincs 116 C2
Stoke Row Oxon 47 A4
Stoke St Gregory Som 28 C3
Stoke St Mary Som 28 C2
Stoke St Michael Som 29 A6
Stoke St Milborough Shrops 94 C3
Stoke sub Hamdon Som 29 D4
Stoke Talmage Oxon 66 D1
Stoke Trister Som 30 C1
Stoke Wake Dorset 16 A1
Stokeford Dorset 16 C2
Stokeham Notts 132 B2
Stokeinteignhead Devon 13 D4
Stokenchurch Bucks 66 D2
Stokenham Devon 8 C2
Stokesay Shrops 94 C2
Stokesby Norf 121 D6
Stokesley N Yorks 158 A4
Stolford Som 28 A2
Ston Easton Som 43 D5
Stondon Massey Essex 69 C5
Stone Bucks 66 B2
Stone Glos 62 D2
Stone Kent 38 C1
Stone Kent 50 B2
Stone Staffs 112 B3
Stone S Yorks 131 A5
Stone Worcs 95 D6
Stone Allerton Som 42 D3
Stone Bridge Corner P'boro 101 A4
Stone Chair W Yorks 139 A4
Stone Cross E Sus 22 B4
Stone Cross Kent 53 D5
Stone-edge Batch N Som 42 B3
Stone House Cumb 155 C6
Stone Street Kent 36 A3
Stone Street Suff 87 D5
Stone Street Suff 105 C4
Stonebroom Derbys 131 D4
Stoneferry Hull 151 D4
Stonefield S Lnrk 194 A1
Stonegate E Sus 37 D4
Stonegate N Yorks 159 A6
Stonegrave N Yorks 159 D5
Stonehaugh Northumb 177 B5
Stonehaven Aberds 245 D5
Stonehenge, Amesbury Wilts 31 A5
Stonehouse Glos 63 C4
Stonehouse Northumb 177 D4
Stonehouse S Lnrk 194 B2
Stoneleigh Warks 97 D6
Stonely Cambs 84 A3
Stoner Hill Hants 33 C6
Stone's Green Essex 71 A5
Stonesby Leics 115 C6
Stonesfield Oxon 65 B4
Stonethwaite Cumb 163 C5
Stoney Cross Hants 31 D6
Stoney Middleton Derbys 130 B2
Stoney Stanton Leics 98 B1
Stoney Stoke Som 29 B7
Stoney Stratton Som 29 B6
Stoney Stretton Shrops 94 A1
Stoneybreck Shetland 285 L3
Stoneyburn W Loth 208 D2
Stoneygate Aberds 257 C5
Stoneygate Leicester 98 A3
Stoneyhills Essex 70 D3
Stoneykirk Dumfries 170 B2
Stoneywood Aberdeen 245 A5
Stoneywood Falk 207 B5
Stonganess Shetland 284 C7
Stonham Aspal Suff 88 B2
Stonnall Staffs 96 A3
Stonor Oxon 47 A5
Stonton Wyville Leics 99 B4
Stony Cross Hereford 79 C5
Stony Stratford M Keynes 83 C4
Stonyfield Highld 264 C2
Stoodleigh Devon 27 D4
Stopes S Yorks 130 A2
Stopham W Sus 20 A3
Stopsley Luton 67 A6
Stores Corner Suff 89 C4
Storeton Mers 126 A3
Stornoway W Isles 288 D5
Stornoway Airport W Isles 288 D5
Storridge Hereford 79 C5
Storrington W Sus 20 A3
Storrs Cumb 154 B2
Storth Cumb 154 C3
Storwood E Yorks 149 C6
Stotfield Moray 266 B3
Stotfold Beds 84 D4
Stottesdon Shrops 95 C4
Stoughton Leics 98 A3
Stoughton Sur 34 A2
Stoughton W Sus 33 D7
Stoul Highld 235 A6
Stoulton Worcs 80 C2
Stour Provost Dorset 30 C1
Stour Row Dorset 30 C2
Stourbridge W Mid 96 C2
Stourhead Garden Wilts 30 B1
Stourpaine Dorset 16 A2
Stourport on Severn Worcs 95 D6
Stourton Staffs 95 C6
Stourton Warks 81 D5
Stourton Wilts 30 B1
Stourton Caundle Dorset 29 D7
Stove Orkney 282 D7
Stove Shetland 285 L6
Stoven Suff 105 C5
Stow Borders 196 B3
Stow Lincs 132 A3
Stow Lincs 116 B3
Stow Bardolph Norf 102 A2
Stow Bedon Norf 103 B5
Stow cum Quy Cambs 85 A7
Stow Longa Cambs 100 D3
Stow Maries Essex 70 D2
Stow-on-the-Wold Glos 64 A2
Stowbridge Norf 102 A2
Stowe Shrops 93 D7
Stowe-by-Chartley Staffs 112 C4
Stowe Green Glos 62 C1
Stowe House and Gardens, Buckingham Bucks 82 D3
Stowell Som 29 C6
Stowford Devon 11 C5
Stowlangtoft Suff 87 A5
Stowmarket Suff 87 B6
Stowting Kent 38 A3
Stowupland Suff 87 B6
Straad Argyll 203 B5
Strachan Aberds 244 C3
Stradbroke Suff 104 D3
Stradishall Suff 86 B3
Stradsett Norf 102 A2
Stragglethorpe Lincs 133 D4
Straid S Ayrs 180 B3
Straith Dumfries 183 D6
Straiton Edin 209 D5
Straiton S Ayrs 181 A5
Straloch Aberds 256 D3
Straloch Perth 230 B4
Stramshall Staffs 113 B4
Strang I o M 152 D3
Stranraer Dumfries 170 A2
Stratfield Mortimer W Berks 47 C4
Stratfield Saye Hants 47 C4
Stratfield Turgis Hants 47 D4
Stratford London 49 A6
Stratford Racecourse Warks 81 B4
Stratford St Andrew Suff 89 A4
Stratford St Mary Suff 87 D6
Stratford Sub Castle Wilts 31 B5
Stratford Tony Wilts 31 C4
Stratford-upon-Avon Warks 81 B4
Strath Highld 281 C4
Strath Highld 261 C4
Strathan Highld 238 C3
Strathan Highld 277 B6
Strathan Highld 270 B3
Strathaven S Lnrk 194 B2
Strathblane Stirl 205 A5
Strathcanaird Highld 271 D4
Strathcarron Highld 249 B6
Strathcoil Argyll 225 C5
Strathdon Aberds 243 A6
Strathellie Aberds 269 C5
Strathkinness Fife 221 C4
Strathmashie House Highld 240 C3
Strathmiglo Fife 220 C2
Strathmore Lodge Highld 280 D3
Strathpeffer Highld 251 A6
Strathrannoch Highld 263 C5
Strathtay Perth 230 C3
Strathvaich Lodge Highld 263 C5
Strathwhillan N Ayrs 191 B6
Strathy Highld 279 B4
Strathyre Stirl 217 C5
Stratton Corn 10 A3
Stratton Dorset 15 B6
Stratton Glos 63 C6
Stratton Audley Oxon 65 A7
Stratton on the Fosse Som 43 D5
Stratton St Margaret Swindon 45 A5
Stratton St Michael Norf 104 B3
Stratton Strawless Norf 120 C4
Stravithie Fife 221 C5
Streat E Sus 21 A6
Streatham London 49 B6
Streatley Beds 67 A5
Streatley W Berks 46 A3
Street Lancs 145 B5
Street N Yorks 159 A6
Street Som 29 B4
Street Dinas Shrops 110 B2
Street End Kent 52 D3
Street End W Sus 20 C1
Street Gate T & W 179 D4
Street Lydan Wrex 110 B3
Streethay Staffs 113 D5
Streetlam N Yorks 157 B7
Streetly W Mid 96 B3
Streetly End Cambs 86 C2
Strefford Shrops 94 C2
Strelley Notts 114 A3
Strensall York 149 A5
Stretcholt Som 28 A2
Strete Devon 8 C2
Stretford Gtr Man 137 D7
Strethall Essex 85 D6
Stretham Cambs 101 D7
Strettington W Sus 20 B1
Stretton Ches 127 D4
Stretton Derbys 130 C3
Stretton Rutland 116 D2
Stretton Staffs 112 D2
Stretton Staffs 113 C6
Stretton Warr 127 A6
Stretton Grandison Hereford 79 C4
Stretton-on-Dunsmore Warks 97 D7
Stretton-on-Fosse Warks 81 D5
Stretton Sugwas Hereford 78 C2
Stretton under Fosse Warks 98 C1
Stretton Westwood Shrops 94 B3
Strichen Aberds 269 D4
Strines Gtr Man 129 A4
Stringston Som 28 A1
Strixton Northants 83 A6
Stroat Glos 62 D1
Stromeferry Highld 249 C5
Stromemore Highld 249 C5
Stromness Orkney 283 G3
Stronaba Highld 239 D6
Stronachlachar Stirl 216 C4
Stronchreggan Highld 237 B4
Stronchrubie Highld 271 C5
Strone Argyll 215 D4
Strone Highld 252 D1
Strone Highld 239 D5
Strone Invclyd 204 A2
Stronmilchan Argyll 227 D6
Stronsay Airport Orkney 282 E7
Strontian Highld 236 C2
Strood Medway 51 C4
Strood Green Sur 35 B5
Strood Green W Sus 34 D3
Strood Green W Sus 35 C4
Stroud Glos 63 C4
Stroud Hants 33 C6
Stroud Green Essex 70 D2
Stroxton Lincs 116 B2
Struan Highld 246 A2
Struan Perth 230 B2
Strubby Lincs 135 A4
Strumpshaw Norf 104 A4
Strutherhill S Lnrk 194 B2
Struy Highld 251 C5
Stryt-issa Wrex 110 A1
Stuartfield Aberds 257 B4
Stub Place Cumb 153 A1
Stubbington Hants 19 A4
Stubbins Lancs 137 B6
Stubbs Cross Kent 38 B1
Stubb's Green Norf 104 B3
Stubbs Green Norf 105 B4
Stubhampton Dorset 30 D3
Stubton Lincs 115 A6
Stuckgowan Argyll 215 B6
Stuckton Hants 31 D5
Stud Green Windsor 48 B1
Studham Beds 67 B5
Studland Dorset 17 C4
Studley Warks 80 A3
Studley Wilts 44 B3
Studley Roger N Yorks 157 D6
Stump Cross Essex 85 C7
Stuntney Cambs 102 D1
Sturbridge Staffs 112 B2
Sturmer Essex 86 C2
Sturminster Marshall Dorset 16 A3
Sturminster Newton Dorset 30 D1
Sturry Kent 52 C3
Sturton N Lincs 142 C1
Sturton by Stow Lincs 132 A3
Sturton le Steeple Notts 132 A2
Stuston Suff 104 D2
Stutton N Yorks 148 C3
Stutton Suff 88 D2
Styal Ches 128 A3
Styrrup Notts 140 D4
Suainebost W Isles 288 A6
Suardail W Isles 288 D5
Succoth Aberds 255 C5
Succoth Argyll 215 B6
Suckley Worcs 79 B5
Suckquoy Orkney 283 K5
Sudborough Northants 99 C6
Sudbourne Suff 89 B5
Sudbrook Lincs 116 A2
Sudbrook Mon 43 A4
Sudbrooke Lincs 133 B5
Sudbury Derbys 113 B5
Sudbury London 49 A4
Sudbury Suff 87 C4
Suddie Highld 252 A2
Sudeley Castle and Gardens Glos 63 A6
Sudgrove Glos 63 C5
Suffield Norf 120 B4
Suffield N Yorks 160 B3
Sugnall Staffs 112 B1
Suladale Highld 258 C3
Sulaisiadar W Isles 288 D6
Sulby I o M 152 B3
Sulgrave Northants 82 C2
Sulham W Berks 47 B4
Sulhamstead W Berks 47 C4
Sulland Orkney 282 C6
Sullington W Sus 20 A3
Sullom Shetland 284 F5
Sullom Voe Oil Terminal Shetland 284 F5
Sully V Glam 41 E6
Sumburgh Shetland 285 N6
Sumburgh Airport Shetland 285 M5
Summer Bridge N Yorks 147 A6
Summer-house Darl 167 D5
Summercourt Corn 4 B3
Summerfield Norf 119 B4
Summergangs Hull 151 D4
Summerleaze Mon 42 A3
Summerlee Heritage Centre, Coatbridge N Lnrk 207 D5
Summersdale W Sus 20 B1
Summerseat Gtr Man 137 B6
Summertown Oxon 65 C6
Summit Gtr Man 138 C2
Sunbury-on-Thames Sur 48 C4
Sundaywell Dumfries 183 D6
Sunderland Argyll 200 B2
Sunderland Cumb 163 A4
Sunderland T & W 179 D5
Sunderland Bridge Durham 167 B5
Sundhope Borders 196 D2
Sundon Park Luton 67 A5
Sundown Adventure Land, Rampton Notts 132 B2
Sundridge Kent 36 A2
Sunipol Argyll 224 A2
Sunk Island E Yorks 143 B4
Sunningdale Windsor 48 C2
Sunninghill Windsor 48 C2
Sunningwell Oxon 65 C5
Sunniside Durham 166 B4
Sunniside T & W 179 D4
Sunnyhurst Blkburn 137 A5
Sunnylaw Stirl 207 A5
Sunnyside W Sus 36 C1
Sunton Wilts 45 D6
Surbiton London 49 C4
Surby I o M 152 D2
Surfleet Lincs 117 C5
Surfleet Seas End Lincs 117 C5
Surlingham Norf 104 A4
Sustead Norf 120 B3
Susworth Lincs 141 C6
Sutcombe Devon 24 D4
Suton Norf 104 B1
Sutors of Cromarty Highld 265 D4
Sutterby Lincs 134 B3
Sutterton Lincs 117 B5
Sutton Beds 84 C4
Sutton Cambs 101 D6
Sutton London 49 C5
Sutton Kent 39 A5
Sutton Mers 136 D4
Sutton Norf 121 C5
Sutton Notts 115 B5
Sutton Notts 132 A1
Sutton N Yorks 140 A2
Sutton Oxon 65 C5
Sutton P'boro 100 B2
Sutton Shrops 95 C5
Sutton Shrops 111 B5
Sutton Som 29 B6
Sutton Staffs 111 C6
Sutton Suff 88 C4
Sutton Sur 34 B4
Sutton S Yorks 140 B3
Sutton W Sus 20 A2
Sutton at Hone Kent 50 B2
Sutton Bassett Northants 99 B4
Sutton Benger Wilts 44 B3
Sutton Bonington Notts 114 C3
Sutton Bridge Lincs 118 C1
Sutton Cheney Leics 97 A7
Sutton Coldfield W Mid 96 B4
Sutton Courtenay Oxon 65 D6
Sutton Crosses Lincs 118 C1
Sutton Grange N Yorks 157 D6
Sutton Green Sur 34 A3
Sutton Howgrave N Yorks 157 D7
Sutton In Ashfield Notts 131 D4
Sutton-in-Craven N Yorks 147 C4
Sutton in the Elms Leics 98 B2
Sutton Ings Hull 151 D4
Sutton Lane Ends Ches 129 B4
Sutton Leach Mers 136 D4
Sutton Maddock Shrops 95 A5
Sutton Mallet Som 28 B3
Sutton Mandeville Wilts 30 C3
Sutton Manor Mers 136 D4
Sutton Montis Som 29 C6
Sutton on Hull Hull 151 D4
Sutton on Sea Lincs 135 A5
Sutton-on-the-Forest N Yorks 149 A4
Sutton on the Hill Derbys 113 B6
Sutton on Trent Notts 132 C2
Sutton St Edmund Lincs 117 D6
Sutton St James Lincs 117 D6
Sutton St Nicholas Hereford 78 C3
Sutton Scarsdale Derbys 131 C4
Sutton Scotney Hants 32 B3
Sutton under Brailes Warks 81 D6
Sutton-under-Whitestonecliffe N Yorks 158 C3
Sutton upon Derwent E Yorks 149 C6
Sutton Valence Kent 37 B6
Sutton Veny Wilts 30 A2
Sutton Waldron Dorset 30 D2
Sutton Weaver Ches 127 B5
Sutton Wick Bath 43 D4
Swaby Lincs 134 B3
Swadlincote Derbys 113 D7
Swaffham Norf 103 A4
Swaffham Bulbeck Cambs 86 A1
Swaffham Prior Cambs 86 A1
Swafield Norf 121 B4
Swainby N Yorks 158 A3
Swainshill Hereford 78 C2
Swainsthorpe Norf 104 A3
Swainswick Bath 43 C6
Swalcliffe Oxon 81 D6
Swalecliffe Kent 52 C3
Swallow Lincs 142 C3
Swallowcliffe Wilts 30 C3
Swallowfield Wokingham 47 C5
Swallownest S Yorks 131 A4
Swallows Cross Essex 69 D6
Swan Green Ches 128 B2
Swan Green Suff 104 D3
Swanage Dorset 17 D4
Swanage Railway Dorset 17 D4
Swanbister Orkney 283 G4
Swanbourne Bucks 66 A3
Swanland E Yorks 142 A1
Swanley Kent 50 C2
Swanley Village Kent 50 C2
Swanmore Hants 33 D4
Swannery, Abbotsbury Dorset 15 C5
Swannington Leics 114 D2
Swannington Norf 120 D3
Swanscombe Kent 50 B3
Swansea = Abertawe Swansea 57 C6
Swanton Abbott Norf 121 C4
Swanton Morley Norf 120 D2
Swanton Novers Norf 120 B2
Swanton Street Kent 37 A6
Swanwick Derbys 131 D4
Swanwick Hants 18 A4
Swarby Lincs 116 A3
Swardeston Norf 104 A3
Swarister Shetland 284 E7
Swarkestone Derbys 114 C1
Swarland Northumb 189 C4
Swarland Estate Northumb 189 C4
Swarthmoor Cumb 153 C3
Swathwick Derbys 130 C3
Swaton Lincs 116 B4
Swavesey Cambs 85 A5
Sway Hants 18 B1
Swayfield Lincs 116 C2
Swaythling Soton 32 D3
Sweet Green Worcs 79 A4
Sweetham Devon 12 B3
Sweethouse Corn 5 A5
Sweffling Suff 88 A4
Swepstone Leics 114 D1
Swerford Oxon 81 D6
Swettenham Ches 128 C3

Swetton N Yorks 157 D5
Swffryd Bl Gwent 60 D4
Swiftsden E Sus 37 D5
Swilland Suff 88 B2
Swillington W Yorks 148 D2
Swimbridge Devon 25 C7
Swimbridge Newland Devon 25 B7
Swinbrook Oxon 64 B3
Swinderby Lincs 132 C3
Swindon Glos 63 A5
Swindon Staffs 95 B6
Swindon Swindon 45 A5
Swine E Yorks 151 D4
Swinefleet E Yorks 141 A5
Swineshead Beds 84 A2
Swineshead Lincs 117 A5
Swineshead Bridge Lincs 117 A5
Swiney Highld 275 A6
Swinford Leics 98 D2
Swinford Oxon 65 C5
Swingate Notts 114 A3
Swingfield Minnis Kent 39 A4
Swingfield St Kent 39 A4
Swinhoe Northumb 189 A5
Swinhope Lincs 143 D4
Swining Shetland 284 G6
Swinithwaite N Yorks 156 C4
Swinnow Moor W Yorks 147 D6
Swinscoe Staffs 113 A5
Swinside Hall Borders 187 B6
Swinstead Lincs 116 C3
Swinton Borders 198 B2
Swinton Gtr Man 137 C6
Swinton N Yorks 157 D6
Swinton N Yorks 159 D6
Swinton S Yorks 140 D2
Swintonmill Borders 198 B2
Swithland Leics 114 D3
Swordale Highld 264 D1
Swordland Highld 238 C1
Swordly Highld 278 B3
Sworton Heath Ches 128 A1
Swydd-ffynnon Ceredig 75 B5
Swynnerton Staffs 112 B2
Swyre Dorset 15 C5
Sychtyn Powys 92 A3
Syde Glos 63 B5
Sydenham London 49 B6
Sydenham Oxon 66 C2
Sydenham Damerel Devon 11 D5
Syderstone Norf 119 B5
Sydling St Nicholas Dorset 15 B6
Sydmonton Hants 46 D2
Syerston Notts 115 A5
Syke Gtr Man 138 B1
Sykehouse S Yorks 140 B4
Sykes Lancs 145 B6
Syleham Suff 104 D3
Sylen Carms 57 B5
Symbister Shetland 285 G7
Symington S Ayrs 192 B3
Symington S Lnrk 195 C4
Symonds Yat Hereford 62 B1
Symondsbury Dorset 14 B4
Synod Inn Ceredig 73 A7
Syon Park & House London 49 B4
Syre Highld 278 D2
Syreford Glos 63 A6
Syresham Northants 82 C3
Syston Leics 115 D4
Syston Lincs 116 A2
Sytchampton Worcs 79 A6
Sywell Northants 83 A5

T

Taagan Highld 262 D2
Tàbost W Isles 288 A6
Tabost W Isles 288 F4
Tackley Oxon 65 A5
Tacleit W Isles 288 D2
Tacolneston Norf 104 B2
Tadcaster N Yorks 148 C3
Taddington Derbys 129 B6
Taddiport Devon 25 D5
Tadley Hants 47 C4
Tadlow Beds 85 C4
Tadmarton Oxon 81 D6
Tadworth Sur 35 A5
Tafarn-y-gelyn Denb 126 C1
Tafarnau-bach Bl Gwent 60 B3
Taff's Well Rhondda 41 C6
Tafolwern Powys 91 B6
Tai Conwy 124 C2
Tai-bach Powys 109 C6
Tai-mawr Conwy 109 A4
Tai-Ucha Denb 125 D5
Taibach Neath 40 C2
Taigh a Ghearraidh W Isles 287 G2
Tain Highld 264 B3
Tain Highld 280 B4
Tainant Wrex 110 A1
Tainlon Gwyn 107 A4
Tai'r-Bull Powys 60 A1
Tairbeart = Tarbert W Isles 288 G2
Tairgwaith Neath 59 D4
Takeley Essex 69 A5
Takeley Street Essex 69 A5
Tal-sarn Ceredig 75 C4
Tal-y-bont Ceredig 91 D4
Tal-y-Bont Conwy 124 C2
Tal-y-bont Gwyn 123 C6
Tal-y-bont Gwyn 107 D5
Tal-y-cafn Conwy 124 B2
Tal-y-llyn Gwyn 91 B5
Tal-y-wern Powys 91 B6
Talachddu Powys 77 D4
Talacre Flint 125 A6
Talardd Gwyn 108 C3
Talaton Devon 13 B5
Talbenny Pembs 54 C4
Talbot Green Rhondda 41 C5
Talbot Village Poole 17 B4
Tale Devon 13 A5
Talerddig Powys 92 A3
Talgarreg Ceredig 74 C3
Talgarth Powys 77 D5
Talisker Highld 246 A2
Talke Staffs 128 D3
Talkin Cumb 176 D3
Talla Linnfoots Borders 195 D6
Talladale Highld 261 C6
Tallarn Green Wrex 110 A3
Tallentire Cumb 163 A4
Talley Carms 58 B3
Tallington Lincs 100 A2
Talmine Highld 277 B6
Talog Carms 73 D6
Talsarn Carms 59 C4
Talsarnau Gwyn 107 C6
Talskiddy Corn 4 A4
Talwrn Anglesey 123 C4
Talwrn Wrex 110 A1
Talybont-on-Usk Powys 60 A3
Talygarn Rhondda 41 C5
Talyllyn Powys 60 A3
Talysarn Gwyn 107 A4
Talywain Torf 61 C4
Tame Bridge N Yorks 158 A4
Tamerton Foliot Plym 6 A3
Tamworth Staffs 97 A5
Tan Hinon Powys 91 D6
Tan-lan Conwy 124 C2
Tan-lan Gwyn 107 B6
Tan-y-bwlch Gwyn 107 B6
Tan-y-fron Conwy 125 C4
Tan-y-graig Anglesey 123 C5
Tan-y-graig Gwyn 106 C3
Tan-y-groes Ceredig 73 B5
Tan-y-pistyll Powys 109 C5
Tan-yr-allt Gwyn 107 A4
Tandem W Yorks 139 B4
Tanden Kent 37 C7
Tandridge Sur 35 A6
Tanerdy Carms 73 D7
Tanfield Durham 178 D3
Tanfield Lea Durham 178 D3
Tangasdal W Isles 286 G2
Tangiers Pembs 55 C5
Tangley Hants 46 D1
Tanglwst Carms 73 C6
Tangmere W Sus 20 B2
Tangwick Shetland 284 F4
Tank Museum, Bovington Dorset 16 C2
Tankersley S Yorks 139 C6
Tankerton Kent 52 C3
Tannach Highld 281 D5
Tannachie Aberds 245 D4
Tannadice Angus 232 C2
Tannington Suff 88 A3
Tansley Derbys 130 D3
Tansley Knoll Derbys 130 C3
Tansor Northants 100 B2
Tantobie Durham 178 D3
Tanton N Yorks 168 D3
Tanworth-in-Arden Warks 96 D4
Tanygrisiau Gwyn 107 B6
Tanyrhydiau Ceredig 75 B6
Taobh a Chaolais W Isles 286 E3
Taobh a Thuath Loch Aineort W Isles 286 D3
Taobh a Tuath Loch Baghasdail W Isles 286 D3
Taobh a'Ghlinne W Isles 288 F4
Taobh Tuath W Isles 287 F4
Taplow Bucks 48 A2
Tapton Derbys 130 B3
Tarbat Ho. Highld 264 C3
Tarbert Argyll 213 D4
Tarbert Argyll 202 B3
Tarbert Argyll 202 C1
Tarbert = Tairbeart W Isles 288 G2
Tarbet Argyll 215 B6
Tarbet Highld 276 D2
Tarbet Highld 238 C1
Tarbock Green Mers 127 A4
Tarbolton S Ayrs 193 C4
Tarbrax S Lnrk 195 A5
Tardebigge Worcs 80 A3
Tarfside Angus 232 A2
Tarland Aberds 244 B1
Tarleton Lancs 136 A3
Tarlogie Highld 264 B3
Tarlscough Lancs 136 B3
Tarlton Glos 63 D5
Tarnbrook Lancs 145 B5
Tarporley Ches 127 C5
Tarr Som 27 B6
Tarrant Crawford Dorset 16 A3
Tarrant Gunville Dorset 30 D3
Tarrant Hinton Dorset 30 D3
Tarrant Keyneston Dorset 16 A3
Tarrant Launceston Dorset 16 A3
Tarrant Monkton Dorset 16 A3
Tarrant Rawston Dorset 16 A3
Tarrant Rushton Dorset 16 A3
Tarrel Highld 265 B4
Tarring Neville E Sus 22 B2
Tarrington Hereford 79 C4
Tarsappie Perth 219 B6
Tarskavaig Highld 247 D4
Tarves Aberds 256 C3
Tarvie Highld 251 A6
Tarvie Perth 230 B4
Tarvin Ches 127 C4
Tasburgh Norf 104 B3
Tasley Shrops 95 B4
Taston Oxon 65 A4
Tate Gallery London 49 B5
Tate Gallery, Albert Dock Mers 126 A3
Tate Modern London 49 B6
Tate St Ives Corn 2 A3
Tatenhill Staffs 113 C6
Tathall End M Keynes 83 C5
Tatham Lancs 145 A6
Tathwell Lincs 134 A3
Tatling End Bucks 48 A3
Tatsfield Sur 36 A2
Tattenhall Ches 127 D4
Tattenhoe M Keynes 83 D5
Tatterford Norf 119 C5
Tattersett Norf 119 B5
Tattershall Lincs 134 D2
Tattershall Bridge Lincs 134 D1
Tattershall Thorpe Lincs 134 D2
Tattingstone Suff 88 D2
Tatton House, Knutsford Ches 128 A2
Tatworth Som 14 A3
Taunton Som 28 C2
Taunton Racecourse Som 28 C2
Taverham Norf 120 D3
Tavernspite Pembs 56 A1
Tavistock Devon 11 D5
Taw Green Devon 12 B1
Tawstock Devon 25 C6
Taxal Derbys 129 B5
Tay Bridge Dundee 220 B4
Tayinloan Argyll 202 D1
Taymouth Castle Perth 230 D1
Taynish Argyll 213 D5
Taynton Glos 62 A3
Taynton Oxon 64 B3
Taynuilt Argyll 227 C5
Tayport Fife 221 B4
Tayvallich Argyll 213 D5
Tealby Lincs 142 D3
Tealing Angus 220 A4
Teangue Highld 247 D5
Teanna Mhachair W Isles 287 H2
Tebay Cumb 155 A5
Tebworth Beds 67 A4
Tedburn St Mary Devon 12 B3
Teddington Glos 80 D2
Teddington London 49 B4
Tedstone Delamere Hereford 79 B4
Tedstone Wafre Hereford 79 B4
Teeton Northants 98 D3
Teffont Evias Wilts 30 B3
Teffont Magna Wilts 30 B3
Tegryn Pembs 73 C5
Teigh Rutland 115 D6
Teigncombe Devon 12 C1
Teigngrace Devon 12 D3
Teignmouth Devon 13 D4
Telford Telford 95 A4
Telham E Sus 23 A5
Tellisford Som 44 D2
Telscombe E Sus 22 B2
Telscombe Cliffs E Sus 22 B1
Templand Dumfries 184 D3
Temple Corn 10 D2
Temple Glasgow 205 B5
Temple Midloth 196 A2
Temple Balsall W Mid 97 D5
Temple Bar Ceredig 75 C4
Temple Bar Carms 57 A5
Temple Cloud Bath 43 D5
Temple Combe Som 29 C7
Temple Ewell Kent 39 A4
Temple Grafton Warks 80 B4
Temple Guiting Glos 64 A1
Temple Herdewyke Warks 81 B6
Temple Hirst N Yorks 140 A4
Temple Normanton Derbys 131 C4
Temple Sowerby Cumb 165 C4
Templehall Fife 209 A5
Templeton Devon 26 D3
Templeton Pembs 55 C7
Templeton Bridge Devon 26 D3
Templetown Durham 178 D3
Tempsford Beds 84 B3
Ten Mile Bank Norf 102 B2
Tenbury Wells Worcs 78 A3
Tenby = Dinbych-y-Pysgod Pembs 56 B1
Tendring Essex 71 A5
Tendring Green Essex 71 A5
Tenston Orkney 282 F3
Tenterden Kent 37 C6
Terling Essex 70 B1
Ternhill Shrops 111 B5
Terregles Banks Dumfries 174 A2
Terrick Bucks 66 C3
Terrington N Yorks 159 D5
Terrington St Clement Norf 118 D2
Terrington St John Norf 118 D2
Teston Kent 37 A5
Testwood Hants 32 D2
Tetbury Glos 63 D4
Tetbury Upton Glos 63 D4
Tetchill Shrops 110 B2
Tetcott Devon 10 B4
Tetford Lincs 134 B3
Tetney Lincs 143 C5
Tetney Lock Lincs 143 C5
Tetsworth Oxon 66 C1
Tettenhall W Mid 96 A1
Teuchan Aberds 257 C5
Teversal Notts 131 C4
Teversham Cambs 85 B6
Teviothead Borders 186 C3
Tewel Aberds 245 D5
Tewin Herts 68 B2
Tewkesbury Glos 80 D1
Tewkesbury Abbey Glos 80 D1
Teynham Kent 51 C6
Thackthwaite Cumb 163 B4
Thainston Aberds 233 A4
Thakeham W Sus 21 A4
Thame Oxon 66 C2
Thames Ditton Sur 49 C4
Thames Haven Thurrock 51 A4
Thamesmead London 50 A1
Thanington Kent 52 D3
Thankerton S Lnrk 195 C4
Tharston Norf 104 B2
Thatcham W Berks 46 C3
Thatto Heath Mers 136 D4
Thaxted Essex 86 D2
The Aird Highld 259 C4
The All England Jumping Course, Hickstead W Sus 21 A5
The Arms Norf 103 B4
The Bage Hereford 77 C6
The Balloch Perth 218 C3
The Barony Orkney 282 E3
The Bluebell Railway, Sheffield Park E Sus 36 D2
The Bog Shrops 94 B1
The Bourne Sur 33 A7
The Braes Highld 247 A4
The Broad Hereford 78 A2
The Burrell Collection Glasgow 205 B5
The Butts Som 30 A1
The Camp Glos 63 C5
The Camp Herts 67 C6
The Chequer Wrex 110 A3
The City Bucks 66 D2
The Common Wilts 31 B6
The Craigs Highld 263 A6
The Cronk I o M 152 B3
The Dell Suff 105 B5
The Den N Ayrs 204 C3
The Dinosaur Museum, Dorchester Dorset 15 B7
The Eals Northumb 177 A5
The Eaves Glos 62 C2
The Flatt Cumb 176 B3
The Four Alls Shrops 111 B5
The Friars, Aylesford Kent 37 A5
The Garths Shetland 284 B8
The Green Cumb 153 B2
The Green Wilts 30 B2
The Grove Dumfries 174 A2
The Hall Shetland 284 D8
The Haven W Sus 34 C3
The Heath Norf 120 C3
The Heath Suff 88 D2
The Hill Cumb 153 B2
The Howe Cumb 154 C3
The Howe I o M 152 E1
The Hundred Hereford 78 A3
The Lee Bucks 67 C4
The Lhen I o M 152 A3
The Living RainForest W Berks 46 B3
The Long Man of Wilmington E Sus 22 B3
The Lost Gardens of Heligan, Mevagissey Corn 5 C4
The Lowry, Salford Gtr Man 137 D7
The Marsh Powys 93 B7
The Marsh Wilts 45 A4
The Middles Durham 179 D4
The Moor Kent 37 D5
The Moors Centre, Danby N Yorks 159 A6
The Mumbles = Y Mwmbwls Swansea 57 D6
The Murray S Lnrk 205 C6
The National Archives, Kew London 49 B4
The National Tramway Museum, Crich Derbys 130 D3
The Needles Old Battery I o W 18 C1
The Neuk Aberds 245 C4
The Oval Bath 43 C6
The Oval Cricket Ground London 49 B6
The Oxford Story, Oxford Oxon 65 C6
The Pole of Itlaw Aberds 268 D1
The Quarry Glos 62 D3
The Rhos Pembs 55 C6
The Rock Telford 95 A4
The Ryde Herts 68 C2
The Sands Sur 34 B1
The Stocks Kent 37 D7
The Tales of Robin Hood Nottingham 114 B3
The Throat Wokingham 47 C6
The Tutankhamun Exhibition, Dorchester Dorset 15 B6
The Vauld Hereford 78 C3
The Vyne Hants 47 D4
The World of Beatrix Potter, Bowness-on-Windermere Cumb 154 B3
The Wyke Shrops 95 A5
Theakston N Yorks 157 C7
Thealby N Lincs 141 B6
Theale Som 29 A4
Theale W Berks 47 B4
Thearne E Yorks 150 D3
Theberton Suff 89 A5
Theddingworth Leics 98 C3
Theddlethorpe All Saints Lincs 135 A4
Theddlethorpe St Helen Lincs 135 A4
Thelbridge Barton Devon 26 D2
Thelnetham Suff 103 D6
Thelveton Norf 104 C2
Thelwall Warr 127 A6
Themelthorpe Norf 120 C2
Thenford Northants 82 C2
Therfield Herts 85 D5
Thetford Lincs 116 D4
Thetford Norf 103 C4
Theydon Bois Essex 68 D4
Thickwood Wilts 44 B2
Thimbleby Lincs 134 C2
Thimbleby N Yorks 158 B3
Thingwall Mers 126 A2
Thirdpart N Ayrs 204 D1
Thirlby N Yorks 158 C3
Thirlestane Borders 197 B4
Thirn N Yorks 157 C6
Thirsk N Yorks 158 C3
Thirsk Racecourse N Yorks 158 C3
Thirtleby E Yorks 151 D4
Thistleton Lancs 144 D4
Thistleton Rutland 116 D2
Thistley Green Suff 102 D2
Thixendale N Yorks 150 A1
Thockrington Northumb 178 B1
Tholomas Drove Cambs 101 A5
Tholthorpe N Yorks 148 A3
Thomas Chapel Pembs 55 D7
Thomas Close Cumb 164 A2
Thomastown Aberds 255 C6
Thompson Norf 103 B5
Thomshill Moray 266 D3
Thong Kent 50 B3
Thongsbridge W Yorks 139 C4
Thoralby N Yorks 156 C4
Thoresway Lincs 142 D3
Thorganby Lincs 143 D4
Thorganby N Yorks 149 C5
Thorgill N Yorks 159 B6
Thorington Suff 105 D5
Thorington Street Suff 87 D6
Thorlby N Yorks 146 B3
Thorley Herts 69 B4
Thorley Street Herts 69 B4
Thorley Street I o W 18 C2
Thormanby N Yorks 158 D3
Thornaby on Tees Stockton 168 D2
Thornage Norf 120 B2
Thornborough Bucks 83 D4
Thornborough N Yorks 157 D6
Thornbury Devon 11 A5
Thornbury Hereford 79 B4
Thornbury S Glos 62 D2
Thornbury W Yorks 147 D5
Thornby Northants 98 D3
Thorncliffe Staffs 129 D5
Thorncombe Dorset 14 A3
Thorncombe Dorset 16 A2
Thorncombe Street Sur 34 B3
Thorncote Green Beds 84 C3
Thorncross I o W 18 C3
Thorndon Suff 88 A2
Thorndon Cross Devon 11 B6
Thorne S Yorks 141 B4
Thorne St Margaret Som 27 C5
Thorner W Yorks 148 C2
Thorney Notts 132 B3
Thorney P'boro 101 A4
Thorney Crofts E Yorks 143 A4
Thorney Green Suff 87 A6
Thorney Hill Hants 17 B5
Thorney Toll Cambs 101 A5
Thornfalcon Som 28 C2
Thornford Dorset 29 D6
Thorngumbald E Yorks 143 A4
Thornham Norf 119 A4
Thornham Magna Suff 104 D2
Thornham Parva Suff 104 D2
Thornhaugh P'boro 100 A2
Thornhill Caerph 41 C6
Thornhill Cumb 162 D3
Thornhill Derbys 130 A1
Thornhill Dumfries 183 C6
Thornhill Soton 32 D3
Thornhill Stirl 207 A4
Thornhill W Yorks 139 B5
Thornhill Edge W Yorks 139 B5
Thornhill Lees W Yorks 139 B5
Thornholme E Yorks 151 A4
Thornley Durham 166 B4
Thornley Durham 167 B6
Thornliebank E Renf 205 C5
Thorns Suff 86 B3
Thorns Green Ches 128 A2
Thornsett Derbys 129 A5
Thornthwaite Cumb 163 B5
Thornthwaite N Yorks 147 B5
Thornton Angus 232 D1
Thornton Bucks 83 D4
Thornton E Yorks 149 C6
Thornton Fife 209 A5
Thornton Lancs 144 C3
Thornton Leics 98 A1
Thornton Lincs 134 C2
Thornton Mers 136 C2
Thornton M'bro 168 D2
Thornton Northumb 198 B3
Thornton Pembs 55 D5
Thornton W Yorks 147 D5
Thornton Curtis N Lincs 142 B2
Thornton Heath London 49 C6
Thornton Hough Mers 126 A3
Thornton in Craven N Yorks 146 C3
Thornton-le-Beans N Yorks 158 B2
Thornton-le-Clay N Yorks 149 A5
Thornton-le-Dale N Yorks 160 C2
Thornton le Moor Lincs 142 D2
Thornton-le-Moor N Yorks 158 C2
Thornton-le-Moors Ches 127 B4
Thornton-le-Street N Yorks 158 C3
Thornton Rust N Yorks 156 C3
Thornton Steward N Yorks 157 C5
Thornton Watlass N Yorks 157 C6
Thorntonhall S Lnrk 205 C5
Thorntonloch E Loth 211 C4
Thorntonpark Northumb 198 B3
Thornwood Common Essex 69 C4
Thornydykes Borders 197 B5
Thoroton Notts 115 A5
Thorp Arch W Yorks 148 C3
Thorpe Derbys 129 D6
Thorpe E Yorks 150 C2
Thorpe Lincs 135 A4
Thorpe Norf 105 B5
Thorpe Notts 115 A5
Thorpe N Yorks 147 A4
Thorpe Sur 48 C3
Thorpe Abbotts Norf 104 D2
Thorpe Acre Leics 114 C3
Thorpe Arnold Leics 115 C5
Thorpe Audlin W Yorks 140 B2
Thorpe Bassett N Yorks 160 D2
Thorpe Bay Sthend 51 A6
Thorpe by Water Rutland 99 B5
Thorpe Common Suff 88 D3
Thorpe Constantine Staffs 97 A5
Thorpe Culvert Lincs 135 C4
Thorpe End Norf 121 D4
Thorpe Fendykes Lincs 135 C4
Thorpe Green Essex 71 A5
Thorpe Green Suff 87 B5
Thorpe Hesley S Yorks 140 D1
Thorpe in Balne S Yorks 140 B3

Thorpe in the Fallows Lincs 133 A4
Thorpe Langton Leics 99 B4
Thorpe Larches Durham 167 C6
Thorpe-le-Soken Essex 71 A5
Thorpe le Street E Yorks 150 C1
Thorpe Malsor Northants 99 D5
Thorpe Mandeville Northants 82 C2
Thorpe Market Norf 120 B4
Thorpe Marriot Norf 120 D3
Thorpe Morieux Suff 87 B5
Thorpe on the Hill Lincs 133 C4
Thorpe Park, Chertsey Sur 48 C3
Thorpe St Andrew Norf 104 A3
Thorpe St Peter Lincs 135 C4
Thorpe Salvin S Yorks 131 A5
Thorpe Satchville Leics 115 D5
Thorpe Thewles Stockton 168 C2
Thorpe Tilney Lincs 133 D6
Thorpe Underwood N Yorks 148 B3
Thorpe Waterville Northants 100 C2
Thorpe Willoughby N Yorks 149 D4
Thorpeness Suff 89 B5
Thorrington Essex 71 A4
Thorverton Devon 13 A4
Thrandeston Suff 104 D2
Thrapston Northants 100 D1
Thrashbush N Lnrk 207 D5
Threapland Cumb 163 A4
Threapland N Yorks 146 A3
Threapwood Ches 110 A3
Threapwood Staffs 112 A4
Threave Gardens Dumfries 173 B5
Three Ashes Hereford 61 A7
Three Bridges W Sus 35 C5
Three Burrows Corn 4 C2
Three Chimneys Kent 37 C6
Three Cocks Powys 77 D5
Three Counties Showground, Malvern Worcs 79 C5
Three Crosses Swansea 57 C5
Three Cups Corner E Sus 36 D4
Three Holes Norf 101 A7
Three Leg Cross E Sus 37 C4
Three Legged Cross Dorset 17 A4
Three Oaks E Sus 23 A6
Threehammer Common Norf 121 D5
Threekingham Lincs 116 B3
Threemile Cross Wokingham 47 C5
Threemilestone Corn 4 C2
Threemiletown W Loth 208 C3
Threlkeld Cumb 163 B6
Threshfield N Yorks 146 A3
Thrigby Norf 121 D6
Thringarth Durham 166 C2
Thringstone Leics 114 D2
Thrintoft N Yorks 157 B7
Thriplow Cambs 85 C6
Throckenholt Lincs 101 A5
Throcking Herts 85 D5
Throckley T & W 178 C3
Throckmorton Worcs 80 C2
Throphill Northumb 178 A3
Thropton Northumb 188 C3
Throsk Stirl 207 A6
Throwleigh Devon 12 B1
Throwley Kent 52 D1
Thrumpton Notts 114 B3
Thrumster Highld 281 D5
Thrunton Northumb 188 B3
Thrupp Glos 63 C4
Thrupp Oxon 65 B5
Thrushelton Devon 11 C5
Thrussington Leics 115 D4
Thruxton Hants 32 A1
Thruxton Hereford 78 D2
Thruxton Motor Racing Circuit Hants 32 A1
Thrybergh S Yorks 140 D2
Thulston Derbys 114 B2
Thundergay N Ayrs 202 D3
Thundersley Essex 51 A4
Thundridge Herts 68 B3
Thurcaston Leics 114 D3
Thurcroft S Yorks 131 A4
Thurgarton Norf 120 B3
Thurgarton Notts 115 A4
Thurgoland S Yorks 139 C5
Thurlaston Leics 98 B2
Thurlaston Warks 98 D1
Thurlbear Som 28 C2
Thurlby Lincs 116 D4
Thurlby Lincs 133 C4
Thurleigh Beds 84 B2
Thurlestone Devon 7 C5
Thurloxton Som 28 B2
Thurlstone S Yorks 139 C5
Thurlton Norf 105 B5
Thurlwood Ches 128 D3
Thurmaston Leics 98 A3
Thurnby Leics 98 A3
Thurne Norf 121 D6
Thurnham Kent 37 A6
Thurnham Lancs 145 B4
Thurning Norf 120 C2
Thurning Northants 100 C2
Thurnscoe S Yorks 140 C2
Thurnscoe East S Yorks 140 C2
Thursby Cumb 175 C6
Thursford Norf 120 B1
Thursford Collection, Fakenham Norf 120 B1
Thursley Sur 34 C2
Thurso Highld 280 B3
Thurso East Highld 280 B3
Thurstaston Mers 126 A2
Thurston Suff 87 A5
Thurstonfield Cumb 175 C6
Thurstonland W Yorks 139 B4
Thurton Norf 104 A4
Thurvaston Derbys 113 B6
Thuxton Norf 103 A6
Thwaite N Yorks 156 B2
Thwaite Suff 88 A2
Thwaite St Mary Norf 104 B4
Thwaites W Yorks 147 C4
Thwaites Brow W Yorks 147 C4
Thwing E Yorks 160 D4
Tibbermore Perth 219 B5
Tibberton Glos 62 A3
Tibberton Telford 111 C5
Tibberton Worcs 80 B2
Tibenham Norf 104 C2
Tibshelf Derbys 131 C4
Tibthorpe E Yorks 150 B2
Ticehurst E Sus 37 C4
Tichborne Hants 33 B4
Tickencote Rutland 100 A1
Tickenham N Som 42 B3
Tickhill S Yorks 140 D3
Ticklerton Shrops 94 B2
Ticknall Derbys 114 C1
Tickton E Yorks 150 C3
Tidcombe Wilts 45 D6
Tiddington Oxon 66 C1
Tiddington Warks 81 B5
Tidebrook E Sus 36 D4
Tideford Corn 6 B2
Tideford Cross Corn 6 A2
Tidenham Glos 62 D1
Tideswell Derbys 129 B6
Tidmarsh W Berks 47 B4
Tidmington Warks 81 D5
Tidpit Hants 31 D4
Tidworth Wilts 31 A6
Tiers Cross Pembs 55 C5
Tiffield Northants 82 B3
Tifty Aberds 256 B2
Tigerton Angus 232 B3
Tigh-na-Blair Perth 218 C2
Tighnabruaich Argyll 203 A4
Tighnafiline Highld 261 B5
Tigley Devon 7 A6
Tilbrook Cambs 84 A2
Tilbury Thurrock 50 B3
Tilbury Juxta Clare Essex 86 C3
Tile Cross W Mid 97 C4
Tile Hill W Mid 97 D5
Tilehurst Reading 47 B4
Tilford Sur 34 B1
Tilgate W Sus 35 C5
Tilgate Forest Row W Sus 35 C5
Tillathrowie Aberds 255 C5
Tilley Shrops 111 C4
Tillicoultry Clack 208 A2
Tillingham Essex 70 C3
Tillington Hereford 78 C2
Tillington W Sus 34 D2
Tillington Common Hereford 78 C2
Tillyarblet Angus 232 B3
Tillybirloch Aberds 244 B3
Tillycorthie Aberds 257 D4
Tillydrine Aberds 244 C3
Tillyfour Aberds 244 A2
Tillyfourie Aberds 244 A3
Tillygarmond Aberds 244 C3
Tillygreig Aberds 256 D3
Tillykerrie Aberds 256 D3
Tilmanstone Kent 53 D5
Tilney All Saints Norf 118 D2
Tilney High End Norf 118 D2
Tilney St Lawrence Norf 118 D2
Tilshead Wilts 31 A4
Tilstock Shrops 111 B4
Tilston Ches 127 D4
Tilstone Fearnall Ches 127 C5
Tilsworth Beds 67 A4
Tilton on the Hill Leics 99 A4
Timberland Lincs 133 D6
Timbersbrook Ches 128 C3
Timberscombe Som 27 A4
Timble N Yorks 147 B5
Timperley Gtr Man 128 A2
Timsbury Bath 43 D5
Timsbury Hants 32 C2
Timsgearraidh W Isles 287 A5
Timworth Green Suff 87 A4
Tincleton Dorset 16 B1
Tindale Cumb 176 D4
Tingewick Bucks 82 D3
Tingley W Yorks 139 A5
Tingrith Beds 84 D2
Tingwall Orkney 282 E4
Tinhay Devon 11 C4
Tinshill W Yorks 147 D6
Tinsley S Yorks 140 D2
Tintagel Corn 9 C6
Tintagel Castle Corn 9 C6
Tintern Abbey Mon 62 C1
Tintern Parva Mon 62 C1
Tintinhull Som 29 D5
Tintwistle Derbys 138 D3
Tinwald Dumfries 184 D3
Tinwell Rutland 100 A2
Tipperty Aberds 257 D4
Tipsend Norf 101 B7
Tipton W Mid 96 B2
Tipton St John Devon 13 B5
Tiptree Essex 70 B2
Tir-y-dail Carms 57 A6
Tirabad Powys 59 A5
Tiraghoil Argyll 224 D2
Tiree Airport Argyll 222 C2
Tirley Glos 63 A4
Tirphil Caerph 41 A6
Tirril Cumb 164 C3
Tisbury Wilts 30 C3
Tisman's Common W Sus 34 C3
Tissington Derbys 130 D1
Titchberry Devon 24 C3
Titchfield Hants 18 A4
Titchmarsh Northants 100 D2
Titchwell Norf 119 A4
Tithby Notts 115 B4
Titley Hereford 78 A1
Titlington Northumb 189 B4
Titsey Sur 36 A2
Tittensor Staffs 112 B2
Tittleshall Norf 119 C5
Tiverton Ches 127 C5
Tiverton Devon 27 D4
Tivetshall St Margaret Norf 104 C2
Tivetshall St Mary Norf 104 C2
Tividale W Mid 96 B2
Tivy Dale S Yorks 139 C5
Tixall Staffs 112 C3
Tixover Rutland 99 A6
Toab Orkney 283 G6
Toab Shetland 285 M5
Toadmoor Derbys 130 D3
Tobermory Argyll 225 A4
Toberonochy Argyll 213 B5
Tobha Mor W Isles 286 C3
Tobhtarol W Isles 288 D2
Tobson W Isles 288 D2
Tocher Aberds 256 C1
Tockenham Wilts 44 B4
Tockenham Wick Wilts 44 A4
Tockholes Blkburn 137 A5
Tockington S Glos 43 A5
Tockwith N Yorks 148 B3
Todber Dorset 30 C2
Todding Hereford 94 D2
Toddington Beds 67 A5
Toddington Glos 80 D3
Todenham Glos 81 D5
Todhills Cumb 175 B6
Todlachie Aberds 244 A3
Todmorden W Yorks 138 A2
Todrig Borders 186 B3
Todwick S Yorks 131 A4
Toft Cambs 85 B5
Toft Lincs 116 D3
Toft Hill Durham 167 C4
Toft Hill Lincs 134 C2
Toft Monks Norf 105 B5
Toft next Newton Lincs 133 A5
Toftrees Norf 119 C5
Tofts Highld 281 B5
Toftwood Norf 120 D1
Togston Northumb 189 C5
Tokavaig Highld 247 C5
Tokers Green Oxon 47 B5
Tolastadh a Chaolais W Isles 288 D2
Tolastadh bho Thuath W Isles 288 C6
Toll Bar S Yorks 140 C3
Toll End W Mid 96 B2
Toll of Birness Aberds 257 C5
Tolland Som 27 B6
Tollard Royal Wilts 30 D3
Tollbar End W Mid 97 D6
Toller Fratrum Dorset 15 B5
Toller Porcorum Dorset 15 B5
Tollerton Notts 115 B4
Tollerton N Yorks 148 A4
Tollesbury Essex 70 B3
Tolleshunt D'Arcy Essex 70 B3
Tolleshunt Major Essex 70 B3
Tolm W Isles 288 D5
Tolpuddle Dorset 16 B1
Tolvah Highld 241 C6
Tolworth London 49 C4
Tomatin Highld 253 D4
Tombreck Highld 252 C2
Tomchrasky Highld 239 A6
Tomdoun Highld 239 B5
Tomich Highld 251 D5
Tomich Highld 264 C2
Tomich House Highld 252 B1
Tomintoul Aberds 242 C4
Tomintoul Moray 243 A4
Tomnaven Moray 255 C5
Tomnavoulin Moray 254 D3
Ton-Pentre Rhondda 41 B4
Tonbridge Kent 36 B3
Tondu Bridgend 40 C3
Tonfanau Gwyn 90 B3
Tong Shrops 95 A5
Tong W Yorks 147 D6
Tong Norton Shrops 95 A5
Tonge Leics 114 C2
Tongham Sur 34 B1
Tongland Dumfries 173 C4
Tongue Highld 277 C6
Tongue End Lincs 117 D4
Tongwynlais Cardiff 41 C6
Tonna Neath 40 B2
Tonwell Herts 68 B3
Tonypandy Rhondda 41 B4
Tonyrefail Rhondda 41 C5
Toot Baldon Oxon 65 C6
Toot Hill Essex 69 C5
Toothill Hants 32 D2
Top of Hebers Gtr Man 138 C1
Topcliffe N Yorks 158 D3
Topcroft Norf 104 B3
Topcroft Street Norf 104 B3
Toppesfield Essex 86 D3
Toppings Gtr Man 137 B6
Topsham Devon 13 C4
Torbay Torbay 8 B3
Torbeg N Ayrs 191 C5
Torboll Farm Highld 264 A3
Torbrex Stirl 207 A5
Torbryan Devon 8 A2
Torcross Devon 8 C2
Tore Highld 252 A2
Torinturk Argyll 202 B3
Torksey Lincs 132 B3
Torlum W Isles 286 A3
Torlundy Highld 237 B5
Tormarton S Glos 43 B6
Tormisdale Argyll 200 C1
Tormitchell S Ayrs 181 B4
Tormore N Ayrs 191 B4
Tornagrain Highld 252 B3
Tornahaish Aberds 243 B5
Tornaveen Aberds 244 B3
Torness Highld 252 D1
Toronto Durham 167 B4
Torpenhow Cumb 163 A5
Torphichen W Loth 208 C2
Torphins Aberds 244 B3
Torpoint Corn 6 B3
Torquay Torbay 8 A3
Torquhan Borders 196 B3
Torran Argyll 214 B1
Torran Highld 248 B2
Torran Highld 264 C3
Torrance E Dunb 205 A6
Torrans Argyll 224 D3
Torranyard N Ayrs 204 D3
Torre Torbay 8 A3
Torridon Highld 249 A6
Torridon Ho. Highld 249 A5
Torrin Highld 247 B4
Torrisdale Highld 278 B2
Torrisdale-Square Argyll 190 B3
Torrish Highld 274 C3
Torrisholme Lancs 145 A4
Torroble Highld 272 D3
Torry Aberdeen 245 B6
Torry Aberds 255 C5
Torryburn Fife 208 B3
Torterston Aberds 257 B5
Torthorwald Dumfries 174 A3
Tortington W Sus 20 B3
Tortworth S Glos 62 D3
Torvaig Highld 259 D4
Torver Cumb 154 B1
Torwood Falk 207 B6
Torworth Notts 131 A6
Tosberry Devon 24 C3
Toscaig Highld 249 C4
Toseland Cambs 84 A4
Tosside N Yorks 146 B1
Tostock Suff 87 A5
Totaig Highld 258 C2
Totaig Highld 249 D5
Tote Highld 259 D4
Totegan Highld 279 B4
Tothill Lincs 135 A4
Totland I o W 18 C2
Totnes Devon 8 A2
Toton Notts 114 B3
Totronald Argyll 223 B4
Totscore Highld 258 B3
Tottenham London 68 D3
Tottenhill Norf 118 D3
Tottenhill Row Norf 118 D3
Totteridge London 68 D2
Totternhoe Beds 67 A4
Tottington Gtr Man 137 B6
Totton Hants 32 D2
Touchen End Windsor 48 B1
Tournaig Highld 261 B5
Toux Aberds 269 D4
Tovil Kent 37 A5
Tow Law Durham 166 B4
Toward Argyll 203 B6
Towcester Northants 82 C3
Towcester Racecourse Northants 83 C4
Towednack Corn 2 B2
Tower End Norf 118 D3
Tower Knowe Visitor Centre, Kielder Water Northumb 177 A4
Tower of London London 49 A6
Towersey Oxon 66 C2
Towie Aberds 244 A1
Towie Aberds 268 C3
Towiemore Moray 255 B4
Town End Cambs 101 B6
Town End Cumb 154 C3
Town Row E Sus 36 C3
Town Yetholm Borders 187 A7
Townend W Dunb 205 A4
Towngate Lincs 116 D4
Townhead Cumb 164 B3
Townhead Dumfries 173 D4
Townhead S Ayrs 181 A4
Townhead S Yorks 139 C4
Townhead of Greenlaw Dumfries 173 B5
Townhill Fife 208 B4
Townsend Bucks 66 C2
Townsend Herts 67 C6
Townshend Corn 2 B3
Towthorpe York 149 B5
Towton N Yorks 148 D3
Towyn Conwy 125 B4
Toxteth Mers 126 A3
Toynton All Saints Lincs 134 C3
Toynton Fen Side Lincs 134 C3
Toynton St Peter Lincs 135 C4
Toy's Hill Kent 36 A2
Trabboch E Ayrs 193 C4
Traboe Corn 3 C5
Tradespark Highld 253 A4
Tradespark Orkney 283 G5
Trafford Park Gtr Man 137 D6
Trago Mills, Newton Abbot Devon 12 D3
Trallong Powys 59 C6
Tranent E Loth 209 C7
Tranmere Mers 126 A3
Trantlebeg Highld 279 C4
Trantlemore Highld 279 C4
Tranwell Northumb 178 A3
Trapp Carms 57 A6
Traprain E Loth 210 C2
Traquair Borders 196 C2
Trawden Lancs 146 D3
Trawsfynydd Gwyn 108 B2
Tre-Gibbon Rhondda 60 C1
Tre-Taliesin Ceredig 91 C4
Tre-vaughan Carms 73 D7
Tre-wyn Mon 61 A5
Trealaw Rhondda 41 B5
Treales Lancs 144 D4
Trearddur Anglesey 122 C2
Treaslane Highld 258 C3
Trebah Garden, Mawnan Smith Corn 3 C5
Trebanog Rhondda 41 B5
Trebanos Neath 40 A2
Trebartha Corn 10 D3
Trebarwith Corn 9 C6
Trebetherick Corn 9 D5
Treborough Som 27 B5
Trebudannon Corn 4 A3
Trebullett Corn 10 D4
Treburley Corn 10 D4
Trebyan Corn 5 A5
Trecastle Powys 59 C5
Trecenydd Caerph 41 C6
Trecwn Pembs 55 A5
Trecynon Rhondda 41 A4
Tredavoe Corn 2 C2
Treddiog Pembs 55 B4
Tredegar Bl Gwent 60 C3
Tredegar Newydd = New Tredegar Caerph 41 A6
Tredington Glos 63 A5
Tredington Warks 81 C5
Tredinnick Corn 9 D5
Tredomen Powys 77 D5
Tredunnock Mon 61 D5
Tredustan Powys 77 D5
Treen Corn 2 C1
Treeton S Yorks 131 A4
Tref-y-Clawdd = Knighton Powys 93 D6
Trefaldwyn = Montgomery Powys 93 B6
Trefasser Pembs 72 C1
Trefdraeth Anglesey 123 C4
Trefdraeth = Newport Pembs 72 C3
Trefecca Powys 77 D5
Trefechan Ceredig 90 D3
Trefeglwys Powys 92 B3
Trefenter Ceredig 75 B5
Treffgarne Pembs 55 B5
Treffynnon Pembs 54 B4
Treffynnon = Holywell Flint 126 B1
Trefgarn Owen Pembs 55 B4
Trefil Bl Gwent 60 B3
Trefilan Ceredig 75 C4
Trefin Pembs 54 A4
Treflach Shrops 110 C1
Trefnanney Powys 109 D7
Trefnant Denb 125 B5
Trefonen Shrops 110 C1
Trefor Anglesey 122 B3
Trefor Gwyn 106 B3
Treforest Rhondda 41 C5
Trefriw Conwy 124 C2
Trefynwy = Monmouth Mon 61 B7
Tregadillett Corn 10 C3
Tregaian Anglesey 123 C4
Tregare Mon 61 B6
Tregaron Ceredig 75 C5
Tregarth Gwyn 123 D6
Tregeare Corn 10 C3
Tregeiriog Wrex 109 B6
Tregele Anglesey 122 A3
Tregidden Corn 3 C5
Treglemais Pembs 54 B4
Tregole Corn 10 B2
Tregonetha Corn 5 A4
Tregony Corn 4 C4
Tregoss Corn 5 A4
Tregoyd Powys 77 D6
Tregroes Ceredig 73 B7
Tregurrian Corn 4 A3
Tregynon Powys 93 B4
Trehafod Rhondda 41 B5
Treharris M Tydf 41 B5
Treherbert Rhondda 40 B4
Trekenner Corn 10 D4
Treknow Corn 9 C6
Trelan Corn 3 D5
Trelash Corn 10 B2
Trelassick Corn 4 B3
Trelawnyd Flint 125 B5
Trelech Carms 73 C5
Treleddyd-fawr Pembs 54 B3
Trelewis M Tydf 41 B6
Treligga Corn 9 C6
Trelights Corn 9 D5
Trelill Corn 9 D6
Trelissick Corn 4 D3
Trelissick Garden, Feock Corn 4 D3
Trellech Mon 61 C7
Trelleck Grange Mon 61 C6
Trelogan Flint 125 A6
Trelystan Powys 93 A6
Tremadog Gwyn 107 B5
Tremail Corn 10 C2
Tremain Ceredig 73 B5
Tremaine Corn 10 C3
Tremar Corn 6 A1
Trematon Corn 6 B2
Tremeirchion Denb 125 B5
Trenance Corn 4 A3
Trenarren Corn 5 C5
Trench Telford 111 D5
Treneglos Corn 10 C3
Trenewan Corn 5 B6
Trent Dorset 29 D5
Trent Vale Stoke 112 A2
Trentham Stoke 112 A2
Trentham Gardens, Newcastle-under-Lyme Staffs 112 A2
Trentishoe Devon 26 A1
Treoes V Glam 40 D4
Treorchy = Treorci Rhondda 41 B4
Treorci = Treorchy Rhondda 41 B4
Tre'r-ddôl Ceredig 91 C4
Trerule Foot Corn 6 B2
Tresaith Ceredig 73 A5
Tresawle Corn 4 C3
Trescott Staffs 95 B6
Trescowe Corn 2 B3
Tresham Glos 62 D3
Tresillian Corn 4 C3
Tresinwen Pembs 72 B1
Treskinnick Cross Corn 10 B3
Tresmeer Corn 10 C3
Tresparrett Corn 10 B2
Tresparrett Posts Corn 10 B2
Tressait Perth 230 B2
Tresta Shetland 285 H5
Tresta Shetland 284 D8
Treswell Notts 132 B2
Trethosa Corn 4 B4
Trethurgy Corn 5 B5
Tretio Pembs 54 B3
Tretire Hereford 62 A1
Tretower Powys 60 A3
Treuddyn Flint 126 D2
Trevalga Corn 10 C1
Trevalyn Wrex 126 D3
Trevanson Corn 9 D5
Trevarren Corn 4 A4

Trevarrian Corn 4 A3
Trevarrick Corn 5 C4
Trevaughan Carms 56 A1
Treveighan Corn 9 D6
Trevellas Corn 4 B2
Treverva Corn 4 D2
Trevethin Torf 61 C4
Trevigro Corn 6 A2
Treviscoe Corn 4 B4
Trevone Corn 9 D4
Trewarmett Corn 9 C6
Trewassa Corn 10 C2
Trewellard Corn 2 B1
Trewen Corn 10 C3
Trewennack Corn 3 C4
Trewern Powys 110 D1
Trewethern Corn 9 D6
Trewidland Corn 6 B1
Trewint Corn 10 C3
Trewint Corn 10 B2
Trewithian Corn 4 D3
Trewoofe Corn 2 C2
Trewoon Corn 5 B4
Treworga Corn 4 C3
Treworlas Corn 4 D3
Treyarnon Corn 9 D4
Treyford W Sus 33 D7
Trezaise Corn 5 B4
Triangle W Yorks 138 A3
Trickett's Cross Dorset 17 A4
Triffleton Pembs 55 B5
Trimdon Durham 167 B6
Trimdon Colliery Durham 167 B6
Trimdon Grange Durham 167 B6
Trimingham Norf 121 B4
Trimley Lower Street Suff 88 D3
Trimley St Martin Suff 88 D3
Trimley St Mary Suff 88 D3
Trimpley Worcs 95 D5
Trimsaran Carms 57 B4
Trimstone Devon 25 A5
Trinafour Perth 229 B6
Trinant Caerph 41 A7
Tring Herts 67 B4
Tring Wharf Herts 67 B4
Trinity Angus 233 B4
Trinity Jersey 6
Trisant Ceredig 75 A6
Trislaig Highld 237 B4
Trispen Corn 4 B3
Tritlington Northumb 189 D5
Trochry Perth 230 D3
Trodigal Argyll 190 C2
Troed-rhiwdalar Powys 76 B3
Troedyraur Ceredig 73 B6
Troedyrhiw M Tydf 41 A5
Tromode I o M 152 D3
Trondavoe Shetland 284 F5
Troon Corn 3 B4
Troon S Ayrs 192 B3
Trosaraidh W Isles 286 E3
Trossachs Hotel Stirl 217 D5
Troston Suff 103 D4
Trottiscliffe Kent 50 C3
Trotton W Sus 34 D1
Troutbeck Cumb 154 A3
Troutbeck Cumb 164 C1
Troutbeck Bridge Cumb 154 A3
Trow Green Glos 62 C1
Trowbridge Wilts 44 D2
Trowell Notts 114 B2
Trowle Common Wilts 44 D2
Trowley Bottom Herts 67 B5
Trows Borders 197 C5
Trowse Newton Norf 104 A3
Trudoxhill Som 30 A1
Trull Som 28 C2
Trumaisgearraidh W Isles 287 G3
Trumpan Highld 258 B2
Trumpet Hereford 79 D4
Trumpington Cambs 85 B6
Trunch Norf 121 B4
Trunnah Lancs 144 C3
Truro Corn 4 C3
Truro Cathedral Corn 4 C3
Trusham Devon 12 C3
Trusley Derbys 113 B6
Trusthorpe Lincs 135 A5
Trysull Staffs 95 B6
Tubney Oxon 65 D5
Tuckenhay Devon 8 B2
Tuckhill Shrops 95 C5
Tuckingmill Corn 3 A4
Tuddenham Suff 102 D3
Tuddenham St Martin Suff 88 C2
Tudeley Kent 36 B4
Tudhoe Durham 167 B5
Tudorville Hereford 62 A1
Tudweiliog Gwyn 106 C2
Tuesley Sur 34 B2
Tuffley Glos 63 B4
Tufton Hants 32 A3
Tufton Pembs 55 B6
Tugby Leics 99 A4
Tugford Shrops 94 C3
Tullibardine Perth 218 C4
Tullibody Clack 207 A6
Tullich Argyll 214 A3
Tullich Highld 252 D2
Tullich Muir Highld 264 C3
Tullie House, Carlisle Cumb 175 C6
Tulliemet Perth 230 C3
Tulloch Aberds 233 A5
Tulloch Aberds 256 C3
Tulloch Perth 219 B5
Tulloch Castle Highld 264 D1
Tullochgorm Argyll 214 C2
Tulloes Angus 232 D3
Tullybannocher Perth 218 B2
Tullybelton Perth 219 A5
Tullyfergus Perth 231 D6
Tullymurdoch Perth 231 C5
Tullynessle Aberds 244 A2
Tumble Carms 57 A5
Tumby Woodside Lincs 134 D2
Tummel Bridge Perth 229 C6
Tunga W Isles 288 D5
Tunstall E Yorks 151 D6
Tunstall Kent 51 C5
Tunstall Lancs 155 D5
Tunstall Norf 105 A5
Tunstall N Yorks 157 B6
Tunstall Stoke 128 D3
Tunstall Suff 89 B4
Tunstall T & W 179 D5
Tunstead Derbys 129 B6
Tunstead Gtr Man 138 C3
Tunstead Norf 121 C4
Tunworth Hants 33 A5
Tupsley Hereford 78 C3
Tupton Derbys 130 C3
Tur Langton Leics 99 B4
Turgis Green Hants 47 D4
Turin Angus 232 C3
Turkdean Glos 64 B2
Turleigh Wilts 44 C2
Turn Lancs 137 B7
Turnastone Hereford 78 D1
Turnberry S Ayrs 192 E2
Turnditch Derbys 113 A6
Turners Hill W Sus 35 C6
Turners Puddle Dorset 16 B2
Turnford Herts 68 C3
Turnhouse Edin 209 C4
Turnworth Dorset 16 A2
Turriff Aberds 268 D2
Turton Bottoms Blkburn 137 B6
Turves Cambs 101 B5
Turvey Beds 83 B6
Turville Bucks 66 D2
Turville Heath Bucks 66 D2
Turweston Bucks 82 D3
Tushielaw Borders 185 A6
Tutbury Staffs 113 C6
Tutnall Worcs 96 D2
Tutshill Glos 62 D1
Tuttington Norf 120 C4
Tutts Clump W Berks 46 B3
Tuxford Notts 132 B2
Twatt Orkney 282 E3
Twatt Shetland 285 H5
Twechar E Dunb 207 C4
Tweedmouth Northumb 198 A3
Tweedsmuir Borders 195 D5
Twelve Heads Corn 4 C2
Twemlow Green Ches 128 C2
Twenty Lincs 117 C4
Twerton Bath 43 C6
Twickenham London 49 B4
Twickenham Stadium London 48 B4
Twigworth Glos 63 A4
Twineham W Sus 21 A5
Twinhoe Bath 43 D6
Twinstead Essex 87 D4
Twinstead Green Essex 87 D4
Twiss Green Warr 137 D5
Twiston Lancs 146 C2
Twitchen Devon 26 B2
Twitchen Shrops 94 D1
Two Bridges Devon 11 D7
Two Dales Derbys 130 C2
Two Mills Ches 126 B3
Twycross Leics 97 A6
Twycross Zoo, Ashby-de-la-Zouch Leics 97 A6
Twyford Bucks 66 A1
Twyford Derbys 114 C1
Twyford Hants 32 C3
Twyford Leics 115 D5
Twyford Lincs 116 C2
Twyford Norf 120 C2
Twyford Wokingham 47 B5
Twyford Common Hereford 78 D3
Twyn-y-Sheriff Mon 61 C6
Twynholm Dumfries 173 C4
Twyning Glos 80 D1
Twyning Green Glos 80 D2
Twynllanan Carms 59 C4
Twynmynydd Carms 57 A6
Twywell Northants 99 D6
Ty-draw Conwy 124 D3
Ty-hen Carms 73 D6
Ty-hen Gwyn 106 C1
Ty-mawr Anglesey 123 B4
Ty Mawr Carms 58 A2
Ty Mawr Cwm Conwy 108 A4
Ty-nant Conwy 109 A4
Ty-nant Gwyn 108 C4
Ty-uchaf Powys 109 C5
Tyberton Hereford 78 D1
Tyburn W Mid 96 B4
Tycroes Carms 57 A6
Tycrwyn Powys 109 D6
Tydd Gote Lincs 118 D1
Tydd St Giles Cambs 118 D1
Tydd St Mary Lincs 118 D1
Tyddewi = St David's Pembs 54 B3
Tyddyn-mawr Gwyn 107 B5
Tye Green Essex 86 D1
Tye Green Essex 70 A1
Tye Green Essex 69 C4
Tyldesley Gtr Man 137 C5
Tyler Hill Kent 52 C3
Tylers Green Bucks 67 D4
Tylorstown Rhondda 41 B5
Tylwch Powys 92 C3
Tyn-y-celyn Wrex 109 B6
Tyn-y-coed Shrops 110 C1
Tyn-y-fedwen Powys 109 B6
Tyn-y-ffridd Powys 109 B6
Tyn-y-graig Powys 76 B4
Ty'n-y-groes Conwy 124 B2
Ty'n-y-maes Gwyn 123 D6
Tyn-y-pwll Anglesey 123 B4
Ty'n-yr-eithin Ceredig 75 B5
Tyncelyn Ceredig 75 B5
Tyndrum Stirl 216 A3
Tyne Tunnel T & W 179 C5
Tyneham Dorset 16 C2
Tynehead Midloth 196 A2
Tynemouth T & W 179 C5
Tynemouth Sea Life Centre T & W 179 B5
Tynewydd Rhondda 40 B4
Tyninghame E Loth 210 C3
Tynron Dumfries 183 C6
Tynygongl Anglesey 123 B5
Tynygraig Ceredig 75 B5
Tŷ'r-felin-isaf Conwy 124 C3
Tyrie Aberds 269 C4
Tyringham M Keynes 83 C5
Tythecott Devon 25 D5
Tythegston Bridgend 40 D3
Tytherington Ches 129 B4
Tytherington S Glos 43 A5
Tytherington Som 30 A1
Tytherington Wilts 30 A3
Tytherleigh Devon 14 A3
Tywardreath Corn 5 B5
Tywyn Conwy 124 B2
Tywyn Gwyn 90 B3

U

Uachdar W Isles 286 A3
Uags Highld 249 C4
Ubbeston Green Suff 104 D4
Ubley Bath 43 D4
Uckerby N Yorks 157 A6
Uckfield E Sus 36 D2
Uckington Glos 63 A5
Uddingston S Lnrk 207 D4
Uddington S Lnrk 194 C3
Udimore E Sus 23 A6
Udny Green Aberds 256 D3
Udny Station Aberds 257 D4
Udston S Lnrk 194 A1
Udstonhead S Lnrk 194 B2
Uffcott Wilts 45 B5
Uffculme Devon 27 D5
Uffington Lincs 100 A2
Uffington Oxon 45 A7
Uffington Shrops 111 D4
Ufford P'boro 100 A2
Ufford Suff 88 B3
Ufton Warks 81 A6
Ufton Nervet W Berks 47 C4
Ugadale Argyll 190 C3
Ugborough Devon 7 B5
Uggeshall Suff 105 C5
Ugglebarnby N Yorks 160 A2
Ughill S Yorks 139 D5
Ugley Essex 69 A5
Ugley Green Essex 69 A5
Ugthorpe N Yorks 169 D5
Uidh W Isles 286 G2
Uig Argyll 215 D4
Uig Highld 258 B3
Uig Highld 258 C1
Uigen W Isles 287 A5
Uigshader Highld 259 D4
Uisken Argyll 224 E2
Ulbster Highld 281 D5
Ulceby Lincs 135 B4
Ulceby N Lincs 142 B3
Ulceby Skitter N Lincs 142 B3
Ulcombe Kent 37 B6
Uldale Cumb 163 A5
Uley Glos 62 D3
Ulgham Northumb 189 D5
Ullapool Highld 262 A3
Ullenhall Warks 80 A4
Ullenwood Glos 63 B5
Ulleskelf N Yorks 148 C4
Ullesthorpe Leics 98 C2
Ulley S Yorks 131 A4
Ullingswick Hereford 78 C3
Ullinish Highld 246 A2
Ullock Cumb 162 B3
Ulnes Walton Lancs 136 B4
Ulpha Cumb 153 A2
Ulrome E Yorks 151 B4
Ulsta Shetland 284 E6
Ulva House Argyll 224 C3
Ulverston Cumb 154 D1
Ulwell Dorset 17 C4
Umberleigh Devon 25 C7
Unapool Highld 271 A5
Unasary W Isles 286 D3
Underbarrow Cumb 154 B3
Undercliffe W Yorks 147 D5
Underhoull Shetland 284 C7
Underriver Kent 36 A3
Underwood Notts 131 D4
Undy Mon 42 A3
Unifirth Shetland 285 H4
Union Cottage Aberds 245 C5
Union Mills I o M 152 D3
Union Street E Sus 37 C5
University Museum, Oxford Oxon 65 C6
Unst Airport Shetland 284 C8
Unstone Derbys 130 B3
Unstone Green Derbys 130 B3
Unthank Cumb 164 B2
Unthank Cumb 165 A4
Unthank End Cumb 164 B2
Up Cerne Dorset 15 A6
Up Exe Devon 13 A4
Up Hatherley Glos 63 A5
Up Holland Lancs 136 C4
Up Marden W Sus 33 D6
Up Nately Hants 47 D4
Up Somborne Hants 32 B2
Up Sydling Dorset 15 A6
Upavon Wilts 45 D5
Upchurch Kent 51 C5
Upcott Hereford 78 B1
Upend Cambs 86 B2
Upgate Norf 120 D3
Uphall W Loth 208 C3
Uphall Station W Loth 208 C3
Upham Devon 12 A3
Upham Hants 32 C4
Uphampton Worcs 79 A6
Uphill N Som 42 D2
Uplawmoor E Renf 205 C4
Upleadon Glos 62 A3
Upleatham Redcar 168 D4
Uplees Kent 52 C1
Uploders Dorset 15 B5
Uplowman Devon 27 D5
Uplyme Devon 14 B3
Upminster London 50 A2
Upnor Medway 51 B4
Upottery Devon 14 A2
Uppark, Petersfield Hants 33 D6
Upper Affcot Shrops 94 C2
Upper Ardchronie Highld 264 B2
Upper Arley Worcs 95 C5
Upper Arncott Oxon 65 B7
Upper Astrop Northants 82 D2
Upper Badcall Highld 276 D2
Upper Basildon W Berks 46 B3
Upper Beeding W Sus 21 A4
Upper Benefield Northants 100 C1
Upper Bighouse Highld 279 C4
Upper Boddington Northants 82 B1
Upper Borth Ceredig 90 D4
Upper Boyndlie Aberds 269 C4
Upper Brailes Warks 81 D6
Upper Breakish Highld 247 B5
Upper Breinton Hereford 78 C2
Upper Broadheath Worcs 79 B6
Upper Broughton Notts 115 C4
Upper Bucklebury W Berks 46 C3
Upper Burnhaugh Aberds 245 C5
Upper Caldecote Beds 84 C3
Upper Catesby Northants 82 B2
Upper Chapel Powys 76 C4
Upper Church Village Rhondda 41 C5
Upper Chute Wilts 45 D6
Upper Clatford Hants 32 A2
Upper Clynnog Gwyn 107 B4
Upper Cumberworth W Yorks 139 C5
Upper Cwm-twrch Powys 59 D4
Upper Cwmbran Torf 61 D4
Upper Dallachy Moray 267 C4
Upper Dean Beds 84 A2
Upper Denby W Yorks 139 C5
Upper Denton Cumb 176 C4
Upper Derraid Highld 253 C6
Upper Dicker E Sus 22 B3
Upper Dovercourt Essex 88 D3
Upper Druimfin Argyll 225 A4
Upper Dunsforth N Yorks 148 A3
Upper Eathie Highld 264 D3
Upper Elkstone Staffs 129 D5
Upper End Derbys 129 B5
Upper Farringdon Hants 33 B6
Upper Framilode Glos 62 B3
Upper Glenfintaig Highld 239 D6
Upper Gornal W Mid 96 B2
Upper Gravenhurst Beds 84 D3
Upper Green Mon 61 B5
Upper Green W Berks 46 C1
Upper Grove Common Hereford 62 A1
Upper Hackney Derbys 130 C2
Upper Hale Sur 34 B1
Upper Halistra Highld 258 C2
Upper Halling Medway 50 C3
Upper Hambleton Rutland 99 A5
Upper Hardres Court Kent 52 D3
Upper Hartfield E Sus 36 C2
Upper Haugh S Yorks 140 D2
Upper Heath Shrops 94 C3
Upper Hellesdon Norf 120 D4
Upper Helmsley N Yorks 149 B5
Upper Hergest Hereford 77 B6
Upper Heyford Northants 82 B3
Upper Heyford Oxon 65 A5
Upper Hill Hereford 78 B2
Upper Hopton W Yorks 139 B4
Upper Horsebridge E Sus 22 A3
Upper Hulme Staffs 129 C5
Upper Inglesham Swindon 64 D3
Upper Inverbrough Highld 253 C4
Upper Killay Swansea 57 C5
Upper Knockando Moray 254 B2
Upper Lambourn W Berks 45 A7
Upper Leigh Staffs 112 B4
Upper Lenie Highld 251 D7
Upper Lochton Aberds 244 C3
Upper Longdon Staffs 113 D4
Upper Lybster Highld 275 A6
Upper Lydbrook Glos 62 B2
Upper Maes-coed Hereford 78 D1
Upper Midway Derbys 113 C6
Upper Milovaig Highld 258 D1
Upper Minety Wilts 63 D6
Upper Mitton Worcs 95 D6
Upper North Dean Bucks 66 D3
Upper Obney Perth 219 A5
Upper Ollach Highld 247 A4
Upper Padley Derbys 130 B2
Upper Pollicott Bucks 66 B2
Upper Poppleton York 149 B4
Upper Quinton Warks 81 C4
Upper Ratley Hants 32 C2
Upper Rissington Glos 64 B3
Upper Rochford Worcs 79 A4
Upper Sandaig Highld 238 A1
Upper Sanday Orkney 283 G6
Upper Sapey Hereford 79 A4
Upper Seagry Wilts 44 A3
Upper Shelton Beds 84 C1
Upper Sheringham Norf 120 A3
Upper Skelmorlie N Ayrs 204 B2
Upper Slaughter Glos 64 A2
Upper Soudley Glos 62 B2
Upper Stondon Beds 84 D3
Upper Stowe Northants 82 B3
Upper Stratton Swindon 45 A5
Upper Street Hants 31 D5
Upper Street Norf 121 D5
Upper Street Norf 121 D5
Upper Street Suff 88 D2
Upper Strensham Worcs 80 D2
Upper Sundon Beds 67 A5
Upper Swell Glos 64 A2
Upper Tean Staffs 112 B4
Upper Tillyrie Perth 219 D6
Upper Tooting London 49 B5
Upper Tote Highld 259 C5
Upper Town N Som 43 C4
Upper Treverward Shrops 93 D6
Upper Tysoe Warks 81 C6
Upper Upham Wilts 45 B6
Upper Wardington Oxon 82 C1
Upper Weald M Keynes 83 D4
Upper Weedon Northants 82 B3
Upper Wield Hants 33 B5
Upper Winchendon Bucks 66 B2
Upper Witton W Mid 96 B3
Upper Woodend Aberds 244 A3
Upper Woodford Wilts 31 B5
Upper Wootton Hants 46 D3
Upper Wyche Worcs 79 C5
Upperby Cumb 175 C7
Uppermill Gtr Man 138 C2
Uppersound Shetland 285 J6
Upperthong W Yorks 139 C4
Upperthorpe N Lincs 141 C5
Upperton W Sus 34 D2
Uppertown Derbys 130 C3
Uppertown Highld 281 A5
Uppertown Orkney 283 H5
Uppingham Rutland 99 B5
Uppington Shrops 95 A4
Upsall N Yorks 158 C3
Upshire Essex 68 C4
Upstreet Kent 53 C4
Upthorpe Suff 103 D5
Upton Cambs 100 D3
Upton Ches 127 C4
Upton Corn 10 A3
Upton Dorset 16 C1
Upton Dorset 16 B3
Upton Hants 32 D2
Upton Hants 46 D1
Upton Leics 97 B6
Upton Lincs 132 A3
Upton Mers 126 A2
Upton Norf 121 D5
Upton Notts 132 D2
Upton Notts 132 B2
Upton Northants 83 A4
Upton Oxon 46 A3
Upton P'boro 100 A3
Upton Slough 48 B2
Upton Som 27 C4
Upton W Yorks 140 B2
Upton Bishop Hereford 62 A2
Upton Cheyney S Glos 43 C5
Upton Cressett Shrops 95 B4
Upton Cross Corn 10 D3
Upton Grey Hants 33 A5
Upton Hellions Devon 12 A3
Upton House Warks 81 C6
Upton Lovell Wilts 30 A3
Upton Magna Shrops 111 D4
Upton Noble Som 29 B7
Upton Pyne Devon 13 B4
Upton St Leonard's Glos 63 B4
Upton Scudamore Wilts 30 A2
Upton Snodsbury Worcs 80 B2
Upton upon Severn Worcs 79 C6
Upton Warren Worcs 80 A2
Upwaltham W Sus 20 A2
Upware Cambs 102 D1
Upwell Norf 101 A6
Upwey Dorset 15 C6
Upwood Cambs 101 C4
Uradale Shetland 285 K6
Urafirth Shetland 284 F5
Urchfont Wilts 44 D4
Urdimarsh Hereford 78 C3
Ure Shetland 284 F4
Ure Bank N Yorks 157 D7
Urgha W Isles 288 H2
Urishay Common Hereford 77 D7
Urlay Nook Stockton 167 D6
Urmston Gtr Man 137 D6
Urpeth Durham 179 D4
Urquhart Highld 252 A1
Urquhart Moray 266 C3
Urquhart Castle, Drumnadrochit Highld 252 D1
Urra N Yorks 159 A4
Urray Highld 251 A7
Ushaw Moor Durham 167 A5
Usk = Brynbuga Mon 61 C5
Usselby Lincs 142 D2
Usworth T & W 179 D5
Utkinton Ches 127 C5
Utley W Yorks 147 C4
Uton Devon 12 B3
Utterby Lincs 143 D5
Uttoxeter Staffs 113 B4
Uttoxeter Racecourse Staffs 113 B5
Uwchmynydd Gwyn 106 D1
Uxbridge London 48 A3
Uyeasound Shetland 284 C7
Uzmaston Pembs 55 C5

V

Valley Anglesey 122 C2
Valley Truckle Corn 10 C1
Valleyfield Dumfries 173 C4
Valsgarth Shetland 284 B8
Valtos Highld 259 B5
Van Powys 92 C3
Vange Essex 51 A4
Varteg Torf 61 C4
Vatten Highld 258 D2
Vaul Argyll 222 C3
Vaynor M Tydf 60 B2
Veensgarth Shetland 285 J6
Velindre Powys 77 D5
Vellow Som 27 B5
Veness Orkney 282 E6
Venn Green Devon 25 D4
Venn Ottery Devon 13 B5
Vennington Shrops 94 A1
Venny Tedburn Devon 12 B3
Ventnor I o W 19 D4
Ventnor Botanic Garden I o W 19 D4
Vernham Dean Hants 46 D1
Vernham Street Hants 46 D1
Vernolds Common Shrops 94 C2
Verwood Dorset 17 A4
Veryan Corn 4 D4
Vicarage Devon 14 C2
Vickerstown Cumb 153 D2
Victoria Corn 5 A4
Victoria S Yorks 139 C4
Victoria and Albert Museum London 49 B5
Vidlin Shetland 284 G6

Viewpark N Lnrk 207 D5
Vigo Village Kent 50 C3
Vinehall Street E Sus 37 D5
Vine's Cross E Sus 22 A3
Viney Hill Glos 62 C2
Virginia Water Sur 48 C3
Virginstow Devon 11 B4
Vobster Som 29 A7
Voe Shetland 285 G6
Voe Shetland 284 E5
Vowchurch Hereford 78 D1
Voxter Shetland 284 F5
Voy Orkney 282 F3

W

Wackerfield Durham 167 C4
Wacton Norf 104 B2
Wadbister Shetland 285 J6
Wadborough Worcs 80 C2
Waddesdon Bucks 66 B2
Waddesdon Manor, Aylesbury Bucks 66 B2
Waddingham Lincs 142 D1
Waddington Lancs 146 C1
Waddington Lincs 133 C4
Wadebridge Corn 9 D5
Wadeford Som 28 D3
Wadenhoe Northants 100 C2
Wadesmill Herts 68 B3
Wadhurst E Sus 36 C4
Wadshelf Derbys 130 B3
Wadsley S Yorks 139 D6
Wadsley Bridge S Yorks 139 D6
Wadworth S Yorks 140 D3
Waen Denb 125 C6
Waen Denb 125 C4
Waen Fach Powys 109 D7
Waen Goleugoed Denb 125 B5
Wag Highld 274 B4
Wainfleet All Saints Lincs 135 D4
Wainfleet Bank Lincs 135 D4
Wainfleet St Mary Lincs 135 D5
Wainfleet Tofts Lincs 135 D4
Wainhouse Corner Corn 10 B2
Wainscott Medway 51 B4
Wainstalls W Yorks 138 A3
Waitby Cumb 155 A6
Waithe Lincs 143 C4
Wake Lady Green N Yorks 159 B5
Wakefield W Yorks 139 A6
Wakehurst Place Garden, Crawley W Sus 35 C6
Wakerley Northants 99 B6
Wakes Colne Essex 70 A2
Walberswick Suff 105 D5
Walberton W Sus 20 B2
Walbottle T & W 178 C3
Walcot Lincs 116 B3
Walcot N Lincs 141 A6
Walcot Shrops 94 C1
Walcot Telford 111 D4
Walcot Swindon 45 A5
Walcot Green Norf 104 C2
Walcote Leics 98 C2
Walcote Warks 80 B4
Walcott Lincs 133 D6
Walcott Norf 121 B5
Walden N Yorks 156 C4
Walden Head N Yorks 156 C3
Walden Stubbs N Yorks 140 B3
Waldersey Cambs 101 A6
Walderslade Medway 51 C4
Walderton W Sus 33 D6
Walditch Dorset 15 B4
Waldley Derbys 113 B5
Waldridge Durham 179 D4
Waldringfield Suff 88 C3
Waldringfield Heath Suff 88 C3
Waldron E Sus 22 A3
Wales S Yorks 131 A4
Walesby Lincs 142 D3
Walesby Notts 132 B1
Walford Hereford 94 D1
Walford Hereford 62 A1
Walford Shrops 110 C3
Walford Heath Shrops 110 D3
Walgherton Ches 111 A5
Walgrave Northants 99 D5
Walhampton Hants 18 B2
Walk Mill Lancs 146 D2
Walkden Gtr Man 137 C6
Walker T & W 179 C4
Walker Art Gallery Mers 136 D2
Walker Barn Ches 129 B4
Walker Fold Lancs 145 C6
Walkerburn Borders 196 C2
Walkeringham Notts 141 D5
Walkerith Lincs 141 D5
Walkern Herts 68 A2
Walker's Green Hereford 78 C3
Walkerville N Yorks 157 B6
Walkford Dorset 17 B6
Walkhampton Devon 7 A4
Walkington E Yorks 150 D2
Walkley S Yorks 130 A3
Walkley Clogs, Hebden Bridge W Yorks 138 A3
Wall Northumb 177 C7
Wall Staffs 96 A4
Wall Bank Shrops 94 B3
Wall Heath W Mid 96 C1
Wall under Heywood Shrops 94 B3
Wallaceton Dumfries 183 D6
Wallacetown S Ayrs 181 A4
Wallacetown S Ayrs 192 C3
Wallands Park E Sus 22 A2
Wallasey Mers 136 D2
Wallcrouch E Sus 37 C4
Wallingford Oxon 47 A4
Wallington London 49 C5
Wallington Hants 19 A4
Wallington Herts 85 D4
Wallington House, Ponteland Northumb 178 A2
Wallis Pembs 55 B6
Walliswood Sur 35 C4
Walls Shetland 285 J4
Wallsend T & W 179 C4
Wallston V Glam 41 D6
Wallyford E Loth 209 C6
Walmer Kent 53 D5
Walmer Bridge Lancs 136 A3
Walmersley Gtr Man 137 B7
Walmley W Mid 96 B4
Walney Island Airport Cumb 153 C2
Walpole Suff 105 D4
Walpole Cross Keys Norf 118 D2
Walpole Highway Norf 118 D2
Walpole Marsh Norf 118 D1
Walpole St Andrew Norf 118 D2
Walpole St Peter Norf 118 D2
Walsall W Mid 96 B3
Walsall Arboretum W Mid 96 B3
Walsall Wood W Mid 96 A3
Walsden W Yorks 138 A2
Walsgrave on Sowe W Mid 97 C6
Walsham le Willows Suff 103 D5
Walshaw Gtr Man 137 B6
Walshford N Yorks 148 B3
Walsoken Cambs 118 D1
Walston S Lnrk 195 B5
Walsworth Herts 84 D4
Walters Ash Bucks 66 D3
Walterston V Glam 41 D5
Walterstone Hereford 61 A5
Waltham Kent 38 A3
Waltham NE Lincs 143 C4
Waltham Abbey Essex 68 C3
Waltham Chase Hants 33 D4
Waltham Cross Herts 68 C3
Waltham on the Wolds Leics 115 C6
Waltham St Lawrence Windsor 47 B6
Walthamstow London 49 A6
Walton Cumb 176 C3
Walton Derbys 130 C3
Walton Leics 98 C2
Walton Mers 136 D2
Walton M Keynes 83 D5
Walton P'boro 100 A3
Walton Powys 77 B6
Walton Som 29 B4
Walton Staffs 112 B2
Walton Suff 88 D3
Walton Telford 111 D4
Walton Warks 81 B5
Walton W Yorks 139 B6
Walton W Yorks 148 C3
Walton Cardiff Glos 80 D2
Walton East Pembs 55 B6
Walton Hall Warr 127 A6
Walton-in-Gordano N Som 42 B3
Walton-le-Dale Lancs 137 A4
Walton-on-Thames Sur 48 C4
Walton on the Hill Staffs 112 C3
Walton on the Hill Sur 35 A5
Walton-on-the-Naze Essex 71 A6
Walton on the Wolds Leics 114 D3
Walton-on-Trent Derbys 113 D6
Walton West Pembs 55 C4
Walwen Flint 126 B2
Walwick Northumb 177 B7
Walworth Darl 167 D5
Walworth Gate Darl 167 C5
Walwyn's Castle Pembs 55 C4
Wambrook Som 14 A2
Wanborough Sur 34 B2
Wanborough Swindon 45 A6
Wandsworth London 49 B5
Wangford Suff 105 D5
Wanlockhead Dumfries 183 A6
Wansford E Yorks 150 B3
Wansford P'boro 100 B2
Wanstead London 49 A7
Wanstrow Som 29 A7
Wanswell Glos 62 C2
Wantage Oxon 46 A1
Wapley S Glos 43 B6
Wappenbury Warks 81 A6
Wappenham Northants 82 C3
Warbleton E Sus 22 A4
Warblington Hants 19 A6
Warborough Oxon 65 D6
Warboys Cambs 101 C5
Warbreck Blkpool 144 D3
Warbstow Corn 10 B3
Warburton Gtr Man 128 A2
Warcop Cumb 165 D5
Ward End W Mid 96 C4
Ward Green Suff 87 A6
Warden Kent 52 B2
Warden Northumb 177 C7
Wardhill Orkney 282 E7
Wardington Oxon 82 C1
Wardlaw Borders 185 A5
Wardle Ches 127 D6
Wardle Gtr Man 138 B2
Wardley Rutland 99 A5
Wardlow Derbys 130 B1
Wardy Hill Cambs 101 C6
Ware Herts 68 B3
Ware Kent 53 C4
Wareham Dorset 16 C3
Warehorne Kent 38 B1
Waren Mill Northumb 199 C5
Warenford Northumb 189 A4
Warenton Northumb 199 C5
Wareside Herts 68 B3
Waresley Cambs 84 B4
Waresley Worcs 95 D6
Warfield Brack 48 B1
Warfleet Devon 8 B2
Wargrave Wokingham 47 B5
Warham Norf 119 A6
Warhill Gtr Man 138 D2
Wark Northumb 177 B6
Wark Northumb 198 C2
Warkleigh Devon 26 C1
Warkton Northants 99 D5
Warkworth Northants 82 C1
Warkworth Northumb 189 C5
Warlaby N Yorks 158 B2
Warland W Yorks 138 A2
Warleggan Corn 5 A6
Warlingham Sur 35 A6
Warmfield W Yorks 140 A1
Warmingham Ches 128 C2
Warmington Northants 100 B2
Warmington Warks 81 C7
Warminster Wilts 30 A2
Warmlake Kent 37 A6
Warmley S Glos 43 B5
Warmley Tower S Glos 43 B5
Warmonds Hill Northants 83 A6
Warmsworth S Yorks 140 C3
Warmwell Dorset 16 C1
Warndon Worcs 80 B1
Warnford Hants 33 C5
Warnham W Sus 35 C4
Warninglid W Sus 35 D5
Warren Ches 128 B3
Warren Pembs 55 E5
Warren Heath Suff 88 C3
Warren Row Windsor 47 A6
Warren Street Kent 51 D6
Warrington M Keynes 83 B5
Warrington Warr 127 A6
Warsash Hants 18 A3
Warslow Staffs 129 D5
Warter E Yorks 150 B1
Warthermarske N Yorks 157 D6
Warthill N Yorks 149 B5
Wartling E Sus 23 B4
Wartnaby Leics 115 C5
Warton Lancs 136 A3
Warton Lancs 154 D3
Warton Northumb 188 C3
Warton Warks 97 A5
Warwick Warks 81 A5
Warwick Bridge Cumb 176 D2
Warwick Castle Warks 81 A5
Warwick on Eden Cumb 176 D2
Warwick Racecourse Warks 81 A5
Wasbister Orkney 282 D4
Wasdale Head Cumb 163 D4
Wash Common W Berks 46 C2
Washaway Corn 5 A5
Washbourne Devon 8 B1
Washfield Devon 27 D4
Washfold N Yorks 157 A4
Washford Som 27 A5
Washford Pyne Devon 26 D3
Washingborough Lincs 133 B5
Washington T & W 179 D5
Washington W Sus 21 A4
Wasing W Berks 46 C3
Waskerley Durham 166 A3
Wasperton Warks 81 B5
Wasps Nest Lincs 133 C5
Wass N Yorks 159 D4
Watchet Som 27 A5
Watchfield Oxon 64 D3
Watchfield Som 28 A3
Watchgate Cumb 154 B4
Watchhill Cumb 175 D4
Watcombe Torbay 8 A3
Watendlath Cumb 163 C5
Water Devon 12 C2
Water Lancs 138 A1
Water End E Yorks 149 D6
Water End Herts 67 B5
Water End Herts 68 C2
Water Newton Cambs 100 B3
Water Orton Warks 97 B4
Water Stratford Bucks 82 D3
Water Yeat Cumb 154 C1
Waterbeach Cambs 85 A6
Waterbeck Dumfries 175 A5
Watercress Line (Mid Hants Railway), Alton Hants 33 B5
Waterden Norf 119 B5
Waterfall Staffs 129 D5
Waterfoot E Renf 205 C5
Waterfoot Lancs 138 A1
Waterford Hants 18 B2
Waterford Herts 68 B3
Waterhead Cumb 154 A2
Waterhead Dumfries 185 C4
Waterheads Borders 196 A1
Waterhouses Durham 167 A4
Waterhouses Staffs 129 D5
Wateringbury Kent 37 A4
Waterloo Gtr Man 138 C2
Waterloo Highld 247 B5
Waterloo Mers 136 D2
Waterloo N Lnrk 194 A3
Waterloo Norf 120 D4
Waterloo Perth 219 A5
Waterloo Poole 17 B4
Waterloo Shrops 111 B4
Waterloo Port Gwyn 123 D4
Waterlooville Hants 19 A5
Watermeetings S Lnrk 184 A2
Watermillock Cumb 164 C2
Watermouth Castle, Ilfracombe Devon 25 A6
Waterperry Oxon 66 C1
Waterrow Som 27 C5
Water's Nook Gtr Man 137 C5
Waters Upton Telford 111 D5
Watersfield W Sus 20 A3
Watershed Mill Visitor Centre, Settle N Yorks 146 A2
Waterside Aberds 257 D5
Waterside Blkburn 137 A6
Waterside Cumb 175 D5
Waterside E Ayrs 182 B2
Waterside E Ayrs 205 D4
Waterside E Dunb 207 C4
Waterside E Renf 205 C5
Waterstock Oxon 66 C1
Waterston Pembs 55 D5
Watford Herts 67 D6
Watford Northants 82 A3
Watford Gap W Mid 96 A4
Wath N Yorks 147 A5
Wath N Yorks 157 D7
Wath N Yorks 159 D5
Wath Brow Cumb 162 C3
Wath upon Dearne S Yorks 140 C2
Watley's End S Glos 43 A5
Watlington Norf 118 D3
Watlington Oxon 66 D1
Watnall Notts 114 A3
Watten Highld 280 C4
Wattisfield Suff 103 D6
Wattisham Suff 87 B6
Wattlesborough Heath Shrops 110 D2
Watton E Yorks 150 B3
Watton Norf 103 A5
Watton at Stone Herts 68 B3
Wattston N Lnrk 207 C5
Wattstown Rhondda 41 B5
Wauchan Highld 238 D3
Waulkmill Lodge Orkney 283 G4
Waun Powys 91 B6
Waun-y-clyn Carms 57 B4
Waunarlwydd Swansea 57 C6
Waunclunda Carms 58 B3
Waunfawr Gwyn 107 A5
Waungron Swansea 57 B5
Waunlwyd Bl Gwent 60 C3
Wavendon M Keynes 83 D6
Waverbridge Cumb 175 D5
Waverton Ches 127 C4
Waverton Cumb 175 D5
Wavertree Mers 126 A3
Wawne E Yorks 150 D3
Waxham Norf 121 C6
Waxholme E Yorks 143 A5
Way Kent 53 C5
Way Village Devon 26 D3
Wayfield Medway 51 C4
Wayford Som 14 A4
Waymills Shrops 111 A4
Wayne Green Mon 61 B6
Wdig = Goodwick Pembs 72 C2
Weachyburn Aberds 268 D1
Weald Oxon 64 C4
Weald and Downland Open Air Museum, Chichester W Sus 20 A1
Wealdstone London 49 A4
Weardley W Yorks 148 C1
Weare Som 42 D3
Weare Giffard Devon 25 C5
Wearhead Durham 165 B6
Weasdale Cumb 155 A5
Weasenham All Saints Norf 119 C5
Weasenham St Peter Norf 119 C5
Weatherhill Sur 35 B6
Weaverham Ches 127 B6
Weaverthorpe N Yorks 160 D3
Webheath Worcs 80 A3
Wedderlairs Aberds 256 C3
Wedderlie Borders 197 A5
Weddington Warks 97 B6
Wedgwood Visitor Centre, Barlaston Staffs 112 B2
Wedhampton Wilts 45 D4
Wedmore Som 28 A4
Wednesbury W Mid 96 B2
Wednesfield W Mid 96 A2
Weedon Bucks 66 B3
Weedon Bec Northants 82 B3
Weedon Lois Northants 82 C3
Weeford Staffs 96 A4
Week Devon 26 D2
Week St Mary Corn 10 B3
Weeke Hants 32 B3
Weekley Northants 99 C5
Weel E Yorks 150 D3
Weeley Essex 71 A5
Weeley Heath Essex 71 A5
Weem Perth 230 D2
Weeping Cross Staffs 112 C3
Weethley Gate Warks 80 B3
Weeting Norf 102 C3
Weeting Heath NNR Norf 102 C3
Weeton E Yorks 143 A5
Weeton Lancs 144 D3
Weeton N Yorks 148 C1
Weetwood Hall Northumb 188 A3
Weir Lancs 138 A1
Weir Quay Devon 6 A3
Welborne Norf 120 E2
Welbourn Lincs 133 D4
Welburn N Yorks 149 A6
Welburn N Yorks 159 C5
Welbury N Yorks 158 A2
Welby Lincs 116 B2
Welches Dam Cambs 101 C6
Welcombe Devon 24 D3
Weld Bank Lancs 137 B4
Weldon Northumb 189 D4
Welford Northants 98 C3
Welford W Berks 46 B2
Welford-on-Avon Warks 81 B4
Welham Leics 99 B4
Welham Notts 132 A2
Welham Green Herts 68 C2
Well Hants 33 A6
Well Lincs 135 B4
Well N Yorks 157 C6
Well End Bucks 48 A1
Well Heads W Yorks 147 D4
Well Hill Kent 50 C1
Well Town Devon 13 A4
Welland Worcs 79 C5
Wellbank Angus 221 A4
Welldale Dumfries 175 B4
Wellesbourne Warks 81 B5
Welling London 50 B1
Wellingborough Northants 83 A5
Wellingham Norf 119 C5
Wellingore Lincs 133 D4
Wellington Cumb 162 D3
Wellington Hereford 78 C2
Wellington Som 27 C6
Wellington Telford 111 D5
Wellington Heath Hereford 79 C5
Wellington Hill W Yorks 148 D2
Wellow Bath 43 D6
Wellow I o W 18 C2
Wellow Notts 131 C6
Wellpond Green Herts 68 A4
Wells Som 29 A5
Wells Cathedral Som 29 A5
Wells Green Ches 128 D1
Wells-Next-The-Sea Norf 119 A6
Wellsborough Leics 97 A6
Wellswood Torbay 8 A3
Wellwood Fife 208 B3
Welney Norf 102 B1
Welsh Bicknor Hereford 62 B1
Welsh End Shrops 111 B4
Welsh Frankton Shrops 110 B2
Welsh Highland Railway, Caernarfon Gwyn 123 D4
Welsh Highland Railway, Porthmadog Gwyn 107 C5
Welsh Hook Pembs 55 B5
Welsh National Velodrome Newport 42 A2
Welsh Newton Hereford 61 B6
Welsh St Donats V Glam 41 D5
Welshampton Shrops 110 B3
Welshpool = Y Trallwng Powys 93 A6
Welton Cumb 164 A1
Welton E Yorks 142 A1
Welton Lincs 133 B5
Welton Northants 82 A2
Welton Hill Lincs 133 A5
Welton le Marsh Lincs 135 C4
Welton le Wold Lincs 134 A2
Welwick E Yorks 143 A5
Welwyn Herts 68 B2
Welwyn Garden City Herts 68 B2
Wem Shrops 111 C4
Wembdon Som 28 B2
Wembley London 49 A4
Wembley Stadium London 49 A4
Wembury Devon 7 C4
Wembworthy Devon 12 A1
Wemyss Bay Invclyd 204 B1
Wenallt Ceredig 75 A5
Wenallt Gwyn 109 A4
Wendens Ambo Essex 85 D7
Wendlebury Oxon 65 B6
Wendling Norf 119 D6
Wendover Bucks 66 C3
Wendron Corn 3 B4
Wendy Cambs 85 C5
Wenfordbridge Corn 10 D1
Wenhaston Suff 105 D5
Wennington Cambs 100 D4
Wennington London 50 A2
Wennington Lancs 155 D5
Wensley Derbys 130 C2
Wensley N Yorks 157 C4
Wentbridge W Yorks 140 B2
Wentnor Shrops 94 B1
Wentworth Cambs 101 D6
Wentworth S Yorks 140 D1
Wenvoe V Glam 41 D6
Weobley Hereford 78 B2
Weobley Marsh Hereford 78 B2
Wereham Norf 102 A2
Wergs W Mid 95 A6
Wern Powys 109 D4
Wern Powys 110 D1
Wernffrwd Swansea 57 C5
Wernyrheolydd Mon 61 B5
Werrington Corn 10 C4
Werrington P'boro 100 A3
Werrington Staffs 112 A3
Wervin Ches 127 B4
Wesham Lancs 144 D4
Wessington Derbys 130 D3
West Acre Norf 119 D4
West Adderbury Oxon 82 D1
West Allerdean Northumb 198 B3
West Alvington Devon 7 C6
West Amesbury Wilts 31 A5
West Anstey Devon 26 C3
West Ashby Lincs 134 B2
West Ashling W Sus 19 A7
West Ashton Wilts 44 D2
West Auckland Durham 167 C4
West Ayton N Yorks 160 C3
West Bagborough Som 27 B6
West Barkwith Lincs 133 A6
West Barnby N Yorks 169 D6
West Barns E Loth 210 C3
West Barsham Norf 119 B6
West Bay Dorset 15 B4
West Beckham Norf 120 B3
West Bedfont Sur 48 B3
West Benhar N Lnrk 208 D1
West Bergholt Essex 70 A3
West Bexington Dorset 15 C5
West Bilney Norf 119 D4
West Blatchington Brighton 21 B5
West Bowling W Yorks 147 D5
West Bradford Lancs 146 C1
West Bradley Som 29 B5
West Bretton W Yorks 139 B5
West Bridgford Notts 114 B3
West Bromwich W Mid 96 B3
West Buckland Devon 26 B1
West Buckland Som 28 C1
West Burrafirth Shetland 285 H4
West Burton N Yorks 156 C4
West Burton W Sus 20 A2
West Butterwick N Lincs 141 C6
West Byfleet Sur 48 C3
West Caister Norf 121 D7
West Calder W Loth 208 D3
West Camel Som 29 C5
West Challow Oxon 46 A1
West Chelborough Dorset 15 A5
West Chevington Northumb 189 D5
West Chiltington W Sus 20 A3
West Chiltington Common W Sus 20 A3
West Chinnock Som 29 D4
West Chisenbury Wilts 45 D5
West Clandon Sur 34 A3
West Cliffe Kent 39 A5
West Clyne Highld 274 D2
West Clyth Highld 275 A6
West Coker Som 29 D5
West Compton Dorset 15 B5
West Compton Som 29 A5

West Cowick E Yorks 140 A4
West Cranmore Som 29 A6
West Cross Swansea 57 D6
West Cullery Aberds 245 B4
West Curry Corn 10 B3
West Curthwaite Cumb 175 D6
West Darlochan Argyll 190 C2
West Dean Wilts 31 C6
West Dean W Sus 20 A1
West Deeping Lincs 100 A3
West Derby Mers 136 D2
West Dereham Norf 102 A2
West Didsbury Gtr Man 138 D1
West Ditchburn Northumb 189 A4
West Down Devon 25 A6
West Drayton London 48 B3
West Drayton Notts 132 B2
West Ella E Yorks 142 A2
West End Beds 84 B1
West End E Yorks 150 D2
West End E Yorks 151 D4
West End Hants 32 D3
West End Lancs 137 A6
West End Norf 103 A5
West End Norf 121 D7
West End N Som 42 C3
West End N Yorks 147 B5
West End Oxon 65 C5
West End S Lnrk 195 B4
West End Suff 105 C5
West End Sur 48 C2
West End S Yorks 141 C4
West End Wilts 30 C3
West End Wilts 44 B3
West End W Sus 21 A5
West End Green Hants 47 C4
West Farleigh Kent 37 A5
West Felton Shrops 110 C2
West Fenton E Loth 210 B1
West Ferry Dundee 221 A4
West Firle E Sus 22 B2
West Ginge Oxon 46 A2
West Grafton Wilts 45 C6
West Green Hants 47 D5
West Greenskares Aberds 268 C2
West Grimstead Wilts 31 C6
West Grinstead W Sus 35 D4
West Haddlesey N Yorks 140 A3
West Haddon Northants 98 D3
West Hagbourne Oxon 46 A3
West Hagley Worcs 96 C2
West Hall Cumb 176 C3
West Hallam Derbys 114 A2
West Halton N Lincs 141 A7
West Ham London 49 A7
West Handley Derbys 130 B3
West Hanney Oxon 65 D5
West Hanningfield Essex 70 D1
West Hardwick W Yorks 140 B2
West Harnham Wilts 31 C5
West Harptree Bath 43 D4
West Hatch Som 28 C2
West Head Norf 102 A1
West Heath Ches 128 C3
West Heath Hants 34 A1
West Heath Hants 46 D3
West Helmsdale Highld 274 C4
West Hendred Oxon 46 A2
West Heslerton N Yorks 160 D3
West Hill Devon 13 B5
West Hill E Yorks 151 A4
West Hill N Som 42 B3
West Hoathly W Sus 35 C6
West Holme Dorset 16 C2
West Horndon Essex 50 A3
West Horrington Som 29 A5
West Horsley Sur 34 A3
West Horton Northumb 198 C4
West Hougham Kent 39 A4
West Houlland Shetland 285 H4
West-houses Derbys 131 D4
West Huntington York 149 B5
West Hythe Kent 38 B3
West Ilsley W Berks 46 A2
West Itchenor W Sus 19 A6
West Keal Lincs 134 C3
West Kennett Wilts 45 C5
West Kilbride N Ayrs 204 D2
West Kingsdown Kent 50 C2
West Kington Wilts 44 B2
West Kinharrachie Aberds 257 C4
West Kirby Mers 126 A2
West Knapton N Yorks 160 D2
West Knighton Dorset 16 C1
West Knoyle Wilts 30 B2
West Kyloe Northumb 199 B4
West Lambrook Som 28 D4
West Langdon Kent 39 A5
West Langwell Highld 273 D4
West Lavington Wilts 44 D4
West Lavington W Sus 34 D1
West Layton N Yorks 157 A5
West Lea Durham 168 A2
West Leake Notts 114 C3
West Learmouth Northumb 198 C2
West Leigh Devon 12 A1
West Lexham Norf 119 D5
West Lilling N Yorks 149 A5
West Linton Borders 195 A6
West Liss Hants 33 C6
West Littleton S Glos 43 B6
West Looe Corn 6 B1
West Luccombe Som 26 A3
West Lulworth Dorset 16 C2
West Lutton N Yorks 150 A2
West Lydford Som 29 B5
West Lyng Som 28 C3
West Lynn Norf 118 C3
West Malling Kent 37 A4
West Malvern Worcs 79 C5
West Marden W Sus 33 D6
West Marina E Sus 23 B5
West Markham Notts 132 B2
West Marsh NE Lincs 143 B4
West Marton N Yorks 146 B2
West Meon Hants 33 C5
West Mersea Essex 71 B4
West Midlands Safari Park, Kidderminster Worcs 95 D6
West Milton Dorset 15 B5
West Minster Kent 51 B6
West Molesey Sur 48 C4
West Monkton Som 28 C2
West Moors Dorset 17 A4
West Morriston Borders 197 B5
West Muir Angus 232 B3
West Ness N Yorks 159 D5
West Newham Northumb 178 B2
West Newton E Yorks 151 D4
West Newton Norf 118 C3
West Norwood London 49 B6
West Ogwell Devon 12 D3
West Orchard Dorset 30 D2
West Overton Wilts 45 C5
West Park Hrtlpl 168 B2
West Parley Dorset 17 B4
West Peckham Kent 36 A4
West Pelton Durham 179 D4
West Pennard Som 29 B5
West Pentire Corn 4 A2
West Perry Cambs 84 A3
West Putford Devon 25 D4
West Quantoxhead Som 27 A6
West Rainton Durham 167 A6
West Rasen Lincs 133 A5
West Raynham Norf 119 C5
West Retford Notts 132 A1
West Rounton N Yorks 158 A3
West Row Suff 102 D2
West Rudham Norf 119 C5
West Runton Norf 120 A3
West Saltoun E Loth 210 D1
West Sandwick Shetland 284 E6
West Scrafton N Yorks 157 C4
West Sleekburn Northumb 179 A4
West Somerset Railway, Minehead Som 27 A4
West Somerton Norf 121 D6
West Stafford Dorset 16 C1
West Stockwith Notts 141 D5
West Stoke W Sus 20 B1
West Stonesdale N Yorks 156 A2
West Stoughton Som 28 A4
West Stour Dorset 30 C1
West Stourmouth Kent 53 C4
West Stow Suff 103 D4
West Stowell Wilts 45 C5
West Strathan Highld 277 B6
West Stratton Hants 32 A4
West Street Kent 37 A7
West Tanfield N Yorks 157 D6
West Taphouse Corn 5 A6
West Tarbert Argyll 202 B3
West Thirston Northumb 189 D4
West Thorney W Sus 19 A6
West Thurrock Thurrock 50 B2
West Tilbury Thurrock 50 B3
West Tisted Hants 33 C5
West Tofts Norf 103 B4
West Tofts Perth 219 A6
West Torrington Lincs 133 A6
West Town Hants 19 B6
West Town N Som 42 C3
West Tytherley Hants 32 C1
West Tytherton Wilts 44 B3
West Walton Norf 118 D1
West Walton Highway Norf 118 D1
West Wellow Hants 32 D1
West Wemyss Fife 209 A6
West Wick N Som 42 C2
West Wickham Cambs 86 C2
West Wickham London 49 C6
West Williamston Pembs 55 D6
West Willoughby Lincs 116 A2
West Winch Norf 118 D3
West Winterslow Wilts 31 B6
West Wittering W Sus 19 B6
West Witton N Yorks 157 C4
West Woodburn Northumb 177 A6
West Woodhay W Berks 46 C1
West Woodlands Som 30 A1
West Worldham Hants 33 B6
West Worlington Devon 26 D2
West Worthing W Sus 21 B4
West Wratting Cambs 86 B2
West Wycombe Bucks 66 D3
West Wylam Northumb 178 C3
West Yell Shetland 284 E6
Westacott Devon 25 B6
Westbere Kent 52 C3
Westborough Lincs 115 A6
Westbourne Bmouth 17 B4
Westbourne Suff 88 C2
Westbourne W Sus 19 A6
Westbrook W Berks 46 B2
Westbury Bucks 82 D3
Westbury Shrops 94 A1
Westbury Wilts 44 D2
Westbury Leigh Wilts 44 D2
Westbury-on-Severn Glos 62 B3
Westbury on Trym Bristol 43 B4
Westbury-sub-Mendip Som 29 A5
Westby Lancs 144 D3
Westcliff-on-Sea Sthend 51 A5
Westcombe Som 29 B6
Westcote Glos 64 A3
Westcott Bucks 66 B2
Westcott Devon 13 A5
Westcott Sur 35 B4
Westcott Barton Oxon 65 A5
Westdean E Sus 22 C3
Westdene Brighton 21 B5
Wester Aberchalder Highld 252 D1
Wester Balgedie Perth 219 D6
Wester Culbeuchly Aberds 268 C1
Wester Dechmont W Loth 208 D3
Wester Denoon Angus 232 D1
Wester Fintray Aberds 245 A5
Wester Gruinards Highld 263 A7
Wester Lealty Highld 264 C2
Wester Milton Highld 253 A5
Wester Newburn Fife 220 D4
Wester Quarff Shetland 285 K6
Wester Skeld Shetland 285 J4
Westerdale Highld 280 C3
Westerdale N Yorks 159 A5
Westerfield Shetland 285 H5
Westerfield Suff 88 C2
Westergate W Sus 20 B2
Westerham Kent 36 A2
Westerhope T & W 178 C3
Westerleigh S Glos 43 B6
Westerton Angus 233 C4
Westerton Durham 167 B5
Westerton W Sus 20 B1
Westerwick Shetland 285 J4
Westfield Cumb 162 B2
Westfield E Sus 23 A6
Westfield Hereford 79 C5
Westfield Highld 279 B6
Westfield N Lnrk 207 C5
Westfield Norf 103 A5
Westfield W Loth 208 C2
Westfields Dorset 15 A7
Westfields of Rattray Perth 231 D5
Westgate Durham 166 B2
Westgate N Lincs 141 C5
Westgate Norf 119 A5
Westgate Norf 119 A6
Westgate on Sea Kent 53 B5
Westhall Aberds 256 D1
Westhall Suff 105 C5
Westham Dorset 15 D6
Westham E Sus 22 B4
Westham Som 28 A4
Westhampnett W Sus 20 B1
Westhay Som 28 A4
Westhead Lancs 136 C3
Westhide Hereford 78 C3
Westhill Aberds 245 B5
Westhill Highld 252 B3
Westhope Hereford 78 B2
Westhope Shrops 94 C2
Westhorpe Lincs 117 B5
Westhorpe Suff 87 A6
Westhoughton Gtr Man 137 C5
Westhouse N Yorks 155 D5
Westhumble Sur 35 A4
Westing Shetland 284 C7
Westlake Devon 7 B5
Westleigh Devon 25 C5
Westleigh Devon 27 D5
Westleigh Gtr Man 137 C5
Westleton Suff 89 A5
Westley Shrops 94 A1
Westley Suff 87 A4
Westley Waterless Cambs 86 B2
Westlington Bucks 66 B2
Westlinton Cumb 175 B6
Westmarsh Kent 53 C4
Westmeston E Sus 21 A6
Westmill Herts 68 A3
Westminster London 49 B6
Westminster Cathedral London 49 B5
Westmuir Angus 232 C1
Westness Orkney 282 E4
Westnewton Cumb 174 D4
Westnewton Northumb 198 C3
Westoe T & W 179 C5
Weston Bath 43 C6
Weston Ches 128 D2
Weston Devon 13 C6
Weston Dorset 15 D6
Weston Halton 127 A5
Weston Hants 33 C6
Weston Herts 85 D4
Weston Lincs 117 C5
Weston Notts 132 C2
Weston Northants 82 C2
Weston N Yorks 147 C5
Weston Shrops 94 B3
Weston Shrops 111 C4
Weston Staffs 112 C3
Weston W Berks 46 B1
Weston Beggard Hereford 78 C3
Weston by Welland Northants 99 B4
Weston Colville Cambs 86 B2
Weston Coyney Stoke 112 A3
Weston Favell Northants 83 A4
Weston Green Cambs 86 B2
Weston Green Norf 120 D3
Weston Heath Shrops 112 D1
Weston Hills Lincs 117 C5
Weston-in-Gordano N Som 42 B3
Weston Jones Staffs 111 C6
Weston Longville Norf 120 D3
Weston Lullingfields Shrops 110 C3
Weston-on-the-Green Oxon 65 B6
Weston-on-Trent Derbys 114 C2
Weston Park Staffs 112 D2
Weston Patrick Hants 33 A5
Weston Rhyn Shrops 110 B1
Weston-Sub-Edge Glos 80 C4
Weston-super-Mare N Som 42 C2
Weston Turville Bucks 66 B3
Weston under Lizard Staffs 112 D2
Weston under Penyard Hereford 62 A2
Weston under Wetherley Warks 81 A6
Weston Underwood Derbys 113 A6
Weston Underwood M Keynes 83 B5
Westonbirt Glos 44 A2
Westonbirt Arboretum, Tetbury Glos 44 A2
Westoncommon Shrops 110 C3
Westoning Beds 84 D2
Westonzoyland Som 28 B3
Westow N Yorks 149 A6
Westport Argyll 190 C2
Westport Som 28 D3
Westray Airport Orkney 282 B5
Westrigg W Loth 208 D2
Westruther Borders 197 B5
Westry Cambs 101 B5
Westville Notts 114 A3
Westward Cumb 175 D5
Westward Ho! Devon 25 C5
Westwell Kent 38 A1
Westwell Oxon 64 C3
Westwell Leacon Kent 38 A1
Westwick Cambs 85 A6
Westwick Durham 166 D3
Westwick Norf 121 C4
Westwood Devon 13 B5
Westwood Wilts 44 D2
Westwoodside N Lincs 141 D5
Wetheral Cumb 176 D2
Wetherby W Yorks 148 C3
Wetherby Racecourse W Yorks 148 C3
Wetherden Suff 87 A6
Wetheringsett Suff 88 A2
Wethersfield Essex 86 D3
Wethersta Shetland 284 G5
Wetherup Street Suff 88 A2
Wetley Rocks Staffs 112 A3
Wettenhall Ches 127 C6
Wetton Staffs 129 D6
Wetwang E Yorks 150 B2
Wetwood Staffs 111 B6
Wexcombe Wilts 45 D6
Wexham Street Bucks 48 A2
Weybourne Norf 120 A3
Weybread Suff 104 C3
Weybridge Sur 48 C3
Weycroft Devon 14 B3
Weydale Highld 280 B3
Weyhill Hants 32 A2
Weymouth Dorset 15 D6
Weymouth Sea Life Park Dorset 15 C6
Whaddon Bucks 83 D5
Whaddon Cambs 85 C5
Whaddon Glos 63 B4
Whaddon Wilts 31 C5
Whale Cumb 164 C3
Whaley Derbys 131 B5
Whaley Bridge Derbys 129 A5
Whaley Thorns Derbys 131 B5
Whaligoe Highld 281 D5
Whalley Lancs 146 D1
Whalsay Airport Shetland 284 G7
Whalton Northumb 178 A3
Wham N Yorks 146 A1
Whaplode Lincs 117 C6
Whaplode Drove Lincs 117 D6
Whaplode St Catherine Lincs 117 C6
Wharfe N Yorks 146 A1
Wharles Lancs 144 D4
Wharncliffe Side S Yorks 139 D5
Wharram le Street N Yorks 150 A1
Wharton Ches 127 C6
Wharton Green Ches 127 C6
Whashton N Yorks 157 A5
Whatcombe Dorset 16 A2
Whatcote Warks 81 C6
Whatfield Suff 87 C6
Whatley Som 14 A3
Whatley Som 30 A1
Whatlington E Sus 23 A5
Whatstandwell Derbys 130 D3
Whatton Notts 115 B5
Whauphill Dumfries 171 C6
Whaw N Yorks 156 A3
Wheatacre Norf 105 B5
Wheatcroft Derbys 130 D3
Wheathampstead Herts 68 B1
Wheathill Shrops 95 C4
Wheatley Devon 13 B4
Wheatley Hants 33 A6
Wheatley Oxon 65 C6
Wheatley S Yorks 140 C3
Wheatley W Yorks 138 A3
Wheatley Hill Durham 167 B6
Wheaton Aston Staffs 112 D2
Wheddon Cross Som 27 B4
Wheedlemont Aberds 255 D5
Wheelerstreet Sur 34 B2
Wheelock Ches 128 D2
Wheelock Heath Ches 128 D2
Wheelton Lancs 137 A5
Wheen Angus 232 A1
Wheldrake York 149 C5
Whelford Glos 64 D2
Whelpley Hill Bucks 67 C4
Whempstead Herts 68 A3
Whenby N Yorks 149 A5
Whepstead Suff 87 B4
Wherstead Suff 88 C2
Wherwell Hants 32 A2
Wheston Derbys 129 B6
Whetsted Kent 37 B4
Whetstone Leics 98 B2
Whicham Cumb 153 B2
Whichford Warks 81 D6
Whickham T & W 179 C4
Whiddon Down Devon 12 B1
Whigstreet Angus 232 D2
Whilton Northants 82 A3
Whim Farm Borders 195 A7
Whimble Devon 11 A4
Whimple Devon 13 B5
Whimpwell Green Norf 121 C5
Whinburgh Norf 103 A6
Whinnieliggate Dumfries 173 C5
Whinnyfold Aberds 257 C5
Whippingham I o W 18 B4
Whipsnade Beds 67 B5
Whipsnade Wild Animal Park, Dunstable Beds 67 B5
Whipton Devon 13 B4
Whirlow S Yorks 130 A3
Whisby Lincs 133 C4
Whissendine Rutland 115 D6
Whissonsett Norf 119 C6
Whistlefield Argyll 215 C4
Whistlefield Argyll 215 C5
Whistley Green Wokingham 47 B5
Whiston Mers 136 D3
Whiston Northants 83 A5
Whiston Staffs 112 D2
Whiston Staffs 112 A4
Whiston S Yorks 131 A4
Whitbeck Cumb 153 B2
Whitbourne Hereford 79 B5
Whitbread Hop Farm, Beltring Kent 37 B4
Whitburn T & W 179 C6
Whitburn W Loth 208 D2
Whitburn Colliery T & W 179 C6
Whitby Ches 126 B3
Whitby N Yorks 169 D6
Whitby Abbey N Yorks 169 D7
Whitbyheath Ches 126 B3
Whitchurch Bath 43 C5
Whitchurch Bucks 66 A2
Whitchurch Cardiff 41 C6
Whitchurch Devon 11 D5
Whitchurch Hants 32 A3
Whitchurch Hereford 62 B1
Whitchurch Oxon 47 B4
Whitchurch Pembs 54 B3
Whitchurch Shrops 111 A4
Whitchurch Canonicorum Dorset 14 B3
Whitchurch Hill Oxon 47 B4
Whitcombe Dorset 15 C7
Whitcott Keysett Shrops 93 C6
White Coppice Lancs 137 B5
White Lackington Dorset 15 B7
White Ladies Aston Worcs 80 B2
White Lund Lancs 144 A4
White Mill Carms 58 C1
White Ness Shetland 285 J5
White Notley Essex 70 B1
White Pit Lincs 134 B3
White Post Notts 131 D6
White Post Farm Centre, Farnsfield Notts 131 D6
White Rocks Hereford 61 A6
White Roding Essex 69 B5
White Waltham Windsor 47 B6
Whiteacen Moray 254 B3
Whiteacre Heath Warks 97 B5
Whitebridge Highld 240 A2
Whitebrook Mon 62 C1
Whiteburn Borders 197 B4
Whitecairn Dumfries 171 B4
Whitecairns Aberds 245 A6
Whitecastle S Lnrk 195 B5
Whitechapel Lancs 145 C5
Whitecleat Orkney 283 G6
Whitecraig E Loth 209 C6
Whitecroft Glos 62 C2
Whitecross Corn 9 D5
Whitecross Falk 208 C2
Whitecross Staffs 112 C2
Whiteface Highld 264 B3
Whitefarland N Ayrs 202 D3
Whitefaulds S Ayrs 192 E2
Whitefield Gtr Man 137 C7
Whitefield Perth 219 A6
Whiteford Aberds 256 D2
Whitegate Ches 127 C6
Whitehall Blkburn 137 A5
Whitehall W Sus 35 D4
Whitehall Village Orkney 282 E7
Whitehaven Cumb 162 C2
Whitehill Hants 33 B6
Whitehills Aberds 268 C1
Whitehills S Lnrk 205 C6
Whitehough Derbys 129 A5
Whitehouse Aberds 244 A3
Whitehouse Argyll 202 B3
Whiteinch Glasgow 205 B5
Whitekirk E Loth 210 B2
Whitelaw S Lnrk 205 D6
Whiteleas T & W 179 C5
Whiteley Bank I o W 19 C4
Whiteley Green Ches 129 B4
Whiteley Village Sur 48 C3
Whitemans Green W Sus 35 D6
Whitemire Moray 253 A5
Whitemoor Corn 5 B4
Whitemore Staffs 128 C3
Whitenap Hants 32 C2
Whiteoak Green Oxon 64 B4
Whiteparish Wilts 31 C6
Whiterashes Aberds 256 D3
Whiterow Highld 281 D5
Whiteshill Glos 63 C4
Whiteside Northumb 177 C5
Whiteside W Loth 208 D2
Whitesmith E Sus 22 A3
Whitestaunton Som 28 D2
Whitestone Devon 12 B3
Whitestone Devon 25 A5
Whitestone Warks 97 C6
Whitestones Aberds 268 D3
Whitestreet Green Suff 87 D5
Whitewall Corner N Yorks 159 D6
Whiteway Glos 63 D4
Whiteway Glos 63 B5
Whitewell Aberds 269 C4
Whitewell Lancs 145 C6
Whitewell Bottom Lancs 138 A1
Whiteworks Devon 11 D7
Whitfield Kent 39 A5
Whitfield Northants 82 D3
Whitfield Northumb 177 D5
Whitfield S Glos 62 D2
Whitford Devon 14 B2
Whitford Flint 125 B6
Whitgift E Yorks 141 A6
Whitgreave Staffs 112 C2
Whithorn Dumfries 171 C6
Whiting Bay N Ayrs 191 C6
Whitkirk W Yorks 148 D2
Whitland Carms 56 A1
Whitletts S Ayrs 192 C3
Whitley N Yorks 140 A3
Whitley Reading 47 B5
Whitley Wilts 44 C2
Whitley Bay T & W 179 B5
Whitley Chapel Northumb 178 D1
Whitley Lower W Yorks 139 B5
Whitley Row Kent 36 A2
Whitlock's End W Mid 96 D4
Whitminster Glos 62 C3
Whitmore Staffs 112 A2
Whitnage Devon 27 D5

Whitnash Warks 81 A6
Whitney-on-Wye Hereford 77 C6
Whitrigg Cumb 163 A5
Whitrigg Cumb 175 C5
Whitsbury Hants 31 D5
Whitsome Borders 198 A2
Whitson Newport 42 A2
Whitstable Kent 52 C3
Whitstone Corn 10 B3
Whittingham Northumb 188 B3
Whittingslow Shrops 94 C2
Whittington Glos 63 A6
Whittington Lancs 155 D5
Whittington Norf 102 B3
Whittington Shrops 110 B2
Whittington Staffs 95 C6
Whittington Staffs 97 A4
Whittington Worcs 80 B1
Whittle-le-Woods Lancs 137 A4
Whittlebury Northants 82 C3
Whittlesey Cambs 101 B4
Whittlesford Cambs 85 C6
Whittlestone Head Blkburn 137 B6
Whitton Borders 187 A6
Whitton N Lincs 141 A7
Whitton Northumb 188 C3
Whitton Powys 77 A6
Whitton Shrops 94 D3
Whitton Stockton 167 C6
Whitton Suff 88 C2
Whittonditch Wilts 45 B6
Whittonstall Northumb 178 D2
Whitway Hants 46 D2
Whitwell Derbys 131 B5
Whitwell Herts 68 A1
Whitwell I o W 18 D4
Whitwell N Yorks 157 B6
Whitwell Rutland 99 A6
Whitwell-on-the-Hill N Yorks 149 A6
Whitwell Street Norf 120 C3
Whitwick Leics 114 D2
Whitwood W Yorks 140 A2
Whitworth Lancs 138 B1
Whixall Shrops 111 B4
Whixley N Yorks 148 B3
Whoberley W Mid 97 D6
Whorlton Durham 166 D4
Whorlton N Yorks 158 A3
Whygate Northumb 177 B5
Whyle Hereford 78 A3
Whyteleafe Sur 35 A6
Wibdon Glos 62 D1
Wibsey W Yorks 147 D5
Wibtoft Leics 98 C1
Wichenford Worcs 79 A5
Wichling Kent 37 A7
Wick Bmouth 17 B5
Wick Devon 13 A6
Wick Highld 281 C5
Wick S Glos 43 B6
Wick Shetland 285 K6
Wick V Glam 40 D4
Wick Wilts 31 C5
Wick Worcs 80 C2
Wick W Sus 20 B3
Wick Airport Highld 281 C5
Wick Hill Wokingham 47 C5
Wick St Lawrence N Som 42 C2
Wicken Cambs 102 D1
Wicken Northants 83 D4
Wicken Bonhunt Essex 85 D6
Wicken Green Village Norf 119 B5
Wickenby Lincs 133 A5
Wickersley S Yorks 140 D2
Wickford Essex 70 D1
Wickham Hants 33 D4
Wickham W Berks 46 B1
Wickham Bishops Essex 70 B2
Wickham Market Suff 88 B4
Wickham St Paul Essex 87 D4
Wickham Skeith Suff 88 A1
Wickham Street Suff 86 B3
Wickham Street Suff 88 A1
Wickhambreux Kent 53 D4
Wickhambrook Suff 86 B3
Wickhamford Worcs 80 C3
Wickhampton Norf 105 A5
Wicklewood Norf 104 A1
Wickmere Norf 120 B3
Wicksteed Park, Kettering Northants 99 D5
Wickwar S Glos 43 A6
Widdington Essex 86 D1
Widdrington Northumb 189 D5
Widdrington Station Northumb 189 D5
Wide Open T & W 179 B4
Widecombe in the Moor Devon 12 D2
Widegates Corn 6 B1
Widemouth Bay Corn 10 A3
Widewall Orkney 283 H5
Widford Essex 69 C6
Widford Herts 68 B4
Widham Wilts 45 A4
Widmer End Bucks 66 D3
Widmerpool Notts 115 C4
Widnes Halton 127 A5
Wigan Gtr Man 137 C4
Wigan Pier Gtr Man 137 C4
Wiggaton Devon 13 B6
Wiggenhall St Germans Norf 118 D2
Wiggenhall St Mary Magdalen Norf 118 D2
Wiggenhall St Mary the Virgin Norf 118 D2
Wigginton Herts 67 B4
Wigginton Oxon 81 D6
Wigginton Staffs 97 A5
Wigginton York 149 B4
Wigglesworth N Yorks 146 B2
Wiggonby Cumb 175 C5
Wiggonholt W Sus 20 A3
Wighill N Yorks 148 C3
Wighton Norf 119 B6
Wigley Hants 32 D2
Wigmore Hereford 78 A2
Wigmore Medway 51 C5
Wigsley Notts 132 B3
Wigsthorpe Northants 100 C2
Wigston Leics 98 B3
Wigthorpe Notts 131 A5
Wigtoft Lincs 117 B5
Wigton Cumb 175 D5
Wigtown Dumfries 171 B6
Wigtwizzle S Yorks 139 D5
Wike W Yorks 148 C2
Wike Well End S Yorks 141 B4
Wilbarston Northants 99 C5
Wilberfoss E Yorks 149 B6
Wilberlee W Yorks 138 B3
Wilburton Cambs 101 D6
Wilby Norf 103 C6
Wilby Northants 83 A5
Wilby Suff 104 D3
Wilcot Wilts 45 C5
Wilcott Shrops 110 D2
Wilcrick Newport 42 A3
Wilday Green Derbys 130 B3
Wildboarclough Ches 129 C4
Wilden Beds 84 B2
Wilden Worcs 95 D6
Wildfowl and Wetland Centre, Martin Mere Lancs 136 B3
Wildhern Hants 46 D1
Wildhill Herts 68 C2
Wildlife & Dinosaur Park, Combe Martin Devon 25 A6
Wildmoor Worcs 96 D2
Wildsworth Lincs 141 D6
Wilford Notts 114 B3
Wilkesley Ches 111 A5
Wilkhaven Highld 265 B5
Wilkieston W Loth 208 D4
Willand Devon 27 D5
Willaston Ches 126 B3
Willaston Ches 128 D1
Willen M Keynes 83 C5
Willenhall W Mid 97 D6
Willenhall W Mid 96 B2
Willerby E Yorks 150 D3
Willerby N Yorks 160 D4
Willersey Glos 80 D4
Willersley Hereford 77 C7
Willesborough Kent 38 A2
Willesborough Lees Kent 38 A2
Willesden London 49 A5
Willett Som 27 B6
Willey Shrops 95 B4
Willey Warks 98 C1
Willey Green Sur 34 A2
Williamscott Oxon 82 C1
Willian Herts 84 D4
Willingale Essex 69 C5
Willingdon E Sus 22 B3
Willingham Cambs 101 D6
Willingham by Stow Lincs 132 A3
Willington Beds 84 C3
Willington Derbys 113 C6
Willington Durham 167 B4
Willington T & W 179 C5
Willington Warks 81 D5
Willington Corner Ches 127 C5
Willisham Tye Suff 87 B6
Willitoft E Yorks 149 D6
Williton Som 27 A5
Willoughbridge Staffs 111 A6
Willoughby Lincs 135 B4
Willoughby Warks 82 A2
Willoughby-on-the-Wolds Notts 115 C4
Willoughby Waterleys Leics 98 B2
Willoughton Lincs 142 D1
Willows Green Essex 69 B7
Willsbridge S Glos 43 B5
Willsworthy Devon 11 C6
Wilmcote Warks 81 B4
Wilmington Devon 14 B2
Wilmington E Sus 22 B3
Wilmington Kent 50 B2
Wilminstone Devon 11 D5
Wilmslow Ches 128 A3
Wilnecote Staffs 97 A5
Wilpshire Lancs 145 D6
Wilsden W Yorks 147 D4
Wilsford Lincs 116 A3
Wilsford Wilts 45 D5
Wilsford Wilts 31 B5
Wilsill N Yorks 147 A5
Wilsley Pound Kent 37 C5
Wilsom Hants 33 B6
Wilson Leics 114 C2
Wilsontown S Lnrk 195 A4
Wilstead Beds 84 C2
Wilsthorpe Lincs 116 D3
Wilstone Herts 67 B4
Wilton Borders 186 B3
Wilton Cumb 162 C3
Wilton N Yorks 160 C2
Wilton Redcar 168 D3
Wilton Wilts 31 B4
Wilton Wilts 45 C6
Wilton House, Salisbury Wilts 31 B5
Wimbish Essex 86 D1
Wimbish Green Essex 86 D2
Wimblebury Staffs 112 D4
Wimbledon London 49 B5
Wimbledon All England Tennis Club London 49 B5
Wimblington Cambs 101 B6
Wimborne Minster Dorset 17 B4
Wimborne Minster Dorset 17 B4
Wimborne St Giles Dorset 31 D4
Wimbotsham Norf 102 A2
Wimpole Hall and Home Farm, Royston Cambs 85 B5
Wimpson Soton 32 D2
Wimpstone Warks 81 C5
Wincanton Som 29 C7
Wincanton Racecourse Som 29 C7
Wincham Ches 128 B1
Winchburgh W Loth 208 C3
Winchcombe Glos 63 A6
Winchelsea E Sus 23 A7
Winchelsea Beach E Sus 23 A7
Winchester Hants 32 C3
Winchester Cathedral Hants 32 C3
Winchet Hill Kent 37 B5
Winchfield Hants 47 D5
Winchmore Hill Bucks 67 D4
Winchmore Hill London 68 D3
Wincle Ches 129 C4
Wincobank S Yorks 140 D1
Windermere Cumb 154 B3
Winderton Warks 81 C6
Windhill Highld 252 B1
Windhouse Shetland 284 D6
Windlehurst Gtr Man 129 A4
Windlesham Sur 48 C2
Windley Derbys 113 A7
Windmill Hill E Sus 22 A4
Windmill Hill Som 28 D3
Windrush Glos 64 B2
Windsor N Lincs 141 B5
Windsor Windsor 48 B2
Windsor Castle Windsor 48 B2
Windsor Racecourse Windsor 48 B2
Windsoredge Glos 63 C4
Windygates Fife 220 D3
Windyknowe W Loth 208 D2
Windywalls Borders 197 C6
Wineham W Sus 35 D5
Winestead E Yorks 143 A4
Winewall Lancs 146 C3
Winfarthing Norf 104 C2
Winford I o W 19 C4
Winford N Som 43 C4
Winforton Hereford 77 C6
Winfrith Newburgh Dorset 16 C2
Wing Bucks 66 A3
Wing Rutland 99 A5
Wingate Durham 168 B2
Wingates Gtr Man 137 C5
Wingates Northumb 189 D4
Wingerworth Derbys 130 C3
Wingfield Beds 67 A5
Wingfield Suff 104 D3
Wingfield Wilts 44 D2
Wingham Kent 53 D4
Wingmore Kent 38 A3
Wingrave Bucks 66 B3
Winkburn Notts 132 D2
Winkfield Brack 48 B2
Winkfield Row Brack 48 B1
Winkhill Staffs 129 D5
Winklebury Hants 47 D4
Winkleigh Devon 12 A1
Winksley N Yorks 157 D6
Winkton Dorset 17 B5
Winlaton T & W 178 C3
Winless Highld 281 C5
Winmarleigh Lancs 145 C4
Winnal Hereford 78 D2
Winnall Hants 32 C3
Winnersh Wokingham 47 B5
Winscales Cumb 162 B3
Winscombe N Som 42 D3
Winsford Ches 127 C6
Winsford Som 27 B4
Winsham Som 14 A3
Winshill Staffs 113 C6
Winskill Cumb 164 B3
Winslade Hants 33 A5
Winsley Wilts 44 C2
Winslow Bucks 66 A2
Winson Glos 64 C1
Winson Green W Mid 96 C3
Winsor Hants 32 D2
Winster Cumb 154 B3
Winster Derbys 130 C2
Winston Durham 166 D4
Winston Suff 88 A2
Winston Green Suff 88 A2
Winstone Glos 63 C5
Winswell Devon 25 D5
Winter Gardens Essex 51 A4
Winterborne Bassett Wilts 45 B5
Winterborne Clenston Dorset 16 A2
Winterborne Herringston Dorset 15 C6
Winterborne Houghton Dorset 16 A2
Winterborne Kingston Dorset 16 B2
Winterborne Monkton Dorset 15 C6
Winterborne Monkton Wilts 45 B5
Winterborne Stickland Dorset 16 A2
Winterborne Whitechurch Dorset 16 A2
Winterborne Zelston Dorset 16 B2
Winterbourne S Glos 43 A5
Winterbourne W Berks 46 B2
Winterbourne Abbas Dorset 15 B6
Winterbourne Dauntsey Wilts 31 B5
Winterbourne Down S Glos 43 B5
Winterbourne Earls Wilts 31 B5
Winterbourne Gunner Wilts 31 B5
Winterbourne Steepleton Dorset 15 C6
Winterbourne Stoke Wilts 31 A4
Winterburn N Yorks 146 B3
Winteringham N Lincs 142 A1
Winterley Ches 128 D2
Wintersett W Yorks 140 B1
Wintershill Hants 32 D4
Winterton N Lincs 142 B1
Winterton-on-Sea Norf 121 D6
Winthorpe Lincs 135 C5
Winthorpe Notts 132 D3
Winton Bmouth 17 B4
Winton Cumb 165 D5
Winton N Yorks 158 B3
Wintringham N Yorks 160 D2
Winwick Cambs 100 C3
Winwick Northants 98 D3
Winwick Warr 137 D5
Wirksworth Derbys 130 D2
Wirksworth Moor Derbys 130 D3
Wirswall Ches 111 A4
Wisbech Cambs 101 A6
Wisbech St Mary Cambs 101 A6
Wisborough Green W Sus 34 D3
Wiseton Notts 132 A2
Wishaw N Lnrk 194 A2
Wishaw Warks 97 B4
Wisley Sur 34 A3
Wispington Lincs 134 B2
Wissenden Kent 37 B7
Wissett Suff 105 D4
Wistanstow Shrops 94 C2
Wistanswick Shrops 111 C5
Wistaston Ches 128 D1
Wistaston Green Ches 128 D1
Wiston Pembs 55 C6
Wiston S Lnrk 195 C4
Wiston W Sus 21 A4
Wistow Cambs 101 C4
Wistow N Yorks 149 D4
Wiswell Lancs 146 D1
Witcham Cambs 101 C6
Witchampton Dorset 16 A3
Witchford Cambs 101 D7
Witham Essex 70 B2
Witham Friary Som 30 A1
Witham on the Hill Lincs 116 D3
Withcall Lincs 134 A2
Withdean Brighton 21 B6
Witherenden Hill E Sus 36 D4
Witheridge Devon 26 D3
Witherley Leics 97 B6
Withern Lincs 135 A4
Withernsea E Yorks 143 A5
Withernwick E Yorks 151 C4
Withersdale Street Suff 104 C3
Withersfield Suff 86 C2
Witherslack Cumb 154 C3
Withiel Corn 5 A4
Withiel Florey Som 27 B4
Withington Glos 63 B6
Withington Gtr Man 138 D1
Withington Hereford 78 C3
Withington Shrops 111 D4
Withington Staffs 112 B4
Withington Green Ches 128 B3
Withleigh Devon 27 D4
Withnell Lancs 137 A5
Withybrook Warks 98 C1
Withycombe Som 27 A5
Withycombe Raleigh Devon 13 C5
Withyham E Sus 36 C2
Withypool Som 26 B3
Witley Sur 34 C2
Witnesham Suff 88 B2
Witney Oxon 65 B4
Wittering P'boro 100 A2
Wittersham Kent 37 D6
Witton Angus 232 A3
Witton Worcs 80 A1
Witton Bridge Norf 121 B5
Witton Gilbert Durham 167 A5
Witton-le-Wear Durham 166 B4
Witton Park Durham 167 B4
Wiveliscombe Som 27 C5
Wivelrod Hants 33 B5
Wivelsfield E Sus 35 D6
Wivelsfield Green E Sus 35 D6
Wivenhoe Essex 71 A4
Wivenhoe Cross Essex 71 A4
Wiveton Norf 120 A2
Wix Essex 71 A5
Wixford Warks 80 B3
Wixhill Shrops 111 C4
Wixoe Suff 86 C3
Woburn Beds 83 D6
Woburn Abbey, Woburn Beds 83 D6
Woburn Sands M Keynes 83 D6
Woburn Wild Animal Kingdom Beds 83 D6
Wokefield Park W Berks 47 C4
Woking Sur 34 A3
Wokingham Wokingham 47 C6
Wolborough Devon 12 D3
Wold Newton E Yorks 160 D4
Wold Newton NE Lincs 143 D4
Woldingham Sur 35 A6
Wolfclyde S Lnrk 195 C5
Wolferton Norf 118 C3
Wolfhill Perth 219 A6
Wolf's Castle Pembs 55 B5
Wolfsdale Pembs 55 B5
Woll Borders 186 A3
Wollaston Northants 83 A6
Wollaston Shrops 110 D2
Wollaton Nottingham 114 B3
Wollaton Hall Nottingham 114 B3
Wollerton Shrops 111 B5
Wollescote W Mid 96 C2
Wolsingham Durham 166 B3
Wolstanton Staffs 112 A2
Wolston Warks 97 D7
Wolvercote Oxon 65 C5
Wolverhampton W Mid 96 B2
Wolverhampton Racecourse W Mid 96 A2
Wolverley Shrops 110 B3
Wolverley Worcs 95 D6
Wolverton Hants 46 D3
Wolverton M Keynes 83 C5
Wolverton Warks 81 A5
Wolverton Common Hants 46 D3
Wolvesnewton Mon 61 D6
Wolvey Warks 98 C1
Wolviston Stockton 168 C2
Wombleton N Yorks 159 C5
Wombourne Staffs 95 B6
Wombwell S Yorks 140 C1
Womenswold Kent 53 D4
Womersley N Yorks 140 B3
Wonastow Mon 61 B6
Wonersh Sur 34 B3
Wonson Devon 12 C1
Wonston Hants 32 B3
Wooburn Bucks 48 A2
Wooburn Green Bucks 48 A2
Wood Dalling Norf 120 C2
Wood End Herts 68 A3
Wood End Warks 96 D4
Wood End Warks 97 B5
Wood Enderby Lincs 134 C2
Wood Field Sur 35 A4
Wood Green London 68 D3
Wood Green Animal Shelter, Godmanchester Cambs 85 A4
Wood Hayes W Mid 96 A2
Wood Lanes Ches 129 A4
Wood Norton Norf 120 C2
Wood Street Norf 121 C5
Wood Street Sur 34 A2
Wood Walton Cambs 100 C4
Woodacott Devon 11 A4
Woodale N Yorks 156 D4
Woodbank Argyll 190 D2
Woodbastwick Norf 121 D5
Woodbeck Notts 132 B2
Woodborough Notts 115 A4
Woodborough Wilts 45 D5
Woodbridge Dorset 29 D7
Woodbridge Suff 88 C3
Woodbury Devon 13 C5
Woodbury Salterton Devon 13 C5
Woodchester Glos 63 C4
Woodchurch Kent 38 B1
Woodchurch Mers 126 A2
Woodcombe Som 27 A4
Woodcote Oxon 47 A4
Woodcott Hants 46 D2
Woodcroft Glos 62 D1
Woodcutts Dorset 30 D3
Woodditton Cambs 86 B2
Woodeaton Oxon 65 B6
Woodend Cumb 153 A2
Woodend Northants 82 C3
Woodend W Sus 19 A7
Woodend Green Northants 82 C3
Woodfalls Wilts 31 C5
Woodfield Oxon 65 A6
Woodfield S Ayrs 192 C3
Woodford Corn 24 D3
Woodford Devon 8 B1
Woodford Glos 62 D2
Woodford London 68 D4
Woodford Gtr Man 128 A3
Woodford Northants 99 D6
Woodford Bridge London 68 D4
Woodford Halse Northants 82 B2
Woodgate Norf 120 D2
Woodgate W Mid 96 C2
Woodgate Worcs 80 A2
Woodgate W Sus 20 B2
Woodgreen Hants 31 D5
Woodhall Herts 68 B2
Woodhall Invclyd 204 A3
Woodhall N Yorks 156 B3
Woodhall Spa Lincs 134 C1
Woodham Sur 48 C3
Woodham Ferrers Essex 70 D1
Woodham Mortimer Essex 70 C2
Woodham Walter Essex 70 C2
Woodhaven Fife 220 B4
Woodhead Aberds 256 C2
Woodhey Gtr Man 137 B6
Woodhill Shrops 95 C5
Woodhorn Northumb 179 A4
Woodhouse Leics 114 D3
Woodhouse N Lincs 141 C5
Woodhouse S Yorks 131 A4
Woodhouse W Yorks 148 D1
Woodhouse W Yorks 140 A1
Woodhouse Eaves Leics 114 D3
Woodhouse Park Gtr Man 128 A3
Woodhouselee Midloth 209 D5
Woodhouselees Dumfries 175 A6
Woodhouses Staffs 113 D5
Woodhurst Cambs 101 D5
Woodingdean Brighton 21 B6
Woodkirk W Yorks 139 A5
Woodland Devon 8 A1
Woodland Durham 166 C3
Woodland Leisure Park, Dartmouth Devon 8 B2
Woodlands Aberds 245 C4
Woodlands Dorset 17 A4
Woodlands Hants 32 D2
Woodlands Highld 264 D1
Woodlands N Yorks 148 B2
Woodlands S Yorks 140 C3
Woodlands Park Windsor 47 B6
Woodlands St Mary W Berks 46 B1
Woodlane Staffs 113 C5
Woodleigh Devon 7 C6
Woodlesford W Yorks 139 A6
Woodley Gtr Man 138 D2
Woodley Wokingham 47 B5
Woodmancote Glos 62 D3
Woodmancote Glos 63 C6
Woodmancote Glos 63 A5
Woodmancote W Sus 19 A6
Woodmancote W Sus 21 A5
Woodmancott Hants 33 A4
Woodmansey E Yorks 150 D3
Woodmansterne Sur 35 A5
Woodminton Wilts 31 C4
Woodnesborough Kent 53 D5
Woodnewton Northants 100 B2
Woodplumpton Lancs 145 D5
Woodrising Norf 103 A5
Wood's Green E Sus 36 C4
Woodseaves Shrops 111 B5
Woodseaves Staffs 112 C1
Woodsend Wilts 45 B6
Woodsetts S Yorks 131 A5
Woodsford Dorset 16 B1
Woodside Aberdeen 245 B6
Woodside Aberds 257 B5
Woodside Brack 48 B2
Woodside Fife 220 D4
Woodside Hants 18 B2
Woodside Herts 68 C2

Woodside Perth 220 A2
Woodside Farm and Wildfowl Park, Luton Beds 67 B5
Woodside of Arbeadie Aberds 245 C4
Woodstock Oxon 65 B5
Woodstock Pembs 55 B6
Woodthorpe Derbys 131 B4
Woodthorpe Leics 114 D3
Woodthorpe Lincs 135 A4
Woodthorpe York 149 C4
Woodton Norf 104 B3
Woodtown Devon 25 C5
Woodtown Devon 25 C5
Woodvale Mers 136 B2
Woodville Derbys 113 D7
Woodyates Dorset 31 D4
Woofferton Shrops 78 A3
Wookey Som 29 A5
Wookey Hole Som 29 A5
Wookey Hole Caves & Papermill, Wells Som 29 A5
Wool Dorset 16 C2
Woolacombe Devon 25 A5
Woolage Green Kent 39 A4
Woolaston Glos 62 D1
Woolavington Som 28 A3
Woolbeding W Sus 34 D1
Wooldale W Yorks 139 C4
Wooler Northumb 188 A2
Woolfardisworthy Devon 24 C4
Woolfardisworthy Devon 12 A3
Woolfords Cottages S Lnrk 195 A5
Woolhampton W Berks 46 C3
Woolhope Hereford 79 D4
Woolhope Cockshoot Hereford 79 D4
Woolland Dorset 16 A1
Woollaton Devon 25 D5
Woolley Bath 43 C6
Woolley Cambs 100 D3
Woolley Corn 24 D3
Woolley Derbys 130 C3
Woolley W Yorks 139 B6
Woolmer Green Herts 68 B2
Woolmere Green Worcs 80 A2
Woolpit Suff 87 A5
Woolscott Warks 82 A1
Woolsington T & W 178 C3
Woolstanwood Ches 128 D1
Woolstaston Shrops 94 B2
Woolsthorpe Lincs 115 B6
Woolsthorpe Lincs 116 C2
Woolston Devon 7 C6
Woolston Shrops 94 C2
Woolston Shrops 110 C2
Woolston Soton 32 D3
Woolston Warr 127 A6
Woolstone M Keynes 83 D5
Woolstone Oxon 45 A6
Woolton Mers 127 A4
Woolton Hill Hants 46 C2
Woolverstone Suff 88 D2
Woolverton Som 44 D1
Woolwich London 50 B1
Woolwich Ferry London 50 B1
Woonton Hereford 78 B1
Wooperton Northumb 188 A3
Woore Shrops 111 A6
Wootten Green Suff 104 D3
Wootton Beds 84 C2
Wootton Hants 17 B6
Wootton Hereford 78 B1
Wootton Kent 39 A4
Wootton N Lincs 142 B2
Wootton Northants 83 B4
Wootton Oxon 65 B5
Wootton Oxon 65 C5
Wootton Shrops 94 D2
Wootton Shrops 110 C2
Wootton Staffs 112 C2
Wootton Staffs 113 A5
Wootton Bassett Wilts 45 A4
Wootton Bridge I o W 18 B4
Wootton Common I o W 18 B4
Wootton Courtenay Som 27 A4
Wootton Fitzpaine Dorset 14 B3
Wootton Rivers Wilts 45 C5
Wootton St Lawrence Hants 46 D3
Wootton Wawen Warks 81 A4
Worcester Worcs 79 B6
Worcester Cathedral Worcs 79 B6
Worcester Park London 49 C5
Worcester Racecourse Worcs 79 B6
Wordsley W Mid 96 C1
Worfield Shrops 95 B5
Work Orkney 282 F5
Workington Cumb 162 B2
Worksop Notts 131 B5
Worlaby N Lincs 142 B2
World of James Herriot N Yorks 158 C3
World's End W Berks 46 B2
Worle N Som 42 C2
Worleston Ches 127 D6
Worlingham Suff 105 C5
Worlington Suff 102 D2
Worlingworth Suff 88 A3
Wormald Green N Yorks 148 A2
Wormbridge Hereford 78 D2
Wormegay Norf 118 D3
Wormelow Tump Hereford 78 D2
Wormhill Derbys 129 B6
Wormingford Essex 87 D5
Worminghall Bucks 66 C1
Wormington Glos 80 D3
Worminster Som 29 A5
Wormit Fife 220 B3
Wormleighton Warks 82 B1
Wormley Herts 68 C3
Wormley Sur 34 C2
Wormley West End Herts 68 C3
Wormshill Kent 37 A6
Wormsley Hereford 78 C2
Worplesdon Sur 34 A2
Worrall S Yorks 139 D6
Worsbrough S Yorks 139 C6
Worsbrough Common S Yorks 139 C6
Worsley Gtr Man 137 C6
Worstead Norf 121 C5
Worsthorne Lancs 146 D2
Worston Lancs 146 C1
Worswell Devon 7 C4
Worth Kent 53 D5
Worth W Sus 35 C6
Worth Matravers Dorset 16 D3
Wortham Suff 104 D1
Worthen Shrops 94 A1
Worthenbury Wrex 110 A3
Worthing Norf 120 D1
Worthing W Sus 21 B4
Worthington Leics 114 C2
Worting Hants 47 D4
Wortley S Yorks 139 D6
Wortley W Yorks 147 D6
Worton N Yorks 156 B3
Worton Wilts 44 D3
Wortwell Norf 104 C3
Wotherton Shrops 93 A6
Wotter Devon 7 A4
Wotton Sur 35 B4
Wotton-under-Edge Glos 62 D3
Wotton Underwood Bucks 66 B1
Woughton on the Green M Keynes 83 D5
Wouldham Kent 51 C4
Wrabness Essex 88 D2
Wrafton Devon 25 B5
Wragby Lincs 133 B6
Wragby W Yorks 140 B2
Wragholme Lincs 143 D5
Wramplingham Norf 104 A2
Wrangbrook W Yorks 140 B2
Wrangham Aberds 256 C1
Wrangle Lincs 135 D4
Wrangle Bank Lincs 135 D4
Wrangle Lowgate Lincs 135 D4
Wrangway Som 27 D6
Wrantage Som 28 C3
Wrawby N Lincs 142 C2
Wraxall Dorset 15 A5
Wraxall N Som 42 B3
Wraxall Som 29 B6
Wray Lancs 145 A6
Wraysbury Windsor 48 B3
Wrayton Lancs 155 D5
Wrea Green Lancs 144 D3
Wreay Cumb 164 C2
Wreay Cumb 164 A2
Wrecclesham Sur 34 B1
Wrecsam = Wrexham Wrex 126 D3
Wrekenton T & W 179 D4
Wrelton N Yorks 159 C6
Wrenbury Ches 111 A4
Wrench Green N Yorks 160 C3
Wreningham Norf 104 B2
Wrentham Suff 105 C5
Wrenthorpe W Yorks 139 A6
Wrentnall Shrops 94 A2
Wressle E Yorks 149 D6
Wressle N Lincs 142 C1
Wrestlingworth Beds 85 C4
Wretham Norf 103 C5
Wretton Norf 102 B2
Wrexham = Wrecsam Wrex 126 D3
Wrexham Industrial Estate Wrex 110 A2
Wribbenhall Worcs 95 D5
Wrightington Bar Lancs 136 B4
Wrinehill Staffs 111 A6
Wrington N Som 42 C3
Writhlington Bath 43 D6
Writtle Essex 69 C6
Wrockwardine Telford 111 D5
Wroot N Lincs 141 C5
Wrotham Kent 36 A4
Wrotham Heath Kent 36 A4
Wroughton Swindon 45 A5
Wroxall I o W 19 D4
Wroxall Warks 97 D5
Wroxeter Shrops 94 A3
Wroxham Norf 121 D5
Wroxham Barns, Hoveton Norf 121 C5
Wroxton Oxon 81 C7
Wyaston Derbys 113 A5
Wyberton Lincs 117 A6
Wyboston Beds 84 B3
Wybunbury Ches 111 A6
Wych Cross E Sus 36 C2
Wychbold Worcs 80 A2
Wyck Hants 33 B6
Wyck Rissington Glos 64 A2
Wycoller Lancs 146 D3
Wycomb Leics 115 C5
Wycombe Marsh Bucks 66 D3
Wyddial Herts 85 D5
Wye Kent 38 A2
Wyesham Mon 61 B7
Wyfordby Leics 115 D5
Wyke Dorset 30 C1
Wyke Shrops 95 A4
Wyke Sur 34 A2
Wyke W Yorks 139 A4
Wyke Regis Dorset 15 D6
Wykeham N Yorks 160 C3
Wykeham N Yorks 159 D7
Wyken W Mid 97 C6
Wykey Shrops 110 C2
Wylam Northumb 178 C3
Wylde Green W Mid 96 B4
Wyllie Caerph 41 B6
Wylye Wilts 31 B4
Wymering Ptsmth 19 A5
Wymeswold Leics 115 C4
Wymington Beds 83 A6
Wymondham Leics 115 D6
Wymondham Norf 104 A2
Wyndham Bridgend 40 B4
Wynford Eagle Dorset 15 B5
Wyng Orkney 283 H4
Wynyard Village Stockton 168 C2
Wyre Piddle Worcs 80 C2
Wysall Notts 115 C4
Wythall Worcs 96 D3
Wytham Oxon 65 C5
Wythburn Cumb 163 C6
Wythenshawe Gtr Man 128 A3
Wythop Mill Cumb 163 B4
Wyton Cambs 101 D4
Wyverstone Suff 87 A6
Wyverstone Street Suff 87 A6
Wyville Lincs 116 C1
Wyvis Lodge Highld 263 C6

Y

Y Bala = Bala Gwyn 108 B4
Y Barri = Barry V Glam 41 E6
Y Bont-Faen = Cowbridge V Glam 41 D4
Y Drenewydd = Newtown Powys 93 B5
Y Felinheli Gwyn 123 D5
Y Fenni = Abergavenny Mon 61 B4
Y Fflint = Flint Flint 126 B2
Y Ffôr Gwyn 106 C3
Y-Ffrith Denb 125 A5
Y Gelli Gandryll = Hay-on-Wye Powys 77 C6
Y Mwmbwls = The Mumbles Swansea 57 D6
Y Pîl = Pyle Bridgend 40 C3
Y Rhws = Rhoose V Glam 41 E5
Y Rhyl = Rhyl Denb 125 A5
Y Trallwng = Welshpool Powys 93 A6
Y Waun = Chirk Wrex 110 B1
Yaddlethorpe N Lincs 141 C6
Yafford I o W 18 C3
Yafforth N Yorks 158 B2
Yalding Kent 37 A4
Yanworth Glos 63 B6
Yapham E Yorks 149 B6
Yapton W Sus 20 B2
Yarburgh Lincs 143 D5
Yarcombe Devon 14 A2
Yard Som 27 B5
Yardley W Mid 96 C4
Yardley Gobion Northants 83 C4
Yardley Hastings Northants 83 B5
Yardro Powys 77 B6
Yarkhill Hereford 79 C4
Yarlet Staffs 112 C3
Yarlington Som 29 C6
Yarlside Cumb 153 D3
Yarm Stockton 168 D2
Yarmouth I o W 18 C2
Yarmouth Racecourse Norf 121 D7
Yarnbrook Wilts 44 D2
Yarnfield Staffs 112 B2
Yarnscombe Devon 25 C6
Yarnton Oxon 65 B5
Yarpole Hereford 78 A2
Yarrow Borders 196 D2
Yarrow Feus Borders 196 D2
Yarsop Hereford 78 C2
Yarwell Northants 100 B2
Yate S Glos 43 A6
Yateley Hants 47 C6
Yatesbury Wilts 45 B4
Yattendon W Berks 46 B3
Yatton Hereford 78 A2
Yatton N Som 42 C3
Yatton Keynell Wilts 44 B2
Yaverland I o W 19 C5
Yaxham Norf 120 D2
Yaxley Cambs 100 B3
Yaxley Suff 104 D2
Yazor Hereford 78 C2
Yeading London 48 A4
Yeadon W Yorks 147 C6
Yealand Conyers Lancs 154 D4
Yealand Redmayne Lancs 154 D4
Yealmpton Devon 7 B4
Yearby Redcar 168 C4
Yearsley N Yorks 159 D4
Yeaton Shrops 110 D3
Yeaveley Derbys 113 A5
Yedingham N Yorks 160 D2
Yeldon Beds 84 A2
Yelford Oxon 65 C4
Yelland Devon 25 B5
Yelling Cambs 85 A4
Yelvertoft Northants 98 D2
Yelverton Devon 7 A4
Yelverton Norf 104 A3
Yenston Som 29 C7
Yeo Mill Devon 26 C3
Yeoford Devon 12 B2
Yeolmbridge Corn 10 C4
Yeovil Som 29 D5
Yeovil Marsh Som 29 D5
Yeovilton Som 29 C5
Yerbeston Pembs 55 D6
Yesnaby Orkney 282 F3
Yetlington Northumb 188 C3
Yetminster Dorset 29 D5
Yettington Devon 13 C5
Yetts o'Muckhart Clack 219 D5
Yieldshields S Lnrk 194 A3
Yiewsley London 48 A3
Ynys-meudwy Neath 59 E4
Ynysboeth Rhondda 41 B5
Ynysddu Caerph 41 B6
Ynysgyfflog Gwyn 90 A4
Ynyshir Rhondda 41 B5
Ynyslas Ceredig 90 C4
Ynystawe Swansea 40 A1
Ynysybwl Rhondda 41 B5
Yockenthwaite N Yorks 156 D3
Yockleton Shrops 110 D2
Yokefleet E Yorks 141 A6
Yoker Glasgow 205 B5
Yonder Bognie Aberds 255 B6
York York 149 B4
York Castle Museum York 149 B5
York Minster York 149 B5
York Racecourse York 149 C4
York Town Sur 47 C6
Yorkletts Kent 52 C2
Yorkley Glos 62 C2
Yorkshire Museum York 149 B4
Yorkshire Sculpture Park, Wakefield W Yorks 139 B5
Yorton Shrops 111 C4
Youlgreave Derbys 130 C2
Youlstone Devon 24 D3
Youlthorpe E Yorks 149 B6
Youlton N Yorks 148 A3
Young Wood Lincs 133 B6
Young's End Essex 70 B1
Yoxall Staffs 113 D5
Yoxford Suff 89 A4
Yr Hôb = Hope Flint 126 D3
Yr Wyddgrug = Mold Flint 126 C2
Ysbyty-Cynfyn Ceredig 75 A6
Ysbyty Ifan Conwy 108 A3
Ysbyty Ystwyth Ceredig 75 A6
Ysceifiog Flint 125 B6
Yspitty Carms 57 C5
Ystalyfera Neath 59 E4
Ystrad Rhondda 41 B4
Ystrad Aeron Ceredig 75 C4
Ystrad-mynach Caerph 41 B6
Ystradfellte Powys 59 D6
Ystradffin Carms 76 C1
Ystradgynlais Powys 59 D4
Ystradmeurig Ceredig 75 B6
Ystradowen Carms 59 D4
Ystradowen V Glam 41 D5
Ystumtuen Ceredig 75 A6
Ythanbank Aberds 257 C4
Ythanwells Aberds 256 C1
Ythsie Aberds 256 C3

Z

Zeal Monachorum Devon 12 A2
Zeals Wilts 30 B1
Zelah Corn 4 B3
Zennor Corn 2 B2

www.philips-maps.co.uk

First published in 2006 by
Philip's a division of
Octopus Publishing Group Ltd
2–4 Heron Quays, London E14 4JP
An Hachette Livre UK Company

Third edition 2008
First impression 2008

Cartography by Philip's

Data for the speed cameras provided by PocketGPSWorld.com Ltd.

Information for Tourist Attractions shown on the mapping supplied by VisitBritain

Information for National Parks, Areas of Outstanding Natural Beauty, National Trails and Country Parks in Wales supplied by the Countryside Council for Wales.

Information for National Parks, Areas of Outstanding Natural Beauty, National Trails and Country Parks in England supplied by the Countryside Agency. Data for Regional Parks, Long Distance Footpaths and Country Parks in Scotland provided by Scottish Natural Heritage.

Gaelic name forms used in the Western Isles provided by Comhairle nan Eilean.

Data for the National Nature Reserves in England provided by English Nature. Data for the National Nature Reserves in Wales provided by Countryside Council for Wales. Darparwyd data'n ymwneud â Gwarchodfeydd Natur Cenedlaethol Cymru gan Gyngor Cefn Gwlad Cymru.

Information on the location of National Nature Reserves in Scotland was provided by Scottish Natural Heritage.

Data for National Scenic Areas in Scotland provided by the Scottish Executive Office. Crown copyright material is reproduced with the permission of the Controller of HMSO and the Queen's Printer for Scotland. Licence number C02W0003960.

Printed in China by Toppan

Photographic acknowledgments

Page I *Adrian Beesley / iStockphoto.com* • Page II, top *Mark Bond / Dreamstime.com* • Page III, top right *Andy Hallam / Alamy*; below right *Simon Holdcroft / Alamy*

Distance table

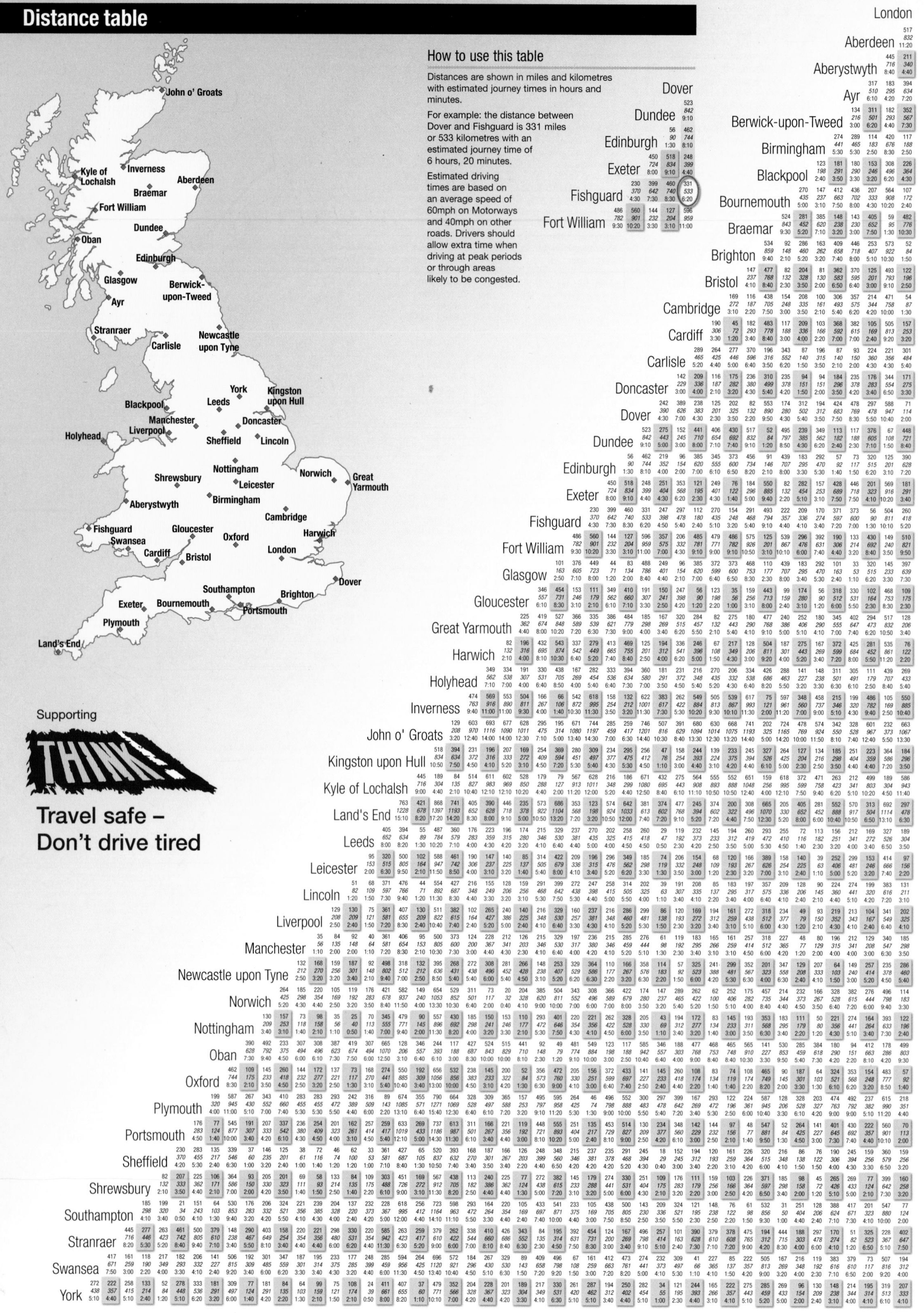

How to use this table

Distances are shown in miles and kilometres with estimated journey times in hours and minutes.

For example: the distance between Dover and Fishguard is 331 miles or 533 kilometres with an estimated journey time of 6 hours, 20 minutes.

Estimated driving times are based on an average speed of 60mph on Motorways and 40mph on other roads. Drivers should allow extra time when driving at peak periods or through areas likely to be congested.

	Fort William	Fishguard	Exeter	Edinburgh	Dundee	Dover
Dundee						523/842/9:10
Edinburgh					56/90/1:30	462/744/8:10
Exeter				450/724/8:00	518/834/9:10	248/399/4:40
Fishguard			230/370/4:30	399/642/7:30	460/740/8:30	331/533/6:20
Fort William		486/782/9:30	560/901/10:20	144/232/3:30	127/204/3:10	596/959/11:00

	Swansea	Stranraer	Southampton	Shrewsbury	Sheffield	Portsmouth	Plymouth	Oxford	Oban	Nottingham	Norwich	Newcastle upon Tyne	Manchester	Liverpool	Lincoln	Leicester	Leeds	Land's End	Kyle of Lochalsh	Kingston upon Hull	John o' Groats	Inverness	Holyhead	Harwich	Great Yarmouth	Gloucester	Glasgow	Fort William	Fishguard	Exeter	Edinburgh	Dundee	Dover	Doncaster	Carlisle	Cardiff	Cambridge	Bristol	Brighton	Braemar	Bournemouth	Blackpool	Birmingham	Berwick-upon-Tweed	Ayr	Aberystwyth	Aberdeen	London
Aberdeen																																																517/832/11:20
Aberystwyth																																															445/716/8:40	211/340/4:40
Ayr																																														317/510/6:10	183/295/4:20	394/634/7:20
Berwick-upon-Tweed																																													134/216/3:00	311/501/6:20	182/293/4:40	352/567/7:30
Birmingham																																												274/441/5:30	289/465/5:30	114/183/2:50	420/676/8:30	117/188/2:50
Blackpool																																											123/198/2:40	181/291/3:50	180/290/3:30	153/246/3:20	308/496/6:20	226/364/4:30
Bournemouth																																										270/435/5:00	147/237/3:10	412/663/7:50	436/702/8:00	207/333/4:30	564/908/10:20	107/172/2:40
Braemar																																									524/843/9:30	281/452/5:20	385/620/7:10	148/238/3:20	143/230/3:00	405/652/7:50	59/95/1:30	482/776/10:30
Brighton																																								534/859/9:40	92/148/2:10	286/460/5:20	163/262/3:20	409/658/7:40	446/718/8:00	253/407/5:10	573/922/10:30	52/84/1:50
Bristol																																							147/237/4:10	477/768/8:40	82/132/2:30	204/328/3:50	81/130/2:00	362/583/6:50	370/595/6:40	125/201/3:00	493/793/9:10	122/196/2:50
Cambridge																																						169/272/3:10	116/187/2:20	438/705/7:50	154/248/3:00	208/335/3:50	100/161/2:10	306/493/5:40	357/575/6:20	214/344/4:20	471/758/10:00	54/87/1:30
Cardiff																																					190/306/3:30	45/72/1:20	182/293/3:40	483/778/8:40	117/188/3:00	209/336/4:00	103/166/2:20	368/592/7:00	382/615/7:00	105/169/2:40	505/813/9:20	157/253/3:20
Carlisle																																				289/465/5:20	264/425/4:40	277/446/5:00	370/596/6:40	196/316/3:50	343/552/6:20	87/140/1:50	196/315/3:50	87/140/2:10	93/150/2:00	224/360/4:30	221/356/4:30	301/484/5:40
Doncaster																																			142/229/3:00	209/336/4:00	116/187/2:10	175/282/3:20	236/380/4:30	310/499/5:40	235/378/4:20	94/151/1:50	94/151/2:00	184/296/3:50	235/378/4:20	176/283/3:40	344/554/6:50	171/275/3:30
Dover																																		242/390/4:30	389/626/7:00	238/383/4:30	125/201/2:30	202/325/3:50	82/132/2:20	553/890/9:50	174/280/4:30	312/502/5:40	194/312/3:50	424/683/7:50	478/769/8:30	297/478/5:50	588/947/10:40	71/114/2:00
Dundee																																	523/842/9:10	275/443/5:00	152/245/3:00	441/710/8:00	406/654/7:10	430/692/7:40	517/832/9:10	52/84/1:20	495/797/8:50	239/385/4:30	349/562/6:20	113/182/2:40	117/188/2:30	376/605/7:10	67/108/1:50	448/721/8:40
Edinburgh																																56/90/1:30	462/744/8:10	219/352/4:00	96/154/2:00	385/620/7:00	345/555/6:10	373/600/6:50	456/734/8:20	91/146/2:10	439/707/8:00	183/295/3:30	292/470/5:30	57/92/1:40	73/117/1:50	320/515/6:20	125/201/3:10	390/628/7:20
Exeter																															450/724/8:00	518/834/9:10	248/399/4:40	251/404/4:30	353/568/6:20	121/195/2:30	249/401/4:30	76/122/1:40	184/296/5:00	550/885/9:40	82/132/2:20	282/454/5:10	157/253/3:10	428/689/7:50	446/718/7:50	201/323/4:10	569/916/10:20	181/291/3:40
Fishguard																														230/370/4:30	399/642/7:30	460/740/8:30	331/533/6:20	247/398/4:50	297/478/5:40	112/180/2:40	270/435/5:10	154/248/3:20	291/468/5:40	493/794/9:10	222/357/4:40	209/336/4:10	170/274/3:40	371/597/7:20	373/600/7:00	56/90/1:30	504/811/10:10	260/418/5:20
Fort William																													486/782/9:30	560/901/10:20	144/232/3:30	127/204/3:10	596/959/11:00	357/575/7:00	206/332/4:30	485/781/9:10	479/771/9:00	486/782/9:10	575/926/10:50	125/201/3:10	539/867/10:10	296/476/6:00	392/631/7:40	190/306/4:40	133/214/3:20	430/692/8:40	149/240/3:50	510/821/9:50
Glasgow																												101/163/2:50	376/605/7:10	449/723/8:00	44/71/1:20	83/134/2:00	488/786/8:40	249/401/4:40	96/154/2:10	385/620/7:00	372/599/6:40	373/600/6:50	468/753/8:30	110/177/2:30	439/707/8:00	183/295/3:40	292/470/5:30	101/163/2:40	33/53/1:10	320/515/6:20	145/233/3:30	397/639/7:30
Gloucester																											346/557/6:10	454/731/8:30	153/246/3:10	111/179/2:10	349/562/6:10	410/660/7:10	191/307/3:30	150/241/2:50	247/398/4:20	56/90/1:20	123/198/2:20	35/56/1:00	159/256/3:10	443/713/8:00	99/159/2:40	174/280/3:10	56/90/1:20	318/512/6:00	330/531/5:50	102/164/2:30	468/753/8:30	109/175/2:30
Great Yarmouth																										225/362/4:40	419/674/8:00	527/848/10:20	366/589/7:20	335/539/6:30	386/621/7:30	484/779/9:00	185/298/4:00	167/269/3:40	320/515/6:20	284/457/5:50	82/132/2:10	275/443/5:40	180/290/4:10	477/768/9:10	240/386/5:00	252/406/5:10	180/290/4:10	345/555/7:00	402/647/7:40	294/473/6:20	517/832/10:50	128/206/3:40
Harwich																									82/132/2:10	196/316/4:00	432/695/8:10	543/874/10:30	337/542/6:40	279/449/5:20	413/665/7:40	469/755/8:40	125/201/2:50	194/312/4:00	336/541/6:20	246/396/5:00	67/108/1:50	217/349/4:30	128/206/3:00	504/811/9:20	187/301/4:00	275/443/5:20	167/269/3:40	372/599/7:20	425/684/8:00	281/452/5:50	535/861/11:20	76/122/2:20
Holyhead																								349/562/7:10	334/538/7:00	191/307/4:00	330/531/6:40	438/705/8:50	167/269/4:00	282/454/5:40	333/536/6:40	394/634/7:30	360/580/7:00	181/291/3:50	231/372/4:50	216/348/5:40	270/435/5:20	206/332/4:30	334/538/6:40	426/686/8:20	288/463/5:50	141/227/3:20	148/238/3:30	311/501/6:30	305/491/6:10	111/179/2:50	439/707/8:40	269/433/5:40
Inverness																							474/763/9:40	569/916/11:00	553/890/11:00	504/811/9:30	166/267/4:00	66/106/1:40	542/872/10:30	618/995/11:30	158/254/3:50	132/212/3:20	622/1001/11:30	383/617/7:30	262/422/5:30	549/884/10:20	505/813/9:30	539/867/10:10	617/993/11:30	75/121/2:00	597/961/11:20	348/560/7:00	458/737/9:00	215/346/5:10	199/320/4:30	486/782/9:40	105/169/2:50	550/885/10:40
John o' Groats																						129/208/3:20	603/970/12:40	693/1116/14:00	677/1090/14:00	628/1011/12:30	295/475/7:10	195/314/5:00	671/1080/13:40	744/1197/14:30	285/459/7:00	259/417/6:30	746/1201/14:40	507/816/10:30	391/629/8:40	680/1094/13:30	630/1014/12:30	668/1075/13:20	741/1193/14:40	202/325/5:00	724/1165/14:20	478/769/10:00	574/924/11:50	342/550/8:10	328/528/7:40	601/967/12:40	232/373/5:50	663/1067/13:30
Kingston upon Hull																					518/834/10:50	394/634/7:50	231/372/4:50	196/316/4:10	207/333/5:20	169/272/3:10	254/409/4:50	369/594/7:20	280/451/5:30	309/497/5:40	234/377/4:30	295/475/5:30	256/412/4:50	47/76/1:10	158/254/3:00	244/393/4:40	139/224/3:10	233/375/4:20	245/394/4:40	327/526/6:10	264/425/5:00	127/204/2:30	134/216/2:50	185/298/3:50	251/404/4:40	223/359/4:40	364/586/7:20	184/296/3:50
Kyle of Lochalsh																				445/716/9:00	189/304/4:40	84/135/2:10	514/827/10:40	611/983/12:10	602/969/12:10	528/850/10:20	179/288/4:40	79/127/2:00	567/913/11:20	628/1011/12:00	216/348/5:20	186/299/4:40	671/1080/12:50	432/695/8:40	275/443/6:10	564/908/11:10	555/893/10:50	552/888/10:50	651/1048/12:40	159/256/4:00	618/995/12:10	372/599/7:50	471/758/9:40	263/423/6:20	212/341/5:10	499/803/10:20	189/304/4:50	586/943/11:40
Land's End																			763/1228/15:10	421/678/8:20	868/1397/17:20	741/1193/14:20	405/652/8:30	390/628/8:00	446/718/9:10	235/378/5:00	573/922/10:50	686/1104/13:20	353/568/7:20	123/198/3:20	574/924/10:50	642/1033/12:00	381/613/7:40	374/602/7:20	477/768/9:10	245/394/5:20	374/602/7:20	200/322/4:40	308/496/7:50	665/1070/12:30	205/330/5:20	405/652/8:00	281/452/6:00	552/888/10:40	570/917/10:50	313/504/6:50	692/1114/13:10	297/478/6:30
Leeds																		405/652/8:00	394/634/8:20	55/89/1:30	487/784/10:20	360/579/7:10	176/283/4:00	223/359/4:30	196/315/4:20	174/280/3:20	215/346/4:10	329/530/6:40	237/381/4:40	270/435/5:00	202/325/4:00	258/415/4:50	260/418/4:50	29/47/0:50	119/192/2:30	232/373/4:20	145/233/2:50	194/312/3:50	260/419/5:00	293/472/5:30	255/410/4:50	72/116/1:40	113/182/2:30	156/251/3:20	212/341/4:00	169/272/3:40	327/526/6:50	189/304/3:50
Leicester																	95/153/2:00	320/515/6:30	500/805/9:50	102/164/2:10	588/947/11:50	461/742/8:50	190/306/4:00	147/237/3:10	140/225/3:20	85/137/1:40	314/505/5:40	422/679/8:00	209/336/4:10	196/315/3:40	296/476/5:20	349/562/6:20	185/298/3:30	74/119/1:30	206/332/3:50	154/248/3:00	68/109/1:20	120/193/2:30	166/267/3:20	389/626/7:00	158/254/3:10	140/225/2:40	39/63/1:10	252/406/5:00	299/481/5:20	153/246/3:20	414/666/7:40	97/156/2:20
Lincoln																51/82/1:20	68/109/1:50	371/597/7:30	476/766/9:40	44/71/1:20	554/892/11:30	427/687/8:30	216/348/4:40	155/249/3:30	128/206/3:20	159/256/3:10	291/468/5:30	399/642/7:50	272/438/5:30	247/398/4:40	258/415/5:00	314/505/5:50	202/325/4:00	39/63/1:10	191/307/3:40	208/335/4:10	85/137/2:20	183/295/3:40	197/317/4:00	357/575/6:40	209/336/4:10	128/206/2:40	90/145/2:10	224/360/4:40	274/441/5:10	199/320/4:20	383/616/7:20	131/211/3:10
Liverpool															129/208/2:50	130/209/2:40	75/121/1:50	361/581/7:20	407/655/8:30	130/209/2:40	511/822/10:40	382/615/7:40	102/164/2:40	265/427/5:20	240/386/5:00	140/225/2:40	216/348/4:10	329/530/6:40	160/257/3:30	237/381/4:30	216/348/4:10	286/460/5:20	299/481/5:30	86/138/1:50	120/193/2:30	169/272/3:20	194/312/3:40	161/259/3:10	272/438/5:10	318/512/6:00	234/377/4:30	49/79/1:20	93/150/2:10	219/352/4:30	213/343/4:10	104/167/2:40	341/549/6:40	202/325/4:10
Manchester														35/56/1:10	84/135/2:00	92/148/2:00	40/64/1:10	361/581/7:20	406/654/8:30	95/153/2:10	500/805/10:30	373/600/7:30	124/200/3:00	228/367/4:40	212/341/4:30	126/203/2:30	215/346/4:10	329/530/6:40	197/317/4:00	236/380/4:20	215/346/4:10	285/459/5:20	276/444/5:10	61/98/1:30	119/192/2:30	183/295/3:40	165/266/3:10	161/259/3:10	257/414/4:50	318/512/6:00	227/365/4:20	48/77/1:20	80/129/2:00	196/315/4:00	212/341/4:00	129/208/3:00	340/547/6:30	185/298/3:50
Newcastle upon Tyne													132/212/2:50	168/270/3:20	159/256/3:20	187/301/3:40	92/148/2:10	498/802/9:40	318/512/7:00	132/212/2:50	395/636/8:50	268/431/5:40	272/438/5:40	308/496/6:00	281/452/5:40	266/428/4:50	148/238/3:10	253/407/5:20	329/529/6:20	364/586/6:30	110/177/2:20	166/267/3:20	358/576/6:30	114/183/2:20	57/92/1:50	325/523/6:00	241/388/4:20	299/481/5:30	352/567/6:30	201/323/4:00	347/558/6:30	129/208/2:40	207/333/4:10	64/103/1:50	149/240/3:00	257/414/5:20	235/378/4:50	286/460/5:40
Norwich												264/425/5:20	185/298/4:30	220/354/4:40	105/169/2:50	119/192/3:20	176/283/3:50	421/678/8:40	582/937/11:50	149/240/4:00	654/1053/13:30	529/852/10:30	311/501/6:40	73/117/2:00	20/32/0:40	204/328/4:10	385/620/9:00	504/811/10:00	343/552/7:00	308/496/6:00	366/589/7:00	422/679/8:00	174/280/3:50	147/237/3:20	289/465/5:40	262/422/5:20	62/100/1:50	252/406/5:10	175/282/4:00	457/735/8:40	214/344/4:40	232/373/4:50	166/267/3:50	328/528/6:40	382/615/7:20	276/444/6:00	496/798/9:40	114/183/3:30
Nottingham											130/209/3:40	157/253/3:10	73/118/1:40	98/158/2:10	35/56/1:10	25/40/0:50	70/113/1:40	345/555/7:00	479/771/9:40	90/145/2:00	557/896/11:30	430/692/8:20	185/298/4:00	150/241/3:20	153/246/3:30	110/177/2:10	293/472/5:30	401/646/7:50	220/354/4:30	221/356/4:10	262/422/4:50	328/528/6:00	205/330/3:50	43/69/1:10	194/312/3:40	172/277/3:20	83/134/1:40	145/233/3:00	193/311/3:50	353/568/6:30	183/295/3:40	111/179/2:20	50/80/1:20	221/356/4:30	274/441/5:10	164/264/3:40	393/633/7:30	122/196/2:40
Oban										390/628/7:30	492/792/9:40	233/375/4:50	307/494/6:00	308/496/6:10	387/623/7:30	419/674/7:50	307/494/6:00	665/1070/12:50	128/206/3:10	346/557/6:40	244/393/6:10	117/188/3:00	427/687/8:30	524/843/10:00	515/829/10:00	441/710/8:10	92/148/2:30	49/79/1:20	481/774/9:10	549/884/10:00	123/198/3:00	117/188/2:50	585/942/10:40	346/557/6:40	188/303/4:00	477/768/9:00	468/753/8:40	465/748/8:40	565/910/10:30	141/227/3:30	530/853/9:50	285/459/5:40	384/618/7:30	180/290/4:20	94/151/2:20	412/663/8:10	178/286/4:20	499/803/9:30
Oxford									462/744/8:30	109/175/2:10	145/233/3:50	260/418/4:50	144/232/2:50	172/277/3:20	137/221/2:50	73/117/1:30	168/270/3:10	274/441/5:40	550/885/10:40	192/309/3:40	656/1056/13:00	532/856/10:00	238/383/4:50	145/233/3:10	200/322/4:20	52/84/1:30	356/573/6:30	472/760/9:00	205/330/4:10	156/251/3:00	372/599/6:40	433/697/7:40	141/227/2:50	145/233/2:40	260/418/4:40	108/174/2:20	83/134/1:40	74/119/1:40	108/174/2:20	465/749/8:20	90/145/2:00	187/301/3:30	64/103/1:30	324/521/6:10	353/568/6:20	154/248/3:20	483/777/8:50	57/92/1:40
Plymouth								199/320/4:00	587/945/11:00	267/430/5:10	343/552/7:00	410/660/7:40	283/455/5:30	283/455/5:30	293/472/5:50	242/389/4:40	316/509/6:00	89/143/2:20	674/1085/13:10	355/571/6:40	790/1271/15:40	664/1069/12:30	328/528/6:40	309/497/6:10	365/588/7:20	157/253/3:20	495/797/9:10	595/958/11:20	264/425/5:30	46/74/1:30	496/798/9:00	552/888/10:00	300/483/5:50	297/478/5:40	399/642/7:20	167/269/3:40	293/472/5:30	122/196/2:50	224/361/6:00	587/945/10:40	128/206/3:30	328/528/6:10	203/327/4:20	474/763/9:00	492/792/9:00	237/382/5:10	615/990/11:20	218/351/4:40
Portsmouth							176/283/4:50	77/124/1:40	545/877/10:00	191/307/3:40	207/333/4:20	337/542/6:10	236/380/4:30	254/409/4:50	201/323/4:00	162/261/3:10	257/414/4:50	259/417/5:40	633/1019/12:10	269/433/5:00	737/1186/14:30	613/987/11:30	311/501/6:10	166/267/3:40	221/356/4:40	119/192/3:00	448/721/8:10	555/893/10:20	251/404/5:00	135/217/2:40	453/729/8:10	514/827/9:00	130/209/2:50	234/377/4:20	348/560/6:10	142/229/3:00	144/232/2:50	97/156/2:10	48/77/1:40	547/881/9:50	52/84/1:30	264/425/4:50	141/227/3:00	401/645/7:30	430/692/7:40	222/357/4:40	560/901/10:10	70/113/2:00
Sheffield						230/370/4:20	283/455/5:30	135/217/2:40	339/546/6:30	37/60/1:00	146/235/3:20	125/201/2:40	38/61/1:00	72/116/1:40	46/74/1:20	62/100/1:20	33/53/1:00	361/581/7:10	427/687/8:40	65/105/1:30	520/837/10:50	393/632/7:40	168/270/3:40	187/301/3:50	166/267/3:40	126/203/2:20	248/399/4:40	348/560/6:50	215/346/4:20	237/381/4:20	235/378/4:20	291/468/5:20	245/394/4:30	18/29/0:40	152/245/3:00	194/312/3:40	120/193/2:20	161/259/3:10	226/364/4:20	320/515/6:00	216/348/4:10	86/138/1:50	76/122/1:50	190/306/4:00	245/394/4:30	159/256/3:30	360/579/6:50	159/256/3:20
Shrewsbury					82/132/2:10	207/333/3:50	225/362/4:40	106/171/2:10	364/586/7:00	93/150/2:00	205/330/4:20	201/323/3:50	69/111/1:40	58/93/1:50	133/214/2:50	84/135/1:40	109/175/2:20	303/488/6:10	451/726/9:00	169/272/3:10	567/912/11:30	438/705/8:20	113/182/2:50	240/386/4:40	225/362/4:40	77/124/1:30	272/438/5:00	382/615/7:20	145/233/3:10	179/288/3:20	274/441/5:00	330/531/6:00	251/404/4:30	109/175/2:10	176/283/3:20	111/179/2:20	159/256/3:00	103/166/2:50	226/364/4:20	371/597/6:50	185/298/3:40	98/158/2:00	45/72/1:20	265/426/5:10	269/433/5:00	77/124/2:10	399/642/7:30	160/258/3:20
Southampton				185/298/4:10	199/320/3:40	21/34/0:50	151/243/4:10	64/103/1:30	530/853/9:40	176/283/3:20	206/332/4:20	324/521/5:50	221/356/4:10	239/385/4:30	204/328/4:00	137/220/2:40	232/373/4:20	228/367/5:00	618/995/12:00	256/412/4:40	723/1164/14:10	598/963/11:10	293/472/5:50	164/264/3:30	220/354/4:40	105/169/2:40	433/697/7:40	541/871/10:00	233/375/4:40	105/169/3:00	438/705/7:50	500/805/8:50	143/230/2:50	209/336/3:50	324/521/5:50	121/195/2:30	148/238/2:50	76/122/2:20	61/98/1:50	532/856/9:30	31/50/1:00	251/404/4:40	128/206/2:40	388/624/7:10	417/671/7:30	201/323/4:10	547/880/10:00	77/124/2:00
Stranraer			445/716/8:20	277/446/5:30	263/423/5:20	461/742/8:40	500/805/9:40	379/610/7:10	148/238/3:40	290/467/5:50	403/649/8:10	158/254/3:40	220/354/4:40	221/356/4:40	298/480/6:00	330/531/6:20	220/354/4:40	585/942/11:30	263/423/6:30	259/417/5:20	379/610/9:00	262/422/6:00	338/544/7:00	410/660/8:10	426/686/8:40	343/552/6:30	84/135/2:30	195/314/4:50	392/631/7:50	454/731/8:30	124/200/3:00	167/269/3:40	496/798/9:10	257/414/5:10	101/163/2:40	390/628/7:30	379/610/7:10	378/608/7:20	475/765/9:00	194/312/4:20	444/715/8:30	188/303/4:00	297/478/6:00	170/274/4:10	51/82/1:20	325/523/6:50	228/367/5:10	402/647/7:50
Swansea		417/671/7:50	161/259/3:00	118/190/2:20	217/349/4:00	182/293/3:30	206/332/4:10	141/227/2:40	506/815/9:20	192/309/3:40	301/485/6:00	347/559/6:20	187/301/3:30	195/314/3:40	233/375/4:30	177/285/3:20	248/399/4:40	285/459/6:00	594/956/11:30	264/425/4:50	696/1120/13:40	572/921/10:40	184/296/4:50	267/430/5:10	329/530/6:30	89/143/1:50	409/658/7:20	496/798/9:20	67/108/1:50	161/259/3:00	412/663/7:20	473/761/8:20	274/441/5:00	232/373/4:10	309/497/5:30	41/66/1:10	227/365/4:10	85/137/1:50	222/357/4:20	505/813/9:00	167/269/3:20	216/348/4:00	119/192/2:30	383/616/7:10	379/610/6:50	73/117/2:00	507/816/9:20	194/312/4:00
York	272/438/5:10	222/357/4:40	258/415/5:10	133/214/2:40	52/84/1:20	278/448/5:10	333/536/6:20	181/291/3:20	309/497/6:00	77/124/1:40	181/291/4:20	84/135/2:20	64/103/1:30	99/159/2:10	75/121/1:50	108/174/2:10	24/39/0:50	411/661/8:00	407/655/8:20	37/60/1:10	479/771/10:10	352/566/7:00	204/328/4:20	228/367/4:40	201/323/4:20	189/304/3:30	217/349/4:10	330/531/6:30	261/420/5:10	287/462/5:10	194/312/3:40	250/402/4:40	282/454/5:10	34/55/1:00	121/195/2:30	244/393/4:40	165/266/3:10	222/357/4:10	275/443/5:10	285/459/5:20	269/433/5:00	96/154/2:00	130/209/2:40	148/238/3:10	214/344/4:00	195/314/4:10	319/513/6:10	207/333/4:10